D1604657

EMPLOYMENT AND LABOR LAW

NINTH EDITION

EMPLOYMENT AND LABOR LAW

NINTH EDITION

PATRICK J. CIHON
Law and Public Policy, Management Department,
Whitman School of Management, Syracuse University

JAMES OTTAVIO CASTAGNERA
Associate Provost/Legal Counsel, Rider University
Adjunct Professor of Law, Drexel University
Managing Director, K&C HR Enterprises

CENGAGE
Learning·

Australia • Brazil • Mexico • Singapore • United Kingdom • United States

Employment and Labor Law, 9e
Patrick J. Cihon and James Ottavio Castagnera

Vice President, General Manager, Social Science & Qualitative Business: Erin Joyner

Product Director: Michael Worls

Associate Product Manager: Tara Singer

Content Developer: Sarah Blasco

Product Assistant: Ryan McAndrews

Marketing Director: Kristen Hurd

Marketing Manager: Katie Jergens

Marketing Coordinator: Christopher Walz

Art and Cover Direction, Production Management, and Composition: Lumina Datamatics, Inc.

Intellectual Property Analyst: Jennifer Nonenmacher

Project Manager: Betsy Hathaway

Manufacturing Planner: Kevin Kluck

Cover Image(s): ©Wesely VanDinter/ Thinkstock

For product information and technology assistance, contact us at
Cengage Learning Customer & Sales Support, 1-800-354-9706

For permission to use material from this text or product, submit all requests online at **www.cengage.com/permissions**
Further permissions questions can be emailed to
permissionrequest@cengage.com

Library of Congress Control Number: 2015956164

ISBN: 978-1-305-58001-5

Cengage Learning
20 Channel Center Street
Boston, MA 02210
USA

Cengage Learning is a leading provider of customized learning solutions with employees residing in nearly 40 different countries and sales in more than 125 countries around the world. Find your local representative at **www.cengage.com.**

Cengage Learning products are represented in Canada by Nelson Education, Ltd.

To learn more about Cengage Learning Solutions, visit **www.cengage.com**

Purchase any of our products at your local college store or at our preferred online store **www.cengagebrain.com**

Printed in the Unites States of America
Print Number: 04   Print Year: 2017

BRIEF CONTENTS

CONTENTS

Chapter 8   Discrimination Based on Religion and National Origin and Procedures Under Title VII 205

Chapter 9   Discrimination Based on Age 255

Chapter 10 Discrimination Based on Disability 279

■ Part 3 LABOR RELATIONS LAW « 349

Chapter 12 The Rise of Organized Labor and Its Regulatory Framework 351

Chapter 13 The Unionization Process 397

Chapter 16 Picketing and Strikes 513

Chapter 17 The Enforcement and Administration of the Collective Agreement 549

Chapter 18 The Rights of Union Members 583

Chapter 19 Public Sector Labor Relations 613

■ Part 4   EMPLOYMENT LAW ISSUES « 653

Chapter 20 Occupational Safety and Health   655

Chapter 21 The Employee's Safety Nets: Unemployment and Workers' Compensation, Social Security, and Retirement Plans   691

PREFACE

Nearly 30 years ago, when we first undertook the writing of an employment and labor law textbook, we had no notion that our creative effort would carve itself such a long-lasting niche in higher education. Clearly, however, the release of this ninth edition, as well as accolades like those below, confirm that *Employment and Labor Law* is now firmly established. Lest this sound as if we were resting on our laurels, allow us to hastily add that this new edition has been significantly revised and updated. A source of particular pride is Part One, expressly intended to bring our "old standard" firmly into the employment and labor firmament of the 21st century. Three issues of critical importance in the new millennium—privacy, globalization, and immigration—are treated specifically and in-depth. Additionally, numerous new cases, case problems, hypotheticals, and The Working Law features ensure that every chapter of this new volume is on the cutting edge of the topic it covers.

> I have practiced labor and employment law for over twenty years and I think this is the best text for a basic labor and employment law class.... It's simple to read and straightforward. I tell my students to keep the book and not sell it because it is quite helpful for the basic questions they will be asked in the work world.
>
> Maris Stella (Star) Swift
> *Grand Valley State University*

> The text is well laid-out, and is written in language that is appropriate for the students; there is no reason for the students to not read the text. The questions that follow the edited cases help to focus the student's analysis of the case in question, its relevance to the topic, and introduce the student to legal concepts and outcomes they tend to neglect or may not fully understand....
>
> Curt M. Weber
> *University of Wisconsin—Whitewater*

> [*Employment and Labor Law* has an] excellent balance of in-depth case-law readings, related ethical considerations, Internet resources and foundational materials for the non-lawyer audience.
>
> Susan F. Alevas
> *New York University*

Hallmark Features

In the constantly changing, often controversial areas of employment and labor law, the ninth edition of *Employment and Labor Law* provides current information in a way that highlights critical thinking, ethical decision-making, and relevance to the business world. The unique hallmark features of this text that have been retained include the following.

Current and Balanced Coverage

This text offers a comprehensive balance of both employment law and labor law topics and includes up-to-date information. This edition specifically examines the revolutionary changes being wrought by the Obama administration with regard to who is an employee under the National Labor Relations Act (NCAA Division I athletes) and the Fair Labor Standards Act, and by the United States Supreme Court (a corporation can hold religious beliefs that trump the Affordable Care Act per the First Amendment). Expanded employee rights under Obamacare, the Family and Medical Leave Act, and the Supreme Court's same-sex-marriage decisions are fully delineated, while the EEOC's challenge to corporate wellness programs is also described.

Readability

In no other area of the law are nonlawyer professionals exposed to such legal regulation, and in no other area do they experience the need for "lawyer-like" skills to the extent that human resources directors and industrial relations specialists do. This book is therefore written to help business and management students, not necessarily lawyers. The straightforward writing style clarifies complex concepts, while pedagogical features help readers develop the legal reasoning and analysis skills that are vital for success in the business world.

The Working Law

Connecting legal concepts and cases to our everyday environment, The Working Law features highlight the relevancy of the law while sparking student interest and bringing concepts to life. Cutting-edge topics like emotional distress via social networking websites and increasing age discrimination claims in today's tough economy, as well as controversial discussions about sweatshops and the landmark Affordable Care Act, are just a few of those considered in this edition.

Ethical Dilemma

What is the extent of global corporate social responsibility? Can employers use genetic information in hiring decisions? What are the boundaries regarding religion and harassment in the workplace? Questions like these, presented in the Ethical Dilemma features in each chapter, address the increasing need for ethical behavior in decision-making. These features can be used to encourage debates in class or as assignments that consider the differences between what is legal and what is ethical.

Guide to Briefing Cases

Students will find the Guide to Briefing Cases to be a valuable reference. It gives a quick overview of how to read a case citation and outlines what information to provide in a brief. While offering an excellent refresher for students who have already taken legal environment or business law courses, it also gives students with no previous legal background an introduction to the basics of case analysis.

Case Treatment

Many new summarized cases, in which the authors outline the facts, issue, and decision of a real case in their own words, have been added to provide more case illustrations that are concise and student-friendly. However, as learning to interpret cases in the language of the court is crucial in developing analytical and critical thinking skills, half of the cases in the text remain excerpted in the words of the courts. These case extracts have been crisply edited to focus attention on the relevant concept, while including occasional dissents and/or concurring opinions, which allow the reader to experience the fact that law develops from the resolution—or at least the accommodation—of differing views. These two different types of case treatment allow for flexibility in approach and depth of coverage.

Concept Summaries

Concept Summaries throughout each chapter reinforce the legal concepts illustrated in applicable sections and provide students with a quick outline to ensure that they understand what they have read.

Key Terms

To help students master the specialized legal terminology and easily identify integral ideas, a Key Terms section is included at the end of each chapter. Page references direct students back to the relevant chapter content and marginal definitions.

End-of-Chapter Problem Types

Each chapter contains five short-answer questions regarding basic chapter comprehension, ten case problems based on real cases, and five hypothetical scenarios to provide students an opportunity to critically analyze real-life situations without a case citation reference. This versatility in the end-of-chapter assignments offers instructors a variety of ways in which to engage students and measure comprehension.

Recent Coverage

The ninth edition of *Employment and Labor Law* includes recent and up-to-date coverage on many topics. Some of the highlights of this edition include the following:

- **Chapter 1:** This cutting-edge chapter provides a broad overview of the employment and labor law landscape covered in the subsequent chapters. Gilbert and Sullivan notwithstanding, the law is not a seamless web. However, the American mosaic of employment and labor laws does present a public-policy picture, which ought to be perceived and considered before embarking on in-depth considerations of its many and diverse pieces.

- **Chapter 4:** Perhaps no issue is of greater concern to employees—after compensation and benefits—than personal privacy in this so-called Information Age. From the possibility of genetic testing for latent medical defects to the ability to monitor our email, our Internet usage, indeed our every move, privacy rights are in jeopardy, while litigation nonetheless increases. Sure to encourage lively debates, this chapter brings privacy issues to the forefront.

- **Chapter 5:** "The world is flat," to quote *New York Times* columnist Thomas Friedman. Employers and employees alike compete against their counterparts in other regions of the globe. No longer is it enough for students of employment and labor law to grasp the major tenets of American statutory and common law. Furthermore, in a 21st-century society that has moved way beyond America's traditional melting pot, knowledge of the rules and regulations applying to immigrants, international students, and foreign workers is critical. This chapter explores these issues.

- **Chapter 7:** This chapter includes coverage of the Patient Protection and Affordable Care Act's provisions regarding nursing mothers, and the Working Law feature updates the legal protections for transgendered persons. Also covered is the Supreme Court's 2014 *Hobby Lobby* decision, according First-Amendment religious freedom to closely held corporations.

- **Chapter 8:** The case of *Lewis v. City of Chicago*, the most recent Supreme Court decision regarding disparate impact discrimination, is included.

- **Chapter 9:** The Supreme Court's decision in *Gross v. FBL Financial Services* is covered.

- **Chapter 10:** A case discussing the Genetic Information Nondiscrimination Act (GINA) and a more detailed discussion of the EEOC's definition of "medical exams and tests" under the ADA are included in this chapter. The EEOC's ADA-based challenge to corporate wellness programs is likewise covered.

- **Chapter 11:** This chapter includes a discussion of the impact of the repeal of the "Don't Ask, Don't Tell" policy.

- **Chapter 14:** An expanded discussion of the recent NLRB decisions regarding employer restrictions on employees' use of social media and the employee status of NCAA Division I football players is included, and the Working Law feature covers the NLRB unfair practice complaint against Boeing for moving production lines to South Carolina. The board's 2015 "quickie election" rules also are discussed.

- **Chapter 16:** A case addressing the legality of the NFL lockout of its players in 2011 is included in this chapter.

- **Chapter 17:** This chapter discusses the recent changes in the NLRB policy of whether to defer to arbitration on unfair labor practice complaints.

- **Chapter 18:** The chapter includes a discussion of employers' obligations to post information regarding employee rights under Executive Order 13496, as well as President Obama's controversial executive orders regarding fair pay for female workers and non-discrimination protection for LGBT employees.

- **Chapter 19:** View significant labor law issues in an everyday, easy-to-relate-to setting with this chapter's updated material on national security and collective bargaining rights for federal employees and TSA airport screens. This chapter has expanded information on the National Security Personnel System, political action committees, the TSA, and current related cases.
- **Chapter 21:** Following market preferences, this chapter combines content on ERISA with that of employee welfare programs like social security, workers' compensation, and unemployment compensation.

Instructor Resources

Instructor's Manual

The Instructor's Manual provides an overview of the chapter, a lecture outline with page references, case synopses for each excerpted case, answers to the case questions, and answers to the end-of-chapter questions, case problems, and hypothetical scenarios.

Test Bank

The Test Bank includes true/false, multiple choice, short answer, and essay questions ready to use for creating tests. The Test Bank is available through Cognero.

Cengage Learning Testing Powered by Cognero is a flexible, online system that allows you to:

- author, edit, and manage test bank content from multiple Cengage Learning solutions
- create multiple test versions in an instant
- deliver tests from your LMS, your classroom or wherever you want

PowerPoint® Slides

PowerPoint® slides offer a basic chapter outline to accompany class lecture. They also highlight the key learning objectives in each chapter—including slides summarizing each legal case and each The Working Law and Ethical Dilemma feature.

Textbook Companion Website

The companion website for this edition of Employment and Labor Law provides access to the Instructor's Manual, Test Bank, and PowerPoint® slides. The website also offers links to the following: a number of important employment and labor law statutes, important labor and employment law sites, labor and employment law blogs, legal forms and documents, free legal research sites (comprehensive and circuit-specific), help in the classroom, labor and employment law directories, departments, agencies, associations, and organizations.

Acknowledgments

The authors wish to thank the many people who contributed to the completion of this book. Pat Cihon wishes to acknowledge the contributions of his research assistants Alex Allport and Katie Goldstein. Jim Castagnera thanks his daughter, Claire Holland, a free-lance writer/editor/illustrator, who contributed significantly to the revision of his chapters.

We also would like to thank all those who have contributed to the preparation and production of this ninth edition. In particular, we wish to acknowledge the contribution and assistance of our editors at Cengage Learning: Product Director Mike Worls, Associate Product Manager Tara Singer, Marketing Manager Katie Jergens, Associate Program Manager Divya Divakaran, and Content Developer Sarah Blasco for her guidance and insights during the revision of this edition.

We wish to thank the following reviewers, whose helpful comments and suggestions were used during the preparation of this and the previous edition of the book:

Ken Gaines
East–West University

Richard Custin
University of San Digeo

Susan F. Alevas
New York University

Bruce-Alan Barnard
Davenport University

Curtiss K. Behrens
Northern Illinois University

Helen Bojarczyk
Baker College—Auburn Hills

Colette Borom Carpenter
Mercy College

Terry Conry
Ohio University

Larry G. Covell
Jefferson Community College

Sandra J. Defebaugh
Eastern Michigan University

Ronald L. Foster
Cornerstone University,
Davenport University

John L. Gilbert
Southern Illinois University—
Edwardsville

Diane M. Pfadenhauer
St. Joseph's College

Veena P. Prabhu
California State University—Los
Angeles

JoDee Salisbury
Baker College

Stephanie R. Sipe
Georgia Southern University

Joe Stauffer
University of Texas of the
Permian Basin

Byron Stuckey
Dallas Baptist University

Maris Stella (Star) Swift
Grand Valley State University

Patsy Thimmig
Mount Mercy College

Donald Lee Vardaman, Jr.,
Troy University

Janette C. Waterhouse
University of Iowa

Curt M. Weber
*University of Wisconsin—
Whitewater*

Kelly Collins Woodford
University of South Alabama.

Lastly, the authors wish to rededicate the book to the memory of their parents, John E. and Marian M. Cihon and James Ottavio and Catherine L. Castagnera.

Professor Patrick J. Cihon
Law and Public Policy, Management Department, Whitman School of Management, Syracuse University

Dr. James Ottavio Castagnera
*Associate Provost/Legal Counsel, Rider University
Adjunct Professor of Law, Drexel University*

GUIDE TO BRIEFING CASES

Reading and understandings cases is required in order to understand and analyze the legal decisions forming the basis of the law. A case is a bit like a parable or a fable. It presents a set of facts and events that led two opposing parties into a conflict requiring resolution by a court or agency. The judge or adjudicator is guided by legal principles developed from statutes or prior cases in the resolution of the dispute. There may be competing legal principles that must be reconciled or accommodated. The case is a self-contained record of the resolution of the dispute between the parties, but it is also an incremental step in the process of developing legal principles for resolution of future disputes.

It is the legal principles—their reconciliation and development—and the reasoning process involved that justify the inclusion of the cases we have selected. The critical task of the reader, therefore, is to sift through the facts of a case and to identify the legal principles underlying that case. In analyzing a case you may find it helpful to ask, after reading the case, "Why was this particular case included at this point in the chapter? What does this case add to the textual material immediately preceding it?"

In analyzing the cases, especially the longer ones, you may find it helpful to "brief" them. Case briefing is a highly useful corollary to efficient legal research. A case brief is nothing more than a specialized outline. As such, a brief summarizes the main feature of a court opinion. A group of briefs, accurately and lucidly constructed, often forms the bridge between the relevant decisions identified by a lawyer's research, on one hand, and the memorandum of law, which is his or her final work product, on the other. The following template should prove useful in outlining the case excerpts published in this textbook.

How to Brief a Case

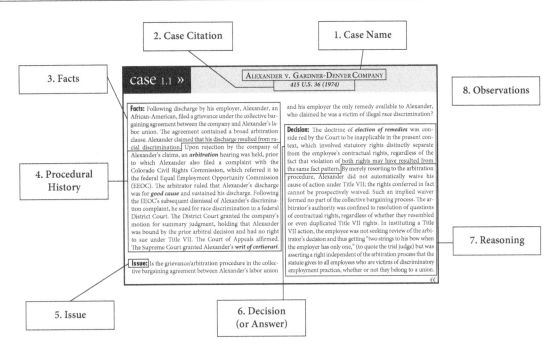

2. Case Citation

1. Case Name

3. Facts

CASE 1.1 »

ALEXANDER V. GARDNER-DENVER COMPANY
415 U.S. 36 (1974)

8. Observations

Facts: Following discharge by his employer, Alexander, an African-American, filed a grievance under the collective bargaining agreement between the company and Alexander's labor union. The agreement contained a broad arbitration clause. Alexander claimed that his discharge resulted from racial discrimination. Upon rejection by the company of Alexander's claims, an *arbitration* hearing was held, prior to which Alexander also filed a complaint with the Colorado Civil Rights Commission, which referred it to the federal Equal Employment Opportunity Commission (EEOC). The arbitrator ruled that Alexander's discharge was for *good cause* and sustained his discharge. Following the EEOC's subsequent dismissal of Alexander's discrimination complaint, he sued for race discrimination in a federal District Court. The District Court granted the company's motion for summary judgment, holding that Alexander was bound by the prior arbitral decision and had no right to sue under Title VII. The Court of Appeals affirmed. The Supreme Court granted Alexander's *writ of certiorari.*

Issue: Is the grievance/arbitration procedure in the collective bargaining agreement between Alexander's labor union

and his employer the only remedy available to Alexander, who claimed he was a victim of illegal race discrimination?

Decision: The doctrine of *election of remedies* was considered by the Court to be inapplicable in the present context, which involved statutory rights distinctly separate from the employee's contractual rights, regardless of the fact that violation of both rights may have resulted from the same fact pattern. By merely resorting to the arbitration procedure, Alexander did not automatically waive his cause of action under Title VII; the rights conferred in fact cannot be prospectively waived. Such an implied waiver formed no part of the collective bargaining process. The arbitrator's authority was confined to resolution of questions of contractual rights, regardless of whether they resembled or even duplicated Title VII rights. In instituting a Title VII action, the employee was not seeking review of the arbitrator's decision and thus getting "two strings to his bow when the employer has only one," (to quote the trial judge) but was asserting a right independent of the arbitration process that the statute gives to all employees who are victims of discriminatory employment practices, whether or not they belong to a union.

«

4. Procedural History

7. Reasoning

5. Issue

6. Decision (or Answer)

1. **Case Name:** The case name need not include a complete list of all the plaintiffs and defendants, where multiple parties were involved. Typically, a decision is identified by the last name of the first-named plaintiff and the last name of the first-named defendant. Organizations which are parties should be identified by their full names, except that terms such as "Corporation" may be abbreviated, for instance as "Corp."

   For the *Alexander* case presented here, the case name would be *Alexander v. Gardner-Denver Company.*

2. **Case Citation:** Published decisions are identified by the reporters in which they are published. Typical citations begin with the volume number, followed by the name of the reporter, and then the page number where the case begins. Following this information will be the date of the decision in parentheses.

   For example, in the *Alexander v. Gardner-Denver Company* case, the citation is 415 U.S. 36 (1974). This tells the reader that the case appears in volume 415 of the official Supreme Court reporter, starting on page 36, and that the Court announced this decision in 1974.

   Citations come in a dizzying variety of forms. They all have one thing in common: A proper citation provides sufficient information for the reader to know the precise place where the full text can be located, the court which issued the decision, and the date it was announced. The "Bible" of case citations is *The Bluebook: A Uniform System of Citation*, published by the editors of the *Harvard Law Review.* It is now available online at https://www.legalbluebook.com.

3. **Facts:** Here a concise summary of the main facts of the case are presented in no more than a couple of paragraphs. Only facts relevant and material to the court's decision should be included.

   In the *Alexander* case, the full legal case has been summarized into relevant facts for you already.

4. **Procedural History:** In a sentence or two the briefer presents an explanation of how the case made its way to the appeals court in which it is now under consideration.

   In the *Alexander* case, the history has been summarized for you already.

5. **Issue:** A critical portion of the brief, this section identifies the precise question that *this* court is being asked to answer. The issue is usually expressed in the form of a question. That question seldom is the ultimate question in the underlying case, such as whether the defendant in a criminal case is guilty, or whether the plaintiff in a civil suit is entitled to damages. Rather the issue before the appellate court is usually a more narrow legal point that is an essential step toward enabling the trial judge or jury to reach a correct decision on the ultimate issues of the lawsuit. The issue on appeal is almost always a question of law, not fact.

   For example, in *Alexander v. Gardner Denver Company*, the U.S. Supreme Court was required to tell the lower federal courts whether a union member (Alexander) was required to submit his discrimination case to a labor arbitrator exclusively or whether he could also pursue his rights under the federal antidiscrimination statutes. The Court was not asked to decide the ultimate issue of whether or not the plaintiff had meritorious discrimination claim.

6. **Decision (or Answer):** Here, in a very few words, the briefer records how the court answered the question that was posed to it.

7. **Reasoning:** The analysis underlying the court's decision should be summarized here. As with the "Facts," this analysis should be no more than a couple of paragraphs in length.

8. **Observations:** This optional section is where the briefer may choose to add his or her own reaction to the court's opinion, some notes on decisions which closely agree or sharply disagree with the outcome of the case, or any other observations that he or she thinks may be useful when it comes time to write the research paper, memorandum of law, or other work product at the end of this research product.

PART 1

COMMON-LAW EMPLOYMENT ISSUES

First the Forest, Then the Trees: An Overview of Employment and Labor Law

Employment and labor are, arguably, as old as recorded history. In the New Testament's parable of the laborers in the vineyard, we find those workers who began picking grapes at dawn complaining to the owner because those he hired at noon received the exact same wage as they got. "What business is it of yours, if I choose to be generous?" he inquires rhetorically.

The parable is a rare recorded case of employer largesse. More often workers' complaints have involved too little pay, lack of benefits, unreasonably long hours, or unsafe workplace conditions. When such complaints have typically been addressed, it was by the workers themselves or the government.

For example, in the Middle Ages—when many Europeans believed the earth was flat—craftsmen formed guilds according to their respective trades. But by the 14th century, as one famous historian has explained, "Once united by a common craft, the guild masters, journeymen, and apprentices had spread apart into entrepreneurs and hired hands divided by class hatred. The guild was now a corporation in which the workers had no voice."[1] Dissatisfaction led to working-class revolts, which in turn resulted in brutal reprisals by the upper classes.[2]

The Black Death, a plague that first decimated Europe's population in the mid-14th century, actually benefited those workers who survived. The labor shortage encouraged demands for higher wages and better conditions. Rulers' responses were swift and severe. In 1339, Britain's king issued a proclamation that required everyone to accept the same wages that they had received two years earlier. The new labor law also established stiff penalties for refusing to work, for leaving a job in search of higher pay, and for an offer of higher wages by an employer. Parliament reissued the proclamation as the Statute of Laborers in 1351, not only denouncing workers who had the temerity to demand higher wages, but especially decrying those who chose "rather to beg in idleness than to earn their bread in labor."[3]

The Industrial Revolution in 19th-century England and America witnessed the rise of the **employment-at-will** doctrine in the **common law**. At-will employment—covered in depth in Chapter 2—meant, in theory, that either the employer or the worker could terminate their

employment-at-will
both the employee and the employer are free to unilaterally terminate the relationship at any time and for any legally permissible reason, or for no reason at all

common law
judge-made law, as opposed to statutes and ordinances enacted by legislative bodies

---

[1] Barbara W. Tuchman, *A Distant Mirror: The Calamitous 14th Century* (New York: Alfred A. Knopf, 1978), p. 39.

[2] *Ibid.*, pp. 383–91.

[3] *Ibid.*, pp. 125–26.

relationship at any time for any reason. In reality, the employers had all the bargaining power; real negotiation of terms and conditions of employment was, for the most part, a myth.

To put the relationship more nearly into balance, workers banded together into labor unions. The reaction of the American judiciary, drawn almost exclusively from the upper, propertied class, was negative. Early court cases concluded that labor organizations were criminal conspiracies.[4]

Labor, however, persisted. The unions' first breakthrough came in 1842, when the Supreme Judicial Court of Massachusetts held that unionized workers could be indicted only if either their means or their ends were illegal, and that the "tendency" of organized labor to diminish the employer's gains and profits was not in itself a crime.[5] Progress was slow but more or less steady thereafter, highlighted by such federal legislation as the Federal Employers Liability Act (1908) and the Railway Labor Act (1926), which allowed for alternative methods of dispute resolution, first in the railroad, and later in the airline industry.

1-1   The New Deal and the Rise of the Modern American Union

Still, nearly a century would elapse before the Great Depression and the subsequent New Deal of President Franklin D. Roosevelt resulted in the enactment of the major federal employment and labor laws, which govern the fundamental features of the employment relationship and unionization to this very day. These statutes include:

- The Social Security Act (1935), which provides modest pensions to retired workers
- The National Labor Relations Act (1935) (NLRA), which sets the ground rules for the give and take between labor unions and corporate managers
- The Walsh-Healy Act (1936), the first of several statutes to set the terms and conditions of employment to be provided by government contractors
- The Merchant Marine (Jones) Act (1936), which provides remedies for injured sailors
- The Fair Labor Standards Act (1938), which sets minimum wages, mandates overtime pay, and regulates child labor

Before these statutes could revolutionize the American workplace, FDR's New Deal had to survive constitutional challenge in the Supreme Court. In the early years of Roosevelt's presidency (1933–1936) the justices repeatedly refused to enforce New Deal legislation, consistently declaring the new laws unconstitutional. Only after FDR threatened to "pack" the court with new appointments from the ranks of his New Deal Democrats did the high court reverse course and declare a piece of labor legislation to be constitutionally legitimate.

In *West Coast Hotel Company v. Parrish*,[6] the challenged law was actually a state statute. Elsie Parrish, a chambermaid working at the Cascadian Hotel in Wenatchee, Washington (owned by the West Coast Hotel Company), sued her employer for the difference between what she was being paid and the $14.50 per 48-hour work week mandated by the state's Industrial Welfare Committee and the Supervisor of Women in Industry, pursuant to a state

---

[4] See, e.g., *Commonwealth v. Pullis*, 3 Commons & Gilmore (Philadelphia Mayor's Court 1806).

[5] *Commonwealth v. Hunt*, 44 Mass. (4 Met.) 111 (1842).

[6] 300 U.S. 379 (1937).

law. The trial court held for the defendant. The Washington Supreme Court, taking the case on a direct appeal, reversed the trial court and found in favor of Mrs. Parrish. The hotel appealed to the U.S. Supreme Court. In a decision that clever pundits labeled "the switch in time that saved the nine" (because it forestalled the president's court-packing plan), the justices asked, "What can be closer to the public interest than the health of women and their protection from unscrupulous and overreaching employers? And if the protection of women is a legitimate end of the exercise of state power, how can it be said that the requirement of the payment of a minimum wage fairly fixed in order to meet the very necessities of existence is not an admissible means to that end?"

The Court majority answered those questions by stating that the legislature of the state was clearly entitled to consider the situation of women in employment, that they were in the class receiving the least pay, that their bargaining power was relatively weak, and that they were the ready victims of those who would take advantage of their necessitous circumstances. Furthermore, continued the Court, the legislature was entitled to adopt measures to reduce the evils of what was known as "the sweating system," which referred to the exploiting of workers at wages so low as to be insufficient to meet the bare cost of living. Deferring to the judgment of the state lawmakers, the Court majority conceded that the legislature had the right to consider that its minimum wage requirements would be an important component of its policy of protecting these highly vulnerable workers. The opinion pointed to the prevalence of similar laws in a growing number of states as evidence of a broadening national consensus that (1) sweatshops were evil and (2) these kinds of laws significantly contributed to their eradication.

While this ruling was directly applicable only to state minimum wage laws—and arguably, only to such statutes as they applied to women—the broader impact was essentially to sweep away judicial opposition to the flood of legislation at both federal and state levels, which was overwhelmingly favorable to workers and their labor organizations. One result was a rush by workers to join labor unions, which organized with legal impunity. Corporations that resisted were charged with unfair labor practices under the NLRA— covered in depth in Part 3—and compelled by the National Labor Relations Board (NLRB) to recognize and bargain with organized labor.

Concept *Summary* 1.1

LABOR DISPUTES ARE AS OLD AS RECORDED HISTORY

1-2   The Post-War Decline of Organized Labor

Several significant issues and trends combined to cause the gradual decline of organized labor in America from its peak in the 1950s, when one in three private-sector employees belonged to a union, to only about seven out of every 100 eligible private-sector workers being unionized in 2010.[7]

Several factors contributed to this precipitous decline. First, many policy makers, especially in the conservative camp, became concerned about labor leaders' abuse of power. One of the worst examples occurred when John L. Lewis, president of the United Mine Workers, violated a "gentlemen's agreement" with the Roosevelt administration during World War II. Sullivan called a strike at the height of the war, making his miners look unpatriotic and selfish in the public eye. Critics, especially politicians aligned with "Big Business," believed the combined American Federation of Labor/Congress of Industrial Organizations (AFL-CIO) had grown to be far too potent. The upshot in 1947 was the Taft-Hartley Act, a federal statute that enacted unfair labor practices for which unions might be punished, such as coercing workers to join against their will.

As the Cold War developed between the U.S. and the U.S.S.R., perceived communist influences in some large and powerful unions, notably the International Longshoremen's Association, placed organized labor in the gun sights of such so-called Red Hunters as the infamous Senator Joseph McCarthy. Similarly, alleged organized-crime ties of other huge unions, especially Jimmy Hoffa's Teamsters, attracted the attention of politicians, ranging from Senator Estes Kefauver in the 1950s to Attorney General Robert F. Kennedy in the early 1960s.

globalization
the integration of national economies into a worldwide economy, due to trade, investment, migration, and information technology

Most destructive of all to organized labor, however, has been **globalization**. American industry's stranglehold on major manufacturing sectors, such as autos and steel, was successfully challenged immediately after World War II—first by a reconstructed Japan, then subsequently by many other Asian and European competitors. The manufacturing sector was the bedrock of unionism. When it declined, organized labor inevitably followed. As in the Middle Ages, the earth is once again flat.[8]

individual employee rights
rights enjoyed by workers as individuals, as against collective rights secured by unionization; sources are statutes and court decisions

Meanwhile, among the many political and social trends of the 1960s was the rise of **individual employee rights**. Leading the way was the Civil Rights Act of 1964. Title VII[9]—covered in detail in Part 2—declared employment discrimination illegal if based on race, sex, religion, or any of several other "protected categories." Other laws and court decisions followed in relatively quick succession, seemingly in inverse proportion to the steady decline of collective bargaining under the auspices of organized labor. Other major examples of individual employee rights laws and legal concepts include the Age Discrimination in Employment Act (1967) and the generalized recognition of theories of wrongful discharge (see Chapter 2) and related employment-related torts (see Chapter 3) in American common law.

These new laws and common-law legal theories have often supplanted labor unions as the main source of legal protection for American workers. In fact, sometimes they actually have conflicted with the legal remedies available to workers under

---

[7] Jerry White, "US trade union membership at lowest level in more than a century," *World Socialist Web Site*, February 3, 2010, available at http://www.wsws.org/en/articles/2010/02/unio-f03.html.

[8] See Thomas L. Friedman, *The World Is Flat: A Brief History of the Twenty-First Century* (New York: Farrar, Strauss and Giroux, 2005).

[9] 42 U.S.C. Sec. 2000e *et seq.*

collective bargaining agreements. For example, under Title VII, an employee alleging illegal discrimination has the right to file a complaint with the Equal Employment Opportunity Commission (EEOC). If he or she is a union member, that same employee has not only a right but an obligation to pursue any such wrong as a grievance under the collective agreement with his or her employer, apparently as the exclusive remedy.

In *Alexander v. Gardner-Denver Company*, 415 U.S. 36 (1974), the Supreme Court was called upon to reconcile this clash between individual and collective worker rights within a decade of Title VII's enactment. The employer wanted to limit the aggrieved employee's remedy to the grievance/arbitration procedures in the collective bargaining agreement that Gardner-Denver had with Alexander's union. More to the point, the company wanted to cut off Alexander's access to Title VII. The Court refused to allow this to happen, holding that the doctrine of **election of remedies** was inapplicable in the present context, which involved statutory rights distinctly separate from the employees' collective contractual rights, regardless of the fact that violation of both rights may have resulted from the same fact pattern. By merely resorting to the arbitration procedure, Alexander did not automatically waive his cause of action under Title VII; the rights conferred in fact could not be prospectively waived. Such an implied waiver formed no part of the collective bargaining process. The arbitrator's authority was confined to resolution of questions of contractual rights, regardless of whether they resembled or even duplicated Title VII rights. It would take 35 years for the high court to reverse this rule in two stages.

election of remedies
the requirement to
choose one out of two
or more means afforded
under the law for the
redress of an injury
to the exclusion of the
other(s)

In *Alexander*, the Supreme Court established a critical distinction between individual and collective employee rights. Perhaps it was not the Court's intention, but the decision had the effect of further undermining the rapidly eroding influence of labor unions in the American workplace. If union members are able to effectively pursue their rights outside of the labor–management relationship, then why should they bother to pay dues to a labor organization?

1-3   The Resurrection of the Arbitration Remedy

The proliferation of individual employee rights soon swamped the state and federal courts. By the 1980s, for example, employment law cases dominated the federal District Court dockets across the country. In their heyday, labor unions diverted much of this court business into their grievance/arbitration processes. The decline of organized labor combined with the Supreme Court's ruling that individual rights—at least those derived from antidiscrimination, **whistleblower**, and other such statutes—could not be automatically ceded to the labor–management dispute-resolution process contributed significantly to the litigation tsunami.

whistleblower
an employee who
reports or attempts
to report employer
wrongdoing or actions
threatening public
health or safety to
government authorities

In 1991, in *Gilmer v. Interstate/Johnson Lane Corporation*, the Supreme Court revisited the issue of whether an agreement to arbitrate employment disputes could ever trump an employee's right to pursue his or her claims under a federal statute that enabled the aggrieved employee to file a complaint with an agency and/or in court. The case involved a standard employment contract that almost all employees in the financial-services industry are required to sign.

Gilmer's impact upon the federal common law was profound. The U.S. trial and appellate courts extended its reach to virtually all types of employment discrimination cases. Simultaneously, federal agencies also embraced alternative dispute resolution (ADR).

» CASE 1.1

GILMER V. INTERSTATE/JOHNSON LANE CORPORATION
500 U.S. 20 (1991)

Facts: Gilmer was required by his employer to register as a securities representative with, among others, the New York Stock Exchange (NYSE). His registration application contained an agreement to arbitrate when required to by NYSE rules. NYSE Rule 347 provided for arbitration of any controversy arising out of a registered representative's employment or termination of employment. The company terminated Gilmer's employment at age 62. He filed a charge with the EEOC and brought suit in the District Court, alleging that he had been discharged in violation of the Age Discrimination in Employment Act of 1967 (ADEA). The company moved to compel arbitration, relying on the agreement in Gilmer's registration application. The court denied the company's motion, based on *Alexander v. Gardner-Denver Co.* In *Alexander*, the court held that an employee's suit under Title VII of the Civil Rights Act of 1964 was not foreclosed by the prior submission of his claim to arbitration under the terms of a collective bargaining agreement. It concluded that Congress intended to protect ADEA claimants from a waiver of the judicial forum. The Court of Appeals reversed the decision, and the company took the case to the Supreme Court, which agreed to hear it.

Issue: Should the rule of *Alexander v. Gardner-Denver Co.* apply to an arbitration provision in an individual contract as opposed to a collective bargaining contract?

Decision: In the opinion, which took many knowledgeable observers by surprise, the Court said it saw no inconsistency between the important social policies furthered by the ADEA and enforcing agreements to arbitrate age-discrimination claims. While arbitration focuses on specific disputes between the parties involved, so too does judicial resolution of claims. Just the same, both can further broader social purposes, and with equal force. The justices pointed out that various other laws, including antitrust and securities laws and the civil provisions of the **Racketeer Influenced and Corrupt Organizations Act (RICO)**, are designed to advance equally important public policies, and yet claims under them are considered by Congress to be appropriate for arbitration. Nor were the majority of justices persuaded that allowing arbitration would somehow undermine the EEOC's role in ADEA enforcement, because an ADEA claimant remained free under the Court's holding to file an EEOC charge. However, claimants were precluded from instituting suit— not an insignificant limit on the rights they would otherwise have had under the statute. This limitation didn't trouble the Court, primarily because it perceived that the ADEA already reflected a flexible approach to claims resolution, such as by permitting the EEOC to pursue informal resolution methods. This suggested to the justices that out-of-court dispute resolution is consistent with the statutory scheme, and that arbitration is consistent with Congress's grant of concurrent jurisdiction over ADEA claims to state and federal courts.

Racketeer Influenced and Corrupt Organizations Act (RICO)
a federal law designed to criminally penalize those that engage in illegal activities as part of an ongoing criminal organization (e.g., the Mafia)

THE **WORKING** LAW

A t the close of 2014, the EEOC sent a sharp signal that the outer limits of deferral to arbitration had been reached and that, indeed, the trend required a strong push in the opposite direction. On September 22, 2014, the discrimination watchdog issued the following press release:

Restaurant Franchiser Unlawfully Barred New Hires from Filing Discrimination Charges, Federal Agency Charges

MIAMI - Doherty Enterprises, Inc., a regional company that owns and operates over 140 franchise restaurants, including Applebee's and Panera Bread locations scattered throughout Florida, Georgia, New Jersey and New York, unlawfully violated its employees' right to file charges of discrimination with the Equal Employment Opportunity Commission (EEOC), the federal agency charged in a lawsuit filed yesterday.

According to the EEOC, Doherty requires each prospective employee to sign a mandatory arbitration agreement as a condition of employment. The agreement mandates that all employment-related claims—which would otherwise allow resort to the EEOC—shall be submitted to and determined exclusively by binding arbitration. The agreement interferes with employees' rights to file discrimination charges, the agency says.

Interfering with these employee rights violates Section 707 of Title VII of the Civil Rights Act of 1964, which prohibits employer conduct that constitutes a pattern or practice of resistance to the rights protected by Title VII. Section 707 permits the EEOC to seek immediate relief without the same presuit administrative process that is required under Section 706 of Title VII, and does not require that the agency's suit arise from a discrimination charge.

The EEOC filed suit in the U.S. District Court for the Southern District of Florida (*EEOC v. Doherty Enterprises, Inc.*, Civil Action No. 9:14-cv-81184-KAM). The suit has been assigned to U.S. District Judge Kenneth A. Marra.

"Employee communication with the EEOC is integral to the agency's mission of eradicating employment discrimination," explained EEOC Regional Attorney Robert E. Weisberg. "When an employer forces all complaints about employment discrimination into confidential arbitration, it shields itself from federal oversight of its employment practices. This practice violates the law, and the EEOC will take action to deter further use of these types of overly broad arbitration agreements."

EEOC District Director Malcolm Medley added, "Preserving access to the legal system is one of the EEOC's six strategic enforcement priorities adopted in its Strategic Enforcement Plan. When an employer seeks to deter people from exercising their federally protected Title VII rights, the EEOC is uniquely situated to seek an end to such unlawful practices, and to ensure the necessary safeguards are in place to allow employees to participate in the EEOC's charge filing process."[10]

Supreme Court Allows Arbitration Clause in Labor Contract to Trump

The EEOC's 2014 policy pronouncement in *Doherty Enterprises* appears to pose a challenge to the Supreme Court's reconsideration of *Alexander* five years earlier. On April 1, 2009, by a vote of 5–4, the Court held that where a provision of a collective bargaining agreement clearly and unmistakably requires union members to arbitrate ADEA claims, the federal courts will enforce this provision. Writing in dissent, Justice Stevens complained, "Notwithstanding the absence of change in any relevant statutory provision, the Court has recently retreated from, and in some cases reversed, prior decisions based on its changed view of the merits of arbitration.… [T]he Court in *Gardner-Denver* held that a clause of a collective bargaining agreement (CBA) requiring arbitration of discrimination claims could not waive an employee's right to a judicial forum for statutory claims.… Today the majority's preference for arbitration again leads it to disregard our precedent."[11]

However, in 2012, the NLRB, dominated by Obama appointees, signaled that they intended to interpret the *14 Penn Plaza* holding very narrowly. Thus, at least so long as a

---

[10] "EEOC Sues Doherty Enterprises over Mandatory Arbitration Agreement," *JDSUPRA Business Advisor*, September 22, 2014, available at http://www.jdsupra.com/legalnews/eeoc-sues-doherty-enterprises-over-manda-72282.

[11] *14 Penn Plaza LL.C. v. Pyett*, 556 U.S. 247, 129 S. Ct. 1456 (2009) is excerpted and discussed in greater depth in Chapter 9.

Democrat occupies the White House (which may be no more than another year and a half as this edition goes to press), the EEOC and NLRB appear to be of one mind where substitution of private ADR remedies for statutory rights and recourse to federal courts and agencies are concerned. This view is essentially opposed to that of the five conservative justices who made up the majority view in *Pyett*.

>> CASE 1.2

IN RE D. R. HORTON, INC.
357 NLRB No. 184 (2012)

Facts: D. R. Horton, Inc. is a homebuilder with operations in more than 20 states. In January 2006, the company began to require on a corporate-wide basis that each new and current employee execute a "Mutual Arbitration Agreement" (MAA) as a condition of employment. The MAA provides in relevant part:

> that all disputes and claims relating to the employee's employment with Respondent (with exceptions not pertinent here) will be determined exclusively by final and binding arbitration, that the arbitrator "may hear only Employee's individual claims" "will not have the authority to consolidate the claims of other employees" and "does not have authority to fashion a proceeding as a class or collective action or to award relief to a group or class of employees in one arbitration proceeding", and that the signatory employee waives "the right to file a lawsuit or other civil proceeding relating to Employee's employment with the Company" and "the right to resolve employment-related disputes in a proceeding before a judge or jury."

In sum, pursuant to the MAA, all employment-related disputes must be resolved through individual arbitration, and the right to a judicial forum is waived. Stated otherwise, employees are required to agree, as a condition of employment, that they will not pursue class or collective litigation of claims in any forum, arbitral or judicial.

Charging party Michael Cuda was employed by the firm as a superintendent from July 2005 to April 2006. Cuda's continued employment was conditioned on his signing the MAA, which he did. In 2008, his attorney, Richard Celler, notified Horton that his firm had been retained to represent Cuda and a nationwide class of similarly situated superintendents. Celler asserted that

respondent Horton was misclassifying its superintendents as exempt from the protections of the Fair Labor Standards Act (FLSA), and he gave notice of intent to initiate arbitration. The respondent's counsel replied that Celler had failed to give an effective notice of intent to arbitrate, citing the language in the MAA that bars arbitration of collective claims.

Cuda filed an unfair labor practice charge, and the general counsel issued a complaint alleging that the respondent violated Section 8(a)(1) by maintaining the MAA provision stating that the arbitrator "may hear only Employee's individual claims and does not have the authority to fashion a proceeding as a class or collective action or to award relief to a group or class of employees in one arbitration proceeding." The complaint further alleged that the respondent violated Sections 8(a)(4) and (1) by maintaining arbitration agreements requiring employees, as a condition of employment, "to submit all employment related disputes and claims to arbitration. thus interfering with employee access to the [NLRB]."

Issue: In light of *Gilmer* and *14 Penn Plaza*, can an arbitration clause cut off employees' collective access to the rights and remedies of the NLRA?

Decision: The board panel found that a class action constitutes protected concerted activity. Therefore, the arbitration clause violated the NLRA. However, the panel was careful to emphasize "the limits of our holding and its basis. Only a small percentage of arbitration agreements are potentially implicated by the holding in this case. First, only agreements applicable to 'employees' as defined in the NLRA even potentially implicate Section 7 rights."

Concept *Summary* 1.2

DECLINE OF LABOR UNIONS AND RISE OF INDIVIDUAL RIGHTS

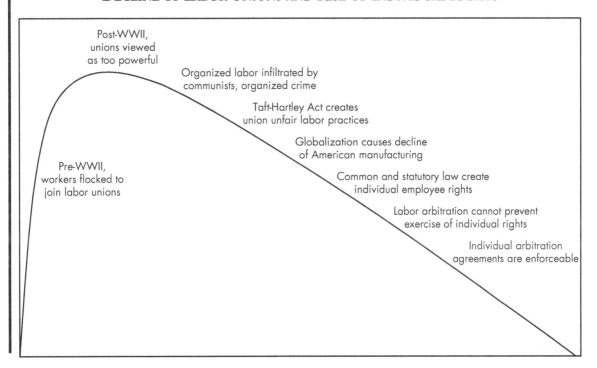

Post-WWII,
unions viewed
as too powerful

Organized labor infiltrated by
communists, organized crime

Taft-Hartley Act creates
union unfair labor practices

Globalization causes decline
of American manufacturing

Pre-WWII,
workers flocked to
join labor unions

Common and statutory law create
individual employee rights

Labor arbitration cannot prevent
exercise of individual rights

Individual arbitration
agreements are enforceable

1-4 Employee Health, Safety, and Welfare

In the preceding section, we charted a sort of "bell curve" in the rise and fall of labor unions. American workers first banded together to increase their bargaining power and improve their working and living conditions. They then turned (or were driven) increasingly away from unions and toward a panoply of individual rights, ranging from statutory prohibitions of employment discrimination to common-law wrongful discharge decisions, all of which is discussed in detail in the chapters that follow.

Also covered thoroughly in their own sections of this text are the major aspects of employee health, safety, and welfare, as they are embodied in our federal and state laws. These include:

- The federal Occupational Safety and Health Act (OSHA) and its many state-law counterparts

- Workers' compensation and unemployment insurance statutes, which are a part of virtually every state's statutory safety net for injured and out-of-work workers

- The U.S. Social Security system, which includes both pensions and support payments for permanently disabled workers who are still too young to retire

- The Employee Retirement Income Security Act (ERISA), which is intended to protect and preserve employee pensions
- The Family and Medical Leave Act (FMLA) and its numerous state and local counterparts, which increasingly require employers to grant leaves of absence (in some states, even paid leaves) for an ever-increasing range of personal issues
- Worker Adjustment and Retraining Notification (WARN) acts, both federal and state, which are aimed at letting employees know when a plant closing or mass layoff is in the offing
- The Patient Protection and Affordable Care Act (PPACA), commonly called Obamacare after the president during whose first term it was enacted. This act dramatically revised the American health care system, notably by mandating that all Americans buy health insurance or pay a tax penalty.

As extensive as this web of federal, state, and local laws may seem to be, some notable gaps, which are very troubling to many people, remain in the American labor and employment law system. No national statute requires private employers to provide their employees with either health insurance or a pension plan, for example (although Obamacare ensures that all Americans now have access to some form of health insurance).

THE **WORKING** LAW

From 2011 to 2015 Public-Employee Labor Unions, the Remaining Strongholds of Labor's Power in the United States, Have Been Targeted by Conservative Governors, Legislators, and the U.S. Supreme Court

After the November 2010 mid-term elections, the switch from liberal Democrats to conservative Republicans in many governors' mansions saw several states move toward ending collective bargaining by public employees. This initiative, most visible and confrontational in Wisconsin and Ohio, led the American Federation of State, County and Municipal Employees (AFSCME) to issue the following comment: "The radical proposals by the governors in Wisconsin and Ohio would not just gut public services and jobs, they would take away the rights of workers to collectively bargain and the basic freedom to join a union—effectively eliminating public employee unions. The goals of these efforts are simple: reduce the tax bills of the ultra-rich, privatize public services and deflect blame away from corporations for the reckless behavior that caused the economy to tank."[12]

The Wisconsin Case
On March 11, 2011, Wisconsin's governor Scott Walker signed the 2011 Wisconsin Act 10, a controversial bill that limits the collective bargaining power of the state's public employees (except for firefighters, police, and State Patrol troopers) and requires state employees to pay more for their health care and pensions. The new law is labeled "An Act relating to: state finances, collective bargaining for public employees, compensation and fringe benefits of public employees, the state civil service system, the Medical Assistance program."

[12] AFSCME, http://www.afscme.org.

Simultaneously canceling 1,500 scheduled public employee layoffs, Governor Walker remarked, "While tough budget choices certainly still lie ahead, both state and local units of government will not have to do any mass layoffs or direct service reductions because of the reforms contained in the budget repair bill. The reforms contained in this legislation, which require modest health care and pension contributions from all public employees, will help put Wisconsin on a path to fiscal sustainability."

On March 18, 2011, Dane County Circuit judge Maryann Sumi granted a restraining order, temporarily preventing the Wisconsin secretary of state from publishing the law, which remained the subject of bitter controversy and litigation as this edition went to press.

On June 14, 2011, the Supreme Court ordered the reinstatement of Governor Walker's bill. The Court overruled the restraining order granted by Sumi, finding that the legislature did not violate the Wisconsin Constitution; the committee of lawmakers was not subject to the state's open meetings law and therefore did not violate that law when it approved the governor's bill and allowed the Senate to take it up. The Court ruled that Sumi's ruling exceeded her jurisdiction and was *void ab initio*, or "invalid from the outset."

While Republicans praised the Court's decision, Democrats decried it for the Court's finding that lawmakers do not have to follow the open meetings law, as the committee did not give the required 24-hour notice prior to the meeting, essentially saying that the legislature is above the law.

As a result of the new bill, the city projected savings of at least $25 million a year—and as much as $36 million in 2012—from health care benefit changes it didn't have to negotiate with unions. Still, in March 2012 union supporters from around the world gathered in Wisconsin to rally for the governor's recall, and a record number of educators retired after the bill was signed into law. The Wisconsin state pension fund received 18,780 retirement applications from state and local governments and school districts in 2011, representing a 79 percent increase from the average in each of the previous seven years.

Less than a year later, the governor was faced with an unprecedented recall election. On March 30, 2012, the state's election commission ruled that the governor's adversaries had met the requirements for the recall vote, which was scheduled for June 2012. Come June, the voters allowed the governor to remain in office.

Meanwhile, the legal challenge to the law continued. On April 25, 2013, a Wisconsin appellate court held the state in contempt of the trial court's partial summary judgment in favor of the union and urged the state's supreme court to review the case.[13]

Responding to the appellate court's plea, the Wisconsin Supreme Court reviewed the case. In a November 2013 opinion, the high court held that the appellate court's contempt order impermissibly interfered with the Supreme Court's own jurisdiction. Opined the majority, "We are mindful of the pressures a circuit court can face from aggressive litigation in high-profile cases. However, when the appeal of a circuit court's prior decision is pending before this court, the circuit court must take care to avoid actions that may interfere with the pending appeal. Once an appeal had been perfected, the circuit court should not have taken any action that significantly altered its judgment. Accordingly, in order to assure the orderly administration of justice in the pending appeal, we elect to apply our superintending authority and vacate the circuit court's contempt order."

---

[13] *Madison Teachers, Inc. v. Walker*, 2013 WL 1760805 (Wis. App. Apr. 25, 2013).

Two dissenting justices retorted, "The order today essentially serves as a backdoor ruling on a substantive matter with no mention of the far-reaching effects of its order. The order creates a springboard for future uncertainty and litigation. Three glaring questions stand out: how will this affect (1) the unions that did not follow WERC's rules, relying on the declaratory judgment, (2) the unions that *did* follow WERC's rules, and (3) the contempt proceeding pending at the court of appeals?... The court's order today fails to grapple with these unknown practical and legal implications. The per curiam reaches its result. Satisfied, the opinion foregoes any consideration of the collateral damage it has wrought."[14]

In December 2013, under the requirements of the new law, some 400 school-district unions—mostly representing teachers, but also some custodial staff—sought recertification. About 80 of these locals failed to secure majorities and therefore were decertified.

The Ohio Case

On March 3, 2011, the Ohio legislature passed a massive revision of the state's public sector collective bargaining act. The chief changes are described as follows:

1. S.B. 5 places significant restrictions on the subjects that can be brought to the bargaining table for public employees. Specifically, bargaining will not be permitted about health insurance benefits, employer assistance toward the employee share of pension contributions, privatization of public services, staffing levels, and certain other management rights.

2. S.B. 5 prohibits strikes by all public employees. Previously, Ohio collective bargaining law prohibited strikes only by police officers, firefighters, and other specified employees whose jobs have a direct impact on public safety. S.B. 5 makes it illegal for all public employees to strike and imposes extraordinary penalties if public employees do strike. Striking employees can be terminated and can be subjected to substantial financial penalties.

3. S.B. 5 establishes a new procedure for dispute resolution in bargaining. Under existing law, if contract negotiations reach a stalemate, the parties typically first have a hearing before a neutral "fact-finder." The fact-finder issues recommendations for resolving the dispute, but either the union or the employer can reject those recommendations. In the case of police, firefighters, and other specified safety employees who are prohibited from striking, the dispute then goes to a hearing before another neutral person whose decision is binding. The theory is that since those employees do not have the leverage of the threat of a strike, there has to be a neutral person to break the deadlock in the bargaining. S.B. 5 eliminates the binding arbitration step and prohibits all employees from striking. In cases where bargaining reaches a stalemate, the fact-finding proceeding will be followed first. If either party rejects the fact-finder's report, the employer's last best offer and the union's last best offer will be presented to the legislative body (i.e., City Council in the case of a municipality), which will conduct a public hearing and then vote to accept either the last best offer of the union or the last best offer of the employer.

---

[14] *Madison Teachers, Inc. v. Walker*, 351 Wis.2d 237, 839 N.W.2d 388 (2013).

On November 8, 2011, Ohioans voted to repeal the law, with 63 percent of voters against the bill, and a union-backed committee that formed to repeal the law raised approximately $30 million for the effort. This marked a major setback for Ohio governor John Kasich and those with similar initiatives.

However, not to be entirely dissuaded, in the wake of an NLRB regional director's ruling in early April 2014 that Northwestern University's Division I football players were employees eligible to organize and strike, the Ohio House of Representatives moved to enact legislation that would forestall any such organizing effort by student athletes at Ohio public universities, such as Ohio State.[15]

The Supreme Court Case

In June 2014, overruling a longstanding legal precedent, the U.S. Supreme Court held in yet another 5–4 split between conservative and liberal justices that public employees who do not choose to join the union that represents their bargaining unit need not necessarily pay their "fair share" contributions to that labor organization—even though they inevitably benefit from the favorable terms and conditions of employment won by the union. The decision[16] is widely viewed as a major setback to public-employee unions in states where membership is a matter of choice, rather than a requirement, for employees in the units that such unions represent.

ethical DILEMMA

IS PRESIDENT OBAMA'S "GO IT ALONE" STRATEGY CONSTITUTIONAL?

In 2010 the Republican Party won control of the House of Representatives in the mid-term national elections. In 2014, the GOP also (more narrowly) wrested control of the Senate from Democrats. These reversals of fortune presented President Obama with the prospect of being unable to win passage of any of his legislative agenda. Even achieving Senate consent for his presidential appointments became problematic. The president increasingly has sought to circumvent this congressional roadblock by "going it alone," that is, using his ability to issue executive orders to outmaneuver his opponents. The following are examples, most notably in the employment law arena:

- An April 2014 executive order forbids government contractors to discipline employees who discuss their wages and benefits among themselves. An accompanying memorandum explains that the order is intended to assist female workers, especially women of color, to close the gender gap in employee compensation.

---

[15] See Emily Rorris, "College Athletes Are Not Employees Under Ohio State Law," April 8, 2014, available at http://woub.org/2014/04/08/college-athletes-are-not-employees-under-ohio-state-law.

[16] *Harris v. Quinn*, 134 S.Ct. 2618 (2014).

- In July 2014, a second such order extended job-discrimination protection under federal government contracts to lesbian, gay, bisexual, and transgender (LGBT) employees.

Most controversial of all is the president's late 2014 executive actions on immigration, summarized by the U.S. Citizenship and Immigration Service as follows:

On November 20, 2014, the President announced a series of executive actions to crack down on illegal immigration at the border, prioritize deporting felons not families, and require certain undocumented immigrants to pass a criminal background check and pay taxes in order to temporarily stay in the U.S. without fear of deportation.

These initiatives include:

- *Expanding the population eligible for the Deferred Action for Childhood Arrivals (DACA) program to people of any current age who entered the United States before the age of 16 and lived in the United States continuously since January 1, 2010, and extending the period of DACA and work authorization from two years to three years*
- *Allowing parents of U.S. citizens and lawful permanent residents to request deferred action and employment authorization for three years, in a new Deferred Action for Parents of Americans and Lawful Permanent Residents program, provided they have lived in the United States continuously since January 1, 2010, and pass required background checks*
- *Expanding the use of provisional waivers of unlawful presence to include the spouses and sons and daughters of lawful permanent residents and the sons and daughters of U.S. citizens*
- *Modernizing, improving and clarifying immigrant and nonimmigrant visa programs to grow our economy and create jobs*
- *Promoting citizenship education and public awareness for lawful permanent residents and providing an option for naturalization applicants to use credit cards to pay the application fee.[17]*

Congressional opponents immediately saw this executive action as an attempt to cut them out of immigration-reform initiatives that all parties seem to agree are necessary. Many also saw it as a usurpation of congressional power. Most significantly, in December 2014 a 25-state coalition, led by Texas Attorney General (now governor) Greg Abbott, sued the president.

Attorney General Ken Paxton: President Obama's Amnesty for Illegal Immigrants Tramples on U.S. Constitution

AUSTIN – Texas Attorney General Ken Paxton today issued the following statement after Texas led a 25-state coalition at a hearing in U.S. District Court in Brownsville on the states' enforcement action against President Barack Obama's unilateral execution action on immigration:

"No individual is above the law, not even the President of the United States. President Obama's brazenly lawless action in November trampled on the U.S. Constitution. It is a clear violation of the Take Care Clause and federal statutory law. As the President himself had repeatedly admitted, he lacks the authority to impose this unilateral amnesty. The President's action makes clear that he has decided that the rule of law no longer applies to his Administration. President Obama's action violates the separation of powers and goes beyond prosecutorial discretion to the point of unilaterally creating and enforcing legislation—bypassing the people's duly-elected representatives in Congress entirely."

The multistate coalition led by Texas includes: Alabama, Arizona, Arkansas, Florida, Georgia, Idaho, Indiana, Kansas, Louisiana, Maine, Michigan, Mississippi, Montana, Nebraska, North Carolina, North Dakota, Ohio, Oklahoma, South Carolina, South Dakota, Tennessee, Utah, West Virginia, and Wisconsin.[18]

Undeterred, as this edition went to press, President Obama promised that 2015 would be another "Year of Action."

---

[17] "Executive Actions on Immigration," U.S. Citizenship and Immigration Services, available at http://www.uscis.gov/immigrationaction.

[18] "Attorney General Ken Paxton: President Obama's Amnesty for Illegal Immigrants Tramples on U.S. Constitution," The Attorney General of Texas, January 15, 2015, available at https://www.texasattorneygeneral.gov/oagnews/release.php?id=4928.

Concept *Summary* 1.3

EMPLOYEE HEALTH, SAFETY, AND WELFARE

- The web of federal and state laws includes:
  - OSHA
  - ERISA
  - FMLA
  - WARN
  - PPACA

- Gaps:
  - Pensions (protected but not mandated by ERISA)
  - Health care (if the Supreme Court invalidates the PPACA)

CHAPTER REVIEW

» Key Terms

employment-at-will	3	individual employee rights	6	Racketeer Influenced and Corrupt Organizations Act (RICO)	8
common law	3	election of remedies	7		
globalization	6	whistleblower	7		

» Summary

- Anglo-American labor and employment law can be traced back at least to 14th-century England. Laws tended to be heavily pro-employer well into the 19th century, when courts decriminalized labor unions and workers were able to combine and thus counterbalance corporate power.

- While some federal and state labor and employment reforms occurred prior to 1930, the first era of significant pro-employee legislation was the New Deal of the Great Depression. The National Labor Relations Act and the Fair Labor Standards Act were among the many statutes enacted by Congress during the 1930s. As a result, labor unions proliferated and prospered.

- After World War II, unions went into a slow but inexorable decline due to unfavorable legislation, the decline of American manufacturing, and the rise of individual employee rights. The Supreme Court decided in the 1970s that union grievance and arbitration procedures could not strip union members of their individual rights, especially where federal antidiscrimination laws were concerned.

- In the 1980s, as the federal courts were deluged with employment cases, the Supreme Court reversed course somewhat, endorsing the use of arbitration clauses in individual employment contracts. The Court in 2009 extended this endorsement to cover arbitration provisions in collective bargaining agreements, provided the parties expressly state their intent to preclude court and agency remedies.

- Employee health, safety, and welfare laws have proliferated at the federal and state levels, notably OSHA, ERISA, FMLA, and WARN. The PPACA (Obamacare) mandates the purchase of health insurance by all Americans by 2014 but may be invalidated by the Supreme Court. A gap remains in the area of mandatory pensions, which are not required under U.S. law.

» Problems

» Questions

1. Can you think of any public policy reasons why the courts developed the concept of employment-at-will in 19th-century America? In thinking about this question, consider that the U.S. Congress made huge land grants to companies willing to undertake the building of the nation's railroads. Can you see how both employment-at-will and public financial support of private enterprise might rise from the same underlying policy considerations?

2. How did new technologies combine with the arrival of millions of unskilled immigrants from Ireland, and later southern and eastern Europe, to impact the relative bargaining power of capitalists and workers in 19th-century America? What do you think were some reasons why the courts at first tended to support capital against labor? Why do you think that view gradually changed?

3. Imagine that the Supreme Court during the 1930s had staunchly refused to change its view and continued to declare almost all New Deal labor and employment laws to be unconstitutional, as the Court did at first. What do you think might have been some of the results of such intransigence on the Court's part?

4. Granting that organized labor has been guilty of abusing its power, and that when it was on top, some unions were aligned at times with the Mafia or with the American Communist Party, on balance do you think that labor unions are a blessing or a curse to American society?

5. Explain the Supreme Court's attempts in the *Alexander*, *Gilmer*, and *Pyett* cases to balance private arbitration with public legal remedies, such as government agency and court cases. Do you think the Court has struck the right balance? If not, do you favor the EEOC/NLRB approach? Why? Or do you believe that the policy considerations at stake here are trumped by political interests, that is, conservatives (represented by the five right-leaning Supreme Court justices) versus liberals (as embodied in the Obama administration's bureaucracy)?

6. One reason that U.S. workers, especially in the manufacturing sector, have a hard time competing with competitors in China, Southeast Asia, and India is wage differentials. And one reason (though not the only one) that labor costs are so much lower in some of America's major competitors, such as Japan and Korea, is that the governments of these countries provide substantial pensions for workers, so that the employers do not need to bear this expense. While providing such a pension (which would have to be significantly larger than current Social Security retirement benefits) would not address wage differentials between the U.S. and its many competitors in Asia and Latin America, this would help level the playing field with others, such as Japan, Korea, and perhaps some of the European Union nations. Should the U.S. Congress consider enacting such an expanded federal pension benefit? What are the pros and cons? Alternatively, should Uncle Sam *require* U.S. employers to establish employee pension plans? What are the pros and cons of doing this?

7. Putting aside partisan politics, what are the pros and cons of attempts by the governors and legislators in Ohio and Wisconsin to eliminate public employees' collective bargaining rights and decertify their labor unions? In answering this question, consider the current fiscal pressures under which many, if not most, states are suffering. Consider, too, that public employees enjoy protections under the 14th Amendment to the U.S. Constitution, which do not apply to private-sector employees.

8. Explain the roles that the courts play in creating and/or implementing labor and employment law. Do any of the roles you can identify amount to unreasonable intrusions into the roles of Congress and the state legislatures? Private enterprise?

9. Having considered and, hopefully, discussed the ethical dilemma posed by President Barack Obama's aggressive use of executive orders to achieve policy goals in the face of congressional roadblocks, do you feel that the separation of powers, so carefully crafted by the nation's founders in the U.S. Constitution, has become too much an impediment to progress in the "Flat Earth" environment in which America (and American workers) must compete? If so, how would you amend the Constitution to deal with this governmental gridlock?

10. Along these same lines, do you believe, as do many conservatives, that labor unions have outlived their usefulness in our "Flat Earth" economic environment? Or, alternatively, do you believe they still play an important role in the American democracy? If so, what would you do to encourage more American workers to rally to organized labor?

CHAPTER 2

Employment Contracts and Wrongful Discharge

This chapter and the one that follows are a survey of several major areas of the law where the federal and state legislatures have not fully populated the field with statutes and, therefore, the courts are still, by and large, sovereign. This type of law is referred to as common law. These include employment-at-will and wrongful discharge, as well as express and implied employment contracts.

2-1   Employment-at-Will and Its Exceptions

employment-at-will
both the employee and the employer are free to unilaterally terminate the relationship at any time and for any legally permissible reason, or for no reason at all

To appreciate how far the courts have come, it is necessary to look back to where they were just decades ago. In the 19th century, virtually every state court subscribed to the doctrine of **employment-at-will**. In its raw form, employment-at-will holds that an employee who has not been hired for an express period of time (say a year) can be fired at any time for any reason—or for no reason at all.

State and federal laws have narrowed this sweeping doctrine in many ways. The National Labor Relations Act (NLRA) forbids firing employees for engaging in protected concerted activities. Title VII forbids discharge on the basis of race, color, gender, creed, or national origin. The Age Discrimination in Employment Act (ADEA) protects older workers from discriminatory discharge. The Occupational Safety and Health Act (OSHA) makes it illegal to fire an employee in retaliation for filing a safety complaint.

Although employers may complain that employment regulation is pervasive, these laws leave broad areas of discretion for private-sector employers to discharge at-will employees. Although federal government workers are protected from such discrimination, there is no federal law that specifically outlaws workplace discrimination on the basis of sexual orientation in the private sector (i.e., the law allows an employer to discharge an employee if the company does not approve of an employee being homosexual or transgender). However, a growing number of states have enacted laws that prohibit sexual-orientation discrimination in both public- and private-sector jobs. Furthermore, some cities and counties prohibit discrimination on the basis of sexual orientation on a local level. And in 2014, President Obama issued an executive order forbidding LGBT discrimination by federal government contractors and subcontractors.

whistleblower
employee who reports
or attempts to report
employer wrongdoing
or actions threatening
public health or
safety to government
authorities

Whistleblowers—employees who bring intra-organizational wrongdoing to the attention of the authorities—have often been fired. This has frequently occurred in spite of ostensible legal protection for whistleblowers. However, as we shall see later in this chapter, much tougher protections were put into place by the U.S. Congress in the wake of one of the financial-industry debacles of the 21st century. Sometimes an employee gets fired simply because the boss does not like him or her. In such situations, the employee is not covered by any of the federal and state labor laws previously discussed. Should the employee be protected? If so, how?

Advocates of the employment-at-will doctrine defend it by pointing out that

- the employee is likewise free to sever the working relationship at any time and
- in a free market, the worker with sufficient bargaining power can demand an employment contract for a set period of time if so desired.

The trouble with the second point, in the view of most workers, is that as individuals they lack the bargaining power to command such a deal. This is one reason that in this age of globalization, labor unions continue to claim a role in securing workers' rights and job security, despite a plethora of federal and state statutes. Unless and until a federal statute creates a "just cause" requirement (discussed later in the chapter) for all employment terminations—something that is not even on the national agenda—many workers' best bet for job security is unionization. Indeed, making unionization easier is a priority item on the Obama administration's legislative agenda.

The first of these arguments is not so easily dismissed. If the employee is free to quit at any time with or without notice, why should the employer be denied the same discretion in discharging employees? One answer to this troublesome question—an answer given by a majority of the state courts at this time—is, "The firing of an at-will employee is permitted, except if the discharge undermines an important public policy."

2-2   Wrongful Discharge Based on Public Policy

**public policy
exception**
although the employee
is employed at-will,
termination is illegal if
a clear and significant
mandate of law
(statutory or common)
is damaged if the
firing is permitted to
stand unchallenged

The most commonly adopted exception to the pure employment-at-will rule (the employee can be fired at any time for any reason) is the **public policy exception**. If a statute creates a right or a duty for the employee, he or she may not be fired for exercising that legal right or fulfilling that legal duty. A widely adopted example is jury duty. The courts of most states agree that an employer cannot fire an employee who misses work to serve on a jury (provided, of course, that the employee gives the employer proper notice).

Many courts accepting this exception, however, have kept it narrow by holding that the right or duty must be clearly spelled out by statute. For instance, in the seminal case of *Geary v. United States Steel Corporation*,[1] the Pennsylvania Supreme Court upheld the dismissal of a lawsuit brought by a salesman who was fired for refusing to sell what he insisted to management was an unsafe product. The court noted, "There is no suggestion that he possessed any expert qualifications or that his duties extended to making judgments in matters of product safety." Most courts applying *Geary* have required the plaintiff-employee to point to some precise statutory right or duty before ruling the discharge wrongful.

---

[1] 456 Pa. 171, 319 A.2d 174, 115 L.R.R.M. (BNA) 4665, Pa., March 25, 1974.

Additionally, if the statute itself provides the employee with a cause of action, the courts are reluctant to recognize an alternative remedy in the form of a lawsuit for wrongful discharge. Thus, several Pennsylvania courts agree that an employee fired on the basis of gender or race discrimination in Pennsylvania has, as his or her exclusive state law remedy, the Pennsylvania Human Relations Act (PHRA), which requires that the employee initially seek redress with the commission created by that act. If the employee fails to file with the commission, thus losing the right of action under the PHRA, that person cannot come into court with the same grievance claiming wrongful discharge. Many other states' courts have reached similar conclusions regarding their states' antidiscrimination, workers' compensation, and work safety laws.

tort
a private or civil wrong or injury, caused by one party to another, either intentionally or negligently

By contrast, California courts are willing to entertain a wrongful-discharge **tort** claim that is grounded in a plaintiff's allegation of sexual harassment. The question tackled in a 2014 Court of Appeals decision was whether the burden of proof placed on the plaintiff should parallel the standard set out in discrimination cases.

CASE 2.1

MENDOZA V. WESTERN MEDICAL CENTER SANTA ANA
222 Cal. App. 4th 1334, 166 Cal.Rptr.3d 720 (2014)

A jury voted 9–3 to award $238,328 to plaintiff Romeo Mendoza, who claimed he was fired in retaliation for reporting allegations of sexual harassment. The court instructed the jury with the 2012 version of CACI No. 2430 and a special verdict form consistent therewith. Case law issued subsequent to the judgment leads us to conclude the court committed prejudicial error in doing so. We reject, however, defendants' contention that they are entitled to a defense judgment as a matter of law. Accordingly, we reverse the judgment for a new trial.

First hired as a staff nurse in 1990, Mendoza was employed at a hospital for more than 20 years. By 2010, Mendoza was an intermediate-level supervisor on the overnight shift and even filled in periodically as the person in charge at the hospital ("House Supervisor"). By all accounts, and as reflected by his long term of service and march up the ranks of authority, Mendoza was an excellent nurse. As defense counsel stated during a pretrial hearing, "we will stipulate he was a fine employee, he was performing his job competently, he received awards, he received commendations.... This is not a case where Mr. Mendoza was terminated because he performed his job in a substandard manner[,] because he made medical errors or anything of that nature."

In late October 2010, Mendoza reported to a House Supervisor that he was being sexually harassed by Del Erdmann, a per diem House Supervisor hired by defendants in April 2010. Whenever Mendoza and Erdmann worked the same shift, Erdmann was Mendoza's supervisor. After the complaint was passed up the chain of command, the matter was referred to the human resources department and an investigation ensued.

Mendoza and Erdmann are both gay men. The gist of Mendoza's accusation was that Erdmann, on numerous occasions, harassed Mendoza on the job with inappropriate comments (e.g., "I know you want me in your ass"), physical contact (e.g., Erdmann blowing air in Mendoza's ear), and lewd displays (e.g., Erdmann showing his genitals to Mendoza). According to Mendoza's testimony, this behavior began in August 2010 with words and culminated in October with Erdmann exposing himself. Mendoza denied he consented to Erdmann's behavior. Mendoza denied he had ever willingly engaged in flirtatious or lewd conduct with Erdmann. Mendoza told Erdmann to stop. Mendoza admitted that he violated defendants' policy by not immediately reporting Erdmann's behavior. Mendoza ultimately complained about Erdmann's conduct after a second incident in which Erdmann exposed himself and said, "I know you want this in your ass."

Erdmann, on the other hand, testified (and stated during defendants' investigation) that Mendoza consented to Erdmann's conduct and participated in other mutual interactions (e.g., Mendoza would bend over provocatively in front of Erdmann, Mendoza requested that Erdmann display his genitals, Mendoza assisted Erdmann in exposing his genitals). Indeed, Erdmann claimed he was a reluctant participant in conduct initiated by Mendoza. At both the investigation stage and at trial, Mendoza and Erdmann were the only two individuals identified with personal knowledge of what occurred between them at the hospital.

Mendoza's expert witness took issue with the quality of the investigation process. Defendants did not prepare a formal investigation plan. Defendants did not take written statements from Mendoza or Erdmann. Defendants did not immediately interview Erdmann, and suspended the investigation while Mendoza missed work for several weeks following a bicycle accident. When Mendoza returned to work, Mendoza and Erdmann were interviewed simultaneously rather than separately. Defendants did not interview anyone other than Mendoza and Erdmann (such as coworkers who might provide insights as to the credibility of the two men). The individual charged with completing the investigation was not a trained human resources employee, but was instead the supervisor of Erdmann and Mendoza. On cross-examination, Mendoza's expert conceded he was unaware of any specific information that would have been uncovered had defendants conducted a proper (in the expert's view) investigation. But a subsequent witness (an employee who conducted Erdmann's orientation) testified that he noticed Erdmann making sexual innuendos during the orientation.

Upon the completion of the investigation, defendants fired both Mendoza and Erdmann on December 14, 2010. The written notice of termination provided by defendants to Mendoza cited "unprofessional conduct" as the reason for Mendoza's dismissal. According to their testimony, the individuals participating in the decision concluded that both Mendoza and Erdmann were complicit in inappropriate and unprofessional behavior. There is a progressive discipline system in place at the hospital, subject to which an employee could be verbally warned, warned in writing, suspended, or terminated. Defendants claim to have considered but rejected a lesser punishment for Mendoza.

Mendoza sued defendants for wrongful termination in violation of public policy. Answering a special verdict form, the jury found defendants liable for wrongful termination in violation of public policy. The jury determined that Mendoza suffered $93,328 in past economic loss and $145,000 in past

emotional distress. The court subsequently entered judgment in favor of Mendoza and against defendants in the total amount of $238,328, plus interest from the date of judgment and costs. Defendants filed a timely notice of appeal.

Analysis

With one exception, the elements of Mendoza's claim are undisputed by the parties on appeal. Mendoza was discharged by his ex-employers, defendants, after Mendoza accused a supervisor, Erdmann, of sexual harassment. The public policy invoked by Mendoza supports his claim in the abstract (i.e., a common-law wrongful termination action may be based on the firing of an employee because the employee reports sexual harassment to the employer). Mendoza suffered harm as a result of his termination (and the amount of damages awarded by the jury is not challenged on appeal).

The crux of the case is causation, a slippery concept in tort law generally and employment law in particular.

Mendoza claims his report of sexual harassment caused defendants to fire him. In other words, defendants retaliated against Mendoza for accusing his superior (Erdmann) of sexual harassment. On the other hand, defendants cite their belief that Mendoza willingly participated in sexual misconduct on the job as their motivation for firing Mendoza. From defendants' perspective, Mendoza's report only "caused" his firing in the sense that it alerted defendants to Mendoza's misconduct. Defendants concede it is against public policy to fire employees because they report actual sexual harassment. But defendants posit it is not against public policy for employers to fire employees after the employer determines in good faith that the employee actually participated in sexual misconduct on the job.

On appeal, defendants attack the judgment by pointing to alleged instructional error with regard to the element of causation. Defendants also assert there is insufficient evidence in the record to support the jury's causation findings.

Prejudicial Instructional Error Occurred Requiring Reversal

Initially, defendants obtained a very favorable jury instruction and special verdict form on the issue of causation. The jury was instructed as follows: "3. That Romeo Mendoza's report of sexual harassment by Del Erdmann was the motivating reason for Romeo Mendoza's discharge." This instruction included a slight (but important) modification of the 2012 version of CACI No. 2430 ("the motivating reason" rather than "a motivating reason"). The special verdict form submitted to the jury was even starker: "Was Romeo

Mendoza's report of sexual harassment by Del Erdman the reason for [defendants'] decision to discharge Romeo Mendoza." This differed from the special verdict language used in the 2012 version of CACI No. VF–2406 ("a motivating reason"). A jury tasked with deciding whether the report of sexual harassment was "the motivating reason" or "the reason" might logically conclude that this element could only be satisfied if there were only one reason motivating the decision to fire Mendoza.

In the midst of its deliberations, the jury submitted the following question about the causation interrogatory on the special verdict form: "Does this question ... imply that the report was the only reason for the termination? Does this mean they retaliated?" Over defendants' objection, the court submitted a written response to the jury's inquiry: "Pursuant to the Jury Instruction ..., the plaintiff must prove that his report of Sexual Harassment was a motivating reason for his discharge. (That instruction incorrectly refers to 'the motivating reason'. It should say 'a motivating reason'). Please consider this answer in any vote or deliberations." The jury marked out the word "the" and inserted the word "a" on both the relevant jury instruction and the special verdict form.

Defense counsel opposed the court's response to the jury on the grounds that the initial instruction and special verdict form were correct. Defense counsel added that "the clarification would, at a minimum, have to say, 'a primary reason. A substantial motivating reason.'" The court responded, "[i]f CACI is right, then we are right."

The 2012 versions of CACI Nos. 2430 and VF–2406 were not right, at least in the view of the Judicial Council in 2013. Effective June 2013, CACI No. 2430 provides the following with regard to causation: "That [insert alleged violation of public policy ...] was a substantial motivating reason for [name of plaintiff]'s discharge." The corresponding special verdict form also inserted updated language ("a substantial motivating reason").

These changes were inspired by *Harris*, a February 2013 case in which the plaintiff alleged her employer fired her because she was pregnant. Our Supreme Court held that CACI No. 2500 (the FEHA disparate treatment/discrimination instruction) did not accurately state the law in calling for the jury "to determine whether discrimination was 'a motivating factor/reason' for Harris's termination.... [T]he jury should instead determine whether discrimination was 'a substantial motivating factor/reason.'" "Requiring the plaintiff to show that discrimination was a substantial motivating factor, rather than simply a motivating factor, more effectively ensures that liability will not be imposed

based on evidence of mere thoughts or passing statements unrelated to the disputed employment decision. At the same time, ... proof that discrimination was a substantial factor in an employment decision triggers the deterrent purpose of the FEHA and thus exposes the employer to liability, even if other factors would have led the employer to make the same decision at the time." (*Ibid.*) *Harris* makes clear (at least with regard to CACI No. 2500) that the initial instruction in this case ("the motivating reason") and the court's amended instruction ("a motivating reason") were incorrect.

Even more recently, an appellate court held "that the trial court prejudicially erred in instructing the jury with the former versions of CACI Nos. 2430, 2500, 2505, and 2507 because the proper standard of causation in a FEHA discrimination or retaliation claim is not 'a motivating reason,' as used in the [former] CACI instructions, but rather 'a substantial motivating' reason, as set forth in Harris." Following her termination, the Alamo plaintiff (who had recently taken a "pregnancy-related leave of absence") sued under a variety of theories, including wrongful termination in violation of public policy. The Alamo court rejected the contention "that a jury in an employment discrimination case would not draw any meaningful distinction between 'a motivating reason' and 'a substantial motivating reason' in deciding whether there was unlawful discrimination [because] the Supreme Court reached a contrary conclusion in Harris."

The directions for use included with the current version of CACI No. 2430 state that "[w]hether the FEHA standard [as explicated in *Harris*] applies to cases alleging a violation of public policy has not been addressed by the courts." But the Alamo case, issued in August 2013, has answered this question in the affirmative. We agree with Alamo. It would be nonsensical to provide a different standard of causation in FEHA cases and common law tort cases based on public policies encompassed by FEHA. Mendoza tries to distinguish the instant case from Alamo by noting that he abandoned his statutory FEHA claims before the case was submitted to the jury. This is a distinction without a difference for purposes of crafting appropriate jury instructions.

It is therefore clear that the court erred in its instruction of the jury. The court should have instructed the jury to determine whether Mendoza's report of sexual harassment was a substantial motivating reason for Mendoza's discharge. Following Harris and Alamo, we conclude this error was prejudicial. The jury's verdict in favor of Mendoza was extremely close (a nine to three vote). No other instructions provided to the jury could have cured the erroneous instruction with regard to the contested element. Viewing the evidence "in the light most favorable" to defendants, there is a reasonable probability that the instructional error prejudicially affected the verdict.

Holding

There is sufficient evidence in the record for the jury to conclude that a substantial motivating reason for Mendoza's firing was his report of sexual harassment. Defendants terminated an excellent, long term employee soon after he reported sexual harassment by a recent hire, Erdmann. Accepting Mendoza's testimony as true (as we must for this purpose), Mendoza was not complicit in sexual misconduct at the hospital. Instead, Erdmann harassed Mendoza while Erdmann was acting as Mendoza's supervisor at the hospital. After being confronted by defendants, Erdmann confirmed part of Mendoza's story (i.e., that improper activity occurred) but accused Mendoza of being the instigator and willing participant. With nothing to go on besides their respective statements, defendants claim they chose to believe Erdmann's characterization of the incidents rather than Mendoza's complaint.

Importantly, in combination with the foregoing facts, Mendoza's expert witness testified that there were numerous shortcomings in the investigation conducted by defendants following Mendoza's complaint. The lack of a rigorous investigation by defendants is evidence suggesting that defendants did not value the discovery of the truth so much as a way to clean up the mess that was uncovered when Mendoza made his complaint. Defendants point to the expert's concession that additional facts would not necessarily have been discovered had the alleged flaws in the investigation been addressed. But the question for the jury was defendants' subjective motivation in deciding to fire Mendoza, not whether defendants actually had all available material before them. Moreover, a more thorough investigation might have disclosed additional character and credibility evidence for defendants to consider before making their decision.

In sum, substantial evidence supports the judgment. Thus, on remand, it will be up to a jury to decide whether the expert's characterization of the investigation is accurate and whether to infer from that characterization that defendants had retaliatory animus. Similarly, it will be up to a jury to determine whether defendants' termination of Mendoza was substantially motivated by improper considerations.

The judgment is reversed. In the interests of justice, the parties shall bear their own costs incurred on appeal.

Case Questions

1. Explain the California court's ruling. Did it find in the employer's favor? If yes, how so?

2. Why did the court rule that the plaintiff had to show that discrimination was a substantial motivating factor rather than simply a motivating factor? Explain the difference between the two.

3. In its opinion, the court states, "The crux of the case is causation." Explain that statement and how it relates to the court's ruling.

Concept *Summary* 2.1

EMPLOYMENT-AT-WILL AND WRONGFUL DISCHARGE

- Justifications for at-will employment:
  - Freedom of contract
  - Free enterprise in a competitive marketplace
- Problems with at-will employment:
  - Disparities of bargaining power between employer and employee
  - Potential for unfair treatment falling outside statutory protections
- Exceptions to at-will employment:
  - Statutory exceptions, such as antidiscrimination laws
  - Employment contracts containing set lengths of employment
  - Public policy exception

2-3   Express and Implied Contracts of Employment

express contract
a contract in which the terms are explicitly stated, usually in writing but perhaps only verbally, and often in great detail. In interpreting such a contract, the judge and/ or the jury is asked only to determine what the explicit terms are and to interpret them according to their plain meaning

implied contract
a contractual relationship, the terms and conditions of which must be inferred from the contracting parties' behavior toward one another

Some employees have express contracts of employment, usually for a definite duration. Others fall within the coverage of a collective bargaining agreement negotiated for them by their union. Most workers, however, have no express agreement as to the term of their employment, and some were given an oral promise of a fixed term in a state in which the statute of frauds requires that contracts for performance extending for a year or more be written. Such employees have sometimes tried to convince the courts that they have been given implied promises that take them outside the ranks of their at-will coworkers. An **express contract** has terms spelled out by the parties, usually in writing. **Implied contracts** are contracts that the courts infer from company policies (such as those published in employee handbooks) and the behavior of the parties, or that are implied from the law.

If a company provides its employees with a personnel handbook, and that handbook says that employees will be fired only for certain enumerated infractions of work rules, or that the firm will follow certain procedures in disciplining them, a worker may later argue that the manual formed part of his or her employment contract with the firm. An increasing number of state and federal courts agree.

Many employers in turn have responded by adding clauses to their employee handbooks that reserve the firm's right to make unilateral changes or to vary the application of particular policies to fit the unique circumstances of each new situation. The following cases involve determinations of if and when an employer can withdraw a unilaterally promulgated policy or employment agreement and replace it with another, thus unilaterally altering the employment relationship or deviate from a policy's particular terms in a specific instance.

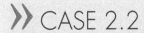 CASE 2.2

Serri v. Santa Clara University
226 Cal. App. 4th 830, 172 Cal.Rptr.3d 732 (2014)

Facts: A university's former director of affirmative action, Conchita Franco Serri, brought her action against the university and the university's officers and attorneys for breach of her employment contract, among other claims, after being terminated from her position. The university claimed it terminated her employment because she failed to produce Affirmative Action Plans for three consecutive years, even though her job required that she produce an Affirmative Action Plan annually. The university also terminated her employment because she allegedly made misrepresentations about the plans that she had failed to prepare.

Issue: Serri's fourth cause of action for breach of contract alleged that she was not an at-will employee and that her employment contract with the university was "partially oral, partially written in the form of [the university's] Staff Policy Manual." Serri alleged that her employment contract contained promises that she would not be discharged except for good cause and that she would be afforded progressive discipline or remediation if there were problems with her job performance. She alleged that the university breached her employment contract when it terminated her without good cause and without an opportunity to correct any improper conduct.

Decision: Based on all of the admissible evidence in the case, the court concluded that the university met its burden of establishing that it acted in good faith and had reasonable grounds for believing Serri engaged in gross misconduct, when it decided to terminate her and that its decision was based on "fair and honest reasons." It could not be reasonably asserted that termination for misrepresenting the status of an important report that impacted the work of other university departments was "trivial, arbitrary or capricious" or unrelated to the university's business needs or goals. Thus, the university was within its rights in not affording the plaintiff progressive discipline.

» CASE 2.3

KILLINGSWORTH V. HOUSING AUTHORITY OF CITY OF DALLAS

447 S.W.3d 480 Tex. App. Dallas (2014)

Facts: A prospective employee, Jerry Killingsworth, contended that the Housing Authority of the City of Dallas (DHA) backed out of a deal to hire him as the DHA's President and Chief Executive Officer. Killingsworth claimed that despite having a written employment contract offering him the position, the DHA yielded to political pressure to retain then-DHA President Ann Lott and refused to allow him to assume the duties of the position. He sued the DHA for breach of an employment contract and violations of his civil rights.

Issue: Did the alleged employment agreement constitute an enforceable contract? And did DHA breach an employment contract by rescinding its offer of employment?

Decision: No to both questions. The court concluded that the letter agreement required subsequent approval by the DHA Board after it was presented to Killingsworth. The summary-judgment evidence conclusively demonstrated that the Board did not approve the letter agreement, and so Killingsworth could not prove the existence of a valid contract. His breach-of-contract claim fails as a matter of law, and the trial court properly granted summary judgment for the DHA on the claim.

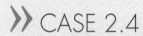

» CASE 2.4

STEGALL V. ORR MOTORS OF LITTLE ROCK, INC.

121 So.3d 684 La. App. 2d Cir. (2013)

Facts: A parts and service manager at a car dealership was made aware via email from the owner that the profit margins for the parts and service departments were low in comparison to other dealerships. The owner set sales requirements for the parts department and advised that failing to meet the requirements would result in a one percent deduction in commissions from the parts department. The owner then unilaterally modified the manager's pay plan in writing, but it was unsigned by the parties. The new pay plan removed the manager's base salary provision and set out that his compensation would be based solely on commissions from exceeding net profit goals, as well as the opportunity to earn other commissions based on certain benchmark sales numbers. Although the manager continued working at the dealership under the modified pay plan, he was dissatisfied with the modifications and later resigned.

The manager brought an action for breach of employment contract, seeking unpaid wages.

Issue: Can the employer apply modifications to the employment contract unilaterally, without a formal written contract?

Decision: No. The trial court heard the conflicting testimony of the manager and the owner and determined that the manager's testimony was more credible. The trial court chose to believe the manager's testimony that pay plans in his line of work are reduced to writing and any modifications should be handled in the same manner. The owner applied modifications unilaterally, sometimes without notice and not in a formal, written contract. The new pay plan was unsigned by the parties, and the trial court therefore found that the original pay plan should remain the controlling document. The finding by the trial court that the owner improperly modified the manager's pay plan was not manifestly erroneous or clearly wrong.

These three case decisions indicate that the employer retains considerable control over the terms of the employment relationship, but this control is not unlimited. While an employer, for example, may exercise discretion in its disciplinary procedures, this discretion is not unlimited. Furthermore, changes in such fundamental terms of employment as compensation, when contractually set, cannot be arbitrarily modified.

THE **WORKING** LAW

Model Employment Termination Act

The National Conference of Commissioners on Uniform State Laws was organized in the 1890s as part of a movement in the American Bar Association for the reform and unification of American law. Currently, the conference's list comprises 99 uniform acts and 24 model acts, which the states are encouraged to adopt. In 1987, the conference established a drafting committee to create a Uniform Employment Termination Act to provide employees with statutory protection against wrongful discharge. By 1991, the conference had approved a "model" act. However, division among the commissioners has prevented the act from achieving the status of "uniform." Consequently, states are encouraged to modify the model to suit each jurisdiction's particular social, economic, and legal needs. So far, only a handful of states have done so.

The heart and soul of the Model Employment Termination Act (META) in its present form is Section 3(a), which states "an employer may not terminate the employment of an employee without good cause." "Good cause" is defined in one of two ways. The employee's own inadequate or improper conduct in the performance of the job is the first. The second involves the economic or institutional goals of the employer. If the employer's goals require reorganization, discontinuing functions, and/or changing the size and character of its work force, employees discharged as a result are discharged with "good cause."

Section 3(b) limits application of the good cause limitation on employment-at-will to workers who have been with the particular employer for at least one year. Section 4(c) adds another possible exception, stating that employer and employee may substitute a severance pay agreement for the good cause standard, and the good cause standard is inapplicable to situations where termination comes at the expiration of an express oral or written contract containing a fixed duration for the employment relationship.

If a qualified employee is terminated without good cause, META provides remedies. Remedies that may be sought under META include reinstatement, back pay, lost benefits, or, alternatively, a lump-sum severance payment. META excludes recovery for pain and suffering, emotional distress, defamation, fraud, punitive damages, compensatory damages, or any other monetary award. Attorney's fees are recoverable, so that employees with modest incomes have an opportunity to obtain legal assistance in bringing legitimate claims.

Enforcement in META is conducted solely by arbitration. Judicial review of arbitration awards is permitted only for abuses of the discretion or office of the arbitrators.

Finally, META also provides protections to employees who participate in termination proceedings. Employers are barred from retaliating against an employee who files a complaint, provides testimony, or otherwise lawfully participates in proceedings under META.

The META suggests that claims under it be subject to binding arbitration with arbitral awards being issued within 30 days of hearings. Section 10 forbids retaliation against employees who make claims or who testify under the procedural provisions of the META.[2]

Concept *Summary* 2.2

EMPLOYMENT CONTRACTS AND EMPLOYEE HANDBOOKS

- Common-law presumption of at-will employment can be overcome by an express contract or by implication, for instance, based on a policy in an employee handbook
- American courts remain reluctant to infer terms and conditions of employment when the employer has not expressly awarded the right to its employees or where the relevant employment documents, or even the reasonable passage of time, indicate the employer set limits on its obligations to the employee(s)

2-4   Protection for Corporate Whistleblowers

On July 30, 2002, Congress passed and the president signed the Sarbanes-Oxley Act (SOX). SOX amended the creaky Securities and Exchange Acts of 1933 and 1934, as well as the more recent-vintage Employee Retirement Income Security Act (ERISA), plus the Investment Advisers Act of 1940 and the U.S. Criminal Code. SOX includes two provisions, one criminal and the other civil, for the protection of employees who report improper conduct by corporate officials concerning securities fraud and corruption.

Dozens of federal laws, such as the Occupational Safety and Health Act (OSHA) and Title VII, protect employees who blow the whistle on illegal practices or who cooperate in investigations and testify at hearings from employer retaliation, such as employment termination. Dozens of states have jumped on the whistleblower bandwagon, adding a dizzying variety of whistleblower laws to the panoply of rules and regulations that human resource managers and employment lawyers must consider before initiating "industrial capital punishment" (i.e., firing a miscreant worker). In those increasingly rare jurisdictions or circumstances in which no federal or state antiretaliation rule is implicated, the courts often have shown themselves willing to carve out a public policy exception to employment-at-will, where the plaintiff provides proof that he or she was fired for reporting or restricting illegal supervisory activity. But the proliferation of such laws and court rulings has often fallen short of protecting whistleblowers, because of either poor enforcement procedures or ineffectual remedies. SOX is unique in making whistleblower retaliation a federal crime that can result in officer/director defendants actually going to prison.

---

[2] See, e.g., Montana Wrongful Discharge from Employment Act, Mont. Code Ann. Sections 39-2-901 through 39-2-915. A summary of the META's status across the U.S. is provided by the Uniform Law Commission, available at http://www.uniformlaws.org/Act.aspx?title=Employment%20Termination%20Act,%20Model.

Perhaps the scariest aspect of SOX's criminal provision is that it can be used to punish retaliation against persons who provide information to law enforcement officials relating to the possible commission of any federal offense, not just securities fraud, albeit securities fraud was the catalyst for the legislation. The provision makes it a crime to "knowingly, with the intent to retaliate, take . . . any action harmful to any person, including interference with lawful employment or livelihood of any person, for providing a law enforcement officer any truthful information relating to the commission or possible commission of any Federal offense." Individuals found guilty under this proviso may be fined up to a quarter-million dollars and imprisoned up to 10 years. Corporate defendants can face up to a half-million dollar fine if convicted.

2-4a Civil Liability Under SOX

A child of corporate greed and accounting scandals, SOX's legislative history indicates that its whistleblower provisions are intended primarily to protect employees of publicly traded companies acting in the public interest to try to prevent officer/director wrongdoing and "to encourage and protect those who report fraudulent activity that can damage innocent investors in publicly traded companies." The following case exemplifies the limits of this new federal whistleblower cause of action.

» CASE 2.5

LAWSON V. FMR LLC
134 S.Ct. 1158 U.S. (2014)

Facts: In these two consolidated cases, plaintiffs Jackie Hosang Lawson and Jonathan M. Zang separately sued their corporate employers; private companies that advise managers of mutual funds, pursuant to the Investment Company Act of 1940. FMR LLC., one of a family of named defendants, shared both suits, leading the district judge to deal with the two cases in common. The defendants provided management services under contract to the Fidelity of family of mutual funds, which are owned by their shareholders, are registered with the SEC, and which have board members but no employees of their own.

Plaintiff Zang was employed by Fidelity Management & Research Co. and later by FMR Co., Inc., which was formed as a subsidiary of Fidelity Management & Research Co. These Fidelity Management companies had entered into contracts with certain of the Fidelity mutual funds to serve as investment advisers or sub-advisers. As investment advisers to the funds, the Fidelity Management companies were subject to the provisions of the Investment Advisers

Act of 1940. They were subsidiaries, directly or indirectly, of FMR LLC.

Zang's employment was terminated in July 2005. On September 15, 2005, he filed a complaint with the Occupational Safety and Health Administration (OSHA) of the Department of Labor (DOL), based on 18 U.S.C. § 1514A(b)(1)(A), which allows a person who alleges discharge or discrimination in violation of SOX to seek relief by filing a complaint with the Secretary of Labor. Zang alleged that he had been terminated by the Fidelity Management companies in retaliation for raising concerns about inaccuracies in a draft revised registration statement for certain Fidelity funds. Zang alleged that he reasonably believed these inaccuracies violated several federal securities laws.

OSHA dismissed Zang's complaint, finding that he was a covered employee within the meaning of § 1514A(a). This is to say, he was an employee "covered" by the whistleblower protections, but that he had not engaged in conduct protected by that subsection. Zang objected and had a hearing before an Administrative Law Judge. The Fidelity Management companies moved for a summary decision, contending, among other things, that Zang was not a covered employee. After allowing limited discovery on the issue, the ALJ granted the summary-decision motion for the Fidelity Management companies on that basis and dismissed. Interpreting § 1514A(a), the ALJ concluded that merely being an employee of a privately held contractor to a fund was insufficient to come within the term "employee."

Zang petitioned for review of the ALJ decision by the DOL's Administrative Review Board (ARB). He then gave notice to the DOL of his intention to file an action in federal court and filed his complaint against the Fidelity Management companies in the district court, terminating his appeal with the ARB. Under SOX, a claimant may seek *de novo* review in federal district court, if the DOL has not issued a final decision on a complaint within 180 days of its filing.

Plaintiff Lawson was employed by Fidelity Brokerage Services, LLC, a private subsidiary of FMR Corp., which was succeeded by FMR LLC. Together these companies operated under the trade name Fidelity Investments. Lawson filed SOX complaints against her employer and its parent with OSHA pursuant to § 1514A(b)(1)(A) in 2006, while she was still employed. She alleged retaliation against her for raising concerns primarily relating to cost accounting methodologies. She resigned her employment in September 2007, claiming that she had been constructively discharged. One year after filing, Lawson notified OSHA that she intended to seek review of her SOX claim in federal court. Her claims, which had been consolidated, were closed by the DOL, and she filed a complaint against her employers in the district court.

The defendants, all private companies, filed motions to dismiss under Rule 12(b)(6), arguing that the plaintiffs were not covered employees under § 1514A(a) and, in the alternative, that they had not engaged in protected activity under § 1514A(a)(1). The district court denied the motions to dismiss as to the plaintiffs' claims alleging retaliation in violation of § 1514A, which denial became the subject of this appeal.

The First Circuit panel reversed the decision of the lower court. Noting that the whistleblower provisions are just a small part of the SOX Act, the appellate judges added that they saw their job as a straightforward statutory interpretation task. Section 1514A of SOX says,

"(a) Whistleblower protection for employees of publicly traded companies.—No company with a class of securities registered under section 12 of the Securities Exchange Act of 1934 (15 U.S.C. § 78 l), or that is required to file reports under section 15(d) of the Securities Exchange Act of 1934 (15 U.S.C. § 78 o(d)), or any officer, employee, *contractor, subcontractor,* or agent of such company, *may discharge, demote, suspend, threaten, harass, or in any other manner discriminate against an employee* in the terms and conditions of employment because of any lawful act done by the employee—

"(1) to provide information, cause information to be provided, or otherwise assist in an investigation regarding any conduct which the employee reasonably believes constitutes a violation of section 1341 [mail fraud], 1343 [wire fraud], 1344 [bank fraud], or 1348 [securities or commodities fraud], any rule or regulation of the Securities and Exchange Commission, or any provision of Federal law relating to fraud against shareholders, when the information or assistance is provided to or the investigation is conducted by—

"(A) a Federal regulatory or law enforcement agency;

"(B) any Member of Congress or any committee of Congress; or

"(C) a person with supervisory authority over the employee (or such other person working for the employer who has the authority to investigate, discover, or terminate misconduct); or

"(2) to file, cause to be filed, testify, participate in, or otherwise assist in a proceeding filed or about to be filed (with any knowledge of the employer) relating to an alleged violation of section 1341, 1343, 1344, or 1348, any rule or regulation of the Securities and Exchange Commission, or any provision of Federal law relating to fraud against shareholders." [Emphasis added.]

Rejecting the position taken by not only the plaintiffs, but also the SEC as *amici,* the judges originally held, "Although there is a close relationship between the private investment adviser defendants and their client mutual funds, as pointed out by the plaintiffs and the SEC as amicus curiae, the two entities are separate because Congress wanted it that way. Had Congress intended to ignore that separation and cover the employees of private investment advisers for whistleblower protections, it would have done so explicitly in § 1514A(a). However, it did not."

However, the case was then considered by the Supreme Court.

Issue: Are the plaintiffs covered by the SOX whistleblower provisions?

Decision: The Supreme Court held that whistleblower protection under Sarbanes-Oxley extended to employees of private contractors and subcontractors serving public companies. The Supreme Court stated, "We hold, based on the text of § 1514A, the mischief to which Congress was responding, and earlier legislation Congress drew upon, that the provision shelters employees of private contractors and subcontractors, just as it shelters employees of the public company served by the contractors and subcontractors. We first summarize our principal reasons, then describe this controversy and explain our decision more comprehensively.

"Plaintiffs below, petitioners here, are former emp-loyees of private companies that contract to advise or manage mutual funds. The mutual funds themselves are public companies that have no employees. Hence, if the whistle is to be blown on fraud detrimental to mutual fund investors, the whistleblowing employee must be on another company's payroll, most likely, the payroll of the mutual fund's investment adviser or manager.

"Taking the allegations of the complaint as true, both plaintiffs blew the whistle on putative fraud relating to the mutual funds and, as a consequence, suffered adverse action by their employers. Plaintiffs read § 1514A to convey that '[n]o ... contractor ... may ... discriminate against [its own] employee [for whistleblowing].' We find that reading consistent with the text of the statute and with common sense. Contractors are in control of their own employees, but are not ordinarily positioned to control someone else's workers. Moreover, we resist attributing to Congress a purpose to stop a contractor from retaliating against whistleblowers employed by the public company the contractor serves, while leaving the contractor free to retaliate against its own employees when they reveal corporate fraud.

"In the Enron scandal that prompted the Sarbanes-Oxley Act, contractors and subcontractors, including the accounting firm Arthur Andersen, participated in Enron's fraud and its coverup. When employees of those contractors attempted to bring misconduct to light, they encountered retaliation by their employers. The Sarbanes-Oxley Act contains numerous provisions aimed at controlling the conduct of accountants, auditors, and lawyers who work with public companies. Given Congress' concern about contractor conduct of the kind that contributed to Enron's collapse, we regard with suspicion construction of § 1514A to protect whistleblowers only when they are employed by a public company, and not when they work for the public company's contractor.

"Congress borrowed § 1514A's prohibition against retaliation from the wording of the 2000 Wendell H. Ford Aviation Investment and Reform Act for the 21st Century (AIR 21), 49 U.S.C. § 42121. That Act provides: 'No air carrier or contractor or subcontractor of an air carrier may discharge an employee or otherwise discriminate against an employee with respect to compensation, terms, conditions, or privileges of employment' when the employee provides information regarding violations 'relating to air carrier safety' to his or her employer or federal authorities. § 42121(a)(1). AIR 21 has been read to cover, in addition to employees of air carriers, employees of contractors and subcontractors of the carriers. Given the parallel statutory texts and whistleblower protective aims, we read the words 'an employee' in AIR 21 and in § 1514A to have similar import."

Case Questions

1. Why did the Supreme Court reverse the decision of the lower court?

2. Explain what "employee" means within the scope of the Sarbanes-Oxley Act and as defined in this court ruling.

3. Whose position do you favor on the basis of the law as it is written, the Supreme Court's or the lower court's?

4. Whose position do you favor on the basis of the con-gressional policy underlying the Sarbanes-Oxley Act?

5. Whose position furthers the interests of the investing public the most?

ethical DILEMMA

THE FIRST AMENDMENT AND UNPROTECTED EMPLOYEE SPEECH

A director of a community youth program conducted an audit of the program's expenses, and in doing so, discovered that a state legislator on the program's payroll has not been reporting for work. Consequently, the director terminated the state lawmaker's employment. Shortly after that, federal authorities indicted the state representative on charges of mail fraud and theft concerning a program receiving federal funds. The director testified, under subpoena, regarding the events that led to his terminating the state legislator. She in fact was convicted and sentenced to 30 months in prison.

Meanwhile, the youth program had experienced significant budget shortfalls. The president of the program's sponsoring university terminated the director along with 28 other employees in a claimed effort to address the financial difficulties. A few days later, however, the president rescinded all but two of the 29 terminations—those of the director and one other employee. The director sued the president in his individual and official capacities, alleging that the president violated the First Amendment by firing him in retaliation for testifying in court. The president made a motion for summary judgment, claiming that the director's testimony was not entitled to First Amendment protection. He claimed the director spoke as an employee and not as a citizen because he acted pursuant to his official duties when he investigated and terminated the state representative's employment.

Consider: Should the First Amendment protect a public employee who provides truthful sworn testimony, compelled by subpoena, of an organization's corruption? Or was the director's testimony unprotected employee speech? What are some policy considerations pushing in each direction?

Concept *Summary* 2.3

WHISTLEBLOWERS

- A whistleblower is an employee who calls attention to the employer's illegal or unethical activities
- Many federal and state statutes seek to protect whistleblowers by making retaliation an illegal act
- The most significant whistleblower-protection law of the 21st century is the federal Sarbanes-Oxley Act, which protects employees who blow the whistle on illegal financial transactions
- Whistleblowers' rights may conflict with the privacy rights of others

CHAPTER REVIEW

» Key Terms

employment-at-will	2 1	public policy exception	2 2	express contract	2 7
whistleblower	2 2	tort	2 3	implied contract	2 7

» Summary

- The employment-at-will doctrine became the norm in 19th-century American common law. The at-will doctrine holds that, unless the parties expressly agree on a specific duration, the employment relationship may be severed by either the employee or the employer at any time and for any reason.

- During the second half of the 20th century, American courts narrowed the at-will doctrine by carving out several common-law exceptions. The most common of these is the public policy exception, which holds that an employer cannot fire an employee if that termination would undermine a clear mandate of public policy. For example, many states have punished employers for firing workers who were absent from work because they had been called to jury duty.

- Another exception to the at-will rule is the legal doctrine of an implied contract. While the parties may not have agreed expressly to a duration of the employment relationship, an employee handbook or other employer policy may state that employees will not be fired except for good cause. Or such a company document may accord employees certain procedural rights, such as arbitration, before a job termination becomes final.

- Under the doctrine of good faith and fair dealing, which only a minority of American courts have adopted as a limitation on at-will employment, a terminated worker may bring a wrongful discharge action whenever the employer has failed to deal in good faith. For instance, an employer who fires a salesperson simply to escape paying commissions might run afoul of this common-law rule.

- The Model Employment Termination Act seeks to make "good cause" the basis for all employment terminations and to provide the parties with arbitration as their remedy when the propriety of a firing is in dispute. So far, only a handful of states have adopted all or some of the model act.

- Whistleblowers, who are ostensibly protected from retaliation under many federal and state laws, nevertheless have often been victimized by their employers, discovering too late that the laws on which they relied lacked the teeth to properly protect them. The federal Sarbanes-Oxley Act of 2002 makes such retaliation against those reporting a federal crime itself a crime that can result in the imprisonment of corporate officers.

» Problems

» Questions

1. What were some of the socioeconomic conditions in 19th-century America that led the majority of state courts to adopt the legal principle of employment-at-will?

2. How do advocates of the employment-at-will doctrine defend it, and what is the opposing reasoning? Which do you believe is in the best interests of the public?

3. List and explain the three most widely adopted exceptions to the employment-at-will doctrine.

4. Is it preferable to change the law by enacting a statute, such as the Model Employment Termination Act, or for a state's supreme court to make the change by judicial fiat in a court decision?

5. What is the reasoning behind limiting the Sarbanes-Oxley Act's protections to public employees?

» Case Problems

6. A loss-prevention manager employed by a general store was terminated for pursuing a shoplifter outside of the store and throwing the shoplifter's phone onto the roof of the store. The manager filed a complaint in superior court, claiming breach of contract and wrongful termination. He claimed that the store's loss-prevention policies and procedures were part of his employment contract and that the store breached those contractual provisions when it terminated his employment without notice.

   The store moved for summary judgment. The company argued that its loss-prevention policy manual was not a binding contract and that, even if it were, the store's actions did not violate company policy. The superior court agreed that the company's policy manual was not a contract, and that the manager's employment was, therefore, terminable at will. Accordingly, the court granted the motion for summary judgment and dismissed the manager's claims. The manager appealed.

Do you think the company's loss-prevention policy manual created a binding contract that would support the employee's breach of contract claim? What facts, above, suggest that the policy couldn't have covered the plaintiff's conduct? [See *Becker v. Fred Meyer Stores, Inc.*, 335 P.3d 1110 (Alaska 2014).]

7. A radiologist's employment with a hospital was terminated for "four incidents of scanning exams incorrectly, alleged delay in patient care, scanning the wrong anatomy, alleged complaint on a patient survey, peer reviews of which [plaintiff] knew nothing, and alleged complaints from co-workers." The radiologist filed suit against the hospital for numerous claims, including breach of contract. The radiologist did not allege that a contract specifying a definite period of employment existed between her and the hospital. Instead, she asserted that certain contractual rights regarding termination and grievance procedures arose out of the hospital's employee handbook. The hospital's failure to follow those procedures in terminating her employment, she argued, constituted a breach of contract.

   The radiologist alleged that, as part of employee orientation, she was required to acknowledge in writing the receipt of the employee handbook that set forth the grievance procedures that were available to employees of the hospital and that she was likewise required to acknowledge in writing the receipt of Standards of Performance for Employees.

   Do you think that these stipulations in the employee handbook's grievance procedures were sufficient to create a contract? [See *Horne v. Cumberland County Hosp. System, Inc.*, 746 S.E.2d 13 (N.C. App. 2013).]

8. A former employee worked as a part-time building inspector and then as a full-time code enforcement officer for the town of Cedar Lake. By ordinance, Cedar Lake adopted a 60-page "Town of Cedar Lake Policy and Procedure Manual" ("Manual"), which stated up front that it was not a contract of employment. The Manual also contained a lengthy at-will employment provision, a progressive disciplinary policy provision, and an employee appeal

provision. The employee acknowledged receipt of the Manual.

Cedar Lake later notified the former employee of a disciplinary job action against him; the recommended discipline was employment termination. Alleging violations of the Procedure Manual and the Town Code of Conduct, the town administrator advised the former employee that, in accordance with the Manual, he was entitled to request an administrative hearing before the Town Council. A hearing was held, and after demoting the former employee, his employment was eventually terminated altogether.

The former employee filed a complaint against the town. In part, he asked the trial court to declare that the disciplinary procedure violated of the due process rights afforded him under the town's personnel policy. The town moved for summary judgment and filed a supporting memorandum of law, arguing that the former employee had no constitutionally protected property interest in his job. The former employee identified three "state-law sources" of his purported property interest, all of which stemmed from the Manual.

Do you think the Manual created a contract of employment, supporting the former employee's breach of contract claim? If so, did the defendant fulfill its contractual obligations under the agreement? [See *Wynkoop v. Town of Cedar Lake*, 970 N.E.2d 230 (Ind. App. 2012).]

9. A former employee brought an action against his employer, alleging that the employer, in demoting him out of management, had breached enforceable provisions of the employer's code of conduct. The code was a one-page document that every employee must sign every year, certifying understanding and compliance. It began with a general statement of high ethical aspirations (i.e., "The highest standards of ethical business conduct are required of Boeing employees in the performance of their company responsibilities. Employees will not engage in conduct or activity that may raise questions as to the company's honesty, impartiality, reputation or otherwise cause embarrassment to the company."). The code then enumerated eight specific employee obligations and encouraged employees to report

violations. It concluded by stating, "Every employee has the responsibility to ask questions, seek guidance and report suspected violations of this Code of Conduct. Retaliation against employees who come forward to raise genuine concerns will not be tolerated."

Does this in any way create an implied contract between the former employee and his employer? Or is the code merely a statement of corporate aspirations? [See *Quedado v. Boeing Co.*, 168 Wash. App. 363, 276 P.3d 365 (Div. 1 2012).]

10. A former employee brought an action against his former employer alleging unlawful retaliation in violation of Title VII of the Civil Rights Act of 1964 and wrongful discharge contrary to Wisconsin law. The employee claimed his discharge was pretextual and that he was actually terminated for opposing alleged sexual harassment of a colleague (rumors about a sexual affair and a hair-pulling incident), in violation of Title VII's antiretaliation provision. Additionally, he claimed his termination was wrongful under Wisconsin law because in meetings with supervisors he stated he would testify truthfully if ever questioned about certain tax and antitrust matters that he believed could expose the employer company to liability. The former employee gave no specific instances of the company directing him to violate tax or antitrust statutes. The company contended it eliminated the former employee's position as a cost-saving move in response to an economic downturn.

Has the plaintiff in this case articulated public policies sufficient to support his wrongful-discharge case? If so, do you think he articulated facts sufficient to support his allegation that firing him violated these public policies? [See *Lewis v. Bay Industries, Inc.*, — F.Supp.3d —, 2014 WL 4925483 (E.D. Wis. 2014).]

11. A former security guard and at-will employee sued the university for which he worked for wrongful discharge, premised upon the theory that he was fired in violation of public policy. The security guard argued he was fired simply for enforcing the criminal laws of the state when he attempted to arrest a student who he thought was fighting with another student. The university contended that it only terminated his employment after he refused

a transfer. The former employee concedes that he was an at-will employee at the time but believes he was fired in violation of public policy, making his discharge unlawful.

What do you think? What additional facts might persuade you that the plaintiff has a valid wrongful-discharge action? [See *Lloyd v. Drake University*, 686 N.W.2d 225 (Iowa 2014).]

12. The maintenance director, Rick Carter, for Lee County brought allegations against the county when it terminated his employment. He claimed that he was wrongfully discharged from employment, and the termination violated the state whistleblower statute. Carter claimed he revealed to the public what he believed to be Lee County's "troubling pattern of irresponsible money management" and health and safety violations, and his termination was precluded by Iowa Code section 70A.29 (2011), a statute prohibiting reprisals against employees of political subdivisions who disclose negative information. The Lee County supervisors, however, said that Carter was an insubordinate employee who demonstrated "a proclivity to ad hominem attacks on any one disagreeing with him."

Carter never took his complaints regarding the board's alleged wrongdoing to other officials. When asked on cross-examination to whom he blew the whistle, he admitted he did not report his concerns about safety and health violations to agencies such as the Occupational Safety and Health Administration or the Department of Natural Resources. Instead he testified that he "whistled all the goddamn day to the Board and everybody that would listen."

Do you think Carter should have a case? [See *Carter v. Lee County*, Slip Copy, 2015 WL 161833 (Iowa App. 2015).]

13. Former union employees brought actions against the construction worker union, alleging that their indefinite layoff from employment at the union was unlawful retaliation under the Whistleblowers' Protection Act (WPA) for contacting the U.S. Department of Labor about their suspicions of unlawful activity by managers. The union alleged that the employees' claims were preempted by the Labor-Management Reporting and Disclosure Act (LMRDA; see Chapter 18).

Congress enacted the LMRDA in 1959 as "the product of congressional concern with widespread abuses of power by union leadership." It also provides union members with procedural protections against discipline by the union. However, in *Finnegan v. Leu*, the Supreme Court explained that "[i]t is readily apparent, both from the language of these provisions and from the legislative history . . ., that it was rank-and-file union members—not union officers or employees, as such—whom Congress sought to protect," nor was the act meant to allow union officers to use their discretion as a shield to hide alleged criminal misconduct.

With that in mind, would you find that the LMRDA preempts the employees' claims in this case? [See *Henry v. Laborers' Local 1191*, 495 Mich. 260, 848 N.W.2d 130 (2014).]

» Hypothetical Scenarios

14. Deborah, a registered nurse, was a member of the "Blue Team" in the ER of her hospital. The team's supervising physician believed strongly that team cohesion and *esprit de corps* were essential to the efficient and safe functioning of the team, as if it were a well-oiled machine. To help foster this attitude among team members, the doctor annually organized an overnight outdoor "adventure." This year she arranged for the team members to go whitewater rafting together on a nearby river. During the overnight campout, the alcohol flowed liberally and teammates took part in impromptu karaoke and skits. Deborah was dragged up from the campfire to participate with two other female team members in a raucous rendition of "Moon River," which ended with the singers "mooning" their colleagues seated around the fire. Deborah refused to bare her bottom. Not much was said that night or the next day, but in the weeks that followed the outing, her supervisor was markedly chilly toward her. When it was time for her annual review, Deborah found that she was given a less-than-satisfactory score for

"cooperation"; a few months later she was denied a promotion she expected to receive. Furthermore, her colleagues took their lead from the supervisor and became generally unfriendly to Deborah, making her day-to-day work experience highly unpleasant. She took the hint and updated her résumé. She found a job at another hospital, albeit at a reduced salary.

Does Deborah have a claim of constructive discharge (i.e., that her treatment at the hands of her employer was so intolerable as to leave her no choice but to resign, thus amounting in effect to a wrongful discharge)? If so, what public policy can she claim was violated by her constructive discharge? Does the employer have a *bona fide* business reason with which to counter Deborah's claim?

15. Boris was a physician on the staff of a city hospital. He was an at-will employee. He was a recent immigrant from an East European country that had a health-care system that was years behind that of the U.S. in terms of technology and equipment. Consequently, equipment that was deemed to be obsolete in Boris's hospital was often considered to be nearly state-of-the-art in his homeland. A number of such pieces of lab equipment were targeted for disposal by his department at the hospital. Without seeking permission, Boris rented a truck and, with the help of a friend, took the equipment from the hospital's rear loading dock and, easily finding a buyer, shipped the equipment off to a health-care facility in his homeland. When the hospital learned what Boris had done, he was fired. The hospital also called the police and filed a criminal complaint. However, when the local district attorney studied the police report, she determined that the equipment had been abandoned by the hospital and therefore no crime had been committed.

Does Boris have a claim of wrongful discharge? Does your answer change if the hospital's employee handbook said that employees would be fired only for "good cause"?

Does your answer change if Boris had salvaged equipment like this before, but with the advance permission of the head of his department, and

he assumed that he had standing permission to continue doing so?

16. Stanley sold prefabricated steel sheds. One day he learned that a shed similar to those he sold had collapsed, killing a worker who was inside the structure at the time. Stanley went to his supervisor and indicated his concern that he was selling an unsafe product. The supervisor assured him that the shed in question had collapsed because the buyer's employees had assembled it incorrectly. Not satisfied with this answer, Stanley went over his boss's head to the vice president of sales, who likewise assured him that the sheds were safe and even gave him a copy of a report that seemed to confirm this. Still unsatisfied, Stanley attempted to see the president of the company. At this point, out of patience with Stanley, his supervisor and the vice president conferred with HR and fired him.

Does Stanley have a claim of wrongful discharge? If the federal Occupational Safety and Health Act has regulations relating to the safe construction of steel sheds, might these regulations help strengthen Stanley's case?

17. Mindy and Fred work for a large retail chain. The chain's billionaire owner is a staunch fundamentalist Christian. He requires his stores to enforce rules of conduct that include forbidding adultery between members of the sales staff. As sales associates, Mindy and Fred ran afoul of this rule when they began a relationship while Mindy's divorce was still pending. When word got around about their affair, both sales associates were fired. Do Mindy and Fred have wrongful discharge claims against the company?

If they were unaware of the rule against adultery, would your answer be any different?

18. Janice signed an employment contract under which she agreed to be the CEO of a new company, which planned to provide some very advanced software programs to the financial services industry. She also signed a shareholders' agreement, which provided her with a substantial number of stock options, which could be exercised

"at such time as the company surpassed $100 million in annual sales" provided "said employee is at that time an active member of the management team." The contract was for a term of three years, renewable by mutual agreement of the parties. At the end of the three-year term, the company notified Janice that it had decided not to renew her contract. Three months after Janice involuntarily left the company, a huge software deal with Wells Fargo pushed sales for the year past the $100 million mark.

Does Janice have a breach of contract claim against her former employer? Does she have a wrongful discharge claim against the company?

CHAPTER **3**

Commonly Committed Workplace Torts

With increased frequency in the final decades of the 20th century, legal actions for wrongful termination were embellished by accompanying counts accusing employers of (and seeking additional damages for) defamation, invasion of privacy, infliction of emotional distress, and other forms of alleged improper conduct. Less frequently, employers and their defense counsels encountered such claims standing on their own. This trend did not diminish in the first decade and a half of this new century. In this chapter and the next (which focuses on employee privacy rights, a matter of special concern in our Internet age), we look at some of the major personal injury claims that plaintiff-employees pursue.

tort
a private or civil wrong or injury, caused by one party to another, either intentionally or negligently

The word **tort** derives from the French influence upon the English language and the English common law. It means a civil wrong not based upon a preexisting contractual relationship. By and large, tort law is the law of personal injury. Its application to employer–employee relationships is affected by workers' compensation insurance (see Chapter 21), which immunizes the employer from some tort liabilities. The extent of this immunity varies widely from state to state. In an effort to circumvent such employer immunity and defeat that affirmative defense, plaintiffs sometimes contend that they were not employees at all but rather independent contractors not covered by state workers' compensation statutes.

Additionally, where the work force is unionized (see Chapters 12–18) or where the employer is a public entity (see Chapter 19), the employee/plaintiff's right to bring a common-law tort action against the employer may be subject to significant restrictions. These may include National Labor Relations Act preemption, a requirement to submit the claim to binding arbitration (even non-unionized companies may add arbitration clauses to their employment contracts to ward off these proliferating claims), and sovereign immunity, where public employers are targeted.

Furthermore, employers are turning the tables and using the tort of trade secret theft as a means of guarding their valuable intellectual property from misappropriation by disgruntled, departing employees.

3-1   Defamation: Libel and Slander

defamation
an intentional,
false, and harmful
communication

One of the most commonly committed workplace torts is **defamation**. The tort of defamation has been defined as follows:

> A communication is defamatory if it tends so to harm the reputation of another as to lower him in the estimation of the community or to deter third persons from associating or dealing with him.[1]

Expanding on this bare-bones definition, it is said that language is defamatory:

> … if it tends to expose another to hatred, shame, obloquy, contempt, ridicule, aversion, ostracism, degradation, or disgrace, or to induce an evil opinion of one in the minds of right-thinking persons and to deprive him of their confidence and friendly intercourse in society.[2]

libel
a written falsehood

slander
a spoken falsehood

Defamation is subdivided into the torts of **libel** and **slander**, the former being defamation by writing and the latter defamation through speech. These two torts may be further divided into the libel or slander that is per se and the libel or slander that is not per se. What makes this distinction critical in some cases is that libel or slander per se requires no showing of specific damages for the plaintiff to recover a judgment, whereas libel or slander that is not per se demands such a showing from the injured party. The term "per se" connotes that the third person to whom the defamation is communicated (and indeed the court) can recognize the damaging nature of the communication without being apprised of the contextual setting (innuendo) in which the communication was made. Professor Prosser, the greatest scholar of tort law, has identified the commonly recognized forms of per se defamation as:

> … the imputation of crime, of a loathsome disease, and those affecting the plaintiff in his business, trade, profession, office or calling …[3]

Business defamation thus may be defined as defamation per se having the following characteristics:

> False spoken or written words that tend to prejudice another in his business, trade, or profession are actionable without proof of special damage if they affect him in a manner that may, as a necessary consequence, or do, as a natural consequence, prevent him from deriving therefrom that pecuniary reward which probably otherwise he might have obtained.[4]

strict liability
plaintiff prevails without
proving negligence

This definition leaves the door to the courtroom wide open to the defamed employee, whose job is his or her "business, trade, or profession." Indeed, since business defamation is a per se tort, it can amount to strict liability once the plaintiff has proved that the damaging statement was published. This use of the words **strict liability** is not to say that no defenses are available. On the contrary, it is possible to identify several. One can dispute the contention that one published the statement or that it is defamatory. Or one can try to prove that

---

[1] *Black's Law Dictionary*, 6th ed. (St. Paul, MN: West, 1991), p. 288.
[2] *Ibid.*
[3] *Ibid.*
[4] *Ibid.*

qualified privilege
immunity from a suit in
the absence of malice

the statement is true. Failing these, the defendant may be able to argue successfully that the statement was made from behind the shield of a privilege.

The law recognizes **qualified privilege**. When a person is protected by qualified privilege, the remarks made will be immune from a defamation suit if the person made them in good faith. If the remarks were made with malice, or in bad faith, they will not be privileged. The law generally recognizes a qualified privilege where one person communicates with another who has a legitimate need to know the information. For example, comments concerning an employee's performance made to a supervisor, and communicated through the organizational structure, are privileged if made in good faith. In addition, assessments of an employee, communicated by a former employer to a prospective employer, made in good faith, are privileged. But comments or remarks, if not made in good faith and/or communicated to persons who have no legitimate need to know, are subject to a defamation action.

The following case is a good example of a case of qualified privilege, and how it can affect a defamation claim.

≫ CASE 3.1

TOLER V. SÜD-CHEMIE, INC.
— S.W.3d —, 2014 WL 7238202 (Ky. Supreme Ct. 2014)

Facts: Süd–Chemie manufactured catalysts used in various chemical operations. Toler began working for the company in 1976 at its southern Louisville plant, one of two it operates in the area. After nearly 25 years of employment with the company, Toler was promoted to a supervisory role. By all accounts, Toler excelled at his role in management until the incidents that were the subject of this litigation.

The company's human resources director, Scott Hinrichs, received reports from some employees regarding Toler's use of racist language in the workplace. Perhaps highlighting the obvious, Toler's statements were rather offensive. And Hinrichs was duty-bound under company policy to investigate any reports of racist language because the company had a zero-tolerance standard concerning the use of such language in the workplace. Accordingly, Hinrichs reviewed the written reports submitted by the employees and then sat down with each employee to discuss the allegations.

During this investigation, the employees all acknowledged and affirmed the written statement submitted to Hinrichs. Going further, the employees were unequivocal in confirming Toler had indeed uttered the offensive statements. Hinrichs, along with the company's plant manager, then met with Toler to hear his side of the story. At the meeting, Toler was provided with the names of the employees as well as the nature of the accusations levied against him. By Toler's account, he was not provided with the employees' actual written statements until the pretrial discovery process. Toler denied making such statements in the workplace and, in an attempt to explain the employees' motive, alleged he was the target of a "union gang-up" as a result of his disagreement with another employee named Allen Trice.

The disagreement with Trice, an African American employee working under Toler, stemmed from an incident in which Trice allegedly failed to follow Toler's instruction. As a result, Toler, acting within the company's protocol, sent Trice home. In the end, the company terminated Trice's employment. A short time after Trice's termination, Trice filed a racial-discrimination claim with the Equal Employment Opportunity Commission. As it happens, the company learned of Trice's EEOC complaint the day after it received the employees' written statements about Toler. Members of the local workers' union, according to Toler, became upset with him over his handling of Trice. For each of the complaining employees, Toler provided an account of a disagreement that, in his view, essentially prompted a vendetta aimed at ousting him as a supervisor. The company terminated Toler's employment the day after his meeting with Hinrichs and the company's plant manager. Toler then filed the present case, arguing the employees had fabricated the allegations resulting in his termination, and, as a result, had defamed him.

Analysis: The Court of Appeals relied heavily on a Kentucky Supreme Court precedent to reach the conclusion that, generally speaking, the determination of whether a defendant abused its qualified privilege is a question of fact properly reserved for the jury. It therefore reversed the trial judge's grant of the company's motion for a directed verdict. But, continued the Supreme Court, its prior decision in no way altered the proof required for a party opposing a directed verdict motion—Toler in this case—to be successful in that opposition. Not only was the analysis undertaken by the Court of Appeals incorrect, it seemed especially curious to the justices in light of a decision of that Court of Appeals in another case that it announced on the same day as its opinion in the Toler case. That other case, *Harstad v. Whiteman*, was applauded by the justices as a thorough, accurate review of Kentucky case law and the proper analytical approach to qualified-privilege defamation cases.

The Court of Appeals in *Harstad* made a number of important observations regarding the burden of proof carried by the plaintiff in a defamation case involving the qualified privilege. In the words of the *Harstad* court:

> "It was Harstad's burden to present some evidence that would incline a reasonable person to believe that Lowe's perception was not simply the product of mistaken observation, but the result of malice, i.e., some evidence that Lowe knew she was lying or making wholly unfounded statements without regard to their truth or falsity."

In this case, Toler simply had not presented any evidence indicating the company's malicious publication. To be sure, conceded the Justices, Toler wove a "dramatic narrative filled with collusion and rumor." But simply alleging union retaliation without any further proof could not support a jury verdict against the company, and, therefore, could not defeat its directed-verdict motion. The majority of Toler's allegations revolved around the retaliatory motivations of the employees in publishing the statements to the company, rather than any maliciousness behind the company's publication during the meeting with Toler.

The company, on the other hand, acted prudently within the scope of its qualified privilege by investigating the claims levied against Toler, meeting with Toler to discuss the claims, and simply enforcing a well-known, understood, and reasonable corporate policy of not permitting such offensive statements in the workplace. Toler presented no evidence that the company excessively published the material or otherwise abused its privilege. Instead, this case presents a "paradigmatic example of why the qualified privilege is recognized: society benefits when employers, or others who share common interests, are permitted to discuss matters freely, even if those discussions are found to be based on erroneous beliefs or misinformation."

Finally, concluded the high court, Toler's argument failed because merely alleging falsity is not enough to defeat a directed-verdict motion based on the qualified privilege. As the Harstad court noted, "[e]ven were we to conclude that each of these inconsistencies was both material and indicative of a specific falsehood, we could not reasonably conclude from their falsity alone that they were malicious utterances as opposed to mistaken observations." Added the justices, "We are in much the same position with Toler's claims. And Toler 'was required to do more than assert that these statements were false; people are sometimes wrong without even suspecting it.' The qualified privilege, it should be remembered, requires evidence of malice in fact, i.e., actual malice, and 'not every erroneous statement is expressed with malice.'"

Further expounding on malice, they wrote that the abuse-of-privilege question typically is one for the jury, as are a great many determinations in tort law. But the submission of the question to the jury is not automatic. A jury is entitled to draw all reasonable inferences from the evidence, but when insufficient evidence is presented to enable a jury to infer an issue "in accordance with reason or sound thinking and within the bounds of common sense without regard to extremes or excess" a reasonable inference cannot be drawn. In other words, providing evidence permitting a jury to perform mere guesswork—"making a judgment without adequate information, or to conjecture, or to speculate"—does not defeat a directed-verdict motion.

Decision: Simply put, held the high court, Toler failed to produce any evidence tending to show that the company acted toward him with malice. The trial court's directed verdict was appropriate. Any finding of malice on the company's part would have been nothing more than conjecture or speculation. Toler was required to put forth evidence sufficient to support a jury verdict founded on reason rather than emotion or prejudice. Accordingly, in light of the company's qualified privilege, the Kentucky Supreme Court reversed the decision of the Court of Appeals and reinstated the trial court's directed verdict in favor of the company.

Case Questions

1. Why did the plaintiff claim that the company abused its qualified privilege? Why did the Supreme Court disagree and reinstate the verdict in favor of the firm? How would you rule on the matter if you were one of the justices?

2. What are the social and economic policies that underlie the creation by the courts of a qualified privilege in the business environment?

3. A plaintiff in a defamation action opposing a directed-verdict motion made by a defendant claiming a qualified privilege must produce some evidence of the defendant's actual malice to survive a directed verdict. Where did this plaintiff fail in his argument?

Concept *Summary* 3.1

DEFAMATION

- Two types:
  - Libel: written lies
  - Slander: spoken lies

- Defamation gives rise to damages if the lies harm, among other things, the plaintiff's career

- Defenses include:
  - Truth
  - Privilege
  - Immunity

- Privilege can be absolute or qualified
  - Public employers may enjoy an absolute privilege or sovereign immunity from suit
  - Private employers have a qualified privilege, meaning they are protected from suit if they speak without malice

3-2   Tortious Infliction of Emotional Distress

intentional infliction of emotional distress
purposely outrageous conduct causing emotional harm

The elements of a prima facie case of **intentional infliction of emotional distress** are:

- extreme and outrageous conduct by the defendant;
- the defendant's intention of causing, or reckless disregard of the likelihood of causing, emotional distress;
- the plaintiff's suffering of severe emotional distress; and
- as a direct result of the defendant's extreme and outrageous conduct.

negligent infliction of emotional distress
carelessly outrageous conduct causing emotional harm

A minority of jurisdictions also recognize the tort of **negligent infliction of emotional distress**. In these states, a defendant may be liable in damages for unreasonable behavior that results in severe emotional harm to the plaintiff, even though the defendant never meant to inflict any harm.

The following case involves a claim of intentional infliction of emotional distress.

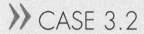

» CASE 3.2

NELSON V. TARGET CORPORATION
334 P.3d 1010 (Utah Ct. App. 2014)

Nelson began working at a Target retail store in Orem, Utah, in January 1997. Nelson was fired on February 25, 2011, after Target security officers determined that she took a customer's wallet. The customer had contacted Target's security department on February 18 to report that her wallet was missing and that she may have left it at a checkout lane after paying for her groceries. Target's security team reviewed the store's video surveillance footage to determine what had happened. Video footage from a checkout location showed Nelson putting the customer's wallet in her purse. In the video, Nelson, who was shopping after her shift ended that day, took her own wallet out of her purse to pay for groceries. Nelson noticed another wallet a previous customer apparently left at the checkout stand near the credit card reader, glanced at the cashier as the cashier turned away, picked up the customer's wallet with her right hand while her own wallet was still in her left, and quickly placed it in her purse, which was in the shopping cart next to her. Nelson then finished paying for her groceries with her own wallet still in her hand, put her wallet back in her purse on top of the customer's wallet, and left the store.

A Target security officer called Nelson at home after reviewing the video. Nelson confirmed that she had the wallet, and the security officer asked her to return it. The officer stated in a deposition that Nelson seemed surprised by his question and returned the wallet within 10 minutes. Nelson claimed that she put the wallet in her purse because she mistook it for her own.

Jason Turner, Target's store security chief, investigated the wallet incident. He interviewed the security officer and viewed several store surveillance videos of the event. After reviewing "the video over and over and over again to eliminate any of the possibilities that it could have been an accident," Turner concluded that there was "no way" Nelson could have taken the wallet by mistake.

Turner interviewed Nelson about the incident on February 25, 2011. As required by company policy, a human resources representative was also present at the interview. After some initial questioning, Turner left the room to allow Nelson time to complete a written statement explaining why she took the wallet. Nelson wrote that she took the wallet inadvertently and did not realize she had it until she got home. Turner returned, reviewed Nelson's statement, listened to Nelson explain her version of the incident, and told Nelson he did not believe her. After Nelson refused to amend her written statement, Turner left the room and returned with a supervisor who informed Nelson that Target was dismissing her.

In April 2011, Nelson sued Target for intentional infliction of emotional distress, among other claims. In the complaint, Nelson alleged that "she inadvertently picked up a wallet, resembling her own," and "immediately returned" it when she realized her mistake. She further alleged that Turner "interrogated [her] at length and repeatedly accused [her] of being dishonest" even though he knew or should have known that Nelson was telling the truth. Nelson claimed that Turner's questioning caused her "to suffer emotional distress," along with other claims.

Target moved for summary judgment on all of Nelson's claims. Nelson opposed the motion, filed a discovery motion requesting leave to depose two additional witnesses, and moved to amend her complaint to add a claim for breach of the covenant of good faith and fair dealing. The court granted Target's motion for summary judgment on each claim. With respect to the emotional distress claim, the court concluded that "the facts do not demonstrate any conduct by [Target], or [its] agent, Mr. Turner, so outrageous and intolerable that it would offend accepted standards of morality and decency."

The Court of Appeals found that the trial judge properly denied Nelson's claim of intentional infliction of emotional distress. Nelson argued that because Turner, the store security chief, admitted that he "conducted the interrogation after he had determined that Nelson had intentionally taken the wallet and was to be terminated, ... the interview served no legitimate purpose other than to inflict emotional distress or to extract an admission from Nelson through intimidation in order to attempt to insulate Target from liability." But, wrote the appellate judges, even if Turner intended to cause Nelson some distress, Nelson must still show that Turner's conduct during the interview was "outrageous and intolerable in that [it] offend[s] against the generally accepted standards of decency and morality." Conduct that is merely "unreasonable, unkind, or unfair" does not qualify. Rather, the plaintiff must identify behavior so extreme that it "evoke[s] outrage or revulsion."

Here, concluded the court, Turner told Nelson that he did not believe she had taken the wallet by mistake and gave her several opportunities to explain herself. The interview was private and, according to company policy, conducted in the presence of a human resources representative. There was no evidence that Turner was verbally abusive or unprofessional. To the extent Nelson alleged that Turner interviewed her so that Target could avoid liability for her termination, such a purpose was perfectly legitimate and did not support Nelson's claim that Target deliberately caused her emotional distress. And the fact that Turner had already concluded that Nelson intentionally took the wallet and interviewed her for the sole purpose of persuading Nelson to admit it simply did not offend "generally accepted standards of decency and morality." Consequently, the district court did not err when it determined that Turner's conduct was not sufficiently outrageous for Nelson's claim to withstand summary judgment.

Case Questions

1. Explain why the court did not find that the defendant's interview with the plaintiff constituted intentional infliction of emotional distress.

2. The case summary states that the plaintiff needed to show conduct that was "outrageous and intolerable in that [it] offend[s] against the generally accepted standards of decency and morality" in order to prove her claim of intentional infliction of emotional distress. Was there any evidence offered by the plaintiff that supported her contention? More specifically, should the security officer have been required to terminate the interrogation once the plaintiff provided her signed statement?

3. Why is this a contended case of *intentional* infliction of emotional distress, and not *negligent* infliction of emotional distress?

THE **WORKING** LAW

Infliction of Emotional Distress via Social Networking Sites

On April 19, 2006, Anna Draker, a vice-principal at Clark High School in Texas, was advised by a coworker that some students had created a website on MySpace.com. The website, which appeared to have been created by Draker, contained her name, photo, and place of employment, as well as explicit and graphic sexual references. It was subsequently discovered that Benjamin Schreiber and Ryan Todd, at the time both minors and students at Clark High School, were responsible for creating the website. Draker sued the students and their parents, alleging, among other things, intentional infliction of emotional distress.

The Texas Court of Appeals said of her emotional distress claim, "The Internet capabilities of modern society present numerous opportunities for individuals to engage in extreme and outrageous conduct that can produce severe emotional distress.[5] There appears to be little civil remedy for the injured targets of these Internet communications. Intentional infliction of emotional distress would seem to be one option. But as it has developed, the tort is nearly impossible to establish. The citizens of Texas would be better served by a fair and workable framework in which to present their claims, or by an honest statement that there is, in fact, no remedy for their damages." See *Draker v. Schreiber*, 271 S.W.3d 318 (Tex. App. 2008).

---

[5] See *Layshockv Hermitage Sch. Dist.*, 496 F. Supp. 2d 587, 590-91(W.D. Pa. 2007) (discussing a student's creation of a false MySpace profile of his high school principal); David L. Hudson, Jr., *Taming the Gossipmongers*, 94 A.B.A.J. 19 (2008) (reviewing the use of the 1996 Communications Decency Act to protect Web publishers, such as juicycampus.com, from liability for content created by third parties); John Seigenthaler, Op-Ed, "A False Wikipedia 'Biography,'" *USA Today*, November 29, 2005, available at http://www.usatoday.com/news/opinion/editorials/2005-11-29-wikipedia-edit_x.htm (detailing the "Internet character assassination" of a former government official with an Internet "biography" reference, indicating that the official was suspected of involvement in the assassinations of President John Kennedy and Attorney General Robert Kennedy); and Linda Deutsch, "Woman Pleads Not Guilty in Internet Suicide Case," *USA Today*, June 16, 2008, available at http://www.usatoday.com/news/nation/2008-06-16-327594069_x.htm (discussing a 13-year-old girl's suicide after receiving more than a dozen cruel messages from a nonexistent teen boy via a false MySpace profile).

Concept *Summary* 3.2

INFLICTION OF EMOTIONAL DISTRESS

- May be intentionally or negligently inflicted
  - Intentional infliction requires outrageous conduct by defendant with the intent and result of causing severe emotional distress to the plaintiff
  - Negligent infliction requires similarly extreme behavior by the defendant, who, though lacking a bad intent, carelessly causes severe emotional harm to the plaintiff
- Many courts shy away from this tort, particularly the negligent variety, because of problems of proving the extent of the plaintiff's suffering, and/or the causal connection, particularly where the defendant never intended to cause the harm
- Social networking sites, such as Facebook and Myspace, have vastly expanded the potential for causing harm, because the hapless target potentially may be exposed to the entire universe of cyberspace

3-3   Tortious Interference with Contract

tortious interference with contract
unprivileged intrusion into a contractual relationship

Another tort worth noting, based upon its common occurrence in the context of employment law, is **tortious interference with contract**. It is a claim that is sometimes available to plaintiff-employees against third parties, who sometimes are named as additional defendants along with the plaintiff's employer in cases of alleged wrongful termination or breach of an employment contract. Following are some recent examples of how this tort plays out in real-world situations.

CASE 3.3

BULWER V. MOUNT AUBURN HOSP.
86 Mass. App. Ct. 316, 16 N.E.3d 1090 (2014)

Facts: An employee, who was an experienced physician and a black man from Belize, brought his action against his hospital employer after he was terminated from the residency program, alleging discrimination and retaliation based on his race and national origin, breach of contract, defamation, and tortious interference with contractual relationship. He had joined the residency program under a one-year contract, with the possibility of advancement to a second year of residency upon successful completion of the first. Eight months into the program, he was told that the hospital would not extend a second-year contract to him because of concerns in the areas of patient care, interpersonal and communication skills, and practice-based learning (based on observation and interviews by hospital supervisors). However, he would be allowed to continue his residency through the end of his first year. One month later, however, he was terminated. He sued and, following discovery, the Superior Court granted summary judgment in favor of the employer. Bulwer appealed.

Issue: Did the individually named defendants (the employee's supervisors at the hospital) intentionally interfere with the employee's contractual relationship with the hospital?

Decision: To prove that the defendants intentionally interfered with his contractual relationship with the hospital, the plaintiff had to prove that they acted "malevolently, i.e., for a spiteful malignant purpose unrelated to the legitimate corporate interest." Although the appellate court concluded that the record was sufficient to put the claim of discrimination to a jury, that record did not suffice to raise a genuine issue of fact regarding malevolence on the part of the three individual defendants.

CASE 3.4

DUTY V. BOYS AND GIRLS CLUB OF PORTER COUNTY
— N.E.3d —, 2014 WL 7201770 (Ind. Ct. App. 2014)

Facts: A former employee, Dawn Duty, brought action against her former employer, the Boys and Girls Club of Porter County (BGC), and a former coworker, Charles R. Leer, alleging wrongful discharge and tortious interference with a contractual relationship, claiming that the employer violated its policy to protect employees from retaliation under the employee handbook's whistleblower policy and that the coworker persuaded the employer to terminate her employment. The superior court dismissed all the claims, and the employee appealed.

Issue: Did the plaintiff prove a tortious interference claim against the defendants?

Decision: The court's reading of Duty's allegations led to the conclusion that they were sufficiently specific regarding Leer's alleged wrongful and unjustified conduct. First, Duty's second amended complaint alleged that Leer "engaged in statements and conduct with [the] purpose and intent[ ] to persuade and induce [BGC] … to terminate [Duty] as an employee of [BGC]." Under 'notice pleading', Duty did not have to describe those statements and conduct with more specificity than that. Moreover, Duty alleged that Leer's statements and conduct were "in retaliation for [her] invocation of the Whistleblower policy of [BGC] with the intent[ ] to induce [BGC] to terminate its employment of [Duty]" and that Leer's actions were "vindictive against [Duty] for what he thought were damaging [sic] to his reputation[.]" The court observed that vindictiveness is, by its very nature, malicious. Thus, Duty pled facts sufficient to show that the alleged breach was malicious and exclusively directed to the injury and damage of Duty. The judges held that Duty stated a claim upon which relief could be granted for tortious interference with a contractual relationship. They reinstated her case.

» CASE 3.5

OLIVER V. ORLEANS PARISH SCHOOL BD.

133 So.3d 38 (La. App. 4 Cir. 2014)

Facts: Employees of a parish school district, who were terminated by a reduction in force (RIF) after failing schools in the parish were transferred to the Recovery School District (RSD), filed a class action against the board and the Louisiana Department of Education (LDOE) for wrongful termination and also asserted a claim against LDOE for tortious interference with their employment contracts. Following a bench trial, the civil district court judge entered judgment for the employees, and the defendants sought appellate review.

Issue: Do the plaintiffs have a tortious interference with contract claim against the defendant, because it terminated their employment?

Decision: The trial court relied on a precedent called *9 to 5 Fashions v. Spurney*, in determining that the state had intentionally and tortiously interfered with the appellees' vested property rights in continued employment. However, the appellate court disagreed, finding that the appellees failed to establish the necessary elements to prove a claim of tortious interference.

In *9 to 5*, the Louisiana Supreme Court had set forth five elements that must be proven to succeed in a claim for tortious interference of contract: (1) the existence of a contract or a legally protected interest between the plaintiff and the corporation; (2) the corporate officer's knowledge of the contract; (3) the officer's intentional inducement or causation of the corporation to breach the contract or his intentional rendition of its performance impossible or more burdensome; (4) absence of justification on the part of the officer; and (5) causation of damages to the plaintiff by the breach of contract or difficulty of its performance brought about by the officer.

In order to find that there was a tortious interference with contract, all five elements must be proven. In its discussion on the wrongful termination, the appellate panel acknowledged that the appellees had a vested property right in their employment. However, the judges also recognized that the right is not absolute. They found that ACT 35 (which allowed for the automatic transfer of a failing school to the RSD, if that school was in a district that was "academically in crisis") together with the Board's policy provided the authority to implement an RIF. In the same manner, they found that ACT 35 provided the state with the power and authority to transfer funding and facilities to the RSD. Therefore, the trial court's determination that the defendant's actions were unauthorized and unjustified was "clearly wrong," which defeats the tortious interference with contract claim.

Concept *Summary* 3.3

TORTIOUS INTERFERENCE WITH CONTRACT

- A cause of action aimed at a third party who allegedly causes the plaintiff to be fired or interferes with his or her ability to get a job

- The third party must interfere for an improper reason, such as animosity toward the plaintiff, and not for a valid business reason, in order to be held responsible for this tort

- In at least some jurisdictions, if the third party acts out of mixed motives, such as both malice and a legitimate business reason, the plaintiff will not have a cause of action for tortuous interference

ethical DILEMMA

WHEN AN EMPLOYEE–LAWYER SUES HIS OWN LAW FIRM

In September 2010, a California attorney sued his own law firm, claiming that his pay had been docked because he refused to attend a weekend-long "New Warrior" personal-development seminar that allegedly would include the men disrobing and passing around a wooden phallus. According to the lawyer's complaint, filed in the Orange County Superior Court, the event was hosted by the ManKind Project. The organization's website[6] states,

> The ManKind Project flies in the face of rigid stereotypes about the "Sensitive New Age Man" AND the "Macho Man". We ask men to go right up to the edge—and beyond it—in a culture that seems to be comfortable with mediocrity and passivity from men. We ask men to stop living a vicarious adventure through their TV's and step into a real time adventure to win back their passion for life. We ask men to confront the real issues, to get 100% honest about who they are. Some men have a really hard time doing that. Many of us did too, but we took the risk anyway.

The website describes the "New Warrior Training Adventure" as "a modern male initiation and self-examination. We believe that this is crucial to the development of a healthy and mature male self, no matter how old a man is. It is the 'hero's journey' of classical literature and myth that has nearly disappeared in modern culture. We ask men to stop living vicariously through movies, television, addictions and distractions and step up into their own adventure—in real time and surrounded by other men."[7]

In a news story about the lawsuit, the executive director of the ManKind Project was cited as saying that nudity was optional, as was the exercise of which the plaintiff complained.[8]

The plaintiff-attorney claimed he was being paid $15,000 a month until he refused to attend the event. The defendant-firm countered that his six-month contract wasn't renewed because his performance was sub-par. The attorney's complaint pled every cause of action discussed in this chapter, and then some:

1. Sexual harassment
2. Retaliation
3. Failure to pay wages
4. Failure to provide itemized statements (of wages)
5. Constructive termination
6. Intentional interference with economic advantage
7. Breach of written contract

---

[6] http://mankindproject.org.

[7] http://mankindproject.org/new-warrior-training-adventure.

[8] See David Lat, "Lawsuit of the Day: Pass the Wooden Dildo, Please," Above the Law, October 11, 2010, available at http://abovethelaw.com/2010/10/lawsuit-of-the-day-pass-the-wooden-dildo-please; and Ray Sanchez, "Calif. Lawyer Sues over Attending All-Male Mountain Retreat," ABC News, September 30, 2010, available at http://abcnews.go.com/Business/lawyer-sues-attending-male-retreat/story?id=11760666#.T6VgJe0qNT6.

8. Breach of oral contract
9. Intentional infliction of emotional distress[9]

Putting aside the potential merits of the case, is it ethically inappropriate for an attorney to sue his own law firm? Put another way, would it be more appropriate for the plaintiff to have brought ethics charges against the firm and its attorneys before the California bar association? What are the pros and cons of such a public policy, if it were adopted by the state's supreme court and imposed by the court on the state's legal profession?

Putting aside the ethical issue for a moment, taking the facts as stated above, which—if any—of the plaintiff's causes of action seem potentially meritorious to you?

[9] See *Eggleston v. Bisnar/Chase LLP*, Case No. 00404255 (Cal. Superior Ct., Orange County, Aug. 31, 2010), available at http://www.courthousenews.com/2010/09/03/Sensitivity.pdf.

3-4 Retaliatory Demotion

retaliatory demotion
reduction in rank, salary, or job title as a punishment

Students also should alert themselves to the less-commonly encountered cause of action called **retaliatory demotion**, a tort that echoes the wrongful discharge cause of action considered in Chapter 2. The elements of the tort are much the same as with a wrongful discharge. Consequently, if firing the employee would be illegal under the circumstances, the chances are good that a demotion is equally illegitimate in the eyes of the courts.

Concept *Summary* 3.4

RETALIATORY DEMOTION

- The rules governing wrongful discharge (Chapter 2) generally apply with equal force to retaliatory demotions

- Retaliatory demotion cases are somewhat more delicate than wrongful discharge suits, because the plaintiff remains an employee of the defendant-firm, unless the latter takes the next step and actually fires him or her

- This fact creates complex ethical issues for the parties and the courts to sort out

3-5 Theft of Trade Secrets

trade secret
proprietary information protected by common law or state statute

In all of the foregoing cases, the plaintiffs were employees and former employees, while the defendants were companies that were accused by these plaintiffs of tortious behavior that allegedly injured these workers. Less frequently, employers sue their own employees. One area of tort law in which such suits are becoming increasingly more common is **trade secrets**. In this Information Age, a knowledgeable and unscrupulous employee can walk off the employer's premises with immensely valuable trade secrets encapsulated on a single compact disc. The common law will protect employers from such misappropriations by allowing judges to issue injunctions and award damages. Sometimes employers reinforce their common-law rights by requiring employees to sign confidentiality and noncompetition agreements at the time of hire. These latter agreements expressly forbid such employees from joining a competitor for a specified period of time after leaving the company. In some states, such illicit employee behavior is also a crime.

≫ CASE 3.6

TSG FINISHING, LLC v. BOLLINGER

--S.E.2d--, 2014 WL 7463824 (N.C. App. 2014), motion for temporary stay granted, --S.E.2d--, 2015 WL 246016 (N.C. Supr. Ct. 2015)

Facts: TSG Finishing is in the business of fabric finishing. It has three plants in Catawba County, North Carolina. Rather than manufacturing fabrics, TSG applies chemical coatings to achieve whichever result is desired by the customer, such as coloring, stiffening, deodorizing, and abrasion resistance.

The defendant began working in the field of fabric finishing for Geltman Corporation after graduating from high school in 1982. He had no formal education beyond high school. TSG, the plaintiff's predecessor firm, acquired Geltman in 1992, and the defendant stayed on to work for TSG, Inc. By the late 1990s, he was promoted to quality control manager.

Bollinger was responsible for assessing a customer's finishing needs and developing a finishing protocol for that customer. He also helped in the creation of a "style data card" for each customer. The style data cards contained information on each step of the finishing process.

TSG expended great effort to keep its customer and finishing information confidential. Specifically, according to the court, it used a code system in its communications with customers that allowed the customer to identify the type of finish it wanted, but did not reveal the chemicals or processes involved in creating that finish. TSG had confidentiality agreements in place with many of its customers. Third parties were required to sign confidentiality agreements and received a temporary identification badge when visiting TSG's facilities. TSG's computers were password protected, with additional passwords being required to access the company's production information.

In 2007, TSG, and the defendant entered into a nondisclosure and noncompete agreement. In exchange for an annual increase in compensation of $1,300.00 and a $3,500.00 signing bonus, the defendant agreed not to disclose TSG's confidential and proprietary trade secrets and further assented to employment restrictions after his tenure at the company ended.

TSG filed for bankruptcy in 2009. By a plan approved by the United States Bankruptcy Court on May 1, 2011, the company transferred its interests to the plaintiff, previously a wholly owned operating subsidy of TSG, which remained in operation. According to the defendant, every aspect of his day-to-day job remained the same after the bankruptcy reorganization.

In July 2013, Bollinger and a direct competitor of TSG, American Custom Finishing, LLC ("ACF"), began negotiations regarding the defendant's potential to leave TSG and work for ACF. According to TSG Finishing, the defendant resigned from his position on November 21, 2013 and announced that he was leaving to become plant manager for ACF at a plant five miles away from TSG Finishing. Bollinger claimed that he gave the plaintiff two weeks' notice on November 21, 2013 but was terminated immediately and escorted off of the premises. He began working for ACF the following Monday. During his deposition, Bollinger testified that TSG Finishing and ACF shared certain customers, and that he was responsible for performing similar customer evaluations for ACF as he did at TSG.

TSG Finishing filed suit against the defendant on January 16, 2014, alleging claims for breach of contract, misappropriation of trade secrets, and unfair and deceptive practices. The plaintiff also moved for a preliminary injunction to prevent the defendant from breaching his noncompete agreement and misappropriating TSG Finishing's trade secrets. A confidential hearing was held on the plaintiff's motion, and by order entered on February 20, 2014, the trial court denied the motion for a preliminary injunction. The plaintiff filed its timely notice of appeal.

Analysis: The plaintiff argued that the trial court erred by concluding that it had not demonstrated a likelihood of success on the merits of its claim for trade secret misappropriation. After careful review, the appellate court agreed.

The Trade Secrets Protection Act ("TSPA") in North Carolina allows for a private cause of action where a plaintiff can prove the "acquisition, disclosure, or use of a trade secret of another without express or implied authority or consent, unless such trade secret was arrived at by independent development, reverse engineering, or was obtained from another person with a right to disclose the trade secret." A trade secret under this statute

"a. Derives independent actual or potential commercial value from not being generally known or readily ascertainable through independent development or reverse engineering by persons who can obtain economic value from its disclosure or use; and

b. Is the subject of efforts that are reasonable under the circumstances to maintain its secrecy."

To determine what information should be treated as a trade secret for the purposes of protection under the TSPA, the Court should consider the following factors:

"(1) the extent to which the information is known outside the business;
(2) the extent to which it is known to employees and others involved in the business;
(3) the extent of measures taken to guard secrecy of the information;
(4) the value of the information to business and its competitors;
(5) the amount of effort or money expended in developing the information; and
(6) the ease or difficulty with which the information could properly be acquired or duplicated by others."

Misappropriation of a trade secret is prima facie established by the introduction of substantial evidence that the person against whom relief is sought both:

"(1) Knows or should have known of the trade secret; and

(2) Has had a specific opportunity to acquire it for disclosure or use or has acquired, disclosed, or used it without the express or implied consent or authority of the owner."

Here, the trial court determined that the plaintiff failed to demonstrate a likelihood of success on the merits of its misappropriation of trade secrets claim for the following reasons: (1) the plaintiff asserted that its finishing process "as a whole" was the trade secret for which it sought protection, and under the holding of a 2002 North Carolina Supreme Court case, *Analog Devices, Inc. v. Michalski*, general processes were deemed to be too vague to receive TSPA protection; and (2) the defendant's familiarity with customer preferences was "more akin to general knowledge and skill acquired on the job than any trade secret maintained by [p]laintiff." For the following reasons, the appellate panel disagreed with the trial court's conclusions.

First, contrary to the trial court's assessment of the preliminary injunction hearing, the plaintiff did not "continually assert" that it was the "combination of [the] components," or the "process as a whole," for which it sought protection. Although TSG Finishing's Chief Executive Officer Jack Rosenstein did say that the entire equation of processes was a trade secret in and of itself, he also testified that the particular steps in the process were also trade secrets. As an example, Rosenstein high-lighted the needle punch technique on a style data card that Bollinger had worked on during his time at TSG. The customer initially requested that the fabric be put through the needle punch machine one time at a specific setting. Through trial and error, the defendant discovered that the customer's desired result could not be accomplished by running the needle punch machine one time at this setting, so he changed the process after experimenting with varying settings. Rosenstein testified the needle punch research for this client, as well as similar types of experimentation done to various processes throughout the finish equation, were trade secrets.

Therefore, held the appeals court, it was not just the process as a whole, but the specific knowledge defendant gained as to each discrete step in the process, that TSG Finishing sought to protect.

Based on the *Analog Devices, Inc.* decision, the trial court concluded that the plaintiff had failed to "put forward enough facts to support trade secret protection over the process as a whole or any particular component such that the [trial court] would be justified in granting the injunction sought." However, the court in *Analog*

Devices, Inc. upheld the denial of a preliminary injunction in part because the differences between the defendant's former and new employers "render[ed] the alleged trade secrets largely non-transferable." Furthermore, the court determined that the plaintiff did not carry its burden of producing evidence specifically identifying the trade secrets it sought to protect. The evidence before that court showed that some of the plaintiff's production techniques were "easily and readily reverse engineered," while others were "either generally known in the industry, are process dependent so as to preclude misappropriation, or are readily ascertainable by reverse engineering." Finally, regarding the processes used by the plaintiff, the court found that there were substantial differences between the products of the two companies that would "require new experimentation and development of new ways to effectively identify efforts that will lead to successful development." Thus, the court affirmed the trial court's denial of the preliminary injunction.

The court found the facts of this case readily distinguishable from *Analog Devices, Inc.*, holding that they demonstrated that TSG Finishing would likely prevail on the merits of its claim for misappropriation of trade secrets. TSG Finishing presented sufficient evidence on its specific trade secrets to warrant protection. First, Rosenstein testified that the company spent $500,000.00 per year on research and development in order to create unique finishes and applications for its customers.

Bollinger himself testified that the results of his experimentation at TSG Finishing regarding specific process refinements were not known outside the firm. Rosenstein also testified that the defendant's work was not something that anyone else in the industry would know without years of trial and error by experienced technicians. Security measures were in place such that only top-level employees were familiar with the proprietary information defendant was in charge of developing. The trial court acknowledged in its order that the plaintiff "maintains significant security measures over its finishing process." In fact, TSG made its employees, customers, and facility visitors sign confidentiality forms to protect this information. Additionally, Rosenstein testified that the defendant's disclosure of the trade secrets would give ACF the opportunity to save "untold amounts of hours, days, weeks, and months to come up with these finishes and these applications." Rosenstein testified that the defendant could help ACF achieve the customers' desired results, which they sometimes shared with the company, without spending the money on research and development that TSG Finishing invested. The record reflected that Bollinger admitted as much in his deposition when he testified that he performed many of the same duties for ACF for some of the same customers that he formerly served at TSG Finishing. Therefore, unlike in *Analog Devices, Inc.*, there was significant evidence showing that TSG Finishing's trade secrets were transferrable to ACF. Over the past two decades, TSG had invested millions of dollars to develop and protect the information the defendant compiled through his years of employment. The director of operations at TSG Finishing testified in his deposition that the defendant would sometimes work for more than a year on a process in order to achieve a desired result. There was no indication in the record that these processes were able to be "reverse engineered" like those in *Analog Devices, Inc.*, and it was undisputed that they were not generally known throughout the industry.

In sum, each of the relevant factors weighed in the plaintiff's favor. The company specifically identified the production factors for which it claimed trade secret protection. Bollinger acknowledged during his deposition that he performed research and development for these factors during his time at TSG and TSG Finishing and was responsible for keeping customer- and fabric-specific proprietary information regarding these processes on the style data cards. Therefore, the appellate court concluded that the plaintiff carried its burden of presenting evidence sufficient to identify the specific trade secrets protected by the TSPA.

Additionally, the judges held that the plaintiff presented prima facie evidence of misappropriation of its trade secrets. "Direct evidence ... is not necessary to establish a claim for misappropriation of trade secrets; rather, such a claim may be proven through circumstantial evidence." Bollinger testified that he was being asked to perform similar duties for ACF as he did at TSG and TSG Finishing, including evaluating customer needs and organizing production processes. The defendant acknowledged that TSG Finishing and ACF shared customers and that he was currently working with multiple customers for ACF that he had served at TSG. Specifically, he admitted that he had done independent research and experimentation for TSG on the needle punch, finish, and heating processes for one specific customer that he now served at ACF, and that he talked about the various components of the TSG-style data cards with ACF management personnel. This, concluded the court, was precisely the type of threatened misappropriation, if not actual misappropriation, that the TSPA aims to prevent through issuance of a preliminary injunction.

Based on the foregoing, the court concluded that the plaintiff demonstrated a likelihood of success on the merits of his claim for trade secret misappropriation.

NOTE: As this edition was being prepared for press in 2015, the North Carolina Supreme Court had granted the defendant's motion to stay the injunction while it considered hearing his appeal.

Case Questions

1. Should a defendant such as Bollinger be prohibited from making use of the experience of a working lifetime in trying to better his career with another employer? Given that he voluntarily entered into noncompete and nondisclosure agreements, do you think he was paid enough in return to justify the restrictions placed on his future?

2. Do you think the plaintiff presented prima facie evidence of misappropriation of its trade secrets under the North Carolina state statute? Or did it simply show that the defendant's own hard work and ingenuity made him an experienced, and therefore very attractive, target for the plaintiff's competitor?

3. Can you conceive of a middle ground that could have set a better way to balance the parties' conflicting interests in lieu of years of costly litigation?

Concept *Summary* 3.5

THEFT OF TRADE SECRETS

- This is a rare area in which the employer or former employer appears in the guise of plaintiff rather than defendant

- The term "trade secrets" often is synonymous with "proprietary information"

- The common law of most states imposes an obligation upon employees to respect and protect the trade secrets of their employers
    - Confidentiality and noncompetition agreements often are required by employers at the time of hire in order to bolster their common-law protections
    - In some states, such misappropriation of trade secrets also is a crime

- Employers whose employees misappropriate trade secrets for their own use or for the benefit of a new employer, are entitled to obtain an injunction (court order) putting a stop to such illegal behavior

CHAPTER REVIEW

» Key Terms

tort	4 1	qualified privilege	4 3	tortious interference with contract	4 8
defamation	4 2	intentional infliction of emotional distress	4 5	retaliatory demotion	5 2
libel	4 2			trade secret	5 2
slander	4 2	negligent infliction of emotional distress	4 5		
strict liability	4 2				

Summary

- Defamation can be verbal (slander) or written (libel). Many states recognize a qualified business privilege—that commercial efficiency demands that employers be able to share information about employees and applicants without undue fear of litigation. The qualified privilege requires the plaintiff-employee, who claims employer defamation, to prove the employer spoke falsely out of malice—that is, knew or should have known what was communicated was false.

- Infliction of emotional distress is a tort, which usually requires proof by the plaintiff-employee that the employer's actions, which caused severe emotional distress, were outrageous. The normal stress involved in being fired from one's job, without something more, normally will not support this tort claim.

  - Third parties are sometimes named as defendants in wrongful discharge suites, where the plaintiff-employee claims that the third party maliciously interfered with his or her employment contract or future job opportunities.

  - Closely affiliated with wrongful discharge is the lesser offense of retaliatory demotion. Most courts approach the latter tort similarly to assessing the merits of a wrongful termination claim. However, these cases are often somewhat trickier than wrongful firings, because the parties typically remain in an employment relationship while the suit proceeds. This situation sometimes causes the employer-defendant to give in to the urge to convert the demotion into an actual job termination. Complex ethical issues, such as the plaintiff's duty of loyalty to his or her employer, make the decisions of both employer and employee extremely difficult.

- In this Information Age, not only are employees suing their employers for a variety of alleged torts, but increasingly employers are suing their former employees, accusing them of theft of the company's trade secrets. Some states treat misappropriation as garden-variety theft, whereas others have criminal statutes expressly directed to this particular offense. Either way, such theft is also a subset of the tort of conversion of another's property. Because the employer usually alleges irreparable harm, injunctions are a typical part of the court's remedy when the plaintiff-employer prevails.

» Problems

» Questions

1. How does one prove qualified privilege? Give an example in which a defendant would not meet the requirements for qualified privilege.

2. Give some examples of absolute and qualified privilege with regard to invasion of privacy and defamation as they may occur in the workplace.

3. What remedies are available to an employer looking to stop an employee or former employee who misappropriates trade secrets?

4. What defenses are available in a strict liability case?

5. Are there circumstances in which a demotion could constitute a breach of contract, whether or not the demotion is retaliatory?

» Case Problems

6. In 1995, Robert Reeves's law firm employed Hanlon as an attorney. In 1997, the firm employed Greene as an associate attorney. In 1998, Reeves entered into an agreement with Hanlon whereby Hanlon could earn an equity position in a law firm to be formed; thereafter, the firm's name was changed to "Reeves and Hanlon, Professional Law Corporation." On or about June 30, 1999, both Hanlon and Greene resigned from Reeves's firm without notice or warning to form their own firm, Hanlon & Greene (H & G). They persuaded the plaintiffs' employees to join H & G, and personally solicited the plaintiffs' clients to discharge the plaintiffs and to instead obtain services from H & G, among other claims. The complaint asserted several causes of action, including tortious interference with contractual relations with the law firm's at-will employees, as well as misappropriation of trade secrets.

    Based on what you learned in this chapter, do you think the defendants were liable for tortious interference in this case? Explain why or why not. Further, do you think the defendants

misappropriated their former employers' trade secrets by using their client list to convince clients to obtain services from H&G? Explain why or why not. [See *Reeves v. Hanlon*, 33 Cal. 4th 1140, 95 P.3d 513 (2004).]

7. Triangle Fire was a fire equipment provider and service company that had employed Andres Davila as a sales representative. As part of his employment contract, Davila signed a noncompetition and nonsolicitation agreement. Davila left Triangle Fire and began working for a rival fire equipment service company, Sea Coast Fire. Triangle Fire ultimately brought suit against both Davila and Sea Coast Fire.

    In the course of the litigation, Triangle Fire submitted interrogatories and requests for production seeking information regarding Sea Coast Fire's customer lists, customer contact information, and pricing information. Sea Coast Fire objected and filed a motion for a protective order. It alleged that Triangle Fire sought trade secret information. Triangle Fire contended the requested materials were not trade secrets. Without conducting an "in camera" inspection of the requested information or holding an evidentiary hearing, the trial court ordered the production of the discovery. Two days later, the court entered a second order limiting the discovery to certain dates.

    Do you think the materials sought by Triangle Fire in their discovery request constituted trade secrets? Explain why or why not. [See *Sea Coast Fire, Inc. v. Triangle Fire, Inc.*, --- So.3d ----, 2014 WL 6679018 Fla. App. 3 Dist. (2014).]

8. A former tenured professor brought an action against the university and its assistant vice president (AVP) for human resources for defamation. The defamation claim was predicated on the fact that the AVP sent a letter to the former professor, directing him to participate in a fit-for-duty evaluation, which listed the frightening behavior people had attributed to him in the previous weeks, and then sent a copy of that letter to the doctor who would perform the evaluation. The court granted the university a nonsuit on the defamation action, based on

qualified common interest privilege, which protects "a communication, without malice, to a person interested therein ... by one who is also interested."

Do you think the court correctly granted the nonsuit? Or do you think the former professor had a case for defamation against his former employers? If not, what additional evidence might have swayed the judge to find for the professor? [See *Kao v. University of San Francisco*, 229 Cal. App. 4th 437, 177 Cal.Rptr.3d 145 1 Dist. (2014).]

9. A former employee filed a wrongful termination complaint against his employer. The employer filed a motion to dismiss the complaint, which resulted in a hearing that received widespread media attention. After the hearing, the *Wall Street Journal* published an online article about the case. According to the article, the employer provided an e-mail response to the *Journal*'s inquiry that allegedly said:

> While I have largely stayed silent on the matter to this point, the recycling of his allegations must be addressed.... We have a substantial list of reasons why [the employee] was fired for cause and interestingly he has not refuted a single one of them. Instead, he has attempted to explain his termination by using outright lies and fabrications which seem to have their origins in delusion.

The plaintiff subsequently amended his complaint, adding a claim for defamation per se against the employer. The amended complaint alleged that the statements published in the *Wall Street Journal* were false and defamatory, unprivileged, published maliciously and known to be false or in reckless disregard of the truth, and necessarily injurious to the employee's professional reputation.

The employer filed motions to dismiss the defamation claim, arguing that the statements were absolutely privileged communications made in the course of judicial proceedings or, in the alternative, were protected by the conditional privilege of reply. Would you side with the employer or the employee in this case? Explain why. [See *Jacobs v. Adelson*, 325 P.3d 1282 Nev. (2014).]

10. A public accounting firm executed an asset purchase agreement with another public accounting firm, Lloyd and Company C.P.A., P.C., that contained

covenants by the shareholders of Lloyd that they would not solicit specified clients of the plaintiff. The agreement also contemplated that the plaintiff firm would thereafter employ Lloyd shareholders, and defendant Kelly A. Dawson, a Lloyd shareholder, entered into an employment agreement with the plaintiff that included a provision that she would continue to be bound by the nonsolicitation covenants in the agreement. Dawson thereafter left the plaintiff's employ to work for defendant John S. Trussalo, Certified Public Accountants, P.C., a competitor of the plaintiff.

The plaintiff commenced an action alleging, among other things, that Dawson solicited certain clients in violation of the agreement. The complaint alleged, among other claims, tortious interference with contract by Trussalo.

Based on what you know about tortious interference with a contract, do you think Trussalo should be held liable for hiring Dawson? [See *Buffamante Whipple Buttafaro, Certified Public Accountants, P.C. v. Dawson*, 118 A.D.3d 1283, 988 N.Y.S.2d 341 N.Y.A.D. 4 Dept. (2014).]

11. Plaintiff Michael Battaglia was a long-term employee of defendant United Parcel Service, Inc. (UPS), serving in a variety of positions and eventually reaching the supervisory ranks. Although he accepted a change in his position with UPS that involved his temporary relocation to another state, he soon returned to New Jersey and, as a result, became a subordinate to defendant Wayne DeCraine, a man he had formerly supervised.

In September 2005, the plaintiff was demoted. The plaintiff contended that his demotion was retaliatory because it was the company's response to complaints he made both orally to DeCraine and in an anonymous letter he sent to human resources personnel in January 2005. The plaintiff's complaints included alleged offensive and derogatory comments about female employees made by DeCraine and the improper use of credit cards at the company. The plaintiff testified that he never learned about any action being taken in response to his anonymous letter; however, he contended that DeCraine and others, including Wiltz, were aware of the letter. He testified that DeCraine mentioned the letter and asked the plaintiff if he had written it, an assertion that DeCraine denied. The plaintiff also testified that Wiltz made a sarcastic comment to let the plaintiff know that his complaint was not truly anonymous.

UPS asserted that the demotion was justified by the plaintiff's violation of company confidentiality policies, his abusive treatment of other employees, and insubordination.

Considering the timing and circumstances of the plaintiff's demotion, do you think the plaintiff has made a case for retaliatory demotion? [See *Battaglia v. United Parcel Service, Inc.*, 214 N.J. 518, 70 A.3d 602 (2013).]

12. Penny Fox, the plaintiff, filed a complaint against Sara Lee Corporation and John Ziekle, alleging that she had been sexually assaulted by coworker Ziekle, and, as a result, suffered severe mental health problems that led to the loss of her job with Sara Lee. The plaintiff asserted a claim against defendant Sara Lee for intentional infliction of emotional distress, based upon Sara Lee's alleged ratification of Mr. Ziekle's conduct.

The plaintiff contended that the following proved that Sara Lee ratified Ziekle's conduct: (1) Prudy Yates was the plaintiff's immediate supervisor at the time of the incident; (2) manager Yates told the plaintiff not to report the Ziekle assault; (3) manager Yates never reported the Ziekle assault; and (4) manager Yates's instructions to not report the Ziekle assault and her failure to immediately report the assault herself were done in the line of duty and within the scope of manager Yates's employment.

Do you think the employer ratified the tortious actions of its employee, and thus is liable for intentional infliction of emotional distress? What about negligent infliction? [See *Fox v. Sara Lee Corp.*, 764 S.E.2d 624 N.C. App. (2014).]

13. A former employee, Michael Onderko, made a workers' compensation claim based on an injury that he claimed (but could not prove) he sustained during the course of his employment. The claim was denied, and Onderko did not appeal the decision, stating that he did not file because he was already back at work and just wanted the ordeal to be over.

One month later, Onderko's employment was terminated. Prior to his termination, Onderko had received three performance bonuses, had no discipline write-ups, and had no unexcused absences. Onderko claimed his employer told him he was being terminated due to the workers' compensation outcome. The employer, for his part, stated in his affidavit that Onderko was terminated "for his deceptive attempt to obtain Workers' Compensation benefits for a non-work related injury." Onderko then initiated claims for retaliatory discharge and for intentional infliction of emotional distress.

As to the claim for intentional infliction of emotional distress, the employer argued that it was entitled to summary judgment because its act of terminating Onderko for deceptively attempting to collect benefits for a non-work-related injury was not "extreme and outrageous" conduct, especially where Onderko was employed "at-will." Onderko responded by arguing that he did not lie about his workers' compensation claim, and that his claim was supported by the medical report of Dr. Ahn and by the statements of three coworkers who reported that Onderko told them he had aggravated his knee while moving cabinets in the shop.

Assuming Onderko proves his retaliatory discharge claim, do you think that conduct is enough to make a claim for intentional infliction of emotional distress as well? [See *Onderko v. Sierra Lobo, Inc.*, 20 N.E.3d 322 Ohio App. 6 Dist. (2014).]

14. A former employee, Howard Pierce, started working for Atlantic Group, Inc. in 2001, and held numerous positions with Atlantic. Pierce reported to both Atlantic and Duke Energy. In February 2009, Pierce received a memorandum from Duke Energy alerting employees that new regulations would affect crane operators and riggers, requiring them to be certified. Pierce brought the memorandum to the attention of his supervisors and proposed a process by which the operators could be trained and certified in a way which would not interfere with the operations of the plant during its busiest times. Pierce did not receive a response to his proposal but continued to raise the issue on a weekly basis.

In late March 2009, Pierce was demoted to a lower position and pay rate. Pierce continued to be concerned about the certification issue and "feared that [Atlantic's] explanations for his demotion in pay were a pretext in order to remove him from a supervisor position."

On August 24, 2009, Pierce called Duke Energy's "ethics hotline" and reported the alleged "retaliatory treatment" he had received. Pierce believed the hotline was a confidential resource but was asked to provide his identity and the names of "persons who concerned him."

During September 2010, Pierce felt that "workplace conditions became increasingly adverse." Specifically, Pierce felt that his schedule was being arbitrarily changed and interrupted, such that he could not get sufficient hours to support his family. He began to experience serious on- and off-the-job stress, severely affecting his relationship with his wife and family members. He was later terminated altogether.

Do you think Pierce has grounds for a claim of intentional or negligent infliction of emotional distress? Explain. [See *Pierce v. Atlantic Group, Inc.*, 219 N.C. App. 19, 724 S.E.2d 568 (2012).]

» Hypothetical Scenarios

15. Fred, an off-duty police officer, became a bit intoxicated in his local bar one Saturday evening, and shot off his mouth. Among other things, he told everyone within hearing distance that his precinct captain was "probably on the take, just like every other hotshot on the force." When this comment got back to his captain, the captain reported it to the police commissioner. Fred was given a written reprimand and demoted from sergeant to corporal, and the captain filed a lawsuit for defamation.

    Based on these facts, was Fred actually guilty of defaming his captain? What obstacles to proving a case of defamation and recovering money from Fred does the captain face? If Fred is a member of a police officers' union and could be disciplined only for good cause, what arguments does the union have in a grievance situation to contest Fred's drop in rank?

16. Super Saver is a convenience store chain. Maggie Jones is a clerk who works the night shift in one of the company's many stores. She and other employees who work nights have often asked to have hidden alarms placed under the front counter in case of robberies. The company, not wanting to spend the money, has never complied with the request.

    Last Saturday night, an armed robber entered the store while Maggie was working the night shift alone. He put a loaded revolved directly in her face and ordered her to lie on the floor. He then tied her hands behind her back and shouted, "One peep out of you, girl, and I'll blow whatever brains you have right out of your head!" He then robbed the register, loaded a trash bag with cigarettes and exited the store. Maggie lay on the floor, weeping hysterically, until a customer came in a half-hour later and called the police on his cell phone. Although physically unharmed, Maggie was hospitalized overnight. At the hospital, she was sedated. Since the incident, she has been unable to work in a convenience store and has been under the care of a psychologist.

    Does Maggie have a viable cause of action for infliction of emotional distress against her former employer?

17. Barney is the winningest basketball coach in the history of Central State University. His five-year contract is set to expire at the end of this season. The university's athletic director (AD) has been authorized by the board to offer Barney a new five-year contract with a substantial salary increase, plus greater flexibility in cutting his own deals for product endorsements. Having reviewed and signed the new contract, Barney stopped by the AD's office to drop it off. But before he can remove the signed contract from his briefcase, he's told by the AD that the latter had a conversation with his counterpart at Eastern State, and that Eastern State really wants to hire Barney for their own floundering program. Barney asked his AD what he thought he should do. The AD relied, "If I were you, I'd hold onto that contract and give Eastern a call." Barney followed that advice, was subsequently offered a better deal, and signed with Eastern.

Is Central's AD guilty of tortuous interference with Barney's contract with the university? If so, what should Central's remedy be?

18. Dana was a highly conscientious environmental health and safety manager at Fiberoptics Corporation. One day a janitorial employee reported to Dana that he found a brown paper bag in a corner of the men's changing room inside the plant. Dana went to the changing room and confirmed the presence of the bag. She called the local fire department, which sent a first-responder unit to the plant. The plant was shut down and evacuated, while the first responders examined the mysterious parcel. It turned out to contain a bagel with cream cheese and a latte. The company lost more than $10,000 due to lost employee time and lost production, and the fire company sent the firm a bill for $2,000. The CEO told Dana, "I know you meant well, but you clearly overreacted. I'm not firing you, but I am demoting you to a position in the HR department. You'll keep your salary."

Is Dana the victim of a retaliatory demotion? If so, what are her damages?

19. Nancy Drew worked for Sam Spade as an assistant private detective. Sam generously taught her everything he knew about good detective work. He also allowed her to handle assignments for some of his best corporate clients. Fly By Night, Inc., a local airline company, loved Nancy's work. The commercial carrier also realized that as a hungry young neophyte, she would work more cheaply than Sam. Management therefore told her that they would lend her some seed money to start her own agency and that they would give her a three-year contract to work on retainer for the airline. Nancy submitted her resignation to Sam. A week later, he heard from Fly By Night that his services were no longer needed.

Does Sam have an action against Nancy for theft of trade secrets? How about for tortuous interference with contract?

CHAPTER 4

Employee Privacy Rights in the 21ˢᵗ Century

Do we, as workers, have privacy rights in our places of employment? We often ask our students, most of whom hold part-time jobs, this question. Instinctively, they answer "yes," but seem unsure about the accuracy of their answer or their support of it.

The idea of a legal right to privacy originated in America. Louis Brandeis (later a Supreme Court justice) and another young lawyer, Samuel D. Warren, published an article titled "The Right to Privacy" in the *Harvard Law Review* in 1890, in which they argued that the Constitution and the common law implied a general "right to privacy." Their efforts were never entirely successful. It took the renowned tort scholar Dean Prosser to postulate some decades later that the "privacy" umbrella covered four separate torts, the only unifying element of which is "the right to be left alone." These four elements of common-law privacy are:

- Appropriating the plaintiff's identity for the defendant's benefit
- Placing the plaintiff in a false light in the public eye
- Publicly disclosing private facts about the plaintiff
- Unreasonably intruding upon the seclusion or solitude of the plaintiff

In *Griswold v. Connecticut*,[1] the Supreme Court for the first time expressly acknowledged a right of privacy implicit in the Constitution. Griswold was executive director of the Planned Parenthood League of Connecticut. Fellow-appellant Buxton was a licensed physician and a professor at the Yale Medical School and served as medical director for the League at its center in New Haven. The center operated from November 1 to November 10, 1961, when the two appellants were arrested. They gave information, instruction, and medical advice to *married persons* as to the means of preventing conception. They examined the woman and prescribed the best contraceptive device or material for her use. Fees were usually charged, although not always.

---

[1] 381 U.S. 479, 85 S.Ct. 1678, 14 L.Ed.2d 510 (1965).

The statute involved in the case provided:

Any person who uses any drug, medicinal article or instrument for the purpose of preventing conception shall be fined not less than fifty dollars or imprisoned not less than sixty days nor more than one year or be both fined and imprisoned.

Any person who assists, abets, counsels, causes, hires or commands another to commit any offense may be prosecuted and punished as if he were the principal offender.

The appellants were found guilty as accessories and fined $100 each. They appealed, contending that the accessory statute as so applied violated the Fourteenth Amendment. They argued that their services concerned a relationship (marriage) that lay within the zone of privacy created by several fundamental constitutional guarantees. In forbidding the use of contraceptives rather than merely regulating their manufacture or sale, they claimed that the law sought to achieve its goals by having a maximum destructive impact upon that relationship. Such a law, they said, could not stand in light of the principle that a governmental purpose to control or prevent activities constitutionally subject to state regulation may not be achieved by means which sweep unnecessarily broadly and thereby invade the area of protected freedoms.

Justice William O. Douglas, writing for the majority of the Court, asked the rhetorical question, "Would we allow the police to search the sacred precincts of marital bedrooms for telltale signs of the use of contraceptives?" His answer: "The very idea is repulsive to the notions of privacy surrounding the marriage relationship."

Declaring the law unconstitutional and reversing the convictions, he wrote, "We deal with a right of privacy older than the Bill of Rights—older than our political parties, older than our school system. Marriage is a coming together for better or for worse, hopefully enduring, and intimate to the degree of being sacred. It is an association that promotes a way of life, not causes; a harmony in living, not political faiths; a bilateral loyalty, not commercial or social projects. Yet it is an association for as noble a purpose as any involved in our prior decisions."

While this decision had the marital bed as its focus, its impact has been far broader, as it has claimed to find a generalized right of privacy between the lines of the Bill of Rights.

4-1   Privacy Rights in the Employment Area

Clearly, public employees enjoy the protection accorded to all of us by the Fourth Amendment of the U.S. Constitution against unreasonable searches and seizures by governmental entities. This important constitutional right is extended to state and municipal employees by the Fourteenth Amendment's "due process" clause. Public employers, unquestionably, are state actors for the purposes of the Fourth and Fourteenth Amendments' restrictions.

What about employees working for private firms? Labor lawyers commonly counsel their clients that "the Bill of Rights stops at the factory door." This is generally true. All the same, employees of private corporations do have significant common-law and statutory privacy protections. In the words of one widely read employment law expert, "The most common way employers invade their employees' privacy is to intrude on their seclusion, solitude, or private affairs. There is a delicate balance between the employer's legitimate need for the intrusion versus the employees' legitimate expectations of privacy regarding the intrusion."[2] This expert suggests that the common ways in which employers (both public and private) intrude upon their employees' privacy include surveillance and eavesdropping, monitoring and reviewing computer information and use, requests for information from third parties, requests for medical information, and conducting internal investigations.[3]

4-2   Surveillance and Eavesdropping

surveillance
monitoring of behavior

eavesdropping
surreptitiously listening
to others' conversations

The word **surveillance** is commonly used to describe "observation from a distance by means of electronic equipment or other technological means. However, surveillance also includes simple, relatively no- or low-technology methods such as direct observation, observation with binoculars, postal interception, or similar methods."[4] **Eavesdropping**, on the other hand, is "the act of surreptitiously listening to a private conversation."[5] Both techniques are commonly associated with police, spies, and military intelligence. As such, they are the subjects of many laws and much controversy, especially in our post-9/11 world of international terrorism, the USA Patriot Act, and the Department of Homeland Security.

Employers often are tempted to observe and eavesdrop on employees to ensure quality of customer service, to prevent inventory and intellectual property thefts, and to discourage wasting time on Internet abuses—to name just a few motives. Not surprisingly, such activities have generated much litigation, especially when the employer's intrusion on employee privacy resulted in employee discipline. Following are several cases that exemplify the types of incidents that give rise to privacy-based lawsuits.

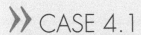 CASE 4.1

KOEPPEL V. SPEIRS
808 N.W.2d 177 (Iowa 2011)

Facts: An employee who discovered a hidden video camera in a workplace bathroom brought an invasion of privacy action against her employer, an insurance agent who secretly installed the camera. The district court entered summary judgment in the employer's favor based upon evidence showing that the camera was inoperable at the time of its discovery due to a weak radio wave signal to the receiver in the employer's office. The court of appeals reversed and the employer petitioned for review, which was granted.

Issue: When are invasions of privacy intentional?

Decision: The trial judge concluded that the district court erred in granting the employer's motion for summary judgment. An electronic invasion occurs under the intrusion on solitude or seclusion component of the tort of invasion of privacy when the plaintiff establishes by a preponderance of evidence that the electronic device or equipment used by a defendant could have invaded privacy in some way.

---

[2] Labor lawyer Mark R. Filipp in Filipp & Castagnera, *Employment Law Answer Book*, 8th ed. (NY: Aspen Law and Business, 2013), pp. 5–13.

[3] *Ibid.*, pp. 5–15.

[4] http://en.wikipedia.org/wiki/Surveillance.

[5] http://en.wikipedia.org/wiki/Eavesdropping.

» CASE 4.2

LIEBESKIND V. RUTGERS UNIVERSITY
– A.3d –, 2015 WL 7662032 (N.J. Superior 2015)

Facts: Suspecting that the plaintiff, a university employee, was spending a disproportionate amount of working time surfing on his office computer, his supervisor decided to investigate his Internet-browsing history. The supervisor used an application called "IEHistoryView" to extract browsing history based on data maintained by Internet Explorer. The investigation did not attempt to gather any information about the plaintiff's personal communications that might have been conducted on his work computer. Nor did the supervisor's foray attempt to gather any of the plaintiff's personal online accounts or websites. Nevertheless, the investigation yielded a report that reflected numerous visits to nonwork websites.

Although the supervisor took no immediate disciplinary action following this investigation, when termination of the plaintiff was under consideration for a variety of performance issues, computer misuse issue was put into the mix. Ultimately, the plaintiff received a letter which read, "It is with sincere regret that I must inform you that your employment at Rutgers University as Unit Computing Specialist is being terminated due to the lack of skill set needed to perform the required duties. Over the past few weeks I have observed your work and find it to be inadequate to effectively perform your duties. Your constant reliance for help to perform basic troubleshooting tasks and poor attitude does not meet our expectations and basic position requirements."

The plaintiff subsequently sued, challenging his termination on a number of grounds, including invasion of privacy. With regard to this cause of action he claimed his firing offended New Jersey's Wiretapping & Surveillance Control Act, N.J. Stat. Ann. 2A:156A-1, as well as the garden state's Computer Related Offenses Act, NJ. Stat. Ann. 2A:38A-1. He also pointed to the Fourth and Fourteenth Amendments, because Rutgers University is a "state actor."

On the defendant's summary judgment motion, the trial court dismissed this cause of action.

Issue: Was the trial judge correct in dismissing the plaintiff's "invasion of privacy" cause of action?

Decision: The Appellate Division of the New Jersey Superior Court held that, particularly in light of the university's Acceptable Use Policy for Computing and Information Technology Resources, the plaintiff did not have the reasonable expectation of privacy with regard to his work computer that is required to trigger a violation of the "search and seizure" protections of the U.S. Constitution.

Additionally, the court found that the two state statutes were inapplicable to his claim. The court suggested that the plaintiff may have had a stronger case if he had managed to prove certain allegations that were never factually supported. "Plaintiff also alleges, based on the dates in one field of the browsing history report that Masforroll actually hacked into plaintiff's personal email and other personal accounts and put over 1500 false entries into the report. Plaintiff declined to get an expert to prove this claim concerning the specifics of a computer software application. The trial judge appropriately dismissed this claim as an expert is required where, as here, the subject matter is so esoteric that jurors of common knowledge and experience cannot form a valid opinion without it."

» CASE 4.3

HUSTON V. COSSETTE
– A.3d –, 2015 WL 601216 (Conn. Super. 2015)

Facts: The plaintiff alleged the following facts: In April of 2011, he was employed as a police officer with the Meriden Police Department. On or about April 8, 2011, the defendant Chief of Police, knowing that the plaintiff was an officer in his police department, "maliciously, and/or recklessly released information from the plaintiff's personnel file to the press during an interview with reporters of the local newspaper." The plaintiff alleged that the defendant "opened up plaintiff's personnel file" and told reporters about a letter of reprimand the plaintiff received in 2007. The plaintiff also alleged that the letter should have been removed from the personnel file after two years but never was. The defendant also disclosed to the gathered reporters that the plaintiff was arrested in 2007, although the arrest was later dismissed. The plaintiff argued that the information revealed by the defendant was not subject to disclosure and was an invasion of personal privacy based upon intrusion into his right to seclusion. He also stated that as a result of these actions, he has suffered injury to his reputation, economic loss, and severe emotional distress. He asked for compensatory damages, punitive damages, and costs.

Issue: Did the Chief intrude upon the plaintiff's right to seclusion, thus committing an invasion of privacy?

Decision: In this case, the court explained that the crux of the tort of intrusion upon seclusion is the manner of the invasion, not the subsequent dissemination resulting from it. As the Restatement of Torts states, it is the intrusion itself, not the publication, which makes a party subject to liability for this tort. Here, the court found nothing in the pleadings argued that the method of obtaining the information was objectionable. In fact, there was nothing pleaded concerning the method of obtaining the information at all. At best, read in the light most favorable to the plaintiff, the manner of the intrusion was the opening of the file, and reading aloud of its contents. Thus, the plaintiff was not objecting to the *manner* in which the information was disseminated, but the fact that the information was disclosed to the press, thus publicizing the plaintiff's personnel information and causing anxiety and distress. The court found that the conduct alleged, namely, the opening of the file and reading of its contents, did not rise to the level of invasion typically found in violations of this tort. [*See* Restatement of Torts, § 652B (invasion described as physical intrusion into a place in which the plaintiff has secluded himself, looking through windows with binoculars or tapping phones, opening private and personal mail or forging a court order in order to obtain private documents)], and therefore the count alleging intrusion upon seclusion was pleaded sufficiently and had to be stricken.

Liebeskind is a classic case of computer surveillance by the employer to ascertain if the employee, whose performance was under par, might be spending working time surfing the Internet. The lesson of the case is that an employer can shield itself against subsequent invasion of privacy actions by promulgating a policy that makes its surveillance rights crystal clear. As the case suggests, neither statutory nor constitutional rights are likely to avail the worker who has been placed on notice by an express written policy that she or he has no reasonable expectation of privacy where her or his desktop computer is concerned.

Koeppel and *Huston* are companion cases concerning intrusion into the plaintiffs' right of seclusion. In the first case, the plaintiff prevailed. The employer had no right to intrude upon her bathroom breaks. In the latter, however, the Chief of Police had every right to open the plaintiff's personnel file. Thus, the nature of the intrusion, as well as where it occurs, will be determinative in these kinds of cases. Analogizing to *Liebeskind*, we also can characterize these outcomes in terms of the reasonable expectation of privacy that permeates so many of these cases. The plaintiff in *Koeppel* could reasonably expect her employer to keep its cameras out of the restrooms. Huston, however, could hardly expect the Chief to never open his personnel file.

Concept *Summary* 4.1

SURVEILLANCE AND EAVESDROPPING

- Surveillance: Monitoring of behavior

- Eavesdropping: Surreptitiously listening to others' conversations
  - Can include:
    - Email
    - Instant messages
    - Text messages

4-3 Monitoring and Reviewing Computer Information and Use

information technology
the study, design, development, implementation, support, or management of computer-based information systems

Although private employers, and even public employers with an appropriate notice that trumps employees' privacy expectations, are free to monitor and review employee use of employer-owned computers, some employers have voluntarily—or under pressure from a labor union—limited their own access to such devices and the information stored in them. The policy below, adopted by a northeastern university, where the faculty and clerical staff are both represented by labor unions, seeks a balance between protecting the integrity of the institution's **information technology** and the employees' (especially the tenured faculty's) privacy interests.

THE **WORKING** LAW

Rights and Responsibilities of Users of the Rider University Computer Network

network
group of computers, all interconnected to one another

This policy governs the use of computers and networks at Rider University. As a user of these resources, you are responsible for reading and understanding this document. This policy exists to protect the users of computing resources, computing hardware and **networks**, system administrators, other University employees and the University itself. The University reserves the right to change this policy in accordance with applicable University procedures....

Rider University is committed to protecting the rights of students, faculty, and staff to freedom of expression and to free academic inquiry and experimentation. Concomitantly, users must respect the rights of other users, respect the integrity of the systems and related physical resources, and observe all relevant laws, regulations, and contractual obligations....

While users do not own their accounts on the University computer network, they are granted the exclusive use of those accounts. Users therefore are entitled to privacy regarding computer communication and stored data. Subject to the exceptions set out below, users have reason to expect the same level of privacy for their files on the University's computer (i.e., files in a user's home directory) as users have in any space under their personal control.

system administrator
person employed by an organization's IT department to manage and oversee a network of computers

Private communications by computer (e-mail) will be treated to the same degree of privacy as any private communication. Users should note that by adopting this policy the University does not assume an affirmative responsibility of insuring the privacy or integrity of users e-mail....

System administrators or other University employees will access user files without permission of the user only when immediate action is necessary to protect the integrity of the computer network or when subject to a search by law enforcement agencies acting under the order of a court of appropriate jurisdiction. In the event of an order by a court, or a governmental agency with subpoena authority, the user of that file will be notified of that order prior to the University providing access to those files to the extent permitted by applicable law. Copies of all user files stored on the network may be routinely backed up for disaster recovery purposes. Such copying shall not be considered to be in violation of this policy as long as such operations are purely mechanical and do not involve the viewing of those files. However, ultimate responsibility for the back-up of files in personal accounts, local disks, and personal computers, lies with the account holder.

academic freedom
the college professors' right to take unpopular positions in the classroom and in scholarly work without fear of reprisals by the university

While Rider University is committed to intellectual and **academic freedom** and to the application of those freedoms to computer media and facilities, the University is also committed to protecting the privacy and integrity of computer data belonging to the University and to individual users....

This policy sets a balance that tips in favor—some would say heavily in favor—of the employee. As such, it reflects the power that the employee unions, especially the faculty union, wielded at the institution. Most organizations have not gone so far in according their employees such a broad expectation of privacy with regard to their workplace computers—and for good reason. Such a policy as this can make it difficult for an organization not only to investigate allegations of employee wrongdoing, but also even to defend itself under some circumstances, such as where the computer files of a hostile ex-employee are required and the disgruntled individual refuses to cooperate.

Concept *Summary* 4.2

MONITORING COMPUTER INFORMATION AND USE

- Information technology: The study, design, development, implementation, support or management of computer-based information systems

- Networks: Group of computers, all interconnected to one another

- System administrators: Persons employed by an organization's IT department to manage and oversee a network of computers

- Sources of employee privacy rights and computers:
  - Public employees: First and Fourteenth Amendments
  - College professors: Academic freedom
  - Private employees: Tort of invasion of privacy
  - Unionized employees: Collective bargaining agreement

4-4 Requests for Information from Third Parties

malice
knowledge or reckless disregard of the falsity of a communication

Privacy concerns arise in the context of third-party information requests primarily at the hiring stage. Communications between former and prospective employers regarding an employee typically are protected by a qualified privilege, provided such communications are conducted in the absence of malice. While malice in the generic sense usually implies animosity toward somebody, **malice** in the context of defamation[6] and invasion of privacy means knowledge that your statement is false or a reckless disregard of its truth or falsity.

Some employers, often on the advice of legal counsel, have opted in recent years to limit responses to reference requests to confirming the dates of the former employee's employment, his or her salary or wage rate, and job title. While this approach generally is the safest, it inhibits the free flow of information required for the hiring employer to make an informed and intelligent decision. And while this policy may protect the former employer from tort liability in most circumstances, where the former employee was fired for serious cause, withholding this knowledge from a potential new employer may actually open the former employer to more significant liability than if he or she had spoken up.

The following is an actual reference policy adopted by an organization in the health care industry. Try to articulate reasons why this organization chose to institute this policy:

> When you terminate employment, you may use this hospital as a reference when seeking other employment. However, by law we can only give limited information from your file to your prospective employer unless you sign a release form. Letters of recommendation for terminating employees, therefore, cannot be given. We recommend that you retain your personal copies of your [evaluation forms] to share with prospective employers.

negligent hiring
when an employer hires an employee that the employer knows (or should have known through reasonable checks) could cause injury to others

Faced with such restrictive reference policies, employers often take it upon themselves to learn as much as they can about prospective employees. Increases in incidents of workplace violence, and concomitant increases in **negligent hiring** lawsuits by customers and coworkers of violent employees, have added urgency to this effort. Applicants, therefore, are often asked to authorize extensive background investigations before they are offered employment. A typical authorization policy looks something like this:

BACKGROUND SCREENING POLICY

ABC Company is committed to providing a safe and secure working environment for its employees, vendors, and customers. To this end, the company's selection process includes background checks of all potential employees. ABC Company will follow all applicable state, federal, and local laws governing employment and background screening in all respects. The following procedures will be followed to ensure compliance with our background screening policy:

---

[6] See Chapter 3, "Commonly Committed Workplace Torts."

Applicants

As part of the selection process, all applicants will be required to sign a release for the completion of a background check when being considered for potential employment. The following information will be verified:

- Social Security trace
- Criminal search
- Employment verification
- Education verification
- Motor vehicle report (if the position requires a valid driver's license)

Procedures

1. The Human Resources Department will initiate background checks at the time a CONTINGENT employment offer is made to an applicant. No offer of employment is binding until completion of a background check and notification from HR to the hiring manager that a final offer can be made.

2. Human Resources will confirm to the hiring manager that the background screen is complete and that the applicant meets ABC Company's criteria for employment. In the event that adverse information is discovered, the offer will be retracted and the selection process and next steps will be determined on a case-by-case basis.

3. The external vendor will notify the applicant of any information that cannot be verified through customary search methods to obtain another source of verification such as W2s, paycheck stubs, or diploma. Any material information that cannot be verified will result in a disposition of "not recommended."

4. Any prospective employee who receives a "not recommended" result will receive communications consistent with Fair Credit Reporting Act (FCRA) requirements. Should you have any questions regarding this process, please feel free to contact your recruiting consultant.

Background checks, especially of the criminal variety, are a sore point for many employees and labor unions. With regard to criminal background investigations, unions often observe that in the absence of a unified national clearinghouse, investigators are limited to checking the records of the states and counties where the applicant admits to having previously resided. This means that less than full disclosure by the applicant can result in a serious offense being entirely overlooked. Employees and labor organizations also object to the discretion that is often exercised by human resources professionals in determining whether a revealed offense will disqualify the applicant. That determination is necessarily a judgment call, taking into consideration the seriousness of the crime, the recency or remoteness of the conviction, and the direct or indirect relationship of the crime to the employer's business.

Concept *Summary* 4.3

REQUESTS FOR INFORMATION FROM THIRD PARTIES

- Types of privileges:
  - Absolute: Congress; courtroom testimony
  - Qualified: Business privilege; journalist's privilege

- Elements of qualified privilege:
  - Bona fide reason
  - Absence of malice

4-5 Requests for Medical Information

**protected health
information (PHI)**
information specifically
identified by federal
law as subject to
privacy protection

The federal Health Insurance Portability and Accountability Act (HIPAA), enacted in 1998 and having taken full effect some five years later, mandates—among other things[7]—stringent policies and procedures aimed at preventing the unauthorized use or disclosure of health and medical information, commonly called **protected health information (PHI)** in the relevant regulations. In general, the privacy regulations promulgated pursuant to HIPAA apply to health care and health insurance providers. Covered entities include:

- Health care plans
- Health care clearinghouses
- Health care providers

The regulations are aimed at restricting access to health care information and tracking the use and disclosure of such information.

The Department of Health and Human Services' Office of Civil Rights 2002 Guidelines pointed out that the regulations address disclosure of information by covered entities to a noncovered entities.[8] As a matter of fact, one of the express purposes of HIPAA's privacy provisions is to prevent employers from using PHI for personnel decisions. Furthermore, if an employer, as the sponsor of an employee health insurance plan, wants to receive PHI from covered health care providers in order to administer the plan, then the employer has to place itself under the HIPAA umbrella. Consequently, many thousands of private employers are subject to HIPAA and its implementing regulations. Employers subject to HIPAA must:

- Create a "firewall" between employees who administer health insurance plans and all other employees to prevent illegal dissemination of PHI
- Amend health insurance plan documents to describe how PHI will be handled and by whom
- Certify in writing that they will comply with HIPAA's regulations

---

[7] Not least among these other things is the worker's ability to maintain health insurance coverage between and among different employers.

[8] 45 C.F.R. Section 164.504(f)(3)(iv).

- Designate a privacy official who will be specifically responsible for policing compliance
- Notify plan participants of the company's use and disclosure policies under HIPAA

Additionally, the Americans with Disabilities Act (ADA) also protects employees and applicants, who may suffer from physical and mental disabilities, from discriminatory use of their medical records to deny them employment and advancement. Jose Rosenberg, director of the Greensboro Office of the U.S. Equal Employment Opportunity Commission, drew a distinction between offering someone a job contingent on his or her passing a physical, which is legal, and asking for medical information in general, which is not.[9]

ethical DILEMMA

USE OF GENETIC INFORMATION

genetic testing
examination of chromosomes, genes, and proteins in human cells in a search for defects

One of the most pressing ethical dilemmas facing employers today is if, and if so how, to use genetic information that is readily available. DNA testing can tell an employer and/or its health and life insurance carriers the likelihood that an employee or applicant will contract a wide range of serious medical conditions, which pose potentially catastrophic claims under the firm's health and life insurance plans. However, **genetic testing** is undoubtedly among the most serious intrusions into an employee's privacy that an employer might make. Below is a policy aimed at addressing this issue. Do you think it balances the two parties' interests?

Policy Against Use of Genetic Information
[Company Name] does not collect, consider or make employment or benefit decisions based on genetic information.

[Company Name] does not use genetic information or genetic testing to identify individuals (applicants or employees) who are especially susceptible to general workplace risks, who may become unable to work, or who are likely to incur significant health care costs for either themselves or their dependents.

Accordingly, applicants for employment or employees of [Company Name] will not be required to undergo any genetic testing or reveal genetic information to [Company Name].

Limited Toxic Chemicals Exception
Testing prior to exposure. There is only one exception to our "no genetic information" policy. Employees may be asked to submit to genetic testing before working around certain toxic chemicals in the workplace. [Company Name] may require genetic testing to determine the individual's susceptibility to or level of exposure of certain toxic chemicals that occur in the workplace. Work in a specified toxic area will not be permitted until testing demonstrates that the individual does not have sensitivity to the chemicals.

Informed, written consent required. Although genetic testing may be required, it will only be conducted after the individual's informed, written consent has been

---

[9] News & Record, http://www.news-record.com/blogs.

obtained. If testing consent is not obtained, the individual will not be permitted to work in the specified area.

No retaliation. No adverse reaction may be taken against an employee as a result of the genetic test; however, the genetic test may disqualify the individual from work in the toxic area.

There will be no retaliation against any applicant or employee who refuses to take a genetic test or refuses to reveal the results of a genetic test to [Company Name].

Confidentiality. Any genetic information obtained for this purpose will be stored in confidential files, not in the employee's regular employment record. [Company Name] will not, except upon the individual's informed, written consent, give the results to anyone else.

A number of state equal employment opportunity laws prohibit use of genetic testing and also "predisposing genetic characteristics" as a basis of employment decisions.[10] Genetic testing raises the specter of eugenics, the now-discredited science that sought to control the direction of human evolution. In the infamous case of *Buck v. Bell*,[11] no less a liberal jurist than Oliver Wendell Homes, declaring Virginia's compulsory-sterilization law constitutional, infamously wrote, "Three generations of imbeciles are enough." Any tattered shred of credibility eugenics still had was destroyed by the revelations of ghastly medical experiments carried out by Nazi doctors in the Third Reich's concentration camps. Novels like Aldous Huxley's *Brave New World*, which postulated a future in which humans were designed and engineered in labs, also helped discredit eugenics.

On the other hand, as medical science learns more about our DNA, the possibility for the prevention or cure of many horrible diseases, including cancer, makes the science of genetics a valuable area of human knowledge. Therefore, genetic testing is an area of increased interest to many people. However, employers who seek to forestall costly medical claims by identifying genetically vulnerable applicants up front are unlikely to find much sympathy in American courtrooms.

Concept *Summary* 4.4

REQUESTS FOR MEDICAL INFORMATION

- Relevant laws:
  - HIPAA
  - ADA
  - Genetic-testing statutes
- Covered entities:
  - Health care plans
  - Health care clearinghouses
  - Health care providers
  - Employers

---

[10] See NY Human Rights Law, [NY Exec. Law, s. 296(1)(a)].

[11] 274 U.S. 200 (1927).

4-6   **Internal Investigations**

drug testing
testing of human blood and/or urine for the presence of controlled or illegal substances

Perhaps the aspect of internal investigation that has instigated the greatest amount of litigation is **drug testing**. The federal Drug-Free Workplace Act[12] mandates drug testing for employers receiving federal funding. Yet, in all cases, drug testing raises significant privacy issues. One way to insulate an organization from liability is to promulgate a reasonable policy. Read the following example of a substance abuse policy, consider the reasoning behind its provisions, and evaluate its potential effectiveness in solving the problem(s) it is intended to address while avoiding employer liability.

reasonable suspicion
justifiably suspecting a person, based on facts or circumstances, of inappropriate or criminal activities

substance abuse
long-term use or dependence on alcohol or drugs

ACTIVE EMPLOYEE SUBSTANCE ABUSE TESTING POLICY

Employees may be required to submit to drug and/or alcohol testing at a laboratory chosen by the company if there is a cause for **reasonable suspicion** of substance abuse.

Whenever possible, the supervisor should have the employee observed by a second supervisor or manager before requiring testing. Employees who refuse substance testing under these circumstances will be terminated.

Circumstances that could be indicators of a **substance abuse** problem and considered reasonable suspicion are:

1. Observed alcohol or drug abuse during work hours on company premises.
2. Apparent physical state of impairment.
3. Incoherent mental state.
4. Marked changes in personal behavior that are otherwise unexplainable.
5. Deteriorating work performance that is not attributable to other factors.
6. Accidents or other actions that provide reasonable cause to believe the employee may be under the influence.

Employee Assistance Program (EAP)
includes a range of psychological, health, fitness and legal services aimed at helping employees solve problems that interfere with job performance

If the test results are positive, the employee may be administratively referred to the **Employee Assistance Program (EAP)**. If the employee refuses treatment, or does not comply with the treatment recommended by the EAP, termination will result.

If the tests are positive and if an employee is granted a leave of absence for substance abuse rehabilitation, he or she will be required to participate in all recommended after-care and work rehabilitation programs. Upon successful completion of all or part of these required programs, the employee may be released to resume work but must agree to random substance abuse testing and close performance monitoring to ensure that he or she remains drug free.

Likewise, many employers mandate a pre-employment drug test. Ultimate employment is contingent upon passing of the test.

---

[12] 41 U.S.C. Section 702 et seq. P.L. 100-690 (1988).

Pre-Employment Drug Testing Policy

All job applicants at this company will undergo screening for the presence of illegal drugs or alcohol as a condition for employment.

Applicants will be required to voluntarily submit to a urinalysis test at a laboratory chosen by the company, and by signing a consent agreement, will release the company from liability.

Any applicant with positive test results will be denied employment at that time but may initiate another inquiry with the company after six months.

The company will not discriminate against applicants for employment because of past abuse of drugs or alcohol. It is the current abuse of drugs or alcohol that prevents employees from properly performing their jobs that the company will not tolerate.

4-7   False Light Invasion of Privacy

In a pair of related 2015 decisions, sister courts in the state of Michigan issued back-to-back January/February 2015 decisions in a high-profile case involving the attorney general's office and the University of Michigan. In these cases, the central figure, a former assistant attorney general, turned up in the guise of a defendant being sued for "false light" invasion of privacy by a third party and of a plaintiff, suing his former employer for wrongful termination, which the attorney general based upon plaintiff's alleged false light privacy invasion of the third party. Fresh as yesterday's headlines, the twin decisions aptly illustrate the complexity of such cases in this age of social networking and "viral" Internet blogging.

CASE 4.4

ARMSTRONG V. SHIRVELL

– Fed. Appx. –, 2015 WL 410545 (6th Cir., February 2, 2015)

Andrew Shirvell, an alumnus of the University of Michigan and a former Assistant Attorney General for the State of Michigan, engaged in an online and in-person "campaign" against Christopher Armstrong, the former president of the University of Michigan's student council. Shirvell appeals many aspects of the proceedings in the district court, which resulted in the jury finding him liable for defamation, false light invasion of privacy, intentional infliction of emotional distress, and stalking. Most of Shirvell's objections lack merit, and we therefore affirm in part. The district court committed plain error, however, in its treatment of the compensatory damages for false light. We therefore reverse in part, vacate the judgment, and remand with instructions for the court to enter judgment in Armstrong's favor for the

reduced amount of $3.5 million. This represents the total sum that the jury awarded, less the damages for false light.

I.

In 2010, Christopher Armstrong was elected president of the student council at the University of Michigan in Ann Arbor. The student council does not make University policy, but it works with, reports to, and advises the University on a range of issues.

Andrew Shirvell, a 2002 graduate of the University, worked as an Assistant Attorney General for the State of Michigan. In early 2010, Shirvell learned via an online newspaper report of Armstrong's election and also learned that Armstrong was openly gay. Shirvell began posting on his Facebook page about Armstrong, whom he had never met. Among other comments, Shirvell called Armstrong "dangerous" and a "radical homosexual activist" and a "major-league fanatic who is obsessed with imposing the radical homosexual agenda on the student body." Shirvell also set up a Facebook "fan page," entitled "Michigan Alumni and Others Against Chris Armstrong's Radical MSA Agenda," which purported to "expos[e] the real Chris Armstrong." He urged others, via Facebook and email, to join the "pro-family" group in order to "fight[ ] against Satan's representative." Shirvell took to his personal Facebook page to express outrage when Facebook deleted his "fan page" about Armstrong. He wrote: "I will not be SILENCED by the likes of Armstrong. You're going down fruity-pebbles." His self-proclaimed "outrage" continued from there: "I better not see Chris Armstrong at MY [church] parish in Charlotte—that's all I got to say." He claimed that Armstrong was scared of him and—in commenting on another story involving gay students—"remember[ed] the good old days when 'guys' like this would get their asses kicked at school."

Not content with Facebook posting, Shirvell then established a blog entitled "Chris Armstrong Watch," which discussed Armstrong's "character and his agenda and other items." The blog purported to be a "watch site," providing "testimony" and "an expose of the REAL Chris Armstrong." The blog was accessible to the public from April 2010 until September 30, 2010, when Shirvell removed it from public view. The blog featured a picture of Armstrong's face next to a swastika. It called Armstrong "a radical homosexual activist, racist, elitist, & liar." It attributed to Armstrong a "Nazi-like hatred of the First Amendment," explaining, "Much like Nazi Germany's leaders, many of whom were also homosexuals, Armstrong believes that any and all opposition must be suppressed by whatever means necessary." The blog further stated that Armstrong "mocks Christians," and called Armstrong an "anti-Christian bigot[ ]." One entry claimed that Armstrong attended an event "whose intent was to encourage underage drinking," and that Armstrong "spent most of this time [after the semester ended] engaging in underage binge-drinking." The blog made repeated references to Armstrong's participation in—and facilitation of—underage drinking. It alleged that Armstrong showed contempt toward law enforcement. Shirvell—re-posting online conversations between Armstrong and another student at the University—claimed that these conversations revealed Armstrong's "tendency toward sexual promiscuity," and thus labeled Armstrong "a perverted homosexual exhibitionist." Shirvell interpreted another online conversation as demonstrating that Armstrong

had previously hosted an "orgy" in his college dormitory, at which "homosexual shenanigans" were rampant. Days after this entry, Shirvell authored another blog post proclaiming: "Armstrong engages in sexual escapades at 'churches & children's playgrounds.'" He linked Armstrong to "possible involvement" in violent attacks against places of worship in the wake of California's passage of Proposition 8. He alleged that Armstrong used his welcome to freshmen as "a thinly veiled attempt to cause sexually confused, and perhaps some impressionable, 17- and 18-year-olds to experiment sexually with members of their own gender."

Shirvell also reported on an alleged romantic relationship between Armstrong and another student. Shirvell claimed that the other student was "not out of the closet," but that Armstrong "basically seduced" the student and quickly became obsessed with him. Explaining that the other student, "[t]hanks in large part to Armstrong's influence... has indeed morphed into a proponent of the radical homosexual agenda," Shirvell called Armstrong "a very, very twisted sick individual who is manipulative and cunning in a most devilish way."

Shirvell also appeared on television to rant about Armstrong. In September 2010, in an interview on local station WXYZ, he said that Armstrong held the presidential position in order "to promote special rights for homosexuals at the cost of... heterosexual students." Shirvell later appeared in front of a national audience with CNN's Anderson Cooper. Standing by his blog and Facebook posts, Shirvell told Cooper that he had "gotten stuff from third-party sources," and argued that Armstrong was not giving interviews because "he can't defend what's on the blog." When Cooper suggested that Shirvell was a bigot, Shirvell retorted, "The real bigot here is Chris Armstrong." Two days later, back before a national audience on Comedy Central's *The Daily Show*, Shirvell said that Chris was "acting like a gay Nazi," and that this explained his decision to include a picture of Armstrong next to a swastika on the blog.

Across these various forums, Shirvell attempted to justify his commentary by pointing to several purportedly legitimate concerns. Shirvell, a proud Roman Catholic, apparently feared that Armstrong would discriminate against Christian, pro-life, and pro-family people. In one post, Shirvell warned that these groups would be "violently persecuted." Second, he claimed that "Armstrong's radical agenda includes mandating 'gender-neutral' housing" at the University, an initiative that Shirvell opposed. Third, he believed that Armstrong would use his platform as president to "promote the homosexual lifestyle." Finally, Shirvell opposed Armstrong's membership in a student group known as the Order of the Angell, an organization that—according to Shirvell—was known as "the University of Michigan's version of the KKK," and had "a well-documented history of racism and elitism." Shirvell claimed that Armstrong lied before the election about his intentions to join the group.

In addition to broadcasting his views, Shirvell tracked Armstrong down in Ann Arbor. At first, Shirvell posted flyers around campus and in students' mailboxes. He soon discovered Armstrong's off-campus residence and made an appearance at a party there. On several occasions, he marched up and down the street outside Armstrong's house, protesting. Fearing for his safety and that of his roommates when they needed to leave their home, Armstrong called the campus Department of Public Safety and received an escort. Shirvell later followed Armstrong to two campus events in the space of a day, holding a sign that branded Armstrong a racist liar and advertised the Chris Armstrong Watch blog. On one occasion, Shirvell stood outside Armstrong's residence while Armstrong was hosting a party, called police to complain about the noise, then filmed the ensuing proceedings and posted about the party on his blog. On one occasion, while Armstrong was speaking at a rally, Shirvell heckled him and took pictures of him. After discovering online that Armstrong planned to attend a friend's birthday party, Shirvell went, uninvited, to the party. Armstrong and his friends became concerned.

Shirvell approached students outside of an Ann Arbor night club on one occasion while holding a sign saying "Chris Armstrong is a racist liar," and quizzed them about their online conversations. Shirvell told one student that he planned to go to her house the following day because he had heard she was hosting a party. The friend, afraid that Shirvell might endanger her guests, decided to cancel the party. Another time, Shirvell learned that Armstrong's friends were celebrating a birthday at a bar. He showed up at the bar, then followed the group to another bar around a mile away. When confronted, he lied about his identity, then asked for Armstrong. Shirvell believed Armstrong was supposed to be with the group, and produced a printed Facebook invitation to prove it.

Shirvell continued to monitor Armstrong's activities even while Armstrong was off campus. In the summer of 2010, Shirvell learned that Armstrong was working as an intern in Washington, D.C., in the office of then-Speaker Nancy Pelosi. In a blog post entitled "Pelosi's Office Reconsiders Armstrong's Internship; Currently Investigating His Ties to Racist Student Group," Shirvell explained that he personally contacted a Pelosi aide, provided him with documents about Armstrong's membership in the Order of the Angell, and was assured that the aide would investigate further. In several phone calls and messages to Pelosi's office, Shirvell accused Armstrong of being a racist and of having lied to minority students' faces.

University authorities were concerned about Shirvell's actions. Beginning in June 2010, University police reports detail Shirvell's ongoing harassment of Armstrong. Ann Arbor police also became involved. In July 2010, police asked Shirvell to stop contacting Armstrong, but Shirvell continued, undeterred. In the fall of 2010, the University police issued Shirvell a trespass warning, banning Shirvell from the University campus. The warning was later modified, allowing Shirvell onto campus, but still requiring him to avoid contact with Armstrong. The police were familiar with peaceful protests on campus but believed Shirvell's conduct was different. The Deputy Chief of the University police testified that the warning was necessary because Shirvell was "obsessed with" Armstrong, and was perceived as a threat to him. Despite this, the prosecutor's office declined to issue a criminal warrant against Shirvell. The Deputy Chief believed that Shirvell's sole reason for focusing on Armstrong was "that he was against him being gay." Even at the time of trial—after Armstrong had graduated and the trespass warning had expired—the Deputy Chief remained concerned about Armstrong's safety.

In April 2011, Armstrong sued Shirvell in Michigan state court for defamation, intentional infliction of emotional distress, abuse of process, false light, intrusion, and stalking. Shirvell removed the case to federal court. Armstrong later dismissed the abuse of process claim and the court granted summary judgment on the intrusion claim. The court denied Shirvell's motion for summary judgment on the remaining claims. Armstrong requested that Shirvell retract certain statements, but Shirvell refused....

The jury awarded $750,000 in compensatory damages and $500,000 in exemplary damages for defamation, $1,000,000 in compensatory damages for casting Armstrong in a false light, $1,750,000 in compensatory damages for intentional infliction of emotional distress, and $100,000 in compensatory damages and $400,000 in exemplary damages for stalking.

***

Armstrong argues that the jury separated the verdicts for defamation and false light and that there was no basis for assuming that double recovery resulted. But it is difficult to see how this verdict could represent anything other than double recovery. The jury was assessing the same harm caused by the same statements and awarded a lump-sum figure for both. There appears to be no plausible way in which the jury could have awarded damages for distinct harms. The court should consider the verdict form in combination with the jury instructions.

SHIRVELL V. DEPARTMENT OF ATTORNEY GENERAL
– N.W.2d –, 2015 WL 114608 (Mich. App., January 8, 2015)

In these consolidated appeals, in Docket Nos. 314223 and 314227, the Department of Attorney General (the Department), and the Department of Licensing and Regulatory Affairs/Unemployment Insurance Agency (UIA), respectively, appeal by leave granted a circuit court order reversing the Michigan Compensation Appellate Commission's (MCAC's) order affirming the UIA's denial of claimant Andrew Shirvell's claim for unemployment benefits. In Docket No. 316146, Shirvell appeals by leave granted a circuit court order affirming a Civil Service Commission (the Commission) order denying Shirvell's grievance and holding that the Department had just-cause to terminate Shirvell's employment under the Civil Service Rules (CSRs) for conduct unbecoming a state employee. For the reasons set forth in this opinion, in Docket Nos. 314223 and 314227, we reverse the circuit court's order and remand for reinstatement of the MCAC's order and in Docket No. 316146, we affirm the circuit court's order.

[NOTE: The facts presented in the court's opinion are substantially the same as those in *Armstrong v. Shirvell* above.]

Finally, on November 8, 2010, following a disciplinary hearing, the Department terminated Shirvell's employment for "conduct unbecoming a state employee." The Department issued a termination letter to Shirvell that listed the reasons for the termination as follows:

> Engaging in inappropriate conduct by targeting individual members of the public both in person and through electronic media, which could reasonably be construed to be an invasion of privacy, slanderous, libelous, and tantamount to stalking behavior unbecoming an Assistant Attorney General….

IV. CONCLUSION

To summarize, we conclude that Shirvell's speech was not protected under the First Amendment for purposes of these proceedings. Although Shirvell may have spoken as a private citizen on a matter of public concern, the Department introduced evidence at both proceedings to show that its interests in the efficient provision of governmental services outweighed Shirvell's speech interests. Accordingly, neither termination of Shirvell's employment nor denial of unemployment benefits offended the constitution. Therefore, in Docket No. 316146 we affirm the circuit court's order wherein the court properly held that there was competent, material, and substantial evidence on the whole record to support that there was just cause to terminate Shirvell and properly held that the termination was not arbitrary or capricious. However, in Docket Nos. 314223 and 314227, we reverse the circuit court order wherein the court erred in concluding that Shirvell did not engage in misconduct that disqualified him for unemployment benefits under the MESA. Shirvell's speech was not protected and there was competent, material, and substantial evidence introduced at the unemployment compensation hearing to support the UIA's determination that Shirvell engaged in misconduct such that he was disqualified for benefits under MCL 421.29(1)(b); therefore, remand for reinstatement of the MCAC's order in that case is appropriate.

Case Questions

1. As plaintiff Armstrong was "openly gay" according to the court in his case against Shirvell, how was Shirvell guilty of portraying the plaintiff "in a false light"?

2. If Shirvell in no way defamed Armstrong, could a jury still properly have found Shirvell liable to Armstrong for false light invasion of privacy?

3. In the second of these two cases, the Michigan state court affirmed Shirvell's firing for—among other things—invading Armstrong's privacy. As Armstrong obviously had his own remedy in court for this alleged privacy invasion, what business was it of the attorney general to get involved in this dispute?

4. If the jury in the first case and the attorney general in the second are both right that Shirvell portrayed Armstrong in a false light, what facts support their conclusion? And wasn't the general public entitled to know the facts that Shirvell was revealing?

《《

Concept *Summary* 4.5

INTERNAL INVESTIGATIONS

- Reasons for drug tests:
  - Required by law in some industries
  - Reasonable suspicion
  - Random
  - Prior history (e.g., return to work)
  - Workplace accident

4-8   Personnel Files

Personnel files pose two major issues for employers regarding what should be placed and retained in the employee's file and which employees should have access to personnel files. Typical items in a personnel file include applications, references and letters of recommendation, performance evaluations, disciplinary actions, and attendance records. (Health records usually are maintained in separate human resources files, as is appropriate under HIPAA and the ADA, as noted earlier.) Access to such files should be limited to human resources and legal department employees, direct supervisors, and senior management. "Need to know" is the operative principle here.

So, what about the employee's access to his or her own personnel file? A typical company policy might look something like this:

POLICY: EMPLOYEE ACCESS TO THEIR PERSONNEL FILES

Employee files are maintained by the Human Resources department and are considered confidential. Managers and supervisors other than Human Resources may only have access to personnel file information on a need-to-know basis. A manager or supervisor considering the hire of a former employee or transfer of a current employee may be granted access to the file.

[Company Name] shall provide access to personnel files by current or former employees in accordance with applicable laws.

Representatives of government or law enforcement agencies, in the course of their business, may be allowed access to file information. This decision will be made at the discretion of the Human Resources department in response to the request, a legal subpoena, or court order.

Many states have statutes dealing with access by current and former employees to their files. Pennsylvania's law is a good example:

An employer shall, at reasonable times, upon request of an employee, permit that employee or an agent designated by the employee to inspect his or her own personnel files used to determine his or her own qualifications for employment, promotion, additional compensation, termination or disciplinary action. The employer shall make these records available during the regular business hours of the office where these records are usually and ordinarily maintained, when sufficient time is available during the course of a regular business day, to inspect the personnel files in question. The employer may require the requesting employee or the agent designated by the employee to inspect such records on the free time of the employee or agent. At the employer's discretion, the employee may be required to file a written form to request access to the personnel file or files or to indicate a designation of agency for the purpose of file access and inspection. This form is solely for the purpose of identifying the requesting individual or the designated agent of the requesting individual to avoid disclosure to ineligible individuals. To assist the employer in providing the correct records to meet the employee's need, the employee shall indicate in his written request, either the purpose for which the inspection is requested, or the particular parts of his personnel record which he wishes to inspect or have inspected by the employee's agent.[13]

Note, too, that the sample policy in the adjoining box allows access to "government or law enforcement agencies." Who else should be entitled to access an employee's personnel file and under what circumstances? Company human resources, legal, and management employees are often confronted with process servers delivering subpoenas related to everything from personal injury actions to child-support orders to criminal cases. How should employee privacy interests be balanced with the justice system's interest in fair and expeditious processes? In the *Commonwealth* case that follows, a defendant on trial for murder attempted to obtain access to the personnel files of the arresting officers for purposes of cross-examination at trial.

CASE 4.5

MARKEN V. SANTA MONICA-MALIBU UNIFIED SCHOOL DIST.

202 Cal. App. 4th 1250, 136 Cal.Rptr.3d 395 (2012)

A high school teacher, Marken, brought action against the school district for declaratory, injunctive, and writ relief challenging the district's planned disclosure to a student's parent of records concerning the district's investigation and finding that the teacher violated the district's sexual harassment policy. The Superior Court denied preliminary injunction and denied the parent's application to intervene. The teacher and the parent appealed.

On December 14, 2010 Chwe, a professor of political science at UCLA and the father of two children who attend Santa Monica High School, made a CPRA request to the District, seeking "copies of all public records ... concerning the investigation of Santa Monica High School teacher Mr. Ari Marken and the resulting decision to place him on leave in December 2008 for sexually harassing a thirteen-year-old girl, in violation of SMMUSD policy 5145.7." The request attached a copy of a letter dated December 4, 2008 from a District assistant superintendent to the mother of the student who had initiated the complaint against Marken, which stated, in part, "[T]he District hired an Independent Investigator to examine this complaint. The District found that Mr. Marken did violate Board Policy 5145.7 [on sexual harassment] and

[13] 43 Pa. Stat. Section 1322.

has taken appropriate action." The request also sought other public records regarding any substantial complaints about Marken's improper behavior toward students.

On February 8, 2011 Marken filed a lawsuit against the District, captioned verified complaint for: temporary restraining order, preliminary and permanent injunction, declaratory relief; petition for writ of mandate. Marken alleged the District's decision to disclose the November 25, 2008 investigation report and the November 26, 2008 letter of reprimand in response to Chwe's request was not authorized under the CPRA because the sexual harassment complaint was neither substantial in nature nor well founded. Marken further alleged the District's intended disclosure of his confidential personnel records, unless enjoined, would violate his rights of privacy protected by the California Constitution and the Education and Government Codes and cause him irreparable harm. Concurrently with the filing of his complaint/petition for writ of mandate, Marken filed an ex parte application for a temporary restraining order and an application for an order to show cause re preliminary injunction, which were supported by a memorandum of points and authorities and related declarations.

The Court of Appeal held that: the agency's decision to release confidential documents under California Public Records Act (CPRA) is reviewable by petition for writ of mandate; the district's planned disclosure did not violate the teacher's right to privacy under state constitution; but the denial of the student's parent's ex parte application for leave to intervene was not appealable.

Judgment affirmed, and appeal from order denying intervention dismissed.

Case Questions

1. As a general proposition, which legal interest should outweigh the other in a case like this: the employee's privacy interests or the interests of the minor involved in the investigation?

2. Does the fact that the employee, whose files were sought here, was a teacher change your answer to question 1?

3. Assuming the court was correct in denying the defendant's request for access to the personnel files, what more, if anything, might the defendant have alleged that could have tipped the balance in his favor, persuading the judge to grant access?

4. Does the fact that a minor was involved in the investigation and subsequent records in question sway your opinion on any of these questions?

Concept *Summary* 4.6

PERSONNEL FILES

- Issues:
  - What should be in a personnel file?
  - Who can see the file?
  - Who can make copies?
  - Who can take notes?
  - When is information released to third parties?

- Factors:
  - Federal and state laws
  - Qualified privilege
  - Legal process (e.g., subpoena)
  - Collective bargaining agreement
  - Company policies

CHAPTER REVIEW

» Key Terms

surveillance	65	academic freedom	69	drug testing	75
eavesdropping	65	malice	70	reasonable suspicion	75
information technology	68	negligent hiring	70	substance abuse	75
network	68	protected health information (PHI)	72	Employee Assistance Program (EAP)	75
system administrator	69	genetic testing	73		

» Summary

- The tort of invasion of privacy is a relatively recent addition to American common law. A broad and generalized privacy right grounded in the U.S. Constitution's Bill of Rights is an even more recent arrival on the American legal scene.

- The four general grounds for an invasion of privacy lawsuit recognized by most American courts today are:
  - Appropriating the plaintiffs identity for the defendant's benefit
  - Placing the plaintiff in a false light in the public eye
  - Publicly disclosing private facts about the plaintiff

  - Unreasonably intruding upon the seclusion or solitude of the plaintiff.

- The major areas where an employer is likely to risk liability for invading the privacy of its employees in the modern U.S. workplace are:
  - Surveillance and eavesdropping
  - Monitoring and reviewing computer information and use
  - Requests for information from third parties
  - Requests for medical information, and
  - Conducting internal investigations.

» Problems

» Questions

1. What is the most important factor that distinguishes the tort of invasion of privacy from the tort of defamation?

2. Taking into account all the new technologies in the workplace, as compared to even 15 or 20 years ago, and considering the events of September 11, 2001, in general, is employee privacy or workplace safety the more important consideration for the average employer today?

3. Does genetic testing have any legitimate place in a company's human resource policies today?

4. When should an employer refer the investigation of alleged employee wrongdoing to outside experts, such as attorneys, human resources consultants, or private investigators? When should the matter be referred to a law enforcement agency?

5. What are the pros and cons of placing a written record of every counseling session between a supervisor and his/her subordinate into the subordinate's personnel file?

» Case Problems

6. In this chapter, we briefly examined several cases in which the employer's surveillance was challenged as an alleged invasion of employees' privacy. Are there circumstances under which an employer's failure to provide surveillance will support tort liability? In one recent case, Dean, a mentally disabled but "very dedicated" Whataburger employee of 14 years, was murdered when he was shot in the face by Marshall, who was, at the direction of Love, attempting to rob the Whataburger restaurant at which Love served as manager. In the wrongful death suit brought by Dean's estate against Whataburger, the plaintiffs' expert "emphasized that Whataburger was the only fast-food chain of which he was aware that had 'failed to develop a comprehensive robbery prevention program to protect its employees.'" At the time of the capital murder of Dean, Whataburger had no security manual or methodology in place. There were no minimum standards published or training provided to managers, and "Whataburger's conduct of not addressing workplace violence and robbery prevention fell below the standard of care and constituted malice or conscious indifference to the magnitude of the risk of harm and disregard for the safety of its employees. This conduct was a proximate cause of Christopher Dean's death." The expert focused in particular on the "lack of security guards, alarms, bullet-resistant barriers, and surveillance equipment," and cited "a combination of surveillance camera and hold-up alarm system as significant deterrents."

Should Whataburger be found liable for Dean's death? [See *Barton v. Whataburger, Inc.*, 2009 WL 417292 (Tex. App., February 13, 2009).]

7. What if the plaintiff-employee, who is suing her employer, is guilty of eavesdropping? In a recent case, female firefighters filed employment discrimination action against city and individual defendants, asserting claims include hostile-environment sexual harassment and disparate-treatment discrimination. One plaintiff alleged that while assigned to a fire station, she became the object of severe harassment, consisting of repeated verbal assault and sexual innuendo. When she reported this harassment to her superiors, she was rebuked for her part in precipitating trouble in the work environment. Subsequent complaints about what she perceived as demeaning and hostile statements in her presence resulted in her being accused by the employer of eavesdropping.

If the plaintiff is guilty of eavesdropping on her coworkers and/or supervisors, (1) should her testimony about what she heard be admitted at trial; and (2) if she was disciplined for eavesdropping, should this discipline be admitted as evidence of employer retaliation? [See *Stachura v. Toledo*, 177 Ohio App. 3d 481, 895 N.E.2d 202 (2008).]

8. Television writers filed class-action lawsuits against studios, networks, production companies, and talent agencies, asserting an industry-wide pattern and practice of age discrimination. The writers served subpoenas on third parties, including the Writers Guild of America, seeking data on Writers Guild members from which they could prepare a statistical analysis to support their claims of age discrimination. A privacy notice was sent to 47,000 Writers Guild members, advising them of their right to object to disclosure of personal information on privacy grounds. Some 7,700 individuals filed objections. The writers moved to overrule the objections. The trial court sustained the objections in their entirety. The writers sought a writ directing the trial court to vacate its order and allow access to certain of the requested information, arguing the information was critical to proving their claims and privacy concerns were minimal.

On balance, who has the stronger claim, the TV writers who want the information, or the companies and the union who want to keep the information confidential? [See *Alch v. Superior Court*, 165 Cal. App. 4th 1412, 82 Cal.Rptr.3d 470 (2008).]

9. Two employees sued an employer, who had placed a surveillance video camera in an office that employees shared, for invasion of privacy, intentional infliction of emotional distress, and negligent infliction of emotional distress. The employer, a facility for abused children, defended on the grounds that (1) the plaintiffs were not recorded or viewed by the surveillance equipment defendants placed in their office; and (2) all employees of the facility had a diminished expectation of privacy that was overcome by defendants' need to protect the children residing at their facility.

    Does the fact that the employees were never actually recorded let the employer off the liability hook? Did the nature of the employer's business diminish the employees' expectation of privacy to the point where their privacy interest could not support an invasion of privacy lawsuit? [See *Hernandez v. Hillsides, Inc.*, 48 Cal.Rptr.3d 780 (Cal. App. 2006).]

10. On February 6, 1991, the decedent Daniel Boyle, a police officer for the city of Philadelphia, died as a result of a gunshot wound to the head, sustained in the course and scope of his employment. On March 17, 1992, Patricia Rossa filed a fatal-claim petition on behalf of her daughter with the state's workers' compensation board, and the matter was assigned to Workers' Compensation Judge Lundy, who placed the matter in indefinite postponement status to allow the parties the opportunity to file a paternity claim in the court of common pleas. The claimant presented the testimony of Rossa, Patricia J. Ranalli, Claimant's grandmother and Rossa's mother, Raymond Ranalli, Rossa's stepfather, Louis Rossa, Rossa's brother, and Ethel Weir, Rossa's grandmother, all to the effect that Officer Boyle was the father of her daughter.

    The employer—the City of Philadelphia—petitioned to do genetic testing before the workers' comp claim was allowed. Should the court order such genetic tests? [See *Rossa ex rel. Rossa v. W.C.A.B. (City of Philadelphia)*, 794 A.2d 919 (Pa. Commonwealth Ct. 2002).]

11. Wahkiakum School District required its student athletes to refrain from using or possessing alcohol or illegal drugs. Beginning in 1994, the school district implemented myriad ways to combat drug and alcohol use among the student population. Nevertheless, drug and alcohol problems persisted. Acting independently of the school district, the Wahkiakum Community Network (community network) began surveying district students. From these surveys, the community network ranked teen substance abuse as the number one problem in Wahkiakum County. The community network's surveys showed that in 1998, 40 percent of sophomores reported previously using illegal drugs and 19 percent of sophomores reported illegal drug use within the previous 30 days, while 42 percent of seniors reported previously using illegal drugs and 12.5 percent reported illegal drug use within the previous 30 days. As a result, the school district decided to implement random drug testing, where all students may be tested initially and then subjected to random drug testing during the remainder of the season. The school district formed the Drug and Alcohol Advisory Committee (now the "Safe and Drug Free Schools Advisory Committee") to help deal with the student substance abuse problems. The committee evaluated the effectiveness of its previous programs, and contemplated adopting Policy 3515, which would require random drug testing of student athletes. Parents sued to block the policy.

    On balance, which concern should be accorded greater judicial weight, preventing drug abuse or student-athletes' privacy rights? Does the balance change if the athletes are NCAA Division I athletes at a major university? Does the balance change if the athletes are professional athletes employed by major league teams? [See *York v. Wahkiakum School District*, 163 Wash.2d 297, 178 P.3d 995 (2008).]

12. The University of Wyoming employed Corrine Sheaffer for more than 25 years. However, in February 2004, UW terminated Sheaffer from her

position as transportation and parking services manager. UW's position was that Sheaffer was terminated "for cause" for her role in a secret audiotape recording of a meeting of the UW Traffic Appeals Committee (TAC). Sheaffer's reason for taping the meeting was centered on the number of appeals that were being granted and a general lack of consistency in the handling of the appeals. There was a generalized perception by Sheaffer that the members of the TAC were biased in favor of faculty, administration, and student athletes. Sheaffer believed that the only way to get the upper administration to sit up and take notice was to make them hear exactly what went on in the meetings. She also complained that the language used in the hearings created an abusive work environment amounting to sexual harassment. When she was fired, she charged retaliatory discharge.

Absent any justification for the eavesdropping, was Sheaffer guilty of an invasion of her colleagues' privacy that was deserving of employer discipline? If she was trying to collect evidence of a sexually hostile work environment, did this justify her conduct? If Wyoming has a whistleblower statute, do you think she should qualify as a protected whistleblower? [See *Sheaffer v. State ex rel. University of Wyoming*, 2009 WL 387269 (Wyoming Supreme Court, February 18, 2009).]

13. The State of Vermont appealed the Vermont Labor Relations Board's decision, reinstating grievant Lawrence Rosenberger to his position as a game warden and awarding him back pay after he was discharged for falsifying a time report to obtain compensation for work not done. One of the main issues for the Board to resolve at the grievance hearing in this case was how to remedy the employer's violation of a collective bargaining agreement provision requiring state employers to inform employees of their right to union representation before being called to a meeting that might lead to disciplinary action. The state argued that the board erred by adopting the criminal law doctrines—the exclusionary rule and its companion fruit-of-the-poisonous-tree corollary—to exclude from the grievance hearing not only the grievant's admissions during an initial interview without union

representation, but also his admissions during later investigative interviews when accompanied by a union representative.

Should the employer's error invalidate the results of its internal investigation? [See *In re Rosenberger, 2009*, WL 350631 (Vermont Supreme Court, February 13, 2009).]

14. Plaintiff Richard and three other Lafayette police officers had performed authorized off-duty security work at Club 410, a nightclub located in downtown Lafayette, Louisiana, for some time. Richard in fact was head of security at Club 410. On the night that other police raided the club and confiscated illegal drugs, Richard received a phone call from the club. On the basis of that call, the 10-year veteran was subjected to a nonrandom drug test, which revealed the use of steroids. He was fired.

Did the employer police department have sufficient reasonable suspicion, based upon the occurrence of the phone call on the night of the raid, to subject Richard to the nonrandom drug test? [See *Richard v. Lafayette Fire and Police Civil Service Board*, 2009 WL 307145 (Louisiana Supreme Court, February 6, 2009).]

15. This action arose from a dispute between political opponents. The plaintiff Derith Smith alleged that Charles Stewart, the village manager, wrongfully terminated her during her employment with the Village of Suttons Bay. However, she did not file suit against the village because she obtained other employment as the elected supervisor of Elmwood Township. On May 17, 2005, the plaintiff received an anonymous mailing while serving as Elmwood Township supervisor. This mailing consisted of a document written by Stewart that was contained in her personnel file but was never brought to her attention or discussed during her employment. The document raised various issues regarding the plaintiff's employment, such as whether she inappropriately paid herself a higher wage and whether she misrepresented her status as an employee when she was in fact an independent contractor. Someone had added a caption to the document that read, "Attention: Suttons Bay Villagers Alledged [*sic*] Misuse of Village Taxpayer Funds?" and "Subject: Personnel meeting scheduled for August 10,

2004...." The plaintiff sued, alleging that the mailing defamed her, invaded her privacy, constituted an injurious falsehood, and was a violation of her free speech rights.

What do you think are her chances of prevailing on the invasion of privacy count in the complaint? If she has a valid cause of action, against whom does she have it? [See *Smith v. Anonymous Joint Enterprise*, 2009 WL 249415 (Mich. Ct. App., February 3, 2009).]

» Hypothetical Scenarios

16. Assume that an employer's computer-use policy permits employees to use their company-owned laptops for personal emails and web searches, provided such use does not interfere with company business. Assume further that, when members of the company's outside sales force have their laptops collected and replaced by newer models, the IT department in the act of inspecting the old computers and sweeping their hard drives for redistribution to clerical workers, discovers Internet pornography on a salesman's hard drive. If, as is the case with some corporations such as Wal-Mart, the company has a policy against pornography entering its premises, should the salesman be reported to human resources and disciplined? Suppose that some of the material appears to be "kiddy porn" that violates federal law. Does this change your answer? If the salesman is fired, does he have the basis for a wrongful discharge action? If he is prosecuted for possessing "kiddy porn," does he have a viable Fourth/Fourteenth Amendment search-and-seizure defense?

17. Suppose that a 25-year-old woman, whose mother and aunts all were afflicted with breast cancer by the time they were 45, has a genetic test conducted at her own expense. The test reveals that she has inherited her mother's genetic susceptibility to breast cancer. After applying for employment and being given the position, her human resources orientation includes registration for employer-paid health insurance. The insurance questionnaire asks if she suffers from any preexisting medical condition. What should the new employee answer? Suppose that, later on, she desires to take advantage of the employer's wellness program. This includes free annual breast examinations. Should she reveal to the health care provider that she has a genetic susceptibility to breast cancer? If she does so, what obligations does the health care provider have (1) to the employee, (2) to the employer, and (3) to the insurance carrier?

18. A web site reads as follows: "Need to pass a Drug test? Our detox online store is here to help you! Pass a drug test now! Results are guaranteed!!! Our drug detoxification products are produced by the best manufactures and based on alternative or herbal methods of flushing toxins from your system. Nowadays, popular trade publications such as *Men's Health, Glamour, Muscle Media, Whole Foods*, and many others have mentioned these cleansing products as very effective and safe. Pass your drug test with rapid detox now. We take care of our customers and respect privacy! All products will be shipped in plain boxes. Just to let you know—You are not alone!!! Shop with confidence. Do not be afraid to log in and create an account. Overnight shipping is available. Place your order by 2 pm EST and your order will be shipped the same day!" How can an employer guard against employee use of such products to defeat the employer's drug-testing program? Be sure to consider whether your proposed solution(s) themselves create additional privacy concerns for the employer. See http://www.stardetox.com.

19. Beginning a mere week after the terrorist attacks of September 11, 2001, envelopes packed with anthrax spores started turning up in people's mailboxes. Two of those people were sitting U.S. senators Tom Daschle of South Dakota and Patrick Leahy of Vermont. The *National Enquirer* in Florida and TV network offices in New York also were targeted. The envelopes were all postmarked in the Trenton/Princeton (NJ) area. The FBI visited the biology labs on every college campus along the Route One corridor between New York and Philadelphia. The bureau also intensely investigated Uncle Sam's own

bio-weapons facilities, including Fort Detrick in Frederick, Maryland. The investigation proved to be one of needles and haystacks. Eventually, FBI suspicions focused on a bio-weapons researcher named Steven Hatfill. Indeed, after years of investigating, the agency's only "person of interest" was this Fort Detrick alumnus. Although never indicted, Hatfill's person of interest status was enough to make him a leper to his profession, essentially unemployable. Hatfill eventually was cleared and suspicion shifted to another scientist at the same government facility. That suspect actually committed suicide before being indicted and tried. Should Hatfill be permitted to sue his former employer, the federal government? If so, what legal theories presented in this chapter might apply? On balance, whose interests were more important here, Hatfill's or Uncle Sam's? Did both parties have important privacy interests in this case? At some point in the FBI's investigation, did the balance shift from one of them to other?

20. Pat was a certified registered nurse anesthetist who worked at a hospital. Pat met with his supervisor regarding his job performance. His supervisor told Pat of complaints he had received from members of the hospital staff, including complaints that Pat was often late for surgeries, did not make proper patient status reviews, and failed to review EKG and lab results in a timely manner. The supervisor warned Pat that his repeated failure to perform patient work-ups in advance of surgery and his careless attitude would no longer be tolerated. No mention of the meeting was placed in Pat's personnel file. Should Pat have a right to see the written records of the alleged complaints? Does your answer change if the complaints are placed in Pat's personnel file? Does your answer to this second question depend in any way upon applicable state law(s)?

CHAPTER 5

The Global Perspective: International Employment Law and American Immigration Policy

Before 1964, an American labor lawyer need only have known the National Labor Relations Act to practice competently. Beginning in that fateful year, nearly a half-century ago, federal and state statutory and common law greatly complicated the employment and labor law landscape. Still, a competent employment law lawyer's expertise had no need to extend beyond U.S. borders. As businesses continue to evolve, employemt lawyers and human resources executives must be versed in both international law and the employment laws and policies of the world's major nations. Additionally, a working knowledge of U.S. immigration law is virtually a "must," as new arrivals and employees of overseas subsidiaries increasingly figure into the work forces of American-based firms.

5-1 International Employment Law and Policy

International Labor Organization (ILO)
a United Nations subsidiary agency dealing with international labor standards, workers' rights, and global employment issues

The **International Labor Organization (ILO)** is the branch of the United Nations charged with developing and promulgating uniform labor and employment standards internationally, encouraging member nations to adopt those universal standards, and monitoring compliance by those nations which have adopted them. The ILO, which is based in Geneva, has promulgated a vast scheme of labor and employment laws, regulations, and guidelines. These ILO "laws" cannot supersede an individual nation's sovereignty unless that nation affirmatively adopts any such laws. The United States is not a signatory to many ILO enactments or pronouncements; however, U.S. labor and employment laws in many instances are equal or superior to the ILO scheme in according rights and remedies to workers within our borders (exceptions involve labor organization rights and employment security versus employment at will). However, Americans doing business globally must be mindful of ILO legal principles adopted by the nations in which they are operating and employing personnel. U.S. embassies and consulates should be consulted not only about the labor and employment laws of the host nation but also about any relevant ILO rules and regulations.

convention
international law,
usually sponsored by
the United Nations
or other multinational
organizations, to which
a number of nations
agree to adhere

Conventions are "pacts or agreements between states or nations in the nature of a treaty."[1] In the context of international employment law, conventions are the uniform codes of procedure and standards of conduct that the ILO seeks to promulgate and enforce in order to establish international standards for the fair treatment of workers among all member nations of the United Nations. International conventions to which the United States is a signatory that should be noted when doing business abroad, and that can affect international labor relations and employment litigation, include:

- *Convention on the Service Abroad of Judicial and Extrajudicial Documents in Civil or Commercial Matters.* Facilitates and standardizes the service of legal processes, such as complaints, summons, and subpoenas, in pursuit of litigation, including labor and employment litigation.

- *Convention on the Recognition and Enforcement of Foreign Arbitral Awards.* Ensures that signatory states will enforce arbitral awards, including labor and employment arbitration awards, against parties found within their jurisdictions.

- *Convention on the Taking of Evidence Abroad in Civil or Commercial Matters.* A judicial authority (*e.g.*, a court) in one contracting state may request its counterpart in another contracting state to facilitate such discovery activities as the taking of depositions or sworn statements in support of litigation, including labor and employment litigation.

- *Convention on the Civil Aspects of International Child Abduction.* Aims to control and eliminate exploitation of child labor.

The major conventions on labor and employment, adopted under the auspices of the United Nations and the ILO, most of which have not been signed by the United States (primarily because they may conflict with existing U.S. labor and employment laws), involve the abolition of forced labor (signed by the U.S.), employment discrimination, and collective bargaining.

**global corporate
responsibility**
philosophy which says
that corporations should
behave as good global
citizens

The fact that more and more business is being conducted across borders has led to a growing concern about how companies with differing policies should act. **Global corporate responsibility** signifies the notion, held by many advocates of workers' rights and environmental issues, that multinational corporations have the ethical obligation to behave in fair and humane ways toward their workers and to pursue "green" policies and practices to protect the environments in which they operate.

ethical DILEMMA

SHOULD MULTINATIONAL CORPORATIONS RECOGNIZE THEIR EMPLOYEES' SAME-SEX MARRIAGES, REGARDLESS OF WHERE THE EMPLOYEES ARE LOCATED?

In June 2013, the U.S. Supreme Court declared the federal Defense of Marriage Act (DOMA) to be unconstitutional. [*United States v. Windsor*, 133 S.Ct. 2675 (2013).]

---

[1] *Black's Law Dictionary.*

This set off a domino effect across the country, as one court after another declared states' "Baby-DOMAs" equally unconstitutional. As of February 2015, same-sex marriage was legal in 30 states, plus the District of Columbia. The climactic event was the U.S. Supreme Court's June 26, 2015 decision [*Obergefell v. Hodges*, 135 S.Ct. 2584] that held (1) the right to marry is a fundamental 14th Amendment right of which same-sex couples may not be deprived by state laws, and (2) states must recognize same-sex marriages legally performed in sister states. These common-law developments have dramatically altered U.S. policy regarding same-sex marriages among immigrants. Less than two months after the Supreme Court's 2013 decision was announced, U.S. Immigration and Customs Enforcement (ICE) issued the following notice to U.S. employers and universities:

> *The Department of State, Bureau of Consular Affairs has advised consulates that their officials may issue derivative visas based on same-sex marriage if the marriage is "recognized in the place of celebration." That is, if the country where the couple married recognizes same-sex marriage as legal, then the U.S. government will recognize the union as legal for visa issuance, irrespective of where the couple plans to reside. The Department of State will be updating the reciprocity tables to 9 FAM 41.105 to identify what types of marriages are available to same-sex couples.*

What should employers of H-1B nonimmigrant workers and other legal alien employees in the United States anticipate? According to immigration attorney Matthew I. Hirsch of Wayne, Pennsylvania, "In practical terms, the decision means that married same-sex couples will have the same rights as traditional married couples in such areas as income tax, estate tax, health privacy and other federally regulated areas—including immigration." Confirming Hirsch's prediction, on June 20, 2014, the U.S. Department of Labor, the Social Security Administration, and the Department of Veterans Affairs announced that benefits extended to heterosexual married couples will be extended to same-sex married couples.[2]

Within a month of the U.S. Supreme Court's 2013 DOMA decision, Britain legalized same-sex marriage. Other nations fall along a broad spectrum in their treatment of discrimination against LGBT employees. For example, Canada is among the most advanced nations in the world for eradicating discrimination based on sexual orientation. Section 15(1) of the Canadian Constitution reads much like Title VII of the Civil Rights Act of 1964:

> *Every individual is equal before and under the law and has the right to the equal protection and equal benefit of the law without discrimination and, in particular, without discrimination based on race, national or ethnic origin, colour, religion, sex, age or mental or physical disability.*

As early as 1995, the Supreme Court of Canada held that the enumerated grounds for finding illegal discrimination were only examples and not limiting categories, and further that sexual orientation is implicitly included among the protected categories.[3]

In Britain, LGBT rights were spotty and varied across England, Scotland, Wales, and Northern Ireland. The Equality Act of 2010 uniformly extended protection against discrimination to eight specific categories of persons, including gender reassignment and sexual orientation.[4]

---

[2] Michael D. Shear, "Obama Extends Marriage Benefits to Gay Couples," *New York Times*, June 20, 2014, available at http://www.nytimes.com/2014/06/21/us/politics/obama-to-extend-array-of-marriage-benefits-to-gay-couples.html?_r=0.

[3] *Egan v. Canada*, 2 S.C.R 513 (1995).

[4] Equality Act 2010, The National Archives, available at http://www.legislation.gov.uk/ukpga/2010/15/contents.

By 2015, the following nations recognized same-sex marriage:

Scotland (2014)
Luxembourg (2014)
Brazil (2013)
England/Wales (2013)
France (2013)
New Zealand (2013)
Uruguay (2013)
Denmark (2012)
Argentina (2010)
Iceland (2010)
Portugal (2010)
Norway (2009)
Sweden (2009)
South Africa (2006)
Spain (2005)
Canada (2005)
Belgium (2003)
The Netherlands (2000)[5]

Of course, many more nations do not.

5-1a   The Alien Tort Claims Act and International Workers' Rights

Alien Tort Claims Act
federal statute that
provides a cause of
action for aggrieved
aliens in U.S. courts

The **Alien Tort Claims Act**[6] was enacted in 1789 as part of the original Judiciary Act. In its original form, it simply said that "[t]he district courts shall have original jurisdiction of any civil action by an alien for a tort only, committed in violation of the law of nations or a treaty of the United States." For almost two centuries, the statute lay relatively dormant, supporting jurisdiction in only a handful of cases. In recent years, however, the statute has been rediscovered by attorneys seeking to vindicate the rights of foreign workers allegedly oppressed by U.S. multinational corporations.

For example, two United States Courts of Appeals decisions were announced in December 2008, interpreting the Alien Tort Claims Act as it may or may not apply to labor-related claims. The two decisions offer mixed messages but, by and large, bode well for multinational corporate-defendants.

One knowledgeable observer, viewing the two circuit court decisions with an eye fixed on the potential of the two federal statutes' applicability in the global environmental arena, commented, "Like the earlier 9th Cir. case, this [11th Circuit] case demonstrates that the use of the Alien Tort Statute to establish jurisdiction and the use of the Torture Act will be difficult in the context of environmental and toxic tort matters occurring

---

[5] "Same-sex marriage: Where in the world is it legal?" CNN Wires, February 10, 2015, available at http://fox2now.com/2015/02/10/same-sex-marriage-where-in-the-world-is-it-legal/.

[6] 28 U.S.C. 1350.

» CASE 5.1

SAREI V. RIO TINTO, PLC
2008 WL 5220286 (9th Cir. 2008)

Facts: Bougainville is an island in the South Pacific located just off the main island of Papua New Guinea (PNG). Rich in natural resources, including copper and gold, the island was targeted as a prime mining site by defendants Rio Tinto, PLC, a British and Welsh corporation, and Rio Tinto Limited, an Australian corporation (collectively "Rio Tinto"). Rio Tinto was part of an international mining group that operated more than 60 mines and processing plants in 40 countries, including the United States. To operate a mine on Bougainville, Rio Tinto required and received the assistance of the PNG government. According to the plaintiffs' complaint, beginning in the 1960s Rio Tinto displaced villages; razed massive tracts of rain forest; intensely polluted the land, rivers, and air (with extensive collateral consequences including fatal and chronic illness, death of wildlife and vegetation, and failure of farm land); and systematically discriminated against its Bougainvillian workers, who lived in slave-like conditions.

In November 1988, some Bougainville residents revolted; they sabotaged the mine and forced its closure. After Rio Tinto demanded that the PNG government quash the uprising, the government complied and sent in troops. PNG forces used helicopters and vehicles supplied by Rio Tinto. On February 14, 1990, the country descended into a civil war after government troops slaughtered many Bougainvillians in what has come to be known as the St. Valentine's Day Massacre.

Unable to resume mining, Rio Tinto threatened to abandon its operations and halt all future investment in PNG unless the government took military action to secure the mine. In April 1990, the PNG government imposed a military blockade on the island that lasted almost a decade. The blockade prevented medicine, clothing, and other necessities from reaching the residents. Under further pressure from Rio Tinto, according to the complaint, the government engaged in aerial bombardment of civilian targets, wanton killing and acts of cruelty, village burning, rape, and pillage. As a result, an estimated 15,000 Bougainvillians, including many children, died. Of the survivors, tens of thousands are displaced and many suffer health problems. In March 2002, the PNG Parliament formalized a peace accord that ended the civil war.

In November 2000, nearly a year and a half before the civil war formally ended, the plaintiffs filed their class action, raising numerous claims under the Alien Tort Statute, 28 U.S.C. Section 1350:

- crimes against humanity resulting from the blockade;
- war crimes for murder and torture;
- violation of the rights to life, health, and security of the person resulting from the environmental damage;
- racial discrimination in destroying villages and the environment, and in working conditions;
- cruel, inhuman, and degrading treatment resulting from the blockade, environmental harm, and displacement;
- violation of international environmental rights resulting from building and operating the mine; and
- a consistent pattern of gross violations of human rights resulting from destruction of the environment, racial discrimination, and PNG military activities. The plaintiffs also raised various non–Alien Tort Statute claims ranging from negligence to public nuisance.

A model of brevity, the Alien Tort Act says, simply, "The district courts shall have original jurisdiction of any civil action by an alien for a tort only, committed in violation of the law of nations or a treaty of the United States." In *Sosa v. Alvarez-Machain*,[1] the high court held, "Though the Alien Tort Statute (ATS) . . . is a jurisdictional statute, which does not create a statutory cause of action for aliens, it was not intended to lie fallow until specific causes of action were authorized by further legislation, but was meant to have practical effect from the moment that it became law, by providing a basis for district courts to exercise jurisdiction over a modest number of causes of action recognized under the law of nations, such as for offenses against ambassadors, violations of safe conduct, and possibly for piracy." The Court also indicated that plaintiffs should first exhaust causes of action available to them under local law.

Issue: Should the plaintiffs be required to exhaust their other available remedies before being permitted to sue in a U.S. court under the Alien Tort Statute?

Decision: In *Sarei*, the Ninth Circuit, sitting en banc, considered the significance of this exhaustion requirement. The plurality opinion noted that, "As the Supreme Court directed in *Sosa*, exhaustion of local remedies should 'certainly' be considered in the 'appropriate case' for claims brought under the ATS.[2] This is an appropriate case for such consideration under both domestic prudential standards and core principles of international law."

Six judges then went on to hold, "As a preliminary matter, to 'exhaust,' it is not sufficient that a plaintiff merely initiate a suit, but rather, the plaintiff must obtain a final decision of the highest court in the hierarchy of courts in the legal system at issue, or a show that the state of the law or availability of remedies would make further appeal futile. . . . Another basic element is that the remedy must be available, effective, and not futile. To measure effectiveness, a court must look at the circumstances surrounding the access to a remedy and the ultimate utility of the remedy to the petitioner. In

addition, '[w]hen a person has obtained favorable decision in a domestic court, but that decision has not been complied with, no further remedies need be exhausted.' A judgment that cannot be enforced is an incomplete, and thus ineffective, remedy. The adequacy determination will also necessarily include an assessment of any delay in the delivery of a decision. We remand to the district court for the limited purpose to determine in the first instance whether to impose an exhaustion requirement on plaintiffs."

---

[1] 124 S.Ct. 2739, 542 U.S. 692, 159 L.Ed.2d 718 (2004). This colorful case concerned a Mexican physician accused by U.S. authorities of participating in the torture and death of a U.S. Drug Enforcement Administration officer south of the border. The doctor was kidnapped by the famous bounty hunter Duane "Dog" Chapman—http://www.dogthebountyhunter.com—and brought back to Texas to stand trial.

[2] 542 U.S. at 733 n. 21.

CASE 5.2
ROMERO V. DRUMMOND COMPANY, INC.
2008 WL 5274192 (11th Cir. 2008)

A Colombian labor union sued executives of Drummond, Ltd., the Colombian subsidiary of an American coal mining company located principally in Alabama, which paid paramilitary operatives to torture and assassinate leaders of the union, SINTRAMIENERGETICA. In 2002 and 2003, the union and several of its leaders and relatives of deceased leaders sued Drummond and its parent company and executives under the Alien Tort Statute and the Torture Victim Protection Act of 1991. The Torture Act establishes a separate cause of action for victims of torture and extrajudicial killing. The district court consolidated the complaints and later granted partial summary judgment against them; one claim for relief—that Drummond aided and abetted the killings, which were war crimes—remained. At a trial of that claim, the jury returned a verdict for Drummond. The plaintiffs appealed the partial summary judgment and a series of discovery and evidentiary rulings made before and during the trial. Long after the discovery deadline had been extended and later expired, the plaintiffs moved for continuances and the admission of the testimonies of several new witnesses, and some of those

requests were denied. Drummond challenged the subject-matter jurisdiction of the district court.

In the underlying complaints in this case, the union, its leaders, and relatives of its leaders complained that Augusto Jimenez, the president of the mining operations of Drummond, Ltd., with the knowledge of company executives in the United States, hired paramilitaries affiliated with the United Self-Defense Forces of Colombia to torture union leaders Juan Aquas Romero, Jimmy Rubio Suarez, and Francisco Ruiz Daza and to kill union leaders Valmore Locarno Rodriquez, Victor Hugo Orcasita Amaya, and Gustavo Soler Mora. The complaints included claims of torture, extrajudicial killing, and denials of the right to associate, lodged under the Alien Tort Statute; claims of torture and extrajudicial killing, grouped under the Torture Act; a claim of wrongful death under Colombian law; and claims for assault, intentional infliction of emotional distress, negligent infliction of emotional distress, negligent supervision, and false imprisonment under Alabama law.

On these complex facts and complicated legal issues, the appellate court held:

(1) the Torture Victim Protection Act allows suits against corporate defendants;

(2) the Alien Tort Statute contains no express exception for corporations, and the statute grants jurisdiction over complaints of torture against corporate defendants;

(3) the plaintiffs failed to satisfy the "state action" requirement of the Torture Victim Protection Act;

(4) the district court did not abuse its discretion in refusing to exercise supplemental jurisdiction over the plaintiffs' wrongful death claim under Colombian law;

(5) the district court did not abuse its discretion in denying plaintiffs' motion for additional continuance when they were not able to complete the letter rogatory process to secure witness's testimony for rescheduled trial date;

(6) the district court did not abuse its discretion in excluding the testimony of late-disclosed witnesses; and

(7) the district court did not abuse its discretion in refusing to allow the plaintiffs' proffered experts to testify.

In sum, the panel affirmed the district judge, essentially defeating the plaintiffs' claims.

Case Questions

1. Why didn't the plaintiffs seek to secure justice in their own countries?

2. In *Romero*, the plaintiffs sought to have the U.S. federal judge take jurisdiction of their wrongful death claim, brought under Colombian law. Wouldn't a Colombian court be better equipped to adjudicate this claim? Why did they prefer to bring it into an American courtroom?

3. If a multinational corporation strictly abides by the laws of each country in which it does business, affording its workers in each country whatever rights and benefits are required by local law, shouldn't this be sufficient to insulate such company from legal liability? Don't the shareholders of such a corporation have the right to expect management to take advantage of business-favorable laws and policies to maximize the firm's profits?

4. In these two cases, are the unions' and workers' grievances so closely connected to the fundamental labor-relations policies of the their respective countries that a U.S. court would be intruding upon foreign policy issues, which are the exclusive realm of the executive branch of our government, if it were to adjudicate these cases?

5. Why does the court in *Sarei* suggest that the plaintiffs should first have to exhaust their local (i.e., home-country) remedies before coming into a U.S. courtroom?

«

in third countries."[7] Given that each case enjoys a strong nexus to labor and employment law, we must conclude that this commentator's conclusion applies with equal force to foreign labor unions and labor leaders, as well as classes of workers, who had hopes of bringing tort claims into American federal courts against multinational corporations headquartered in the U.S. Like the ILO conventions, most of which the U.S. has declined to sign, and the idealistic concept of corporate responsibility, discussed earlier (see the Ethical Dilemma), the Alien Tort Statute is unlikely to have a high impact upon the way U.S. corporations deal with their overseas employees. For workers and reformers seeking to impact American multinationals, especially in nations that lack meaningful human rights and labor legislation, global labor organizations may present the highest prospect of success.

---

[7] Thomas H. Clarke, Jr., "Like the earlier reported 9th Circuit case, this recent 11th Circuit case shows that using the Alien Tort Statute or the Torture Act in an environmental context will be quite difficult," LexisNexis Environmental Law Blog, December 26, 2008, available at http://www.lexisnexis.com/legalnewsroom/environmental/b/environmental-law-blog/archive/2008/12/26/like-the-earlier-reported-9th-circuit-case_2c00_-this-recent-11th-circuit-case-shows-that-using-the-alien-tort-statute-or-the-torture-act-.aspx.

In a 2012 decision, *Mohamad v. Palestinian Authority*,[8] the issues were the same: do the human rights laws at issue apply to someone other than a natural person? In this case, the widow and sons of a U.S. citizen allegedly tortured and killed in Israel brought suit against three individuals, the Palestinian Authority, and the Palestine Liberation Organization for violations under the Torture Victim Protection Act and the Alien Tort Statute. The Supreme Court affirmed the decision of the lower court, finding that only a natural person is an "individual" who can be held liable.

Most recently, in 2014, the Supreme Court considered a case in which 22 residents of Argentina filed suit in California Federal District Court, naming as a defendant DaimlerChrysler Aktiengesellschaft, a German public stock company that was the predecessor to Daimler AG, the defendant in this case. Their complaint alleged that Mercedes-Benz Argentina, an Argentinian subsidiary of Daimler, collaborated with state security forces during Argentina's 1976–1983 "Dirty War" to kidnap, detain, torture, and kill certain Mercedes-Benz Argentinian workers, among them the plaintiffs or persons closely related to the plaintiffs. Based on those allegations, the plaintiffs asserted claims under the Alien Tort Claims Act and the Torture Victim Protection Act of 1991, as well as under California and Argentina law. Personal jurisdiction over Daimler was predicated on the California contacts of Mercedes-Benz USA, LLC (MBUSA), another Daimler subsidiary, one incorporated in Delaware with its principal place of business in New Jersey. MBUSA distributed Daimler-manufactured vehicles to independent dealerships throughout the United States, including California. Daimler moved to dismiss the action for want of personal jurisdiction. Opposing that motion, the plaintiffs argued that jurisdiction over Daimler could be founded on the California contacts of MBUSA. The District Court granted Daimler's motion to dismiss. Reversing the District Court's judgment, the Ninth Circuit held that MBUSA, which it assumed to fall within the California courts' all-purpose jurisdiction, was Daimler's "agent" for jurisdictional purposes, so that Daimler, too, should generally be answerable to suit in that State.

In a unanimous opinion penned by liberal Justice Ginsburg, the high court held that Fifth Amendment due process rules prevented the federal courts in California from exercising jurisdiction over the defendant corporation on behalf of the Argentinian plaintiffs. Wrote Justice Ginsburg, "Here, neither Daimler nor MBUSA is incorporated in California, nor does either entity have its principal place of business there. If Daimler's California activities sufficed to allow adjudication of this Argentina-rooted case in California, the same global reach would presumably be available in every other State in which MBUSA's sales are sizable. Such exorbitant exercises of all-purpose jurisdiction would scarcely permit out-of-state defendants 'to structure their primary conduct with some minimum assurance as to where that conduct will and will not render them liable to suit.' *Burger King Corp.*, 471 U.S., at 472, 105 S.Ct. 2174 (internal quotation marks omitted)."

Justice Ginsburg added, "The Ninth Circuit, moreover, paid little heed to the risks to international comity its expansive view of general jurisdiction posed. Other nations do not share the uninhibited approach to personal jurisdiction advanced by the Court of Appeals in this case. In the European Union, for example, a corporation may generally be sued in the nation in which it is 'domiciled,' a term defined to refer only to the location of the corporation's 'statutory seat,' 'central administration,' or 'principal place of business.' European Parliament and Council Reg. 1215/2012, Arts. 4(1), and 63(1), 2012 O.J. (L. 351) 7, 18."[9]

---

[8] 132 S.Ct. 1702 (U.S. 2012).

[9] *Daimler AG v. Bauman*, 134 S.Ct. 746 (2014).

5-2 Global Labor Unions

global unions
international labor organizations, which typically attempt to organize employees of globalized industries

Recently the international trade union movement has begun to use the term **global unions** as an umbrella designation. The components of global unions include the International Confederation of Free Trade Unions, which represents national trade union centers around the globe, and the Union Network International.

5-2a Union Network International (UNI)

Union Network International (UNI) is an organization aimed at meeting the globalization of corporations, trade, and manufacturing head on. Reasoning that the global labor market no longer recognizes or is confined within the borders of traditional nation-states, UNI seeks to organize workers on an international scale. The organization targets multinational corporations, seeking to apply global pressure in order to organize local and regional corporate facilities. "When companies are local, unions can be local; when companies are national, unions must be national; when companies are global, unions must be global. Our aim is to build more effective alliances in multinationals," UNI explains.[10]

At its August 2005 Chicago convention, UNI announced that signing global agreements with targeted companies would be that organization's focus going forward. In 2007, UNI expanded its attention to monitoring private equity funds. In a March 2007 press release, UNI stated:

> In the furor that has enveloped private equity these past weeks, one of the criticisms of their way of doing business is the absence of any regard to corporate social responsibility (CSR). UNI Global Union has had a look at the websites of a range of the key private equity funds and has found precious few, if any, references to CSR, to the ILO core conventions, the UN Global Compact or the UN Principles for Responsible Investment (UNPRI). We are struck by the lack of any commitment to these global principles, which have been forged to improve the accountability and responsibility of the business community to all shareholders. . . . It is challenging to find even a minor reference to CSR matters among fund managers or those who spend time assessing trends in private equity funds. Issues of human rights, labor standards, environment and even corporate governance are seldom discussed as pros and cons of private equity. The fact that private equity funds closely guard their information represents a substantial impediment to actively analyzing the CSR performance of companies they hold. In the weeks to come, we will be keeping a close watch on whether there will be a shift towards more transparency, disclosure or any commitment to CSR principles.

UNI claims to hold the allegiance of approximately 15 million workers in 900 unions in 150 countries, representing employees in the following economic sectors:

- Commerce
- Electricity
- Finance
- Gaming
- Graphical
- Hair and beauty

---

[10] UNI, http://www.uniglobalunion.org.

- IBITS (industry, business services, and information and computer technology)
- Media, entertainment, and the arts
- Postal
- Property services (cleaning and security)
- Social insurance
- Telecom
- Tourism[11]

UNI has targeted a list of 100 multinational employers. As of early 2009, UNI had achieved labor contracts with the following targeted corporations:

- Carrefour (a Paris-based food retailer)
- Hennes & Mauritz of Sweden (trading as H&M stores in the United States)
- Falck (a Danish rescue, health care, and safety-training organization)
- Internet Security Systems (based in Atlanta, Georgia)
- Metro AG of Germany
- OTE (Greek telecommunications company)
- Telefónica (the Spanish telecom provider)[12]

In total, according to UNI's general secretary Philip Jennings, the organization now boasts 50 signed collective agreements and another 50 in various stages of negotiation.[13]

THE **WORKING** LAW

Workers Uniting Claims to Represent Three Million Members Worldwide, Uses the Social Net to Organize

Workers Uniting is a new international labor organization created through the combination of Unite, the largest union in the United Kingdom and Ireland, and the United Steelworkers, North America's largest private sector union. The amalgamation claims the loyalty of some three million members. Its goal is to promote "global union activism," including "[c]ommon political strategies to fight right-wing cuts in pensions and social services and attacks on workers' fundamental right to organize and join unions, and to rebuild our economies through investment in manufacturing industry,

---

[11] UNI, http://www.uniglobalunion.org.

[12] UNI, http://www.union-network.org/UNIsite/In_Depth/Multinationals/Multinationals.html.

[13] UNI's contact information is as follows:
Union Network International
8–10 Avenue Reverdil
CH-1260 Nyon, Switzerland
Tel. +41 22 365 21 00
Fax: +41 22 365 21 21
Email: contact@union-network.org
Website: http://www.uniglobalunion.org

infrastructure and green jobs … [and] [j]oint collective bargaining efforts with common employers in our industries."

This mega-union explains its *raison d'etre* with four key points:

1. The economy is globalizing. From Brussels to Beijing, decisions about our economy are increasingly made far from home. A global union can provide us a voice in those decisions.

2. Politics is globalizing. Right-wing politicians are using the same vicious tactics to undermine our livelihoods in the UK as they are in the U.S. and Canada. A global union can help us support progressive politics on both sides of the Atlantic.

3. Our employers are globalizing. A couple decades ago, only a few of our employers operated in more than one country. Now, nearly all of them do. A global union can help us stand up to our employers wherever they operate.

4. The movement is globalizing. Whether it's standing up for fair trade or fighting back against bank bailouts, progressive groups are mobilizing and uniting everywhere. A global union can helps us join them in the fight for a better world.

Like nearly all organizations today, Workers Uniting has a social-network presence.[14] Additionally, the union supports an online news service called "United Live."[15]

Source: Workers Uniting, http://www.workersuniting.org.

Concept *Summary* 5.1

INTERNATIONAL LABOR AND EMPLOYMENT LAW AND POLICY

- Sources:
  - Corporate responsibility: Ethical principle incorporated into some nations' law and policy
  - International Labor Organization: UN agency that promulgates international conventions
  - Alien Tort Claims Act: Old U.S. statute subject to 21st-century interpretations
  - Global Labor Unions: Seek to foster workplace justice through collective bargaining agreements (labor contracts)

5-3   Immigration Law and Policy

The fundamental U.S. immigration statute is the Immigration and Nationality Act (INA) of 1952. Prior to its passage, U.S. immigration was governed by a variety of federal statutes, which were not collected under a single title of the U.S. Code.

---

[14] Workers Uniting Facebook, https://www.facebook.com/WorkersUniting.

[15] UNITElive, http://unitelive.org/workers-uniting.

5-3a   Immigration Reform and Control Act of 1986

The last major overhaul of the U.S. immigration statutory scheme, founded upon the 1952 law, occurred more nearly a quarter of a century ago. The purposes of the **Immigration Reform and Control Act (IRCA) of 1986** were to:

- Provide a solution for controlling illegal immigration to the United States;
- Make some changes in the U.S. system of legal immigration; and
- Provide a controlled legalization program for undocumented aliens who entered the United States before 1982.

Primarily by the creation of civil and criminal penalties for employers who hire undocumented (illegal) aliens, IRCA intended to stem the flow of illegal immigrants. IRCA altered several immigration provisions of the INA of 1952. First, a new immigrant category for dependents of employees of international organizations was created. IRCA recognized the unique position of children and spouses of long-term international organization employees when those employees die, transfer, or retire. It is often difficult for children and spouses to become reoriented to their original society and culture. For all purposes, these individuals are "Americanized." The special immigrant category recognizes their Americanization and allows the individuals to remain in this country if they meet certain residence requirements.

Second, IRCA restricted the ability of many foreign students to adjust their status to that of lawful permanent resident aliens. This modification was aimed at reducing the number of foreign students who remain in the United States. IRCA also altered the allocation of visas and created a visa waiver program.

Finally, IRCA modified the former H-2 program for temporary workers by adding the H-2A program for temporary agricultural workers. It also established a mechanism by which "special agricultural workers" are admitted to perform field work in perishable crops. Under this mechanism, agricultural workers move freely between employers without penalty and are fully protected under all federal, state, and local labor laws. This mechanism creates a legal workforce without decreasing the number of workers available to harvest perishable crops.

IRCA also provided a one-shot amnesty program under which illegal aliens who entered the United States before January 1, 1982, could become legalized. Applications for the amnesty program were accepted for an 18-month period that ended in April 1988. IRCA "grandfathered" workers hired prior to November 6, 1986; however, although the employers were not subject to sanctions, the grandfather provisions of IRCA did not make it lawful for an unauthorized alien to accept employment. Consequently, the alien was (and is) still subject to deportation for accepting employment.

Today, experts estimate that more than 12 million illegal aliens are living in the U.S., and some pundits predict that the number is substantially higher.

5-3b   Employer Compliance with IRCA

Employers must verify the employment eligibility of any employee hired. The preemployment question that must be asked is: Is the employee a U.S. citizen or lawfully authorized to work in the United States? To comply with verification requirements, an employer must show that it has examined documents that establish both:

- the employment authorization, and
- the identity of the employee.

A U.S. passport, certificate of U.S. citizenship, certificate of naturalization, or certain resident alien cards establish both. Employment authorization documents include a Social Security card or a birth certificate. Identity documents include a driver's license, other state-issued card, or under certain circumstances, other documentation approved by the attorney general.

One of the proposals afloat in the Congress for immigrant verification and control is an electronic employment-verification system aimed at screening approximately 54 million new hires annually. The Government Accountability Office estimates that creation, dissemination, and operation of this proposed system could cost $11.7 billion. Employer cost per employee is expected to run somewhere between $10 and $50. One thing seems certain: the seldom-enforced requirement of the Immigration Reform and Control Act of 1986 (passed the last time the United States granted amnesty to its illegal aliens) that employers verify the legitimacy of their workers will no longer be winked at by the federal government, regardless of what other provisions a new immigration statute may contain.

DOCUMENTS HR OFFICES MAY USE TO VERIFY NEW EMPLOYEES' ELIGIBILITY

For identity:

- Driver's license
- Other state-issued I.D. card (e.g., a Pennsylvania Liquor Control Board I.D. card)

For employment authorization:

- Social Security card
- Birth certificate

For satisfaction of both categories:

- U.S. passport
- Certificate of U.S. citizenship
- Certificate of naturalization
- Certain resident-alien cards
- Unexpired foreign passport with attached visa authorizing U.S. employment
- Alien registration card with photo

The employer is expected to examine the proffered documents. If they appear reasonably on their face to be genuine and to relate to the person presenting them, they are to be accepted. To refuse to accept such documents, in fact, may be viewed by the INS as an unfair immigration-related employment practice. On the other hand, if the document does not appear reasonably on its face to be genuine or to relate to the person presenting it, the employer is expected to refuse to accept it. Instead, that employer should contact the local INS office closest to the employer's facility and request assistance. Under these circumstances, that employer will not be guilty of a verification violation and, all else being equal, should not be charged. If charged, the employer can raise the "good faith" defense, as the employer did not knowingly hire an illegal alien. Only original documents are acceptable. The one exception to this hard-and-fast rule is a certified copy of a birth certificate.

An employee who fails to provide required documentation within three business days of being hired may be terminated from employment. If the employee claims the documents were lost or stolen, a receipt for a request for replacement documents will suffice for the time being. In that case, the employee has an additional 90 days in which to present those replacement documents to the employer, whose human resources department should make sure that there is a follow-up request should the employee fail to proffer the replacement documents within the time allotted by law. Remember, these policies must be applied uniformly to all employees in order to avoid a charge of immigrant-related discrimination.

5-3c Who Enforces U.S. Immigration Laws?

- **U.S. Citizenship and Immigration Services:** In the wake of the 9/11 terrorist attacks, in 2003, service and benefit functions of the U.S. Immigration and Naturalization Service (INS) transitioned into the Department of Homeland Security (DHS) as the U.S. Citizenship and Immigration Services (USCIS). The president nominated Eduardo Aguirre to lead the USCIS; he was confirmed by the Senate on June 19, 2003. The USCIS is responsible for the administration of immigration and naturalization adjudication functions and establishing immigration services policies and priorities. These functions include:
  - o   adjudication of immigrant visa petitions;
  - o   adjudication of naturalization petitions;
  - o   adjudication of asylum and refugee applications;
  - o   adjudications performed at the service centers; and
  - o   all other adjudications performed by the INS.[16]

- **U.S. Immigration and Customs Enforcement:** Also created in 2003 as a reaction to the INS's failure to detect and deal with the 9/11 terrorists, Immigration and Customs Enforcement (ICE) remains in 2015 the largest investigative branch of the DHS. The agency was created after September 11, 2001, by combining the law enforcement arms of the former INS and the former U.S. Customs Service, to more effectively enforce U.S. immigration and customs laws so as to protect the United States against terrorist attacks. ICE does this by targeting illegal immigrants: the people, money, and materials that support terrorism and other criminal activities. ICE is a key component of the DHS layered defense approach to protecting the nation.[17]

- **U.S. Department of Justice:** The DOJ mission statement provides this list of responsibilities: "to enforce the law and defend the interests of the United States according to the law; to ensure public safety against threats foreign and domestic; to provide federal leadership in preventing and controlling crime; to seek just punishment for those guilty of unlawful behavior; and to ensure fair and impartial administration of justice for all Americans."

---

[16] USCIS, http://www.uscis.gov.

[17] ICE, http://www.ice.gov.

The Office of Special Counsel for Immigration-Related Unfair Employment Practices (OSC), in the Civil Rights Division, is responsible for enforcing the antidiscrimination provisions of the INA, 8 U.S.C. § 1324b, which protect U.S. citizens and legal immigrants from employment discrimination based upon citizenship or immigration status and national origin, from unfair documentary practices relating to the employment eligibility verification process, and from retaliation.[18]

- **U.S. Social Security Administration:** The Social Security Administration (SSA) is headquartered in Baltimore, Maryland, and has 10 regional offices and 1,300 local offices nationwide. The agency pays retirement, disability, and survivors benefits to workers and their families and administers the Supplemental Security Income program. It also issues Social Security numbers.[19]

- **Federal Bureau of Investigation:** Since the tragic events of September 11, 2001, one week into its new director's term, the Bureau became responsible for spearheading what is perhaps the most extensive reorganization the FBI has experienced since its conception. By May 2002, the director articulated 10 top FBI priorities:

  o protecting the United States from terrorist attacks, from foreign intelligence operations, and from cyber-based attacks and high-technology crimes;
  o combating public corruption at all levels;
  o protecting civil rights;
  o combating international and national organized crime, major white-collar crime, and significant violent crime;
  o supporting our law enforcement and intelligence partners; and
  o upgrading FBI technology.

  "While we remain committed to our other important national security and law enforcement responsibilities, the prevention of terrorism takes precedence in our thinking and planning; in our hiring and staffing; in our training and technologies; and, most importantly, in our investigations," the director has said.[20]

- **U.S. Department of Labor:** The Department of Labor fosters and promotes the welfare of the job seekers, wage earners, and retirees of the United States by improving their working conditions, advancing their opportunities for profitable employment, protecting their retirement and health care benefits, helping employers find workers, strengthening free collective bargaining, and tracking changes in employment, prices, and other national economic measurements. In carrying out this mission, the department administers a variety of federal labor laws, including those that guarantee workers' rights to safe and healthful working conditions, a minimum hourly wage and overtime pay, freedom from employment discrimination, unemployment insurance, and other income support.

  The INA sets forth the conditions for the temporary and permanent employment of aliens in the United States and includes provisions that address employment

---

[18] DOJ, http://www.justice.gov.

[19] SSA, http://www.ssa.gov.

[20] FBI, http://www.fbi.gov.

eligibility and employment verification. These provisions apply to all employers. The DOL provides a wide variety of resources to aid employers with compliance.[21]

- **U.S. Department of State:** The Department of State's mission statement reads as follows: "Create a more secure, democratic, and prosperous world for the benefit of the American people and the international community."[22] The Bureau of Consular Affairs within the State Department manages the visa process.[23]

5-3d Anatomy of an ICE Raid

During the first week of March 2007, ICE agents raided a leather factory in New Bedford, Massachusetts. Supported by local law enforcement, ICE arrested 361 workers. Most were female sewing-machine operators from Guatemala or El Salvador. The Michael Bianco plant employed a total of 500 workers, who made backpacks and vests for the U.S. military under an $83 million federal contract.

The detainees were taken to Fort Devens, a former army base near Ayer, Massachusetts. The following day, some 60 women, sole caretakers of their children, were released. The remaining workers were dispersed to detention centers and jails for processing of their cases.

Also arrested were factory owner Francesco Insola and four plant managers. They were soon released on bail.

The arrests were hardly completed before the public relations war commenced. In a public statement, the U.S. attorney characterized the illegal immigrants as "exploited workers with low-paying jobs and horrible working conditions." At a gathering in a local church, relatives of those arrested confirmed the U.S. attorney's claims of exploitative conditions in the factory. One speaker was quoted in the media as saying, "They are only allowed two minutes to use the bathrooms and threatened with a fine of $20 if they return late to the job."

Ultimately, the war of words made its way into a federal courthouse. By November 2007, the detainees' main case had climbed all the way up into the lofty realm of the U.S. Court of Appeals for the Second Circuit, sitting in Boston.

CASE 5.3

AGUILAR V. U.S. IMMIGRATION AND CUSTOMS ENFORCEMENT
510 F.3d 1 (U.S. Ct. App. 1st Cir.)

On March 6, 2007, federal officers conducted a raid as part of "Operation United Front." The raid targeted Michael Bianco, Inc., a Department of Defense contractor suspected of employing large numbers of illegal aliens. Immigration and Customs Enforcement (ICE) agents, armed with search and arrest warrants, appeared unannounced at the factory, arrested five executives on immigration-related criminal charges, and took more than 300 rank-and-file employees into custody for civil immigration infractions. The ICE agents cast a wide net and paid little attention to the detainees' individual or family circumstances.

[21] Department of Labor, http://www.dol.gov.

[22] U.S. Department of State, http://www.state.gov.

[23] Information on all types of visas can be found at http://usvisas.state.gov.

The government's subsequent actions regarding the undocumented workers who were swept up in the net lie at the epicenter of this litigation. After releasing dozens of employees determined either to be minors or to be legally residing in the United States, ICE transported the remaining detainees to Fort Devens (a holding facility in Ayer, Massachusetts). Citing a shortage of available bed space in Massachusetts, ICE then began transferring substantial numbers of aliens to faraway detention and removal operations centers (DROs). For example, on March 7, 90 detainees were flown to a DRO in Harlingen, Texas, and the next day 116 more were flown to a DRO in El Paso, Texas.

ICE attempted to coordinate its maneuvers with the Massachusetts Department of Social Services (DSS) to ensure the proper care of family members. It took steps to address concerns about child welfare and released several detainees for humanitarian reasons. Still, the petitioners allege (and, for present purposes, we accept) that ICE gave social welfare agencies insufficient notice of the raid, that caseworkers were denied access to detainees until after the first group had been transferred, and that various ICE actions temporarily thwarted any effective investigation into the detainees' needs. As a result, a substantial number of the detainees' minor children were left for varying periods of time without adult supervision.

With respect to the detainees themselves, the petitioners averred that ICE inhibited their exercise of the right to counsel. According to the petitioners, a squad of volunteer lawyers who had offered to provide the detainees with guidance was turned away from Fort Devens on March 7. The next day, the lawyers were allowed to meet with those detainees (some thirty in number) who had expressly requested legal advice. The petitioners allege that, notwithstanding this largesse, some detainees were denied access to counsel after they arrived in Texas.

On the afternoon of March 8, the Guatemalan consul, acting as next friend of the detainees (many of whom were Guatemalan nationals), filed a petition for a writ of habeas corpus and a complaint for declaratory and injunctive relief in the United States District Court for the District of Massachusetts. The action sought the detainees' immediate release or, in the alternative, a temporary restraining order halting further transfers. The district court enjoined ICE from moving any of the remaining detainees out of Massachusetts pending further order of the court. . . .

The district court patiently sorted through them and, in a thoughtful rescript, eventually dismissed the action for want of subject matter jurisdiction. . . . We have scoured the case law for any authority suggesting that claims similar to those asserted here are actionable under the substantive component of the Due Process Clause, and we have found none. That chasm is important because, given the scarcity of 'guideposts for responsible decision-making in this uncharted area,' courts must be 'reluctant to expand the concept of substantive due process.'[24]

This unfortunate case is a paradigmatic example of an instance in which the prudential principle announced by the *Collins* Court should be heeded. Accordingly, we dismiss the petitioners' substantive due process claims for failure to satisfy the prerequisites of Federal Rule of Civil Procedure 12(b)(6). . . .

We are sensitive to the concerns raised by the petitioners and are conscious that undocumented workers, like all persons who are on American soil, have certain inalienable rights. But in the first instance, it is Congress—not the judiciary—that has the responsibility of prescribing a framework for the vindication of those rights. When Congress speaks clearly and formulates a regime that satisfies constitutional imperatives, the courts must follow Congress's lead. In that sense, it does not matter whether a court approves or disapproves of an agency's *modus operandi*.

We add only two comments. First, we applaud the able district judge for the skill and sensitivity with which he handled this highly charged case. Second, we express our hope that ICE, though it has prevailed, nonetheless will treat this chiaroscuro series of events as a learning experience in order to devise better, less ham-handed ways of carrying out its important responsibilities.

Case Questions

1.   The due process clauses of the Fifth and Fourteenth Amendments decree that "no person" may be deprived of life, liberty, or property without due process of law. If the detainees in this case, who clearly are persons, if not U.S. citizens, cannot secure their due process rights in a federal court, where do you think they will be secured?

---

[24] *Washington v. Glucksberg*, 521 U.S. 702, 720, 117 S.Ct. 2258, 138 L.Ed.2d 772 (1997) (quoting *Collins v. Harker Heights*, 503 U.S. 115, 125, 112 S.Ct. 1061, 117 L.Ed.2d 261 (1992)).

2. Assuming that, following dismissal of their federal court case, the detainees are afforded an opportunity to be heard in some other forum, such as in front of an immigration judge,[25] do you think it would be more fair to place the burden of proving their right to stay in the U.S., or lack of such a right, upon the detainees or the ICE agency?

3. In what ways, if any, do you think that the ICE agency (in the words of the court) was "ham-handed"?

4. If the detainees ultimately are found to be illegal aliens, what penalty should be imposed upon them? What if some of them are found to be repeat offenders? What if they can prove they have children who were born in the United States?

5. Does this case suggest to you that the U.S. system for dealing with illegal-alien workers requires reforming? If so, what policy recommendations would you make to President Obama, if asked?

Aftermath

On November 4, 2007, the *Boston Globe* reported, "The New Bedford leather goods company that helped push deportation methods into the national spotlight when it was raided by federal immigration agents in March has been sold to a Missouri-based manufacturer of military and law enforcement gear. Michael Bianco Inc., whose top officers were indicted in August for allegedly taking overt steps to shield illegal workers from authorities and help them stay in this country, was sold to Eagle Industries Inc., a longtime competitor, according to David Costello, the buyer's Boston-based spokesman." The *Globe* added, "Following the raid, the federal Occupational Safety and Health Administration fined Bianco $45,000 after identifying 15 violations, including chemical, mechanical, and electrical hazards."[26]

The U.S. attorney's press release, announcing the indictments of the managers, stated, "If convicted, INSOLIA, COSTA and MELO each face a maximum sentence of 10 years in prison, a $250,000 fine, a $100 special assessment, and at least two years of supervised release on the charge of conspiring to harbor illegal aliens; and 6 months in prison, a $100 special assessment, and $10,000 fine for each illegal alien hired by MBI on the conspiracy to hire illegal aliens charge."

5-3e   State and Local Involvement with Illegal Immigrants

As a general proposition, immigration law and policy are deemed to be the exclusive provinces of the federal government. State and local governments are usually deemed to be preempted from intruding into this area of the law. However, in recent years, many state and local governments have become frustrated with federal inaction or ineffectiveness in the face of rapidly rising numbers of illegal-immigrant workers, who make claims upon public services and, allegedly, increase crime rates in communities where they settle. Most of these state statutes and municipal ordinances have fallen to constitutional challenges.

---

[25] See Office of the Chief Immigration Judge, DOJ, http://www.usdoj.gov/eoir/ocijinfo.htm.

[26] Kathy McCabe, "New Bedford factory is sold; was site of immigration raid," *Boston Globe*, November 4, 2007, available at http://boston.com/news/local/articles/2007/11/04/new_bedford_factory_is_sold_was_site_of_immigration_raid.

5-3f   The Legal Arizona Workers Act

One state statute, which stands out from the crowd by virtue of having so far survived all legal challenges, is the Legal Arizona Workers Act.[27] In May of 2011, the Supreme Court of the United States made a decision upholding the law.

 CASE 5.4

CHAMBER OF COMMERCE OF U.S. V. WHITING
131 S.Ct. 1968 (U.S. 2011)

Facts: The Chamber of Commerce and various business and civil rights organizations brought action challenging the validity of Arizona's unauthorized alien employment law, which allowed the suspension and revocation of business licenses for employing unauthorized aliens and required every employer to verify the employment eligibility of hired employees through a specific Internet-based system. The United States District Court for the District of Arizona upheld the statute, and the plaintiffs appealed. The United States Court of Appeals for the Ninth Circuit affirmed the decision. Certiorari was granted.

Issue: Is the Legal Arizona Workers Act preempted by federal immigration law?

Decision: The Supreme Court affirmed the decision of the lower court and held that:

(1) the provision of Arizona law allowing suspension and revocation of business licenses fell within the Immigration Reform and Control Act's (IRCA) savings clause;

(2) the provision of Arizona law allowing suspension and revocation of business licenses was not impliedly preempted for conflicting with federal law; and

(3) the Arizona law's requirement that every employer verify the employment eligibility of hired employees through a specific Internet-based system did not conflict with federal law.

In the wake of the Ninth's Circuit's 2007 blessing on the act, the Arizona Attorney General moved forward with its implementation.[28] According to the official legislative notice to employers, "A judicial determination of a violation of this new state law will subject the employer to probation, and may subject the employer to a suspension or revocation of all licenses as defined in section 23–211, Arizona Revised Statutes, depending on the following conditions:

- For a first violation of an employer *knowingly* hiring an unauthorized alien, the court shall order mandatory three years' probation and may suspend all licenses held by the employer for a maximum of 10 days. The employer must file a signed sworn affidavit with the county attorney within three business days, stating that the employer has fired all unauthorized aliens and that the employer will not intentionally or knowingly employ any unauthorized alien.

- For a first violation of an employer *intentionally* hiring an unauthorized alien, the court shall order a mandatory five years' probation and order the appropriate licensing

---

[27] Ariz. Rev. Stats. §§ 23–211 to 23–216.

[28] See Legal Arizona Workers Act, Arizona Attorney General, http://www.azag.gov/LegalAZWorkersAct/FAQ .html.

agencies to suspend all licenses held by the employer for a minimum often days. The employer must file a signed sworn affidavit, stating that the employer has fired all unauthorized aliens and that the employer will not intentionally or knowingly employ any unauthorized alien with the county attorney. A license that is suspended will remain suspended until the employer files a signed sworn affidavit.

- For a second violation of this new state law committed during a period of probation, the court will order the appropriate licensing agencies to permanently revoke all licenses that are held by the employer."[29]

- Licenses that can be lost under the law include, "any agency permit, certificate, approval, registration, charter or similar form of authorization that is required by law and that is issued by any agency for the purposes of operating a business in this state."[30]

A year later, the Supreme Court was less kind to another Arizona statute, this one aimed at criminalizing the activities of illegal aliens in a variety of ways.

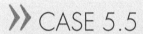

» CASE 5.5

ARIZONA V. UNITED STATES
132 S.Ct. 2492 (U.S. 2012)

Facts: An Arizona statute known as S.B. 1070 was enacted in 2010 to address pressing issues related to the large number of unlawful aliens in the State. The United States sought to enjoin the law as preempted. The District Court issued a preliminary injunction preventing four of its provisions from taking effect. Section 3 makes failure to comply with federal alien-registration requirements a state misdemeanor; § 5(C) makes it a misdemeanor for an unauthorized alien to seek or engage in work in the State; § 6 authorizes state and local officers to arrest without a warrant a person "the officer has probable cause to believe ... has committed any public offense that makes the person removable from the United States"; and § 2(B) requires officers conducting a stop, detention, or arrest to make efforts, in some circumstances, to verify the person's immigration status with the Federal Government. The Ninth Circuit affirmed, agreeing that

the United States had established a likelihood of success on its preemption claims.

Decision: The Supreme Court held that

(1) the provision making failure to comply with federal alien-registration requirements a state misdemeanor was preempted;

(2) the provision making it a misdemeanor for unauthorized alien to seek or engage in work in Arizona was preempted;

(3) the provision authorizing arrests for a removable offense was preempted; but

(4) the preliminary injunction against the provision requiring officer conducting stop, detention, or arrest to verify person's immigration status with the federal government if the officer had suspicion that the person was unlawfully in the United States was improper.

«

5-3g   President Obama's Executive Order

In 2014, immigrant-advocacy groups clamored for reform at the national level, while Congress dithered. Hispanics in particular called upon President Barack Obama to institute

---

[29] Notice available at http://www.azleg.gov/Employer_Notice.asp.

[30] Ariz. Rev. Stats. §§ 23-211 (9)(a).

reform measures. He, too, hesitated, as the November national elections loomed and many Democratic senators and representatives up for reelection feared a backlash by their non-Hispanic constituencies. Despite the president's restraint, his party lost the mid-term elections and control of the Senate. Finally, with both houses of Congress in Republican hands, a frustrated President Obama acted unilaterally, issuing an executive order on November 20, 2014. His order mandated a number of initiatives by the federal bureaucracy, the major ones being:

- Expanding the population eligible for the Deferred Action for Childhood Arrivals (DACA) program to people of any current age who entered the United States before the age of 16 and lived in the United States continuously since January 1, 2010, and extending the period of DACA and work authorization from two years to three years;

- Allowing parents of U.S. citizens and lawful permanent residents to request deferred action and employment authorization for three years, in a new Deferred Action for Parents of Americans and Lawful Permanent Residents program, provided they have lived in the United States continuously since January 1, 2010, and pass required background checks;

- Expanding the use of provisional waivers of unlawful presence to include the spouses and sons and daughters of lawful permanent residents and the sons and daughters of U.S. citizens;

- Modernizing, improving, and clarifying immigrant and nonimmigrant visa programs to grow the economy and create jobs; and

- Promoting citizenship education and public awareness for lawful permanent residents and providing an option for naturalization applicants to use credit cards to pay the application fee.[31]

On December 3, 2014, 17 states joined together in a suit aimed at blocking the president's executive order.[32]

Concept *Summary* 5.2

IMMIGRATION LAW AND ENFORCEMENT

- Major federal statutes:
  - Immigration and Nationality Act of 1952 is the foundational statute upon which U.S. immigration policy, following the Second World War, was built.
  - Immigration Reform and Control Act of 1986 is the single most sweeping revision of the 1952 statute. Significantly, it was intended to stem the flow of illegal immigrants into the U.S. labor market.

---

[31] Executive Actions on Immigration, USCIS, http://www.uscis.gov/immigrationaction.

[32] *Texas v. Johnson*, United States District Court, Southern District of Texas (complaint available at https://www .texasattorneygeneral.gov/files/epress/files/20141203ImmigrationExecutiveOrderLawsuit.pdf).

- Major federal agencies:
  - Department of Homeland Security
    - U.S. Immigration and Customs Enforcement (ICE): the immigration police
    - U.S. Citizenship and Immigration Service (USCIS): processes applications for immigrant and nonimmigrant presence in the United States.
  - Department of Justice
    - Federal Bureau of Investigation (FBI): Assists Home Security with domestic law enforcement, for instance, terrorists
    - Drug Enforcement Administration: Assists where drug smuggling is a factor
  - Department of Labor: Processes labor determinations related to temporary worker visas
  - Department of State: Issues visas, supervises exchange-visitor programs

CHAPTER REVIEW

» Key Terms

International Labor Organization (ILO) 89	**global corporate responsibility** 90	**global unions** 97
convention 90	**Alien Tort Claims Act** 92	**Immigration Reform and Control Act (IRCA) of 1986** 100

» Summary

- The principle source of international labor and employment law is the International Labor Organization (ILO), which develops conventions covering significant topics in labor and employment law and policy. Sovereign nations are free to adopt or decline to adopt these conventions. The United States has adopted some, but far from all, the ILO's conventions. In some areas, the U.S. decision not to sign onto particular conventions is grounded in the belief that U.S. labor law and policy are superior to the international options.

- Corporate social responsibility is more of an aspiration or ideal than it is an actual example of international employment law. However, some nations have incorporated notions of corporate social responsibility into their laws.

- The Alien Tort Claims Act is one of the oldest U.S. statutes on the books and for many years was little used. However, in the 21st century workers and labor unions in foreign countries have rediscovered the statute and are attempting to use it—with mixed results—against U.S.-based multinational companies.

- International labor unions are attempting to organize the employees of multinational corporations on a global scale.

- U.S. immigration law's most recent major overhaul took place in 1986. A major goal of Congress at that time was to staunch the flow of illegal immigrants into the country. However, limited resources and lack of will resulted in only limited, spotty enforcement of the new statutory scheme. The result has been an enormous influx of illegal aliens into the U.S. during the past two decades.

- After September 11, 2001, the Department of Homeland Security was created and the Immigration and Naturalization Service (INS) was split into an enforcement branch, Immigration and Customs Enforcement (ICE), and a services-oriented branch, the U.S. Citizenship and Immigration Service (USCIS). ICE has been more active than the predecessor INS in enforcing the laws, including increased raids of workplaces known to employ numerous undocumented immigrants.

- Nevertheless, many states and municipalities, frustrated by the failure of the federal government to staunch the flow and employment of illegal immigrants, have enacted their own statutes and ordinances to deal with the problem on the local level. These laws have been subjected to court challenges. Recently some of them have survived these challenges and remain in effect.

» Problems

» Questions

1. Can an argument be made that even underpaid and exploited workers in so-called sweatshops in under-developed nations are better off than if no such sweatshops existed?

2. If your answer to question 1 is "yes," does this justify the exploitation of these workers?

3. If a foreign nation chooses not to enact or enforce humane wage and hour, health and safety, and other human resources laws for the benefit of its citizens, why should an American company, doing business in that nation, be expected to do any better?

4. If menial and dirty jobs which American citizens have no interest in performing are filled primarily by illegal aliens, isn't the best policy for all concerned to ignore the presence of these workers in the U.S.?

5. Granting that it is probably unrealistic to round up and deport the estimated 12 million illegal immigrants in the U.S., what social services should these illegal residents in the U.S. be permitted to have: Welfare and/or unemployment compensation when they are out of work? Emergency room services? Public school for their children? The right to join a labor union? The right to file a health and safety complaint with an appropriate federal or state agency? The right to sue for unpaid wages or job-related injury?

» Case Problems

6. The plaintiff, a private citizen, sought to obtain for Native Americans "just compensation for the minerals mined in the Black Hills of South Dakota." He averred that the Black Hills belonged to Native Americans and were taken from them in violation of the Fifth Amendment of the U.S. Constitution. He also asserted in one of several consolidated complaints that American companies that operate sweatshops "should not be allowed to enter into international trade with the United States," and asked that the court enjoin such trade. Additionally, he contended that the "globalization of the auto industry violate[s] the Sherman Anti-Trust Act." In yet another complaint, he contended that the U.S. Food and Drug Administration is "in violation of the Treaty of Unification of

Pharmacopeial Formulas for Patent Drugs." Finally, he pled that the "U.S.A.," presumably the federal government, is "trading in fur seals in violation of [a] treaty."

How should the federal district judge assigned to these consolidated cases resolve them? Why? [See *Demos v. U.S.*, 2007 WL1492413 (CIT), 29 ITRD 1926 (U.S. Court of International Trade 2007).]

7. The plaintiffs, current and former residents of the Republic of the Sudan, filed a class action suit against Talisman Energy, Inc. and Sudan, alleging violations of international law stemming from oil exploration activities conducted in that country. Specifically, the plaintiffs alleged that the defendants collaborated to commit gross human rights violations, including extrajudicial killing, forcible displacement, war crimes, confiscation and destruction of property, kidnapping, rape, and enslavement for forced labor. Collectively, the plaintiffs claimed that these activities amounted to genocide. Talisman moved to dismiss this action on the basis of lack of subject matter jurisdiction, lack of personal jurisdiction, lack of plaintiffs' standing, *forum non conveniens*, international comity, act of state doctrine, political question doctrine, failure to join necessary and indispensable parties, and because equity does not require a useless act.

Based upon what you have read in this chapter, is there a basis in U.S. law for the plaintiffs to proceed with their case? [See *Presbyterian Church of Sudan v. Talisman Energy, Inc.*, 244 F. Supp. 2d 289 (S.D.N.Y. 2003).]

8. The plaintiffs were seven Guatemalan citizens currently residing in the United States. Del Monte is a Delaware company; its principal place of business is in Coral Gables, Florida. In Guatemala, the plaintiffs were officers in SITRABI, a national trade union of plantation workers. At the time in question, they represented workers on a Bandegua banana plantation that was a wholly owned subsidiary of Del Monte. SITRABI and Bandegua were negotiating a new collective bargaining agreement for workers at the plantation. While those negotiations were ongoing, Bandegua terminated 918

workers. SITRABI responded by filing a complaint in the Labor Court of Guatemala. The plaintiffs allege that on October 13, 1999, Bandegua hired a private, armed security force. (Private security forces are permitted and regulated in Guatemala.) According to the plaintiffs, Del Monte agents met with the security force "to plan violent action against the Plaintiffs and other SITRABI leaders." According to the plaintiffs, at 5:45 p.m., the security force, which is described as "a gang of over 200 heavily armed men," arrived at SITRABI's headquarters. There, the security force held two plaintiffs hostage, threatened to kill them, and shoved them with guns. Throughout the evening, other SITRABI leaders were lured, abducted, or otherwise forced to the headquarters and similarly detained. The plaintiffs, at gunpoint, announced the labor dispute was over and that they were resigning.

Do the plaintiffs have a cause of action against Del Monte in federal court? [See *Aldana v. Del Monte Fresh Produce, NA, Inc.*, 416 F.3d 1242 11th Cir. 2005).]

9. San Juan Pueblo is a federally recognized Indian tribe, which is to say an independent Indian nation, located in New Mexico. Most of its 5,200 members live on tribal lands that are held in trust by the United States for the Pueblo. The Pueblo is governed by a tribal council, which is vested with legislative authority over tribal lands. Through federally approved leases, the Pueblo leases portions of its tribal land to nontribal businesses as a source of generating tribal income and as a means of employment for tribal members. On November 6, 1996, the San Juan Pueblo Tribal Council enacted Tribal Ordinance No. 96-63. The ordinance in substance is a so-called "right-to-work" measure (see Chapter 14). The Pueblo asserts that the ordinance is a valid exercise of its inherent sovereign authority. As amended, the ordinance prohibits the making of agreements containing union-security clauses covering any employees, whether tribal members or not. Section 6(a) of the ordinance reads:

> No person shall be required, as a condition of employment or continuation of employment on Pueblo lands, to: (i) resign or refrain from voluntary

membership in, voluntary affiliation with, or voluntary financial support of a labor organization; (ii) become or remain a member of a labor organization; (iii) pay dues, fees, assessments or other charges of any kind or amount to a labor organization; (iv) pay to any charity or other third party, in lieu of such payments any amount equivalent to or a pro-rata portion of dues, fees, assessments or other charges regularly required of members of a labor organization; or (v) be recommended, approved, referred or cleared through a labor organization.

Should the tribal law be considered preempted by the National Labor Relations Act, or should the tribal council be recognized as a sovereign government body outside the reach of the NLRA? What policy reasons can you think of that favor one or the other of these outcomes? [See *NLRB v. Pueblo of San Juan*, 276 F.3d 1186 (10th Cir. 2002).]

10. During August to October 2002, Cianbro Corporation applied to the United States Department of Labor and the Maine Department of Labor for H-2B temporary labor certifications for as many as 120 foreign workers to be employed as structural and pipe welders on two giant oil rigs known as the Amethyst 4 and 5 that were under construction in the harbor of Portland, Maine. To make their determinations, the DOL and the Maine DOL were required to calculate prevailing wages and working conditions for the jobs for which Cianbro sought temporary labor certifications pursuant to a DOL regulation, 20 C.F.R. § 656.40. Federal regulations (8 C.F.R. § 214.2(h)(6)(iii)(A)) provided that before filing a petition with the INS (now USCIS) director in whose jurisdiction a petitioning employer intends to employ an H-2B nonagricultural temporary worker, the employer must apply for a temporary labor certification with the Secretary of Labor. The Secretary of Labor's temporary labor certification provided advice to the INS director on "whether or not United States workers capable of performing the temporary services or labor are available and whether the alien's employment will adversely affect the wages and working conditions of similarly employed United States workers." Many qualified and available U.S. workers applied for positions with Cianbro

as structural and pipe welders during the period when the DOL was supposed to be reevaluating the matter after receipt of the relevant union's letter, opposing the company's application; however, none was offered employment by Cianbro. Meanwhile the federal and state agencies proposed to issue more than 50 H-2B visas. On March 21, 2003 the relevant unions filed an application for a temporary restraining order.

Should the court grant this TRO, blocking the issuance of the H-2B visas, pending resolution of the unions' objections? What policy considerations should the judge take into account on both sides of the controversy when making this decision? [See *Maine State Building and Construction Council v. Chao*, 265 F. Supp.2d 105 (D. Maine 2003).]

11. JAL was a Japanese commercial air carrier based in Tokyo. HACS, a Hawaii corporation with its principal place of business in Honolulu, provided contract flight crews to JAL. Plaintiffs Ventress and Crawford were employed by HACS to perform services for JAL flights. The plaintiffs' employment agreements with HACS contained mandatory arbitration provisions. In December 2002, Ventress and Crawford jointly filed a complaint against JAL and HACS in the U.S. District Court for the Central District of California, alleging that JAL required a seriously ill pilot to fly in June 2001, in violation of American and Japanese aviation laws as well as JAL's own operations manual. Crawford expressed his concern to a JAL official in Honolulu in July 2001. Afterward, he experienced harassment from his superiors, including repeated performance checks, questions, and homework assignments. In December 2001, HACS informed Crawford that his assignment to JAL was canceled because of unsatisfactory performance. That same month, Ventress submitted reports on the June incidents to JAL, HACS, and aviation regulators. Ventress claimed repeated harassment from JAL thereafter, including demands to undergo psychiatric evaluations. Ventress was not allowed to fly after September 2001.

The complaint sought recovery for violation of California's whistleblower statute, wrongful termination in violation of the public policy protecting whistleblowers, and emotional distress. The California whistleblower law states in pertinent part, "An employer may not retaliate against an employee for disclosing information to a government or law enforcement agency, where the employee has reasonable cause to believe that the information discloses a violation of state or federal statute, or a violation or noncompliance with a state or federal regulation." Cal. Labor Code § 1102.5(b). The defendant claimed that the plaintiffs' claims were preempted by the Friendship, Commerce, and Navigation Treaty (U.S.–Japan, April 2, 1953). The treaty was primarily designed to protect the right of employers on both sides of the Pacific to "utilize the services of their own nationals in managerial, technical, and confidential capacities to be critical." The court here was faced with three choices:

(1) dismiss the case as preempted by the treaty;

(2) stay the proceedings and require the plaintiffs to pursue arbitration under the express terms of their employment contracts; or

(3) permit the action to proceed under the California Whistleblower Law.

What policy considerations can you come up with in favor of or against each of these options? [See *Ventress v. Japan Airlines*, 486 F.3d 1111 (9th Cir. 2007).]

12. The governor of Missouri issued a press release, which included the following announcements:

> KINGSTON—Gov. Matt Blunt today highlighted his tough new directives in the fight against illegal immigration in Missouri in a visit to the Caldwell County Sheriff's Office, where on an average day the facility holds approximately 55 immigration detainees. "With Washington failing to enact policies to enforce our federal immigration laws it is necessary for our state to take action," Gov. Blunt said. "We support and welcome lawful immigrants into Missouri but will also continue to take a tough stand against illegal immigration in our state."

Governor Blunt has offered his support to local prosecutors in their efforts in the fight against illegal immigration and reminds prosecutors that state law makes the receipt of tax credits by employers of il-

legal aliens who are ineligible for state tax credits, tax abatements, or loans a class A misdemeanor, punishable by up to a year in prison. In a letter to prosecutors, the governor notes that since the attorney general has yet to bring a case to enforce this law, it is left to them to enforce the law in their counties.

Governor Blunt also called on his administration to work with ICE for authority under Section 287g of the Immigration and Nationality Act that would deputize state law enforcement officers to enforce federal laws and protect Missourians against illegal immigration. The agreement will allow select troopers, capitol police, and water patrol officers to help enforce immigration laws. The governor has directed his staff to examine the costs associated with the 287g designation and plans to seek funding in next year's budget to help state and local law enforcement agencies pursue the cooperative agreement and help enhance public safety.

The governor also directed state law enforcement agencies to verify the immigration status of every criminal presented for incarceration.

In addition, he took significant steps to shield taxpayers' money from supporting building projects that employ illegal workers including:

• Conducting random on-site inspections of all projects accompanied by the tax credit recipient to monitor and retrieve documentation regarding the legal status of all workers on the job. The inspections will include direct employees of the tax credit recipient, contracted or subcontracted agents, and both general contractors and their subcontractors.

• Performing a Compliance by Written Demand action for all tax credit recipients that requires all workers' proof of legal status, including contractors and subcontractors, to be submitted within 30 days of the date of the receipt of the written request.

Based upon what you have learned in this chapter, evaluate the legality of the governor's various proposals in light of (1) federal preemption and (2) due process of law considerations.

13. David Rodriguez, a citizen of Mexico, entered the United States without inspection at El Paso, Texas,

on or about July 22, 1996. During his time in the United States, he lived in Minnesota and fraudulently obtained a Texas birth certificate, a Minnesota driver's license and a social security card in the name of Oscar Martinez, and a social security card and legal resident card in the name of David Rodriguez Silva. He sought to obtain employment with a private employer by checking a box on a Form I-9 indicating that he was a "citizen or national of the United States" and by submitting the fraudulent Martinez driver's license and social security card as support for his claim. On April 19, 2001, Rodriguez married Veronica Vazquez, a U.S. citizen. On April 24, 2001, he submitted an immediate relative immigrant visa petition, which the Immigration and Naturalization Service (now the USCIS) approved. The INS informed Rodriguez that he would be considered for lawful permanent residence status subject to his application for adjustment of status. On February 26, 2002, Rodriguez and his wife appeared for an interview with a district adjudications officer as part of the process to adjust his status. Rodriguez brought the fraudulent documents. After the interview, the adjudications officer prepared a sworn statement that included the questions and answers from the interview. Rodriguez reviewed and signed the statement. In the interview and in his resulting sworn statement, Rodriguez admitted that he knew that with the use of the fraudulent documents he had made a claim to a government agency that he was a citizen of the United States. The INS denied Rodriguez's application for adjustment of status because he had made a false claim that he was a U.S. citizen. On appeal of the agency's decision, the court can either affirm the decision—in which case Rodriguez will be deported back to Mexico—or overlook his earlier employment history and order his change of status based upon his marriage to an American citizen.

What are the ethical considerations favoring each of these outcomes? What would you do, if you were the judge and had discretion to rule either way? [See *Rodriguez v. Mukasey*, 519 F.3d 773 (8th Cir. 2008).]

14. Petitioner Agri Processor Co. was a wholesaler of kosher meat products based in Brooklyn, New York. In September 2005, the company's employees voted to join the United Food and Commercial Workers union. When the company refused to bargain, the union filed an unfair labor practice charge with the National Labor Relations Board. The company defended its refusal, arguing that most of those who voted were undocumented aliens. The company argues that undocumented aliens are prohibited from unionizing because they do not qualify as "employees" protected by the National Labor Relations Act. The NLRA states, "The term 'employee' shall include any employee . . ., but shall not include any individual employed as an agricultural laborer, or in the domestic service of any family or person at his home, or any individual employed by his parent or spouse, or any individual having the status of an independent contractor, or any individual employed as a supervisor, or any individual employed by an employer subject to the Railway Labor Act . . ., or by any other person who is not an employer as herein defined."

How should the court rule in this case? Does the statutory definition compel an outcome, or is there sufficient ambiguity for the court to go either way? If so, what are the public policy considerations that the court ought to weigh in reaching a determination of the case? [See *Agri Processor, Inc. v. NLRB*, 514 F.3d 1 (D.C. Cir. 2008).]

15. Yu owned and operated the Great Texas Employment Agency along with his girlfriend, Ya Cao. Great Texas was in the business of supplying Chinese restaurants in several states with immigrant workers. Yu advertised Great Texas to Chinese restaurant owners through direct mailings and in the Midwest edition of a Chinese periodical, agreeing to supply "Hispanic and Middle Southern American workers" for "odd jobs" or positions such as "dishwashers" or "busboys." Upon receiving an order from a restaurant owner, Great Texas would recruit immigrant workers from Texas and arrange for their transportation to the restaurants.

Authorities began investigating Yu after a border patrol agent encountered two men riding bicycles on Interstate 29 in North Dakota in June 2004. The two men admitted that they were Mexican citizens who were in the country illegally and who had been working at a Chinese restaurant in Grand Forks, North Dakota. One of the men had an employment contract, written in both Chinese and Spanish, which provided that the employee would receive a salary of $1,000 per month. The contract also listed a 312 area code telephone number for an employment agency. Agents asked to interview Yu, and he consented. After receiving his *Miranda* warnings, Yu explained that he lived at the residence with Ya Cao (whom he referred to as Lily) and that Ya Cao and a Spanish-speaking recruiter would go to street corners to find workers to fill requests. He said that he paid $20 for each worker recruited. Yu admitted that some of the workers were illegal but said that he assumed most were legal and that the restaurants would check on the workers' immigration status. After he was indicted, he contested the charges and sought to have his statement excluded on the ground that he spoke poor English and did not understand what rights he was giving up.

    If you were the trial judge, how would you rule on Yu's motion to suppress the confession? [See *U.S. v. Shan Wei Yu*, 484 F.3d 979 (8th Cir. 2007).]

» Hypothetical Scenarios

16. One well-known approach to corporate responsibility is the so-called "triple bottom line." Traditionally, a corporation's bottom line referred to the company's net profits. "In practical terms, triple-bottom-line accounting means expanding this traditional reporting framework to take into account ecological and social performance in addition to financial performance. The phrase was coined by John Elkington in 1994. It was later expanded and articulated in his 1998 book *Cannibals with Forks: The Triple Bottom Line of 21st Century Business.* Sustainability, itself, was first defined by the Brundtland Commission of the United Nations in 1987. The concept of TBL demands that a company's responsibility be to stakeholders rather than shareholders. In this case, "stakeholders" refers to anyone who is influenced, either directly or indirectly, by the actions of the firm. According to the stakeholder theory, the business entity should be used as a vehicle for coordinating stakeholder interests instead of maximizing shareholder (owner) profit" (http://en.wikipedia .org/wiki/Triple_bottom_line). Assume that an American corporation decides to adopt the triple-bottom-line approach with regard to its environmental and labor relations policies worldwide. What are the pros and cons of this decision for the firm's traditional bottom line? What response should shareholders make to this decision? Does your answer to the second question depend upon whether the particular shareholder happens to be

(1) an individual investor,

(2) a university endowment fund, or

(3) an employee pension fund?

17. Villagers from Myanmar's Tenasserim region, the rural area through which an American oil company built a new pipeline, alleged that the Myanmar military forced them, under threat of violence, to work on and serve as porters for the project. For instance, John Doe IX testified that he was forced to build a helipad near the pipeline site in 1994 that was then used by company officials who visited the pipeline during its planning stages. John Doe VII and John Roe X described that the helipads constructed at Eindayaza and Po Pah Pta, both of which were near the pipeline site, were used to ferry executives and materials to the construction site, and were constructed using the forced labor of local villagers, including Plaintiffs John Roes VIII and IX, as well as John Does I, VIII, and IX, who testified that they were forced to work on building roads leading to the pipeline construction area. Finally, John Does V and IX testified that they were required to serve as "pipeline porters"—workers who performed menial tasks such as such as hauling materials and cleaning the army camps for the soldiers guarding the pipeline construction. Plaintiffs also alleged, in furtherance of the forced labor program just described, that the Myanmar military subjected them to acts of murder, rape, and torture. For instance, Jane Doe I testified that after her husband, John Doe I, attempted to escape the forced labor program, he was shot at by soldiers, and, in retaliation for his attempted escape, that she and her baby were thrown into

a fire, resulting in injuries to her and the death of the child. Other witnesses described the summary execution of villagers who refused to participate in the forced labor program or who grew too weak to work effectively. Several plaintiffs testified that rapes occurred as part of the forced labor program. For instance, both Jane Does II and III testified that while conscripted to work on pipeline-related construction projects, they were raped at knife-point by Myanmar soldiers who were members of a battalion that was supervising the work. Plaintiffs finally allege that the American firm's conduct gives rise to liability for these abuses. What must these plaintiffs prove in order to pursue an Alien Tort Claims Act case against the U.S. oil company? What must the U.S. try to show in order to successfully defend itself? Should the law impose an obligation on the oil company to "police" how the host country's military fulfills a national agreement to assist the oil company in building the pipeline?

18. A European labor union succeeded in organizing the workers at a facility in Germany that was owned and operated by a U.S.-headquartered and incorporated multinational corporation. After successfully negotiating a first contract for the German workers, the union presented the corporation's board of directors with a demand that they recognize the union as the collective bargaining representative for all workers holding similar rank-and-file jobs worldwide. Without trying to deal with the National Labor Relations Act, which you'll learn about further on in this book, what are the equitable considerations that, let's say, a world court should consider in

deciding whether or not the multinational corporation ought to be required to recognize the union globally? Are there any possible advantages to the corporation in voluntarily agreeing to do so?

19. In a U.S. ICE raid on a Midwestern meat packing plant, federal agents round up dozens of illegal aliens employed at the plant. Assuming that an immigration judge has the authority to do, how much weight should he or she give to the following factors in deciding whether to repatriate these illegal workers to their countries of origin:

(1) length of time in the U.S.;

(2) children born in the U.S.;

(3) clean criminal and credit records;

(4) skill level and value to the employer; and

(5) membership in a U.S, labor union?

20. In assessing penalties against the employer in question 19 above, and again assuming that the court has broad discretion whether to impose severe or mild penalties, what weight should a judge give each of the following factors in determining punishment:

(1) availability or lack of American workers to fill the jobs held by the alien workers;

(2) level of compensation and benefits provided to the illegal workers;

(3) the health and safety conditions to which the illegal workers were subjected; and

(4) the handling of payroll deductions or lack of such payroll "formalities"?

PART 2

EQUAL EMPLOYMENT OPPORTUNITY

CHAPTER **6**

Title VII of the Civil Rights Act and Race Discrimination

Ideally, employers should hire those employees best qualified for the particular jobs being filled; an employee should be selected because of his or her ability to perform the job. Determining the qualifications required for the job, however, may be difficult. In fact, required qualifications that have no relationship to job performance may disqualify prospective employees who are capable of performing satisfactorily. In addition, some employers may be influenced in their selection of employees by their biases—conscious or unconscious—regarding certain groups of people. All of these factors are part of the problem of discrimination in employment.

Discrimination in employment, both intentional and unintentional, has been a major concern of many people who believe that our society has not lived up to its ideal of equality of opportunity for all people. The glaring inequities in our society sparked violent protests during the civil rights movement of the 1960s. African Americans, Hispanic Americans, and Native Americans constituted a disproportionate share of those living in poverty. Women of all races and colors found their access to challenging and well-paying jobs limited; they were frequently channeled into lower paying occupations traditionally viewed as "women's work."

6-1 Title VII of the Civil Rights Act of 1964

To help remedy these discrimination problems, Congress passed the Civil Rights Act of 1964, which was signed into law by President Lyndon Johnson on July 2, 1964. The Civil Rights Act was aimed at discrimination in a number of areas of our society: housing, public accommodation, education, and employment. Title VII of the Civil Rights Act deals with discrimination in employment. It became the foundation of modern federal equal employment opportunity (EEO) law.

Title VII has been amended several times since its passage; the amendments made in 1968, 1972, and 1991 were substantial. The 1991 amendments, made by that year's Civil Rights Act, were intended to reverse several U.S. Supreme Court decisions that were perceived as making it more difficult for plaintiffs to bring suit under Title VII. Congress again amended Title VII in 2009 to reverse another Supreme Court decision dealing with the time limit for bringing pay-discrimination claims.

This part of our textbook focuses on the statutory provisions requiring equal opportunity in employment. This chapter deals with the provisions of Title VII, as they apply to discrimination based on race. Chapter 7 will discuss employment discrimination based on gender, including Title VII and other gender-related EEO legislation. Chapter 8 will discuss discrimination based on religion and national origin, the enforcement of Title VII, and the remedies available under it. Chapter 9 will discuss the Age Discrimination in Employment Act and EEO laws dealing with discrimination based on disability. Finally, Chapter 10 will focus on miscellaneous federal and state EEO legislation.

6-1a Coverage of Title VII

Title VII of the Civil Rights Act of 1964
legislation that outlawed discrimination in terms and conditions of employment based on race, color, sex, religion, or national origin

Title VII of the Civil Rights Act of 1964 took effect on July 2, 1965. It prohibits the refusal or failure to hire any individual, the discharge of any individual, or the discrimination against any individual with respect to compensation, terms, conditions, or privileges of employment, because of that individual's race, color, religion, sex, or national origin.

Title VII, as amended, applies to employers, labor unions, and employment agencies. An employer under Title VII is defined as a person, partnership, corporation, or other entity engaged in an industry affecting commerce that has 15 or more employees. In *Walters v. Metropolitan Educational Enterprises, Inc.*,[1] the Supreme Court held that the "payroll method" is used to determine the number of employees for coverage of Title VII. This criterion requires that the employer have at least 15 employees on its payroll, whether they actually worked or not, for each working day of 20 or more calendar weeks in the current or preceding calendar year. According to the Supreme Court decision in *Clackamas Gastroenterology Associates, P.C. v. Wells*,[2] common-law principles should have been applied in determining whether managing directors and/or physician-shareholders of professional corporations are employees for the purpose of determining coverage under Title VII. Such common-law principles include:

- whether the organization can hire or fire the individual or set the rules and regulations of the individual's work;
- whether, and to what extent, the organization supervises the individual's work;
- whether the individual reports to someone higher in the organization;
- whether, and to what extent, the individual is able to influence the organization;
- whether the parties intended that the individual be an employee, as expressed in written agreements or contracts; and
- whether the individual shares in the profits, losses, and liabilities of the organization.

The question of whether the employer meets the 15-employee requirement is an element of the plaintiff's claim for relief under the statute; an employer that fails to raise the issue during the trial cannot seek to raise it after the trial is completed.[3]

---

[1] 519 U.S. 202 (1997).

[2] 538 U.S. 440 (2003).

[3] *Arbaugh v. Y & H Corporation*, 546 U.S. 500 (2006).

State and local governments are also covered by Title VII; the federal government and wholly owned U.S. government corporations are covered under separate provisions of Title VII. Subsequent legislation extended the coverage of Title VII to other federal employees: (1) The Congressional Accountability Act of 1995[4] extended the statute to the employees of the House of Representatives, the Senate, the Capitol Guide Service, the Capitol Police, the Congressional Budget Office, the Office of the Architect of the Capitol, the Office of the Attending Physician, and the Office of Technology Assessment; and (2) the Presidential and Executive Office Accountability Act[5] extended coverage to the Executive Office of the President, the Executive Residence at the White House, and the official residence of the Vice President. Title VII does not apply to tax-exempt private membership clubs.

The 1991 amendments to Title VII extended the coverage of the act to American employers that employ U.S. citizens abroad. Foreign corporations that are controlled by American employers are also covered with regard to the employment of U.S. citizens. For such employers, compliance with Title VII is not required if this compliance would force the employer to violate the law of the country where the workplace is located. The effect of this amendment was to overturn the Supreme Court decision in *EEOC v. Arabian American Oil Co.*[6]

Labor unions with at least 15 members or that operate a hiring hall are subject to Title VII. Unions are prohibited from discriminating in employment opportunities or status against their members or applicants on the basis of race, color, religion, gender, or national origin. Employment agencies violate Title VII by discriminating on prohibited bases in announcing openings, interviewing applicants, or referring applicants to employers.

6-1b Administration of Title VII

Title VII is administered by the Equal Employment Opportunity Commission (EEOC), a five-member commission appointed by the president that works with the commission's Office of General Counsel. The EEOC is empowered to issue binding regulations and nonbinding guidelines in fulfillment of its responsibility for administering and enforcing the act. Although the EEOC generally responds to complaints of discrimination filed by individuals, it can also initiate an action on its own if it finds a "pattern or practice" of discrimination in employment.

The regulations and guidelines under Title VII require that employers, unions, and employment agencies post EEOC notices summarizing the act's requirements. Failure to display such notices is punishable by a fine of not more than $100 per violation. The act further requires that those covered keep records relevant to the determination of whether unlawful employment practices have been, or are being, committed. Covered employers must maintain payroll records and other records relating to applicants and to employee promotion, demotion, transfer, and discharge.

---

[4] 2 U.S.C. §1301.

[5] 3 U.S.C. §§402, 411.

[6] 499 U.S. 244 (1991).

THE **WORKING** LAW

African American Workers Sue Mickey D's for Race Discrimination

On January 22, 2015, 10 former McDonald's employees sued three Virginia locations of the fast-food giant. Nine black and one Hispanic plaintiff locked arms, alleging "rampant racial and sexual harassment" at store locations in Clarksville and South Boston, Virginia. Their complaint alleged a dozen employees of color were precipitously let go because they "didn't fit the profile" that supervisors were seeking. They claim they were to "get the ghetto out of the store." On other occasions, according to the federal court complaint, managers complained of "too many black people," and administered discipline disparately.

The high-profile lawsuit was dropped on McDonald's at a time when the mega-franchise is already under fire for alleged mistreatment of its workers. According to Kendall Falls, organizing director of Fast Food Forward (http://strikefastfood.org), "This is a problem that goes far beyond these stores in Virginia—it's a problem with McDonald's business model itself when workers at the company have nowhere to turn."

The corporation for its part retorts that it can't police behavior at every one of its thousands of outlets. The plaintiffs' pleading counters that the home office controls "nearly every aspect of its restaurant operations." But, litigant Pamela Marable claims, "The company told us to take our concerns to the franchise—the same franchise that just fired us!" She added, "McDonald's closely monitors everything we do, from the speed of the drive-through line, to the way we smile and fold customers' bags—but when we try to tell that we're facing discrimination, they ignore us and say it's not their problem."

Source: Nadia Prupis, "Former McDonald's Workers Sue Over Racial Discrimination, Sexual Harassment," *Common Dreams*, January 22, 2015, available at http://www.commondreams.org/news/2015/01/22/former-mcdonalds-workers-sue-over-racial-discrimination-sexual-harassment.

6-1c   Discrimination Under Title VII

Section 703 of Title VII states that it shall be an unlawful employment practice for an employer "to fail or refuse to hire or to discharge any individual, or otherwise to discriminate against an individual with respect to his compensation, terms, condition, or privileges of employment, because of such individual's race, color, religion, sex or national origin." It should be clear from the wording of Section 703 that Title VII prohibits intentional discrimination in employment on the basis of race, color, religion, sex, or national origin. An employer who refuses to hire African Americans, or who will only hire women for clerical positions rather than for production jobs, is in violation of Title VII. Likewise, a union that will not accept Hispanic Americans as members, or that maintains separate seniority lists for male and female members, violates the act. Such intentional discrimination, called **disparate treatment**, means the particular employee is subject to different treatment because of that employee's race, color, gender, religion, or national origin.

In the years immediately following the passage of Title VII, some people believed that the act was intended to protect only minority or female employees. That idea was specifically rejected by the Supreme Court in the 1976 case of *McDonald v. Santa Fe Trail*

disparate treatment when an employee is treated differently from others due to race, color, religion, gender, or national origin

bona fide occupational qualification (BFOQ)
an exception to the civil rights law that allows an employer to hire employees of a specific gender, religion, or national origin when business necessity—the safe and efficient performance of the particular job—requires it

Transportation Co.[7] The case arose when three employees of a trucking company were caught stealing cargo from the company. Two of the employees, who were white, were discharged; the third, an African American, was given a suspension but was not discharged. The employer justified the difference in disciplinary penalties on the ground that Title VII protected the African American employee. The white employees filed suit under Title VII. The Supreme Court emphasized that Title VII protects all employees; every individual employee is protected from any discrimination in employment because of race, color, sex, religion, and national origin. The employer had treated the white employees differently because of their race, and the employer was therefore in violation of Title VII.

Concept *Summary* 6.1

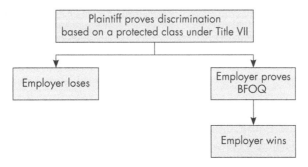

SHOWING DISPARATE TREATMENT

6-1d   Bona Fide Occupational Qualifications (BFOQs)

Although Title VII prohibits intentional discrimination in employment, it does contain a limited exception that allows employers to select employees on the basis of gender, religion, or national origin when the employer can establish that being of a particular gender, religion, or national origin is a **bona fide occupational qualification (BFOQ)**. To establish that a particular characteristic is a BFOQ, the employer must demonstrate that **business necessity**—the safe and efficient operation of the business—requires that employees be of a particular gender, religion, or national origin. Employer convenience, customer preference, or coworker preference will not support the establishment of a BFOQ. Title VII recognizes BFOQs only on the basis of gender, religion, and national origin; the act provides that race and color can never be used as BFOQs. (BFOQs will be discussed in more detail in the next chapter.)

business necessity
the safe and efficient performance of the business or performance of a particular job requires that employees be of a particular sex, religion, or national origin

6-2   Unintentional Discrimination: Disparate Impact

It should be clear that intentional discrimination in employment on the basis of race, religion, gender, color, or national origin (the "prohibited grounds"), apart from a BFOQ, is prohibited, but what about unintentional discrimination? An employer may specify certain requirements

---

[7] 427 U.S. 273 (1976).

disparate impact
the discriminatory effect
of apparently neutral
employment criteria

for a job that operate to disqualify otherwise capable prospective employees. Although the employer is allowed to hire those employees best able to do the job, what happens if the specified requirements do not actually relate to the employee's ability to perform the job but do have the effect of disqualifying a large proportion of minority applicants? This discriminatory effect of apparently neutral requirements is known as a **disparate impact**. Should the disparate impact of such neutral job requirements be prohibited under Title VII?

Concept *Summary* 6.2

DISCRIMINATION UNDER TITLE VII

Disparate Treatment

Intentional discrimination in terms or conditions of employment

The employer intentionally treats employees or applicants differently because of their race, color, sex,* religion,* or national origin*

----

* May be subject to BFOQ exception.

Disparate Impact

The discriminatory effect of apparently neutral employment criteria or selection devices; does not require intention to discriminate on the part of the employer

The employment criteria or selection device disproportionately disqualifies employees based on race, color, sex, religion, or national origin

Frequently, the neutral requirement at issue may be a test used by the employer to screen applicants for a job. Title VII does allow the use of employment testing. Section 703(h) provides, in part,

> ... [i]t shall not be an unlawful employment practice for an employer to give and act upon the results of any professionally developed ability test provided that such test, its administration or action upon the results is not designed, intended or is used to discriminate because of race, color, religion, sex, or national origin.

The effect of that provision and the legality of using job requirements that have a disparate impact were first considered by the Supreme Court in the seminal case *Griggs v. Duke Power Company*.

CASE 6.1

GRIGGS V. DUKE POWER COMPANY
401 U.S. 424 (1971)

Background

Duke Power Company is an electrical utility company operating in North Carolina. Prior to July 2, 1965, the effective date of Title VII of the Civil Rights Act of 1964, the

Company discriminated on the basis of race in the hiring and assigning of employees at its Dan River plant. The plant was organized into five operating departments: (1) Labor, (2) Coal Handling, (3) Operations, (4) Maintenance, and (5) Laboratory and Test. African Americans were only employed in the Labor Department where the highest paying jobs paid less than the lowest paying jobs in the other four operating departments in which only whites were employed.

Promotions were normally made within each department on the basis of job seniority. Transferees into a department usually began in the lowest position. In 1955 the Company instituted a policy of requiring a high school education for initial assignment to any department except Labor, and for transfer from the Coal Handling to any "inside" department (Operations, Maintenance, or Laboratory). When the Company abandoned its policy of restricting African Americans to the Labor Department in 1965, it instituted a requirement of having a high school diploma in order to transfer from the Labor Department to any other department. However, the white employees hired before the adoption of the high school diploma requirement continued to perform satisfactorily and achieve promotions in the various operating departments. The U.S. Census Bureau data from the 1960 census indicated that approximately 34 percent of white males in North Carolina had a high school diploma, compared to about 12 percent of African American males in North Carolina who had completed high school. The Company added a further requirement for new employees on July 2, 1965, the date on which Title VII became effective. To qualify for placement in any but the Labor Department it became necessary to register satisfactory scores on two professionally prepared aptitude tests, as well as to have a high school education. However, employees with a high school diploma who had been hired prior to the adoption of the aptitude test requirements were still eligible for transfer to the four desirable departments from which African Americans had been excluded. In September 1965 the Company began to permit incumbent employees who lacked a high school education to qualify for transfer from Labor or Coal Handling to an "inside" job by passing two tests—the Wonderlic Personnel Test, which purports to measure general intelligence, and the Bennett Mechanical Comprehension Test. Neither was directed or intended to measure the ability to learn to perform a particular job or category of jobs. The requisite scores used for both initial hiring and transfer approximated the national median for high school graduates. For the employees who took the tests, the pass rate for white employees was 58 percent, while the pass rate for African American employees was 6 percent.

Griggs and a group of other African-American employees brought suit against Duke Power, alleging that the high school diploma requirement and the aptitude test requirements violated Title VII because they made it more difficult for African-American employees to be promoted from the Labor Department, and had the effect of continuing the previous job segregation. The District Court had found that while the Company previously followed a policy of overt racial discrimination prior to the passage of Title VII, such conduct had ceased. The District Court also concluded that Title VII was intended to be prospective only and not retroactive, and therefore, the impact of prior discrimination was beyond the reach of the Act. On appeal, the U.S. Court of Appeals for the Fourth Circuit concluded that the intent of the employer should govern, and that in this case there was no showing of intentional discrimination in the company's adoption of the diploma and test requirements. The Court of Appeals concluded there was no violation of the Act. Griggs then appealed to the U.S. Supreme Court.

Burger, Chief Justice

We granted the [appeal] in this case to resolve the question whether an employer is prohibited by ... Title VII from requiring a high school education or passing of a standardized general intelligence test as a condition of employment in or transfer to jobs when (a) neither standard is shown to be significantly related to successful job performance, both requirements operate to disqualify Negroes at a substantially higher rate than white applicants, and the jobs in question formerly had been filled only by white employees as part of a longstanding practice of giving preference to whites....

The objective of Congress in the enactment of Title VII ... was to achieve equality of employment opportunities and remove barriers that have operated in the past to favor an identifiable group of white employees over other employees. Under the Act, practices, procedures, or tests neutral on their face, and even neutral in terms of intent, cannot be maintained if they operate to "freeze" the status quo of prior discriminatory employment practices.

The Court of Appeals' opinion ... agreed that, on the record in the present case, "whites register far better on the Company's alternative requirements" than Negroes. This consequence would appear to be directly traceable to race. Basic intelligence must have the means of articulation to manifest itself fairly in a testing process. Because they are Negroes, petitioners have long received inferior education in segregated schools and this Court expressly recognized these differences ... Congress did not intend by Title VII, however, to guarantee a job to every person regardless of qualifications. In short, the Act does not command that any person be hired simply because he was formerly the subject of discrimination, or because he is a member of a minority group.... What is required by Congress is the removal of artificial, arbitrary, and unnecessary barriers to employment when the barriers operate invidiously to discriminate on the basis of racial or other impermissible classification.

Congress has now provided that tests or criteria for employment or promotion may not provide equality of opportunity merely in the sense of the fabled offer of milk to the stork and the fox. On the contrary, Congress has now required that the posture and condition of the job-seeker be taken into account. It has—to resort again to the fable—provided that the vessel in which the milk is proffered be one all seekers can use. The Act proscribes not only overt discrimination but also practices that are fair in form, but discriminatory in operation. The touchstone is business necessity. If an employment practice which operates to exclude Negroes cannot be shown to be related to job performance, the practice is prohibited.

On the record before us, neither the high school completion requirement nor the general intelligence test is shown to bear a demonstrable relationship to successful performance of the jobs for which it was used. Both were adopted, as the Court of Appeals noted, without meaningful study of their relationship to job-performance ability. Rather, a vice president of the Company testified, the requirements were instituted on the Company's judgment that they generally would improve the overall quality of the work force.

The evidence, however, shows that employees who have not completed high school or taken the tests have continued to perform satisfactorily and make progress in departments for which the high school and test criteria are now used. The promotion record of present employees who would not be able to meet the new criteria thus suggests the possibility that the requirements may not be needed even for the limited purpose of preserving the avowed policy of advancement within the Company....

The Court of Appeals held that the Company had adopted the diploma and test requirements without any "intention to discriminate against Negro employees." We do not suggest that either the District Court or the Court of Appeals erred in examining the employer's intent; but good intent or absence of discriminatory intent does not redeem employment procedures or testing mechanisms that operate as "built-in headwinds" for minority groups and are unrelated to measuring job capability.

... Congress directed the thrust of the Act to the consequences of employment practices, not simply the motivation. More than that, Congress has placed on the employer the burden of showing that any given requirement must have a manifest relationship to the employment in question....

The Company contends that its general intelligence tests are specifically permitted by § 703(h) of the Act. That section authorizes the use of "any professionally developed ability test" that is not "designed, intended or used to discriminate because of race...."

The Equal Employment Opportunity Commission, having enforcement responsibility, has issued guidelines interpreting § 703(h) to permit only the use of job-related tests. The administrative interpretation of the Act by the enforcing agency is entitled to great deference....Since the Act and its legislative history support the Commission's construction, this affords good reason to treat the guidelines as expressing the will of Congress.

... Nothing in the Act precludes the use of testing or measuring procedures; obviously they are useful. What Congress has forbidden is giving these devices and mechanisms controlling force unless they are demonstrably a reasonable measure of job performance.... Far from disparaging job qualifications as such, Congress has made such qualifications the controlling factor, so that race, religion, nationality, and sex become irrelevant. What Congress has commanded is that any tests used must measure the person for the job and not the person in the abstract.

The judgment of the Court of Appeals ... is reversed.

Case Questions

1. What is the significance of the fact that Duke Power had intentionally discriminated against African Americans in hiring prior to the passage of Title VII?

2. Why did the high school diploma requirement and the aptitude tests requirement operate to disqualify African Americans from eligibility for transfer at a greater rate than whites? Explain your answer.

3. Why does the court say that the high school diploma requirement and the aptitude test requirements were "unrelated to measuring job capability"?

4. Does Title VII allow an employer to use applicants' scores on professionally developed aptitude tests as criteria for hiring? Explain your answer.

5. What is the fable of the stork and the fox that Chief Justice Burger refers to? How does it relate to this case?

The *Griggs* case dealt with objective employment selection requirements—a high school diploma and passing two aptitude tests—but in *Watson v. Fort Worth Bank & Trust*,[8] the Supreme Court held that a claim of disparate impact discrimination may be brought against an employer using a subjective employment practice, such as an interview rating. The plaintiff alleging a disparate impact claim must identify the specific employment practice being challenged, and the plaintiff must offer statistical evidence sufficient to show that the challenged practice has a disparate impact on applicants for hiring or promotion because of their membership in a protected group.

6-2a   Section 703(k) and Disparate Impact Claims

The 1991 amendments to Title VII added Section 703(k), which deals with disparate impact claims and requires that the plaintiff demonstrate that the employer uses a particular employment practice that causes a disparate impact on one of the bases prohibited by Title VII. If such a showing is made, the employer must then demonstrate that the practice is job related for the position in question and is consistent with business necessity. Even if the employer makes such a showing, if the plaintiff can demonstrate that an alternative employment practice—one without a disparate impact—is available, and the employer refuses to adopt it, the employer is still in violation of the act. Section 703(k) states that a plaintiff shall demonstrate that each particular employment practice that is challenged causes a disparate impact unless the plaintiff can demonstrate that the elements of the decision-making process are not capable of separation for analysis. If the employer demonstrates that the challenged practice does not have a disparate impact, then there is no need to show that the practice is required by business necessity. Work rules that bar the employment of individuals using or possessing illegal drugs are exempt from disparate impact analysis; such rules violate Title VII only when they are adopted or applied with an intention to discriminate on grounds prohibited by Title VII.

If the employment practice at issue is shown to be sufficiently job related, and the plaintiff has not shown that alternative practices without a disparate impact are available, then the employer may continue to use the challenged employment practice because it is necessary to perform the job. Nothing in Title VII prohibits an employer from hiring only those persons who are capable of doing the job. The 1991 amendments to Title VII added Section 703(k)(2), which states that demonstrating that an employment practice is required by business necessity is not a defense to a claim of intentional discrimination under Title VII. Most of the cases dealing with disparate impact discrimination involve race, gender, or national origin discrimination, although the language of Section 703(k) is not limited to only those bases of discrimination.

Uniform Guidelines on Employee Selection Procedures regulations adopted by the EEOC and other federal agencies that provide for methods of demonstrating a disparate impact and for validating employee selection criteria

The Uniform Guidelines on Employee Selection

How can a plaintiff demonstrate a claim of disparate impact? How can an employer demonstrate that a requirement is job-related? The **Uniform Guidelines on Employee Selection Procedures**,[9] a series of regulations adopted by the EEOC and other federal agencies, provide some answers to those questions.

---

[8] 487 U.S. 977 (1988).

[9] 29 C.F.R. Part 1607 (1978).

Showing a Disparate Impact

The Supreme Court held in *Watson v. Fort Worth Bank & Trust* that a plaintiff must "offer statistical evidence of a kind and degree sufficient to show that the practice in question has caused the exclusion of applicants for jobs or promotions because of their membership in a protected group. In *Wards Cove Packing Co. v. Atonio*,[10] the Supreme Court described one way to demonstrate that hiring practices had a disparate impact on nonwhites by comparing the composition of the employer's work force with the composition of the labor market from which applicants are drawn:

> The "proper comparison [is] between the racial composition of [the at-issue jobs] and the racial composition of the qualified ... population in the relevant labor market." It is such a comparison—between the racial composition of the qualified persons in the labor market and the persons holding at-issue jobs—that generally forms the proper basis for the initial inquiry in a disparate impact case. Alternatively, in cases where such labor market statistics will be difficult if not impossible to ascertain, we have recognized that certain other statistics—such as measures indicating the racial composition of "otherwise-qualified applicants" for at-issue jobs—are equally probative for this purpose.

Four-Fifths Rule
a mathematical formula developed by the EEOC to demonstrate disparate impact of a facially neutral employment practice on selection criteria

The Uniform Guidelines, adopted before the *Watson* and *Wards Cove* decisions, set out another way to demonstrate the disparate impact of a job requirement. This procedure, known as the **Four-Fifths Rule**, compares the selection rates (the rates at which applicants meet the requirements or pass the test) for the various protected groups under Title VII. The Four-Fifths Rule states that a disparate impact will be demonstrated when the proportion of applicants from the protected group with the lowest selection rate (or pass rate) is less than 80 percent of the selection rate (pass rate) of the group with the highest selection rate.

For example, a municipal fire department requires that applicants for firefighter positions be at least five feet, six inches tall and weigh at least 130 pounds. Of the applicants for the positions, 5 of 20 (25 percent) of the Hispanic applicants meet the requirements, while 30 of 40 (75 percent) of the white applicants meet the requirements. To determine whether the height and weight requirements have a disparate impact on Hispanics, the pass rate for Hispanics is divided by the pass rate for whites. Since 0.25/0.75 = 0.33, or 33 percent, a disparate impact according to the Four-Fifths Rule exists. Stating the rule in equation form, disparate impact exists when:

$$\frac{\text{Pass rate for group with lowest pass rate}}{\text{Pass rate for group with highest pass rate}} < 0.80$$

Using the numbers from our example:

$$\frac{0.25 \ (\text{Hispanic pass rate})}{0.75 \ (\text{White pass rate})} = 0.33; \ 033 \ < 0.80$$

Therefore, a disparate impact exists, establishing a prima facie case of employment discrimination. To continue using such a test, the employer must satisfy the court that the test is sufficiently job related.

---

[10] 490 U.S. 642 (1989).

6-2b Validating Job Requirements

The fire department must demonstrate that the height and weight requirements are job related in order to continue using them in selecting employees. The Uniform Guidelines provide several methods to show that the height and weight requirements are job related. The Uniform Guidelines also require a showing of a statistical correlation demonstrating that the requirements are necessary for successful job performance. In our example, the fire department would have to show that the minimum height and weight requirements screen out those applicants who would be unable to perform safely and efficiently the tasks or duties of a firefighter.

When the job requirements involve passing an examination, it must be shown that a passing score on the exam has a high statistical correlation with successful job performance. The Uniform Guidelines set out standards for demonstrating such a correlation (known as test validity) developed by the American Psychological Association. The standards may be classified into three types: content validity, construct validity, and criterion-related validity.

Content Validity

content validity
a method of demonstrating that an employment selection device reflects the content of the job for which employees are being selected

Content validity is a means of measuring whether the requirement or test actually evaluates abilities required on the job. The fire department using the height and weight requirements would have to show that the requirements determine abilities needed to do the job—that anyone shorter than five feet, six inches or weighing less than 130 pounds would be unable to do the job. That would be difficult to do, but to validate the requirements as job related, such a showing is required by the Uniform Guidelines. If the job of firefighter requires physical strength, then using a strength test as a selection device would be valid. (Height and weight requirements are sometimes used instead of a physical strength test, but they are much more difficult to validate than strength tests.) The strength test used to screen applicants should reflect the actual tasks of the job—for example, carrying large fire hoses while climbing a ladder. For the job of typist, a spelling and typing test would likely have a high content validity because these tests measure abilities actually needed on the job. A strength test for a typist, on the other hand, would have a low content validity rating because physical strength has little relationship to typing performance. The Uniform Guidelines set out statistical methods to demonstrate the relationship (if any) of the requirements to job performance. An employer seeking to validate such requirements must follow the procedures and conditions in the Uniform Guidelines.

Construct Validity

construct validity
a method of demonstrating that an employment selection device selects employees based on the traits and characteristics that are required for the job in question

Construct validity is a means of isolating and testing for specific traits or characteristics that are deemed essential for job performance. Such traits, or constructs, may be based on observations but cannot be measured directly. For example, a teacher may be required to possess the construct "patience," or an executive may be required to possess "leadership" or "judgment." Such traits, or constructs, cannot be measured directly, but they may be observed based on simulations of actual job situations. The Uniform Guidelines set out procedures and methods for demonstrating that certain constructs are really necessary to the job and that means used to test for or identify these constructs actually do measure them.

Criterion-Related Validity

criterion-related validity
a method of demonstrating that an employment selection device correlates with the skills and knowledge required for successful job performance

Criterion-related validity concerns the statistical correlation between scores received on tests ("paper-and-pencil" tests) and job performance. An employer who administers an

IQ test to prospective employees must establish that there is a high statistical correlation between successful performance on the test and successful performance on the job. That correlation may be established by giving the test to current employees and comparing their test scores with their job performance; the correlation coefficient so produced is then used to predict the job performance of other current or prospective employees taking the same test. The Uniform Guidelines provide specific procedures and requirements for demonstrating the criterion-related validity of tests used for employment selection. Failure to comply with the requirements of the Uniform Guidelines will prevent an employer from establishing that a test is job related. If the test has not been validated, its use for employment purposes will violate Title VII if such a test has a disparate impact. Furthermore, a test validated for one group, such as Hispanic Americans, may have to be separately validated for one or more other groups, such as African Americans or Asian Americans.

Concept *Summary* 6.3

PROVING JOB RELATEDNESS

Content Validity Studies	**Construct Validity Studies**	**Criterion-Related Validity Studies**
Is the selection device or test an accurate sample of the job's requirements?	Does the selection device test for traits or characteristics essential for job performance?	Does the employment test identify skills or knowledge necessary for successful job performance?
Employers need to show that the selection device or test reflects important tasks or aspects of the job	Employers must show that they are accurately screening for constructs identified as essential for successful job performance	Employers must show that the test has a high statistical correlation between success on the test and success on the job

In *Ricci v. DeStefano*,[11] the New Haven Fire Department administered an exam to candidates for promotion, but decided not to use the exam results because of a perceived disparate impact on African Americans. A group of white firefighters who would have been promoted based on the exam results filed suit, claiming that the employer's action was race-based discrimination against them. A divided Supreme Court held that the employer had violated Title VII because it did not have a "strong basis in evidence" to justify taking race-conscious action to reject the exam results. Justice Kennedy, writing for the majority, held that the exam was job related, and that fear of litigation alone was not a sufficient reason for setting aside the exam results.

In light of the *Ricci* case, employers should ensure that any exams or other employment selection devices have been validated as being job related. If the exam or selection device is job related, employers may continue to use it even if the exam has a disparate impact on

---

[11] 129 S.Ct. 2658 (2009).

a protected group (as long as there is no available alternative exam or selection device that does not have a disparate impact).

The following case deals with an employer's attempt to justify a strength test used to select applicants for hiring in a meatpacking plant.

>> CASE 6.2

EQUAL EMPLOYMENT OPPORTUNITY COMMISSION V. DIAL CORP.
469 F.3d 735 (8th Cir. 2006)

Facts: A Dial plant located in Fort Madison, Iowa, produces canned meats. Entry-level employees at the plant are assigned to the sausage packing area, where workers daily lift and carry up to 18,000 pounds of sausage, walking the equivalent of four miles in the process. They are required to carry approximately thirty-five pounds of sausage at a time and must lift and load the sausage to heights between thirty and sixty inches above the floor. Employees who worked in the sausage packing area experienced a disproportionate number of injuries as compared to the rest of the workers in the plant. Dial implemented several measures to reduce the injury rate starting in late 1996. In 2000, Dial also instituted a strength test used to evaluate potential employees, called the Work Tolerance Screen (WTS). In this test, job applicants were asked to carry a thirty-five pound bar between two frames, approximately thirty and sixty inches off the floor, and to lift and load the bar onto these frames. The applicants were told to work at their "own pace" for seven minutes. An occupational therapist watched the process, documented how many lifts each applicant completed, and recorded her own comments about each candidate's performance. Starting in 2001, the plant nurse, Martha Lutenegger, also watched and documented the process. Lutenegger reviewed the test forms and had the ultimate hiring authority.

Women and men had worked together, doing the same jobs, in the sausage packing area for years. In the three years before the WTS was adopted, 46 percent of the new hires were women, but the number of female hires dropped to 15 percent after the WTS test was implemented. The percentage of women who passed the test decreased each year the TWS was used, with only 8 percent of the women applicants passing in 2002. Overall, 38 percent of female applicants passed, while 97 percent of the male applicants passed. While injuries

among sausage workers declined consistently after 2000 when the WTS was adopted, the downward trend in injuries had begun in 1998 after the company had instituted other measures to reduce injuries.

Paula Liles applied to Dial in January 2000 and was one of the first applicants to take the WTS test. She was not hired, even though the occupational therapist administering the WTS test told her that she had passed. Liles filed a discrimination complaint with the EEOC in August 2000. On September 24, 2002, EEOC brought this action on behalf of Liles and fifty-three other women who had applied to work at Dial and were denied employment after taking the WTS. The EEOC claimed that the use of the WTS test had an unlawful disparate impact on female applicants.

At the trial, the EEOC presented an expert on industrial organization who testified that the WTS was significantly more difficult than the actual job that workers performed at the plant. He explained that although workers did 1.25 lifts per minute on average and rested between lifts, applicants who took the WTS performed six lifts per minute on average, usually without any breaks. He also testified that in two of the three years before Dial had implemented the WTS, the women's injury rate had been lower than that of the male workers. EEOC's expert also analyzed the company's written evaluations of the applicants and testified that more men than women were given offers of employment even when they had received similar comments about their performance on the WTS. EEOC also introduced evidence that the occupational nurse marked some women as failing despite their having completed the full seven-minute test.

Dial presented an expert in work physiology, who testified that in his opinion the WTS effectively tested skills which were representative of the actual job, and an industrial and organizational psychologist, who testified that the WTS measured the requirements of the job and that the decrease in injuries could be attributed to the test. Dial also called plant nurse Martha Lutenegger who testified that although she and other Dial managers knew the WTS was screening out more women than men, the decrease in injuries warranted its continued use.

The trial court held that Dial was in violation of Title VII because the WTS had a discriminatory effect on female applicants, that Dial had not demonstrated that the WTS was a business necessity or shown either content or criterion validity, and that Dial had not effectively controlled for other variables that may have caused the decline in injuries, including other safety measures that Dial had implemented starting in 1996. Dial was ordered to pay back pay and benefits to the female applicants.

Dial appealed to the U.S. Court of Appeals for the Eighth Circuit. Dial attacked the trial court's findings of disparate impact, and claimed that it had proved that the WTS was a business necessity.

Issue: Has Dial proven that use of the WTS to screen applicants for employment was a business necessity because it reduced the number of injuries in the sausage production area?

Decision: In a disparate impact case, once the plaintiff establishes a prima facie case, the employer must then show the challenged practice is "related to safe and efficient job performance and is consistent with business necessity." An employer using the business necessity defense must prove that the practice was related to the specific job and the required skills and physical requirements of the position. Although a validity study of an employment test can be sufficient to prove business necessity, it is not necessary if the employer demonstrates the procedure is sufficiently related to safe and efficient job performance. If the employer demonstrates business necessity, the plaintiff can still prevail by showing that there is a less discriminatory alternative available.

Dial claimed that the WTS was shown by its experts to have both content and criterion validity. Under EEOCs Uniform Guidelines, "A content validity study should consist of data showing that the content of the selection procedure is representative of important aspects of performance on the job for which the candidates are to

be evaluated." Dial's physiology expert testified that the WTS was highly representative of the actions required by the job. The trial court was persuaded by the testimony of the EEOCs expert in industrial organization "that a crucial aspect of the WTS is more difficult than the sausage-making jobs themselves" and that the average applicant had to perform four times as many lifts as current employees and had no rest breaks. There was also evidence that in a testing environment where hiring is contingent upon test performance, applicants tend to work as fast as possible during the test in order to outperform the competition.

Dial argued that the WTS had criterion validity because both overall injuries and strength-related injuries decreased dramatically following the implementation of the WTS. The Uniform Guidelines establish that criterion validity can be shown by "empirical data demonstrating that the selection procedure is predictive of or significantly correlated with important elements of job performance." Despite Dial's claims that the decrease in injuries showed that the WTS enabled it to predict which applicants could safely handle the strenuous nature of the work, the evidence showed that the sausage plant injuries started decreasing before the WTS was implemented. Moreover, the injury rate for women employees was lower than that for men in two of the three years before Dial implemented the WTS. The evidence did not require the district court to find that the decrease in injuries resulted from the implementation of the WTS instead of the other safety mechanisms Dial started to put in place in 1996.

Dial also argued that the district court improperly gave it the burden to establish that there was no less discriminatory alternative to the WTS, instead of holding that the EEOC had the burden as part of the burden-shifting framework in disparate impact cases. Because Dial failed to demonstrate that the WTS was a business necessity, however, the EEOC never was required to show the presence of a nondiscriminatory alternative. Part of the employer's burden to establish business necessity is to demonstrate the need for the challenged procedure, and the court found that Dial had not shown that its other safety measures could not produce the same results.

The Court of Appeals upheld the district court findings of a disparate impact on female applicants and that Dial had not shown that the WTS was required as business necessity. The court affirmed the trial court finding that Dial was liable for back pay and benefits.

《《

Concept *Summary* 6.4

SHOWING DISPARATE IMPACT

Plaintiff shows that a neutral requirement has a disparate impact—using the Four-Fifths Rule or other statistical evidence

Employer loses

Employer shows that the requirement is job related—using validity studies or other statistical evidence—or that it is consistent with business necessity, the safe and efficient performance of the job

Employer wins

Employee proves an alternative option was available and was not offered

Employer loses

6-3   Seniority and Title VII

seniority
the length of service on the job

Seniority, the length of service on the job, is frequently used to determine entitlement to employment benefits, promotions, or transfers, and even job security itself. Seniority systems usually provide that worker layoffs be conducted on the basis of inverse seniority; those with the least length of service, or seniority, are laid off before those with greater seniority. Seniority within a department may also be used to determine eligibility to transfer to a different department.

Seniority could have had a discriminatory effect when an employer, prior to the adoption of Title VII, refused to hire women or minority workers. If, after Title VII's adoption, the employer did hire them, those workers would have enjoyed the least seniority. In the event of a layoff, the workers who lost their jobs would necessarily be women and minorities, whereas white males retained their jobs. The layoffs by inverse seniority thus had a disparate impact on women and minorities. Did this mean the seniority system is in violation of Title VII, as in *Griggs*?

Section 703(h) of Title VII dealt with the problem by providing an exemption for bona fide seniority systems. That section still states, in part,

> Notwithstanding any other provision of this title, it shall not be an unlawful employment practice for an employer to apply different standards of compensation or different terms, conditions, or privileges of employment pursuant to a bona fide seniority or merit system provided that such differences are not the result of an intention to discriminate because of race, color, religion, sex or national origin.

Section 706(e)(2), added to Title VII by the 1991 amendments, addresses the time limits for a challenge to a seniority system that allegedly is used intentionally to discriminate in violation of Title VII. According to that section, a claim may be filed after the allegedly discriminatory seniority system is adopted, after the plaintiff becomes subject to the seniority system, or after the plaintiff is injured by the application of the seniority system. Section 706(e)(2) was intended to reverse the Supreme Court decision in *Lorance v. AT&T Technologies, Inc.*,[12] which held that the time limit for challenging a seniority system ran from the date on which the system was adopted, even if the plaintiff was not subjected to the system until five years later.

The other side of the "seniority coin" is manifested in employer decisions that appear to have ignored seniority, suggesting that the firm had an illegal motive for terminating long-timers. Here's just such a case, decided by a U.S. Court of Appeals in 2015.

CASE 6.3

FULLER V. EDWIN B. STIMPSON CO. INC.
—Fed. Appx. —, 2015 WL 294112 (11th Cir. 2015)

Per Curiam

Elzie Fuller, III, an African-American male, appeals the district court's grant of defendant Edwin B. Stimpson Company, Inc.'s ("Stimpson Co.") motion for summary judgment as to Fuller's claims alleging race discrimination in violation of Title VII of the Civil Rights Act of 1964 ("Title VII"), 42 U.S.C. § 2000e–2(a), and the Florida Civil Rights Act ("FCRA"), Fla. Stat. § 760.10, arising out of his long-term employment with Stimpson and his termination in 2009 as part of a reduction in force ("RIF"). On appeal, Fuller argues that: (1) he established a prima facie case of race discrimination; and (2) the district court abused its discretion by denying his motion for reconsideration. After thorough review, we affirm....

First, we find no merit to Fuller's race discrimination claim. Title VII provides that it is unlawful for an employer "to discharge any individual, or otherwise to discriminate against any individual ... because of such individual's race ..." 42 U.S.C. § 2000e–2(a)(1). The FCRA is modeled after Title VII, and claims brought under it are analyzed under the same framework, so FCRA claims do not need separate discussion and their outcome is the same as the federal claims. ... In evaluating disparate treatment claims supported by circumstantial evidence, we use the framework of *McDonnell Douglas Corp. v. Green*, 411 U.S. 792 (1973). *Wilson*, 376 F.3d at 1087. Under *McDonnell Douglas*, the plaintiff must initially establish a prima facie case, which generally consists

of the following: (1) the plaintiff was a member of a protected class; (2) he was qualified to do the job; (3) he was subjected to an adverse employment action; and (4) he was treated less favorably than similarly situated individuals outside his protected class. ... "In order to satisfy the similar offenses prong, the comparator's misconduct must be nearly identical to the plaintiff's in order to prevent courts from second-guessing employers' reasonable decisions and confusing apples with oranges." *Silvera v. Orange County Sch. Bd.*, 244 F.3d 1253, 1259 (11th Cir.2001) (quotations omitted).

In situations involving a reduction in force, a modified prima facie formulation may apply, which allows a case of discrimination to be established by presenting evidence showing, not dissimilar treatment, but that the employer intended to discriminate against the plaintiff in making the discharge decision. ... To establish intent, a plaintiff must proffer evidence that the defendant (1) consciously refused to consider retaining the plaintiff because of his race or (2) regarded race as a negative factor in such consideration....

Executive Order 11246 prohibits federal contractors and subcontractors from discriminating in employment decisions on the basis of race, color, religion, sex, or national origin, and requires certain federal contractors and subcontractors to take affirmative action to ensure that an equal opportunity for employment is provided in all respects of their employment. Exec. Order No. 11246 § 202(1), 41

---

[12] 490 U.S. 900 (1989).

C.F.R. § 60–1.1 (1965); *see also* http://www.dol.gov/compliance/laws/comp-eeo.htm. It requires government contractors and subcontractors to have in place an acceptable affirmative-action program that identifies problem areas. *See* 41 C.F.R. § 60–1.3 (including subcontractors in the definition of "contractor"); *id.* § 60–2.17 (listing required elements of affirmative action programs). In meeting this requirement, the contractor or subcontractor must "perform in-depth analyses of its total employment process to determine whether and where impediments to equal employment opportunity exist." *Id.* § 60–2.17(b). The contractor or subcontractor must evaluate, among other things,

1. The workforce by organizational unit and job group to determine whether there are problems of minority or female utilization (i.e., employment in the unit or group), or of minority or female distribution (i.e., placement in the different jobs within the unit or group);
2. Personnel activity (applicant flow, hires, terminations, promotions, and other personnel actions) to determine whether there are selection disparities; ...

Affirmative-action programs must include an internal audit and reporting system that "[m]onitor[s] records of all personnel activity, including ... terminations ..., at all levels to ensure the nondiscriminatory policy is carried out." *Id.* § 60–2.17(d). Executive Order 11246 has the force and effect of law....

Here, the district court did not err by concluding that Fuller failed to establish a prima facie case of race discrimination. As for the four comparators Fuller identifies on appeal, only employee Jack Shuck was identified in Fuller's motion for partial summary judgment as a comparator regarding attendance. In any event, Fuller was either late to work or left early on 57 occasions in 2008, whereas none of the four individuals identified here had more than 16 total late arrivals and early departures that year, so they are not valid comparators....

Moreover, the record does not support Fuller's contentions that (1) the court granted summary judgment without considering the statistical evidence and Dr. Pearson's analysis, and (2) Dr. Pearson's analysis supports a prima facie case of discrimination. Instead, the court determined that, despite any statistical analysis performed by Fuller's expert, Dr. Pearson, the actual decisions made by Stimpson Co. refuted discriminatory intent. As the district court determined, and the record revealed, the termination decisions that Stimpson Co. modified following a review of the Workforce Review spreadsheet—which listed all employees and their department, job classification, race, gender, age, and years of service, among other information—revealed that, if anything, being African-American was regarded as a positive factor in Stimpson Co.'s termination decisions.

Thus, Fuller failed to establish the requisite discriminatory intent for a prima facie case of discrimination in a RIF.

As for Fuller's arguments that the statistical evidence and Fuller's seniority bear on the issue of pretext, the district court did not need to reach the pretext step of the test since Fuller did not establish a prima facie case of race discrimination.... In any event, Executive Order 11246 required Stimpson Co. to prepare the information contained in the Workforce Review spreadsheet, including its groupings of employees by race. Therefore, the court properly concluded that Stimpson's creation of the spreadsheet could not serve as evidence of discrimination or pretext. Without the Workforce Review spreadsheet, and considering Fuller's poor attendance record in 2008, Fuller's seniority alone does not establish the requisite discriminatory intent for a prima facie case of discrimination in a RIF.... Accordingly, the district court properly granted summary judgment as to Fuller's race discrimination claim.

We are also unpersuaded by Fuller's claim that the district court abused its discretion by denying his motion for reconsideration. A court may only grant a Rule 59 motion based on "newly-discovered evidence or manifest errors of law or fact." *Arthur v. King*, 500 F.3d 1335, 1343 (11th Cir. 2007). "[A] Rule 59(e) motion [cannot be used] to relitigate old matters, raise argument or present evidence that could have been raised prior to the entry of judgment." *Id.* (brackets in original) (quotations omitted).

Here, the record shows that Fuller did not present any newly-discovered evidence or manifest errors of law or fact in his motion for reconsideration. In particular, he failed to point out errors in the district court's original decision that would have changed its ultimate conclusion. Thus, the district court did not abuse its discretion in denying Fuller's motion for reconsideration.

AFFIRMED.

Case Questions

1. According to the company, why was the plaintiff selected to be part of the RIF?

2. Why did the court find the company's articulation of a legitimate business reason for selecting the plaintiff to be part of the RIF persuasive?

3. Was there inferential evidence that race played no part in picking the plaintiff to be part of the RIF?

4. Do you think the court was wrong in refusing to give the plaintiff's seniority more weight than it did?

5. Why were the plaintiff's proffered "comparators" of no help to his case?

Concept *Summary* 6.5

BONA FIDE SENIORITY SYSTEM

- Section 703(h) immunizes employment actions taken pursuant to a bona fide seniority system.

- To be bona fide within the meaning of Section 703(h), the seniority system:
  - Must be neutral on its face—apply equally to all groups
  - Must have its origin free from intentional discrimination
  - Must have been negotiated and maintained free from intentional discrimination
  - Must have its basis be reasonable in light of industry practice

6-4 Mixed-Motive Cases Under Title VII

In *Price Waterhouse v. Hopkins*,[13] the Supreme Court held that when a plaintiff shows that the employer has considered an illegal factor under Title VII (race, sex, color, religion, or national origin) in making an employment decision, the employer must demonstrate that it would have reached the same decision if it had not considered the illegal factor. According to the Supreme Court, if the employer can show this, the employer can escape liability under Title VII; that is, it will not have violated the statute.

The 1991 amendments to Title VII addressed this "mixed-motive" situation and partially overruled the *Price Waterhouse* decision. Section 703(m) now states that "an unlawful employment practice is established when the complaining party demonstrates that race, color, religion, sex, or national origin was a motivating factor for any employment practice, even though other factors also motivated the practice." That is, the employer violates Title VII when an illegal factor is considered, even though there may have been other factors also motivating the decision or practice. If the employer is able to show that it would have reached the same decision in the absence of the illegal factor, then the employer's liability for remedy under Title VII is reduced under Section 706(g)(2)(B). Section 706(g)(2)(B), also added by the 1991 amendments, states that the employer is subject to a court order to cease violating Title VII and is liable for the plaintiff's legal fees but is not required to pay damages or to reinstate or hire the plaintiff. In *Desert Palace, Inc. v. Costa*,[14] the Supreme Court held that a plaintiff need only "demonstrate" that the defendant used a prohibited factor (race, color, gender, religion, or natural origin) as one of the motives for an employment action. That demonstration can be made either by circumstantial evidence or direct evidence; the act does not require direct evidence to raise the mixed motive analysis under Section 703(m).

6-5 Retaliation Under Title VII

Section 704(a) of Title VII prohibits retaliation by an employer, union, or employment agency against an employee or applicant because that person has opposed any practice that

---

[13] 490 U.S. 228 (1989).
[14] 539 U.S. 90 (2003).

is prohibited by Title VII (known as the "opposition clause") or because that person has taken part in or assisted any investigation, hearing, or proceeding under Title VII (known as the "participation clause"). To demonstrate a case of retaliation under Section 704(a), plaintiffs must demonstrate that:

(1) they were engaged in an activity or activities protected under Title VII;

(2) they suffered an adverse employment decision or action; and

(3) there was a causal link between the protected activity and the adverse employment decision.

The "protected activity" must be related to either the participation clause or the opposition clause of Section 704. An employee who voluntarily cooperated with an employer's internal investigation of a sexual harassment complaint was protected under the opposition clause of Section 704 even though she did not make a complaint to the employer or file a formal charge under Title VII; the Supreme Court held that her subsequent discharge by the employer violated Title VII, according to *Crawford v. Metropolitan Govt. of Nashville & Davidson City*.[15] In *Burlington Northern & Santa Fe Railroad Co. v. White*,[16] the U.S. Supreme Court held that retaliation under Title VII is not limited to ultimate employment decisions such as promotion or termination, but rather includes any action that a reasonable employee would find to be materially adverse—such that it might dissuade a reasonable worker from making or supporting a charge under Title VII. Section 704(a) also protects former employees from retaliation, according to *Robinson v. Shell Oil Company*.[17] In that case, an employer gave a former employee a negative reference because the employee had filed a Title VII charge against the employer; the Supreme Court ruled that giving the negative reference was retaliation in violation of Section 704(a).

THE **WORKING** LAW

Building Contractor Ignored Complaints of Racial Harassment and Fired Black Employees in Retaliation, Federal Agency Charges

MEMPHIS, Tenn.–Skanska USA Building, Inc., a building contractor headquartered in Parsippany, N.J., will pay $95,000 to settle a racial harassment and retaliation lawsuit brought by the U.S. Equal Employment Opportunity Commission (EEOC), the agency announced today.

According to the EEOC's suit, Skanska violated federal law by allowing workers to subject a class of black employees who were working as buck hoist operators to racial harassment, and by firing them for complaining to Skanska about the misconduct. Skanska served as the general contractor on the Methodist Le Bonheur Children's Hospital in Memphis, where the incidents in this lawsuit took place. The class of black employees worked for C-1, Inc. Construction Company, a minority-owned subcontractor for Skanska. Skanska awarded a subcontract to C-1 to provide buck hoist operations for the construction site and thereafter supervised all C-1 employees while at the work site.

---

[15] 129 S.Ct. 846 (2009).

[16] 548 U.S. 53 (2006).

[17] 519 U.S. 337 (1997).

The EEOC charged that Skanska failed to properly investigate complaints from the buck hoist operators that white employees subjected them to racially offensive comments and physical assault. The EEOC alleged that after Maurice Knox, one of the buck hoist operators, complained about having urine and feces thrown on him at the job site, Skanska cancelled its contract with C-1 Inc., and immediately fired all of its black buck hoist operators. With assistance from the Memphis Minority Business Council's president, Skanska reinstated the contract with C-1 and recalled the black buck hoist operators to work. The white employees, however, continued to subject the buck hoist operators to racial harassment on a daily basis.

The EEOC filed suit (*EEOC v. Skanska USA Building, Inc.*, Civil Action No. 2:10-cv-02717) in U.S. District Court for the Western District of Tennessee after first attempting to reach a pre-litigation settlement through its conciliation process.

During litigation, Skanska asserted that it did not employ the sub-contracted buck hoist operators. The U.S. District Court for the Western District of Tennessee ruled in favor of Skanska, granting summary judgment. After the EEOC appealed, the U.S. Court of Appeals for the Sixth Circuit reversed the ruling and remanded the case. The Sixth Circuit acknowledged that it had not previously applied the joint employer theory in a Title VII case. According to the joint employer theory, two separate entities are considered to be joint employers if they share or co-determine essential terms and conditions of employment. The Sixth Circuit adopted the joint employer theory in the Title VII context and held that there was sufficient evidence to hold Skanska liable as a joint employer because Skanska supervised and controlled the day-to-day activities of the buck hoist operators.

Besides the $95,000 in monetary relief, the three-year consent decree settling the lawsuit enjoins Skanska from subjecting employees to racial harassment or retaliating against any employee who lodges a discrimination complaint. The consent decree also requires defendant to provide in-person training on race discrimination and retaliation, maintain records of any complaints of racial harassment, and provide annual reports to the EEOC. Knox intervened in the EEOC's lawsuit and settled his claim separately for an undisclosed amount.

Source: EEOC Press Release, January 30, 205, accessed at http://www.jdsupra.com/legalnews/skanska-usa-building-to-pay-95000-to-s-20035.

Concept *Summary* 6.6

RETALIATION UNDER TITLE VII

- To demonstrate retaliation under Title VII, plaintiffs must show the following:
  - They were engaged in an activity protected under Title VII or opposed a practice prohibited by Title VII;
  - They suffered an adverse employment decision or employment action;

AND

  - There was a casual link between the protected activity and the adverse employment decision.

6-6 Affirmative Action and Reverse Discrimination

Affirmative action has been an extremely controversial and divisive legal and political issue since Title VII was enacted in 1964. Critics of affirmative action argue that it benefited individuals who were not, themselves, victims of illegal discrimination, and operated to discriminate against persons (usually white males) who were not personally guilty of illegal discrimination. Supporters argue that affirmative action is necessary to overcome the legacy of prior discrimination and that our society is still not free from racism and sexism.

Affirmative action programs in employment involve giving some kind of preference in hiring or promotion to qualified female or minority employees. Employees who are not members of the group being accorded the preference (usually white males) may therefore be at a disadvantage for hiring or promotion. Recall that *McDonald v. Santa Fe Trail* held that Title VII protected every individual employee from discrimination because of race, sex, color, religion, or national origin. Is the denial of preferential treatment to employees not within the preferred group (defined by race or sex) a violation of Title VII? Affirmative action programs by public sector employers raise legal issues under the U.S. Constitution as well as under Title VII: Does the affirmative action program violate the constitutional prohibitions against intentional discrimination contained in the Equal Protection Clause? The discussion of affirmative action in this chapter focuses mainly on affirmative action under Title VII. Chapter 11 will also discuss affirmative action under the Constitution.

Title VII does not require employers to enact affirmative action plans; however, the courts have often ordered affirmative action when the employer has been found in violation of Title VII. The courts have consistently held that remedial affirmative action plans—plans set up to remedy prior illegal discrimination—are permissible under Title VII because such plans may be necessary to overcome the effects of the employer's prior illegal discrimination.

But if the plan is voluntary and the employer has not been found guilty of prior discrimination, does it violate Title VII by discriminating on the basis of race or gender? In *United Steelworkers of America v. Weber*,[18] the Court held that such voluntary plans do not necessarily run afoul of Title VII. Such a plan, the majority of justices held, comported philosophically with Title VII's goals. Provided white workers were not absolutely barred from advancement and the plan did not unreasonably trammel their interests, it *might* pass legal muster.

The next case is a variation on this theme. Here, the Supreme Court considered a municipal employer's decision to ignore the results of a promotional exam for its firefighters, because it believed that certifying the scores would have a disparate impact on African American test-takers. The question posed to the Court can be characterized as, "Could the city engage in the *ad hoc* affirmative action of disregarding the test results in order to avoid a perceived Title VII 'disparate impact' violation?"

---

[18] 443 U.S. 193 (1979).

» CASE 6.4

RICCI V. DESTEFANO
557 U.S. 557 (2009)

Facts: New Haven, Connecticut, used objective examinations to identify those firefighters best qualified for promotion. When the results of such an exam to fill vacant lieutenant and captain positions showed that white candidates had outperformed minority candidates, a rancorous public debate ensued. Confronted with arguments both for and against certifying the test results— and threats of a lawsuit either way—the City threw out the results based on the statistical racial disparity. Petitioners, white and Hispanic firefighters who passed the exams but were denied a chance at promotions by the City's refusal to certify the test results, sued the City and city officials, alleging that discarding the test results discriminated against them based on their race in violation of Title VII. The defendants responded that had they certified the test results, they could have faced Title VII liability for adopting a practice having a disparate impact on minority firefighters. The District Court granted summary judgment for the defendants, and the Second Circuit affirmed.

Issue: Did the City's affirmative action of discarding the test results amount to disparate treatment of the successful white and Hispanic test-takers on the basis of race and in violation of Title VII?

Decision: The Supreme Court explained that under Title VII, before an employer can engage in intentional discrimination for the asserted purpose of avoiding or remedying an unintentional disparate impact, the employer must have a strong basis in evidence to believe it will be subject to disparate-impact liability if it fails to take the race-conscious, discriminatory action. The Court's analysis began with the premise that the City's actions would violate Title VII's disparate-treatment prohibition absent some valid defense. All the evidence demonstrated that the City rejected the test results because the higher-scoring candidates were white. Without some other justification, this express, race-based decision making was prohibited. The question, therefore, was whether the purpose to avoid disparate-impact liability excused what otherwise would be prohibited disparate-treatment discrimination.

The Court majority did not find such an excuse. The problem for the City, said Justice Kennedy's majority opinion, was that showing a significant statistical disparity between white and black test-takers, standing on its own, was not a solid enough basis for tossing the tests. That, he continued, is because the City could be liable for disparate-impact discrimination only if the exams at issue were not job related and consistent with business necessity, or if there existed an equally valid, less discriminatory alternative that served the City's needs but that the City refused to adopt. Based on the record before the Court, there was no substantial basis in the evidence that the test was deficient in either respect.

The Court in *Ricci* ruled that an employer must have solid evidence that it would be breaking the law, if it operationalized the results of a race-neutral promotion exam. A significant statistical disparity between how the two races performed on the assessment, standing alone, was not deemed to be sufficient to carry the day. So, just when is an employer justified in initiating a voluntary affirmative action program? What kind of evidence must the employer demonstrate to support the adoption of the affirmative action plan? What evidence must an individual who alleges discriminatory treatment by an employer acting pursuant to an affirmative action program demonstrate to establish a claim under Title VII?

In *Johnson v. Transportation Agency, Santa Clara County, California*,[19] the U.S. Supreme Court held that an employer can justify the adoption of an affirmative action plan by

[19] 480 U.S. 616 (1987).

showing that "a conspicuous … imbalance in traditionally segregated job categories" exists in its work force. A plaintiff challenging an employment decision based on an affirmative action plan has the burden of showing that the affirmative action plan is not valid. In *Johnson*, the Court upheld the legality of an affirmative action plan that granted a relative preference to women and minorities in hiring for positions in traditionally male-dominated jobs. The fact that the employer's plan had no definite termination date was not a problem, according to the court, because it did not set aside a specific number of positions. The plan used a flexible, case-by-case approach and was designed to attain a more balanced work force. The affirmative action plan, therefore, met the criteria set out in *Weber*: It furthered the purposes of Title VII by overcoming a manifest imbalance in traditionally segregated job categories, and it did not "unnecessarily trammel" the interests of the nonpreferred employees.

Both *Ricci* and *Johnson* involved suits under Title VII. When considering the legality of affirmative action programs under the U.S. Constitution, the approach used by the courts is slightly different from the approach used in Title VII cases. In *Wygant v. Jackson Board of Education*[20] and in *Adarand Constructors, Inc. v. Pena*,[21] the U.S. Supreme Court held that affirmative action plans by public sector employers must pass the strict scrutiny test under the U.S. Constitution. The strict scrutiny test, a two-part test, requires that (1) the affirmative action plan must serve a "compelling governmental interest," and (2) it must be "narrowly tailored" to further that compelling interest. Although the language of the test for the legality of affirmative action under Title VII and the test under the Constitution is similar, the Supreme Court has emphasized that the tests are distinct and different. In two cases that dealt with the constitutionality of using affirmative action criteria for admissions to the University of Michigan, and not with employment, *Grutter v. Bollinger*[22] and *Gratz v. Bollinger*,[23] a majority of the Supreme Court held that achieving the educational benefits of a diverse student body was a compelling governmental interest.[24] Those cases indicated that achieving the benefits of a diverse work force may be a sufficiently compelling governmental interest to justify the use of affirmative action programs for hiring or promotion decisions by public sector employers.

However, in 2013 the Supreme Court considered the legality of the University of Texas–Austin's policy of admitting the top 10 percent of all high school graduating classes. As the institution intended, this practice ensured the enrollment of a large number of students from minority-dominated school districts. The Court majority refrained from ruling on the legality of the scheme. Instead, it remanded the case to the U.S. Court of Appeals, instructing that the most rigorous standard of review—strict scrutiny—had to be applied to the university's facially neutral admission policy.[25] Many observers expected the lower court to reverse its earlier ruling in the university's favor, given the tough test of

---

[20] 476 U.S. 267 (1986).

[21] 515 U.S. 200 (1995).

[22] 539 U.S. 306 (2003).

[23] 539 U.S. 244 (2003).

[24] However, in the 2007 decision of *Parents Involved in Community Schools v. Seattle School Dist. No.1*, 127 S.Ct. 2738 (2007), the Supreme Court held that a public school system's goal of achieving racial diversity in schools did not justify the use of race as a factor in assigning pupils to a particular school.

[25] *Fisher v. University of Texas, at Austin*, 133 S.Ct. 2411 (2013).

legality dictated by the Supreme Court. To the contrary, in 2014, the U.S. Court of Appeals for the Fifth Circuit affirmed its ruling on the defendant's favor.[26] As this textbook went to press, the plaintiff's petition for a second trip up to the Supreme Court had been filed and remained pending.

Meanwhile, it is important to note that in addition to being justified by a compelling governmental interest, the affirmative action program must also be narrowly tailored to achieve that purpose. The courts have held that affirmative action programs that give a relative preference rather than an absolute one—race or gender is used as a "plus factor" rather than as the determinative factor—are narrowly tailored. Programs that are temporary and that will cease when the employer achieves a more diverse work force have also been held to be narrowly tailored. However, an affirmative action program that required laying off or firing nonminority employees was held to be unconstitutional in *Wygant v. Jackson Board of Education*.

The following case discusses the legality of an affirmative action plan under both Title VII and the Constitution.

CASE 6.5

UNIVERSITY AND COMMUNITY COLLEGE SYSTEM OF NEVADA V. FARMER

113 Nev. 90, 930 P.2d 730 (Nev. Sup. Ct. 1997), *cert. denied*, 523 U.S. 1004 (March 9, 1998)

Background

Between 1989 and 1991, only one percent of the University of Nevada's full-time faculty were black, while eighty-seven to eighty-nine percent of the full-time faculty were white; twenty-five to twenty-seven percent of the full-time faculty were women. In order to remedy this racial imbalance, the University instituted the "minority bonus policy," an unwritten amendment to its affirmative action policy which allowed a department to hire an additional faculty member following the initial placement of a minority candidate.

In 1990, the University advertised for an impending vacancy in the sociology department. The announcement of the position vacancy emphasized a need for proficiency in social psychology and mentioned a salary range between $28,000.00 and $34,000.00, dependent upon experience and qualifications. The University's hiring guidelines require departments to conduct more than one interview; however, this procedure may be waived in certain cases. Yvette Farmer was one of the three finalists chosen by the search committee for the position but the University obtained a waiver to interview only one candidate, Johnson Makoba, a black

African male emigrant. The department chair recalled that the search committee ranked Makoba first among the three finalists. Because of a perceived shortage of black Ph.D. candidates, coupled with Makoba's strong academic achievements, the search committee sought approval to make a job offer to Makoba at a salary of $35,000.00, with an increase to $40,000.00 upon completing his Ph.D. This initial offer exceeded the advertised salary range for the position; even though Makoba had not accepted any competing offers, the University justified its offer as a method of preempting any other institutions from hiring Makoba. Makoba accepted the job offer. Farmer was subsequently hired by the University the following year; the position for which she was hired was created under the "minority bonus policy." Her salary was set at $31,000.00 and a $2,000.00 raise after completion of her dissertation.

Farmer sued the University and Community College System of Nevada ("the University") claiming violations of Title VII of the Civil Rights Act, the Equal Pay Act and for breach of an employment contract. Farmer alleged that despite the fact that she was more qualified, the University

---

[26] *Fisher v. University of Texas at Austin*, 758 F.3d 274 (5th Cir. 2014), rehearing denied, 771 F.3d 274 (5th Cir. 2014).

hired a black male (Makoba) as an assistant professor of sociology instead of her because of the University's affirmative action plan. After a trial on her claims, the trial court jury awarded her $40,000 in damages, and the University appealed to the Supreme Court of Nevada. The issue on appeal was the legality of the University's affirmative action plan under both Title VII and the U.S. Constitution.

Steffen, Chief Justice

... Farmer claims that she was more qualified for the position initially offered to Makoba. However, the curriculum vitae for both candidates revealed comparable strengths with respect to their educational backgrounds, publishing, areas of specialization, and teaching experience. The search committee concluded that despite some inequalities, their strengths and weaknesses complemented each other; hence, as a result of the additional position created by the minority bonus policy, the department hired Farmer one year later.…

The University contends that the district court made a substantial error of law by failing to enter a proposed jury instruction which would have apprised the jury that Title VII does not proscribe race-based affirmative action programs designed to remedy the effects of past discrimination against traditionally disadvantaged classes. The University asserts that the district court's rejection of the proposed instruction left the jury with the impression that all race-based affirmative action programs are proscribed.…

Farmer … asserts that the University's unwritten minority bonus policy contravenes its published affirmative action plan. Finally, Farmer alleges that all race-based affirmative action plans are proscribed under Title VII of the Civil Rights Act as amended in 1991; therefore, the University discriminated against her as a female, a protected class under Title VII.

Tension exists between the goals of affirmative action and Title VII's proscription against employment practices which are motivated by considerations of race, religion, sex, or national origin, because Congress failed to provide a statutory exception for affirmative action under Title VII. Until recently, the Supreme Court's failure to achieve a majority opinion in affirmative action cases has produced schizophrenic results.…

United Steelworkers of America v. Weber is the seminal case defining permissible voluntary affirmative action plans [under Title VII].… Under *Weber*, a permissible voluntary affirmative action plan must: (1) further Title VII's statutory purpose by "break[ing] down old patterns of racial segregation and hierarchy" in "occupations which have been traditionally closed to them"; (2) not "unnecessarily trammel the interests of white employees"; (3) be "a temporary measure; it is not intended to maintain racial balance, but simply to eliminate a manifest racial imbalance." …

Most recently, in *Adarand Constructors, Inc. v. Pena*, the Supreme Court revisited [the issue of the constitutionality of] affirmative action in the context of a minority set-aside program in federal highway construction. In the 5–4 opinion, the Court held that a reviewing court must apply strict scrutiny analysis for all race-based affirmative action programs, whether enacted by a federal, state, or local entity.… [T]he Court explicitly stated "that federal racial classifications, like those of a State, must serve a compelling governmental interest, and must be narrowly tailored to further that interest." …

Here, in addition to considerations of race, the University based its employment decision on such criteria as educational background, publishing, teaching experience, and areas of specialization. This satisfies [the previous cases'] commands that race must be only one of several factors used in evaluating applicants. We also view the desirability of a racially diverse faculty as sufficiently analogous to the constitutionally permissible attainment of a racially diverse student body.…

The University's affirmative action plan conforms to the *Weber* factors [under Title VII]. The University's attempts to diversify its faculty by opening up positions traditionally closed to minorities satisfies the first factor under *Weber*. Second, the plan does not "unnecessarily trammel the interests of white employees." The University's 1992 Affirmative Action Report revealed that whites held eighty-seven to eighty-nine percent of the full-time faculty positions. Finally, with blacks occupying only one percent of the faculty positions, it is clear that through its minority bonus policy, the University attempted to attain, as opposed to maintain, a racial balance.

The University's affirmative action plan … [also] passes constitutional muster. The University demonstrated that it has a compelling interest in fostering a culturally and ethnically diverse faculty. A failure to attract minority faculty perpetuates the University's white enclave and further limits student exposure to multicultural diversity. Moreover, the minority bonus policy is narrowly tailored to accelerate racial and gender diversity. Through its affirmative action policies, the University achieved greater racial and gender diversity by hiring Makoba and Farmer. Of note is the fact that Farmer's position is a direct result of the minority bonus policy.

Although Farmer contends that she was more qualified for Makoba's position, the search committee determined that Makoba's qualifications slightly exceeded Farmer's. The record, however, reveals that both candidates were equal in most respects. Therefore, given the aspect of subjectivity involved in choosing between candidates, the University must be given the latitude to make its own employment decisions provided that they are not discriminatory.

[The court then rejected Farmer's claim that the 1991 amendments to Title VII prohibit affirmative action.]

... we conclude that the jury was not equipped to understand the necessary legal basis upon which it could reach its factual conclusions concerning the legality of the University's affirmative action plan. Moreover, the undisputed facts of this case warranted judgment in favor of the University as a matter of law. Therefore, even if the jury had been properly instructed, the district court should have granted the University's motion for judgment notwithstanding the [jury's] verdict. Reversal of the jury's verdict on the Title VII claim is therefore in order.

The University ... has adopted a lawful race-conscious affirmative action policy in order to remedy the effects of a manifest racial imbalance in a traditionally segregated job category....

The University has aggressively sought to achieve more than employment neutrality by encouraging its departments to hire qualified minorities, women, veterans, and handicapped individuals. The minority bonus policy, albeit an unwritten one, is merely a tool for achieving cultural diversity and furthering the substantive goals of affirmative action.

For the reasons discussed above, the University's affirmative action policies pass constitutional muster. Farmer has failed to raise any material facts or law which would render the University's affirmative action policy constitutionally infirm....

Young and Rose, JJ., concur.
Springer, J., dissenting [omitted]

Case Questions

1. Why did the university adopt its affirmative action plan and the "minority bonus policy"?

2. How was Farmer injured or disadvantaged under the university's affirmative action plan?

3. How does the Court here apply the Weber test for legality of affirmative action under Title VII to the facts of this case? Explain your answer.

4. According to the Court, how does the constitutional "strict scrutiny" test apply to the facts of the case here? Explain your answer.

The affirmative action plan in the previous case was a voluntary plan; that is, it was not imposed upon the employer by a court to remedy a finding of illegal discrimination. The affirmative action plans in the *Weber*, *Johnson*, and *Wygant* cases were also voluntary plans. Title VII specifically mentions affirmative action as a possible remedy available under §706(g)(1). In *Local 28, Sheet Metal Workers Int. Ass'n. v. EEOC*,[27] the Supreme Court held that Title VII permits a court to require the adoption of an affirmative action program to remedy "persistent or egregious discrimination." The Court in *U.S. v. Paradise*[28] upheld the constitutionality of a judicially imposed affirmative action program to remedy race discrimination in promotion decisions by the Alabama State Police.

ethical DILEMMA

You are the human resource manager for Wydget Corporation, a small manufacturing company. Wydget's assembly plant is located in an inner-city neighborhood, and most of its production employees are African Americans and Hispanics,

---

[27] 478 U.S. 421 (1986).
[28] 480 U.S. 149 (1987).

as well as some Vietnamese and Laotians who live nearby. Wydget's managers are white males who sometimes have difficulty relating to the production workers. The board of directors of Wydget is considering whether to establish a training program to groom production workers for management positions, targeting women and minorities in particular. The CEO has asked you to prepare a memo to guide the board of directors in its decision about the training program. Should you establish such a program? How can you encourage minority employees to enter the program without discouraging the white employees? What criteria should be used for determining admission into the training program? Address these issues in a short memo, explaining and supporting your position.

6-7 Other Provisions of Title VII

The 1991 amendments to Title VII added two other provisions to the act. One addresses the ability to challenge affirmative action programs and other employment practices that implement judicial decisions or result from consent decrees. Section 703(n) now provides that such practice may not be challenged by any person who had notice of such decision or decree and had an opportunity to present objections or by any person whose interests were adequately represented by another person who had previously challenged the judgment or decree on the same legal ground and with a similar factual situation. Challenges based on claims that the order or decree was obtained through fraud or collusion, is "transparently invalid," or was entered by a court lacking jurisdiction are not prevented by Section 703(n).

The other added provision deals with the practice known as "race norming." Race norming refers to the use of different cutoff scores for different racial, gender, or ethnic groups of applicants or adjusting test scores or otherwise altering test results of employment-related tests on the basis of race, color, religion, sex, or national origin. Section 703(l) makes race norming an unlawful employment practice under Title VII.

CHAPTER REVIEW

» Key Terms

» Summary

- Equal employment opportunity (EEO) legislation represents a statutory limitation on the employment-at-will doctrine. The EEO laws prohibit termination and other forms of employment discrimination because of an employee's race, color, gender, religion, or national origin. Title VII of the Civil Rights Act of 1964, as amended, protects all individuals from intentional discrimination (known as disparate treatment) as well as the unintentionally discriminatory effect of apparently neutral criteria that are not job related (known as disparate impact).

- Employers are free to hire employees who can effectively perform the job. The Uniform Guidelines on Employee Selection define methods for employers to demonstrate that employment selection criteria are job related; employers can use content-related, criterion-related, or construct-related validity studies to meet the requirements of Section 703(k). Employers are also free to use seniority for employment decisions, as long as the seniority system is bona fide under Section 703(h) of Title VII.

- Affirmative action, giving some employees preferential treatment because of their race, color, or gender, has become more controversial in recent years. Remedial affirmative action, designed to remedy the lingering effects of prior illegal discrimination, has been endorsed by the courts; the *Weber* and *Johnson* decisions allow voluntary affirmative action under Title VII when it is consistent with the purposes of the act and does not unduly harm those persons who are not of the preferred group. More recent decisions of the U.S. Supreme Court indicate that the Court will look very closely at an employer's justification for adopting an affirmative action program.

» Problems

» Questions

1. What are the main provisions of Title VII of the Civil Rights Act? Which employers are subject to Title VII? What employees or applicants are protected from employment discrimination by Title VII?

2. What is meant by a bona fide occupational qualification (BFOQ)? What must be shown to establish that job-selection requirements are a BFOQ?

3. What is meant by disparate treatment? What is meant by disparate impact? What is the difference between disparate treatment and disparate impact? How can a claim of disparate impact be demonstrated?

4. When is a seniority system protected against challenge under Title VII? When is a seniority system bona fide under Title VII?

5. What are the Uniform Guidelines for Employee Selection? What is the Four-Fifths Rule, and how is it used?

» Case Problems

6. Southeastern Pennsylvania Transportation Authority (SEPTA) is a regional mass transit authority in the Philadelphia area. SEPTA sought to upgrade the fitness level of its transit police by adopting a requirement that, in order to be hired as transit police, job applicants must be able to run 1.5 miles in 12 minutes or less.

   The requirement was developed by a consultant to SEPTA, Dr. Paul Davis, after he studied the job of transit officer for several days. He felt that completion of the 1.5-mile run within the required time would ensure that the applicant possessed sufficient aerobic capacity to perform the job. SEPTA also tested transit officers hired prior to the adoption of the 1.5-mile run requirement, and discovered that a significant percentage of the incumbents could not complete the run within the required time limit. Some of the incumbent employees who failed the run requirement had been awarded special recognition and commendations for their job performance. One female employee, hired by mistake after she had failed the requirement, was nominated for Officer of the Year awards because of her job performance.

After the adoption of the 1.5-mile run requirement, only 12 percent of the female applicants successfully passed it, while 56 percent of the male applicants passed it; SEPTA employed 234 transit police officers, but only 16 of the officers were female. A group of female applicants who failed the 1.5-mile run requirement filed suit against SEPTA under Title VII, alleging that the 1.5-mile run requirement had a disparate impact on women. SEPTA argued that the more physically fit officers are, the better they are able to perform their job.

Will the plaintiffs be successful in their suit, or can SEPTA establish that the 1.5-mile run requirement is job related? Explain your answer. [See *Lanning v. Southeastern Pennsylvania Transportation Authority*, 181 F.3d 478 (3d Cir. 1999), *cert. denied*, 528 U.S. 1131 (Mem. 2000).]

7. The defendant's foreman on a series of terrazzo-flooring installations apparently treated all of his subordinates "abominably," according to the court. Plaintiff Jesse Thompson, the only African American worker on the crew, testified that the foreman belittled him for being "cool" with the "white mother fuckers" who were his coworkers. He allegedly called Thompson an "F'ing Uncle Tom" and "whitewash." He also allegedly called Thompson a "nigger." In fact, the evidence suggested he did so frequently. The foreman likewise called Thompson's Latino coworkers "mother fucking wetbacks," and did so "all the time." By the same token, he referred to Plaintiff Vitaliy Ostapyuk, a Caucasian born in Ukraine, as a "fucking Russian."

Because the foreman apparently was an "equal opportunity harasser," is it possible that his language did not violate Title VII? [See *Thompson v. North American Terrazzo, Inc.*, 2015 WL 926575 (W.D. Wash. 2015).]

8. The plaintiff was a Guyanese male of Indian ancestry. A crane operator, he worked for the defendant on projects involving the New York City subway system. When the contract was lost to a competitor, the plaintiff and all his coworkers were hired by the successful bidder. But when the defendant won the contract back, the company declined to bring the plaintiff back, although it rehired all of his coworkers. The plaintiff complained that he was the Indian and one of only two employees of color in his job category. The company countered his claims by articulating its business justification, namely, that it chose to bring back only operators who had experience working on a specific part of the project. Labeling this reason a pretext, the plaintiff proffered the demographic data he had regarding the racial composition of the defendant's workforce. The company objected, arguing that without an expert to explain the numbers, this evidence had to be excluded.

Do you believe that the plaintiff should be permitted to show a jury how underrepresented was his race in the defendant's workforce? Or, alternatively, should his case of race discrimination have to rise or fall on whatever evidence of disparate treatment he is able to produce? [See *Singh v. Bay Crane Service Inc.*, 2015 WL 918678 (E.D.N.Y. 2015).]

9. The plaintiff was an African American woman working as a licensed practical nurse working in the defendant hospital. She was initially assigned to a white patient, identified by the court as Patient X. When patient X objected to receiving healthcare from people of color, the plaintiff was reassigned. According to the court, the plaintiff "by all accounts" was a perfectly competent LPN. The evidence also indicated that Patient X, a Hispanic female, was hospitalized due to a mugging inflicted by a black male. The hospital had antidiscrimination policies in place, and there was no evidence that the plaintiff's reassignment at Patient X's request formed any sort of a pattern of racial matching in assignments of caregivers to patients.

On these facts, did the hospital violate Title VII by reassigning the plaintiff? [See *Dysart v. Palms of Passedna Hospital, LP*, --- F. Supp. 3d ---, 2015 WL 864881 (M.D. Fla. 2015).]

10. The plaintiff, a black female, worked as a molding supervisor for the defendant. She sued, complaining that she was paid less than her counterparts, all

white males. The company responded that the disparity was based on her fellow supervisors' technical skills, such as the ability to tear down molds, repair and adjust the molding machines, work with resins, and engage in troubleshooting. Labeling this explanation a pretext for discrimination, the plaintiff argued that these skills were irrelevant to the essential functions of her supervisory position. To the contrary, while she admitted lacking such a skill set, she claimed to have been told not to tinker with the machines.

Assuming that the plaintiff was able to prove she competently performed all her supervisory duties, but the defendant proved that handling the machinery was a useful, though not essential, aspect of the job, do you think the firm has borne its burden of articulating a legitimate business reason for paying the plaintiff less than her white colleagues? [See *Henderson v. Mid-South Electronics, Inc.*, 2015 WL 875381 (N.D. Ala. 2015).]

11. The plaintiff, an African American, claimed that a white coworker informed her that the manager of the restaurant where she worked told this coworker she wouldn't be safe at that location because the staff was "mostly black." The plaintiff further alleged that when she went over the manager's head and filed a complaint, her hours were cut back.

If here allegations are accurate, has the plaintiff articulated a prima facie case of race discrimination? Of retaliation? [See *Johnson v. River Road Restaurants, LLC*, 2015 WL 853461 (N.D. Ohio 2015).]

12. Wal-Mart's Transportation Division includes approximately 8,000 drivers in 47 field transportation offices nationwide. The hiring process for drivers at every transportation office is identical. First, new drivers are recruited almost exclusively through the "word of mouth" referral by current Wal-Mart drivers. Wal-Mart provides current drivers with a "1-800 card" to pass out to prospective applicants. The card lists the minimum driver qualifications and a 1-800 number drivers can call to request an application. Wal-Mart does little advertising of its over-the-road (OTR) driver

positions in addition to the 1-800 cards. Potential applicants who call the 1-800 number, regardless of the transportation office to which they wish to apply, are initially processed and screened at Wal-Mart's Bentonville headquarters. An application is then sent to the potential applicant. The applicant is instructed to return the completed application to the Bentonville headquarters. If the application is completed and the applicant meets the minimum requirements, and if the applicant's preferred transportation office is currently hiring, the application is then forwarded to the appropriate transportation office. Sometimes an applicant submits an application directly to a transportation office. After the application is forwarded from the Bentonville headquarters to the appropriate transportation office, a screening committee, consisting of current drivers at the transportation office, decides which applicants will be granted an interview, and then interviews those applicants. A management committee then interviews applicants who successfully complete the screening committee interview.

Wal-Mart has no written or objective criteria to guide the driver screening committees when those committees analyze applicants during the hiring process. Wal-Mart does require each driver screening committee to be 50 percent diverse, but that does not guarantee that any member of the screening committee is African American.

Tommy Armstrong and Darryl Nelson are African American truck drivers who applied for positions as OTR truck drivers at transportation offices operated by Wal-Mart; their applications were rejected. They discover that African Americans represent 8.4 percent of Wal-Mart's OTR drivers nationwide; a study prepared for the American Trucking Association using U.S. Census Bureau data indicates that African Americans represent about 15 percent of persons employed as "driver/sales workers or truck drivers" in the "truck transportation" industry nationwide in the United States. Armstrong and Nelson decide to file a suit under Title VII against Wal-Mart.

Would their claim involve disparate impact or disparate treatment discrimination? What problems may be raised by the "word of mouth" referral system for recruiting new drivers? What defenses could Wal-Mart raise in response to their suit? [See *Nelson v. Mal-Mart Stores, Inc.*, 2009 WL 88550 (E.D. Ark. Jan. 13, 2009).]

13. The plaintiff sued, alleging race discrimination, after he was denied what he characterized as a "promotion." The defendant countered the claim with evidence that the position for which the plaintiff applied was in effect a mere "lateral move," and not a promotion at all.

    If the court agrees with the defendant that the position sought by the plaintiff was no better than a lateral move, should the company prevail, whether or not race discrimination underlay the denial of his application? [See *Merriweather v. Charter Communications, LLC*, 2015 WL 790771 (M.D. Ala. 2015).]

14. The plaintiff, a white male, applied for an "At-Home Adviser" job in the defendant's customer service division. After his application was reviewed, he was offered an audio-visual interview using Skype. The plaintiff didn't get the job. In his complaint he claimed that the scheduled 20-minute interview was terminated in under 10 minutes, because as soon as the Hispanic interviewer ascertained the plaintiff was white, he cut the session short. The defendant, for its part, countered that the plaintiff came across as "cold." Disputing this characterization, the plaintiff testified that he was "fantastic," projecting his "amazing ability to work with people."

    How should the court go about resolving this credibility dispute? [See *Shomo v. Apple, Inc.*, 2015 WL 777620 (W.D. Va. 2015).]

15. The plaintiff was employed by the Postal Service since 1999. During that decade and a half, he compiled a history of suing his employer several times. This time around he challenged a warning letter and a suspension without pay, alleging that both were acts of race discrimination.

    How much weight should the court place on his prior litigious history in weighing the merits of this case? Should his success or failure record be a factor in this determination? [See *Avillan v. Donahoe*, 2015 WL 728169 (S.D.N.Y. 2015).]

» Hypothetical Scenarios

16. Cantor Enterprises is a public relations and advertising agency; its clerical and administrative staff are represented by a union. A number of the clerical staff are college graduates with marketing or advertising degrees who hope to be promoted into a copywriter or account manager position; however, such workers become discouraged if there are no higher positions open, and their job performance deteriorates or they quit. The result is a high turnover rate for the clerical and administrative positions. Cantor and the union decide that the company will no longer hire college graduates for entry-level clerical and administrative positions. Does this "no college degree" rule violate Title VII? Explain your answer.

17. Stith, Inc. operates a small manufacturing plant. In order to upgrade its workforce, Stith's human resources manager decides as of January 1, 2009, to adopt a requirement that the company will only hire applicants with a high school diploma or equivalent. Previously, Stith had only required applicants to complete a simple aptitude test, and a number of current employees are not high school graduates. Does the new requirement raise any problems under Title VII? Explain.

18. Cratchit worked as a staff accountant for Scrooge & Partners. Scrooge asks Cratchit to interview the applicants for an administrative assistant position, but tells him not to hire any African American applicants. Cratchit reminds Scrooge that Title VII prohibits race discrimination, and Scrooge immediately removes Cratchit from the interview process and cuts his working hours from 40 hours per week to 30 hours per week. Has Scrooge violated Title VII? Why? Is Cratchit protected by Title VII in this situation? Explain.

19. A local call center is seeking to expand its work force. Because of the nature of its work, the call center decides to hire only persons who speak perfect English and not to hire any person who has a noticeable accent or, in the words of the call center manager, "who sounds too much like a minority." Does the call center hiring policy violate Title VII? Explain your answer.

20. HomeCare provides healthcare aides who work in the homes of its clients, who are generally elderly or disabled persons. Some of the clients are bedridden and require total personal care. HomeCare screens applicants for employment by using a strength test—the applicants must be able to lift a dummy weighing 150 pounds. The strength test disqualifies most female applicants, as well as a majority of Asian and Hispanic male applicants. What must HomeCare do to show that the strength test has validity under the Uniform Guidelines? Should HomeCare use a construct validity, a content validity, or a criterion-related validity approach for the strength test? Explain.

CHAPTER 7

Gender and Family Issues: Title VII and Other Legislation

The preceding chapter introduced Title VII of the Civil Rights Act of 1964 and discussed its prohibitions on employment discrimination based on race. This chapter focuses on discrimination based on gender, family-related issues, and the relevant provisions of Title VII and other legislation.

7-1 Gender Discrimination

bona fide occupational qualification (BFOQ)
an exception to the civil rights law that allows an employer to hire employees of a specific gender, religion, or national origin when business necessity— the safe and efficient performance of the particular job—requires it

Title VII prohibits any discrimination in terms or conditions of employment because of an employee's sex; it also prohibits limiting, segregating, or classifying employees or applicants in any way that would deprive individuals of employment opportunities or otherwise adversely affect their status as employees because of their sex. (While some people may argue that sex is a biological or physical construct and gender is a psychological and sociological construct, the courts have generally treated the terms "sex" and "gender" as interchangeable.) Title VII protects all individuals from employment discrimination based on sex or gender; this means both men and women are protected from sex discrimination in employment. Employers who refuse to hire an individual for a particular job because of that individual's gender violate Title VII unless the employer can demonstrate that being of a particular gender is a **bona fide occupational qualification (BFOQ)** for that job. The act also prohibits advertising for male or female employees in help-wanted notices (unless it is a BFOQ) or maintaining separate seniority lists for male and female employees. Unions that negotiate such separate seniority lists or refuse to admit female members also violate Title VII.

7-1a Dress Codes and Grooming Requirements

The act prohibits imposing different working conditions or requirements on similarly situated male and female employees because of the employee's gender. Some cases have involved employer dress codes and grooming standards. Employers need not have identical dress code or grooming requirements for men and women. For example, men may be required to wear a necktie while women are not, *Fountain v. Safeway Stores, Inc.*[1]; men may be required to wear suits while women must wear "appropriate business attire," *Baker v. California Land Title Co.*[2]; or women may be permitted to wear long hair while males are not permitted to have hair below the collar, *Willingham v. Macon Tel. Publishing Co.*[3] The key is that the standards are related to commonly accepted social norms and are reasonably related to legitimate business needs; however, an employer who requires women to wear a uniform but has no such requirement for men violates Title VII, *Carroll v. Talman Federal Savings & Loan Assoc.*[4]

7-1b Gender as a BFOQ

As mentioned in Chapter 6, the act does allow employers to hire only employees of one sex, or of a particular religion or national origin, if that trait is a BFOQ; most BFOQ cases involve BFOQs based on gender. Section 703(e)(1), which defines the BFOQ exemption, states that

> . . . it shall not be an unlawful employment practice for an employer to hire and employ employees, for an employment agency to classify, or refer for employment any individual, for a labor organization to classify its membership or to classify or refer for employment any individual . . . on the basis of his religion, sex, or national origin in those certain instances where religion, sex, or national origin is a bona fide occupational qualification reasonably necessary to the normal operation of that particular business or enterprise. . . .

The statute requires that an employer justify a BFOQ on the basis of business necessity. In other words, the safe and efficient performance of the job in question requires that the employee be of a particular gender, religion, or national origin. Employer convenience, customer preference, or coworker preference is not sufficient to support a BFOQ. The additional costs to provide bathroom facilities for female workers was also not a sufficient basis to establish a BFOQ. What must an employer demonstrate to establish a claim of business necessity? The following case illustrates the approach taken by the courts when an employer claims a BFOQ based on gender.

» CASE 7.1

AMBAT V. CITY AND COUNTY OF SAN FRANCISCO
757 F.3d 1017 (9th Cir. 2014)

Facts: In October 2006, the San Francisco Sheriff's Department implemented a new policy prohibiting male deputies from supervising female inmates in the housing units of the jails operated by the county. Single-sex staffing policies in correctional facilities are not new, and the court noted that it had considered before whether such polices violate Title VII by impermissibly discriminating on the basis of sex. [*See Breiner v. Nevada Dep't of Corr.*, 610 F.3d

---

[1] 555 F.2d 753 (9th Cir. 1977).

[2] 507 F.2d 895 (9th Cir. 1974), *cert. denied*, 422 U.S. 1046 (1975).

[3] 507 F.2d 1084 (5th Cir. 1975).

[4] 604 F.2d 1028 (7th Cir. 1979), *cert. denied*, 445 U.S. 929 (1980).

1202 (9th Cir. 2010) (holding policy violated Title VII); *Robino v. Iranon*, 145 F.3d 1109 (9th Cir. 1998) (per curiam) (holding policy did not violate Title VII).]

The adoption of the policy coincided with SFSD's plan to consolidate all of its female inmates within a single facility, County Jail 8 ("CJ8"). CJ8 had a "direct supervision" design, meaning that its housing units, or "pods," were composed of cells or sleeping bays arrayed around a central congregation space. Each pod had two tiers and between 56 and 88 beds. At the center of the pod was a podium from which a deputy could see into common areas and into the cells and sleeping bays. Each pod was staffed by two deputies, one of whom remain at the podium while the other made rounds. Female inmates filled some, but not all, of the available housing pods in CJ8. Even though CJ8 was not single-sex, all of its pods were single-sex. This was consistent with SFSD's long-standing practice of segregating female and male inmates.

Although housing pods were single-sex, CJ8's pod for inmates receiving medical or psychiatric care was not sex-segregated. Male deputies were not permitted under the Policy to work with female inmates in the housing pods; however, male deputies might be assigned to the mixed-sex medical pod or assigned to transport female inmates between CJ8 and other locations. Male deputies might also enter female housing pods in some circumstances, such as to assist with feeding female inmates.

According to San Francisco Sheriff Michael Hennessey, who had held his position since 1980, he adopted the policy for four reasons: (1) to protect the safety of female inmates from sexual misconduct perpetrated by male deputies, (2) to maintain the security of the jail in the face of female inmates' ability to manipulate male deputies and of the deputies' fear of false allegations of sexual misconduct by the inmates, (3) to protect the privacy of female inmates, and (4) to promote the successful rehabilitation of female inmates.

Issue: Did the SFSD articulate a bona fide occupational qualification for its rule forbidding male guards from supervising female inmates?

Decision: The justifications offered by the county in support of the policy each spoke to extremely important concerns, according to the court, which added that "the Sheriff is to be commended for his attention to the welfare of female inmates in San Francisco's jails." However, continued the appellate judges, the fact that the policy sought to advance such important goals as inmate safety was not, by itself, sufficient to permit discrimination on the basis of sex. When moving for summary judgment, the county bore the heavy burden of showing that there were no genuine issues of material fact as to whether excluding male deputies because of their sex was a legitimate substitute for excluding them because they were actually unfit to serve in the female housing pods. On the record before the appeals court, the county had not made such a showing.

Therefore, the case was remanded to the trial judge for further proceedings to resolve the disputed facts identified in this decision.

《

In *Dothard v. Rawlinson*,[5] the U.S. Supreme Court held that the dangers presented by the conditions in Alabama maximum security prisons, characterized as "rampant violence" and "a jungle atmosphere," would reduce the ability of female guards to maintain order and would pose dangers to the female guards and to other prisoners. The Court therefore upheld as a BFOQ an Alabama state regulation restricting guard positions in maximum security prisons to persons of the same gender as the prisoners being guarded. The *Ambat* case perhaps suggests that in 2015 federal judges are less willing to exclude an entire gender category on the basis of generalized concerns; the Ninth Circuit seems to be saying that employees' fitness for the job must be ascertained on a case-by-case basis rather than under a broad BFOQ determination. As the following item illustrates, even the U.S. military is prepared to adopt a case-by-case determination over a BFOQ resolution.

---

[5] 433 U.S. 321 (1977).

THE **WORKING** LAW

Corps' Top Leaders Address Lifting of Combat Exclusion Policy

Defense Secretary Leon E. Panetta officially announced the end of the 1994 Direct Ground Combat Definition and Assignment Rule excluding women from assignment to units and positions whose primary mission is to engage in direct ground combat, Jan. 24.

"This milestone reflects the courageous and patriotic service of women through more than two centuries of American history and the indispensable role of women in today's military," said President Barack Obama.

Rescinding the exclusion opens about 237,000 positions to women Department of Defense-wide. Of the DoD total, 54,721 are Marine positions: 38,445 in combat-related military occupational specialties and 15,276 in assignments with ground combat units.

SgtMaj Micheal P. Barrett, the 17th Sergeant Major of the Marine Corps, addressed Marines in a video regarding the ending of the exclusion policy, stressing that the rescinding of this policy will not impair readiness, degrade combat effectiveness or cohesion.

"Our plan is deliberate, measured, and responsible," he said. "We will not lower our standards."

"The decision as to whether or not to do this has passed," said Lt. Gen. Robert Milstead, the Deputy Commandant, Manpower and Reserve Affairs. "We are doing this the right way.

"Does this mean that we're immediately going to open every MOS? No. MOSs like infantry, reconnaissance and Marine special operations will not be immediately opened."

For well over the past year, the Secretary of Defense has been working closely with the Chairman of the Joint Chiefs of Staff, and all of the military service chiefs, to examine how to expand the opportunities for women in the armed services.

"It's clear to all of us that women are contributing in unprecedented ways to the military's mission of defending the nation," Panetta said. "They're serving in a growing number of critical roles on and off the battlefield. The fact is that they have become an integral part of our ability to perform our mission."

Goals and milestones have been established by DoD to support of the elimination of unnecessary gender-based barriers to women's service to provide the time necessary to institutionalize the changes and integrate women into occupational fields in a climate where they can succeed and flourish.

"As our Corps moves forward with this process, our focus will remain on combat readiness and generating combat-ready units while simultaneously ensuring maximum success for every Marine," said Gen. James F. Amos, the 35th Commandant of the Marine Corps. "The talent pool from which we select our finest warfighters will consist of all qualified individuals, regardless of gender."

Source: Sgt Megan Angel, "Corps' top leaders address lifting of Combat Exclusion Policy," Marines Blog, February 19 2013, available at http://www.marines.com/news/-/news-story/detail /NEWS_19FEB2013_LEADERSADDRESSCOMBATEXCLUSIONPOLICY_MARINESBLOG.

7-1c   Gender Stereotyping

If an employer refuses to promote a female employee because, despite her excellent performance, she is perceived as being too aggressive and unfeminine, has the employer engaged in sex discrimination in violation of Title VII? This question was addressed by the Supreme Court in the following case.

CASE 7.2

PRICE WATERHOUSE V. ANN B. HOPKINS

490 U.S. 228 (1989)

[Ann Hopkins, a senior manager in an office of Price Waterhouse, was proposed for partnership in 1982. She was neither offered nor denied admission to the partnership; instead, her candidacy was held for reconsideration the following year. When the partners in her office later refused to repropose her for partnership, she sued under Title VII of the Civil Rights Act of 1964, charging that the firm had discriminated against her on the basis of sex in its decisions regarding partnership. The trial court ruled in her favor on the question of liability, and the U.S. Court of Appeals for the District of Columbia Circuit affirmed. Price Waterhouse then appealed to the U.S. Supreme Court, which granted *certiorari* to hear the appeal.]

Brennan, J.

At Price Waterhouse, a nationwide professional accounting partnership, a senior manager becomes a candidate for partnership when the partners in her local office submit her name as a candidate. All the other partners in the firm are then invited to submit written comments on each candidate—either on a "long" or a "short" form, depending on the partner's degree of exposure to the candidate. Not every partner in the firm submits comments on every candidate. After reviewing the comments and interviewing the partners who submitted them, the firm's Admissions Committee makes a recommendation to the Policy Board. This recommendation will be either that the firm accept the candidate for partnership, put her application on "hold," or deny her the promotion outright. The Policy Board then decides whether to submit the candidate's name to the entire partnership for a vote, to "hold" her candidacy, or to reject her. The recommendation of the Admissions Committee, and the decision of the Policy Board, are not controlled by fixed guidelines: a certain number of positive comments from partners will not guarantee a candidate's admission to the partnership, nor will a specific quantity of negative comments necessarily defeat her application. . . .

Ann Hopkins had worked at Price Waterhouse's Office of Government Services in Washington, D.C. for five years when the partners in that office proposed her as a candidate for partnership. Of the 662 partners at the firm at that time, 7 were women. Of the 88 persons proposed for partnership that year, only 1—Hopkins—was a woman. Forty-seven of these candidates were admitted to the partnership, 21 were rejected, and 20—including Hopkins—were "held" for reconsideration the following year. Thirteen of the 32 partners who had submitted comments on Hopkins supported her bid for partnership. Three partners recommended that her candidacy be placed on hold, eight stated that they did not have an informed opinion about her, and eight recommended that she be denied partnership.

In a jointly prepared statement supporting her candidacy, the partners in Hopkins' office showcased her successful 2-year effort to secure a $25 million contract with the Department of State, labeling it "an outstanding performance" and one that Hopkins carried out "virtually at the partner level." . . . Judge Gesell specifically found that Hopkins had "played a key role in Price Waterhouse's successful effort to win a multi-million dollar contract with the Department of State." Indeed, he went on, "[n]one of the other partnership candidates at Price Waterhouse that year had a comparable record in terms of successfully securing major contracts for the partnership." The partners in Hopkins' office praised her character as well as her accomplishments, describing her in their joint statement as "an outstanding professional" who had a "deft touch," a "strong character, independence and integrity."

Clients appear to have agreed with these assessments. . . . Evaluations such as these led Judge Gesell to conclude that Hopkins "had no difficulty dealing with clients and her clients appear to have been very pleased with her work" and that she "was generally viewed as a highly competent project leader who worked long hours, pushed vigorously to meet deadlines and demanded much from the multidisciplinary staffs with which she worked."

On too many occasions, however, Hopkins' aggressiveness apparently spilled over into abrasiveness. Staff members seem to have borne the brunt of Hopkins' brusqueness. Long before her bid for partnership, partners evaluating her work had counseled her to improve her relations with staff members. Although later evaluations indicate an improvement, Hopkins' perceived shortcomings in this important area eventually doomed her bid for partnership. Virtually all of the partners' negative remarks about Hopkins—even those of partners supporting her—had to do with her "interpersonal skills." Both "[s]upporters and opponents of her candidacy," stressed Judge Gesell, "indicated that she was sometimes overly aggressive, unduly harsh, difficult to work with and impatient with staff."

There were clear signs, though, that some of the partners reacted negatively to Hopkins' personality because she was a woman. One partner described her as "macho"; another suggested that she "overcompensated for being a woman"; a third advised her to take "a course at charm school." Several partners criticized her use of profanity; in response, one partner suggested that those partners objected to her swearing only "because it[']s a lady using foul language." Another supporter explained that Hopkins "ha[d] matured from a tough-talking somewhat masculine hard-nosed mgr to an authoritative, formidable, but much more appealing lady ptr candidate." But it was the man who, as Judge Gesell found, bore responsibility for explaining to Hopkins the reasons for the Policy Board's decision to place her candidacy on hold who delivered the *coup de grace*: in order to improve her chances for partnership, Thomas Beyer advised, Hopkins should "walk more femininely, talk more femininely, dress more femininely, wear make-up, have her hair styled, and wear jewelry."

Dr. Susan Fiske, a social psychologist and Associate Professor of Psychology at Carnegie-Mellon University, testified at trial that the partnership selection process at Price Waterhouse was likely influenced by sex stereotyping. Her testimony focused not only on the overtly sex-based comments of partners but also on gender-neutral remarks, made by partners who knew Hopkins only slightly, that were intensely critical of her. One partner, for example, baldly stated that Hopkins was "universally disliked" by staff, and another described her as "consistently annoying and irritating"; yet these were people who had had very little contact with Hopkins. According to Fiske, Hopkins' uniqueness (as the only woman in the pool of candidates) and the subjectivity of the evaluations made it likely that sharply critical remarks such as these were the product of sex stereotyping. . . .

In previous years, other female candidates for partnership also had been evaluated in sex-based terms. As a general matter, Judge Gesell concluded "[c]andidates were viewed favorably if partners believed they maintained their femin[in]ity while becoming effective professional managers"; in this environment, "[t]o be identified as a 'women's lib[b]er' was regarded as [a] negative comment." In fact, the judge found that in previous years "[o]ne partner repeatedly commented that he could not consider any woman seriously as a partnership candidate and believed that women were not even capable of functioning as senior managers—yet the firm took no action to discourage his comments and recorded his vote in the overall summary of the evaluations."

Judge Gesell found that Price Waterhouse legitimately emphasized interpersonal skills in its partnership decisions, and also found that the firm had not fabricated its complaints about Hopkins' interpersonal skills as a pretext for discrimination. Moreover, he concluded, the firm did not give decisive emphasis to such traits only because Hopkins was a woman; although there were male candidates who lacked these skills but who were admitted to partnership, the judge found that these candidates possessed other, positive traits that Hopkins lacked.

The judge went on to decide, however, that some of the partners' remarks about Hopkins stemmed from an impermissibly cabined view of the proper behavior of women, and that Price Waterhouse had done nothing to disavow reliance on such comments. He held that Price Waterhouse had unlawfully discriminated against Hopkins on the basis of sex by consciously giving credence and effect to partners' comments that resulted from sex stereotyping. Noting that Price Waterhouse could avoid equitable relief by proving by clear and convincing evidence that it would have placed Hopkins' candidacy on hold even absent this discrimination, the judge decided that the firm had not carried this heavy burden. . . .

Congress' intent to forbid employers to take gender into account in making employment decisions appears on the face of the statute. . . . We take these words [of Title VII] to mean that gender must be irrelevant to employment decisions. . . . The critical inquiry, the one commanded by the words of Section 703(a)(1), is whether gender was a factor in the employment decision *at the moment it was made*. Moreover, since we know that the words "because of do not mean "solely because of," we also know that Title VII meant to condemn even those decisions based on a mixture of legitimate and illegitimate considerations. When, therefore, an employer considers both gender and legitimate factors at the time of making a decision, that decision was "because of sex and the other, legitimate considerations—even if we may say later, in the context of litigation, that the decision would have been the same if gender had not been taken into account. . . .

. . . The central point is this: while an employer may not take gender into account in making an employment decision (except in those very narrow circumstances in which gender is a BFOQ), it is free to decide against a woman for other reasons . . . the employer's burden is most appropriately deemed an affirmative defense: the plaintiff must persuade the factfinder on one point, and then the employer, if it wishes to prevail, must persuade it on another.

. . . our assumption always has been that if an employer allows gender to affect its decision making process, then it must carry the burden of justifying its ultimate decision. . . .

In saying that gender played a motivating part in an employment decision, we mean that, if we asked the employer at the moment of the decision what its reasons were and if we received a truthful response, one of those reasons would be that the applicant or employee was a woman. In the specific context of sex stereotyping, an employer who acts on the basis of a belief that a woman cannot be aggressive, or that she must not be, has acted on the basis of gender. . . .

As to the existence of sex stereotyping in this case, we are not inclined to quarrel with the District Court's conclusion that a number of the partners' comments showed sex stereotyping at work. As for the legal relevance of sex stereotyping, we are beyond the day when an employer could evaluate employees by assuming or insisting that they matched the stereotype associated with their group, for "[i]n forbidding employers to discriminate against individuals because of their sex, Congress intended to strike at the entire spectrum of disparate treatment of men and women resulting from sex stereotypes." An employer who objects to aggressiveness in women but whose positions require this trait places women in an intolerable and impermissible Catch-22: out of a job if they behave aggressively and out of a job if they don't. Title VII lifts women out of this bind.

Remarks at work that are based on sex stereotypes do not inevitably prove that gender played a part in a particular employment decision. The plaintiff must show that the employer actually relied on her gender in making its decision. In making this showing, stereotyped remarks can certainly be evidence that gender played a part. In any event, the stereotyping in this case did not simply consist of stray remarks. On the contrary, Hopkins proved that Price Waterhouse invited

partners to submit comments; that some of the comments stemmed from sex stereotyping; that an important part of the Policy Board's decision on Hopkins was an assessment of the submitted comments; and that Price Waterhouse in no way disclaimed reliance on the sex-linked evaluations. This is not, as Price Waterhouse suggests, "discrimination in the air"; rather, it is, as Hopkins puts it, "discrimination brought to ground and visited upon" an employee. . . .

In finding that some of the partners' comments reflected sex stereotyping, the District Court relied in part on Dr. Fiske's expert testimony. . . .

Indeed, we are tempted to say that Dr. Fiske's expert testimony was merely icing on Hopkins' cake. It takes no special training to discern sex stereotyping in a description of an aggressive female employee as requiring "a course at charm school." Nor, turning to Thomas Beyer's memorable advice to Hopkins, does it require expertise in psychology to know that, if an employee's flawed "interpersonal skills" can be corrected by a soft-hued suit or a new shade of lipstick, perhaps it is the employee's sex and not her interpersonal skills that has drawn the criticism.

. . . Hopkins showed that the partnership solicited evaluations from all of the firm's partners; that it generally relied very heavily on such evaluations in making its decision; that some of the partners' comments were the product of stereotyping; and that the firm in no way disclaimed reliance on those particular comments, either in Hopkins' case or in the past. Certainly a plausible—and, one might say, inevitable—conclusion to draw from this set of circumstances is that the Policy Board in making its decision did in fact take into account all of the partners' comments, including the comments that were motivated by stereotypical notions about women's proper deportment. . . .

. . . The District Judge acknowledged that Hopkins' conduct justified complaints about her behavior as a senior manager. But he also concluded that the reactions of at least some of the partners were reactions to her as a woman manager. Where an evaluation is based on a subjective assessment of a person's strengths and weaknesses, it is simply not true that each evaluator will focus on, or even mention, the same weaknesses. Thus, even if we knew that Hopkins had "personality problems," this would not tell us that the partners who cast their evaluations of Hopkins in sex-based terms would have criticized her as sharply (or criticized her at all) if she had been a man. It is not our job to review the evidence and decide that the negative reactions to Hopkins were based on reality; our perception of Hopkins' character is irrelevant. We sit not to determine whether Ms. Hopkins is nice, but to decide whether the partners reacted negatively to her personality because she is a woman.

[The Supreme Court affirmed the trial court and court of appeals' decision that employment decisions based on sex stereotypes may constitute sex discrimination in violation of Title VII.]

Case Questions

1. Was Hopkins qualified for promotion to partner? Explain your answer. What reasons did Price Waterhouse offer for its refusal to promote Hopkins to partner?

2. How did the partners' comments about Hopkins reflect gender stereotyping? What was the relevance of those comments? Does it matter that Price Waterhouse also had legitimate reasons for its reluctance to promote Hopkins?

3. Does an employer action based upon mixed motives, some of which include sex or race discrimination, violate Title VII? What defenses can an employer offer under such circumstances?

On remand from the Supreme Court, the district court in *Hopkins* found that Ann Hopkins had been a victim of sex discrimination and ordered that Price Waterhouse make her a partner.[6] Following the Supreme Court decision in *Price Waterhouse v. Hopkins*, the federal courts of appeals have held that discrimination against a male employee with gender identity disorder because he did not conform to the employer's expectations of how a male should act and behave was discrimination based on stereotypical gender norms and violated Title VII.[7] In *Nichols v. Azteca Restaurant Enterprises, Inc.*[8] the court held that abuse and ridicule by coworkers and managers directed at a male employee because he appeared effeminate and did not conform to a male stereotype was discrimination "because of sex" for the purposes of establishing a claim under Title VII.

The most recent "gender identity disorder" cases have involved transgender prisoners. In the 2015 case of *Druley v. Patton*[9] for example, the plaintiff, an Oklahoma state prisoner, sought a court order requiring the department of corrections to provide her with the hormone shots her sex change required, as well as provision of female undergarments. The court of appeals affirmed the trial court's denial of an injunction, finding that the plaintiff's medical evidence was insufficient and that the defendant had articulated a rational relationship between its treatment of the plaintiff and legitimate penal requirements.

7-1d "Gender-Plus" Discrimination

An employer who places additional requirements on employees of a certain gender but not on employees of the opposite gender violates Title VII. For example, an employer who refuses to hire females having preschool-aged children but who does hire males with preschool-aged children is guilty of an unlawful employment practice under Title VII.[10] Such discrimination is known as gender-plus discrimination. The additional requirement (no preschool-aged children) becomes an issue only for employees of a certain gender (female). Because similarly situated employees (men and women both with preschool-aged children) are treated differently because of their gender, the employer is guilty of gender discrimination.

---

[6] See *Hopkins v. Price Waterhouse*, 737 F. Supp. 1202, (D.D.C. 1990), *aff'd.*, 920 F.2d 967 (D.C. Cir. 1990).

[7] *Smith v. City of Salem, Ohio*, 369 F.3d 912 (6th Cir. 2004).

[8] 256 F.3d 864 (9th Cir. 2001).

[9] --- Fed. Appx. ---, 2015 WL 430770 (10th Cir. 2015).

[10] *Phillips v. Martin Marietta Corp.*, 400 U.S. 542 (1971).

Concept *Summary* 7.1

GENDER DISCRIMINATION

- Gender discrimination
  - Title VII prohibits discrimination because of sex
    - Applies to both men and women
  - Examples of gender discrimination
    - Advertising for male/female employees in help-wanted ads
    - Maintaining separate male/female seniority lists
    - Requiring dress codes that are not equally enforced
      - Note that dress codes need not be identical for men and women
  - Exceptions
    - If sex is a BFOQ for a job
      - Gender stereotyping
  - Occurs when a person is treated differently because he or she does not conform to the typical social norms expected of his or her gender
  - Examples of gender stereotyping
    - Overly aggressive women
    - Effeminate men
      - Sex-plus discrimination
  - Occurs when a person is treated differently because of additional requirements beyond gender
  - Examples of gender-plus discrimination
    - Refusing to hire women with preschool-aged children, but hiring men with preschool-aged children

7-2   Gender Discrimination in Pay

Both Title VII and the Equal Pay Act apply to gender discrimination in pay. There is some overlap between Title VII and the Equal Pay Act, which was passed in 1963, a year before the passage of Title VII. There are also some differences in coverage, procedures, and remedies. This section discusses both the Equal Pay Act and the Title VII provisions relating to gender-based pay differentials.

Equal Pay Act of 1963
federal legislation that requires that men and women performing substantially equal work be paid equally

7-2a   The Equal Pay Act

The **Equal Pay Act of 1963** requires that men and women performing substantially equal work be paid equally. The act does not reach other forms of gender discrimination or discrimination on grounds other than gender.

Coverage

The Equal Pay Act was enacted as an amendment to the Fair Labor Standards Act, which regulates minimum wages and maximum hours of employment. The Equal Pay Act's coverage is therefore similar to that of the Fair Labor Standards Act. The act applies to all employers "engaged in commerce (interstate commerce)," and it applies to all employees of an "enterprise engaged in commerce." Virtually all substantial business operations are covered.

The act also covers state and local government employees. The Congressional Accountability Act of 1995[11] extended the coverage of Fair Labor Standards Act, including the Equal Pay Act, to federal employees of these offices:

- House of Representatives
- Senate
- Capitol Guide Service
- Capitol Police
- Congressional Budget Office
- Office of the Architect of the Capitol
- Office of the Attending Physician
- Office of Technology Assessment

The Equal Pay Act coverage does not depend on a minimum number of employees. Hence, the act may apply to firms having fewer than the 15 employees required for Title VII coverage.

There are some exceptions to the coverage of the Equal Pay Act. These exceptions deal with operations that are exempted from the Fair Labor Standards Act. For example, certain small retail operations and small agricultural operations are excluded. Seasonal amusement operations and the fishing industry are also exempted from the act.

Provisions

The Equal Pay Act prohibits discrimination by an employer:

> between employees on the basis of sex by paying wages to employees in such establishment at a rate less than the rate at which he pays wages to employees of the opposite sex . . . for equal work on jobs the performance of which requires equal skill, effort, and responsibility, and which are performed under similar working conditions.

A plaintiff claiming violation of the Equal Pay Act must demonstrate that the employer is paying lower wages to employees of the opposite sex who are performing equal work in the same establishment. Note that the act does not require paying equal wages for work of equal value, known as comparable worth. The act requires only "equal pay for equal work." Work that is equal, or substantially equivalent, involves equal skills, effort, and responsibilities and is performed under similar working conditions.

Equal Work When considering whether jobs involve substantially equivalent work under the Equal Pay Act, the courts do not consider job titles, job descriptions, or job classifications

---

[11] 2 U.S.C. § 1301.

to be controlling. Rather, they evaluate each job on a case-by-case basis, making a detailed inquiry into the substantial duties and facts of each position.

Effort   Equal effort involves substantially equivalent physical or mental exertion needed for performance of the job. If an employer pays male employees more than female employees because of additional duties performed by the males, the employer must establish that the extra duties are a regular and recurring requirement and that they consume a substantial amount of time. Occasional or infrequent assignments of extra duties do not warrant additional pay for periods when no extra duties are performed. The employer must also show that the extra duties are commensurate with the extra pay. The employer who assigns extra duties only to male employees may face problems under Title VII unless the employer can demonstrate that being male is a BFOQ for performing the extra duties. Unless the employer can make the requisite showing of business necessity to justify a BFOQ, the extra duties must be available to both male and female employees.

Skill   Equal skill includes substantially equivalent experience, training, education, and ability. The skill, however, must relate to the performance of actual job duties. The employer cannot pay males more for possessing additional skills that are not used on the job. The act requires equal or substantially equivalent skills, not identical skills. Differences in the kinds of skills involved will not justify differentials in pay when the degree of skills required is substantially equal. For example, male hospital orderlies and female practical nurses may perform different duties requiring different skills, but if the general nature of their jobs is equivalent, the degree of skills required by each is substantially equal according to *Hodgson v. Brookhaven General Hospital.*[12]

Responsibility   Equal responsibility includes a substantially equivalent degree of accountability required in the performance of a job, with emphasis on the importance of the job's obligations. When work of males and females is subject to similar supervisory review, the responsibility of males and females is equal. But when females work without supervision, whereas males are subject to supervision, the responsibility involved is not equal.

When considering the responsibility involved in jobs, the courts focus on the economic or social consequences of the employee's actions or decisions. Minor responsibility such as making coffee or answering telephones may not be an indication of different responsibility. The act does not require identical responsibility, only substantially equivalent responsibility. For instance, if a male employee is required to compile payroll lists and a female employee must make and deliver the payroll, the responsibilities may be substantially equivalent.

Working Conditions   The act requires that the substantially equivalent work be performed under similar working conditions. According to the 1974 Supreme Court decision in *Corning Glass Works v. Brennan,*[13] working conditions include the physical surroundings and hazards involved in a job. Exposures to heat, cold, noise, fumes, dust, risk of injury, or poor ventilation are examples of working conditions. Work performed outdoors involves different working conditions from work performed indoors. Work performed during the

---

[12] 436 F.2d 719 5th Cir. (1972).

[13] 417 U.S. 188 (1974).

night shift, however, is not under different working conditions from the performance of the same work during the day.

The Equal Pay Act does not reach pay differentials for work that is not substantially equal in skill, effort, responsibility, and working conditions.

7-2b   Defenses Under the Equal Pay Act

Although a plaintiff may establish that an employer is paying different wages for men and women performing work involving equivalent effort, skills, responsibility, and working conditions, the employer may not be in violation of the Equal Pay Act because the act provides several defenses to claims of unequal pay for equal work. When the pay differentials between the male and female employees are due to a seniority system, a merit pay system, a productivity-based pay system, or "a factor other than sex," the pay differentials do not violate the act.

Employers justifying pay differentials on seniority systems, merit pay systems, or production-based pay systems must demonstrate that the system is bona fide and applies equally to all employees. A merit pay system must be more than an *ad hoc* subjective determination of employees' merit, especially if there is no listing of criteria considered in establishing an employee's merit. Any such systems should be formal and objective to justify pay differentials.

The "factor other than sex" defense covers a wide variety of situations. A "shift differential," for example, involves paying a premium to employees who work during the afternoon or night shift. If the differential is uniformly available to all employees who work a particular shift, it qualifies as a "factor other than sex." But if females are precluded from working the night shift, a night-shift pay differential is not defensible under the act. A training program may be the basis of a pay differential if the program is bona fide. Employees who perform similar work but are in training for higher positions may be paid more than those not in the training program. The training program should be open to both male and female employees unless the employer can establish that gender is a BFOQ for admission to the program. In *Kouba v. Allstate Insurance Co.*,[14] the U.S. Court of Appeals for the Ninth Circuit held that using an employee's prior salary to determine pay for employees in a training program was not precluded by the Equal Pay Act.

The following case is a good illustration of the court's inquiry into the alleged equality of jobs involved in an Equal Pay Act complaint.

» CASE 7.3

BLACKMAN V. FLORIDA DEPT. OF BUSINESS AND PROFESSIONAL REGULATION
– Fed. Appx. –, 2015 WL 689622 (11th Cir. 2015)

Facts: After starting as a typist for the DBPR in 1986, Jill Blackman worked her way up the organization in the Division of Pari–Mutuel Wagering. In 1998, she earned a bachelor's degree in political science and a certificate in public administration. Approximately four years later, she was promoted to her first management position in the DPMW as a Senior Management Analyst II.

---

[14] 691 F.2d 873 (1982).

When her predecessor, Mr. Royal Logan, retired in 2006, Blackman was promoted to Bureau Chief of Operations. Upon being promoted, she received a 14% raise to a salary of approximately $57,700. Soon thereafter, she received a legislatively-mandated three percent raise, bringing her salary to approximately $59,500. In 2007, however, the state stopped providing legislatively-mandated annual raises, and Blackman's salary remained static until January of 2012, when she received a 3.4% discretionary salary increase to $61,500.

In July of 2010, Blackman viewed a public website with state salary information and learned that the DBPR was paying her less than two male DPMW bureau chiefs and one of her male subordinates. Believing that the differences stemmed from gender discrimination, Blackman submitted a charge of discrimination to the Florida Commission on Human Relations and the Equal Employment Opportunity Commission. After receiving a right to sue letter from the EEOC, she filed a complaint in Florida state court. The DBPR removed the case to federal district court.

Blackman alleged that she was being paid less than five male employees on the basis of her gender in violation of Title VII and the Equal Pay Act, specifically: (1) Logan, the former Chief of Operations and her predecessor; (2) Steven Kogan, the Chief of Investigations; (3) Dewayne Baxley, the Chief Auditing Officer; (4) John Karr, the Regional Program Administrator and her subordinate; and (5) Joel White, a Special Projects Advisor to the DBPR Secretary. The district court granted summary judgment to the DBPR. It concluded that Blackman failed to establish a *prima facie* case of discrimination because her male colleagues, other than Logan, were not proper comparators under Title VII or the EPA due to differences in their job responsibilities and skill sets. In addition, the district court ruled that the DBPR had established legitimate, nondiscriminatory reasons for the pay disparities between Blackman and her male colleagues, including Logan.

Issue: Was the disparity between the plaintiff's salary and those of her alleged male counterparts a violation of the Equal Pay Act?

Decision: The court held, "We agree with the district court that Mr. Logan, Ms. Blackman's predecessor as Chief of Operations, was a proper comparator under Title VII [and the EPA]. We also agree with the district court, however, that the DBPR provided legitimate, nondiscriminatory explanations for the salary differential between Mr. Logan and Ms. Blackman. First, the record indicates that Mr. Logan, who held a bachelor's degree in business management and a master's degree in management and supervision, had better qualifications for the position than Ms. Blackman, who only had a bachelor's degree in political science. Second, and more importantly, Mr. Logan, unlike Ms. Blackman, benefitted from legislatively-mandated annual raises (which were gender-neutral) during his entire 13-year tenure as Chief of Operations. As a result, Mr. Logan, who was making a salary of $52,780 in 2000, was earning $72,000 at the time of his retirement in July of 2006.

"Ms. Blackman concedes that it was not discriminatory for her to make less than Mr. Logan when she first started as Chief of Operations. . . . Rather, she argues that her salary in 2012 should have come close to Mr. Logan's 2006 salary, because his salary increased from $52,780 to $72,000 over the course of six years—approximately the same amount of time that Ms. Blackman held the same position. . . . But, as the DBPR correctly argues, Ms. Blackman's salary would have been closer to Mr. Logan's salary at retirement if Ms. Blackman had benefitted from annual legislatively mandated raises from 2007 to 2012. Indeed, had Ms. Blackman received these annual pay raises, as Mr. Logan did, she would have been making approximately $71,000 at the time she filed her complaint in 2012 (assuming a 3% annual increase). In short, the salary difference is a function of the annual raises (and compound interest) from which Mr. Logan benefited, and Ms. Blackman did not."

《《

7-2c   Procedures Under the Equal Pay Act

The Equal Pay Act is administered by the Equal Employment Opportunity Commission (EEOC). Prior to 1979, it was administered by the Department of Labor, but in July 1979, the EEOC became the enforcement agency. The act provides for enforcement actions by individual employees (Section 16), or by the U.S. Secretary of Labor (Section 17), who has transferred that power to the EEOC.

There is no requirement that an individual filing a suit under the Equal Pay Act must file first with the EEOC. If the EEOC has filed a suit, it precludes individual suits on the

Concept *Summary* 7.2

THE EQUAL PAY ACT

- Requires employers to pay equal wages for equal work
- Work is equal when male and female employees perform work involving equivalent:
  - Skill
  - Effort
  - Responsibilities
  - Working conditions
- Unless the pay differentials are due to:
  - Seniority system
  - Merit pay system
  - Productivity-based pay system
  - A "factor other than sex"

same complaint. An individual suit must be filed within two years of the alleged violation. An Equal Pay Act violation will be held to be continuing for each payday in which unequal pay is received for equal work.

In a case decided under Title VII, *Ledbetter v. Goodyear Tire & Rubber Co.*,[15] a divided Supreme Court held that the receipt of individual paychecks reflecting a discriminatory performance evaluation system did not constitute a separate violation of Title VII but simply reflected the effects of the discriminatory evaluation system. The *Ledbetter* decision meant that an employee alleging sex discrimination in pay would have to file suit within 180 days (or, in some cases, 300 days) from the employer's adoption of the discriminatory pay policies. If the employee did not become aware of the discriminatory pay practice or policy until a year or more after it was adopted, it was too late to file suit under Title VII. However, *Ledbetter* was overruled by legislation signed into law by President Obama in early 2009. The **Lilly Ledbetter Fair Pay Act**[16] amended Title VII (and the Age Discrimination in Employment Act, the Americans with Disabilities Act, and the Rehabilitation Act) to provide that the time limit for filing suit alleging discrimination in pay begins either:

Lilly Ledbetter Fair Pay Act
statute that extends time in which an employee may file suit under several federal employment statutes

- when the discriminatory pay practice or policy is adopted;
- when the employee becomes subject to the discriminatory pay policy or practice; or
- when the employee is affected by the application of the discriminatory pay practice or policy.

The act makes it clear that each payment of wages, benefits, or other compensation (*i.e.*, each time the employee receives the discriminatory pay) paid under the discriminatory pay practice or policy is a separate violation. Employees filing pay discrimination

---

[15] 550 U.S. 618 (2007).

[16] P.L. 111-2 (January 29, 2009).

suits under Title VII can recover back pay for up to two years prior to the date they filed a complaint with the EEOC.

7-2d Remedies

An individual plaintiff's suit under the Equal Pay Act may recover the unpaid back wages due and may also receive an amount equal to the back wages as liquidated damages under the act. The trial court has discretion to deny recovery of the liquidated damages if it finds that the employer acted in good faith. An employer claiming to act in good faith must show some objective reason for its belief that it was acting legally.

The back pay recovered by a private plaintiff can be awarded for the period from two years prior to the suit. However, if the court finds the violation was "willful," it may allow recovery of back pay for three years prior to filing suit. According to *Laffey*, a violation is willful when the employer was aware of the appreciable possibility that its actions might violate the act. A successful private plaintiff also is awarded legal fees and court costs.

The remedies available under a government suit include injunctions and back pay with interest. The act does not provide for the recovery of liquidated damages in a government suit.

Unlike Title VII, the Equal Pay Act does not allow recovery of punitive damages. However, the potential recovery of liquidated damages for up to three years (in the case of willful violations) may offer recovery beyond that available under Title VII because of its limitations on punitive damages. Therefore, in certain cases, the remedies available under the Equal Pay Act may exceed those recoverable under Title VII.

7-2e Title VII and the Equal Pay Act

As in *Laffey*, plaintiffs often file suit under both Title VII and the Equal Pay Act. Generally, conduct that violates the Equal Pay Act also violates Title VII. However, Title VII's coverage extends beyond that of the Equal Pay Act.

An employer paying different wages to men and women doing the same job is violating the law unless the pay differentials are due to a bona fide seniority system, a merit pay system, a productivity-based pay system, or a "factor other than sex." The Equal Pay Act prohibits paying men and women different rates if they are performing substantially equivalent work unless the difference in pay is due to one of the four factors just listed. Section 703(h) of Title VII also allows pay differentials between employees of different sexes when the differential is due to seniority, merit or productivity-based pay systems, or a factor other than sex. That provision of Section 703(h) is known as the **Bennett Amendment**.

Bennett Amendment
the provision of Section 703(h) that allows pay differentials between employees of different sexes when the pay differential is due to seniority, merit pay, productivity-based pay, or a factor other than sex

The Equal Pay Act applies only when male and female employees are performing substantially equivalent work. Can Title VII be used to challenge pay differentials between men and women when they are not performing equal work? What is the effect of the Bennett Amendment?

In *County of Washington v. Gunther*,[17] the Supreme Court held that the Bennett Amendment incorporates the defenses of the Equal Pay Act into Title VII. In other words, pay differentials due to a seniority system, merit pay system, productivity-based pay system, or a factor other than sex do not violate Title VII.

---

[17] 452 U.S. 161 (1981).

The *Gunther* case also held that Title VII prohibits intentional gender discrimination in pay even when the male and female employees are not performing equivalent work. In *Gunther*, the plaintiffs were able to establish a prima facie case of intentional discrimination by the employer in setting pay scales for female employees. In *Spalding v. University of Washington*[18] and *A.F.S.C.M.E. v. State of Washington*,[19] the U.S. Court of Appeals for the Ninth Circuit held that a plaintiff bringing a *Gunther*-type claim under Title VII must establish evidence of intentional discrimination (known as disparate treatment). The court held that statistical evidence purporting to show gender-based disparate salary levels for female professors, standing alone, was not sufficient to establish intentional discrimination as required by *Gunther*.

Comparable Worth

comparable worth
a standard of equal pay for jobs of equal value; not the same as equal pay for equal work

Some commentators felt that the *Gunther* decision was, in effect, an endorsement of the idea of **comparable worth**—that is, that employees should receive equal pay for jobs of equal value. Notice that comparable worth is different from the equal-pay-for-equal-work requirements of the Equal Pay Act. The Supreme Court in *Gunther* emphasized that it was not endorsing comparable worth; it held simply that Title VII prohibited intentional discrimination on the basis of gender for setting pay scales. The courts of appeals have consistently maintained that Title VII does not require comparable worth standards. An employer need not pay equal wages for work of equal value as long as the pay differential is not due to intentional gender discrimination by the employer. In *Lemons v. Denver*,[20] the U.S. Court of Appeals for the Tenth Circuit held that Title VII did not prohibit a public employer from paying public health nurses salaries based on the private sector wage rates for nurses, even though the public health nurses were paid less than the predominantly male jobs of garbage collector or tree trimmer. The employer was not guilty of gender discrimination simply by following the "market," even if the "market" wages for nurses reflected the effects of historical discrimination against women. Several states, however, have adopted laws requiring comparable worth pay for public sector employees.

While the comparable-worth theory has been largely debunked and rejected by American courts, the theory is alive and well elsewhere. For example, in 2014 the New Zealand Court of Appeal held that paying women in predominantly female occupations less than men in other occupations with similar skills and responsibilities may be a violation of that nation's Equal Pay Act of 1972.[21]

7-2f   Gender-Based Pension Benefits

Women, on the average, live longer than men. Such differences in life expectancy are used by actuaries in determining the premium and benefit levels for annuities purchased

---

[18] 740 F.2d 686 (1984).

[19] 770 F.2d 1401 (1985).

[20] 620 F.2d 228 (1980).

[21] *See* Simon Collins, "Battle to close the pay gap," *The New Zealand Herald*, December 6, 2014, available at http://www.nzherald.co.nz/business/news/article.cfm?c_id=3&objectid=11369631; and Jim Rose, "Will comparable worth increase the pay of male prison guards?" *Utopia—You Are Standing in It!,* March 4, 2015, available at http://utopiayouarestandinginit.com/2015/03/04/will-comparable-worth-increase-the-pay-of-male-prison-guards.

by individuals. Gender-based actuarial tables used to determine premiums and benefits for pensions would require that women pay higher premiums to receive the same levels of benefits as men of the same age. Does an employer who uses gender-based actuarial tables to determine entitlement to pensions offered as an employment benefit violate Title VII? This question was addressed by the Supreme Court in the following case.

CASE 7.4
CITY OF LOS ANGELES V. MANHART
435 U.S. 702 (1978)

[As a class, women live longer than men. The Los Angeles Department of Water and Power [the Department] administered its own retirement, disability, and death benefit programs for its employees. Because women, as a class, live longer than men, the Department required its female employees to make larger contributions to its pension fund than its male employees. Upon retirement, male and female employees of the same age, seniority, and salary received the same monthly pension benefits, but before retirement the female employees were required to pay contributions to the pension fund that were 14.84 percent higher than those paid by males. This differential was based on actuarial mortality tables and the experience of the Department, which indicated that women on average live longer than men and thus would receive more retirement benefit payments. A group of female employees filed suit against the Department, alleging that the practice of making female employees pay higher contributions to receive equal benefits upon retirement violated Title VII. The trial court held for the employees, ruling that the Department's practice was illegal sex discrimination; upon appeal, the U.S. Court of Appeals for the Ninth Circuit affirmed the trial court's verdict. The Department then appealed to the U.S. Supreme Court.]

Stevens, J.

The Department . . . [contends] that . . . the differential in take-home pay between men and women was not discrimination within the meaning of Section 703(a)(1) because it was offset by a difference in the value of the pension benefits provided to the two classes of employees . . . [and] in any event, the retroactive monetary recovery is unjustified. We consider these contentions in turn. . . .

It is now well recognized that employment decisions cannot be predicated on mere "stereotyped" impressions about the characteristics of males or females. . . . This case does not, however, involve a fictional difference between men and women. It involves a generalization that the

parties accept as unquestionably true: women, as a class, do live longer than men. The Department treated its women employees differently from its men employees because the two classes are in fact different. It is equally true, however, that all individuals in the respective classes do not share the characteristic that differentiates the average class representatives. Many women do not live as long as the average man and many men outlive the average woman. The question, therefore, is whether the existence or nonexistence of "discrimination" is to be determined by comparison of class characteristics or individual characteristics. A "stereotyped" answer to that question may not be the same as the answer which the language and purpose of the statute command.

The statute makes it unlawful "to discriminate against any *individual* with respect to his compensation, terms, conditions, or privileges of employment, because of such *individual's* race, color, religion, sex, or national origin." [emphasis added] The statute's focus on the individual is unambiguous. It precludes treatment of individuals as simply components of [a] racial, religious, sexual, or national class. If height is required for a job, a tall woman may not be refused employment merely because, on the average, women are too short. Even a true generalization about the class is an insufficient reason for disqualifying an individual to whom the generalization does not apply.

That proposition is of critical importance in this case because there is no assurance that any individual woman working for the Department will actually fit the generalization on which the Department's policy is based. Many of those individuals will not live as long as the average man. While they were working, those individuals received smaller paychecks because of their sex, but they will receive no compensating advantage when they retire.

It is true, of course, that while contributions are being collected from the employees, the Department cannot know which individuals will predecease the average woman.

Therefore, unless women as a class are assessed an extra charge, they will be subsidized, to some extent, by the class of male employees. It follows, according to the Department, that fairness to its class of male employees justifies the extra assessment against all of its female employees.

But the question of fairness to various classes affected by the statute is essentially a matter of policy for the legislature to address. Congress has decided that classifications based on sex, like those based on national origin or race, are unlawful. Actuarial studies could unquestionably identify differences in life expectancy based on race or national origin, as well as sex. But a statute that was designed to make race irrelevant in the employment market, . . . could not reasonably be construed to permit a take-home pay differential based on a racial classification.

Even if the statutory language were less clear, the basic policy of the statute requires that we focus on fairness to individuals rather than fairness to classes. Practices which classify employees in terms of religion, race, or sex tend to preserve traditional assumptions about groups rather than thoughtful scrutiny of individuals. The generalization involved in this case illustrates the point. Separate mortality tables are easily interpreted as reflecting innate differences between the sexes; but a significant part of the longevity differential may be explained by the social fact that men are heavier smokers than women.

Finally, there is no reason to believe that Congress intended a special definition of discrimination in the context of employee group insurance coverage. It is true that insurance is concerned with events that are individually unpredictable, but that is characteristic of many employment decisions. Individual risks, like individual performance, may not be predicted by resort to classifications proscribed by Title VII. Indeed, the fact that this case involves a group insurance program highlights a basic flaw in the Department's fairness argument. For when insurance risks are grouped, the better risks always subsidize the poorer risks. Healthy persons subsidize medical benefits for the less healthy; unmarried workers subsidize the pensions of married workers; persons who eat, drink, or smoke to excess may subsidize pension benefits for persons whose habits are more temperate. Treating different classes of risks as though they were the same for purposes of group insurance is a common practice that has never been considered inherently unfair. To insure the flabby and the fit as though they were equivalent risks may be more common than treating men

and women alike; but nothing more than habit makes one "subsidy" seem less fair than the other.

An employment practice which requires 2,000 individuals to contribute more money into a fund than 10,000 other employees simply because each of them is a woman, rather than a man, is in direct conflict with both the language and the policy of the Act. Such a practice does not pass the simple test of whether the evidence shows "treatment of a person in a manner which but for the person's sex would be different." It constitutes discrimination and is unlawful unless exempted by the Equal Pay Act or some other affirmative justification. . . . The Department argues that the different contributions exacted from men and women were based on the factor of longevity rather than sex. It is plain, however, that any individual's life expectancy is based on a number of factors, of which sex is only one. The record contains no evidence that any factor other than the employee's sex was taken into account in calculating the 14.84 percent differential between the respective contributions by men and women. We agree with Judge Duniway's observation that one cannot "say that an actuarial distinction based entirely on sex is 'based on any other factor other than sex.' Sex is exactly what it is based on."

. . .

[W]e recognize that in a case of this kind it may be necessary to take special care in fashioning appropriate relief. . . . Although Title VII was enacted in 1964, this is apparently the first litigation challenging contribution differences based on valid actuarial tables. Retroactive liability could be devastating for a pension fund. The harm would fall in large part on innocent third parties. If, as the courts below apparently contemplated, the plaintiffs' contributions are recovered from the pension fund, the administrators of the fund will be forced to meet unchanged obligations with diminished assets. If the reserve proves inadequate, either the expectations of all retired employees will be disappointed or current employees will be forced to pay not only for their own future security but also for the unanticipated reduction in the contributions of past employees. . . .

[The practice of requiring female employees to pay more into the pension system in order to receive the same benefits upon retirement violated Title VII's prohibition on sex discrimination in pay, but the Supreme Court directed that its decision would not have retroactive effect.]

So ordered.

Case Questions

1. What factors determine a person's longevity? What factors did the department's pension plan take into consideration in determining premiums employees had to pay?

2. Does Title VII allow a "reasonable cost differential" defense to a charge of gender discrimination?

3. How can an employer comply with *Manhart*'s requirement of equal treatment between male and female employees for pensions? If women live longer than men, won't men be paid less under a unisex pension? Would that violate Title VII? Explain.

《

The Supreme Court noted in *Manhart* that it did not want to revolutionize the insurance industry. In the subsequent case of *Arizona Governing Committee v. Norris*,[22] the Supreme Court held that a deferred compensation plan for state employees, administered by a private insurance company that used gender-based actuarial tables to determine monthly benefit payments, violated Title VII. The Court held that its ruling would apply prospectively only, not retroactively.

7-3   Pregnancy Discrimination

Pregnancy Discrimination Act of 1978
an act that amended Title VII to include pregnancy discrimination in the definition of sex discrimination

In *General Electric v. Gilbert*,[23] the Supreme Court held that General Electric's refusal to cover pregnancy or related conditions under its sick-pay plan, even though male-specific disabilities such as vasectomies were covered, did not violate Title VII. In response to the *General Electric v. Gilbert* decision, Congress passed the **Pregnancy Discrimination Act of 1978**, which amended Title VII by adding Section 701(k) to Title VII. Section 701(k) provides:

The terms "because of sex" or "on the basis of sex" include, but are not limited to, because of or on the basis of pregnancy, childbirth, or related medical conditions; and women affected by pregnancy, childbirth, or related medical conditions shall be treated the same for all employment-related purposes, including receipt of benefits under fringe benefit programs, as other persons not so affected but similar to their ability or inability to work. . . .

Simply stated, the amendment to Title VII requires that an employer treat a pregnant employee the same as any employee suffering a non-pregnancy-related, temporary disability (unless, in a relatively rare instance, the employer can establish a BFOQ for pregnancy-related discrimination). If the employer's sick-leave pay benefits cover temporary disabilities, it must also provide coverage for pregnancy-related leaves. In *Newport News Shipbuilding and Dry Dock Co. v. EEOC*,[24] the Supreme Court held that an employer's medical insurance plan covering 80 percent of the cost of hospital treatment for employees' spouses or dependents, but which limited coverage of spouses' pregnancy-related costs to

---

[22] 463 U.S. 1073 (1983).

[23] 429 U.S. 125 (1976).

[24] 462 U.S. 669 (1983).

$500, was in violation of the pregnancy discrimination provisions of Title VII. Title VII required the employer to provide coverage for spouses' pregnancy-related conditions equal to the coverage of spouses' or dependents' other medical conditions.

Employers who fire pregnant employees are clearly in violation of Title VII, as are employers who fire pregnant employees because of the assumption that the employees will likely be absent from work for lengthy periods.[25] Discriminating against an employee who has had an abortion, or who is contemplating having an abortion, is also prohibited by Title VII.[26] The act also prohibits discharging an employee because of her efforts to become pregnant by in vitro fertilization.[27] An employer that transferred a successful sales representative to an undesirable sales territory because of her desire to start a family despite having several miscarriages was held to have violated Title VII in *Goss v. Exxon Office Systems Co.*[28] The exclusion of prescription contraceptives from an employer's otherwise comprehensive prescription drug plan has also been held to violate Title VII.[29]

7-3a Pregnancy and Hazardous Working Conditions

On-the-job exposure to harsh substances or potentially toxic chemicals may pose a hazard to the health of employees. The risk of such hazards may be greatly increased when pregnant employees are exposed to them; the hazards may also affect the health of the fetus carried by the pregnant employee. An employer wishing to avoid potential health problems for female employees and their offspring may prohibit women of childbearing age from working in jobs that involve exposure to hazardous substances. Do such restrictions violate Title VII, or may they be justified as BFOQs?

The U.S. Supreme Court in *U.A.W. v. Johnson Controls, Inc.*[30] held that the employer's restrictions were gender discrimination in violation of Title VII. For an employer to establish a BFOQ would require showing that the employee's pregnancy interfered with the employee's ability to perform the job. The Court noted:

> . . . women as capable of doing their jobs as their male counterparts may not be forced to choose between having a child and having a job. . . . Johnson Controls' professed moral and ethical concerns about the welfare of the next generation do not suffice to establish a BFOQ of female sterility. Decisions about the welfare of future children must be left to the parents who conceive, bear, support, and raise them rather than to the employers who hire those parents. . . . Johnson Controls has attempted to exclude women because of their reproductive capacity. Title VII (and the pregnancy discrimination amendments) simply do not allow a woman's dismissal because of her failure to submit to sterilization.

---

[25] *Maldonado v. U.S. Bank*, 186 F.3d 759 (7th Cir. 1999).

[26] *Turic v. Holland Hospitality*, 85 F.3d 1211 (6th Cir. 1996).

[27] *Pacourek v. Inland Steel Co.*, 858 F. Supp. 1393 (N.D. Ill. 1994).

[28] 33 B.N.A. FEP Cas. 21 (E.D. Pa. 1983).

[29] *Erickson v. The Bartell Drug Co.*, 141 F. Supp. 2d 1266 (W.D. Wash. 2001); *EEOC v. United Parcel Service, Inc.*, 141 F. Supp. 2d 1216 (D. Minn. 2001).

[30] 499 U.S. 187 (1991).

7-4   The Family and Medical Leave Act

The Family and Medical Leave Act (FMLA),[31] signed into law by President Clinton in 1993, allows eligible employees to take up to 12 weeks unpaid leave in any 12 months because of:

- the birth, adoption, or foster care of a child;
- the need to care for a child, spouse, or parent with a serious health condition; or
- the employee's own serious health condition makes the employee unable to perform functions of his or her job.

The FMLA was amended in 2008 and 2009 to allow employees to take up to 26 weeks' leave to care for members of the armed forces and recent veterans who have a serious injury or illness, or 12 weeks' leave to deal with situations arising from the fact that a child, spouse, or parent is called to active military duty or is deployed to a foreign country.

7-4a   FMLA Coverage

The FMLA applies to private sector employers with 50 or more employees; public sector employers are covered without regard to the number of employees. Employees employed at work sites with less than 50 employees may still be covered if the employer employs at least 50 employees within 75 miles of the work site. In *Hackworth v. Progressive Casualty Insurance Co.*,[32] the Department of Labor's interpretation that the 75 miles should be measured in surface miles (using surface transportation over public streets and roads) rather than linear miles ("as the crow flies") was upheld. In *Nevada Dept. of Human Resources v. Hibbs*,[33] the Supreme Court held that the Eleventh Amendment of the Constitution does not grant the states immunity from suits for damages by employees under the FMLA.

Employees of covered employers are eligible for leave under the act if they have been employed by the employer for at least 12 months and have worked at least 1,250 hours of the 12-month period immediately preceding commencement of the leave. The employer may designate "key employees" who may be denied leave under the act; key employees are those whom it would be necessary for the employer to replace in order to prevent substantial and grievous economic injury to the operation of business. The employer must give written notice to key employees at the time such employees give notice of leave and may deny reinstatement to key employees who take leave. Key employees must be salaried employees and must be among the highest paid 10 percent of the employees at the work site. No more than 10 percent of the employees at a work site can be designated key employees.

---

[31] 29 U.S.C. § 2611 *et seq.*

[32] 468 F.3d 722 (10th Cir. 2006).

[33] 538 U.S. 721 (2003).

7-4b Entitlement to Medical Leave

Serious Health Condition

The regulations under the FMLA[34] define a serious health condition as:

- an illness, injury, or condition that requires inpatient hospital care, or
- that lasts more than three days and requires continuing treatment by a health-care provider, or
- that involves pregnancy, or
- a long-term or permanently disabling health condition, or
- absences for receiving multiple treatments for restorative surgery, or
- for a condition that would likely result in a period of incapacity of more than three days if it were not treated.

An employee's food poisoning that required one visit to a doctor but did not require hospitalization was not a serious health condition under the FLMA, nor was a child's ear infection that lasted only one day and required only a single visit to the doctor. However, a child's throat and upper respiratory infection that incapacitated the child for more than three days did qualify as a serious health condition under the FLMA.

Leave Provisions

The leave may be taken all at once, or in certain cases, intermittently, or the employee may work at a part-time schedule. An employee or the employer may choose to substitute paid leave such as vacation or sick leave for part or all of the FMLA leave if the employee is entitled to such paid leave. The employee's ability to substitute paid leave is determined by the terms of the employer's normal leave policy. Under certain circumstances, the employee may take the leave on an intermittent basis—that is, taking the leave in separate blocks of time or through a reduced work schedule for the employee. If the leave is for planned medical treatment, the employee must make a reasonable effort to schedule the medical treatment so not to unduly disrupt the employer's operation. If both parents are employed by the same employer, the leave because of childbirth or to care for a sick child may be limited to a total of 12 weeks between both parents. The employee's health benefits must be maintained during leave if the health coverage was provided to the employee before the leave; if the employee fails to return to work after the leave, the employer may recover the premiums it paid to maintain the employee's health benefits. The employee has the right to return to the same or an equivalent position, and the leave cannot result in the loss of any benefit by the employee. In *Ragsdale v. Wolverine World Wide, Inc.*,[35] the employer granted an employee a medical leave of 30 weeks, but the employer failed to notify the employee that the leave would count against the employee's FMLA leave. According to a regulation under the FMLA, adopted by the Department of Labor, the employer's failure to provide such a notice would require the employer to grant the employee an additional 12-week leave. The Supreme Court held that the regulation was invalid because it was contrary to the FMLA legislation and it went beyond the authority of the Secretary of Labor under the FMLA.

---

[34] 29 C.F.R. § 825.100 *et seq.*

[35] 535 U.S. 81 (2002).

7-4c Military Leave Provisions

The 2008 National Defense Authorization Act[36] amended the FMLA to allow employees to take up to 12 weeks of unpaid leave during a 12-month period for "qualifying exigencies" arising out of an employee's spouse, child, or parent being on active duty service or deployed to a foreign country, or called to active-duty service as a member of the National Guard or Reserves. The amended FMLA also allows employees to take "military caregiver leave" of up to 26 weeks of unpaid leave to care a child, spouse, parent, or next of kin who is a current member of the armed forces (including the National Guard or Reserves) or a veteran within five years of discharge and who suffers a serious illness or injury. The 2010 National Defense Authorization Act again amended the FMLA; in 2013 the U.S. Department of Labor issued new regulations operationalizing these amendments. Along with the Final Rule, the Department of Labor issued a set of Frequently Asked Questions.

Q. **Why is the Department of Labor revising the Family and Medical Leave Act regulations?**

A. The Department is revising the regulations to implement and interpret two statutory amendments to the Family and Medical Leave Act (FMLA): the National Defense Authorization Act for Fiscal Year 2010 (FY 2010 NDAA) and the Airline Flight Crew Technical Corrections Act (AFCTCA).

Q. **How did the FY 2010 NDAA change the military leave entitlements?**

A. The FY 2010 NDAA amended the FMLA's military family leave provisions to expand the availability of military caregiver leave and qualifying exigency leave. The FY 2010 NDAA extended military caregiver leave to eligible employees whose family members are recent veterans with serious injuries or illnesses, including conditions that do not arise until after the veteran has left the military. The FY 2010 NDAA also expanded the definition of a serious injury or illness for both current servicemembers and veterans to include serious injuries or illnesses that result from a condition that existed before the servicemember's active duty service and was aggravated by service in the line of duty on active duty.

In addition, the FY 2010 NDAA expanded qualifying exigency leave to eligible employees with family members serving in the Regular Armed Forces, in addition to the National Guard and Reserves. The FY 2010 NDAA also added the requirement that for all qualifying exigency leave the military member (National Guard, Reserves, Regular Armed Forces) must be deployed to a foreign country.

Q. **How does the Final Rule change the military caregiver leave provisions?**

A. Military caregiver leave entitles an eligible employee who is the spouse, parent, son, daughter, or next of kin of a covered servicemember with a serious illness or injury to take up to a total of 26 workweeks of unpaid, job-protected leave during any single 12-month period to care for the servicemember. Before the FY 2010 NDAA was enacted, military caregiver leave was limited to eligible employees who were the family members of current servicemembers with a serious injury or illness incurred in the line of duty on active duty. The Final Rule expands military caregiver leave to eligible employees who are the family members of certain

---

[36] P.L. 110-181 (2008).

veterans with a serious injury or illness incurred or aggravated in the line of duty on active duty and that manifested before or after the veteran left active duty. The Final Rule expands the definition of serious injury or illness for a current service-member to include injuries or illnesses that existed prior to the servicemember's active duty but were aggravated in the line of duty on active duty.

Q. Has the definition of a serious injury or illness for a current servicemember changed?

A. Yes. The Final Rule expands the definition of serious injury or illness for current servicemembers to include preexisting conditions that were aggravated by service in the line of duty on active duty.

Q. Have the medical certification requirements for military caregiver leave changed?

A. Yes. The Final Rule expands the list of health care providers who can provide a medical certification to support FMLA military caregiver leave to include health care providers who are not affiliated with the military. If a medical certification is obtained from a health care provider who is not affiliated with the military, the employer may request a second (or third) opinion from the employee. The Final Rule retains the provisions that healthcare certifications obtained from healthcare providers associated with the military may not be subject to second and third opinions. In either situation, employers are not permitted to request recertifications.

The Final Rule also allows eligible employees to submit a copy of a VASRD rating determination or documentation of enrollment in the Program of Comprehensive Assistance for Family Caregivers from the Department of Veterans' Affairs to certify that the veteran has a serious injury or illness. However, if an employee submits such documents, the employee may still be required to provide additional information.

Q. How does the Final Rule change the qualifying exigency leave provisions?

A. Qualifying exigency leave entitles an eligible employee whose spouse, son, daughter, or parent is a military member on covered active duty to take unpaid, job-protected leave to address any of the qualifying exigencies listed in the regu-lations. Before the FY 2010 NDAA was enacted, qualifying exigency leave was limited to eligible employees whose family member was a military member of the National Guard and Reserves. The Final Rule implements the FY 2010 NDAA amendments expanding qualifying exigency leave to eligible employees with a spouse, son, daughter, or parent in the Regular Armed Forces on covered active duty. The Final Rule also includes a foreign country deployment requirement in the definition of covered active duty for both members of the Regular Armed Forces and members of the National Guard and Reserves.

In addition, the Final Rule adds a new category of qualifying exigency that allows employees to take qualifying exigency leave for certain activities related to the care of the military member's parent who is incapable of self-care where those activities arise from the military member's covered active duty. The Final Rule also increases the amount of time from five days to up to 15 calendar days that an eligible employee may take to spend with his or her military family member during the military member's Rest and Recuperation leave.

Source: United States Department of Labor, "Frequently Asked Questions," available at http://www.dol.gov/whd/fmla/2013rule/militaryFR_FAQs.htm.

The following case deals with the issue of whether an employee's absences qualified for FMLA leave or could be counted against the employee under the employer's attendance policy.

>> CASE 7.5

NOVAK V. METROHEALTH MEDICAL CENTER
503 F.3d 572 (6th Cir. 2007)

Facts: Donna Novak was employed by MetroHealth Medical Center. MetroHealth maintained a "point-based" attendance policy that assigned points to employees based on the number of hours of unexcused absence. Employees were terminated if they accumulated 112 points during a twelve-month period (leave authorized under the FMLA was not included in the point total). Novak was absent from work a number of times in late March 2004. She called MetroHealth each day that she was absent to provide an explanation. Some absences were because she was experiencing back pain; others were because she was helping care for her eighteen-year-old daughter, Victoria, who had recently given birth. She said that her daughter was suffering from "postpartum depression" and that she had to help her care for the baby (Novak's grandson).

Novak's absences resulted in her accumulating more than 112 points, and she faced termination. She requested that MetroHealth grant her leave under the FMLA. Novak consulted a Dr. Patil about her back pain, but she had been treated by a Dr. Wloszek in the past. MetroHealth required Novak to submit a FMLA certification form that was to be completed by the physician of record, Dr. Wloszek, and not by Dr. Patil. Dr. Wloszek completed the form, but because she had not examined Novak since October 2003, Dr. Wloszek omitted information on the description of the medical facts and the likely duration of Novak's condition. Novak then asked Boda, Wloszek's assistant, to complete the remainder of the form and fax it to MetroHealth. MetroHealth questioned the authenticity of Dr. Wloszek's certification forms, and contacted Dr. Wloszek, who told them that she completed the form based on secondhand information from Novak about her condition. Novak also submitted certification forms for her absences to help her daughter care for the baby.

On April 16, 2004, MetroHealth determined that Novak's March absences did not qualify for the FMLA leave.

Her absences were not authorized and, as a result, MetroHealth terminated her employment. Novak filed suit against MetroHealth, alleging interference with her FMLA rights and retaliation under the FMLA. The trial court held that there was no basis for the FMLA claims, and dismissed them with prejudice. Novak appealed to the U.S. Court of Appeals for the Sixth Circuit.

Issue: Was Novak entitled to FMLA leave because of her back pain and/or her caring for her daughter and her grandson?

Decision: An employer may require an employee requesting FMLA leave to provide a doctor's certification confirming the existence of a serious health condition. A doctor's certification of a serious health condition is sufficient if it states:

* the date on which the serious health condition began;
* the probable duration of the condition;
* the appropriate medical facts within the health care provider's knowledge; and
* a statement that the employee is unable to perform her job duties.

An employer may show that the certification is invalid or inauthentic.

The court of appeals agreed that Novak's certification forms from Dr. Wloszek were insufficient to establish the existence of a serious health condition for purposes of the FMLA. MetroHealth had established that the certification was unreliable and it acted reasonably in refusing to grant FMLA leave on that basis.

Novak also claimed that she was entitled to FMLA leave to care for her daughter, who was suffering from short-term postpartum depression. The FMLA permits an employee to take leave to care for a parent, spouse, or child suffering from a serious health condition. However, the FMLA authorizes leave to care for a child eighteen years of age or older only if that child is "disabled" within the definition of the Americans with Disabilities Act. Because Novak did not establish that her adult daughter suffered from a disability, the FMLA did not authorize Novak's leave to care for her. Novak offered evidence about her daughter's difficulty in caring for the baby and Novak's need to help with the care of her grandchild. But the FMLA does not entitle an employee to take leave to care for a grandchild, only for a parent, spouse, or child.

The court of appeals held that Novak was not entitled to FMLA leave. The court therefore affirmed the dismissal of Novak's FMLA claims.

Concept *Summary* 7.3

THE FMLA

Family and Medical Leave Act

- Qualified employees may take up to 12 weeks' unpaid leave for:
  - Birth and care of a child
  - Adoption or placement of a child into foster care
  - Care for self or a spouse, child, or parent with a serious health condition
  - Qualifying exigencies arising from the call to active military duty of a spouse, child, or parent
- Qualified employees may take up to 26 weeks' unpaid leave for:
  - Care for a spouse, child, parent, or next of kin who suffers a serious illness or injury in the line of active military duty

7-4d   Effect of Other Laws on the FMLA

The FMLA does not preempt or supersede any state or local law that provides for greater family or medical leave rights than those granted under the FMLA. In addition, employers are required to comply with any collective bargaining agreement or employee benefit program that provides for greater rights than those given under the FMLA.

7-4e   State Legislation

The California Fair Employment and Housing Act Law requires employers to provide pregnant employees up to four months of unpaid pregnancy leave and to reinstate female employees returning from pregnancy leave to the job they held prior to the leave.

However, if the job is unavailable due to business necessity, the employer is required to make a good-faith effort to provide a substantially similar job. The California law does not require the employer to offer such treatment to employees returning from other temporary disability leaves. California Federal Savings and Loan, a California bank, alleged that the California law violated the Pregnancy Discrimination Act because it required the employer to treat pregnant employees differently from other temporarily disabled employees. In *California Federal Savings and Loan v. Guerra*,[37] the Supreme Court upheld the California law. The majority reasoned that the Pregnancy Discrimination Act amendments to Title VII were intended merely to create a minimum level of protection for pregnant employees that could be supplemented by state legislation as long as the state laws did not conflict with the terms or policies of Title VII. The Court also noted that the California law did not prevent employers from extending the right of reinstatement to employees on other temporary disability leaves; hence, the law did not require that pregnant employees be treated more generously than nonpregnant employees on temporary disability leave.

THE **WORKING** LAW

A Growing Number of Cities and States Mandate Paid Family Leave

In 2004, the state of California became the first state to provide for temporary paid family leave through the state's disability insurance program. Workers who take time off to care for a seriously ill child, spouse, domestic partner, or who take time off to bond with a newborn child, adopted child, or child placed through foster care are eligible for up to six weeks of "family temporary disability insurance benefits." The worker must make a claim for the benefits with the state Disability Insurance Program and will begin receiving benefits after a seven-day waiting period. No more than six weeks of benefits may be received within any 12-month period. Workers who are already receiving unemployment compensation, state disability benefits, or any other temporary disability benefits under state or federal law are not eligible to receive family temporary disability insurance benefits. Workers who are entitled to a leave under the federal Family and Medical Leave Act or the California Family Rights Act must take the family temporary disability insurance leave at the same time as the leave under those laws.

In 2015, California, Rhode Island, and New Jersey lead the nation in offering broad paid family and medical leave insurance programs for their residents, with significant positive impacts. In addition, Ohio, Virginia, and Illinois offer paid parental leave for state employees, while Washington, D.C.; St. Paul and Brooklyn Park, Minnesota; St. Petersburg, Florida; San Francisco, California; Chicago, Illinois; and Austin, Texas offer these benefits for their municipal employees. The U.S. Department of Labor claimed, "Offering such benefits for municipal employees can help city government as an employer to attract and retain a talented workforce, maximizing efficiency and saving on hiring and turnover costs."

Sources: California's Unemployment Insurance Code, §§ 3300-3303; and "Cities and states are leading on paid family and medical leave," U.S. Department of Labor, available at http://www.dol.gov/wb/PaidLeave/PaidLeave.htm.

---

[37] 479 U.S. 272 (1987).

7-5   Sexual Harassment

sexual harassment
unwelcome sexual advances, requests for sexual favors, or other verbal or physical conduct of a sexual nature that the employee is required to accept as a condition of employment, the employee's response to such conduct is used as a basis for employment decisions, or such conduct creates a hostile working environment

quid pro quo harassment
harassment where the employee's response to the harassment is considered in granting employment benefits

hostile environment harassment
harassment which may not result in economic detriment to the victim, but which subjects the victim to unwelcome conduct or comments and may interfere with the employee's work performance

Sexual harassment is one of the most significant employment problems facing our society. It imposes significant costs on both employers and employees. Victims of sexual harassment may experience severe emotional anguish, physical and mental stress, frustration, humiliation, guilt, withdrawal and dysfunction in family and social relationships, medical expenses, loss of sick leave and vacation, and litigation costs. Employers suffer from absenteeism, higher turnover of employees, replacement and retraining costs, morale problems, losses in productivity, and of course, litigation expenses and damages.

The language of Title VII does not specifically mention sexual harassment, and in some early cases, the courts had difficulty determining whether sexual harassment was within the Title VII prohibition on gender discrimination. Now, however, the courts are clear on the position that sexual harassment is gender discrimination prohibited by Title VII. The EEOC has issued guidelines defining sexual harassment and declaring that sexual harassment constitutes gender discrimination in violation of Title VII. **Sexual harassment** is defined as unwelcome sexual advances, requests for sexual favors, or other verbal or physical conduct of a sexual nature, where the employee is required to accept such conduct as a condition of employment; the employee's response to such conduct is used as a basis for employment decisions such as promotion, bonuses, or retention; or such conduct unreasonably interferes with the employee's work performance or creates a hostile working environment. The Title VII protections against sexual harassment apply to all individuals—both men and women—covered by Title VII. (Note that Title VII also prohibits harassment based on race, color, religion, or national origin.)

The EEOC Guidelines and the courts have recognized two general categories of sexual harassment: quid pro quo harassment and hostile environment harassment. In **quid pro quo harassment**, the employee's response to the request for sexual favors is considered in granting employment benefits, such as a male supervisor promising a female employee that she will be promoted or receive a favorable performance rating if she sleeps with him. Such harassment was held to violate Title VII in *Barnes v. Costle*.[38] In **hostile environment harassment**, an employee may not suffer any economic detriment but is subjected to unwelcome sexual comments, propositions, jokes, or conduct that have the effect of interfering with the employee's work performance or creating a hostile work environment. The Supreme Court held hostile environment sexual harassment was prohibited by Title VII in *Meritor Savings Bank, FSB v. Vinson*.[39]

EEOC Guidelines on Sexual Harassment

Section 1604.11 Sexual Harassment

(a) Harassment on the basis of sex is a violation of § 703 of Title VII.[40] Unwelcome sexual advances, requests for sexual favors, and other verbal or physical conduct of

---

[38] 561 F.2d 983 (D.C. Cir. 1977).

[39] 477 U.S. 57 (1986).

[40] The principles involved here continue to apply to race, color, religion, or national origin.

a sexual nature constitute sexual harassment when (1) submission to such conduct is made either explicitly or implicitly a term or condition of an individual's employment; (2) submission to or rejection of such conduct by an individual is used as the basis for employment decisions affecting such individual; or (3) such conduct has the purpose or effect of unreasonably interfering with an individual's work performance or creating an intimidating, hostile, or offensive working environment.

(b) In determining whether alleged conduct constitutes sexual harassment, the Commission will look at the record as a whole and at the totality of the circumstances, such as the nature of the sexual advances and the context in which the alleged incidents occurred. The determination of the legality of a particular action will be made from the facts, on a case-by-case basis.

(c) Applying general Title VII principles, an employer, employment agency, joint apprenticeship committee or labor organization (hereinafter collectively referred to as "employer") is responsible for its acts and those of its agents and supervisory employees with respect to sexual harassment regardless of whether the specific acts complained of were authorized or even forbidden by the employer and regardless of whether the employer knew or should have known of their occurrence. The Commission will examine the circumstances of the particular employment relationship and the job functions performed by the individual in determining whether an individual acts in either a supervisory or agency capacity.

(d) With respect to conduct between fellow employees, an employer is responsible for acts of sexual harassment in the workplace where the employer (or its agents or supervisory employees) knows or should have known of the conduct, unless it can show that it took immediate and appropriate corrective action.

(e) An employer may also be responsible for the acts of nonemployees with respect to sexual harassment of employees in the workplace, where the employer (or its agents or supervisory employees) knows or should have known of the conduct and fails to take immediate and appropriate corrective action. In reviewing these cases, the Commission will consider the extent of the employer's control and any other legal responsibility which the employer may have with respect to the conduct of such non-employees.

(f) Prevention is the best tool for the elimination of sexual harassment. An employer should take all steps necessary to prevent sexual harassment from occurring, such as affirmatively raising the subject, expressing strong disapproval, developing appropriate sanctions, informing employees of their rights and procedures for raising the issue of harassment under Title VII, and developing methods to sensitize all concerned.

(g) Other related practices: Where employment opportunities or benefits are granted because of an individual's submission to the employer's sexual advances or requests for sexual favors, the employer may be held liable for unlawful sex discrimination against other persons who were qualified for but denied that employment opportunity or benefit.

7-5a   Quid Pro Quo Harassment

To establish a case of quid pro quo harassment, a plaintiff must show five things:

- She or he belongs to a protected group
- She or he was subject to unwelcome sexual harassment
- The harassment was based on sex
- Job benefits were conditioned on the acceptance of the harassment, and if appropriate,
- There is some basis to hold the employer liable

The essence of quid pro quo harassment is that the employee's submission to such conduct is made either explicitly or implicitly a term or condition of an individual's employment or that submission to or rejection of such conduct by the employee is used as the basis for employment decisions affecting the employee.

The case of *Tomkins v. Public Service Electric & Gas Co.*[41] is a classic example of quid pro quo sexual harassment. Tomkins was told by her male supervisor that she should have sex with him if she wanted him to give her a satisfactory evaluation and recommend her for promotion. When she refused, she was subjected to a demotion, negative evaluations, and disciplinary suspensions, and was ultimately fired. The U.S. Court of Appeals held that Title VII is violated when a supervisor makes sexual advances or demands toward a subordinate employee and conditions the employee's continued employment or possible promotion on a favorable response to those advances or demands.

The EEOC Guidelines on sexual harassment also provide that when an employer rewards one employee for entering a sexual relationship, other employees denied the same reward or benefit may have a valid harassment complaint. In *King v. Palmer*,[42] a supervisor promoted a nurse with whom he was having an affair rather than one of several more qualified nurses. The court held that the employer was guilty of gender discrimination against the superior nurses who were denied the promotion.

7-5b   Hostile Environment Harassment

Unlike quid pro quo harassment, hostile environment harassment does not involve the conditioning of any job status or benefit on the employee's response to the harassment. Rather, the unwelcome harassment has the effect of interfering with the employee's work performance or creating a hostile work environment for the employee. Because no employment consequences are conditioned on the employee's response to the harassing conduct, some courts refused to hold that hostile environment harassment violated Title VII. The Supreme Court rejected that approach and upheld the EEOC Guidelines that declare hostile environment harassment to be sex discrimination in violation of Title VII in the case of *Meritor*. After that decision, the lower courts addressed the question of just how severe the harassing conduct has to be, and how hostile the work environment must become, before such harassment is found to violate Title VII. That issue was finally settled by the Supreme Court in the following decision.

---

[41] 568 F.2d 1044 (3d Cir. 1977).

[42] 778 F.2d 878 (D.C. Cir. 1985).

CASE 7.6
HARRIS V. FORKLIFT SYSTEMS, INC.
510 U.S. 17 (1993)

O'Connor, J.

Teresa Harris worked as a manager at Forklift Systems, Inc., an equipment rental company, from April 1985 until October 1987. Charles Hardy was Forklift's president. . . . [T]hroughout Harris' time at Forklift, Hardy often insulted her because of her gender and often made her the target of unwanted sexual innuendos. Hardy told Harris on several occasions, in the presence of other employees, "You're a woman, what do you know" and "We need a man as the rental manager"; at least once, he told her she was "a dumbass woman." Again in front of others, he suggested that the two of them "go to the Holiday Inn to negotiate [Harris'] raise." Hardy occasionally asked Harris and other female employees to get coins from his front pants pocket. He threw objects on the ground in front of Harris and other women, and asked them to pick the objects up. He made sexual innuendos about Harris' and other women's clothing.

In mid-August 1987, Harris complained to Hardy about his conduct; Hardy said he was surprised that Harris was offended, claimed he was only joking, and apologized. He also promised he would stop, and based on this assurance Harris stayed on the job. But in early September, Hardy began anew: While Harris was arranging a deal with one of Forklift's customers, he asked her, again in front of other employees, "What did you do, promise the guy . . . some [sex] Saturday night?" On October 1, Harris collected her paycheck and quit.

Harris then sued Forklift, claiming that Hardy's conduct had created an abusive work environment for her because of her gender. The [trial] Court found this to be a "close case," but held that Hardy's conduct did not create an abusive environment. The court found that some of Hardy's comments "offended [Harris], and would offend the reasonable woman," but that they were not "so severe as to be expected to seriously affect [Harris'] psychological well being." [On appeal, the U.S. Court of Appeals for the Sixth Circuit affirmed the trial court decision. Harris then appealed to the U.S. Supreme Court.] We granted certiorari to resolve a conflict among [the federal courts of appeals] . . . on whether conduct, to be actionable as "abusive work environment" harassment (no quid pro quo harassment issue is presented here), must "seriously

affect [an employee's] psychological well-being" or lead the plaintiff to "suffer injury". . . .

Title VII of the Civil Rights Act of 1964 makes it "an unlawful employment practice for an employer . . . to discriminate against any individual with respect to his compensation, terms, conditions, or privileges of employment, because of such individual's race, color, religion, sex, or national origin." As we made clear in *Meritor Savings Bank v. Vinson* . . . this language "is not limited to 'economic' or 'tangible' discrimination. The phrase 'terms, conditions, or privileges of employment' evinces a congressional intent 'to strike at the entire spectrum of disparate treatment of men and women' in employment," which includes requiring people to work in a discriminatorily hostile or abusive environment. When the workplace is permeated with "discriminatory intimidations, ridicule, and insult," that is "sufficiently severe or pervasive to alter the conditions of the victim's employment and create an abusive working environment," Title VII is violated. . . .

But Title VII comes into play before the harassing conduct leads to a nervous breakdown. A discriminatorily abusive work environment, even one that does not seriously affect employees' psychological well-being, can and often will detract from employees' job performance, discourage employees from remaining on the job, or keep them from advancing in their careers. Moreover, even without regard to these tangible effects, the very fact that the discriminatory conduct was so severe or pervasive that it created a work environment abusive to employees because of their race, gender, religion, or national origin offends Title VII's broad rule of workplace equality.

. . . We therefore believe the District Court erred in relying on whether the conduct "seriously affected plaintiff's psychological well-being" or led her to "suffer injury." Such an inquiry may needlessly focus the factfinder's attention on concrete psychological harm, an element Title VII does not require. Certainly Title VII bars conduct that would seriously affect a reasonable person's psychological well-being, but the statute is not limited to such conduct. So long as the environment would reasonably be perceived, and is perceived, as hostile or abusive, there is no need for it also to be psychologically injurious.

This is not, and by its nature cannot be, a mathematically precise test. We need not answer today all the potential questions it raises, nor specifically address the EEOC's new regulations on this subject . . . But we can say that whether an environment is "hostile" or "abusive" can be determined only by looking at all the circumstances. These may include the frequency of the discriminatory conduct; its severity; whether it is physically threatening or humiliating, or a mere offensive utterance; and whether it unreasonably interferes with an employee's work performance. The effect on the employee's psychological well-being is, of course, relevant to determining whether the plaintiff actually found the environment abusive. But while psychological harm, like any other relevant factor, may be taken into account, no single factor is required.

Forklift, while conceding that a requirement that the conduct seriously affect psychological well being is unfounded, argues that the District Court nonetheless correctly applied the *Meritor* standard. We disagree. Though the District Court did conclude that the work environment was not "intimidating or abusive to [Harris]," it did so only after finding that the conduct was not "so severe as to be expected to seriously affect plaintiff's psychological

well-being" and that Harris was not "subjectively so offended that she suffered injury." The District Court's application of these incorrect standards may well have influenced its ultimate conclusion, especially given that the court found this to be a "close case."

We therefore reverse the judgment of the Court of Appeals, and remand the case for further proceedings consistent with this opinion.

So ordered.

Case Questions

1. How did the harassment directed against Harris affect her economically? How did the harassment directed against Harris affect her emotionally? Did it interfere with her work performance? Explain your answers.

2. How severe must hostile environment sexual harassment be before it violates Title VII?

3. Is the standard used to determine when sexual harassment becomes severe enough to create a hostile environment a subjective or an objective standard? Explain your answer.

Reasonable Person or Reasonable Victim?

In cases involving claims of hostile environment harassment, the courts have dealt with the question of which standard should be used to determine whether the challenged conduct was sufficiently severe and hostile. Most courts have used the "reasonable person" standard. That is, would a reasonable person find the conduct to be offensive and severe enough to create a hostile environment or to interfere with the person's work performance? The EEOC issued a policy statement declaring that courts should also consider the perspective of the victim to avoid perpetuating stereotypical notions of what behavior was acceptable to persons of a specific gender.

In response to that, some courts adopted the "reasonable victim" or "reasonable woman" standard, recognizing that men and women were likely to perceive and react differently to certain behaviors. In *Ellison v. Brady*,[43] the court held that the reasonable woman standard should be used to determine whether a series of unsolicited love letters sent to a female employee by a male coworker had the effect of creating a hostile work environment. Even when courts did adopt the reasonable woman standard, they emphasized that the standard was not totally subjective but was to be based on whether an objective reasonable woman would find the conduct offensive or would have been detrimentally affected.

---

[43] 924 F.2d 872 (9th Cir. 1991).

The Supreme Court, although not specifically addressing the issue of whether to use the reasonable person or reasonable woman standard, used the reasonable person standard in *Harris v. Forklift Systems, Inc.*

7-5c   Employer Liability for Sexual Harassment

The EEOC Guidelines state that employers are liable for sexual harassment by supervisory or managerial employees and may also be liable for harassment by coworkers or even nonemployees under certain circumstances. The Supreme Court in *Meritor* rejected the EEOC Guidelines' position on employer liability for supervisors or managerial employees and instead held that employer liability should be determined according to traditional common-law agency principles; that is, was the harasser acting as an agent of the employer?

Concept *Summary* 7.4

SEXUAL HARASSMENT

- Sexual harassment is:
  - Unwelcome:
    - Sexual advances
    - Requests for sexual favors
    - Verbal or physical conduct of a sexual nature
  - Where the employee is required to accept such conduct as a condition of employment
- Quid pro quo harassment
  - The employee's response to sexual harassment is used as a basis for employment decisions
    - Examples: A male supervisor promising a female employee a promotion if she sleeps with him
- Hostile work environment
  - Sexual harassment unreasonably interferes with the employee's work performance or creates a hostile working environment
    - Example: Coworkers or supervisors continually subject an employee to unwelcome sexual comments or requests for sexual favors.

Agency Relationships

Whether an agency relationship is created is a question of fact to be determined on the specifics of a particular situation. Supervisors or managerial employees, acting in the course of their employment, are generally held to be agents of the employer; that is, they act with the actual, or apparent, authorization of the employer. An agency relationship can also be created by an employer's acceptance of, tolerance of, acquiescence to, or after-the-fact ratification of an employee's conduct, such as when the employer becomes aware of harassment and fails to take action to stop it.

Employer Liability for Supervisors

When is an employer liable under Title VII for sexual harassment by a supervisor or managerial employee? The courts have consistently held an employer liable for quid pro quo sexual harassment by a manager or supervisor because such conduct is related to the supervisor's or manager's job status. But courts have differed over holding an employer liable for hostile environment harassment by a supervisor or manager. Some courts held an employer liable only when the harassment was somehow aided by the supervisor's job status, while other courts held that the employer was liable when it knew or should have known of the harassment. The U.S. Supreme Court settled the issue of employer liability for hostile environment harassment by a supervisor or manager in *Faragher v. City of Boca Raton*.[44] Subsequent to that decision, the EEOC issued a question-and-answer document to guide employers seeking to insulate themselves from vicarious liability.

---

1. When does harassment violate federal law?

Harassment violates federal law if it involves discriminatory treatment based on race, color, sex (with or without sexual conduct), religion, national origin, age, disability, genetic information, or because the employee opposed job discrimination or participated in an investigation or complaint proceeding under the EEO statutes. Federal law does not prohibit simple teasing, offhand comments, or isolated incidents that are not extremely serious. The conduct must be sufficiently frequent or severe to create a hostile work environment or result in a "tangible employment action," such as hiring, firing, promotion, or demotion.

2. Does the guidance apply only to sexual harassment?

No, it applies to *all* types of unlawful harassment.

3. When is an employer legally responsible for harassment by a supervisor?

An employer is always responsible for harassment by a supervisor that culminated in a tangible employment action. If the harassment did not lead to a tangible employment action, the employer is liable unless it proves that: (1) it exercised reasonable care to prevent and promptly correct any harassment *and* (2) the employee unreasonably failed to complain to management or to avoid harm otherwise.

4. Who qualifies as a "supervisor" for purposes of employer liability?

An individual qualifies as an employee's "supervisor" if the individual has the authority to recommend tangible employment decisions affecting the employee *or* if the individual has the authority to direct the employee's daily work activities.

5. What is a "tangible employment action"?

A "tangible employment action" means a significant change in employment status. Examples include hiring, firing, promotion, demotion, undesirable reassignment, a decision causing a significant change in benefits, compensation decisions, and work assignment.

---

[44] 524 U.S. 775 (1998).

6. How might harassment culminate in a tangible employment action?

This might occur if a supervisor fires or demotes a subordinate because she rejects his sexual demands, or promotes her because she submits to his sexual demands.

7. What should employers do to prevent and correct harassment?

Employers should establish, distribute to all employees, and enforce a policy prohibiting harassment and setting out a procedure for making complaints. In most cases, the policy and procedure should be in writing.

8. What should an anti-harassment policy say?

An employer's anti-harassment policy should make clear that the employer will not tolerate harassment based on race, sex, religion, national origin, age, disability, or genetic information, or harassment based on opposition to discrimination or participation in complaint proceedings. The policy should also state that the employer will not tolerate retaliation against anyone who complains of harassment or who participates in an investigation.

9. What are important elements of a complaint procedure?

The employer should encourage employees to report harassment to management before it becomes severe or pervasive.

The employer should designate more than one individual to take complaints, and should ensure that these individuals are in accessible locations. The employer also should instruct all of its supervisors to report complaints of harassment to appropriate officials.

The employer should assure employees that it will protect the confidentiality of harassment complaints to the extent possible.

10. Is a complaint procedure adequate if employees are instructed to report harassment to their immediate supervisors?

No, because the supervisor may be the one committing harassment or may not be impartial. It is advisable for an employer to designate at least one official outside an employee's chain of command to take complaints, to assure that the complaint will be handled impartially.

11. How should an employer investigate a harassment complaint?

An employer should conduct a prompt, thorough, and impartial investigation. The alleged harasser should not have any direct or indirect control over the investigation.

The investigator should interview the employee who complained of harassment, the alleged harasser, and others who could reasonably be expected to have relevant information. The Guidance provides examples of specific questions that may be appropriate to ask.

Before completing the investigation, the employer should take steps to make sure that harassment does not continue. If the parties have to be separated, then the separation should not burden the employee who has complained of harassment. An involuntary transfer of the complainant could constitute unlawful retaliation. Other examples of interim measures are making scheduling changes to avoid contact between the parties or placing the alleged harasser on non-disciplinary leave with pay pending the conclusion of the investigation.

12. How should an employer correct harassment?

If an employer determines that harassment occurred, it should take immediate measures to stop the harassment and ensure that it does not recur. Disciplinary measures should be proportional to the seriousness of the offense. The employer also should correct the effects of the harassment by, for example, restoring leave taken because of the harassment and expunging negative evaluations in the employee's personnel file that arose from the harassment.

13. Are there other measures that employers should take to prevent and correct harassment?

An employer should correct harassment that is clearly unwelcome regardless of whether a complaint is filed. For example, if there is graffiti in the workplace containing racial or sexual epithets, management should not wait for a complaint before erasing it.

An employer should ensure that its supervisors and managers understand their responsibilities under the organization's anti-harassment policy and complaint procedures.

An employer should screen applicants for supervisory jobs to see if they have a history of engaging in harassment. If so, and the employer hires such a candidate, it must take steps to monitor actions taken by that individual in order to prevent harassment.

An employer should keep records of harassment complaints and check those records when a complaint of harassment is made to reveal any patterns of harassment by the same individuals.

14. Does an employee who is harassed by his or her supervisor have any responsibilities?

Yes. The employee must take reasonable steps to avoid harm from the harassment. Usually, the employee will exercise this responsibility by using the employer's complaint procedure.

15. Is an employer legally responsible for its supervisor's harassment if the employee failed to use the employer's complaint procedure?

No, unless the harassment resulted in a tangible employment action or unless it was reasonable for the employee not to complain to management. An employee's failure to complain would be reasonable, for example, if he or she had a legitimate fear of retaliation. The employer must prove that the employee acted unreasonably.

Source: EEOC, "Questions and answers for small employers on employer liability for harassment by supervisors," available at http://www.eeoc.gov/policy/docs/harassment-facts.html.

Employer Liability for Coworkers and Nonemployees

For both quid pro quo harassment and hostile environment harassment by nonsupervisory or nonmanagerial employees, an employer will be liable if it knew of, or should have known of, the harassing conduct and failed to take reasonable steps to stop it. An employer may even be liable for harassment by nonemployees if the employer had some control over the harasser and failed to take reasonable steps to stop it once the employer became aware of, or should have been aware of, the harassment.

Individual Liability

The courts have held that individual employees are not liable for damages under Title VII; this means that the employee doing the harassing will not be held personally liable for damages under Title VII. They are subject to court injunctions to cease and desist from such conduct. But harassers or potential harassers should be aware that they may be held personally liable under the various state EEO laws or under common-law tort claims. The damages under state EEO laws and tort claims may include compensatory and punitive damages in addition to employment-related damages and legal fees.

Public employees who engage in sexual harassment may, in addition to the foregoing remedies, be subject to suits for damages under 42 U.S.C. § 1983 and criminal prosecution under 18 U.S.C. § 242.

Concept *Summary* 7.5

LIABILITY FOR SEXUAL HARASSMENT

- Employer liability
  - Employers are liable for employees acting in the course of their employment, including:
    - Managerial/supervisors
    - Coworkers—if the employer knows or should have known about the harassment and fails to take action to stop it
    - Nonemployees—if the employer knows or should have known about the harassment and fails to take action to stop it
- Individual liability
  - Individual harassers are not liable for damages under Title VII
  - Individuals may face damages under certain state EEO laws or common-law tort claims
  - Public employees may also be subject to criminal prosecution

7-5d Employer Responses to Sexual Harassment Claims

Employers have several defenses to raise against claims of sexual harassment. Prevention is probably the best defense to stop sexual harassment before any legal problems develop.

Prevention

As the Supreme Court decision in *Faragher* stated, the best way for an employer to avoid liability for sexual harassment is to take active steps to prevent it. Both the EEOC Guidelines and the Supreme Court emphasize the importance of having a policy against sexual harassment and of following that policy whenever a complaint arises. According to the EEOC Guidelines and court decisions, the sexual harassment policy should define sexual harassment and give practical, concrete examples of such conduct. The policy must also make it very clear that such conduct by anyone in the organization will not be tolerated, and it should specify the penalties, up to and including termination, for violations of the policy. The policy should spell out the procedures for filing complaints of sexual harassment, designate specific (preferably managerial) employees who are responsible for receiving and investigating complaints, and include reassurances that employees who file complaints will be protected from retaliation or reprisals.

The policy must be communicated to all employees, who should be educated about the policy through training and workshops; all employees must understand the policy and be aware of the employer's commitment to the policy. Above all, the employer must take steps to enforce the policy immediately upon receipt of a complaint of sexual harassment because the policy is effective only if it is followed. If the employer acts promptly to enforce the policy whenever a complaint of sexual harassment is received, it will generally avoid liability for such conduct, according to *Faragher*.

Defenses

In addition to the preventive approach and the defense set out in *Faragher*, employers have a few other defenses to raise when faced with charges of sexual harassment. The definition of sexual harassment indicates that the conduct complained of must be unwelcome and of a sexual nature, and it must either be quid pro quo or serious enough to create a hostile working environment. Generally, the courts will not consider isolated incidents or trivial comments to constitute sexual harassment. As the Supreme Court indicated in *Harris v. Forklift Systems*, factors to consider in determining whether the challenged conduct amounts to sexual harassment include its frequency, severity, whether it is physically threatening or humiliating or a mere offensive utterance, and whether it unreasonably interferes with an employee's work performance. In *Scott v. Sears, Roebuck & Co.*,[45] the court held that one pat on the buttocks, winks, one dinner invitation, and an offer by one employee to give a female employee a rubdown did not create a hostile environment. In *Rabidue v. Osceola Refining Co.*[46] the court held that the display of pin-up photos and posters of nude or scantily clad women did not seriously affect female employees, but in *Barbetta v. Chemlawn Services Corp.*[47] the court held that a proliferation of pornographic material featuring nude women did create a hostile working environment for female employees.

The fact that the harassed employee failed to file a complaint through the employer's sexual harassment complaint procedure does not automatically protect the employer from liability. The employer may still be held liable if it knew of, or had reason to know of, the harassment.[48]

Unwelcome

Conduct of a sexual nature must be unwelcome to be sexual harassment; the target of the harassment must indicate that it is unwelcome. In *Meritor*, the Supreme Court held that as long as the victim indicates that the conduct is unwelcome, it is still sexual harassment, even if the victim voluntarily complies with the harassment. A consensual sexual relationship, instigated by a female employee in an attempt to advance in her job, was held not to be sexual harassment in *Perkins v. General Motors Corporation*.[49]

---

[45] 798 F.2d 210 (7th Cir. 1986).

[46] 805 F.2d 611 (6th Cir. 1986).

[47] 669 F. Supp. 569 (W.D. N.Y. 1987).

[48] *Burlington Industries, Inc. v. Ellerth*, 542 U.S. 742 (1998).

[49] 709 F. Supp. 1487 (W.D. Mo. 1989).

Provocation

Meritor also indicated that the employer can raise the defense of provocation by the victim: Did the victim instigate the allegedly harassing conduct through her or his own style of dress, comments, or conduct? The issue of provocation goes to whether the conduct was unwelcome: If the victim has encouraged the allegedly harassing conduct, is it really unwelcome? In *McLean v. Satellite Technology Services, Inc.*,[50] where a female employee regularly offered to engage in sexual acts with other employees and often lifted her skirt to show her supervisor that she was not wearing undergarments, a single attempt by her supervisor to hug and kiss her was held not to be sexual harassment. However, the fact that an employee had posed nude for a national magazine did not automatically mean that she would find her boss's sexual advances welcome,[51] nor did the fact that a female employee swore "like a drunken sailor" mean that she welcomed harassing conduct.[52]

Conduct of a Sexual Nature

In order to be sexual harassment, the conduct complained of must be based on the employee's sex. Tasteless comments or jokes or annoying behavior, while offensive, may not be sexual harassment. A supervisor who is obnoxious and verbally abusive to all employees is not guilty of sexual harassment as long as the abuse is not based on sex. In *Holman v. State of Indiana*,[53] the U.S. Court of Appeals for the Seventh Circuit held that a supervisor's harassment and solicitation of sexual favors of both male and female employees was not conduct "because of sex."

Concept *Summary* 7.6

DEFENSES TO SEXUAL HARASSMENT CLAIMS

- Prevention
  - Employers should have a policy that:
    - Defines harassment
    - Outlines penalties and procedures for filing complaints
    - Protects employees who file complaints from retaliation

- Defenses
  - Conduct was isolated incident—not frequent or severe enough to cause unreasonable interference with work performance
  - Employee did not indicate that conduct was unwelcome
  - "Victim" provoked harassment through his or her own conduct

---

[50] 673 F. Supp. 1458 (E.D. Mo. 1987).

[51] *Burnes v. McGregor Electronic Industries, Inc.*, 989 F.2d 959 (8th Cir. 1993).

[52] *Steiner v. Showboat Operating Co.*, 25 F.3d 1459 (9th Cir. 1994).

[53] 211 F.3d 399 (7th Cir. 2000).

7-5e   Same-Sex Harassment

The Supreme Court decision in *Oncale v. Sundowner Offshore Services, Inc.*[54] resolved a split among the Courts of Appeals regarding whether same-sex harassment was prohibited by the sexual harassment prohibition of Title VII. The Supreme Court held that Title VII prohibits discrimination because of sex in terms or conditions of employment, including sexual harassment by employees of the same sex as the victim of the harassment. Oncale, a worker on an offshore oil platform, alleged that his male coworkers had subjected him to sexual assault and sex-related humiliating actions and had threatened him with rape. His supervisors failed to take any remedial action when he complained. The Supreme Court decision emphasized that Title VII does not reach conduct tinged with offensive sexual overtones but does forbid conduct of a sexual nature that creates a hostile work environment, conduct so severe as to alter the conditions of the victim's employment. The Court stated:

> We see no justification in the statutory language or our precedents for a categorical rule excluding same-sex harassment claims from the coverage of Title VII. As some courts have observed, male-on-male sexual harassment in the workplace was assuredly not the principal evil Congress was concerned with when it enacted Title VII. But statutory prohibitions often go beyond the principal evil to cover reasonably comparable evils, and it is ultimately the provisions of our laws rather than the principal concerns of our legislators by which we are governed. Title VII prohibits "discriminat [ion] . . . because of . . . sex" in the "terms" or "conditions" of employment. Our holding that this includes sexual harassment must extend to sexual harassment of any kind that meets the statutory requirements.
>
> We have emphasized, moreover, that the objective severity of harassment should be judged from the perspective of a reasonable person in the plaintiff's position, considering "all the circumstances." [citing *Harris*] In same-sex, (as in all) harassment cases, that inquiry requires careful consideration of the social context in which particular behavior occurs and is experienced by its target. A professional football player's working environment is not severely or pervasively abusive, for example, if the coach smacks him on the buttocks as he heads onto the field—even if the same behavior would reasonably be experienced as abusive by the coach's secretary (male or female) back at the office. The real social impact of workplace behavior often depends on a constellation of surrounding circumstances, expectations, and relationships which are not fully captured by a simple recitation of the words used or the physical acts performed. Common sense, and an appropriate sensitivity to social context, will enable courts and juries to distinguish between simple teasing or roughhousing among members of the same sex, and conduct which a reasonable person in the plaintiff's position would find severely hostile or abusive.

According to *Hamner v. St. Vincent Hospital and Health Care Center, Inc.*,[55] Title VII's prohibition on sexual harassment does not include harassment based on sexual orientation or sexual preference. However, a male employee who was harassed by managers and coworkers because he was perceived as being effeminate and did not conform to a male stereotype established a case of hostile environment sexual harassment.[56]

---

[54] 523 U.S. 75 (1998).

[55] 224 F.3d 701 (7th Cir. 2000).

[56] *Nichols v. Azteca Restaurant Enterprises, Inc.*, 256 F.3d 864 (9th Cir. 2001).

7-5f   Remedies for Sexual Harassment

Remedies for sexual harassment available under Title VII include injunctions to stop the harassment and to refrain from such conduct in the future, lost wages and benefits, compensatory and punitive damages for intentional conduct, and legal fees and reinstatement (if appropriate). Employment-related damages, such as back pay, benefits, seniority, and so on, are recoverable in their entirety. Compensatory damages (such as damages for emotional trauma and/or medical expenses) and punitive damages are available in cases of intentional violations of Title VII. Sexual harassment is generally held to be intentional conduct, so such damages are generally available to successful plaintiffs; however, there are statutory limits on the amount of compensatory and punitive damages under Title VII based on the size of the employer. In addition to Title VII, sexual harassment may also be challenged under state EEO laws and common-law torts such as intentional infliction of emotional distress, invasion of privacy, battery, and assault. Compensatory and punitive damages may be available under the various state EEO laws and are usually available under tort law; there are generally no statutory limitations on such damages available under state EEO laws and tort claims.

In addition to Title VII, state EEO laws, and tort claims, federal and state constitutional provisions may also apply to public sector employers guilty of sexual harassment. Public employees who engage in sexual harassment may be subject to suits for damages under 42 U.S.C. § 1983, which allows civil suits for damages against persons who act, under the color of law, to deprive others of legally protected rights. In *United States v. Lanier*,[57] the Supreme Court upheld the criminal prosecution of a public employee guilty of sexual harassment under 18 U.S.C. § 242, which provides for criminal penalties of fines and prison terms of up to 10 years for persons who, under the color of law, willfully subject another person to the deprivation of legally protected rights.

ethical DILEMMA

Your office cubicle is next to that of Mona Leslie, a newly hired female employee in your department. Her male supervisor seems to be devoting a lot of attention to her and drops by her cubicle many times a day. You can hear the supervisor's conversations—and they include some off-color jokes and comments. You have also heard, on several occasions, the supervisor ask Mona to go to lunch with him or to go out for a drink after work. Mona always politely declines his invitations, but at times she appears to be distressed and agitated after the supervisor's visits. In a conversation with Mona, you inform her that you believe that the supervisor's conduct is in violation of the company's sexual harassment policy. She responds that she is a new employee and doesn't want to "make waves" because she really needs her job. What should you do—inform the human resources department of the supervisor's behavior? Explain your response.

---

[57] 520 U.S. 259 (1997).

7-5g Sexual Orientation, Sexual Preference, and Sexual Identity Discrimination

Title VII and Other EEO Legislation

Prior to the U.S. Supreme Court decision in *Price Waterhouse v. Hopkins*, the federal courts had consistently held that Title VII's prohibition of discrimination based on gender does not extend to discrimination against homosexuals or lesbians.[58] Similar decisions held that Title VII did not protect transvestites and transsexuals from employment discrimination.[59] As well, the Rehabilitation Act and the Americans with Disabilities Act specifically exclude homosexuality, bisexuality, transvestism, transsexualism, and other sexual behavior conditions from their protection against discrimination based on disability or handicap as well. Recall, however, that in *Price Waterhouse*, the U.S. Supreme Court held that Title VII's prohibition of sex discrimination included discrimination based on sex stereotypes. In light of that decision, could a male transsexual bring a claim of sex discrimination against the employer who fired him because he did not meet the employer's perceptions of how a male should look and behave? That is the issue addressed in the following case.

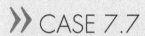

>> CASE 7.7

SMITH V. CITY OF SALEM, OHIO
378 F.3d 566 (6th Cir. 2004)

Facts: Smith had been a lieutenant in the Salem Fire Department for seven years. His service had been without any negative incidents. Smith, a male by birth, was a transsexual and had been diagnosed with gender identity disorder ("GID"), which the American Psychiatric Association characterizes as a disjunction between an individual's sexual organs and sexual identity. After being diagnosed with GID, Smith began expressing a more feminine appearance on a full-time basis, including at work, in accordance with international medical protocols for treating GID. As a result, Smith's coworkers began questioning him about his appearance and commenting that his appearance and mannerisms were not "masculine enough." Smith notified his supervisor, Eastek, about his GID diagnosis and treatment. He also informed Eastek of

the likelihood that his treatment would eventually include a complete physical transformation from male to female. Smith had approached Eastek in order to answer any questions Eastek might have concerning his appearance and manner and so that Eastek could address Smith's coworkers' comments and inquiries. Smith specifically asked Eastek not to divulge the conversation to any of his superiors, particularly to Greenamyer, chief of the fire department. However, Eastek told Greenamyer about Smith's behavior and his GID.

Greenamyer then met with other city officials and arranged a meeting of the City's executive body to discuss Smith and devise a plan for terminating his employment. During the meeting, Greenamyer and the mayor agreed to arrange for the Salem Civil Service Commission to require

---

[58] *DeSantis v. Pacific Telephone and Telegraph Co.*, 608 F.2d 327 (9th Cir. 1979); *Williamson v. A.G. Edwards & Sons, Inc.*, 876 F.2d 69 (8th Cir. 1989).

[59] *Holloway v. Arthur Andersen & Co.*, 566 F.2d 659 (9th Cir. 1977); *Sommers v. Budget Marketing Inc.*, 667 F.2d 748 (8th Cir. 1982); *Ulane v. Eastern Airlines, Inc.*, 742 F.2d 1081 (7th Cir. 1984).

Smith to undergo three separate psychological evaluations. They hoped that Smith would either resign or refuse to comply. If he refused, they could terminate his employment for insubordination. Another official who attended the meeting telephoned Smith afterwards to inform him of the plan.

Two days later, Smith's lawyer telephoned the mayor to advise him of Smith's legal representation and the potential legal problems for the city if it followed through on the plan. Four days later, Greenamyer suspended Smith for one 24-hour shift, based on his alleged infraction of a city and/or fire department policy. Smith challenged his suspension to the city's Civil Service Commission, and ultimately before the county court, which reversed the suspension because the regulation Smith was alleged to have violated was not in effect.

Smith had previously filed a complaint under Title VII with the EEOC, which granted him a right to sue letter. Smith filed suit in the federal district court alleging sex discrimination and retaliation in violation of Title VII. The trial court dismissed Smith's suit on the ground that he failed to state a claim for sex stereotyping pursuant to *Price Waterhouse v. Hopkins.* The trial court held that his claim was really based upon his transsexuality and that Title VII does not prohibit discrimination based on an individual's transsexualism. Smith then appealed to the U.S. Court of Appeals for the Sixth Circuit, claiming that he was a victim of sex discrimination both because of his gender-nonconforming conduct and because of his identification as a transsexual.

Issue: Has Smith established a claim of sex discrimination because of sex stereotyping, under the Supreme Court decision in *Price Waterhouse?*

Decision: Smith claimed that Price Waterhouse applied to his case. He stated that his conduct and mannerisms did not conform to his employers' and coworkers' sex stereotypes of how a man should look and behave, and the discrimination he experienced was a direct result of this. The court of appeals held that Smith had established claims of sex stereotyping and gender discrimination and that the trial court erred in relying on a series of pre–*Price Waterhouse* cases holding that transsexuals were not protected by Title VII.

The Supreme Court decision in *Price Waterhouse* held that Title VII protected a woman who failed to conform to social expectations concerning how a woman should look and behave and established that Title VII's reference to "sex" encompasses both the biological differences between men and women, and gender discrimination based on a failure to conform to stereotypical gender norms. It follows that employers who discriminate against men because they *do* wear dresses and makeup, or otherwise act femininely, are also engaging in sex discrimination, because the discrimination would not occur except for the victim's sex. Sex stereotyping based on a person's gender nonconforming behavior is discrimination in violation of Title VII.

The court of appeals held that Smith had stated a claim of sex discrimination under Title VII. The court reversed the trial court decision and remanded the case back to that court.

《《

Other courts have taken the same approach as the Sixth Circuit did in *Smith*. In *Nichols v. Azteca Restaurant Enterprises, Inc.*,[60] the U.S. Court of Appeals for the Ninth Circuit held that a male employee who was subjected to abuse and ridicule by managers and coworkers because of his effeminate appearance had established a claim under Title VII.

State EEO Legislation

While no federal legislation expressly protects homosexuals, a number of state EEO laws, including those of California, Colorado, Connecticut, Delaware, Hawaii, Illinois, Iowa, Maine, Maryland, Massachusetts, Minnesota, Nevada, New Hampshire, New Jersey, New Mexico, New York, Oregon, Rhode Island, Vermont, Washington,

---

[60] 256 F.3d 864 (9th Cir. 2001).

Wisconsin, and the District of Columbia, prohibit discrimination based on sexual preference or sexual orientation. Other states, including Louisiana, Michigan, Ohio, and Pennsylvania, prohibit sexual orientation or sexual preference discrimination by public sector employers under executive orders issued by the governor. In addition, some large cities such as New York City and San Francisco have human rights ordinances that prohibit discrimination based on sexual orientation or sexual preference. The state EEO laws of California, Colorado, Minnesota, New Jersey, New Mexico, Oregon, Rhode Island, Washington, and the District of Columbia also prohibit employment discrimination based on gender identity or gender expression, which means that transsexuals and persons who have undergone sex-change operations are protected from discrimination on those grounds.

There are some limits to the coverage of the state laws against discrimination based on sexual orientation or sexual preference. In *Boy Scouts of America v. Dale*,[61] the U.S. Supreme Court held that applying the New Jersey Law Against Discrimination's prohibition of discrimination based on sexual orientation to the Boy Scouts violated their constitutional right of expressive association under the First Amendment. The Court stated that prohibiting the Boy Scouts from dismissing a gay assistant scoutmaster would undermine the Boy Scouts' mission of instilling values in young people.

Constitutional Protection

Public employers who discriminate on the basis of homosexuality are subject to the equal protection provisions of the U.S. Constitution, which prohibit arbitrary or "invidious" discrimination. However, that has not stopped public employers from discriminating against homosexuals. The courts have generally allowed public employers to refuse to hire homosexuals when the employer can show that the ban on homosexuals has some legitimate relationship to valid employment-related concerns. In *Doe v. Gates*,[62] the court upheld the CIA's dismissal of a gay clerk typist because he "posed a threat to national security" based on the fact that he hid information about his homosexuality. The FBI's refusal to hire a lesbian as a special agent was upheld because homosexual conduct was illegal in the country in which she would have worked, and the agent would have been subject to blackmail to protect herself or her partner.[63] The Georgia state attorney general's refusal to hire a lesbian as a staff attorney was affirmed on similar grounds in *Shahar v. Bowers*.[64]

A number of cases dealing with discrimination against homosexuals have involved the armed services' refusal to admit homosexuals. In several decisions, the courts have upheld this general policy but have required the military to demonstrate that an individual has engaged in homosexual conduct in order to bar that person from military service.[65] Under President Clinton, the military adopted a "don't ask, don't

---

[61] 530 U.S. 640 (2000).

[62] 981 F.2d 1316 (D.C. Cir. 1993).

[63] *Padula v. Webster*, 822 F.2d 97 (D.C. Cir. 1987).

[64] 114 F.3d 1097 (11th Cir. 1997).

[65] *Watkins v. U.S. Army*, 875 F.2d 699 (9th Cir. 1989); *Meinhold v. United States Dept. of Defense*, 34 F.3d 1469 (9th Cir. 1994).

tell" policy, under which persons will be barred from service if they engage in homosexual conduct or demonstrate a propensity to engage in such conduct. The policy focuses on conduct rather than a person's status. A person's declaration about his or her sexual orientation alone is not sufficient to bar that person from the military. The "don't ask, don't tell" policy has been upheld in several decisions, such as *Phillips v. Perry*[40] and *Thomasson v. Perry*.[41] It must be noted that the constitutional cases discussed above were decided prior to the Supreme Court decision in *Lawrence v. Texas*.[42] In *Lawrence*, which was a criminal law case and not an employment case, the Court, by a 6–3 vote, declared unconstitutional state laws making it a crime for adults of the same sex to engage in consensual sexual activity in the privacy of their home. The majority held that such laws infringed upon the constitutionally protected liberty interests of homosexuals. Some commentators argue that the *Lawrence* case may signal the end of government discrimination against homosexuals. Others claim that the case is more limited and deals only with laws that criminalized private, consensual sexual conduct between adults.

A related case was triggered by a number of law schools that refused to allow military recruiters access to their campuses as a protest over the military's policies regarding homosexuals. Congress reacted by passing legislation (known as the Solomon Amendment) that would cut off federal funds to schools if they did not allow military recruiters campus access. Several of the schools involved filed suit, challenging the Solomon Amendment. The Supreme Court held that the Solomon Amendment did not violate law schools' First Amendment freedom of expressive association.[43]

THE **WORKING** LAW

Rape and Sexual Assault: A Call to Action

Introduction

The numbers alone are stunning: nearly 1 in 5 women—or almost 22 million—have been raped in their lifetimes.

And the numbers don't begin to tell the whole story. They don't tell of the physical, emotional and psychological scars that a victim can carry for life. They don't speak to the betrayal and broken trust when the attacker is a friend, a trusted colleague, or a family member. And they don't give voice to the courage of survivors who work every day to put their lives back together.

Twenty years ago, then-Senator Joe Biden authored the Violence Against Women Act (VAWA) to bring the problem of domestic violence and sexual assault out from the shadows and into the national spotlight. In the intervening decades, help has come: rape crisis centers have been built; hotlines are up and running; dedicated activists,

---

[66] 106 F.3d 1420 (9th Cir. 1997).

[67] 80 F.3d 915 (4th Cir. 1996).

[68] 539 U.S. 558 (2003).

[69] *Rumsfeld v. Forum for Academic and Institutional Rights, Inc.*, 547 U.S. 47 (U.S. 2006).

advocates and service providers have more resources; states have passed tough new laws; and more abusers and sex offenders have been put behind bars.

In 2010, President Obama called upon all federal agencies to make domestic and sexual violence a priority. And in March 7, 2013, he signed the third reauthorization of VAWA, which provides states, tribes, and local communities with unprecedented resources to combat sexual assault. This and other federal programs put federal dollars where they are most needed and effective: for crisis intervention, counseling, criminal justice advocacy, forensic evidence-gathering, medical and social services, law enforcement training and prosecutorial resources. In 2012, President Obama directed federal agencies to develop policies to address domestic violence, sexual assault, and stalking in the federal workplace.

Federal agencies have heeded the President's call to action in many innovative and wide-ranging ways. Among other initiatives, the Administration has issued new guidance to help schools, colleges and universities better understand their obligations to prevent and respond to sexual assault on their campuses; promulgated a series of executive actions to better protect our service members from military sexual assault; developed a national, best-practices protocol for conducting sexual assault forensic examinations; modernized the definition of "rape" for nationwide data collection, ensuring a more accurate accounting of the crime; launched new technologically advanced ways for young women to get help; and enlisted men and boys to take an active stand against sexual violence. And today, the President is establishing a White House Task Force to Protect Students from Sexual Assault—which will go even further to make our schools safer for all students.

More of the Administration's efforts are catalogued in this report—and they are making a real difference.

But despite all the progress, too many of our friends, wives, sisters, daughters and sons are still raped or sexually assaulted every day.

A new generation of anti-rape activists, both women and men, are having a national conversation about rape and sexual assault—and about attitudes toward victims and the role of the criminal justice system in holding offenders accountable.

This report aims to be part of that conversation. It provides an overview of the scope of the problem, identifies those most at risk, describes the costs of this violence (both to survivors and society as a whole), and takes a look at the response of the criminal justice system. The report discusses steps this Administration has taken to address rape and sexual assault, and identifies challenging new fronts on which we should set our sights.

Source: "Rape and Sexual Assault: A Call to Action," The White House Council on Women and Girls, January 2014, available at https://www.whitehouse.gov/sites/default/files/docs/sexual_assault _report_1-21-14.pdf.

CHAPTER REVIEW

» Key Terms

» Summary

- Title VII allows employers to select employees based on their gender, religion, or national origin when these criteria are bona fide occupational qualifications (BFOQs) that are necessary for the safe and efficient operation of the business. The courts will look closely at the particular job in question and the employer's justification for the BFOQ. Title VII does not allow the use of race or color as a BFOQ.

- Employers need to ensure that all aspects of the employment process are free from gender discrimination. Promotions and work assignments must not be based on stereotypical assumptions about men's and women's roles or capabilities. Pay and benefits must comply with the Equal Pay Act and with Title VII, and employers must not restrict the job opportunities of females because of concerns about potential hazards to pregnant women or their children. The Family and Medical Leave Act requires larger employers to allow employees unpaid leave for childbirth, adoption, and medical conditions; for issues arising from the call to active military service; and to care for injuries or illness suffered during military service.

- Sexual harassment in the workplace can pose serious legal and morale problems; employers should take positive steps to inform employees that sexual harassment will not be tolerated and that the employer has a policy in place to resolve sexual complaints fairly and effectively. Title VII does not prohibit discrimination based on sexual orientation or sexual preference, but some states do outlaw such discrimination. The equal protection clause of the U.S. Constitution may restrict sexual orientation or sexual preference discrimination by public sector employers.

» Problems

» Questions

1. Can customer preference be used to support a restaurant's decision to hire only male waiters? What must an employer demonstrate to justify using gender as a BFOQ for hiring?

2. Must an employer offer paid pregnancy leave for employees under Title VII? How do the Pregnancy Discrimination Act provisions of Title VII affect employment benefits?

3. Under what circumstances can an employer be held liable for a supervisor's sexual harassment of another employee? For sexual harassment by a coworker? For sexual harassment by a nonemployee?

4. When can Title VII be used to challenge gender-based pay differentials for jobs that are not equivalent? Is there a difference between coverage of the Equal Pay Act and that of the pay discrimination prohibitions of Title VII? Explain your answers.

5. Are all employees entitled to take leave under the Family and Medical Leave Act? Explain.

» Case Problems

6. Anderson, a female attorney, was hired as an associate in a large law firm in 2001. She had accepted the position based on the firm's representations that associates would advance to partnership after five or six years and that being promoted to partner "was a matter of course" for associates who received satisfactory evaluations. The firm also maintained that promotions were made on a "fair and equal basis." Anderson consistently received satisfactory evaluations, yet her promotion to partnership was rejected in 2007. She again was considered and rejected in 2008. The firm's rules state that an associate passed over for promotion must seek employment elsewhere. Anderson was therefore terminated by the firm on December 31, 2008. The firm, with more than 50 partners, has never had a female partner. Anderson filed a complaint alleging gender discrimination against the firm. The firm replied that the selection of partners is not subject to Title VII because it entails a change in status "from employee to employer."

   Does Title VII apply to such partnership selection decisions? Does Anderson's complaint state a claim under Title VII? [See *Hishon v. King & Spaulding*, 467 U.S. 69 (U.S. Sup. Ct. 1984).]

7. Pin Ups is an adult entertainment club that features nude dancers. Its main form of entertainment is female performers who remove their clothes and dance for the customers. Pin Ups requires that performers be attractive and remain fit. While it has no rule concerning pregnancy, for both appearance and safety reasons, the club's owners will ask pregnant employees to leave until they "terminate the pregnancy or carry it out." The plaintiff told her "house mom" at the club that she was pregnant. The house mom told her not to dance. When she appeared on the stage anyway, she was fired. The plaintiff claims she is a victim of sex and pregnancy discrimination. The club's owner is defending on the basis that appearance is a BFOQ.

   How should the federal court rule? [See *Berry v. Great American Dream, Inc.*, 2014 WL 7906860 (U.S. Dist. Ct., N.D. Ga., 2014).]

8. A group of nurses employed by the state of Illinois filed a complaint charging the state with gender discrimination in classification and compensation of employees. The nurses alleged that the state had refused to implement the changes in job classifications and wage rates recommended by an evaluation study conducted by the state. The study suggested that changes in pay and classification for some female-dominated job classes should be more equitable.

   Does the nurses' complaint state a claim under Title VII? Explain your answer. [See *American Nurses Association v. Illinois*, 783 F.2d 716 (7th Cir. 1986).]

9. Baker, a female, was employed as a history teacher by More Science High School for three years. Although she received good evaluation reviews for her first two years, her third-year review was poor. Her contract of employment was not renewed after the end of her third year. During Baker's third year, the coach of the boys' basketball team had given notice of his resignation, which was effective at the end of that school year. Baker was replaced by Dan Roundball, who was also hired as the coach of the boys' basketball team. Baker filed a complaint with the EEOC, alleging that her contract was not renewed because the school wanted to replace her with a man who would also coach the basketball team.

   Is More Science High School guilty of violating Title VII's prohibition on gender discrimination? Explain your answer. [See *Carlile v. South Routt School Dist.*, 739 F.2d 1496 (10th Cir. 1984).]

10. Linda Collins worked for Bowers Corp. for several years; in the past year, she had received 12 informal and 4 formal warnings for deficient attendance. Shortly after receiving the latest warning, she called in sick for two days. She simply informed her employer that she was "sick"; she did not provide any additional information or describe the nature of her sickness. Because of her prior attendance problems, Collins's employer fired her. She then filed suit under the FMLA, offering evidence that she suffered from depression and was being treated by Dr. Ronald K. Leonard. Dr. Leonard testified that Collins is incapacitated by depression between 10 percent and 20 percent of the time, and that episodes may occur without warning. The employer claimed that the notice given by Collins was not adequate to trigger protection under the FMLA.

   Has the employer violated the FMLA by firing Collins? Explain your answer. [See *Linda S. Collins v. NTN-Bower Corp.*, 272 F.3d 1006 (7th Cir. 2001).]

11. In October 2006, Rebecca Thomas was hired as a personnel assistant by Cooper Industries, a plant that manufactures hammers, axes, and other hand tools. In February 2007, Thomas was promoted to personnel supervisor. Her boss, the plant's employee relations manager, was fired in March 2007, whereupon she filled his job in an acting capacity. The plant manager gave her the highest possible rating on her performance evaluation, but corporate officials repeatedly refused to interview her for permanent award of the position. According to testimony, the plant manager was told by the company vice president that there was "no way" a female employee relations manager could stand up to the union. A male was ultimately hired to fill the job on a permanent basis.

   Is this an example of gender discrimination? Explain your answer. [See *Thomas v. Cooper Industries, Inc.*, 627 F. Supp. 655 (W.D. N.C. 1986).]

12. Alvie Thompkins was employed as a full-time instructor of mathematics at Morris Brown College. Her classes were scheduled in academic year 2007–2008 in such a way that she was able to hold down a second full-time post as a math instructor at Douglas High School. Only one other faculty member, Thompkins's predecessor at Morris Brown College, ever held down two concurrent full-time jobs, and the college's vice president for academic affairs testified that he had never been aware of this earlier situation. Some male part-time faculty of the college were employed full-time elsewhere. Although labeled part-timers, some of these faculty sometimes taught 9 to 12 credit hours per semester, which was about the same as many "full-time" faculty. Thompkins was told to choose between her two full-time jobs. When she refused to make a choice, she was fired.

   Is this a case of gender discrimination? Explain your answer. [See *Thompkins v. Morris Brown College*, 752 F.2d 558, 37 F.E.P. Cases 24 (11th Cir. 1985).]

13. Diane L. Matthews served in the U.S. Army for four years as a field communication equipment mechanic. She received numerous awards and high performance ratings and ultimately was promoted to sergeant. After she was honorably discharged,

she enrolled in the University of Maine and joined the Reserve Officers Training Corps program on campus. Her ROTC instructor learned that she had attended a student senate meeting, which had been called to discuss the budget for the WildeStein Club. Upon inquiring as to the nature of the club, he was told by Matthews that it was the campus homosexual organization. On further inquiry, she told the officer she was a lesbian. Although her commander did not attempt to interfere with Matthews's continued membership in the club, he reported Matthews's disclosure to his supervisor. An investigation was conducted, and she was disenrolled from the ROTC program.

Was Matthews a victim of gender discrimination? Explain your answer. [See *Matthews v. Marsh*, 755 F.2d 182, 37 F.E.P. Cases 126 (1st Cir. 1985).]

14. Wilson, a male, applied for a job as a flight attendant with Southwest Airlines. Southwest refused to hire him because the airline hires only females for those positions. Southwest, a small commuter airline in the southwestern United States, must compete against larger, more established airlines for passengers. Southwest, which has its headquarters at Love Field in Dallas, decided that the best way to compete with those larger airlines was to establish a distinctive image. Southwest decided to base its marketing image as the "Love Airline"; its slogan is, "We're spreading love all over Texas." Southwest requires its flight attendants and ticket clerks, all female, to wear a uniform consisting of a brief halter top, hot pants, and high boots. Its quick ticketing and check-in flight counters are called "quickie machines," and the in-flight snacks and drinks are referred to as "love bites" and "love potions." Southwest claims that it is identified with the public through its "youthful, feminine" image; it cites surveys of its passengers to support its claim that business necessity requires it to hire only females for all public contact positions. The surveys asked passengers the reasons that they chose to fly with Southwest; the reason labeled "courteous and attentive hostesses" was ranked fifth in importance, after reasons relating to lower fares, frequency of flights, on-time departures, and helpful reservations personnel.

Has Southwest established that its policy of hiring only females in flight attendant and ticket clerk positions is a bona fide occupational qualification? [See *Wilson v. Southwest Airlines Co.*, 517 F. Supp. 292 (N.D. Texas 1981).]

15. George Vorman was being recruited by the National Aeronautics and Space Administration (NASA) as a defense intelligence coordinator; that position involved access to classified intelligence and national security information. After the preliminary round of interviews, NASA required him to undergo extensive psychological testing and expanded security clearance investigation far beyond those normally required of recruits. Vorman was informed that the expanded investigation and testing were required because he was suspected of being homosexual. Vorman refused to either affirm or deny that he was homosexual because he felt that it was irrelevant to his qualifications for the job. NASA ultimately refused to hire Vorman; he filed suit, claiming he was discriminated against because of NASA's perception of his sexual orientation.

On what legal provisions can Vorman base his suit? Is he likely to win? Would the outcome be different if Vorman applied for a flight engineer position that did not involve classified national security information? Explain your answers. [See *Norton v. Macy*, 417 F.2d 1161 (D.C. Cir. 1969); and *High Tech Gays v. Defense Industry Security Clearance Office*, 895 F.2d 563 (9th Cir. 1990).]

» Hypothetical Scenarios

16. Carol Lee was a local sales representative for CableCo, a national cable TV network. When a vacancy in the position of regional sales manager arose, Carol applied for the job. Her supervisor told her that the job involved a lot of overnight travel, and because she had small children, it "wouldn't be right" for her. The position was given instead to Tom Matthews, a single male with no children. Has Lee's employer violated Title VII's prohibitions against sex discrimination? Explain.

17. When Tom Berks asks his employer if the firm's health insurance benefits cover same-sex partners, he is fired. Under what laws, if any, does Berks have a legal claim? Why?

18. Nancy Carter's son, a soldier stationed in Afghanistan, was injured in combat and will have to undergo a lengthy rehabilitation. Carter asks her employer, the Denver Public School District, for a leave to help her son during his rehabilitation. Is Carter entitled to such leave? Explain. What must Carter provide the employer to support her request for the leave?

19. Mark Morris is a professor at Enormous State University. Every morning he greets the department secretary, Mollie Bloom, by saying, "Hello, sexy!" Bloom has become increasingly annoyed by Morris's comments, but whenever she complains to Gilman, the department chair, he ignores her complaints or tells her she needs to develop a sense of humor. Does Bloom have a legitimate complaint of sexual harassment? What must she show to establish such a claim? Would the university be held liable for Morris's conduct? How would your answer change if Bloom were Morris's graduate student instead of an employee of the university?

20. Linda Brown and Ralph Williams are recent law school graduates hired as first-year associates by Dewey, Cheatem, and Howe, a large Boston law firm. Brown graduated from Suffolk Law School, while Williams graduated from Harvard Law School. Over coffee one day, Brown discovers that Williams is being paid $20,000 more than she is. Is Dewey, Cheatem, and Howe violating the law by paying Brown less than Williams? Explain.

CHAPTER 8

Discrimination Based on Religion and National Origin and Procedures Under Title VII

The preceding chapters dealt with Title VII of the Civil Rights Act of 1964 and its prohibitions on employment discrimination based on race and sex. This chapter deals with the Title VII provisions and procedures regarding discrimination based on religion and national origin. The section dealing with religion also touches upon recent developments involving the Religious Freedom Restoration Act (RFRA).[1]

8-1   Discrimination on the Basis of Religion

Title VII prohibits employment discrimination because of religion. The definition of religion under Title VII is fairly broad; it includes "... all aspects of religious observance and practice, as well as belief...." Harassment because of an individual's religious beliefs (or lack thereof) that creates a hostile work environment is also prohibited under Title VII. Title VII protection extends to the beliefs and practices connected with organized religions but also includes what the EEOC Guidelines[2] define as a person's moral or ethical beliefs as to what is right and wrong which are sincerely held with the strength of traditional religious views." Such personal moral or ethical beliefs are protected even if the beliefs are not connected with any formal or organized religion. Atheism is included under the Title VII definition of religion according to *Young v. Southwestern Savings & Loan Association*,[3] but personal political or social ideologies are not protected. The racist and anti-Semitic beliefs of the Ku Klux Klan do not fall under the definition of religion,[4] and harassment of an individual because of that person's self-identification as a member of the Ku Klux Klan was not harassment because of religion and did not give rise to a claim under Title VII.[5]

---

[1] 42 U.S.C. 2000bb through 2000bb-4.

[2] 29 C.F.R. § 1605.1.

[3] 509 F.2d 140 (5th Cir. 1975).

[4] *Bellamy v. Mason's Stores, Inc.*, 368 F. Supp. 1025 (W.D. Va. 1973), *aff'd on other grounds*, 508 F.2d (4th Cir. 1974).

[5] *Swartzentruber v. Gunite Corp.*, 99 F. Supp. 2d 976 (N.D. Ind. 2000).

8-1a   Exceptions for Religious Preference and Religious Employers

Constitutional Issues

Government action involving religion raises issues under the First Amendment of the U.S. Constitution. The U.S. Constitution regulates the relationship between the government and the governed. That means that public sector employers, in addition to being covered by Title VII, are also subject to the constitutional protections for freedom of religion under the First Amendment of the U.S. Constitution. The First Amendment prohibits the establishment of religion by government (generally interpreted as government conduct favoring or promoting religion) and also prohibits undue government interference with the free exercise of religion. The Supreme Court has broadly interpreted religion in determining the scope of protection under the First Amendment, requiring only that the plaintiff demonstrate that her belief is "religious" in her own scheme of things and that it is sincerely held with the strength of traditional religious beliefs.[6] The case of *Lemon v. Kurtzman*[7] (discussed in the *Amos* case, see Case 8.1) set out a three-part test to determine if government action affecting religion violates the First Amendment:

- Does the government action have a secular purpose?
- Does the action neither advance nor inhibit religion?
- Does the government action involve "entanglement" of church and state?

In *Estate of Thornton v. Caldor, Inc.*,[8] the Supreme Court held that a Connecticut statute requiring employers to allow employees to take off work on their religious Sabbath was unconstitutional. That statute violated the First Amendment because it advanced a religious purpose: It gave Sabbath observers an unqualified right not to work, and it ignored the interests and convenience of the employer and other employees who did not observe a Sabbath.

In 1993, believing that the Supreme Court's so-called "*Lemon* Test" gave government entities too much leeway in enforcing laws against religious entities, Congress overwhelmingly enacted bipartisan legislation, known as the Religious Freedom Restoration Act (RFRA). The statute, signed by President Clinton, was soon declared unconstitutional to the extent that its provisions applied to state and local laws. However, the statute remains operative with regard to the federal government. In 2014, the Supreme Court heard the case of a closely held corporation, the family shareholders of which objected to providing certain contraceptives to their employees under the company's group health-insurance plan.

THE **WORKING** LAW

A Divided Supreme Court Holds that RFRA Trumps Obamacare

Hobby Lobby Stores, Inc. began out of founder David Green's garage and has grown from one 300-square-foot store to more than 550 stores across the country, becoming one of the nation's leading arts and crafts retailers.

---

[6] *Welsh v. United States*, 398 U.S. 333 (1970); *United States v. Seeger*, 380 U.S. 163 (1965); and *Frazee v. Illinois Dept. of Employment Security*, 489 U.S. 829 (1989).

[7] 403 U.S. 602 (1971).

[8] 472 U.S. 703 (1985).

Devout Christians, the Green family believes that "it is by God's grace and provision that Hobby Lobby has endured." Therefore, the Greens seek to honor God by "operating their company in a manner consistent with Biblical principles."

Believing their employees should have the opportunity to spend Sundays with their families, the company is closed on Sundays and only operates 66 hours per week. Indeed, the Greens strive to apply the Christian teachings on respect and fairness to their employees, increasing the pay of Hobby Lobby's full- and part-time hourly workers for four years in a row. Full-time hourly workers now start at 90 percent above the federal minimum wage.

The Hobby Lobby success story is a true example of the American dream. Now the Greens want to live another American dream: that every American, including business owners like the Greens, should be free to live and do business according to their beliefs.

The HHS mandate requires the family-owned business to provide insurance coverage for potentially life-terminating drugs and devices, contrary to the Greens' religious convictions—or pay fines to the IRS.

The Green family has no moral objection to the use of 16 of 20 preventive contraceptives required in the mandate, and Hobby Lobby will continue its longstanding practice of covering these preventive contraceptives for its employees. However, the Green family cannot provide or pay for four potentially life-threatening drugs and devices. These drugs include Plan B and Ella, the so-called morning-after pill and the week-after pill. Covering these drugs and devices would violate their deeply held religious belief that life begins at the moment of conception, when an egg is fertilized.

The Greens believe that Hobby Lobby cannot fulfill its mission while paying for drugs and devices that conflict with their beliefs. That is why Hobby Lobby filed suit to defend its constitutional freedom to carry out its mission, consistent with its owners' religious principles. Their case has now gone all the way to the Supreme Court.

The Green family respects the religious convictions of all Americans, including those who do not agree with them. All they are asking is that the government give them the same respect by not forcing them to violate their religious beliefs.

The Supreme Court heard oral argument in this case on March 25, 2014. On June 30, the Court ruled 5–4 in favor of David and Barbara Green and their family business, Hobby Lobby.

Source: *Burwell v. Hobby Lobby*, The Becket Fund for Religious Liberty, available at http://www.becketfund.org/hobbylobby.

Ministerial Exemption Under Title VII

Religious organizations, like individuals, enjoy the right of free exercise of religion under the First Amendment. Subjecting the actions of religious organizations to the provisions of Title VII could involve "excessive entanglement" of the government into the affairs of the religious organization. To avoid such constitutional concerns, and to avoid government interference with the free exercise rights of the religious organization, the federal courts have created a "ministerial exemption" under Title VII when a discrimination complaint involves personnel decisions of religious organizations regarding who would perform spiritual functions and about how those functions would be organized. For example, in

Petruska v. Gannon University,[9] a female chaplain of a private Catholic university was removed from her position and replaced by a male. She claimed that the action was prompted by her gender and by the fact that she had complained about the university's response to sexual harassment claims. The U.S. Court of Appeals for the Third Circuit held that university's actions were protected by the "ministerial exception" because the position of chaplain served a spiritual function, and the religious institution was free to determine how to structure or reorganize that spiritual position. Most courts have limited the ministerial exemption to employment decisions of the religious employer—such as the Catholic Church's ban on female priests. Actions such as sexual harassment or retaliation by a religious employer may not be exempt because they do not involve protected employment decisions, according to *Elvig v. Calvin Presbyterian Church*.[10]

Statutory Provisions for Religious Preference

In addition to the ministerial exemption created by the courts under Title VII, the act contains several statutory provisions that allow employers to exercise religious preference in certain situations.

Religion as a BFOQ Section 703(e)(1) of Title VII includes religion within the BFOQ exception. Religion, as with gender or national origin, may be used as a BFOQ when the employer establishes that business necessity (the safe and efficient performance of the job) requires hiring individuals of a particular religion. Only rarely will a private sector business be able to establish a BFOQ based on religion. For example, an employer who is providing helicopter pilots under contract to the Saudi Arabian government to fly Muslim pilgrims to Mecca may require that all pilots be of the Muslim religion because Islamic law prohibits non-Muslims from entering the holy areas of the city of Mecca. The penalty for violating the prohibition is beheading. The employer could therefore refuse to hire non-Muslims or require all pilots to convert to Islam.[11]

Educational Institutions Under Section 703(e)(2)

Religiously affiliated schools, colleges, universities, or other educational institutions are permitted to give preference to members of their particular religion in hiring. This exception is broader than that available under the BFOQ provisions. Under Section 703(e)(2), the educational institution does not have to demonstrate business necessity to give preference to members of its religion when hiring employees. Therefore, a Hebrew day school can require that all of its teachers be Jewish, and a Catholic university like Notre Dame can require that the university president be Catholic. However, it is important to note that other federal agencies, such as the National Labor Relations Board, accord educational institutions with religious affiliations a lesser level of exemption from their jurisdiction.[12]

Section 702(a)

In addition to the exception granted to religious schools or colleges under Section 703(e)(2), Section 702(a) provides an exception under Title VII to all

[9] 462 F.3d 294 (3d Cir. 2006).
[10] 375 F.3d 951 (9th Cir. 2004).
[11] See the case of *Kern v. Dynalectron Corp.*, 577 F. Supp. 1196 (N.D. Texas 1983).
[12] See Chapter 12.

- religious societies;

- religious corporations;

- religious educational institutions; or

- religious associations.

This exception covers all religious entities and is wider than that under Section 703(e)(2), which is limited to religious educational institutions. Section 702(a) states:

> This Title shall not apply to … a religious corporation, association, educational institution, or society with respect to the employment of individuals of a particular religion to perform work connected with the carrying on by such corporation, association, educational institution or society of its activities.

But how broad is the scope of the exemption under Section 702(a)? Does it extend to all activities of a religious corporation, even those that are not really religious in character? The Supreme Court considered that question in the next case.

CASE 8.1

CORPORATION OF THE PRESIDING BISHOP OF THE CHURCH OF JESUS CHRIST OF LATTER-DAY SAINTS V. AMOS

483 U.S. 327 (1987)

[Note that this case was decided prior to the 1991 amendments to Title VII, when Section 702(a) was simply Section 702.]

White, J.

Section 702 of the Civil Rights Act of 1964, as amended, exempts religious organizations from Title VII's prohibition against discrimination in employment on the basis of religion. The question presented is whether applying the Section 702 exemption to the secular nonprofit activities of religious organizations violates the Establishment Clause of the First Amendment. The District Court held that it does, and the case is here on direct appeal.

The Deseret Gymnasium (Gymnasium) in Salt Lake City, Utah, is a nonprofit facility, open to the public, run by the Corporation of the Presiding Bishop of The Church of Jesus Christ of Latter-day Saints (CPB), and the Corporation of the President of The Church of Jesus Christ of Latter-day Saints (COP). The CPB and the COP are religious entities associated with The Church of Jesus Christ of Latter-day Saints (Church), an unincorporated religious association sometimes called the Mormon or LDS Church.

Mayson worked at the Gymnasium for some 16 years as an assistant building engineer and then building engineer.

He was discharged in 1981 because he failed to qualify for a temple recommend; that is, a certificate that he is a member of the Church and eligible to attend its temples.

Mayson and others purporting to represent a class of plaintiffs brought an action against the CPB and the COP alleging, among other things, discrimination on the basis of religion in violation . . . of the Civil Rights Act of 1964. . . . The defendants moved to dismiss this claim on the ground that Section 702 shields them from liability. The plaintiffs contended that if construed to allow religious employers to discriminate on religious grounds in hiring for nonreligious jobs, Section 702 violates the Establishment Clause [of the First Amendment].

The District Court first considered whether the facts of this case require a decision on the plaintiffs' constitutional argument. Starting from the premise that the religious activities of religious employers can permissibly be exempted under Section 702, the court developed a three-part test to determine whether an activity is religious. Applying this test to Mayson's situation, the court found: first, that the Gymnasium is intimately connected to the Church financially and in matters of management; second, that there is no clear connection between the primary function which the Gymnasium performs and the religious beliefs and tenets of the Mormon Church or church administration; and third, that none of Mayson's duties at the Gymnasium are "even tangentially related to any conceivable religious belief or ritual of the Mormon Church or church administration," ... The court concluded that Mayson's case involves nonreligious activity.

The court next considered the plaintiffs' constitutional challenge to Section 702. Applying the three-part test set out in *Lemon v. Kurtzman* . . ., the court first held that Section 702 has the permissible secular purpose of "assuring that the government remains neutral and does not meddle in religious affairs by interfering with the decision-making process in religions. . . ." The court concluded, however, that Section 702 fails the second part of the *Lemon* test because the provision has the primary effect of advancing religion. Among the considerations mentioned by the court were: that Section 702 singles out religious entities for a benefit, rather than benefiting a broad grouping of which religious organizations are only a part; that Section 702 is not supported by long historical tradition; and that Section 702 burdens the free exercise rights of employees of religious institutions who work in nonreligious jobs. Finding that Section 702 impermissibly sponsors religious organizations by granting them "an exclusive authorization to engage in conduct which can directly and immediately advance religious tenets and practices," the court declared the statute unconstitutional as applied to secular activity. The court entered summary judgment in favor of Mayson and ordered him reinstated with backpay. Subsequently, the court vacated its judgment so that the United States could intervene to defend the constitutionality of Section 702. After further briefing and argument the court affirmed its prior determination and reentered a final judgment for Mayson. . . .

We find unpersuasive the District Court's reliance on the fact that Section 702 singles out religious entities for a benefit. Although the Court has given weight to this consideration in its past decisions, it has never indicated that statutes that give special consideration to religious groups are *per se* invalid. That would run contrary to the teaching of our cases that there is ample room for accommodation of religion under the Establishment Clause.

Where, as here, government acts with the proper purpose of lifting a regulation that burdens the exercise of religion, we see no reason to require that the exemption come packaged with benefits to secular entities. We are also unpersuaded by the District Court's reliance on the argument that Section 702 is unsupported by long historical tradition. There was simply no need to consider

the scope of the Section 702 exemption until the 1964 Civil Rights Act was passed, and the fact that Congress concluded after eight years that the original exemption was unnecessarily narrow is a decision entitled to deference, not suspicion.

Appellees argue that Section 702 offends equal protection principles by giving less protection to the employees of religious employers than to the employees of secular employers.

... In a case such as this, where a statute is neutral on its face and motivated by a permissible purpose of limiting governmental interference with the exercise of religion, we see no justification for applying strict scrutiny to a statute that passes the *Lemon* test. The proper inquiry is whether Congress has chosen a rational classification to further a legitimate end. We have already indicated that Congress acted with a legitimate purpose in expanding the Section 702 exemption to cover all activities of religious employers.... it suffices to hold—as we now do—that as applied to the nonprofit activities of religious employers, Section 702 is rationally related to the legitimate purpose of alleviating significant governmental interference with the ability of religious organizations to define and carry out their religious missions.

It cannot be seriously contended that Section 702 impermissibly entangles church and state; the statute effectuates a more complete separation of the two and avoids the kind of intrusive inquiry into religious belief that the District Court engaged in this case. The statute easily passes muster under the third part of the *Lemon* test.

The judgment of the District Court is reversed, and the case is remanded for further proceedings consistent with this opinion.

It is so ordered.

Brennan, J., with whom Marshall, J. joins (concurring)

... my concurrence in the judgment rests on the fact that this case involves a challenge to the application of Section 702's categorical exemption to the activities of a nonprofit organization. I believe that the particular character of nonprofit activity makes inappropriate a case-by-case determination whether its nature is religious or secular....

... I concur in the Court's judgment that the nonprofit Deseret Gymnasium may avail itself of an automatic exemption from Title VII's proscription on religious discrimination.

O'Connor, J. (concurring)

... I emphasize that under the holding of the Court, and under my view of the appropriate Establishment Clause analysis, the question of the constitutionality of the Section 702 exemption as applied to for-profit activities of religious organizations remains open.

Case Questions

1. What is the relevance of the three-part test set out in *Lemon v. Kurtzman* to a claim under Title VII?

2. What, according to the Supreme Court, was the rationale for the enactment of the Section 702(a) exemption for religious organizations? How does that purpose relate to the three-part test from *Lemon v. Kurtzman*?

3. Does the Section 702(a) exemption apply to all activities of religious organizations, even to commercial activities? Does the exemption allow religious organizations to discriminate on the basis of race or gender? Explain your answers.

Reasonable Accommodation

Even when religion is not a BFOQ and the employer is not within the Section 702 exemption, the prohibition against discrimination on the basis of religion is not absolute. Section 701(j) defines religion as:

> includ[ing] all aspects of religious observance and practice, as well as belief, unless an employer demonstrates that he is unable to reasonably accommodate to an employee's religious observance or practice without undue hardship on the conduct of the employer's business.

An employer must make reasonable attempts to accommodate an employee's religious beliefs or practices, but if such attempts are not successful or involve undue hardship, the employer may discharge the employee. The following case explores the extent to which an employer is required to accommodate an employee's beliefs.

CASE 8.2

TRANS WORLD AIRLINES V. HARDISON

432 U.S. 63 (1977)

White, J.

Petitioner Trans World Airlines (TWA) operates a large maintenance and overhaul base in Kansas City, Mo. On June 5, 1967, respondent Larry G. Hardison was hired by TWA to work as a clerk in the Stores Department at its Kansas City base. Because of its essential role in the Kansas City operation, the Stores Department must operate 24 hours per day, 365 days per year, and whenever an employee's job in that department is not filled, an employee must be shifted from another department, or a supervisor must cover the job, even if the work in other areas may suffer.

Hardison, like other employees at the Kansas City base, was subject to a seniority system contained in a collective-bargaining agreement which TWA maintains with petitioner International Association of Machinists and Aerospace Workers (IAM).

The seniority system is implemented by the union steward through a system of bidding by employees for particular shift assignments as they become available. The most senior employees have first choice for job and shift assignments, and the most junior employees are required to work when the union steward is unable to find enough people willing to work at a particular time or in a particular job to fill TWA's needs.

In the spring of 1968 Hardison began to study the religion known as the Worldwide Church of God. One of the tenets of that religion is that one must observe the Sabbath by refraining from performing any work from sunset on Friday until sunset on Saturday. The religion also proscribes work on certain specified religious holidays.

When Hardison informed Everett Kussman, the manager of the Stores Department, of his religious conviction regarding observance of the Sabbath, Kussman agreed that the union steward should seek a job swap for Hardison or a change of days off; that Hardison would have his religious holidays off whenever possible if Hardison agreed to work the traditional holidays when asked; and that Kussman would try to find Hardison another job that would be more compatible with his religious beliefs. The problem was temporarily solved when Hardison transferred to the 11 P.M.–7 A.M. shift. Working this shift permitted Hardison to observe his Sabbath.

The problem soon reappeared when Hardison bid for and received a transfer from Building 1, where he had been employed, to Building 2, where he would work the day shift. The two buildings had entirely separate seniority lists; and while in Building 1 Hardison had sufficient seniority to observe the Sabbath regularly, he was second from the bottom on the Building 2 seniority list.

In Building 2 Hardison was asked to work Saturdays when a fellow employee went on vacation. TWA agreed to permit the union to seek a change of work assignments for Hardison, but the union was not willing to violate the seniority provisions set out in the collective-bargaining contract, and Hardison had insufficient seniority to bid for a shift having Saturdays off.

A proposal that Hardison work only four days a week was rejected by the company. Hardison's job was essential, and on weekends he was the only available person on his shift to perform it. To leave the position empty would have impaired Supply Shop functions, which were critical to airline operations; to fill Hardison's position with a supervisor or an employee from another area would simply have undermanned another operation; and to employ someone not regularly assigned to work Saturdays would have required TWA to pay premium wages.

When an accommodation was not reached, Hardison refused to report for work on Saturdays. . . . [Hardison was fired by TWA.]

The Court of Appeals found that TWA had committed an unlawful employment practice under Section 703(a)(1) of the Act. . . .

In 1967 the EEOC amended its guidelines to require employers "to make reasonable accommodations to the religious needs of employees and prospective employees where such accommodations can be made without undue hardship on the conduct of the employer's business." The Commission did not suggest what sort of accommodations are "reasonable" or when hardship to an employer becomes "undue."

This question—the extent of the required accommodation—remained unsettled. . . . Congress [then]

included the following definition of religion in its 1972 amendments to Title VII:

> The term "religion" includes all aspects of religious observance and practice, as well as belief, unless an employer demonstrates that he is unable to reasonably accommodate to an employee's or prospective employee's religious observance or practice without undue hardship on the conduct of the employer's business. [Section 701(j)] . . .

The Court of Appeals held that TWA had not made reasonable efforts to accommodate Hardison's religious needs. . . .

We disagree. . . .

. . . As the record shows, Hardison himself testified that Kussman was willing, but the union was not, to work out a shift or job trade with another employee.

. . . it appears to us that the [seniority] system itself represented a significant accommodation to the needs, both religious and secular, of all of TWA's employees. As will become apparent, the seniority system represents a neutral way of minimizing the number of occasions when an employee must work on a day that he would prefer to have off. . . .

We are also convinced, contrary to the Court of Appeals, that TWA cannot be faulted for having failed itself to work out a shift or job swap for Hardison. Both the union and TWA had agreed to the seniority system; the union was unwilling to entertain a variance over the objections of men senior to Hardison. . . .

Had TWA nevertheless circumvented the seniority system by relieving Hardison of Saturday work and ordering a senior employee to replace him, it would have denied the latter his shift preference so that Hardison could be given his. The senior employee would also have been deprived of his contractual rights under the collective-bargaining agreement.

Title VII does not contemplate such unequal treatment. . . . we conclude that Title VII does not require an employer to go that far.

. . . [T]he Court of Appeals suggested that TWA could have replaced Hardison on his Saturday shift with other available employees through the payment of premium wages. Both of these alternatives would involve costs to TWA, either in the form of lost efficiency in other jobs or as higher wages.

To require TWA to bear more than a *de minimis* cost in order to give Hardison Saturdays off is an undue hardship. . . .

As we have seen, the paramount concern of Congress in enacting Title VII was the elimination of discrimination in employment. In the absence of clear statutory language or legislative history to the contrary, we will not readily construe the statute to require an employer to discriminate against some employees in order to enable others to observe their Sabbath.

Reversed.

Case Questions

1. Did Hardison's religious beliefs present a scheduling problem when he was hired? Is the employer required to accommodate religious beliefs if a conflict arises only after the employee has been hired? Explain your answers.

2. Did the union's refusal to grant Hardison a variance from the seniority requirements of the collective bargaining agreement violate the union's duty to accommodate Hardison's beliefs under Title VII? Explain.

3. Why was TWA unwilling to pay some other employee overtime to work for Hardison on Saturdays? Was TWA required to do so under Title VII? Explain.

The Duty of Reasonable Accommodation

As the *Hardison* case illustrates, the prohibition of religious discrimination under Title VII is not absolute. An employee may not be protected under Title VII if the employer is unable to make reasonable accommodation to the employee's religious beliefs or practices without undue hardship to the employer's business. The determination of what accommodation is reasonable, and whether it would impose an undue hardship on the employer, is to be based on each individual case and the facts of each situation. The EEOC Guidelines indicate that the following factors will be considered in determining what a reasonable accommodation is and whether it results in undue hardship:

- The size of the employer's work force and the number of employees requiring accommodation
- The nature of the job or jobs that present a conflict
- The cost of the accommodation
- The administrative requirements of the accommodation
- Whether the employees affected are under a collective bargaining agreement
- What alternatives are available and have been considered by the employer.

The employee seeking accommodation must first inform the employer of the conflict with his or her religious beliefs or practices and must request accommodation. The employee is also required to act reasonably in considering the alternative means of accommodation available.[13]

 CASE 8.3

WEBB V. CITY OF PHILADELPHIA
562 F.3d 256 (3d Cir. 2009)

Facts: Kimberlie Webb, a practicing Muslim, was a police officer for the City of Philadelphia. She requested permission to wear a traditional headscarf (known as a *khimar* or *hijaab*) with her uniform while on duty. The commanding officer denied the request because of Philadelphia Police Department Directive 78, which defines the approved

---

[13] *Jordan v. North Carolina National Bank*, 565 F.2d 72 (4th Cir. 1977).

Philadelphia police uniforms and prohibits the wearing of any religious symbols or garb as part of the uniform. Webb then filed a complaint of religious discrimination under Title VII with the Pennsylvania Human Relations Commission and the federal Equal Employment Opportunity Commission. While her complaint was pending before the EEOC, Webb arrived for work wearing the headscarf. She refused requests to remove it, and was sent home for failing to comply with Directive 78. The department ultimately suspended her for 13 days for insubordination. Webb filed suit against the City of Philadelphia, alleging violations of Title VII because of religious discrimination, hostile work environment, and retaliation. The trial court granted the city's motion for summary judgment. The court stated that Directive 78 prevents any accommodation for religious symbols and attire not only because of the need for uniformity but also to enhance cohesiveness, cooperation, and the *esprit de corps* of the police force. The court also held that the city would suffer an undue hardship if forced to permit officers to wear religious symbols or clothing or ornamentation with their uniforms. Webb appealed to the U.S. Court of Appeals for the Third Circuit.

Issue: Would allowing Webb to wear a headscarf while on duty constitute an undue hardship on the Philadelphia Police Department?

Decision: Once the plaintiff has established a prima facie case, the employer then has the burden to show that it made a good faith effort to accommodate the employee's religious belief or that such an accommodation would work an undue hardship upon the employer's business. According to *Trans World Airlines, Inc. v. Hardison*, an accommodation would cause an undue hardship if it imposes more than a de minimis cost on the employer. Noneconomic costs such as violations of the seniority provisions of a collective agreement or the threat of possible criminal sanctions could also pose an undue hardship on employers. The U.S. Supreme Court has considered the importance of dress regulations for law enforcement personnel and for the military in *Goldman v. Weinberger*.[1] The Court there stated that the standardization of uniforms encourages "the subordination of personal preferences and identities in favor of the overall group mission." In *Daniels v. City of Arlington*,[2] the court held that a police department could refuse to allow a police officer to wear a gold cross on his uniform in violation of an official "no pins" policy. The court held that the department's uniform standards were proper and that an accommodation of the officer's religious belief would have imposed an undue hardship. Here, the city demonstrated that the strict enforcement of Directive 78 was essential to the values of impartiality, religious neutrality, uniformity, and the subordination of personal preference necessary to the proper functioning of the police department.

The Third Circuit held that the uniform requirements were crucial to the safety of officers, to their morale and *esprit de corps*, and to public confidence in the police. The court of appeals therefore affirmed the trial court grant of summary judgment to the city.

---

[1] 475 U.S. 503 (1986).
[2] 246 F.3d 500 (5th Cir. 2001).

《《

Some employees may find a coworker's exercise of his or her religious beliefs offensive. How should the employer accommodate the employee's right to express her or his religious beliefs with the concerns of the coworkers? Must the employer allow an employee continually to ask coworkers if they "have been born again" or to invite them to attend religious services when the coworkers have made it clear that they find such conduct offensive? In *Wilson v. U.S. West Communications*,[14] an employee insisted on wearing an antiabortion button featuring a color photo of a fetus as an expression of her religious beliefs. She also occasionally wore a T-shirt with a color image of a fetus. Other employees found the button and the T-shirt offensive or disturbing. Their reactions to the button and T-shirt caused disruptions at work, and the employer documented a 40 percent decline in productivity of the unit after the employee began wearing the button. The employer offered the employee three choices:

• she could wear the button while she was in her cubicle, but must take it off when she moved around the office;

---

[14] 58 F.3d 1337 (8th Cir. 1995).

- she could cover the button while at work; or
- she could wear a different antiabortion button without the photograph.

The employee refused, insisting that she had to wear the button to be a "living witness" to her religious beliefs. The employer ultimately fired the employee, and the former employee filed suit under Title VII, alleging religious discrimination. She argued that the disruption in the workplace was caused by the reaction of the coworkers, not by her wearing the button. The court of appeals held that the employer did not violate Title VII by firing the employee. Title VII requires that an employer reasonably accommodate an employee's religious beliefs but does not require that the employer allow that employee to impose her or his religious views on others.

If there are several ways to accommodate the employee's religious beliefs, is the employer required to provide the accommodation that is preferred by the employee? In *Ansonia Board of Education v. Philbrook*,[15] the Supreme Court held the following:

> … We find no basis in either the statute or its legislative history for requiring an employer to choose any particular reasonable accommodation. By its very terms the statute directs that any reasonable accommodation by the employer is sufficient to meet its accommodation obligation. The employer violates the statute unless it "demonstrates that [it] is unable to reasonably accommodate … an employee's … religious observance or practice without undue hardship on the conduct of the employer's business." Thus, where the employer has already reasonably accommodated the employee's religious needs, the statutory inquiry is at an end. The employer need not further show that each of the employee's alternative accommodations would result in undue hardship. As *Hardison* illustrates, the extent of undue hardship on the employer's business is at issue only where the employer claims that it is unable to offer any reasonable accommodation without such hardship. Once the Court of Appeals assumed that the school board had offered to Philbrook a reasonable alternative, it erred by requiring the board to nonetheless demonstrate the hardship of Philbrook's alternatives…. We accordingly hold that an employer has met its obligation under Section 701(j) when it demonstrates that it has offered a reasonable accommodation to the employee.

ethical DILEMMA

ALLAH IN THE WORKPLACE?

A small group of employees at Wydget are Muslims; some wear turbans and burkas (robes covering their body). They have asked you, the human resource manager, to allow them to conduct religious prayer services in the plant cafeteria during their morning and afternoon coffee breaks and their lunch break. In general, those employees are good workers, and you do not want to do anything that would undermine their morale. However, a number of other Wydget employees have complained to you that they are suspicious of such meetings, which they fear may be a cover for terrorist or subversive activities. You are concerned that if you allow the lunchtime prayer services, other employees who are Buddhists, Hindus, or Christians may also seek to conduct religious or prayer services.

---

[15] 479 U.S. 60 (1986).

Should you allow the Muslim employees to hold the prayer services? What arguments can you make in favor of allowing the services? What arguments can you make against allowing them? How should you respond to the fears and perceptions of the other employees? Can Wydget allow the prayer services for the Muslims while refusing other employees the right to hold their own prayer services? Prepare a memo for the CEO on this question. The memo should list the arguments in favor of, and against, allowing the prayer services and should recommend a decision, with appropriate explanation and justification, for the CEO.

See the EEOC's "Questions and Answers About Employer Responsibilities Concerning the Employment of Muslims, Arabs, South Asians and Sikhs" at http://www.eeoc.gov/facts/backlash-employer.html.

Concept *Summary* 8.1

DISCRIMINATION BASED ON RELIGION

- Religion includes:
  - All aspects of religious observance, practice, and belief

- Exceptions:
  - Constitutional protections (First Amendment)
    - *Lemon* test
  - Religion as a BFOQ (Section 703(e)(1))
  - Religious organizations (Section 702 (a))
  - Religiously affiliated educational institutions (Section 703(e)(2))
  - Religious societies, corporations, associations (Section 702 (a))

- Employer's duty of reasonable accommodation of religion:
  - Employee must inform employer of religious belief or conduct in conflict with work requirement
  - Employer must then attempt to make reasonable accommodation to belief or conduct—or show that accommodation would impose undue hardship
  - Undue hardship—employer not required to:
    - Pay more than minimal costs
    - Regularly pay overtime or premium wages
    - Act in violation of the seniority provisions of a collective agreement

8-2 Discrimination Based on National Origin

Title VII prohibits employment discrimination against any applicant or employee because of national origin, although it does recognize that national origin may be a BFOQ, where the employer demonstrates that hiring employees of a particular ethnic or national origin is a business necessity for the safe and efficient performance of the job in question. The government's response to the terrorist attacks on the World Trade Center and the Pentagon on September 11, 2001, and the public's heightened awareness regarding security and fear of potential threats led to increased scrutiny of individuals who appeared to be Muslims or of Middle Eastern origin. Incidents of "ethnic profiling" were common; persons (primarily males) perceived to be from Middle Eastern countries were subjected to security checks, searches, interrogation by authorities, and general public suspicion. Is such ethnic profiling permissible under Title VII? In general, no. Any employment discrimination against an individual because of that individual's (actual or perceived) national origin, ethnicity, or religion is a violation of Title VII unless it is justified by a BFOQ.

Following the events of September 11, 2001, the EEOC reported an increase in complaints alleging discrimination against individuals because they were perceived as being Muslim, Arabic, Middle Eastern, South Asian, or Sikh. More than 800 complaints of "backlash" discrimination were filed by individuals who alleged that they were discriminated against because of their religion or national origin. Most of the complaints involved discharge or harassment. EEOC enforcement efforts have resulted in nearly 100 individuals receiving over $1.45 million in benefits as resolution of employment discrimination complaints related to the September 11 attacks. The EEOC has also conducted numerous outreach and education efforts for employers to promote voluntary compliance with Title VII.[16] In recent years, the number of national origin discrimination complaints filed with the EEOC has been increasing, from 8,025 in its fiscal year (FY) 2001, to 10,601 in FY 2008. The EEOC recovered damage settlements of $22.8 million for national origin discrimination claims in FY 2007, and $25.4 million in FY 2008.[17] During the years 2009 to 2012, EEOC charges based on allegations of Muslim discrimination have hovered steadily around 800 per year, or a bit more than 20 percent of all religious discrimination charges.[18]

8-2a   Definition

National origin discrimination includes any discrimination based upon the place of origin of an applicant or employee or his or her ancestor(s) and any discrimination based upon the physical, cultural, or linguistic characteristics of an ethnic group. Title VII's prohibition on national origin discrimination includes harassment of employees because of their national origin and extends to discrimination based upon reasons related to national origin or ethnic considerations, such as:

- a person's marriage to a person of, or association with persons of, an ethnic or national origin group;

- a person's membership in, or association with, an organization identified with or seeking to promote the interests of any ethnic or national origin group;

---

[16] EEOC Press Release, 7/17/2003, "Muslim pilot fired due to religion and appearance, EEOC says in post-9/11 backlash discrimination suit," available at http://www.EEOC.gov/press/7-17-03a.html.

[17] Equal Employment Opportunity Commission, "National origin-based charges FY 1997–FY 2014," available at http://www.eeoc.gov/eeoc/statistics/enforcement/origin.cfm.

[18] Equal Employment Opportunity Commission, "Religion-based charges filed from 10/01/2000 through 9/30/2011," available at http://www.eeoc.gov/eeoc/events/9-11-11_religion_charges.cfm.

- a person's attendance or participation in schools, churches, temples, or mosques generally used by persons of an ethnic or national origin group; or
- a person's name, or the name of the person's spouse, which is associated with an ethnic or national origin group.

An employer may violate the statute by discriminating against an applicant or employee whose education or training is foreign or, conversely, by requiring that training or education be done abroad. Title VII does allow employers to hire employees based on legitimate business, safety, or security concerns. Employers may impose heightened background screening for employees or applicants, as long as such requirements are related to legitimate job concerns and are applied uniformly to the employees in similar situations or job classes. Section 703(g) states that it is not a violation of Title VII for an employer to refuse to hire or to discharge an employee who is unable to meet the requirements for a national security clearance where federal law or regulations require such a clearance for the job in question.

As the following case illustrates, employers must also ensure that employees are not subjected to harassment based on their national origin.

CASE 8.4

EQUAL EMPLOYMENT OPPORTUNITY COMMISSION V. WC&M ENTERPRISES, INC.

496 F.3d 393 (5th Cir. 2007)

[Mohommed Rafiq was born in India and was a practicing Muslim. He was a car salesman at WC&M Enterprises' Honda dealership in Conroe, Texas. After the September 11, 2001, terrorist attacks, Rafiq began to be subjected to ongoing harassment based on his religion and national origin by his managers and coworkers. When Rafiq arrived at work for his afternoon shift on 9/11, a number of his coworkers and managers, including Matthew Kiene (a coworker), Kevin Argabrite (a finance manager), Jerry Swigart (Rafiq's direct supervisor), and Richard Burgoon (the general manager of the dealership), were watching television coverage of the attacks. Upon seeing Rafiq, Kiene called out, "Hey, there's Mohommed," and Argabrite said, "Where have you been?" in a mocking way, at which point everyone began to laugh. Rafiq inferred from these comments that the supervisors and colleagues were implying that he had participated in the terrorist attacks. After the U.S. began military action against Afghanistan, his coworkers and some managers began calling Rafiq "Taliban." Rafiq repeatedly asked them to stop calling him "Taliban," to no avail. He also complained a number of times to the managers without any real success.

Coworkers and some managers also ridiculed and harassed Rafiq in other ways, such as asking him, "Why don't you just go back where you came from since you believe what you believe?" and mocking Rafiq's religious dietary restrictions and his need to pray during the workday. They also often referred to Rafiq as an "Arab," even though Rafiq told them on numerous occasions that he was from India. This harassment continued through the end of his employment.

On October 16, 2002, Rafiq got into a dispute with his manager, Swigart, after being told that it was mandatory for all employees to attend a United Way meeting. When Rafiq questioned what, if any, connection there was between the United Way and his job, Swigart said, "This is America. That's the way things work over here. This is not the Islamic country where you come from." After the confrontation, Swigart issued Rafiq a written warning, which stated that Rafiq "was acting like a Muslim extremist" and that he could not work with Rafiq because of his "militant stance." On October 26, 2002, Argabrite "banged" on the partition separating Rafiq's office space from the sales floor; Argabrite did this to try to startle Rafiq whenever he walked by his office. This time, however, Rafiq responded by banging on the partition himself and saying, "Don't do that." Argabrite then confronted Rafiq and told Rafiq that he was a manager, so Rafiq could not tell him what to do. Rafiq later complained to Burgoon about Argabrite's continual harassment.

Two days later, Rafiq was fired. Rafiq filed a charge of discrimination with the EEOC, and the EEOC filed suit against the employer, alleging that WC&M subjected Rafiq to a hostile work environment on the basis of his religion and national origin, in violation of Title VII. The district court granted summary judgment to the employer, stating that the EEOC could not establish that Rafiq was harassed on the basis of his national origin, that the EEOC did not establish the existence of severe and pervasive harassment, and the EEOC had not shown that Rafiq's emotional distress or mental anguish from the harassment was so severe that it interrupted his daily life. The EEOC appealed to the U.S. Court of Appeals for the Fifth Circuit.]

Dennis, Circuit Judge

In this case involving allegations of a hostile work environment, the Equal Employment Opportunity Commission ("EEOC") appeals the district court's decision to enter summary judgment in favor of the defendant-appellee, WC&M Enterprises, Inc....

... the district court made two findings that essentially disposed of the EEOC's hostile work environment claim on the merits: (1) that the EEOC had not shown that Rafiq lost sales as a result of the alleged harassment that he suffered; and (2) that the EEOC could not bring a claim based on Rafiq's national origin because none of the harassing comments specifically referred to the fact that Rafiq was from India. The EEOC argues that the district court erred in each respect....

The Supreme Court has emphasized that Title VII's prohibition "is not limited to 'economic' or 'tangible' discrimination." Rather, "[w]hen the workplace is permeated with 'discriminatory intimidation, ridicule, and insult' that is 'sufficiently severe or pervasive to alter the conditions of the victim's employment and create an abusive working environment,' Title VII is violated." [*Harris v. Forklift Sys.*] ...

For harassment to be sufficiently severe or pervasive to alter the conditions of the victim's employment, the conduct complained of must be both objectively and subjectively offensive.... As the Supreme Court stated, "even without regard to ... tangible effects, the very fact that the discriminatory conduct was so severe or pervasive that it created a work environment abusive to employees because of their race, gender, religion, or national origin offends Title VII's broad rule of workplace equality."

Under the totality of the circumstances test, a single incident of harassment, if sufficiently severe, could give rise to

a viable Title VII claim as well as a continuous pattern of much less severe incidents of harassment....

Here, the district court held that even if Rafiq could prove that any harassment occurred, "he has not shown that it was so severe that it kept him from doing his job." In so holding, the district court applied an incorrect legal standard. Whether Rafiq lost sales as a result of the alleged harassment is certainly relevant to his hostile work environment claim; but it is not, by itself, dispositive. The district court erred in concluding otherwise.

Applying the totality of the circumstances test, we conclude that the EEOC has presented sufficient evidence to create an issue of fact as to whether the harassment that Rafiq suffered was so severe or pervasive as to alter a condition of his employment. The evidence showed that Rafiq was subjected to verbal harassment on a regular basis for a period of approximately one year. During that time, Rafiq was constantly called "Taliban" and referred to as an "Arab" by Kiene and Argabrite, who also mocked his diet and prayer rituals. Moreover, Rafiq was sporadically subjected to additional incidents of harassment ...

Although no single incident of harassment is likely sufficient to establish severe or pervasive harassment, when considered together and viewed in the light most favorable to the EEOC, the evidence shows a long-term pattern of ridicule sufficient to establish a claim under Title VII....

In addition, the evidence is sufficient to show that the harassment Rafiq suffered was based on his religion and national origin.

Indeed, the EEOC's guidelines on discrimination define "discrimination based on national origin" broadly, to include acts of discrimination undertaken "because an individual has the physical, cultural or linguistic characteristics of a national origin group." Nothing in the guidelines requires that the discrimination be based on the victim's actual national origin. The EEOC's final guidelines make this point clear:

> In order to have a claim of national origin discrimination under Title VII, it is not necessary to show that the alleged discriminator knew the particular national origin group to which the complainant belonged.... [I]t is enough to show that the complainant was treated differently because of his or her foreign accent, appearance, or physical characteristics....

... In this case, the evidence that the EEOC presented supports its claim that Rafiq was harassed based on his national origin. Indeed, several of the challenged statements refer to national origin generally (even though they do not accurately describe Rafiq's actual country of origin): (1) Kiene's comment to Rafiq, "Why don't you just go back where you came from since you believe what you believe?"; (2) Swigart's statement, "This is America. That's the way things work over here. This is not the Islamic country where you come from"; and (3) Kiene's and Argabrite's practice of referring to Rafiq as "Taliban" and calling him an "Arab."

Accordingly, we conclude that the EEOC has submitted sufficient evidence to support its claim that Rafiq was subjected to a hostile work environment both on the basis of religion and on the basis of national origin.

... Rafiq testified at his deposition that the alleged harassment caused problems with his family life that led him to seek counseling from several mosques, that he had difficulty sleeping, lost 30 pounds, and suffered gastrointestinal problems. Although Rafiq equivocated about whether his gastrointestinal problems were attributable to the harassment, the record evidence is sufficient to show that the harassment caused some discernible injury to his mental state even when those symptoms are not considered.

Accordingly, the district court erred in concluding that the EEOC could not recover for any mental anguish that Rafiq suffered.

... [W]e reverse the district court's grant of summary judgment in favor of the defendant . . . and remand this matter to the district court for proceedings consistent with this opinion.

Reversed and Remanded.

Case Questions

1. On what basis was Rafiq being harassed? What evidence supports his claim that the harassment was based on national origin and religion?

2. How did the harassing conduct here affect Rafiq? Must Rafiq show that the harassment caused him to lose sales or otherwise affected his work performance? Explain.

3. What is an employer's obligation under Title VII to prevent workplace harassment based on race, color, sex, national origin, or religion? What had the employer done in this case to stop the harassment?

≪

8-2b Disparate Impact

Employers should avoid arbitrary employment criteria, such as height or weight requirements, for applicants or employees because such requirements may have a disparate impact on national origin. They have the effect of excluding large numbers of certain ethnic groups. For example, height requirements may exclude most persons of Asian or Hispanic origin, and the refusal to recognize educational qualifications from foreign institutions may exclude foreign-born applicants. If such requirements or practices have a disparate impact, they constitute discrimination in violation of Title VII, unless they can be shown to be required for the effective performance of the job in question.

THE **WORKING** LAW

EEOC Sues Rhino Eastern for National Origin Discrimination and Retaliation

Mining Company Fired Foreman Because He Complained About Pervasive Harassment Based on His Polish Ancestry, Federal Agency Says

BECKLEY, W.V.–Mining company Rhino Eastern LLC violated federal law when it subjected a mine foreman to pervasive national origin discrimination and retaliated against him for his opposition to the harassment, the U.S. Equal Employment Opportunity Commission (EEOC) charged in a lawsuit it announced today.

The EEOC says that supervisory and non-supervisory personnel regularly subjected Michael Jagodzinski to degrading and humiliating comments, taunts and slurs based on his Polish ancestry. The harassment included calling Jagodzinski a "stupid Polack," a "dumb Polack," and other offensive names, displaying offensive graffiti about Jagodzinski on mine walls and elsewhere in the workplace, and taunting Jagodzinski with derogatory remarks about his national origin, the EEOC charged.

Despite Jagodzinksi's complaints about, and Rhino Eastern's knowledge of, the hostile work environment, the company failed to prevent or correct the harassment, the EEOC said. Instead, the company retaliated against Jagodzinski by issuing a pretextual disciplinary action and then firing him.

Such alleged conduct violates Title VII of the Civil Rights Act of 1964, which prohibits discrimination and harassment based on national origin. Title VII also forbids employers from firing or otherwise disciplining an employee because he or she complained about discriminatory conduct. The EEOC filed suit (*EEOC v. Rhino Energy WV LLC d/b/a Rhino Eastern LLC*, Civil Action No 5:14-cv-26250) in the U.S. District Court for the Southern District of West Virginia, Beckley Division, after first attempting to reach a voluntary pre-litigation settlement through its conciliation process.

"No employee should be subjected to degrading and humiliating harassment in order to earn a living," said Philadelphia District Director Spencer H. Lewis, Jr. "The EEOC will take action when employers fail to protect employees from a hostile work environment or retaliate against those who oppose it."

Debra M. Lawrence, regional attorney of the EEOC's Philadelphia District Office, said, "As we celebrate the 50th anniversary of Title VII this year, it is unfortunate that some employers still permit pervasive national origin harassment to continue unchecked in the workplace and punish an employee who complains about the unlawful misconduct instead of taking action against the wrongdoers."

The Philadelphia District Office of the EEOC oversees Pennsylvania, Maryland, Delaware, West Virginia, and parts of New Jersey and Ohio. The legal staff of the Philadelphia District Office of the EEOC also prosecutes discrimination cases arising from Washington, D.C. and parts of Virginia.

Source: EEOC Press Release, September 30, 2014, available at http://www.eeoc.gov/eeoc /newsroom/release/9-30-14f.cfm.

8-2c   English-Only Rules

An employer may violate Title VII by denying employment opportunities because of an applicant's or employee's foreign accent or inability to communicate well in English, unless the job in question involves public contact (such as sales clerks or receptionists). One issue of specific concern to the EEOC is the use by employers of **English-only rules**, which prohibit employees from speaking any language but English at work. Absolute or "blanket" English-only rules, requiring employees to speak English exclusively during all their time in the workplace, are generally more difficult to justify than more limited English-only rules, which require employees to speak English only at certain times—such as when they are with customers—or in certain places—such as the sales floor or other "public contact" areas. The employer must clearly notify the employees of when and where the restriction applies.

English-only rules employer work rules requiring that employees speak English in the workplace during working hours

The EEOC Guidelines on Discrimination Because of National Origin[19] take the position that blanket English-only rules violate Title VII unless they are required by business necessity. The EEOC believes that such rules may create an "atmosphere of inferiority, isolation, and intimidation" based on an employee's ethnicity, which could result in a discriminatory working environment and tend to be "a burdensome term and condition of employment." However, not all courts have agreed with the EEOC position on blanket English-only rules, as the following case illustrates.

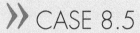

≫ CASE 8.5

CASTILLO V. WELLS FARGO BANK, N.A.
554 Fed. Appx. 646 (9th Cir. 2014)

Facts: The *Wells Fargo Team Member Handbook* states at page 132, "English is the business language for Wells Fargo's U.S. operations. At the same time, we recognize that we serve a highly diverse customer base, and in some cases, it's both necessary and desirable to conduct business in languages other than English. In fact, some of our team members have been hired specifically because of their multilingual business skills.

"So, while business communications in the United States should be in English, it is recognized that the specific business needs of a unit or position may periodically dictate otherwise. By establishing this language policy, we don't intend to prevent team members from using other languages in appropriate business or social communications. In fact, Wells Fargo encourages an environment that supports our diverse workforce as well as our multicultural customer base. We respect our team members' desire to communicate in languages other than English.

"However, this policy allows managers to limit non-English communications if they interfere with clear business communications or with efficient work performance."[20]

Plaintiff Martha Castillo challenged this Wells Fargo rule on the basis of national origin discrimination. The trial judge granted the defendant's motion for summary judgment and Castillo appealed.

Issue: Does the "English only" rule violate Title VII?

Decision: The district court granted summary judgment on Castillo's claims on the bases that (1) Wells Fargo's enforcement of its language policy against Castillo was not racially discriminatory; (2) Castillo failed to exhaust administrative remedies as to her Title VII retaliation claims; (3) Castillo failed to put Wells Fargo on notice of her § 1981 claims regarding her eventual termination and the denial of her transfer request; and (4) Castillo's remaining § 1981 claims lacked merit because the incidents alleged are not actionable retaliation.

The appellate judges agreed that Wells Fargo's language policy was a "limited, reasonable and business-related English-only rule" that Wells Fargo enforced against "an employee who can readily comply with the rule [but] voluntarily chooses not to observe it as a matter of individual preference." *Jurado v. Eleven–Fifty Corp.*, 813 F.2d 1406, 1411 (9th Cir. 1987). Wells Fargo's enforcement of its language policy against Castillo was not racially discriminatory.

With regard to Castillo's retaliation claim, the court found that (1) Wells Fargo's verbal counseling did not rise to the level of an adverse employment action, while the denial of a transfer request, coming 15 months after she filed her EEOC complaint, was not sufficiently proximate to support the charge.

---

[19] 29 C.F.R. § 1606.

[20] *Wells Fargo Team Member Handbook*, January 2015, available at http://teamworks.wellsfargo.com/handbook/HB_Online.pdf.

Citizenship

Title VII protects all individuals, both citizens and noncitizens, who reside in or are employed in the United States from employment discrimination based on race, color, religion, sex, or national origin. However, the Supreme Court in *Espinoza v. Farah Mfg. Co.*[21] held that Title VII's prohibition on national origin discrimination does not include discrimination on the basis of citizenship. Section 703(g) of Title VII also allows employers to refuse to hire applicants who are denied national security clearances for positions subject to federal security requirements.

8-2d   The Immigration Reform and Control Act of 1986 and Discrimination Based on National Origin or Citizenship

The Immigration Reform and Control Act of 1986 (IRCA) prohibits employment discrimination because of national origin or citizenship against applicants or employees, other than illegal aliens, with respect to hiring, recruitment, discharge, or referral for a fee. Employers may, however, discriminate based upon citizenship when it is necessary to comply with other laws or federal, state, or local government contracts or when determined by the attorney general to be essential for an employer to do business with a government agency. Employers are permitted under the IRCA to give a U.S. citizen preference over an alien when both the citizen and the alien are "equally qualified" for the job for which they are being considered.

The Immigration Act of 1990 expanded the protection of the IRCA to cover seasonal agricultural workers. It is unlawful to intimidate, threaten, coerce, or retaliate against any person for the purpose of interfering with the rights secured under the IRCA's antidiscrimination provisions. Employers are also prohibited from requesting more or different employment-eligibility documents than are required under the IRCA and from refusing to honor documents that reasonably appear to be genuine.

The IRCA is enforced by the Department of Justice through the Special Counsel for Immigration-Related Unfair Employment Practices, a position created by the act. The nondiscrimination provisions of the IRCA apply to employers with more than three employees, but they do not extend to national origin discrimination that is prohibited by Title VII. Consequently, employers who are subject to Title VII (those with 15 or more employees) are not subject to the IRCA's provisions on national origin discrimination. However, because Title VII does not expressly prohibit discrimination based upon citizenship, all employers with more than three employees are covered by the IRCA's provisions against discrimination based upon citizenship.

Concept *Summary* 8.2

DISCRIMINATION BASED ON NATIONAL ORIGIN

- National origin discrimination includes discrimination based upon:
  - The place of origin of an applicant or employee (or his or her ancestors)
  - The physical, cultural, or linguistic characteristics of an ethnic group

---

[21] 414 U.S. 86 (1973).

- Associating with persons of a particular ethnic group or membership in organizations associated with particular ethnic groups
- Refusal to recognize or credit foreign education or professional credentials

- Language
  - Title VII prohibits discrimination based on accents or fluency unless job requires public contact
  - English-only rules are allowed if required for business necessity
  - Employers can refuse to hire persons denied national security clearances (Section 703(g))

- Coverage
  - Title VII—Discrimination based on national origin
    - Employers with at least 15 employees
    - Citizens and noncitizens residing or working in the United States
    - Hiring or harassment
  - IRCA—Discrimination based on national origin or citizenship
    - Employers with more than three employees
    - Hiring, recruitment, discharge, or referral for a fee
    - Employers may set citizenship requirements if required by other laws, government contracts, or government agency

8-3   Enforcement of Title VII

This section focuses on the procedures for filing and resolving complaints of employment discrimination that arise under Title VII.

8-3a   The Equal Employment Opportunity Commission

Title VII is administered and enforced by the Equal Employment Opportunity Commission (EEOC). The EEOC is headed by a five-member commission; the commissioners are appointed by the president with Senate confirmation. The general counsel of the EEOC is also appointed by the president, also with Senate confirmation.

Unlike the National Labor Relations Board (NLRB; another federal enforcement agency discussed in Chapter 12) the EEOC does not adjudicate, or decide, complaints alleging violations of Title VII, nor is it the exclusive enforcement agency for discrimination complaints. The EEOC staff investigates complaints filed with it and attempts to settle such complaints voluntarily. If a settlement is not reached voluntarily, the EEOC may file suit against the alleged discriminator in the federal courts.

The EEOC also differs from the NLRB in that the EEOC may initiate complaints on its own when it believes a party is involved in a "pattern or practice" of discrimination. In these cases, the EEOC need not wait for an individual to file a complaint with it. When a complaint alleges discrimination by a state or local government, Title VII requires that the Department of Justice initiate any court action against the public sector employer.

8-3b Procedures Under Title VII

Filing a Complaint

Title VII, unlike the National Labor Relations Act (discussed in Chapter 12), does not give the federal government exclusive authority over employment discrimination issues. Section 706(c) of Title VII requires that an individual filing a complaint of illegal employment discrimination must first file with a state or local agency authorized to deal with the issue, if such an agency exists. The EEOC may consider the complaint only after the state or local agency has had the complaint for 60 days or ceased processing the complaint, whichever occurs first.

State Agency Role

A number of states and municipalities have created equal employment opportunity agencies, also known as "fair employment" or "human rights" commissions. Some state agencies have powers and jurisdiction beyond those given to the EEOC. The New York State Human Rights Division enforces the New York State Human Rights Law. In addition to prohibiting discrimination in employment on the basis of race, color, religion, gender, and national origin, the New York legislation also prohibits employment discrimination on the basis of age, marital status, disability, and criminal record. The Pennsylvania Human Relations Act established the Human Rights Commission, which is empowered to hold hearings before administrative law judges to determine whether the act has been violated. The Pennsylvania legislation goes beyond Title VII's prohibitions by forbidding employment discrimination on the basis of disability.

Filing with the EEOC

When the complaint must first be filed with a state or local agency, Section 706(e) requires that it be filed with the EEOC within 300 days of the act of alleged discrimination. If there is no state or local agency, the complaint must be filed with the EEOC within 180 days of the alleged violation. By contrast, the limitation for filing a complaint under the New York State Human Rights Law is one year and under the Pennsylvania Human Relations Act is 90 days.

As noted earlier, an individual alleging employment discrimination must first file a complaint with the appropriate state or local agency, if such an agency exists. Once the complaint is filed with the state or local agency, the complainant must wait 60 days before filing the complaint with the EEOC. If the state or local agency terminates proceedings on the complaint prior to the passage of 60 days, the complaint may then be filed with the EEOC. This means that the individual filing the complaint with the state or local agency must wait for that agency to terminate proceedings or for 60 days, whichever comes first. *Mohasco Corp. v. Silver*[22] involved a situation in which an individual filed a complaint alleging that he was discharged because of religious discrimination with the New York Division of Human Rights 291 days after the discharge. The state agency began to process and investigate the complaint; the EEOC began to process the complaint some 357 days after the discharge. The Supreme Court held that the complaint had not been properly filed with the EEOC within the 300-day limit. The Court held that the EEOC has a duty,

---

[22] 447 U.S. 807 (1980).

under the statute, to begin processing a complaint within 300 days of the alleged violation. In order to allow the state agency the required 60 days for processing, the complaint must have been filed with the state agency within 240 days so that, when the EEOC began to process the complaint, it would be within the 300-day limit. However, as noted, when the state or local agency terminates proceedings on the complaint before 60 days have passed, the EEOC may begin to process the complaint upon the other agency's termination.

8-3c EEOC Procedure and Its Relation to State Proceedings

The EEOC has entered into "work-sharing" agreements with most state equal employment opportunity agencies to deal with the situation that arose in the *Mohasco* decision. Under such agreements, the agency that initially receives the complaint processes it. When the EEOC receives the complaint first, it refers the complaint to the appropriate state agency. The state agency then waives its right to process the complaint and refers it back to the EEOC. The state agency does retain jurisdiction to proceed on the complaint in the future, after the EEOC has completed its processing of the complaint. The EEOC treats the referral of the complaint to the state agency as the filing of the complaint with the state agency, and the state's waiver of the right to process the complaint is treated as termination of state proceedings, allowing the filing of the complaint with the EEOC under Section 706(c) of Title VII.

In *EEOC v. Commercial Office Products Co.*,[23] the complainant filed a sex discrimination complaint with the EEOC on the 289th day after her discharge. The EEOC, under a work-sharing agreement, sent the complaint to the state agency, which returned the complaint to the EEOC after indicating that it waived its right to proceed on the complaint. The EEOC then began its investigation into the complaint and ultimately brought suit against the employer. The trial court and the court of appeals held that Section 706(c) required that either 60 days must elapse from the filing of the complaint with the state agency, or the state agency must both commence and terminate its proceedings, before the complaint could be deemed to have been filed with the EEOC. The Supreme Court, on appeal, reversed the court of appeals. The Supreme Court held that the state agency's waiver of its right to proceed on the complaint constituted a termination of the state proceedings under Section 706(c), allowing the EEOC to proceed with the complaint. As a result of this decision, in states where the EEOC and the state agency have work-sharing agreements, a complaint filed with the EEOC anytime within the 300-day time limit will be considered properly filed, and the EEOC can proceed with its processing of the complaint.

When Does the Violation Occur?

Because the time for filing a complaint under Title VII is limited, it is important to determine when the alleged violation occurred. In most situations, it is not difficult to determine the date of the violation from which the time limit begins to run, but in some instances, it may present a problem. The Supreme Court, in *Delaware State College v. Ricks*,[24] held that the time limit for a Title VII violation begins to run on the date that the individual is aware of, or should be aware of, the alleged violation, not on the date that the alleged violation

---

[23] 486 U.S. 107 (1988).

[24] 449 U.S. 250 (1982).

has an adverse effect on the individual. Following the rationale in the Ricks decision, the Supreme Court in *Ledbetter v. Goodyear Tire and Rubber Co.*[25] held that the time limit to challenge pay discrepancies based on a sexually discriminatory performance evaluation begins when the evaluation is made, not when paychecks reflecting that discriminatory evaluation are received. However, Congress overruled the *Ledbetter* decision by legislation signed into law by President Obama in 2009. The **Lilly Ledbetter Fair Pay Act** of 2009[26] added Section 706(e)(3)(A) to Title VII,[27] which states:

Lilly Ledbetter Fair Pay Act
statute that extends time in which an employee may file suit under several federal employment statutes

> For purposes of this section, an unlawful employment practice occurs, with respect to discrimination in compensation in violation of this subchapter, when a discriminatory compensation decision or other practice is adopted, when an individual becomes subject to a discriminatory compensation decision or other practice, or when an individual is affected by application of a discriminatory compensation decision or other practice, including each time wages, benefits, or other compensation is paid, resulting in whole or in part from such a decision or other practice.

Concept *Summary* 8.3

FILING A CHARGE OF DISCRIMINATION

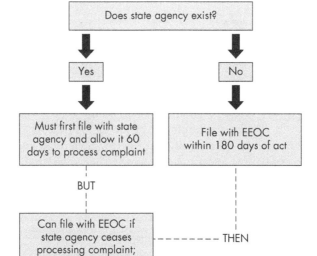

---

[25] 550 U.S. 618 (2007).

[26] 2009 Pub. L. 111-2, § 3(A), 123 Stat. 5-6.

[27] 42 U.S.C. § 2000e-5(e)(3)(A).

The effect of the Lilly Ledbetter Fair Pay Act is to allow an employee to file a complaint with the EEOC within 180 days (or 300 where a state or local EEO agency exists) from the latest of three dates:

- when the discriminatory pay policy is adopted;
- when the employee becomes subject to the discriminatory pay policy; or
- when the employee is affected by the policy.

The act also specifies that each time the employee receives a paycheck reflecting the discriminatory pay policy, it is a new violation of Title VII. In deciding *Ledbetter v. Goodyear Tire and Rubber Co.*, the Supreme Court majority relied upon *Lorance v. AT&T Technologies, Inc.*[28] (see Chapter 6), where the Supreme Court ruled that the time limit for filing a complaint against an allegedly discriminatory change to a seniority system begins to run at the time the actual change is made—not when the employee becomes subject to the system or when the seniority system has an adverse effect on the employee. But just as was the case with the *Ledbetter*, the decision in *Lorance* was reversed by Congress as part of the 1991 amendments to Title VII. Section 706(e)(2) now provides that for claims involving the adoption of a seniority system for allegedly discriminatory reasons, the violation can occur when the seniority system is adopted, when the complainant becomes subject to the seniority system, or when the complainant is injured by the application of the seniority system.

Continuing Violation

In *Bazemore v. Friday*,[29] the plaintiffs challenged a pay policy that discriminated against African American employees. The pay policy had its origins in the era of racial segregation, prior to the date that Title VII applied to the employer, but the Supreme Court held that the violation was a continuing one—a new violation occurred every time the employees received a paycheck based on the racially discriminatory policy. Where the plaintiff alleges a continuing violation of Title VII, the plaintiff need only file within 180 or 300 days (depending on whether there is an appropriate local or state agency involved) of the latest incident of the alleged continuing violation. As noted above, the Lilly Ledbetter Fair Pay Act reaffirms the decision in *Bazemore* by stating that each paycheck reflecting the discriminatory pay policy is a new and separate violation of Title VII.

Hostile Environment Harassment

Employees alleging harassment creating a hostile environment in violation of Title VII must file their complaint with the EEOC within 180 days (if there is no state or local agency involved) or 300 days (it there is an appropriate state and local agency) of the most recent discrete incident of harassment, according to *National Railroad Passenger Corp. v. Morgan*.[30]

---

[28] 490 U.S. 900 (1989).

[29] 478 U.S. 385 (1986).

[30] 536 U.S. 101 (2002).

8-3d   EEOC Procedure for Handling Complaints

Upon receipt of a properly filed complaint, the EEOC has 10 days to serve a notice of the complaint with the employer, union, or agency alleged to have discriminated (the respondent). Following service upon the respondent, the EEOC staff conducts an investigation into the complaint to determine whether reasonable cause exists to believe it is true. If no reasonable cause is found, the charge is dismissed. If reasonable cause to believe the complaint is found, the commission will attempt to settle the complaint through voluntary conciliation, persuasion, and negotiation. If the voluntary procedures are unsuccessful in resolving the complaint after 30 days from its filing, the EEOC may file suit in a federal district court.

If the EEOC dismisses the complaint or decides not to file suit, it notifies the complainant that he or she may file suit on his or her own. The complainant must file suit within ninety days of receiving the right-to-sue notice.

When the EEOC has not dismissed the complaint but has also not filed suit or acted upon the complaint within 180 days of its filing, the complainant may request a right-to-sue letter. Again, the complainant has ninety days from the notification to file suit. The suit may be filed:

- in the district court in the district where the alleged unlawful employment practice occurred;
- where the relevant employment records are kept; or
- where the complainant would have been employed.

In *Yellow Freight System, Inc. v. Donnelly*,[31] the Supreme Court held that the federal courts do not have exclusive jurisdiction over Title VII claims; state courts are competent to adjudicate claims based on federal law such as Title VII. This means that the individual may file suit in either the federal or appropriate state court.

Because the complainant may be required to file first with a state or local agency and may file his or her own suit if the EEOC has not acted within 180 days, several legal proceedings involving the complaint may occur at the same time. What is the effect of a state court decision dismissing the complaint on a subsequent suit filed in federal court? In *Kremer v. Chemical Construction Co.*,[32] the U.S. Supreme Court held that a plaintiff who loses a discrimination suit in a state court is precluded from filing a Title VII suit based on the same facts in federal court. According to *Kremer*, the complainant who is unsuccessful in the state courts does not get a second chance to file a suit based on the same facts in federal court because of the full-faith-and-credit doctrine. However, the holding in *Kremer* was limited only to the effect of a state court decision.

What is the effect of a negative determination by a state administrative agency on the complainant's right to sue in federal court? In *University of Tennessee v. Elliot*,[33] the Supreme Court held that the full-faith-and-credit doctrine did not apply to state administrative agency decisions. Hence, a negative determination by the state agency would not

---

[31] 494 U.S. 820 (1990).

[32] 456 U.S. 461 (1982).

[33] 478 U.S. 788 (1986).

preclude the complainant from suing in federal court under Title VII. (The Court in *Elliot* did hold that the findings of fact made by the state agency should be given preclusive effect by the federal courts in suits filed under 42 U.S. 1981 and 1983.)

Concept *Summary* 8.4

EEOC PROCEDURE FOR HANDLING COMPLAINTS

```
        ┌─────────────────────────────────┐
        │  Serve respondent notice        │
        │  of complaint within 10 days    │
        └─────────────────────────────────┘
                       │
                       ▼
        ┌─────────────────────────────────┐
        │  EEOC conducts investigation    │
        └─────────────────────────────────┘
                       │
                       ▼
        ┌─────────────────────────────────┐
        │  Reasonable cause for complaint?│
        └─────────────────────────────────┘
              │                      │
              ▼                      ▼
          ┌───────┐              ┌───────┐
          │  Yes  │              │  No   │
          └───────┘              └───────┘
              │                      │
              ▼                      ▼
    ┌──────────────────┐    ┌──────────────────┐
    │ Attempt to settle│    │ Right-to-sue     │
    │ through          │    │ letter issued    │
    │ voluntary        │    │ to complainant   │
    │ procedures       │    │                  │
    └──────────────────┘    └──────────────────┘
              │                      │
              ▼                      ▼
    ┌──────────────────┐    ┌──────────────────┐
    │ EEOC may file in │    │ Complainant must │
    │ a federal        │    │ file within 90   │
    │ district court   │    │ days of right-to-│
    │                  │    │ sue              │
    └──────────────────┘    └──────────────────┘
```

The Relationship Between Title VII and Other Statutory Remedies

In *Tipler v. E. I. du Pont de Nemours*,[34] the U.S. Court of Appeals for the Sixth Circuit held that the NLRB's rejection of an unfair labor practice charge alleging racial discrimination does not preclude the filing of a Title VII suit growing out of the same situation. However, if an employee had voluntarily accepted reinstatement with back pay in settlement of his or her grievance against the employer, the U.S. Court of Appeals for the Fifth Circuit held that the employee had waived his or her right to sue under Title VII on the same facts.[35]

In the case of *Johnson v. Railway Express Agency*,[36] the Supreme Court held that an action under Title VII is separate and distinct from an action alleging race discrimination under the Civil Rights Act of 1866, 42 U.S.C., Section 1981 (see Chapter 11).

---

[34] 433 F.2d 125 (1971).

[35] *Strozier v. General Motors*, 635 F.2d 424 (1981).

[36] 421 U.S. 454 (1975).

8-4   Burdens of Proof: Establishing a Case

Once the complaint of an unlawful employment practice under Title VII has become the subject of a suit in a federal district court, the question of the burden of proof arises. What must the plaintiff show to establish a valid claim of discrimination? What must the defendant show to defeat a claim of discrimination?

prima facie case
a case "on the face of it" or "at first sight"; often used to establish that if a certain set of facts is proven, then it is apparent that another fact is established

The plaintiff in a suit under Title VII always carries the burden of proof; that is, the plaintiff must persuade the trier of fact (the jury or the judge if there is no jury) that there has been a violation of Title VII. To do this, the plaintiff must establish a **prima facie case** of discrimination—enough evidence to raise a presumption of discrimination. If the plaintiff is unable to establish a prima facie case of discrimination, the case will be dismissed. The specific elements of a prima facie case, or the means to establish it, will vary depending on whether the complaint involves disparate treatment (intentional discrimination) or disparate impact (the discriminatory effects of apparently neutral criteria).

The plaintiff may use either anecdotal evidence or statistical evidence to establish the prima facie case. In *Bazemore v. Friday*, the plaintiffs offered a statistical multiple-regression analysis to demonstrate that pay policies discriminated against African American employees. The employer argued that the multiple-regression analysis did not consider several variables that were important in determining employees' pay. The trial court and the court of appeals refused to admit the multiple-regression analysis as evidence because it did not include all relevant variables. On appeal, however, the Supreme Court held that the multiple-regression-analysis evidence should have been admitted. The failure of the analysis to include all relevant variables affects its probative value (the weight given to it by the trier of fact), not its admissibility.

According to the U.S. Supreme Court decision in *Desert Palace, Inc. v. Costa*,[37] a plaintiff seeking to establish a mixed-motive case under Section 703(m) of Title VII need only demonstrate that the defendant used a prohibited factor (race, color, gender, religion, or natural origin) as one of the motives for an employment action. That demonstration can be made either by circumstantial evidence or direct evidence. The act does not require direct evidence to raise the mixed-motive analysis under Section 703(m).

8-4a   Disparate Treatment Claims

Claims of disparate treatment involve allegations of intentional discrimination in employment. A plaintiff alleging disparate treatment must establish that he or she was subjected to less favorable treatment because of his or her race, color, religion, gender, or national origin. The specific elements of a prima facie case of disparate treatment under Title VII are discussed in the following case.

---

[37] 539 U.S. 90 (2003).

CASE 8.6
McDonnell Douglas Corp. v. Green
411 U.S. 792 (1973)

Powell, J.

The case before us raises significant questions as to the proper order and nature of proof in actions under Title VII of the Civil Rights Act of 1964.

Petitioner, McDonnell Douglas Corporation, is an aerospace and aircraft manufacturer headquartered in St. Louis, Missouri, where it employs over 30,000 people. Respondent, a black citizen of St. Louis, worked for petitioner as a mechanic and laboratory technician from 1956 until August 28, 1964 when he was laid off in the course of a general reduction in petitioner's work force.

Respondent, a long-time activist in the civil rights movement, protested vigorously that his discharge and the general hiring practices of petitioner were racially motivated. As part of this protest, respondent and other members of the Congress on Racial Equality illegally stalled their cars on the main roads leading to petitioner's plant for the purpose of blocking access to it at the time of the morning shift change. The District Judge described the plan for, and respondent's participation in, the "stall-in" as follows:

> ... five teams, each consisting of four cars, would "tie-up" five main access roads into McDonnell at the time of the morning rush hour. The drivers of the cars were instructed to line up next to each other completely blocking the intersections or roads. The drivers were also instructed to stop their cars, turn off the engines, pull the emergency brake, raise all windows, lock the doors, and remain in their cars until the police arrived. The plan was to have the cars remain in position for one hour....

... On July 2, 1965, a "lock-in" took place wherein a chain and padlock were placed on the front door of a building to prevent the occupants, certain of petitioner's employees, from leaving. Though respondent apparently knew beforehand of the "lock-in," the full extent of his involvement remains uncertain.

Some three weeks following the "lock-in," on July 25, 1965, petitioner publicly advertised for qualified mechanics, respondent's trade, and respondent promptly applied for reemployment. Petitioner turned down respondent, basing its rejection on respondent's participation in the "stall-in" and "lock-in." Shortly thereafter, respondent filed a formal complaint with the Equal Employment Opportunity Commission, claiming that petitioner had refused to rehire him because of his race and persistent involvement in the civil rights movement in violation of Sections 703(a)(1) and 704(a).... The former section generally prohibits racial discrimination in any employment decision while the latter forbids discrimination against applicants or employees for attempting to protest or correct allegedly discriminatory conditions of employment.

The Commission made no finding on respondent's allegation of racial bias under Section 703(a)(1), but it did find reasonable cause to believe petitioner had violated Section 704(a) by refusing to rehire respondent because of his civil rights activity. After the Commission unsuccessfully attempted to conciliate the dispute, it advised respondent in March 1968, of his right to institute a civil action in federal court within 30 days.

On April 15, 1968, respondent brought the present action, claiming initially a violation of Section 704(a) and, in an amended complaint, a violation of Section 703(a)(1) as well. The District Court dismissed the latter claim of racial discrimination in petitioner's hiring procedures.... The District Court also found that petitioner's refusal to rehire respondent was based solely on his participation in the illegal demonstrations and not on his legitimate civil rights activities. The court concluded that nothing in Title VII or Section 704 protected "such activity as employed by the plaintiff in the 'stall-in' and 'lock-in' demonstrations."

... On appeal, the Eighth Circuit affirmed that unlawful protests were not protected activities under Section 704(a), but reversed the dismissal of respondent's Section 703(a)(1) claim relating to racially discriminatory hiring practices ... The court ordered the case remanded for trial of respondent's claim under Section 703(a)(1).

... The critical issue before us concerns the order and allocation of proof in a private, single-plaintiff action challenging employment discrimination. The language of Title VII makes plain the purpose of Congress to assure equality of employment opportunities and to eliminate those discriminatory practices and devices which have fostered racially stratified job environments to the disadvantage of minority citizens.

As noted in [*Griggs v. Duke Power Co.*]:

Congress did not intend Title VII, however, to guarantee a job to every person regardless of qualifications. In short, the Act does not command that any person be hired simply because he was formerly the subject of discrimination, or because he is a member of a minority group. Discriminatory preference for any group, minority or majority, is precisely and only what Congress has proscribed. What is required by Congress is the removal of artificial, arbitrary, and unnecessary barriers to employment when the barriers operate invidiously to discriminate on the basis of racial or other impermissible classification….

There are societal as well as personal interests on both sides of this equation. The broad, overriding interest shared by employer, employee, and consumer, is efficient and trustworthy workmanship assured through fair and racially neutral employment and personnel decisions. In the implementation of such decisions, it is abundantly clear that Title VII tolerates no racial discrimination, subtle or otherwise.

In this case, respondent, the complainant below, charges that he was denied employment "because of his involvement in civil rights activities" and "because of his race and color." Petitioner denied discrimination of any kind, asserting that its failure to re-employ respondent was based upon and justified by his participation in the unlawful conduct against it. Thus, the issue at the trial on remand is framed by those opposing factual contentions….

The complainant in a Title VII trial must carry the initial burden under the statute of establishing a prima facie case of racial discrimination. This may be done by showing (i) that he belongs to a racial minority; (ii) that he had applied and was qualified for a job for which the employer was seeking applicants; (iii) that, despite his qualifications, he was rejected; and (iv) that, after his rejection, the position remained open and the employer continued to seek applicants from persons of complainant's qualifications. In the instant case, we agree with the Court of Appeals that respondent proved a prima facie case…. Petitioner sought mechanics, respondent's trade, and continued to do so after respondent's rejection. Petitioner, moreover, does not dispute respondent's qualifications and acknowledges that his past work performance in petitioner's employ was "satisfactory."

The burden then must shift to the employer to articulate some legitimate, nondiscriminatory reason for respondent's rejection. We need not attempt in the instant case to detail every matter which fairly could be recognized as a reasonable basis for a refusal to hire. Here petitioner has assigned respondent's participation in unlawful conduct against it as the cause for his rejection. We think that this suffices to discharge petitioner's burden of proof at this stage and to meet respondent's prima facie case of discrimination.

The Court of Appeals intimated, however, that petitioner's stated reason for refusing to rehire respondent was a "subjective" rather than objective criterion which "carries little weight in rebutting charges of discrimination." Regardless of whether this was the intended import of the opinion, we think the court below seriously underestimated the rebuttal weight to which petitioner's reasons were entitled. Respondent admittedly had taken part in a carefully planned "stall-in," designed to tie up access and egress to petitioner's plant at a peak traffic hour. Nothing in Title VII compels an employer to absolve and rehire one who has engaged in such deliberate, unlawful activity against it….

… Petitioner's reason for rejection thus suffices to meet the prima facie case, but the inquiry must not end here. While Title VII does not, without more, compel rehiring of respondent, neither does it permit petitioner to use respondent's conduct as a pretext for the sort of discrimination prohibited by Section 703(a)(1). On remand, respondent must, as the Court of Appeals recognized, be afforded a fair opportunity to show that petitioner's stated reason for respondent's rejection was in fact pretextual. Especially relevant to such a showing would be evidence that white employees involved in acts against petitioner of comparable seriousness to the "stall-in" were nevertheless retained or rehired. Petitioner may justifiably refuse to rehire one who was engaged in unlawful, disruptive acts against it, but only if this criterion is applied alike to members of all races.

Other evidence that may be relevant to any showing of pretextuality includes facts as to the petitioner's treatment of respondent during his prior term of employment, petitioner's reaction, if any, to respondent's legitimate civil rights activities, and petitioner's general policy and practice with respect to minority employment. On the latter point, statistics as to petitioner's employment policy and practice may be helpful to a determination of whether petitioner's refusal to rehire respondent in this case conformed to a general pattern of discrimination against blacks. In short, on the retrial respondent must be given a full and fair opportunity to demonstrate by competent evidence that the presumptively valid reasons for his rejection were in fact a coverup for a racially discriminatory decision....

Case Questions

1. How can a plaintiff establish a prima facie case of disparate treatment discrimination?

2. What was McDonnell Douglas's reason for refusing to rehire Green? Why did Green argue that the reason was a pretext for illegal discrimination?

3. How could Green convince the Court that McDonnell Douglas's reason was a pretext? What evidence would be relevant to such a showing? What would be the effect of such a showing?

Defendant's Burden

If the plaintiff is successful in establishing a prima facie case of disparate treatment, the defendant must then try to overcome the plaintiff's claims. Is the defendant required to disprove those claims, prove that there was no discrimination, or merely explain the apparent discrimination? What is the nature of the defendant's burden in a disparate treatment case? In *Texas Department of Community Affairs v. Burdine*,[38] the U.S. Supreme Court stated:

> The nature of the burden that shifts to the defendant should be understood in light of the plaintiffs ultimate and intermediate burdens. The ultimate burden of persuading the trier of fact that the defendant intentionally discriminated against the plaintiff remains at all time with the plaintiff.... The burden that shifts to the defendant, therefore, is to rebut the presumption of discrimination by producing evidence that the plaintiff was rejected, or someone else was preferred, for a legitimate, nondiscriminatory reason. The defendant need not persuade the court that it was actually motivated by the proffered reasons. It is sufficient if the defendant's evidence raises a genuine issue of fact as to whether it discriminated against the plaintiff. To accomplish this, the defendant must clearly set forth, through the introduction of admissible evidence, the reasons for the plaintiff's rejection. The explanation provided must be legally sufficient to justify a judgment for the defendant. If the defendant carries this burden of production, the presumption raised by the prima facie case is rebutted....

According to *Burdine*, the defendant need only "articulate" some legitimate justification for its actions; the burden of proof—of persuading the trier of fact—remains with the plaintiff. Although the defendant need not *prove* that there was no discrimination, the nondiscriminatory justification or explanation offered by the defendant must be believable. Obviously, if the defendant's justification is not credible, then the plaintiff's prima facie case will not be rebutted, and the plaintiff will prevail.

Plaintiff's Burden of Showing Pretext

After the defendant has advanced a legitimate justification to counter, or rebut, the plaintiff's prima facie case, the focus of the proceeding shifts back to the plaintiff. The plaintiff, as was discussed in the *McDonnell Douglas* case, must be afforded an opportunity to show that the employer's justification is a mere pretext, or cover-up. This can be shown either directly, by persuading the court that a discriminatory reason likely motivated the defendant, or indirectly, by showing that the offered justification is not worthy of credence. The burden of showing that the defendant's offered justification is a pretext for discrimination is

---

[38] 450 U.S. 248 (1979).

a very difficult one. According to the Supreme Court decision in *St. Mary's Honor Center v. Hicks*,[39] the plaintiff, in addition to demonstrating that the defendant's justification is false, still has to convince the trier of fact that the defendant was motivated by illegal discrimination. In *Reeves v. Sanderson Plumbing Products, Inc.*,[40] when the plaintiff has established a prima facie case of discrimination, and in doing so has provided enough evidence for the trier of fact (jury or judge) to reject the employer's offered excuse as false, there was sufficient evidence to support a finding that the employer had intentionally discriminated against the plaintiff. (Note that the *Reeves* case involved a claim under the Age Discrimination in Employment Act, which is discussed in the next chapter, but the burden of proof analysis is also applicable under Title VII.)

8-4b Disparate Impact Claims

Unlike a disparate treatment claim, a claim of disparate impact does not involve an allegation of intentional discrimination. Rather, as in *Griggs v. Duke Power Co.*, it involves a claim that neutral job requirements have a discriminatory effect. The plaintiff, in order to establish a prima facie case, must show that the apparently neutral employment requirements or practices have a disproportionate impact upon a class protected by Title VII.

The Supreme Court in the *Wards Cove Packing Co. v. Atonio* and *Watson v. Fort Worth Bank & Trust* decisions (see Chapter 6) held that a plaintiff alleging a disparate impact claim must "offer statistical evidence of a kind and degree sufficient to show that the practice in question has caused the exclusion of applicants for jobs or promotions because of their membership in a protected group."

Four-Fifths Rule

As discussed in Chapter 6, one way to establish proof of a disproportionate impact is by using the Four-Fifths Rule from the EEOC Guidelines. The rule states that a disparate impact will be presumed to exist when the selection or pass rate for the protected class with the lowest selection rate is less than 80 percent of the selection or pass rate of the protected class with the highest rate. The Four-Fifths Rule is used primarily when challenging employment tests or requirements such as a high school diploma or minimum height and weight requirements.

Using Statistics

Another method of establishing a disparate impact may be by making a statistical comparison of the minority representation in the employers' work force and the minority representation in the population as a whole (or in the relevant area or labor market). When a job requires specific skills and training, the population used for comparison with the work force may be limited to available qualified individuals within the relevant area or labor market. The court may require specific demographic and geographic comparisons when using statistical evidence, as demonstrated in *Hazelwood School Dist. v. U.S.*[41]

---

[39] 509 U.S. 502 (1993).

[40] 530 U.S. 133 (2000).

[41] 433 U.S. 299 (1977).

Defendant's Burden

When the plaintiff has established a prima facie case of disparate impact, the defendant has two methods of responding. The defendant may challenge the statistical analysis, the methods of data collection, or the significance of the plaintiff's evidence. The defendant may also submit alternative statistical proof that leads to conclusions that contradict those of the plaintiff's evidence.

Rather than attacking the plaintiff's statistical evidence, the defendant alternatively may show that the employment practice, test, or requirement having the disparate impact is job related.

Although the Supreme Court decisions in *Watson v. Fort Worth Bank & Trust* and *Wards Cove Packing Co. v. Atonio* both held that the employer need only show some business justification for the challenged practice, and the plaintiff has the burden of persuasion for showing that the challenged practice is not job related, the 1991 amendments to Title VII overruled those cases. Section 703(k) requires that, once the plaintiff has demonstrated that the challenged practice has a disparate impact, the employer has the burden of persuasion for convincing the court that the practice is job related.

A defense of job relatedness can be established by using the methods of demonstrating validity set out in the Uniform Guidelines for Employee Selection. (The methods of demonstrating that a test or requirement is content valid, construct valid, or criterion valid are described in Chapter 6.)

If the defendant establishes that the practice, requirement, or test is job related, the plaintiff may still prevail by showing that other tests, practices, or requirements that do not have disparate impacts on protected classes are available and would satisfy the defendant's legitimate business concerns. The plaintiff may also try to show that the job-related justification is really just a pretext for intentional discrimination.

Concept *Summary* 8.5

BURDEN OF PROOF: ESTABLISHING A CASE OF DISCRIMINATION UNDER TITLE VII

Disparate Treatment	Disparate Impact
Plaintiff must present evidence raising presumption of discrimination	Plaintiff must show neutral requirement or that selection device has disparate impact on a protected group
↓	↓
Defendant must then offer nondiscriminatory reason or explanation of conduct	Defendant must then show that requirement or selection device is job related
↓	↓
Plaintiff can demonstrate that offered reason is pretext for discrimination	Plaintiff can then show alternative requirement or selection device without disparate impact

After-Acquired Evidence

after-acquired evidence
evidence, discovered after an employer has taken an adverse employment action, that the employer uses to justify the action taken

What happens when the employer, after an employee who was allegedly fired for discriminatory reasons has filed a Title VII claim, discovers that the employee had falsified credentials on the application for employment? Does the evidence of the plaintiff employee's misconduct (known as **after-acquired evidence**) preclude the right of the plaintiff to sue? In *McKennon v. Nashville Banner Publishing Co.*,[42] the Supreme Court held that the after-acquired evidence does not preclude the plaintiff's suit but rather goes to the issue of the remedies available. If the employer can demonstrate that the employee's wrongdoing is severe enough to result in termination had the employer known of the misconduct at the time the alleged discrimination occurred, the court must then consider the effect of the wrongdoing on the remedies available to the plaintiff. In such a case, the Supreme Court held that reinstatement would not be appropriate, and back pay may be awarded from the date of the alleged discrimination by the employer to the date upon which the plaintiff's misconduct was discovered. *McKennon* involved a suit under the Age Discrimination in Employment Act, but the after-acquired evidence rule has also been applied in Title VII suits, like *Wallace v. Dunn Construction Co.*[43] Evidence of the plaintiff's misconduct that occurs after the plaintiff was terminated was not relevant to the plaintiff's claim of discrimination and was excluded by the court in *Carr v. Woodbury County Juvenile Detention Center.*[44]

8-4c Arbitration of Statutory EEO Claims

Unions and employers generally agree that any disputes arising under their collective agreements will be settled through arbitration. More recently, an increasing number of employers whose employees are not unionized are requiring their employees to agree to settle any employment disputes through arbitration rather than litigation in the courts. Employers tend to favor arbitration because it is generally quicker than litigation, it is confidential while court decisions are public, and the remedies available under arbitration may be less generous than those available through the courts. What is the effect of such arbitration agreements on the employee's ability to bring a suit under Title VII or other EEO legislation?

In *Alexander v. Gardner Denver Co.*,[45] the Supreme Court held that an arbitration proceeding under a collective agreement did not prevent an employee from filing suit alleging a violation of Title VII. The employee had lost in an arbitration challenging his discharge under the collective agreement but was still permitted to bring a Title VII suit in court. The Supreme Court held that the arbitration dealt with the employee's rights under the collective agreement, which were distinct from the employee's statutory rights under Title VII.

Seventeen years later, in *Gilmer v. Interstate/Johnson Lane Corp.*,[46] the Supreme Court held that a securities broker was required to arbitrate, rather than litigate, his age discrimination claim because he had signed an agreement to arbitrate all disputes arising from his employment. The arbitration agreement was included in Gilmer's registration with the New York Securities Exchange, which was required for him to work as a broker. The Supreme

---

[42] 513 U.S. 352 (1995).

[43] 62 F.3d 374 (11th Cir. 1995).

[44] 905 F. Supp. 619 (N.D. Iowa 1995), *aff'd by*, 97 F.3d 1456 (8th Cir. 1996).

[45] 415 U.S. 147 (1974).

[46] 500 U.S. 20 (1991).

Court in *Gilmer* held that the individual agreement to arbitrate, voluntarily agreed to by *Gilmer*, was enforceable under the Federal Arbitration Act (FAA) and required Gilmer to submit all employment disputes, including those under EEO legislation, to arbitration. The agreement to arbitrate did not waive Gilmer's rights under the statutes but simply required that those rights be determined by the arbitrator rather than the courts. The Court in *Gilmer* emphasized that it involved a different situation from *Alexander v. Gardner Denver*, which continued to apply when arbitration under a collective agreement was involved.

The distinctions between the *Alexander* case and the *Gilmer* case need to be emphasized. In *Gilmer*, the individual employee had agreed, as part of an agreement connected with his employment, to arbitrate all disputes growing out of that employment. In *Alexander*, the union and the employer had agreed, as part of a collective agreement, to arbitrate employment disputes arising under that collective agreement. The individual employee, while subject to the collective agreement, had not personally agreed to arbitrate any disputes.

THE **WORKING** LAW ▬▬▬▬▬▬▬▬▬▬▬▬▬▬

Equal Employment Opportunity Commission Adopts Mediation

Mediation

Mediation is an informal and confidential way for people to resolve disputes with the help of a neutral mediator who is trained to help people discuss their differences. The mediator does not decide who is right or wrong or issue a decision. Instead, the mediator helps the parties work out their own solutions to problems.

Note: Federal agencies are required to have an alternative dispute resolution program. Most use mediation, but not necessarily the EEOC process.

Benefits of Mediation

One of the greatest benefits of mediation is that it allows people to resolve the charge in a friendly way and in ways that meet their own unique needs. Also, a charge can be resolved faster through mediation. While it takes less than 3 months on average to resolve a charge through mediation, it can take 6 months or longer for a charge to be investigated. Mediation is fair, efficient and can help the parties avoid a lengthy investigation and litigation.

EEOC's Mediation Process

Shortly after a charge is filed, we may contact both the employee and employer to ask if they are interested in participating in mediation. The decision to mediate is completely voluntary. If either party turns down mediation, the charge will be forwarded to an investigator. If both parties agree to mediate, we will schedule a mediation, which will be conducted by a trained and experienced mediator. If the parties do not reach an agreement at the mediation, the charge will be investigated like any other charge. A written signed agreement reached during mediation is enforceable in court just like any other contract.

Duration and Cost of Mediation

A mediation session usually lasts from 3 to 4 hours, although the time can vary depending on how complicated the case is. There is no charge to either party to attend the mediation.

Who Should Attend the Mediation

All parties to the charge should attend the mediation session. If you are representing the employer, you should be familiar with the facts of the charge and have the authority to settle the charge on behalf of the employer. Although you don't have to bring an attorney with you to the mediation, either party may choose to do so. The mediator will decide what role the attorney will play during the mediation.

Learn More About Mediation

If you would like to learn more about mediation, we have extensive information about EEOC's Mediation Program available.

Source: EEOC, "Employees & Applicants: Mediation," available at http://www.eeoc.gov/employees/mediation.cfm.

Arbitration Clauses in Collective Agreements

The U.S. Supreme Court took a step toward resolving the distinction between *Gilmer* and *Alexander* when it decided the case of *14 Penn Plaza v. Pyett*.[47] That case involved age discrimination claims filed by employees covered by a collective agreement that included an arbitration clause that specifically covered any claims under Title VII, the Age Discrimination in Employment Act, and other EEO legislation. The Court held that the employees were required to arbitrate their age discrimination claims. The Court noted that *Alexander* rationale that arbitration dealt with contractual rights while litigation dealt with the employee's statutory rights did not apply where the collective bargaining agreement's arbitration provision expressly includes statutory claims as well as contractual claims arising under the terms of the collective agreement. The effect of the decision in *14 Penn Plaza v. Pyett* may not be to completely overrule *Alexander*, however, because the Court specifically refrained from holding that employees must arbitrate their statutory EEO claims when the union controls access to arbitration and may prevent the employees from pursuing their EEO claims through arbitration.

Individual Agreements to Arbitrate Employment Discrimination Disputes

The *Gilmer* case involved a claim of age discrimination under the Age Discrimination in Employment Act, but courts soon applied its reasoning to discrimination claims under Title VII and other federal and state employment discrimination legislation.

The FAA requires federal courts to enforce agreements to arbitrate if they are voluntary and knowing. However, Section 1 of the FAA states that it does not apply to "contracts of employment of seamen, railroad employees, or any other class of workers engaged in foreign or interstate commerce." How broadly should the courts read the exception for "contracts of employment" in Section 1 of the FAA? Does it encompass all employment contracts, or is it limited to the specific kinds of contracts mentioned? This issue, which was not directly addressed by the *Gilmer* case, was decided by the U.S. Supreme Court in the case of *Circuit City Stores, Inc. v. Adams*.[48] The Supreme Court held that Section 1 of the FAA excludes only contracts of employment of the specific classes of workers listed in the statute. In *Circuit*

---

[47] 129 S.Ct. 1456 (2009).

[48] 532 U.S. 105 (2001).

City, the employer's application for employment contained a dispute resolution agreement requiring employees to submit all employment disputes to binding arbitration. Applicants who refused to sign the dispute resolution agreement were not hired. The Supreme Court held that such an agreement is enforceable under the FAA and that employees signing the agreement are precluded from suing the employer over employment disputes. While individual employees may be bound by arbitration agreements in their contracts of employment, the individual arbitration agreements do not prevent the EEOC from bringing suit against an employer to enforce EEO laws according to *EEOC v. Waffle House, Inc.*[49] The EEOC can bring legal action to enforce the EEO statutes and may also seek individual remedies (such as back pay and reinstatement) for the employee who had signed the arbitration agreement.

Challenges to the Enforceability of Agreements to Arbitrate

The *Circuit City* decision means that employers may insist upon employees agreeing to arbitrate employment disputes as a condition of employment; applicants or employees who refuse to agree to such provisions will not be hired or will be fired. Because employers can force such arbitration agreements upon employees, a court asked to enforce an agreement to arbitrate must be satisfied that the agreement is knowing and reasonable. In *Brisentine v. Stone & Webster Engineering Corp.*,[50] the U.S. Court of Appeals for the Eleventh Circuit stated that, for an arbitration agreement to be enforced, it must meet three requirements:

- The employee must have individually agreed to the arbitration provision
- The arbitration must authorize the arbitrator to resolve the statutory EEO claims
- The agreement must give the employee the right to insist on arbitration if the statutory EEO claim is not resolved to his or her satisfaction in any grievance procedure or dispute resolution process of the employer

Most courts now take the position that an agreement to arbitrate, knowingly and voluntarily agreed to by an employee, is binding and requires the employee to arbitrate EEO claims instead of taking them to court. Arbitration agreements that were not knowingly agreed to will not be enforced, as shown in *Prudential Insurance Co. v. Lai*,[51] nor will the courts enforce agreements that are not binding upon the employer or that are unfair to the employee, according to *Hooters of America, Inc. v. Phillips*[52] and *Floss v. Ryan's Family Steak Houses*.[53] The courts will also refuse to enforce arbitration agreements that restrict remedies available to employees less than those remedies available under the appropriate EEO statute.[54] The California Supreme Court, in the case of *Armendariz v. Foundation Health Psychcare Services, Inc.*,[55] set out requirements for enforcing agreements requiring arbitration of claims under California state employment discrimination legislation:

- the arbitration must be by a neutral arbitrator;
- the arbitration procedures must allow the parties access to witnesses and essential documents;

---

[49] 534 U.S. 279 (2003).

[50] 117 F.3d 519 (11th Cir. 1997).

[51] 42 F.3d 1299 (9th Cir. 1994).

[52] 173 F.3d 933 (4th Cir. 1999).

[53] 211 F.3d 306 (6th Cir. 2000).

[54] *Circuit City Stores, Inc. v. Adams*, 279 F.3d 889 (9th Cir. 2002), *cert. denied*, 535 U.S. 1112 (2002).

[55] 99 Cal. Rptr.2d 745, 24 Cal. 4th 83 (2000).

- the arbitrator must provide a written decision;

- the remedies available under the arbitration must be similar to those available in court; and

- the employee may not be required to pay any arbitrators' fees or expenses or any unreasonable costs as a condition of going to arbitration.

While *Armendariz* deals with state law, some federal courts have adopted its analysis with regard to enforcing mandatory agreements to arbitrate.

Costs of Arbitration

Some challenges to the enforceability of arbitration agreements involve the question of cost: Does the arbitration agreement require the employee to bear unreasonable costs? As mentioned in *Armendariz*, arbitration agreements that impose excessive costs on employees could operate to deter those employees from bringing complaints of employment discrimination. Because the employees may be required to arbitrate rather than litigate their claims, they are effectively denied the protection of the EEO laws. As a result, the courts have refused to enforce arbitration agreements that require the employee to bear unreasonable expenses associated with the arbitration. In *Green Tree Financial Corp. v. Randolph*,[56] which was not an employment case, the Supreme Court held that the party seeking to invalidate an arbitration agreement because it would be prohibitively expensive has the burden of demonstrating the likelihood of incurring such costs.

After *Green Tree*, the federal courts have struggled with the question of when the cost requirements of arbitration become prohibitively or unreasonably expensive. Plaintiffs who file EEO suits in the federal courts are required to pay a filing fee (currently less than $300) and must also bear the cost of legal representation. Attorneys for plaintiffs are likely to take such cases on a contingency basis (they will only charge legal fees if the plaintiff wins the suit). Title VII also provides that successful plaintiffs may recover legal fees as part of the statutory remedies available. In contrast, the employee filing for arbitration will be required to pay a filing fee and will also generally be held to pay at least half of the arbitrator's fees and expenses. There may be additional fees for administrative costs, for discovery proceedings, and for subpoenas of witnesses. One study estimated that the costs of filing for arbitration (based on holding three days of hearings) ranged between $3,950 and $10,925.[57] Requiring an employee to pay such expenses to pursue an employment discrimination claim may have the effect of deterring the employee from doing so. Some employers may have an incentive to impose arbitration requirements with high costs to prevent employees from filing employment discrimination claims. As a result, the courts have been sensitive to claims that the arbitration agreement imposes unreasonable costs on the employee.

In *Armendariz v. Foundation Health Psychcare Services, Inc.*, the California Supreme Court held that an arbitration agreement that required the employee to pay any expenses beyond that which would be required to file a suit in court would be unreasonable and not enforceable. In *Morrison v. Circuit City Stores, Inc.*,[58] the court held that a "fee-splitting clause (which required the employee and the employer to split the costs of the arbitration

---

[56] 531 U.S. 79 (2000).

[57] "The Costs of Arbitration," Public Citizen, April 2002.

[58] 317 F.3d 646 (6th Cir. 2003) *(en banc)*.

and the arbitrator's fees) would be unreasonable and unenforceable when it would deter a substantial number of potential claimants from exerting their statutory rights.

The court, in making such a determination, should consider the employee's income and resources available, the potential costs of arbitration, and the costs of litigation as an alternative to arbitration. Such an approach may yield different results for different employees: For highly paid executive employees, fee-splitting requirements would be affordable and therefore enforceable, but for lower-level employees, such cost requirements would not be enforceable. In the *Morrison* case, the court required the employee to arbitrate her claim but held that the employer had to pay the costs of the arbitration. Other courts have held fee-splitting clauses unreasonable per se. Such requirements are unenforceable because, by requiring the employee to pay at least some of the costs of arbitration, they automatically limit the remedies that would be available to the employee under Title VII.[59]

8-4d Private Settlement and Release Agreements

In 2014, the EEOC took the position that private settlement-and-release agreements between employers and current or former employers are unenforceable to the extent that they potentially interfere with the employee's future access to the agency and/or future ability to cooperate in agency investigations. On February 7, 2014, the EEOC sued CVS for unlawfully violating employees' right to communicate with the agency and to file charges.

> According to the EEOC, CVS conditioned the receipt of severance benefits for certain employees on an overly broad severance agreement set forth in five pages of small print. The agreement interfered with employees' right to file discrimination charges and/or communicate and cooperate with the EEOC, the agency said.
>
> Interfering with these employee rights violates Section 707 of Title VII of the Civil Rights Act of 1964, which prohibits employer conduct that constitutes a pattern or practice of resistance to the rights protected by Title VII, the EEOC said. Section 707 permits the agency to seek immediate relief without the same pre-suit administrative process that is required under Section 706 of Title VII, and does not require that the agency's suit arise from a discrimination charge.[60]

8-4e Remedies Under Title VII

Plaintiffs under Title VII are entitled to a jury trial on their claims. The remedies available to a successful plaintiff under Title VII are spelled out in Section 706(g). These remedies include:

* Judicial orders requiring hiring or reinstatement of employees
* Awarding of back pay and seniority

---

[59] *Perez v. Globe Airport Security Services*, 253 F.3d 1280 (11th Cir. 2001); *Circuit City Stores, Inc. v. Adams*, 279 F.3d 889 (9th Cir. 2002), *cert. denied*, 535 U.S. 1112 (2002); and *Ingle v. Circuit City Stores, Inc.*, 328 F.3d 1165 (9th Cir. 2003).

[60] EEOC Press Release, February 7, 2014, available at http://www.eeoc.gov/eeoc/newsroom/release/2-7-14.cfm.

- Injunctions against unlawful employment practices
- "Such affirmative action as may be appropriate"

Section 706(k) provides that the court, in its discretion, may award legal fees to a prevailing party other than the EEOC or the United States. The Civil Rights Act of 1991 added the right to recover compensatory and punitive damages for intentional violations of Title VII. Individual employees, even those in supervisory or managerial positions, are not personally liable under Title VII.[61]

Back Pay

Section 706(g) states that the court may award back pay to a successful plaintiff. Back-pay orders spelled out by that section have some limitations, however. Section 706(g) provides that no back-pay order shall extend to a period prior to two years before the date of the filing of a complaint with the EEOC. It also provides that "interim earnings or amounts earnable with reasonable diligence by the person or persons discriminated against shall operate to reduce the back pay otherwise allowable." That section imposes a duty to mitigate damages upon the plaintiff.

Although Section 706(g) states that a court may award back pay, it does not require that such an award always be made. What principles should guide the court on the issue of whether to award back pay?

According to the Supreme Court in *Albemarle Paper Co. v. Moody*,[62] Title VII is remedial in nature and is intended to "make whole" victims of discrimination. Therefore, a successful plaintiff should be awarded back pay as a matter of course. Back pay should be denied only in exceptional circumstances, such as when it would frustrate the purpose of Title VII.

In *Ford Motor Co. v. EEOC*,[63] the Supreme Court held that an employer's back-pay liability may be limited to the period prior to the date of an unconditional offer of a job to the plaintiff, even though the offer did not include seniority retroactive to the date of the alleged discrimination. The plaintiff's rejection of the offer, in the absence of special circumstances, would end the accrual of back-pay liability of the employer.

In addition, Section 706(g)(2)(B), added by the 1991 amendments to Title VII, limits an employer's liability in mixed-motive cases, provided that the employer can demonstrate that it would have reached the same decision even without consideration of the illegal factor. In these situations, the employer is subject to the court's injunctive or declaratory remedies and is liable for legal fees but is not liable for back pay or other damages, nor is the employer required to hire or reinstate the complainant.

Front Pay

front pay
monetary damages awarded to a plaintiff instead of reinstatement or hiring

In some cases, if a hiring or reinstatement order may not be appropriate or if there is excessive animosity between the parties, the court may award the plaintiff **front pay**—monetary damages in lieu of reinstatement or hiring. The question of whether front pay is appropriate is a question for the judge, as is the determination of the amount of front pay. The amount of front pay depends upon the circumstances of each case. The court will consider factors such as the employability of the plaintiff and the likely duration of the employment.

---

[61] *Tomka v. The Seiler Corp.*, 66 F.3d 1295 (2d Cir. 1995).

[62] 422 U.S. 405 (1975).

[63] 456 U.S. 923 (1982).

Any front pay awarded to the plaintiff by the court is separate from any compensatory and punitive damages awarded. The front-pay award is not subject to the statutory limits (discussed in the next section) placed on the compensatory and punitive damages awards, according to the Supreme Court decision in *Pollard v. E. I. du Pont de Nemours & Co.*[64]

8-4f   Compensatory and Punitive Damages

The right to recover compensatory and punitive damages for intentional violations of Title VII was created by the Civil Rights Act of 1991, which amended Title VII. The 1991 act allows claims for compensatory and punitive damages, in addition to any remedies recoverable under Section 706(g) of Title VII, to be brought under 42 U.S.C. Section 1981, as amended by the 1991 act. Section 1981 (discussed in detail in Chapter 11) allows recovery of damages for intentional race discrimination. The Civil Rights Act of 1991 added a section to 42 U.S.C. Section 1981 that allows damages suits for intentional discrimination in violation of Title VII, for which the plaintiff could not recover under Section 1981 (i.e., discrimination because of gender, religion, or national origin).

If the plaintiff can demonstrate that a private sector defendant (not a governmental unit, agency, or other public sector entity) has engaged "in a discriminatory practice or discriminatory practices with malice or with reckless indifference to the federally protected rights of an aggrieved individual," the plaintiff can recover compensatory and punitive damages. Punitive damages are not recoverable against public sector defendants. The compensatory and punitive damages are separate from, and in addition to, any back pay, interest, front pay, legal fees, or other remedies recovered under Section 706(g) of Title VII.

The compensatory and punitive damages recoverable under the amended Section 1981 are subject to statutory limits, depending on the number of employees of the defendant-employer:

- For employers with more than 14 but fewer than 101 employees, the damages recoverable are limited to $50,000

- For defendants with more than 100 but fewer than 201 employees, the limit is $100,000

- For more than 200 but fewer than 501 employees, it is $200,000

- For employers with more than 500 employees, the limit is $300,000

The number of people employed by a defendant-employer is determined by considering the number employed in each week of 20 or more calendar weeks in the current or preceding year.

Plaintiffs bringing a claim for damages under the amended Section 1981 have the right to a jury trial. As noted, punitive and compensatory damages are not recoverable against a public sector employer; punitive and compensatory damages are only recoverable for intentional discrimination and not for claims of disparate impact discrimination. Punitive and compensatory damages under the amended Section 1981 are also recoverable for intentional violations of the Americans with Disabilities Act of 1990 (discussed in Chapter 10.)

When an employee has convinced the court that there was hostile environment harassment (based on race, sex, religion, or national origin) in violation of Title VII, the employer may be held liable for damages for all the acts that contributed to the hostile environment,

---

[64] 532 U.S. 843 (2001).

even though some of those acts may have occurred more than 300 days (or 180 days, if appropriate) prior to the date on which the employee filed the complaint according to *National Railroad Passenger Corp. v. Morgan.*[65]

The federal courts of appeals have split on the question of whether a plaintiff who prevails under state law in a state agency and state court can file suit in federal court under Title VII to recover remedies that were not available under state law. In *Nestor v. Pratt & Whitney,*[66] the U.S. Court of Appeals for the Second Circuit allowed a plaintiff alleging sex discrimination to bring a suit under Title VII to recover compensatory and punitive damages. The plaintiff had been awarded back pay under Connecticut legislation, which did not provide for compensatory and punitive damages. The U.S. Court of Appeals for the Eighth Circuit, in *Jones v. American State Bank,*[67] and the U.S. Court of Appeals for the Seventh Circuit, in *Patzer v. Board of Regents,*[68] have also allowed such suits. However, the U.S. Court of Appeals for the Fourth Circuit has held a plaintiff who is successful before a state administrative agency may not file suit under Title VII to recover remedies that were not available under the state law.[69]

Limitations on Remedies for Mixed Motive Discrimination

In cases involving mixed motive discrimination claims under Section 703(m) of Title VII [see the discussion of the *Hopkins* case and Section 703(m) in Chapter 6], Section 706(g)(2)(B) provides that an employer will not be liable for damages when the employer can demonstrate that it would have reached the same decision even without consideration of the illegal factor. Where the employer has met the "same decision" test, the court will only issue a declaration or injunction and award the plaintiff legal fees. The plaintiff is not entitled to be hired, reinstated, or receive back pay, front pay, or compensatory and punitive damages.

Employer Liability for Punitive Damages Under Title VII

Prior to being amended in 1991, Title VII did not provide for the recovery of punitive or compensatory damages. Successful plaintiffs were limited to recovering wages, benefits, and legal fees. The Civil Rights Act of 1991 amended Title VII to allow recovery of punitive damages in cases in which the employer has engaged in intentional discrimination and has done so "with malice or with reckless indifference to the federally protected rights of an aggrieved individual." Under what circumstances should employers be held liable for punitive damages under Title VII? Are there any defenses that employers may raise to avoid liability for punitive damages? In *Kolstad v. American Dental Association,*[70] the Supreme Court answered those questions:

> The employer must act with "malice or with reckless indifference to [the plaintiffs] federally protected rights." The terms "malice" or "reckless indifference" pertain to the employer's knowledge that it may be acting in violation of federal law, not its awareness that it is engaging in discrimination…. An employer must at least discriminate in the face of a perceived risk that its actions will violate federal law to be liable in punitive damages. There will be circumstances

---

[65] 536 U.S. 101 (2002).

[66] 466 F.3d 65 (2d Cir. 2006).

[67] 857 F.2d 494 (8th Cir. 1988).

[68] 763 F.2d 851 (7th Cir. 1985).

[69] *Chris v. Tenet,* 221 F.3d 648 (4th Cir. 2000).

[70] 527 U.S. 526 (1999).

where intentional discrimination does not give rise to punitive damages liability under this standard. In some instances, the employer may simply be unaware of the relevant federal prohibition. There will be cases, moreover, in which the employer discriminates with the distinct belief that its discrimination is lawful. The underlying theory of discrimination may be novel or otherwise poorly recognized, or an employer may reasonably believe that its discrimination satisfies a bona fide occupational qualification defense or other statutory exception to liability.... Holding employers liable for punitive damages when they engage in good faith efforts to comply with Title VII, however, is in some tension with the very principles underlying common law limitations on vicarious liability for punitive damages—that it is "improper ordinarily to award punitive damages against one who himself is personally innocent and therefore liable only vicariously." Where an employer has undertaken such good faith efforts at Title VII compliance, it "demonstrates] that it never acted in reckless disregard of federally protected rights."

... We agree that, in the punitive damages context, an employer may not be vicariously liable for the discriminatory employment decisions of managerial agents where these decisions are contrary to the employer's "good-faith efforts to comply with Title VII."

8-4g   Remedial Seniority

The *Teamsters* case, discussed in Chapter 6, held that a bona fide seniority system is protected by Section 703(h), even when it perpetuates the effects of prior discrimination. If the court is prevented from restructuring the bona fide seniority system, how can the court remedy the prior discrimination suffered by the plaintiffs? In *Franks v. Bowman Transportation Co.*,[71] the Supreme Court held that remedial seniority may be awarded to the victims of prior discrimination to overcome the effects of discrimination perpetuated by the bona fide seniority system. The Court stated that "the denial of seniority relief to victims of illegal ... discrimination in hiring is permissible 'only for reasons which, if applied generally, would not frustrate the central statutory purposes of eradicating discrimination ... and making persons whole for injuries suffered through past discrimination....'"

The granting of remedial seniority may be necessary to place the victims of discrimination in the position they would have been in had no illegal discrimination occurred.

8-4h   Legal Fees

Section 706(k) provides that the court, in its discretion, may award "reasonable attorney's fees" under Title VII. The section also states that the United States or the EEOC may not recover legal fees if they prevail, but shall be liable for costs "the same as a private person" if they do not prevail.

In *New York Gaslight Club v. Carey*,[72] the Supreme Court held that an award of attorney's fees under Section 706(k) can include fees for the legal proceedings before the state or local agency when the complainant is required to file with that agency by Section 706(c).

Section 706(k) does not require that attorney's fees be awarded to a prevailing party; the award is at the court's discretion. In *Christianburg Garment Co. v. EEOC*,[73] the Supreme Court held that a successful plaintiff should generally be awarded legal fees except in special circumstances. A prevailing defendant should be awarded legal fees only when the court determines that the plaintiff's case was frivolous, unreasonable, vexatious, or meritless. A case is meritless, according to the Court, not simply because the plaintiff lost, but

---

[71] 424 U.S. 747 (1976).

[72] 447 U.S. 54 (1980).

[73] 434 U.S. 412 (1978).

where the plaintiff's case was "groundless or without foundation." Why should prevailing defendants be treated differently than prevailing plaintiffs under Title VII?

8-4i   Class Actions

The rules of procedure for the federal courts allow an individual plaintiff to sue on behalf of a whole class of individuals allegedly suffering the same harm. Rule 23 of the Federal Rules of Civil Procedure allows such suits, known as *class actions*, when several conditions are met. First, the number of members of the class is so numerous that it would be "impracticable" to have them join the suit individually. Second, there must be issues of fact or law common to the claims of all members. Third, the claims of the individual seeking to represent the entire class must be typical of the claims of the members of the class. Finally, the individual representative must fairly and adequately protect the interests of the class.

When these conditions are met, the court may certify the suit as a class-action suit on behalf of all members of the class. Individuals challenging employment discrimination under Title VII may sue on behalf of all individuals affected by the alleged discrimination by complying with the requirements of Rule 23. In *General Telephone Co. of the Southwest v. Falcon*,[74] the Supreme Court held that an employee alleging that he was denied promotion due to national origin discrimination is not a proper representative of the class of individuals denied hiring by the employer due to discrimination. The plaintiff had not suffered the same injuries allegedly suffered by the class members.

The EEOC need not seek certification as a class representative under Rule 23 to seek classwide remedies under Title VII, according to the Supreme Court decision in *General Telephone v. EEOC*.[75] The EEOC, said the Court, acts to vindicate public policy and not just to protect personal interests.

Remedies in Class Actions

Classwide remedies are appropriate under Title VII according to the Supreme Court's holding in *Franks v. Bowman Transportation Co.*,[76] which authorized such classwide "make whole" orders. In *Local 28, Sheet Metal Workers v. EEOC* (see Chapter 6), the Supreme Court upheld court-ordered affirmative action to remedy prior employment discrimination. The Court specifically said affirmative relief may be available to minority group members who were not personally victimized by the employer's prior discrimination. Additionally, in *Local 93, Int'l Ass'n. of Firefighters v. Cleveland* (see Chapter 11), the Supreme Court approved a consent decree that imposed affirmative action to remedy prior discrimination, again upholding the right of nonvictims to benefit from the affirmative remedy.

8-4j   Public Employees Under Title VII

Title VII was amended in 1972 to cover the employees of state and local employers. These employees are subject to the same procedural requirements as private employees. However, Section 706(f)(1) authorizes the U.S. attorney general, rather than the EEOC, to file suit under Title VII against a state or local public employer.

---

[74] 457 U.S. 147 (1982).

[75] 446 U.S. 318 (1980).

[76] 424 U.S. 747 (1976).

Most federal employees are covered by Title VII but are subject to different procedural requirements. Section 701(b) excludes the United States, wholly owned federal government corporations, and any department or agency of the District of Columbia subject to civil service regulations from the definition of "employer" under Title VII. Section 717 of the act does provide, however, that "All personnel actions affecting employees or applicants for employment … in positions under the federal civil service, the D.C. Civil Service and the U.S. Postal Service … shall be made free from any discrimination based on race, color, religion, sex or national origin."

Section 717 also designated the federal Civil Service Commission as the agency having jurisdiction over complaints of discrimination by federal employees. However, that authority was transferred to the EEOC under Reorganization Plan No. 1 of 1978. The EEOC adopted procedural regulations regarding Title VII complaints by federal employees. A federal employee alleging employment discrimination must first consult with an Equal Employment Opportunity (EEO) counselor within the employee's own agency. If the employee is not satisfied with the counselor's resolution of the complaint, the employee can file a formal complaint with the agency's designated EEO official. The EEO official, after investigating and holding a hearing, renders a decision. That decision can be appealed to the head of the agency. If the employee is not satisfied with that decision, he or she can either seek judicial review of it or file an appeal with the EEOC. If the employee chooses to file with the EEOC, the complaint is subject to the general EEOC procedures. The employee has 90 days from receiving notice of the EEOC taking final action on the complaint to file suit. The employee may file suit, as well, when the EEOC has not made a decision on the complaint after 180 days from its filing with the EEOC.

Employees of Congress and the White House

The Civil Rights Act of 1991 extended the coverage of Title VII to employees of Congress. Employees of the following offices are subject to Title VII through the Congressional Accountability Act of 1995:

- House of Representatives
- Senate
- Capitol Guide Service
- Capitol Police
- Congressional Budget Office
- Office of the Architect of the Capitol
- Office of the Attending Physician
- Office of Technology Assessment

Those employees can file complaints of illegal discrimination with the Office of Compliance, created by the act, within 180 days of the alleged violation. The Office of Compliance initially attempts to resolve the complaint through counseling and mediation. If the complaint is still unresolved after the counseling and mediation period, the employee may either seek administrative resolution of the complaint through the Office of Compliance or file suit in federal court. Employees of the executive office of the president, the executive residence at the White House, and the official residence of the vice president are subject to Title VII through the Presidential and Executive Office Accountability Act. Complaints by those employees of violations of Title VII are subject to an initial counseling and mediation period. The employee may then choose to pursue the complaint with the EEOC or file suit in federal court.

CHAPTER REVIEW

» Key Terms

English-only rules	2 2 1	prima facie case	2 3 1	front pay	2 4 3
Lilly Ledbetter Fair Pay Act	2 2 7	after-acquired evidence	2 3 7		

» Summary

- The protection that Title VII provides for employees from religious discrimination is not absolute. Religion may be a BFOQ, and the employer is not required to accommodate an employee's religious beliefs or practices if doing so would impose undue hardship on the employer, as defined in the *Hardison* case. Religious corporations and religiously affiliated educational institutions may give preference in employment to members of their particular religion according to Section 702(a) of Title VII and the *Amos* decision. Public sector employers are also subject to the First Amendment of the U.S. Constitution, which may further restrict their dealings with employees' religious beliefs and practices.

- Title VII prohibits employment discrimination based on national origin, although national origin may be used as a BFOQ when necessary for safe and efficient performance of the particular job. Employer English-only rules may also present problems under Title VII, unless supported by specific business justification. Title VII does not prohibit discrimination based on citizenship, but the Immigration Reform and Control Act of 1986 prohibits employment discrimination based on citizenship or national origin.

- The enforcement procedures under Title VII require that individuals claiming illegal discrimination go first to the appropriate state or local agency and then file their complaint with the Equal Employment Opportunity Commission (EEOC) after 60 days or the termination of proceedings at the state or local level, whichever comes first. The EEOC may decide to file suit on the complaint, and if it chooses not to sue, the individual may do so. Title VII suits can be brought in either federal or state courts. The plaintiff in a suit under Title VII must establish a prima facie case of discrimination; the defendant must then offer some legitimate explanation for the apparently discriminatory action to rebut the plaintiff's claims. If the defendant does offer a legitimate explanation for the challenged conduct, the plaintiff still has the opportunity to demonstrate that the employer's explanation was a pretext for illegal discrimination. Successful plaintiffs under Title VII may get an order of reinstatement, may recover back pay and benefits, legal fees, and in cases of intentional discrimination, can recover compensatory and punitive damages up to the appropriate statutory limit. Prevailing defendants may recover legal fees if the plaintiff's case was frivolous, groundless, or brought in bad faith. Plaintiffs claiming discrimination may be required to take their cases to arbitration rather than sue in court if they have knowingly and voluntarily agreed to arbitrate such complaints.

» Problems

» Questions

1. How does Title VII's prohibition of religious discrimination differ from the prohibition of discrimination based on race or color? Explain your answer.

2. What is meant by national origin under Title VII? Does Title VII prohibit discrimination based on ancestry? Explain.

3. What is the effect of a state court's dismissal of a discrimination complaint on the complainant's right to file suit in federal court? What is the effect of a state EEO agency's dismissal of a discrimination complaint on the right of the complainant to file suit in federal court?

4. What remedies are available to a successful plaintiff under Title VII? When are punitive damages recoverable?

5. Must a complainant always file a complaint of illegal discrimination with the relevant state or local agency before filing a complaint with the EEOC? Explain.

» Case Problems

6. Morgan was an untenured faculty member at Ivy University. In February 2013, he was informed that the Faculty Tenure Committee recommended that he not be offered a tenured position with the university. Failure to achieve tenure requires that the faculty member seek employment else-where. The university offers such faculty members a one-year contract following denial of tenure. At the expiration of the one-year contract, the faculty member's employment is terminated.

   Morgan appealed to the tenure committee for reconsideration. The committee granted him a one-year extension for reconsideration. In February 2014, the committee denied Morgan tenure at Ivy University. The university board of trustees affirmed the committee's decision. Morgan was informed of the trustees' decision and offered a one-year contract on June 26, 2014.

   Morgan accepted the one-year contract, which would expire on June 30, 2015. On June 1, 2015, Morgan filed charges with the EEOC alleging race and sex discrimination by Ivy University in denying him tenure. The one-year contract expired on June 30, 2015, and Morgan's employment was terminated.

   Assuming no state or local EEOC agency is involved, is Morgan's complaint validly filed with the EEOC? What employment practice is he challenging? When did it occur? [See *Delaware State College v. Ricks*, 449 U.S. 250 (1980).]

7. Cohen, a college graduate with a degree in journalism, applied for a position with *The Christian Science Monitor*, a daily newspaper published by the Christian Science Publishing Society, a branch of the Christian Science Church. The church board of directors elects the editors and managers of the *Monitor* and is responsible for the editorial content of the *Monitor*. The church subsidizes the *Monitor*, which otherwise would run at a significant loss. The application for employment at the *Monitor* is the same one used for general positions with the church. It contains many questions relating to membership in the Christian Science Church and to its religious affiliation.

   Cohen, who is not a member of the Christian Science Church, was rejected for employment with the *Monitor*. He filed a complaint with the EEOC alleging that his application was not given full consideration by the *Monitor* because he is not a member of the Christian Science Church. The *Monitor* claimed that it can apply a test of religious qualifications to its employment practices.

   Is the *Monitor* in violation of Title VII? Explain your answer. [See *Feldstein v. Christian Science Monitor*, 555 F. Supp. 974 (D.C. Mass. 1983).]

8. Dewhurst was a female flight attendant with Sub-Central Airlines. Sub-Central's employment

policies prohibited female attendants from being married, but married male employees were employed by Sub-Central. Dewhurst was married on June 15, 2012. She was discharged by Sub-Central the next day. Sub-Central, under pressure from the EEOC, eliminated the "no-married females" rule in March 1982.

Dewhurst was rehired by Sub-Central on February 1, 2015. Sub-Central refused to recognize her seniority for her past employment with Sub-Central as the company's policy is to refuse to recognize prior service for all former employees who are rehired. Dewhurst filed a complaint with the EEOC on March 1, 2015, alleging that Sub-Central's refusal to credit her with prior seniority violated Title VII.

Is her complaint validly filed with EEOC? [See *United Airlines v. Evans*, 431 U.S. 553 (1977).]

9. Smith, Washington, and Bailey are African American bricklayers. They had applied for work with Constructo Co., a brick and masonry contractor. Constructo refused their applications for the reason that company policy is to hire only bricklayers referred by Constructo employees. The three filed charges with the EEOC, which decided not to file suit against Constructo. The bricklayers then filed suit in federal court against Constructo, alleging race discrimination in hiring.

At the trial, the three presented evidence of their rejection by Constructo. Constructo denied any racial discrimination in hiring and introduced evidence showing that African Americans make up 13 percent of its work force. Only 5.7 percent of all certified bricklayers in the greater metropolitan area are African American.

Has Constructo met its burden under Title VII? Have the three African Americans met their burden under Title VII? [See *Furnco Construction Co. v. Waters*, 438 U.S. 567 (1978); see also *Brown v. Bibb County Properties, LLC*, --- Fed. Appx. ---, 2015 WL 1003619 (11th Cir. 2015) (plaintiffs complained that Hispanic employees averaged 7.3 hours more overtime than their African American coworkers).]

10. Walker is a clerk with the U.S. Postal Service. The Postal Service distributes the materials for the draft registration required of young men. Walker, although not a formal member of the Society of Friends (known as Quakers), had a long history of involvement with the Quakers. She therefore refused to distribute draft registration materials when she was working. The Postal Service fired her.

Is Walker's refusal to distribute the draft registration materials protected by Title VII? Explain your answer. [See *McGinnis v. U.S. Postal Service*, 512 F. Supp. 517 (U.S. Dist. Ct., N.D. Cal. 1980).]

11. Kim Cloutier was employed by Costco Corp. When she was hired, she had several tattoos and wore multiple earrings. When she was transferred to Costco's deli department, she was informed that Costco's dress code prohibited food handlers, including deli workers, from wearing any jewelry. Her supervisor instructed her to remove her earrings. Cloutier refused to do so, and requested a transfer to a cashier position. She was transferred, and worked as a cashier for several years. During her time as a cashier, she underwent several facial and eyebrow piercings and wore various types of facial jewelry. In 2001, Costco revised its dress code to prohibit all facial jewelry except earrings. Cloutier continued to wear her facial jewelry for several months. In June, 2001, Costco began enforcing its ban on facial jewelry. Cloutier's supervisor informed her that she must remove her facial jewelry and eyebrow piercing. Cloutier returned to work the next day wearing the facial jewelry and eyebrow piercing, and when confronted by her supervisor, she insisted that she was a member of the Church of Body Modification (see http://www.uscobm.com), and wearing the facial jewelry was part of her religion. Costco then offered to let her wear plastic retainers (to keep her piercings open) or to cover the eyebrow piercing with a band-aid. Cloutier rejected that offer, stating that her beliefs required her to display all of her facial piercings at all times. She maintained that the only acceptable accommodation would be to excuse her from Costco's dress code and allow her to wear facial jewelry while at work. Costco replied that such an accommodation would interfere with its ability to maintain a professional appearance and would thus create an undue hardship on Costco's business. Cloutier filed a complaint

with the EEOC, alleging religious discrimination in violation of Title VII. After receiving a right to sue letter from the EEOC, Cloutier filed suit against Costco under Title VII.

How should the court rule on her suit? Explain your answer. [See *Cloutier v. Costco Wholesale Corp.*, 390 F.3d 126 (1st Cir. 2004).]

12. Elizabeth Westman was employed by Valley Technologies as an engineering technician. On June 15, 2014, she was terminated after being informed by her supervisor that the company was experiencing financial difficulties and could no longer afford to employ her. Westman subsequently learned, on May 15, 2015, that she was terminated so that her supervisor could hire a less qualified male technician in her place. Upon learning of the real reason for her discharge, Westman immediately filed a complaint with the EEOC. The employer argued that her complaint should be dismissed because it was not filed within the time limit required under Title VII.

Will her complaint be dismissed, or was it properly filed? Explain your answer. [See *Reeb v. Economic Opportunity Atlanta, Inc.*, 516 F.2d 924 (5th Cir. 1975); cf., *Kwai Fun Wong v. Beebe*, 732 F.3d 1030 (9th Cir. 2013).]

13. This case required the court to consider plaintiff Deborah Malin's experience over several years as an employee with Hospira's information technology department, which was reorganized in 2006. Malin offered evidence that she was effectively demoted as part of the 2006 reorganization. She also offered evidence that would allow a reasonable jury to find that the demotion was (a) part of a manager's long-term effort at retaliation for a sexual harassment complaint she made over his vociferous objection in 2003, or (b) in retaliation for her use of FMLA leave during the reorganization, or (c) both. Although three years is a significant period of time, Malin offered evidence of other retaliatory behavior between her 2003 sexual harassment complaint and the 2006 reorganization and demotion that bridged the gap between the two events.

How should the court rule on whether a jury should be allowed to consider all of the plaintiff's allegations, going back to 2003? Explain your answer. [See *Malin v. Hospira, Inc.*, 762 F.3d 552 (7th Cir. 2014).]

14. Bernardo Huerta, an employee of the Adams Corp., was transferred to a position that prevented him from being eligible for overtime work. Huerta filed a complaint with the EEOC alleging that he had been discriminated against because of his national origin. After negotiations subsequent to the filing of the complaint, Huerta and the Adams Corp. reached a settlement agreement on his complaint. A year later, Huerta claimed that Adams had broken the settlement agreement, and he filed suit in federal court. The court granted judgment for Huerta, and he asked the court to award him legal fees. Adams Corp. argued that the action to enforce the settlement agreement was not the same as an action under Title VII. Therefore, Huerta should not be awarded legal fees as a prevailing party under Title VII.

Should the court award Huerta legal fees? Explain your answer. [See *Robles v. United States*, 54 Emp. Prac. Dec. (CCH) P 40, 193 (D.D.C. 1990).]

15. Marjorie Reiley Maguire was a professor in the theology department at Marquette University, a Roman Catholic institution. Approximately half of the 27 members of the department were Jesuits, and only one other member was female at the time Maguire came up for tenure. The school denied her tenure because of her pro-choice view on the abortion issue—that is, because she favored personal choice rather than the Church's strict ban on abortions.

Was she a victim of gender discrimination? [See *Maguire v. Marquette University*, 814 F.2d 1213 (7th Cir. 1987).]

» Hypothetical Scenarios

16. Covert Communications provides interpreters and linguistic analysts to federal law enforcement agencies on a contract basis. Much of the work performed for its government clients by Covert involves national security matters, and the clients

require that the Covert employees must have government security clearances. Because of the security clearance requirement, Covert will not hire applicants who are not U.S. citizens. Farik Al Quran speaks Arabic and Pashto fluently but is refused a job with Covert because he is not a U.S. citizen. Does Covert's refusal to hire Al Quran violate Title VII? Explain.

17. Raji Gobendar is a practicing Sikh, an Asian religion that requires adult males to wear a turban on their head and to grow beards. He is hired by Security Systems as a private security guard. Security Systems requires its security guards to wear a uniform, including a hat, and company policy prohibits facial hair and beards. Gobendar is told that he must shave his beard and must wear the uniform hat rather than his turban when he is on duty. Security Systems refuses to allow any exceptions to its uniform and facial hair policies, and violations of the policies could result in termination. Must Security Systems grant an exception to its policies because of Gobendar's religious beliefs? Explain.

18. Your boss, the human resources manager for Springfield Enterprises, asks you to research and

prepare a report on whether the company should require employees to sign an agreement to arbitrate all employment disputes that might arise. Would such a requirement be acceptable under Title VII? How would the arbitration requirement benefit the employer? What would be the effect of the requirement on the employees?

19. Wang's Mandarin Palace is a Chinese restaurant in Rochester, New York. The restaurant only hires persons of Chinese ancestry as employees because the owner believes that customers would be uncomfortable with employees who are not of Chinese origin. Does the restaurant's hiring policy qualify as a BFOQ under Title VII? Explain.

20. Thrivent Financial for Lutherans is a fraternal benefit society that provides financial services and offers service and educational programs to members of the Lutheran Church. Harris is a CPA who applies for a job with Thrivent Financial. Thrivent Financial refuses to hire Harris because he is a member of the Southern Baptist Church, and Thrivent Financial only hires Lutherans. Which, if any, provisions of Title VII can Thrivent Financial use to justify its hiring policy? Explain.

CHAPTER 9

Discrimination Based on Age

Title VII of the Civil Rights Act, which was discussed in the preceding chapters, prohibits employment discrimination based on race, color, religion, gender, and national origin. In addition to Title VII, other federal legislation deals with employment discrimination because of other factors. This chapter covers the Age Discrimination in Employment Act, which prohibits employment discrimination based on age.

9-1 The Age Discrimination in Employment Act

Discrimination in terms or conditions of employment because of age is prohibited by the Age Discrimination in Employment Act of 1967 (ADEA). The act's prohibitions, however, are limited to age discrimination against employees aged 40 and older. It was intended to protect older workers, who were more likely to be subjected to age discrimination in employment. (Although the ADEA's protection is limited to older workers, state equal employment opportunity laws may provide greater protection against age discrimination. The New York Human Rights Law, for example, prohibits age discrimination in employment against persons 18 and older.)

9-1a Coverage

The ADEA applies to employers, labor unions, and employment agencies. Employers involved in an industry affecting commerce, with 20 or more employees, are covered by the act. U.S. firms that employ American workers in a foreign country are subject to the ADEA. Labor unions are covered if they operate a hiring hall or if they have 25 or more members and represent the employees of an employer covered by the act.

The definition of *employer* under the ADEA includes state and local governments; the U.S. Supreme Court upheld the inclusion of state and local governments under the ADEA in *EEOC v. Wyoming*.[1] However, in the case of *Kimel v. Florida Board of Regents*,[2] decided in 2000, the Supreme Court held that the Eleventh Amendment of the U.S. Constitution provides state governments with immunity from suits by private individuals under the ADEA.

---

[1] 460 U.S. 226 (1983).

[2] 528 U.S. 62 (2000).

Concept *Summary* 9.1

THE AGE DISCRIMINATION IN EMPLOYMENT ACT

• The ADEA prohibits discrimination in employment based on age against employees aged 40 or older

• ADEA coverage:
  ◦ Employers with 20 or more employees
  ◦ Labor unions operating a hiring hall or with 25 or more members
  ◦ Employment agencies
  ◦ Federal government employees

9-1b Provisions

The ADEA prohibits the refusal or failure to hire, the discharge, or any discrimination in compensation, terms, conditions, or privileges of employment because of an individual's age (40 and older). The act applies to employers, labor unions, and employment agencies. The main effect of the act is to prohibit the mandatory retirement of employees. The act does not affect voluntary retirement by employees. It does provide for some limited exceptions and recognizes that age may be a bona fide occupational qualification (BFOQ).

A plaintiff alleging a violation of the ADEA must establish a prima facie case that the employer has discriminated against the employee because of age. The plaintiff must demonstrate that age was "the determining factor" in the employer's action. In *Gross v. FBL Financial Services, Inc.*,[3] the Supreme Court held that the language of the ADEA does not allow for "mixed motive" cases. Rather than showing that age was "a determining factor," the plaintiff must show that age was the "but-for cause" of the employer's action. The Court in *Gross* specifically rejected the "mixed motive" approach used under Title VII (see Chapter 6).

The process for establishing a claim under the ADEA is as follows: the plaintiff must establish a prima facie case of age discrimination; the employer-defendant must then offer a legitimate justification for the challenged action; and if the defendant offers such a justification, the plaintiff can still show that the proffered justification is a pretext for age discrimination.

Examples of violations of the ADEA include:

• The mandatory retirement of workers over age 55 while allowing workers under 55 to transfer to another plant location or

• The denial of a promotion to a qualified worker because the employee is over 50.

While discrimination against older workers is prohibited by the ADEA, according to *General Dynamics Land Systems, Inc. v. Cline*,[4] an employer that eliminated health insurance for workers under 50 but continued health insurance for the employees over 50 was held not to have violated the ADEA. What must a plaintiff alleging that he was fired because of his

---

[3] 129 S.Ct. 2343 (2009).

[4] 540 U.S. 581 (2004).

age show to establish a prima facie case of age discrimination? Must the employee demonstrate that the employer replaced him with a person under 40 (i.e., someone not protected by the ADEA)? The U.S. Supreme Court addressed that question in *O'Connor v. Consolidated Coin Caterers Corp.*,[5] holding that whether the replacement was over or under 40 years of age was irrelevant. Because the ADEA prohibits discrimination on the basis of age, the fact that a replacement is substantially younger than the plaintiff is a far more reliable indicator of age discrimination than is the fact that the plaintiff was replaced by someone outside, as opposed to inside, the class protected by the ADEA (i.e., someone under 40 versus someone who happens to be over 40). Subsequently, a number of lower courts have dealt with similar cases, wherein the plaintiff's replacement was also a member of ADEA's protected class but also was significantly younger than the plaintiff. The following case is a relatively recent example.

» CASE 9.1

HARMON V. EARTHGRAINS BAKING COMPANIES, INC.
2009 WL 332705 (U.S. Ct. App. 6th Cir. 2009)

Facts: Beginning in 2002, Michael Harmon managed Earthgrains's facility in Bowling Green, Kentucky, in its West Tennessee Zone. In October 2005, Earthgrains hired 32-year-old Bradley Jordan as vice-president of the West Tennessee Zone. Jordan supervised Harmon. At the time of Jordan's hire, Harmon's employee file contained no negative entries.

During parts of November and December 2005, Harmon missed work for health-related reasons. When Harmon returned to work in December 2005, he and Jordan toured various stores in the Bowling Green area to evaluate Harmon's performance. During that review, Jordan told him: "I bet you think that your older people are your best people.... well, they're not. They're not your best people."

Jordan's assessment of Harmon's performance in December 2005 was negative. The evaluation cited numerous areas requiring improvement, including poor product displays, products that were outdated and out of stock, and lack of "pride."

While reviewing Earthgrains's profit and loss statements in February 2006, Jordan learned that an Earthgrains delivery truck in Bowling Green had been involved in two separate accidents, in December 2005 and January 2006. In the first accident, the truck, operated by employee Lewis Geron, struck a deer. In the second accident, the truck, operated

by employee Chuck (Casper) Glass, hit a doghouse that fell from another vehicle. The employee drivers reported both accidents to mechanics in Earthgrains's in-house repair garage in Nashville. Although the truck sustained damage after each accident, the mechanics advised the Bowling Green employees that the truck remained functional until they could make the required repairs. Accordingly, employees in Bowling Green continued to drive it.

On February 8, 2006, Jordan confronted Harmon about the accidents. Jordan asked Harmon why he did not complete an accident report after each collision, which would have notified Jordan of the incidents. Jordan allegedly informed him for the first time that Earthgrains's policy required that all accidents be reported to the "zone leadership team," including accidents that did not involve injuries or liability issues. Jordan suspended Harmon pending further investigation, documenting his concern that Harmon permitted the damaged truck to be driven by employees on both occasions without first ensuring that it was safe to drive. The next day, Danny Gaither, zone human resources manager, notified Lisa Millisor, Earthgrains's human resources director in Atlanta, that he intended to terminate Harmon.

Earthgrains did not fill the vacancy created by Harmon's termination; rather, it assigned Mark Carter, an existing

---

[5] 517 U.S. 308 (1996).

district manager in Glasgow, Kentucky, who was 10 years younger than Harmon (aged 58 at the time), to manage the area previously supervised by Harmon. Carter not only absorbed permanently all of Harmon's job responsibilities, but he also continued to serve as district manager in Glasgow, thereby increasing his workload. As part of the realignment, Earthgrains also assigned four truck routes managed previously by Carter in Leitchfield, Kentucky, to another existing district manager, Joe Kocher. According to the affidavit of Mitchel Cox, regional vice-president of Sara Lee's South Region, Earthgrains decided to make these adjustments before it terminated Harmon. It also announced its restructuring plans four months before Harmon filed the present lawsuit.

Issue: Given that Harmon's replacement was also over 40 years of age, and given that he absorbed plaintiff's duties into his current job, rather than actually taking Harmon's job as such, did the plaintiff have a viable ADEA case?

Decision: Without citing *O'Connor*, the court of appeals seems to have had no hesitancy to rule for the defendant on these facts. Because Harmon was not replaced by Carter, the appellate panel held that he failed to present a prima facie case of age discrimination. Nor did the judges buy the plaintiff's contention that the company's so-called "reorganization" was a pretext to disguise its discriminatory termination of the plaintiff in favor of his younger counterpart, Carter.

Observed the court, "Simply stated, Harmon failed to demonstrate that Earthgrains's articulated reason for not replacing him—its plan to restructure its zones and personnel—was intended to conceal its alleged prior discriminatory conduct and defeat his prima facie case. Mitchel Cox, Sara Lee's regional vice president, stated in his affidavit that Sara Lee's decision to restructure Earthgrains's zones and move the Bowling Green depot and two other depots from Earthgrains's West Tennessee Zone to its Kentucky/Indiana Zone was made *before* Earthgrains terminated Harmon and *before* it became aware that Harmon intended to file a lawsuit. According to Cox, Earthgrains made a PowerPoint presentation announcing its restructuring decision *four months before* Harmon filed suit. Cox also confirmed that Carter's absorption of Harmon's duties were permanent and that no new district manager positions were created as a result of the vacancy left by Harmon. Carter verified in his affidavit that he did absorb Harmon's duties, that his overall job responsibilities increased as a result, and that 'they remain so to this day.'"

Thus, the fact that the 58-year-old Harmon's workload was picked up by the 48-year-old Carter was of no relevance one way or the other. The relevant facts were that (1) Harmon was never actually replaced (either by a younger person or anybody else, for that matter), and (2) the reorganization under which Harmon's duties were reassigned to a current employee—some of whose existing duties likewise were reassigned—was a *fait accompli* before Harmon's termination.

THE **WORKING** LAW

14 Former General Mills Employees File Class Action ADEA Suit

Overview

1. This pattern or practice age discrimination action case presents the issue of whether employees can knowingly and voluntarily waive federal Age Discrimination in Employment Act (ADEA) claims and their rights to a jury trial and to proceed collectively with other similarly situated persons if their former employer secured a purported waiver of those claims and rights without complying with the minimum requirements of the Older Workers Benefit Protection Act (OWBPA).

2. In June 2012, General Mills announced a mass layoff of about 850 employees. The layoffs resulted from a companywide initiative called "Project Refuel."

3. Approximately half of those persons who lost their jobs as a result of General Mills' Project Refuel were based in the Twin Cities. Concurrently with the terminations, General Mills was hiring and promoting younger employees to replace the Plaintiffs and other employees similarly situated whom General Mills terminated as part of Project Refuel.

4. The Project Refuel terminations, as discussed more fully below, adversely affected employees age 40 or over at much higher rates than younger employees. In this action, fourteen persons who were employed with General Mills in the Twin Cities as of June 1, 2012, and who were involuntarily terminated from employment later that year as part of the Project Refuel program, assert claims for intentional and disparate impact age discrimination against General Mills under the Age Discrimination in Employment Act of 1967 ("ADEA"), 29 U.S.C. § 621, *et seq.*, both in behalf of themselves as well in behalf of other employees similarly situated.

5. General Mills informed employees terminated as part of Project Refuel that, to receive any severance pay, they were required to sign and return a "Release Agreement" form, drafted by General Mills, which was the same or essentially the same for all terminated employees.

6. In connection with its request that terminated employees execute its Release Agreement form, General Mills provided Project Refuel terminated employees who were age 40 or over with certain information about the job titles and ages of some employees terminated and retained as part of that program. General Mills did not, however, provide individual employees with disclosures that provided information about the full scope of the Project Refuel termination program, and instead provided each with only a portion of that information. When the partial data given to various terminated employees is aggregated, it shows that employees age 40 and over were terminated at exceptionally higher rates than younger employees, and that the risk of involuntary termination as part of Project Refuel increased dramatically with increased age.

7. The General Mills-produced data about its 2012 Project Refuel employee terminations, when combined, shows the exceptionally strong correlation between higher age and increased risk of termination. A statistical p-value calculation performed on the data to ascertain the likelihood that this correlation between age and rates of termination could have occurred if age (or a factor closely-related to age) were not used in making the termination selection decisions generates a very tiny p-value of only 0.0000000000 00000000000000000000000000000, whereas any p-value smaller than 0.05 is deemed to be statistically significant and any p-value smaller than 0.01 is deemed to be highly statistically significant by professional statisticians.

8. The "Release Agreement" form that General Mills required employees to sign as a condition of receipt of severance pay, and which was later signed by the above-named Plaintiffs, includes one paragraph that sets forth a broad release by the employee of "causes of action" and "claims" against General Mills. Another paragraph on the same page in the same agreement states that the employee agrees that "any dispute or claim arising out of or relating to the above release of claims, including, without limitation, any dispute about the validity or enforceability of the release or the assertion of any claim covered by the release," "will be resolved exclusively through a final and binding arbitration on an individual basis and not in any form of class, collective or representative proceeding." This latter paragraph thus purports to waive two important rights granted to employees under the ADEA: the right to a trial by jury on disputed issues of fact related to their claims for age discrimination and the right to proceed collectively in one action with others who are similarly situated.

9. Unlike other U.S. anti-discrimination statutes, the ADEA, through a 1990 amendment known as the Older Workers Benefit Protection Act ("OWBPA"), provides in plain

language that "[a]n individual may not waive *any right or claim* under this chapter unless the waiver is knowing and voluntary" (emphasis added), and the ADEA sets out mandatory minimum requirements that must be satisfied for a waiver of "any right or claim" under the ADEA to "knowing and voluntary." 29 U.S.C. § 626(f).

10. In this case, in addition to asserting claims for age discrimination under federal law as referenced above, the above-named Plaintiffs, in behalf of themselves and others similarly situated, seek declaratory relief from the Court. In particular, Plaintiffs seek a declaration that, in connection with its Project Refuel Termination Program, General Mills failed to satisfy the mandatory minimum statutory requirements for an employer to obtain from a discharged employee a "knowing and voluntary" waiver of "any right or claim" under the ADEA and that, as a result, the "Release Agreement" signed by all of the above-named Plaintiffs and by other similarly situated persons was and is not "knowing and voluntary" under the ADEA and thus was and is ineffective as a matter of law to waive "any right or claim" of any such individual under the ADEA, including the rights to a jury trial and to proceed collectively in pursuing relief under the ADEA.

11. If there is any dispute of fact related to whether General Mills can meet its affirmative burden to prove that the "Release Agreement" forms signed by the Plaintiffs and others similarly situated are "knowing and voluntary," and thus whether they could constitute valid waivers of any right or claim under the ADEA of the employees who signed them, Plaintiffs demand a jury trial on such issues. The right to a jury trial on issues of fact relating to the validity or lack thereof of what is alleged to be a binding agreement to arbitrate is specifically provided for in the U.S. Federal Arbitration Act, 9 U.S.C. § 1, *et seq.* ("FAA"). The FAA states that when a "party aggrieved by the alleged failure" of another party to arbitrate "under a written agreement for arbitration" brings a petition to compel arbitration, and when there is a dispute about the "making of the arbitration agreement," if the party opposing arbitration demands a jury trial, "upon such demand the court shall make an order referring the issue or issues to a jury in the manner provided by the Federal Rules of Civil Procedure or may specially call a jury for that purpose." 9 U.S.C. § 4. The statute further provides that arbitration will not be compelled "[i]f the jury find that no agreement in writing for arbitration was made."

12. While it may be the case for employees who signed it that the General Mills "Release Agreement" form constitutes a valid waiver of rights or claims of other types, the "Release Agreements" signed by the above-named Plaintiffs and others similarly situated were not "knowing and voluntary" under the ADEA because General Mills did not satisfy the minimum "knowing and voluntary" requirements set forth in 29 U.S.C. § 626(f) and in related regulations, and were thus ineffective as a matter of law to waive or impair any right or claim under the ADEA of any such person who signed it.

Source: Complaint, *McLeod et al. v. General Mills, Inc.*, No. 0:15-cv-00494, February 11, 2015, accessed at 2015 WL 574341.

Defenses

When the plaintiff has established a prima facie case of age discrimination, the defendant must articulate some legitimate justification for the challenged action. The ADEA provides some specific exemptions and defenses on which the defendant may rely. The following are not violations:

- actions pursuant to a bona fide seniority system, retirement, pension, or benefit system,
- for good cause, or
- for a "reasonable factor other than age."

The act also recognizes that age may be a BFOQ and permits the mandatory retirement of certain executive employees at age 65.

The ADEA was amended in 1990 to provide an additional defense for employers: Where the employer employs American workers in a foreign country and compliance with the ADEA would cause the employer to violate foreign law, the employer is excused from complying with the ADEA. In *Mahoney v. RFE/RL Inc.*,[6] the employer's compliance with German law requiring employees to enforce a labor contract setting retirement age at 65 was held to be a defense under the foreign law exception of the ADEA.

Bona Fide Seniority or Benefit Plan

The ADEA allows an employer to observe the terms of a bona fide seniority system or employee benefit plan, such as a retirement or pension plan, as long as the plan or system is not "subterfuge to evade the purpose of this Act." The ADEA provides, however, that no seniority system or benefit plan "shall require or permit the involuntary retirement of any individual."

In *Public Employees' Retirement System of Ohio v. Betts*,[7] the Supreme Court held that the ADEA exception protected any age-based decisions taken pursuant to a bona fide benefit plan as long as the plan did not require mandatory retirement. In response to that decision, Congress passed the Older Workers Benefit Protection Act, which became law in October 1990. The law amended the ADEA to require that any differential treatment of older employees under benefit plans must be "cost-justified." That is, the employer must demonstrate that the reduction in benefits is only to the extent required to achieve approximate cost equivalence in providing benefits to older and younger employees. General claims that the cost of insuring individuals increases with age are not sufficient; the employer must show that the specific level of reductions for older workers in a particular benefit program is no greater than necessary to compensate for the higher cost of providing such benefits for older workers.

Reasonable Factor Other Than Age

The ADEA allows employers to differentiate between employees when the differentiation is based on a reasonable factor other than age. For example, an employer may use a productivity-based pay system, even if older employees earn less than younger employees because they do not produce as much as younger employees. The basis for determining pay would be the employees' production, not their age. Similarly, when a work force reduction is carried out pursuant to an objective evaluation of all employees, it does not violate the act simply because a greater number of older workers than younger workers were laid

[6] 47 F.3d 447 (D.C. Cir. 1995).
[7] 492 U.S. 158 (1989).

off according to *Mastie v. Great Lakes Steel Co.*[8] In addition, the employer is permitted to discipline or discharge employees over 40 for good cause. In *Hazen Paper Co. v. Biggins,*[9] the Supreme Court held that discrimination directed against an employee because of his years of service is not the same as discrimination because of age; hence, the employer's conduct in allegedly firing an employee to prevent him from becoming eligible for vesting under the pension plan was based on a factor other than age.

The Supreme Court's decision in *Hazen Paper* was based on the fact that the ADEA has a specific exemption for employer actions based on a factor other than age. The Court did not decide the question of whether a disparate impact claim may be brought under the ADEA. Disparate impact claims, you recall, involve challenges to apparently neutral employment criteria that have a disproportionate impact on a protected group of employees—in the case of the ADEA, employees 40 and older. After the *Hazen Paper* decision, the federal courts of appeals have differed on the question of whether an age discrimination claim based on the disparate impact theory is possible. In the following decision, the Supreme Court considered whether a disparate impact claim of age discrimination is available under the ADEA.

CASE 9.2

SMITH V. CITY OF JACKSON, MISSISSIPPI
544 U.S. 228 (2005)

[The City of Jackson, Mississippi adopted a pay plan in May 1999 that was intended to bring the starting salaries of police officers up to the average of other police departments in the region. The city granted raises to all police officers, but the officers with less than five years of tenure received proportionately greater raises than officers with more than five years of tenure. Most of the officers who were older than 40 years of age had more than five years tenure. A group of older officers filed suit against the city, alleging that the differential raise policy violated the Age Discrimination in Employment Act. They alleged that the city had engaged in intentional age discrimination, and also that the pay raise policy had a disparate impact against the older officers. The trial court dismissed the suit, and the U.S. Court of Appeals affirmed the dismissal. The officers then appealed to the U.S. Supreme Court.]

Stevens, J.

... [This] suit raises the question whether the "disparate-impact" theory of recovery announced in *Griggs v. Duke*

Power Co. for cases brought under Title VII of the Civil Rights Act of 1964, is ... [available] under the ADEA....

As enacted in 1967, § 4(a)(2) of the ADEA ... provided that it shall be unlawful for an employer "to limit, segregate, or classify his employees in any way which would deprive or tend to deprive any individual of employment opportunities or otherwise adversely affect his status as an employee, because of such individual's age...." Except for substitution of the word "age" for the words "race, color, religion, sex, or national origin," the language of that provision in the ADEA is identical to that found in § 703 (a)(2) of the Civil Rights Act of 1964 (Title VII). Other provisions of the ADEA also parallel the earlier statute. Unlike Title VII, however, § 4(f)(1) of the ADEA contains language that significantly narrows its coverage by permitting any "otherwise prohibited" action "where the differentiation is based on reasonable factors other than age" [the RFOA provision].

In determining whether the ADEA authorizes disparate-impact claims, we begin with the premise that when Congress uses the same language in two statutes having

---

[8] 424 F. Supp. 1299 (E.D. Mich. 1976).

[9] 507 U.S. 604 (1993).

similar purposes, particularly when one is enacted shortly after the other, it is appropriate to presume that Congress intended that text to have the same meaning in both statutes.... In *Griggs*, a case decided four years after the enactment of the ADEA, we considered whether § 703 of Title VII prohibited an employer "from requiring a high school education or passing of a standardized general intelligence test as a condition of employment in or transfer to jobs when (a) neither standard is shown to be significantly related to successful job performance, (b) both requirements operate to disqualify Negroes at a substantially higher rate than white applicants, and (c) the jobs in question formerly had been filled only by white employees as part of a long-standing practice of giving preference to whites." Accepting the Court of Appeals' conclusion that the employer had adopted the diploma and test requirements without any intent to discriminate, we held that good faith "does not redeem employment procedures or testing mechanisms that operate as 'built-in headwinds' for minority groups and are unrelated to measuring job capability."

We explained that Congress had "directed the thrust of the Act to the *consequences* of employment practices, not simply the motivation." ... We thus squarely held that § 703(a)(2) of Title VII did not require a showing of discriminatory intent.... While our opinion in *Griggs* relied primarily on the purposes of the Act, buttressed by the fact that the EEOC had endorsed the same view, we have subsequently noted that our holding represented the better reading of the statutory text as well. Neither § 703(a)(2) nor the comparable language in the ADEA simply prohibits actions that "limit, segregate, or classify" persons; rather the language prohibits such actions that "deprive any individual of employment opportunities or *otherwise adversely affect* his status as an employee, because of such individual's" race or age.... Thus the text focuses on the *effects* of the action on the employee rather than the motivation for the action of the employer.

Griggs, which interpreted the identical text at issue here, thus strongly suggests that a disparate-impact theory should be cognizable under the ADEA. Indeed, for over two decades after our decision in *Griggs*, the Courts of Appeal uniformly interpreted the ADEA as authorizing recovery on a "disparate-impact" theory in appropriate cases. IT WAS ONLY AFTER our decision in *Hazen Paper Co. v. Biggins* that some of those courts concluded that the ADEA did not authorize a disparate-impact theory of liability. Our opinion in *Hazen Paper*, however, did not address or comment on the issue we decide today. In that case, we held that an

employee's allegation that he was discharged shortly before his pension would have vested did not state a cause of action under a *disparate-treatment* theory. The motivating factor was not, we held, the employee's age, but rather his years of service, a factor that the ADEA did not prohibit an employer from considering when terminating an employee. While we noted that disparate-treatment "captures the essence of what Congress sought to prohibit in the ADEA," we were careful to explain that we were not deciding "whether a disparate impact theory of liability is available under the ADEA.... In sum, there is nothing in our opinion in *Hazen Paper* that precludes an interpretation of the ADEA that parallels our holding in *Griggs*.

The Court of Appeals' categorical rejection of disparate-impact liability [in this case] ... rested primarily on the RFOA provision and the majority's analysis of legislative history. As we have already explained, we think the history of the enactment of the ADEA ... supports the *pre-Hazen Paper* consensus concerning disparate-impact liability. And *Hazen Paper* itself contains the response to the concern over the RFOA provision.

The RFOA provision provides that it shall not be unlawful for an employer "to take any action otherwise prohibited under subsectio[n] (a) ... where the differentiation is based on reasonable factors other than age discrimination...." In most disparate-treatment cases, if an employer in fact acted on a factor other than age, the action would not be prohibited under subsection (a) in the first place....

In disparate-impact cases, however, the allegedly "otherwise prohibited" activity is not based on age.... It is, accordingly, in cases involving disparate-impact claims that the RFOA provision plays its principal role by precluding liability if the adverse impact was attributable to a nonage factor that was "reasonable." Rather than support an argument that disparate impact is unavailable under the ADEA, the RFOA provision actually supports the contrary conclusion.

The text of the statute, as interpreted in *Griggs*, the RFOA provision, and the EEOC regulations all support petitioners' view. We therefore conclude that it was error for the Court of Appeals to hold that the disparate-impact theory of liability is categorically unavailable under the ADEA.

Two textual differences between the ADEA and Title VII make it clear that even though both statutes authorize recovery on a disparate-impact theory, the scope of disparate-impact liability under ADEA is narrower than under Title VII. The first is the RFOA provision, which we have already identified. The second is the amendment to Title VII contained in the Civil Rights Act of 1991. One of the purposes of that amendment was to modify the Court's holding in *Wards Cove Packing Co. v. Atonio*, a case in which we narrowly construed the employer's exposure to liability on a disparate-impact theory. While the relevant 1991 amendments expanded the coverage of Title VII, they did not amend the ADEA or speak to the subject of age discrimination. Hence, *Wards Cove*'s pre-1991 interpretation of Title VII's identical language remains applicable to the ADEA.

Congress' decision to limit the coverage of the ADEA by including the RFOA provision is consistent with the fact that age, unlike race or other classifications protected by Title VII, not uncommonly has relevance to an individual's capacity to engage in certain types of employment....

Turning to the case before us, we initially note that petitioners have done little more than point out that the pay plan at issue is relatively less generous to older workers than to younger workers. They have not identified any specific test, requirement, or practice within the pay plan that has an adverse impact on older workers. As we held in *Wards Cove*, it is not enough to simply allege that there is a disparate impact on workers, or point to a generalized policy that leads to such an impact. Rather, the employee is "'responsible for isolating and identifying the specific employment practices that are allegedly responsible for any observed statistical disparities.'" Petitioners have failed to do so.... In this case not only did petitioners thus err by failing to identify the relevant practice, but it is also clear from the record that the City's plan was based on reasonable factors other than age.

The plan divided each of five basic positions—police officer, master police officer, police sergeant, police lieutenant, and deputy police chief—into a series of steps and half-steps. The wage for each range was based on a survey of comparable communities in the Southeast. Employees were then assigned a step (or half-step) within their position that corresponded to the lowest step that would still give the individual a 2% raise. Most of the officers were in the three lowest ranks; in each of those ranks there were officers under age 40 and officers over 40. In none did their age affect their compensation. The few officers in the two highest ranks are all over 40. Their raises, though higher in dollar amount than the raises given to junior officers, represented a smaller

percentage of their salaries, which of course are higher than the salaries paid to their juniors. They are members of the class complaining of the "disparate impact" of the award.

Petitioners' evidence established two principal facts: First, almost two-thirds (66.2%) of the officers under 40 received raises of more than 10% while less than half (45.3%) of those over 40 did. Second, the average percentage increase for the entire class of officers with less than five years of tenure was somewhat higher than the percentage for those with more seniority. Because older officers tended to occupy more senior positions, on average they received smaller increases when measured as a percentage of their salary. The basic explanation for the differential was the City's perceived need to raise the salaries of junior officers to make them competitive with comparable positions in the market.

While there may have been other reasonable ways for the City to achieve its goals, the one selected was not unreasonable. Unlike the business necessity test, which asks whether there are other ways for the employer to achieve its goals that do not result in a disparate impact on a protected class, the reasonableness inquiry includes no such requirement.

Accordingly, while we do not agree with the Court of Appeals' holding that the disparate-impact theory of recovery is never available under the ADEA, we affirm its judgment.

It is so ordered.

Case Questions

1. How did the city's pay raise plan affect older police officers? Why did the city adopt such a pay raise plan?

2. According to Justice Stevens, what provisions of the ADEA allow plaintiffs to bring a disparate impact claim of age discrimination?

3. How does a claim of disparate impact age discrimination under the ADEA differ from a claim of disparate impact discrimination under Title VII of the Civil Rights Act of 1964?

4. Why did the Supreme Court dismiss the plaintiff's disparate impact age discrimination claim fail here? Explain.

In *Meacham v. Knolls Atomic Power Laboratory*,[10] a case decided following *Smith*, the Supreme Court held that an employer raising the "reasonable factor other than age" defense has to demonstrate that it relied on the "factor other than age," and has the burden of persuading the court that the factor was "reasonable."

---

[10] 128 S.Ct. 2395 (2008).

Executive Exemption

Section 631(c) of the ADEA allows the mandatory retirement of executive employees who are over the age of 65. To qualify under this exemption, the employee must have been in a bona fide executive or high policy-making position for at least two years and, upon retirement, must be entitled to nonforfeitable retirement benefits of at least $44,000 annually. An employee who is within the executive exemption can be required to retire upon reaching age 65; mandatory retirement of such executives prior to 65 is still prohibited.

State or Local Government Firefighters or Law Enforcement Officers

Section 623(j) of the ADEA allows state and local governments to set, by law, retirement ages for firefighters and law enforcement officers. Where the state or local retirement age law was in effect as of March 3, 1983, the retirement age set by that law may be enforced. Where the state or local legislation setting the retirement age was enacted after September 30, 1996, the retirement age must be at least 55. This original version of this exception was inserted into the ADEA in response to the Supreme Court decision in *Johnson v. Mayor and City Council of Baltimore*,[11] but that provision expired at the end of 1993. The current version of this exception was added to the ADEA in 1996.

Bona Fide Occupational Qualification (BFOQ)

The ADEA does recognize that age may be a BFOQ for some jobs. The act states that a BFOQ must be reasonably necessary to the normal operation of the employer's business. In *Hodgson v. Greyhound Lines, Inc.*,[12] the court held that Greyhound could refuse to hire applicants for bus driver positions if the candidates were over 35 years old because of passenger safety considerations. However, a test pilot could not be mandatorily retired at age 52 according to *Houghton v. McDonnell Douglas Corp.*[13] The Supreme Court considered the question of what is required to qualify as a BFOQ under the ADEA in *Western Airlines v. Criswell*,[14] where it affirmed the court of appeals' decision that Western had not established the mandatory retirement of flight engineers was a BFOQ. However, in 2014 the U.S. Court of Appeals reached a different conclusion in a case concerning mandatory retirement of corporate pilots.

» CASE 9.3

E.E.O.C. v. EXXON MOBILE CORPORATION
560 Fed. Appx. 282 (5th Cir. 2014)

Facts: In 1959, the FAA adopted a rule prohibiting pilots from flying in any operations in Part 121 of the FAA's regulations if the pilot was over the age of 60 ("Age 60 Rule"). Part 121 applied to "large commercial passenger aircraft, smaller propeller aircraft with 10 or more passenger seats, and common carriage operations of all-cargo aircraft with a payload capacity of 7,500 pounds." The FAA supported this Age 60 Rule because:

> *there is a progressive deterioration of certain important physiological and psychological functions with age, that significant medical defects attributable to this*

---

[11] 472 U.S. 353 (1985).

[12] 499 F.2d 859 (7th Cir. 1974).

[13] 553 F.2d 561 (8th Cir. 1977).

[14] 472 U.S. 400 (1985).

degenerative process occur at an increasing rate as age increases, and that sudden incapacity due to such medical defects becomes significantly more frequent in any group reaching age 60.

Such incapacity, due primarily to heart attacks and strokes, cannot be predicted accurately as to any specific individual on the basis of presently available scientific tests and criteria.... Other factors, even less susceptible to precise measurement as to their effect but which must be considered in connection with safety in flight, result simply from aging alone and are, with some variations, applicable to all individuals. These relate to loss of ability to perform highly skilled tasks rapidly, to resist fatigue, to maintain physical stamina, to perform effectively in a complex and stressful environment, to apply experience, judgment and reasoning rapidly in new, changing and emergency situations, and to learn new techniques, skills and procedures.

Borrowing a page from the FAA play book, Defendant Exxon adopted a similar retirement-at-60 rule for its corporate pilots. The EEOC challenged this rule in court.

Issue: Is Exxon's mandatory retirement rule a valid BFOQ?

Decision: The EEOC argued that genuine issues of material fact remained, precluding summary judgment based on the incongruity between the two occupations (commercial airline pilot and corporate pilot) at issue. The agency asserted that the record refuted Exxon's contentions that, because its pilots fly in the same airspace, with the same air traffic sectors, under identical weather conditions, and in the same congested domestic international airports, the occupations are congruent. Specifically, the EEOC stated that the piloting duties, planes, and operations of an Exxon pilot were materially different from that of a commercial pilot. In response, Exxon argued that

these distinctions were not material. More importantly, according to Exxon, the EEOC improperly narrowed the issue by ignoring the fact that pilots covered by Part 121 are not solely commercial pilots. Part 121 also included those flying cargo planes and smaller commuter planes. Exxon stated that its pilots must be compared to the wide range of piloting covered by Part 121, not solely large commercial aircrafts.

The appellate court agreed with Exxon that the occupations were substantially similar and congruent. They held that Exxon had put forth significant evidence demonstrating that its pilots flew similar planes, in similar conditions, and in the same airspace and airports as commercial pilots. Additionally, aspects of Exxon's piloting were more onerous than Part 121 piloting. Exxon's pilots had to obtain some of their own pre-flight information, fly with little advance warning, allow passengers to change itineraries mid-flight, and occasionally fly into and out of unfamiliar, remote airports. Although Exxon's pilots might face different regulations, certifications, and testing, the essence of their occupation—piloting Exxon's corporate aircraft—was congruent to the essence of commercial piloting and other piloting covered by Part 121.

The EEOC failed to address the fact that Part 121 covered a wide range of operations and to distinguish Exxon's operations. Instead, the EEOC's evidence compared only commercial piloting to Exxon piloting or corporate piloting generally. When compared to commercial pilots, the EEOC was correct that corporate pilots might fly fewer hours, operate on a varying schedule, and only fly in certain weather conditions. However, these distinctions were "distinctions without difference." Exxon's operations functioned in much the same manner as commercial, commuter, or cargo operations, all types of piloting covered by Part 121. Thus, the EEOC had not shown a genuine dispute of material fact that the occupations lack congruence.

Summary judgment for Exxon was affirmed.

Early Retirement and Work Force Reductions

The ADEA does not prohibit voluntary retirement as long as it is truly voluntary. The Older Workers Benefit Protection Act of 1990, which amended the ADEA, contained several provisions concerning work force reductions. Employers seeking to reduce their work force may offer employees early retirement incentives, such as subsidized benefits for early retirees or paying higher benefits until retirees are eligible for social security, as long as the practice is a permanent feature of a plan that is continually available to all who meet eligibility requirements and participation in the early retirement program is voluntary. Severance pay made available because of an event unrelated to age (such as a plant closing or work force reduction) may be reduced by the amount of health benefits or additional benefits received by individuals eligible for an immediate pension.

Waivers

Under the Older Workers Benefits Protection Act (1990), employers may require employees receiving special benefits upon early retirement to execute a waiver of claims under the ADEA if the waiver is knowing and voluntary and the employees receive additional compensation for the waiver, over and above that to which they are already entitled. The waivers must be in writing and must specifically refer to rights under the ADEA. The waivers do not operate to waive any rights of the employee that arise after the waiver is executed. The employees required to execute a waiver must be advised, in writing, to consult an attorney about the waiver and must be given at least 21 days to consider the matter before deciding whether to execute the waiver. The employees must also be allowed to revoke the waivers up to seven days after signing. If the waivers are part of a termination incentive program offered to a group or class of employees, the employer must give the employees 45 days to consider the waiver. If the early retirement and waiver are offered to a class of employees, the employer must provide employees with the following information:

• A list of the class eligible for early retirement

• The factors to determine eligibility for early retirement

• The time limits for deciding upon early retirement

• Any possible adverse action if the employee declines to accept early retirement and the date of such possible action

For any waiver involving a claim that is already before the EEOC or a court, employees must be given "reasonable time" to consider the waiver. No waiver affects an employee's right to contact the EEOC or the EEOC's right to pursue any claim under the ADEA. In any suit involving a waiver of ADEA rights, the burden of proving that the waiver complies with ADEA requirements is on the person asserting that the waiver is valid (usually the employer).

When an employee accepts an employer's offer of severance benefits in return for signing a waiver that does not comply with the waiver requirements set out in the ADEA, does the employee's retention of those benefits operate to "ratify" the waiver and make it effective? The U.S. Supreme Court addressed that question in the following case.

CASE 9.4

OUBRE V. ENTERGY OPERATIONS, INC.
522 U.S. 422 (1998)

Kennedy, Justice

Petitioner Dolores Oubre worked as a scheduler at a power plant in Killona, Louisiana, run by her employer, respondent Entergy Operations, Inc. In 1994, she received a poor performance rating. Oubre's supervisor met with her on January 17, 1995, and gave her the option of either improving her performance during the coming year or accepting a voluntary arrangement for her severance. She received a packet of information about the severance agreement and had 14 days to consider her options, during which she consulted with attorneys. On January 31, Oubre decided to accept. She signed a release, in which she "agree[d] to waive, settle, release, and discharge any and all claims, demands, damages, actions, or causes of action ... that I may have against Entergy...." In exchange, she received six installment payments over the next four months, totaling $6,258.

The Older Workers Benefit Protection Act (OWBPA) imposes specific requirements for releases covering ADEA claims. In procuring the release, Entergy did not comply with the OWBPA in at least three respects: (1) Entergy did not give Oubre enough time to consider her options, (2) Entergy did not give Oubre seven days after she signed the release to change her mind, and (3) the release made no specific reference to claims under the ADEA.

Oubre filed a charge of age discrimination with the Equal Employment Opportunity Commission, which dismissed her charge on the merits but issued a right-to-sue letter. She filed this suit against Entergy in the United States District Court for the Eastern District of Louisiana, alleging constructive discharge on the basis of her age in violation of the ADEA and state law. Oubre has not offered or tried to return the $6,258 to Entergy, nor is it clear she has the means to do so. Entergy moved for summary judgment, claiming Oubre had ratified the defective release by failing to return or offer to return the monies she had received. The District Court agreed and entered summary judgment for Entergy. The Court of Appeals affirmed....

The employer rests its case upon general principles of state contract jurisprudence. As the employer recites the rule, contracts tainted by mistake, duress, or even fraud are voidable at the option of the innocent party. The employer maintains, however, that before the innocent party can elect avoidance, she must first tender back any benefits received under the contract. If she fails to do so within a reasonable time after learning of her rights, the employer contends, she ratifies the contract and so makes it binding. The employer also invokes the doctrine of equitable estoppel. As a rule, equitable estoppel bars a party from shirking the burdens of a voidable transaction for as long as she retains the benefits received under it. Applying these principles, the employer claims the employee ratified the ineffective release (or faces estoppel) by retaining all the sums paid in consideration of it. The employer, then, relies not upon the execution of the release but upon a later, distinct ratification of its terms....

In 1990, Congress amended the ADEA by passing the OWBPA. The OWBPA provides: "An individual may not waive any right or claim under [the ADEA] unless the waiver is knowing and voluntary.... [A] waiver may not be considered knowing and voluntary unless at a minimum" it satisfies certain enumerated requirements....

The statutory command is clear: An employee "may not waive" an ADEA claim unless the waiver or release satisfies the OWBPA's requirements. The policy of the Older Workers Benefit Protection Act is likewise clear from its title: It is designed to protect the rights and benefits of older workers. The OWBPA implements Congress' policy via a strict, unqualified statutory stricture on waivers, and we are bound to take Congress at its word. Congress imposed specific duties on employers who seek releases of certain claims created by statute. Congress delineated these duties with precision and without qualification: An employee "may not waive" an ADEA claim unless the employer complies with the statute. Courts cannot with ease presume ratification of that which Congress forbids.

The OWBPA sets up its own regime for assessing the effect of ADEA waivers, separate and apart from contract law. The statute creates a series of prerequisites for knowing and voluntary waivers and imposes affirmative duties of disclosure and waiting periods. The OWBPA governs the effect under federal law of waivers or releases on ADEA claims and incorporates no exceptions or qualifications. The text of the OWBPA forecloses the employer's defense, notwithstanding how general contract principles would apply to non-ADEA claims.

The rule proposed by the employer would frustrate the statute's practical operation as well as its formal command. In many instances a discharged employee likely will have spent the monies received and will lack the means to tender their return. These realities might tempt employers to risk noncompliance with the OWBPA's waiver provisions, knowing it will be difficult to repay the monies and relying on ratification. We ought not to open the door to an evasion of the statute by this device.

Oubre's cause of action arises under the ADEA, and the release can have no effect on her ADEA claim unless it complies with the OWBPA. In this case, both sides concede the release the employee signed did not comply with the requirements of the OWBPA. Since Oubre's release did not comply with the OWBPA's stringent safeguards, it is unenforceable against her insofar as it purports to waive or release her ADEA claim. As a statutory matter, the release cannot bar her ADEA suit, irrespective of the validity of the contract as to other claims....

It suffices to hold that the release cannot bar the ADEA claim because it does not conform to the statute. Nor did the employee's mere retention of monies amount to a ratification equivalent to a valid release of her ADEA claims, since the retention did not comply with the OWBPA any more than the original release did. The statute governs the effect of the release on ADEA claims, and the employer cannot invoke the employee's failure to tender back as a way of excusing its own failure to comply.

We reverse the judgment of the Court of Appeals and remand for further proceedings consistent with this opinion.

It is so ordered.

Appendix to Opinion of the Court

Older Workers Benefit Protection Act, §201, 104 Stat. 983, 29 U.S.C. §626(f)

(f) Waiver

(1) An individual may not waive any right or claim under this chapter unless the waiver is knowing and voluntary. Except as provided in paragraph (2), a waiver may not be considered knowing and voluntary unless at a minimum—

(A) the waiver is part of an agreement between the individual and the employer that is written in a manner calculated to be understood by such individual, or by the average individual eligible to participate;

(B) the waiver specifically refers to rights or claims arising under this Act;

(C) the individual does not waive rights or claims that may arise after the date the waiver is executed;

(D) the individual waives rights or claims only in exchange for consideration in addition to anything of value to which the individual already is entitled;

(E) the individual is advised in writing to consult with an attorney prior to executing the agreement;

(F) (i) the individual is given a period of at least 21 days within which to consider the agreement; or

(ii) if a waiver is requested in connection with an exit incentive or other employment termination program offered to a group or class of employees, the individual is given a period of at least 45 days within which to consider the agreement;

a. the agreement provides that for a period of at least 7 days following the execution of such agreement, the individual may revoke the agreement, and the agreement shall not become effective or enforceable until the revocation period has expired;

b. if a waiver is requested in connection with an exit incentive or other employment termination program offered to a group or class of employees, the employer (at the commencement of the period specified in subparagraph (F)) informs the individual in writing in a manner calculated to be understood by the average individual eligible to participate, as to—

(i) any class, unit, or group of individuals covered by such program, any eligibility factors for such program, and any time limits applicable to such program; and

(ii) the job titles and ages of all individuals eligible or selected for the program, and the ages of all individuals in the same job classification or organizational unit who are not eligible or selected for the program.

(2) A waiver in settlement of a charge filed with the Equal Employment Opportunity Commission, or an action filed in court by the individual or the individual's representative, alleging age discrimination of a kind prohibited under section 4 or 15 may not be considered knowing and voluntary unless at a minimum—

(A) subparagraphs (A) through (E) of paragraph (1) have been met; and

(B) the individual is given a reasonable period of time within which to consider the settlement agreement.

(3) In any dispute that may arise over whether any of the requirements, conditions, and circumstances set forth in subparagraph (A), (B), (C), (D), (E), (F), (G), or (H) of paragraph (1), or subparagraph (A) or (B) of paragraph (2), have been met, the party asserting the validity of a waiver shall have the burden of proving in a court of competent jurisdiction that a waiver was knowing and voluntary pursuant to paragraph (1) or (2).

(4) No waiver agreement may affect the Commission's rights and responsibilities to enforce this Act. No waiver may be used to justify interfering with the protected right of an employee to file a charge or participate in an investigation or proceeding conducted by the Commission.

Case Questions

1. Why was the waiver signed by Oubre not valid under the ADEA?

2. Did Entergy argue that the waiver did comply with the ADEA? Why did Entergy argue that the waiver should be binding on Oubre?

3. Must Oubre return the money Entergy gave her for signing the waiver before she can sue Entergy under the ADEA? Explain your answer.

ethical DILEMMA

You are the manager of a small financial planning and consulting firm in Little Rock, Arkansas. The firm has been experiencing a slowdown in business lately, and because of the decline in business, you are forced to eliminate one of two financial planner positions. One of the financial planners is 55 and has been with the company for years. She is one of the highest paid employees. She is married and has two children in college. Because her husband has severe medical problems, he is unable to work and depends on her medical benefits for his medical treatment. The other financial planner is 27. He is single and lives with his parents. You must choose which of the two financial planners to lay off. How should you make the decision? What criteria should you use in making the decision? Note that Arkansas does not have any state law prohibiting age discrimination by private sector employers, but your firm is subject to the federal Age Discrimination in Employment Act.

Concept *Summary* 9.2

EXCEPTIONS UNDER THE ADEA

- Exceptions under the ADEA:
  - Age as a BFOQ
  - Actions under a bona fide seniority system or benefit plan
  - Actions based on a "reasonable factor other than age"
  - Executive exemption:
    - Employees in bona fide executive position for at least two years
    - Entitled to retirement benefits of at least $44,000
    - Can be required to retire at age 65
  - State or local government firefighters or law enforcement officers can be required to retire at age 55

9-1c   Procedures Under the ADEA

The ADEA is enforced and administered by the EEOC. The EEOC acquired the enforcement responsibility from the Department of Labor pursuant to a reorganization in 1978. The ADEA allows suits by private individuals as well as by the EEOC.

An individual alleging a violation of the ADEA must file a written complaint with the EEOC and with the state or local equal employment opportunity (EEO) agency if one exists. Unlike Title VII, however, the individual may file simultaneously with both the EEOC and the state or local agency. There is no need to go to the state or local agency prior to filing with the EEOC. The complaint must be filed with the EEOC within 180 days of the alleged violation if no state or local agency exists. If such an agency does exist, the complaint must be filed with the EEOC within 30 days of the termination of proceedings by the state or local agency, and it must be filed no later than 300 days from the alleged violation.

After filing with the EEOC and the state or local EEO agency, the individual must wait 60 days before filing suit in federal court. Although there is no requirement that the individual wait for a right-to-sue notice from the EEOC, the 60-day period is to allow time for a voluntary settlement of the complaint. If the EEOC dismisses the complaint or otherwise terminates proceedings on the complaint, it is required to notify the individual filing the complaint. The individual then has 90 days from receipt of the notice to file suit. Even though the individual must wait at least 60 days from filing with the agencies before bringing suit in court, the court suit must be filed no later than 90 days from receiving the right-to-sue notice from the EEOC. An individual can file an age discrimination suit in federal court even if the state or local EEO agency has ruled that the employee was not the victim of age discrimination according to the Supreme Court decision in *Astoria Federal Savings & Loan v. Solimino*.[15] If the EEOC files suit under the ADEA, the EEOC suit supersedes any ADEA suit filed by the individual or any state agency. As with Title VII, the ADEA allows for a jury trial.

After-Acquired Evidence

In *McKennon v. Nashville Banner Publishing Co.*,[16] the employer discovered that an employee allegedly fired because of her age had copied confidential documents prior to her discharge. The employer argued that the evidence of the plaintiff/employee's misconduct (known as **after-acquired evidence**) precluded the right of the plaintiff to sue under the ADEA. The Supreme Court held that the after-acquired evidence does not preclude the plaintiff's suit but rather goes to the issue of what remedies are available. If the employer can demonstrate that the employee's wrongdoing was severe enough to result in termination had the employer known of the misconduct at the time the alleged discrimination occurred, the court must then consider the effect of the wrongdoing on the remedies available to the plaintiff. In such a case, reinstatement might not be appropriate, and back pay could be awarded only from the date of the alleged discrimination by the employer to the date upon which the plaintiff's misconduct was discovered.

after-acquired evidence
evidence, discovered after an employer has taken an adverse employment action, that the employer uses to justify the action taken

---

[15] 501 U.S. 104 (1991).

[16] 513 U.S. 352 (1995).

Arbitration of ADEA Claims

In *Gilmer v. Interstate/Johnson Lane Corp.*,[17] the Supreme Court held that a securities broker was required to arbitrate, rather than litigate, his age discrimination claim because he had signed an agreement to arbitrate all disputes arising from his employment. The individual agreement to arbitrate, voluntarily agreed to by Gilmer, was enforceable under the Federal Arbitration Act and required Gilmer to submit all employment disputes, including those under EEO legislation, to arbitration. The agreement to arbitrate did not waive Gilmer's rights under the statutes but simply required that those rights be determined by the arbitrator rather than the courts. In general, agreements to arbitrate ADEA claims will be enforced when they were voluntarily and knowingly agreed to by the employees, but such arbitration agreements do not prevent the EEOC from bringing a suit on behalf of the individual employees subject to the arbitration agreements. The employees covered by a collective agreement that contained an arbitration clause that specifically included age discrimination claims were required to arbitrate their ADEA claims rather than litigate them, according to the Supreme Court decision in *14 Penn Plaza v. Pyett*.[18] (See the discussion of the arbitration of EEO claims in Chapter 8.)

Suits by Federal Employees

Despite the fact that the federal government is not included in the ADEA's definition of employer, Section 15 of the act provides that personnel actions in most federal government positions shall be made free from discrimination based on age. The ADEA protects federal workers "who are at least 40 years of age."

Complaints of age discrimination involving federal employees are now handled by the EEOC. A federal employee agency must file the complaint with the EEOC within 180 days of the alleged violation. The employee may file suit in federal court after 30 days from filing with the EEOC. The ADEA provides only for private suits in cases involving complaints by federal employees. No provision is made for suits by the EEOC.

Government Suits

In addition to private suits, the ADEA provides for suits by the responsible government agency (now the EEOC, formerly the secretary of labor) against nonfederal employers. The EEOC must attempt to settle the complaint voluntarily before filing suit. There is no specific time limitation for this required conciliation effort. Once conciliation has been attempted, the EEOC may file suit.

The 1991 amendments to the ADEA eliminated the previous time limits spelled out for suits by the EEOC. As a result, at present, the courts are split on the question of when the EEOC suit must be filed. Some courts have held that there is no specific statute of limitations on ADEA suits filed by the EEOC, as with *EEOC v. Tire Kingdom*;[19] other courts have held that the EEOC is also subject to the 90-day limitation, as with *McConnell v. Thomson Newspapers, Inc.*[20]

---

[17] 500 U.S. 20 (1991).

[18] 129 S.Ct. 1456 (2009).

[19] 80 F.3d 449 (11th Cir. 1996).

[20] 802 F. Supp. 1484 (E.D. Tex. 1992).

Concept *Summary* 9.3

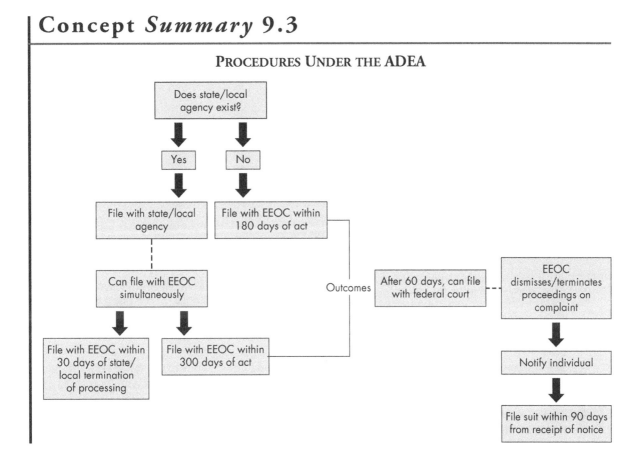

PROCEDURES UNDER THE ADEA

- Does state/local agency exist?
  - Yes → File with state/local agency
  - No → File with EEOC within 180 days of act
- File with state/local agency ⇢ Can file with EEOC simultaneously
  - File with EEOC within 30 days of state/local termination of processing
  - File with EEOC within 300 days of act
- Outcomes
  - After 60 days, can file with federal court
  - EEOC dismisses/terminates proceedings on complaint → Notify individual → File suit within 90 days from receipt of notice

9-1d Remedies Under the ADEA

The remedies available under the ADEA are similar to those available under the Equal Pay Act. Successful private plaintiffs can recover any back wages owing and legal fees. They may also recover an equal amount as liquidated damages if the employer acted "willfully." The Supreme Court, in the 1985 case of *Trans World Airlines, Inc. v. Thurston*,[21] held that an employer acts willfully when "the employer either knew or showed reckless disregard for the matter of whether its conduct was prohibited by the ADEA." Injunctive relief is also available, and legal fees and costs are recoverable by the successful private plaintiff. Back pay and liquidated damages recovered under the ADEA are subject to income taxation according to *Commissioner of IRS v. Schleier*.[22] Remedies in suits by the EEOC may include injunctions and back pay. Liquidated damages, however, are not available in such suits.

---

[21] 469 U.S. 111 (1985).

[22] 515 U.S. 323 (1995).

CHAPTER REVIEW

» Key Terms

after-acquired evidence   271

» Summary

- The Age Discrimination in Employment Act (ADEA) prohibits discrimination in employment based on age. The ADEA protects only employees aged 40 and older from such discrimination, but some state laws protect employees aged 18 and older. Mandatory retirement is prohibited, except where age is a BFOQ necessary for the safe and efficient performance of the job in question; the *Western Air Lines* case interprets the BFOQ provisions of the ADEA. Exceptions under the ADEA allow certain executives to be retired at age 65 and allow public sector employers to establish retirement ages for law enforcement officers and firefighters. Employers may differentiate among employees because of age in the provision of employment benefits, as long as the differentiation is cost justified and pursuant to a bona fide benefits plan. Voluntary early retirement is not prohibited, and employers may offer supplemental benefits as an inducement for early retirement. The ADEA imposes certain requirements on employers who require employees to sign a waiver as a condition of receiving early retirement incentives.

» Problems

» Questions

1. What, if any, incentives can an employer offer employees to retire voluntarily? Can an employer require employees to waive their rights under the ADEA as a condition of receiving such incentives? Explain your answers.

2. What must an employer show to establish a BFOQ under the ADEA? What other defenses are available to an employer under the ADEA?

3. Many ADEA suits arise from workforce reductions. What factors should an employer consider to determine which employees to be laid off?

4. When can an employer institute a mandatory retirement age for employees?

5. What must a plaintiff demonstrate to make a disparate impact claim under the ADEA? What defense can an employer raise in an ADEA disparate impact case?

» Case Problems

6. Springfield Power Co. lost a major electricity customer when General Motors closed several auto factories in Springfield's service area. Because of the loss of business, Springfield decided to reduce its workforce. Managers were instructed to rate their workers on the factors of "performance, flexibility, and critical skills." Using those discretionary ratings, combined with points for years of service, the company then decided which workers would be laid off. Of the 31 workers who were laid off, 30 of them were over the age of 40. Several of the employees who were laid off file suit against Springfield under the ADEA.

Can the workers establish a prima facie case of age discrimination? What defense can the employer raise here? [See *Meacham v. Knolls Atomic Power Lab.*, 128 S.Ct. 2395 (2008).]

7. Davis, an Indiana State Police officer, resigned to take another job when he was aged 42. Two months later he asked to be reinstated to his old position. The Indiana State Police refused because of its policy that ex-troopers seeking reinstatement must meet all the requirements for new applicants. The Indiana State Police required that applicants be over the age of 21 and under 40—no applicant 40 or over will be hired. Davis points out that the Indiana State Police allows officers to work until age 65, so that had he not resigned, he would have been able to continue working at age 43, or 55, or even 64. However, because of a two-month break in his service, he is now disqualified from serving because of his age. He files suit, alleging that refusal to rehire him violates the ADEA.

Is Indiana's policy of not rehiring officers over the age of 40 in violation of the ADEA? Explain. [See *Davis v. Indiana State Police*, 541 F.3d 760 (7th Cir. 2008).]

8. Wholesale Grocers, Inc. is shutting down several warehouses in upstate New York. The company's pension plan provides that employees are entitled to a non-forfeitable pension upon retirement after working for the company for five years. When closing the warehouses, the company decided to offer severance pay to workers under the age of 55, while workers aged 55 or older were offered early retirement but no severance pay.

Does the denial of severance pay violate the ADEA? Explain. [See *E.E.O.C. v. Great Atlantic and Pacific Tea Co.*, 618 F. Supp. 115 (D.C. Ohio 1985); see also *Widmar v. Sun Chemical Corp.*, 772 F.3d 457 (7th Cir. 2014) (former employee's assertion that a short-term employee who was terminated for cause and was under the age of 40 had received severance pay, alone, was insufficient to establish a claim of age discrimination in severance pay).]

9. Burns, aged 64, and Smithers, aged 38, were applicants for the position of postmaster at the Shelbyville Post Office. Burns had been the assistant postmaster for several years and was seeking promotion to postmaster as the final step in his career. After interviewing both candidates, the Postal Service Management Selection Board decided to promote Smithers because they felt he had "management potential to advance beyond Shelbyville."

Can Burns establish a prima facie case of age discrimination under the ADEA? What defenses are available to the employer? Explain. [See *Smithers v. Bailar*, 629 F.2d 892 (3d Cir. 1980).]

10. The city of Memphis is experiencing a budget shortfall. By abolishing the rank of captain, the chief of police demonstrates that the Memphis Police Department will save $1,400,000. Unlike promotion to other ranks, which is based on merit, officers are promoted to captain automatically when they achieve 30 years of service with the department. Captains perform the same duties as lower ranked officers but receive higher pay because of their rank as captain. Officers who are captains were given the choice of returning to their prior lower rank and having their pay reduced, or retiring. Several officers who had been captains file suit against the city, alleging age discrimination.

What must they show to establish a claim of disparate impact age discrimination? What defenses are available to the city? Explain. [See *Aldridge v. City of Memphis*, 2007 WL 4370707 (W.D. Tenn. Dec. 10, 2007).]

11. Ann Lindsey and Linda York, both over 40 years old, were employed as head waitresses shortly after the opening of the Cabaret Royale, an upscale gentlemen's club in Dallas. Its facilities include a gourmet restaurant, conference room with office services, a boutique, wide-screen viewing of sports events, and topless dancing. Lindsey was hired in January 1989. Two months later, she sought promotion to dancer. She spoke with one of the managers, and that same evening, she was summoned into the office of the general manager, Brian Paul, and told that she was "too old" to be a dancer. York was present at the time. In ensuing weeks, several younger waitresses were promoted to dancer. Finally, on May 8, 1989, Lindsey resigned and immediately became employed as a dancer at the Million Dollar Saloon. Cabaret Royale contends that Lindsey was not qualified to be one of its dancers because she failed to meet its attractiveness standard; specifically, she was not "beautiful, gorgeous, and sophisticated." York also began working as a waitress in January 1989. On May 8, 1989, she left work around 1:30 a.m. claiming to be ill. As she left, she saw a regular customer, Kevin Hale, waiting for a cab and gave him a ride home. When she returned to work two days later, she was informed that she was fired. She maintains that no reasons were assigned for her dismissal. Cabaret Royale responds that she was terminated because she violated the club's prohibition against leaving with customers. York counters that younger waitresses were not disciplined for identical behavior. The Cabaret employed only one other nonmanagement female over age 40, Joy Tarver, a dancer who also was terminated at the same time. York and Lindsey filed suit under the ADEA.

Can they establish a prima facie case of age discrimination? Are they likely to be successful in their claim? Explain your answers. [See *Lindsey v. Prive Corp.*, 987 F.2d 324 (5th Cir. 1993); see also *Berry v. Great American Dream, Inc.*, --- F. Supp. 3d ---, 2015 WL 751650 (N.D. Ga. 2015) (discussing whether "sex appeal" is a legitimate BFOQ for exotic dancers, and if so, whether terminating a pregnant dancer violated federal antidiscrimination laws).]

12. Giles Parkinson had been chief general counsel for Cordmaker, Inc., for a number of years. He was nearly 60 years old. After experiencing financial difficulties and a severe downturn in business, Cordmaker eliminated Parkinson's position and informed him that he was being terminated. Most of his duties were reassigned to other employees, including a 37-year-old attorney. Parkinson informed the board of directors of Cordmaker that he believed their decision to fire him was illegal and that he would file suit. Parkinson was then placed on a leave of absence and paid full salary for six months and 70 percent of his salary for three months thereafter. He requested that he be able to use his former office, and the company's phones and computers, to conduct a job search but was barred from using any company facilities. Parkinson filed suit under the ADEA and the New York Human Rights Law, alleging that Cordmaker had discriminated against him because of his age and had retaliated against him for complaining of age discrimination by denying him use of company facilities.

How should the court rule on his suit? Explain your answer. [See *Wanamaker v. Columbian Rope Co.*, 108 F.3d 462 (2d Cir. 1997).]

13. Gerald Woythal was chief engineer for Tex-Tenn Corp. He was one of the company's original employees and 62 years old. His boss was Operating Manager James Carico. Carico found it difficult to communicate with Woythal, whom he characterized as having a negative attitude, being apathetic about the company's future and sometimes unavailable when Carico needed to talk to him. The company was experiencing rapid growth, and Carico was concerned about the Engineering Department's ability to meet the increased demands placed upon it. He decided to hire an additional engineer to serve as Woythal's assistant. Woythal showed no interest in the hiring decision or in recruiting the new engineer. When Carico asked Woythal about his plans for the future and what he wanted to do for Tex-Tenn, Woythal simply replied that he would work until he was 70. When Carico pressed Woythal about his plans for the Engineering Department, Woythal was uninterested and evasive. Carico then

called Woythal into his office for a discussion and told him that "the company needed his participation, and if he chose not to participate, he would not be needed." Carico then asked Woythal if he intended to be an active participant in the company and told him to make his mind up by the end of the month. Woythal interpreted Carico's remarks to mean that he was fired, and he left the company at the end of the month. Tex-Tenn hired a younger engineer to replace Woythal. Woythal then filed suit under the ADEA, alleging age discrimination.

Can Woythal establish a legitimate claim of age discrimination? What defenses can Tex-Tenn raise? How should the court rule on the suit? Explain your answers. [See *Woythal v. Tex-Tenn Corp.*, 112 F.3d 243 (6th Cir. 1997).]

14. Ralph Sheehan was an assistant editor at Racing Form, Inc., a publisher that prints horse racing newsletters, programs, and tout sheets. Racing Form decided to computerize its operations, which would eliminate several jobs. The company human resources manager prepared a list of the jobs to be eliminated and the employees occupying those jobs, the jobs to be retained and the employees filling those jobs, and the birth dates of those employees. Sheehan, age 50, was informed that his job would be eliminated. He noticed from the listing that most of the employees losing their jobs were older, while those being retained were younger. Sheehan filed an age discrimination complaint and argued that including the employees' birth dates was evidence of age discrimination.

Is the court likely to agree with Sheehan? Are there other legitimate reasons for including the employees' birth dates on the listing? Explain. [See *Sheehan v. Daily Racing Form*, 104 F.3d 940 (7th Cir. 1997).]

15. In 1989, Ms. Castillo, born February 22, 1967, in the Dominican Republic, began working for Allegro, a company that oversees all of the marketing and promotions for several brands of all-inclusive resorts in Aruba, Costa Rica, the Dominican Republic, and Mexico, including Occidental. Through the years, Allegro promoted Ms. Castillo several times. She had two children and took maternity leave each time, but she continued to fulfill her duties at Allegro. On May 29, 2009, with management citing a reduction in force, Ms. Castillo was terminated. She was 42 years old. According to the complaint, Allegro's global vice president, Luis Namnum, and its vice president of North America, Jorn Kaee, began harassing her in September 2006 (when she was 39 years old) and terminated her on May 29, 2009, because she is female and in her late 30s to early 40s. On September 1, 2006, while Ms. Castillo was working from home on maternity leave, Mr. Namnum criticized her work and told her, "Brigitte, I want a young boy in your position." He told her he would think about what to do with her. Then, on October 20, 2006, Ms. Castillo returned to her Miami office from maternity leave to find a young man named Carlos in her office awaiting training. A couple of weeks later, Mr. Namnum sent Carlos to Ms. Castillo for additional training, telling her that Carlos would take over a portion of her work and stating, "I know it is hard to give your job away, but you must grow even against your will."

If the company fires Ms. Castillo, are there sufficient facts here to support an ADEA claim? If so, is this a case that can be disposed by the judge's summary judgment, or must a jury make credibility determinations before judgment can be rendered? [See *Castillo v. Allegro Resort Marketing*, --- Fed. Appx. ---, 2015 WL 1214057 (11th Cir. 2015).]

» Hypothetical Scenarios

16. DeLormer is sales manager for Fast Freddy's Auto Sales, a local car dealer selling Kia, Hyundai, and Subaru cars. Fred Fischer, the owner of Fast Freddy's, decides to reorganize his work force due to slumping auto sales. Fischer tells DeLormer, who is 60, that his job will be eliminated and the position's duties will be consolidated with those of the service manager position. Fischer also tells DeLormer that the new position will be filled by Gaines, the current service manager, who is 42. DeLormer feels that he is being terminated because of his age.

Can DeLormer establish a prima facie case of age discrimination based on these facts? Explain.

17. Rotert, age 59, worked as a mortgage processing officer. Her manager told her that her duties were being changed to those of a loan consultant and that she would be transferred to another, more distant branch office. The manager told Rotert that her salary would be the same. Rotert protested the new work assignment and resigned. She filed a claim for unemployment benefits, which was denied because she was not "constructively discharged" due to the new assignment. Rather, the state agency held, she had voluntarily quit. When Rotert filed an ADEA complaint, again stating that she was constructively discharged in favor of a younger employee who took her former job as mortgage processing officer, the company argued for dismissal because the issue of "constructive discharge" had already been decided against her by the state agency. How should the court rule? Why?

18. The City of Rochester will not accept applications for positions with the city's fire department and police department from persons over the age of 30. The city also has a mandatory retirement age for police officers and firefighters of age 55. The city maintains that the strenuous nature of the work of the firefighters and police officers requires that employees be in good physical shape, and that experience on the job can help offset the effects of aging on the employees up until about the age of 55. However, after age 55, the effects of aging on the cardiovascular system are more likely to cause potential problems for the employees. Has the city established that the age limit for applicants and the mandatory retirement age are BFOQs under the ADEA? Explain.

19. Kentucky's state pension system requires that police officers who are disabled after reaching the age of 55 to retire and receive normal retirement benefits, while officers who become disabled prior to age 55 receive disability benefits until they reach the normal retirement age of 60, and then begin receiving pension benefits. Officer Wiggums and his partner are injured after crashing their patrol car during a high speed chase. Wiggums, aged 56, is required to retire and take his pension, while his partner, aged 53, will receive disability benefits until he reaches the age of 60, and then will begin receiving his pension. Does Kentucky's pension system violate the ADEA? Explain.

20. Watkins Co. was looking to hire an administrative secretary, and after viewing the applications of various candidates, selected two applicants for personal interviews. When the manager interviewed Sue Phillips, aged 47, he asked her how comfortable she felt working with computers, using various software programs and the Internet. The manager also made a note on Phillips's application that she "seemed too old and inflexible." The same manager next interviewed Sonya Glass, aged 33, but simply asked her about her prior work experience. The manager decided to hire Glass for the position. Does Phillips have a claim under the ADEA? Explain.

CHAPTER **10**

Discrimination Based on Disability

The legislation prohibiting employment discrimination because of disability is more recent than the other equal employment opportunity legislation. The Rehabilitation Act of 1973 prohibits discrimination because of disability by the federal government, by government contractors, and by recipients of federal financial assistance. The Americans with Disabilities Act of 1990 (ADA) also prohibits discrimination in employment because of disability. The ADA is patterned after the Civil Rights Act of 1964. The coverage of the ADA is much broader than the Rehabilitation Act. The ADA covers all employers with 15 or more employees. This chapter discusses both the ADA and the Rehabilitation Act.

10-1   The Americans with Disabilities Act

The ADA is a comprehensive piece of civil rights legislation for individuals with disabilities. Title I of the act, which applies to employment, prohibits discrimination against individuals who are otherwise qualified for employment. The act became law on July 26, 1990, effective two years after that date for employers with 25 or more employees and three years from that date for employers with 15 or more employees. In 2009, the act was amended by the Americans with Disabilities Act Amendment Act (ADAAA), which broadened the definition of covered disabilities to include a wide range of life activities that previously had been declared outside the ADA by a series of Supreme Court decisions, which the ADAAA in effect overruled.

10-1a   Coverage

The ADA applies to both private and public sector employers with 15 or more employees but does not apply to most federal government employers, American Indian tribes, or bona fide private membership clubs. The Congressional Accountability Act of 1995[1] extended the coverage of the ADA and the Rehabilitation Act to the employees of the following offices:

*   House of Representatives
*   Senate

---

[1] Pub. L. 104-1, 109 Stat. 3.

- Capitol Guide Service
- Capitol Police
- Congressional Budget Office
- Office of the Architect of the Capitol
- Office of the Attending Physician
- Office of Technology Assessment

The Presidential and Executive Office Accountability Act[2] extended coverage of the ADA and the Rehabilitation Act to:

- the executive office of the president;
- the executive residence at the White House; and
- the official residence of the vice president.

U.S. employers operating abroad or controlling foreign corporations are covered with regard to the employment of U.S. citizens, unless compliance with the ADA would cause the employer to violate the law of the foreign country in which the workplace is located.

In *Board of Trustees of the University of Alabama v. Garrett*,[3] the U.S. Supreme Court, in a 5–4 decision, ruled that the Eleventh Amendment of the U.S. Constitution gave the states immunity from individual suits for damages under the ADA. The Court's reasoning in *Garrett* was consistent with its earlier decision in *Kimel v. Florida Board of Regents*.[4]

10-1b Provisions

The ADA prohibits covered employers from discriminating in any aspect of employment because of disability against an otherwise qualified individual with a disability. Illegal discrimination under the ADA includes:

> … limiting, segregating, or classifying employees or applicants in a way that adversely affects employment opportunities because of disability, using standards or criteria that have the effect of discriminating on the basis of disability or perpetuating discrimination against others, excluding or denying jobs or benefits to qualified individuals because of the disability of an individual with whom a qualified individual is known to associate, failing to make reasonable accommodation to the known limitations of an otherwise qualified individual unless such accommodation would impose an undue hardship, failing to hire an individual who would require reasonable accommodation, and failing to select or administer employment tests in the most effective manner to ensure that the results reflect the skills of applicants or employees with disabilities.

The ADA also prohibits retaliation against any individual because the individual has opposed any act or practice unlawful under the ADA or because the individual has filed a charge or participated in any manner in a proceeding under the ADA. The act also prohibits coercion or intimidation of, threats against, or interference with an individual's exercise of or enjoyment of any rights granted under the act.

---

[2] Pub. L. 104-331, 110 Stat. 4053.

[3] 531 U.S. 356 (2001).

[4] 528 U.S. 62 (2000).

10-2   Qualified Individual with a Disability

qualified individual with a disability
an individual with a disability who is able to perform, with reasonable accommodation, the requirements of the job in question, despite the disability

The ADA and the Rehabilitation Act impose obligations not to discriminate against an otherwise **qualified individual with a disability**. According to the Supreme Court decision in *Southeastern Community College v. Davis*,[5] a person is a qualified individual with a disability if the person "is able to meet all … requirements in spite of his disability." The individual claiming to be qualified has the burden of demonstrating his or her ability to meet all physical requirements legitimately necessary for the performance of duties. An employer is not required to hire a person with a disability who is not capable of performing the duties of the job. However, the regulations under the act require the employer to make "reasonable accommodation" to the disabilities of individuals.

The ADA defines "qualified individual with a disability" as "an individual with a disability who, with or without reasonable accommodation, can perform the essential functions of the employment position that such individual holds or desires." When determining the essential functions of a job, the court or the Equal Employment Opportunity Commission (EEOC), which administers and enforces the ADA, is to consider the employer's judgment as to what is essential. If a written job description is used for advertising the position or interviewing job applicants, that description is to be considered evidence of the essential functions of the job.

In *Cleveland v. Policy Management Systems*,[6] the Supreme Court held that an individual who applies for Social Security disability benefits may still be a "qualified individual with a disability" within the meaning of the ADA. In *Albertsons, Inc. v. Kirkingburg*,[7] the Supreme Court held that a truck driver who was not able to meet federal safety standards for commercial motor vehicle operators was not "a qualified individual with a disability" under the ADA. The employer was not required to participate in an experimental program that would have waived the safety standards.

10-3   Definition of Disability

The ADA defines "individual with a disability" very broadly. Disability means, with respect to an individual:

(a)   a physical or mental impairment that substantially limits one or more of the major life activities of such individual;

(b)   a record of such an impairment; or

(c)   being regarded as having such an impairment.

10-3a   The ADA Amendments Act of 2008

The ADA was amended, effective January 1, 2009,[8] to indicate that the definition of disability should be construed in favor of broad coverage of individuals under the ADA. Spe-

---

[5] 442 U.S. 397 (1979).
[6] 526 U.S. 795 (1999).
[7] 527 U.S. 555 (1999).
[8] Pub. L. 110-325, 122 Stat. 3553.

cifically, the amendments expanded the definition of "major life activities" to include, but not be limited to:

• Caring for oneself	• Walking	• Learning
• Performing manual tasks	• Standing	• Reading
• Seeing	• Lifting	• Concentrating
• Hearing	• Bending	• Thinking
• Eating	• Speaking	• Communicating
• Sleeping	• Breathing	• Working

The amended ADA also states that "major life activity" also includes the operation of a major bodily function, including but not limited to:

• Functions of the immune system	• Bowel	• Respiratory
• Normal cell growth	• Bladder	• Circulatory
• Digestion	• Neurology	• Endocrine
	• Brain	• Reproduction

Individuals can establish that they are "regarded as having such an impairment" if they show that they have been subjected to discriminatory treatment because of an actual or perceived physical or mental impairment, whether or not the impairment limits or is perceived to limit a major life activity.

In cases decided before the 2009 ADAAA, the Supreme Court restricted the scope of the ADA's definition of disability. In *Sutton v. United Air Lines, Inc.*,[9] the Court held that when determining whether an individual has a disability that substantially limits one or more major life activities, a court must also consider the existence of corrective, mitigating, or remedial measures that may reduce the effect of the disability. In *Toyota Motor Manufacturing, Kentucky, Inc. v. Williams*,[10] the Court stated that when assessing the impact of a disability on the major life activity of performing manual tasks, the central inquiry must be whether the individual is unable to perform the variety of tasks central to most people's daily lives, not whether the individual is unable to perform the tasks associated with her specific job.

The 2009 amendments specifically overrule those two decisions and set out rules of construction for the definition of disability. The ADA now provides that "[a]n impairment that substantially limits one major life activity need not limit other major life activities in order to be considered a disability" and that "[a]n impairment that is episodic or in remission is a disability if it would substantially limit a major life activity when active." The amendments also state that when determining whether an impairment substantially limits a major life activity, the court is not to consider the ameliorative effects of mitigating measures, assistive devices, or aids other than eyeglasses or contact lenses.

Employees who use illegal drugs are not protected by the ADA, nor are alcoholics who use alcohol at the workplace or who are under the influence of alcohol at the workplace. Individuals who are former drug users or recovering drug users, including persons participating in a supervised rehabilitation program and individuals "erroneously regarded" as using drugs but who do not use drugs, are under the ADA's protection.

---

[9] 527 U.S. 471 (1999).

[10] 534 U.S. 184 (2002).

The definition of disability under the ADA includes infectious or contagious diseases, unless the disease presents a direct threat to the health or safety of others and that threat cannot be eliminated by reasonable accommodation. Temporary or short-term nonchronic conditions, with little or no long-term or permanent impact, are usually not considered disabilities. The 2009 amendments to the ADA specifically state that the "being regarded as having an impairment" aspect of the definition of disability shall not apply to impairments that are transitory (defined as an impairment with an actual or expected duration of six months or less) and minor. The act's protection does not apply to an individual who is a transvestite, nor are homosexuality, bisexuality, or sexual behavior disorders such as exhibitionism or transsexualism considered disabilities. Compulsive gambling, kleptomania, pyromania, and psychoactive substance use disorders resulting from current illegal use of drugs are also not within the definition of disability.

≫ CASE 10.1

JACOBS V. N.C. ADMINISTRATIVE OFFICE OF THE COURTS
– F.3d –, 2015 WL 1062673 (4th Cir. 2015)

Facts: Christina Jacobs worked as a deputy clerk at a courthouse in New Hanover County, North Carolina. Although she allegedly suffered from social anxiety disorder, her employer assigned her to provide customer service at the courthouse front counter. Believing that her mental illness hindered her ability to perform this inherently social task, Jacobs requested an accommodation to be assigned to a role with less direct interpersonal interaction. Her employer waited three weeks without acting on her request and then terminated her.

Jacobs had suffered from mental illness since childhood. At 10, Jacobs was diagnosed with severe situational performance anxiety. At 12, she was hospitalized for several days after threatening to harm herself and others. During her hospitalization, she was diagnosed with mood disorder and selective mutism, and was prescribed antidepressants. At the age of 18, she received an additional diagnosis of social anxiety disorder for which she has been treated intermittently by several physicians.

Social anxiety disorder is characterized by a "marked and persistent fear of ... social or performance situations in which [a] person is exposed to unfamiliar people or to possible scrutiny by others." [Am. Psychiatric Ass'n, *Diagnostic and Statistical Manual of Mental Disorders* 456 (4th ed. 2000)]. A person suffering from social anxiety disorder either "avoid[s]" the feared social or performance situations, or

"endure[s them] with intense anxiety or distress." *Id.* A person can only be diagnosed with social anxiety disorder when the "avoidance, anxious anticipation, or distress in the feared social or performance situation(s) interferes significantly with the person's normal routine, occupational ... functioning, or social activities or relationships...." *Id.* The American Psychiatric Association (APA) notes that social anxiety disorder can create a "vicious cycle of anticipatory anxiety leading to fearful cognition and anxiety ..., which leads to actual or perceived poor performance ..., which leads to embarrassment and increased anticipatory anxiety...."

Issue: Under the expanded definition of "disability" created by the ADAAA, is Jacobs a covered person with a qualifying disability?

Holding: The Fourth Circuit panel held that the trial judge erred by concluding that Jacobs was not disabled within the meaning of the ADA. During the course of discovery both parties produced expert testimony by mental health specialists on this issue. After examining Jacobs, forensic psychologist Dr. Claudia Coleman concluded that "her mental disorders, Social Phobia and Anxiety Disorder, ... constitute a disability as defined by the [ADA]." Forensic psychiatrist Dr. George Corvin, the AOC's expert, did not examine Jacobs. Instead, Dr. Corvin based his report on a review of her medical records, social media use, employment records, and the report of a private investigator who observed Jacobs while she was at work at a new job. Dr. Corvin concluded that it was possible that Jacobs met the diagnostic criteria for social anxiety disorder but that "her medical records alone are insufficient to establish such a diagnosis." He also determined from the private investigator's report that Jacobs was currently succeeding in a new customer service job, and thereby inferred that she had not experienced "any significant level of anxiety or other psychiatric impairment" while working at the AOC.

The judges noted that the EEOC regulations operationalizing the ADAAA define a substantially limiting impairment as one that "substantially limits the ability of an individual to perform a major life activity as compared to most people in the general population."[11] Based on that definition, Jacobs had articulated a covered disability. That being said, the parties clearly faced a material issue of fact regarding the extent of the plaintiff's disability.

The court concluded that, therefore, the defendant was not entitled to summary judgment with regard to the plaintiff's claim of failure to accommodate her disability by transferring her to a less socially demanding job.

THE **WORKING** LAW

The Genetic Information Nondiscrimination Act

Congress passed the Genetic Information Nondiscrimination Act (GINA) in 2008; its employment-related provisions took effect in November 2009. The legislation prohibits discrimination based on genetic information by employers with 15 or more employees, employment agencies, labor organizations, and joint labor–management committees. GINA defines genetic information as an individual's genetic tests, the genetic tests of an individual's family members, and the "manifestation of a disease or disorder." Discrimination in hiring, firing, compensation, or any other terms of employment based on genetic information is prohibited. Labor unions cannot exclude, expel, or otherwise discriminate against individuals based on genetic information. Employers are prohibited from inquiring about genetic information of applicants or employees and from requesting, requiring, collecting, or purchasing genetic information regarding an individual or an individual's family members. Employers must maintain the confidentiality of any genetic information. Employers may ask employees to provide genetic information as part of a voluntary wellness program, and employers that are forensic laboratories for law enforcement purposes may require employees to provide genetic information only to be used to detect sample contamination for analysis of DNA identification markers. Voluntary wellness programs may not require employee participation, nor may the employee be penalized for not participating. The employee must give written authorization describing the genetic information to be obtained, the general purposes for which it will be used, and the restrictions on disclosure of the information. Employers may conduct genetic monitoring of the biological effects of toxic substances in the workplace if the employer gives written notice of the monitoring, the employee gives written authorization, the employee is given the individual monitoring results, and the employer receives only aggregate monitoring results not identifying individuals.

[11] 29 CFR 1630.2(j)(1)(ii).

›› CASE 10.2

CHALFANT V. TITAN DISTRIBUTION, INC.

475 F.3d 982 (8th Cir. 2007)

Facts: Titan Distribution had contracted with Quintak, Inc. to run its tire mounting and distribution operation. Quintak employees worked at Titan's building using Titan's equipment. In July 2002, Titan decided to end the contract with Quintak and run the operation itself. Titan announced it would hire some of Quintak's employees, but they would have to apply and have a qualifying physical. Titan managers Barucic and Luthin were in charge of the application process.

Robert Chalfant had worked for Quintak as a second shift supervisor. His duties included loading trucks with a forklift. Chalfant had been working for Quintak for five years. In the past, Chalfant had suffered a heart attack and had undergone carpal tunnel surgery and heart bypass surgery, and he had arthritis in his back, neck, ankle, and hands. He applied for the same position with Titan that he had had with Quintak, second shift supervisor. In his application, Chalfant stated that he was physically handicapped.

The physical examination was conducted by Dr. Anthony Sciorrota, who determined that Chalfant could work in his current capacity, including driving a forklift. Dr. Sciorrota also wrote on the exam record that Chalfant would need to have a functional capacity examination if he was required to do heavy lifting. Barucic received the exam record and wrote "OK for lift driving" on the top of the record and sent it to Luthin with the application. While his application was pending, Chalfant continued working as a second shift supervisor in the tire and wheel mounting division as an employee of Labor Ready, a temporary work service used by Titan during the application period.

During the first week of August 2002, Chalfant was told by a Titan manager that he was included in a list of Quintak employees to be retained by Titan, but on August 8, 2002, he was told that he had failed the physical and would not be hired. Within two months, Chalfant took a job with AMPCO Systems, a parking ramp management company. At AMPCO, Chalfant performed general service work. His job there involved walking up to five miles a day and lifting more than he did as a Quintak employee.

Chalfant sued Titan for disability discrimination under the Americans with Disabilities Act. After a trial, the jury found for Chalfant on the disability discrimination claims and awarded $60,000 in back pay and $100,000 in punitive damages. The district court then awarded $18,750 in front pay. Titan appealed.

Issue: Has Chalfant demonstrated sufficient evidence to establish that Titan regarded him as disabled under the ADA?

Decision: Titan regarded Chalfant as disabled because it mistakenly believed that his physical ailments substantially limited his ability to work in a broad range of jobs. Chalfant wrote in his application packet that he considered himself physically handicapped because of his ailments. Titan therefore knew about the ailments. The physician who conducted the physical exam did not find that Chalfant had failed the physical and that he could operate a forklift. The doctor did recommend that Chalfant undergo a functional capacity examination if he was required to do heavy lifting. Chalfant applied for the second shift supervisor position, a position that did not require unique or strenuous lifting. Titan employees testified that there was no lifting requirement, or even a job description, for the second shift supervisor position. Chalfant also testified that he had not been required to do any heavy lifting when he was the second shift supervisor for Quintak and Labor Ready.

The court of appeals held that there was sufficient evidence for a reasonable jury to conclude that Titan believed Chalfant's impairments substantially restricted his ability to work in a class of jobs or a broad range of jobs despite the fact that he was able to perform the essential functions of the second shift supervisor position. Titan accepted that Chalfant passed his physical, notified him that he would be hired, then changed the results of his physical to "failed" and notified him that he would not be hired. Titan's inconsistent behavior could lead a reasonable jury to infer that Titan knew it might be acting in violation of federal law. There was sufficient evidence to support the submission of the issue of punitive damages to the jury.

The court of appeals affirmed the trial court verdict and the award of punitive damages to Chalfont.

‹‹

10-4   Medical Exams and Tests

The ADA limits the ability of an employer to test for or inquire into the disabilities of job applicants and employees. Employers are prohibited from asking about the existence, nature, or severity of a disability. However, an employer may ask about the individual's ability to perform the functions and requirements of the job. Employers are likewise not permitted to require preemployment medical examinations of applicants. However, once an offer of a job has been extended to an applicant, employers can require a medical exam, provided that such an exam is required of all entering employees. Current employees are similarly protected from inquiries or exams, unless those requirements can be shown to be "job-related and consistent with business necessity." The act does not consider a drug test to be a medical examination, and it does not prohibit an employer from administering drug tests to its employees or from making employment decisions based on the results of such tests.

10-5   Reasonable Accommodation

The definition of a "qualified individual with a disability" includes the individual who is capable of performing the essential functions of a job with reasonable accommodation on the part of the employer. The ADA and the Rehabilitation Act impose on employers the obligation to make reasonable accommodations for such individuals or employees, unless the accommodation would impose "undue hardship" on the employer. Examples of accommodations listed in the ADA include:

- Making facilities accessible to disabled individuals
- Restructuring jobs
- Providing part-time or modified work schedules
- Acquiring or modifying equipment
- Adjusting or modifying examinations, training materials, or policies
- Providing qualified readers or interpreters

Failure to make such reasonable accommodation (which would not impose an undue hardship), or failure to hire an individual because of the need to make accommodation for that individual, is included in the definition of illegal discrimination under the act. Employers are not required to create a new position for the disabled applicant or employee, nor are they required to offer the individual the most expensive means of accommodation.

A number of courts have held that extending a medical leave beyond the 12-week leave available under the Family and Medical Leave Act (discussed in Chapter 7) can be a reasonable accommodation to an employee's disability under the ADA. The courts have considered whether the extended leave would create an undue hardship for the employer, and whether the leave would permit the employee eventually to perform the essential functions of her or his job, as in *Nunes v. Wal-Mart Stores*[12] and *Cehrs v. Northeast Ohio Alzheimer's Research*

---

[12] 164 F.3d 1243 (9th Cir. 1999).

Center.[13] According to *Smith v. Blue Cross/Blue Shield of Kansas, Inc.*,[14] an accommodation that would eliminate an essential function of the employee's job is not reasonable, and an employer is not required to wait indefinitely for an employee to return to work.

When an employee requests an accommodation that conflicts with the seniority provisions of a collective bargaining agreement, the employer ordinarily need only demonstrate the conflict to establish that the accommodation is unreasonable. However, according to the Supreme Court decision in *U.S. Airways, Inc. v. Barnett*,[15] the employee may present evidence of special circumstances that would make an exception to the seniority rules reasonable under the particular facts.

Reasonable accommodations may include the minimal realignment or assignment of job duties or the provision of certain assistance devices. For example, an employer could reassign certain filing or reception duties from the requirements of a typist position to accommodate an individual confined to a wheelchair. An employer could also be required to equip telephones with amplifiers to accommodate an employee's hearing disability. Although the extent of accommodation required must be determined case by case, drastic realignment of work assignments or the undertaking of severe financial costs by an employer would be considered "unreasonable" and would not be required. In *PGA Tour, Inc. v. Martin*[16] (which involved the public accommodation provisions of Title III of the ADA and not the ADA's employment-related provisions under Title I), the Court held that allowing a disabled golfer to ride in a golf cart rather than walk during a golf tournament, was a reasonable accommodation that did not fundamentally alter the nature of the event.

How should an employer respond to an employee's request for reasonable accommodation? This is discussed in the following case.

CASE 10.3

HUMPHREY V. MEMORIAL HOSPITALS ASSOCIATION

239 F.3d 1128 (9th Cir. 2001)

Background

[Carolyn Humphrey worked for Memorial Hospitals Association (MHA) as a medical transcriptionist from 1986 until her termination in 1995. Humphrey's transcription performance was generally evaluated as excellent. In 1989, she began to experience problems getting to work on time or at all. She began engaging in a series of obsessive rituals that prevented her from arriving at work on time. She felt compelled to wash, rinse, and brush her hair for up to three hours. She would also feel compelled to dress very slowly, to repeatedly check for papers she needed, and to pull out strands of her hair and examine them closely because she felt as though something was crawling on her scalp.

MHA gave Humphrey a disciplinary warning in June 1994 because of her tardiness and absenteeism, but her obsessions and peculiar rituals grew worse after the warning, and her attendance record did not improve. In December 1994, she received a "Level III" warning, because she was

---

[13] 155 F.3d 775 (6th Cir. 1998).

[14] 102 F.3d 1075 (10th Cir. 1996), *cert. denied*, 522 U.S. 811 (1997).

[15] 535 U.S. 391 (2002).

[16] 532 U.S. 661 (2001).

tardy four days and absent one day in a two-week period. Humphrey began to suspect that her debilitating symptoms and inability to get to work on time might be related to a medical condition.

In May 1995, after a diagnostic evaluation and psychological testing, Dr. John Jacisin diagnosed her with obsessive-compulsive disorder (OCD). He sent a letter explaining that diagnosis to her supervisor on May 18, 1995, telling her that Humphrey's OCD "is directly contributing to her problems with lateness." The letter also stated that Jacisin would like to see Humphrey continue to work, but it may be necessary for her to take some time off until her symptoms are under better control.

On June 7, 1995, Humphrey met with her supervisor to review Dr. Jacisin's letter. What happened at this meeting is disputed: MHA claimed that Humphrey rejected the leave of absence alluded to in the doctor's letter, but Humphrey claimed that she was never offered a leave of absence and never rejected one. Humphrey wanted to try to keep working, if possible, and the supervisor told her that she could have an "accommodation" that would allow her to do so. The supervisor suggested a flexible start time arrangement, and Humphrey accepted, but she continued to miss work. MHA never suggested modifying the accommodation.

On September 18, 1995, Humphrey sent her supervisor an email request that she be allowed to work from her home as a new accommodation. MHA did allow some medical transcriptionists to work out of their homes, but MHA denied Humphrey's request because of her disciplinary warnings for tardiness and absenteeism. The supervisor did not suggest an alternative accommodation or reassess its arrangements to accommodate Humphrey in light of the failure of the flexible work schedule arrangement.

Sometime later Humphrey asked about working at home but was told that she would have to be free of attendance problems for a year before she could be considered for an at-home transcriptionist position. Humphrey was absent two more times, and was fired on October 10, 1995, because of her history of tardiness and absenteeism. Humphrey testified that after learning of her termination, she went across the hall to her supervisor's office and asked if she might take a leave of absence instead, but her request was refused. MHA concedes that it would have granted the request if Humphrey had asked for a leave of absence prior to her termination, as MHA had a policy of permitting medical leaves of absence to employees with disabilities.

Humphrey filed suit against MHA under the ADA. The district court granted MHA's motion for summary judgment, and Humphrey appealed to the U.S. Court of Appeals for the Ninth Circuit.]

Reinhardt, Circuit Judge

Humphrey contends that MHA violated the ADA and the FEHA by failing to reasonably accommodate her disability and by terminating her because of that disability…. To prevail on a claim of unlawful discharge under the ADA, the plaintiff must establish that he is a qualified individual with a disability and that the employer terminated him because of his disability…. It is undisputed that Humphrey had the skills, training, and experience to transcribe medical records…. Humphrey is a "qualified individual" under the ADA so long as she is able to perform the essential functions of her job "with or without reasonable accommodation." Either of two potential reasonable accommodations might have made it possible for Humphrey to perform the essential functions of her job: granting her a leave of absence or allowing her to become a "home-based transcriptionist." …

Working at home is a reasonable accommodation when the essential functions of the position can be performed at home and a work-at-home arrangement would not cause undue hardship for the employer. [EEOC Enforcement Guidance: Reasonable Accommodation and Undue Hardship Under the Americans with Disabilities Act, FEP (BNA) 405:7601, at 7626 (March 1, 1999).] Humphrey does not dispute that regular and predictable performance of the job is an essential part of the transcriptionist position because many of the medical records must be transcribed within twenty-four hours, and frequent and unscheduled absences would prevent the department from meeting its deadlines. However, physical attendance at the MHA offices is not an essential job duty; in fact … MHA permits some of its medical transcriptionists to work at home.

MHA denied Humphrey's application for a work-at-home position because of her disciplinary record, which consisted of … warnings for tardiness and absenteeism prior to her diagnosis of OCD. It would be inconsistent with the purposes of the ADA to permit an employer to deny an otherwise reasonable accommodation because of past disciplinary action taken due to the disability sought to be accommodated. Thus, Humphrey's disciplinary record does not constitute an appropriate basis for denying her a work-at-home accommodation….

… We conclude, as a matter of law, that … MHA had an affirmative duty under the ADA to explore further methods of accommodation before terminating Humphrey.

Once an employer becomes aware of the need for accommodation, that employer has a mandatory obligation under the ADA to engage in an interactive process with the employee to identify and implement appropriate reasonable accommodations. "An appropriate reasonable accommodation must be effective, in enabling the employee to perform the duties of the position." The interactive process requires communication and good-faith exploration of possible accommodations between employers and individual employees, and neither side can delay or obstruct the process. Employers, who fail to engage in the interactive process in good faith, face liability for the remedies imposed by the statute if a reasonable accommodation would have been possible.

Moreover, we have held that the duty to accommodate "is a 'continuing' duty that is 'not exhausted by one effort.'" ... the employer's obligation to engage in the interactive process extends beyond the first attempt at accommodation and continues when the employee asks for a different accommodation or where the employer is aware that the initial accommodation is failing and further accommodation is needed. This rule fosters the framework of cooperative problem-solving contemplated by the ADA, by encouraging employers to seek to find accommodations that really work, and by avoiding the creation of a perverse incentive for employees to request the most drastic and burdensome accommodation possible out of fear that a lesser accommodation might be ineffective.

... Even if we assume that Humphrey turned down the leave of absence in June in favor of a flexible start-time arrangement, her attempt to perform her job functions by means of a less drastic accommodation does not forfeit her right to a more substantial one upon the failure of the initial effort.

By the time of her annual performance review in September, it was abundantly clear to MHA that the flexible start time accommodation was not succeeding; Humphrey had accumulated six unreported absences in each of the months of August and September, and her evaluation stated that her attendance record was "unacceptable." At this point, MHA had a duty to explore further arrangements to reasonably accommodate Humphrey's disability.

Humphrey also realized that the accommodation was not working, and requested a work-at-home position. When it received that request, MHA could have either granted it or initiated discussions with Humphrey regarding other alternatives. Instead, MHA denied her request without suggesting any alternative solutions, or

exploring with her the possibility of other accommodations. Rather than fulfill its obligation to engage in a cooperative dialogue with Humphrey, Pierson's e-mail suggested that the matter was closed: "During our 6/7/95 meeting, you requested to be accommodated for your disability by having a flexible start-time, stating that you would have no problems staying for a full shift once you arrived. You were given this flexible start time accommodation which continues to remain in effect." ... [A]n employer fails to engage in the interactive process as a matter of law where it rejects the employee's proposed accommodations by letter and offers no practical alternatives. Similarly, MHA's rejection of Humphrey's work-at-home request and its failure to explore with Humphrey the possibility of other accommodations, once it was aware that the initial arrangement was not effective, constitutes a violation of its duty regarding the mandatory interactive process.

Given MHA's failure to engage in the interactive process, liability is appropriate if a reasonable accommodation without undue hardship to the employer would otherwise have been possible. As we have already discussed, a leave of absence was a reasonable accommodation for Humphrey's disability. Ordinarily, whether an accommodation would pose an undue hardship on the employer is a factual question. Here, however, MHA has conceded that granting a leave of absence would not have posed an undue hardship. MHA had a policy of granting leaves to disabled employees, and admits that it would have given Humphrey a leave had she asked for one at any time before her termination. MHA's ultimate position, therefore, is simply that Humphrey is not entitled to a leave of absence because she failed to ask for one before she was fired. As we have explained, however, MHA was under a continuing duty to offer a reasonable accommodation. Accordingly, we hold as a matter of law ... that MHA violated the ADA's reasonable accommodation requirement.

Unlike a simple failure to accommodate claim, an unlawful discharge claim requires a showing that the employer terminated the employee because of his disability.... In this case, MHA's stated reason for Humphrey's termination was absenteeism and tardiness. For purposes of the ADA, with a few exceptions, conduct resulting from a disability is considered to be part of the disability, rather than a separate basis for termination. The link between the disability and termination is particularly strong where it is the employer's failure to reasonably accommodate a known disability that leads to discharge for performance inadequacies resulting from that disability.... Humphrey has presented sufficient evidence to create a triable issue of fact as to whether her attendance problems were caused by OCD. In sum, a jury could reasonably find the requisite causal link between a disability of OCD and Humphrey's absenteeism and conclude that MHA fired Humphrey because of her disability.

For the foregoing reasons, the district court's grant of summary judgment to MHA on Humphrey's ADA and FEHA claims is hereby REVERSED and the case is REMANDED for proceedings consistent with this opinion.

It is so ordered.

Case Questions

1. How did Humphrey's condition affect her ability to perform her job? Was Humphrey "an otherwise qualified individual with a disability" under the ADA? Explain your answers.

2. What accommodation did the employer initially offer to Humphrey? Was the accommodation effective? Explain.

3. What accommodation did Humphrey then request from her employer? How did the employer respond to her request? Why?

4. Was the employer's decision to terminate Humphrey a violation of the ADA? Explain your answer.

A court's consideration of what would be a reasonable accommodation to the individual's disability is to be done on a case-by-case basis. What may be a reasonable accommodation in one situation may not be reasonable under differing circumstances. In *Vande Zande v. State of Wisconsin Dept. of Administration*,[17] the court held that an employer's refusal to allow a disabled employee to work at home was not a violation of the ADA. The court there stated:

> Most jobs in organizations public or private involve teamwork under supervision rather than solitary unsupervised work, and teamwork under supervision generally cannot be performed at home without a substantial reduction in the quality of the employee's performance. This will no doubt change as communications technology advances, but is the situation today. Generally, therefore, an employer is not required to accommodate a disability by allowing the disabled worker to work, by himself, without supervision, at home.... An employer is not required to allow disabled workers to work at home, where their productivity inevitably would be greatly reduced.

10-5a Undue Hardship

undue hardship
an accommodation that requires significant difficulty or expense for the employer

An employer is not required to make accommodation for an individual if that accommodation would impose "undue hardship on the operation of the business of the covered entity." The ADA provides a complex definition of what constitutes an **undue hardship**, including a list of factors to be considered in determining the impact of the accommodation on the employer. An accommodation imposes an undue hardship if it requires significant difficulty or expense when considered in light of the following factors:

*   the nature and cost of the accommodation needed under this act;

*   the overall financial resources of the facility or facilities involved in the provision of the reasonable accommodation; the number of persons employed at such facility; the effect

---

[17] 44 F.3d 538 (7th Cir. 1995).

on expenses and resources; or the impact otherwise of such accommodation upon the operation of the facility;

- the overall financial resources of the covered entity; the overall size of the business of a covered entity with respect to the number of its employees; the number, type, and location of its facilities; and

- the type of operation or operations of the covered entity, including the composition, structure, and functions of the work force of such entity; the geographic separateness, administrative, or fiscal relationship of the facility or facilities in question to the covered entity.

It should be obvious that the definition of undue hardship is intended to be flexible. What would be a reasonable accommodation for Microsoft could be a significant expense or difficulty for a much smaller employer.

Concept *Summary* 10.1

DISCRIMINATION BASED ON DISABILITY

- The Americans with Disabilities Act (Title I) prohibits employment discrimination based on disability against otherwise qualified individuals with a disability
- ADA applies to public and private sector employers with 15 or more employees
- ADA requires employers to make reasonable accommodation to otherwise qualified individuals with a disability, unless accommodation would impose undue hardship on employer

10-6 Defenses Under the ADA

In addition to the defense of undue hardship, the ADA sets out four other possible defenses for employers.

10-6a Direct Threat to Safety or Health of Others

Employers may refuse to hire or accommodate an individual if that individual's condition poses a "direct threat" to the health or safety of others in the workplace. Direct threat is defined as a "significant risk to the health or safety of others that cannot be eliminated by reasonable accommodation." The definition of disability under the act includes infectious or contagious diseases. According to *School Board of Nassau County, Florida v. Arline*,[18] in determining if such a disease presents a direct threat to others, the employer's considerations must be based on objective and accepted public health guidelines, not on stereotypes or public attitudes or fears. An employer would probably not be required to hire an individual with an active case of hepatitis or tuberculosis,

---

[18] 480 U.S. 273 (1987).

but could not discriminate against an individual who has been treated for cancer, has been exposed to the HIV virus (associated with AIDS), or has had a history of mental illness. According to *Chevron, U.S.A. v. Echazabal*,[19] an employer may refuse to hire an individual when performance of the job would endanger the individual's own health due to an existing disability.

10-6b Job-Related Criteria

Employers may hire, select, or promote individuals based on tests, standards, or criteria that are job related or are consistent with business necessity. Employers could refuse to hire or promote individuals with a disability who are unable to meet such standards, tests, or criteria or when performance of the job cannot be accomplished by reasonable accommodation. For example, an employer would be justified in refusing to hire a blind person for a bus driver position.

10-6c Food Handler Defense

An employer in the food service industry may refuse to assign or transfer to a job involving food handling any individual who has an infectious or communicable disease that can be transmitted to others through the handling of food, when the risk of infection cannot be eliminated by reasonable accommodation. The ADA requires the secretary of Health and Human Services to develop a list of diseases that can be transmitted through food handling. Only the diseases on that list (which is to be updated annually) may be used as a basis for refusal under this defense. The secretary of Health and Human Services has stated that HIV infection (associated with AIDS) cannot be transmitted through food handling.[20]

10-6d Religious Entities

Title I of the ADA does not prohibit a religious corporation, association, educational institution, or society from giving preference in employment to individuals of a particular religion to perform work connected with the carrying on by such corporation, association, educational institution, or society of its activities. As discussed in Chapter 8, a gymnasium operated by the Church of Jesus Christ of Latter-day Saints could discharge an employee who failed to meet the requirements for continued membership in the Mormon church. More specifically, the Court held that the religious-organization exemption in Title VII extends to the auxiliary operations of a church, and that exemption does not offend the "establishment" clause of the First Amendment.

In the following case, the Supreme Court was asked to decide whether the so-called ministerial exception applies to a retaliation claim brought under the ADA.

---

[19] 536 U.S. 73 (2002).

[20] See "How to Comply with the Americans with Disabilities: A Guide for Restaurants and Other Food Service Employers," available at http://www.eeoc.gov/facts/restaurant_guide.html.

» CASE 10.4

HOASANNA-TABOR EVANGELICAL LUTHERAN CHURCH AND SCHOOL V. E.E.O.C.

132 S.Ct. 694 (2012)

Facts: The Equal Employment Opportunity Commission brought this action against the member congregation of the Lutheran Church, alleging that the "called" teacher at its school had been fired in retaliation for threatening to file an Americans with Disabilities Act (ADA) lawsuit. The teacher intervened, claiming unlawful retaliation under both the ADA and state law.

Perich, the called teacher, developed narcolepsy and began the 2004–2005 school year on disability leave. In January 2005, she notified the school principal that she would be able to report to work in February. The principal responded that the school had already contracted with a lay teacher to fill Perich's position for the remainder of the school year. The principal also expressed concern that Perich was not yet ready to return to the classroom. The congregation subsequently offered to pay a portion of Perich's health insurance premiums in exchange for her resignation as a called teacher. Perich refused to resign. In February, Perich presented herself at the school and refused to leave until she received written documentation that she had reported to work. The principal later called Perich and told her that she would likely be fired. Perich responded that she had spoken with an attorney and intended to assert her legal rights. In a subsequent letter, the chairman of the school board advised Perich that the congregation would

consider whether to rescind her call at its next meeting. As grounds for termination, the letter cited Perich's "insubordination and disruptive behavior," as well as the damage she had done to her "working relationship" with the school by "threatening to take legal action." The congregation voted to rescind Perich's call, and Hosanna-Tabor sent her a letter of termination.

Issue: Is the called teacher a minister, and if so, does the ministerial exception prevent the EEOC and the teacher from pursuing a retaliation claim against the defendant under the ADA?

Holding: Chief Justice Roberts wrote his opinion on behalf of a unanimous Court. In it, he held that (1) the First Amendment bars suits by ministers against their churches, claiming termination in violation of employment discrimination laws; (2) the called teacher in effect was a minister for purposes of this rule, notwithstanding that she performed many duties equivalent to what lay teachers in the church's school also performed; and (3) this ministerial exception extends not only to the ADA but to all employment discrimination statutes.

Thus, the defendant in this case enjoyed a viable affirmative defense to the EEOC's suit.

Concept *Summary* 10.2

DEFENSES UNDER THE ADA

- Defenses under the ADA:
  - Individual's condition poses a direct threat to the health or safety of the individual or others in the workplace
  - Employers can hire based on job-related criteria
  - Employers in the food service industry can refuse to hire individuals with diseases that can be communicated through handling of food
  - Religious entities can give preference to members of a particular religion.

10-7   Enforcement of the ADA

The ADA is enforced by the EEOC. The act specifically provides that the procedures and remedies under Title VII of the Civil Rights Act of 1964 shall be those used or available under the ADA. This means that an individual must first file a complaint with a state or local agency, where appropriate, and then with the EEOC. The EEOC, or the individual if the EEOC declines, may file suit against an employer. Remedies available include injunctions, a hiring or reinstatement order (with or without back pay), and attorney fees. The Civil Rights Act of 1991 amended 42 U.S.C. Section 1981A to allow suits for compensatory and punitive damages against parties accused of intentional discrimination in violation of the ADA.

Such damages are not available where the alleged discrimination involves provision of a reasonable accommodation of an individual's disability and the employer demonstrates that it made a good-faith effort to accommodate the individual's disability. Punitive damages are not available against public sector employers. The ADA also directs the EEOC to develop and issue regulations to enforce the act.

10-8   The Rehabilitation Act

The Rehabilitation Act of 1973 protects the employment rights of individuals with a disability. The act's provisions prohibit discrimination against otherwise qualified individuals with a disability. The definition of "individual with a disability" under the Rehabilitation Act is similar to that under the ADA:

> any person who (a) has a physical or mental impairment, which substantially limits one or more of such person's major life activities, (b) has a record of such an impairment, or (c) is regarded as having such an impairment.

The Supreme Court decision in *School Board of Nassau County, Fla. v. Arline*[21] held that the definition of disability under the Rehabilitation Act included contagious diseases; the employee with an infectious disease is "otherwise qualified" within the meaning of the act if the threat posed to others by the disease can be eliminated or avoided through reasonable accommodation by the employer.

The Civil Rights Restoration Act of 1988, passed by Congress over President Reagan's veto, amended the definition of "individual with a disability" under the Rehabilitation Act to exclude a person with:

> a currently contagious disease or infection and who, by reason of such disease or infection, would constitute a direct threat to the health or safety of other individuals or who, by reason of the currently contagious disease or infection, is unable to perform the duties of the job.

10-8a   Provisions

The Rehabilitation Act imposes obligations not to discriminate against otherwise qualified individuals with a disability. According to *Southeastern Community College v. Davis*, a person is "an otherwise qualified individual with a disability" under the Rehabilitation Act

---

[21] 480 U.S. 273 (1987).

(as with the ADA) if the person is able to meet the requirements of the position in spite of the disability or with reasonable accommodation of the disability. The individual claiming to be qualified has the burden of demonstrating her or his ability to meet all physical requirements legitimately necessary for the performance of the duties of the position. An employer is not required to hire a person with a disability who is not capable of performing the duties of the position. However, the employer is required to make reasonable accommodation to the disability of the individual if such accommodation will allow the individual to perform the job and does not impose undue hardship on the employer.

Three main provisions of the Rehabilitation Act deal with discrimination against otherwise qualified individuals with a disability:

*   Section 501 prohibits such discrimination by federal government employers
*   Section 503 prohibits such discrimination by employers with federal contracts
*   Section 504 prohibits the denial of participation in, or the benefits of, any federally funded activity to an otherwise qualified individual with a disability

Section 501: Federal Government Employers

Section 501 of the Rehabilitation Act prohibits discrimination on the basis of disability by federal executive agencies, departments, and instrumentalities. It also requires them to develop affirmative action plans for the hiring, placement, and advancement of individuals with disabilities. The plans are to be updated annually and reviewed and approved by the EEOC.

Enforcement of Section 501

Section 505(a) of the act provides that Section 501 is enforced through the provisions under Title VII of the Civil Rights Act of 1964, as amended. While federal executive employees with complaints of alleged violations may bring a private suit, they must first seek review of the alleged violation with their agency's equal employment opportunity (EEO) counselor, whose decision is subject to a formal review through the agency's EEO complaint procedures. The employee can then either seek judicial review of the final decision of the agency or appeal the action to the EEOC. If the employee elects to seek judicial review, a civil action may be filed in federal court within 90 days of receipt of notice of the agency's final decision or within 180 days of filing with the agency if there has been no decision. Employees choosing to refer the complaint to the EEOC may file a civil action within 90 days of receipt of the EEOC's notice of final action or within 180 days of filing with the EEOC if there has been no EEOC decision within that time.

Remedies available include injunctions; orders directing hiring or reinstatement, with or without back pay and interest; attorney fees; and expert witness fees. In addition to the remedies under the Civil Rights Act, plaintiffs alleging intentional discrimination in violation of Section 501 can bring an action seeking compensatory damages under 42 U.S.C. Section 1981A. Such damages are not available when the alleged discriminatory practice involves reasonable accommodation and the respondent showed good-faith efforts. Punitive damages under 42 U.S.C. Section 1981A are not available against public sector employers.

Section 503: Federal Contractors

Section 503 of the Rehabilitation Act prohibits discrimination on the basis of disability by federal contractors with annual contracts in excess of $10,000. Federal contractors with contracts of $50,000 or more are also required to develop affirmative action plans as to the hiring of otherwise qualified individuals with a disability. Enforcement of Section 503 is through the administrative procedures of the Office of Federal Contract Compliance Programs (OFCCP) under the Department of Labor. Aggrieved individuals must file a complaint with the OFCCP. There is no individual right to file suit under Section 503. Employers found in violation of Section 503 may be subject to injunctions, withholding of progress payments under the contract, termination of the contract, or debarment from future contracts. Remedies available under the administrative procedures for individuals who are victims of discrimination in violation of Section 503 include hiring or reinstatement, back pay, and benefits.

Section 504: Federally Assisted Programs

Section 504 of the Rehabilitation Act prohibits discrimination on the basis of disability against otherwise qualified individuals with a disability by persons or entities operating or administering any federally funded programs. To be covered by Section 504, the entities must be the direct recipient of federal financial assistance. According to *U.S. Department of Transportation v. Paralyzed Veterans of America*,[22] indirect beneficiaries are not recipients within the meaning of the section. The statutory language provides that "No otherwise qualified individual with a disability ... shall ... (solely by reason of the disability) be excluded from participation in, be denied the benefits of, or be subjected to discrimination under ..." any program receiving federal financial assistance. If any part of the entity receives any federal funding, the nondiscrimination requirement applies to the entire entity. There is no minimum funding amount required for coverage under Section 504. While the language of Section 504 does not specifically refer to employment, its prohibition against discrimination extends to employment discrimination, even though the primary purpose of the federal financial assistance is not providing employment, according to the Supreme Court decision in *Consolidated Rail Corp. v. Darrone*.[23]

Employers are required to make reasonable accommodation to the otherwise qualified employee's or applicant's condition. Any employment requirements that adversely affect disabled persons must be directly and substantially related to business necessity and safe job performance. In *Southeastern Community College v. Davis*, the Supreme Court upheld the college's refusal to admit a woman with a severe hearing disability to the registered nurses training program. The woman's disability was not correctable with a hearing aid and would create problems in carrying out her duties during the clinical portions of her training. The college was not required to redesign the program to accommodate her disability because the components of the nursing program were required by state law.

Enforcement of Section 504

The regulations under Section 504 make the agencies administering the funding the primary enforcement authority for complaints against the recipients of such funding. Most agencies have developed their own administrative procedures for investigating and adjudicating claims of discrimination. The federal Department of Education coordinates and oversees enforcement of Section 504 by the other federal agencies. Unlike Section 503,

---

[22] 477 U.S. 597 (1986).

[23] 465 U.S. 624 (1984).

there is an individual right to sue under Section 504. Persons claiming a violation of Section 504 may seek equitable relief and recover back pay, monetary damages, and legal fees; they are not required to pursue the agency's administrative procedures before filing suit. Punitive damages are not recoverable in private suits brought under Section 504, according to *Barnes v. Gorman*.[24]

Concept *Summary* 10.3

THE REHABILITATION ACT

- Section 501 prohibits disability discrimination by federal government employers
- Section 503 prohibits disability discrimination by federal contractors with annual contracts over $10,000
- Section 504 prohibits disability discrimination by persons or entities operating any program receiving federal financial assistance

10-8b   AIDS and the Disability Discrimination Legislation

Recall that the definition of disability under both the ADA and the Rehabilitation Act includes contagious diseases, such as AIDS. Although AIDS is contagious, medical authorities agree that it is not transmitted through the casual contact likely to occur in the workplace. The courts have consistently held that persons who are HIV-positive suffering from AIDS or AIDS-related conditions are individuals with a disability under the Rehabilitation Act and the ADA. Therefore, employers are required to make reasonable accommodation for employees with AIDS or related conditions, as long as the employees are capable of performing the essential functions of the job and do not present a direct threat to the health or safety of others.

The nature of the risk posed by the employee's HIV-positive status or AIDS infection depends on the nature of the job in question. In *Chalk v. U.S. District Court*,[25] a teacher who was diagnosed with AIDS was granted an injunction against transfer to an administrative position because the risk of AIDS transmission in the classroom was minimal. However, in *Doe v. University of Md. Medical Systems Corp.*,[26] an HIV-positive neurosurgeon was not entitled to continue his residency because he posed a significant risk to his patients, and in *Doe v. Washington University*,[27] an HIV-positive dental student was not permitted to continue his dental education. *Severino v. North Fort Meyers Fire Control Dist.*[28] held that a firefighter who was HIV-positive was reasonably accommodated under the Rehabilitation Act by being reassigned to light duties because the medical evidence indicated a risk of transmission of his disease to others during rescue operations. In *Leckelt*

---

[24] 536 U.S. 181 (2002).

[25] 840 F.2d 701 (9th Cir. 1988).

[26] 50 F.3d 1261 (4th Cir. 1995).

[27] 780 F. Supp. 628 (E.D. Mo. 1991).

[28] 935 F.2d 1179 (11th Cir. 1991).

v. Board of Comm. of Hosp. District No. 1,[29] a licensed practical nurse who refused to report the results of an HIV test was legally discharged for violating a hospital policy requiring employees to report any infectious disease to protect patients, coworkers, and the infected employees themselves.

Because the definition of an individual with a disability under both the ADA and the Rehabilitation Act includes an individual regarded as having a physical or mental condition that impairs a major life activity, an employee who is discharged because of a false and unfounded rumor that he or she was infected with HIV is protected as an individual with a disability. Do individuals who are HIV positive, but who do not present any evidence of impairment and who suffer from no ailments that affect the manner in which they live, fall under the definition of "individual with a disability" under the ADA or the Rehabilitation Act? The U.S. Supreme Court, in *Bragdon v. Abbott*[30] held that asymptomatic HIV was a disability within the meaning of the ADA because it was a medical condition that impaired the major life activity of reproduction.

10-8c   State Disability Discrimination Legislation

All 50 states have laws that prohibit discrimination against individuals with disabilities. The coverage of such laws varies; some cover both private and public sector employers, while others apply only to the public sector. The provisions of such laws generally parallel those of the ADA but in some instances go beyond the ADA protections. The California Fair Employment and Housing Act requires only that physical and mental disabilities place a "limitation" on a major life activity, rather than the "substantial limitation" required under the ADA. Some states have specific legislation prohibiting discrimination against individuals with specific conditions, such as the sickle cell trait, Tay-Sachs disease, HIV, or AIDS. Kentucky, for example, prohibits employers from requiring that applicants or employees take an HIV test, unless the employer can establish that the absence of HIV infection is a bona fide occupational qualification (BFOQ) for the job in question. New York, New Jersey, and North Carolina prohibit discrimination against applicants or employees because of genetic traits or conditions and prohibit requiring individuals to undergo genetic testing as a condition of employment.

10-8d   Drug Abuse and Drug Testing

Neither the ADA nor the Rehabilitation Act prohibits drug testing by employers. The ADA specifically states that drug tests are not considered medical exams under its provisions. Section 104 of the ADA specifically excludes from the definition of "qualified individual with a disability" any persons who are currently engaged in the illegal use of drugs and allows employers to prohibit the use of alcohol and illegal drugs at the workplace. The Rehabilitation Act also excludes from its protection individuals who are alcoholics or drug abusers whose current use of alcohol or drugs prevents them from performing the duties of the job or whose employment constitutes a direct threat to the property or safety of others.

---

[29] 909 F.2d 820 (5th Cir. 1990).

[30] 524 U.S. 624 (1998).

Note that the ADA and the Rehabilitation Act refer to the current use of drugs or alcohol. Both laws specifically protect:

- former drug users who have successfully been rehabilitated;

- persons who are participating in or have completed a supervised drug rehabilitation program and who no longer use drugs; and

- persons who are "erroneously regarded" as using illegal drugs but who do not actually use such drugs.

The following case deals with the question of whether an employee who was addicted to cocaine and who voluntarily entered a drug rehabilitation program is protected under the ADA.

CASE 10.5

BROWN v. LUCKY STORES, INC.
246 F.3d 1182 (9th Cir. 2001)

[Karen Brown was employed by Lucky Stores. She was arrested for drunk driving, possession of methamphetamine, and being under the influence of an illegal controlled substance. Because she could not post bail, she remained in jail from November 10 to November 15, 1996. She then appeared in court and was convicted of driving under the influence of intoxicants and possession of methamphetamine. The court conditioned suspension of her sentence on her participation in a round-the-clock 90-day drug and alcohol rehabilitation program. She attended the rehabilitation program from November 15, 1996, to February 12, 1997.

On the day of her arrest, Brown called Rebecca Caldeira, her sister-in-law, and asked her to inform John Hunt, Brown's manager at Lucky Stores, that she was in jail and could not make it to work that day. Caldeira called Hunt on November 10 and informed him of Brown's incarceration. Brown did not report for work on November 10, 11, and 16 because she was either in jail or attending the rehabilitation program. Lucky Stores fired Brown for abandoning her job. The collective bargaining agreement (CBA) governing Brown's employment authorized the discharge of an employee for "improper conduct," and a company policy provided that an employee who misses three consecutive shifts for an unauthorized reason will be terminated from employment.

Brown filed suit against Lucky Stores and Hunt alleging discrimination based on her alcoholism under the ADA, Rehabilitation Act, FEHA, and various state tort and contract claims. The trial court granted summary judgment in favor of Lucky Stores and Hunt on the ADA, Rehabilitation Act, and FEHA claims. The court concluded that an employer is permitted to terminate an alcoholic employee for violating a rational rule of conduct even if the misconduct was related to the employee's alcoholism. The court further concluded Lucky Stores did not have a duty to accommodate Brown because she never requested an accommodation.]

Fisher, Circuit Judge

Karen L. Brown appeals the district court's grant of summary judgment in favor of Lucky Stores and John Hunt on her claims that she was terminated because of her alcoholism in violation of the Americans with Disabilities Act ("ADA"), the Rehabilitation Act and California's Fair Employment and Housing Act ("FEHA")…. This appeal requires us to address the scope of the ADA's so-called "safe harbor" provision [42 U.S.C. § 12114(b)(2)] which extends the Act's protections to an individual "participating in a supervised rehabilitation program, and … no longer engaging in" the illegal use of drugs. We hold that the "safe harbor" provision applies only to employees who have refrained from using drugs for a significant period of time….

Although alcoholism is a protected disability under the ADA, … Brown has not presented any evidence that she was terminated because of her status as an alcoholic, as is required to prove her ADA claim. Rather, the evidence shows that Lucky Stores terminated her pursuant to its general policy under which three consecutive unexcused absences from work warrant termination. The ADA clearly states that an employer:

> may hold an employee who engages in the illegal use of drugs or who is an alcoholic to the same qualification standards for employment or job performance and behavior that such entity holds other employees, even if any unsatisfactory performance or behavior is related to the drug use or alcoholism of such employee. [42 U.S.C. § 12114(c)(4)]

Thus, Lucky Stores' termination of Brown did not violate the ADA.

Brown argues that her absence from work on November 16 was protected by 42 U.S.C. § 12114(b)(2). Section 12114(a) of the statute specifies that an employee or applicant "currently engaging in the use of illegal drugs" is not covered by the ADA, while section 12114(b) clarifies that section (a) does not apply to an individual who "has successfully completed a supervised drug rehabilitation program and is no longer engaging in the illegal use of drugs, or has otherwise been rehabilitated successfully and is no longer engaging in such use," [42 U.S.C. § 12114(b)(1)], nor to one who "is participating in a supervised rehabilitation program and is no longer engaging in such use" [§ 12114(b)(2)]. Mere participation in a rehabilitation program is not enough to trigger the protections of § 12114(b); "refraining from illegal use of drugs also is essential. Employers are entitled to seek reasonable assurances that no illegal use of drugs is occurring or has occurred recently enough so that continuing use is a real and ongoing problem." Brown's continuing use of drugs and alcohol was clearly an ongoing problem at least until November 10, as demonstrated by her incarceration for driving while intoxicated and possession of methamphetamine. Because she had not refrained from the use of drugs and alcohol for a sufficient length of time, she was not entitled to the protections of the ADA's safe-harbor provision.

Brown also claims that Lucky Stores had a duty to provide a reasonable accommodation for her disability by excusing her absence from her November 16 shift in order to attend the rehabilitation program.... Neither Brown nor her sister-in-law asked for an accommodation, however. Brown testified that she never believed she needed rehabilitation while working for Lucky Stores. That, coupled with the absence of evidence that she ever requested an accommodation, leads us to conclude Lucky Stores was under no affirmative obligation to provide an accommodation for her. *Barnett v. U.S. Air, Inc.* [228 F.3d 1105 (9th Cir. 2000)] does not alter our conclusion. In *Barnett*, we held that the

interactive process for finding a reasonable accommodation may be triggered by the employer's recognition of the need for such an accommodation, even if the employee does not specifically make the request. The exception to the general rule that an employee must make an initial request applies, however, only when the employer "(1) knows that the employee has a disability, (2) knows, or has reason to know, that the employee is experiencing workplace problems because of the disability, and (3) knows, or has reason to know, that the disability prevents the employee from requesting a reasonable accommodation." *Barnett* went on to explain that the employer is required to initiate the interactive process only when "an employee is unable to make such a request" and "the company knows of the existence of the employee's disability." The record does not show that Brown was unable to request a reasonable accommodation, or that Lucky Stores knew or had reason to know that Brown had a disability preventing her from making such a request.

In sum, we conclude that Lucky Stores did not terminate Brown in violation of the ADA, she was not entitled to the protections of the ADA's "safe harbor" provision and Lucky Stores had no duty to provide an accommodation for her, given that she never requested one.

The Rehabilitation Act is restricted in application to "any program or activity receiving Federal financial assistance or under any program or activity conducted by any Executive agency or by the United States Postal Service." [29 U.S.C. § 794(a)] Plaintiff has made no showing that Lucky Stores receives federal funds or is otherwise under executive agency control. Accordingly, her Rehabilitation Act claim fails....

We affirm the district court's judgment as to Brown's ADA, FEHA and Rehabilitation Act claims and its dismissal of the state law tort claims without prejudice....

Case Questions

1. What is the "safe harbor" provision of the ADA that Brown claims should apply to her case? How does the court of appeals interpret that provision—does it provide protection for Brown? Explain why or why not.

2. Did Brown's participation in a drug rehabilitation program shield her from adverse employment action by her employer? Explain.

3. Must employers treat alcoholic employees the same as employees who use illegal drugs for purposes of the ADA? Are there some reasons that might justify treating alcoholic employees differently? Explain.

An employer's policy against rehiring former employees discharged for workplace misconduct was a legitimate, nondiscriminatory reason for refusing to rehire a former employee who was discharged after testing positive for cocaine use and was not a violation of the ADA, according to *Raytheon Co. v. Hernandez.*[31]

Federal Drug Testing Legislation

Drug testing by employers is not generally prohibited by any federal legislation. Indeed, federal laws or regulations may require that certain employees, such as those in the airline or transportation industry, undergo periodic or random drug testing. The Drug-Free Workplace Act, passed by Congress in 1988, requires that government contractors doing more than $25,000 of business annually and recipients of federal grants of more than $25,000 establish written drug-free workplace policies and establish drug-free awareness programs.

State Drug Testing Legislation

A number of states have passed legislation regarding drug testing of employees. Most such laws set mandatory procedural requirements for employers who subject employees or applicants to drug testing. In general, these laws require that employers:

- provide employees with a written statement of their drug testing policy;
- require confirmatory tests in the case of an initial positive test result;
- allow employees or applicants who have tested positive to have the sample retested at their own expense;
- offer employees who test positive the opportunity to enroll in a drug rehabilitation program; and
- allow termination of employees testing positive only when they refuse to participate in such a program, fail to complete such a program, or violate the terms of the rehabilitation program.

Several states, including Connecticut and West Virginia, require employers to have reasonable grounds to suspect that employees are using drugs before subjecting employees (other than employees in safety-sensitive positions or subject to federal drug testing requirements) to drug tests.

Drug Testing by Private Sector Employers

As noted, neither the ADA nor the Rehabilitation Act prohibits drug testing by employers. Private sector employers may be subject to federal laws or regulations that require drug testing of certain employees and may be required by the Drug-Free Workplace Act to establish a drug-free workplace policy. In general, federal and state laws do not prohibit drug testing by private sector employers, though such testing may be subject to the procedural requirements of any relevant state laws. Employers whose work forces are unionized are required to bargain in good faith with the union representing their employees before instituting a drug testing program for those employees.

---

[31] 540 U.S. 44 (2003).

Drug Testing by Public Sector Employers

In addition to the legal issues that may arise under specific drug testing laws, drug testing of employees or applicants by a public sector employer could raise questions of its legality under the Constitution. In *New York City Transit Authority v. Beazer*,[32] a case that arose prior to the passage of the ADA, the Supreme Court upheld the constitutionality of a New York City Transit Authority rule prohibiting the employment of persons using methadone. The rule was held to serve the purposes of safety and efficiency and was a policy choice that the public sector employer was empowered to make.

The constitutional challenges to public sector drug testing are based on the Fourth Amendment, which forbids unreasonable searches or seizures by the government. Drug testing is considered a search. The general requirement under the Fourth Amendment is that the government must show some reasonable cause to justify the drug testing. In *Skinner v. Railway Labor Executives' Association*,[33] the Supreme Court upheld the constitutionality of Federal Railroad Administration regulations that required drug tests of all railroad employees involved in accidents, regardless of whether there was any reason to suspect individual employees of drug use. The Supreme Court held that the testing program served a compelling government interest by regulating conduct of railroad employees to ensure public safety, and that interest outweighed the privacy concerns of the employees. The fact that the employees had been involved in an accident was sufficient reason to subject them to drug testing.

In *National Treasury Employees Union v. Von Raab*,[34] the Supreme Court upheld rules of the U.S. Customs Service that required drug tests of all employees in, or applicants for, positions that involved the interdiction of drug smuggling, carrying a firearm, or access to classified materials. The government interest in public safety and in preventing law enforcement officials from being subjected to bribery or blackmail because of their own drug use justified the drug testing program under the Fourth Amendment. The unique mission of the Customs Service and the important government interests served by the testing justified the testing of all employees in the particular positions even without any showing of individualized suspicion that they were using drugs.

Subsequent to its decisions in *Skinner* and *Von Raab*, the Supreme Court held in *Chandler v. Miller*[35] that a Georgia law that required all candidates for state political offices to pass a drug test was unconstitutional because there was no evidence of a drug problem among elected officials, and the political offices did not involve high-risk or safety-sensitive positions or drug-interdiction efforts.

A number of lower federal court decisions have also dealt with drug testing by public sector employers. In *American Fed. of Govt. Employees v. Thornburgh*,[36] the court confined drug testing by the Immigration and Naturalization Service to the job classes specified in *Von Raab*: those employees involved directly in drug interdiction, carrying firearms, and with access to classified information. In *AFGE v. Thornburgh (Bureau of Prisons)*,[37] the court

---

[32] 440 U.S. 568 (1979).

[33] 489 U.S. 602 (1989).

[34] 489 U.S. 656 (1989).

[35] 520 U.S. 305 (1997).

[36] 713 F. Supp. 359 (N.D. Cal. 1989).

[37] 720 F. Supp. 154 (N.D. Cal. 1989).

enjoined the Bureau of Prisons' program of mandatory random testing of all employees, regardless of their job function, because the employer had failed to demonstrate a special need for the testing, as required by the Supreme Court decisions. *NTEU v. Watkins*[38] upheld the Department of Energy's drug testing of employees in "sensitive" positions:

- Those with access to sensitive information
- Presidential appointees
- Law enforcement officers
- Those whose duties pertain to law enforcement or national security or to protection of lives or property
- Those occupied with public health or safety
- Those positions involved with a high degree of trust

The court in *Watkins* also held that testing employees carrying firearms was not justified unless they also had law enforcement duties, and merely holding a security clearance does not decrease one's privacy expectation to justify testing with no other justification present.

In *Harmon v. Thornburgh*,[39] the court held that the *Von Raab* and *Skinner* public safety rationale to justify testing focuses on the immediacy of the threat posed. Therefore, the Department of Justice program of random drug testing of prosecutors, those with access to grand jury proceedings, and those with top-secret security clearances was not justified here. The court did allow the testing of employees with access to top-secret national security information. In *AFGE v. Skinner*,[40] the Department of Transportation's drug testing of employees in jobs with a direct impact on public health, safety, or national security, such as air traffic controllers, safety inspectors, aircraft mechanics, and motor vehicle operators, was upheld by the court of appeals.

In the case of *Georgia Association of Educators v. Harris*,[41] a federal court in Georgia issued an injunction against the enforcement of Georgia legislation requiring drug tests of all applicants for state employment. The court held that the testing requirement could not stand under the standards set out in *Von Raab*.

Drug Testing and the NLRB

A number of National Labor Relations Board (NLRB) decisions have dealt with drug testing. An employer's mandatory drug testing program for all employees who suffered work-related injuries was held to be a mandatory bargaining subject in *Johnson–Bateman Co.*,[42] requiring that employers must bargain in good faith with the union(s) representing their employees before instituting drug testing requirements. In *Oil, Chemical and Atomic Workers Int. Union, Local 2-286 v. Amoco Oil Co.*,[43] the court of appeals issued an injunction to prevent an employer from unilaterally implementing a drug testing program, pending the

---

[38] 722 F. Supp. 766 (D.D.C. 1989).

[39] 878 F.2d 484 (D.C. Cir. 1989).

[40] 885 F.2d 884 (D.C. Cir. 1989).

[41] 749 F. Supp. 1110 (N.D. Ga. 1990).

[42] 295 NLRB No. 26, 131 L.R.R.M. 1393 (1989).

[43] 885 F.2d 697 (10th Cir. 1989).

outcome of arbitration over whether the collective agreement gave the employer the right to institute such a program. However, drug testing of job applicants is not a mandatory bargaining subject according to *Star Tribune*,[44] which means that employers may unilaterally adopt drug testing for applicants for employment.

Medical Marijuana Laws

As of 2014, 23 states and the District of Columbia had enacted laws that (1) remove criminal sanctions for the medicinal use of marijuana, (2) define eligibility for its use, and (3) enable some means of access.[45] In 2009, the U.S. Attorney General issued guidelines regarding medical marijuana. AG Eric Holder announced in a press release,

> The guidelines make clear that the focus of federal resources should not be on individuals whose actions are in compliance with existing state laws, while underscoring that the Department will continue to prosecute people whose claims of compliance with state and local law conceal operations inconsistent with the terms, conditions, or purposes of those laws.
>
>   "It will not be a priority to use federal resources to prosecute patients with serious illnesses or their caregivers who are complying with state laws on medical marijuana, but we will not tolerate drug traffickers who hide behind claims of compliance with state law to mask activities that are clearly illegal," Holder said. "This balanced policy formalizes a sensible approach that the Department has been following since January: effectively focus our resources on serious drug traffickers while taking into account state and local laws."[46]

In light of these developments, how should the courts deal with disability discrimination cases in which medical marijuana is implicated? Here is one federal court's answer to this tricky question.

» CASE 10.6

THOMPSON V. MCHUGH
2014 WL 5320637 (U.S. Dist. Ct., D. Ariz., 2014)

Facts: Plaintiff Reuben James Thompson was a truck driver employed by a U.S. Army in Afghanistan. While working in Afghanistan, he was cited for driving under the influence of alcohol. Subsequent to his return to the United States he was found to be in possession of marijuana and paraphernalia. He claimed to be disabled and legally in possession of the alleged contraband. The Army nonetheless proceeded with the termination, and Thompson sued.

Issue: If Thompson can prove that he is disabled and that the marijuana was legitimately in his possession as a prescribed treatment for his disability, is he entitled to pursue his disability discrimination case against the Army?

Holding: Since his employer was a federal agency, concluded the court, he was potentially protected by Section 504 of the Rehabilitation Act. However,

---

[44] 295 NLRB No. 63, 131 L.R.R.M. 1404 (1989).

[45] "The Twenty-Three States and One Federal District With Effective Medical Marijuana Laws," Marijuana Policy Project (2014), available at https://www.mpp.org/issues/medical-marijuana /state-by-state-medical-marijuana-laws/summary-of-medical-marijuana-laws.

[46] "Attorney General Announces Formal Medical Marijuana Guidelines," U.S. Department of Justice, October 19, 2009, available at http://www.justice.gov/opa/pr /attorney-general-announces-formal-medical-marijuana-guidelines.

marijuana remains on the Controlled Substances Act's list of illegal drugs. Notwithstanding Thompson's possession of Arizona and California medical-marijuana authorization cards, the federal government has not yet recognized the legitimate medical use of marijuana. Citing a 2010 decision of the U.S. Court of Appeals for the Ninth Circuit[47] as precedent for that conclusion, the federal judge continued that, assuming that the plaintiff was disabled within the meaning of the Rehabilitation Act, and that he could make out a prima facie case of discrimination, the Army nevertheless produced evidence that Plaintiff was terminated for a "legitimate, nondiscriminatory reason[s]," i.e., his possession of illegal narcotics and previous discipline in Afghanistan. Thompson had not carried his burden of demonstrating that the stated reason was pretextual.

Consequently, the judge granted the Secretary of the Army's motion for summary judgment.

Concept *Summary* 10.4

DRUG ABUSE AND DRUG TESTING

- Coverage
  - The ADA and Rehabilitation Act do not cover individuals currently using drugs or alcohol
  - The acts do cover:
    - Former drug users who have been successfully rehabilitated
    - Persons participating in or who have completed a supervised drug rehabilitation program and no longer use drugs
    - Persons erroneously regarded as using illegal drugs
  - Testing
  - Drug testing is not prohibited by federal or state legislation or the ADA or Rehabilitation Act
  - Public employers requiring drug testing may face problems under the Fourth Amendment
  - Private sector employers requiring drug testing may be subject to state laws

- Legislation
  - The Drug-Free Workplace Act requires government contractors with contracts of more than $25,000 and recipients of federal grants of more than $25,000 to establish drug-free workplaces
  - State drug testing laws require that employers:
    - Provide written statement of drug testing policy
    - Require confirmatory tests if initial test result is positive
    - Allow employees and applicants who have tested positive to have the sample retested at their own expense
    - Offer employees who test positive the opportunity to enroll in a drug rehabilitation program
    - Allow termination of employees testing positive only when they refuse to participate in, fail to complete, or violate the terms of such a program

---

[47] *United States v. $186,416 in United States Currency*, 590 F.3d 942 (9th Cir. 2010).

CHAPTER REVIEW

» Key Terms

qualified individual with a disability   2 8 1   **undue hardship**   2 9 0

» Summary

- Both the Americans with Disabilities Act (ADA) and the Rehabilitation Act prohibit employment discrimination against otherwise qualified individuals with a disability. Both acts have the same broad definition of disability. Persons otherwise qualified, but who are perceived by others as having a disability, are protected under both acts. Persons with AIDS or who are HIV-positive have generally been held to be protected from employment discrimination under both acts. The Rehabilitation Act covers only employers who are government contractors or who operate or administer federally funded activities. The ADA covers both public and private employers with 15 or more employees. Both acts require employers to make reasonable accommodation to the conditions of otherwise qualified individuals with a disability, as discussed in the *Humphrey* case.

- Neither the ADA nor the Rehabilitation Act requires or forbids drug testing of employees, although the ADA does protect employees who have successfully completed a drug rehabilitation program or who are "erroneously regarded as using drugs." Public employers who require employees to be tested for drugs may face problems under the Fourth Amendment of the U.S. Constitution. Private sector employers who impose drug testing programs may be subject to appropriate state laws.

» Problems

» Questions

1. How does the coverage of the Americans with Disabilities Act differ from that of the Rehabilitation Act? Is there any overlap between the coverage of the acts? Explain your answers.

2. What constitutes a disability under the ADA? Are all individuals with disabilities protected under the ADA?

3. Under what circumstances can public sector employers require their employees to take drug tests? How do the circumstances under which private sector employers may require employees to take drug tests differ from those of public sector employers?

4. What are the differences in the procedures for filing complaints under Section 503 and Section 504 of the Rehabilitation Act?

5. Is alcoholism a disability under the ADA? Are alcoholics protected under the ADA? Explain.

» Case Problems

6. When Finan began to have seizures, his employer, Good Earth Tools, temporarily suspended him from his sales position because it required him to drive. Finan's doctor diagnosed him as having epilepsy but determined that his seizures could be controlled with proper medication. The doctor also told Finan that he would be able to drive after he had been free from seizures for six months. Good Earth restored Finan to the sales position but restricted him to telephone and Internet sales rather than driving. Because of the restrictions on his sales activity, Finan's sales performance declined significantly. After six months, he was permitted to make sales calls in person, but one month later Good Earth placed him on probation because of poor sales performance. Two months later, Good Earth fired him. Finan sued Good Earth under the ADA.

    Can Finan establish a *prima facie* case of disability discrimination under the ADA? What, if any, defenses can Good Earth raise here? Explain. [See *Finan v. Good Earth Tools, Inc.*, 2009 WL 1375135 (8th Cir., May 19, 2009).]

7. Michael Mengine was employed by the United States Postal Service (USPS) as a letter carrier. Following hip surgery, he was no longer able to perform the duties of a letter carrier, which required prolonged walking and substantial lifting. Mengine went on sick leave, but after exhausting his leave, he requested assignment to light duty work. The USPS assigned him to temporary light duty work for a month, but after the expiration of that temporary position, the Postal Service informed him that there were no permanent light duty positions available. Mengine asked the USPS to create a permanent light duty position for him, but that request was refused and Mengine ultimately took disability retirement. He then filed suit under the ADA, alleging that the USPS refused to offer him a reasonable accommodation.

    Has the USPS violated the ADA? Explain. [See *Mengine v. Runyon*, 114 F.3d 415 (3d Cir. 1997).]

8. Allan Peden, a Detroit police officer, suffered a heart attack and underwent successful heart surgery.

His physician approved his return to work on indefinite restricted duty conditions, and for 10 years he continued working in clerical positions with the police department's Crime Analysis Unit (CAU). The Detroit Police Department decided to update the written job description for police positions based on a list of "24 Essential Job Functions of a Law Enforcement Officer" developed by the Michigan Law Enforcement Officers Training Council. The list included such tasks as pursuing suspects in foot chases, engaging in vehicle pursuits, effecting forcible arrests, overcoming violent resistance, and qualifying with a firearm. The police department described the duties of police officers as including patrolling an assigned post, enforcing laws, apprehending violators of the law, transporting sick and injured people to hospitals, and serving warrants. The police department physicians reviewed Peden's medical records and determined that he was unable to perform the required tasks on the job description. The police department then placed Peden on involuntary disability retirement. The department claimed that he was incapable of performing the essential functions of a police officer position, but Peden argued that the job description did not accurately reflect the nature of his previous position.

    Will the court rule for Peden or the police department? Why? [See *Peden v. City of Detroit*, 470 Mich. 195, 680 N.W.2d 857 (Mich. 2004).]

9. Gaul worked for AT&T as a senior technical associate. He was diagnosed as suffering from depression and anxiety-related disorders but was able to control his condition for more than a year with antidepressant drugs. He then suffered a nervous breakdown and was hospitalized for several weeks. He was absent from work for approximately three months. After receiving treatment, his condition appeared under control, but he later suffered a relapse after an unfavorable performance review from his manager and again went out on disability leave. Gaul asked that AT&T assign him to a "low stress" position, but AT&T ignored his request, and Gaul was placed on disability retirement.

    Is Gaul a "qualified individual with a disability" within the meaning of the ADA? Does AT&T have a duty to accommodate Gaul's condition? Explain. [See *Gaul v. Lucent Technologies, Inc.*, 134 F.3d 576 (3d Cir. 1998).]

10. Steven Anders was a waste hauler employed by Waste Management. When he arrived at work one morning, he had a disagreement with his supervisor over the route he was assigned for the day. He decided to leave work, claiming that he felt sick. Rather than going to his home, Anders went to the employer's regional office to speak to the managers there. Anders entered the office, but while waiting to speak to a manager, he began to shake, and his head and chest ached, so he went outside to get some fresh air. The managers then went outside to get Anders, but when they talked to him, Anders began to pound his fists on his car and smashed his cell phone on the ground. Anders became short of breath, and the managers tried to escort him back into the building. Anders then attempted to attack one of the managers but was restrained. He calmed down but then became violent and threatened the manager again. Anders was terminated by the employer; he then filed suit under the ADA, claiming that he suffered from "panic disorder" which caused his behavior. He had previously asked for time off work under the Family and Medical Leave Act but was denied such leave.

    How should the court rule on Anders' ADA claim? Explain. [See *Anders v. Waste Management of Wisconsin*, 463 F.3d 670 (7th Cir. 2006).]

11. Alan Labonte was hired as executive director of the Hutchins & Wheeler law firm in June 1992. In his first year in the position, he created a time-keeping system that saved the firm $13,000 per month, negotiated leases to lower rental payments by $43,000, lowered client disbursement costs by $200,000, and reduced overtime costs by $40,000. The firm's partners gave him a performance evaluation stating that they were "very satisfied" with his performance, and he received a raise of $4,600. After about a year, Labonte developed a limp. When he consulted a doctor about the problem, he was informed that he had multiple sclerosis. After his diagnosis, he informed the firm and requested that the partners meet with his doctors to determine

what measures could be taken to accommodate his condition. One partner had a brief lunch meeting with one doctor, who suggested that the firm limit the amount of walking that Labonte would be required to do.

The firm made no effort to limit Labonte's walking, to move his office, or to rearrange his job. Instead, the firm assigned additional duties to him and pressured him to cancel a personal trip to Florida that he had planned. On one occasion, a partner told him to go home if he was tired, so he wouldn't wear himself out and become ineffective. In January 1994, the firm terminated Labonte because his condition affected his performance. The firm claimed that his thinking was "not as crisp as it needed to be." After he was terminated, Labonte applied for, and was granted, disability benefits under the firm's insurance policy, stating that he was "unable to work long hours in a stressful job" and "needed a flexible work schedule." He then worked as a consultant and enrolled in a graduate program at a local university. Labonte brought a claim of disability discrimination against the firm under both state and federal law. After following the administrative procedures, he filed suit in federal court. The firm argued that Labonte was precluded from bringing suit because he accepted disability benefits.

How should the court rule on his claim? Can he pursue the suit despite accepting disability benefits? Why should that matter for his claim? Explain your answers. [See *Labonte v. Hutchins & Wheeler*, 424 Mass. 813, 678 N.E.2d 853 (Mass. Sup. Ct. 1997).]

12. Dura Automotive Systems operates a factory manufacturing auto glass window units through a manufacturing process involving high temperature injection molds and cutting machines. Lately there had been a high rate of workplace accidents at the facility, and managers suspect that drug use by the workers was the cause. Dura hired FFS, a consulting firm, to implement a comprehensive drug testing program. The program would test for 12 substances which the parties believed could create a safety risk in a manufacturing facility. Some of the substances were found in legal prescription drugs. The drug testing involved an initial screening

test of urine samples provided by the employees. If the initial screen tested positive for one of the banned substances, the employee's sample was then subjected to a confirmatory test. The results of the confirmatory test were then reviewed by a licensed medical review officer, who would contact the employee to determine if there was a medical explanation for the positive result. If the employee provided a valid medical explanation and documentation—such as a medical prescription for a drug containing one of the banned substances—the medical review officer would change the test results from "positive" to "negative" and forward the results to FFS, who then relayed the results to Dura.

Dura management, however, regarded the confirmatory testing as irrelevant—they required any employee whose initial test result was positive to provide a list of all the medications that the employee was taking. Dura then sent letters to the employees taking such medications, informing them that they were placed on 30-day leave to allow them to transition to a different medication or to stop using the medication altogether. Dura ignored letters from employees' physicians stating that the medications would not affect the employees' performance and were necessary for the employees' health. Employees who failed the initial drug test were permitted to take another test within 30 days—and if the second test was negative, the employee was allowed to return to work. But if the second test was positive, the employee was placed on indefinite layoff and was terminated after six months. Dura also implemented random and "post layoff return" drug testing, and any employee failing such test could be terminated immediately.

Several Dura employees who failed an initial drug test because they were taking legally prescribed medications containing one of the banned substances had their initial "positive" results changed to "negative" by the medical review officer after documenting their medical need for the prescription drug; however, Dura would not allow them to return to work, and they were ultimately terminated by Dura. Those seven employees file suit against Dura under the ADA.

Is Dura's drug testing policy a violation of the ADA? Explain. [See *Bates v. Dura Automotive Systems, Inc.*, 2009 WL 1108479 (M.D. Tenn., April 23, 2009).]

13. Bonnie Cook applied for employment as an attendant at a Rhode Island hospital for the developmentally disabled. She had previously worked at the hospital and had a good work record but left voluntarily. She was not rehired because she was extremely obese. She was five feet two inches tall and weighed more than 320 pounds. The hospital's human resources director stated that she felt Cook's obesity would limit her ability to evacuate patients in case of an emergency and make her more susceptible to developing serious health problems. Cook sued the hospital under the ADA.

Is Cook's obesity a disability under the ADA? Does her obesity prevent her from being an "otherwise qualified individual with a disability" under the ADA? Does it matter that Cook's weight may change? How should the court decide this case? Explain your answers. [See *Cook v. State of Rhode Island Dept. of Mental Health, Retardation and Hospitals*, 10 F.3d 17 (1st Cir. 1993).]

14. Bultemeyer was a custodian for the Fort Wayne Community Schools (FWCS), but he developed serious mental illnesses, including bipolar disorder, anxiety attacks, and paranoid schizophrenia. Bultemeyer went on disability leave for several months while undergoing treatment for his condition. He was then contacted by the employee relations director of FWCS to see if he was ready to return to work. When he answered that he was, she told him that there was an open position at Northrop School, the largest of the schools operated by FWCS. She told him that in order to begin working again, he would have to take a physical examination that was required of all employees returning from disability leave. She then informed him that he would not receive any special accommodations. He was directed to work at Northrop and told that if he did not, his employment would be terminated. Bultemeyer reported as directed, but after touring Northrop School with the custodial foreman, he told the employee relations director

that he could not work at Northrop; however, he also told her that he was not resigning. Bultemeyer was also afraid to take the physical exam, because he thought that if he passed, he would have to work at Northrop, and if he worked there, he would be unable to perform his tasks and would get fired. So Bultemeyer did not take the physical, and he did not report for work as directed. He did contact his psychiatrist, who wrote a letter to FWCS stating that it would be in Bultemeyer's best interest to return to a school that might be less stressful than Northrop School. In response, FWCS notified him that his employment with FWCS was terminated because he had not reported for work and had not taken the physical. Bultemeyer filed suit against FWCS, alleging that FWCS had violated the ADA by failing to make reasonable accommodations for his mental disability.

Has FWCS violated the ADA? Explain. [See *Bultemeyer v. Fort Wayne Community Schools*, 100 F.3d 1281 (7th Cir. 1996).]

15. The administrators at Wayzatta Central High School, in Wayzatta, Mississippi, were concerned about rumors of illegal drug use by the high school students. The school administrators decided to require all high school varsity athletes to undergo drug tests. Although there was no specific evidence that the athletes were using drugs, the administration reasoned that athletes tend to be role models and opinion leaders for the student body. Hence, requiring them to take drug tests would also send a strong antidrug message to the rest of the students. When some students complained that the faculty were not subject to the drug testing, the administration adopted a policy that also required all faculty and staff at the school to take drug tests, despite the fact that there was no evidence of drug use by the faculty. Anyone testing positive would be discharged. The teachers protested the drug testing policy and decided to file suit to challenge it.

On what grounds can the teachers challenge the drug testing policy? Is their legal challenge likely to be successful? Is the drug testing of the student athletes legal? Explain. [See *Board of Education of Indpt. School Dist. No. 92 of Pottawatomie County*

v. Earls, 536 U.S. 822 (2002); *Georgia Assoc. of Educators v. Harris*, 749 F. Supp. 1110 (N.D. Ga. 1990); and *Vernonia School Dist. v. Acton*, 515 U.S. 646 (1995).]

» Hypothetical Scenarios

16. The City of Auburn, a public employer, decides that it wants its employees to participate in a health risk assessment program as a condition of being eligible for the employer's health plan. The program involves the employees filling out a health-related questionnaire, taking a blood pressure test, and giving a blood sample for screening. The results of the tests were only given to the employees, and the employer only received aggregate results. Employees who did not participate in the assessment were not eligible for coverage under the employer's health plan. Does the employer violate the ADA by requiring participation in the health risk assessment as a condition of participating in the health plan? Explain.

17. Zenor worked as a pharmacist at El Paso Medical Center. Her job requires that she work with restricted narcotics, sedatives, pain relievers, and other prescription medications. Zenor had developed an addiction to cocaine, and on the night of August 15, after injecting herself with cocaine, she suffered a mild seizure and was unable to report for work the next morning. She called the pharmacy manager and told him she was unable to work because of a "drug reaction." When asked what drug was involved, she admitted that it was cocaine. The manager reminded her of the employer's drug-free policy and advised her to check into a rehabilitation program. Zenor made arrangements to enroll on a residential 90-day rehabilitation program. She notified the manager of her participation in the rehabilitation program, and the manager promised to arrange a medical leave to cover the time in the rehabilitation program. After Zenor completed half of the rehabilitation program, her manager informed her that her employment would be terminated at the end of the rehabilitation program.

Is Zenor protected under the ADA? Has her employer violated the ADA? Explain.

18. Bonds tested positive for cocaine and was fired by Selig, Inc., for violating its drug-free workplace policy. Bonds then enrolled in a drug rehabilitation program and was able to end his drug abuse. He was drug-free for over two years, and reapplied to Selig to be rehired. To support his application, he provided letters from his pastor about his active church participation and from an Alcoholics Anonymous counselor about his regular attendance at meetings and his recovery. Selig refused to rehire Bonds because of its policy against rehiring employees who are terminated for workplace misconduct. Bonds claims the "no rehire" policy violates the ADA. Does it? Explain.

19. Deborah Friend applied to enroll in the nursing program at Rockland Community College, a public college that received financial aid funding from the federal government. In addition to the academic courses, the nursing program also required students to complete a clinical program. After being notified that she was accepted into the nursing program, Friend was asked by the director of the nursing program to list any medical conditions that might affect her ability to complete the clinical portions of the nursing program. Friend suffers from diminished hearing, but she has a cochlear implant that allows her to hear normally. She informed the director of her condition, who told her that her admission into the program was withdrawn because her condition would prevent her from performing the clinical requirements. Has Rockland Community College violated the Rehabilitation Act? Explain.

20. Rosen had worked for many years as a waiter at Café Boeuf, an elegant French restaurant in Minneapolis. When Rosen was interviewed on a community television program about living with HIV, he admitted that he was HIV-positive but was asymptomatic. Upon learning about his TV appearance, the restaurant fired him. Rosen filed suit against the Café Boeuf under the ADA. Is Rosen protected by the ADA? Has Café Boeuf violated the ADA? Explain.

CHAPTER **11**

Other EEO and Employment Legislation: Federal and State Laws

In addition to the legislation discussed in the preceding chapters, there are other legal provisions that can be used to attack discrimination in employment. Those other provisions include the Civil Rights Acts of 1866 and 1870, Executive Order 11246, the Uniformed Services Employment and Reemployment Act, the National Labor Relations Act, the Constitution, and the various state EEO laws. This chapter discusses these provisions in some detail.

11-1 The Civil Rights Acts of 1866 and 1870

The Civil Rights Acts of 1866 and 1870 were passed during the Reconstruction era immediately following the Civil War. They were intended to ensure that the newly freed slaves were granted the full legal rights of U.S. citizens. The acts are presently codified in Sections 1981, 1983, and 1985 of Chapter 42 of the U.S. Code (referred to as 42 U.S.C. Sections 1981, 1983, 1985).

11-1a Section 1981

Section 1981 provides, in part, that:

> All persons within the jurisdiction of the United States shall have the same right in every State and Territory to make and enforce contracts … as is enjoyed by white citizens …

The Supreme Court held in *Jones v. Alfred H. Mayer Co.*[1] that the acts could be used to attack discrimination in private employment. Following *Jones*, Section 1981 was increasingly used, in addition to Title VII, to challenge employment discrimination. In *Johnson v. Railway Express Agency*,[2] the Supreme Court held that Section 1981 provided for an independent cause of action (right to sue) against employment discrimination. A suit under Section 1981 was separate and distinct from a suit under Title VII.

---

[1] 392 U.S. 409 (1968).
[2] 421 U.S. 454 (1975).

In the 1989 decision of *Patterson v. McLean Credit Union,*[3] the Supreme Court held that Section 1981 covered only those aspects of racial discrimination in employment that related to the formation and enforcement of contracts and did not cover harassment based on race. The Civil Rights Act of 1991 amended Section 1981 and effectively overturned the *Patterson* decision by adding Section 1981(b), which states:

> For the purposes of this section, the term "make and enforce contracts" includes the making, performance, modification, and termination of contracts, and the enjoyment of all benefits, privileges, terms and conditions of the contractual relationship.

The 1991 act also added Section 1981A, which gives the right to sue for compensatory and punitive damages to victims of intentional discrimination in violation of Title VII, the Americans with Disabilities Act of 1990, and the Rehabilitation Act.

The wording of Section 1981 ("… as is enjoyed by white citizens …") seems to indicate a concern with racial discrimination. In *Saint Francis College v. Al-Khazraji,*[4] a college professor alleged that he was denied tenure because he was an Arab. The college argued that Arabs are members of the Caucasian (white) race and that the professor was therefore not a victim of race discrimination subject to Section 1981. In determining whether Section 1981 applied to the professor's claim, the Supreme Court held that:

> Based on the history of Section 1981, we have little trouble in concluding that Congress intended to protect from discrimination identifiable classes of persons who are subjected to intentional discrimination solely because of their ancestry or ethnic characteristics. Such discrimination is racial discrimination that Congress intended Section 1981 to forbid, whether or not it would be classified as racial in terms of modern scientific theory. The Court of Appeals was thus quite right in holding that Section 1981, "at a minimum," reaches discrimination against an individual "because he or she is genetically part of an ethnically and physiognomically distinctive sub-grouping of *homo sapiens*." It is clear from our holding, however, that a distinctive physiognomy is not essential to qualify for Section 1981 protection. If respondent on remand can prove that he was subjected to intentional discrimination based on the fact that he was born an Arab, rather than solely on the place or nation of his origin, or his religion, he will have made out a case under Section 1981.

Based on *Al-Khazraji,* the courts now interpret "race" under Section 1981 broadly to include claims of ethnic discrimination that are racial in character, such as claiming that an individual was treated differently because he was Hispanic rather than "Anglo," as in *Lopez v. S. B. Thomas, Inc.*[5] Plaintiffs may bring suits under Section 1981 to challenge racial or ethnic harassment or retaliation, according to *Manatt v. Bank of America, N.A.*[6]

11-1b   Section 1983

Section 1983 of 42 U.S.C. provides that:

> Every person who, under the color of any statute, ordinance, regulation, custom or usage, of any State or Territory, subjects, or causes to be subjected, any citizen of the United States or other person within the jurisdiction thereof to the deprivation of any rights, privileges, or immunities secured

---

[3] 91 U.S. 164 (1989).

[4] 481 U.S. 604 (1987).

[5] 831 F.2d 1184 (2d Cir. 1987).

[6] 339 F.3d 792 (9th Cir. 2003).

by the Constitution and laws, shall be liable to the party injured in an action at law equity, or other proper proceeding for redress.

As with Section 1981, Section 1983 is restricted to claims of intentional discrimination. But unlike Section 1981, the prohibitions of Section 1983 extend to the deprivation of any rights guaranteed by the Constitution or by law. In *Maine v. Thiboutot*,[7] the Supreme Court held that Section 1983 encompasses claims based on deprivation of rights granted under federal statutory law. This means that claims alleging discrimination on grounds prohibited by federal law, such as gender, age, religion, national origin, and so forth, can be brought under Section 1983. But because of the wording of Section 1983 ("… under the color of any statute, … of any state"), claims under Section 1983 are restricted to cases in which the alleged discrimination is by someone acting (or claiming to act) under government authority. That means employment discrimination by public employers is subject to challenge because such employers act under specific legal authority. In general, claims against private sector employers can rarely be filed under Section 1983. Any claims against private employers under Section 1983 must establish that the employer acted pursuant to some specific government authority; this is the "state action" requirement. In addition, in *Brown v. GSA*,[8] the Supreme Court held that the only remedy available to federal government employees complaining of race discrimination in employment is provided by Section 717 of Title VII.

11-1c   Section 1985(c)

Section 1985(c) of 42 U.S.C. prohibits two or more persons from conspiring to deprive a person or class of persons "of the equal protection of the laws, or of equal privileges and immunities under the law." The provision was enacted in 1871 to protect African Americans from the violent activities of the Ku Klux Klan.

In *Griffin v. Breckenridge*,[9] the Supreme Court held that a group of African Americans alleging that they were attacked and beaten by a group of whites could bring suit under Section 1985(c). It appeared that the provision could be used to attack intentional discrimination in private employment when two or more persons were involved in the discrimination. But in 1979, the Supreme Court held in *Great American Federal Savings & Loan Ass'n. v. Novotny*[10] that Section 1985(c) could not be used to sue for violation of a right created by Title VII. Relying on *Novotny*, lower courts have held that Section 1985(c) cannot be used to challenge violations of the Equal Pay Act or the Age Discrimination in Employment Act.

11-1d   Procedure Under Sections 1981 and 1983

A suit under Section 1981 is not subject to the same procedural requirements as a suit under Title VII. There is no requirement to file a claim with any administrative agency, such as the Equal Employment Opportunity Commission (EEOC), before filing suit under Section 1981 or Section 1983. The plaintiff may file suit in federal district court and is

---

[7] 448 U.S. 1 (1980).

[8] 425 U.S. 820 (1976).

[9] 403 U.S. 88 (1971).

[10] 442 U.S. 366 (1979).

entitled to a jury trial; a successful plaintiff may recover punitive damages in addition to compensatory damages such as back pay, benefits, and legal fees.

The right to sue under Section 1981A for compensatory and punitive damages for intentional violations of Title VII and the Americans with Disabilities Act of 1990 was added by the Civil Rights Act of 1991. The act also set upper limits on the amount of damages recoverable based on the size of the employer (as discussed in Chapter 8). Punitive damages are not recoverable against public sector employers. For claims arising under the provisions added by the 1991 amendments, the limitations period for filing suit is four years, according to *Jones v. R. R. Donnelley & Sons Co.*[11]

Concept *Summary* 11.1

THE CIVIL RIGHTS ACTS OF 1866 AND 1870

- The Civil Rights Acts of 1866 and 1870

    ○ 42 U.S.C. Section 1981: Allows for individual suits for damages for intentional discrimination based on race or color

    ○ Section 1981A: Provides for compensatory and punitive damages for intentional violations of Title VII, the Americans with Disabilities Act, and the Rehabilitations Act

    ○ Section 1983: Allows for individual suits for intentional action "under color of state law" causing deprivation of any rights guaranteed by law

    ○ Section 1985(c): Allows for suits against persons conspiring to deprive persons of rights protected by law

        ■ Does not apply for suits claiming deprivation of rights under Title VII

- Enforcement by individual suits; no administrative enforcement

11-2   Executive Order No. 11246

contract compliance program
regulations which provide that all firms having federal government contracts or subcontracts exceeding $10,000 must include a no-discrimination clause in the contract

Executive Order No. 11246, originally signed by President Johnson in 1965 and amended by President Nixon in 1969, provides the basis for the federal government contract compliance program. Under that executive order, as amended, firms doing business with the federal government must agree not to discriminate in employment on the basis of race, color, religion, national origin, or gender.

11-2a   Equal Employment Requirements

The **contract compliance program** is administered by the U.S. Secretary of Labor through the Office of Federal Contract Compliance Programs (OFCCP).[12] The OFCCP has issued

---

[11] 541 U.S. 369 (2004).

[12] See "Compliance Assistance by Law—the Executive Order No. 11246," available at http://www.dol.gov /compliance/laws/comp-eeo.htm.

extensive regulations spelling out the requirements and procedures under the contract compliance program. The regulations provide that all firms having contracts or subcontracts exceeding $10,000 with the federal government must agree to include a no-discrimination clause in the contract. The clause, which is binding on the firm for the duration of the contract, requires the contractor to agree not to discriminate in employment on the basis of race, color, religion, gender, or national origin. The contractor also agrees to state in all employment advertisements that all qualified applicants will be considered without regard to race, color, religion, gender, or national origin and to inform each labor union representing its employees of its obligations under the program. The contracting firm is also required to include the same type of no-discrimination clause in every subcontract or purchase order pursuant to the federal contract.

The Secretary of Labor, through the OFCCP, may investigate any allegations of violations by contracting firms. Penalties for violation include the suspension or cancellation of the firm's government contract and the disbarment of the firm from future government contracts.

11-2b   Affirmative Action Requirements

affirmative action plan
program which involves giving preference in hiring or promotion to qualified female or minority employees

In addition to requiring the no-discrimination clause, the OFCCP regulations may require that a contracting firm develop a written plan regarding its employees. Firms with contracts of services or supply for over $50,000 and having 50 or more employees are required to maintain formal written programs, called **affirmative action plans**, for the utilization of women and minorities in their work force. Affirmative action plans, which must be updated annually, must contain an analysis of the employer's use of women and minorities for each job category in the work force. When job categories reveal an underutilization of women and minorities—that is, fewer women or minorities employed than would reasonably be expected based on their availability in the relevant labor market—the plan must set out specific hiring goals and timetables for improving the employment of women and minorities. The firm is expected to make a good-faith effort to reach those goals; the goals set are more in the nature of targets than hard-and-fast "quotas." The firms must submit annual reports of the results of their efforts to meet the goals set out in the affirmative action plan.

Firms holding federal or federally assisted construction contracts or subcontracts over $10,000 are also subject to affirmative action requirements. The contracting firm must comply with the goals and timetables for employment of women and minorities set periodically by the OFCCP. Those construction industry goals are set for "covered geographic areas" of the country based on census data for the areas. The "goals and timetables" approach to affirmative action for construction industry employees was held to be constitutional and legal under Title VII in *Contractors Ass'n. of Eastern Pennsylvania v. Shultz.*[13]

11-2c   Procedure Under Executive Order No. 11246

Individuals alleging a violation of a firm's obligations under Executive Order No. 11246 may file complaints with the OFCCP within 180 days of the alleged violation. The OFCCP may refer the complaint to the EEOC for investigation, or it may make its own investigation.

---

[13] 442 F.2d 159 (3d Cir. 1971).

If it makes its own investigation, it must report to the director of the OFCCP within 60 days.

If there is reason to believe that a violation has occurred, the firm is issued a show-cause notice directing it to show why enforcement proceedings should not be instituted; the firm has 30 days to provide such evidence. During this 30-day period, the OFCCP is also required to make efforts to resolve the violation through mediation and conciliation.

If the firm fails to show cause or if the conciliation is unsuccessful, the director of the OFCCP may refer the complaint to the Secretary of Labor for administrative enforcement proceedings or to the Department of Justice for judicial enforcement proceedings. The individual filing the complaint may not file suit privately against the firm alleged to be in violation, but the individual may bring suit to force the OFCCP to enforce the regulations and requirements under the executive order.[14] Administrative enforcement proceedings involve a hearing before an administrative law judge (ALJ). The ALJ's decision is subject to review by the Secretary of Labor; the secretary's decision may be subjected to judicial review in the federal courts.[15]

Firms found to be in violation of the obligations under the executive order, either through the courts or the administrative proceedings, may be subject to injunctions and required to provide back pay and grant retroactive seniority to affected employees. The firm may also have its government contract suspended or canceled and may be declared ineligible for future government contracts. Firms declared ineligible must demonstrate compliance with the executive order's requirements to be reinstated by the director of the OFCCP.

THE **WORKING** LAW

President Obama Signs a New Executive Order to Protect LGBT Workers

"Many of you have worked for a long time to see this day coming."

Those were President Obama's words to the audience in the East Room of the White House this morning, before he signed an Executive Order prohibiting federal contractors from discriminating on the basis of sexual orientation or gender identity.

At the signing, the President explained how, because of their "passionate advocacy and the irrefutable rightness of [their] cause, our government—government of the people, by the people, and for the people—will become just a little bit fairer."

Today's Executive Order amends Executive Order 11246, issued by President Lyndon B. Johnson, adding sexual orientation and gender identity to the list of protected categories in the existing Executive Order covering federal contractors.

"It doesn't make much sense," President Obama said, "but today in America, millions of our fellow citizens wake up and go to work with the awareness that they could lose their job, not because of anything they do or fail to do, but because of who they are—lesbian, gay, bisexual, transgender. And that's wrong."

The President also pointed out that workplace equality is simply good business. Noting that most of the Fortune 500 companies already have nondiscrimination policies on their books, he explained that these policies help companies attract and retain the best talent.

---

[14] *Legal Aid Society v. Brennan*, 608 F.2d 1319 (9th Cir. 1979).

[15] *Firestone Co. v. Marshall*, 507 F. Supp. 1330 (E.D. Texas 1981).

"Despite all that," he said, "in too many states and in too many workplaces, simply being gay, lesbian, bisexual, or transgender can still be a fireable offense. There are people here today who've lost their jobs for that reason."

"I'm going to do what I can, with the authority I have, to act," the President said. "The rest of you, of course, need to keep putting pressure on Congress to pass federal legislation that resolves this problem once and for all."

Source: The White House Blog, July 21, 2015, available at https://www.whitehouse.gov/blog/2014/07/21/president-obama-signs-new-executive-order-protect-lgbt-workers.

Concept *Summary* 11.2

E.O. 11246

- Federal Contractors (> $10K) must agree not to discriminate on race, color, religion, sex, or national origin

- Contractors with contracts for over $50,000 and 50+ employees must have a written affirmative action plan that:
  - Assesses diversity of workforce
  - Sets goals and timetables to remedy any underutilization of women and minorities

11-3   Employment Discrimination Because of Military Service: The Uniformed Services Employment and Reemployment Rights Act

During the recent U.S. military actions in Afghanistan and Iraq, many persons who were members of the National Guard or military reserves were called to active duty; in some instances, the tour of active duty lasted more than one year. What are the legal rights of employees who are called to active duty? Do they have the right to return to their job after their active duty service is over? Federal legislation protects the reemployment rights of employees who serve in the military services or who are members of the reserves and are called into active duty.

11-3a   The Uniformed Services Employment and Reemployment Rights Act

The Uniformed Services Employment and Reemployment Rights Act (USERRA),[16] enacted in 1994, replaced the Veterans' Reemployment Rights Act. USERRA covers both private and public sector employers, including the federal government; it prohibits employers from discriminating against employees because of their service in the military.

---

[16] 38 U.S.C. § 4301 *et seq.*

USERRA applies only to noncareer military service—that is, to employees who are called to active duty from their civilian jobs. It does not apply to career military service, according to *Woodman v. Office of Personnel Management*.[17]

Employees who are absent from employment because they were ordered to active military service are entitled to reinstatement and employment benefits if they meet the following requirements:

- They gave the employer notice of the period of military service
- They are absent for a cumulative total of less than five years
- They submitted an application for reemployment within the designated time period

The time period for submitting the notice of reemployment to the employer depends on the length of the military service. For military service less than 31 days, the employee need only report to work on the first full work day after completion of the service and transportation to the employee's residence. For service longer than 30 days but less than 181 days, the notice must be submitted not later than 14 days after completing the period of military service. For service longer than 180 days, the notice must be submitted not later than 90 days after completion of the period of military service.

Employers are not required to reinstate employees after their military service if:

- the employer's circumstances have changed so that reemployment would be unreasonable or impossible;
- the reemployment would cause undue hardship in accommodation, training, or effort; or
- the initial employment was for a brief, nonrecurring period.

In any such case, the employer has the burden of proving that the denial of reemployment was permissible under the act.

Employees reemployed after military service are entitled to the seniority, rights, and benefits they had as of the date the military service began, plus any seniority, rights, and benefits that they would have received had they remained continuously employed. Persons who are reemployed under the act after military service of more than 180 days may not be discharged without cause within one year of reemployment; persons reemployed after military service of more than 30 days but less than 180 days may not be discharged without cause within 180 days of reemployment. Persons who are affected by alleged violations of the USERRA must file written complaints with the federal Secretary of Labor; the Secretary will investigate any complaint and make reasonable attempts to settle it. If such attempts are unsuccessful, affected persons may request that the secretary refer a complaint to the U.S. Attorney General to take court action to enforce the act or may file legal action themselves in the appropriate federal district court.

Remedies available under such a suit include ordering the employer to comply with the act and compensation for lost wages, benefits, and legal fees. Liquidated damages are available where the employer's violation was willful. According to *Gummo v. Village of Depew, N.Y.*,[18] the employee only needs to show that the military service was a substantial

---

[17] 258 F.3d 1372 (Fed. Cir. 2001).

[18] 75 F.3d 98 (2d. Cir. 1996).

or motivating factor in the employer's decision to discharge the employee; it need not be the sole reason. An employer can escape liability by showing that the employee *would* have been discharged even if the employee had no military service.[19]

The following case involves a claim of termination of a reservist in violation of USERRA and discusses the allocation of the burden of proof under the statute.

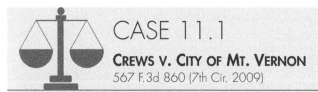

CASE 11.1

CREWS V. CITY OF MT. VERNON
567 F.3d 860 (7th Cir. 2009)

Background

[Ryan Crews had been a member of the Army National Guard since 1988 and an officer of the Mt. Vernon Police Department since 1997. As a member of the Guard, Crews had to attend weekend training and preparedness exercises ("drill") about once a month. The chief of police, Mendenall, has the authority to establish officers' weekly work schedules, which consist of five eight-hour shifts and two days off. For nine years, the City of Mt. Vernon allowed police officers who missed their weekend work shifts to attend National Guard duties to work on their scheduled days off to make up the lost time. The City did not provide a comparable scheduling benefit to non-Guard employees who missed work for nonmilitary activities. Crews's weekend drill obligations frequently conflicted with his work schedule. When such a conflict arose, the city would grant Crews and other Guard employees military leave to attend drill. This leave is unpaid, but Guard employees may turn in their military pay for attending drill and in exchange receive their regular City pay. Guard employees may also allocate their accrued vacation days, personal days, and compensatory time off to cover days missed for drill, thereby collecting City pay and military pay for time spent at drill. The Department also maintained a policy for several years that allowed Guard employees to reschedule work shifts that fell on drill weekends. In a 1997 memorandum, Crews's supervisor told him that he could use the monthly weekend drills as his days off for that week so he would not lose any pay, and he would also collect his military pay. The Department extended this scheduling benefit to three other Guard members who joined the department between 2000 and 2003; non-Guard employees did not have a comparable opportunity to reschedule work shifts missed for outside activities. When the department hired two additional Guard members, Mendenall rescinded

the work scheduling policy. The chief and the assistant chief of police, Deichman, determined that extending the policy to an increasing number of Guard employees would result in too many costly scheduling conflicts, and the cost of maintaining the policy for all current and future Guard employees was increasing. Following the rescission of the scheduling policy, Crews tried to persuade Deichman to continue allowing him to reschedule his work days missed for drill, but Deichman refused. Because of the rescission of the work scheduling policy, Crews was no longer able to collect a full week's pay from the City when he missed a weekend shift for drill, unless he used up his limited days of paid time off. In December 2006, Crews filed a complaint against the City of Mt. Vernon, Mendenall, and Deichman, alleging that the rescission of the work scheduling policy denied him a benefit of employment based on military status, in violation of USERRA, and that Deichman retaliated against him for opposing the rescission of the policy by making negative comments toward Crews and denying him advancement opportunities.]

Tinder, Circuit Judge

… The district court concluded that… the City was not required to give Crews preferential work scheduling benefits not generally available to non-Guard employees. The court also rejected Crews's retaliation claim, concluding that… making negative comments, and noting his negative attitude on a quarterly evaluation were not "materially adverse" employment actions. The court accordingly denied Crews's motion for summary judgment and granted the City's motion for summary judgment. Crews timely appealed.

A. Denial of a "Benefit of Employment"…
USERRA affords broad protections to service members against employment discrimination, providing that members "shall not be denied initial employment, reemployment,

[19] *Dean v. Consumer Product Safety Comm.*, 548 F.3d 1370 (Fed. Cir. 2008).

retention in employment, promotion, or any benefit of employment by an employer on the basis of that membership...." [38 U.S.C. 4311(a)] A "benefit of employment" means "any advantage, profit, privilege, gain, status, account, or interest (other than wages or salary for work performed) that accrues by reason of an employment contract or agreement or an employer policy, plan, or practice and includes ... the opportunity to select work hours or location of employment." [§ 4303(2)]. Under the burden-shifting framework of [USERRA] a plaintiff makes out a prima facie case of discrimination by showing that his service membership was "a motivating factor in the employer's action." The employer must then "prove that the action would have been taken in the absence of such membership."...

... Crews argues that the City violated § 4311 by rescinding an existing policy of providing Guard employees with special work scheduling benefits. According to Crews, while USERRA may not have required the City to establish that policy in the first place, having voluntarily done so, the City cannot now renege.... Crews's interpretation of § 4311 admittedly finds some support in the statutory language of USERRA. [But] the better interpretation is that the "benefit of employment" referenced in § 4311(a) is one provided to both military and nonmilitary employees. Section 4311 is entitled "Discrimination against persons who serve in the uniformed services and acts of reprisal prohibited." Accordingly, courts have indicated that the statute reaches only discriminatory employment actions that provide military employees with fewer benefits....

Given the anti-discriminatory purpose of § 4311, the Department's decision in this case to provide equal work scheduling benefits to all employees does not violate USERRA. The preferential work scheduling policy that the Department previously extended to Guard employees was not a "benefit of employment" within the meaning of § 4311(a), as this benefit was not one generally available to all employees. It follows that the Department's rescission of that policy could not be a "denial" of any "benefit of employment" actionable under § 4311(a).

... The Department's recent decision to revoke those preferences and return to the "floor" requirements, while understandably disappointing to Crews, does not violate USERRA. We add that, if Guard employees like Crews want legal protection against their employer's discretion to unilaterally revoke special benefits, they can negotiate to make those benefits part of a "contract" or "agreement." Here, however, the Department's work scheduling policy for Guard employees was strictly voluntary, and Crews has not claimed that any contract or other provision of law required the defendants to maintain the policy....

B. Retaliation Under USERRA

We turn to Crews's claim that the defendants retaliated against him for voicing his opposition to the rescission of the work scheduling policy. In addition to protecting against discrimination on the basis of service membership, § 4311 prohibits an employer from taking "any adverse employment action against any person because such person ... has taken an action to enforce a protection" provided by USERRA. Although we have not previously discussed the statute's "adverse employment action" requirement in the specific context of a USERRA retaliation claim, our case law on other civil rights statutes describes those employment actions that are sufficiently "adverse" to be actionable retaliation. "An adverse employment action must be materially adverse, not merely an inconvenience or a change in job responsibilities." "An adverse employment action is one that significantly alters the terms and conditions of the employee's job." Materially adverse actions include termination, demotion accompanied by a decrease in pay, or a material loss of benefits or responsibilities, but do not include "everything that makes an employee unhappy." There is no reason to understand "adverse employment action" differently in the USERRA context.

Echoing an argument made in support of his denial-of-benefit claim, Crews argues that applying the "materially adverse" standard from other civil rights statutes to his USERRA retaliation claim fails to appreciate the different purposes of USERRA and conventional civil rights laws.... Requiring material adversity for both types of claims is consistent with the Supreme Court's decision in *Burlington Northern & Santa Fe Railway Co. v. White*, 548 U.S. 53, 126 S.Ct. 2405, 165 L.Ed.2d 345 (2006), in which the Court established the standard for retaliation claims under Title VII. The Court concluded that, although the retaliatory actions prohibited by Title VII are not limited to harms that are employment-related or that occur in the workplace, the action must nonetheless be "materially adverse," such that it "well might have dissuaded a reasonable worker from making or supporting a charge of discrimination." Requiring "material adversity" is important, the Court continued, to discourage civil rights litigation over "trivial harms."

In line with Burlington, we do not think that the protections of USERRA are so sweeping as to provide a remedy for mere "trivial harms." ... Applying the "materially adverse" standard to Crews's claim, it is clear that Crews suffered no actionable retaliation. Crews first points to disparaging comments that Chief Mendenall made to the press about Crews's USERRA lawsuit. However, negative employer comments will support a retaliation claim only if they are "severe and pervasive." The plaintiff must show more than "petty slights or minor annoyances that often take place at work and that all employees experience." Here, the purportedly "disparaging" comments cited by Crews are nothing more than Mendenall's statements to the media that Crews's USERRA lawsuit "had no merit" and that his allegations were "simply untrue." These isolated comments, which occurred outside the workplace and had no impact on Crews's conditions of employment, are not severe enough to be actionable retaliation....

Accordingly, Crews has failed to establish a materially adverse employment action, and the district court properly granted summary judgment for the defendants on Crews's retaliation claim.

Conclusion

For the foregoing reasons, we AFFIRM the district court's grant of summary judgment in favor of the defendants.

Case Questions

1. According to Crews, what actions of the Police Department violated his rights under USERRA?

2. Does USERRA require an employer to provide benefits to employees with military obligations that are not made available to other employees? Does USERRA prohibit an employer from doing so? Explain.

3. What actions are prohibited by the antiretaliation provisions of USERRA? What actions did Crews claim constituted retaliation against him? Did the court agree? Why?

11-3b Military Family Rights Under the FMLA

In 2013, the U.S. Department of Labor (DOL) issued new regulations operationalizing expanded Family and Medical Leave Act rights for members of the armed forces and their families. The DOL's final rule springs from the 2010 Defense Authorization Act and affords significantly expanded leave rights for injured servicemen and women, as well as new intermittent-leave rights for spouses and other family members. The DOL's detailed Q&A publication regarding these new and expanded rights is reproduced in Chapter 7. Note in particular in reviewing this Q&A that caregiver rights under the new regulations extend to situations in which the medical condition arises after the injured, ill, or disabled veteran has separated from the service.

Concept *Summary* 11.3

UNIFORMED SERVICES EMPLOYMENT AND REEMPLOYMENT RIGHTS ACT

- USERRA prohibits employers from discriminating against employees because of their (noncareer) service in the military

- To qualify, employees must:
  - give the employer notice of the period of military service;
  - be absent for a cumulative total of less than five years; and
  - submit an application for reemployment within the designated time period.

- Employers are not required to reinstate employees if:
  - the employer's circumstances have changed so that reemployment would be unreasonable or impossible;
  - the reemployment would cause undue hardship in accommodation, training, or effort; or
  - the initial employment was for a brief, nonrecurring period.

11-4   The National Labor Relations Act

The unfair labor practice prohibitions of the National Labor Relations Act (NLRA) may be used to attack discrimination in employment in some instances. In *United Packinghouse Workers Union v. NLRB*,[20] the court held that racial discrimination by an employer was an unfair labor practice in violation of Section 8(a)(1) of the NLRA. Retaliation against employees who filed charges with the EEOC, by refusing to recall them from layoff, was held to violate Section 8(a)(1) in *Frank Briscoe Inc. v. NLRB*.[21]

Unions that discriminate against African Americans in membership or in conditions of employment are in violation of Section 8(b)(1)(A) and their duty of fair representation of all employees in the bargaining unit according to the Supreme Court decision of *Syres v. Oil Workers*.[22] (See the *Steele v. Louisville & Nashville R.R.* case in Chapter 18.) In *Hughes Tool Co.*[23] the NLRB held that a union's refusal to represent African American workers violated Section 8(b)(1)(A) and was grounds to rescind the union's certification as bargaining agent. Discrimination against female employees by a union also violates Section 8(b)(1)(A) as held in *NLRB v. Glass Bottle Blowers Local 106*.[24] (See Chapter 18 for a discussion of the duty of fair representation.)

Employers and unions that negotiate, or attempt to negotiate, discriminatory provisions in seniority systems, pay scales, or promotion policies may commit unfair labor practices in violation of Section 8(a)(5) or Section 8(b)(3) by refusing to bargain in good faith.

11-5   Constitutional Prohibitions Against Discrimination

Certain provisions of the U.S. Constitution may be used by public sector employees to challenge discrimination in their employment. The Constitution regulates the relationship between the government and individuals; therefore, the Constitution's prohibitions against discrimination apply only to government employers and to private employers acting under government support or compulsion (state action).

11-5a   Due Process and Equal Protection

The primary constitutional provisions used to attack discrimination are the guarantees of due process of law and equal protection found in the Fifth and Fourteenth Amendments. The Fifth Amendment applies to the federal government, and the Fourteenth Amendment applies to state and local governments. In addition, specific enactments such as the First Amendment guarantee of freedom of religion may be used to challenge

---

[20] 416 F.2d 1126 (D.C. Cir. 1969).

[21] 637 F.2d 946 (3d Cir. 1981).

[22] 350 U.S. 892 (1955).

[23] 56 L.R.R.M. 1289 (1964).

[24] 520 F.2d 693 (6th Cir. 1975).

discrimination. In *Brown v. GSA*,[25] the Supreme Court held that the only remedy available to persons complaining of racial discrimination in federal government employment is provided by Section 717 of Title VII. However, not all federal employees are covered by Title VII. For example, members of the armed forces or the personal staff members of elected officials, who are not covered by Title VII, could file constitutional challenges to alleged discrimination.

In the case of *Davis v. Passman*,[26] the Supreme Court held that a member of a congressman's staff, who was not covered by Title VII, could bring a suit under the Fifth Amendment against her employer for discharging her because of intentional gender discrimination.

Challenges to employment discrimination under the due process and equal protection guarantees involve claims that the discriminatory practices deny the victims of the discrimination rights equal, or treatment equal, to those who are not targets of the discrimination. Blanket prohibitions on employment of females, or of members of a minority group, deny those employees due process of law by presuming that all women, or members of the minority group, are unable to perform the requirements of a particular job.

In *Washington v. Davis*,[27] the Supreme Court held that the constitutional prohibitions applied only to invidious, or intentional, discrimination; claims alleging disparate impact could not be brought under the constitutional provisions.

Not all intentional discrimination on the basis of race, gender, and so on is unconstitutional, however. In considering claims of discrimination under the Constitution, the court will first consider the basis of discrimination. Some bases of discrimination, or "classifications" by government action, will be considered **suspect classes**. That is, there is little justification for treating persons differently because they fall within a particular class. For example, racial discrimination involves classifying employees, and treating them differently, by race. Such conduct can rarely be justified. The court will strictly scrutinize any offered justification for such conduct. The government must show that such classification, or treatment, is required because of a compelling government interest, and no less discriminatory alternatives exist. For example, classifying employees by race, while discriminatory, may be justified if the reason is to compensate employees who had been victims of prior racial discrimination.

suspect class
a basis of discrimination, classification, or differential treatment—such as race, color, gender, religion, or national origin—by government action for which there is little legitimate justification for treating persons because of such characteristics

11-5b Affirmative Action and the Constitution

Affirmative action has become an extremely controversial issue in recent years (see the discussion in Chapter 6). The courts have been growing more skeptical about the legality of affirmative action requirements imposed by government entities.

The U.S. Supreme Court, in the 1995 decision *Adarand Constructors, Inc. v. Pena*,[28] held that federal government affirmative action programs giving preferential treatment

---

[25] 425 U.S. 820 (1976).

[26] 442 U.S. 228 (1979).

[27] 426 U.S. 229 (1976).

[28] 515 U.S. 200 (1995).

strict scrutiny test
a constitutional analysis used by courts hearing equal protection claims involving governmental discrimination based on a "suspect class." This test requires the government to demonstrate that the discriminatory treatment was necessary to achieve a compelling government purpose and that the governmental action was "narrowly tailored" to achieve the compelling purpose

based on race or color must be justified under the **strict scrutiny test**. This test requires the government to demonstrate that the affirmative action program was necessary to achieve a compelling government purpose and that the program was "narrowly tailored" to achieve the compelling purpose. It must also show that it did not unduly harm those who were not given the preferential treatment.

A majority of the Supreme Court upheld the use of affirmative action in admissions by a public university, the University of Michigan, in two cases, *Grutter v. Bollinger*[29] and *Gratz v. Bollinger*.[30] In these cases, which did not deal with employment, the Supreme Court held that achieving the educational benefits of a diverse student body was a compelling governmental interest. However, in a more recent case dealing with public schools, *Parents Involved in Community Schools v. Seattle School Dist. No. 1*,[31] the Supreme Court held that diversity in education was not a sufficient justification for the schools' use of racial classifications in assigning students to particular schools.

Extending the rationale of these cases to employment would indicate that achieving the benefits of a diverse work force may be a sufficiently compelling governmental interest to justify the use of affirmative action programs for hiring or promotion decisions by public sector employers. However, an affirmative action program must also be narrowly tailored to achieve the compelling governmental purpose. The courts have held that affirmative action programs that give a relative preference rather than an absolute one—race or gender is used as a "plus factor" rather than as the determinative factor—are narrowly tailored. Programs that are temporary and that will cease when the employer achieves a more diverse work force have also been held to be narrowly tailored.

Wygant v. Jackson Board of Education[32] involved an affirmative action program that was not narrowly tailored. In this case, the collective bargaining agreement between a public school board and the teachers' union contained an affirmative action program in the event that layoffs of teachers were necessary. Layoffs would be based on seniority ("last hired, first fired") unless the effect of the seniority-based layoffs would reduce the percentage of minority teachers at a given school below the percentage of minority students in that school. If that were the case, the affirmative action program would require the layoff of senior nonminority teachers ahead of minority teachers with less seniority. The purpose of the plan was to ensure the presence of minority teachers in the schools so that the minority teachers could serve as role models for minority students and encourage them to get an education. Wygant, a white teacher who lost her job under the affirmative action plan, brought suit, arguing that the plan calling for race-based layoffs was in violation of the Equal Protection Clause of the Fourteenth Amendment. The Supreme Court held that although providing role models for minority students might be a compelling governmental purpose, a plan requiring the layoff of teachers because of their race was "not sufficiently narrowly tailored" to the achievement of that purpose. The Court stated "the … selection of layoffs as the means to accomplish even a valid purpose cannot satisfy the demands of the Equal Protection Clause."

---

[29] 539 U.S. 306 (2003).

[30] 539 U.S. 244 (2003).

[31] 551 U.S. 701 (2007).

[32] 476 U.S. 267 (1986).

Remedial affirmative action programs—that is, programs adopted to remedy illegal discrimination—have generally been held to be constitutional. In *Local 28, Sheet Metal Workers Int. Ass'n. v. EEOC*,[33] the U.S. Supreme Court held that courts may impose affirmative action programs to remedy "persistent or egregious discrimination," even if the affirmative action plan had the effect of benefiting individuals who were not themselves victims of discrimination. The Court emphasized that affirmative action programs should be imposed by a court only as a last resort and such programs should be "tailor[ed] … to fit the nature of the violation" the court seeks to remedy. In *Local 93, Int. Ass'n. of Firefighters v. Cleveland*,[34] the Supreme Court held that the parties in an employment discrimination suit may enter into a settlement agreement (known as a consent decree) requiring an affirmative action program where the employer has been found guilty of discrimination. The consent decree's affirmative action program may benefit minority employees who were not personally victims of illegal employment discrimination.

In *U.S. v. Paradise*,[35] the Supreme Court upheld a court-ordered affirmative action plan that required the Alabama Public Safety Department to promote to corporal one African American state trooper for every white trooper promoted, until either African Americans occupied 25 percent of the corporal positions or until the department instituted a promotion policy that did not have an adverse impact on African American troopers. The majority held that the order was necessary to remedy past "pervasive, systematic and obstinate" discrimination by the department.

11-5c Other Constitutional Issues

non-suspect class
a basis of discrimination, classification, or differential by government action which is neutral with regard to race, color, gender, religion, or national origin, and which is related to legitimate government interests; examples of non-suspect classes are age, veteran status, or personal achievement

Some forms of discrimination involve classifications that may be more neutral than racial classifications. The courts refer to such classifications as **non-suspect classes**. When discrimination is based on non-suspect classes, the court will consider whether the discriminatory classification bears a reasonable relationship to a valid state interest. For example, in *Personnel Administrator of Massachusetts v. Feeney*,[36] the Supreme Court upheld a Massachusetts law that required all veterans to be given preference for state civil service positions over nonveterans, even though the law had the effect of discriminating against women because veterans were overwhelmingly male. The classification of applicants on the basis of veteran status was reasonably necessary for the valid government objective of rewarding veterans for the sacrifices of military service.

In *Cleveland Board of Education v. LaFleur*,[37] the Supreme Court struck down a rule imposing a mandatory maternity leave on teachers reaching the fifth month of pregnancy on grounds that it violated the due process rights of the teachers. The rule denied the teachers the freedom of personal choice over matters of family life, and it was not shown to be sufficiently related to the school-board interests of administrative scheduling and protecting the health of teachers. The rule had the effect of classifying every teacher reaching the fifth

---

[33] 478 U.S. 421 (1986).

[34] 478 U.S. 501 (1986).

[35] 480 U.S. 149 (1987).

[36] 442 U.S. 256 (1979).

[37] 414 U.S. 632 (1974).

month of pregnancy as being physically incapable of performing the duties of the job, when such a teacher's ability or inability to perform during pregnancy is an individual matter.

Personal grooming requirements and restrictions on hair length and facial hair for police officers were upheld by the Supreme Court in *Kelley v. Johnson*[38] because they were reasonably related to the maintenance of discipline among members of the police force. In *Goldman v. Weinberger*,[39] the Supreme Court dismissed a challenge under the First Amendment to an Air Force uniform regulation that prevented an Orthodox Jew from wearing his yarmulke while on duty. Despite the fact that the yarmulke was unobtrusive, the regulations were justified by the Air Force interest in maintaining morale and discipline, which were held to be legitimate military ends. The courts consistently upheld the constitutionality of the military's "don't ask, don't tell" policy barring persons from serving in the military if they engage in homosexual conduct or demonstrate a propensity to engage in such conduct, as in *Phillips v. Perry*[40] and *Homasson v. Perry*.[41] Nevertheless, in December 2011, President Obama signed the Don't Ask, Don't Tell Repeal Act.

THE **WORKING** LAW

President Obama and the LGBT Community

Earlier today, I had the opportunity to meet with a small group of openly gay and lesbian servicemembers, together with several of their partners and spouses. We celebrated the one year anniversary of the repeal of "Don't Ask, Don't Tell."

The servicemembers represented a range of ranks and services. All of them agreed that the most remarkable aspect about their post-repeal service is that, after just one year, serving in the military without DADT feels unremarkable because the transition has been so smooth.

It should come as no surprise to any of us that the men and women of our armed forces have handled the repeal of DADT with the professionalism and class that we have come to expect from the finest fighting force in the world. As a consequence, our national security has been strengthened.

As the President said in a statement issued today, "Gay and lesbian Americans now no longer need to hide who they love in order to serve the country they love. It is a testament to the professionalism of our men and women in uniform that this change was implemented in an orderly manner, preserving unit cohesion, recruitment, retention and military effectiveness."

Earlier this year, I had the opportunity to address the Servicemembers Legal Defense Network National Dinner, and I spoke about the kind of change repeal of DADT has brought:

> Thanks to the work we've done together, if anyone ever asks you what change is all about, you can tell them that change is finally being able to put a family photo on your desk. Change is being able to tell your coworkers what you and your loved one

---

[38] 425 U.S. 238 (1976).

[39] 475 U.S. 503 (1976).

[40] 106 F.3d 1420 (9th Cir. 1997).

[41] 80 F.3d 915 (4th Cir. 1996).

did over the weekend, or what you have planned for your family vacation. Change is being able to share stories about your family with fellow servicemembers while you're away from home, and living with the fear that you may never see them again. Change is knowing that if you make that ultimate sacrifice for your country, someone will be able to notify your loved ones. That's change.

On behalf of President Obama, I want to thank all of the servicemembers, veterans, and military families who fought for the repeal of DADT and who honor us with their service and sacrifice. We will never forget what you've done for America, and we are committed to making sure that we serve you as well as you have served us.

Source: Valerie Jarrett, "Marking One Year Since the Repeal of Don't Ask, Don't Tell," The White House, September 20, 2012, available at https://www.whitehouse.gov/blog/2012/09/20/marking-one-year-repeal-don-t-ask-don-t-tell.

Concept *Summary* 11.4

CONSTITUTIONAL PROHIBITIONS AGAINST DISCRIMINATION

- U.S. Constitution
  - Due process of law and equal protection under the Fifth and Fourteenth Amendments
  - Basis of discrimination considered first

- Affirmative action
  - Strict scrutiny test: Requires the government to demonstrate that an affirmative action plan is necessary to achieve a compelling government purpose and is narrowly tailored to achieve that purpose
  - Remedial affirmative action programs: Programs adopted to remedy illegal discrimination; should be tailored to fit the nature of the violation

11-6   State EEO and Employment Laws

The discussion of EEO law in this and preceding chapters has focused mainly on federal legislation. In addition to the various federal laws, most states also have their own equal employment opportunity legislation or regulations. State laws figure into the enforcement of federal laws. Recall that under Title VII, persons complaining of employment discrimination must file with the appropriate state or local EEO agency before taking their complaint to the federal Equal Employment Opportunity Commission. Such state or local EEO laws may provide greater protection than the federal legislation does. For example, the Michigan Civil Rights Act specifically prohibits discrimination based on height or weight, and the District of Columbia Human Rights Law prohibits discrimination based on personal appearance or political affiliation. The New York State Human Rights Law prohibits age discrimination in employment against employees aged 18 or older (unless age is a bona fide occupational qualification [BFOQ]).

11-6a   Gender Discrimination

All state EEO laws prohibit gender discrimination in terms or conditions of employment, except in those instances where sex may be a BFOQ. Most state laws interpret gender discrimination as including sexual harassment, but some state laws, such as Minnesota's Human Rights Act, specifically prohibit sexual harassment in addition to the general prohibition on gender discrimination. Maine law requires employers to post a notice in the workplace informing employees that sexual harassment is illegal and describing how to file a complaint of sexual harassment with the Maine Human Rights Commission.

11-6b   Sexual Orientation Discrimination

Although federal law does not prohibit discrimination because of sexual orientation or sexual preference, a number of states have legislation prohibiting such discrimination. California, Colorado, Connecticut, Delaware, Hawaii, Illinois, Iowa, Maine, Maryland, Massachusetts, Minnesota, Nevada, New Hampshire, New Jersey, New Mexico, New York, Oregon, Rhode Island, Vermont, Washington, Wisconsin, and the District of Columbia prohibit employment discrimination based on sexual orientation or sexual preference by public and private sector employers. Several other states, including Louisiana, Michigan, Ohio, and Pennsylvania, prohibit public sector employers from discriminating because of sexual orientation or sexual preference through executive orders issued by the governor. In some large cities, including New York City and San Francisco, local ordinances prohibit employment discrimination because of sexual orientation or sexual preference.

By way of contrast, on March 12, 2015, Utah Governor Gary Herbert signed into law Senate Bill 296, known as the Antidiscrimination and Religious Freedom Amendments to the state's statute banning discrimination in employment and housing. The statute, one of a number of state laws enacted here and there across the country in reaction to the Supreme Court's decision that the Defense of Marriage Act was unconstitutional and its negative impact on state DOMAs, reads as follows:

34A-5-102. Definitions—Unincorporated entities
(i)(ii) "Employer" does not include:

(A) a religious organization, a religious corporation sole, a religious association, a religious society, a religious educational institution, or a religious leader, when that individual is acting in the capacity of a religious leader;
(B) any corporation or association constituting an affiliate, a wholly owned subsidiary, or an agency of any religious organization, religious corporation sole, religious association, or religious society; or
(C) the Boy Scouts of America or its councils, chapters, or subsidiaries ...

34A-5-111. Application to the freedom of expressive association and the free exercise of religion.

This chapter may not be interpreted to infringe upon the freedom of expressive association or the free exercise of religion protected by the First Amendment of the United States Constitution and Article I, Sections 1, 4, and 15 of the Utah Constitution. ...

34A-5-112. Religious liberty protections—Expressing beliefs and commitments in workplace—Prohibition on employment actions against certain employee speech.

(1) An employee may express the employee's religious or moral beliefs and commitments in the workplace in a reasonable, non-disruptive, and non-harassing way on equal terms with similar types of expression of beliefs or commitments allowed by the employer in the workplace, unless the expression is in direct conflict with the essential business-related interests of the employer.

(2) An employer may not discharge, demote, terminate, or refuse to hire any person, or retaliate against, harass, or discriminate in matters of compensation or in terms, privileges, and conditions of employment against any person otherwise qualified, for lawful expression or expressive activity outside of the workplace regarding the person's religious, political, or personal convictions, including convictions about marriage, family, or sexuality, unless the expression or expressive activity is in direct conflict with the essential business-related interests of the employer. ...

57-21-3. Exemptions—Sale by private individuals—Nonprofit organizations—Noncommercial transactions. ...

(2) This chapter does not apply to a dwelling or a temporary or permanent residence facility if:

(a) the discrimination is by sex, sexual orientation, gender identity, or familial status for reasons of personal modesty or privacy, or in the furtherance of a religious institution's free exercise of religious rights under the First Amendment of the United States Constitution or the Utah Constitution; and

(b) the dwelling or the temporary or permanent residence facility is:
(i) operated by a nonprofit or charitable organization;
(ii) owned by, operated by, or under contract with a religious organization, a religious association, a religious educational institution, or a religious society;
(iii) owned by, operated by, or under contract with an affiliate of an entity described in Subsection (2)(b)(ii); or
(iv) owned by or operated by a person under contract with an entity described in Subsection (2)(b)(ii).

... (4)(a)(i) Unless membership in a religion is restricted by race, color, sex, or national origin, this chapter does not prohibit an entity described in Subsection (4)(a) (ii) from:

(A) limiting the sale, rental, or occupancy of a dwelling or temporary or permanent residence facility the entity owns or operates for primarily noncommercial purposes to persons of the same religion; or

(B) giving preference to persons of the same religion when selling, renting, or selecting occupants for a dwelling, or a temporary or permanent residence facility, the entity owns or operates for primarily noncommercial purposes.

      (ii) The following entities are entitled to the exemptions described in Subsection (4)(a)(i):

      (A) a religious organization, association, or society; or

      (B) a nonprofit institution or organization operated, supervised, or controlled by or in conjunction with a religious organization, association, or society.

... (7) This chapter does not prohibit a nonprofit educational institution from:

      (a) requiring its single students to live in a dwelling, or a temporary or permanent residence facility, that is owned by, operated by, or under contract with the nonprofit educational institution;

      (b) segregating a dwelling, or a temporary or permanent residence facility, that is owned by, operated by, or under contract with the nonprofit educational institution on the basis of sex or familial status or both:

          (i) for reasons of personal modesty or privacy; or

          (ii) in the furtherance of a religious institution's free exercise of religious rights under the First Amendment of the United States Constitution or the Utah Constitution....

11-6c Family Friendly Legislation

A number of states have legislation similar to the federal Family and Medical Leave Act, which allows employees to take unpaid leave for childbirth, adoption, or serious illness of a child, parent, or spouse. California's Fair Employment and Housing Act requires that an employer reinstate an employee returning from pregnancy leave to her previous job, unless that job was unavailable because of business necessity. In that case, an employer is required to make a reasonable, good-faith effort to provide a similar position for the employee. New Jersey law allows employees to take up to six weeks of paid medical or family care leave under the state's disability insurance program. The District of Columbia requires employers to provide paid medical or family care leave; the amount of leave that employees accrue depends upon the size of the employer and the number of hours worked by the employees.

New York law protects the right of a mother to breast-feed her child in any public or private place where she is authorized to be, and allows employees who are nursing mothers to take reasonable unpaid break time to express breast milk; employers are to make reasonable efforts to provide a room where an employee may express breast milk in privacy. Several states require that employers allow employees time off (without pay) to attend their children's school meetings or conferences if held during normal working hours. The number of hours allowed per year varies by state, and Nevada simply prohibits an employer from discharging an employee for absences due to school conferences or meetings. In each case, the employee is required to give appropriate advance notice to the employer. New York requires employers with 20 or more employees to allow employees leave time to donate blood; such employees may take up to three hours' leave in any 12-month period.

11-7   Other Employment Legislation

11-7a   Whistleblower Laws

whistleblower
employee who reports or attempts to report employer wrongdoing or actions threatening public health or safety to government authorities

A number of federal and state laws provide some protection for **whistleblowers**—employees who report employer wrongdoing or actions threatening public health or safety. The federal Civil Service Reform Act[42] provides general protection for civil service workers from any discipline or retaliation because they have disclosed a violation of laws or regulations, gross mismanagement or a gross waste of funds, or a substantial and specific danger to the public health or safety. The federal Office of Special Counsel is responsible for investigating and pursuing claims of whistleblowers. A number of specific federal laws provide protection from retaliation for employees who report violations of those laws. Examples include the Safe Drinking Water Act, which protects employees who report illegal pollution of water, and the Federal Mine Health and Safety Act, which protects employees reporting mine safety violations.

The Sarbanes-Oxley Act of 2002,[43] which was passed in response to the corporate scandals involving Enron and WorldCom, imposes both civil and criminal penalties for employers who take adverse employment actions against whistleblowers. The legislation applies to corporations whose shares are publicly traded in the U.S. The criminal provisions make it a federal crime to knowingly retaliate against persons who provide information to law enforcement officials relating to the possible commission of any federal offense. Penalties include fines of up to $250,000 and imprisonment of up to 10 years for individual violators and fines of up to $500,000 for corporations. The civil provisions allow suits by employees allegedly retaliated against by their employers for providing information or cooperating in investigations related to violations of specified securities laws, SEC rules or regulations, or any other provision of federal law relating to shareholder fraud.[44] The civil whistleblower provisions are administered by the Department of Labor and provide for remedies including

- Reinstatement
- Back pay
- Legal fees and costs
- Compensatory damages

The whistleblower provisions of Sarbanes-Oxley do not apply to foreign citizens working abroad for foreign subsidiaries of U.S. corporations.[45]

All 50 states and the District of Columbia have some form of whistleblower laws. Some state laws, such as those of Connecticut, Florida, Hawaii, and Maine, cover both private and public sector employees; most such laws, however, cover only public sector workers. In California, Louisiana, and New Jersey, both public and private sector employees who reasonably believe that an employer is acting illegally are protected if they report such actions to the authorities. New York has separate legislation for public and private employers.

---

[42] 5 U.S.C. § 2303.

[43] Pub. L. No. 107-204, 116 Stat. 745.

[44] *Livingston v. Wyeth, Inc.*, 520 F.3d 344 (4th Cir. 2008).

[45] *Carnero v. Boston Scientific Corp.*, 433 F.3d 1 (1st Cir. 2006).

In New York, public sector employees who reasonably believe that their employer has violated the law, and that the violation poses a "substantial and specific danger" to public health or safety, are protected. However, according to *Green v. Saratoga A.R.C.*,[46] the private sector whistleblower law requires that the conduct employees report must be an actual violation of a law, rule, or regulation; a reasonable belief that the conduct was illegal is not sufficient to state a claim under the law.

The following case involves the question of whether testimony in a civil suit is protected activity under the Michigan Whistleblower Protection Act.

» CASE 11.2

HENRY V. CITY OF DETROIT

234 Mich.App. 405, 594 N.W.2d 107 (Mich. Ct. App. 1999), *appeal denied*, 461 Mich. 937, 606 N.W.2d 24 (Mich. 1999)

Facts: Henry was a commander in the Detroit Police Department. After the death of a suspect (Green) in police custody, the department formed a board of review to investigate the death and to recommend whether any officers should be criminally charged. Henry was the chairman of the board of review. McKinnon, the police chief, gave orders that effectively precluded the board of review from performing its obligations. As a result, some innocent officers were falsely accused and disciplined by the police department.

One of those officers, Lessnau, was acquitted of killing Green and then filed a civil suit against the police department. During the trial of Lessnau's suit, Henry was called as a witness and testified that the department rules concerning the board of review were violated and the board of review was not allowed to perform its duties. Henry also testified before the Michigan Employment Relations Commission (MERC) in an unrelated matter.

Less than four months after plaintiff's testimony in the civil suit and less than one month following his testimony before the MERC, Henry was given the choice of taking an early retirement or a demotion. He claimed the forced retirement was in retaliation for his testimony in the civil suit and before the MERC. The city claimed that he was being demoted because of poor job performance and for being out of his precinct during the middle of several work days. Henry filed suit under Michigan's Whistleblower's Protection Act [MWPA, MCL 15.362; MSA 17.428(2)].

After a trial, the jury found that defendants city of Detroit and Police Chief McKinnon retaliated against plaintiff for his testimony in the civil suit and awarded him $1.08 million in damages. The defendants appealed to the Michigan Court of Appeals.

Issue: Has Henry established a prima facie case of retaliation because of his whistleblowing?

Decision: To establish a prima facie violation of the WPA, a plaintiff must show (1) that the plaintiff was engaged in a protected activity as defined by the WPA, (2) that the plaintiff was discharged, and (3) a causal connection existed between the protected activity and the discharge. The plain language of the statute provides protection for two types of "whistleblowers": (1) those who report, or are about to report, violations of law, regulation, or rule to a public body; and (2) those who are requested by a public body to participate in an investigation held by that public body or in a court action. "Type 1" whistleblowers are persons who takes it upon themselves to communicate the employer's wrongful conduct to a public body in an attempt to bring the violation to light to remedy the situation or harm done by the violation. "Type 2" are those who participate in a previously initiated investigation or hearing at the behest of a public body. If the plaintiff falls under either category, then that plaintiff has engaged in "protected activity" for purposes of presenting a prima facie case under the MWPA.

---

[46] 233 A.D.2d 821, 650 N.Y.S.2d 441 (N.Y. App. Div. 1996).

Henry testified that the internal procedures governing the board of review were not followed here. Because the board of police commissioners, pursuant to the city charter, drafted the police manual that set forth the procedures governing the board of review, the board of review was a public body within the meaning of the MWPA. The court held that Henry presented a prima facie case of a violation of the MWPA as a Type 2 whistleblower. By giving a deposition in a civil case, Henry clearly participated in a "court action." The court held that Henry's testimony was activity protected by the MWPA—his attendance and testimony were compelled under state law, and "compelled" is a higher standard than the "requested" language of the MWPA. There was also evidence to support the claim that Henry's testimony was causally connected to his demotion or forced retirement: (1) he was a veteran of the Detroit Police Department and had received several honors and citations; (2) prior to his testimony, he had never been reprimanded or subject to any disciplinary action; and (3) less than four months after his testimony, he was forced to choose between a demotion or retirement.

A reasonable jury could conclude that Henry was subjected to such action because he testified in the *Lessnau* case. The court therefore held that Henry had presented a prima facie violation of the MWPA for consideration by the jury. The court affirmed the trial court's award of damages to Henry.

11-7b   Criminal Record

Federal EEO laws do not specifically prohibit employment discrimination based on criminal record. However, refusing to hire applicants because of their arrest records (as opposed to convictions) may constitute disparate impact discrimination in violation of Title VII.[47] Some states have specific prohibitions on discrimination because of criminal records. The New York State Human Rights Law prohibits employment discrimination because of prior criminal convictions, unless such convictions have a direct and specific relationship to the job being sought or when granting employment to the individual would involve an unreasonable risk to the property or safety of others or the general public. The New York Human Rights Law also specifically prohibits employers from seeking information about arrests that did not result in a conviction; this restriction does not apply to applicants for employment as law enforcement officers or to governmental bodies that grant licenses for guns or firearms.

Some states require that employers conduct criminal record background checks on applicants for certain positions:

- Tennessee law requires applicants for jobs with public schools to disclose any prior convictions
- Texas law allows institutions of higher education to obtain background checks on applicants for security-sensitive positions
- Vermont requires persons employed as private security officers, armed guards or couriers, guard dog handlers, and applicants for private detective licenses to undergo background checks for prior convictions
- Missouri requires criminal background checks for persons working as home care providers, youth service workers, school bus drivers, and nursing home workers
- North Carolina requires a background check for applicants and employees in nuclear power plants

---

[47] *Green v. Missouri Pacific Railroad Co.*, 523 F.2d 1290 (8th Cir. 1975).

- Indiana law requires criminal background checks for employees of the state Lottery Commission

A growing number of states, including Delaware, Florida, Hawaii, Indiana, Missouri, Nebraska, New York, and Virginia, require criminal background checks for employees involved in child care or day care.

11-7c Polygraph Testing

The federal Employee Polygraph Protection Act of 1988 (EPPA)[48] severely restricts the right of private employers to require employees to take polygraph, or "lie detector," tests; many states have similar laws. The EPPA does not apply to public sector employers; it prohibits private sector employers, unless they fall under one of four exceptions, from requiring employees or applicants to submit to polygraph tests as a condition of employment. Employers are also prohibited from disciplining or discharging any employees because they refused to submit to a polygraph test. The exceptions under the EPPA allow polygraph testing under the following circumstances:

- Private employees who are working as consultants to, or employees of, firms that are contractors to federal national security intelligence operations

- Employers engaged in the provision of private security services, armored car services, or the installation and maintenance of security alarm systems may require polygraph testing of certain prospective employees

- Employers whose business involves the manufacture, sale, or distribution of controlled substances (drugs) are authorized to test employees who have direct access to the controlled substances

- Employers who have a reasonable basis to suspect that employees may have been involved in an incident that resulted in economic loss to the employer may request that those employees take polygraph tests

The EPPA requires that any polygraph test must be administered by a validly licensed examiner. An employer that requests employees to submit to a polygraph test under the fourth exception (ongoing investigation into an economic loss) must meet specific procedural requirements:

- The employer must provide the employees with a written statement describing the incident being investigated, specifically identifying the economic loss and the reason for testing the particular employees.

- The employees must be given a written notice of the date, time, and location of the test.

- The employees must read, and sign, a written notice that they cannot be required to submit to the test as a condition of employment.

- The employees have the right to review all questions that will be asked during the test and are informed that they have the right to terminate the test at any time.

---

[48] 29 U.S.C. § 2001–§ 2009.

The EPPA specifically forbids the polygraph operator from asking any questions relating to religious beliefs, beliefs or opinions on racial matters, political beliefs or affiliations, any questions relating to sexual behavior, and any questions relating to beliefs, affiliations, or lawful activities of labor unions.

After the test has been administered, the employer must furnish the employees with a written copy of the examiner's conclusions regarding their test, a copy of questions asked, and their charted responses. The polygraph examiner may only disclose information acquired through the test to the employer requesting the test and to the employees subjected to the test; the employer may only disclose information to the employees involved.

Even when an employer may legally administer a polygraph test under the EPPA, and the employer has complied with the procedural requirements, the employer may not discharge, discipline, or otherwise deny employment to an individual solely on the basis of the polygraph test results. The employer must have additional evidence to support any employment action taken against the tested employees. The EPPA is enforced by the federal Secretary of Labor, who may assess civil penalties of up to $10,000 against violators. In addition, individual employees or applicants who allege violations of the EPPA may bring a civil suit for damages, reinstatement, back pay, benefits, and legal fees. The time limit for bringing such suits is three years from the alleged violation. *Rubin v. Tourneau, Inc.*[49] held that the company performing the polygraph test may be sued, along with the employer, by an employee alleging violations of the EPPA. Failure to comply with the EPPA's procedural requirements is a violation subject to civil suit according to *Mennen v. Easter Stores*[50] and *Long v. Mango's Tropical Cafe, Inc.*[51] The following case addresses the question of whether the employer's actions fall under the exceptions of the EPPA.

>> CASE 11.3

CUMMINGS V. WASHINGTON MUTUAL
650 F.3d 1386 (11th Cir. 2011)

Facts: In February 2007, the manager of the Piedmont Commons branch of Washington Mutual Bank conducted a cash audit and discovered a shortage of approximately $58,000. The entire amount was missing from two teller cash dispenser machines that Cummings, the previous branch manager, had access to during his employment at the branch. The manager hired two fraud investigators to look into the shortage. They reviewed surveillance camera still images that they believed showed Cummings and his employees repeatedly violating the defendant's dual control policy, which requires two persons to be present when cash is handled or certain secure areas are accessed. Several current and former employees at the branch told the investigators that Cummings had repeatedly violated the policy during his

---

[49] 797 F. Supp. 247 (S.D.N.Y. 1992).

[50] 951 F. Supp. 838 (N.D. Iowa 1997).

[51] 958 F. Supp. 612 (S.D. Fla. 1997).

tenure as branch manager. The investigators also interviewed Cummings and then asked him to take a polygraph test; he declined to do so. On March 19, 2007, Cummings's employment was terminated; he was told by his supervisor that he was being terminated because of his violations of the dual control policy and not because he refused to take a polygraph test. After his termination, Cummings filed a complaint against Washington Mutual with the Department of Labor, alleging that Washington Mutual had violated the Employee Polygraph Protection Act (EPPA). After the Department of Labor informed him that his claims could not be substantiated, Cummings filed suit against Washington Mutual alleging, among other claims, that the bank violated the EPPA. The district court granted summary judgment for the bank on all counts. Cummings appealed.

Issue: Did the request by Washington Mutual that Cummings take a polygraph test violate the EPPA?

Decision: Under the EPPA, employers generally cannot "require, request, suggest, or cause any employee ... to take or submit to any lie detector test." But employers can request that an employee take a polygraph test on four conditions:

(1)   the test is administered in connection with an ongoing investigation involving economic loss or injury to the employer's business ...;

(2)   the employee had access to the property that is the subject of the investigation;

(3)   the employer has a reasonable suspicion that the employee was involved in the incident or activity under investigation; and

(4)   the employer executes a statement, provided to the examinee before the test, that is signed and that describes with particularity the employee's alleged misconduct and the basis for the employer's reasonable suspicion.

Cummings did not dispute that the second and fourth conditions were satisfied in this case, but he challenged the trial court's conclusions that an "ongoing investigation" existed and that the employer had a "reasonable suspicion" of Cummings. Under the regulations under the EPPA, the existence of an inventory shortage by itself is not a sufficient basis for administering a polygraph test, but such testing in response to a shortage is permitted where the employer obtains additional evidence through a subsequent investigation of specific items missing and a reasonable suspicion exists that the employee to be polygraphed was involved in the incident under investigation. Here, the employer was investigating a specific incident: the disappearance of $58,000 from the Piedmont Commons branch during the time that the plaintiff managed that branch. The regulations do not require employers to have conclusive evidence of a violation before requesting or administering a polygraph test; they only require "additional evidence" suggesting that the employee in question was involved in the incident. Here the employer had obtained evidence—surveillance images and testimony from other employees—of repeated violations of the dual control policy by Cummings and by the employees he managed. Therefore, the request for polygraph testing was made "in connection with an ongoing investigation."

The regulations under the EPPA also define "reasonable suspicion," which is "an observable, articulable basis in fact which indicates that a particular employee was involved in, or responsible for, an economic loss." Under the totality of the circumstances in this case, the employer had a reasonable suspicion that Cummings was involved in the cash shortage. Only four other employees had access to the areas from which the money was taken, and Cummings, the branch manager, was responsible for all four of those employees. The investigators viewed photographic evidence that they believed showed Cummings and his employees accessing money and secure areas in violation of the dual control policy. Cummings's coworkers corroborated that evidence, telling the investigators that Cummings repeatedly violated the policy. These facts gave the employer reason to believe that Cummings was actually capitalizing on that opportunity. The employer therefore had a "reasonable suspicion" about Cummings's involvement in the shortage. Because the employer requested Cummings to submit to a polygraph test in connection with an "ongoing investigation" of a specific incident in which the employer had a "reasonable suspicion" that Cummings was involved, the court of appeals affirmed the trial court's dismissal of Cummings's EPPA claim.

11-7d   Honesty Testing

honesty test
employment test used by employers as a screening device to evaluate employees or applicants on various workplace behaviors such as truthfulness, perceptions about employee theft, admissions of theft, and drug use

Because federal and state legislation generally prohibits employers from requiring employees to take polygraph tests, some employers have turned to other **honesty tests** in an attempt to evaluate employees or applicants. These are usually "paper-and-pencil" tests and may include psychological profile testing. (Most psychological profile tests are generally not intended to be used as an employment screening device, but employers may choose to use them as part of the hiring process.) The honesty tests seek to measure various workplace behaviors such as

- Truthfulness

- Perceptions about the pervasiveness of employee theft

- Illegal drug use

- Admissions of theft

There is some controversy over the validity of honesty tests: A 1990 study by the federal Office of Technology and Assessment found research on the effectiveness of such tests inconclusive, but a 1991 study by the American Psychological Association was much more positive and favorable.

The federal EPPA does not prohibit honesty testing, and neither does most state legislation. However, Massachusetts specifically prohibits employers from using honesty tests; Rhode Island bars using honesty tests as the primary basis of employment decisions, and Wisconsin also limits the use of honesty tests by employers. The use of psychological profile tests as an employee selection device could possibly raise issues under the Americans with Disabilities Act or state antidiscrimination legislation (see Chapter 10). Employers desiring to use psychological profile tests should have a legitimate, work-related rationale for the testing.

11-7e   Off-Duty Conduct

A number of states protect employees from employment discrimination because of their lawful, off-the-job conduct. This legislation is mainly designed to protect smokers or tobacco users from employment discrimination as long as their tobacco use is off duty. Tennessee law protects the off-duty use of "agricultural products not regulated by the alcoholic beverage commission." New York and Minnesota protect the "legal use of consumable products" off duty, covering alcohol as well as tobacco. States such as Illinois, Minnesota, Montana, New York, North Carolina, South Dakota, West Virginia, Wisconsin, and Wyoming protect off-duty smokers from employment discrimination but do allow employers to differentiate between smokers and nonsmokers in the costs of insurance and medical benefits, as long as the cost differential reflects the actual difference in the cost of coverage. In states such as Michigan that do not have such protective legislation, it is legal for employers to fire or refuse to hire smokers.

ethical	DILEMMA

AN ADDITIONAL CHARGE FOR SMOKERS?

As the Employee Benefits Manager at Immense Multinational Business (IMB), you are responsible for trying to hold down the cost of employee medical insurance while still providing comprehensive quality medical care to IMB employees. Lately, you have noticed that some employees, usually those who smoke, have significantly higher medical claims than nonsmokers. Studies indicate that employees who smoke a pack of cigarettes a day have claims that are 18 percent higher than those of nonsmokers; smokers are 29 percent more likely than nonsmokers to have annual medical claims over $5,000. Estimates by the American Lung Association indicate that the medical benefits for smokers cost at least $1,000 more per year than for nonsmokers.

Based on such information, you are considering whether IMB should impose an additional annual charge of $500 for medical benefits and insurance coverage on employees who are smokers. Would such an additional charge for smokers be legal? What arguments can you make for imposing the additional charge on smokers? What arguments can you make for not imposing the additional charge? Should IMB impose the additional charge? Explain your answers.

Section 201-d of the New York State Labor Law probably goes the furthest in protecting off-the-job activities. It prohibits employers from discriminating against employees because of their legal off-duty recreational or political activities. On the question of whether an employee's affair with a coworker was protected "recreational activity" under the legislation, a split developed among various courts. A state appellate court, in the case of *NYS v. Wal-Mart Stores*,[52] held that dating a coworker was not protected under the legislation, while the Federal District Court for the Southern District of New York in two separate cases, *Pasch v. Katz Media Corp.*[53] and *Aquilone v. Republic Nat'l Bank of New York*,[54] held that dating and cohabitation with a coworker were protected. In the following case, the U.S. Court of Appeals for the Second Circuit resolved the split.

---

[52] 207 A.D.2d 150, 621 N.Y.S.2d 158 (N.Y. A.D. 1995). See also *Carey v. de Souza*, 254 A.D.2d 119, 678 N.Y.S.2d 264 (N.Y. A.D. 1998) (the court assumed that dating is a protected recreational activity for purposes of the decision but did not consider the issue on its merits); and *Bilquin v. Roman Catholic Church, Diocese of Rockville Centre*, No. 0118588/99 (Sup. Ct. Nassau County, Sept. 12, 2000) (the definition of "recreational activities" does not include "personal relationships").

[53] 1995 WL 469710, 1995 U.S. Dist. LEXIS 11153 (S.D.N.Y. Aug. 8, 1995).

[54] 1998 WL 872425, 1998 U.S. Dist. LEXIS 19531 (S.D.N.Y. Dec. 15, 1998).

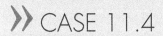

» CASE 11.4

McCAVITT V. SWISS REINSURANCE AMERICA CORPORATION
237 F.3d 166 (2d Cir. 2001) (per curiam)

Facts: McCavitt was employed as an executive by Swiss Reinsurance America Corporation (Swiss Re). He had been involved in a personal relationship with Diane Butler, who was also an executive with Swiss Re. Swiss Re had no formal antifraternization policy, but McCavitt claimed that he was initially denied a promotion and ultimately discharged by Swiss Re because he was dating Butler. McCavitt filed suit against Swiss Re, alleging that his discharge was in violation of New York Labor Law Section 201-d. The trial court dismissed McCavitt's complaint for failure to state a legal claim. McCavitt appealed to the U.S. Court of Appeals for the Second Circuit.

Issue: Is McCavitt protected under New York Labor Law § 201-d from being discharged for dating a co-worker?

Decision: The provisions of § 201-d of New York Labor Law that relate to the issue here state:

2. Unless otherwise provided by law, it shall be unlawful for any employer or employment agency to refuse to hire, employ or license, or to discharge from employment or otherwise discriminate against an individual in compensation, promotion or terms, conditions or privileges of employment because of:...c. an individual's legal recreational activities outside work hours, off of the employer's premises and without use of the employer's equipment or other property.

The statute defines "recreational activities" as:

any lawful, leisure-time activity, for which the employee receives no compensation and which is generally engaged in for recreational purposes, including but not limited to sports, games, hobbies, exercise, reading and the viewing of television, movies and similar material.

While the New York Court of Appeals has not ruled on the question of whether dating was a "recreational activity" protected by § 201-d, several lower courts have. The Appellate Division of the New York Supreme Court held that dating was not a protected activity in *State v. Wal-Mart Stores, Inc.* In *Carey v. de Souza*, the Appellate Division assumed that dating is a protected recreational activity for purposes of the decision but did not consider the issue on its merits. A Nassau County New York Supreme Court in *Bilquin v. Roman Catholic Church, Diocese of Rockville Centre* determined that "recreational activities" did not include "personal relationships."

However, the U.S. District Court for the Southern District of New York has taken the opposite position in two cases. In *Pasch v. Katz Media Corp.*, it held that the New York Court of Appeals would deem cohabitation to be a protected recreational activity under § 201-d; and in *Aquilone v. Republic Nat'l Bank of New York*, it held that an employee's friendship with another person, where contacts between them took place off the employer's premises and not on the employer's time, was protected recreational activity under § 201-d.

The district court here held that it was bound to follow the Third Department's decision in *Wal-Mart*. With regard to interpreting and applying New York state law, the federal courts are bound to apply New York law as interpreted by New York's intermediate appellate courts, unless there is persuasive evidence that the New York Court of Appeals, which has not ruled on this issue, would reach a different conclusion. The court of appeals therefore held that dating a coworker was not protected "recreational activity" under § 201-d. The court overruled the *Pasch* and *Aquilone* cases, and affirmed the trial court's dismissal of McCavitt's suit.

                                                                                              «

In the absence of specific legislative provisions, state tort laws may provide some protection for employees off duty conduct. In *Rulon-Miller v. IBM*,[55] the court awarded an employee damages for invasion of privacy and intentional infliction of emotional distress for her discharge

---

[55] 162 Cal. App. 3d 241, 208 Cal. Rptr. 524 (Cal. Ct. App. 1984).

because she was dating an employee of a competitor. But in *Barbee v. Household Automotive Finance Corporation*,[56] the court held that a supervisor discharged for dating a subordinate did not have a claim for invasion of privacy because he had been repeatedly warned against such conduct and therefore had no reasonable expectation of privacy regarding such conduct.

11-7f   Guns at Work Laws

In *Hansen v. America Online, Inc.*,[57] the Utah Supreme Court rejected a wrongful termination suit brought by several employees who were discharged for violating an employer's policy prohibiting possession of a firearm on the employer's property. The court held that the discharge of the employees was not in violation of public policy and that the private property rights of the employer allowed the employer to ban firearms from its property.

In response to the *Hansen* decision, the National Rifle Association began a lobbying campaign at the state legislature level. As a result of that campaign, a number of states have passed laws that allow employees to bring firearms onto their employer's property, as long as the weapons are kept locked in the employee's vehicle.[58] Oklahoma passed such a law[59] in 2005, making it a criminal offense for any "person, property owner, tenant, employer, or business entity" to prohibit any person, except a convicted felon, from transporting and storing firearms locked in a motor vehicle on "any property set aside for any motor vehicle." The law also provides that property owners who attempt to bar guns from their property are subject to a civil suit to enforce the law and are liable for court costs and legal fees. The law was challenged by a number of employers on the grounds that requiring employers to allow guns on their property would violate the employers' general duty under the federal Occupational Safety and Health Act (OSHA) to provide a safe workplace. The U.S. District Court for the Northern District of Oklahoma agreed with the employers and granted an injunction against enforcement of the law,[60] but on appeal, the U.S. Court of Appeals for the Tenth Circuit reversed the trial court and held that the Oklahoma law was valid and was not in conflict with federal law.[61]

On March 19, 2015, the Texas Senate passed Senate Bill 11, which aims to expand the state's concealed-handgun license to allow holders to carry their weapons into specified buildings on the Lone Star State's public colleges and universities.[62] According to the Law Center to Prevent Gun Violence,[63] as of 2015 approximately half of the 50 states now have laws permitting individuals to be licensed to carry their guns where they will, including in many such statutes into their workplaces.

---

[56] 113 Cal. App. 4th 525, 6 Cal. Rptr. 3d 406 (Cal. Ct. App. 2003).

[57] 96 P.3d 950 (Utah 2004).

[58] States with such laws include Oklahoma, Florida, Georgia, Kansas, Kentucky, Alaska, Minnesota, Mississippi, and Nebraska.

[59] 21 Okla. Stat. § 12897a and § 1290.22.

[60] *ConocoPhillips Co. v. Henry*, 520 F. Supp. 2d 1282 (N.D. Ok. 2007).

[61] *Ramsey Winch, Inc. v. Henry*, 555 F.3d 1199 (10th Cir. 2009).

[62] Sarah Rumpf, "Texas Senate Republicans Cheer Passage of Campus Carry Bill," Breitbart.com, March 19, 2015, available at http://www.breitbart.com/texas/2015/03/19/texas-senate-republicans-cheer-passage-of-campus-carry-bill.

[63] http://smartgunlaws.org.

CHAPTER REVIEW

» Key Terms

contract compliance program	316	**suspect class**	325	**whistleblower**	333
affirmative action plan	317	**strict scrutiny test**	326	**honesty test**	339
		non-suspect class	327		

» Summary

- In addition to the primary EEO laws at the federal level, other legislation protects employees from some other forms of discrimination in employment. The Civil Rights Acts of 1866 and 1870 allow persons who are victims of intentional discrimination to sue for damages: 42 U.S.C. Section 1981 can be used against intentional racial or national origin discrimination, and 42 U.S.C. Section 1983 can be used for intentional discrimination by public sector employers.

- Government contractors are subject to the affirmative action requirements of Executive Order 11246, and employees who serve in the military are protected from employment discrimination by the Uniformed Services Employment and Reemployment Rights Act. The National Labor Relations Act may provide employees with legal remedies against employment discrimination.

- Public sector employers are subject to the constitutional equal protection and due process provisions that prohibit intentional discrimination. The federal courts are becoming increasingly skeptical about governmental affirmative action programs, which entail preferential discrimination based on race or gender. State employment discrimination and employment laws supplement federal legislation and provide additional protection for employees.

» Problems

» Questions

1. Against which kinds of discrimination can 42 U.S.C. Section 1981 be used? What remedies are available to plaintiffs under 42 U.S.C. Section 1981? Against which kinds of discrimination can 42 U.S.C. Section 1983 be used? What remedies are available under 42 U.S.C. Section 1983?

2. When are employees protected from discrimination because of their service in the U.S. military forces? What must the employees do to receive such protection? What remedies are available under the USERRA?

3. When are employers subject to the obligations of E.O. 11246? What does E.O. 11246 require of employers?

4. Can a public sector employer use affirmative action to give hiring preference to female applicants? Can that public sector employer give females preference when deciding which employees to lay off? Explain your answers.

5. Does the U.S. Constitution prohibit all employment discrimination based on race? Explain your answer.

» Case Problems

6. Keller worked for the Maryland Department of Social Services. She sued both the department and the state after she was denied promotion to case worker associate III. She argued that the state had violated Title VII and Section 1983 by refusing to promote her because she was African American. The state moved for dismissal of Keller's Section 1983 count, arguing that Title VII provides a concurrent and more comprehensive remedy and, therefore, preempts Keller from coming under Section 1983.

   How should the court rule? [See *Keller v. Prince George's County Department of Social Services*, 616 F. Supp. 540 (D. Md. 1985).]

7. Marta Davis sued her employer under Section 1981 of the 1866 Civil Rights Act, claiming she was discriminated against because of her Hispanic ancestry. The company contended that Section 1981 was passed in 1866 in response to the enactment of "black codes" in several states, which prevented African Americans from exercising fundamental rights to which they were entitled as part of their newly acquired citizenship. The company asserts that because this was the clear congressional purpose for passing Section 1981, it cannot be stretched to cover national origin discrimination.

   Do you agree? [See *Davis v. Boyle-Midway, Inc.*, 615 F. Supp. 560 (N.D. Ga. 1985).]

8. Bibb County Properties owns and operates a sawmill and mulch processing plant in Grove Hill, Alabama. In July 2011, when each of the plaintiffs still worked at the plant, Jose Victor Zetino became the plant's manager. Zetino is Hispanic; the plaintiffs are African American. They claim that, in the year after Zetino became the plant's manager, the plant's Hispanic employees worked more overtime hours than the plant's non-Hispanic employees. Pointing to payroll data that Bibb provided during discovery, the plaintiffs contend that "Hispanic workers averaged 7.3 hours of overtime per week more than their [African American] counterpart[s]" (and 4.2 hours more per week than their Caucasian counterparts). They attribute the disparity in overtime hours to racial discrimination, contending that Zetino favored his fellow Hispanics when assigning overtime. In support, they assert that Zetino often referred to the plant's Hispanic employees as "my guys" or "my Hispanic guys."

   Can the five plaintiffs, all African Americans, pursue a claim against Bibb under 42 U.S.C. Section 1981? Explain your answer. [See *Brown v. Bibb County Properties LLC*, --- Fed Appx. ---, 2015 WL 1003619 (11th Cir. 2015).]

9. Plaintiff was employed by DK Industries as general manager; she was also a member of the U.S. Army Reserves. Her reserve unit was called up to active duty in Iraq for six months in December 2012, and she gave the employer appropriate notice of her need to be absent from her job for that period. Upon completion of her duty in Bosnia, she returned to the job at DK Industries on July 7, 2012. She was reemployed at the same rate of pay as she received prior to leaving for Bosnia, but the employer did not give her the general pay increase granted by DK to all employees in May 2012. Plaintiff informed the employer that she was entitled to receive the May 2012 pay increase, but the employer refused and told her she was lucky to have a job at all. Three weeks later, plaintiff informed her employer that she was required to attend a two-day training program for the Reserves and that she would be absent from work on August 14 and 15, 2012. The employer complained about the disruption caused by her absence during her service in Bosnia and informed her that her Reserve duty was "too much trouble" and that she was needed on the job. Novak then

presented a copy of her reserve orders to report for the training session, along with a written request for a two-day leave; the employer told her that if she went, she "shouldn't come back." When Novak did not appear for work on August 14, the employer prepared a check for her, with the notation "final pay owing as of termination date, August 14, 2012." The employer presented the check to plaintiff when she reported for work August 18, told her she was fired, and asked for her keys.

What legal remedies can plaintiff pursue against DK Industries? What steps should she take to pursue a claim, and what is her likelihood of success? What remedies can she recover? Explain your answers. [See *Novak v. Mackintosh*, 937 F. Supp. 873 (D.S.D. 1996); and "Job Rights for Veterans and Reserve Component Members," Vets USERRA Fact Sheet 3, U.S. Department of Labor, available at http://www.dol.gov/vets/programs/userra/userra_fs.htm.]

10. Pucci began working as a clerk and typist in 1991. She worked her way up, becoming a probation officer, then a judicial aide, then a clerk of court, and then—in 1995—assistant court administrator. That position was later reclassified as deputy court administrator, and Pucci remained in that role until 2006. In 2001, Pucci began a romantic relationship with Judge William Hultgren, one of the three judges on the Nineteenth District Court. They began living together and became engaged in 2004.

In 2004, Pucci became concerned that Judge Mark W. Somers, one of the other district judges, was expressing religious views in the course of performing his job as a judge. She saw a letter that Somers had written to a potential juror, which contained a biblical passage in the letterhead. She contacted the State Court Administrative Office (SCAO) to report her concern. A SCAO representative contacted Somers to discuss the issue and learned that Somers had apparently already stopped using the letterhead. Pucci also spoke to the SCAO on at least one other occasion about Somers's behavior, including his discussions about religion in open court. When asked about Somers's suitability for the chief judge position, she replied that she would not recommend him because "he mixes religion with the

business of the court." She explained: "[M]y job isn't to critique judges. We have got people in place for that. But as a person, as an individual, as a citizen, I was ... offended."

Somers told the SCAO in the summer of 2006 that he planned to reorganize the Nineteenth District Court and was considering terminating Pucci's employment. He did so in October 2006. Pucci first heard of her termination when she found a memo from Somers in her mailbox. Although the memo did not mention Pucci by name, it stated that "[t]he position of [deputy] court administrator will ... be eliminated effective November 15, 2006." On the envelope, Somers wrote something to the effect of "if you want to discuss this or you have any questions, please let me know." Pucci immediately called Somers, who came to her office. Somers said that her termination was unrelated to her job performance. Pucci suggested various alternatives that would allow her to keep her job. She explained that she had "bumping rights" over Langen, and should therefore be able to take over as clerk of court, but Somers was unmoved. At the end of the conversation, Pucci reports that Somers indicated his willingness to talk again but acknowledged that she would not be able to change his mind. Pucci and Somers had some brief exchanges via email about severance pay and related matters but did not otherwise discuss the termination any further. Attached to Somers's termination memo was a job posting for the court administrator position. Pucci submitted an application, but Somers eventually hired an outside candidate. Pucci's termination was originally scheduled to be effective in mid-November 2006 but eventually took effect in December of that year.

Does Pucci have a Section 1983 complaint? Against whom? And if so, what are her chances of prevailing? Explain. [See *Pucci v. Nineteenth District Court*, --- Fed. Appx. ---, 2015 WL 619613 (6th Cir. 2015).]

11. Joseph K. Bonacorsa had been involved in the harness racing industry for a number of years; he was licensed by the New York State Racing and Wagering Board as both a harness owner and a driver. He had been convicted of perjury for lying

under oath that he and his wife owned several horses. These horses were in fact owned by Gerald Forrest, who had previously been found guilty of conspiring to fix races at harness tracks and was therefore legally barred from owning licensed race horses. When Bonacorsa was convicted of perjury, the New York State Racing and Wagering Board revoked his harness owner and driver license. Bonacorsa served two years in prison and was on probation for a number of years. When his probation period ended, he was issued a certificate of good conduct by the New York Board of Parole. Upon receiving the certificate, Bonacorsa applied to the State Racing and Wagering Board to reinstate his harness owner and driver license. The Racing and Wagering Board refused to reinstate his license because his prior conviction was conduct that "impugned the integrity of racing within the state." Bonacorsa decided to pursue a legal challenge to the board's refusal to grant him a license.

Under what legal provisions can he sue to challenge the refusal to grant him a license? What is his likelihood of success? Explain. [See *Bonacorsa v. Lindt*, 129 A.D.2d 518, 514 N.Y.S.2d 370 (N.Y. A.D. 1987).]

12. Christine Noland was employed as an administrative assistant in the County Assessor's Office in Comanche County, Oklahoma. Her immediate supervisor was Robert McAdoo; McAdoo was initially the county deputy assessor and was later promoted to the assessor position. Throughout the period of her employment, Noland claims that McAdoo subjected her to unwelcome sexual advances, remarks, and physical contact. McAdoo would put his arm around her waist or neck despite the fact that she continually told him to stop. McAdoo would also stand in a doorway so that Noland had to rub against him to pass through. When Noland refused McAdoo's request that he and she attend an out-of-town conference, she was fired. Noland filed suit under 42 U.S.C. Section 1983 against both the county and McAdoo personally, alleging sexual harassment.

Can Noland bring a sexual harassment claim under 42 U.S.C. Section 1983? Can McAdoo personally be held liable under 42 U.S.C. Section 1983? Does Noland have any other statutory remedies available? Explain your answers. [See *Noland v. McAdoo*, 39 F.3d 269 (10th Cir. 1994).]

13. Madden, a member of the U.S. Air Force Reserves, was hired for a temporary 90-day position of process engineer by Rolls-Royce Data Systems at its Indiana facilities. Madden claimed to have an engineering degree from Purdue, but he never graduated. Madden made a number of mistakes on the job, and he was terminated at the end of the 90-day period. When he was told that he would not be considered for a permanent position, his supervisor did not mention Madden's performance but instead referred to Madden's impending call-up to active duty service with the Air Force. Madden later applied for another position with Rolls-Royce, but the human resources manager was unable to verify Madden's degree credentials, and he was not hired. Madden filed suit against Rolls-Royce under USERRA, claiming that his temporary position was not renewed and he was not hired for the other position because of his military service obligations.

What must he demonstrate in order to establish a claim under USERRA? What defenses can the employer raise? Is Madden likely to succeed? Explain. [See *Madden v. Rolls Royce Corp.*, 563 F.3d 636 (7th Cir. 2009).]

14. In 2010, Invesco contracted with two employment agencies, Matrix and ProSource, to fill a temporary job opening for a junior "Siebel developer." When the job opening was not filled after a few months, Invesco instructed Matrix and ProSource to broaden their search to consider candidates qualified for a junior Structured Query Language (SQL) developer position, who Invesco would then train on Siebel. Matrix found plaintiff's résumé on Monster .com, contacted him about the opening, recommended him to Invesco, and forwarded his resume to Rakhee Matlapudi, a senior recruiter at Invesco. Matlapudi determined that, as plaintiff had eight years of SQL experience, he was overqualified for the position and did not send plaintiff's resume to Invesco's hiring manager for further consideration.

Independent of Matrix and Invesco's activities, ProSource contacted plaintiff about the same Invesco job opening. Plaintiff sent ProSource a written application, in which he indicated that he had never "been convicted of a crime" and authorized ProSource to run his criminal background report. By signing the application, plaintiff stated that he "underst[ood] that any misrepresentation, falsification, or omission of information may be grounds for termination of the interview process, refusal to hire, or, if hired, termination of employment." ProSource subsequently interviewed plaintiff, administered a skills test, and contracted with a third-party credit reporting agency for plaintiff's criminal background report. The criminal background report revealed that plaintiff had been convicted of driving with an invalid license in 2006, assault causing bodily injury in 2001, and theft of between $20 and $500 in 1995. ProSource thereafter decided not to refer plaintiff to Invesco for the SQL developer position. Later, without the assistance of Matrix or ProSource, Invesco found and hired a candidate—a woman with one year and eight months of SQL experience—to fill the SQL/Siebel developer position.

Plaintiff sued under Section 1981, as well as Title VII and the Fair Credit Reporting Act, alleging race discrimination based upon the alleged disparate impact of the defendant's rules regarding criminal records and misrepresentation of the same on applications. What are his chances of success? [See *Manley v. Invesco*, 555 Fed. Appx. 344 (5th Cir. 2014).]

15. A New York State constitutional provision and a civil service statute required that military veterans with wartime service be granted extra points on competitive exams for state civil service jobs. Wartime vets received a five-point bonus on the exam, and disabled vets received an extra 10 points. However, this bonus was limited to veterans who were New York residents at the time they entered military service.

Is this affirmative action program permissible under the Constitution and federal statutory law? [See *Attorney General of the State of New York v. Soto-Lopez*, 476 U.S. 898 (1986).]

» Hypothetical Scenarios

16. You are a member of the local health food cooperative retail store (co-op) in Detroit. At the co-op's monthly membership meeting, the manager says the store has adopted a new policy to prohibit hiring any person who smokes. The co-op already prohibits smoking in the workplace (as required by the state's Clean Indoor Air Act). The new policy would bar hiring smokers even if they don't smoke during working hours. Is the proposed policy legal—can the co-op refuse to hire anyone who smokes? Would your answer be different if the co-op was in Buffalo, New York? Explain.

17. Fahran Al Muhammed applied unsuccessfully for a job with the federal Department of Housing and Urban Development (HUD). He believes he was not hired because he is of Iranian descent. He files suit against HUD under 42 U.S.C. § 1981. Is his case likely to succeed? Explain.

18. You work for the local Honda dealership as a sales associate. You love to play softball, but your employer refuses to sponsor a team in the local recreation league. The Ford dealership across the street from your employer has a team and lets you join. When your manager learns that you are playing on the Ford team, he tells you that "it's a conflict of interest" and that you must quit the team or lose your job. Can the manager legally fire you for playing on the Ford softball team? Does your answer depend upon where your employer is located? Explain.

19. As the new audit manager at Immense Multilateral Business, you are responsible for supervising the work of the audit division and for preparing quarterly reports to be filed with the Securities and Exchange Commission (SEC). You discover that the company accounting practices are not consistent with generally accepted accounting principles (GAAP), as required by the SEC regulations, and that the quarterly reports contain inaccurate information. When you inform the CEO about the problem, he tells you to ignore it. When you persist, he asks you "Do you like your job? Do you want to

keep your job?" If you choose to inform the SEC of the problem, what, if any, legal provisions may apply to your situation? Explain.

20. You are the assistant human resources manager at the regional office of Quickie-Mart, Inc., a chain of convenience stores. The store manager at the Dover store informs you that she has noticed a decline in cash receipts of several cashiers over the last month or two. She wants to force the cashiers to take polygraph tests to "see which ones are stealing from us." Can you require the cashiers to take a polygraph test? Can the cashiers who refuse to take a polygraph test be fired? Under what circumstances, if any, can the cashiers be subjected to polygraph testing? Explain.

PART 3

LABOR RELATIONS LAW

349

CHAPTER 12

The Rise of Organized Labor and Its Regulatory Framework

The Industrial Revolution brought about the rise of centralized manufacturing, with factories replacing the cottage industry in which craftsmen produced their own goods. These factories required laborers, who were subjected to harsh conditions and long hours. Despite the hardships that the new Industrial Age presented, it also carried the promise of a vast increase both in wealth and in mass-produced consumer goods. That increase would be sufficient to make possible a greatly improved standard of living for all classes, including the factory workers. It would be necessary, however, for laborers to join together to ensure that they would get their share of the increasing wealth of the nation. Employers reacted to the collective action of the workers by turning to the courts in an attempt to prevent the laborers from improving their lot in life at the expense of the landed class or the employers. Although labor's initial attempts at joining together were held illegal as combinations or conspiracies, the ruling class and public opinion gradually came to recognize the legitimacy of joint action by workers.

12-1 Labor Development in America

The craftsmen and journeymen of late 18th- and early 19th-century America recognized the importance of organized activity to resist employer attempts to reduce wages. The American courts initially reacted to these activities with hostility.

One of the earliest recorded American labor cases is the *Philadelphia Cordwainers* case, decided in 1806. The cordwainers, or shoemakers, formed a club and presented the master cordwainers, their employers, with a rate schedule for production of various types of shoes. The wage increases they demanded ranged from 25 to 75 cents per pair. The employers, however, who were attempting to compete with shoe producers in other cities, sought to lower prices to compete more effectively. The employers took their complaint to the public prosecutor, and the workers were charged with "contriving and intending unjustly and oppressively, to increase and augment the prices and rates usually paid to them" and with preventing, by "threats, menaces, and other unlawful means," other journeymen from working for lower wages. They were also accused of conspiring to refuse to work for any master who employed workers who did not abide by the club's rules.

In directing the jury to consider the case, the judge noted that "… a combination of workmen to raise their wages may be considered in a two-fold point of view: one is to benefit themselves … the other is to injure those who do not join their society. The rule of law condemns both…." The jury found the defendants guilty of conspiracy to raise their wages. The effect of the decision was to render combinations of workers for the purpose of raising wages illegal. The case produced a public outcry by the Jeffersonians and in the press.

Not all of labors activities were held illegal. For example, in *People v. Melvin*,[1] a New York cordwainers' case decided in 1809, the charge of an illegal combination to raise wages was dismissed. The court declared that the journeymen were free to join together, but they could not use means "of a nature too arbitrary and coercive, and which went to deprive their fellow citizens of rights as precious as any they contended for."

criminal conspiracy
a crime that may be committed when two or more persons agree to do something unlawful

Although that language may have sounded promising, the law remained in a most unsettled state. In 1835, the New York Supreme Court in *People v. Fisher*[2] found unionized workers guilty of **criminal conspiracy** under a statute that vaguely stated, "If two or more persons shall conspire … to commit any act injurious to the public health, to public morals, or to trade or commerce; or for the perversion or obstruction of justice or the due administration of the laws—they shall be deemed guilty of a misdemeanor." The workers—again shoemakers organized into a club—had struck to force the discharge of a coworker who had accepted wages below the minimum set by the club. The defendants were guilty of conspiring to commit an act "injurious to trade or commerce," the court reasoned. Artificially high wages meant correspondingly higher prices for boots, which prevented local manufacturers from selling as cheaply as their competitors elsewhere. Furthermore, the court observed, the community was deprived of the services of the worker whose discharge was procured by the shoemakers' union.

Such decisions provoked outrage among workers in the eastern states. In the wake of these trials, mobs of workers sometimes held their own mock trials and hanged unpopular judges in effigy. Despite such popular sentiments, the courts and the law remained major obstacles to organized labor achieving a legitimate place in society. The first step toward that achievement was the law's recognition that a labor organization was not per se an illegal conspiracy. That legal development came in the landmark decision of the Massachusetts Supreme Court in 1842 in the case of *Commonwealth v. Hunt*,[3] which held that union activities were not illegal conspiracies as long as the objectives of those activities, and the means employed to achieve those objectives, were not illegal.

Although *Commonwealth v. Hunt* did not abolish the doctrine of criminal conspiracy with regard to unions, it did make it extremely difficult to apply the doctrine to labor activities. After 1842, the legality of labor unions was accepted by mainstream judicial opinion. Furthermore, in the post–Civil War period, most state appellate courts accepted the legality of peaceful strikes, provided that the purpose of the work stoppage was determined by the court to be legal.

---

[1] 2 Wheeler C.C. 262, Yates Sel. Cas. 112 (1809).

[2] 14 Wend. 9 (1835).

[3] 45 Mass. (4 Met.) 111 (Mass. 1842).

12-1a   The Post–Civil War Period

After *Commonwealth v. Hunt*, the courts grudgingly accorded labor unions a measure of legitimacy, but the labor movement was forced to struggle—sometimes violently—with employers for recognition. The years following the Civil War were a turbulent period for the American labor movement. Those years saw not only a great increase in the growth and development of unions, but they were also marked by violent strikes in several industries.

The last decades of the 19th century saw three centers of labor activity: the Knights of Labor, the socialists, and the American Federation of Labor. Each group sought to rejuvenate organized labor after the declines suffered during the 1870s.

The Knights of Labor

The Noble Order of the Knights of Labor, first developed in Philadelphia in 1869, sought to organize both skilled and unskilled workers. Following the violent railway strike of 1877, workers rushed to join the Knights, which became a national organization. From 1878 to 1884, they conducted a large number of strikes, but their focus on industry-wide organizations rather than craft unions posed problems because the unskilled workers could easily be replaced during a strike. Membership in the Knights grew, but turnover was high, as members were suspended for nonpayment of dues, usually in the wake of unsuccessful strikes. Some locals disbanded when employers, following unsuccessful strikes, forced workers to sign **yellow-dog contracts** (in which they agreed not to join any union). After suffering defeats in a number of strikes, by 1886 the Knights sought to form a political alliance with the agrarian reform movement and the socialists. This turn to political action had only moderate success. The skilled trade unions within the Knights came to believe that they could more effectively achieve their goals through narrowly based organizations emphasizing labor actions rather than political efforts. Those unions pulled out of the Knights of Labor, causing its decline.

yellow-dog contract
an employment contract requiring employees to agree not to join a union

The Socialists

The establishment of the International Workingmen's Association (the First International) by Karl Marx in London in 1864 stirred interest in socialism in the United States. In 1865, the German Workingmen's Union was formed in New York City.[4] The socialist movement initially sought to organize unions, but it turned to political activities in the aftermath of the railway strike of 1877, with its political arm becoming the Socialist Labor Party. The public outcry following the Haymarket Riot in 1886, during which a bomb killed 11 persons, served to undercut the public acceptance and legitimacy of the socialist movement.

The labor activities of the socialist movement came to be represented by the Industrial Workers of the World (the IWW, or "Wobblies") during the early decades of the 20th century. The Wobblies were a radical union that engaged in a number of violent strikes. Their counterpart in the western United States was the Western Federation of Miners, led by William "Big Bill" Haywood, a socialist labor leader. Following the Russian Revolution in 1917, the Wobblies were eclipsed by the American Communist Party, which emphasized political activities. The influence of the Communist Party in labor activities, although important during the Depression, declined during World War II and the late 1940s; the Cold War and the McCarthy "red hunts" in the late 1940s and early 1950s effectively brought an end to organized labor's links to the American Communist Party.

---

[4] It was later reorganized as the Social Party and ultimately became known as Section 2 of the First International.

The American Federation of Labor

The American Federation of Labor (AFL), which ultimately became the dominant organization of the American labor movement, was the rival of both the socialists and the Knights of Labor. The AFL emphasized union activities in contrast to the political activities of the Knights and the socialists. This "pure and simple" trade union movement was started by Samuel Gompers and Adolph Strasser of the Cigarmakers' Union. The AFL adopted a pattern of union organization based on the British trade union system:

- local unions were to be organized under the authority of a national association;
- dues were to be raised to create a large financial reserve; and
- sick and death benefits were to be provided to members.

The national organization's focus was on wages and practical, immediate goals rather than on the ideological and political aims of the Knights of Labor and the Socialists. A federation of trade unions developed. Although the federation was open to unskilled workers, it was dominated by unions representing the skilled trades or crafts. The federation's unions initially faced stiff rivalry from the Knights of Labor, but as the Knights declined, the AFL grew in size and importance. By 1900, organized labor was largely composed of the 500,000 skilled workers in AFL-affiliated unions. For the next few decades, the AFL and its affiliated craft unions dominated the organized labor movement in America.

The Congress of Industrial Organizations

The Congress of Industrial Organizations (CIO) was a federation of unions that sought to organize the unskilled production workers largely ignored by the AFL. It grew out of a renewed interest in industry-wide organizing activity led by the autoworkers, steel workers, and mine workers under John L. Lewis. The AFL opposed the new organization and in 1938 expelled all unions associated with the CIO. The CIO, which emphasized political activity as well as organizing activity, had spectacular success in organizing the workers of the steel, automobile, rubber, electrical, manufacturing, and machinery industries. After years of bitter rivalry, the AFL was finally forced to recognize the CIO; the AFL (with 10.5 million members) merged with the CIO (with 4.5 million members) in 1955. The resulting organization, the AFL-CIO, was the dominant body in the American labor movement.

The Change to Win Coalition

In 2005, seven major unions accounting for nearly six million members broke away from the AFL-CIO to form the Change to Win Coalition:

- The International Brotherhood of Teamsters
- The Service Employees International Union
- The Laborers' International Union of North America
- The United Brotherhood of Carpenters and Joiners of America
- The United Farm Workers of America
- The United Food and Commercial Workers International Union
- Unite Here

The coalition seeks to revitalize the labor movement by putting greater efforts into organizing and adapting to the changing attitudes of 21st-century American workers.

Concept *Summary* 12.1

LABOR DEVELOPMENT IN AMERICA

- 19th-century views:
  - Courts initially reacted to attempts to organize labor with hostility
    - Formation viewed as a criminal conspiracy
  - Legality of labor unions eventually accepted (*Commonwealth v. Hunt*)

- Post–Civil War:
  - Labor unions develop and grow in reaction to the political, social, and economic environment
    - Knights of Labor
    - Socialists
    - American Federation of Labor (AFL)
    - Congress of Industrial Organizations (CIO)
    - Change to Win Coalition

12-1b Recent Trends in the Labor Movement

The years following World War II were boom years for the labor movement. Unions grew in strength in the manufacturing industries until approximately one-third of the American labor force was unionized. Union membership in the private sector reached a peak in the early 1950s and has been slowly declining since then; by 2009, only about 12 percent of the workforce (public and private sector) were unionized. Since the 1960s, unionized employers have faced increasing competition from domestic non-union firms and foreign competitors. The "oil-induced" inflation of the 1970s also increased the economic pressures on manufacturers and employers, making them very sensitive to production costs—of which labor costs are a significant component. The manufacturing sector of the U.S. economy, in which the labor movement's strength was concentrated, has been hit hardest by the changing economic conditions and global competition.

The late 1970s and the 1980s were marked by the "restructuring" of American industry. Mergers, takeovers, plant relocations to the mostly non-union Sun Belt and overseas, and plant closings all became common occurrences, as did collective bargaining, where the employer asked the union for "give backs"—reductions in wages and benefits and relaxation of restrictive work rules. The mid-1980s were characterized by the decline of the manufacturing sector and the rise of the service economy, the indifference (or hostility) of the Reagan administration toward organized labor, and an aggressiveness toward unions on the part of management. The decline of manufacturing in the United States and the outsourcing of jobs to low-wage countries continued through the 1990s and into the first decade of the 21st century, and the economic recession that began in late 2007 resulted in the loss of huge numbers of jobs. The dramatic decline of the U.S. auto industry, marked by General Motors and Chrysler filing for bankruptcy, and the drastic wage and benefits cuts forced upon the United Auto Workers were stark evidence of the decline of organized labor. As of 2009, less than 8 percent of U.S. private sector workers were union members.

While private sector unions have been in decline, unions in the public sector have been growing since the 1960s; by 2009, about 36 percent of government employees were union members. The 1980s were difficult for public sector unions—the "tax revolts" by American voters and the antigovernment attitude of the Reagan and George H. W. Bush administrations put limits on the ability of government employers to improve wages and benefits for public sector employees. The Clinton administration provided unions with a sympathetic ear at the White House, but the Republican-controlled Congress blocked Clinton's ability to make legislative changes and limited the extent to which organized labor could take advantage of the Democratic president's years in office. Any political influence labor enjoyed during the Clinton administration vanished during the eight years of the George W. Bush administration. The election of Barack Obama, and the control of both houses of Congress by the Democrats, brought a renewed hope to the U.S. labor movement, and union officials looked forward to more political influence. However, the Republicans in Congress made it clear that they would oppose any worker-friendly legislation, and filibuster threats in the Senate forced President Obama to resort to using recess appointments to fill vacancies on the National Labor Relations Board. Those recess appointments, which were made during a three-day recess between pro forma sessions of the Senate in 2012, were held to be unconstitutional by the Supreme Court in *National Labor Relations Board v. Noel Canning*.[5] That decision meant that the NLRB lacked a legal quorum from January 4, 2012, until July 30, 2013, and that decisions issued by the NLRB during that period were invalid. A political compromise was reached, and the president subsequently appointed a full complement of members to the NLRB.

12-2 Legal Responses to the Labor Movement

While judicial hostility against union formation decreased over time, employers facing threats of strikes or boycotts by unions sought new legal weapons to use against labor activists. The development of the labor injunction in the late 1880s provided a powerful weapon for use against the activities of organized labor.

12-2a Injunctions

injunction
a court order to provide remedies prohibiting some action or commanding the righting of some wrongdoing

An **injunction** is a court order directing a person to do, or to refrain from doing, specific actions. Injunctions are available whenever monetary damages alone are inadequate and when the plaintiff's interests are facing irreparable harm from the defendant's actions. A defendant who violates the court order is subject to fines and can be jailed for contempt of the court.

Throughout the last decade of the 19th century and the first two decades of the 20th century, the courts willingly granted injunctions against actual or threatened strikes or boycotts by unions. The courts did not require any showing that the strike or boycott

---

[5] 134 S.Ct. 2550 (2014).

actually harmed the employer's business. The courts were also willing to assume that legal remedies such as damage awards were inadequate. Generally, the injunctions granted were written in very broad terms and directed against unnamed persons. The injunctions were often granted in **ex parte proceedings**, so called because they occurred without any representative of the union present.

Once an injunction had been granted, court officers would enforce it against the union. Union members who resisted risked jail terms and/or fines for being in contempt of the court order. In the face of such threatened sanctions, union leaders generally had to comply by stopping the strike or boycott. Therefore, the labor injunction became a potent weapon for management to use against any union pressure tactics.

ex parte proceedings
court hearing in which one party, usually the defendant, is not present and is not able to take part

12-2b Yellow-Dog Contracts

In addition to securing labor injunctions against union activities, employers were able to use the courts to enforce yellow-dog contracts, or contracts of employment that required employees to agree not to join a union. By incorporating the antiunion promise in the contract, employers could legally make nonmembership in unions a condition of employment. Employees who joined a union could be fired for breach of their employment contract.

In the 1917 case of *Hitchman Coal Co. v. Mitchell*,[6] the Supreme Court upheld an injunction against a strike that was intended to force the employer to abandon the yellow-dog contracts. The majority of the Court held that the union, by inducing the workers to break their contracts, was guilty of wrongly interfering with contractual relations. The Court's decision confirmed the importance of the yellow-dog contract as another weapon in the employers' legal arsenal against unions.

12-2c Antitrust Laws

In addition to labor injunctions and yellow-dog contracts, antitrust laws provided yet another legal weapon for employers. Congress passed the Sherman Antitrust Act in 1890 in response to public agitation against such giant business monopolies as the Standard Oil Company and the American Tobacco Company. The act outlawed restraints of trade and monopolizing of trade. Section 1 stated: "Every contract, combination in the form of trust or otherwise, or conspiracy, in restraint of trade or commerce among the several states, or with foreign nations, is hereby declared to be illegal." It provided for criminal penalties—fines and imprisonment—for violations.

Other provisions of the act allowed private parties to sue for damages if they were injured by restraints of trade, and gave the federal courts power to issue injunctions against violators of the act. Most observers assumed the act was limited to business trusts and predatory corporate behavior. *Loewe v. Lawlor*, known as the *Danbury Hatters'* case, however, made it clear that organized labor activities were also subject to the Sherman Act.

---

[6] 245 U.S. 229 (1917).

CASE 12.1

LOEWE V. LAWLOR
208 U.S. 274 (1908)

Facts: The *Danbury Hatters'* case grew out of an AFL boycott of the D. E. Loewe Company of Danbury, Connecticut, that was called to assist efforts by the United Hatters' Union to organize the Loewe workers. The company responded by filing a suit under the Sherman Act in 1903. The company alleged that the boycott was a conspiracy to restrain trade, and it sought damages totaling $240,000 against the individual union members. The district court, rejecting the union's argument that the boycott did not interfere with "trade or commerce among the states," found the defendants liable for damages. The union appealed to the U.S. Supreme Court.

Issue: Are union boycotts attempts to restrain or interfere with trade in violation of the Sherman Act?

Decision: The Supreme Court held that the boycott was a combination in restraint of trade within the meaning of the Sherman Act. The Court refused to read into the act an exemption for labor activities, citing the words of Section 1 that "every… combination or conspiracy in restraint of trade" was illegal.

After the Supreme Court's decision in the *Danbury Hatters'* case, other employers also successfully attacked union boycotts under the Sherman Act. In the face of such actions, the AFL lobbied Congress for legislative relief. The passage of the Clayton Act in 1914 appeared to provide the relief sought by labor.

The key provisions of the Clayton Act, which also amended the Sherman Act, were Sections 6 and 20. Section 6 stated:

> the labor of a human being is not a commodity or article of commerce. Nothing contained in the antitrust laws shall be construed to forbid the existence and operation of labor … organizations, … nor shall such organizations, or the members thereof, be held or construed to be illegal combinations or conspiracies in restraint of trade, under the antitrust laws.

Section 20 restricted the issuance of labor injunctions. It provided that no injunction could be issued against employees unless irreparable harm to the employer's property or property rights was threatened and the legal remedy of monetary damages would be inadequate. Samuel Gompers of the AFL declared those sections to be "labor's Magna Carta."

The effect of those sections was the subject of the following 1921 Supreme Court decision.

CASE 12.2

DUPLEX PRINTING PRESS COMPANY V. DEERING
254 U.S. 443 (1921)

Facts: The Machinists' Union at the Duplex Printing Press Company organized a strike to force the employer to agree to a closed-shop provision, to accept an eight-hour workday, and to adopt a union-proposed wage scale. When the strike proved unsuccessful, the union called for a national boycott of Duplex products. Duplex responded by filing suit for an injunction under the Clayton Act against the officers of the

New York City Local of the Machinists' Union. The union argued that Sections 6 and 20 of the Clayton Act prevented the issuance of an injunction against the union and its officers.

Issue: Do Sections 6 and 20 of the Clayton Act exempt labor union activities from the prohibitions of the Sherman Act?

Decision: A majority of the Supreme Court held that Section 6:

> assumes the normal objects of a labor organization to be legitimate, and declares that nothing in the antitrust laws shall be construed to forbid the existence and operation of such organizations or to forbid their members from lawfully carrying out their legitimate objects…. But there is nothing in the section to exempt such an organization or its members from accountability where it or they depart from its normal and legitimate objects and engage in actual combination of conspiracy in restraint of

> trade. And by no fair or permissible construction can it be taken as authorizing any activity otherwise unlawful, or enabling a normally lawful organization to become a cloak for an illegal combination or conspiracy in restraint of trade as defined by the antitrust laws.

The Court found that Congress did not intend for Section 6 or Section 20 to be a general grant of immunity for conduct that would otherwise violate the antitrust laws and upheld the injunction against the union and its officers. The Court's decision effectively gutted the Clayton Act provisions that had been hailed by Gompers.

The effects of the labor injunction and the *Danbury Hatters'* and *Duplex* cases continued to make things extremely difficult. Labor would have to wait for the effects of the Great Depression, as well as the accession of the Democratic Party to national power, before the legal and judicial impediments to its activities would be removed.

Concept *Summary* 12.2

LEGAL RESPONSES TO THE LABOR MOVEMENT

- Injunctions: Court orders requiring or prohibiting certain actions
  - Employers used injunctions to prevent strikes or boycotts

- Yellow-dog contracts: Employment contracts requiring employees not to join a union
  - Employers could make nonunion membership a condition of employment

- Antitrust laws: Designed to protect free trade and competition
  - Employers used them to challenge union boycotts by seeking damages for interference with trade
    - Sherman Antitrust Act
    - Clayton Act

12-3   The Development of the National Labor Relations Act

Organized labor reacted to the judicial endorsement of employer antiunion tactics by engaging in coordinated political pressure for legislative controls on judicial involvement in labor disputes. This political activity yielded results in 1932 when a federal anti-injunction act, sponsored by Senator Norris and Congressman La Guardia, was enacted.

12-3a   The Norris–La Guardia Act

The Norris–La Guardia Act, in effect, was a legislative reversal of the prevailing view of the judiciary that economic injury inflicted by unions pursuing their economic self-interest

common law
judge-made law as opposed to statutes and ordinances enacted by legislative bodies

was unlawful both at **common law** and under antitrust laws. The act created a laissez-faire environment for organized labor's self-help activities.

Provisions

Section 1 of the Norris–La Guardia Act prohibits the federal courts from issuing injunctions in labor disputes except in strict conformity with the provisions set out in the act. Those provisions, contained in Section 7, require the following:

- The court must hold an open-court hearing, with opportunity for cross-examination of all witnesses and participation by representatives of both sides to the controversy.
- The court can issue an injunction only if the hearing has established that unlawful acts have actually been threatened or committed and will be committed or continue to be committed unless restraints were ordered.
- The party seeking the injunction has to establish that substantial and irreparable injury to its property will follow and that it has no adequate remedy at law.
- The court has to be convinced that the public officials charged with the duty to protect the threatened property are unable or unwilling to provide adequate protection.

Only after complying with this procedure and making such findings can the court issue an injunction in a labor dispute.

Section 4 of the act sets out a list of activities that are protected from injunctions, even when the foregoing safeguards might be observed. The section states that:

No court of the United States shall have jurisdiction to issue any restraining order or temporary or permanent injunction in any case involving or growing out of any labor dispute to prohibit any person or persons participating or interested in such dispute (as these terms are herein defined) from doing, whether singly or in concert, any of the following acts:

(a) Ceasing or refusing to perform any work or to remain in any relation of employment;
(b) Becoming or remaining a member of any labor organization or of any employer organization, regardless of any such undertaking or promise as is described in Section 3 of this act;
(c) Paying or giving to, or withholding from, any person participating or interested in such labor dispute, any strike or unemployment benefits or insurance, or other moneys or things of value;
(d) By all lawful means aiding any person participating or interested in any labor dispute who is being proceeded against in, or is prosecuting, any action or suit in any court of the United States or of any State;
(e) Giving publicity to the existence of, or the facts involved in, any labor dispute, whether by advertising, speaking, patrolling, or by any other method not involving fraud or violence;
(f) Assembling peaceably to act or to organize to act in promotion of their interests in a labor dispute;
(g) Advising or notifying any person of an intention to do any of the acts heretofore specified;
(h) Agreeing with other persons to do or not to do any of the acts heretofore specified; and
(i) Advising, urging, or otherwise causing or inducing without fraud or violence the acts heretofore specified, regardless of any such undertaking or promise as is described in Section 3 of this act.

The term *labor dispute* is defined in Section 13(c) of the act, which states:

The term "labor dispute" includes any controversy concerning the terms or conditions of employment, or concerning the association or representation of persons in negotiating, fixing, maintaining, changing, or seeking to arrange terms or conditions of employment, regardless of whether or not the disputants stand in the proximate relation of employer and employee.

Finally, Section 3 of the act declares that yellow-dog contracts are contrary to public policy of the United States and are not enforceable by any federal court. Nor can the courts use such contracts as the basis for granting any legal or equitable remedies (such as injunctions).

State Anti-injunction Laws

Although the Norris–La Guardia Act applies only to the federal courts, a number of states passed similar legislation restricting their court systems in issuing labor injunctions. These acts are known as "little Norris–La Guardia Acts." The Supreme Court upheld the constitutionality of Wisconsin's little Norris–La Guardia Act in the 1937 decision of *Senn v. Tile Layers' Protective Union*.[7] Although the case did not involve the federal act, it did raise the same legal issues as would an attack on the constitutionality of the federal act; the decision in *Senn* was regarded as settling the question of the federal act's constitutionality.

Validity and Scope of the Norris–La Guardia Act

The following case illustrates the broad scope of the definition of labor dispute under the Norris–La Guardia Act, and the procedural requirements for seeking an injunction.

» CASE 12.3

Pulte Homes, Inc. v. Laborers' International Union of North America
648 F.3d 295 (6th Cir. 2011)

Facts: Pulte Homes, Inc., a successful home builder, sued a national labor union for orchestrating an attack on the company's phone and e-mail systems. The complaint stems from an employment dispute. In September 2009, Pulte fired a construction crew member, Roberto Baltierra, for misconduct and poor performance. Shortly thereafter, the Laborers' International Union of North America [LIUNA] began mounting a national corporate campaign against Pulte—using both legal and allegedly illegal tactics—in order to damage Pulte's goodwill and relationships with its employees, customers, and vendors. LIUNA filed an unfair-labor-practice charge with the National Labor Relations Board [NLRB]. LIUNA claimed that Pulte actually fired Baltierra because he wore a LIUNA t-shirt to work, and that Pulte also terminated seven other crew members in retaliation for their supporting the union. Pulte maintains that it never terminated any of these seven additional employees. LIUNA also began bombarding Pulte's sales offices and three of its executives with thousands of phone calls and e-mails. To generate a high volume of calls, LIUNA both hired an auto-dialing service and requested its members to call Pulte. It also encouraged its members, through postings on its website, to "fight back" by using LIUNA's server to send e-mails to specific Pulte executives. Most of the calls and e-mails concerned Pulte's purported unfair labor practices, though some communications included threats and obscene language. The calls clogged access to Pulte's voicemail system, prevented its customers from reaching its sales offices and representatives, and even forced one Pulte employee to turn off her business cell phone. The e-mails also overloaded

---

[7] 301 U.S. 468 (1937).

Pulte's system, which limits the number of e-mails in an inbox; and this, in turn, stalled normal business operations because Pulte's employees could not access business-related e-mails or send e-mails to customers and vendors.

Four days after LIUNA started its phone and e-mail blitz, Pulte's general counsel contacted LIUNA and requested that LIUNA stop the attack because it prevented Pulte's employees from doing their jobs. When the calls and e-mails continued, Pulte filed this suit alleging several state-law torts and violations of the Federal Computer Fraud and Abuse Act [CFAA, a statute that both criminal-izes certain computer-fraud crimes and allows for civil suit.]

Pulte asked the court to issue a preliminary injunc-tion stopping LIUNA's phone and e-mail campaign. The district court denied Pulte's motion, holding that it lacked jurisdiction under the Norris–LaGuardia Act [NLGA] to issue a preliminary injunction because the suit involves a labor dispute and LIUNA's campaign attempts to publicize that dispute. Pulte appealed to the U.S. Court of Appeals for the Sixth Circuit.

Issue: Is the phone and email campaign by LIUNA within the definition of a labor dispute under the NLGA, so that the court is unable to issue an injunction prohibiting the conduct?

Decision: If a lawsuit involves or grows out of a "labor dispute," the NLGA deprives a court of jurisdiction to issue a preliminary injunction "except in a strict conformity with the provisions" of the NLGA. Among the NLGA's rigid rules are several procedural safeguards. For example, before a court can issue a preliminary injunction, it must hold an evidentiary hearing and make findings of fact, and the plaintiff must post a bond. Because the district court here held that Pulte's

complaint springs from a labor dispute, NLGA's procedural requirements apply. Pulte, however, failed to comply with one of these safeguards: Section 8 of the NLGA. Section 8 prohibits a court from granting an injunction "to any complainant ... who has failed to make every reasonable effort to settle [a labor] dispute ... by negotiation." The court must determine whether the plaintiff's attempts to settle the dispute constitute "every reasonable effort." Pulte's settlement efforts here, because they did not include any attempt to confer with LIUNA's attorneys before filing suit, do not pass the every-reasonable-effort test, and thus prevent the court from issuing an injunction.

Pulte fired Baltierra on September 4th, prompting the onset of LIUNA's communications attack on September 9th. Four days later, on Sunday, September 13th, Pulte's general counsel faxed and overnighted a cease-and-desist letter to LIUNA, in which Pulte demanded that LIUNA stop encouraging the calls and e-mails and that it "use every means available to [it] to put an end to this activity." The letter cautioned that Pulte intended to seek injunctive relief unless LIUNA "promptly provide[d] ... adequate assur-ances that this conduct will cease immediately." When the calls and e-mails did not stop by the morning of Tuesday, September 15, Pulte filed this suit.

Pulte made little to no effort to settle. It transmitted the cease-and-desist letter on a Sunday, did not specify a time to respond, did not offer LIUNA an opportunity to negotiate, and filed suit less than forty-eight hours after sending the letter without even confirming that LIUNA received the letter. This is not "every reasonable effort" to settle the dispute. Because Pulte failed to comply with Section 8 of the NLGA, the district court lacked jurisdic-tion to issue the injunction. The court of appeals affirmed the district court's denial of a preliminary injunction.

12-3b The Railway Labor Act

The Railway Labor Act, passed in 1926, allowed railroad employees to designate bargaining representatives of their own choosing, free from employer interference. This legislation introduced some of the ideas and approaches later incorporated in the National Labor Relations Act (NLRA).

The railroads were one of the earliest industries in which employees were unionized. As noted earlier, the railroads were the target of several violent strikes during the late 19th century. The importance of the railroads for the nation's economic development and the railroads' position as essentially being public utilities made the disruptive effects of labor disputes involving the railroads a subject for government concern. Congress passed several laws aimed at minimizing or avoiding labor strife in the railroad industry.

The Railway Labor Act established a three-step procedure for settling disputes.

- The first step involved using a federal mediation board to attempt to facilitate negotiation of the parties' differences.

- If that failed, the board would then try to induce the parties to arbitrate the dispute. Although not compelled to submit the dispute to arbitration, the parties would be legally bound by the results if they agreed to arbitration.

- Finally, if arbitration was refused, the board could recommend to the president that an emergency board of investigation be created. If the president created the emergency board, the parties in dispute were required to maintain the status quo for 30 days while the investigation proceeded. Even if an emergency board was not appointed, the parties were still required to maintain the status quo for 30 days. This mandatory cooling-off period was designed to allow the dispute to be settled through negotiation. The union retained its right to strike, and the employer could lock out once the cooling-off period expired.

The act also provided that both labor and management had the right to designate bargaining representatives without the "interference, influence or coercion" of the other party. That provision was the subject of the Supreme Court's 1930 decision of *Texas & New Orleans Railroad v. Brotherhood of Railway Clerks*.[8] The union had sought, and was granted, an injunction against employer interference with the employees' designation of a bargaining representative under the act. The railroad argued that the act did not create any legally enforceable right of free choice for employees and that the act's provisions were an unconstitutional interference with management's right to operate the railroad. The Supreme Court upheld the injunction and the constitutionality of the Railway Labor Act, rejecting the railroad's challenges.

The Railway Labor Act was amended by Congress in 1934, 1936, 1951, and 1966. The act was extended to cover airline employees, and a duty to bargain with the duly designated representative of each side was spelled out. The amendments also provided that unions representing the airline or railway employees could bargain for a union shop provision. The National Railroad Adjustment Board was created to arbitrate disputes involving the railroads and unions; its awards are final and binding upon the parties. The amendments also created sanctions for enforcement of the act by declaring violations to be misdemeanors. Such violations included the interference with the designation of representatives by either party, the use of yellow-dog contracts, and the changing of any terms or conditions of employment without complying with the provisions of a collective agreement.

The amendments creating the duty to bargain with representatives of the employees were the subject of a challenge in the 1937 Supreme Court case of *Virginia Railway Co. v. System Federation No. 40*.[9] The Supreme Court held that the act created a mandatory requirement of recognizing and negotiating with the bargaining representatives duly designated by the parties and that this requirement could be enforced by court order.

12-3c The National Industrial Recovery Act

The other statutory predecessor of the NLRA was the National Industrial Recovery Act (NIRA), the centerpiece of President Franklin D. Roosevelt's New Deal. Roosevelt took office

---

[8] 281 U.S. 548 (1930).

[9] 300 U.S. 515 (1937).

in 1933, the fourth year of the Great Depression. Some 15 million people were unemployed, and there was a widespread belief that the nation's economic growth had come to a permanent halt. Roosevelt proposed his New Deal program to pull the nation out of the Depression. It involved government working closely and actively with business to revive the economy.

The NIRA set up a system in which major industries would operate under codes of fair competition, which would be developed by trade associations for each industry. These associations would be under the supervision and guidance of the National Recovery Administration (NRA). The NIRA, in Section 7(a), also provided that the codes of fair competition contain the following conditions:

(1) That employees shall have the right to organize and bargain collectively through representatives of their own choosing, and shall be free from interference, restraint, or coercion of employers of labor, or their agents, in the designation of such representatives or in self-organization or in other concerted activities for the purpose of collective bargaining or other mutual aid or protection;

(2) that no employee … shall be required as a condition of employment to join any company union or to refrain from joining, organizing, or assisting a labor organization of his own choosing; and

(3) that employers shall comply with the maximum hours of labor, minimum rates of pay, and other conditions of employment, approved or prescribed by the President.

The NRA, responsible for administering the codes of fair competition under the NIRA, had to rely on voluntary cooperation from the industries being regulated. The NRA announced that codes containing provisions concerning hours, rates of pay, and other conditions of employment would be subject to NRA approval, although such conditions had not been arrived at through collective bargaining. The practical effect of this announcement was to allow industry to develop such codes unilaterally, without input from organized labor. While employees rushed to join unions, employers refused to recognize and bargain with the unions. A wave of strikes resulted.

President Roosevelt issued a plea for industrial peace and created the National Labor Board (NLB) to "consider, adjust and settle differences and controversies that may arise through differing interpretations" of the NIRA provisions.

12-3d The National Labor Board

The NLB was created in August 1933. It was composed of seven members; three representatives each would be chosen by the NRA's Industrial Advisory Board and Labor Advisory Board. The seventh member was Senator Robert Wagner of New York, who was chairman. The NLB initially functioned as a mediation board, seeking to persuade the parties to settle their differences peacefully.

The weakness of enforcement powers given to the NLB was its most serious drawback. The NLB relied mainly on the power of persuasion, which was effective only as long as an employer was not overtly antagonistic to organized labor. When, in 1934, the nation's automobile manufacturers all refused to recognize the United Automobile Workers Union or to allow the NLB to conduct a representative election, President Roosevelt had General Hugh Johnson, head of the NRA, negotiate a settlement rather than stand behind the NLB order. That decision destroyed what little effectiveness the NLB retained.

Despite its short tenure, the NLB did make several contributions to modern labor law. It evolved from a mediation service into an adjudicative body akin to the present National Labor Relations Board (NLRB). It also established the principles of majority rule and exclusive representation of the employees in a particular bargaining unit. In addition, the NLB developed other rules that have come to be basic principles of labor relations law, among them the following:

- An employer was obligated to bargain with a union that had been chosen as representative by a majority of employees;

- Employers had no right to know of an employee's membership in, or vote for, a union when a secret ballot representation election was held; and

- Strikers remained employees while on strike and were entitled to displace any replacements hired if the strike was the result of employer violations of the NIRA.

12-3e The "Old" National Labor Relations Board

In June 1934, President Roosevelt formulated Public Resolution No. 44. This resolution, which was then passed by Congress, authorized the president to establish a "board or boards" empowered to investigate disputes arising under Section 7(a) of the NIRA and to conduct secret ballot representation elections among employees. Enforcement of Board decisions would remain with the NRA and the Department of Justice. Roosevelt then abolished the NLB and transferred its funds, personnel, and pending cases to the National Labor Relations Board (the "old" NLRB). The NLRB was denied all jurisdiction over disputes in the steel and auto industries. The NLRB reaffirmed the key rulings of the NLB; it also issued guidelines to assist regional offices in handling common types of cases and began organizing its decisions into a body of precedents guiding future action.

When the Supreme Court declared the NIRA to be unconstitutional in its 1935 *Schechter Poultry Corp. v. U.S.*[10] decision, it also destroyed the "old" NLRB.

Concept *Summary* 12.3

THE DEVELOPMENT OF THE NATIONAL LABOR RELATIONS ACT

- The Railway Labor Act: Established dispute settlement procedures for the railroad industry; it was later extended to the airline industry
- The National Industrial Recovery Act (NIRA): Provided protection for employees organizing unions and encouraged collective bargaining
- The National Labor Board (NLB): Mediated labor disputes but had no legal authority
- The "Old" National Labor Relations Board ("old" NLRB): Replaced the NLB, but was dissolved after the Supreme Court declared the NIRA unconstitutional
- The Norris–La Guardia Act: Limited the use of labor injunctions by employers and outlawed yellow-dog contracts

---

[10] 295 U.S. 495 (1935).

12-4   The National Labor Relations Act

Senator Wagner introduced a proposed National Labor Relations Act (NLRA) in the Senate in 1935. Despite initial stiff opposition, the NLRA was passed by Congress and enacted into law in 1935. Because of the doubts over the NLRA's constitutionality, President Roosevelt had difficulty finding qualified people willing to be appointed to the NLRB established under the NLRA. The main concern over the constitutionality of the NLRA was whether it was a valid exercise of the interstate commerce power given to Congress under the commerce clause of the Constitution. In *Schechter Poultry*, the Supreme Court had held that the NIRA was not within the federal government power to regulate interstate commerce. In passing the NLRA, Congress had relied on the power to regulate commerce among the states given to it under the commerce clause. The findings of fact incorporated in Section 1 of the NLRA contained the following statement:

> The denial by employers of the right of employees to organize and the refusal by employers to accept the procedure of collective bargaining lead to strikes and other forms of industrial strife or unrest, which have the intent or the necessary effect of burdening or obstructing commerce....

For more than a year after the passage of the NLRA, there was only limited activity by the NLRB. The Board set out to develop economic data supporting the findings of fact in Section 1 of the NLRA. It also sought the best possible case to take to the Supreme Court to settle the constitutionality issue.

Finally, the NLRB brought five cases to the federal courts of appeals. The cases involved an interstate bus company, the Associated Press news service, and three manufacturing firms. The Board lost all three of the manufacturing company cases in the courts of appeals on the interstate commerce issue. All five of the cases were taken to the Supreme Court and were heard by the Court in February 1937. The NLRB developed its arguments in the *Jones & Laughlin Steel* case, one of the manufacturing cases, almost entirely on the interstate commerce issue. That case became the crucial litigation in the test of the NLRA's constitutionality.

The Supreme Court in its 1937 decision in *NLRB v. Jones & Laughlin Steel Corp.*[11] upheld the constitutionality of the NLRA by a 5–4 vote. The majority opinion, by Chief Justice Hughes, held that the disruption of operations of Jones & Laughlin due to industrial strife would have a serious and direct effect on interstate commerce. In the words of the Court,

> When industries organize themselves on a national scale, making their relation to interstate commerce the dominant factor in their activities, how can it be maintained that their industrial labor relations constitute a forbidden field into which Congress may not enter when it is necessary to protect interstate commerce from the paralyzing consequences of industrial war?

By the slimmest of margins, the Supreme Court had upheld the validity of the National Labor Relations Act. The decision also meant that a labor relations board effectively empowered to deal with disputes between labor and management had finally been established.

12-4a   Overview of the National Labor Relations Act

The passage of the National Labor Relations Act, or the Wagner Act, constituted a revolutionary change in national labor policy. Workers were now legally protected by the federal

---

[11] 301 U.S. 1 (1937).

government in their rights to organize for mutual aid and security and to bargain collectively through representatives of their own choice.

The purpose of the act, as stated in Section 1, was to:

> eliminate the causes of certain substantial obstructions to the free flow of commerce … by encouraging the practice and procedure of collective bargaining and by protecting the exercise by workers of full freedom of association, self-organization, and designation of representatives of their own choosing, for the purpose of negotiating the terms and conditions of their employment or other mutual aid or protection.

The basis of the act was the protection of the rights of employees, defined by Section 7:

> Employees shall have the right to self-organization, to form, join, or assist labor organizations, to bargain collectively through representatives of their own choosing, and to engage in concerted activities for the purpose of collective bargaining or other mutual aid or protection.

To protect these basic rights of employees, the act prohibited certain practices of employers that would interfere with or prevent the exercise of such rights. Those practices were designated unfair labor practices, and the act listed five of them:

1. interference with, or restraint or coercion of, employees in the exercise of their Section 7 rights;
2. domination of, or interference with, a labor organization (including financial or other contributions to it);
3. discrimination in terms or conditions of employment of employees for the purpose of encouraging or discouraging union membership;
4. discrimination against an employee for filing a charge or testifying in a proceeding under the act and;
5. refusal to bargain collectively with the employees' legal bargaining representative.

The act reconstituted the NLRB to enforce and administer the statute. The Board created a nationwide organization, developed a body of legal precedents (drawing heavily upon decisions of its predecessors), and developed and refined its procedures. In its efforts to carry out the policies of the legislation, the Board was frequently criticized for being too pro-union. At the same time, unions were accused of abusing their newly gained power under the act. A 1946 strike by the United Mine Workers, in defiance of a Supreme Court order to remain on the job, seemed to crystallize public opinion that unions had grown too powerful.

This public concern was reflected in congressional action to limit unions' abuse of their powers. Congressional critics were especially concerned over jurisdictional disputes, in which two unions claimed the right to represent the workers of an employer, leaving the employer "trapped" between them, and recognitional picketing, which was aimed at forcing an employer to recognize the union regardless of the sentiments of the employees. These kinds of congressional concerns resulted in the passage of the Taft-Hartley Act in 1947. The Taft-Hartley Act outlawed the **closed shop**, a term describing an employer who agrees to hire only employees who are already union members. It also added a list of unfair labor practices by unions and emphasized that employees had the right, under Section 7, to refrain from collective activity as well as engage in it. The purpose and

closed shop
an employer who agrees to hire only those employees who are already union members

effect of the Taft-Hartley Act were to balance the rights and duties of both unions and employers.

After Taft-Hartley, the National Labor Relations Act[12] was amended several times, the most significant version being the Landrum-Griffin Act of 1959. Landrum-Griffin was passed in response to concerns about union racketeering and abusive practices aimed at union members. The act set out specific rights for individual union members against the union, and it proscribed certain kinds of conduct by union officials, such as financial abuse, racketeering, and manipulation of union-election procedures.

12-5 The National Labor Relations Board

Unless otherwise specified, the discussion throughout this and subsequent chapters will focus on the current National Labor Relations Act and the present National Labor Relations Board's organization, jurisdiction, and procedure.

12-5a Organization

Because the Wagner Act gave little guidance concerning the administrative structure of the newly created agency, the NLRB adopted an administrative organization that made it prosecutor, judge, and jury with regard to complaints under the act. The Board investigated charges of unfair labor practices, prosecuted complaints, conducted hearings, and rendered decisions. Pursuant to its statutory authority, the Board did appoint a general counsel to serve as legal adviser and direct litigation, but the general counsel was subordinate to the Board in virtually all matters.

The combination of prosecutorial and judicial functions was one of the major criticisms leveled by commentators and attorneys against the Board in the years prior to the passage of the Taft-Hartley Act. This issue, not surprisingly, was addressed by Taft-Hartley in 1947. Although Taft-Hartley retained the concept of a single enforcement agency, it made the Office of the General Counsel an independent unit to direct the administrative and enforcement efforts of the NLRB regional offices. The Board itself was expanded from three to five members. It continued to exercise the judicial function of deciding complaints filed under the act.

The newly organized NLRB represented a unique type of administrative agency structure in that it was bifurcated into two independent authorities within the single agency: the five-member Board and the general counsel. Exhibit 12.1 depicts the organization of the two authorities of the bifurcated agency.

---

[12] The Taft-Hartley Act incorporated the National Labor Relations Act. Scholars and labor lawyers differ over whether the modern act should be referred to as the NLRA or the Labor Management Relations Act, or both. For convenience, and since the enforcing agency is still called the NLRB, we will continue to refer to the act as the National Labor Relations Act.

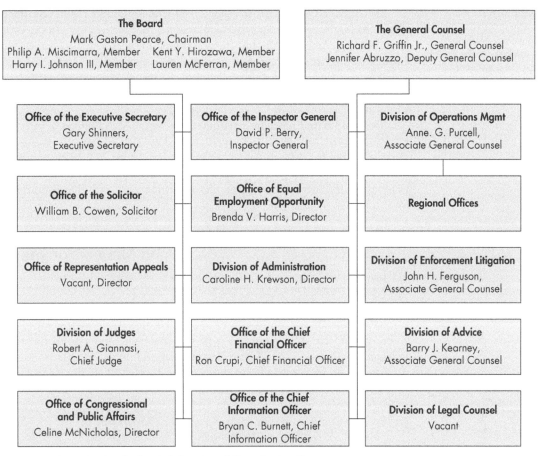

EXHIBIT 12.1   National Labor Relations Board Organization Chart
Source: NLRB, http://www.nlrb.gov/who-we-are/organizational-chart.

The Board

The Board itself is the judicial branch of the agency. The five members of the Board are nominated by the U.S. president and must be confirmed by the Senate. They serve five-year terms. Members of the Board can be removed from office by the president only for neglect of duty or malfeasance in office. One member is to be designated by the president as chairperson. Members have a staff of about 25 legal clerks and assistants to help in deciding the numerous cases that come before them. The executive secretary of the Board is the chief administrative officer, charged with ruling on procedural questions, assigning cases to members, setting priorities in case handling, and conferring with parties to cases that come before the Board. There is also a solicitor, whose function is to advise members on questions of law and policy. Finally, an information director assists the Board on public relations issues.

administrative law judges (ALJs)
formerly called trial examiners, these judges are independent of both the Board and the general counsel

The NLRB also has a branch called the Division of Judges. These **administrative law judges (ALJs)**, formerly called trial examiners, are independent of both the Board and the general counsel. Appointed for life, they are subject to the federal Civil Service Commission rules governing appointment and tenure. This organizational independence is necessary because the ALJs conduct hearings and issue initial decisions on unfair labor practice complaints issued by regional offices throughout the United States, under the authority delegated to these offices by the general counsel.

The Board is prohibited by law from reviewing an ALJ's findings or recommendations before the issuance of the ALJ's formal report. The ALJ's function is that of a specialized trial court judge: to decide unfair labor practice complaints. ALJ decisions may be appealed to the Board, which functions as a specialized court of appeal. After rendering their initial decisions, ALJs (like trial court judges) have nothing to do with the disposition of the case if it is appealed to the Board.

CURRENT MEMBERS OF THE NLRB

The current (January 2015) members of the NLRB are as follows:

- Mark Gaston Pearce was named Chairman of the National Labor Relations Board by President Obama on August 27, 2011. He was sworn in as a Board member on April 7, 2010, following his recess appointment, and was confirmed by the Senate on June 22, 2010, to a term ending on August 27, 2013; he was then reappointed for a second term that expires August 27, 2018. He was a founding partner of the Buffalo, New York, law firm of Creighton, Pearce, Johnsen & Giroux, where he practiced union and plaintiff-side labor and employment law. Prior to entering private practice, he was an attorney and District Trial Specialist in the Buffalo regional office of the NLRB. Pearce received his Juris Doctor from University at Buffalo Law School of the State University of New York, and his bachelor degree from Cornell University.
- Kent Y. Hirozawa was appointed and confirmed by the Senate on July 30, 2013, for a term that expires on August 27, 2016. He was chief counsel to Chairman Pierce until his appointment to the NLRB. He received a B.A. from Yale University and a J.D. from New York University School of Law.
- Harry I. Johnson, III, was appointed to the Board and confirmed by the Senate on August 12, 2013, and his term expires August 27, 2015. He was a partner at the law firm Arent Fox LLP prior to his appointment. He has a B.A. from Johns Hopkins University, an M.A.L.D. from Tufts University's Fletcher School of Law and Diplomacy, and a J.D. from Harvard Law School.
- Lauren McFerran was sworn in on December 17, 2014, for a term ending December 16, 2019. Prior to her appointment to the Board, she served as chief labor counsel for the Senate Committee on Health, Education, Labor and Pensions. She received a B.A. from Rice University and a J.D. from Yale Law School.
- Phillip A. Miscimarra was sworn in as a member of the Board on August 7, 2013, for a term that expires on December 16, 2017. Prior to his appointment, he was a partner with the law firm Morgan Lewis & Bockius LLP, and a senior fellow in

the Center for Human Resources at the Wharton Business School of the University of Pennsylvania. He received a B.A. from Duquesne University, an M.B.A. from the Wharton Business School, and a J.D. from the University of Pennsylvania Law School.

- The current general counsel of the NLRB is Richard F. Griffin, Jr., who was sworn in on November 4, 2013, for a four-year term. He had served as a member of the Board prior to becoming General Counsel. He has a B.A. from Yale University and a J.D. from Northeastern University School of Law.

Source: NLRB, http://www.nlrb.gov/who-we-are.

The General Counsel

The Office of the General Counsel is the prosecutorial branch of the NLRB and is also in charge of the day-to-day administration of the NLRB regional offices. The general counsel is nominated by the president, with Senate confirmation for a four-year term.

The NLRB has 32 regional offices and a number of subregional offices. The staff of each regional office consists of a regional director, regional attorney, field examiners, and field attorneys. Although Section 3(d) of the act gives the general counsel "final authority, on behalf of the Board, in respect of investigation of charges and issuance of complaints ... and in respect of the prosecution of such complaints before the Board," the Office of General Counsel has exercised its statutory right to delegate this power to the regional directors, who make most of the day-to-day decisions affecting enforcement of the act.

Procedures The NLRB handles two kinds of legal questions:

- those alleging that an unfair labor practice has taken place in violation of the act and
- representation questions concerning whether, and if so how, employees will be represented for collective bargaining.

In either type of case, the NLRB does not initiate the proceeding; rather, it responds to a complaint of unfair practice or a petition for an election filed by a party to the case. (The Board refers to unfair practice cases as C cases and to representation cases as R cases.)

Unfair Labor Practice Charges

The filing of an unfair practice charge initiates NLRB proceedings in unfair labor practice cases. The act does not restrict who can file a charge; the most common charging parties are employees, unions, and employers. However, in *NLRB v. Indiana & Michigan Electric Co.*,[13] the Supreme Court held that an individual who was a "stranger" to the dispute could file an unfair labor practice charge. The NLRB has adopted a special form for the filing of unfair practice charges (see Exhibit 12.2). In its fiscal year 2008, there were 22,501 unfair labor practice charges filed with the NLRB.

---

[13] 318 U.S. 9 (1943).

FORM EXEMPT UNDER 44 U.S.C 3512

INTERNET FORM NLRB-501 (2-08)	UNITED STATES OF AMERICA NATIONAL LABOR RELATIONS BOARD **CHARGE AGAINST EMPLOYER**	**DO NOT WRITE IN THIS SPACE**	
		Case No.	Date Filed

INSTRUCTIONS:
File an original with NLRB Regional Director for the region in which the alleged unfair labor practice occurred or is occurring.

1. EMPLOYER AGAINST WHOM CHARGE IS BROUGHT

a. Name of Employer		b. Tel. No.
		c. Cell No.
		f. Fax No.
d. Address *(Street, city, state, and ZIP code)*	e. Employer Representative	g. e-Mail
		h. Number of workers employed
i. Type of Establishment *(factory, mine, wholesaler, etc.)*	j. Identify principal product or service	

k. The above-named employer has engaged in and is engaging in unfair labor practices within the meaning of section 8(a), subsections (1) and *(list subsections)* _____ of the National Labor Relations Act, and these unfair labor practices are practices affecting commerce within the meaning of the Act, or these unfair labor practices are unfair practices affecting commerce within the meaning of the Act and the Postal Reorganization Act.

2. Basis of the Charge *(set forth a clear and concise statement of the facts constituting the alleged unfair labor practices)*

3. Full name of party filing charge *(if labor organization, give full name, including local name and number)*

4a. Address *(Street and number, city, state, and ZIP code)*	4b. Tel. No.
	4c. Cell No.
	4d. Fax No.
	4e. E-mail

5. Full name of national or international labor organization of which it is an affiliate or constituent unit *(to be filled in when charge is filed by a labor organization)*

6. DECLARATION I declare that I have read the above charge and that the statements are true to the best of my knowledge and belief.	Tel. No.
	Office, if any, Cell No.
By _____ _____ *(signature of representative or person making charge)* *(Print/type name and title or office, if any)*	Fax No.
	e-Mail
Address _____ _____ *(date)*	

WILLFUL FALSE STATEMENTS ON THIS CHARGE CAN BE PUNISHED BY FINE AND IMPRISONMENT (U.S. CODE, TITLE 18, SECTION 1001)

PRIVACY ACT STATEMENT

Solicitation of the information on this form is authorized by the National Labor Relations Act (NLRA), 29 U.S.C. § 151 *et seq.* The principal use of the information is to assist the National Labor Relations Board (NLRB) in processing unfair labor practice and related proceedings or litigation. The routine uses for the information are fully set forth in the Federal Register, 71 Fed. Reg. 74942-43 (Dec. 13, 2006). The NLRB will further explain these uses upon request. Disclosure of this information to the NLRB is voluntary; however, failure to supply the information will cause the NLRB to decline to invoke its processes.

EXHIBIT 12.2   Unfair Labor Practice Charge Form

Source: NLRB, http://www.nlrb.gov/resources/forms.

Section 10(b) of the act requires that unfair practice charges must be filed within six months of the occurrence of the alleged unfair practice. Once a charge has been timely filed, the procedure is as follows:

- The charge is investigated by a field examiner. A charge can be resolved at this stage through mutual adjustment, voluntary withdrawal, or agency dismissal for lack of merit.

- If the charge is found to have merit and the case has not been settled by adjustment, a formal complaint is issued by the regional director. (In recent years, approximately one-third of all charges filed were voluntarily withdrawn, another one-third were dismissed as having no merit, and approximately one-third were found to have merit. Of the charges having merit, approximately 60 percent were settled with no formal complaint being issued. Thus, approximately 86 percent of all charges filed were disposed of before reaching the hearing stage in the procedure.)

- A public hearing on the complaint is held in front of an ALJ. (The Taft-Hartley amendments added the requirement that "so far as practicable" this hearing shall be conducted in accordance with the rules of evidence applicable to federal district courts.) At the conclusion of the hearing, the ALJ issues a report with findings of fact and recommendations of law.

- The ALJ's report is served on the parties and forwarded to the Board in Washington, DC. Each party then has 20 days to file exceptions to the report. These exceptions are in effect an appeal to the Board. If no exceptions are taken, the ALJ's report is automatically accepted by the Board as a final order.

- If exceptions have been filed to the ALJ's report by one or more parties, the Board reviews the case and issues a decision and remedial order. The parties will normally have filed briefs with the Board, explaining their respective positions on the exceptions. Sometimes (although rarely) a party will also request and be granted the opportunity to make oral arguments before the Board. Normally, a three-member panel of the Board handles any single case at this stage. (In 40 percent of all the "appeals," the Board approves the ALJ's report in its entirety.)

See Exhibit 12.3 for a summary of unfair labor practice procedures. Orders of the Board are not self-enforcing; if a party against whom an order is issued refuses to comply, the NLRB must ask the appropriate federal circuit court of appeals for a judgment enforcing the order. In addition, any party to the case may seek review of the Board's decision in the appropriate federal court of appeal. The scope of this judicial review of the Board's order is not the same as an appeal from the verdict of a federal trial court; the appeals court is required to accept the Board's findings of fact provided that the findings are supported by substantial evidence in the case record. Any party to the case decided by the federal circuit court of appeals may petition the U.S. Supreme Court to grant certiorari to review the appellate court's decision. The Supreme Court generally restricts its review to cases in which a novel legal issue is raised or in which there is a conflict among the courts of appeal. (Only a minuscule percentage of labor cases reach this final step of the procedure.)

If the regional director refuses to issue a complaint after investigating a charge, that decision can be appealed to the Office of Appeals of the General Counsel in Washington, D.C. Approximately 30 percent of the charges dismissed by the regional offices are appealed

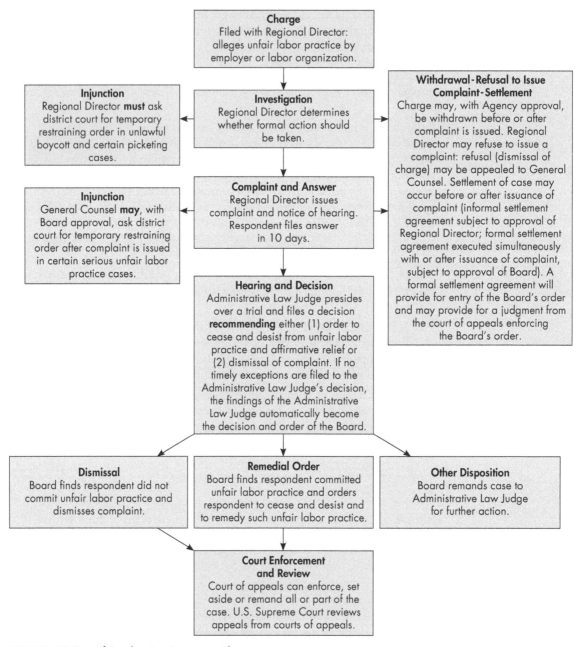

EXHIBIT 12.3   Unfair Labor Practice Process Chart
Source: NLRB, http://www.nlrb.gov/resources/nlrb-process.

to the Office of Appeals of the General Counsel. The Office of Appeals reverses the dismissal by the regional offices only rarely—in less than 10 percent of the cases appealed. The courts have upheld the general counsel's absolute discretion in these decisions; a conclusion that the charge lacks significant merit to issue a complaint cannot be appealed beyond the General Counsel's Office of Appeals. As such, the charging party's statutory rights have been procedurally exhausted and terminated without any hearing or judicial review.

Representation Elections

The other type of cases coming before the NLRB involves representation questions—employees choosing whether or not to be represented by a labor union as their exclusive bargaining agent. In fiscal year 2008, 3,400 representation cases were filed with the NLRB. Although the issues and procedures involved in representation questions are discussed in detail in Chapter 13, a few points are highlighted in this discussion of NLRB procedures.

Representation proceedings are at the very heart of the NLRA because the acceptance or rejection of a union as bargaining agent by a group of employees is the essence of the exercise of the rights guaranteed by Section 7 of the act—to engage in, or refrain from, concerted activity for purposes of collective bargaining or mutual aid or protection. Section 9 of the act outlines the procedures available to employees for exercising their rights under Section 7.

For nearly 25 years, the Board had primary responsibility for the conduct of all representation elections. Then, in 1959, Congress decided that election procedures were sufficiently settled that the Board could delegate its duties in this area to the regional directors. The Board did so in 1961. Specifically, the regional directors are authorized by the Board to

- decide whether a question concerning representation exists;
- determine the appropriate collective bargaining unit;
- order and conduct an election;
- certify the election's results; and
- resolve challenges to ballots by making findings of fact and issuing rulings.

The Board has retained limited review, as the statute suggests, to ensure uniform and consistent application of its interpretation of law and policy. There are four grounds on which the Board will review an election:

- if a significant issue of law or policy is raised due to an absence of or departure from reported Board precedent;
- if the regional director has made a clear error regarding some factual issue and this error is prejudicial to the rights of one of the parties;
- if the procedure involved some error that prejudiced a party; and
- if the Board believes that one of its rules or policies is due for a reconsideration.

Ordinarily, once the regional director has decided that a representation election should be held involving a particular unit of employees, a Notice and a Direction of Election are issued by the regional office, even though one of the parties has appealed some aspect of the director's decision to the Board in Washington. However, unless the parties have waived their right to request Board review, the director will set the election date no earlier than 25 days from the notices. On the other hand, the date will usually not be set any later than 30 days after the director's decision to proceed.

In December 2014, the NLRB adopted a final rule amending the representation election process.[14] The amended procedures are intended to provide for electronic filing of petitions and other documents and to make the process more transparent and uniform across NLRB regional offices. The rules are scheduled to go into effect on April 14, 2015, but several lawsuits challenging the rules change have been filed and are pending in the federal courts.

12-5b Jurisdiction

Under the NLRA, the NLRB is given authority to deal with labor disputes occurring "in commerce" or "affecting commerce" [as defined in Section 2(7) of the act]. Consistent with the federal courts' traditional view of the scope of federal commerce clause powers, the Supreme Court has held that the NLRB can regulate labor disputes in virtually any company, unless the firm's contact with interstate commerce is de minimus (minuscule and merely incidental).

Rather than exercise its jurisdiction to the full extent of the federal commerce power, the NLRB has chosen to set certain minimum jurisdictional standards. These standards specify the limits beyond which the NLRB will decline jurisdiction over any labor dispute. The Landrum-Griffin Act recognized this policy by providing that the NLRB may decline jurisdiction over any labor dispute that would have been outside the NLRB's minimum jurisdictional standards as of August 1, 1959. The NLRB may expand its jurisdictional standards, but it cannot contract them beyond their position as of August 1, 1959. The 1959 amendments to the act also provide that the states under certain circumstances may assert jurisdiction over labor disputes on which the NLRB declines to assert jurisdiction.

General Jurisdictional Standards

The NLRB jurisdictional standards are set in terms of the dollar volume of business that a firm does annually. The current NLRB jurisdictional standards are as follows:

- *General Nonretail Firms.* Sales of goods to consumers in other states, directly or indirectly (termed outflow) or purchases of goods from suppliers in other states, directly or indirectly (termed inflow) of at least $50,000 per year.

- *Retail Businesses.* Annual volume of business of at least $500,000, including sales and excise taxes.

- *Combined Manufacturing and Retail Enterprises.* When an integrated enterprise manufactures a product and sells it directly to the public, either the retail or the nonretail standard can be applied.

- *Combined Wholesale and Retail Companies.* When a company is involved in both wholesale and retail sales, the nonretail standard is applicable.

- *Instrumentalities, Channels, and Links of Interstate Commerce.* Annual income of at least $50,000 from interstate transportation services or the performing of $50,000 or more in services for firms that meet any of the other standards, except indirect inflow and outflow established for nonretail businesses.

---

[14] A description of the new rule is available at NLRB, http://www.nlrb.gov/news-outreach/fact-sheets/nlrb-representation-case-procedures-fact-sheet.

- *National Defense.* Any enterprise having a substantial impact on the national defense.
- *U.S. Territories and the District of Columbia.* Same standards are applied to the territories as to enterprises operating in the 50 states; plenary (total) jurisdiction is exercised in the District of Columbia.
- *Public Utilities.* At least $250,000 total annual volume of business.
- *Newspapers.* At least $200,000 total annual volume of business.
- *Radio, Telegraph, Telephone, and Television Companies.* At least $100,000 total annual volume of business.
- *Hotels, Motels, and Residential Apartment Houses.* At least $500,000 total annual volume of business.
- *Taxicab Companies.* At least $500,000 total annual volume of business.
- *Transit Systems.* At least $250,000 total annual volume of business.
- *Privately Operated Health-Care Institutions.* Nursing homes, visiting nurses' associations, and similar facilities and services, $100,000; all others, including hospitals, $250,000 total annual volume of business.
- *Nonprofit, Private Educational Institutions.* $1 million annual operating expenditures.
- *Multiemployer Bargaining Associations.* Regarded as a single employer for the purpose of totaling up annual business with relation to the above standards.
- *Multistate Establishments.* Annual business of all branches is totaled with regard to the Board's standards.
- *Unions as Employers.* The appropriate nonretail standard.

Exempted Employers

Not all employers—or employees of such employers—meeting the NLRB jurisdictional standards are subject to the provisions of the NLRA. Certain kinds of employers have been excluded from coverage of the act by specific provisions in the act; other employers have been exempted as a result of judicial decisions interpreting the act.

Section 2(2) of the act defines the term *employer* as "including any person acting as an agent of an employer, directly or indirectly," but not including:

- the federal government or any wholly owned government corporation; however, the Board was empowered to assert jurisdiction over the U.S. Postal Service under the Postal Reorganization Act of 1970;
- any state or political subdivision thereof (county, local, or municipal governments);
- railroads, airlines, or related companies that are subject to the Railway Labor Act (In 1996, Congress amended the Railway Labor Act to include Federal Express under its jurisdiction rather than under the NLRA; United Parcel Service, however, remains under the NLRA.); and
- labor organizations in their representational capacity. (Unions are covered by the act in the hiring and treatment of their own employees.)

In addition to these statutory exclusions, judicial decisions have created other exclusions. The NLRB will usually refuse to exercise jurisdiction over an employer that has a close relationship to a foreign government, even if such employers would otherwise come under its jurisdiction. In *Incres S.S. v. Maritime Workers*,[15] the Supreme Court held that the act does not apply to labor disputes of foreign crews on foreign flag vessels temporarily in U.S. ports, even if such ships deal primarily in American contracts. However, when the dispute involves American residents working while the vessel is in port, the dispute is subject to the act. In *Int. Longshore Assoc. v. Allied International, Inc.*,[16] the Supreme Court held that a politically motivated refusal by American longshoremen to service American ships carrying Russian cargo, to protest the Soviet invasion of Afghanistan, was subject to the jurisdiction of the NLRB.

The Supreme Court has also held in *NLRB v. Catholic Bishop*[17] that the NLRB lacked jurisdiction over a parochial high school. The Court stated that its holding was necessary to avoid excessive government entanglement with religion, as prohibited by the First Amendment. The NLRB has taken the position that the Court's decision exempts from NLRB jurisdiction only those organizations devoted principally to the promulgation of the faith of a religion. In December 2015, the NLRB adopted a new standard for determining whether to exert jurisdiction over religious educational institutions in *Pacific Lutheran University*.[18] The NLRB now requires educational institutions claiming that they should be exempted under the *Catholic Bishop* doctrine to first demonstrate that the institution holds itself out as providing a religious educational environment, and then must show that the faculty members that a union seeks to represent perform a specific role in creating or maintaining the institution's religious educational environment, as demonstrated by its representations to current or potential students and faculty members, and the community at large. In *the Pacific Lutheran* decision, the NLRB held that it could assert jurisdiction over the case because the university did not hold those faculty out as performing any religious function, nor did it expect those faculty to contribute anything special to the religious educational environment.

For employers that are not educational institutions, but claim to be religiously affiliated, the NLRB will exempt only those organizations devoted principally to the promulgation of the faith of a religion. The NLRB has refused jurisdiction over a television station owned by a church where more than 90 percent of the station's broadcasts were religious in nature. However, hospitals operated by religious organizations, or religious charity services providing aid to the elderly, have been held subject to NLRB jurisdiction because they were not principally involved with promulgating the religion's faith.

Exempted Employees

Just as with employers, not all employees employed by employers in or affecting commerce are subject to the provisions of the NLRA. These exclusions from coverage are the result of both statutory provisions and judicial decisions.

Statutory Exemptions   Section 2(3) of the NLRA, in its definition of "employee," expressly excludes:

- individuals employed as agricultural laborers;
- individuals employed as domestics within a person's home;

[15] 372 U.S. 24 (1963).
[16] 456 U.S. 212 (1982).
[17] 440 U.S. 490 (1979).
[18] 361 N.L.R.B. No. 157 (Dec. 16, 2014).

- individuals employed by a parent or spouse;

- independent contractors;

- supervisors; and

- individuals employed by employers subject to the Railway Labor Act.

Several of these statutory exclusions require some discussion. For example, the NLRA does not specifically define the term "agricultural laborer"; rather, Congress has directed the NLRB to consider the definition of agriculture found in Section 3(f) of the Fair Labor Standards Act,[19] which is very broad. It includes cultivating, tilling, growing, dairying, producing, or harvesting any agricultural commodity, raising livestock, or any operations or practices performed by a farmer or on a farm as incident to, or in conjunction with, such farming operations. The NLRB considers the facts of each case, looking to the specific duties and the time spent at the duties to determine whether persons are agricultural laborers within the meaning of the NLRA.

In *Holly Farms Corp. v. NLRB*,[20] the Supreme Court (by a 5–4 decision) held that the "live haul" crews of a poultry processor, who drive from the processor's location to independent farms and there collect and cage chickens, lift the cages on a truck, and transport them back to the processor, were not agricultural laborers within the meaning of Section 2(3) and were therefore covered by the NLRA. Agricultural employees exempted from the NLRA may be covered by state legislation; several states, such as California and Arizona, have created agricultural labor relations boards to cover the labor disputes of agricultural laborers.

An **independent contractor** is a person working as a separate business entity; these individuals are not subject to the direction and control of an employer. For example, a person who owns and operates a dump truck and who contracts to provide rubbish disposal service to a firm might be an independent contractor and not an employee of the firm. If the firm used its own truck and directed a worker to haul away its rubbish, the worker would be an employee and not an independent contractor. The NLRB looks to the degree of control and direction exercised by the firm over the worker to determine whether the worker is an employee or an independent contractor.

The term **supervisor** is defined in Section 2(11) of the NLRA as someone who, in the interests of the employer, has the authority to direct, hire, fire, discipline, transfer, assign, reward, responsibly direct, suspend, or adjust the grievances of other employees and who uses independent judgment in the exercise of such authority. The NLRB, applying Section 2(11) to nurses in the health-care industry, held that nurses who directed other employees in patient care were not acting in the interests of their employer and therefore were not supervisors within the meaning of Section 2(11). The Supreme Court rejected the NLRB's decision in *NLRB v. Health Care & Retirement Corporation of America*.[21] The NLRB then held that nurses did not exercise "independent judgment" within the meaning of Section 2(11) because the nurses were exercising "ordinary professional or technical judgment" in directing other employees to deliver patient care in accordance with employer-specified standards.

The following case involves the Supreme Court's consideration of the NLRB's determination that those nurses were not supervisors under the NLRA.

independent contractor
a person working as a separate business entity

supervisor
person with authority to direct, hire, fire, or discipline employees in the interests of the employer

---

[19] 29 U.S.C. § 203(f).

[20] 517 U.S. 392 (1996).

[21] 511 U.S. 571 (1994).

CASE 12.4

NATIONAL LABOR RELATIONS BOARD V. KENTUCKY RIVER COMMUNITY CARE, INC.

532 U.S. 706 (2001)

[Kentucky River Community Care, Inc. (Kentucky River) operates a residential care facility for persons suffering from mental retardation and mental illness. The facility, Caney Creek, employs approximately 110 professional and nonprofessional employees and about 12 managerial or supervisory employees. In 1997, the Carpenters Union petitioned the NLRB to represent a single unit of all 110 potentially eligible employees at Caney Creek. At the hearing on the petition, Kentucky River objected to the inclusion of Caney Creek's six registered nurses in the bargaining unit, arguing that they were supervisors under §2(11) of the Act and therefore were excluded from the class of employees covered by the NLRA and included in the bargaining unit. The Board's regional director initially held that Kentucky River had the burden of proving supervisory status; the regional director then held that Kentucky River had not carried that burden and therefore included the nurses in the bargaining unit. The regional director directed an election to determine whether the union would represent the unit; the union won the election and was certified as the representative of the Caney Creek employees.

Kentucky River then refused to bargain with the union in order to get judicial review of the certification decision. The NLRB's general counsel filed an unfair labor practice complaint under §§8(a)(1) and 8(a)(5) of the Act. The Board granted summary judgment to the general counsel, holding Kentucky River had violated the NLRA. Kentucky River then petitioned the U.S. Court of Appeals for the Sixth Circuit. The Sixth Circuit held that the Board had erred in placing the burden of proving supervisory status on respondent rather than on its general counsel, and it also rejected the Board's determination that the registered nurses did not exercise "independent judgment." The court stated that the Board had erred by classifying the nurses' supervision of nurse's aides in administering patient care as "routine" because the nurses have the ability to direct patient care by virtue of their training and expertise, not because of their connection with management. The NLRB then appealed to the U.S. Supreme Court.]

Scalia, J.

Under the National Labor Relations Act, employees are deemed to be "supervisors" and thereby excluded from the protections of the Act if, *inter alia*, they exercise "independent judgment" in "responsibly … direct[ing]" other employees "in the interest of the employer." This case presents two questions: which party in an unfair-labor-practice proceeding bears the burden of proving or disproving an employee's supervisory status; and whether judgment is not "independent judgment" to the extent that it is informed by professional or technical training or experience…

The Act expressly defines the term "supervisor" in §2(11) … [but] does not, however, expressly allocate the burden of proving or disproving a challenged employee's supervisory status. The Board therefore has filled the statutory gap with the consistent rule that the burden is borne by the party claiming that the employee is a supervisor.…

The Board argues that the Court of Appeals for the Sixth Circuit erred in not deferring to its resolution of the statutory ambiguity, and we agree. The Board's rule is supported by "the general rule of statutory construction that the burden of proving justification or exemption under a special exception to the prohibitions of a statute generally rests on one who claims its benefits. The burden of proving the applicability of the supervisory exception … should thus fall on the party asserting it. In addition, it is easier to prove an employee's authority to exercise 1 of the 12 listed supervisory functions than to disprove an employee's authority to exercise any of those functions, and practicality therefore favors placing the burden on the party asserting supervisory status. We find that the Board's rule for allocating the burden of proof is reasonable and consistent with the Act.…

The text of §2(11) of the Act … sets forth a three-part test for determining supervisory status. Employees are statutory supervisors if (1) they hold the authority to engage in any 1 of the 12 listed supervisory functions, (2) their "exercise of such authority is not of a merely routine or clerical nature, but requires the use of independent judgment," and (3) their authority is held "in the interest of the employer." [*NLRB v. Health Care & Retirement Corp. of America*] The only basis asserted by the Board, before the Court of Appeals and here, for rejecting respondent's proof of supervisory status with respect to directing patient care was the Board's interpretation of the second part of the test—to wit that employees do not use "independent judgment" when they exercise "ordinary professional or technical judgment in directing less-skilled employees to deliver services in accordance with employer-specified standards." The Court of Appeals rejected that interpretation....

The Board ... argues further that the judgment even of employees who are permitted by their employer to exercise a sufficient *degree* of discretion is not "independent judgment" if it is a particular *kind* of judgment, namely, "ordinary professional or technical judgment in directing less-skilled employees to deliver services."... The text, by focusing on the "clerical" or "routine" (as opposed to "independent") nature of the judgment, introduces the question of degree of judgment. ... But the Board's categorical exclusion turns on factors that have nothing to do with the degree of discretion an employee exercises. Let the judgment be significant and only loosely constrained by the employer; if it is "professional or technical" it will nonetheless not be independent. The breadth of this exclusion is made all the more startling by virtue of the Board's extension of it to judgment based on greater " experience" as well as formal training. What supervisory judgment worth exercising, one must wonder, does not rest on "professional or technical skill or experience"? If the Board applied this aspect of its test to every exercise of a supervisory function, it would virtually eliminate "supervisors" from the Act.

As it happens, though, only one class of supervisors would be eliminated in practice, because the Board limits its categorical exclusion with a qualifier: Only professional judgment that is applied "in directing less-skilled employees to deliver services" is excluded from the statutory category of "independent judgment." This second rule is no less striking than the first, and is directly contrary to the text of the statute. *Every* supervisory function listed by the Act is accompanied by the statutory requirement that its exercise " requir[e] the use of independent judgment" before supervisory status will obtain, but the Board would apply its restriction upon "independent judgment" to just 1 of the 12 listed functions: "responsibly to direct." There is no apparent textual justification for this asymmetrical limitation, and the Board has offered none. Surely no conceptual justification can be found in the proposition that supervisors exercise professional, technical, or experienced judgment only when they direct other employees. Decisions "to hire, ... suspend, lay off, recall, promote, discharge, ... or discipline" other employees, must often depend upon that same judgment, which enables assessment of the employee's proficiency in performing his job.... Yet in no opinion that we were able to discover has the Board held that a supervisor's judgment in hiring, disciplining, or promoting another employee ceased to be "independent judgment" because it depended upon

the supervisor's professional or technical training or experience. When an employee exercises one of these functions with judgment that possesses a sufficient degree of independence, the Board invariably finds supervisory status.

The Board's refusal to apply its limiting interpretation of "independent judgment" to any supervisory function other than responsibly directing other employees is particularly troubling because just seven years ago we rejected the Board's interpretation of part three of the supervisory test that similarly was applied only to the same supervisory function. [*NLRB v. Health Care & Retirement Corp. of America*] In *Health Care*, the Board argued that nurses did not exercise their authority "in the interest of the employer," as §2(11) requires, when their "independent judgment [was] exercised incidental to professional or technical judgment" instead of for "disciplinary or other matters, i.e., in addition to treatment of patients." It did not escape our notice that the target of this analysis was the supervisory function of responsible direction. "Under §2(11)," we noted, "an employee who in the course of employment uses independent judgment to engage in 1 of the 12 listed activities, including responsible direction of other employees, is a supervisor. Under the Board's test, however, a nurse who in the course of employment uses independent judgment to engage in responsible direction of other employees is not a supervisor." We therefore rejected the Board's analysis as "inconsistent with ... the statutory language," because it "rea[d] the responsible direction portion of §2(11) out of the statute in nurse cases. " It is impossible to avoid the conclusion that the Board's interpretation of "independent judgment," applied to nurses for the first time after our decision in *Health Care*, has precisely the same object. ... The Labor Management Relations Act, 1947 (Taft-Hartley Act) expressly excluded "supervisors" from the definition of "employees" and thereby from the protections of the Act. §2(3) ... The term "supervisor" means any individual having authority ... "to hire, transfer, suspend, lay off, recall, promote, discharge, assign, reward, or discipline other employees, or responsibly to direct them, or to adjust their grievances." Moreover, the Act assuredly did not incorporate the Board's current interpretation of the term "independent judgment" as applied to the function of responsible direction ... because it had limited the category of supervisors more directly, by requiring functions in *addition* to responsible direction.

... What is at issue is the Board's contention that the policy of covering professional employees under the Act justifies the categorical exclusion of professional judgments from a term, "independent judgment," that naturally includes them. And further, that it justifies limiting this categorical exclusion to the supervisory function of responsibly directing other employees. These contentions contradict both the text and structure of the statute, and they contradict as well the rule of *Health Care* that the test for supervisory status applies no differently to professionals than to other employees. We therefore find the Board's interpretation unlawful....

... the Board's error in interpreting "independent judgment" precludes us from enforcing its order.... Our conclusion that the Court of Appeals was correct to find the Board's test inconsistent with the statute ... suffices to resolve the case. The judgment of the Court of Appeals is affirmed.

It is so ordered.

Case Questions

1. What test determines whether an employee is a supervisor under the NLRA?

2. What is the basis of the NLRB position that nurses who direct other employees in delivering patient care are not exercising independent judgment within the meaning of Section 2(11)? Is the NLRB's position based upon the language of the NLRA? Explain your answers.

3. What is the significance of the determination that the staff nurses are supervisors under the NLRA? What implications does this case have for other professional employees? Explain.

In light of the Supreme Court decision in *NLRB v. Kentucky River Community Care*, the NLRB again considered whether charge nurses were supervisors within the meaning of Section 2(11) in its decision in *Oakwood Healthcare, Inc.*[22] The NLRB majority opinion defined the following terms:

- *Assign:* "... the act designating an employee to a place (such as a location, department, or wing) appointing an employee to a time (such as a shift or overtime period), or giving significant overall duties, i.e., tasks, to an employee.... In the health-care setting, the term 'assign' encompasses the charge nurses' responsibility to assign nurses and aides to particular patients."

- *Responsibly to direct:* whether the "... 'alleged supervisor is held fully accountable and responsible for the performance and work product of the employees' he directs...."

- *Independent judgment:* "professional or technical judgments involving the use of independent judgment are supervisory if they involve one of the 12 supervisory functions of Section 2(11).... Whether the registered nurse is a [Section] 2(11) supervisor will depend on whether his or her responsible direction is performed with the degree of discretion required to reflect independent judgment.... We find that a judgment is not independent if it is dictated or controlled by detailed instructions, whether set forth in company policies or rules, the verbal instructions of a higher authority or in the provisions of a collective bargaining agreement."

In the *Oakwood Healthcare* case, the majority held that employees who permanently served as charge nurses were supervisors under Section 2(11) and were excluded from the bargaining unit, but that the employees who only served as charge nurses when the permanent charge nurses were absent or on vacation were not supervisors under the NLRA and were not excluded from the bargaining unit.

managerial employee person involved in the formulation or effectuation of management policies

Judicial Exemptions In addition to the statutory exclusions of employees from NLRA coverage, the U.S. Supreme Court has created other exemptions. **Managerial employees**,

[22] 348 NLRB 686 (2006).

persons whose positions involve the formulation or effectuation of management policies, were held to be excluded from NLRA coverage in *NLRB v. Textron*.[23] In the 1980 decision in *NLRB v. Yeshiva University*,[24] the Supreme Court held that faculty at a private university, who play a significant role in developing and implementing university academic policies, were managerial employees and thus excluded from the protection of the NLRA. Following *Yeshiva*, the U.S. Court of Appeals for the First Circuit held in *Boston Univ. Chapter, AAUP v. NLRB*[25] that faculty at Boston University were managerial employees. However, where faculty do not have input in developing or implementing policy and exercise no supervisory duties, they have been held to be employees under the coverage of the NLRA, as in *Stevens Inst. v. NLRB*[26] and *Bradford College*.[27]

Recently, in *Pacific Lutheran University*,[28] the NLRB re-examined its approach to the application of the Y*eshiva* decision. The NLRB stated that it will "examine both the breadth and depth of the faculty's authority at the university. In examining the breadth of the faculty's authority, we will give more weight to those areas of policy making that affect the university as a whole, such as the product produced, the terms on which it is offered, and the customers served. In examining the depth of their authority, we seek to determine whether the faculty actually exercise control or make effective recommendations over those areas of policy; this inquiry will necessarily be informed by the administrative structure of the particular university, as well as the nature of the faculty's employment with that university." The NLRB will consider the degree of faculty control of academic programs, enrollment management policies, finances, academic policies, and personnel policies and decisions; the NLRB will put greater weight on the first three of those factors. In the *Pacific Lutheran* decision, the NLRB ruled that adjunct or contingent faculty members did not exercise managerial authority on behalf of the employer and therefore were not exempted from NLRA coverage as managerial employees. Because the NLRA does not cover public sector employers, faculty and staff at public colleges and universities are not subject to NLRB jurisdiction.

The NLRB recently reversed its position on the question of whether graduate students who teach classes and medical residents and interns are employees under the NLRA. In *Brown University*,[29] the NLRB reversed its previous decisions in *Boston Medical Center*[30] and *New York University*.[31] Those decisions had held that medical residents and interns and university graduate teaching assistants were employees under the NLRA. The *Brown University* decision meant that medical residents and interns and graduate assistants are not protected by the NLRA in their efforts to unionize, and their employers are under no legal obligation to recognize and bargain with them if they do form a union. Employees excluded from the act's coverage are not prevented from organizing and attempting to bargain collectively with their employer. There is nothing in the NLRA to prohibit such action. Exclusion means that those employees cannot invoke the act's protection for the exercise

---

[23] 416 U.S. 267 (1974).

[24] 444 U.S. 672 (1980).

[25] 835 F.2d 399 (1987).

[26] 620 F.2d 720 (9th Cir. 1980).

[27] 261 NLRB 565 (1982).

[28] 361 N.L.R.B. No. 157 (Dec. 16, 2015).

[29] 342 NLRB 483 (2004).

[30] 330 NLRB 152 (1999).

[31] 332 NLRB 1205 (2000).

of rights to organize and bargain. There is no requirement that their employer recognize or bargain with their union or even tolerate such activity. Because those employees are denied the act's protections, the employer is free to discipline or discharge excluded employees who attempt to organize and bargain. Therefore, the faculty members in *Boston University* and the graduate assistants in *New York University* may attempt to organize and bargain with their employer, but the university need not recognize and bargain with them.

ethical DILEMMA

FACULTY CONSULTATION RIGHTS AT PRESTIGIOUS UNIVERSITY?

You are the vice president for faculty relations at Prestigious University, a private university in New Jersey. The major portion of your duties involves negotiation and communication with the Prestigious University chapter of the American Association of University Professors (AAUP). The Prestigious chapter of the AAUP has functioned as the representative of the faculty for discussions over salary, benefits, and working conditions for a number of years. Although there is no formal collective agreement between the university administration and the AAUP chapter, the administration has never instituted any policies or changes to benefits or working conditions without first getting the approval of the AAUP chapter.

Because of declining enrollment, increased building maintenance costs, and the expenses of updating computer facilities all across the campus, the university is experiencing financial difficulties. The administration decides to freeze faculty salaries and reduce its contribution to the faculty's medical insurance and pension plans. The AAUP chapter strongly objects to such actions and will not cooperate with the university administration to implement them. The great majority of the faculty at Prestigious University supports the AAUP's position.

Should the university administration continue to work with the AAUP in its capacity as faculty representative, or should the administration impose its financial proposals over the AAUP's objections? The university president has asked you to prepare a memo that outlines the advantages and disadvantages of the two approaches and recommends a course of action. Which approach would you recommend? Why? Prepare the requested memo and explain your position.

confidential employee
person whose job involves access to confidential labor relations information

Confidential employees are neither supervisors nor managerial employees, but those persons whose position involves access to confidential labor relations information. The following case discusses the scope of the confidential employee exemption.

Although managerial employees are excluded from the act's coverage, it is not clear whether "confidential" employees are excluded from the act's coverage or are simply excluded from bargaining units with other employees. If confidential employees, like managers, are excluded from the act's coverage, they are denied the protections of the act. If, however, they are excluded only from bargaining units, they remain employees under the act and are entitled to its statutory protection. The Supreme Court did not specifically address this question in *Hendricks*, nor did the court in *Meenan Oil Co.*

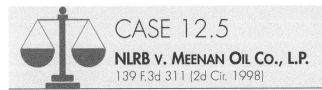

CASE 12.5
NLRB v. Meenan Oil Co., L.P.
139 F.3d 311 (2d Cir. 1998)

Jacobs, Circuit Judge

The National Labor Relations Board (the "Board") petitions for enforcement of its order finding that Meenan Oil Co., L.P. ("Meenan" or the "Company") violated Sections 8 (a) (1) and (5) of the National Labor Relations Act (the "NLRA"), by refusing to bargain with a properly certified union and requiring Meenan to bargain with the union on demand. Meenan contends that the two collective bargaining units at issue were improperly certified because they include employees who are outside the protection of the NLRA. Specifically, Meenan asserts that … its administrator for payroll and personnel matters is … a confidential employee; and the executive secretary to its general manager is a confidential employee.…

Rosemary Gould is [General Manager] Zaweski's executive secretary. She sits outside his office and spends most of her time answering telephones, typing, filing, and performing other clerical tasks. She also opens Zaweski's mail, including items marked "confidential." Gould types documents dealing with employee discipline, including disciplinary notices, termination notices, minutes of union grievance meetings, and grievance settlement documents. Ordinarily, she prepares the documents after a decision has been made, and often after their contents have been disclosed to the relevant employees or union representatives, or discussed with them; copies are generally sent to the employees and union immediately after they are produced. Gould also types some internal memoranda dealing with various personnel issues. These memoranda give her access to intra-management communications that affect union employees generally, even if they do not specifically concern labor issues or strategies. Thus Gould is responsible for typing the Company's annual profit plan, which forecasts the salary increase or decrease planned for every Meenan employee. Meenan asserts that her access to all of these materials makes Gould a confidential employee, and that it was error to include her in a collective bargaining unit.

Angela Gabriel, the Company's payroll/personnel administrator, had worked for the Company for about twelve years at the time of the election.… Gabriel reports to the Company's accounting supervisor on most matters, but reports to Zaweski on issues of personnel. Her primary responsibility is to handle the paperwork for payroll and personnel matters. Specifically, she prepares the weekly payroll figures; collects personnel forms when new employees are hired; receives and files copies of insurance claims, disciplinary notices, and other notices; maintains a complete set of personnel files; calculates and fills out the forms for employees' benefit fund contributions; helps managers keep track of employees' absences and overtime, and is expected to point out any discrepancies she observes; fills out unemployment compensation forms using information provided by the Company's managers; and occasionally copies documents from an employee's file in order to assist a manager who is testifying at an unemployment hearing.

… Gabriel's duties give her access to potentially sensitive information about the Company. Copies of all employees' personnel files are filed in Gabriel's office. She receives employees' drug-test results, though she plays no role in deciding what to do about the results. Gabriel is privy to some union-related information (such as impending layoffs), but she generally acquires that information only when it is in the process of being forwarded to the union. Most important for present purposes, she assists Zaweski with the preparation of the Company's annual profit plan, and in that way has access to the current salary as well as salary changes forecast by the Company for all employees and supervisors, and at least some managers. Because she has access to all of this information, Meenan contends that Gabriel, like Gould, is a confidential employee who for that reason must be excluded from any bargaining unit.…

The Board excludes from collective bargaining units individuals who fit the definition of "confidential employees." *NLRB v. Hendricks County Rural Elec. Membership Corp.*, 454 U.S. 170, 189 (1981).…

The Supreme Court has identified two categories of confidential employees who are excluded from the NLRA's protection: (i) employees who "assist and act in a confidential capacity to persons who formulate, determine, and effectuate management policies in the field of labor relations," and (ii) employees who "regularly have access to confidential information concerning anticipated changes which may result from collective bargaining negotiations."

There are arguably some confidential aspects to many employment relationships, but the Board (for that reason) hews strictly to a narrow definition of a confidential employee.... *In Hendricks County*, the Supreme Court approved the Board's use of this "labor nexus" test; so employees who have access to confidential business information are not for that reason excludible from collective bargaining units. The Board looks to "the confidentiality of the relationship between the employee and persons who exercise managerial functions in the field of labor relations." Moreover, the confidential labor-related information available to the employee must be information that is not already known to the union or in the process of being disclosed to it.

The rationale for the exclusion of confidential employees (as so defined) is that management should not be forced to negotiate with a union that includes employees "who in the normal performance of their duties may obtain advance information of the [c]ompany's position with regard to contract negotiations, the disposition of grievances, and other labor relations matters." An individual who routinely sees data which would enable the union to predict, understand or evaluate the bargaining position of the employer is therefore excluded from union membership.

We conclude that Angela Gabriel, the payroll/personnel administrator, and Rosemary Gould, the executive secretary to the general manager, are confidential employees. Both are in a confidential employment relationship with General Manager Zaweski, who is largely responsible for conducting Meenan's labor relations. Both women fit neatly within the category of confidential employee, identified by the Supreme Court in *Hendricks County*, as those who "assist and act in a confidential capacity to persons who formulate, determine, and effectuate management policies in the field of labor relations."

Zaweski has responsibility for preparing the Company's annual profit plan. Gabriel assists him in that project by filling out forms that show the current salaries and most recent pay raises of the Company's employees, including supervisors and at least some members of management. The forms containing this information, as prepared by Gabriel, are forwarded to the Company's managers, who apply corporate salary increase guidelines to arrive at a recommendation for the timing and size of each employee's next raise, and review these recommendations with Zaweski. A copy of the revised recommendations is then sent to the Company's corporate department, and a copy is retained by Gabriel. If the corporate department revises the figures, Gabriel receives a copy of the updated document. Gabriel thus has knowledge of the proposed salary increase—or decrease—of every Meenan employee. Often she learns of these proposed changes six to seven months before they are implemented.

Zaweski's executive secretary, Rosemary Gould, types the initial draft of the annual profit plan, and in so doing she gets to see the proposed wage and salary figures before they are sent to the corporate department and to Gabriel. Gould testified that she, Gabriel and Zaweski are the only noncorporate employees who see this document.

Because Gabriel and Gould assist Zaweski with the preparation of the Company's annual profit plan, they have access to projected wage and salary data for both union and non-union employees. This information, in the hands of the Union, would give it a significant strategic advantage in negotiations. The Union could predict the size of the raises that management already planned to give both union and non-union employees, prior to any collective bargaining session, and use that level of compensation as a floor for its demands. At the same time, information about the present and projected compensation of managers would afford leverage in bargaining for comparable raises for union members. Even if this information is never mentioned, it would enable the Union to anticipate and gauge management's resistance to its demands.

In summary, the projected wage and salary data contained in the profit plan influences and signals "the [c]ompany's position with regard to contract negotiations." Meenan is not required to bargain with a union whose members have this advantage.

The Board's finding that Gabriel and Gould are not confidential employees is unsupported by substantial evidence, and we therefore decline to enforce the Board's order insofar as Gabriel and Gould are included in the Office Clerical collective bargaining unit....

For the foregoing reasons, we modify the Board's order to remove Meenan's "payroll/personnel administrator" and its "executive secretary" from the Office Clerical collective bargaining unit. The order as modified is enforced.

Case Questions

1. What is the rationale for the exclusion of confidential employees?

2. Does the confidential employee exclusion apply to all employees who have access to the employer's confidential information? What is the "labor nexus" test?

3. What are the key features of Gould's and Gabriel's job duties for the purposes of the "labor nexus" test? Would including Gabriel and Gould in the bargaining unit place the employer at a disadvantage when dealing with the union? Explain.

Unions in the construction industry often try to organize a contractor's workforce by getting some of their organizers to be hired by the contractor. Can persons who are on the payroll of a union as organizers also be employees under the meaning of Section 2(3)? The following case involves that question in the context of the legality of an employer's refusal to hire persons who are also on the union payroll as organizers.

>> CASE 12.6

NLRB v. TOWN & COUNTRY ELECTRIC, INC.
516 U.S. 85 (1995)

Facts: Town & Country Electric, Inc., a non-union electrical contractor, advertised for job applicants, but it refused to interview 10 of 11 union applicants who responded to the ad. Its employment agency hired the one union applicant whom Town & Country interviewed, but he was dismissed after only a few days on the job. Those rejected applicants were members of the International Brotherhood of Electrical Workers, Locals 292 and 343; they filed a complaint with the National Labor Relations Board (NLRB), claiming that Town & Country and the employment agency had refused to interview (or retain) them because of their union membership, a violation of the National Labor Relations Act (NLRA).

An administrative law judge ruled in favor of the union members, and the NLRB affirmed that ruling. The NLRB determined that all 11 job applicants were "employees," as the Act defines that word. The Board recognized that under well-established law, it made no difference that the 10 applicants were never hired; nor did it matter that the union members intended to try to organize the company if they were hired, and that the union would pay them for their organizing. The NLRB held that the company had committed unfair labor practices by discriminating against them on the basis of union membership.

The United States Court of Appeals for the Eighth Circuit reversed the NLRB. It held that the NLRB had incorrectly interpreted the word "employee," and that term "employee" did not include those persons who work for a company while simultaneously being paid by a union to organize that company. The decision of the court of appeals meant that the applicants here were not protected by the NLRA from discrimination because of their union membership. The court refused to enforce the Board's order, and the NLRB appealed to the U.S. Supreme Court.

Issue: Does the definition of "employee" under the NLRA include persons working for a company and, at the same time, being paid by a union to help the union organize the company?

Decision: The National Labor Relations Act definition of "employee" [Section 2(3)] is as follows:

> The term "employee" shall include any employee, and shall not be limited to the employees of a particular employer, unless this subchapter explicitly states otherwise, and shall include any individual whose work has ceased as a consequence of, or in connection with, any current labor dispute or because of any unfair labor practice, and who has not obtained any other regular and substantially equivalent employment, but shall not include any individual employed as an agricultural laborer, or in the domestic service of any family or person at his home, or any individual employed by his parent or spouse, or any individual having the status of an independent contractor, or any individual employed as a supervisor, or any individual employed by an employer subject to the Railway Labor Act, as amended from time to time, or by any other person who is not an employer as herein defined.

The NLRB interpretation of this language to include company workers who are also paid union organizers is consistent with the broad language of the act itself. That language is broad enough to include those company workers whom a union also pays for organizing. The ordinary dictionary definition of "employee" includes any "person who works for another in return for financial or other compensation." The NLRB's broad, literal interpretation of the word "employee" is consistent with the NLRA's purposes of protecting "the right of employees to organize for mutual aid without employer interference" and "encouraging and protecting the collective bargaining process."

Town & Country argues that a worker also being paid as a union organizer is sometimes acting adversely to the company, and the organizer may stand ready to leave the company if so requested by the union. Town & Country claims that means that the union, not the company, would have "the right to control the conduct of the employee" and therefore the worker must be the employee of the union alone. Town & Country's argument fails because the NLRB correctly found that it was not supported by common law. The NLRB concluded that service to the union for pay does not involve abandonment of service to the company. Common sense suggests that a worker going about the ordinary tasks during a working day is subject to the control of the company, whether or not the worker is also paid by the union. The fact that union and company interests may sometimes differ does not matter. The union organizers may limit their organizing to nonwork hours. If that

is so, union organizing, when done for pay but during nonwork hours, would be equivalent to "moonlighting," a practice wholly consistent with a company's control over its workers as to their assigned duties. There are legal remedies for Town & Country's concerns, other than excluding paid or unpaid union organizers from protection under the NLRA. If the company is concerned about employees quitting without notice, it can offer its employees fixed-term contracts rather than hiring them "at will," or it can negotiate with its workers for a notice period. A company faced with unlawful activity by its workers can discipline or dismiss those workers, or file a complaint with the NLRB, or notify law enforcement authorities.

The Supreme Court held the NLRB's interpretation of the word "employee" was lawful, and that the statutory definition of the term does not exclude paid union organizers. The Supreme Court vacated the judgment of the court of appeals, and remanded the case for further proceedings consistent with its opinion.

In *Toering Electric Co.*[32] the NLRB held that when an employer is charged with discriminatorily failing to hire an applicant for employment, the NLRB General Counsel has the burden of proving that the applicant was genuinely interested in working for the employer. The employer can defend itself against the unfair labor practice charge by raising a reasonable question as to the applicant's actual interest in working for the employer. If the employer puts forward such evidence, then the general counsel must establish, by a preponderance of evidence, that the applicant was interested in establishing an employment relationship with the employer. If the general counsel fails to make such a showing, then the employer's refusal to hire the applicant is lawful. This approach has been criticized as not being consistent with the Supreme Court's opinion in *NLRB v. Town & Country Electric, Inc.*

THE **WORKING** LAW

Are College Athletes Employees?

The College Athletics Players Association (CAPA) filed a petition with the NLRB to seek a representation election for the members of the football team at Northwestern University. The NLRB regional director ruled that scholarship players on the team are employees within the meaning of Section 2(3) of the National Labor Relations Act (NLRA).[33] The players seeking union representation stated that their major concerns were ensuring that: (1) the university provided medical treatment for the athletes after their playing days are over, (2) they do not lose their scholarships if they are injured, (3) they are not subject to unnecessary brain trauma, and (4) they are given better opportunities to complete their degrees. The university took the position that the players were students rather than employees.

---

[32] 351 N.L.R.B. No. 18 (2007).

[33] *Northwestern University and College Athletes Players Association*, 2014 WL 1246914 (March 26, 2014).

The regional director's decision that the players were employees under the NLRA was based on the following facts: (1) The players perform valuable services for the university and for which they receive compensation. Northwestern's football program generated revenues of approximately $235 million during the nine year period 2003–2012 through ticket sales, television contracts, merchandise sales, and licensing agreements. (2) The scholarship players are under the strict control and direction of the university—they spend up to 60 hours per week on football-related activities, and the coaches have control over nearly every aspect of the players' private lives by virtue of the fact that there are many rules that they must follow under threat of discipline and/or the loss of a scholarship. (3) The scholarship players are not primarily students because their athletic duties do not constitute a core element of their educational degree requirements, and their athletic duties are not supervised by the university's academic faculty.

The regional director directed that a representation election be held to determine whether the players wish to be represented by CAPA. The bargaining unit was defined as including those football players who receive scholarships and who have not exhausted their playing eligibility at the conclusion of the 2013 football season. The representation election was held on April 25, 2014. However, prior to the election, the university petitioned the NLRB to review the regional director's decision; the Board granted the petition for review on April 24, 2014.[34] The representation election was held on April 25, but the ballots were impounded and will only be counted if the Board upholds the regional director's decision. If the decision is upheld, then the regional director will then determine whether a majority of those voting have chosen to make CAPA their exclusive bargaining agent. The NLRB has not indicated when it will issue its decision, and the question may not finally be resolved for several years.

Jurisdiction over Labor Organizations

Section 2(5) of the NLRA defines "labor organization" as:

> any organization of any kind, or any agency or employee representation committee or plan, in which employees participate and which exists for the purpose, in whole or in part, of dealing with employers concerning grievances, labor disputes, wages, rates of pay, hours of employment, or conditions of work.

NLRB and Supreme Court decisions have held that the words "dealing with" are broad enough to encompass relationships that fall short of collective bargaining. For example, in *NLRB v. Cabot Carbon*,[35] the Supreme Court held that the act encompassed employee committees that functioned merely to discuss with management, but not bargain over, such matters of mutual interest as grievances, seniority, and working conditions. There is also case law to suggest that a single individual cannot be considered a labor organization "in any literal sense."[36]

12-5c　Preemption and the NRLA

Because of the broad reach of NLRB jurisdiction under the federal commerce power, it is important to consider whether the states have any authority to legislate regarding labor relations in the private sector. Although state laws that conflict with federal laws are void under the supremacy clause of Article VI of the Constitution, the Supreme Court has consistently held that states may regulate activities involving interstate commerce where such regulation

---

[34] 2014 WL 1653118 (April 24, 2014).

[35] 360 U.S. 203 (1959).

[36] See *Bonnaz v. NLRB*, 230 F.2d 47 (D.C. Cir. 1956).

is pursuant to a valid state purpose. In such situations, the states have concurrent jurisdiction with the federal government: The regulated firm or activity is subject to both the state and federal regulations. But where an activity is characterized by pervasive federal regulation, the Supreme Court has held that Congress has, under the supremacy clause powers, "occupied the field" so that the federal law preempts any state regulation. One example of such preemption is the regulation of radio and television broadcasting by the Federal Communications Commission. Has Congress, through the enactment of the NLRA, preempted state regulation of private sector labor disputes?

The Supreme Court tried to answer this question in two leading decisions. In *San Diego Building Trades Council v. Garmon*,[37] the Supreme Court held that state and federal district courts are deprived of jurisdiction over conduct that is "arguably subject" to Section 7 or Section 9 of the NLRA. In *Sears Roebuck v. San Diego County District Council of Carpenters*,[38] the Supreme Court held that state courts may deal with matters arising out of a labor dispute when the issue presented to the state court is not the same as that which would be before the NLRB. The Court said it would consider the nature of the particular state interests being asserted and the effect on national labor policies of allowing the state court to proceed. *Sears* involved a trespassing charge filed against picketing by the carpenters; no unfair practice charges were filed with the NLRB by either party to the dispute. The Court upheld the right of the state court to order the picketers to stop trespassing on Sears's property, recognizing that Congress did not preempt all state regulation of matters growing out of a labor dispute.

In *Wisconsin Dept. of Industry, Labor & Human Relations v. Gould*,[39] the Supreme Court held that the NLRA preempted a Wisconsin law that barred any firm violating the NLRA three times within five years from doing business with the state. The Court held that the law sought to supplement the sanctions for violations of the NLRA and so was in conflict with the NLRB's comprehensive regulation of industrial relations.

The Supreme Court summarized the principles of the preemption of state laws by federal labor relations law in the 1993 case of *Building & Construction Trades Council of the Met. Dist. v. Assoc. Builders and Contractors of Mass.*,[40] which upheld a state regulation requiring contractors working on public contracts to abide by the terms of a collective agreement. The Court noted that federal labor relations law preempts state regulation of activities that are protected by Section 7 or are defined as unfair labor practices by the NLRA (as in *San Diego Building Trades v. Garmon*), and state regulation of areas left to the control of market and economic forces (as in *Wisconsin Dept. of Industry, Labor & Human Relations v. Gould*). In *Chamber of Commerce of U.S. v. Brown*,[41] the Supreme Court held that a California state law that prohibited employers that received state grants of more than $10,000 per year from using the funds "to assist, promote, or deter union organizing" was preempted by the NLRA.

President Clinton's Executive Order No. 12954 disqualified firms that hired permanent replacement workers during lawful strikes from federal contracts over $100,000. This order, however, was held to be preempted by the NRLA, which allows employers to hire permanent replacements in economic strikes, according to *Chamber of Commerce v. Reich*.[42]

---

[37] 359 U.S. 236 (1959).

[38] 436 U.S. 180 (1978).

[39] 475 U.S. 282 (1986).

[40] 507 U.S. 218 (1993).

[41] 554 U.S. 60 (2008).

[42] 74 F.3d 1322 (D.C. Cir. 1996), *rehearing denied*, 83 F.3d 439 (D.C. Cir. 1996).

Federal legislation may also expressly preserve the right of the states to regulate activities. For example, Section 103 of the Labor-Management Reporting and Disclosure Act, dealing with internal union affairs, states that "Nothing contained in this title shall limit the rights and remedies of any member of a labor organization under any State … law or before any court or other tribunal.…" Because of this provision, states are free to legislate greater protection for union members vis-à-vis their unions, and state courts are free to hear suits that may arise under such laws.

Concept *Summary* 12.4

THE NATIONAL LABOR RELATIONS BOARD

- Organization
  - Five-member board
  - Division of judges (ALJs)
  - General counsel
- Types of cases
  - Unfair labor practices (ULPs)
  - Representation elections
- Jurisdiction
  - Exempted employers
    - Federal government/government-owned corporations
    - Railroads, airlines, or other companies subject to RLA
    - Representational labor organizations
  - Statutorily exempted employees: The NLRA excludes persons who are:
    - Employed as agricultural laborers
    - Employed in the domestic service of any person or family in a home
    - Employed by a parent or spouse
    - Employed as an independent contractor
    - Employed as a supervisor
    - Employed by an employer subject to the Railway Labor Act, such as railroads and airlines
    - Employed by federal, state, or local government
    - Employed by any other person who is not an employer as defined in the NLRA
  - Judicially exempted employees: The courts have also held the following persons are also excluded from the NLRA:
    - Managerial employees
    - Confidential employees

CHAPTER REVIEW

» Key Terms

criminal conspiracy	352	common law	360	independent contractor	379
yellow-dog contract	353	closed shop	367	supervisor	379
injunction	356	administrative law judge (ALJ)	370	managerial employee	382
ex parte proceeding	357			confidential employee	384

» Summary

- Organized labor developed slowly in the United States, with the post–Civil War industrialization spurring the rise of the Knights of Labor, the socialists, and the American Federation of Labor (AFL). The AFL ultimately developed into the dominant organization of the American labor movement; its merger with the CIO in 1955 marked the high point for organized labor in the United States. Since the mid-1950s, the percentage of the American workforce that is unionized has steadily dwindled, from around 35 percent to the current level of approximately 12 percent. Unions still exert political influence, but there has been no resurgence of the labor movement since the mid-1950s. The U.S. legal system responded to organized labor by initially trying to suppress it through the use of the conspiracy doctrine, the labor injunction, and yellow-dog contracts. The antitrust laws, intended to attack anticompetitive business practices, were also used against union strikes and boycotts.

- It was not until the Great Depression of the 1930s that organized labor received legislative protection. The Norris–La Guardia Act, passed in 1932, greatly limited the use of labor injunctions by the

federal courts. The National Industrial Recovery Act, the centerpiece of Franklin Roosevelt's New Deal, provided protection for employees organizing unions and encouraged collective bargaining. The National Labor Board (NLB) was created in 1933 to mediate labor disputes, but it had to rely on persuasion rather than legal authority. The NLB was replaced by the "old" National Labor Relations Board in 1934. When the Supreme Court declared the National Industrial Recovery Act unconstitutional in 1935, it meant the end of the old NLRB.

- Congress passed the Wagner Act shortly thereafter; the NLRA, and the NLRB it created, survived a constitutional challenge in the 1937 decision of *NLRB v. Jones & Laughlin Steel Corp.* The Wagner Act became the foundation for the development of the current National Labor Relations Act, the legal framework for labor relations in the United States.

- The National Labor Relations Act (NRLA) regulates private sector labor relations; the NLRA is administered by the National Labor Relations Board (NLRB). The NLRA defines the basic rights of employees and prohibits actions by employers or unions that interfere with or restrict those rights—defined as unfair labor practices. The NLRB adjudicates complaints of unfair labor practices under the NLRA and conducts representation elections.

- The NLRA excludes public sector employers, railroads, and airlines subject to the Railway Labor Act from its definition of employer; and the NLRB has adopted guidelines to define the scope of its jurisdiction over private sector employers. The NRLA also excludes certain employees from the act's coverage: agricultural laborers, persons employed as domestics in the homes of others, individuals employed by parents or spouses, independent contractors, supervisors, and employees of Railway Labor Act employers. In addition to the statutory exclusions, the courts have excluded managerial employees and confidential employees.

- The NLRA preempts state laws that purport to regulate conduct protected by or prohibited by the NLRA and that seek to regulate areas left by the NLRA to the market and economic forces.

» Problems

» Questions

1. Why was the labor injunction an effective weapon against union activities?

2. How were the antitrust laws used to deter union activities?

3. What were the main provisions of the Norris–La Guardia Act? How did the Norris–La Guardia Act affect union activities?

4. What were the major provisions of the Wagner Act? What were the effects of this act? What factors led to the passage of the Taft-Hartley Act? What were the effects of this act?

5. Which employers are covered by the NLRA? Which employers are exempt from NLRA coverage? Which employees are excluded from NLRA coverage?

» Case Problems

6. The legislature of West Virginia enacted a law in 1983 (effective July 1, 1984) requiring that at least 40 percent of the board of directors of all nonprofit and local government hospitals in the state be composed of an equal proportion of "consumer representatives" from "small businesses, organized labor, elderly persons, and persons whose income is less than the national median income."

The American Hospital Association joined with a number of West Virginia hospitals in seeking an injunction against enforcement of the law and a declaratory judgment that, among other things, the law interfered with bargaining rights between the hospitals and their employees and was therefore preempted by federal labor law.

If you were arguing for the plaintiff hospitals, how would you contend that this West Virginia law might interfere with the collective bargaining relationship? If you were the federal judge hearing the case, how would you rule and why? [See *American Hospital Association v. Hansbarger*, 600 F. Supp. 465, 118 L.R.R.M. 2389 (N.D. W.Va. 1984).]

7. Spring Valley Farms, Inc. supplied poultry feed to farmers who raised broiler and egg-laying poultry. Sarah F. Jones had the title of feed delivery manager with the company in Cullman, Alabama, and she dispatched the drivers who delivered the feed. Drivers could earn more money on "long hauls" (more than 50 miles from the mill) than on "short hauls." Therefore, Spring Valley Farms instructed Jones to "equalize" the number of long and short hauls so that all drivers would earn approximately the same wages. The company also instructed her to work the drivers as close to 40 hours per week as possible and then to "knock them off" by seniority. It was left to Jones's discretion to devise methods for accomplishing these objectives.

Does Spring Valley Farms fall under the jurisdiction of the NLRB? Is Jones as manager excluded from the Board's jurisdiction? [See *Spring Valley Farms*, 272 NLRB No. 205, 118 L.R.R.M. 1015 (1984).]

8. In 1976, the citizens of New Jersey amended their state constitution to permit the legislative authorization of casino gambling in Atlantic City. Determined to prevent the infiltration of organized crime into its nascent casino industry, the New Jersey legislature enacted the Casino Control Act, which provides for the comprehensive regulation of casino gambling, including the regulation of unions representing industry employees. Sections 86 and 93 of the act specifically impose certain qualification criteria on officials of labor organizations representing casino industry employees. (Section 86, for example, contains a list of crimes, conviction of which disqualifies a union officer from representing casino employees.) A hotel employees' union challenged the state law, arguing that it was preempted by the NLRA, which gives employees the right to select collective bargaining representatives of their own choosing. The case reached the U.S. Supreme Court.

How should the Supreme Court have ruled? Why? [See *Brown v. Hotel Employees Local 54*, 468 U.S. 491, 116 L.R.R.M. 2921 (1984).]

9. The Volunteers of America (VOA) is a religious movement founded in New York City in 1896. Its purpose is "to reach and uplift all segments of the population and to bring them to a knowledge of God." The Denver Post of the VOA, founded in 1898, is an unincorporated association operated under the direction of the national society. It maintains three chapels in the Denver area, at which it conducts regular religious services and Bible study groups. The VOA also operates a number of social programs in Denver, including temporary care, shelter, and counseling centers for women and children.

The United Nurses, Professionals and Health Care Employees Union filed a petition with the NLRB to represent the counselors at these shelters. The VOA argued it was not subject to the Board's jurisdiction because (1) the First Amendment to the U.S. Constitution precludes NLRB jurisdiction over a religious organization, and (2) it received partial funding from the city and county governments under contracts specifying the services it was to perform so that the government, not the VOA, was the true employer. The case reached the Tenth Circuit Court of Appeals.

How should the court have ruled on these two arguments? [See *Denver Post of VOA v. NLRB*, 732 F.2d 769 (10th Cir. 1984); and *Aramark Corp. v. NLRB*, 179 F.3d 872 (10th Cir. 1999).]

10. The *Alcoa Seaprobe* was a U.S.-flagged oceangoing vessel engaged in offshore geophysical and geotechnical research. While berthed in Woods Hole, Massachusetts, its owner, Alcoa Marine Corporation (a Delaware corporation headquartered in Houston, Texas), had contracted with Brazil's national oil company to use *Alcoa Seaprobe* for offshore exploration of Brazil's continental shelf. When Alcoa sent the *Seaprobe* to Brazil, it did not intend to return the vessel to the United States.

The Masters, Mates & Pilots Union (International Longshoremen) filed a petition to represent the crew of *Alcoa Seaprobe*. Alcoa Marine Corporation argued that since *Seaprobe* was not expected to operate in U.S. territorial waters, the NLRA did not apply.

How should the NLRB have ruled? [See *Alcoa Marine Corp.*, 240 NLRB No. 18, 100 L.R.R.M. 1433 (1979).]

11. National Detective Agencies, Inc., of Washington, D.C., provided security officers to various clients in the District of Columbia. Among these clients was the Inter-American Development Bank, "an international economic organization whose purpose is to aid in the economic development and growth of its member nations, who are primarily members of the Organization of American States." The Federation of Special Police petitioned the NLRB to represent National's employees, including those who worked at the bank.

National argued that the bank could require National to issue orders and regulations to its guards and to remove any guard the bank considered unsatisfactory. The bank had the right to interview all job applicants and to suggest wage scales. Consequently, National argued, the bank was a joint employer of the guards and, as an international organization, enjoyed "sovereign immunity" from NLRA jurisdiction. Therefore, these guards should not be included in the proposed bargaining unit.

How do you think the NLRB ruled on this argument? Is this case conceptually distinguishable from the *Alcoa Seaprobe* case in problem 10? [See *National Detective Agencies*, 237 NLRB No. 72, 99 L.R.R.M. 1007 (1978).]

12. Dudczak was employed as a production supervisor at VPA, Inc. until he was fired because his brother and cousin had led a union organizing campaign among the workers at VPA. Dudczak filed an unfair labor practice complaint with the NLRB, alleging that his discharge was a violation of Section 8(a)(1). Subsequent to the firing of Dudczak, VPA agreed to recognize the union as the exclusive bargaining agent of its employees.

How should the NLRB rule on Dudczak's complaint? Explain your answer. [See *Kenrich Petrochemicals v. NLRB*, 893 F.2d 1468 (3d Cir. 1990).]

13. The faculty members at the Universidad Central de Bayamon in Puerto Rico seek to unionize in order to bargain collectively with the university over wages, working conditions, and so on. The university, which describes itself as a "Catholic-oriented civil institution," is governed by a board of trustees, of whom a majority are to be members of the Dominican religious order.

Is the Universidad subject to NLRB jurisdiction, or is it exempt under the *Catholic Bishop* doctrine? What factors would the NLRB consider in making that determination? [See *Pacific Lutheran* University, 361 NLRB No. 157 (2014); and *Universidad Central de Bayamon*, 273 NLRB No. 38 (1984); 778 F.2d 906 (1st Cir.) *rev'd. on rehearing*, 793 F.2d 383 (1985).]

14. Callaghan, an employee of Smith Transportation, is one of the leaders of an effort to unionize the Smith employees. Biggins, the personnel manager of Smith, suspects Callaghan is involved in the organizing campaign and decides to fire him.

Callaghan is given notice on January 15, 2001, that his employment will be terminated on January 31, 2001. On July 20, 2001, Callaghan files a complaint with the appropriate regional office of the NLRB, alleging that he was fired in violation of Sections 8(a) 1 and 3 of the NLRA. Smith Transportation argues that the complaint was not filed within the required six-month limitations period.

Was the complaint filed in a timely fashion? Does the time limit run from when the employee is notified of the impending discharge or from when the discharge becomes effective? [See *United States Postal Service*, 271 NLRB No. 61, 116 L.R.R.M. 1417 (1984).]

15. Speedy Clean Service, Inc. provides janitorial services for office buildings; a number of its employees are Hispanics who have entered the United States illegally. When several employees try to organize a union to represent them, Speedy Clean fires all of its workers. The discharged employees file unfair labor practice charges with the NLRB; the employer argues that the illegal aliens are not entitled to protection under the act.

Are illegal aliens included within the definition of "employee" under Section 2(3)? Explain your answer. [See *Hoffman Plastic Compounds, Inc. v. NLRB*, 535 U.S. 137 (2002).]

» Hypothetical Scenarios

16. The part-time faculty members at Farber College are disturbed by the college administration's decision to freeze their pay. They are paid a flat fee for each course they teach, and that fee has not been raised for the last five years. The part-time faculty does not play any role in developing college policies or in deciding curriculum matters. The part-time faculty members do not have permanent offices and must meet with students in the campus cafeteria or coffee shop. The part-time faculty members decide to form a union to bargain with the college administration. Are the part-time faculty "employees" under the NLRA? Why? Would your answer change if Farber were a public college? Why?

17. Betty Suarez is the administrative assistant for the manager at Mode, Inc., a small fashion design house. She prepares the payroll for the firm and assists the manager with some personnel decisions. The office staff at Mode, Inc. seek to form a union, and Betty is interested in being a part of the union. Are there any legal restrictions on Betty being a member of the bargaining unit? Explain.

18. Cantor, Inc. is a firm that provides counseling and therapy services for children and adolescents with emotional problems. The firm is funded primarily by financial grants from state and local government agencies and charitable foundations, although it does receive a small amount of income from fees paid by clients (or the clients' insurance company). The funding agencies do require that Cantor, Inc. meet certain performance standards, but do not have any role in determining Cantor's employment policies. Is Cantor, Inc. an employer under the NLRA? Explain.

19. The taxi drivers at 4-Star Cabs pay the company a daily rental fee for the use of the company cabs but get to keep all the fares that they earn during their driving shifts. The drivers determine their working hours and must pay for the gas they use during their shifts. The company carries an "umbrella" auto insurance policy that covers the drivers, but it does not provide any benefits to the drivers. Are the drivers "employees" under the NLRA? Explain.

20. Your roommate is a medical resident at St. Olaf's Hospital, which is run by the Lutheran Church. She tells you that the residents are interested in forming a union because they are forced to work long hours for low pay. The residents have graduated from medical school but must complete a certain number of years as residents before they can be certified as licensed medical practitioners. What rights do the residents have under the NLRA? Can they require the hospital administration to discuss working conditions with them? Explain.

CHAPTER **13**

The Unionization Process

In the preceding chapter, we discussed briefly the National Labor Relations Board's (NLRB) administrative structure and procedures in representation (R) cases. In this chapter, we consider in greater detail the mechanisms created by the Board for determining whether a company's employees will be represented by a union for purposes of collective bargaining.

13-1 Exclusive Bargaining Representative

We have seen that Section 7 of the NLRA entitles employees "to bargain collectively through representatives of their own choosing." Section 9(a) adds that:

> Representatives designated or selected for the purposes of collective bargaining by the majority of the employees in a unit appropriate for such purposes, shall be the exclusive representatives of all the employees in such unit for the purposes of collective bargaining in respect to rates of pay, wages, hours of employment, or other conditions of employment.

The position of the union as exclusive bargaining agent supersedes any individual contracts of employment made between the employer and the unit employees. Any dealings with individual unit employees must be in accordance with the collective bargaining agreement.

The Taft-Hartley Act added some protection for minority factions within bargaining units by adding to Section 9(a) the stipulation that:

> any individual or a group of employees shall have the right at any time to present grievances to their employer and to have such grievances adjusted, without the intervention of the bargaining representative, as long as the adjustment is not inconsistent with the terms of a collective bargaining contract or agreement then in effect.

The extent to which this provision allows the employer to deal with individual employee grievances, and its effect on the union's position as exclusive bargaining agent, will be discussed in Chapter 15.

13-1a Employees' Choice of Bargaining Agent

Although the most common method of determining the employees' choice of a bargaining representative is to hold a secret ballot election, the NLRA does not require such procedures.

Employers confronted by a union claiming to have the support of a majority of their employees may recognize the union as the exclusive bargaining agent for those employees. Section 9(a) requires only that the union, in order to become the exclusive bargaining agent, be designated or selected by a majority of the employees. It does not require that an election be held to determine employee choice. The propriety of this method of recognition, called a **voluntary recognition**, is well established, provided that the employer has no reasonable doubt of the employees' preference and that recognition is not granted for the purpose of assisting one particular union at the expense of another seeking to represent the same employees.

voluntary recognition
an employer agreeing to recognize a union with majority support as the exclusive bargaining agent for the workers in the bargaining unit, without holding a certification election

Bargaining status achieved through a voluntary recognition imposes on the employer the duty to bargain with the union in good faith, just the same as with a union victory in a representation election conducted by the Board. But the representation election method has several advantages over the voluntary recognition method. The representation election procedures involve the determination of the bargaining unit—that is, which of the employer's workers should be grouped together for purposes of representation and bargaining. Following a union victory in an election, the employer is obligated to recognize and bargain with the union for at least 12 months following the election. No petitions seeking a new representation (or decertification) election can be filed for that unit of employees during the 12-month period. For a voluntary recognition, the employer is obligated to recognize and bargain with the union only for a "reasonable period" of time, unless a collective bargaining agreement is agreed upon. The NLRB has defined a reasonable period of time to be no less than six months after the parties' first bargaining session and no more than one year.[1] In determining whether a reasonable period has elapsed after six months in a given case, the NLRB will consider the following factors: (1) whether the parties are bargaining for an initial contract; (2) the complexity of the issues being negotiated and of the parties' bargaining processes; (3) the amount of time elapsed since bargaining commenced and the number of bargaining sessions; (4) the amount of progress made in negotiations and how near the parties are to concluding an agreement; and (5) whether the parties are at impasse.[2] The burden is on the General Counsel to prove that a reasonable period of bargaining has not elapsed after six months.

In the absence of an agreement and after the passage of a reasonable period of time, a voluntary recognition will not prevent the filing of a petition seeking a representation election for that same group of employees. In addition, an employer who voluntarily recognizes a union claiming to have majority support commits an unfair labor practice if the union does not actually have the support of a majority of the employees in the bargaining unit. Thus, a representation election conducted by the Board is the method of recognition preferred by the parties in most cases.

Just as filing a charge initiates the administrative process in an unfair labor practice (C) case, so too a petition from an interested party is needed to initiate a Board-sponsored election under Section 9(c)(1)(A). Any employee, group of employees, or labor organization can file such a petition seeking a representation election or a decertification election on behalf of the employees as a whole (see Exhibit 13.1). An employer is entitled to file a petition only after one or more individuals or unions present that employer with a claim for recognition as the bargaining representative according to Section 9(c)(1)(B).

---

[1] *Lamons Gasket Co.*, 357 NLRB No. 72 (2011).

[2] *Lee Lumber & Building Material Corp.*, 334 NLRB 399 (2001), enforced as *Lee Lumber & Building Material Corp. v. N.L.R.B.*, 310 F.3d 209 (D.C. Cir. 2002).

INTERNET FORM
NLRB-502 (2-08)

UNITED STATES GOVERNMENT
NATIONAL LABOR RELATIONS BOARD
PETITION

FORM EXEMPT UNDER 44 U.S.C.

DO NOT WRITE IN THIS SPACE	
Case No.	Date Filed

INSTRUCTIONS: Submit an original of this Petition to the NLRB Regional Office in the Region in which the employer concerned is located.

The Petitioner alleges that the following circumstances exist and requests that the NLRB proceed under its proper authority pursuant to Section 9 of the NLRA.

1. PURPOSE OF THIS PETITION (if box RC, RM, or RD is checked and a charge under Section 8(b)(7) of the Act has been filed involving the Employer named herein, the statement following the description of the type of petition shall not be deemed made.) (Check One)

☐ **RC-CERTIFICATION OF REPRESENTATIVE** - A substantial number of employees wish to be represented for purposes of collective bargaining by Petitioner and Petitioner desires to be certified as representative of the employees.

☐ **RM-REPRESENTATION (EMPLOYER PETITION)** - One or more individuals or labor organizations have presented a claim to Petitioner to be recognized as the representative of employees of Petitioner.

☐ **RD-DECERTIFICATION (REMOVAL OF REPRESENTATIVE)** - A substantial number of employees assert that the certified or currently recognized bargaining representative is no longer their representative.

☐ **UD-WITHDRAWAL OF UNION SHOP AUTHORITY (REMOVAL OF OBLIGATION TO PAY DUES)** - Thirty percent (30%) or more of employees in a bargaining unit covered by an agreement between their employer and a labor organization desire that such authority be rescinded.

☐ **UC-UNIT CLARIFICATION** - A labor organization is currently recognized by Employer, but Petitioner seeks clarification of placement of certain employees:
(Check one) ☐ In unit not previously certified. ☐ In unit previously certified in Case No._____

☐ **AC-AMENDMENT OF CERTIFICATION** - Petitioner seeks amendment of certification issued in Case No._____
Attach statement describing the specific amendment sought.

2. Name of Employer	Employer Representative to contact	Tel. No.

3. Address(es) of Establishment(s) involved (Street and number, city, State, ZIP code)	Fax No.

4a. Type of Establishment (Factory, mine, wholesaler, etc.)	4b. Identify principal product or service	Cell No.
		e-Mail

5. Unit Involved (In UC petition, describe **present** bargaining unit and attach description of proposed clarification.)	6a. Number of Employees in Unit:
Included	Present
Excluded	Proposed (By UC/AC)
	6b. Is this petition supported by 30% or more of the employees in the unit?* ☐ Yes ☐ No *Not applicable in RM, UC, and AC

(If you have checked box RC in 1 above, check and complete EITHER item 7a or 7b, whichever is applicable)

7a. ☐ Request for recognition as Bargaining Representative was made on (Date)_____ and Employer declined recognition on or about (Date)_____ (If no reply received, so state).

7b. ☐ Petitioner is currently recognized as Bargaining Representative and desires certification under the Act.

8. Name of Recognized or Certified Bargaining Agent (If none, so state.)	Affiliation	
Address	Tel. No.	Date of Recognition or Certification
	Cell No.	Fax No. / e-Mail

9. Expiration Date of Current Contract. If any (Month, Day, Year)	10. If you have checked box UD in 1 above, show here the date of execution of agreement granting union shop (Month, Day and Year)

11a. Is there now a strike or picketing at the Employer's establishment(s) involved? Yes ☐ No ☐	11b. If so, approximately how many employees are participating?

11c. The Employer has been picketed by or on behalf of (Insert Name)_____, a labor organization, of (Insert Address)_____ Since (Month, Day, Year)_____

12. Organizations or individuals other than Petitioner (and other than those named in items 8 and 11c), which have claimed recognition as representatives and other organizations and individuals known to have a representative interest in any employees in unit described in item 5 above. (If none, so state)

Name	Address	Tel. No.	Fax No.
		Cell No.	e-Mail

13. Full name of party filing petition (If labor organization, give full name, including local name and number)

14a. Address (street and number, city, state, and ZIP code)	14b. Tel. No. EXT	14c. Fax No.
	14d. Cell No.	14e. e-Mail

15. Full name of national or international labor organization of which Petitioner is an affiliate or constituent (to be filled in when petition is filed by a labor organization)

I declare that I have read the above petition and that the statements are true to the best of my knowledge and belief.

Name (Print)	Signature	Title (If any)
Address (street and number, city, state, and ZIP code)	Tel. No.	Fax No.
	Cell No.	e-Mail

WILLFUL FALSE STATEMENTS ON THIS PETITION CAN BE PUNISHED BY FINE AND IMPRISONMENT (U.S. CODE, TITLE 18, SECTION 1001)
PRIVACY ACT STATEMENT

Solicitation of the information on this form is authorized by the National Labor Relations Act (NLRA), 29 U.S.C. § 151 *et seq.* The principal use of the information is to assist the National Labor Relations Board (NLRB) in processing unfair labor practice and related proceedings or litigation. The routine uses for the information are fully set forth in the Federal Register, 71 Fed. Reg. 74942-43 (Dec. 13, 2006). The NLRB will further explain these uses upon request. Disclosure of this information to the NLRB is voluntary; however, failure to supply the information will cause the NLRB to decline to invoke its processes.

EXHIBIT 13.1   Petition to Initiate NLRB Election

Source: NLRB, http://www.nlrb.gov/resources/forms.

authorization cards cards signed by employees indicating that they authorize the union to act as the employees' bargaining agent and to seek an election on behalf of the employees

forty-eight-hour rule NLRB requirement that a party filing a petition for a representation election must provide evidence to support the petition within 48 hours of the filing

If it is a union or employees who file a petition with the appropriate regional office of the Board, the NLRB will not proceed with the election until the petitioning union or employee group presents evidence that at least 30 percent of the employee group support the election request. (If an employer files the petition under the circumstances outlined above, this rule does not apply.) Usually, this showing of support is reflected in signed and dated **authorization cards** obtained by the union from the individual employees. These cards may simply state that the signatories desire an election to be held, or they may state that the signing employee authorizes the union to be his or her bargaining representative (see Exhibit 13.2). Other acceptable showings of employee interest can include a letter or similar informal document bearing a list of signatures and applications for union membership.

Under the Board's **forty-eight-hour rule**, an employer who files a petition must submit to the regional office proof of a union's recognition demand within two days of filing the petition. Likewise, a petitioning union or employee group has 48 hours after filing in which to proffer authorization cards or other proof of 30 percent employee support for the requested election. Upon the docketing (logging in) of a petition, a written notification of its filing is sent by the regional director to the employer and any labor organizations claiming to represent any employees in the proposed unit or known to have an interest in the case's disposition. Employers are asked to submit the following:

- A payroll list covering the proposed bargaining unit
- Data showing the nature and volume of the company's business for jurisdictional purposes
- A statement of company position on the appropriateness of the requested bargaining unit

Uniting for Change
LOCAL 200UNITED
SEIU
Stronger Together
Syracuse Office
315.424.1750
Buffalo Office
716.631.8940
Rochester Office
585.464.8880
Albany Office
518.438.4206

I hereby request and accept membership in the Service Employees International Union, (S.E.I.U.), Local 200United, and authorize said Union to represent me and, on my behalf, negotiate and conclude, through my elected negotiating committee, any and all agreements regarding my wages, hours and conditions of employment. I understand this card may be used to establish that my Union represents a majority.

Please Print

Name ______ Employer Name ______

Address ______

City ______ State ______ Zip ______ Phone ______

E-Mail ______

Dept./Job title ______ Date of Hire ______ Shift ______

Signature ______ Date ______

EXHIBIT 13.2 Union Authorization Card

The new R case is then assigned to a Board agent, who investigates to determine whether the following conditions exist:

- The employer's operations affect commerce within the act's meaning.

- A question about representation really exists (i.e., no union presently represents the employees and is shielded by the election bar rule, or some similar impediment to the election).

- The proposed bargaining unit is appropriate.

- The petitioning union, if any, has garnered a 30 percent showing of interest among the employees.

If the agent finds some impediment to an election, the regional director can dismiss the petition. The decision to dismiss can be appealed to the Board in Washington, D.C. Conversely, the petitioning party may choose to withdraw the petition. The usual penalty for withdrawal is imposition of a six-month waiting period before the same party can petition again. (If the employer has submitted the petition, the named union may disclaim interest, also leading to dismissal.)

If the petition survives this initial investigation, the parties may still require the resolution of issues raised by the petition. Questions such as the definition of the bargaining unit, the eligibility of certain employees to participate in the election, and the number of polling places need to be settled prior to holding the election. The parties may agree to waive their rights to a hearing on these issues and proceed to a **consent election**. In so doing, they may either agree that all rulings of the regional director on these questions are final and binding, or they may reserve the right to appeal the regional director's decisions to the Board.

consent election
election conducted by the regional office giving the regional director final authority over any disputes

If the parties fail to agree on some of these issues and have not agreed to a consent election, then a representation hearing will be held before a presiding officer, who may be a Board attorney, field examiner, or ALJ. The act does not prescribe rules of evidence to be used in this proceeding (in contrast to the C case hearing); indeed, the Board's rules and regulations state that federal court rules of evidence shall not be controlling.

A second union, with a 10 percent showing of interest from among the employees, is entitled to intervene and participate in the hearing. Such an intervention can also block a consent election and compel a hearing to take place.

Shortly after the hearing, the hearing officer will submit a report to the director, who will then render a decision either to hold an election or to dismiss the petition. This decision can be appealed by a party to the Board in Washington only on the following grounds:

- A Board legal precedent was not followed or should be reconsidered.

- A substantial factual issue is clearly erroneous in the record.

- The conduct of the hearing was prejudicial to the appealing party.

The Board will act expeditiously on the appeal. Meanwhile, the regional director will proceed with plans for the election, which usually occurs 25 to 30 days after it has been ordered. Exhibit 13.3 shows the NLRB representation election process.

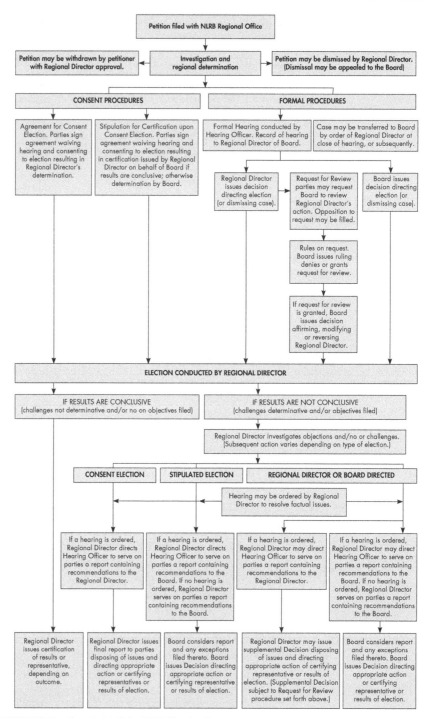

EXHIBIT 13.3 Flowchart of the NLRB Election Process

Source: NLRB, http://www.nlrb.gov/resources/nlrb-process.

The NLRB adopted a rule that would speed up the election process by streamlining and simplifying the procedures and postponing resolution of disputes concerning the eligibility or inclusion of voters that might affect the results of the election. The implementation of the rule was enjoined by the U.S. District Court for the District of Columbia on the grounds that the Board lacked a legal quorum when it adopted the rule.[3] The Board reconsidered and revised the proposed rule, and issued the revised rule on December 12, 2014, to take effect on April 14, 2015.[4] Several legal challenges to this proposed rule have been filed in the federal courts and may result in delaying or preventing the rule from going into effect.

THE **WORKING** LAW

NLRB Issues Final Rule to Modernize Representation-Case Procedures

The National Labor Relations Board has adopted a final rule amending its representation–case procedures to modernize and streamline the process for resolving representation disputes. The rule will be published in the Federal Register on December 15, and will take effect on April 14, 2015.

Of the final rule, Chairman Pearce said, "I am heartened that the Board has chosen to enact amendments that will modernize the representation case process and fulfill the promise of the National Labor Relations Act. Simplifying and streamlining the process will result in improvements for all parties. With these changes, the Board strives to ensure that its representation process remains a model of fairness and efficiency for all."

The final rule was approved by Board Chairman Mark Gaston Pearce and Members Kent Y. Hirozawa and Nancy Schiffer. Board Members Philip A. Miscimarra and Harry I. Johnson III dissented. The rule includes detailed explanations regarding the rule's impact on current procedures and the views of the majority and dissenting members.

The Board believes the rule will enable the agency to more effectively administer the National Labor Relations Act by modernizing its rules in light of modern technology, making its procedures more transparent and uniform across regions, and eliminating unnecessary litigation and delay. With these amendments, the Board will be better able to fulfill its duty to protect employees' rights by fairly, efficiently and expeditiously resolving questions of representation.

Thus, the final rule:

* Provides for electronic filing and transmission of election petitions and other documents;
* Ensures that employees, employers and unions receive timely information they need to understand and participate in the representation case process;
* Eliminates or reduces unnecessary litigation, duplication and delay;

---

[3] *Chamber of Commerce v. NLRB*, 2012 WL 1664028 (May 14, 2012).

[4] The new rules went into effect on April 14. 2015. Information and a detailed description of the rule and procedures, as well as links to revised forms, is available at https://www.nlrb.gov/what-we-do/conduct-elections/representation-case-rules-effective-april-14-2015.

- Adopts best practices and uniform procedures across regions;
- Requires that additional contact information (personal telephone numbers and email addresses) be included in voter lists, to the extent that information is available to the employer, in order to enhance a fair and free exchange of ideas by permitting other parties to the election to communicate with voters about the election using modern technology; and
- Allows parties to consolidate all election-related appeals to the Board into a single appeals process.

Source: "NLRB Representation Case-Procedures Fact Sheet," NLRB Press Release, December 12, 2014, available at http://www.nlrb.gov/news-outreach/fact-sheets/nlrb-representation-case-procedures-fact-sheet.

13-1b Rules That Bar Holding an Election

The philosophy of the NLRB and the courts is that a Board-sponsored election is a serious step, which the affected employees should not be permitted to disavow or over-rule frivolously or hastily. Furthermore, the newly certified bargaining agent should be given a reasonable opportunity to fulfill its mandate by successfully negotiating a collective bargaining agreement with the company. If the Board failed to protect the successfully elected bargaining representative from worker fickleness or rival union challenges, the employer would be encouraged to avoid timely and sincere bargaining in an effort to erode the union's support before an agreement is reached. The Board has, therefore, fashioned several election bar rules.

contract bar rule
a written labor contract
bars an election
during the life of the
bargaining agreement,
subject to the "open-
season" exception

Under the **contract bar rule**, a written labor contract—signed and binding on the parties and dealing with substantial terms and conditions of employment—bars an election among the affected bargaining unit during the life of that bargaining agreement. This rule has two exceptions. First, the Board provides a window, or "open season," during which a rival union can offer its challenge by filing an election petition. This window is open between the 90th day and 60th day prior to the expiration of the current collective bargaining agreement. The rationale here is that a rival union should not be completely prevented from filing an election petition. Otherwise, the employer and incumbent union could continually bargain new contracts regardless of whether the employees wished to continue to be represented by the incumbent union.

If no new petition is filed during the open-season period, then the last 60 days of the contract provide a period during which the parties can negotiate a new agreement insulated from any outside challenges. If a petition is filed during this insulated period, it will be dismissed as untimely. In the event that the employer and the incumbent union fail to reach a new agreement and the old agreement expires, then petitions may be filed any time after the expiration of the existing agreement.

The second exception to the contract bar rule is that a contract for longer than three years will operate only as a bar to an election for three years. In *American Seating Co.*,[5] the Board held that an agreement of excessive duration cannot be used to preclude challenges to

---

[5] 106 NLRB 250 (1953).

the incumbent union indefinitely. Therefore, any contract longer than three years' duration will be treated as if it were three years long for the purposes of filing petitions; that is, the open-season period would occur between the 90th and the 60th day prior to the end of the third year of the agreement.

Section 9(c)(3) of the NLRA provides that when a valid election has been held in a bargaining unit, no new election can be held for a 12-month period for that unit or any subdivision of the unit. When the employees of a unit have voted not to be represented by a union, no other union may file for an election for those employees for 12 months. By the same token, when a union has been certified as the winner of the election, it is free from challenge to its status for at least 12 months. This 12-month period usually runs from the date of certification, but when an employer refuses to bargain with the certified union, the Board may extend the period to 12 months from when good-faith bargaining actually commences. The 12-month period under Section 9(c)(3) applies only when an election has been held.

Concept *Summary* 13.1

RESTRICTIONS ON HOLDING REPRESENTATION ELECTIONS

- A valid election was held within the last 12 months

- A written labor contract covering the terms and conditions of employment exists
  - However, a petition may be filed between the 90th and the 60th day prior to the expiration of the contract
  - For a contract longer than three years, a petition may be filed between the 90th and the 60th day prior to the expiration of the third year of the contract

- When the employer has voluntarily recognized a union, and no challenge to union's status has been filed during the 45-day notice period, the NLRB will not accept a petition for an election for a "reasonable period" of time

13-1c Defining the Appropriate Bargaining Unit

bargaining unit
group of employees being represented by a union

The **bargaining unit** is a concept central to labor relations under both the Railway Labor Act and the NLRA. The bargaining unit is the basic constituency of the labor union; it is the group of employees for which the union seeks to acquire recognition as bargaining agent and to negotiate regarding employment conditions. In order for collective bargaining to produce results fair to both sides, it is essential that the bargaining unit be defined appropriately. The bargaining unit should encompass all employees who share a community of interests regarding working conditions. It should not be so broad as to include divergent or antagonistic interests. Nor should it submerge the interests of a small yet well-defined group of employees within the larger unit.

Section 9(b) of the NLRA provides that the definition of an appropriate bargaining unit is a matter left to the Board's discretion. What constitutes an appropriate bargaining unit is the most commonly disputed issue in representative case hearings. It is also one of the most complex and difficult questions for the Board and the courts to resolve. The Supreme Court in *Packard Motor Car v. NLRB*[6] observed that "The issue as to what unit is appropriate is one for which no absolute rule of law is laid down by statute.... The decision of the Board, if not final, is rarely to be disturbed." This statement is a bit misleading because Section 9(b) of the NLRA does set out some guidelines for the Board in determining the appropriate unit. Section 9(b) states that the goal in defining a bargaining unit is to "assure the employees the fullest freedom in exercising the rights guaranteed by this Act." Section 9(b) also contains the following five provisions:

- The options open to the Board in determining a bargaining unit include an employer-wide unit, a craft unit, a single-plant unit, or a subdivision thereof.

- The unit cannot contain both professional employees [as defined by Section 2(12) of the act] and nonprofessional employees, unless a majority of the professional employees have voted to be included in the unit.

- A craft unit cannot be found to be inappropriate simply on the ground that a different unit (e.g., a plant-wide unit) was established by a previous Board determination, unless a majority of the employees in the proposed craft unit vote against representation in such a separate craft unit.

- A unit including nonguard or nonsecurity employees cannot include plant guards or security personnel; conversely, a union representing plant guards cannot be certified if it also includes workers other than guards as members or if it is directly or indirectly affiliated with a union representing persons other than guards.[7]

- The extent to which employees have already been organized at the time of the filing of the election petition is not to be controlling of the Board's definition of the appropriate bargaining unit.

In addition to the statutory commands, the Board has fashioned a number of other factors to be considered in determining the appropriate unit. Those factors include the following:

- the community of interest of included employees concerning wages, hours, working conditions, the nature of duties performed, and the skills, training, or qualifications required;

- geographical and physical proximity of included workers;

---

[6] 330 U.S. 485 (1947).

[7] By requiring that guards and security personnel be organized in a separate bargaining unit and separate unions, Congress appears to hold the view that the normal duties of plant guards can create conflicts of interest with their union loyalties. Section 9(b) prohibits the NLRB from certifying a "mixed" bargaining unit—one containing guards and nonguards—but it does not preclude voluntary recognition of a union representing a mixed unit, *General Service Employees Union, Local No. 73 v. NLRB*, 230 F.3d 909 (7th Cir. 2000).

- any history of prior collective bargaining tending to prove that a workable relationship exists or can exist between the employer and the proposed unit;

- similarity of the unit to the employer's administrative or territorial divisions, the functional integration of the company's operations, and the frequency of employee interchange; and

- the desires of the employees concerning the bargaining unit, such as might be determined through a secret ballot among workers who have the statutory prerogative of choosing between a plant-wide unit or a separate craft unit. (This right to self-determination by election is referred to as the *Globe* doctrine, after the case in which the standards for such elections were set out, *Globe Machine and Stamping*,[8] pursuant to Section 9(b)(2) of the act.)

Where a company employs temporary workers supplied by a personnel staffing agency in addition to its own employees, the NLRB will only include the temporary workers in a bargaining unit with the firm's employees if both the employer and the staffing agency agree to the multiemployer bargaining unit, according to *Oakwood Care Center*.[9]

In *Macy's Inc.*,[10] the NLRB held that the employer had committed an unfair labor practice by refusing to bargain with the union in order to protest the certification of a bargaining unit defined as including all full-time, regular part-time, and on-call employees who work an average of four hours per week in the cosmetics and fragrances department at the Macy's store in Saugus, Massachusetts.

The following case illustrates the NLRB's application of the "community of interest" test, where the union seeks to represent maintenance workers while the employer argues that the bargaining unit should include both maintenance and production workers.

CASE 13.1

BUCKHORN, INC. AND INTERNATIONAL UNION OF INDUSTRIAL AND INDEPENDENT WORKERS
343 NLRB 201 (Sept. 30, 2004)

Decision on Review and Order by Chairman Battista and Members Schaumber and Meisburg
On December 4, 2003, the Acting Regional Director for Region 25 issued a Decision and Direction of Election in the above-entitled proceeding in which he found appropriate the petitioned-for unit of all maintenance employees employed by the Employer at its Bluffton, Indiana facility. Thereafter …

the Employer filed a timely request for review of the Acting Regional Director's decision. The Employer contends that a separate maintenance unit is not an appropriate unit for bargaining and that the only appropriate unit must include production employees as well as maintenance employees.

On January 14, 2004, the Board granted the Employer's request for review….

---

[8] NLRB 294 (1937).

[9] 343 NLRB 659 (2004).

[10] *Macy's, Inc. and Local 1445 of the United Food and Commercial Workers International Union*, 361 NLRB No. 163 (Jan. 7, 2015).

Facts

The Employer manufactures plastic containers. All aspects of the production process are located within the same facility in Bluffton, Indiana. Manufacturing a container involves conveying plastic pellets from storage silos through an automated system that liquefies the pellets and then delivers the liquid plastic to one of nine presses. The liquefied plastic is poured through nozzles into an individual mold in the shape of a specific product that is installed in the press. After the product is molded, it is removed from the press and readied for shipment to the customer. The nine presses run automatically the majority of the time without the assistance of an employee. When the presses are run on a semiautomatic basis, an employee operates the controls to start the production cycle. The presses have a computerized robot affixed to them that assists in removing the molded product from the press and in placing the product on a conveyer belt, attached to the press, that takes the product to the shipping area. Molds are changed at the conclusion of a product run. Employees remove the existing mold and nozzles and install a new mold and new nozzles for the next product run. The removed mold and nozzles are cleaned, repaired if necessary, and stored.... The Employer operates around the clock, 7 days a week, with the majority of employees assigned to one of four rotating 12-hour shifts. A number of employees work an 8-hour shift, Monday through Friday.

There are approximately 100 hourly paid employees who work at the Bluffton facility, 19 of whom are the maintenance employees the Petitioner [the union] seeks to represent. The remaining employees are production and shipping/receiving/warehouse employees.... The plant manager has overall responsibility for the operation of the plant. A production manager, who reports directly to the plant manager, is responsible for production operations. Reporting to the production manager are four production supervisors, each of whom is assigned to one of the four 12-hour shifts. The maintenance supervisor and the project engineer also report to the production manager.

The maintenance employees the [union] seeks to represent occupy one of five job classifications: skilled maintenance, setup maintenance, tooling associate, tooling technician, and nozzle prep/build associate. The skilled maintenance employees are primarily responsible for the maintenance and upkeep/repair of the presses, as well as for programming the computerized robots. They spend approximately 90 percent of their time on the production floor working on the presses. Additionally, skilled maintenance employees are responsible for the upkeep of the production facility and the automated system that moves the plastic pellets from the storage silos to the presses. They may also help with mold changes. The skilled maintenance employees, currently five in number, report directly to the maintenance supervisor. There is one skilled maintenance employee assigned to each of the four rotating shifts; the fifth skilled maintenance employee works the Monday through Friday schedule.

The remaining maintenance employees, in the job categories of set-up maintenance, tooling associate, tooling technician, and nozzle prep associate, spend the majority of their time performing a variety of functions related to changing molds on the presses. They remove, clean, lubricate, and repair the molds and nozzles which have been removed from the presses, and they install the new mold and nozzles required to produce a new product. These duties involve hydraulic and electrical work. Unlike the skilled maintenance employees, however, these maintenance employees, currently 14 in number, do not report to the maintenance supervisor. Rather, they report directly to the production supervisor responsible for the shift on which they work. Set-up maintenance employees and tooling associates work one of the rotating shifts, while the tooling technicians and the nozzle prep associates work the Monday through Friday schedule.

Production employees include production associates, team leaders, auditors, utility associates, and shipping/warehouse employees.... The production supervisor on each shift supervises the production associates, team leaders, and utility associates, as well as the 14 maintenance employees. Auditors and shipping/repair/warehouse associates have separate supervision.

Nine production employees designated as "helpers" work with the set-up maintenance employees and the tooling associates in the mold change process. These "helpers" regularly perform tasks performed by these maintenance employees, such as removing and installing nozzles, extension blocks, thermocouple wires and hydraulic hoses, as well as operating the crane to remove a mold from the press. Employees in all job classifications have frequent contact and interaction during the day, especially production employees and the skilled maintenance and set-up maintenance employees, who spend almost all their time on the production floor working on the presses doing repairs or production work. Thirteen of the current nineteen maintenance employees were originally hired as production associates, while four current production employees previously held maintenance positions.

The majority of production employees and maintenance employees work similar shifts....

Analysis

It is the Board's longstanding policy, as set forth in American Cyanamid Co. [131 NLRB 909 (1961)] to find petitioned-for separate maintenance department units appropriate where the facts of the case demonstrate the absence of a more comprehensive bargaining history and the petitioned-for maintenance employees have a community of interest separate and distinct from other employees. In determining whether a sufficient community of interest exists, the Board examines such factors as mutuality of interests in wages, hours, and other working conditions; commonality of supervision; degree of skill and common functions; frequency of contact and interchange with other employees; and functional integration. "While many factors may be common to most situations … the effect of any one factor, and therefore the weight to be given it in making the unit determination, will vary from industry to industry and from plant to plant." [*American Cyanamid Co.*, 131 NLRB at 911]

In this case, the [union] contends that the maintenance employees constitute a distinct and homogeneous unit with interests different from those of the production employees. The [union] argues that maintenance employees are in a separate administrative department, are required to have, and do have, skills different from those of production employees, and receive higher wages. The [union] further asserts that there is little job interchange between maintenance and production employees, that maintenance employees are required to take their annual vacation during the summer plant shutdown, unlike other employees, and that they receive training from the Employer that other classifications of employees do not receive.

The Employer contends that a separate unit of maintenance employees is not appropriate, and that an all-inclusive unit of maintenance and production employees is appropriate. The Employer relies on the high degree of functional integration of its operations where, in the Employer's words, "employees work side by side and have daily interaction with each other." The Employer also states that there is a high degree of overlap in job functions. The Employer contends that production employees and maintenance employees throughout its facility share a community of interest based on their common supervision, comparable skills and job functions, frequent interchange, virtually identical terms and conditions of employment, and similar work schedules.

We agree with the Employer that the petitioned-for unit is not an appropriate unit for collective bargaining purposes. Contrary to the Acting Regional Director, we do not find that the petitioned-for maintenance employees constitute a distinct, homogeneous group of employees that would warrant granting the Petitioner's request for a separate unit.

We reach this conclusion based on a number of factors. First, the Employer's operations are highly integrated and there is a significant degree of contact and interaction among the maintenance employees and the production employees. For example, the skilled maintenance and set-up maintenance employees spend virtually all their working time on the production floor, working with production employees on the presses to produce a finished product, and to change the molds on the presses when required. Production employees seek out the assistance of maintenance employees when a mechanical problem arises and routinely perform the same duties as maintenance employees, especially during the mold change process.

Second, there is not a wide disparity in skill level between the maintenance employees and the production employees, except for the five skilled maintenance employees. Although the skilled maintenance position is the highest skilled position in the plant, there are no educational or certification requirements for the job. Further, maintenance employees regularly perform production work. In fact, set-up maintenance employees, who comprise one-half of the maintenance employees, work with and perform the same work as production employees during the mold change process. Both groups of employees regularly assist employees in the shipping/receiving/warehouse area and employees from both groups routinely relieve each other during breaks and can fill in for one another on certain steps in the manufacturing process. Additionally, the production employees designated as "helpers" routinely do the same work as the set-up maintenance employees and tooling associates during the mold change process.

Third, there is evidence of permanent transfers between the two groups of employees. Two-thirds of the current maintenance employees were hired from the ranks of production employees, and four production employees were previously maintenance employees.

A fourth factor weighing against the appropriateness of a separate maintenance unit is that the 19 maintenance employees do not share common supervision: only the 5 skilled maintenance employees are supervised by the maintenance supervisor. Significantly, the maintenance supervisor is not available during all shifts when skilled maintenance employees work; he works Monday through Friday from 7 a.m. to 4 p.m. In his absence, the skilled maintenance employees receive their assignments from the shift production supervisor who has the authority to supersede directions left by the maintenance supervisor. The other classifications of maintenance employees are supervised by the shift production supervisor who also supervises production employees. The production supervisors function as the sole immediate supervisors of 14 of 19 maintenance employees, as well as approximately 70 production employees. While nominally within the maintenance department, 14 maintenance employees are supervised by production supervisors who have authority to hire and discipline them and direct their work.

Finally, in all significant respects, all maintenance employees and production employees share identical terms and conditions of employment, including work rules and policies, work schedules and vacations, lunch facilities, and fringe benefits. Although certain maintenance employees are paid at a higher level than production employees, largely because of their skill level, there is some overlap in wages, just as there is overlap among employees in the exercise of their job skills. While these two factors might appear to favor separate units, we find that the modest discrepancy in wage rates and skill levels is relatively insignificant and is outweighed by all the other factors that clearly demonstrate the broad community of interest that the maintenance employees share with production employees.

Order

Accordingly, we conclude that the petitioned-for unit limited solely to maintenance employees is not an appropriate unit

for the purposes of collective bargaining… We reverse the Acting Regional Director's finding and remand the case to the Regional Director for further appropriate action.

The Acting Regional Director's Decision and Direction of Election is reversed. This proceeding is remanded to the Regional Director for further appropriate action consistent with this Decision on Review and Order.

Case Questions

1. What are the factors that the NLRB considers in determining whether maintenance department employees should be in a bargaining unit separate from production employees? Why would the union seek a unit covering only the maintenance department employees? Why would the employer want a bargaining unit covering both maintenance and production employees?

2. Do the maintenance workers interact with the production employees? Are the maintenance employees subject to separate supervision and separate working conditions? Explain.

3. Did the NLRB decide that a separate unit or an integrated unit is the appropriate bargaining unit in this case? Which factors did the NLRB here consider decisive in making its decision?

Craft Unit Severance

One of the most complex issues in bargaining unit determination involves the questions of craft unit severance: When is it appropriate to certify a craft bargaining unit representing employees who were previously included in a larger bargaining unit? The NLRB decision *Mallinckrodt Chemical Works*[11] is the leading pronouncement on the matter. In that case, the NLRB indicated that it will look to the following factors:

*   if the proposed craft unit consists of skilled crafts workers performing functions on a nonrepetitive basis, or if it is a functionally distinct department;

*   the history of collective bargaining of the employees involved and other plants of the employer;

*   the extent to which the employees in the proposed unit have established and maintained their separate identity during inclusion in the larger unit;

*   the history and pattern of collective bargaining in the industry involved;

*   the degree of integration of the employer's production processes;

---

[11] 162 NLRB 387 (1966).

- the qualifications of the union seeking to represent the separate craft unit; and

- the union's experience in representing employees like those in the proposed craft unit.

Bargaining Unit Definition in the Health-Care Industry

The 1974 amendments to the NLRA extended NLRB jurisdiction over nonprofit health-care institutions. The congressional committee reports accompanying the amending legislation stated that "Due consideration should be given by the Board to preventing proliferation of bargaining units in the health-care industry." The Board issued its final rule for such determinations in 1989.[12] The rule states that the Board will recognize the following eight bargaining units for acute-care hospitals:

- Physicians

- Registered nurses

- Other professional employees

- Medical technicians

- Skilled maintenance workers

- Clerical workers

- Guards

- Other nonprofessional employees

No unit with fewer than six employees will be certified (except for guard units). In determining the eight appropriate units, the Board considered the following factors: the uniqueness of function; training, education and licensing; wages, hours, and working conditions; supervision; employee interaction; and factors related to collective bargaining. The Board also stated that, depending on the particular circumstances of a case, various combinations of the units may be appropriate.

In *American Hospital Association v. NLRB*,[13] the U.S. Supreme Court upheld the NLRB's health-care industry bargaining unit rules and the power of the NLRB to establish bargaining units through its rule-making authority. In certain circumstances, such as where other bargaining units already exist at the health-care facility, or where there are fewer than six employees in any of the specific categories, the NLRB will apply the traditional "community of interest" test for bargaining units, according to *Kaiser Foundation Hospitals*.[14] In *San Miguel Hospital Corp. v. N.L.R.B.*,[15] the D.C. Circuit Court of Appeals upheld the NLRB definition of a bargaining unit comprised of all the hospital's onsite professional and nonprofessional employees, except for guards and physicians. The NLRB also indicated that it will apply the "community of interest" test for determination of bargaining units in nursing homes, rehabilitation facilities, and other nonacute health-care facilities.[16]

---

[12] The final rule was printed in 54 Federal Register 16336 (April 21, 1989).

[13] 499 U.S. 606 (1991).

[14] 312 NLRB 933 (1993).

[15] 697 F.3d 1181 (D.C. Cir. 2012).

[16] *Specialty Healthcare and Rehabilitation Center of Mobile*, 357 NLRB No. 83 (2011), enforced by *Kindred Nursing Center East, LLC v. N.L.R.B.*, 727 F.3d 552 (6th Cir. 2013).

Concept *Summary* 13.2

BARGAINING UNIT ISSUES

- Bargaining unit choices:
  - Single employer or multiemployer unit
  - Single plant or employer-wide unit
  - Industrial or craft unit

- Restrictions on bargaining unit definition:
  - Guards must be in a separate unit
  - Professional employees can only be included in a unit with nonprofessionals if a majority of the professionals vote for inclusion

13-1d   Voter Eligibility

Along with determining the appropriate bargaining unit, the question of which employees are actually eligible to vote in the election must be resolved. Factors to be considered are whether an employee is within the bargaining unit and whether striking employees are able to vote.

In general, when the election has been directed (or agreed to, for consent elections), the Board establishes an eligibility date—that is, the date by which an employee must be on the employer's payroll in order to be eligible to vote. The eligibility date is usually the end of the payroll period immediately preceding the direction of (or agreement to hold) the election. Employees must be on the payroll as of the eligibility date, and they must also continue to be on the payroll on the date the election is held. Employees hired after the eligibility date but before the election date are not eligible to vote.

Employees may be on strike when an election is held. This is most often the case in decertification elections, when the employees not striking seek to get rid of the union. Section 2(3) of the NLRA defines *employee* to include "any individual whose work has ceased as a consequence of … any current labor dispute … and who has not obtained any other regular and substantially equivalent employment." The Board has adopted several rules clarifying the voting rights of striking employees.

The Board distinguishes whether the employees are on an unfair labor practice strike or an economic strike. An **unfair labor practice strike** is a strike by employees in protest of, or precipitated by, employer unfair labor practices. The Board holds that unfair labor practice strikers cannot be permanently replaced by the employer. Unfair labor practice strikers are eligible to vote in any election held during the strike.

Economic strikes are strikes over economic issues, such as grievances or a new contract. Unlike unfair labor strikers, economic strikers may be permanently replaced by the employer. Economic strikers who have not been permanently replaced may vote in any election during the strike, but economic strikers who have been permanently replaced may vote only in elections held within 12 months after the strike begins. After 12 months, they lose

unfair labor practice strike
a strike to protest employer unfair practices

economic strike
a strike over economic issues such as a new contract or a grievance

their eligibility to vote. The employees hired to replace economic strikers may vote if they are permanent replacements—that is, if the employer intends to retain them after the strike is over. Replacements hired on a temporary basis, who will not be retained after the strike ends, are not eligible to vote. As a result of these rules, during the first 12 months of a strike, permanent replacements and all economic strikers may vote. After 12 months, only the permanent replacements and those economic strikers who have not been permanently replaced may vote.

Economic strikers or unfair labor practice strikers who obtain permanent employment elsewhere and who abandon their prior jobs lose their eligibility to vote. Although the Board generally presumes that other employment by strikers during a strike is temporary, they will hold that a striker has lost eligibility to vote if it can be shown that he or she does not intend to return to the prior job. Also, strikers fired for wrongdoing during the strike are not eligible to vote.

According to *O. E. Butterfield, Inc.*,[17] when the eligibility of employees to vote is challenged, the NLRB holds that, in the case of both unfair labor practice strikes and economic strikes, the employer has the burden of proving that replacements hired during the strike are permanent employees in order for the replacements to be qualified to vote in a representation election. Although the Board prefers that challenges to voter eligibility be resolved at a hearing prior to the election, such challenges may also be raised at the time the challenged employee votes. When an employee's right to vote is challenged, the ballot at issue is placed in a sealed envelope rather than in the ballot box. After all employees have voted, the Board first counts the unchallenged ballots. If the results of the election will not be changed by the challenged ballots—because there are not enough of them to change the outcome—the Board will not rule on the challenges. However, if the challenged ballots could affect the election results, the Board will hold a hearing to resolve the challenges, count those ballots from the eligible voters, and then certify the election results.

13-2   Representation Elections

excelsior list
a list of the names and addresses of the employees eligible to vote in a representation election

Within seven days after the regional director approves a consent election or directs that an election be held, the employer must file an election eligibility list with the regional office. This list, called an **Excelsior list** after the decision in which the Board set out this requirement, *Excelsior Underwear, Inc.*,[18] contains the names and home addresses of all employees eligible to vote so that the union can contact them outside their work environment, beyond the boss's observation and control. A Board agent will then arrange a conference with all parties to settle the details of the election. According to *North Macon Health Care Facility*,[19] the NLRB will set aside elections won by the employer where the employer has failed to provide the union with an Excelsior list containing the full first and last names of all employees in the bargaining unit.

---

[17] 319 NLRB 1004 (1995).
[18] 156 NLRB No. 111 (1966).
[19] 315 NLRB 359 (1994).

The election is generally held on company premises; however, if the union objects, it can be held elsewhere. In *San Diego Gas & Electric*,[20] the NLRB held that the regional director may authorize the use of mail-in ballots in cases where:

- the eligible employees are scattered over a wide geographic area because of their job duties;

- the eligible employees are scattered because of their work schedules; or

- there is a strike, lockout, or picketing in progress at the employer's location.

The NLRB agent supervises the conduct of the election, and all parties are entitled to have observers present during the voting. All parties to the election will undoubtedly have engaged in an election campaign prior to the vote. The Board regards such an election as an experiment to determine the employees' choice. The Board therefore strives for **laboratory conditions** in the conduct of the election and requires that neither side engage in conduct that could unduly affect the employees' free choice.

The laboratory conditions can be violated by unfair practices committed by either side. Conduct that does not amount to an unfair practice may also violate the laboratory conditions if the Board believes that wrongful misconduct will unduly affect the employees' choice. **Captive-audience speeches** given by representatives of the employers or mass meetings by the union within 24 hours of an election at which the union promises to waive initiation fees for members who join before the election are examples of such conduct. Elections have been set aside where a supervisor distributed antiunion hats to the employees, as in *Barton Nelson, Inc.*[21]; where the employer offered employees who were not scheduled to work two hours pay to come in to vote, as in *Broward Community Health Corp.*[22]; and where the union used a sound truck to broadcast pro-union songs into the plant on the day of the election, as in *Bro-Tech Corp. v. NLRB.*[23] A supervisor's comment that he would "kick [the employees'] asses" if they voted for the union was grounds to set aside an election according to *Medic One, Inc.*[24] However, according to *Lockheed Martin Skunk Works*,[25] an employer's failure to prevent employees who were urging decertification of the union from sending email messages to the other employees did not invalidate the election, because the union also had access to the employer's email system.

In *Atlantic Limousine, Inc.*,[26] the NLRB adopted a rule barring employers and unions from conducting any election raffles where eligibility to participate in the raffle is tied in any way to voting in the election or being at the election site on election day, or if the raffle is conducted at any time during a period beginning 24 hours before the scheduled opening of the polls and ending with the closing of the polls. Violations of the rule will result in setting aside the election upon filing an objection. The rule against raffles includes announcing a raffle, distributing raffle tickets, identifying raffle winners, and awarding raffle prizes.

Actions by third parties, other than the employer and union, may also violate the laboratory conditions. In one case, the local newspaper in a small southern town printed racially inflammatory articles about the union attempting to organize the work force of a local employer.

laboratory conditions
the conditions under which a representative election is held; the NLRB tries to ensure that neither the employer nor the union unduly affects the employees' free choice

captive-audience speech
meeting or speech held by the employer during working hours, which employees are required to attend

---

[20] 325 NLRB 1143 (1998).

[21] 318 NLRB 712 (1995).

[22] 320 NLRB 212 (1995).

[23] 330 NLRB 37 (1999).

[24] 331 NLRB 464 (2000).

[25] 331 NLRB 852 (2000).

[26] 331 NLRB 1025 (2000).

The Board held that the injection of racial propaganda into the election violated the laboratory conditions and was reason to invalidate the election, which the union lost.

A local pastor who met with employees and discussed possible plant closure if the union won the election was acting as an agent of the employer. In *Southern Pride Catfish*,[27] his comments were held to be an unfair labor practice and were grounds to set aside the election.

The Board will not monitor the truthfulness of the election propaganda of either side. Misrepresentations in campaign promises or propaganda will not, of themselves, be grounds to set aside the election results. The NLRB will intervene, however, if either party uses a forged document that renders the voting employees unable to recognize the propaganda for what it is, as in *NLRB v. St. Francis Healthcare Center*.[28] The Board requires that the parties in an election refrain from formal campaigning for 24 hours prior to the election. This **twenty-four-hour silent period** is intended to give the employees time to reflect upon their choice free from electioneering pressures. Any mass union rallies or employer captive-audience speeches during the silent period will be grounds to set aside the election results, according *to Comet Electric*[29] and *Bro-Tech Corp. v. NLRB*.[30]

Exhibit 13.4 shows a sample ballot for a representation election.

twenty-four-hour silent period
the twenty-four-hour period prior to the representation election, during which the parties must refrain from formal campaign meetings

---

UNITED STATES OF AMERICA
National Labor Relations Board
OFFICIAL SECRET BALLOT
FOR CERTAIN EMPLOYEES OF
SYRACUSE UNIVERSITY
SYRACUSE, NEW YORK

This ballot is to determine the collective bargaining representative, if any, for the unit in which you are employed.

MARK AN "X" IN THE SQUARE OF YOUR CHOICE

INTERNATIONAL UNION, UNITED AUTOMOBILE, AEROSPACE & AGRICULTURAL IMPLEMENT WORKERS OF AMERICA (UAW)	LOCAL 200, SEVICE EMPLOYEES INTERNATIONAL UNION, AFL-CIO-CLC	NEITHER
□	□	□

DO NOT SIGN THIS BALLOT. Fold and drop in ballot box.
If you spoil this ballot return it to the Board Agent for a new one.

EXHIBIT 13.4   Sample NLRB Representation Election Ballot
Source: NLRB poster at 1979 Syracuse University representation election.

---

[27] 331 NLRB 618 (2000).

[28] 212 F.3d 945 (6th Cir. 2000).

[29] 314 NLRB 1215 (1994).

[30] 330 NLRB 37 (1999).

If either party believes the election laboratory conditions were violated, that party may file objections to the other party's conduct with the regional director within five days of the election. Post-election unfair labor practice charges could also result in the election results being set aside.

After the election is held, the parties have five days in which to file any objections with the regional director. If the director finds the objections to be valid, the election will be set aside. If the objections are held to be invalid, the results of the election will be certified. To be victorious, a party to the election must receive a majority of the votes cast; that is, either the union or the no-union choice must garner a majority of the votes cast by the eligible employees. If the election involved more than one union and no choice received a simple majority, the Board will hold a run-off election between the two choices getting the highest number of votes. If a union wins, it will be certified as the bargaining agent for all the employees in the bargaining unit.

Because the conduct of representation elections is a matter subject to the discretion of the regional directors and the Board, only limited judicial review of certification decisions is available. However, as a practical matter, an employer can obtain review of the Board's certification decision by refusing to bargain with the certified union and contesting the issue in the subsequent unfair labor practice proceeding.

13-2a Decertification of the Bargaining Agent

decertification petition
petition stating that a current bargaining representative no longer has the support of a majority of the employees in the bargaining unit

An employee or group of employees, or a union or individual acting on their behalf, may file a **decertification petition** under Section 9(c)(1) of the act, asserting that "the individual or labor organization, which has been certified or is being currently recognized by their employer as the bargaining representative" no longer enjoys the unit's support. The Board also requires the showing of 30 percent employee interest in support of a decertification petition to entertain it. This 30 percent rule has been criticized by some commentators in that the petition signifies nothing more than that fewer than half the employees are unhappy with their representative. Yet the mere filing of the petition can totally disrupt the bargaining process because the employer may refuse to bargain while the petition is pending.

An employer is not permitted to file a decertification petition; the Board will dismiss a decertification petition by employees if it discovers that the employer instigated the filing. However, a company can file an election petition if it can demonstrate by objective evidence that it has reasonable grounds for believing that the incumbent union has lost its majority status. Such petitions must be filed during the open-season periods, just as with petitions seeking representation elections.

Deauthorization Elections

union shop clause
clause in an agreement requiring all present and future members of a bargaining unit to be union members

Section 9(e)(1) of the NLRA provides for the holding of a deauthorization election to rescind the union shop clause in a collective agreement. The **union shop clause**, which may be included in a collective agreement, requires that all present and future members of the bargaining unit become, and remain, union members. They typically must join the union after 30 days from the date on which they were hired. Failure to join the union or to remain a union member is grounds for discharge. The provisions of Section 9(e)(1) state that a petition for a deauthorization election may be filed by an employee or group of employees. The petition must have the support of at least 30 percent of the bargaining unit. If a valid petition is filed, along with the requisite show of support, the Board will conduct a secret ballot election to determine whether a majority of employees in the unit wish to remove the union shop clause from the agreement. As is the case with representation and decertification elections, no deauthorization election can be held for a bargaining unit (or subdivision of the unit) if a valid deauthorization election has been held in the preceding 12-month period. Unlike representation elections and decertification elections, which are determined by a majority of the votes actually cast, deauthorization elections require that a majority of the members in the bargaining unit vote in favor of rescinding the union shop clause for it to be rescinded.

13-2b   Acquiring Representation Rights Through Unfair Labor Practice Proceedings

Unfair labor practice charges filed with the Board while representation proceedings are pending may invoke the Board's blocking charge policy. The filing of such charges usually halts the representation case, and no election will be held pending the resolution of the unfair labor practice charges. An employer may wish to forestall the election and erode the union's support by committing various unfair labor practices, thereby taking unfair advantage of this policy.

A union may wish to proceed with the pending election despite the unfair labor practice charges. It can do so by filing a request-to-proceed notice with the Board. If the union proceeds and wins the election, then the effect of the unfair labor practice charges is not very important. However, if the union loses the election, it may be because of the effect of the employer's illegal actions. In that case, the union could file objections to the election and request that a new election be held. But how could the union overcome the lingering effects of the employer's unfair practices? Rather than seek a new election or proceed with the original election, the union may rely on the unfair practice charges and ask the Board, as a remedy for the unfair labor practices, to order the employer to recognize and bargain with the union without its ever winning an election.

In the case of *NLRB v. Gissel Packing* Co.,[31] the Supreme Court held that the NLRB may issue a bargaining order, requiring the employer to recognize and bargain with the union, as a remedy for the employer's unfair labor practices where those practices were pervasive, outrageous, and precluded the union from ever demonstrating majority support. The Court in *Gissel Packing* also held that a bargaining order might be an appropriate remedy where the employer's unfair labor practices, although not pervasive and outrageous, nevertheless had the effect of preventing any election from being a true demonstration of the employees' desires as to union representation; however, in such situations, a bargaining order should only be granted where the union, at some point during the organizing campaign, had majority support.

The following case illustrates the application of the *Gissel Packing* bargaining order remedy.

---

[31] 395 U.S. 575 (1969).

>> CASE 13.2

NATIONAL STEEL SUPPLY, INC. AND INTERNATIONAL BROTHERHOOD OF TRADE UNIONS, LOCAL 713

344 NLRB No. 121, 2005 WL 1564867 (N.L.R.B.) (2005), enforced by *NLRB v. National Steel Supply, Inc.*, 207 Fed. Appx. 9 (2nd Cir. 2006)

Facts: In response to unfair labor practice charges filed by the union, Local 713, the Administrative Law Judge (ALJ) held that the employer had committed unfair labor practices during a union organizing campaign by unlawfully interrogating employees, discharging an employee because of his union activities, and unlawfully discharging and refusing to reinstate the twenty-seven employees (out of a bargaining unit of thirty-one employees) who engaged in a strike to protest the employer's illegal actions. The ALJ also recommended that the NLRB issue a bargaining order under *Gissel Packing* as a remedy for the unfair labor practices committed by the employer. The employer then sought review of the ALJ decision by the NLRB.

Issue: Is a bargaining order the appropriate remedy in light of the unfair labor practices committed by the employer here?

Decision: The NLRB agreed with the ALJ that the employer violated Section 8(a)(1) on August 13, 2004 by interrogating employee Eric Atalaya about union activities, and violated Section 8(a)(3) and (1) by terminating Atalaya. The NLRB also found that the employer violated Section 8(a)(3) and (1) by issuing a written warning to Atalaya and by refusing to reinstate, and subsequently discharging twenty-seven of the unfair labor practice strikers upon unconditional offer to return to work.

The NLRB agreed with ALJ that the Union had attained the support of a majority of the employees in the bargaining unit, as evidenced by authorization cards signed by the employees.

The Board will issue a *Gissel* bargaining order in two categories of cases, known as "category I" and "category II" cases. Category I involves "exceptional cases" marked by unfair labor practices so "outrageous" and "pervasive" that traditional remedies cannot erase their coercive effects, thus rendering a fair election impossible. Category II involves "less extraordinary cases marked by less pervasive practices which nonetheless still have the tendency to undermine majority strength and impede the election processes." The NLRB here held that the violations were sufficiently outrageous and pervasive to warrant a bargaining order under category I. The employer had interrogated and threatened employees and illegally discharged over 85 percent of the employees in the bargaining unit. Threats of job loss and the actual discharge of union adherents are "hallmark" violations, which are highly coercive because of their potentially long-lasting impact. Terminating a majority of the bargaining unit is unlawful conduct that "goes to the very heart of the Act" and is not likely to be forgotten. The impact of the violations was heightened by the small size of the unit and the direct involvement of the employer's highest officers. The NLRB held that there was a strong likelihood that the employer's unfair labor practices would have a pervasive and lasting effect on the employees' exercise of their Section 7 rights. The NLRB held that traditional unfair labor practice remedies cannot erase the coercive effects of the conduct, making the holding of a fair election impossible. The NLRB therefore ordered the employer to cease and desist from engaging in unfair labor practices, and to recognize and, on request, bargain with the Union as the exclusive representative of the employees in the bargaining unit.

Other Bargaining Order Remedy Issues

The Supreme Court's *Gissel Packing* decision indicated that the NLRB could issue a bargaining order to remedy outrageous and pervasive unfair labor practices by the employer, even if the union never had established majority support of the employees in the appropriate bargaining unit. The U.S. Court of Appeals for the Third Circuit held that the Board had the power to issue such an order in *United Dairy Farmers Co-op. Assoc. v. NLRB.*[32] However, in *Conair Corp. v. NLRB*,[33] the U.S. Court of Appeals for the D.C. Circuit held that it was inappropriate for the Board to issue a bargaining order where the union never established evidence of majority support. The NLRB now takes the position that it will not issue a bargaining order unless the union had, at some point, shown evidence of majority support during the organizing campaign, according to *Gourmet Foods, Inc.*[34]

A second area of dispute over bargaining order remedies is the question of whether the NLRB should consider subsequent events and changed circumstances when determining whether a bargaining order remedy is appropriate: Has the passage of time, the turnover of employees in the unit, or other factors limited the effects of the employer's unfair labor practices? The NLRB takes the position that it will not consider subsequent events or changed circumstances because to do so would allow the employer to capitalize on its misconduct. The courts of appeals are divided on this issue. The Seventh Circuit enforced a bargaining order despite a delay of four years and turnover of most of the bargaining unit employees in America's *Best Quality Coatings v. NLRB*,[35] while the Sixth Circuit, the Second Circuit, and the D.C. Circuit held that the Board must consider subsequent events and the effect of the passage of time when deciding to issue a bargaining order in *DTR Industries v. NLRB*,[36] *Kinney Drugs, Inc. v. NLRB*,[37] and *Charlotte Amphitheater Corp. v. NLRB.*[38]

Employer Response to Union Recognition Demands

The *Gissel Packing* case involved an employer who committed unfair labor practices after the union claimed majority support. But what about the situation in which an employer, after being confronted by the union claiming recognition, simply refuses to recognize the union but refrains from committing any unfair labor practices? Is the employer required to petition for an election or recognize the union? Or is it up to the union to initiate the election process? In *Linden Lumber Div., Summer & Co. v. NLRB*,[39] the U.S. Supreme Court held that an employer who receives a request for voluntary recognition from a union claiming to have the majority support of the employer's employees is not required to recognize the union, provided that the employer has no knowledge of the union's support (independent of the union's claim to have majority support) and does not commit any unfair labor practices. Neither is the employer required to petition the NLRB for a representation election in response to the union's request for recognition; it is then up to the union either to file a petition for an election or to institute unfair labor practice charges. Of course, if the employer does engage in unfair labor practices after receiving the union's request for recognition, the union is free to seek a *Gissel*-type bargaining order from the NLRB as a remedy. Such bargaining orders, however, are granted infrequently.

---

[32] 633 F.2d 1054 (1980).

[33] 721 F.2d 1355 (1983), cert. denied, 467 U.S. 1241 (1984).

[34] 270 NLRB 578 (1984).

[35] 44 F.3d 106, cert. denied, 515 U.S. 1158 (1995).

[36] 39 F.3d 106 (6th Cir. 1994).

[37] 74 F.3d 1419 (2d Cir. 1996).

[38] 82 F.3d 1074 (D.C. Cir. 1996).

[39] 419 U.S. 301 (1974).

ethical	DILEMMA

EMPLOYEE UNION SUPPORT: TO SURVEY OR NOT TO SURVEY?

You are the human resource manager at Southwestco, a small manufacturing company. The office clerical and technical employees at Southwestco are not unionized, but the production employees are. You have heard rumors that some clerical and technical employees are starting a campaign to become unionized, and several employees have specifically told you that they don't want to join. One morning, you receive a letter via certified mail from the union local representing the production workers. The union now claims to have the support of an overwhelming majority of the office clerical and technical employees and requests that the company recognize the union as the exclusive bargaining representative for all clerical and technical employees. How should you respond to the union demand?

You are considering whether to conduct a survey of the clerical and technical employees to determine whether a majority of them support the union. What arguments can you make in favor of conducting such a survey? What arguments can you make against it? Prepare a memo for the board of directors recommending (1) a response to the union demand for recognition and (2) whether to conduct a survey of the employees. Explain and support your positions.

Concept *Summary* 13.3

REPRESENTATION ELECTIONS

- Procedures for holding elections:
  - Employer must give union an Excelsior list to determine all employees eligible to vote in an election
  - Parties must maintain laboratory conditions to ensure that employees can exercise free choice
    - Violations of laboratory conditions include unfair labor practices, captive-audience speeches, incentives (such as raffles), threats, and extreme third-party propaganda
    - The parties must observe the 24-hour silent period prior to the election
  - Decertification petitions can be filed by employees to determine if the union no longer has the majority's support
    - Petitions must meet the 30 percent rule
  - Deauthorization elections can rescind the agency shop clause in a collective agreement

- Unfair labor practice charges
  - Unfair labor practices by employers may delay or halt elections, but unions may choose to proceed despite unfair labor practice charges
  - Under the *Gissel Packing* decision, the NLRB may issue a bargaining order rather than proceed with the election if the unfair labor practices were pervasive and outrageous and the union had majority support at some point

CHAPTER REVIEW

» Key Terms

voluntary recognition	398	bargaining unit	405	captive-audience speech	414
authorization card	400	unfair labor practice strike	412	twenty-four-hour silent period	415
forty-eight-hour rule	400	economic strike	412		
consent election	401	Excelsior list	413	decertification petition	416
contract bar rule	404	laboratory conditions	414	union shop clause	416

» Summary

- The NLRA gives employees the right to determine for themselves whether they wish to be represented by a union. If the majority of the employees in an appropriate bargaining unit indicate that they support a union, the NLRA provides that the union then becomes the exclusive bargaining representative of that bargaining unit. Although representation elections conducted by the NLRB are the most common means through which unions acquire representation rights, an employer may also voluntarily recognize a union as bargaining representative for a group of employees when the union demonstrates majority support.

- Unions, employees, or employers may file a petition with the NLRB seeking a representation election. Unions or employees may file a petition for a decertification election. When a petition is filed, the NLRB will determine whether the contract bar rule precludes holding an election; if not, the NLRB must then determine an appropriate bargaining unit. The NLRB uses the "community of interest" test to define the bargaining unit. While the bargaining unit determination depends on the facts of each case, in the health-care industry the NLRB will apply its rules for bargaining unit determination.

- The NLRB conducts representation elections under "laboratory conditions" to ensure that the election represents the free choice of the employees. Violations of the laboratory conditions or of the 24-hour silent period rule may result in the NLRB invalidating the election results. Representation and decertification elections are by secret ballot, and the winner is determined by a majority of the votes cast. If no choice captures a majority of votes, a runoff election is held between the two choices getting the most votes. For deauthorization elections, which seek to rescind agency shop or union shop dues requirements, the result is determined by whether any choice gets a majority of the votes of all employees in the bargaining unit. Either party may file challenges to votes or to the election itself; valid challenges will be determined after a hearing by either the regional director or the NLRB itself.

- Unions may also acquire representation rights through unfair labor practice proceedings. The NLRB may issue a bargaining order when the effects of unfair labor practices by employers prevent a fair election from being held. Such remedies are the exception, with the NLRB and the courts preferring elections as the means to give effect to employees' right of free choice under the NLRA.

» Problems

» Questions

1. What are the methods by which a union can acquire representation rights for a group of employees?

2. What is a bargaining unit? What factors does the NLRB consider in determining the appropriate bargaining unit?

3. What is the contract bar rule? What are the exceptions to it?

4. Under what conditions are economic strikers ineligible to vote in representation elections? Under what conditions are unfair labor practice strikers ineligible to vote in representation elections?

5. When must an employer recognize a union requesting voluntary recognition?

» Case Problems

6. In 2000, employees of the Kent Corporation elected an independent union as their collective bargaining representative. A collective bargaining agreement was hammered out and ultimately ratified by the employees, effective until December 31, 2003. In November 2003, the two sides again negotiated, the result being a contract to be in effect until December 31, 2006. This agreement was signed by the association committee members but was never ratified by the rank and file. In fact, evidence showed there had been no association membership meetings, no election of officers, no dues ever collected, and no association treasury since 2000.

   In August 2004, the Steelworkers Union filed a representation petition. The NLRB regional director ruled that the association was a defunct union and that its current contract was no bar to an election. The company filed a request for review of the decision with the NLRB in Washington, D.C. The association vice president and a member of the bargaining committee attested to their willingness to continue representing the employees. There was no evidence that the association had ever failed to act on a bargaining unit member's behalf.

   How should the NLRB rule on the association's representative status? [See *Kent Corporation*, 272 NLRB No. 115, 117 L.R.R.M. 1333 (1984).]

7. L&J Equipment Company was engaged in the surface mining of coal, with its principal site in Hatfield, Pennsylvania, and six satellite sites in other parts of western Pennsylvania. In early 2001, the United Mine Workers of America began organizing L&J's mining employees. A few days after the first organizing meeting, a company-owned truck was destroyed by fire. Authorities determined the fire had been deliberately set. Three weeks later, the United Mine Workers filed a petition for an election. The date set for the election was November 4, 2001.

   During the intense election campaign, promanagement employees were threatened. A week before the election, a company-owned barn burned to the ground. The United Mine Workers won the election by a vote of 39–33.

   L&J refused to bargain. The union filed a Section 8(a)(5) charge, and the Board found that L&J was guilty of an unfair labor practice. L&J appealed to the U.S. Court of Appeals for the Third Circuit, claiming that the Board abused its discretion in certifying the union in light of its pre-election improprieties.

   How should the appellate court have ruled on this challenge? [See *NLRB v. L&J Equipment Co.*, 745 F.2d 224, 117 L.R.R.M. 2592 (3rd Cir. 1984).]

8. Action Automotive, Inc., a retail auto parts and gasoline dealer, had stores in a number of Michigan cities. In March 2003, Local 40 of the Retail Store Employees Union filed a petition for a representation election. The union got a plurality of the unchallenged votes. But the challenged ballots could have made the difference.

   The union challenged the ballots of the wife of the company's co-owner/president, who worked as a general ledger clerk at the company's headquarters, and of the mother of the three owners' brother who worked as a cashier in one of the nine stores. The company argued that since neither received any special benefits, neither should be excluded from the employee unit or denied their votes.

   The case reached the U.S. Supreme Court. What arguments could you make to the Court for the union's view? For the company's view? [See *NLRB v. Action Automotive, Inc.*, 469 U.S. 970 (1985).]

9. Micronesian Telecommunications Corporation (MTC) had its principal office on Saipan, a Pacific island held as a U.S. trust territory. Electrical Workers Local 1357 (IBEW) sought to represent the employees of MTC, including its employees on neighboring islands.

   What jurisdictional issues should the NLRB have addressed before asserting jurisdiction of the case? If the Board asserted jurisdiction, what factors should it have considered with respect to whether employees on the neighboring islands belonged in the same bargaining unit with the workers on Saipan? [See *Micronesian Tel. Corp.*, 273 NLRB No. 56, 118 L.R.R.M. 1067 (1984).]

10. Kirksville College in Missouri was a nonprofit corporation providing health-care services, medical education, and medical research. Service Employees Local 50 filed three representation petitions seeking to represent separate units composed, respectively, of all technical, all professional, and all service and maintenance employees at the Kirksville Health Center, an unincorporated subsidiary of the college. The college also had several affiliated hospitals and rural clinics within a 60-mile radius of the main campus.

What factors should the NLRB consider in deciding whether technical, professional, and service employees should be in separate units? What factors must be looked at to decide whether clinic employees should properly have their own bargaining unit(s) or be part of a broader unit taking in (a) the college, (b) affiliated hospitals, and/or (c) satellite facilities? [See *Kirksville College*, 274 NLRB No. 121, 118 L.R.R.M. 1443 (1985).]

11. The Steelworkers Union sought to represent a unit composed of four occupational health nurses in an aluminum plant. The company argued that the nurses were managerial employees, exempt from the act, or in the alternative, professional employees who must be part of a bargaining unit of all the plant's professional employees. The nurses' primary responsibilities were treating employees' injuries and illnesses, administering routine physical examinations to applicants and employees, and maintaining logs and records.

   What additional facts did the NLRB need to decide the issues raised by the company? [See *Noranda Aluminum Inc. v. NLRB*, 751 F.2d 268, L.R.R.M. 2136 (8th Cir. 1984).]

12. Because of the mixture of ethnic groups in the employer's factory, the NLRB conducted the election using a ballot translated from English into Spanish, Vietnamese, and Laotian. Food & Commercial Workers Local 34 won the election 119–112.

   The translations were line-by-line. Some English-reading employees claimed this made it difficult to read. Some of the translations were later found to be somewhat inaccurate. Neither side challenged any ballots.

   How should the NLRB have ruled on the company's challenge to the election outcome based on the flawed ballots? [See *Kraft, Inc.*, 273 NLRB 1484, 118 L.R.R.M. 1242 (1985).]

13. One employee ballot in a close election was marked with a large "X" in the "No Union" box and the word "Yes" written above the box.

Should the NLRB count this ballot? If so, how? [See *NLRB v. Newly Wed Foods Inc.*, 758 F.2d 4, 118 L.R.R.M. 3213 (1st Cir. 1985).]

14. The International Brotherhood of Electrical Workers, Local Unions 605 and 985, AFL-CIO ("the union") have represented a bargaining unit comprised of MP&L's service and maintenance employees since 1938. The most recent collective bargaining agreement concerning these employees is for the term of October 15, 2003, until October 15, 2005. That agreement does not include MP&L's storeroom and warehouse employees.

    In January 2004, the union petitioned the NLRB for certification as bargaining representative of these storeroom and warehouse employees. MP&L opposed the petition, urging that the Board's contract bar rule barred the election required for the union to be certified. MP&L contended that the contract bar rule must be applied to employees intentionally excluded from an existing collective bargaining agreement.

    The regional director rejected MP&L's contention. The Board affirmed this decision. An election was held, and a slim majority of the storeroom and warehouse employees voted to be represented by the union. The NLRB certified the results of the election.

    To obtain judicial review of the Board's decision to permit a representation election, MP&L refused to bargain with the union on behalf of the newly represented employees. The union filed an unfair labor practice charge with the Board.

    How should the Board have ruled on this challenge by MP&L? [See *NLRB v. Mississippi Power & Light Co.*, 769 F.2d 276 (5th Cir. 1985).]

15. The source of dispute was a representation election held at Kusan's Franklin, Tennessee, plant on October 19, 2002. The union, the International Association of Machinists, won that election by a vote of 118–107. Kusan, however, filed objections with the Board over the conduct of the election. The objections charged that the union interfered with the election by conducting a poll of the employees and threatening and coercing employees during the course of the polling.

In December 2002, the regional director of the NLRB investigated Kusan's objections and issued a report recommending that the objections be overruled. The results of the election were certified by the Board in April 2003.

Kusan's objections centered on a petition that Kusan employees who supported the union circulated among their fellow workers prior to the election. The petition, which bore approximately 100 names, read as follows:

We, the undersigned, are voting YES for the IAM. We don't mind being on the firing line because we know it's something that has to be done. Please join with us. VOTE YES and help us to make Kusan, Inc. a better place to work and earn a living.

Kusan contends that the circulation and distribution of the petition constituted impermissible "polling" of the employees by the union.

How should the Board have ruled on Kusan's objections? [See *Kusan Mfg. Co. v. NLRB*, 749 F.2d 362, 117 L.R.R.M. 3394 (6th Cir. 1984).]

» Hypothetical Scenarios

16. The employees in the Parking Services Department at Prestigious University, a large private university in upstate New York, are attempting to organize a union. Some of the Parking Services employees are clerical workers who work in the Parking Office located in the campus Administration Building, while others work as parking lot attendants. The parking lot attendants work out of kiosks located in the various parking lots around the campus. The parking lot attendants control access to the parking lots by checking for appropriate parking permits. They also issue parking tickets to enforce parking regulations and call for tow trucks to take away cars that are in violation of the parking regulations. The union organizing the workers seeks to have all the parking employees in one bargaining unit. The university administration claims that the parking lot attendants are guards within the meaning of Section 9(b)(3) of the NLRA, and must be placed in a separate bargaining unit. Are the parking lot attendants guards within the meaning of Section

9(b)(3)? Should they be in a separate bargaining unit? Explain your answer.

17. The part-time faculty members at Prestigious University are attempting to form a union to represent them in bargaining with the university. In order to get more of the part-time faculty to join, the union organizers promise that faculty members who sign an authorization card before a representation election is held will get a reduction in their union dues for the first year of membership. The union also holds a rally at a campus area pizza restaurant on the night before the representation election. Has the union violated the NLRB election conditions? Explain.

18. The maintenance and food service workers at Prestigious University are represented by the International Brotherhood of Teamsters Union. The union and the university administration have just agreed on a new collective bargaining agreement covering the next four years. A number of workers in the skilled maintenance department are dissatisfied with their union because they feel that the union accepted lower wage raises in return for getting a long-term contract. They contact a representative of the Service Employees International Union to discuss ousting the Teamsters as their bargaining representative. What must the workers do to get the NLRB to hold a decertification election?

19. Glassco manufactures glass containers—bottles and jars—for the food processing industry. Most of the employees work on production lines tending molding machines that extrude the containers. Glassco also employs some skilled glassblowers, who create crystal decanters. The glassblowers are skilled artisans who work in a separate area of the plant and fashion the decanters using molten glass and rudimentary hand tools. Because of their specialized skills, the pay scales for the glassblowers are higher than for the production workers.

All the Glassco employees are represented by the International Molders Union, and are grouped together in one bargaining unit. The glassblowers feel that their interests are not being adequately represented by the union because there are only a few glassblowers, compared to the hundred or so production workers. The glassblowers file a petition with the NLRB to form their own union, the Glass Artisans Guild. Should the NLRB sever the glassblowers from the production bargaining unit? What factors will the NLRB consider in making its decision? Explain.

20. When the NLRB held a deauthorization election for the unionized employees at Shaw Manufacturing Co., only 60 of the 100 members of the bargaining unit actually voted. Of those voting, 25 voted to keep the union shop requirement, and 35 voted to eliminate it. Must the union and the employer rescind the union shop requirement of their collective agreement? Explain.

CHAPTER 14

Unfair Labor Practices by Employers and Unions

unfair labor practices (ULPs)
actions by employers or unions that interfere with the rights of employees under the National Labor Relations Act

The National Labor Relations Act (NLRA) defines a list of **unfair labor practices (ULPs)** by both employers and unions. Such unfair labor practices are various forms of conduct or activities that adversely affect employees in the exercise of their rights under Section 7 of the act. The unfair labor practices by employers in Section 8(a) were in the Wagner Act; the union unfair labor practices in Section 8(b) were added by the Taft-Hartley Act in 1947 and amended by the Landrum-Griffin Act of 1959.

Section 8(a) makes it illegal for an employer to engage in the following conduct:

- interfere with, restrain, or coerce employees in the exercise of rights guaranteed to them by Section 7 of the act;
- dominate, interfere with, or contribute financial or other support to a labor organization;
- discriminate in the hiring or terms or conditions of employment of employees in order to encourage or discourage membership in any labor organization;
- discharge or discriminate against an employee for filing charges or giving testimony under the NLRA; and
- refuse to bargain collectively with the bargaining representatives of the employees, as designated in Section 9(a).

Section 8(b) makes it illegal for unions to engage in the following conduct:

- restrain or coerce employees in the exercise of their rights under Section 7, or restrain or coerce an employer in the selection of a representative for collective bargaining purposes;
- cause or attempt to cause an employer to discriminate against an employee in terms or conditions of employment in order to encourage (or discourage) union membership;
- refuse to bargain collectively with an employer (when the union is the bargaining agent of the employees);
- engage in secondary picketing or encourage secondary boycotts of certain employers;
- require employees to pay excessive or discriminatory union dues or membership fees;
- cause an employer to pay for services that are not performed (feather-bedding); and
- picket an employer in order to force the employer to recognize the union as bargaining agent when the union is not entitled to recognition under the act (recognition picketing).

Because both employer and union unfair practices involve, for the most part, the same kinds of conduct, we examine them together in this chapter. The refusal to bargain by either employer or union will be discussed in Chapter 15, which deals with the duty to bargain in good faith. The union offenses of secondary picketing and recognition picketing will be discussed in Chapter 16, along with other forms of union pressure tactics.

14-1 Section 7: Rights of Employees

Because all unfair practices involve conduct that interferes with employees in the exercise of their rights under Section 7 of the NLRA, it is important to determine the exact rights granted employees by Section 7. Section 7 contains this statement:

> Employees shall have the right to self-organization, to form, join or assist labor organizations, to bargain collectively through representatives of their own choosing, and to engage in other concerted activities for the purpose of collective bargaining or other mutual aid or protection, and shall also have the right to refrain from any or all such activities. . . .

The rights under Section 7 are given to all employees covered by the NLRA; the employees need not be organized union members to enjoy such rights. In addition, because the statutory rights are given to the individual employee, they may not be waived by a union purporting to act on behalf of the employees.

For conduct of employees to be protected under Section 7, it must be concerted, and it must be for the purpose of collective bargaining or other mutual aid or protection. A group of employees discussing the need for a union in order to improve working conditions is obviously under the protection of Section 7, as are employees who attempt to get their coworkers to join a union. But the protection of Section 7 also extends to activities not directly associated with formal unionization. For example, a group of nonunion employees who walked off the job to protest the extremely cold temperatures inside the shop were held to be exercising their Section 7 rights, as was an employee who circulated a petition about the management of the company's credit union. An employee collecting signatures of coworkers on a letter to management protesting the selection of a new supervisor was held to be engaged in protected activity in *Atlantic-Pacific Coast Inc. v. NLRB.*[1] In *NLRB v. Caval Tool Div.*,[2] an employee who challenged a new break policy announced at a company meeting was held to be engaged in concerted activity because she was acting in the interests of all the production workers. Section 7 protects employees in these situations from discipline or discharge for their conduct.

There are, of course, limits to the extent of Section 7 protection. Employees acting individually may not be protected; in addition, conduct not related to collective bargaining or mutual aid or protection purposes is not protected. For example, an employee seeking to have a foreman removed because of a personal "grudge" was held not protected by Section 7, nor was a group of employees striking to protest company sales to South Africa protected.

Perhaps the most difficult aspect of determining whether conduct is protected under Section 7 deals with the "concerted action" requirement: When is an individual employee, acting alone, protected? The following Supreme Court decision addresses this question.

---

[1] 52 F.3d 260 (9th Cir. 1995).

[2] 262 F.3d 184 (2d Cir. 2001).

CASE 14.1

NLRB v. City Disposal Systems
465 U.S. 822 (1984)

Brennan, J.

James Brown, a truck driver employed by respondent, was discharged when he refused to drive a truck that he honestly and reasonably believed to be unsafe because of faulty brakes. Article XXI of the collective-bargaining agreement between respondent and Local 247 of the International Brotherhood of Teamsters, Chauffeurs, Warehousemen and Helpers of America, which covered Brown, provides:

> [T]he Employer shall not require employees to take out on the street or highways any vehicle that is not in safe operating condition or equipped with safety appliances prescribed by law. It shall not be a violation of the Agreement where employees refuse to operate such equipment unless such refusal is unjustified.

The question to be decided is whether Brown's honest and reasonable assertion of his right to be free of the obligation to drive unsafe trucks constituted "concerted activit[y]" within the meaning of Section 7 of the NLRA. The National Labor Relations Board (NLRB) held that Brown's refusal was concerted activity within Section 7, and that his discharge was, therefore, an unfair labor practice under Section 8(a)(1) of the Act. The Court of Appeals disagreed and declined enforcement.

James Brown was assigned to truck No. 245. On Saturday, May 12, 1979, Brown observed that a fellow driver had difficulty with the brakes of another truck, truck No. 244. As a result of the brake problem, truck No. 244 nearly collided with Brown's truck. After unloading their garbage at the landfill, Brown and the driver of truck No. 244 brought No. 244 to respondent's truck-repair facility, where they were told that the brakes would be repaired either over the weekend or in the morning of Monday, May 14.

Early in the morning of Monday, May 14, while transporting a load of garbage to the landfill, Brown experienced difficulty with one of the wheels of his own truck—No. 245—and brought that truck in for repair. At the repair facility, Brown was told that, because of a backlog at the facility, No. 245 could not be repaired that day. Brown reported the situation to his supervisor, Otto Jasmund, who ordered Brown to punch out and go home. Before Brown could leave, however, Jasmund changed his mind and asked Brown to drive truck No. 244 instead. Brown refused explaining that "there's something wrong with that truck. . . . [S]omething was wrong with the brakes . . . there was a grease seal or something leaking causing it to be affecting the brakes." Brown did not, however, explicitly refer to Article XXI of the collective-bargaining agreement or to the agreement in general. In response to Brown's refusal to drive truck No. 244, Jasmund angrily told Brown to go home. At that point, an argument ensued and Robert Madary, another supervisor, intervened, repeating Jasmund's request that Brown drive truck No. 244. Again, Brown refused, explaining that No. 244 "has got problems and I don't want to drive it." Madary replied that half the trucks had problems and that if respondent tried to fix all of them it would be unable to do business. He went on to tell Brown that "[w]e've got all this garbage out here to haul and you tell me about you don't want to drive." Brown responded, "Bob, what are you going to do, put the garbage ahead of the safety of the men?" Finally, Madary went to his office and Brown went home. Later that day, Brown received word that he had been discharged. He immediately returned to work in an attempt to gain reinstatement but was unsuccessful.

. . . Brown filed an unfair labor practice charge with the NLRB, challenging his discharge. The Administrative Law Judge (ALJ) found that Brown had been discharged for refusing to operate truck No. 244, that Brown's refusal was covered by Section 7 of the NLRA, and that respondent had therefore committed an unfair labor practice under Section 8(a)(1) of the Act. The ALJ held that an employee who acts alone in asserting a contractual right can nevertheless be engaged in concerted activity within the meaning of Section 7. . . .

The NLRB adopted the findings and conclusions of the ALJ and ordered that Brown be reinstated with back pay. On a petition for enforcement of the Board's order, the Court of Appeals disagreed with the ALJ and the Board. Finding that Brown's refusal to drive truck No. 244 was an action taken solely on his own behalf, the Court of Appeals concluded that the refusal was not a concerted activity within the meaning of Section 7.

Section 7 of the NLRA provides that "[e]mployees shall have the right to . . . join or assist labor organizations, to bargain collectively through representatives of their own choosing, and to engage in other concerted activities for the purpose of collective bargaining or other mutual aid or protection." The NLRB's decision in this case applied the Board's longstanding "*Interboro* doctrine," under which an individual's assertion of a right grounded in a collective-bargaining agreement is recognized as "concerted activit[y]" and therefore accorded the protection of Section 7. The Board has relied on two justifications for the doctrine: First, the assertion of a right contained in a collective-bargaining agreement is an extension of the concerted action that produced the agreement; and second, the assertion of such a right affects the rights of all employees covered by the collective-bargaining agreement.

Neither the Court of Appeals nor respondent appears to question that an employee's invocation of a right derived from a collective-bargaining agreement meets Section 7's requirement that an employee's action be taken "for purposes of collective bargaining or other mutual aid or protection." As the Board first explained in the Interboro case, a single employee's invocation of such rights affects all the employees that are covered by the collective-bargaining agreement. This type of generalized effect, as our cases have demonstrated, is sufficient to bring the actions of an individual employee within the "mutual aid or protection" standard, regardless of whether the employee has his own interests most immediately in mind.

The term "concerted activit[y]" is not defined in the Act but it clearly enough embraces the activities of employees who have joined together in order to achieve common goals. What is not self-evident from the language of the Act, however, and what we must elucidate, is the precise manner in which particular actions of an individual employee must be linked to the actions of fellow employees in order to permit it to be said that the individual is engaged in concerted activity. We now turn to consider the Board's analysis of that question as expressed in the *Interboro* doctrine.

Although one could interpret the phrase, "to engage in concerted activities," to refer to a situation in which two or more employees are working together at the same time and the same place toward a common goal, the language of Section 7 does not confine itself to such a narrow meaning. In fact, Section 7 itself defines both joining and assisting labor organizations—activities in which a single employee can engage—as concerted activities. Indeed, even the courts that have rejected the *Interboro* doctrine recognize the possibility that an individual employee may be engaged in concerted activity when he acts alone. They have limited their recognition of this type of concerted activity, however, to two situations: (1) that in which the lone employee intends to induce group activity, and (2) that in which the employee acts as a representative of at least one other employee. The disagreement over the *Interboro* doctrine, therefore, merely reflects differing views regarding the nature of the relationship that must exist between the action of the individual employee and the actions of the group in order for Section 7 to apply. We cannot say that the Board's view of that relationship, as applied in the *Interboro* doctrine, is unreasonable.

The invocation of a right rooted in a collective-bargaining agreement is unquestionably an integral part of the process that gave rise to the agreement. That process—beginning with the organization of a union, continuing into the negotiation of a collective-bargaining agreement, and extending through the enforcement of the agreement—is a single, collective activity. Obviously, an employee could not invoke a right grounded in a collective-bargaining agreement were it not for the prior negotiating activities of his fellow employees. Nor would it make sense for a union to negotiate a collective-bargaining agreement if individual employees could not invoke the rights thereby created against their employer. Moreover, when an employee invokes a right grounded in the collective-bargaining agreement, he does not stand alone. Instead, he brings to bear on his employer the power and resolve of all his fellow employees. When, for instance, James Brown refused to drive a truck he believed to be unsafe, he was in effect reminding his employer that he and his fellow employees, at the time their collective-bargaining agreement was signed, had extracted a promise from City Disposal that they would not be asked to drive unsafe trucks. He was also reminding his employer that if it persisted in ordering him to drive an unsafe truck, he could reharness the power of that group to ensure the enforcement of that promise. It was just as though James Brown was reassembling his fellow union members to reenact their decision not to drive unsafe trucks. A lone employee's invocation of a right grounded in his collective-bargaining agreement is, therefore, a concerted activity in a very real sense. . . .

. . . By applying Section 7 to the actions of individual employees invoking their rights under a collective-bargaining agreement, the *Interboro* doctrine preserves the integrity of the entire collective-bargaining process; for by invoking a right grounded in a collective-bargaining agreement, the employee makes that right a reality, and breathes life, not only into the promises contained in the collective-bargaining agreement, but also into the entire process envisioned by Congress as the means by which to achieve industrial peace.

To be sure, the principal tool by which an employee invokes the rights granted him in a collective-bargaining agreement is the processing of a grievance according to whatever procedures his collective-bargaining agreement establishes. . . . Indeed, it would make little sense for Section 7 to cover an employee's conduct while negotiating a collective-bargaining agreement, including a grievance mechanism by which to protect the rights created by the agreement, but not to cover an employee's attempt to utilize that mechanism to enforce the agreement.

. . . As long as the employee's statement or action is based on a reasonable and honest belief that he is being, or has been, asked to perform a task that he is not required to perform under his collective-bargaining agreement, and the statement or action is reasonably directed toward the enforcement of a collectively bargained right, there is no justification for overturning the Board's judgment that the employee is engaged in concerted activity, just as he would have been had he filed a formal grievance. . . .

In this case, the Board found that James Brown's refusal to drive truck No. 244 was based on an honest and reasonable belief that the brakes on the truck were faulty. Brown explained to each of his supervisors his reason for refusing to drive the truck. Although he did not refer to his collective-bargaining agreement in either of these confrontations, the agreement provided not only that "[t]he . . . employer shall not require employees to take out on the streets or highways any vehicle that is not in safe operating condition," but also that "[i]t shall not be a violation of the Agreement where employees refuse to operate such equipment, unless such refusal is unjustified." There is no doubt, therefore, nor could there have been any doubt during Brown's confrontations with his supervisors, that by refusing to drive truck No. 244, Brown was invoking the right granted him in his collective-bargaining agreement to be free of the obligation to drive unsafe trucks. . . . Accordingly, we accept the Board's conclusion that James Brown was engaged in concerted activity when he refused to drive truck No. 244. We therefore reverse the judgment of the Court of Appeals and remand the case for further proceedings consistent with this opinion. . . .

It is so ordered.

Case Questions

1. What is the relationship of the collective bargaining process to the right to refuse to operate unsafe equipment that was invoked by Brown? Did Brown mention the collective agreement when he refused to operate the truck?

2. How was Brown's individual refusal to operate the truck he felt was unsafe "concerted activity" within the meaning of Section 7 of the NLRA? Explain.

3. Under what other circumstances, if any, can individual action be regarded as concerted within the meaning of Section 7?

In *Meyers Industries*,[3] a NLRB decision handed down before the Supreme Court decided *City Disposal Systems*, the Board held that in order for an individual employee's action to be concerted, it would require "that the conduct be engaged in with or on the authority of other employees, and not solely by and on behalf of the employee himself." The case involved an employee who was discharged after refusing to drive his truck and reporting safety problems with his truck to state transportation authorities; the employee had acted alone and the workers were not unionized. Is this holding consistent with the Supreme Court's decision in *City Disposal Systems*?

The U.S. Court of Appeals for the District of Columbia remanded the Board's decision in *Meyers Industries* to the Board for reconsideration.[4] On rehearing, the Board reaffirmed

---

[3] 268 NLRB 493 (1984).

[4] 755 F.2d 941 (1985).

its decision that the employee had not been engaged in concerted activity. When the case again came before the court of appeals in *Prill v. NLRB*,[5] the D.C. Circuit Court upheld the Board's decision, holding that it was a reasonable interpretation of the act. In *Ewing v. NLRB*,[6] the court of appeals upheld the Board in a case similar to *Meyers Industries* on the Board's third try at justifying the conclusion that the employee did not engage in concerted activity.

Even though conduct may be concerted under Section 7, it may not be protected by the act. As noted in the *City Disposal Systems* decision, the employee may not act in an abusive manner. The Board has held that illegal, destructive, or unreasonable conduct is not protected, even if such conduct was concerted and for purposes of mutual aid or protection. For example, workers who engaged in on-the-job slowdowns by refusing to process orders were not protected because they could not refuse to work yet continue to get paid. Threats or physical violence by employees are not protected, nor is the public disparagement of the employer's product by employees or the referral of customers to competitors of the employer. The rights of employees under Section 7 are at the heart of the act; they are enforced and protected through ULP proceedings under Sections 8(a) and 8(b).

Concept *Summary* 14.1

PROTECTED ACTIVITY UNDER SECTION 7

Activity is protected under Section 7 if:

• It is concerted activity
• It is for collective bargaining or mutual aid and protection purposes
• It is not illegal, destructive, or unreasonable

14-2   Sections 8(a)(1) and 8(b)(1): Violation of Employee Rights by Employers or Unions

Interference with, coercion, or restraint of employees in the exercise of their Section 7 rights by employers or unions are prohibited by Section 8(a)(1) and Section 8(b)(1), respectively. While violations of other specific unfair labor practice provisions may also violate Sections 8(a)(1) or 8(b)(1), certain kinds of conduct involve violations of Sections 8(a)(1) or 8(b)(1) only. This section discusses conduct that violates those specific sections only.

The NLRB has held that any conduct that has the natural tendency to restrain or coerce employees in the exercise of their Section 7 rights is a violation; actual coercion or restraint of the employees need not be shown. Intention is not a requirement for a violation of Sections 8(a)(1) and 8(b)(1); the employer or union need not have intended to coerce

---

[5] 835 F.2d 1481 (1987).

[6] 861 F.2d 353 (2d Cir. 1988).

or restrain employees. All that is necessary is that they engage in conduct that the Board believes has the natural tendency to restrain employees in the exercise of their Section 7 rights.

Many employer violations of Section 8(a)(1) occur in the context of union organizing campaigns. Such violations usually involve restrictions on the soliciting activities of employees or coercive or threatening remarks made by the employer. The employer's ability to make antiunion remarks is discussed first.

14-2a Antiunion Remarks by Employer

During a union organizing campaign, the employer might attempt to persuade employees not to support the union. Such attempts may involve statements of opinion regarding the prospects of unionization and may also involve implicit promises or threats of reprisal. The extent to which the employer may communicate its position has been the subject of numerous Board and court decisions. Section 8(c) of the act states that:

> The expressing of any views, argument or opinion . . . shall not constitute or be evidence of an unfair labor practice under any of the provisions of this Act, if such expression contains no threat of reprisal or force or promise of benefit.

It should be clear from the wording of Section 8(c) that explicit threats to fire union sympathizers are not protected by Section 8(c) and are therefore violations of Section 8(a)(1). The Board believes that because employees are economically dependent on the employer for their livelihood, they will be especially sensitive to the views explicitly or implicitly expressed by the employer. The Board will therefore examine closely the "totality of circumstances" of any employer's antiunion remarks to determine if they go beyond the protections of Section 8(c) and thus violate Section 8(a)(1).

In the *Gissel Packing* decision, mentioned in Chapter 13, the Supreme Court defined the limits to which an employer may predict the consequences of unionization. The employer may make a prediction based on objective facts to convey the employer's reasonable belief as to demonstrably probable effects or consequences, provided that such factors are beyond the employer's control. If the employer makes predictions about matters within the control of the employer, the Board is likely to view such statements as implicit threats because the employer is in a position to make those predictions come true. Statements such as, "The union almost put us out of business last time and the new management wouldn't hesitate to close this plant," have been held to be violations of Section 8(a)(1), whereas comments such as, "If the union gets in, it will have to bargain from scratch for everything it gets," have been held to be within Section 8(c)'s protection.

In *American Spring Wire Co.*,[7] the company's president made the following speech to employees in response to rumors that a union was trying to organize the workers:

> . . . We have beaten the Union on two occasions in this plant by overwhelming majorities and I know the majority of us are tired of such activity. The majority of us do not deserve such continuing harassment. We have set up in this Company all the means of communication possible, and to those of you who still think you can win more with the Union than you have

---

[7] 237 NLRB 1551 (1978).

with us in the past nine years, well—you are dead wrong—leave us alone—get the hell out of our plant. . . .

I want to say something to you as clearly as I possibly can. Whether or not ASW has a union is really not significant to the Corporation's future, or to myself, Dave Carruthers, or other major employees of this Company. As far as I am concerned those of us who are loyal to each other as a group can make valve spring wire, music wire, alloy wire, in Moline, Illinois; Saskatchewan, Canada; Puerto Rico; or Hawaii. We don't need Cleveland, Ohio, or all this beautiful property. Remember nine years ago we had nothing. Today our Company has developed a certain amount of wealth and goodwill at the banks, a fantastic organization of people and friends who supply us goods, and above all a long and growing list of customers. These people do business with us, not with this building or this land. We do not intend to have this statement appear as a threat because it is not. It is a statement of fact. Facts are that our real concern regarding a union is with the majority of you who have opposed it in the past, and who would be locked into it should it come to this plant.

With that in mind, I want to tell you that those of us in management do not wish to become involved in another election. We need the time to do the things that will continue to promote our Company, ourselves, and hopefully, you. I am asking you as your friend not to sign union cards, as we don't have the patience to put up with it again. This next battle is yours, not ours. It is up to each one of you who is against the union to stop the card signing before it gets started. I don't care how you do it. Organize yourselves and get it done. . . .

The NLRB held that the statement directing union supporters to ". . . get the hell out of our plant" and telling those employees who opposed the union to ". . . stop the card signing before it gets started. I don't care how you do it. . . ." were threatening and coercive. The statement "We don't need Cleveland, Ohio. . . ." was held to be a clear threat to close the plant if the employees joined a union. The remarks were held to be a violation of Section 8(a)(1). In *NLRB v. Exchange Parts*,[8] the Supreme Court held that the announcement of improved vacation pay and salary benefits during a union organizing campaign violated Section 8(a)(1). The Court reasoned that

The danger inherent in the well-timed increases in benefits is the suggestion of the fist inside the velvet glove. Employees are not likely to miss the inference that the source of benefits now conferred is also the source from which future benefits must flow and which may dry up if it is not obliged.

Why is the promise of benefits not protected under Section 8(c)? How does it interfere with the employees' exercise of Section 7 rights?

In *Heck's, Inc.*,[9] the Board declared that an employer did not commit an unfair labor practice by informing its unionized employees that it was opposed to their union and to unionization in general. However, the employer did commit an unfair labor practice by including its antiunion policy in its employee handbook and unilaterally requesting that all employees sign a statement agreeing to be bound by that policy.

14-2b Employer Limitations on Soliciting and Organizing

For employees to exercise their right, under Section 7, to choose their bargaining representative free from coercion, the employees must have access to information that will enable

---

[8] 375 U.S. 405 (1964).

[9] 293 NLRB 1111, 131 L.R.R.M. 1281 (1989).

them to exercise this right intelligently. Such information may come from fellow employees who are active in union organizing attempts, or it may come from nonemployee union organizers. Although the union may attempt to reach the employees individually at their homes, it is more convenient and more effective to contact the employees at the work site when they are all assembled there. But organizing activities at the workplace may disrupt production and will certainly conflict with the employer's right to control and direct the work force. The employer's property rights at the workplace also include the right to control access to the premises. Clearly, then, the right of employees to organize is in conflict with the employer's property rights over the enterprise. How is such a conflict to be reconciled?

In *NLRB v. Babcock & Wilcox*,[10] the Supreme Court upheld a series of NLRB rules for employer restrictions upon nonemployee access to the premises and soliciting activity of employees. In the following case, the Supreme Court reconsidered the issues raised in *Babcock & Wilcox*.

» CASE 14.2

LECHMERE, INC. V. NLRB
502 U.S. 527 (1992)

Facts: Local 919 of the United Food and Commercial Workers Union was attempting to organize the employees at a Lechmere retail store in Newington, Connecticut. The store was located at the south end of the Lechmere Shopping Plaza, while the main parking lot was to its north. The main entrance to the plaza was on the east side, off of the Berlin Turnpike, a four-lane divided highway. The parking lot is separated from the highway by a forty-six-foot-wide grassy strip, broken only by the Plaza's entrance. To begin the organizing campaign, the union ran a full-page advertisement in a local newspaper, but it drew little response. The union then sent nonemployee organizers into Lechmere's parking lot to place handbills on the windshields of cars parked in a corner of the lot used mostly by employees. Lechmere's manager immediately confronted the organizers, informed them that Lechmere prohibited solicitation or handbill distribution of any kind on its property, and asked them to leave. They left, and Lechmere personnel removed the handbills. The union organizers repeated the handbilling in the parking lot on several other occasions; each time they were asked to leave and the handbills were removed. The organizers then relocated to the public grassy strip, from where they attempted to pass out handbills to cars entering the lot during hours

(before opening and after closing) when the drivers were assumed to be primarily store employees. For one month, the union organizers returned daily to the grassy strip to picket Lechmere; after that, they picketed off and on for another six months. They also recorded the license plate numbers of cars parked in the employee parking area; with the cooperation of the Connecticut Department of Motor Vehicles, and managed to secure the names and addresses of some 41 nonsupervisory employees. The union sent four mailings to these employees and made some attempts to contact them by phone or home visits. These mailings and visits resulted in one signed union authorization card.

The union then filed an unfair labor practice charge with the NRLB, alleging that Lechmere violated the Section 8(a)(1) of NLRA by barring the nonemployee organizers from its property. An administrative law judge (ALJ) ruled in the union's favor, recommending that Lechmere be ordered to cease and desist from barring the union organizers from the parking lot.

On review the NLRB affirmed the ALJ's judgment and adopted the recommended order. Lechmere then sought judicial review, but the U.S. Court of Appeals for the First Circuit denied Lechmere's petition for review and enforced the Board's order. Lechmere then appealed to the U.S. Supreme Court.

---

[10] 351 U.S. 105 (1956).

Issue: Was Lechmere's refusal to allow nonemployee union organizers onto its property to attempt to organize the store's employees an unfair labor practice?

Decision: The NLRA confers rights on employees, not on unions or their nonemployee organizers; however, in *NLRB v. Babcock & Wilcox Co.*, the Supreme Court recognized that the employees' "right of self-organization depends in some measure on [their] ability . . . to learn the advantages of self-organization from others." In that case, the Court held that Section 7 of the NLRA may, in certain circumstances, restrict an employer's right to exclude nonemployee union organizers from its property. As a rule, employers cannot be compelled to allow distribution of union literature by nonemployee organizers on their property. However, there are exceptions to that rule, such as where the location of a plant and the living quarters of the employees place the employees beyond the reach of reasonable union efforts to communicate with them; in such cases, employers' property rights may be "required to yield to the extent needed to permit communication of information on the right to organize." Under the *Babcock & Wilcox Co.* doctrine, the NLRB must accommodate the employees' Section 7 rights and the employer's property rights with as little destruction of the one as is consistent with the maintenance of the other. In *Babcock*, the Court distinguished between the union activities of employees and of nonemployees. In cases involving employee activities, the NLRB allows the employees to receive information on self-organization on the company's property from fellow employees during nonworking time; but Section 7 does not require that nonemployee organizers be granted access to the employer's property except in the rare case where "the inaccessibility of employees makes ineffective the reasonable attempts by nonemployees to communicate with them through the usual channels." Where reasonable alternative means of access exist, the employer does not have to allow the nonemployee organizers on its property.

In the case here, the ALJ held that reasonable alternative means of communicating with the Lechmere employees were available to the union. The NLRB, reviewing the ALJ's decision, however, held that there "was no reasonable, effective alternative means available for the Union to communicate its message" to the employees. The Supreme Court held that the NLRB decision was in error, because the exception to the *Babcock* rule is a narrow one. The employer does not have to allow nonemployees on its property whenever other means of access to employees may be cumbersome or less-than-ideally effective; the employer is required to allow the nonemployee organizers on its property only when "the location of a plant and the living quarters of the employees place the employees beyond the reach of reasonable union efforts to communicate with them." Classic examples include logging camps, mining camps, and mountain resort hotels. The union has the burden of establishing that the employees are inaccessible. Here, because the employees do not reside on Lechmere's property, they are presumed not to be beyond the reach of the union's message. The fact that the employees live in a large metropolitan area does not in itself render them "inaccessible" in the meaning of *Babcock*. The union tried advertising in local newspapers; the NLRB held that this was not reasonably effective because it was expensive and might not reach the employees. Whatever the merits of that conclusion, other alternative means of communication were readily available; access to employees, not success in winning them over, is the critical issue. The union here failed to establish the existence of any unique obstacles that frustrated its access to Lechmere's employees, and the NLRB erred in concluding that Lechmere committed an unfair labor practice by barring the nonemployee organizers from its property. The Supreme Court reversed the decision of the court of appeals, and denied enforcement of the NLRB order.

As the Supreme Court noted in *Lechmere*, under certain circumstances the employer may be required to allow union organizers access to its property when there are no other reasonable alternative means of access available. In *Thunder Basin Coal v. Reich*,[11] the Supreme Court stated that the employer's right to exclude union organizers comes from state property law, not from the NLRA; nothing in the NLRA requires that employers exclude organizers. Where the employer has no state law property right to exclude union organizers, *Lechmere* does not apply, and the employer may not prohibit access by the union, according

---

[11] 510 U.S. 200 (1994).

to *NLRB v. Calkins*.[12] In *United Food and Commercial Workers v. NLRB*,[13] the U.S. Court of Appeals for the D.C. Circuit held that an employer leasing the property had no right, under state law, to deny access to union organizers. An employer's attempts to deny unions access to a temporary sidewalk in front of the employer's hotel and casino violated Section 8(a)(1) of the NLRA because the employer had no property rights to the sidewalk to allow it to exclude people from demonstrating on that sidewalk, as in *Venetian Casino Resort, L.L.C. v. NLRB*.[14]

Restrictions on Employees

Although nonemployees may be barred completely, an employer may place only "reasonable restrictions" on the soliciting activities of employees. Employer rules limiting soliciting activities must have a valid workplace purpose, such as ensuring worker safety or maintaining the efficient operation of the business, and must be applied uniformly to all soliciting, not just to union activities. The employer may limit the distribution of literature where it poses a litter problem. Employee soliciting activity may be limited to nonworking areas such as cafeterias, restrooms, or parking lots. Such activities may also be restricted to "nonworking times" such as coffee breaks and lunch breaks. However, an employer may not completely prohibit such activities.

When the workplace is a department store or hospital, "no-solicitation" rules may present particular problems. An employer will attempt to ensure that soliciting activity does not interfere with customer access or patient care, yet the Board will ensure that the employees are still able to exercise their Section 7 rights. In *Beth Israel Hospital v. NLRB*,[15] the U.S. Supreme Court upheld the Board order allowing a hospital to prohibit soliciting by employees in patient-care areas, but prohibiting the hospital from denying employees the right to solicit in the hospital cafeteria. In *American Baptist Homes of the West d/b/a/ Piedmont Gardens*,[16] the NLRB held that a retirement facility had violated Section 8(a)(1) by posting a sign that prohibited union meetings in an employee break room, by maintaining a policy that prohibited employees from remaining on the premises after their shift unless they were previously authorized by a supervisor, and by enforcing that policy against two employees who sought access to the employer's premises to communicate complaints to management.

In the absence of exceptional circumstances, blanket prohibitions on soliciting have been held unreasonable and in violation of Section 8(a)(1). In *Martin Luther Mem. Home, Inc.*,[17] the Board set out a framework for determining whether an employer's restrictive work rule is in violation of Section 8(a)(1):

- if the work rule explicitly restricts protected activity under Section 7, it is a violation;

- if the rule does not explicitly restrict protected activity, it is still a violation of Section 8(a)(1) if the employees would reasonably construe the language of the rule to prohibit protected activity, or if the rule was promulgated in response to union activity, or if the rule has been applied to restrict the exercise of protected activity.

---

[12] 187 F.3d (9th Cir. 1999).

[13] 222 F.3d 1030 (D.C. Cir. 2000).

[14] 484 F.3d 601 (D.C. Cir. 2007).

[15] 437 U.S. 483 (1978).

[16] 360 NLRB No. 100 (2014).

[17] 343 NLRB 646 (2004).

Employers may not restrict "visual-only" solicitations such as wearing hats, buttons, and so forth in the absence of exceptional circumstances. The U.S. Court of Appeals for the Second Circuit held that a rule by Starbucks Corp allowing employees to wear only one union button did not violate Section 8(a)(1). The court there held that the rule allowed an opportunity for employees to express their pro-union sentiment, while protecting a legitimate managerial interest in displaying a particular public image.[18]

Employer rules requiring that employees get prior approval from the employer for solicitation are overly restrictive and violate Section 8(a)(1) according to *Opryland Hotel*[19] and *Gallup, Inc. v. United Steelworkers of America*.[20] Employers have the right to restrict the use of company bulletin boards and telephones during working time and company email systems, but the employer may not enforce such rules in a discriminatory manner to exclude or restrict union activities.

Employer Social Media Policies and Limitations on Employees' Communications

The Board has generally taken a negative view of employer rules prohibiting employees from discussing work-related matters with fellow workers, holding that they are overly restrictive of protected activity. In *Northeastern Land Services, Inc. v. NLRB*,[21] the U.S. Court of Appeals for the First Circuit upheld the NLRB decision that an employer rule prohibiting employees from discussing terms of employment, including compensation, under penalty of dismissal was a violation of Section 8(a)(1). The U.S. Court of Appeals for the Fifth Circuit upheld that Board's decision that an employer confidentiality policy that prohibited employees from divulging or discussing "financial information, including costs" could be construed as including discussion of wages, in violation of Section 7 rights, because the policy did not indicate that some personnel information, such as wages, was not covered by the policy.[22] An employer that specifically warned an employee not to discuss wages with anyone else, and who fired the employee because the employer believed that the employee had discussed wages with other employees, violated Section 8(a)(1).[23] An employer's informal policy that prohibited employees from discussing disciplinary decisions was held to violate Section 8(a)(1) because employees must be Permitted "to communicate the circumstances of their discipline … so that their colleagues are aware of the nature of discipline being imposed, how they might avoid such discipline, and matters which could be raised in their own defense."[24]

In *Costco Wholesale Corp.*,[25] the Board ruled that an employer's policy that prohibited employees from:

- discussing "private matters of members and other employees . . . includ[ing] topics such as, but not limited to, sick calls, leaves of absence, FMLA call-outs, ADA accommodations, workers' compensation injuries, personal health information, etc.";

---

[18] *NLRB v. Starbucks Corp.*, 679 F.3d 70 (2d Cir. 2012).

[19] 323 NLRB 723 (1997).

[20] 349 NLRB 1213 (2007).

[21] 560 F.3d 36 (1st Cir. 2009).

[22] *Flex Frac Logistics, LLC v. N.L.R.B.*, 746 F.3d 205 (5th Cir. 2014).

[23] *Alternate Energy Applications*, 361 NLRB No. 139 (2014).

[24] *Phillips Electronics North America Corp.*, 361 NLRB No. 16 (2014).

[25] 358 NLRB No. 106 (2012).

- sharing, transmitting, or storing for personal or public use, without prior management approval "[s]ensitive information such as membership, payroll, confidential financial, credit card numbers, social security number or employee personal health information"; and

- sharing "confidential" information such as employees' names, addresses, telephone numbers, and email addresses;

was a violation of Section 8(a)(1) because the broad prohibition clearly encompassed concerted communications protesting working conditions or the employer's treatment of its employees.

Similarly, an employer rule requiring employees to "be courteous, polite and friendly to . . . their fellow employees. No one should be disrespectful or use profanity or any other language which injures the image or reputation of the [employer]" was held to violate Section 8(a)(1) because employees could reasonably construe it as encompassing Section 7 activity such as statements objecting to working conditions and seeking the support of others in improving them.[26] There was no language in the employer's handbook to suggest that communications protected by Section 7 were excluded from the broad reach of the rule. An employer's directive to employees not to discuss matters that were under an internal investigation by the employer was also held to violate Section 8(a)(1) because the employer had not shown a legitimate business justification for the requirement that would outweigh the employees' Section 7 rights.[27] An employer who discharged two employees for their participation in a Facebook discussion complaining that they owed additional income taxes because the employer made mistakes in withholding deductions from their pay; the Board held that employees have a right under Section 7 to act together to improve their terms and conditions of employment, including the use of social media to communicate with each other and with the public.[28]

Can the employer prohibit employees who have access to the company email system in the course of their work from using that email system to engage in workplace communications protected under Section 7 during nonworking time? That question is addressed in the following case.

» CASE 14.3

PURPLE COMMUNICATIONS, INC. AND COMMUNICATIONS WORKERS OF AMERICA, AFL-CIO
361 NLRB No. 126 (N.L.R.B. December 11, 2014)

Facts: Purple Communications, Inc. [the employer] provides sign-language interpretation services. Its employees, known as video relay interpreters, provide two-way, real-time interpretation of telephone communications between deaf or hard-of-hearing individuals and hearing individuals. The interpreters typically use an audio headset to communicate orally with the hearing participant on a call, leaving their hands free to communicate in sign language, via video, with the deaf participant. The interpreters work at 16 call centers that process calls on a nationwide, around-the-clock, "first come, first served" basis.

[26] *Karl Knauz Motors, Inc.*, 358 NLRB No. 164 (2012).
[27] *Banner Health System*, 358 NLRB No. 93 (2012).
[28] *Three D, LLC d/b/a/ Triple Play Sports Bar and Grille,* 361 NLRB No. 31 (2014).

Since June 2012, the company has maintained an employee handbook that contains its electronic communications policy. That policy states:

> Computers, laptops, internet access, voicemail, electronic mail (email), Blackberry, cellular telephones and/or other Company equipment is provided and maintained by the [*sic*] Purple to facilitate Company business. All information and messages stored, sent, and received on these systems are the sole and exclusive property of the Company, regardless of the author or recipient. All such equipment and access should be used for business purposes only. . . .

Prohibited activities

Employees are strictly prohibited from using the computer, internet, voicemail and email systems, and other Company equipment in connection with any of the following activities:

. . . .

2. Engaging in activities on behalf of organizations or persons with no professional or business affiliation with the Company.

. . . .

5. Sending uninvited email of a personal nature.

The interpreters are assigned individual email accounts on the company's email system, and they use those accounts every day that they are at work. They are able to access their company email accounts on the computers at their workstations, as well as on computers in the call centers' break areas and on their personal computers and smartphones. The interpreters have access to the Internet on the break-area computers but very limited access at their workstations. The Communications Workers of America Union [CWA] filed petitions to represent the interpreters, and the Board held elections at seven of the Respondent's call centers. The CWA filed objections to the election results at Purple Communications' Corona and Long Beach facilities; the objections included a charge that the employer's electronic communications policy interfered with the interpreters' freedom of choice in the election. The CWA also filed an unfair labor practice charge regarding the policy.

The ALJ hearing the unfair practice complaint ruled that the electronic communications policy was lawful under the NLRB decision in *Register Guard* [351 NLRB 1110 (2007), enf'd. in relevant part and remanded sub nom. *Guard Publishing v. NLRB*, 571 F.3d 53 (D.C. Cir.

2009)]. The ALJ dismissed the General Counsel's unfair labor practice charge that was based on the electronic communications policy and overruled the CWA's objection to the election results. The General Counsel and CWA filed exceptions to that decision. The National Labor Relations Board granted review of the ALJ decision to address the question concerning employees' use of their employer's email and other electronic communications systems for the purpose of communicating with other employees about union or other Section 7 matters.

Issue: Do employees have a statutory right to use an employer's email system for Section 7 purposes?

Decision: A majority of the NLRB [Chairman Pearce and Members Hirozawa and Schiffer] overruled the Board's decision in *Register Guard* to the extent it holds that employees can have no statutory right to use their employer's email systems for Section 7 purposes. The majority concluded that *Register Guard* had focused too much on an employers' property rights and too little on the importance of email as a means of workplace communication for the employees. Section 7 of the National Labor Relations Act allows employees to effectively communicate with one another at work regarding self-organization and other terms and conditions of employment. The workplace is "uniquely appropriate" and "the natural gathering place" for such communications, and the use of email as a common form of workplace communication has expanded dramatically in recent years. The majority held that, consistent with the purposes and policies of the Act and the obligation to accommodate the competing rights of employers and employees, employee use of email for statutorily protected communications on nonworking time must presumptively be permitted by employers who have chosen to give employees access to their email systems. The *Register Guard* decision failed to adequately protect employees' rights under the Act and avoided the Board's responsibility "to adapt the Act to the changing patterns of industrial life."

Based on Board and Supreme Court precedents, the majority rejected arguments that the presumption that employees have a statutory right to use the email system for Section 7 purposes should apply only if employees would otherwise be entirely deprived of their statutory right to communicate and that employees' alternative means of communication (such as by personal email or social media accounts) made the presumption inappropriate.

The majority emphasized that its decision was limited: (1) it applies only to employees who have already been granted access to the employer's email system in the course of their work and does not require employers to provide such access; (2) an employer may justify a total ban on non-work use of email, including Section 7 use on nonworking time, by demonstrating that special circumstances make the ban necessary to maintain production or discipline; (3) absent justification for a total ban, the employer may apply uniform and consistently-enforced controls over its email system to the extent such controls are necessary to maintain production and discipline; and (4) the decision does not address email access by nonemployees and does not address access to any other type of electronic communications systems.

In separate dissents, Members Miscimarra and Johnson contended that *Register Guard* was correctly decided and should not be overruled. Member Miscimarra argued that the majority's decision improperly presumed that employees need to use employer email systems to engage in protected conduct, and did not properly balance employees' statutory rights against employers' property rights.

Member Johnson argued that the majority undermined employers' rights to own and operate email networks; wrongly rejected precedents stating that employees have no right to use employer equipment; wrongly disregarded employees' alternative means of communication; and violated employers' First Amendment rights by forcing them to subsidize hostile speech.

The rise of email and social media such as Facebook and Twitter poses new questions about whether employee use of such media are protected under Section 7, and if so, to what degree. Employers concerned about their public image are adopting social media policies restricting the posting of negative information about the employer or its policies. The next case involves the legality of a social media policy that prohibited the posting of any information that could "damage the Company . . . or damage any person's reputation."

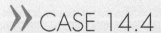 CASE 14.4

COSTCO WHOLESALE CORPORATION AND UNITED FOOD AND COMMERCIAL WORKERS UNION, LOCAL 371
358 NLRB No. 106 (Sept. 7, 2012)

Facts: The employer, Costco Wholesale Corp., included a number of restrictions on employee activity as part of its employee handbook [known as the Costco Employee Agreement]. One rule, section 11.9 of the employee handbook, stated: "Any communication transmitted, stored or displayed electronically must comply with the policies outlined in the Costco Employee Agreement. Employees should be aware that statements posted electronically (such as [to]online message boards or discussion groups) that damage the Company, defame any individual or damage any person's reputation, or violate the policies outlined in the Costco Employee Agreement, may be subject to discipline, up to and including termination of employment." The union representing Costco employees filed an unfair labor practice complaint, and a hearing before an

Administrative Law Judge [ALJ]. The ALJ found that the rule did not violate Section 8(a)(1), stating that employees would not reasonably construe this rule as regulating, and thereby inhibiting, Section 7 conduct. The NLRB General Counsel then sought review of that decision with the NLRB.

Issue: Does the employer's restrictions on what employees may post on social media interfere with, restrain, or coerce the employees' exercise of their Section 7 rights?

Decision: The Board stated that the appropriate inquiry as to whether an employer's work rule violates Section 8(a)(1), the appropriate inquiry is whether the rule would reasonably tend to chill employees in the exercise of their Section 7 rights. If the rule explicitly restricts Section 7

rights, it is unlawful. If it does not impose explicit restrictions on protected activity, the violation is dependent upon a showing of one of the following: (1) that employees would reasonably construe the language to prohibit Section 7 activity; (2) that the rule was promulgated in response to union activity; or (3) that the rule has been applied to restrict the exercise of Section 7 rights.

The Costco at issue here does not explicitly reference Section 7 activity. However, by its terms, the broad prohibition against making statements that "damage the Company, defame any individual or damage any person's reputation" clearly encompasses concerted communications protesting the Respondent's treatment of its employees.

There is nothing in the rule that even arguably suggests that protected communications are excluded from the broad scope of the rule. In these circumstances, employees would reasonably conclude that the rule requires them to refrain from engaging in certain protected communications, such as those that are critical of the employer or its agents. The rule here does not present accompanying language that would tend to restrict its application. It therefore allows employees to reasonably assume that it pertains to, among other things, certain protected concerted activities, such as communications that are critical of Costco's treatment of its employees. The employer's rule thus has a reasonable tendency to inhibit employees' protected activity and violates Section 8(a)(1).

The NLRB General Counsel has issued a memorandum providing guidance for employers in crafting social media policies.[29]

14-2c   Other Section 8(a)(1) Violations

As noted earlier, any conduct by an employer that has the natural tendency to interfere, restrain, or coerce employees in the exercise of their Section 7 rights is a violation of Section 8(a)(1). In *D.R. Horton, Inc.*,[30] the NLRB held that the employer violated Section 8(a)(1) of the act by requiring its employees to sign, as a condition of employment, a mandatory arbitration agreement that did not allow its employees to file joint, class, or collective employment-related claims in any forum, arbitral or judicial. Based on the agreement, the employer had rejected employees' requests for class arbitration of claims under the Fair Labor Standards Act. The Board found that by requiring only individual arbitration of employment-related claims and excluding access to any forum for collective claims, the employer interfered with employees' Section 7 right to engage in "concerted activities for the purpose of collective bargaining or other mutual aid or protection." The collective pursuit of workplace grievances through litigation or arbitration is conduct protected by Section 7 and the right under the NLRA to freedom of association. However, the U.S. Court of Appeals for the Fifth Circuit held that the NLRB's decision did not give proper weight to the Federal Arbitration Act (FAA), and the arbitration agreement had to be enforced according to its terms; however, the court also held that the NLRB properly required employer to clarify with its employees that the arbitration agreement did not eliminate their ability to file unfair labor practice complaints with the NLRB.[31] Despite judicial rejection of the Board's position that mandatory arbitration agreements requiring arbitration of all employment-related claims violated Section 8(a)(1), a majority of the Board reaffirmed that position in *Murphy*

[29] NLRB, the memorandum is available at http://nlrb.gov/news/
acting-general-counsel-releases-report-employer-social-media-policies.

[30] 357 NLRB No. 184 (2012).

[31] *D.R. Horton v. NLRB*, 737 F.3d 344 (5th Cir. 2013).

Oil USA,[32] holding that the employer violated Section 8(a) (1) of the act by requiring its employees to agree to resolve all employment-related claims through individual arbitration. The Board found that mandatory arbitration agreements that bar employees from bringing joint, class, or collective workplace claims in any forum restrict employees' right under Section 7 of the NLRA to improve their working conditions through administrative and judicial forums. The Board majority also found that finding a mandatory arbitration agreement unlawful under the NLRA did not conflict with the FAA because: (1) such agreements extinguish rights guaranteed by Section 7; (2) Section 7 amounts to a "contrary congressional command" overriding the FAA; and (3) the Norris-LaGuardia Act, which prevents enforcement of private agreements that prohibit individuals from participating in lawsuits arising out of labor disputes, indicates that the FAA should yield to accommodate Section 7 rights. The Board majority stated that Section 7 did not guarantee a right to class certification or the equivalent but did create a right to pursue joint, class, or collective claims if and as available, without the interference of an employer-imposed restraint. The Board majority found that the employer also violated Section 8(a)(1) when it sought to compel arbitration under the mandatory individual arbitration agreements of an FLSA claim filed by several employees in federal court.

The NLRB has recently expressed concerns that employers insisting that employees acknowledge broad at-will employment policies may run afoul of Section 8(a)(1).[33]

An employer filing an ultimately unsuccessful suit against unions engaged in protected activity is not automatically in violation of Section 8(a)(1) when there were reasonable grounds for the suit, *BE&K Construction Co. v. NLRB*.[34] Other employer practices likely to produce Section 8(a)(1) complaints may involve interrogation of employees regarding union sympathies and the denial of employee requests to have a representative present during disciplinary proceedings.

Polling and Interrogation

An employer approached by a union claiming to have the support of a majority of employees may wish to get some independent verification of the union's claim. In *Struknes Construction*,[35] the NLRB set out guidelines to reconcile the legitimate interests of an employer in polling employees regarding union support with the tendency of such a poll to restrain employees in the free exercise of their Section 7 rights. The NLRB requires that the

---

[32] 361 NLRB No. 72 (2014).

[33] In one case, *American Red Cross Arizona, Blood Services Region*, 2012 WL 311334 (NLRB Feb. 1, 2012), employees were required to sign an acknowledgment form when receiving a copy of the employee handbook; the form stated that the employees acknowledged receipt of the handbook, and agreed to abide by the rules set forth in it. The handbook noted that the employees were employees at-will, and the acknowledgment form contained language stating, "I further agree that the at-will employment relationship cannot be amended, modified or altered in any way." An administrative law judge held that requiring employees to sign the form violated Section 8(a)(1) because "the clause in question premises employment on an employee's agreement not to enter into any contract, to make any efforts, or to engage in conduct that could result in union representation and in a collective-bargaining agreement, which would amend, modify, or alter the at-will relationship. Clearly such a clause would reasonably chill employees who were interested in exercising their Section 7 rights." The parties entered into a settlement agreement, and the ALJ's decision was not reviewed by the NLRB.

[34] 536 U.S. 516 (2002).

[35] 165 NLRB 1062 (1967).

employer have a "good faith reasonable doubt" about a union's claim of majority support in order to conduct a poll of employees regarding their support of a union. The Supreme Court upheld the Board's "good faith reasonable doubt" requirement in *Allentown Mack Sales and Service, Inc. v. NLRB.*[36] If the employer chooses to poll its employees, the poll must be conducted according to the following guidelines:

- It must be done in response to a union claim of majority support.
- The employees must be informed of the purpose of the poll.
- The employees must be given assurances that no reprisals will result from their choice.
- The poll must be by secret ballot.

In addition, the employer must not have created a coercive atmosphere through unfair labor practices or other behavior; and the poll must not be taken if a representation election is pending. Why should the Board preclude such a poll when an election is pending? In light of *Linden Lumber* (in Chapter 13), what happens when the poll by the employer discloses that the union has majority support?

The employer polling pursuant to the *Struknes* rules needs to be distinguished from the interrogation of employees regarding their union sympathies. Polling is to be done by secret ballot and only in response to a union claim for voluntary recognition. Interrogation may involve confronting individual employees and questioning them about their union sympathies. Such interrogation may be in response to a union organizing campaign or a request for voluntary recognition, and, according to *Johnnie's Poultry Co.*[37] and *Wisconsin Porcelain Co.*,[38] must include reassurances that participation in the interrogation is voluntary and that there will be no reprisals taken against the employees.

The NLRB has held that interrogation of individual employees, even known union adherents, is not an unfair labor practice if it is done without threats or the promise of benefits by the employer in *Rossmore House.*[39] If the interrogation is accompanied by threats against the employees or other unfair labor practices by the employer, however, it may be a violation of Section 8(a)(1).

In *Alliance Rubber,*[40] the Board, in a 2–1 decision, held that two polygraph examiners, hired by the employer to help in an investigation of suspected plant sabotage and drug use, were acting as agents of the employer when they interrogated employees about union activities in the course of administering polygraph exams to the employees. The Board held that the questioning was made even more stressful because of its connection with the investigation into drug use and sabotage, and it implicitly gave the employees the message that engaging in union activity might result in their being suspected of engaging in unlawful activity in the plant. The company vice president's conduct reasonably led employees to believe that the examiners asked the questions about union activities on behalf of the

---

[36] 522 U.S. 359 (1998).

[37] 146 NLRB 770 (1964), enforcement denied by *NLRB v. Johnnie's Poultry Co.*, 344 F.2d 617 (8th Cir. 1965).

[38] 349 NLRB No. 17 (2007).

[39] 269 NLRB 1176 (1984), affirmed sub nom *Hotel & Restaurant Employees Local 11 v. NLRB*, 760 F.2d 1006 (9th Cir. 1985).

[40] 286 NLRB 645 (1987).

employer; therefore, the employer and the polygraph operators were held to have violated Section 8(a)(1).

Weingarten Rights

Weingarten rights
the right of employees to have a representative of their choice present at meetings that may result in disciplinary action against the employees

In *NLRB v. Weingarten*,[41] an employer refused to allow an employee to have a union representative present during the questioning of the employee about thefts from the employer. The Supreme Court upheld the NLRB ruling that such a refusal violated Section 8(a)(1). The Court reasoned "the action of an employee in seeking to have the assistance of his union representative at a confrontation with his employer clearly falls within the literal wording of Section 7 that '[e]mployees shall have the right . . . to engage in concerted activities for the purpose of . . . mutual aid or protection.'" Shortly after its decision in *Weingarten*, the Board extended **Weingarten rights** to nonunion employees as well, as in *Materials Research Corp.*[42] However, in *E. I. DuPont & Co.*,[43] the NLRB decided to restrict such rights to unionized employees only. In 2000, the NLRB again reversed that position and again held that nonunion employees are also entitled to have a representative present during investigatory interviews in *Epilepsy Foundation of Northeast Ohio*.[44] That decision was enforced by the U.S. Court of Appeals for the District of Columbia in *Epilepsy Foundation of Northeast Ohio v. NLRB*.[45]

However, the NLRB once again reversed its position on the question of whether nonunion employees are entitled to *Weingarten* rights in *IBM Corp.*,[46] where the NLRB held that *Weingarten* rights are not available to nonunion workers.

Under present NLRB doctrine, unionized employees have a right to have a representative present applies whenever the meeting with management will have the "probable" result of the imposition of discipline or where such a result is "seriously considered." The NLRB also held that, absent extenuating circumstances, the employee is entitled to the union representative of his or her choice in *Anheuser-Busch v. NLRB*.[47] The Board has set the following two requirements on the exercise of *Weingarten* rights by employees: The employee must actually request the presence of a representative to have the right (see *Montgomery Ward & Co.*[48]) and an employer who violates an employee's *Weingarten rights* is not prevented from disciplining the employee, provided that the employer has independent evidence, not resulting from the "tainted" interview, to justify the discipline (see *ITT Lighting Fixtures, Div. of ITT*).[49]

Violence and Surveillance

One last area of employer violations of Section 8(a)(1) involves violence and surveillance of employees. It should be clear from the wording of Section 8(a)(1) that violence or threats of violence directed against employees by the employer (or agents of the employer) violate

---

[41] 420 U.S. 251 (1975).

[42] 262 NLRB 1010 (1982).

[43] 289 NLRB 627 (1988).

[44] 331 NLRB 676 (2000).

[45] 268 F.3d 1095 (2001), *cert. denied*, 536 U.S. 904 (2002).

[46] 341 NLRB 1228 (2004).

[47] 338 F.3d 267 (4th Cir. 2003).

[48] 269 NLRB 904 (1984).

[49] 261 NLRB 229 (1982).

Section 8(a)(1) because they interfere with the free exercise of the employees' Section 7 rights. Employer surveillance of employee activities, or even creating the impression that the employees are under surveillance, also violates Section 8(a)(1) because such a practice has the natural tendency to restrict the free exercise of the employees' Section 7 rights. An employer photographing or videotaping employees who are engaging in protected activity is a violation of Section 8(a)(1), according to *F. W. Woolworth Co.*[50] In *Allegheny Ludlum Corp. v. NLRB*,[51] an employer asking employees to agree to be filmed for use in an anti-union video was also in violation of Section 8(a)(1).

14-2d   Union Coercion of Employees and Employers

Whereas Section 8(a)(1) prohibits employer interference with employees' Section 7 rights, Section 8(b)(1)(A) prohibits union restraint or coercion of the exercise of Section 7 rights by the employee. It is important to remember that Section 7 also gives employees the right to refrain from concerted activity. (There is an important qualification on the employees' right to refrain from union activities; Section 7 recognizes that a union shop or agency shop provision requiring employees to join the union or to pay union dues may be valid. We discuss these provisions later in this chapter.)

Section 8(b)(1)(A)

In *Radio Officers Union v. NLRB*,[52] the Supreme Court stated that the policy behind Section 7 and Section 8(b) was "to allow employees to freely exercise their right to join unions, be good, bad or indifferent members, or to abstain from joining any union, without imperiling their livelihood."

Union threats or violence directed at employees are clear violations of Section 8(b)(1)(A), as in *United Food and Commercial Workers, Local 7R (ConAgra Foods, Inc.)*,[53] because such actions tend to coerce or interfere with the employees' free choice of whether or not to support the union. But just as with employer actions under Section 8(a)(1), less blatant conduct may also be an unfair labor practice. Where the union has waived its initiation fees for employees who join prior to a representation election, the Board has found a Section 8(b)(1)(A) violation. By the same reasoning, union statements such as, "Things will be tough for employees who don't join the union before the election," were also held to violate Section 8(b)(1)(A). In *Local 466, Int. Brotherhood of Painters and Allied Trades (Skidmore College)*,[54] a union business agent's statement, in response to an internal union investigation into alleged financial improprieties initiated by other union members, which said, "when this is over with, someone's going to get hurt" was held to be a threat of reprisal violating Section 8(b)(1)(A). Union officers photographing or videotaping the license plates and the occupants of vehicles crossing a picket line, when coupled with abusive remarks or other

[50] 10 NLRB 1197 (1993).

[51] 301 F.3d 167 (3d Cir. 2002).

[52] 347 U.S. 17 (1954).

[53] 347 NLRB No. 97 (2006).

[54] 332 NLRB 445 (2000).

conduct having a reasonable tendency to instill fear of retribution in the minds of replacement employees, violates Section 8(b)(1)(A).[55]

Section 8(b)(1)(A) does recognize the need for unions to make rules regarding membership qualifications. A proviso to the section declares "[t]his paragraph shall not impair the right of a labor organization to prescribe its own rules with respect to the acquisition or retention of membership therein." The courts have tended to construe this provision liberally, provided that the union action does not affect the job tenure of an employee. The courts have allowed unions to fine members who refused to go on strike; they have also upheld the right of unions to file suit in state court to collect such fines. However, when a union has expelled a member for filing an unfair labor practice charge with the NLRB without exhausting available internal union remedies, the Supreme Court has found the union in violation of Section 8(b)(1)(A), as in *NLRB v. Industrial Union of Marine and Shipbuilding Workers*.[56] The Court reasoned, "Any coercion used to discourage, retard or defeat that access [to the NLRB] is beyond the legitimate interests of a labor organization."

Section 8(b)(1)(B)

Section 8(b)(1)(B) protects employers from union coercion in their choice of a representative for purposes of collective bargaining or the adjustment of grievances. The legislative history of this section suggests that it was intended to prevent unions from coercing firms into multiemployer bargaining units.

In a number of industries, employers bargain with a union on a multiemployer basis. This is particularly true in industries characterized by a number of small firms and a single large union. Examples are:

- Coal mining

- The trucking industry

- Construction

- The longshoring industry

whipsaw strike
strike by a union selectively pitting one firm in an industry against the other firms

To offset the power of the large union, the employers join together and bargain through an employers' association or multiemployer bargaining unit. This joint bargaining by employers prevents the union from engaging in **whipsaw strikes**—that is, strikes in which the union selectively strikes one firm in the industry. Because that firm's competitors are not struck, they can continue to operate and draw business from the struck firm. The struck firm is under great pressure to concede to union demands to regain lost business. When the firm capitulates, the union repeats the process against other firms. Multiemployer bargaining resists such efforts because all firms bargain together; if the union strikes one firm, the others can lock out their employees to undermine the union's pressure.

In addition to preventing whipsaw strikes, other reasons for engaging in multiemployer bargaining include the following:

- It eases each company's administrative burden by reducing the number of negotiating sessions and aiding information exchange.

---

[55] In re *General Teamsters, Warehousemen and Helpers Union*, 335 NLRB 686 (2001).

[56] 391 U.S. 418 (1968).

- When one large company is the pacesetter in the industry and the union is likely to insist that other firms adopt approximately the same contract terms, smaller employers may have more input into the bargaining process by joining the leader in a multiemployer bargaining arrangement.

- Establishment of uniform wages, hours, and working conditions among the members of the bargaining group means firms will not have to engage in economic competition in the labor market.

Despite the legislative history of Section 8(b)(1)(B), the section does not mention multiemployer bargaining. The Board and the courts have taken the position that multiemployer bargaining cannot be demanded by the interested employers or by the relevant union; rather, it must be consented to by both sides.[57] The union need not agree to bargain with the employers' association, nor can it insist that any company or companies form or join such a bargaining group. However, once the parties have agreed to multiemployer bargaining and negotiations have begun, neither an employer nor the union may withdraw without the consent of the other side, except in the event of "unusual circumstances." This rule prevents one side from pulling out just because the bargaining has taken an undesirable turn. (The Board has held that an impasse, or deadlock in negotiations, does not constitute "unusual circumstances.")

Unions have been found guilty of violating Section 8(b)(1)(B) when they struck to force a company to accept a multiemployer association for bargaining purposes and when they tried to force a firm to enter an individual contract in conflict with the established multiemployer unit. In addition, unions that have insisted on bargaining with company executives rather than an attorney hired by management have been held to violate Section 8(b)(1)(B).

14-2e Section 8(a)(2): Employer Domination of Labor Unions

in-house union
union created and controlled by the employer

In the years just prior to and shortly after the passage of the Wagner Act in 1935, employer-formed and dominated unions were common. Firms that decided they could no longer completely resist worker demands for collective action created **in-house unions**, or captive unions. Such unions or employee associations created an impression of collective bargaining while allowing management to retain complete control. This type of employer domination is outlawed by Section 8(a)(2). That section also outlaws employer interference in the formation or administration of a labor organization, as well as employer support (financial or otherwise) of the same.

As remedies for Section 8(a)(2) violations, the Board may order the employer to cease recognizing the union, to cancel any agreements reached with the union, to cease giving support or assistance to the union, or to disband an in-house or captive union.

Although in-house unions are not a common problem today, the problem of employer support is of continuing interest. Support such as secretarial help, office equipment, or financial aid is prohibited. An employer is permitted by Section 8(a)(2) to allow "employees to confer with him during working hours without loss of time or pay."

---

[57] See *Oakwood Care Center,* 343 NLRB 659 (2004).

An employer who agrees to recognize a union that does not have the support of a majority of employees violates Section 8(a)(2); such recognition is a violation even if the employer acted on a good-faith belief that the union had majority support. An employer is also prohibited from recognizing one union while another union has a petition for a representation election pending before the NLRB. However, in *RCA del Caribe*,[58] the Board held that an employer may continue negotiations with an incumbent union even though a rival union had filed a petition for a representation election. Are these two positions consistent? How can they be reconciled?

In addition to being prohibited from recognizing a nonmajority union, the employer is forbidden from helping a union solicit membership or dues checkoff cards and from allowing a supervisor to serve as a union officer.

One area of interest under Section 8(a)(2) has developed recently as many employers initiated innovative work arrangements among employees. To improve productivity and worker morale, some employers have created autonomous work groups, quality circles, or work teams in which groups of employees are given greater responsibility for determining work schedules, methods, and so forth. When these work groups or teams discuss working conditions, pay, or worker grievances with representatives of the employer, they could be classified as labor organizations under the NLRA. Section 2(5) defines a labor organization as:

> any organization of any kind, or any agency or employee representation committee or plan, in which employees participate and which exists for the purpose, in whole or in part, of dealing with employers concerning grievances, labor disputes, wages, rates of pay, hours of employment, or conditions of work.

The following case deals with the question of whether employer-created "employee action committees" were employer dominated or controlled labor organizations in violation of Section 8(a)(2).

CASE 14.5

ELECTROMATION, INC. V. NLRB
35 F.3d 1148 (7th Cir. 1994)

[Electromation, a manufacturer of small electrical components, employed approximately 200 employees; the employees were not represented by a union. In response to financial losses, the company decided to cut expenses by revising its employee attendance policy and replacing the scheduled wage increases with lump-sum payments based on the length of each employee's service at the company. When Electromation informed its employees of these changes, a number of employees signed a letter to the company expressing their dissatisfaction with the changes and asking the company to reconsider. The company president met with randomly selected employees to discuss wages, bonuses, incentive pay, tardiness, attendance programs, and bereavement and sick leave policy. Following this meeting, the president and supervisors concluded that the company would involve the employees to come up with solutions to these issues through the use of "action committees" of employees and management.

At a meeting to explain the action committees, the employees initially reacted negatively to the concept. They reluctantly agreed to the proposed committees and suggested

---

[58] 262 NLRB 963 (1982).

that they be allowed to sign up for specific committees. The next day, the company informed the employees of the formation of five action committees and posted sign-up sheets for the following committees: (1) Absenteeism/ Infractions; (2) No Smoking Policy; (3) Communication Network; (4) Pay Progression for Premium Positions; and (5) Attendance Bonus Program. Each committee was to consist of employees and one or two members of management, as well as the company's Employee Benefits Manager, Loretta Dickey, who was in charge of the coordination of all the committees. No employees were involved in the drafting of any aspect of the memorandum or the statement of subjects that the committees were to consider. The company then posted a memo announcing the members of each committee and dates of the initial committee meetings. The company's Employee Benefits Manager had determined which employees would participate on each committee. In late January and early February 1989, four of the action committees began to meet, but the No Smoking Policy Committee was never organized.

At the first meeting of the Attendance Bonus Program Committee, management officials solicited employee ideas regarding a good attendance award program. Through the discussions, the committee developed a proposal, but management declared it was too costly and it was not pursued further.

On February 13, 1989, the International Brotherhood of Teamsters, Local Union No. 1049 (the "union") demanded recognition from the company; the company had been unaware that any organizing efforts had occurred. In late February, the president informed Employee Benefits Manager Dickey of the union's demand. Upon the advice of counsel, Dickey announced at the next meeting of each committee that, due to the union demand, the company could no longer participate in the committees, but that the employee members could continue to meet if they so desired. Finally, on March 15, 1989, the president formally announced to the employees that "due to the Union's campaign, the Company would be unable to participate in the committee meetings and could not continue to work with the committees until after the union election."

The election was held on March 31, 1989; the employees voted 95-82 against union representation. On April 24, 1989, a regional director of the Board issued a complaint alleging that Electromation had violated the Act; the NLRB ultimately found that Electromation violated Sections 8(a)(2) and (1) of the NLRA through its establishment and administration of "action committees" consisting of

employees and management. Electromation sought judicial review of the NLRB order.]

Will, J.

. . . In this appeal, we consider a petition to set aside and a cross-petition to enforce an order of the National Labor Relations Board.

. . . An allegation that Electromation has violated Section 8(a)(2) and (1) of the Act raises two distinct issues: first, whether the action committees in this case constituted "labor organizations" within the meaning of Section 2(5); and second, whether the employer dominated, influenced, or interfered with the formation or administration of the organization or contributed financial or other support to it, in violation of Section 8(a)(2) and (1) of the Act. . . .

. . . Under [the] statutory definition [of labor organization, §2(5)] the action committees would constitute labor organizations if: (1) the Electromation employees participated in the committees; (2) the committees existed, at least in part, for the purpose of "dealing with" the employer; and (3) these dealings concerned "grievances, labor disputes, wages, rates of pay, hours of employment, or conditions of work."

In reaching its decision in this case, the Board also noted that "if the organization has as a purpose the representation of employees, it meets the statutory definition of 'employee representation committee or plan' under Section 2(5) and will constitute a labor organization if it also meets the criteria of employee participation and dealing with conditions of work or other statutory subjects." Because the Board found that the employee members of the action committees had acted in a representational capacity, it did not decide whether an employee group could ever be found to constitute a labor organization in the absence of a finding that it acted as a representative of the other employees. . . .

With respect to the first factor, there is no question that the Electromation employees participated in the action committees. Turning to the second factor, which is the most seriously contested on appeal, the Board found that the activities of the action committees constituted "dealing with" the employer.

. . . even if the committees are considered individually, there exists substantial evidence that each was formed and existed for the purpose of "dealing with" the company. It is in fact the shared similarities among the committee structures which compels unitary treatment of them for the purposes of the issues raised in this appeal. . . .

We have previously noted that the broad construction of [the definition of] labor organization applies not only with regard to the "absence of formal organization, [but also to] the type of interchange between parties which may be deemed 'dealing'" with employers. Moreover, an organization may satisfy the statutory requirement that it exists for the purpose in whole or in part of dealing with employers even if it has not engaged in actual bargaining or concluded a bargaining agreement.

. . . the Board here explained that "dealing with" is a bilateral mechanism involving proposals from the employee organization concerning the subjects listed in Section 2(5), coupled with real or apparent consideration of those proposals by management. . . .

. . . the Board did not err in determining that the Electromation action committees constituted labor organizations within the meaning of Sections 2(5) and 8(a)(2) of the Act. Although it is true that [the company] . . . made no guarantees as to the results regarding the employee recommendations, the activities of the action committees nonetheless constituted "dealing with" the employer. Finally, with respect to the third factor, the subject matter of that dealing—for example, the treatment of employee absenteeism and employee bonuses—obviously concerned conditions of employment. We further agree with the Board that the purpose of the action committees was not limited to the improvement of company efficiency or product quality, but rather that they were designed to function and in fact functioned in an essentially representative capacity. Accordingly, given the statute's traditionally broad construction, there is substantial evidence to support the Board's finding that the action committees constituted labor organizations. . . .

. . . [W]e must next consider whether, through their creation and administration of the action committees, the company acted unlawfully in violation of Section 8(a)(2) and (1) of the Act.

. . . the Board focused its analysis on the relationship between Electromation's actions in creating and administering the action committees and the resulting effect upon its employees' rights under the Act. . . . The Board correctly focused on management's participation in the action committees and its effect on the employees and found domination in that the company defined the committee structures and committee subject matters, appointed a manager to coordinate and monitor the committee meetings, structured each committee to include one or two management representatives, and permitted those managers to review and reject committee proposals before they could be presented

to upper level management. The Board's interpretation of Section 8(a)(2) simply does not contravene the statutory language. . . .

As the Board found, substantial evidence supports the finding of company domination of the action committees. First, the company proposed and essentially imposed the action committees upon its employees as the only acceptable mechanism for resolution of their acknowledged grievances regarding the newly announced attendance bonus policies. . . .

The record also clearly shows that the employees were initially reluctant to accept the company's proposal of the action committees as a means to address their concerns; their reaction was "not positive." Nonetheless, the company continued to press the idea until the employees eventually accepted. . . . The company played a pivotal role in establishing both the framework and the agenda for the action committees. Electromation unilaterally selected the size, structure, and procedural functioning of the committees; it decided the number of committees and the topic(s) to be addressed by each. The company unilaterally drafted the action committees' purposes and goal statements, which identified from the start the focus of each committee's work.

. . . Electromation actually controlled which issues received attention by the committees and which did not. . . .

Although the company acceded to the employees' request that volunteers form the committees, it unilaterally determined how many could serve on each committee, decided that an employee could serve on only one committee at a time, and determined which committee certain employees would serve on, thus exercising significant control over the employees' participation and voice at the committee meetings. . . . Also, the company designated management representatives to serve on the committees . . . the management representative[s] . . . reviewed employee proposals, determined whether they were economically feasible, and further decided whether they would be presented to higher management. This role of the management committee members effectively put the employer on both sides of the bargaining table, an avowed proscription of the Act. Finally, the company paid the employees for their time spent on committee activities, provided meeting space, and furnished all necessary supplies for the committees' activities. While such financial support is clearly not a violation of Section 8(a)(2) by itself, . . . in the totality of the circumstances in this case such support may reasonably be characterized to be in furtherance of the company's domination of the action committees. We therefore conclude that there is substantial evidence to support the Board's finding of unlawful employer domination and interference in violation of Section 8(a)(2) and (1).

. . . Accordingly, because we find that substantial evidence supports the Board's factual findings and that its legal conclusions have a reasonable basis in the law, we affirm the Board's findings and enforce the Board's order.

Enforced.

Case Questions

1.   What was the purpose of the action committees created by Electromation? Did the committees constitute labor organizations within the meaning of Section 2(5) of the NLRA? Explain your answer.

2.   When does a labor organization "deal with" an employer within the meaning of Section 2(5)? Did Electromation "deal with" the action committees? Explain.

3.   On what basis did the NLRB and the court determine that Electromation dominated and controlled the action committees?

An employer-created group of managers and employees that discussed matters such as medical benefits, stock ownership plans, and termination policy was held to be an employer-dominated labor organization in violation of Section 8(a)(2) in *Polaroid Corp.*[59] However, an employee committee that exists for the purpose of sharing information with the employer and simply gathers information and makes no proposals to the employer is not a labor organization, according to *NLRB v. Peninsula General Hospital Medical Center.*[60]

ethical DILEMMA

EMPLOYEE INVOLVEMENT GROUP FOR WYDGET?

You are the human resources manager of Wydget Corporation, a small manufacturing firm. The employees of Wydget are not unionized. Because of difficult business conditions, the workers' wages have not increased in several years, and their medical insurance benefits have been reduced. As a result, morale among employees is low, and there has been high turnover in the work force. You are considering creating an employee involvement group to provide an opportunity for workers to share their concerns and ideas with management and to discuss production problems and working conditions. How can you structure the group to ensure that employees feel their role is effective, without running afoul of Section 8(a)(2)? What are the potential problems associated with the creation of such a group? Should you establish the employee involvement group? Explain the reasons for your opinion.

---

[59] 329 NLRB 424 (1999).

[60] 36 F.3d 1262 (4th Cir. 1994).

14-2f   Sections 8(a)(3) and 8(b)(2): Discrimination in Terms or Conditions of Employment

Under Section 8(a)(3) of the NLRA, employers are forbidden to discriminate "in regard to hire or tenure or employment or any term or condition of employment to encourage or discourage membership in any labor organization." Unions, under Section 8(b)(2), are forbidden to:

> cause or attempt to cause an employer to discriminate against an employee in violation of Subsection 8(a)(3) or to discriminate against an employee with respect to whom membership in such organization has been denied or terminated on some ground other than . . . failure to tender the periodic dues and the initiation fees uniformly required as a condition of . . . membership. . . .

The intent of these sections is to insulate an employee's employment from conditions based on his or her union sympathies or lack thereof. If an employee is to have the free choice, under Section 7, to join or refrain from joining a union, then that employee must not be made to suffer economically for his or her choice. The wording of Sections 8(a)(3) and 8(b)(2) indicates that a violation of these sections has two elements.

- First, there must be some discrimination in the terms or conditions of employment— either a refusal to hire, discharge, lay off, or discipline—or a union attempt to get the employer to so discriminate.

- Second, the discrimination or attempt to cause discrimination must be for the purpose of encouraging or discouraging union membership.

For example, in *USF Red Star, Inc.*,[61] a union's efforts to get the employer to discharge an employee because of his internal union activities violated Section 8(b)(2) and Section 8(b)(1)(A); when the employer discharged the employee because of the union's demands, it violated Section 8(a)(3) and Section 8(a)(1).

Because the discrimination (or attempt to cause it) must be for the purpose of encouraging or discouraging union membership, intention is a necessary part of a violation of these sections. If an employer (or union) states that an employee should be fired because of participation in union activities (or lack of participation), demonstrating the requisite intention for a violation is no problem. But most complaints involving Section 8(a)(3) or Section 8(b)(2) are not as clear-cut. For example, what happens if an employee who supports the union's organizing campaign also has a poor work record? How should the Board and the courts handle a case in which the employer or union has mixed motives for its actions? That is the subject of the following case.

CASE 14.6

NLRB v. Transportation Management Corp.

462 U.S. 393 (1983)

White, J.

The National Labor Relations Act makes unlawful the discharge of workers because of union activity, but employers retain the right to discharge workers for any number of other reasons unrelated to the employee's union activities. When the General Counsel of the National Labor

---

[61] 330 NLRB 53 (1999).

Relations Board (Board) files a complaint alleging that an employee was discharged because of his union activities, the employer may assert legitimate motives for his decision. In *Wright Line* . . . the National Labor Relations Board reformulated the allocation of the burden of proof in such cases. It determined that the General Counsel carried the burden of persuading the Board that an anti-union animus contributed to the employer's decision to discharge an employee, a burden that does not shift, but that the employer, even if it failed to meet or neutralize the General Counsel's showing, could avoid the finding that it violated the statute by demonstrating by a preponderance of the evidence that the worker would have been fired even if he had not been involved with the Union. The question presented in this case is whether the burden placed on the employer in *Wright Line* is consistent with Sections 8(a)(1) and 8(a)(3), as well as with Section 10(c) of the NLRA, which provides that the Board must prove an unlawful labor practice by a "preponderance of the evidence."

Prior to his discharge, Sam Santillo was a bus driver for respondent Transportation Management Corporation. On March 19, 1979, Santillo talked to officials of the Teamster's Union about organizing the drivers who worked with him. Over the next four days Santillo discussed with his fellow drivers the possibility of joining the Teamsters and distributed authorization cards. On the night of March 23, George Patterson, who supervised Santillo and the other drivers, told one of the drivers that he had heard of Santillo's activities. Patterson referred to Santillo as two-faced, and promised to get even with him.

Later that evening Patterson talked to Ed West who was also a bus driver for respondent. Patterson asked, "What's with Sam and the Union?" Patterson said that he took Santillo's actions personally, recounted several favors he had done for Santillo, and added that he would remember Santillo's activities when Santillo again asked for a favor. On Monday, March 26, Santillo was discharged. Patterson told Santillo that he was being fired for leaving his keys in the bus and taking unauthorized breaks.

Santillo filed a complaint with the Board alleging that he had been discharged because of his union activities, contrary to Sections 8(a)(1) and 8(a)(3) of the NLRA. The General Counsel issued a complaint. The administrative law judge (ALJ) determined by a preponderance of the evidence that Patterson clearly had an anti-union animus and that Santillo's discharge was motivated by a desire to discourage union activities. The ALJ also found that the asserted reasons for the discharge could not withstand scrutiny. Patterson's

disapproval of Santillo's practice of leaving his keys in the bus was clearly a pretext, for Patterson had not known about Santillo's practice until after he had decided to discharge Santillo; moreover, the practice of leaving keys in buses was commonplace among respondent's employees. Respondent identified two types of unauthorized breaks; coffee breaks and stops at home. With respect to both coffee breaks and stopping at home, the ALJ found that Santillo was never cautioned or admonished about such behavior, and that the employer had not followed its customary practice of issuing three written warnings before discharging a driver. The ALJ also found that the taking of coffee breaks during working hours was normal practice, and that respondent tolerated the practice unless the breaks interfered with the driver's performance of his duties. In any event, said the ALJ, respondent had never taken any adverse personnel action against an employee because of such behavior. While acknowledging that Santillo had engaged in some unsatisfactory conduct, the ALJ was not persuaded that Santillo would have been fired had it not been for his union activities.

The Board affirmed, adopting with some clarification the ALJ's findings and conclusions and expressly applying its *Wright Line* decision. It stated that respondent had failed to carry its burden of persuading the Board that the discharge would have taken place had Santillo not engaged in activity protected by the Act. The First Circuit Court of Appeals, relying on its previous decision rejecting the Board's *Wright Line* test . . . refused to enforce the Board's order and remanded for consideration of whether the General Counsel had proved by a preponderance of the evidence that Santillo would not have been fired had it not been for his union activities. . . .

As we understand the Board's decisions, they have consistently held that the unfair labor practice consists of a discharge or other adverse action that is based in whole or in part on anti-union animus—or as the Board now puts it, that the employee's protected conduct was a substantial or motivating factor in the adverse action. The General Counsel has the burden of proving these elements under Section 10(c). But the Board's construction of the statute permits an employer to avoid being adjudicated a violator by showing what his actions would have been regardless of his forbidden motivation. It extends to the employer what the Board considers to be an affirmative defense but does not change or add to the elements of the unfair labor practice that the General Counsel has the burden of proving under Section 10(c). The Board has instead chosen to recognize, as it insists it has done for many years, what it designates as an affirmative defense that the employer has the burden of sustaining. We are unprepared to hold that this is an impermissible construction of the Act. "[T]he Board's construction here, while it may not be required by the Act, is at least permissible under it . . ." and in these circumstances its position is entitled to deference.

The Board's allocation of the burden of proof is clearly reasonable in this context. . . . The employer is a wrong-doer; he has acted out of a motive that is declared illegitimate by the statute. It is fair that he bear the risk that the influence of legal and illegal motives cannot be separated, because he knowingly created the risk and because the risk was created not by innocent activity but by his own wrongdoing.

For these reasons, we conclude that the Court of Appeals erred in refusing to enforce the Board's orders, which rested on the Board's Wright Line decision.

The Board was justified in this case in concluding that Santillo would not have been discharged had the employer not considered his efforts to establish a union. At least two of the transgressions that purportedly would have in any event prompted Santillo's discharge were common-place, and yet no transgressor had ever before received

any kind of discipline. Moreover, the employer departed from its usual practice in dealing with rules infractions; indeed, not only did the employer not warn Santillo that his actions would result in being subjected to discipline, it never even expressed its disapproval of his conduct. In addition, Patterson, the person who made the initial decision to discharge Santillo, was obviously upset with Santillo for engaging in such protected activity. It is thus clear that the Board's finding that Santillo would not have been fired even if the employer had not had an anti-union animus was "supported by substantial evidence on the record considered as a whole". . . . Accordingly, the judgment is

Reversed.

Case Questions

1.   What reasons did the employer offer to justify Santillo's discharge? What, according to Santillo, prompted his discharge?

2.   What evidence did the NLRB present to challenge the employer's reasons for the discharge?

3.   When does the NLRB's *Wright Line* test apply? What does it require? Does the Supreme Court uphold the *Wright Line* test?

Can an employer refuse to hire an applicant whom the employer suspects is really a union organizer (known as a "salt" or "union salt"), or is such a refusal to hire a violation of Section 8(a)(3)? In *Toering Electric Co.*,[62] the NLRB held that when an employer is charged with discriminatorily failing to hire an applicant for employment, the employer can defend itself against the unfair labor practice charge by raising a reasonable question as to the applicant's actual interest in working for the employer. If the employer puts forward such evidence, then the general counsel must establish, by a preponderance of evidence, that the applicant was genuinely interested in establishing an employment relationship with the employer. If the general counsel fails to make such a showing, then the employer's refusal to hire the applicant is lawful; if the general counsel succeeds in making such a showing, then the employer is in violation of Sections 8(a)(3) and 8(a)(1).

union security agreement
contract provisions requiring employees to join the union or pay union dues

14-2g   Discrimination in Employment to Encourage Union Membership and Union Security Agreements

Although Section 8(a)(3) and Section 8(b)(2) prohibit discrimination to encourage or discourage union membership, there is an important exception regarding the "encouragement" of union membership. That exception deals with **union security agreements**—when

---

[62] 351 NLRB No. 18 (2007).

an employer and union agree that employees must either join the union or at least pay union dues in order to remain employees. This exception requires some discussion.

Prior to the Taft-Hartley Act of 1947, unions and employers could agree that an employer would hire only employees who were already union members. These agreements, called closed shop agreements, had the effect of encouraging (or requiring) workers to join unions if they wished to get a job. Such agreements clearly restrict the employee's free exercise of Section 7 rights; for that reason, they were prohibited. But the Taft-Hartley amendments did not completely prohibit all "union security" arrangements. Section 8(a)(3), as amended by Taft-Hartley, contains the following provision:

> Provided, that nothing in this Act . . . shall preclude an employer from making an agreement with a labor organization . . . to require as a condition of employment membership therein on or after the thirtieth day following the beginning of such agreement, whichever is later. . . .

Section 8(a)(3) also provides that an employer can justify discharging an employee for nonmembership in a union only if membership was denied or terminated because of the employee's failure to pay the dues and initiation fees required of all members.

union shop agreement
agreement requiring employees to join the union after a certain period of time

agency shop agreement
agreement requiring employees to pay union dues, but not requiring them to join the union

The effect of these provisions is to allow an employer and union to agree to a union shop or agency shop provision. A **union shop agreement** requires that all employees hired by the employer must join the union after a certain period of time, not less than 30 days. Although employees need not be union members to be hired, they must become union members if they are to remain employed past the specified time period. An **agency shop agreement** does not require that employees actually join the union, but they must at least pay the dues and fees required of union members.

Although Section 8(a)(3) states that an employer and a union can agree "to require as a condition of employment membership" in the union on or after 30 days of hiring, Section 8(b)(2) and the second proviso to Section 8(a)(3) state that an employee cannot be fired except for failure to pay dues and initiation fees. In effect, this latter language has the legal effect of reducing all union shops to the level of agency shops. Under an agency shop agreement, remember, employees need not become formal members of the union but must pay union dues. Under the language of Section 8(b)(2), formal union members cannot be fired for disobeying the union's internal rules or failing to participate in union affairs. The only difference is that they may be fined by the union for these infractions, and the fines may be enforceable in a state court. Furthermore, the law is clear that an employee who pays dues but refuses to assume full union membership cannot be held to these rules and sanctions.

Unions argue that union security provisions are needed to prevent "free riders"; because all members of the bargaining unit get the benefits of the union's agreement, whether or not they are union members, they should be required to pay the costs of negotiating and administering the agreement—union dues. Only by paying the costs of such union representation can free riders be prevented.

Although such agreements do prevent free riders, they are also coercive to the extent that they may override an employee's free choice of whether or not to join a union. For that reason, the act permits states to outlaw such union security agreements. Section 14(b) states that

> Nothing in this Act shall be construed as authorizing the execution or application of agreements requiring membership in a labor organization as a condition of employment in any state or territory in which such execution or application is prohibited by State or Territorial law.

right-to-work laws
laws which prohibit union security agreements

This section allows for the passage of **right-to-work laws**, which prohibit such union security agreements. In states that have passed such a law, the union shop and agency shop agreements are illegal. A number of states, mainly in the South and West (the Sun Belt), have passed such laws. It is also worth noting that Section 19 of the act was amended to allow employees with bona fide religious objections to joining unions or paying union dues to make arrangements to pay the required fees or dues to a charitable organization.

When a union security agreement is in effect, the employer must discharge an employee, upon the union's request, if the employee has been denied membership in or expelled from the union for failure to pay the required union dues or fees. Under Section 8(b)(2), the union cannot legally demand the discharge of an employee for refusing to pay "back dues" or "reinstatement fees" after a lapse of membership in a prior job. Other examples of union violations of Section 8(b)(2) include:

- Forcing an employer to agree to hire only applicants satisfactory to the union

- Causing an employee to be discharged for opposition to the manner in which internal union affairs are conducted

- Causing an employee to be discharged because the worker was disliked or considered a troublemaker by the union leadership

Hiring Halls

hiring hall
a job-referral mechanism operated by unions whereby unions refer members to prospective employers

In some industries, employers rely on unions to refer prospective employees to the various employers. Such arrangements, known as **hiring halls**, are common in industries such as trucking, construction, and longshoring. Hiring halls and other job-referral mechanisms operated by unions may have the effect of encouraging membership in the union because an employee must go through the union to get a job. The NLRB and the Supreme Court have held such hiring halls or referral mechanisms to be legal as long as they meet the following conditions:

- The union must not discriminate on grounds of union membership for job referrals.

- The employer may reject any applicant referred by the union.

- A notice of the nondiscriminatory operation of the referral service must be posted in the hiring hall.

It is also legal for the union to set skill levels necessary for membership or for referral to employers through a hiring hall.

Preferential Treatment for Union Officers: Super Seniority

In some collective agreements, an employer will agree to give union officers or stewards preferential treatment in the event of layoffs or recall of employees. Such provisions, known as super seniority because layoff and recall are usually done on the basis of seniority, may have the effect of encouraging union membership. Yet they also serve to ensure that employees responsible for the enforcement and administration of the collective agreement remain on the job to ensure the protection of all employees' rights under the contract. However, preferential treatment that goes beyond layoff and recall rights is not so readily justified. For that reason, and because it clearly discriminates in employment conditions to encourage union activity, broad super seniority clauses may involve violations of Sections 8(a)(3) and 8(b)(2).

14-2h Discrimination in Employment to Discourage Union Membership

Just as discrimination in terms or conditions of employment to encourage union membership violates Section 8(a)(3), so does discrimination that is intended to discourage union membership or activities. Most complaints alleging discrimination to discourage such activities occur in the context of union organizing campaigns or strikes.

Activity protected under Section 7 includes union organizing activity as well as strikes over economic issues or to protest unfair labor practices. The employer that refuses to hire, or discharges, lays off, or disciplines an employee for such activity is in violation of Section 8(a)(3). Although the employer must have acted with the intention of discouraging union membership, the Board has held that specific evidence of such an intention need not be shown if the employer's conduct is inherently destructive of the employee's Section 7 rights.

As noted earlier, several reasons may be behind an employer's action; antiunion motives may play a part, along with legitimate work-related reasons. Recall that in *NLRB v. Transportation Management*, the Supreme Court upheld the Board practice of requiring the employer to show that the discipline or discharge would have occurred even without the employee's protected conduct. If the employer can meet that burden, then it is not a violation of Section 8(a)(3). However, if there are no legitimate business reasons for the employer's actions, then the conduct is a violation, according to *Huck Store Fixture Co. v. NLRB*.[63]

An employer who fires employees for engaging in a union organizing campaign is in violation of Section 8(a)(3). Firing employees for striking over economic demands is also a violation. Other examples of Section 8(a)(3) violations include:

- layoffs that violate seniority rules and that fall mainly upon union supporters;
- disproportionately severe discipline of union officers or supporters;
- discharging a union supporter without the customary warning prior to discharge;
- discharging a union supporter based on past misconduct that had previously been condoned; and
- selective enforcement of rules against union supporters.

14-2i Strikes as Protected Activity

Strikes by employees are the essence of concerted activity; workers agree to withhold their labor from the employer in order to pressure the employer to accept their demands. A strike for collective bargaining purposes or for purposes of mutual aid and protection comes under the protection of Section 7. However, despite the purposes of the strike, if it violates the collective agreement or if workers are attempting to strike while still collecting their pay, the strike may not be protected.

When discussing the rights of strikers under the NLRA and the employer's response to the strike, the Board and the courts distinguish between economic strikes and unfair labor practice strikes. As discussed in Chapter 13, an *economic strike* is called to pressure the employer to accept the union's negotiating demands. It occurs after the old collective

---

[63] 327 F.3d 528 (7th Cir. 2003).

agreement has expired and negotiations for a new agreement break down. By contrast, an *unfair labor practice strike* is called to protest an employer's illegal actions. It does not involve contract demands or negotiations. The rights of strikers thus may depend on whether the strike is an unfair labor practice or economic strike. An economic strike may be converted into an unfair labor practice strike by an employer's unfair practices that are committed during the strike, as in *Ryan Iron Works, Inc.*[64]

Unfair Labor Practice Strikes

The Supreme Court has held, in *Mastro Plastics v. NLRB*,[65] that unfair labor practice strikes are protected activity under the act. This means that unfair labor practice strikers may not be fired for going on strike, nor may they be permanently replaced. Strikes that begin as economic strikes may become unfair labor practice strikes if the employer commits serious unfair labor practices during the strike. For example, if the employer refused to bargain with the union over a new agreement and discharged the strikers, the strike would become an unfair labor practice strike. An employer may hire workers to replace the strikers during an unfair labor practice strike, but the strikers must be reinstated when the strike is over. In *National Steel Supply, Inc.*,[66] an employer who terminated or permanently replaced workers striking to protest the illegal termination of an employee violated Section 8(a)(3). Although misconduct on the picket line may normally be a sufficient reason for an employer to discharge a striker, the Board has held in prior decisions that severe misconduct (such as physical assault) is needed to justify the discharge of an unfair labor practice striker.

However, in *Clear Pine Mouldings, Inc.*,[67] the Board held that the existence of an unfair labor practice strike:

> does not in any way privilege those employees [on strike] to engage in other than peaceful picketing and persuasion. . . . There is nothing in the statute to support the notion that striking employees are free to engage in or escalate violence or misconduct in proportion to their estimates of the degree of seriousness of an employer's unfair labor practices.

Economic Strikes

Economic strikes, as previously noted, are work stoppages by the employees designed to force the employer to meet their bargaining demands for increased wages or other benefits. As with unfair labor practice strikes, economic strikes are protected activity; however, the protections afforded economic strikers are not as great as those given unfair labor practice strikers. As mentioned earlier in the discussion of protected activity under Section 7, on-the-job slowdowns are not protected, and employees who engage in such conduct may be discharged. In addition, economic strikes in violation of the collective agreement are not protected.

When the economic strike is protected, the striking employees may not be discharged for going on strike; however, the employer may hire permanent replacements for the striking employees. The right to hire permanent replacements was affirmed by the Supreme Court in

---

[64] 332 NLRB 506 (2000).

[65] 350 U.S. 270 (1956).

[66] 344 NLRB 973 (2005).

[67] 268 NLRB 1044 (1984).

1938 in the case of *NLRB v. MacKay Radio & Telegraph*.[68] Replacement workers hired on an at-will basis may be considered permanent replacements by the NLRB where the employer explicitly indicated to them that the employer intended to hire them as permanent replacements, according to *Jones Plastic & Engineering Co.*[69] Although the striking employees may be permanently replaced, they still retain their status as "employees" under the act. [See the definition of employee in Section 2(3).] Because they retain their status as employees, the strikers are entitled to be reinstated if they make an unconditional application for reinstatement and if vacancies are available. If no positions are available at the time of their application, even if the lack of vacancies is due to the hiring of replacements, the employer need not reinstate the strikers. However, if the strikers continue to indicate an interest in reinstatement, the employer is required to rehire them as positions become available. This requirement was upheld by the Supreme Court in *NLRB v. Fleetwood Trailers Co.*[70]

In *Laidlaw Corp.*,[71] the NLRB held that economic strikers who had made an unconditional application for reinstatement and who continued to make known their availability for employment were entitled to be recalled by the employer prior to the employer's hiring of new employees.

In *David R. Webb Co., Inc. v. NLRB*,[72] the Court of Appeals held that the employer's duty to reinstate strikers continues until the strikers have been reinstated to their former positions or to substantially equivalent positions. Reinstating them to lower positions does not satisfy the employer's obligation. The following case discusses when, if ever, the employer may have a legitimate justification to refuse to reinstate strikers.

The NLRB has held that a union may waive the right of strikers to be reinstated with full seniority in exchange for an end to a strike, as in *Gem City Ready Mix*[73] and *NLRB v. Harrison Ready Mix Concrete*.[74] The following case deals with an employer's justification for refusing to reinstate strikers in their former positions or other available equivalent positions.

» CASE 14.7

DIAMOND WALNUT GROWERS, INC. v. NLRB
113 F.3d 1259 (D.C. Cir. 1997) (en banc), cert. denied, 523 U.S. 1020 (1998)

Facts: Following the expiration of their collective bargaining agreement, nearly 500 of Diamond Walnut Growers permanent and seasonal employees went on strike. Diamond hired replacement workers to continue operations. The strike was bitter, and the union encouraged a public boycott of Diamond's products to exert economic pressure on Diamond. The boycott included a well-publicized national bus tour during which union members publicly distributed leaflets describing Diamond's work force as "scabs" who packaged walnuts contaminated with "mold, dirt, oil, worms and debris."

---

[68] 304 U.S. 333 (1938).

[69] 351 NLRB No. 11 (2007).

[70] 389 U.S. 375 (1967).

[71] 171 NLRB 1366 (1968).

[72] 888 F.2d 501 (7th Cir. 1990).

[73] 279 NLRB 191, 116 L.R.R.M. 1266 (1984).

[74] 770 F.2d 78 (6th Cir. 1985).

One year into the strike, the NLRB held a representation election. The union lost but filed objections with the NLRB, and the NLRB ordered that a new election be held in October 1993. Two weeks prior to the new election, four striking employees approached Diamond with an unconditional offer to return to work. Because their former jobs and other substantially equivalent jobs were not available for three of the returning strikers at the time of their return, Diamond placed them in seasonal jobs. The union lost the rerun election.

The NLRB General Counsel then filed a complaint alleging that Diamond had violated Sections 8(a)(3) and 8(a)(1) of the National Labor Relations Act by unlawfully discriminating against the three reinstated strikers by refusing to put them in certain seasonal position because of their protected activity. After a hearing, the ALJ recommended that the charges be dismissed because, while he found that Diamond had discriminated against the employees, the discrimination was not unlawful because no vacancies in their former jobs or in substantially equivalent jobs were available when they sought reinstatement.

On review, the NLRB reversed the ALJ's decision. The Board held that, while Diamond was under no legal obligation to reinstate the strikers, once it decided to reinstate them, it was required to act in a nondiscriminatory fashion toward them. The NLRB held that Diamond had discriminated against the three strikers because of their union status and/or because of certain protected activity they engaged in while on strike. The Board rejected Diamond's justifications for placing the three returning strikers as it did: the employer's concern that the replacement workers might instigate violence against the three and that the placements were justified by their participation in the boycott and the circulation of disparaging leaflets. The NLRB held that Diamond had failed to justify its discrimination and was guilty of unfair labor practices. Diamond sought judicial review of the NLRB decision in the U.S. Court of Appeals for the D.C. Circuit.

Issue: Did the employer provide an adequate business justification for its refusal to reinstate the three strikers in their former, or equivalent, positions?

Decision: The court held that this case was governed by *Fleetwood Trailers*. The general counsel must make out a prima facie case that the employer discriminated in its treatment of the returning strikers because of their protected activity. A struck employer faced with an unconditional offer to return to work is obliged to treat the returning employee like any other applicant for work, unless the employee's former job or its substantial equivalent is available, in which case the employee is preferred to any other applicant. But here the returning strikers were not treated like any other applicants. Diamond admitted that it took into account the returnees' protected activity in choosing to place them in jobs that were objectively less desirable than those for which they were qualified.

Under *Fleetwood Trailers*, once discrimination is shown, the burden shifts to the employer to establish that its treatment of the employees has a legitimate and substantial business justification. Diamond declined to place the returnees in their former jobs or equivalent positions for which they were qualified because of two concerns: potential hostility against them by the replacements workers, and because the returnees had participated in the union boycott activities, they might be tempted to engage in sabotage or to let defective nuts get through inspection or to contaminate the packaged walnuts. The Board concluded that the possibility of the returnees engaging in future sabotage was simply not a sufficient risk to constitute a substantial business justification for their treatment. As for the employer's concern for the safety of a few returning strikers, put in the midst of a majority of replacements in a strike marked by violence, it may be genuine; but the Board insisted that the employer provide evidence of a concrete threat to those strikers. Otherwise, an employer's generalized concern could easily serve as a handy pretext for disfavoring returning strikers. If there were evidence of such a threat, the employer might well be obliged to take adequate preventative measures against those who threatened the violence, rather than against those who were threatened. Strikes tend to be hard struggles, and although this one may have been more bitter than most, there is always a potential danger that returning strikers may engage in some form of sabotage, especially while the strike is still in progress. There is undeniably some risk in employing returning strikers during a strike, but an employer is forced to assume such risk of sabotage, because otherwise, the employer would not be required to take back strikers at all. There may well be situations in which an employer could produce compelling grounds for a relatively unfavorable assignment of a returning striker. The Board here implied that a serious threat of violence against the striker might suffice. The Board must consider whatever special circumstances are presented by an employer asserting the defense of substantial justification, and it may not summarily reject an employer's specific and persuasive explanation.

Other Strike-Related Issues

Recall that under Section 7, employees have the right to refrain from concerted activity, which includes the right to remain working rather than go on strike. As noted in the discussion of Section 8(b)(2), a union may impose some disciplinary sanctions upon union members who refuse to go on strike, but they may not cause an employer to discriminate against such employees in terms or conditions of employment. Nor may the employer offer incentives or benefits to the replacements or those employees not going on strike when such benefits are not available to the strikers. In the case of *NLRB v. Erie Resistor Co.*,[75] the Supreme Court held that the employer's granting of 20 years' seniority to all replacements violated Section 8(a)(3). The effect of such seniority was to insulate the replacements from layoff, while exposing employees who went on strike to layoff. This effect would continue long after the strike was over; it would place the former strikers at a disadvantage simply because they went on strike. Although *Erie Resistor* involved rather severe actions by the employer, the NLRB has held that any preferential treatment in terms or conditions of employment accorded to the nonstrikers or replacements, and not to the strikers, violates Section 8(a)(3).

A 1983 Supreme Court decision involved the rights of the workers hired to replace economic strikers. In *Belknap v. Hale*,[76] the Court held that replacements hired under the promise of permanent employment could sue the employer for breach of contract if they were laid off at the end of the strike. Does *Belknap v. Hale* undermine the rights of strikers to be reinstated?

Employer Response to Strike Activity

lockout
an employer's temporary withdrawal of employment to pressure employees to agree to the employer's bargaining proposals

Just as employees are free to go on strike to promote their economic demands, employers are free to withdraw employment from employees to pressure them to accept the employer's demands. This tactic, called a **lockout**, is the temporary withdrawal of employment to pressure employees to agree to the employer's bargaining proposals. A lockout needs to be distinguished from a permanent closure of a plant to avoid unionization.

When the employees have not gone on strike and are willing to continue working, the employer may be reluctant to "lock them out." However, employers seeking to pressure unions to accept bargaining changes may resort to a lockout. The National Hockey League owners locked out the players for the entire 2004–2005 season in an attempt to force the players' union to accept a proposal linking player salaries to league revenue. The NHL again resorted to a lockout at the beginning of the 2012–2013 season.

In addition, when the threat of a "quickie strike" or unannounced walkout poses the prospect of damage to equipment or disruption of business, the employer may lock out the employees to avoid such problems. The Board has consistently held that such "defensive" lockouts are not unfair labor practices. Lockouts by the employers in a multiemployer bargaining unit, to avoid a whipsaw strike by the union, have been held legal by the Board and the Supreme Court. What about the situation in which an employer locks out the unionized employees and hires replacements? This issue is addressed in the following Supreme Court decision.

Whereas *Brown* dealt with a defensive lockout in response to a strike against one employer, the Supreme Court, in *American Shipbuilding Co. v. NLRB*,[77] held that an

---

[75] 373 U.S. 221 (1963).

[76] 463 U.S. 491 (1983).

[77] 380 U.S. 300 (1965).

employer is free to lock out employees in anticipation of the union going on strike. That decision allows the employer to use a lockout as an offensive weapon to promote its bargaining position; the employer need not wait for the union to strike first. An employer may not engage in a lockout unless negotiations have reached an impasse, or deadlock, and exceptional circumstances are required by the Board to justify lockouts prior to a bargaining impasse. In *Ancor Concepts, Inc.*,[78] the NLRB held that the use of permanent replacements after a lockout was a violation of Section 8(a)(3). How does that situation differ from *NLRB v. Brown*? The NLRB upheld the use of temporary replacements after an offensive lockout in *Harter Equipment.*[79]

CASE 14.8

NLRB v. BROWN
380 U.S. 278 (1965)

Facts: Five employers operated six retail grocery stores. The employers were members of a multiemployer bargaining unit that was represented by Local 462 of the Retail Clerks International Association. When the negotiations to renew the collective agreement covering the multiemployer unit stalled, the union went on strike against Food Jet, one of the five employers. The other four employers immediately locked out all their employees represented by the union, telling them and the Local that they would be recalled to work when the strike against Food Jet ended. All the employers continued to operate their businesses using temporary replacement workers. The replacement employees were told that they were hired only as long as the union was on strike. A new agreement was reached and the strike ended, and the employers immediately released the temporary replacements and restored the strikers and the locked out employees to their jobs. The union filed a complaint with the NLRB over the lockout and hiring of replacement workers. The NLRB held that the employers violated Sections 8(a)(1) and (3) of the NLRA by locking out their regular employees and using temporary replacements to carry on business. The Court of Appeals for the Tenth Circuit disagreed and refused to enforce the Board's order. The NLRB then appealed to the U.S. Supreme Court.

Issue: Have the employers violated Sections 8(a)(1) and (3) of the NLRA by locking out their regular employees

and hiring temporary replacements during the strike against one of the employers in the multiemployer bargaining unit?

Decision: Under the NLRA, there are a number of economic weapons the parties can use in seeking to force acceptance of their bargaining demands. Absent proof of unlawful motivation, employers may resort to various economic weapons to blunt the effectiveness of an anticipated strike by stockpiling inventories, readjusting contract schedules, or transferring work from one plant to another. Employers are also able to use a lockout as a legitimate economic weapon in various circumstances. The Court here held that the employers' continued operations and the use of temporary replacements did not demonstrate any hostile motivation, nor was it inherently more destructive of employee rights than the lockout itself. The lockout and use of temporary replacements was part of the employers' defensive measure to preserve the multiemployer group in the face of the whipsaw strike. Because Food Jet legitimately continued business operations during the strike, it was only reasonable to regard the employers' actions as an attempt to preserve the integrity of the multiemployer bargaining unit that was threatened unless they stayed open for business during the lockout. If Food Jet had been able to stay open for business while the other stores were closed, the whipsaw strike could succeed in breaking up the multiemployer bargaining unit. Given the very competitive nature of the retail grocery business,

---

[78] 323 NLRB 742 (1997), enforcement denied, 166 F.3d 55 (2d Cir. 1999).

[79] 280 NLRB 597 (1986).

the employers' use of temporary replacements during the lockout was consistent with a legitimate business purpose.

In order to find that conduct violated Section 8(a)(3) there must be discrimination that would discourage union membership, but the added element of antiunion intent is also required. While the use of temporary replacement workers in preference to the locked-out union members was discriminatory, the Court here held that any resulting tendency to discourage union membership was comparatively remote, and that the use of temporary workers was reasonably related to a legitimate business purpose. The use of replacement workers was temporary, only for the duration of the strike; the replacements did not threaten the jobs of the striking employees. The striking employees could end the strike and terminate the lockout at any time simply by agreeing to the employers' contract terms and returning to work on a regular basis. As well, the new collective agreement contained a union-shop provision that had been carried forward from the prior agreement, so a union member would have nothing to gain and much to lose by quitting the union. Given those circumstances, the Court held that the employers' actions here did not tend to discourage union membership. The employers' attempt to remain open for business using temporary replacements was a measure reasonably related to the legitimate business purpose of preserving the integrity of the multiemployer bargaining unit. In the absence of any evidentiary findings of hostile motive, there is no support for the NLRB determination that the employers violated Section 8(a)(1) or 8(a)(3). The Supreme Court therefore affirmed the court of appeals' refusal to enforce the NLRB decision.

Plant Closing to Avoid Unionization

The preceding discussion dealt with an employer's response to the economic demands of organized workers; the employer is free to lock out to avoid union bargaining demands. But what about the situation in which the employees are just in the process of forming a union? Can the employer shut down the plant to avoid unionization? Recall that Section 8(a)(1) prohibits threats of closure or layoff to dissuade employees from joining a union. Should it make any difference whether the shutdown to avoid unionization is complete (the entire operation) or partial (only part of the operation)? In *Textile Workers Union v. Darlington Mfg. Co.*,[80] the Supreme Court held that a total shutdown of a business, even if done for antiunion motivation, was not an unfair labor practice, but that a partial shutdown, done with the intent to deter workers from forming a union, was a violation of Section 8(a)(3).

runaway shop
situation in which an employer closes in one location and opens in another to avoid unionization

The Court in Darlington noted that a complete shutdown to avoid unionization is different from a **runaway shop**, in which the employer closes in one location and opens in another to avoid unionization. Such runaway conduct is in violation of Section 8(a)(3). However, the motive requirement under Section 8(a)(3) may pose a problem in determining whether the relocation of the operation violates the act. If the employer raises some legitimate business reasons for the relocation, the NLRB counsel must demonstrate that the runaway would not have happened except for the employees' unionizing efforts. (See the *Transportation Management* case discussed earlier in this chapter.)

As remedy for a runaway shop, the Board will order that the offending employer offer the old employees positions at the new location. The employer must also pay the employees' moving or travel expenses. If the employer has shut down part of the operation, the Board may order the employer to reopen the closed portion or to reinstate the affected employees in the remaining parts of the operation. The employees will also be awarded back pay lost because of the employer's violation. Remedies are discussed more fully later in this chapter.

---

[80] 380 U.S. 263 (1965).

THE **WORKING** LAW ▮▮▮▮▮▮▮▮▮▮▮▮▮▮▮▮

NLRB Office of the General Counsel Issues Consolidated Complaints Against McDonald's Franchisees and their Franchisor McDonald's, USA, LLC as Joint Employers

The National Labor Relations Board Office of the General Counsel has issued complaints against McDonald's franchisees and their franchisor, McDonald's USA, LLC, as joint employers. The complaints allege that McDonald's USA, LLC and certain franchisees violated the rights of employees working at McDonald's restaurants at various locations around the country by, among other things, making statements and taking actions against them for engaging in activities aimed at improving their wages and working conditions, including participating in nationwide fast food worker protests about their terms and conditions of employment during the past two years.

The Office of the General Counsel informed McDonald's franchisees and their franchisor, McDonald's USA, LLC, that, of 291 charges filed since November 2012, 86 cases have been found meritorious, and therefore, complaints would issue regarding those meritorious cases, absent settlement. While representatives of the Office of the General Counsel have been engaged in efforts to settle the matter with the parties, thus far, those efforts have largely been unsuccessful. Therefore, the Regional Offices, where meritorious charges were filed and not settled, issued complaints against the alleged joint employers today. General Counsel representatives will continue efforts to settle the meritorious charges, notwithstanding issuance of the complaints. Additionally, of the 291 charges filed, 11 cases were resolved and 71 cases remain under investigation.

13 complaints involving 78 charges against McDonald's USA, LLC, McDonald's USA franchisees and/or McDonald's franchisees and their franchisor, McDonald's USA, LLC as joint employers issued in the below Regional offices.

- Region 2 – Manhattan
- Region 4 – Philadelphia
- Region 7 – Detroit
- Region 10 – Atlanta
- Region 13 – Chicago
- Region 14 – St. Louis
- Subregion 17 – Kansas City
- Region 15 – New Orleans
- Region 18 – Minneapolis
- Region 20 – San Francisco
- Region 25 – Indianapolis
- Region 28 – Phoenix
- Region 31 – Los Angeles

Meritorious allegations of unlawful conduct committed by McDonald's franchisees and/or their franchisor, McDonald's USA, LLC, occurring in more than one, and often multiple, locations around the country include: discriminatory discipline, reductions in hours, discharges, and other coercive conduct directed at employees in response to union and protected concerted activity, including threats, surveillance, interrogations, promises of benefit, and overbroad restrictions on communicating with union representatives or with other employees about unions and the employees' terms and conditions of employment.

In the interest of conserving public and private resources and to avoid unnecessary delay, the NLRB has scheduled consolidated hearings in three Regional locations in the Northeast, Midwest and West to address violations that require remedial relief as soon as possible. Absent settlement, the initial litigation will commence on March 30, 2015, and will involve allegations of unlawful actions committed against employees at McDonald's restaurants in the jurisdiction of six Regional Offices.

Specifically, the hearing will begin in Region 2 – Manhattan to address allegations in the complaints of Region 2 and Region 4, then will move to Region 13 – Chicago to address allegations in the complaints of Region 13 and Region 25, and will conclude in Region 31 – Los Angeles to address allegations in the complaints of Region 20 and 31. It is anticipated that hearings involving the allegations in the complaints issued by the other seven Regional offices will be scheduled after the initial litigation before an Administrative Law Judge, if those allegations cannot be resolved through settlement.

Source: NLRB, December 19, 2014, available at http://www.nlrb.gov/news-outreach/news-story/nlrb-office-general-counsel-issues-consolidated-complaints-against.

14-3   Other Unfair Labor Practices

In addition to the unfair labor practices already discussed, the NLRA prohibits several other kinds of conduct. Refusing to bargain in good faith, the subject of Section 8(a)(5) and Section 8(b)(3), will be discussed in Chapter 15, and union unfair practices involving picketing and secondary boycotts will be dealt with in Chapter 16. The remaining unfair labor practices are the focus of this section.

14-3a   Employer Reprisals Against Employees

Section 8(a)(4) prohibits an employer from discharging or otherwise discriminating against an employee who has filed charges or given testimony under the act. Because employees must be free to avail themselves of the act's procedures to give effect to their Section 7 rights, reprisals against employees for exercising their rights must also infringe on those rights. Violations of Section 8(a)(4) include the discharge or disciplining of an employee filing unfair practice charges and the layoff of such employees. Refusing to consider an employee for promotion because that employee filed unfair practice charges is also a violation.

In *BE&K Construction Co.*,[81] the NLRB held that it was not an unfair labor practice when an employer files a lawsuit against employees because they engaged in activity protected by the NLRA if the lawsuit had a reasonable basis in law, even if the employer's motivation for bringing the suit was a desire to retaliate against the employees. Section 8(a)(4) is directed only against employers; union reprisals against employees for exercising their statutory rights are dealt with under Section 8(b)(1)(A).

14-3b Excessive Union Dues or Membership Fees

Section 8(b)(5) prohibits a union from requiring excessive dues or membership fees of employees covered by a union security agreement. Because a union security agreement requires that employees join the union (or at least pay all dues and fees) to retain their jobs, some protection against union abuse or extortion must be given to the affected employees. In deciding a complaint under Section 8(b)(5), the Board is directed by the act to consider "the practices and customs of labor organizations in the particular industry, and the wages currently paid to the employees affected."

14-3c Featherbedding

Section 8(b)(6) makes it unfair labor practice for a union "to cause or attempt to cause an employer to pay or deliver or agree to pay or deliver any money or other thing of value, in the nature of an extraction, for services which are not performed or not to be performed." The practice of getting paid for services not performed or not to be performed is known as **featherbedding**.

featherbedding
the practice of getting paid for services not performed or not to be performed

Although this statutory prohibition may seem straightforward, it may not be easy to discern featherbedding from legal activities. For instance, a union steward may be employed to run a drill press. In reality, she may be spending much of her time assisting coworkers for the union's benefit and may even draw additional compensation for this service from the union. If the collective bargaining agreement allows for this activity, then it is legal.

In another situation, the employer may pay for work that is not really needed—because, for instance, of technological innovations in the industry—but through industrial custom and usage, the work is still performed by union members. This, too, is legal under the NLRA.

In *American Newspaper Publisher's Assoc. v. NLRB*,[82] the Supreme Court held that Section 8(b)(6) is limited only to payment (or demanding of payment) for services not actually rendered. In that case, the payment by the employers for the setting of type that was not needed did not violate the act because the services, although not needed, were actually performed. Because of increasing economic competition from nonunionized firms and because of labor-saving technological developments, complaints of union featherbedding under Section 8(b)(6) are relatively rare today.

[81] 351 NLRB No. 29 (2007).
[82] 345 U.S. 100 (1953).

Concept *Summary* 14.2

| | **UNFAIR LABOR PRACTICES** | |
Activity	**By Employers**	**By Unions**
• Interfering with, coercing, or restraining employees in the exercise of Section 7 rights	Section 8(a)(1)	Section 8(b)(1)(A)
• Coercing or restraining an employer in the selection of a bargaining representative	X	Section 8(b)(1)(B)
• Discriminating in hiring or terms or conditions of employment to encourage or discourage union membership	Section 8(a)(3)	X
• Causing or attempting to cause an employer to discriminate against an employee to encourage or discourage union membership	X	Section 8(b)(2)
• Reprisals against employees for exercising rights under the NLRA	Section 8(a)(4)	Section 8(b)(1)(A)

14-3d Remedies for Unfair Labor Practices

Under Section 10 of the NLRA, the NLRB is empowered to prevent any person from engaging in any unfair labor practice. Section 10(a) authorizes the Board to:

- investigate charges;
- issue complaints; and
- order hearings in unfair labor practice cases.

If the ALJ (or the Board on review) finds that an employer or union has been or is engaging in unfair labor practices, the NLRB will so state in its findings and issue a cease-and-desist order with regard to those practices. If the employer (or union) chooses not to comply with the order, the Board will petition the appropriate federal court of appeals for enforcement of its order as provided in Section 10(e).

The Board may also order the offending party to take affirmative action in the wake of the unfair labor practices. For instance, when an employee has been discriminatorily discharged in violation of Section 8(a)(1), (3), or (4), the Board will commonly require that the employee be reinstated, usually with back pay.

Finally, under Section 10(j) of the act, the Board in its discretion may seek an injunction in a federal district court to put a halt to unfair labor practices while the parties to a dispute await its final resolution by the Board.[83] The purpose is to preserve the status quo while the adjudicative process works itself out. The NLRB obtained an injunction against the Major League Baseball owners for their refusal to bargain in good faith with the Major

---

[83] See "Utilization of Section 10(j) Proceedings," Memorandum of the General Counsel, Memorandum GC02-07, August 9, 2002, available at http://www.nlrb.gov/reports-guidance/general-counsel-memos, and search GC 02-07.

League Baseball Players' Association in 1995, in *Silverman v. Major League Baseball Player Relations Committee, Inc.*[84] That injunction forced the owners back to the bargaining table with the players' union and was instrumental in getting the parties to settle the baseball strike in April 1995. Section 10(l) requires the Board to seek a temporary restraining order from a court when a union is engaging in a secondary boycott, hot cargo agreements, recognitional picketing, or a jurisdictional dispute. (Those unfair practices will be discussed in Chapter 16.)

14-3e Reinstatement

When an employee has been discharged or laid off in violation of the act, the Board is empowered by Section 10(c) to order reinstatement with back pay. However, Section 10(c) also states that the Board shall not order reinstatement of, or back pay for, an employee who has been discharged "for cause." Therefore, an employee guilty of misconduct may not be entitled to reinstatement. This provision is of particular interest in strike situations. Employees on an economic strike may be discharged for misconduct such as violence, destruction of property, and so on. In a 1984 decision, the Board held that verbal threats alone may justify discharge when they "reasonably tend to coerce or intimidate employees in the exercise of rights protected under the Act." The Board had held that in the case of unfair practice strikers, more severe misconduct is required to justify discharge. But in *Clear Pine Mouldings*,[85] the Board stated that unfair practice strikers are not given any privilege to engage in misconduct or violence just because they are on strike over employer unfair labor practices. In any situation, physical assaults or violence will not be tolerated by the Board.

What should the NLRB do when an employee who was fired illegally by the employer has lied under oath in the NLRB hearing? Is the employee entitled to be reinstated, or should the misconduct of lying justify dismissal? That is the question in the following case.

front pay
monetary damages
awarded to a plaintiff
instead of reinstatement
or hiring

While the NLRB generally seeks reinstatement for employees discharged illegally, there are some instances when it may seek **front pay** rather than reinstatement. Front pay is a monetary award for loss of anticipated future earnings because of the unfair labor practice. The Board's general counsel[86] has indicated that front pay may be appropriate where:

- the unfair labor practice has impaired the ability of the employee to return to work;
- the employer or other employees remain hostile to the discharged employee; or
- the discharged employee is close to retirement.

Front pay may also be used as a substitute for a "preferential hire" list.

---

[84] 67 F.3d 1054 (2d Cir. 1995).

[85] 268 NLRB 1044 (1984).

[86] See "Guideline Memorandum Concerning Frontpay," Office of the General Counsel, February 3, 2000, available at http://www.nlrb.gov/reports-guidance/general-counsel-memos, and search GC 00-01.

CASE 14.9

ABF FREIGHT SYSTEM, INC. V. NLRB

510 U.S. 317 (1994)

Stevens, J.

. . . Michael Manso gave his employer a false excuse for being late to work and repeated that falsehood while testifying under oath before an Administrative Law Judge (ALJ). Notwithstanding Manso's dishonesty, the National Labor Relations Board (Board) ordered Manso's former employer to reinstate him with back pay. Our interest in preserving the integrity of administrative proceedings prompted us to grant certiorari to consider whether Manso's misconduct should have precluded the Board from granting him that relief.

Manso worked as a casual dockworker at petitioner ABF Freight's (ABF's) trucking terminal in Albuquerque, New Mexico, from the summer of 1987 to August 1989. He was fired three times. The first time, Manso was one of 12 employees discharged in June 1988 in a dispute over a contractual provision relating to so-called "preferential casual" dockworkers. The grievance Manso's union filed eventually secured his reinstatement; Manso also filed an unfair labor practice charge against ABF over the incident.

Manso's return to work was short-lived. Three supervisors warned him of likely retaliation from top management—alerting him, for example, that ABF was "gunning" for him, and that "the higher echelon was after [him]". . . . Within six weeks ABF discharged Manso for a second time on pretextual grounds—ostensibly for failing to respond to a call to work made under a stringent verification procedure ABF had recently imposed upon preferential casuals. Once again, a grievance panel ordered Manso reinstated.

Manso's third discharge came less than two months later. On August 11, 1989, Manso arrived four minutes late for the 5 A.M. shift. At the time, ABF had no policy regarding lateness. After Manso was late to work, however, ABF decided to discharge preferential casuals—though not other employees—who were late twice without good cause. Six days later Manso triggered the policy's first application when he arrived at work nearly an hour late for the same shift. Manso telephoned at 5:25 A.M. to explain that he was having car trouble on the highway, and repeated that excuse when he arrived. ABF conducted a prompt investigation, ascertained that he was lying, and fired him for tardiness under its new policy on lateness.

Manso filed a second unfair labor practice charge. In the hearing before the ALJ, Manso repeated his story about the car trouble that preceded his third discharge. The ALJ credited most of his testimony about events surrounding his dismissals, but expressly concluded that Manso lied when he told ABF that car trouble made him late to work. Accordingly, although the ALJ decided that ABF had illegally discharged Manso the second time because he was a party to the earlier union grievance, the ALJ denied Manso relief for the third discharge based on his finding that ABF had dismissed Manso for cause.

The Board affirmed the ALJ's finding that Manso's second discharge was unlawful, but reversed with respect to the third discharge. Acknowledging that Manso lied to his employer and that ABF presumably could have discharged him for that dishonesty, the Board nevertheless emphasized that ABF did not in fact discharge him for lying and that the ALJ's conclusion to the contrary was "a plainly erroneous factual statement of [ABF]'s asserted reasons." Instead, Manso's lie "established only that he did not have a legitimate excuse for the August 17 lateness." The Board focused primarily on ABF's retroactive application of its lateness policy to include Manso's first time late to work, holding that ABF had "seized upon" Manso's tardiness "as a pretext to discharge him again and for the same unlawful reasons it discharged him on June 19." In addition, though the Board deemed Manso's discharge unlawful even assuming the validity of ABF's general disciplinary treatment of preferential casuals, it observed that ABF's disciplinary approach and lack of uniform rules for all dockworkers "raise[d] more questions than they resolve[d]." The Board ordered ABF to reinstate Manso with back pay.

The Court of Appeals enforced the Board's order. Its review of the record revealed "abundant evidence of anti-union animus in ABF's conduct towards Manso," including "ample evidence" that Manso's third discharge was not for cause. . . .

. . . We assume that the Board correctly found that ABF discharged Manso unlawfully in August 1989. We also assume, more importantly, that the Board did not abuse its discretion in ordering reinstatement even though Manso gave ABF a false reason for being late to work. We are concerned only with the ramifications of Manso's false testimony under oath in a formal proceeding before the ALJ. We recognize that the Board might have decided that such misconduct disqualified Manso from profiting from the proceeding, or it might even have adopted a flat rule precluding reinstatement when a former employee so testifies . . . however, the issue is not whether the Board might adopt such a rule, but whether it must do so.

False testimony in a formal proceeding is intolerable. We must neither reward nor condone such a "flagrant affront" to the truth seeking function of adversary proceedings.

ABF submits that the false testimony of a former employee who was the victim of an unfair labor practice should always preclude him from winning reinstatement with back pay. . . . The Act expressly authorizes the Board "to take such affirmative action including reinstatement of employees with or without back pay, as will effectuate the policies of [the Act]." Only in cases of discharge for cause does the statute restrict the Board's authority to order reinstatement. This is not such a case.

When Congress expressly delegates to an administrative agency the authority to make specific policy determinations, courts must give the agency's decision controlling weight unless it is "arbitrary, capricious, or manifestly contrary to the statute." Because this case involves that kind of express delegation, the Board's views merit the greatest deference. This has been our consistent appraisal of the Board's remedial authority throughout its long history of administering the Act. . . .

Notwithstanding our concern about the seriousness of Manso's ill-advised decision to repeat under oath his false excuse for tardiness, we cannot say that the Board's remedial order in this case was an abuse of its broad discretion or that it was obligated to adopt a rigid rule that would foreclose relief in all comparable cases. Nor can we fault the Board's conclusions that Manso's reason for being late to work was ultimately irrelevant to whether anti-union animus actually motivated his discharge and that ordering effective relief in a case of this character promotes a vital public interest. Notably, the ALJ refused to credit the testimony of several ABF witnesses . . . and the Board affirmed those credibility findings. The unfairness of sanctioning Manso while indirectly rewarding those witnesses' lack of candor is obvious. Moreover, the rule ABF advocates might force the Board to divert its attention from its primary mission and devote unnecessary time and energy to resolving collateral disputes about credibility. Its decision to rely on "other civil and criminal remedies" for false testimony rather than a categorical exception to the familiar remedy of reinstatement is well within its broad discretion. The judgment of the Court of Appeals is affirmed.

It is so ordered.

Case Questions

1. What was ABF's justification for discharging Manso the third time? Did the ALJ find that discharge illegal under the NLRA? Did the ALJ order that Manso be reinstated? Why?

2. Did the NLRB agree with the ALJ's decision as to what remedy Manso is entitled? Why?

3. Why does the Supreme Court uphold the NLRB's decision? Does the Court's decision encourage or reward lying under oath? Explain.

14-3f Back Pay

When calculating back-pay awards due employees under Section 10(c), the Board requires that the affected employees mitigate their damages. The Board will deduct from the back-pay wages to reflect income that the employee earned or might have earned while the case was pending. (Welfare benefits and unemployment insurance payments are not deducted from back-pay awards by the Board.) When an employer challenges a proposed back-pay award on grounds that the affected employee had not made efforts to find other, equivalent, employment, the Board's general counsel has the burden of introducing evidence of the employee's job search efforts, according to the NLRB decision in *St. George Warehouse*.[87] The Board also requires that interest (at a rate based on the Treasury bills index) be paid on back-pay awards under the act.

---

[87] 351 NLRB No. 42 (2007).

The Internal Revenue Service considers back-pay awards to be taxable income for the year in which the award is received. In some instances, an employee receiving a lump-sum back-pay award representing more than one year's worth of pay may have increased income tax liability due to the award. In such cases, the NLRB has indicated that it will seek an additional monetary award to cover the additional income taxes owed by the employee because of the lump sum-award, plus interest.[88]

The NLRB is precluded by the Immigration Reform and Control Act of 1986 (discussed in Chapter 5) from awarding back pay to an undocumented alien who is not legally entitled to work in the United States, as in *Hoffman Plastic Compounds, Inc. v. NLRB*.[89]

The general wording of Section 10(c) allows the Board great flexibility in fashioning remedies in various unfair practice cases. Such flexibility is exemplified by the bargaining order remedy in *Gissel Packing*, considered in Chapter 13. Furthermore, the Board has required the guilty party to pay the legal fees of the complainant in cases involving severe or blatant violations. In one case involving an employer's unfair practices that destroyed a union's majority support, the Board ordered the employer to pay the union's organizing expenses for those employees.

14-3g   Extraordinary Remedies

Where an employer that was found guilty of "egregious and pervasive violations" of the NLRA, over a period of 10 years, including two injunctions under Section 10(j) of the NLRA, and having been found guilty of contempt of court for violating a federal court injunction, still had not complied with the Board's remedial orders, the Board imposed an array of enhanced remedies, including: (1) requiring the employer to pay the attorneys' fees and costs incurred by both the NLRB general counsel and the union involved; (2) ordering the employer to pay the union's bargaining expenses to the extent that they exceeded "normal expenses" due to the employer's violations; (3) requiring the employer to post the Board's notice of violation, the Board's decision in the case, and an explanation of the rights of employees under the NLRA for a period of three years, rather than the normal posting period of 60 days; (4) requiring the employer to mail the Board's decision and order and the explanation of rights of employees to all employees, including managers and supervisors; (5) requiring the employer to give the Board's notice and explanation of the rights of employees to all newly hired employees, supervisors, and managers for a period of three years; (6) requiring the employer to read the notice and explanation of the rights of employees to all employees, supervisors, managers, and senior executives at a series of meetings; and (7) requiring the employer to rescind all unlawful unilateral changes made by the employer to the terms and conditions of employment.[90]

---

[88] See "Reimbursement for Excess Federal and State Income Taxes which Discriminatees Owe as a Result of Receiving a Lump-sum Backpay Award," Office of the General Counsel, September 22, 2000, available at http://www.nlrb.gov/reports-guidance/general-counsel-memos, and search GC 00-07.

[89] 535 U.S. 137 (2002). See *Mezonos Maven Bakery*, 357 NLRB No. 57 (2011). See also "Procedures and Remedies for Discriminatees Who May Be Undocumented Aliens After Hoffman Plastic Compounds, Inc.," Memorandum of the General Counsel, Memorandum GC02-06, July 19, 2002, available at http://www.nlrb.gov/reports-guidance/general-counsel-memos, and search GC 02-06.

[90] *HTH Corp., Pacific Beach Corp., and KOA Management, LLC, d/b/a Pacific Beach Hotel*, 361 NLRB No. 65 (2014).

14-3h Delay Problems in NLRB Remedies

Although the NLRB has rather broad remedial powers under the NLRA, the delays involved in pursuing the Board's remedial procedures limit somewhat the effectiveness of its powers. The increasing caseload of the Board has delayed the procedural process to the point at which a determined employer can dilute the effectiveness of any remedy in a particular case.

Because unfair practice cases take so long to resolve, the affected employees may be left financially and emotionally exhausted by the process. Furthermore, the remedy, when it comes, may be too little, too late. One study found that when reinstatement was offered more than six months after the violation of the act occurred, only 5 percent of those discriminatorily discharged accepted their old jobs back.

Indeed, the final resolution of the back-pay claims of the employees in the *Darlington* case (presented earlier) did not occur until 1980—24 years from the closing of their plant—to avoid the union!

Obviously, a firm that can afford the litigation expenses may find it advantageous to delay a representation election by committing unfair practices or refusing to bargain with a certified union in violation of Section 8(a)(5), reasoning that the lawyers' fees plus any back-pay awards will total less of a cost of doing business than will increased wages and fringes under a collective bargaining agreement.

CHAPTER REVIEW

» Key Terms

unfair labor practices (ULPs)	427	union shop agreement	456	runaway shop	464
Weingarten rights	445	agency shop agreement	456	featherbedding	467
whipsaw strike	447	right-to-work laws	457	front pay	469
in-house union	448	hiring hall	457		
union security agreement	455	lockout	462		

» Summary

- Section 7 of the NLRA provides protection for employees who engage in concerted activity for collective bargaining or for mutual aid and protection. All employees under the NLRA enjoy the right to engage in protected activity; conduct by employers or unions that undercuts or interferes with employees' Section 7 rights is an unfair labor practice.

- Section 8 of the NLRA defines a list of unfair labor practices by employers and by unions. Restrictions on employees' organizing or soliciting activity may violate Section 8(a)(1) or 8(b)(1); employer support, domination, or control of a labor organization [as defined by Section 2(5)] may be in violation of Section 8(a)(2). Employers that discriminate in terms or conditions of employment against employees either to encourage or discourage union membership violate Section 8(a)(3), and unions that attempt to get an employer to engage in such discrimination against employees violate Section 8(b)(2). The NLRA does allow employers and unions to adopt union security provisions such as an agency shop or union shop agreement; however, closed shop agreements, which require that a person be a union member to be hired, are prohibited under the NLRA.

- Economic strikes are protected activities under the NLRA, but economic strikers may be permanently replaced and are not guaranteed to get their jobs back after the strike. Unfair labor practice strikes are also protected activities, and unfair labor practice strikers may not be permanently replaced. An employer may lock out employees in a bargaining dispute but may not permanently replace the locked-out workers.

- The NLRB has broad powers to remedy unfair labor practices, but in practice, the procedures for resolving unfair labor practice complaints may take a long time. Such delays may operate to undermine the effectiveness of the remedies available and the intent of the NLRA in protecting the free choice of employees.

» Problems

» Questions

1. What kind of activity is protected by Section 7 of the NLRA? What is the effect of such protection? When can an individual acting alone be considered to be engaged in concerted activity under Section 7 of the NLRA?

2. To what extent may an employer limit union soliciting by employees? By nonemployees?

3. What is the relevance of motive under Section 8(a)(1)? What is the relevance of motive under Section 8(a)(3)? Explain.

4. What are union security provisions? Why would unions want to negotiate such provisions? Why are closed shop agreements outlawed?

5. To what extent is an economic strike protected activity? To what extent is an unfair labor practice strike protected activity? What is the practical significance of the difference in the treatment of the different types of strikers under the NLRA?

» Case Problems

6. Sandra Falcone was employed as a dental hygiene assistant. During a staff meeting, Dr. Trufolo discussed some work-related problems. Falcone and a coworker interrupted the meeting several times to disagree with Dr. Trufolo's comments. After the meeting, the office manager reprimanded Falcone and her coworker for disrupting the meeting by questioning Dr. Trufolo and by giggling and elbowing each other. On the following Monday, Falcone presented a list of grievances to the office manager, which Falcone had discussed with coworkers. Shortly thereafter, she was fired.

    Based on these facts, did the employer commit an unfair labor practice by discharging Falcone? Upon what facts should the NLRB determine the true motive for the discharge? [See *Joseph DeRario*, DMD, P.A., 283 NLRB No. 86, 125 L.R.R.M. 1024 (1987).]

7. Potter Manufacturing Co. laid off 15 employees because of economic conditions and lack of business. The union representing the employees at

Potter subsequently discovered that the employer had laid off employees that the employer believed were most likely to honor a picket line in the event of a strike. The union filed an unfair labor practice complaint with the NLRB, alleging that the layoffs violated Sections 8(a)(1) and 8(a)(3).

How should the NLRB rule on the complaint? [See *National Fabricators*, 295 NLRB No. 126, 131 L.R.R.M. 1761 (1989).]

8. Shortly after the union won a representation election in a Philadelphia-area hospital, the hospital fired the union steward, allegedly for failing to report to work. Some 18 months after the discharge, and while the unfair labor practice charge was still in litigation, a majority of the bargaining unit presented the president of the hospital with a petition requesting that the president withdraw recognition from the union and cease bargaining with it. Pursuant to the petition, after confirming the authenticity of the signatures and that it contained a majority of the bargaining unit members, the president withdrew recognition. The union filed another unfair labor practice charge.

If the hospital was found guilty of discriminatorily discharging the union steward, can you make an argument that it committed a second unfair labor practice by withdrawing recognition from the union while the unfair labor practice charge was pending? Do you reach a different result if at the time the petition was presented the hospital had been found guilty of the discriminatory discharge but was in the process of appealing the Board's decision? Would the result be different if the hospital had been found guilty but had immediately remedied the illegal action by reinstating the employee with back pay? [See *Taylor Hospital v. NLRB*, 770 F.2d 1075 (3d Cir. 1985).]

9. During a strike by the employees at Gillen, Inc., the picketers carried signs referring to the company and its president as "scabs." The president of Gillen, Inc., D. C. Gillen, filed a defamation suit against the union for its picketing and signs. Gillen sought $500,000 in damages, despite the fact that he could identify no business losses because of the picketing and signs. Gillen's suit was dismissed by the court as "groundless." The union then filed an unfair labor practice complaint against Gillen, Inc., alleging that filing the suit against the picketing and signs served to coerce the employees in the exercise of their rights under Section 7.

How should the NLRB rule on the complaint? Explain your answer. [See *H. S. Barss Co.*, 296 NLRB No. 151, 132 L.R.R.M. 1339 (1989).]

10. Rubber Workers District No. 8 began an organizing campaign at Bardcor Corporation, a small manufacturing company in Guthrie, Kentucky, during the summer of 1981. Shortly after the campaign began, the president of the corporation began taking pictures of workers in the plant. Employee Maxine Dukes asked supervisor Mike Loreille why the pictures were being taken. Loreille responded that the president wanted something to remember the employees by after he fired them for union activity.

A majority of the company's 37 employees signed union authorization cards. The next day, the employer discharged eight workers, seven of whom had signed cards. After the discharge, the union filed a series of unfair labor practice charges. The company was able to justify the discharges for economic reasons and argued that the picture-taking incident and Loreille's comment were nothing but jokes.

What provision of the NLRA did the company allegedly violate by the picture-taking incident and the supervisor's comment to Ms. Dukes? Try to formulate an argument for and against finding a violation of the act by the employer in one or both of these actions. Could the picture-taking incident alone violate the act? Did the supervisor's comment alone violate the act? [See *Bardcor Corporation*, 270 NLRB No. 157 (1984).]

11. Nicole Wright worked as a supply clerk at White Oak Manor, a long-term care facility. After getting a terrible haircut, she wore a hat to work to cover her hair. She had worn the hat at work for a week, when her supervisor told her that wearing the hat at work violated the facility's dress code, and directed her to remove the hat. Wright refused, and the supervisor reported her to the director of nursing for insubordination. Wright was then told to remove the hat or go home. Wright protested that other employees wore hats without any consequences, and then left work for the day. She returned to work the next day, which was the facility's

Halloween celebration; the employees wore costumes at work. Wright's costume included a hat, and she was asked to remove it; she complied with the request. Later that day, Wright was called to a meeting with her supervisor and the facility administrator. Wright complained that the dress code was not enforced evenly, but the administrator told her to "worry only about herself." At the end of the meeting, the administrator gave her a written warning for insubordination.

Over the next few weeks, Wright noticed a number of employees wearing hats or displaying tattoos, in violation of the dress code, but management didn't take any action. Wright began talking to her fellow employees about the uneven enforcement of the dress code, and they expressed support for her complaint. Wright also used her cell phone to take pictures of employees who were dressed contrary to the dress code, and shared the photos with coworkers, who again supported her actions. A few days later, the facility's business manager informed the administrator that Wright had showing the pictures to coworkers. The administrator again called Wright in for a meeting and told her she had violated the facility's policy prohibiting taking photos inside the facility without prior authorization. The administrator then discharged Wright for taking pictures without authorization or permission. Wright's discharge was the first time any employee had been disciplined for violating the policy prohibiting taking pictures without authorization. Wright filed an unfair labor practice complaint with the regional office of the NLRB, claiming that her discharge violated Section 8(a)(1).

Was Wright's activity protected under Section 7? Explain. Did her termination violate the NLRA? Explain. [See *NLRB v. White Oak Manor*, 2011 WL 5110235 (4th Cir. 2011).]

12. Flex Logistics requires all of its employees to sign a one page at-will-employment agreement. The agreement includes a section entitled "Confidential Information," which states:

> Employees deal with and have access to information that must stay within the Organization. Confidential Information includes, but is not limited to, information that is related to: our customers, suppliers, distributors; our organization management and marketing processes, plans and ideas, processes and plans; our financial information, including costs, prices; current and future business plans, our computer and software systems and processes; personnel information and documents, and our logos, and art work. No employee is permitted to share this Confidential Information outside the organization, or to remove or make copies of any of our records, reports or documents in any form, without prior management approval. Disclosure of Confidential Information could lead to termination, as well as other possible legal action.

The agreement prohibits employees from engaging in "disclosure of personnel information and documents" to persons "outside the organization," and violations of it will result in discipline, including possible termination, or legal action against the violator. Proctor, a newly hired Flex employee, feels that the nondisclosure requirement is too broad and restrictive. She files a complaint with the regional NLRB office.

Does the nondisclosure requirement violate the NLRA? Explain your answer. [See *Flex Frac Logistics, LLC*, 358 NLRB No. 127 (2012).]

13. In response to rumors that the employees of Tristeel Fabrication, Inc. were seeking to join a union, Strodel, the plant manager, held a meeting with the employees. Strodel informed them that if they voted to join a union, "things will no longer be the same—they could get stricter. Any collective bargaining would start from scratch, with no guarantee that the company would agree to continue any of the benefits the employees presently had. Everything will be conducted by the book (meaning the collective agreement)."

Do Strodel's comments constitute an unfair labor practice? Explain. [See *Jamaica Towing, Inc.*, 236 NLRB No. 223 (1978); and *Fidelity Telephone Co.*, 236 NLRB No. 26 (1978).]

14. Santos Diaz, Antonio Lopez, Rafael Naraes, and Jose Rivera worked on the dock crew for Mike Yurosek & Son, Inc., a vegetable packing company. Each had been employed by Yurosek for between 9 and 15 years. In early September 1990, warehouse manager Juan Garza announced to the dock

crew members that he was reducing their hours to approximately 36 a week. Some of the employees complained that the new schedule would not provide enough time to finish their work. Garza apparently responded: "That's the way it's going to be. . . . You are going to punch [out] . . . exactly at the time that I tell you."

On September 24, pursuant to the new schedule, the crew was scheduled to work from 10:00 a.m. to 4:30 p.m. Shortly before 4:30, foreman Jaime Ortiz approached each of the four employees individually and instructed each to work an additional hour. All four employees refused to stay. They told Ortiz that they were required to follow the new schedule imposed by Garza. The employees then proceeded to punch out. Ortiz met them at the time clock and instructed them not to punch in the next morning but to meet him in the company dining hall.

The following day, the four employees were asked to wait in the company waiting room. Each employee was then individually called in turn into the personnel office and questioned by Garza, Ortiz, and three other company officers. When each employee was asked why he did not work the extra hour, each responded that he was adhering to the new schedule posted by Garza. After the interviews, the employees waited while the company officials discussed the matter. Each employee was then individually called back into the office and terminated for insubordination. The employees filed an unfair labor practice complaint with the NLRB over their termination.

Was their conduct protected under Section 7? Was it concerted? How should the NLRB rule on their complaint? Explain. [See *NLRB v. Mike Yurosek & Son, Inc.*, 53 F.3d 261 (9th Cir. 1995).]

15. Lawson runs 700 convenience food stores in Ohio, Indiana, Pennsylvania, and Michigan. Following the murder of an employee in a Lawson store, the United Food and Commercial Workers Union (UFCW) began to organize Lawson sales assistants in northeastern Ohio. Some employees refused to report to work for two days after the murder as a protest against lax security measures.

In response to the complaints, Lawson installed outdoor lights at its stores, adopted a policy that no one would be required to work alone at night, and began paying overtime for work done after closing hours.

Following the initiation of the UFCW campaign, Lawson placed no-solicitation signs in all its stores and told employees that anyone violating the no-solicitation rule would be subject to discharge.

When the UFCW filed a representation petition with the NLRB, seeking an election, employees were told that the stores would close if they voted in the union. One store manager told employees not to discuss the union at work because Lawson planned to install listening devices in the stores.

What, if any, unfair labor practices has Lawson committed? [See *The Lawson Co. v. NLRB*, 753 F.2d 471 (6th Cir. 1985).]

Hypothetical Scenarios

16. Citywatcher.com, a video surveillance company, has issued a work rule requiring its employees to have radio frequency identification chips embedded in their forearms, in order to monitor the employees' movements while they are working. The employees feel that such a rule is overly intrusive and would inhibit the employees' willingness to discuss working conditions among themselves. Does the new work rule violate Section 8(a)(1) of the NLRA? Would it make a difference if the employer adopted the rule because it was aware that the employees had been discussing joining a union? Explain.

17. Gonzales worked in the meat department of Groceries-R-Us, and also served as a union steward at the store. When he learned that he had been scheduled to work on Saturdays, Gonzales confronted his supervisor. During this confrontation, Gonzales angrily threw his meat hook over his shoulder, narrowly missing an employee. He also threw a 40-pound piece of meat into a saw (breaking its blade), threw his knife into a box, threatened his supervisor, and refused to follow the store manager's order to leave the store. The employer terminated Gonzales, based on his threatening and violent behavior. Gonzales filed a complaint

with the NLRB alleging that he was subjected to a more severe disciplinary penalty because he was a union steward. How should the NLRB rule on his complaint? Explain.

18. Decker, the regional manager for Aquatics, Inc., called Ali, one of the company's sales representatives, into his office for a one-on-one meeting. Decker asked Ali how the local management was treating him. Ali responded that he was being treated fine but some of the managers needed to go back to training as they were treating the employees "real bad." Decker then told him that there was a rumor that the sales representatives were threatening to organize a union. Ali said he knew nothing about that. Decker then asked Ali if anyone had approached him with a card to sign and he said "No." During the course of this meeting they also discussed an anticipated employee bonus that had been drastically reduced and Decker explained that this was dependent on how the company performed. Near the end of the meeting, Decker asked Ali whether he, as a loyal employee, would be willing to let management know if someone approached him to sign a union card. Decker stated that he was going to get to the "bottom" of the union campaign. He also took notes during the course of the meeting, and told Ali that anything they discussed would "have to stay in the room" and "not to mention the meeting to anyone." Did Decker's meeting with Ali violate the NLRA? Explain.

19. St. Pancras Medical Center, an acute-care hospital, issued a memorandum prohibiting its nursing and patient care employees from wearing buttons that read "RNs Organized to Promote Patient Care." The buttons were an effort to show support for the nurses' union in contract negotiations with the hospital. The hospital directed the employees not to wear any buttons in any areas of the hospital where they might encounter patients or patients' family members. The hospital claimed that wearing the buttons could cause "unease and worry among patients and their families," and disturb the tranquil hospital atmosphere that is necessary for successful patient care. The union feels that the rule is overly restrictive, and files an unfair labor practice complaint with the NLRB. Under which section of the NLRA should the union file its complaint? Is the rule valid, or does it violate the NLRA? Why?

20. Watkins is a member of the bargaining unit at Stith, Inc., and has been very vocal in his criticism of the performance of the union's leadership in the last contract negotiations. Ronnie Elder, the union's chief steward, is fed up with Watkins' complaints, and meets with Kay Alston, Stith's human resources director, to discuss terminating Watkins. Has Elder committed an unfair labor practice? If so, which section of the NLRA has Elder violated? If Alston fires Watkins, has she committed an unfair labor practice? If so, which section of the NLRA has Alston violated?

CHAPTER 15

Collective Bargaining

collective bargaining
process by which a
union and employer
meet and confer with
respect to wages,
hours, and other terms
and conditions of
employment

Employees join unions to gain some influence over their working conditions and wages; that influence is achieved through the process called **collective bargaining**. Section 8(d) of the National Labor Relations Act (NLRA) defines collective bargaining as

> [t]he performance of the mutual obligation of the employer and the representative of the employees to meet at reasonable times and confer in good faith with respect to wages, hours, and other terms and conditions of employment, or the negotiation of an agreement or any question arising thereunder. . . .

This process of meeting and discussing working conditions is actually a highly stylized and heavily regulated form of economic conflict. Within the limits of conduct spelled out by the National Labor Relations Board (NLRB) under the NLRA, the parties exert pressure on each other to force some concession or agreement. The union's economic pressure comes from its ability to withhold the services of its members—a strike. The employer's bargaining pressure comes from its potential to lock out the employees or to permanently replace striking workers. The NLRB and the courts, through their interpretation and administration of the NLRA, have limited the kinds of pressure either side may exert and how such pressure may be applied. This chapter examines the collective bargaining process and the legal limits placed on that process.

15-1 The Duty to Bargain

An employer is required to recognize a union as the exclusive bargaining representative of its employees when a majority of those employees support the union. The union may demonstrate its majority support either through signed authorization cards or by winning a representation election. Once aware of the union's majority support, the employer must recognize and bargain with the union according to the process spelled out in Section 8(d). Section 8(a)(5) makes it an unfair labor practice for an employer to refuse to bargain with the representative of its employees, and Section 8(b)(3) makes it an unfair practice for a union representing a group of employees to refuse to bargain with their employer.

Although the NLRA imposes an obligation to bargain collectively upon both employer and union, it does not control the results of the bargaining process. Section 8(d) makes it clear that the obligation to bargain "does not compel either party to agree to a proposal or require the making of a concession." The act thus reflects an ambivalence regarding the duty to bargain in good faith. The parties, to promote industrial relations harmony, are required to come together and negotiate, but in deference to the principle of freedom of contract, they are not required to reach an agreement. This tension between the goal of promoting industrial peace and the principle of freedom of contract underlies the various NLRB and court decisions dealing with the duty to bargain. The accommodation of these conflicting ideas makes the area a difficult and interesting aspect of labor relations law.

If the parties are required to negotiate, yet are not required to reach an agreement or even to make a concession, how can the Board determine whether either side is bargaining in good faith? Section 8(d) requires that the parties meet at reasonable times to discuss wages, hours, and terms and conditions of employment. It also requires that any agreement reached must be put in writing if either party so requests. But Section 8(d) does not speak to bargaining tactics. Is either side free to insist upon its proposal as a "take-it-or-leave-it" proposition? Can either side refuse to make any proposal? These questions must be addressed in determining what constitutes bargaining in good faith.

15-1a   Bargaining in Good Faith

Section 8(a)(5) requires that the employer bargain with a union that is the representative of its employees according to Section 9(a). Section 9(a) states that a union that has the support of a majority of employees in a bargaining unit becomes the exclusive bargaining representative of all employees in the unit. That section also states that the employer may address the grievances of individual employees as long as it is done in a manner consistent with the collective agreement and the union has been given an opportunity to be present at such adjustment. That provision raises the question of how far the employer can go in dealing with individuals rather than the union. In *J. I. Case Co. v. NLRB*,[1] the Supreme Court held that contracts of employment made with individual employees were not impediments to negotiating a collective agreement with the union. J. I. Case had made it a practice to sign yearly individual contracts of employment with its employees. When the union, which won a representation election, requested bargaining over working conditions, the company refused. The employer argued that the individual contracts covered those issues and no bargaining could take place until those individual contracts had expired. The Supreme Court held that the individual contracts must give way to allow the negotiation of a collective agreement. Once the union is certified as the exclusive bargaining representative of the employees, the employer cannot deal with the individual employees in a manner inconsistent with the union's status as exclusive representative. To allow individual contracts of employment to prevent collective bargaining would undercut the union's position.

What about the situation in which individual employees attempt to discuss their grievances with the employer in a manner inconsistent with the union's role as exclusive representative? How far does the Section 9(a) proviso go to allow such discussion? That question is addressed in the following Supreme Court decision.

---

[1] 321 U.S. 332 (1944).

CASE 15.1

EMPORIUM CAPWELL CO. V. WESTERN ADDITION COMMUNITY ORGANIZATION

420 U.S. 50 (1975)

[Emporium Capwell Co. operates a department store in San Francisco. The company had a collective bargaining agreement with the Department Store Employees Union. The agreement, among other things, included a prohibition of employment discrimination because of race, color, religion, national origin, age, or sex. The agreement also set up a grievance and arbitration process to resolve any claimed violation of the agreement, including a violation of the nondiscrimination clause.]

Marshall, J.

This litigation presents the question whether, in light of the national policy against racial discrimination in employment, the National Labor Relations Act protects concerted activity by a group of minority employees to bargain with their employer over issues of employment discrimination. . . .

On April 3, 1968, a group of Company employees covered by the agreement met with the Secretary-Treasurer of the Union, Walter Johnson, to present a list of grievances including a claim that the Company was discriminating on the basis of race in making assignments and promotions. The Union official agreed to take certain of the grievances and to investigate the charge of racial discrimination. He appointed an investigating committee and prepared a report on the employees' grievances, which he submitted to the Retailer's Council and which the Council in turn referred to the Company. The report described "the possibility of racial discrimination" as perhaps the most important issue raised by the employees and termed the situation at the Company as potentially explosive if corrective action were not taken. It offered as an example of the problem the Company's failure to promote a Negro stock employee regarded by other employees as an outstanding candidate but a victim of racial discrimination.

Shortly after receiving the report, the Company's labor relations director met with Union representatives and agreed to "look into the matter" of discrimination and see what needed to be done. Apparently unsatisfied with these representations, the Union held a meeting in September attended by Union officials, Company employees, and representatives of the California Fair Employment Practices Committee (FEPC) and the local antipoverty agency.

The Secretary-Treasurer of the Union announced that the Union had concluded that the Company was discriminating, and that it would process every such grievance through to arbitration if necessary. Testimony about the Company's practices was taken and transcribed by a court reporter, and the next day the Union notified the Company of its formal charge and demanded that the joint union-management Adjustment Board be convened "to hear the entire case."

At the September meeting some of the Company's employees had expressed their view that the contract procedures were inadequate to handle a systemic grievance of this sort; they suggested that the Union instead begin picketing the store in protest. Johnson explained that the collective agreement bound the Union to its processes and expressed his view that successful grievants would be helping not only themselves but all others who might be the victims of invidious discrimination as well. The FEPC and antipoverty agency representatives offered the same advice. Nonetheless, when the Adjustment Board meeting convened on October 16, James Joseph Hollins, Tom Hawkins, and two other employees whose testimony the Union had intended to elicit refused to participate in the grievance procedure. Instead, Hollins read a statement objecting to reliance on correction of individual inequities as an approach to the problem of discrimination at the store and demanding that the president of the Company meet with the four protestants to work out a broader agreement for dealing with the issue as they saw it. The four employees then walked out of the hearing.

Hollins attempted to discuss the question of racial discrimination with the Company president shortly after the incidents of October 16. The president refused to be drawn into such a discussion but suggested to Hollins that he see the personnel director about the matter. Hollins, who had spoken to the personnel director before, made no effort to do so again. Rather, he and Hawkins and several other dissident employees held a press conference on October 22 at which they denounced the store's employment policy as racist, reiterated their desire to deal directly with "the top management" of the Company over minority employment conditions, and announced their intention to picket and institute a boycott of the store. On Saturday, November 2,

Hollins, Hawkins, and at least two other employees picketed the store throughout the day and distributed at the entrance handbills urging consumers not to patronize the store. Johnson encountered the picketing employees, again urged them to rely on the grievance process, and warned that they might be fired for their activities. The picketers, however, were not dissuaded, and they continued to press their demand to deal directly with the Company president.

On November 7, Hollins and Hawkins were given written warnings that a repetition of the picketing or public statements about the Company could lead to their discharge. When the conduct was repeated the following Saturday, the two employees were fired.

Respondent Western Addition Community Organization, a local civil rights association of which Hollins and Hawkins were members, filed a charge against the Company with the National Labor Relations Board. After a hearing the NLRB Trial Examiner found that the discharged employees had believed in good faith that the Company was discriminating against minority employees, and that they had resorted to concerted activity on the basis of that belief. He concluded, however, that their activity was not protected by Section 7 of the Act and that their discharges did not, therefore, violate Section 8(a)(1).

The Board, after oral argument, adopted the findings and conclusions of its Trial Examiner and dismissed the complaint. Among the findings adopted by the Board was that the discharged employees' course of conduct:

> . . . was no mere presentation of a grievance, but nothing short of a demand that the [Company] bargain with the picketing employees for the entire group of minority employees.

Central to the policy of fostering collective bargaining, where the employees elect that course, is the principle of majority rule. If the majority of a unit chooses union representation, the NLRA permits them to bargain with their employer to make union membership a condition of employment, thereby imposing their choice upon the minority. . . . In establishing a regime of majority rule, Congress sought to secure to all members of the unit the benefits of their collective strength and bargaining power, in full awareness that the superior strength of some individuals or groups might be subordinated to the interest of the majority.

In vesting the representatives of the majority with this broad power Congress did not, of course, authorize a tyranny of the majority over minority interests. . . . we have held,

by the very nature of the exclusive bargaining representative's status as representative of all unit employees, Congress implicitly imposed upon [the union] a duty fairly and in good faith to represent the interests of minorities within the unit. And the Board has taken the position that a union's refusal to process grievances against racial discrimination, in violation of that duty, is an unfair labor practice. . . .

Plainly, national labor policy embodies the principles of nondiscrimination as a matter of highest priority . . . These general principles do not aid respondent, however, as it is far from clear that separate bargaining is necessary to help eliminate discrimination. Indeed, as the facts of this case demonstrate, the proposed remedy might have just the opposite effect. The collective bargaining agreement in this case prohibited without qualification all manner of invidious discrimination and made any claimed violation a grievable issue. The grievance procedure is directed precisely at determining whether discrimination has occurred. That orderly determination, if affirmative, could lead to an arbitral award enforceable in court. Nor is there any reason to believe that the processing of grievances is inherently limited to the correction of individual cases of discrimination. The decision by a handful of employees to bypass the grievance procedure in favor of attempting to bargain with their employer, by contrast, may or may not be predicated upon the actual existence of discrimination. An employer confronted with bargaining demands from each of several minority groups would not necessarily, or even probably, be able to agree to remedial steps satisfactory to all at once. Competing claims on the employer's ability to accommodate each group's demands, e.g., for reassignments and promotions to a limited number of positions, could only set one group against the other even if it is not the employer's intention to divide and overcome them. Having divided themselves, the minority employees will not be in position to advance their cause unless it be by recourse seriatim to economic coercion, which can only have the effect of further dividing them along racial or other lines. Nor is the situation materially different where, as apparently happened here, self-designated representatives purport to speak for all groups that might consider themselves to be victims of discrimination. Even if in actual bargaining the various groups did not perceive their interests as divergent and further subdivide themselves, the employer would be bound to bargain with them in a field largely preempted by the current collective bargaining agreement with the elected bargaining representatives. . . .

. . . The policy of industrial self-determination as expressed in Section 7 does not require fragmentation of the bargaining unit along racial or other lines in order to consist with the national labor policy against discrimination. And in the face of such fragmentation, whatever its effect on discriminatory practices, the bargaining process that the principle of exclusive representation is meant to lubricate could not endure unhampered. . . .

Respondent objects that reliance on the remedies provided by Title VII is inadequate effectively to secure the rights conferred by Title VII. . . .

Whatever its factual merit, this argument is properly addressed to the Congress and not to this Court or the NLRB. In order to hold that employer conduct violates Section 8(a)(1) of the NLRA because it violates Section 704(a) of Title VII, we would have to override a host of consciously made decisions well within the exclusive competence of the Legislature. This obviously, we cannot do.

Reversed.

Case Questions

1. What were the complaints of the minority employees against the company? How did the union respond to their complaints?

2. Why did the employees reject using the procedures under the collective bargaining agreement? What happened to them when they insisted on picketing the store to publicize their complaints?

3. Did the NLRB hold that their conduct was protected under Section 7? Why? Did the Supreme Court protect their conduct? Why?

Although the employer in *J. I. Case* and the employees in *Emporium Capwell* were held to have acted improperly, there is some room for individual discussions of working conditions and grievances. Where the collective agreement permits individual negotiation, an employer may discuss such matters with individual employees. Examples of such agreements are the collective agreements covering professional baseball and football players; the collective agreement sets minimum levels of conditions and compensation, while allowing the athletes to negotiate salary and other compensation on an individual basis.

Procedural Requirements of the Duty to Bargain in Good Faith

A union or employer seeking to bargain with the other party must notify that other party of its desire to bargain at least 60 days prior to the expiration of the existing collective agreement or, if no agreement is in effect, 60 days prior to the date it proposes the agreement to go into effect. Section 8(d) requires that such notice must be given at the proper time; failure to do so may make any strike by the union or lockout by the employer an unfair labor practice. Section 8(d) also requires that the parties must continue in effect any existing collective agreement for 60 days from the giving of the notice to bargain or until the agreement expires, whichever occurs later. Strikes or lockouts are prohibited during this 60-day "cooling-off" period. Employees who go on an economic strike during this period lose their status as "employees" and the protections of the act. Therefore, if the parties have given the notice to bargain later than 60 days prior to the expiration of the contract, they must wait the full 60 days to go on strike or lockout, even if the old agreement has already expired.

When negotiations result in matters in dispute, the party seeking contract termination must notify the Federal Mediation and Conciliation Service (FMCS) and the appropriate state mediation agency within 30 days from giving the notice to bargain. Neither side may resort to a strike or lockout until 30 days after the FMCS and state agency have been notified.

The NLRA provides for longer notice periods when the collective bargaining involves the employees of a health-care institution. In that case, the parties must give notice to bargain at least 90 days prior to the expiration of the agreement. No strike or lockout can take place for at least 90 days from the giving of the notice or the expiration of the agreement, whichever is later. Furthermore, the FMCS and state agency must be notified 60 days prior to the termination of the agreement. Finally, Section 8(g) requires that a labor organization seeking to picket or strike against a health-care institution must give both the employer and the FMCS written notice of its intention to strike or picket at least 10 days prior to taking such action. Why should a labor organization be required to give health-care institutions advance notice of any strike or picketing?

As noted, Section 8(d) prohibits any strike or lockout during the notice period. Employees who go on strike during that period are deprived of the protection of the act. In *Mastro Plastics Co. v. NLRB*,[2] the Supreme Court held that the prohibition applied only to economic strikes—strikes designed to pressure the employer to "terminate or modify" the collective agreement. Unfair labor practice strikes, which are called to protest the employer's violation of the NLRA, are not covered by the Section 8(d) prohibition. Therefore, the employees in *Mastro Plastics* who went on strike during the 60-day cooling-off period to protest the illegal firing of an employee were not in violation of Section 8(d) and were not deprived of the protection of the act.

Concept *Summary* 15.1

THE DUTY TO BARGAIN IN GOOD FAITH

Procedural Requirements: Section 8(d)

- The party seeking to begin negotiations must give notice of desire to bargain at least 60 days prior to the expiration of the collective agreement, or 60 days prior to the date the agreement will go into effect
- Any existing agreement must be kept in effect for 60 days from giving notice, or until its expiry date (whichever occurs later)
- Strikes and lockouts are prohibited during the 60-day notice period
- If the negotiations result in a dispute, the party seeking contract termination must notify the FMCS and state mediation agency within 30 days from giving the notice to bargain; no strike or lockout can occur until after 30 days from giving notice to the FMCS and state agency

Creation of the Duty to Bargain

As has been discussed, the duty to bargain arises when the union gets the support of a majority of the employees in a bargaining unit. When a union is certified as the winner of a representation election, the employer is required by Section 8(a)(5) to bargain with it. (An employer with knowledge of a union's majority support, independent of the union's claim of such support, must also recognize and bargain with the union without resort to an election.) Because the NLRA does not provide a means of having a court review

---

[2] 350 U.S. 270 (1956).

a certification decision by the NLRB, employers who seek to challenge a certification decision may refuse to bargain with the union, thereby forcing the union to file unfair labor practices under Section 8(a)(5). Because NLRB unfair labor practice decisions are subject to judicial review by the federal courts of appeals, the employer can then raise the issue of the union's improper certification as a defense to the charge of refusing to bargain in good faith with the union.

When an employer is approached by two unions, each claiming to represent a majority of the employees, how should the employer respond? One way would be to refuse to recognize either union (provided, of course, that the employer had no independent knowledge of either union's majority support) and to insist on an election. Can the employer recognize voluntarily one of the two unions claiming to represent the employees?

In *Bruckner Nursing Home*,[3] the NLRB held that an employer may recognize a union that claims to have majority support of the employees in the bargaining unit even though another union is also engaged in an organizing campaign, as long as the second union has not filed a petition for a representation election. The Board reasoned that the rival union, unable to muster even the support of 30 percent of the employees necessary to file a petition, should not be permitted to prevent the recognition of the union with majority support. If, however, a valid petition for a representation election has been filed, then the employer must refrain from recognizing either union and must wait for the outcome of the election to determine if either union has majority support.

The *Bruckner Nursing Home* decision dealt with a situation in which the employees were not previously represented by a union. When an incumbent union's status has been challenged by a rival union that has petitioned for a representation election, is the employer still required to negotiate with the incumbent union? In *RCA del Caribe*,[4] the Board held that:

> the mere filing of a representation petition by an outside, challenging union will no longer require or permit an employer to withdraw from bargaining or executing a contract with an incumbent union. Under this rule . . . an employer will violate Section 8(a)(5) by withdrawing from bargaining based solely on the fact that a petition has been filed by an outside union. . . .
>
> If the incumbent prevails in the election held, any contract executed with the incumbent will be valid and binding. If the challenging union prevails, however, any contract executed with the incumbent will be null and void. . . .

The Bruckner Nursing Home and *RCA del Caribe* decisions were departures from prior Board decisions, which required that an employer stay neutral in the event of rival organizing campaigns or when the incumbent union faced a petition filed by a challenging union. Which approach do you think is more likely to protect the desires of the individual employees? Do *Bruckner Nursing Home* and *RCA del Caribe* make it more difficult to unseat an incumbent union?

A nonincumbent union that accepts recognition from an employer while its own petition for a representation election is pending violates Section 8(b)(1)(A), and the employer granting such recognition is in violation of Section 8(a)(2).[5] In *NLRB v. Matros Automated*

---

[3] 262 NLRB 955 (1982).

[4] 262 NLRB 963 (1982).

[5] *NLRB v. Katz Delicatessen*, 80 F.3d 755 (2d Cir. 1996).

Electrical Construction Corp.,[6] an employer was held to violate Section 8(a)(2) where it recognized a union as bargaining agent for its employees while a rival union's challenges to the results of a representation election were still pending, and the union accepting recognition was held to violate Section 8(b)(1)(A).

When craft employees who had previously been included in a larger bargaining unit vote to be represented by a craft union, and a smaller craft bargaining unit is severed from the larger one, what is the effect of the agreement covering the larger unit? In *American Seating Co.*,[7] the NLRB held that the old agreement no longer applies to the newly severed bargaining unit, and the old agreement does not prevent the employer from negotiating with the craft union on behalf of the new bargaining unit. Is this decision surprising? (Recall the *J. I. Case* decision discussed earlier and reexamine the wording of Section 8(d) in its entirety.)

Duration of the Duty to Bargain

When the union is certified as bargaining representative after winning an election, the NLRB requires that the employer recognize and bargain with the union for at least a year from certification, regardless of any doubts the employer may have about the union's continued majority support. This one-year period applies only when no collective agreement has been made. When an agreement exists, the employer must bargain with the union for the term of the agreement. Unfair labor practices committed by the employer, such as refusal to bargain in good faith, may have the effect of extending the one-year period, as the Board held in *Mar-Jac Poultry*.[8]

When a union acquires bargaining rights by voluntary recognition rather than certification, the employer is required to recognize and bargain with the union only for "a reasonable period of time" if no agreement is in effect. What constitutes a reasonable period of time depends on the circumstances in each case. If an agreement has been reached after the voluntary recognition, then the employer must bargain with the union for the duration of the agreement.

After the one-year period or a reasonable period of time—whichever is appropriate—has expired, and no collective agreement is in effect, the employer may refuse to bargain with the union if the employer can establish that the union has lost the support of the majority of the bargaining unit, according to *Levitz Furniture Co. of the Pacific*.[9] The employer's evidence to support the fact that the union has lost majority support must have a reasonable basis in fact and, in the case of a certified union, must be based only on events that occur after the expiration of the one-year period from the certification of the union, as held in *Chelsea Industries*.[10] In a successorship situation (see Chapter 17), the incumbent union is entitled to a rebuttable presumption of continuing majority support.[11] In *Allentown Mack Sales and Services, Inc. v. NLRB*,[12] the U.S. Supreme Court upheld the NLRB's requirement

---

[6] 366 Fed. Appx. 184, 2010 WL 456755 (2d Cir. Feb. 11, 2010).

[7] 106 NLRB 250 (1953).

[8] 136 NLRB 785 (1962).

[9] 333 NLRB 717 (2001).

[10] 331 NLRB 1648 (2000), enforced by 285 F.3d 1077 (D.C. Cir. 2002).

[11] *Lamons Gasket Co.*, 357 NLRB No. 72 (2011).

[12] 522 U.S. 359 (1998).

that the employer have a "good faith reasonable doubt" about the union's majority support in order to take a poll of employees about their support of the union. The Board held in *NLRB v. Flex Plastics*[13] that filing a decertification petition alone does not suffice to establish a reason to doubt the union's majority support. When the employer can establish some reasonable factual basis for its claim that the union has lost majority support, it may refuse to negotiate with the union. To find a violation of Section 8(a)(5), the Board must then prove that the union in fact represented a majority of the employees on the date the employer refused to bargain.

What happens if the union employees go on strike and are permanently replaced by the employer? Must the employer continue to recognize and bargain with the union? In *Pioneer Flour Mills*,[14] the NLRB held that economic strikers must be considered members of the bargaining unit for the purpose of determining whether the union has majority support for the first 12 months of the strike. After 12 months, if they have been permanently replaced, the strikers need not be considered part of the bargaining unit by the employer. Unfair labor practice strikers may not be permanently replaced and must be considered members of the bargaining unit.

Where an employer has hired replacements during an economic strike and now seeks to determine whether the union still has majority support, can the employer presume that the replacement workers oppose the union? The NLRB takes the position that it will not presume the replacements oppose the union, but rather will consider each case on its own facts: Has the employer presented sufficient objective evidence to indicate that the replacements do not support the union? The NLRB's approach was upheld by the Supreme Court in *NLRB v. Curtin Matheson Scientific, Inc.*[15]

What happens if the employer agrees with the union on a contract but then tries to raise a claim that the union has lost majority support? That is the subject of the following case.

» CASE 15.2

AUCIELLO IRON WORKS, INC. V. NLRB
517 U.S. 781 (1996)

Facts: Auciello Iron Works had 23 production and maintenance employees, all represented by the Shopmen's Local No. 501 of the International Association of Bridge, Structural, and Ornamental Iron Workers. When the collective bargaining agreement expired on September 25, 1988, and negotiations for a new one were unsuccessful, the employees went on strike. On November 17, 1988, Auciello presented the union with a contract proposal. The union stopped picketing the next day, and nine days

later the union telegraphed its acceptance of the offer. The day after the union indicated its acceptance of the offer, Auciello told the union that it doubted that a majority of the bargaining unit's employees supported the union. Auciello disavowed the collective bargaining agreement and denied it had any duty to continue negotiating with the union. Auciello based its doubt about the union's majority support to knowledge acquired before the union accepted the contract offer, including the facts that nine employees

---

[13] 726 F.2d 272 (6th Cir. 1984).
[14] 174 NLRB 1202 (1969).
[15] 494 U.S. 775 (1990).

had crossed the picket line, that 13 employees had given it signed forms indicating their resignation from the union, and that 16 had expressed dissatisfaction with the union.

The union filed unfair labor practice charges with the NLRB. An administrative law judge found that a contract existed between the parties and that Auciello's withdrawal from it violated Sections 8(a)(1) and (5) of the NLRA. The Board affirmed the administrative law judge's decision. The Board treated Auciello's claim of good faith doubt as irrelevant and ordered Auciello to reduce the collective bargaining agreement to a formal written instrument. The Court of Appeals enforced the order and Auciello appealed to the Supreme Court.

Issue: Can an employer disavow a collective bargaining agreement because of a good faith doubt about a union's majority status at the time the contract was made, when the doubt arises from facts known to the employer before its contract offer had been accepted by the union?

Decision: The NLRB has adopted several presumptions about the existence of majority support for a union within a bargaining unit, required for its status of exclusive bargaining representative. The first two are conclusive presumptions:

- A union "usually is entitled to a conclusive presumption of majority status for one year following" certification as such exclusive bargaining representative by the NLRB; and
- a union is also entitled to a conclusive presumption of majority status during the term of any collective bargaining agreement, up to three years in length.

The NLRB also has a third presumption, though it is not a conclusive one. At the end of the certification year or upon expiration of the collective bargaining agreement, the presumption of majority status becomes a rebuttable one. An employer may overcome that presumption (when, for example, defending against an unfair labor practice charge) by showing that, at the time of its refusal to bargain, either:

- the union did not in fact enjoy majority support; or
- the employer had a "good faith" doubt, founded on a sufficient objective basis, about the union's majority support.

Auciello has raised the "good faith doubt" defense after a collective bargaining contract was reached upon the union's acceptance of an employer's outstanding offer.

The NLRB rejected Auciello's claim of an exception for an employer with doubts arising from facts antedating the contract. The NLRB said that such an exception would allow an employer to control the timing of its assertion of good faith doubt and thus to "'sit' on that doubt and . . . raise it after the offer is accepted." The Board held that giving employers such unilateral control over a vital part of the collective bargaining process would undermine the stability of the collective bargaining relationship. The NLRB presumptions generally allow companies an adequate chance to act on their preacceptance doubts before contract formation, just as Auciello could have acted effectively under the Board's rule in this case. Auciello knew that the picket line had been crossed and that a number of its employees had expressed dissatisfaction with the union at least nine days before the contract's acceptance, and all of the resignation forms Auciello received were dated at least five days before the acceptance date. Auciello had at least three alternatives to doing nothing:

- it could have withdrawn the outstanding offer and then petitioned for a representation election;
- following withdrawal, it could also have refused to bargain further on the basis of its good faith doubt, leaving it to the union to charge an unfair labor practice; and
- it could have withdrawn its offer to allow it time to investigate while it continued to fulfill its duty to bargain in good faith with the union.

The company thus had generous opportunities to avoid the presumption before the moment of acceptance.

The Supreme Court upheld the NLRB decision that an employer's pre-contractual, good faith doubt was inadequate to support an exception to the conclusive presumption that arises at the moment a collective bargaining contract offer has been accepted. The Court affirmed the judgment of the Court of Appeals for the First Circuit.

15-2   The Nature of the Duty to Bargain in Good Faith

After having considered how the duty to bargain in good faith arises and how long it lasts, we now turn to exactly what it means: What is "good faith" bargaining?

As we have seen, the wording of Section 8(d) states that making concessions or reaching agreement is not necessary to good faith bargaining. The imposition of such requirements would infringe upon either party's freedom of contract and would destroy the voluntary nature of collective bargaining, which is essential to its success. What is required for good faith bargaining, according to the NLRB, is that the parties enter negotiations with "an open and fair mind" and "a sincere purpose to find a basis of agreement."

As long as the parties bargain with an intention to find a basis of agreement, the breakdown or deadlock of negotiations is not a violation of the duty to bargain in good faith. When talks reach a deadlock—known as an **impasse**—as a result of sincere bargaining, either side may break off talks on the deadlocked issue. In determining whether an impasse exists, the Board considers the totality of circumstances: the number of times the parties have met, the likelihood of progress on the issue, the use of mediation, and so on. The Board considers that a change in the position of either party or a change in the circumstances may break an impasse; in that case, the parties would not be able to break off all talks on the issue.

When the impasse results from a party's rigid insistence upon a particular proposal, it is not a violation of the duty to bargain if the proposal relates to wages, hours, or terms and conditions of employment. In *NLRB v. American National Insurance Co.*,[16] the Supreme Court held that the employer's insistence upon contract language giving it discretionary control over promotions, discipline, work scheduling, and denying arbitration on such matters was not in violation of the duty to bargain in good faith. In *NLRB v. General Electric Co.*,[17] the Court of Appeals held that take-it-or-leave-it bargaining is not, by itself, in violation of the duty to bargain. But when an employer engages in other conduct indicating lack of good faith—such as refusing to sign a written agreement, attempting to deal with individual employees rather than the union, and refusing to provide the union with information regarding bargaining proposals—then the combined effect of the employer's conduct is to violate the duty to negotiate in good faith. But hard bargaining, in and of itself, is not a violation. At some point in negotiations, either side may make a "final" offer and hold to it firmly.

While negotiations are being conducted, is either side free to engage in tactics designed to pressure the other into making a concession? Is such pressure during bargaining consistent with negotiating in good faith? In *NLRB v. Insurance Agents International Union*,[18] the U.S. Supreme Court held that the use of economic pressure such as a "work to rule" and "on the job slow-downs" is not inconsistent with the duty of bargaining in good faith; indeed, the use of economic pressure is "part and parcel" of the collective bargaining process.

The duty to bargain in good faith under Section 8(d) also includes the obligation to execute a written contract incorporating any agreement, if requested by either party. An employer may not refuse to abide by the agreement because it objects to the ratification process used by the union, according to *Valley Central Emergency Veterinary Hospital*.[19]

impasse
a deadlock in negotiations

---

[16] 343 U.S. 395 (1952).

[17] 418 F.2d 736 (2d Cir. 1969), *cert. denied*, 397 U.S. 965 (1970).

[18] 361 U.S. 477 (1960).

[19] 349 NLRB 1126 (2007).

15-3 Subject Matter of Bargaining

As the preceding cases indicate, the NLRB and the courts are reluctant to control the bargaining tactics available to either party. This reluctance reflects a philosophical aversion to government intrusion into the bargaining process. Yet some regulation of bargaining is necessary if the bargaining process is to be meaningful. Some control is required to prevent the parties from making a charade of the process by holding firmly to arbitrary or frivolous positions. One means of control is the distinction between mandatory and permissive subjects of bargaining.

15-3a Mandatory Bargaining Subjects

mandatory bargaining subjects
those matters that vitally affect the terms and conditions of employment of the employees in the bargaining unit; the parties must bargain in good faith over such subjects

Mandatory bargaining subjects, according to the Supreme Court decision in *Allied Chemical & Alkali Workers v. PPG*,[20] are those subjects that "vitally affect the terms and conditions of employment" of the employees in the bargaining unit. The Supreme Court in *PPG* held that changes in medical insurance coverage of former employees who were retired were not a mandatory subject, and the company need not bargain over such changes with the union. The fact that the company had bargained over these issues in the past did not convert a permissive subject into a mandatory one; the company was free to change the insurance policy coverage unilaterally.

The NLRB and the Court have broadly interpreted the matters subject to mandatory bargaining as being related to "wages, hours, terms and conditions of employment" specified in Sections 8(d) and 9(a). Wages have been held to include all forms of employee compensation and fringe benefits, including items such as pensions, stock options, annual bonuses, employee discounts, shift differentials, and incentive plans. Hours and terms and conditions of employment have received similar broadening. The Supreme Court, in *Ford Motor Co. v. NLRB*,[21] held that the prices of food sold in vending machines in the plant cafeteria were mandatory subjects for bargaining when the employer had some control over pricing. In *California Newspapers Partnership d/b/a ANG Newspapers*,[22] the Board held that an employer was required to bargain over the employer's revisions to the email use policy for employees; the employer's unilateral implementation of the policy violated the duty to bargain in good faith under the NLRA. In *Alan Ritchey, Inc.*,[23] the Board held that a unionized employer must give the union notice and an opportunity to bargain before imposing discretionary disciplinary actions involving demotions, suspensions, and terminations when the applicable collective agreement does not establish a grievance-arbitration process. (Grievance arbitration will be discussed in Chapter 17.)

The aspect of mandatory bargaining subjects that has attracted the most controversy has been the duty to bargain over management decisions to subcontract work or to close down a plant. In *Fibreboard Paper Products v. NLRB*,[24] the Supreme Court held that an

---

[20] 404 U.S. 157 (1971).

[21] 441 U.S. 488 (1979).

[22] 350 NLRB 1175 (2007).

[23] 359 NLRB No. 40 (2012).

[24] 379 U.S. 203 (1964).

employer must bargain with the union over a decision to subcontract out work previously done by bargaining unit employees. Later, NLRB and Court decisions held that subcontracting that had never been done by bargaining unit employees was not a mandatory issue. In addition, decisions to change the corporate structure of a business or to terminate manufacturing operations were not mandatory subjects but rather were inherent management rights. Even the decision to go out of business entirely is not a mandatory subject of bargaining. But while the employer need not discuss such decisions with the union, the Board has held that the effects of such decisions upon the employees are mandatory bargaining subjects. The employer must therefore discuss the effects of such decisions with the union, including matters such as:

- Severance pay
- Transfer policies
- Retraining
- The procedure to be used for layoffs

The following case illustrates the test used to determine whether a managerial decision, such as the decision to close part of the firm's operations, is a mandatory bargaining subject.

CASE 15.3

FIRST NATIONAL MAINTENANCE CORP. v. NLRB

452 U.S. 666 (1981)

Blackmun, J.

Must an employer, under its duty to bargain in good faith "with respect to wages, hours, and other terms and conditions of employment," Sections 8(d) and 8(a)(5) of the National Labor Relations Act, negotiate with the certified representative of its employees over its decision to close a part of its business? In this case, the National Labor Relations Board (Board) imposed such a duty on petitioner with respect to its decision to terminate a contract with a customer, and the United States Court of Appeals, although differing over the appropriate rationale, enforced its order.

Petitioner, First National Maintenance Corporation (FNM), is a New York corporation engaged in the business of providing housekeeping, cleaning maintenance, and related services for commercial customers in the New York City area. It contracts for and hires personnel separately for each customer, and it does not transfer employees between locations.

During the spring of 1977, petitioner was performing maintenance work for the Greenpark Care Center, a nursing home in Brooklyn. Petitioner employed approximately 35 workers in its Greenpark operation.

Petitioner's business relationship with Greenpark, seemingly, was not very remunerative or smooth. In March 1977, Greenpark gave petitioner the 30 days' written notice of cancellation specified by the contract, because of "lack of efficiency." This cancellation did not become effective, for FNM's work continued after the expiration of that 30-day period. Petitioner, however, became aware that it was losing money at Greenpark. On June 30, by telephone, it asked that its weekly fee be restored at the $500 figure, and, on July 6, it informed Greenpark in writing that it would discontinue its operations there on August 1 unless the increase were granted. By telegram on July 25, petitioner gave final notice of termination.

While FNM was experiencing these difficulties, District 1199, National Union of Hospital and Health Care Employees, Retail, Wholesale and Department Store Union, AFLCIO (Union), was conducting an organization campaign among petitioner's Greenpark employees. On March 31, 1977, at a Board-conducted election, a majority of the employees selected the union as their bargaining agent.

Petitioner neither responded nor sought to consult with the union.

On July 28, petitioner notified its Greenpark employees that they would be discharged three days later.

With nothing but perfunctory further discussion, petitioner on July 31 discontinued its Greenpark operation and discharged the employees.

The union filed an unfair labor practice charge against petitioner, alleging violations of the Act's Section 8(a)(1) and (5). After a hearing held upon the Regional Director's complaint, the Administrative Law Judge made findings in the union's favor. . . . [H]e ruled that petitioner had failed to satisfy its duty to bargain concerning both the decision to terminate the Greenpark contract and the effect of that change upon the unit employees.

The Administrative Law Judge recommended an order requiring petitioner to bargain in good faith with the union about its decision to terminate its Greenpark service operation and its consequent discharge of the employees, as well as the effects of the termination. He recommended, also, that petitioner be ordered to pay the discharged employees back pay from the date of discharge until the parties bargained to agreement, or the bargaining reached an impasse, or the union failed timely to request bargaining or the union failed to bargain in good faith.

The National Labor Relations Board adopted the Administrative Law Judge's findings without further analysis, and additionally required petitioner, if it agreed to resume its Greenpark operations, to offer the terminated employees reinstatement to their former jobs or substantial equivalents; conversely, if agreement was not reached, petitioner was ordered to offer the employees equivalent positions, to be made available by discharge of subsequently hired employees, if necessary, at its other operations.

The United States Court of Appeals for the Second Circuit, with one judge dissenting in part, enforced the Board's order. . . .

Although parties are free to bargain about any legal subject, Congress has limited the mandate or duty to bargain to matters of "wages, hours, and other terms and conditions of employment." Congress deliberately left the words "wages, hours, and other terms and conditions of employment" without further definition, for it did not intend to deprive the Board of the power further to define those terms in light of specific industrial practices.

Nonetheless, in establishing what issues must be submitted to the process of bargaining, Congress had no expectation that the elected union representative would become an equal partner in the running of the business enterprise in which the union's members are employed.

Some management decisions, such as choice of advertising and promotion, product type and design, and financing arrangements, have only an indirect and attenuated impact on the employment relationship. Other management decisions, such as the order of succession of layoffs and recalls, production quotas, and work rules, are almost exclusively" an aspect of the relationship" between employer and employee. The present case concerns a third type of management decision, one that had a direct impact on employment, since jobs were inexorably eliminated by the termination, but had as its focus only the economic profitability of the contract with Greenpark, a concern under these facts wholly apart from the employment relationship. This decision, involving a change in the scope and direction of the enterprise, is akin to the decision whether to be in business at all, "not in [itself] primarily about conditions of employment, though the effect of the decision may be necessarily to terminate employment." At the same time this decision touches on a matter of central and pressing concern to the union and its member employees: the possibility of continued employment and the retention of the employees' very jobs.

Petitioner contends it had no duty to bargain about its decision to terminate its operations at Greenpark. This contention requires that we determine whether the decision itself should be considered part of petitioner's retained freedom to manage its affairs unrelated to employment. The aim of labeling a matter a mandatory subject of bargaining, rather than simply permitting, but not requiring, bargaining, is to "promote the fundamental purpose of the Act by bringing a problem of vital concern to labor and management within the framework established by Congress as most conducive to industrial peace." The concept of mandatory bargaining is premised on the belief that collective discussions backed by the parties' economic weapons will result in decisions that are better for both management and labor and for society as a whole. This will be true, however, only if the subject proposed for discussion is amenable to resolution through the bargaining process. Management must be free from the constraints of the bargaining process to the extent essential for the running of a profitable business. It also must have some degree of certainty beforehand as to when it may proceed to reach decisions without fear of later evaluations labeling its conduct an unfair labor practice. Congress did not explicitly state what issues of mutual concern to union and management it intended to exclude from mandatory bargaining. Nonetheless, in view of an employer's need for unencumbered decisionmaking, bargaining over management decisions that have a substantial impact on the continued availability of employment should be required only if the benefit, for labor-management relations and the collective-bargaining process, outweighs the burden placed on the conduct of the business.

Both union and management regard control of the decision to shut down an operation with the utmost seriousness. As has been noted, however, the Act is not intended to serve either party's individual interest, but to foster in a neutral manner a system in which the conflict between these interests may be resolved. It seems particularly important, therefore, to consider whether requiring bargaining over this sort of decision will advance the neutral purposes of the Act.

A union's interest in participating in the decision to close a particular facility or part of an employer's operations springs from its legitimate concern over job security. The Court has observed: "The words of [Section 8(d)] . . . plainly cover termination of employment which . . . necessarily results" from closing an operation. The union's practical purpose in participation, however, will be largely uniform: it will seek to delay or halt the closing. No doubt it will be impelled, in seeking these ends, to offer concessions, information, and alternatives that might be helpful to management or forestall or prevent the termination of jobs. It is unlikely, however, that requiring bargaining over the decision itself, as well as its effects, will augment this flow of information and suggestions. There is no dispute that the union must be given a significant opportunity to bargain about these matters of job security as part of the "effects" bargaining mandated by Section 8(a)(5). A union, pursuing such bargaining rights, may achieve valuable concessions from an employer engaged in a partial closing.

Management's interest in whether it should discuss a decision of this kind is much more complex and varies with the particular circumstances. If labor costs are an important factor in a failing operation and the decision to close, management will have an incentive to confer voluntarily with the union to seek concessions that may make continuing the business profitable. At other times, management may have great need for speed, flexibility, and secrecy in meeting business opportunities and exigencies. It may face significant tax or securities consequences that hinge on confidentiality, the timing of a plant closing, or a reorganization of the corporate structure. The publicity incident to the normal process of bargaining may injure the possibility of a successful transition or increase the economic damage to the business. The employer also may have no feasible alternative to the closing, and even good faith bargaining over it may both be futile and cause the employer additional loss.

There is an important difference, also, between permitted bargaining and mandated bargaining. Labeling this type of decision mandatory could afford a union a powerful tool for achieving delay, a power that might be used to thwart management's intentions in a manner unrelated to any feasible solution the union might propose.

We conclude that the harm likely to be done to an employer's need to operate freely in deciding whether to shut down part of its business purely for economic reasons outweighs the incremental benefit that might be gained through the union's participation in making the decision, and we hold that the decision itself is not part of Section 8(d)'s "terms and conditions," over which Congress has mandated bargaining. . . .

Case Questions

1. Why did First National Maintenance decide to close its operations at Greenpark? Could bargaining with the union affect those reasons? Explain your answer.

2. What test does the Supreme Court use to determine whether the decision to close operations is a mandatory bargaining subject? How does that test apply to the facts of this case?

3. What is the significance of labeling a decision a mandatory bargaining subject? Is the employer completely prohibited from acting alone on a mandatory

Subsequent to the First National Maintenance decision, the NLRB has interpreted the "balancing test" set out by the court as focusing on whether the employer's decision is based on labor costs. A decision to relocate production to another plant was not a mandatory subject because the decision did not turn on labor costs, according to *Local 2179, United Steelworkers of America v. NLRB*.[25] In short, the question whether the employer must

_____

[25] 822 F.2d 559 (5th Cir. 1987).

bargain with the union over a management decision such as plant closing, work relocation, or corporate reorganization is whether or not the decision is motivated by a desire to reduce labor costs or to escape the collective bargaining agreement. If the decision is based on other business considerations, apart from labor costs, then the employer's duty to bargain is limited to the effects of the decision on the employees rather than the decision itself.

What is the effect of labeling a subject as a mandatory bargaining issue upon the employer's ability to make decisions necessary to the efficient operation of the enterprise? The Supreme Court opinion in *First National Maintenance* was concerned about placing burdens on the employer that would interfere with the need to act promptly. But rather than preventing employer action over mandatory subjects, the duty to bargain requires only that the employer negotiate with the union. If the union agrees or makes concessions, then the employer is free to act. If the union fails to agree and an impasse results from good faith bargaining, the employer is then free to implement the decision. The duty to bargain over mandatory subjects requires only that the employer bargain in good faith to the point of impasse over the issue. Once impasse has been reached, the employer is free to act unilaterally. In the case of *NLRB v. Katz*,[26] the Supreme Court stated that an employer may institute unilateral changes on mandatory subjects after bargaining to impasse. However, when the impasse results from the employer's failure to bargain in good faith, any unilateral changes would be an unfair labor practice in violation of Section 8(a)(5).

In *WKYC-TV, Inc.*,[27] the Board held that an employer is required to continue to deduct union dues from employees' paychecks despite the expiration of the collective agreement that contained the dues check-off provision; the terms and effects of the old collective bargaining agreement continue in effect until the union and employer reach a new agreement, or a valid impasse allows the employer to take unilateral action. An employer that unilaterally discontinued the annual 3 percent pay raises pursuant to a collective agreement when that agreement expired was held to be in violation of Sections 8(a)(1) and 8(a)(5).[28]

Even if an employer has bargained to impasse over a mandatory subject and is free to implement changes, the changes made must be consistent with the proposal offered to the union. To institute changes unilaterally that are more generous than the proposals the employer was willing to offer the union is a violation of Section 8(a)(5), according to the Supreme Court decision in *NLRB v. Crompton-Highland Mills*.[29] Thus, the employer is not free to offer replacements wages that are higher than those offered to the union before the union went on strike. In some very exceptional circumstances, when changes must be made out of business necessity, the employer may institute unilateral changes without reaching an impasse, but those changes must be consistent with the offers made to the union, as held in *Raleigh Water Heating*.[30] The following case involves the application of the *Katz* decision.

---

[26] 369 U.S. 736 (1962).

[27] 359 NLRB No. 30 (2012).

[28] *The Finley Hospital*, 359 NLRB No. 9 (2012).

[29] 337 U.S. 217 (1949).

[30] 136 NLRB 76 (1962).

» CASE 15.4

VISITING NURSE SERVICES OF WESTERN MASSACHUSETTS, INC. v. NLRB
177 F.3d 52 (1st Cir. 1999), *cert. denied*, 528 U.S. 1074 (2000)

Facts: VNS is a corporation that provides home-based nursing services. The collective bargaining agreement between VNS and the union representing its employees expired on October 31, 1992. Negotiations for a new agreement continued through March 1997. VNS proposed a 2 percent wage increase and to change from a weekly to a biweekly payroll system, to become effective on November 6, 1995. The union rejected the proposal but expressed a willingness to bargain about various proposed changes to the job classifications for the firm's nurses.

VNS presented a substantially identical proposal on December 6, 1995, but this proposal also granted VNS the sole and unqualified right to designate job classifications as it deemed necessary based on operational needs. On February 29, 1996, VNS again offered the union a 2 percent wage increase, effective retroactively to November 6, 1995, in return for the union's agreement to its proposals for a biweekly payroll system and the job classification changes. The union again rejected the proposal. Nevertheless, on March 21, 1996, VNS notified the union that it intended to implement both the wage increase and the biweekly pay proposals. The union replied that it opposed the unilateral implementation of the biweekly payroll system. VNS implemented the wage increase on April 7, 1996, and the biweekly payroll system on May 3, 1996.

On June 18, 1996, VNS presented another proposal that included the proposed job classification changes and a second 2 percent wage increase, and two new provisions: on transforming three holidays into "floating" holidays to be taken at a time requested by the employee, and the implementation of a "clinical ladders" program. VNS also proposed a smaller, alternative package (the "mini package") that also included a second 2 percent wage increase along with the proposals on floating holidays and the clinical ladders program. The parties did not reach an agreement on either proposal, but VNS advised the union that it was contemplating implementing the "mini package." The union again informed VNS that it opposed the unilateral implementation of these proposals. VNS then sent a memo to the employees (but not to the union) informing them that it had implemented the mini package with the wage increase to be applied retroactively

to July 7, 1996. Ten days later, VNS notified the union that the wage increase had already been implemented and that the floating holidays and clinical ladders were "already in process."

The union filed unfair labor practice charges with the NLRB, which ultimately found that VNS violated Sections 8(a)(1) and (5) of the NLRA by unilaterally implementing:

- a bi-weekly payroll system on or about May 3, 1996;
- changes in holidays on or about September 6, 1996;
- a clinical ladder program on or about September 6, 1996; and
- changes in job classifications at some time subsequent to May 3, 1996.

VNS made these changes to mandatory subjects while it was still bargaining with the union and had not yet reached an impasse. VNS then sought review of the NLRB decision with the U.S. Court of Appeals for the First Circuit.

Issue: Did VNS's unilateral changes to mandatory bargaining subjects violate Sections 8(a)(1) and 8(a)(5) of the NLRA?

Decision: Before the NLRB, VNS argued that once it had given the union notice of its position on a particular issue and an opportunity to respond, it was free to unilaterally declare impasse on specific issues and to take action. The NLRB held when parties are engaged in negotiations for a collective bargaining agreement, an employer has the obligation to refrain from unilateral changes in the absence of an impasse. There are two limited exceptions to that general rule:

- when a union, in response to an employer's diligent and earnest efforts to engage in bargaining, insists on continually avoiding or delaying bargaining; or
- when economic exigencies or business emergencies compel prompt action by the employer.

The NLRB found that neither exception applied. The Supreme Court decision in *NLRB v. Katz* held that an employer must bargain to impasse before making unilateral changes to mandatory bargaining subjects. In *Litton*

Financial Printing Div. v. NLRB, the Court reaffirmed that "an employer commits an unfair labor practice if, without bargaining to impasse, it effects a unilateral change of an existing term or condition of employment."

The Court of Appeals rejected VNS's argument that parties are at impasse when the union rejects or does not accept the employer's position on a particular issue. Whether there is an impasse is an intensely fact-driven question, with the initial determination to be made by the NLRB. The Court of Appeals' role is to review the NLRB's factual determinations to determine whether they are supported by substantial evidence in the record as a whole. An impasse occurs when, after good faith bargaining, the parties are deadlocked so that any further bargaining would be futile. Collective bargaining involves give and take on a number of issues, and the effect of VNS's position would be to permit the employer to remove, one by one, issues from the table and impair the ability to reach an overall agreement through compromise on particular items. In addition, it would undercut the role of the union as the collective bargaining representative, effectively communicating that the union lacked the power to keep issues at the table. The Court of Appeals enforced the NLRB's order.

15-3b Permissive Bargaining Subjects

permissive bargaining subjects
those matters that are neither mandatory nor illegal; the parties may, but are not required to, bargain over such subjects

The previous discussion dealt with mandatory bargaining subjects; the Supreme Court in *NLRB v. Wooster Div. of Borg-Warner Corp.*[31] also recognized that there are permissive subjects and prohibited subjects. **Permissive bargaining subjects** are those matters not directly related to wages, hours, or terms and conditions of employment, and not prohibited. Either party may raise permissive items in bargaining, but such matters cannot be insisted upon to the point of impasse. If the other party refuses the permissive-item proposal, it must be dropped. *Borg-Warner* held that insisting upon permissive items to impasse and conditioning agreement on mandatory subjects upon agreement to permissive items was a violation of the duty to bargain in good faith. An interest arbitration clause in the collective bargaining agreement, which would require that all future contract disputes be settled by an arbitrator rather than by a strike or lockout, was held to be a permissive bargaining subject. The employer's insistence that the union agree to the interest arbitration clause as a condition of the employer signing the collective bargaining agreement was a violation of Section 8(a)(5), according to *Laidlaw Transit, Inc.*[32] Other examples of permissive items are proposals regarding:

- Union procedure for ratifying contracts
- Attempts to modify the union certification
- Strike settlement agreements
- Corporate social or charitable activities
- Requiring a transcript of all bargaining sessions
- Employer participation in an industry-wide promotion campaign

Matters that are "inherent management rights" or "inherent union rights" are also permissive subjects. An employer is under no duty to bargain over changes in permissive subjects; according to the Supreme Court opinion in *Allied Chemical & Alkalai Workers v. PPG*, cited earlier, and unilateral changes on permissive subjects are not unfair practices.

---

[31] 356 U.S. 342 (1958).

[32] 323 NLRB 867 (1997).

15-3c   Prohibited Bargaining Subjects

Prohibited bargaining subjects are proposals that involve violations of the NLRA or other laws. Examples would be a union attempt to negotiate a closed shop provision or to require an employer to agree to a "hot cargo clause" prohibited by Section 8(e) of the act. Any attempt to bargain over a prohibited subject may violate Section 8(a)(5) or Section 8(b)(3); any agreement reached on such items is null and void. It should be clear that prohibited subjects may not be used to precipitate an impasse.

Concept *Summary* 15.2

BARGAINING SUBJECTS

Mandatory Bargaining Subjects	Permissive Bargaining Subjects	Prohibited Bargaining Subjects
Matters related to wages, hours, terms and conditions of employment	Anything that is neither a mandatory nor a prohibited bargaining subject	Proposals that involve a violation of the NLRA or other laws
Parties cannot make a unilateral change of a mandatory subject until bargaining in good faith to impasse	Parties cannot insist on permissive subjects to the point of impasse	Any attempt to bargain over a prohibited subject is a violation of the duty to bargain in good faith

15-3d   Modification of Collective Agreements

Section 8(d) of the act prohibits any modifications or changes in a collective agreement's provisions relating to mandatory bargaining subjects during the term of the agreement unless both parties to the agreement consent to such changes. (When the agreement has expired, either party may implement changes in the mandatory subjects covered by the agreement after having first bargained, in good faith, to impasse.)

In *Milwaukee Spring Div. of Illinois Coil Spring*,[33] the question before the NLRB was whether the employer's action to transfer its assembly operations from its unionized Milwaukee Spring facility to its nonunion operations in Illinois during the term of a collective agreement was a violation of Sections 8(a)(1), 8(a)(3), and 8(a)(5). The transfer of operations was made because of the higher labor costs of the unionized operations. As a result of the transfer, the employees at Milwaukee Spring were laid off. Prior to the decision to relocate operations, the employer had advised the union that it needed reductions in wages and benefit costs because it had lost a major customer, but the union had rejected any concessions. The employer had also proposed terms upon which it would retain operations in Milwaukee, but again, the union had rejected the proposals and declined to bargain further over alternatives to transfer. The NLRB had initially held that the actions constituted a violation of Sections 8(a)(1), 8(a)(3), and 8(a)(5); but on rehearing, the Board reversed the prior decision and found no violation. The majority of the Board reasoned that the decision to transfer operations did not constitute a unilateral modification of the collective

---

[33] 268 NLRB 601 (1984).

agreement in violation of Section 8(d) because no term of the agreement required the operations to remain at the Milwaukee Spring facility. Had there been a work-preservation clause stating that the functions the bargaining unit employees performed must remain at the Milwaukee plant, the employer would have been guilty of a unilateral modification of the collective agreement, in violation of Section 8(d). The employer's offers to discuss concessions and the terms upon which it would retain operations in Milwaukee satisfied the employer's duty to bargain under Section 8(a)(5). The majority also held that the layoff of the unionized employees after the operations were transferred did not violate Section 8(a)(3). The effect of their decision, reasoned the majority, would be to encourage "realistic and meaningful collective bargaining that the Act contemplates." The dissent argued that the employer was prohibited from transferring operations during the term of the agreement without the consent of the union. The Court of Appeals for the D.C. Circuit affirmed the majority's decision in *U.A.W. v. NLRB.*[34]

Plant Closing Legislation

Because of concerns over plant closings, Congress passed the Worker Adjustment and Retraining Notification Act (WARN) in August 1988. The law, which went into effect February 4, 1989, requires employers with 100 or more employees to give 60 days' advance notice prior to any plant closings or mass layoffs. The employer must give written notice of the closing or mass layoff to the employees or their representative, to the state economic development officials, and to the chief elected local government official. WARN defines a plant closing as being when 50 or more employees lose their jobs during any 30-day period, because of a permanent plant closing, or a temporary shutdown exceeding six months. A plant closing may also occur when 50 or more employees experience more than a 50 percent reduction in the hours of work during each month of any six-month period. **Mass layoffs** are defined as layoffs creating an employment loss during any 30-day period for 500 or more employees or for 50 or more employees who constitute at least one-third of the full-time labor force at a unit of the facility. The act also requires a 60-day notice when a series of employment losses adds up to the requisite levels over a 90-day period. The notice requirement has two exceptions. One exception is the so-called **failing firm exception**, when the employer can demonstrate that giving the required notice would prevent the firm from obtaining capital or business necessary to maintain the operation of the firm. The other exception is when the work loss is due to "unforeseen circumstances."

Although the legislation speaks of plant closings, and Congress had industrial plant closings as a primary concern when passing WARN, the courts have held that it applies to employers such as law firms, brokerage firms, hotels, and casinos. The act imposes a penalty for failure to give the required notice; the employer is required to pay each affected employee up to 60 days' pay and benefits if the required notice is not given. The act also provides for fines of up to $500 for each day the notice is not given, up to a maximum of $30,000. However, the fines can be imposed only in suits brought by local governments against the employer. WARN does not create any separate enforcement agency, nor does it give any enforcement authority to the Department of Labor.

The act requires only that advance notice of the plant closings or mass layoffs be given; it does not require that the employer negotiate over the decision to close or lay off. To that

mass layoffs
layoffs creating an employment loss during any 30-day period for 500 or more employees or for 50 or more employees who constitute at least one-third of the full-time labor force at a unit of the facility

failing firm exception
an exception to the WARN notice requirement for layoffs that occurs when the employer can demonstrate that giving the required notice would prevent the firm from obtaining capital or business necessary to maintain the operation of the firm

---

[34] 765 F.2d 175 (1985).

extent, WARN does not affect the duty to bargain under the NLRA or the results of the *First National Maintenance* decision.

ethical DILEMMA

POSSIBLE PLANT CLOSINGS—TO MEET OR NOT TO MEET?

You are the human resource manager at Immense Multinational Business's production facility located in Utica, New York. The Utica plant is 75 years old. The plant is profitable, but barely so. Its production costs are the highest in the corporation's manufacturing division. The workers at the Utica facility are unionized, and the wages at Utica are higher than at most of the company's other manufacturing plants. But the utility costs, real estate taxes, and New York workers' compensation and unemployment insurance payroll taxes at the Utica plant are very high and are the main reasons for the plant's high production costs.

The company has recently opened a manufacturing plant in Puerto Rico. Corporate headquarters is considering expanding the production at that facility by transferring production from the Utica plant. The Utica workers have heard rumors that the plant will be closed. The officials of the local union at the Utica plant offer to meet with you to discuss the plant closing rumors and concessions that they are willing to make to keep the Utica plant open. Should you meet with them to discuss the plant closing and possible concessions? What arguments can you make for meeting with the union? What arguments can you make for not meeting with the union? Would refusing to meet and discuss those matters with the union be an unfair labor practice? Prepare a memo for corporate headquarters addressing these questions.

The Duty to Furnish Information

In *NLRB v. Truitt Mfg.*,[35] the Supreme Court held that an employer that pleads inability to pay in response to union demands must provide some financial information in an attempt to support that claim. The Court reasoned that such a duty was necessary if bargaining was to be meaningful; the employer is not allowed to "hide behind" claims that it cannot afford the union's pay demands. The rationale behind this requirement is that the union will be able to determine if the employer's claims are valid. If so, the union will moderate its demands accordingly.

The *Truitt* requirement to furnish information is not a "truth-in-bargaining" requirement. It relates only to claims of financial inability to meet union proposals. If the employer pleads inability to pay, the union must make a good faith demand for financial information supporting the employer's claim. In responding to the union request, the employer need not provide all the information requested by the union, but it must provide financial information in a reasonably usable and accessible form.

---

[35] 351 U.S. 149 (1956).

While the *Truitt* duty relates to financial information when the employer has pleaded inability to pay, another duty to furnish information is far greater in scope. Information relating to the enforcement and administration of the collective agreement must be provided to the union. This information is necessary for the union to perform its role as collective representative of the employees. This duty continues beyond negotiations to cover grievance arbitration during the life of the agreement as well. Such information includes:

- Wage scales

- Factors entering into compensation

- Job rates

- Job classifications

- Statistical data on the employer's minority employment practices

- A list of the names and addresses of the employees in the bargaining unit

The employer's refusal to provide the union with a copy of the contract for the sale of the employer's business was a violation of Section 8(a)(5) when the union sought the contract to determine whether the employees were adequately provided for after the sale and the union had agreed to keep the sales information confidential and to allow the employer to delete the sale price from the contract, according to *NLRB v. New England Newspapers, Inc.*[36] Employers using toxic substances have been required to furnish unions with information on the generic names of substances used, their health effects, and toxicological studies. Employers are not required to turn over medical records of identified individual employees. To safeguard the privacy of individual employees, the courts have required that individual employees must consent to the disclosure of individual health records and scores on aptitude or psychological tests. An employer is entitled, however, to protect trade secrets and confidential information such as affirmative action plans or privately developed psychological aptitude tests.

Information provided to the union does not have to be in the exact format requested by the union, but it must be in a form that is not burdensome to use or interpret. An employer may not prohibit union photocopying of the information provided, according to *Communications Workers Local 1051 v. NLRB.*[37] However, in *SDBC Holdings, Inc. v. NLRB,*[38] the court of appeals held that an employer had satisfied its obligation to provide information by allowing the union multiple opportunities to examine the company's audited financial statement, and was not required to allow the union to retain a copy of that financial statement.

We have seen that the requirements of the duty to bargain in good faith reflect a balance between promoting industrial peace and recognizing the principle of freedom of contract. To preserve the voluntary nature of collective bargaining, the Board and the courts will not require either party to make a concession or agree to a proposal.

When the violation of Section 8(a)(5) or Section 8(b)(3) involves specific practices, such as the refusal to furnish information or the refusal to sign an already agreed-upon

---

[36] 856 F.2d 409 (1st Cir. 1988).

[37] 644 F.2d 923 (1st Cir. 1981).

[38] 711 F.3d 281 (2d Cir. 2013).

contract, the Board orders the offending party to comply. Likewise, when an employer has illegally made unilateral changes, the Board requires that the prior conditions be restored and any reduction in wages or benefits be paid back. However, if the violation of the duty to bargain in good faith involves either side's refusal to recognize or negotiate seriously with the other side, the Board is limited in remedies available. In such cases, the Board will issue a "cease-and-desist" order directing the offending party to stop the illegal conduct and a "bargaining order" directing the party to begin to negotiate in good faith. But the Board cannot require that the parties make concessions or reach an agreement; it can only require that the parties return to the bargaining table and make an effort to explore the basis for an agreement. The following case deals with the limits on the Board's remedial powers in bargaining-order situations.

CASE 15.5

H. K. PORTER CO. V. NLRB
397 U.S. 99 (1970)

Black, J.

After an election, respondent United Steelworkers Union was, on October 5, 1961, certified by the National Labor Relations Board as the bargaining agent for the employees at the Danville, Virginia, plant of the H. K. Porter Co. Thereafter negotiations commenced for a collective bargaining agreement. Since that time the controversy has seesawed between the Board, the Court of Appeals for the District of Columbia Circuit, and this Court. This delay of over eight years is not because the case is exceedingly complex, but appears to have occurred chiefly because of the skill of the company's negotiators in taking advantage of every opportunity for delay in an Act more noticeable for its generality than for its precise prescriptions. The entire lengthy dispute mainly revolves around the union's desire to have the company agree to "check off" the dues owed to the union by its members, that is, to deduct those dues periodically from the company's wage payments to the employees. The record shows, as the Board found, that the company's objection to a check off was not due to any general principle or policy against making deductions from employees' wages. The company does deduct charges for things like insurance, taxes, and contributions to charities, and at some other plants it has a check off arrangement for union dues. The evidence shows, and the court below found, that the company's objection was not because of inconvenience, but solely on the ground that the company was "not going to aid and comfort the union." Based on this and other evidence

the Board found, and the Court of Appeals approved the finding that the refusal of the company to bargain about the check off was not made in good faith, but was done solely to frustrate the making of any collective bargaining agreement. In May 1966, the Court of Appeals upheld the Board's order requiring the company to cease and desist from refusing to bargain in good faith and directing it to engage in further collective bargaining, if requested by the union to do so, over the check off.

In the course of that opinion, the Court of Appeals intimated that the Board conceivably might have required petitioner to agree to a check off provision as a remedy for the prior bad-faith bargaining, although the order enforced at that time did not contain any such provision. In the ensuing negotiations the company offered to discuss alternative arrangements for collecting the union's dues, but the union insisted that the company was required to agree to the check off proposal without modification. Because of this disagreement over the proper interpretation of the court's opinion, the union, in February 1967, filed a motion for clarification of the 1966 opinion. The motion was denied by the court on March 22, 1967, in an order suggesting that contempt proceedings before the Board would be the proper avenue for testing the employer's compliance with the original order. A request for the institution of such proceedings was made by the union, and in June 1967, the Regional Director of the Board declined to prosecute a contempt charge, finding that the employer had "satisfactorily complied with the affirmative requirements of the Order.". . . The union then filed in the Court of Appeals a motion for reconsideration of the earlier motion to clarify the 1966 opinion. The court granted that motion and issued a new opinion in which it held that in certain circumstances a "check off may be imposed as a remedy for bad-faith bargaining. The case was then remanded to the Board and on July 3, 1968, the Board issued a supplemental order requiring the petitioner to "[g]rant to the Union a contract clause providing for the check off of union dues. . . . The Board had found that the refusal was based on a desire to frustrate agreement and not on any legitimate business reason. On the basis of that finding the Court of Appeals approved the further finding that the employer had not bargained in good faith, and the validity of that finding is not now before us. Where the record thus revealed repeated refusals by the employer to bargain in good faith on this issue, the Court of Appeals concluded that ordering agreement to the check off clause "may be the only means of assuring the Board, and the court, that [the employer] no longer harbors an illegal intent."

In reaching this conclusion the Court of Appeals held that Section 8(d) did not forbid the Board from compelling agreement. That court felt that "Section 8(d) defines collective bargaining and relates to a determination of whether a . . . violation has occurred and not to the scope of the remedy which may be necessary to cure violations which have already occurred." We may agree with the Court of Appeals that as a matter of strict, literal interpretation of that section it refers only to deciding when a violation has occurred, but we do not agree that that observation justifies the conclusion that the remedial powers of the Board are not also limited by the same considerations that led Congress to enact Section 8(d). It is implicit in the entire structure of the Act that the Board acts to oversee and referee the process of collective bargaining, leaving the results of the contest to the bargaining strengths of the parties. It would be anomalous indeed to hold that while Section 8(d) prohibits the Board from relying on a refusal to agree as the sole evidence of bad faith bargaining, the Act permits the Board to compel agreement in that same dispute. The Board's remedial powers under Section 10 of the Act are broad, but they are limited to carry out the policies of the Act itself. One of these fundamental policies is freedom of contract. While the parties' freedom of contract is not absolute under the Act, allowing the Board to compel agreement when the parties themselves are unable to do so would violate the fundamental premise on which the Act is based—private bargaining under governmental supervision of the procedure alone, without any official compulsion over the actual terms of the contract.

In reaching its decision, the Court of Appeals relied extensively on the equally important policy of the Act that workers' rights to collective bargaining are to be secured. In this case the Court apparently felt that the employer was trying effectively to destroy the union by refusing to agree to what the union may have considered its most important demand. Perhaps the court, fearing that the parties might resort to economic combat, was also trying to maintain the industrial peace that the Act is designed to further. But the Act, as presently drawn, does not contemplate that unions will always be secure and able to achieve agreement even when their economic position is weak, nor that strikes and lockouts will never result from a bargaining to impasse. It cannot be said that the Act forbids an employer or a union to rely ultimately on its economic strength to try to secure what it cannot obtain through bargaining. It may well be true, as the Court of Appeals felt, that the present remedial powers of the Board are insufficiently broad to cope with important labor problems. But it is the job of Congress, not the Board or the courts, to decide when and if it is necessary to allow governmental review of proposals for collective bargaining agreements and compulsory submission to one side's demands. The present Act does not envision such a process.

The judgment is reversed and the case is remanded to the Court of Appeals for further action consistent with this opinion.

Reversed and remanded.

Case Questions

1. Had the employer agreed to the union dues check-off clause? Why did the court of appeals hold that the NLRB had the power to impose a check-off clause on the employer?

2. Does the Supreme Court agree that the NLRB has the power to impose the check-off clause? Why?

3. In light of this Supreme Court decision, what is the extent of the NLRB's power to remedy violations of the duty to bargain in good faith?

Because of the limitations on the NLRB's remedial powers in bargaining cases, an intransigent party can effectively frustrate the policies of the NLRA. If a union or employer is willing to incur the legal expenses and possible contempt-of-court fines, it can avoid reaching an agreement with the other side. Although unions are occasionally involved in such situations, most often employers have more to gain from refusing to bargain. The legal fees and fines may amount to less money than the employer would be required to pay in wages under a collective agreement (and the legal expenses are tax deductible). Perhaps the most extreme example of such intransigence was the J. P. Stevens Company. In the late 1970s, the company was found guilty of numerous unfair practices and was subjected to a number of bargaining orders, yet in only one case did it reach a collective agreement with the union.

Extreme cases like J. P. Stevens are the exception, however. Despite the Board's remedial shortcomings, most negotiations culminate in the signing of a collective agreement. That fact is a testament to the vitality of the collective bargaining process and a vindication of a policy emphasis on the voluntary nature of the process.

THE **WORKING** LAW

NLRB Office of the General Counsel Memorandum GC 14-03

April 30, 2014

TO: All Regional Directors, Officers-in-Charge and Resident Officers
FROM: Richard F. Griffin, Jr., General Counsel
SUBJECT: Affirmation of 10(j) Program

An important priority of mine is to ensure that we continue our efforts to obtain immediate relief in those unfair labor practice cases that present a significant risk of remedial failure. Section 10(j) of the Act provides the tool to ensure that employees' Section 7 rights will be adequately protected from such failure. During my tenure as General Counsel, I intend to aggressively seek 10(j) relief where necessary to preserve the status quo and the efficacy of final Board orders, and I thank you for your continued dedication and effort in working to achieve this goal.

I am pleased to follow the most recent General Counsel and Acting General Counsel in emphasizing the need to seek 10(j) relief in particular types of cases. Specifically, in 2006, former General Counsel Meisburg instructed Regional Offices to "focus particular attention on remedies for violations that occur during the period after certification when parties are or should be bargaining for an initial collective bargaining agreement." Similarly, former Acting General Counsel Solomon re-affirmed that priority, instructing Regional Offices in 2011 to "continue to consider the propriety of 10(j) relief in all first-contract bargaining cases," and he also initiated a program "to ensure that effective remedies are achieved as quickly as possible when employees are unlawfully discharged or [become] victims of other serious unfair labor practices because of union organizing at their workplaces," establishing specific timelines to streamline processing of those cases.

These initiatives have led to extremely positive results. For instance, in fiscal years 2012 and 2013, we sought 10(j) relief in 19 first-contract bargaining cases and obtained bargaining orders in 16 of those cases for an average success rate of 84%.

. . . I fully endorse the initiatives of my predecessors and, based on the prior successes, I expect to obtain similar results. . . .

Effective enforcement of the Act requires that we protect employees' right to exercise their free choice regarding unionization, to participate in an election free of coercion, and to have their elected representative negotiate a first contract unencumbered by the impact of unfair labor practices. Cases involving a discharge during an organizing campaign or arising during negotiations for a first contract frequently require the most expeditious relief to ensure that employees are not irreparably deprived of those rights.

. . . I have a particular interest in seeking injunctive relief in appropriate cases involving a successor's refusal to bargain and, more importantly, successor refusal-to-hire cases. In many ways, successor cases present the same need for protection as those with a newly certified union. In both, the status of the employees' chosen collective-bargaining successor's refusal to bargain, unlawful conduct by a new employer that undermines the representative will lead to employee disaffection, concomitant loss of bargaining power, and loss of employee benefits that cannot be restored by a final Board order. And in cases where a successor employer refuses to hire employees to avoid bargaining with an incumbent union, the potential scattering of those employees creates an even greater risk that a final Board order will not effectively restore the parties to establish a good faith bargaining relationship. Because these types of cases should be given special emphasis, Regions should submit to the Injunction Litigation Branch a recommendation with respect to whether to seek 10(j) relief in all successorship cases in which a determination has been made to issue complaint. . . .

Thank you again for ensuring that our 10(j) program remains robust and successful so we can continue to provide timely, effective relief to the victims of unfair labor practices.
R.F.G.

Source: NLRB, Memorandum GC 14-03, http://www.nlrb.gov/reports-guidance/general-counsel-memos.

15-4   Antitrust Aspects of Collective Bargaining

When a union and a group of employers agree upon specified wages and working conditions, the effect may be to reduce competition among the employers with respect to those wages or working conditions. In addition, when the parties negotiate limits on subcontracting work or the use of prefabricated materials, the effect may be to reduce or prevent competition among firms producing these materials. Although the parties may be pursuing legitimate goals of collective bargaining, those goals may conflict with the policies of the antitrust laws designed to promote competition.

In the case of *U.S. v. Hutcheson*,[39] the Supreme Court held that a union acting in its self-interest, which does not combine with nonlabor groups, is exempt from the antitrust laws. *Hutcheson* involved union picketing of Anheuser-Busch and a call for a boycott of Anheuser-Busch products as a result of a dispute over work-assignment decisions. The Court ruled that such conduct was legal as long as it was not done in concert with nonlabor groups.

The scope of the labor relations exemption from the antitrust laws was further clarified by the Supreme Court in *Amalgamated Meat Cutters v. Jewel Tea Co.*[40] In that case, the

[39] 312 U.S. 219 (1941).
[40] 381 U.S. 676 (1965).

union and a group of grocery stores negotiated restrictions on the hours its members would work, since the contract required the presence of union butchers for fresh meat sales. The effect of the agreement was to restrict the hours during which the grocery stores could sell fresh (rather than prepackaged) meat. Jewel Tea argued that such a restriction of competition among the grocery stores violated the Sherman Antitrust Act. The Supreme Court held that since the union was pursuing its legitimate interests—that is, setting hours of work through a collective bargaining relationship—and did not act in concert with one group of employers to impose restrictions on another group of employers, the contract did not violate the Sherman Act.

Despite the broad scope of the antitrust exemption for labor relations activities, several cases have held unions in violation of the antitrust laws. In *United Mine Workers v. Pennington*,[41] the union agreed with one group of mine operators to impose wage and pension demands on a different group of mines. The union and the first group of mine owners were held by the Court to have been aware that the second group, composed of smaller mining operations, would be unable to meet the demands and could be forced to cease operations. The Supreme Court stated that if the union had agreed with the first group of employers in order to eliminate competition from the smaller mines, the union would be in violation of the antitrust laws. Although the union, acting alone, could attempt to force the smaller mines to agree to its demands, the union lost its exemption from the antitrust laws when it combined with one group of employers to force demands on the second group.

In *Connell Construction Co. v. Plumbers Local 100*,[42] a union attempted to force a general contractor to agree to hire only plumbing subcontractors who had contracts with the union. The general contractor did not itself employ any plumbers, and the union did not represent the employees of the general contractor. The effect of the union demand would be to restrict competition among plumbing subcontractors. Nonunion firms, and even unionized firms that had contracts with other unions, would be denied access to plumbing jobs. The Supreme Court held that the union conduct was not exempt from the antitrust laws because the union did not have a collective bargaining relationship with Connell, the general contractor. Although a union may attempt to impose restrictions on employers with whom it has a bargaining relationship, it may not attempt to impose such restrictions on employers outside that bargaining relationship.

In *Brown v. Pro Football, Inc.*,[43] the U.S. Supreme Court held that the nonstatutory exemption from the antitrust laws continued past the expiration of the collective agreement and the point of impasse and lasted as long as a collective bargaining relationship existed. The Court therefore upheld the legality of salary restrictions imposed by the members of a multiemployer bargaining unit—the teams of the National Football League—unilaterally after the expiration of their collective agreement and after bargaining in good faith to impasse. The NFL rule requiring a player to wait for at least three full football seasons after high school graduation before being eligible to enter the NFL draft was held to be within the nonstatutory exemption from the antitrust laws in *Clarett v. National Football League*.[44] In

---

[41] 381 U.S. 657 (1965).

[42] 421 U.S. 616 (1975).

[43] 518 U.S. 231 (1996).

[44] 369 F.3d 124 (2d Cir. 2004).

summary, then, the parties are generally exempt from the antitrust laws when they act alone to pursue legitimate concerns within the context of a collective bargaining relationship. If a union agrees with one group of employers to impose demands on another group or if it attempts to impose work restrictions on employers outside a collective bargaining relationship, it is subject to the antitrust laws.

Concept *Summary* 15.3

UNION BARGAINING AND ANTITRUST LAW

Union Activity Exempt from Antitrust Law
Unions pursuing legitimate labor concerns in the context of a collective bargaining relationship

Unions acting in self-interest and not combining with nonlabor groups

Union Activity Subject to Antitrust Law
Unions attempting to impose restrictions outside of a collective bargaining relationship

Unions agreeing with one group of employers to impose restrictions on another group of employers

CHAPTER REVIEW

» Key Terms

collective bargaining	479	mandatory bargaining subjects	490	mass layoffs	498
impasse	489	permissive bargaining subjects	496	failing firm exception	498

» Summary

• The duty to bargain in good faith arises under Section 9(a) of the NLRA because of a union's status as exclusive bargaining agent. When a union demonstrates the support of a majority of the employees in the bargaining unit, both the union and the employer are required to bargain in good faith, as defined in Section 8(d).

• The NLRB presumptions regarding the union's majority status require that the employer recognize and bargain with the union for at least one year following the union's victory in a representation election or for a reasonable period of time following a voluntary recognition of the union by the employer. If the parties have negotiated a collective bargaining agreement, the presumption of union majority support continues for the length of the collective agreement or for the first three years of the agreement if it is for a longer term. After the expiration of the collective agreement, the employer must demonstrate a good faith doubt as to the union's majority support, based on some objective evidence, to refuse to bargain with the union.

- Bargaining in good faith, as defined in Section 8(d), requires that the parties meet and discuss matters with an open mind to explore the basis of an agreement. The parties are not required to make concessions or to reach an agreement.

- The NLRB has classified bargaining subject matter as either mandatory, permissive, or illegal. Attempts to negotiate illegal subjects, or taking an illegal subject to impasse, are a violation of the duty to bargain in good faith. Mandatory subjects are those that directly affect the wages, hours, and terms and conditions of employment of the employees in the bargaining unit; the parties are required to discuss such issues and, after reaching impasse, may strike or lock out over mandatory subjects. Permissive subjects are those that are neither mandatory nor illegal; while the parties are free to discuss these matters, they cannot take permissive subjects to impasse.

- The NLRB's remedies for violations of the duty to bargain in good faith are limited to cease-and-desist orders; the NLRB cannot order parties to reach an agreement, nor can it impose contractual terms on the parties.

» Problems

» Questions

1. Under what circumstances may an employer whose employees are unionized bargain legally with individual employees?

2. Must an employer refuse to bargain with either union when two unions are seeking to represent the employer's workers? Explain your answer.

3. What are mandatory bargaining subjects? What is the significance of an item being classified as a mandatory bargaining subject?

4. When is an employer required to provide financial information to a union?

5. What conduct by unions is subject to the antitrust laws?

» Case Problems

6. During bargaining, the employer reached an impasse on (a) a detailed "management rights" clause, (b) a broad "zipper" clause, (c) a waiver-of-past-practices provision, and (d) a no-strike provision. The employer's final economic offer consisted of an increase of 10 cents per hour for seven of the nine bargaining unit employees and a wage review for the remaining two.

Based on these facts, the NLRB concluded that the employer had engaged in mere surface bargaining and condemned the employer's final proposals as "terms which no self respecting union could be expected to accept." The company appealed the case to the Ninth Circuit.

If you had sat on the panel at the appellate court level, would you have agreed or disagreed with the board's conclusions? [See *NLRB v. Tomco Communications, Inc.*, 567 F.2d 871, 97 L.R.R.M. 2660 (9th Cir. 1978).]

7. The personnel department at an electrical utility had a policy of giving all new employees a "psychological aptitude test." The union demanded access to the test questions, answers, and individual scores for the employees in the bargaining unit. The union pointed out that among similar types of information that the NLRB had ordered disclosed in other cases were seniority lists, employees' ages, names

and addresses of successful and unsuccessful job applicants, information about benefits received by retirees under employer's pension and insurance plans, information on employee grievances, and information on possible loss of work due to a proposed leasing arrangement.

The company claimed that if it released the information the union sought, its test security program would be severely compromised. Furthermore, employee confidence in the confidentiality of the testing program would be shattered.

How do you think the NLRB would rule in this case? [See *Detroit Edison Co. v. NLRB*, 440 U.S. 301, 100 L.R.R.M. 2728 (1979).]

8. During negotiations for renewing the collective agreement, the union representing the employees at Mercy Hospital presented a proposal that the hospital cafeteria be open for all employees from the hours of 6:30 a.m.–8:00 p.m. and 2:00 a.m.–4:00 a.m. The cafeteria had been open for those hours for the past ten years, but the hospital had considered closing it overnight. The union argued that there were approximately 175 employees working the overnight shift, and many of them used the cafeteria for lunch and breaks. The hospital responded that the cafeteria had been losing money during the 2:00 a.m.–4:00 a.m. operations. The union proposal was made on May 15, 2007; on May 19, without any notice to and discussions with the union, the hospital closed the cafeteria overnight. The hospital installed additional vending machines and provided a toaster and microwave for use by the employees. The union filed an unfair labor practice complaint with the NLRB over the hospital's closing of the cafeteria overnight.

How should the NLRB rule on the complaint? Was the hospital required to bargain with the union over the decision to close the cafeteria overnight? Why? [See *Mercy Hospital of Buffalo*, 311 NLRB 869 (1993).]

9. Sonat Marine was engaged in the business of transporting petroleum and petrochemical products. The Seafarers International Union (SIU) represented two separate bargaining units of Sonat's employees. One unit consisted of licensed employees—that is, the tugboat masters, mates, and pilots. In 2004, Sonat advised the union that it intended to withdraw recognition of the SIU as the bargaining representative of these licensed personnel at the expiration of the current collective bargaining agreement. Sonat's stated reason was that it had determined that these personnel were supervisors who were not subject to the NLRA as employees. The union demanded information on the factual basis for Sonat's position. Sonat refused to provide a response.

The union filed an unfair labor practice charge, asserting that Sonat was not bargaining in good faith. Was the union right? [See *Sonat Marine, Inc.*, 279 NLRB 100 (1986).]

10. Pratt-Farnsworth, Inc., a unionized construction contractor in New Orleans, owned a nonunion subsidiary, Halmar. During negotiations of a new collective bargaining agreement with Pratt Farnsworth, the Carpenters' Union demanded that the company provide information concerning Halmar's business activities; the union was suspicious that the subsidiary was being used by the parent to siphon off work that could have been done by union members.

If you represented the union, what arguments would you make to support your demand for information? If you were on the company's side, how would you respond? [See *Carpenters Local 1846 v. Pratt-Farnsworth, Inc.*, 690 F.2d 489, 111 L.R.R.M. 2787 (5th Cir. 1982).]

11. The company and the union commenced collective bargaining in April 2003. After four sessions, the company submitted, on June 15, a contract package for union ratification. Two days later, the union's membership rejected the package. No strike ensued.

Following rejection, the union's chief negotiator contacted the company and pointed out four stumbling blocks to ratification: union security, wages, overtime pay, and sickness and accident benefits. On July 7, the company resubmitted its original contract package unchanged. The union agreed to put it to a second ratification vote. However, before the vote took place, the company's president withdrew the package from the bargaining table. His reasoning was that the union's failure to strike indicated that the company had earlier overestimated the union's economic power. When in subsequent bargaining sessions the company proposed wages and benefits below those in the original package, the union charged it with bad faith bargaining.

How should the NLRB have ruled on this complaint? [See *Pennex Aluminum Corp.*, 271 NLRB 1205 (1984).]

12. For more than 30 years without challenge by the union, the Brod & McClung-Pace Co.'s bargaining unit employees performed warranty work at customers' facilities. Then the international union altered its constitution to forbid its members to do such warranty work. Pursuant to this constitutional change, the local union, which was subject to the international's constitution, sought a midterm modification of its collective bargaining agreement with the company to eliminate the warranty work. When the firm refused, the union sought to achieve a unilateral change by threatening its members with court-collectible fines if they continued to perform the work.

Did the union violate the NLRA? If so, how? [See *Sheet Metal Workers Int'l. Ass'n., Local 16*, 270 NLRB 116 (1984).]

13. After five sessions of multiemployer bargaining, the Carpenters' Union and the Lake Charles District of the Associated General Contractors of Louisiana reached a new agreement. However, the printed contract inadvertently omitted a "weather clause," which was to state that an employee who reported for work but was sent home because of inclement weather would get four hours' pay, and an employee sent home because of weather after having started work would get paid only for hours actually worked, but not less than two hours. When the omission was discovered, the contract was already ratified and signed. The union refused to add the clause. The company then asked to reopen bargaining over the wage and reporting clauses that were affected by the omission. The union refused.

Who, if anyone, has committed an unfair labor practice? [See *International Brotherhood of Carpenters Local 1476*, 270 NLRB 1432 (1984).]

14. The production workers at Molded Products Co., represented by the Allied Workers Union, went on strike in June 2002, after their collective agreement expired. The strike lasted two months, and during the strike, almost half of the 150 workers crossed the picket line and returned to work. When the

strike ended, the company recalled 60 of the strikers and operated with a work force of 135. Some of the workers then circulated a petition stating that they no longer wished to be represented by the union, and 70 of the workers signed it. The company then notified the union that it was withdrawing recognition and refused to bargain with the union over renewing the collective agreement. The union filed a complaint with the NLRB, arguing that the company's withdrawal of recognition violated Sections 8(a)(1) and (5).

How should the NLRB rule on the complaint? Why? Explain your answer. [See *Quazite Div. of Morrison Molded Fiberglass Co. v. NLRB*, 87 F.3d 493 (D.C. Cir. 1996).]

15. Plymouth Stamping, an automotive parts company located in Michigan, decided to contract out its parts assembly operations in response to deteriorating sales and financial conditions. It notified the union on February 11, 2008, of its plans to subcontract. The notice stated that the operation would be discontinued as of February 15, that the assembly operation employees would be either laid off or transferred, and that the action was necessary "due to economic and business reasons." The union requested a meeting, which was held on February 14, 2008. At this meeting, the company explained that the action was the result of a number of factors, including declining sales, noncompetitive wage rates, burdensome state taxes, and high workers' compensation costs. The company, in response to a question concerning possible ways to retain the jobs, stated that the union would have to accept substantial wage cuts, a cost-of-living freeze, a reduction in some benefits, and a modification in work rules. The union requested that the company delay any action until at least the following week; the company, while stating that its decision was not final, requested a reply from the union by February 15 as to whether it would agree to concessions. The union failed to respond by February 15, and over the weekend (February 16 and 17), the company moved its assembly equipment to a plant in Ohio. Meanwhile, unbeknownst to the company, the union, in a letter dated February 14, had requested information regarding the specifics

of the decision. The company received the union's letter on February 20. The company responded to the union's letter on March 11; it stated that the decision was not irreversible and that it was prepared to discuss the matter with the union. The company repeated that the decision to subcontract was taken because "assembly operations are labor intensive and the costs (wages/benefits) associated with supporting this labor group have made the company noncompetitive." On March 1, the company entered into a formal leasing agreement with the subcontracting company; the lease allowed the company to terminate the lease and repossess the equipment and gave the subcontractor the option to purchase the equipment. The subcontractor purchased the equipment on July 1, 1980. The union filed an unfair labor practice complaint with the NLRB, charging the company with violations of Sections 8(a)(1) and 8(a)(5) for failing to bargain over a mandatory subject of bargaining and making a unilateral change in a mandatory subject without bargaining to impasse.

How should the NLRB decide the union's complaint? What would have been the effect of the WARN law if it had applied to this case? [See *NLRB v. Plymouth Stamping Division, Eltec Corp.*, 870 F.2d 1112 (6th Cir. 1989).]

» Hypothetical Scenarios

16. During the negotiations between the employer, Spina Mfg., and the union representing Spina's employees, the union representative noted that the company did not have an employee assistance program (EAP), although it did have a drug and alcohol policy. Parker, Spina's manager replied that the company's health insurance program addressed such employee issues and said that he did not favor instituting an EAP. After a fatal employee accident in the workplace, Parker contacted TriCity Family Services, a local social services agency, to launch an EAP for employees. Parker did not notify the union about the EAP before agreeing with TriCity to set up the program. At the next

negotiation session, Parker gave the union representatives a brochure and related information about the EAP, and told them that he instituted the program as result of the workplace accident. At the negotiation session held the next day, Parker asked the union representatives whether they had read the EAP information. The union representatives answered that they had not yet done so. The union did not offer a counterproposal to the EAP established by Parker. The union filed an unfair labor practice charge with the NLRB, alleging that the employer's unilateral decision to create the EAP was in violation of Section 8(a)(5). Spina's managers responded that its actions in creating the EAP were motivated solely by the desire to provide the employees with immediate grief counseling in light of the death of one of their fellow employees in the workplace accident. They also said that they did notify the union that they were willing to discuss and negotiate the program during their ongoing negotiations. Did Spina's unilateral creation of the EAP violate Section 8(a)(5)? Explain your answer.

17. Rodgers Graphics, a commercial printer, refused to bargain with the Communications Workers of America, Local 14, after its collective bargaining agreement expired. The company claimed that it had a good faith reasonable doubt of the union's majority status, based on the following facts:

    • The company's president, Doyle McDonald, gathered from frequent conversations with various employees that the employees were not happy with the union.

    • Cynthia Termath, an employee who served as one of two union stewards, told McDonald that most employees had lost confidence in the union, did not think it was representing them well, no longer wanted the union to represent them, and were generally dissatisfied with it. Termath gained her information from her conversations with about 60 other employees.

    • Ignacio Burgos, the other union steward, also told McDonald that the employees were dissatisfied with the union.

- Company managers informed McDonald that there was a "lack of interest" in the union among employees.

Does Rodgers's refusal to bargain with the union violate Sections 8(a)(1) and 8(a)(5) of the NLRA? Explain your answer.

18. Lakeland Bus Lines, Inc. is a private bus company whose drivers are represented by the Amalgamated Transit Union, Local 164. The parties' collective agreement expired on January 31, 2007. In February, when negotiations on a new agreement stalled, the company gave a final offer to the union. On the same day, Lakeland's president sent a letter to the bargaining unit employees detailing the company's bargaining position and its financial difficulties. The union then requested that the company provide financial information to verify that it could not afford any contract terms that exceeded the costs of its final offer. Company representatives refused to furnish any of the requested information. Lakeland's employees subsequently rejected the company's final offer, and the company unilaterally implemented the terms of its final offer. The union filed unfair labor practice charges with the NLRB, claiming that Lakeland had failed to bargain in good faith by refusing to provide financial information requested by the union and by unilaterally imposing the terms of its final offer. How should the NLRB rule on the union's complaint? Why?

19. Callahan Construction Co. and the Carpenters' Union had concluded negotiations for a new collective agreement covering Callahan's employees, when the union representative informed Callahan that the union would not agree to the final contract wage proposal unless the employer joined the Green Builders Association and agreed to promote energy-efficient and environmentally friendly construction techniques. Does the union's demand violate the duty to bargain in good faith? Explain your answer.

20. Local No. 580 of the Teamsters Union was certified by the NLRB as the exclusive bargaining representative for the employees of Adams Potato Chip Co. At subsequent negotiations for a collective agreement covering the employees, the union negotiators indicated that they would accept the company's proposal if the company agreed to change its offer of three weeks' vacation for workers with at least 15 years of service to three weeks' vacation after 10 years of service. The company's lead negotiator agreed to the change and the parties held that the negotiations were completed. The company president later refused to sign the written agreement, claiming that the company negotiator lacked authority to agree to the change in vacation policy. Has the company violated Section 8(a)(5)? Explain.

CHAPTER **16**

Picketing and Strikes

Collective bargaining involves economic conflict: Each party to the negotiations seeks to protect its economic interests by extracting concessions from the other side. Both union and management back up their demands with the threat of pressure tactics that would inflict economic harm upon the other party. If the negotiations reach an impasse, the union may go on strike, or the employer may lock employees out to force concessions. This chapter discusses the limitations placed on the use of such pressure tactics.

16-1 Pressure Tactics

pressure tactics
union pressure tactics involve strikes and calls for boycotts, while employers may resort to lockouts

picketing
placing persons outside an employer's premises to convey information to the public via words, signs, or distributing literature

patrolling
the movement of persons back and forth around an employer's premises

strike
the organized withholding of labor by workers—the traditional weapon by which workers attempt to pressure employers

Pressure tactics include:

- Picketing
- Patrolling
- Strikes
- Boycotts by unions
- Lockouts by employers

Picketing is the placing of persons outside the premises of an employer to convey information to the public. The information may be conveyed by words, signs, or the distribution of literature. Picketing is usually accompanied by **patrolling**, which is the movement of persons back and forth around the premises of an employer. A **strike**—the organized withholding of labor by workers—is the traditional weapon by which workers attempt to pressure employers. If the strike is successful, the economic harm resulting from the cessation of production will force the employer to accede to the union's demands. Strikes are usually accompanied by picketing and patrolling as means of enforcing the strike. Unions may also instigate a *boycott* of the employer's product to increase the economic pressure upon the employer.

Employers are free to replace employees who go on strike. If the strike is an economic strike, replacement may be permanent. Employers are also free to lock out the employees—that is, to intentionally withhold work from them—to force the union to make concessions. An employer may resort to a lockout only after bargaining in good faith to an impasse. However, the bargaining dispute must be over a mandatory bargaining subject. Limitations on the right of an employer to lock out are discussed in Chapter 14 in the cases of *NLRB v. Brown* and *American Shipbuilding v. NLRB*.

Strikes may be economic strikes or unfair labor practice strikes. (The rights of the striking workers to reinstatement and their protection under the National Labor Relations Act [NLRA] is discussed in Chapter 14.) Strikes in violation of contractual no-strike clauses may give rise to union liability for damages and to judicial "back-to-work" orders. (The enforcement of no-strike clauses is discussed in Chapter 17.) The focus in this chapter is on economic strikes and picketing. When the word "strike" is used, it refers to an economic strike unless otherwise specified.

16-1a Strikes in the Health-Care Industry

Section 8(g) of the NLRA provides that any union must give written notice of any strike, picketing, or any other concerted refusal to work against any health-care institution at least 10 days prior to the beginning of the strike or picketing. The notice must be given to the employer and to the Federal Mediation and Conciliation Service and must indicate the date and time the strike or picketing will commence. The purpose of this notice requirement is to allow the health-care institution to make arrangements for patient care that could be affected by the strike or picketing. The notice may be extended by the written agreement of both the union and the health-care employer. A union that unilaterally delays the start of a strike beyond the time specified in the written notice violates Section 8(g). Employees who engage in a strike in violation of the notice requirements of Section 8(g) lose their status as employees under the NLRA, and may be discharged for such conduct, as in *Minnesota Licensed Practical Nurses Assn.*[1] A union giving only four days' notice before its members collectively declined to work overtime was held to have violated Section 8(g).[2]

However, in *Civil Service Employees Association, Local 1000 v. National Labor Relations Board*,[3] employees who participated in peaceful picketing at a health-care institution without giving the appropriate notice did not lose status as employees under the NLRA because they were not engaged in a strike.

16-2 The Legal Protection of Strikes

There is no constitutional right to strike. In fact, courts have traditionally held strikes to be criminal conspiracies (see Chapter 12). Constitutional restrictions, however, apply only to government activity; private-sector strikes generally raise no constitutional issues. Strikes by private-sector employees are regulated by the NLRA and are protected activity under Section 7 of the act. For public-sector employees, there may be no right to strike (see Chapter 19).

Although there is no recognized constitutional right to strike, there is a constitutional right to picket. The courts have held that picketing involves the expression and communication of opinions and ideas and is therefore protected under the First Amendment's freedom of speech. In *Thornhill v. Alabama*,[4] the Supreme Court held a state statute that

---

[1] 406 F.3d 1020 (8th Cir. 2005).

[2] *SEIU, United Healthcare Workers-West v. N.L.R.B.*, 574 F.3d 1213 (9th Cir. 2009).

[3] 569 F.3d 88 (2d Cir. 2009).

[4] 310 U.S. 88 (1940).

prohibited all picketing, including even peaceful picketing, to be unconstitutional. Courts did, however, recognize that picketing involves conduct apart from speech so that there may be some reason for limitations upon the conduct of picketing. In *Teamsters Local 695 v. Vogt*,[5] the Supreme Court held that picketing, because it involves speech plus patrolling, may be regulated by the government more readily than pure speech activity.

16-2a   The Norris-La Guardia Act

As you recall from Chapter 12, the Norris-La Guardia Act, passed in 1932, severely restricted the ability of federal courts to issue injunctions in labor disputes. The act did not "protect" strikes; it simply restricted the ability of federal courts to issue injunctions. The act defines "labor dispute" very broadly to cover disputes even when the parties are not in an employer–employee relationship. Furthermore, the dispute need not be the result of economic concerns, as illustrated by *Jacksonville Bulk Terminals v. ILA*,[6] which held that the Norris-La Guardia Act does not exempt labor disputes that spring from political protests. Does the Norris-La Guardia Act apply to a suit by employees alleging that a lockout by their employers violates the antitrust laws? That question is addressed in the following case.

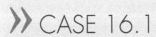

» CASE 16.1

Brady v. National Football League
644 F.3d 661 (8th Cir. 2011)

Facts: The National Football League [NFL] recognized the NFL Players Association [NFLPA] as the exclusive bargaining representative of all NFL players in 1968. Since then, the relationship between the League and its players has been punctuated by both collective bargaining agreements and antitrust lawsuits. The collective bargaining agreement [CBA] entered into by the NFL and NFLPA in 2006 was scheduled to continue through the end of the 2012–2013 season; the CBA also allowed either party to opt out of the final two years of it upon giving the other party written notice. In May 2008, the NFL gave the NFLPA written notice that it would opt out of the final two years of the CBA because of concerns about operating costs and other elements of the agreements. As a result, the CBA was scheduled to expire in early March 2011. Although the NFL and the NFLPA engaged in more than two years of negotiations toward a new CBA, the League and the players were unable to reach an agreement. On March 11, 2011,

the CBA expired. The NFL had announced that it would lockout the players if a new agreement was not reached before the expiration date; during the lockout the players would not be paid or permitted to use club facilities. The players, aware of the League's strategy, opted to terminate the union's status as their collective bargaining agent as of 4:00 p.m. on March 11, just before the agreement expired. Later that day, the players filed suit alleging that the lockout planned by the League would constitute a group boycott and price-fixing agreement that would violate § 1 of the Sherman Antitrust Act. The players also alleged other violations of the antitrust laws and state common law. The NFL instituted the lockout on March 12, 2011. The players sought a preliminary injunction in the federal district court, asking the court to enjoin the lockout as an unlawful group boycott. The district court granted a preliminary injunction, and the NFL appealed. On appeal, the NFL argued that the Norris-La Guardia Act [NLGA] prohibited

---

[5] 354 U.S. 284 (1957).

[6] 457 U.S. 702 (1982).

the district court from issuing an injunction. The players argued that the NLGA did not apply here because there was no union involved, and they were alleging violations of the antitrust laws.

Issue: Does the Norris-La Guardia Act apply to a suit seeking an injunction under the antitrust laws when no union is involved?

Decision: The NLGA was enacted by Congress in 1932. It limits the authority of federal district courts to issue injunctions in labor disputes except in the very limited circumstances set out in the act. The impetus for the NLGA was dissatisfaction with injunctions entered against workers in labor disputes, but the act also requires that an injunction against an employer participating in a labor dispute must conform to the provisions of the NLGA. The district court here held that the NLGA did not apply in this case because it did not involve or grow out of a labor dispute. Section 13(c) of the NLGA states that "[t]he term 'labor dispute' includes any controversy concerning terms or conditions of employment, or concerning the association or representation of persons in negotiating, fixing, maintaining, changing, or seeking to arrange terms or conditions of employment, regardless of whether or not the disputants stand in the proximate relation of employer and employee."). This suit involves a controversy concerning terms or conditions of employment. The players are seeking broad relief that would affect the terms or conditions of employment for the entire industry of professional football. In particular, they urge the court to declare unlawful and to enjoin several features of the relationship between the NFL

and the players, including the limit on compensation that can be paid to rookies, the salary cap, the "franchise player" designation, and the "transition player" designation, all of which the players assert are anticompetitive restrictions that violate § 1 of the Sherman Act. The district court did not appear to question this point.

The Supreme Court has observed that the NLGA definition of a labor dispute is extremely broad. Section 13(a) of the NLGA states that "[a] case shall be held to involve or grow out of a labor dispute when the case involves persons who are engaged in the same industry, trade, craft, or occupation." This case, involves persons engaged in the "same industry," namely, professional football. The statute continues that such a case "shall be held to involve or grow out of a labor dispute" when "such dispute is . . . between one or more employers or associations of employers and one or more employees or associations of employees." The dispute here is between one or more employers or associations of employers (the NFL and the NFL teams) and one or more employees (the players under contract). By the plain terms of the NLGA, this case "shall be held to involve or grow out of a labor dispute." In *New Negro Alliance v. Sanitary Grocery Co.* [303 U.S. 552] the Supreme Court ruled that the NLGA definition of a labor dispute is not limited to controversies involving unions or unionized employees. Because the NLGA does not require the present existence of a union to establish a labor dispute, the district court could only issue an injunction in compliance with the procedural requirements set out in the act. Because the district court did not comply with the NLGA, the court of appeals vacated the district court's injunction, and remanded the case to the district court.

Section 8 of the Norris-La Guardia Act also prohibits federal courts from issuing an injunction in a labor dispute if the employer seeking an injunction has failed to comply with any obligation imposed by law which is involved in the labor dispute in question, or has failed to make "every reasonable effort to settle such dispute either by negotiation or with the aid of any available governmental machinery of mediation or voluntary arbitration."[7]

The Norris-La Guardia Act applies only to federal courts, but a number of states passed similar legislation restricting the issuance of labor injunctions by their courts.

Some exceptions to the Norris-La Guardia restrictions have been recognized. Sections 10(j) and 10(l) of the NLRA authorize the National Labor Relations Board (NLRB) to seek injunctions against unfair labor practices. Section 10(h) of the NLRA provides that

---

[7] 29 U.S.C. § 108.

Norris-La Guardia does not apply to actions brought under Sections 10(j) and 10(l) or to actions to enforce NLRB orders in the courts. The Supreme Court upheld this exemption in the case of *Bakery Sales Drivers, Local 33 v. Wagshal.*[8] The ability to initiate or maintain an action for an injunction under Sections 10(j) or 10(l) is restricted to the NLRB, according to *Solien v. Misc. Drivers & Helpers Union, Local 610.*[9] Another exception to the Norris-La Guardia restrictions has been recognized when a union strikes over an issue that is subject to arbitration. That exception is discussed in Chapter 17.

16-2b The National Labor Relations Act

The National Labor Relations Act, as mentioned earlier, makes strikes protected activity. The NLRA also contains several provisions that deal with picketing. Section 8(b)(4) outlaws secondary boycotts, and Section 8(b)(7) prohibits recognitional picketing in some situations. In *NLRB v. Drivers, Chauffeurs, Helpers Local 639,*[10] the Supreme Court held that the NLRB may not regulate peaceful picketing that does not run afoul of Section 8(b)(4) or Section 8(b)(7). Section 8(b)(1)(A) may be used to prohibit union violence on the picket line, but it does not extend to peaceful picketing. As a result, NLRB regulation of picketing under the NLRA is limited to specific situations such as recognition picketing or secondary picketing.

State Regulation of Picketing

Although the NLRB role in regulating picketing is limited, the states enjoy a major role in the legal regulation of picketing. *Thornhill v. Alabama*, mentioned earlier, prohibited the states from banning all picketing, including peaceful picketing. In *Teamsters Local 695 v. Vogt*, also mentioned earlier, the Supreme Court held that the states may regulate picketing when it conflicts with valid state interests. The state's interest in protecting the safety of its citizens and enforcing the criminal law justifies state regulation of violent picketing. State courts may issue injunctions against acts of violence by strikers, but an outright ban on all picketing because of violence can be justified only when "the fear generated by past violence would survive even though future picketing might be wholly peaceful" according to the Supreme Court in *Milk Wagon Drivers, Local 753 v. Meadowmoor Dairies, Inc.*[11]

State courts may also issue injunctions against *mass picketing*—picketing in which pickets march so closely together that they block access to the plant—even though it is peaceful, as in *Westinghouse Electric Co. v. U.E., Local 410.*[12] Picketing intended to force an employer to join a conspiracy in violation of state antitrust laws may be enjoined by a state court, according to *Giboney v. Empire Storage & Ice Co.*[13] According to *Linn v. United Plant Guard Workers Local 114,*[14] state courts may also enjoin the use of language by pickets that constitutes fraud, misrepresentation, libel, or inciting a breach of the peace.

---

[8] 333 U.S. 437 (1948).

[9] 440 F.2d 124 (8th Cir. 1971), *cert. denied*, 403 U.S. 905 (1971), *rehearing denied*, 405 U.S. 996 (1972).

[10] 362 U.S. 274 (1960).

[11] 312 U.S. 287 (1941).

[12] 139 N.J. Eq. 97 (1946).

[13] 336 U.S. 490 (1949).

[14] 383 U.S. 53 (1966).

All of these cases involved picketing activity on public property. Can trespass laws be used to prohibit peaceful picketing on private property? That is the question addressed by the following case.

CASE 16.2

HUDGENS V. NLRB
424 U.S. 507 (1976)

Stewart, J.

The petitioner, Scott Hudgens, is the owner of the North DeKalb Shopping Center, located in suburban Atlanta, Ga. The center consists of a single large building with an enclosed mall. Surrounding the building is a parking area which can accommodate 2,640 automobiles. The shopping center houses 60 retail stores leased to various business. One of the lessees is the Butler Shoe Co. Most of the stores, including Butler's, can be entered only from the interior mall.

In January 1971, warehouse employees of the Butler Shoe Co. went on strike to protest the company's failure to agree to demands made by their union in contract negotiations. The strikers decided to picket not only Butler's warehouse but its nine retail stores in the Atlanta area as well, including the store in the North DeKalb Shopping Center. On January 22, 1971, four of the striking warehouse employees entered the center's enclosed mall carrying placards which read: "Butler Shoe Warehouse on Strike, AFL-CIO, Local 315." The general manager of the shopping center informed the employees that they could not picket within the mall or on the parking lot and threatened them with arrest if they did not leave. The employees departed but returned a short time later and began picketing in an area of the mall immediately adjacent to the entrances of the Butler store. After the picketing had continued for approximately 30 minutes, the shopping center manager again informed the pickets that if they did not leave they would be arrested for trespassing. The pickets departed.

The union subsequently filed with the Board an unfair labor practice charge against Hudgens, alleging interference with rights protected by Section 7 of the Act. Relying on this Court's decision in *Food Employees v. Logan Valley Plaza*, the Board entered a cease-and-desist order against Hudgens, reasoning that because the warehouse employees enjoyed a First Amendment right to picket on the shopping center property, the owner's threat of arrest violated Section 8(a)(1) of the Act. Hudgens filed a petition for review in the Court of Appeals for the Fifth Circuit. Soon thereafter this Court

decided *Lloyd Corp. v. Tanner, and Central Hardware Co. v. NLRB*, and the Court of Appeals remanded the case to the Board for reconsideration in light of those two decisions.

The Board, in turn, remanded to an Administrative Law Judge, who made findings of fact, recommendations, and conclusions to the effect that Hudgens had committed an unfair labor practice by excluding the pickets. This result was ostensibly reached under the statutory criteria set forth in *NLRB v. Babcock & Wilcox Co.*, a case which held that union organizers who seek to solicit for union membership may intrude on an employer's private property if no alternative means exist for communicating with the employees. But the Administrative Law Judge's opinion also relied on the Court's constitutional decision in *Logan Valley* for a "realistic view of the facts." The Board agreed with the findings and recommendations of the Administrative Law Judge, but departed somewhat from his reasoning. It concluded that the pickets were within the scope of Hudgens' invitation to members of the public to do business at the shopping center, and that it was, therefore, immaterial whether or not there existed an alternative means of communicating with the customers and employees of the Butler store.

Hudgens again petitioned for review in the Court of Appeals for the Fifth Circuit, and there the Board changed its tack and urged that the case was controlled not by Babcock & Wilcox, but by *Republic Aviation Corp. v. NLRB*, a case which held that an employer commits an unfair labor practice if he enforces a no-solicitation rule against employees on his premises who are also union organizers, unless he can prove that the rule is necessitated by special circumstances. The Court of Appeals enforced the Board's cease-and-desist order but on the basis of yet another theory. While acknowledging that the source of the pickets' rights was Section 7 of the Act, the Court of Appeals held that the competing constitutional and property right considerations discussed in *Lloyd Corp. v. Tanner*, "burde[n] the General Counsel with the duty to prove that other locations less intrusive upon Hudgens' property rights than picketing inside the mall were either unavailable or ineffective," and that the Board's General Counsel had met that burden in this case.

In this Court the petitioner Hudgens continues to urge that *Babcock & Wilcox Co.* is the controlling precedent, and that under the criteria of that case the judgment of the Court of Appeals should be reversed. The respondent union agrees that a statutory standard governs, but insists that, since the Section 7 activity here was not organizational as in *Babcock* but picketing in support of a lawful economic strike, an appropriate accommodation of the competing interests must lead to an affirmance of the Court of Appeals' judgment. The respondent Board now contends that the conflict between employee picketing rights and employer property rights in a case like this must be measured in accord with the commands of the First Amendment, pursuant to the Board's asserted understanding of *Lloyd Corp. v. Tanner*, and that the judgment of the Court of Appeals should be affirmed on the basis of that standard.

As the above recital discloses, the history of this litigation has been a history of shifting positions on the part of the litigants, the Board, and the Court of Appeals. It has been a history, in short, of considerable confusion, engendered at least in part by decisions of this Court that intervened during the course of the litigation. In the present posture of the case the most basic question is whether the respective rights and liabilities of the parties are to be decided under the criteria of the National Labor Relations Act alone, under a First Amendment standard, or under some combination of the two. It is to that question, accordingly, that we now turn.

It is, of course, a commonplace that the constitutional guarantee of free speech is a guarantee only against abridgment by government, federal or state.... [T]he rights and liabilities of the parties in this case are dependent exclusively upon the National Labor Relations Act. Under the Act the task of the Board, subject to review by the courts, is to resolve conflicts between Section 7 rights and private property rights, "and to seek a proper accommodation between the two." What is "a proper accommodation" in any situation may largely depend upon the content and the context of the Section 7 rights being asserted. The task of the Board and the reviewing courts under the Act, therefore, stands in conspicuous contrast to the duty of a court in applying the standards of the First Amendment, which requires "above all else" that expression must not be restricted by government "because of its message, its ideas, its subject matter, or its content."

In the *Central Hardware* case, and earlier in the case of *NLRB v. Babcock & Wilcox Co.*, the Court considered the nature of the Board's task in this area under the Act. Accommodation between employees' Section 7 rights and employers' property rights, the Court said in Babcock & Wilcox, "must be obtained with as little destruction of one as is consistent with the maintenance of the other."

Both *Central Hardware* and *Babcock & Wilcox* involved organizational activity carried on by nonemployees on the employers' property. The context of the Section 7 activity in the present case was different in several respects which may or may not be relevant in striking the proper balance. First, it involved lawful economic strike activity rather than organizational activity. Second, the Section 7 activity here was carried on by Butler's employees (albeit not employees of its shopping center store), not by outsiders. Third, the property interests impinged upon in this case were not those of the employer against whom the Section 7 activity was directed, but of another.

The *Babcock & Wilcox* opinion established the basic objective under the Act: accommodation of Section 7 rights and private property rights "with as little destruction of one as is consistent with the maintenance of the other." The locus of that accommodation, however, may fall at differing points along the spectrum depending on the nature and strength of the respective Section 7 rights and private property rights asserted in any given context. In each generic situation, the primary responsibility for making this accommodation must rest with the Board in the first instance. . . .

For the reasons stated in this opinion, the judgment is vacated and the case is remanded to the Court of Appeals with directions to remand to the National Labor Relations Board, so that the case may be there considered under the statutory criteria of the National Labor Relations Act alone.

It is so ordered.

Case Questions

1. With whom does the union have the dispute? Where is the union picketing? Who seeks to prevent the union from picketing there? What is the purpose of the union's picketing there?

2. According to the *Babcock & Wilcox* decision (see Chapter 14), what factors should the court consider in determining whether a union can picket on private property?

3. Are the picketers employees of Butler Shoe Co.? How does the picketing affect the employer's property rights?

Concept *Summary* 16.1

REGULATION OF PICKETING

- The Norris-La Guardia Act prohibits the federal courts from issuing injunctions in labor disputes
- The National Labor Relations Act allows the NLRB to seek injunctions in federal courts in certain situations:
  - The NLRB *must* seek an injunction when a complaint alleges violations of:
    - Section 8(b)(4)
    - Section 8(b)(7)
    - Section 8(e)
  - Section 10(j) provides that the NLRB *may* seek an injunction in other unfair labor practice cases
- State courts *may* issue injunctions against picketing in certain situations:
  - Violent picketing
  - Mass picketing
  - Use of picket signs involving language that constitutes fraud, misrepresentation, libel, or inciting a breach of the peace

16-2c Picketing Under the NLRA

As has been noted, Sections 8(b)(4) and 8(b)(7) of the NLRA prohibit certain kinds of picketing. Peaceful picketing is protected activity under the NLRA. However, violent picketing and mass picketing, as well as threatening conduct by the picketers, are not protected under Section 7. Employees who engage in such conduct may be disciplined or discharged by the employer and may also be subject to injunctions, criminal charges, and civil tort suits. Section 8(b)(7) regulates picketing by unions for organizational or recognitional purposes. Section 8(b)(4) deals with secondary boycotts—certain union pressure tactics aimed at employers that are not involved in a labor dispute with the union.

Section 8(b)(7): Recognitional and Organizational Picketing

Section 8(b)(7) was added to the NLRA by the 1959 Landrum-Griffin Act. It prohibits recognitional picketing by an uncertified union in certain situations. Section 8(b)(7) contains the following provisions:

> [It is an unfair practice for a labor organization] (7) to picket or cause to be picketed, or threaten to picket or cause to be picketed, any employer where an object thereof is forcing or requiring an employer to recognize or bargain with a labor organization as the representative of his employees, or forcing or requiring the employees of an employer to accept or select such labor organization as their collective-bargaining representative, unless such labor organization is currently certified as the representative of such employees:
>
> (A) where the employer has lawfully recognized in accordance with this Act any other labor organization and a question concerning representation may not appropriately be raised under Section 9(c) of this Act,
>
> (B) where within the preceding twelve months a valid election under Section 9(c) of this Act has been conducted, or

(C) where such picketing has been conducted without a petition under Section 9(c) being filed within a reasonable period of time not to exceed thirty days from the commencement of such picketing: *Provided*, That when such a petition has been filed the Board shall forthwith, without regard to the provisions of Section 9(c)(1) or the absence of a showing of a substantial interest on the part of the labor organization, direct an election in such unit as the Board finds to be appropriate and shall certify the results thereof: *Provided further*, That nothing in this subparagraph (C) shall be construed to prohibit any picketing or other publicity for the purpose of truthfully advising the public (including consumers) that an employer does not employ members of, or have a contract with, a labor organization, unless an effect of such picketing is to induce any individual employed by any other person in the course of his employment, not to pick up, deliver or transport any goods or not to perform any services.

Nothing in this paragraph (7) shall be construed to permit any act which would otherwise be an unfair labor practice under this Section 8(b).

The interpretation of Section 8(b)(7) and its application to recognitional picketing are the subjects of the following case.

If a union pickets in violation of Section 8(b)(7)(C), the employer may request that the NLRB hold an expedited election. The NLRB will determine the appropriate bargaining unit and hold an election. No showing of interest on the part of the union is necessary. The NLRB will certify the results of the election; if the union is certified, the employer must bargain with it. If the union loses, continued picketing will violate Section 8(b)(7)(B). Why? Section 10(1) requires the board to seek an injunction against the picketing when it issues a complaint for an alleged Section 8(b)(7) violation. In *International Transp. Serv. v. NLRB*,[15] a union picketing to force the employer to recognize a one-person bargaining unit

CASE 16.3

SMITLEY V. NLRB
327 F.2d 351 (U.S. Court of Appeals, 9th Cir. 1964)

[After the NLRB dismissed a complaint that the union had violated Section 8(b)(7)(C), the company sought judicial review of the Board's decision.]

Duniway, J.
The findings of the Board as to the facts are not attacked. It found, in substance, that the unions picketed the cafeteria for more than thirty days before filing a representation petition under Section 9(c) of the act, that an object of the picketing was to secure recognition, that the purpose of the picketing was truthfully to advise the public that petitioners employed nonunion employees or had no contract with the unions, and that the picketing did not have the effect of inducing any stoppage of deliveries or services to the cafeteria by employees of any other employer. . . . We conclude that the views of the Board, as stated after its second consideration of the matter, are correct, and that the statute has not been violated. . . .

It will be noted that Subdivision (7) of Subsection (b), Section 8, starts with the general prohibition of picketing "where an object thereof is forcing or requiring an employer to recognize or bargain with a labor organization" (this is often called

---

[15] 449 F.3d 160 (D.C. Cir. 2006).

recognitional picketing) "… or forcing or requiring the employees of an employer to accept or select such labor organization…." (this is often called organizational picketing), "…unless such labor organization is currently certified as the representative of such employees…." This is followed by three subparagraphs, (A), (B), and (C). Each begins with the same word, "where." (A) deals with the situation "where" the employer has lawfully recognized another labor organization and a question of representation cannot be raised under Section 9(c). (B) refers to the situation "where," within the preceding 12 months, a valid election under Section 9(c) has been conducted. (C) with which we are concerned, refers to a situation "where" there has been no petition for an election under Section 9(c) filed within a reasonable period of time, not to exceed thirty days, from the commencement of the picketing. Thus, Section 8(b)(7) does not purport to prohibit all picketing having the named "object" of recognitional or organizational picketing. It limits the prohibition of such picketing to three specific situations.

There are no exceptions or provisos in subparagraphs (A) and (B), which describe two of those situations. There are, however, two provisos in subparagraph (C). The first sets up a special procedure for an expedited election under Section 9(c).

The second is one with which we are concerned. It is an exception to the prohibition of "such picketing," i.e., recognitional or organizational picketing, being a proviso to a prohibition of such picketing "where" certain conditions exist. . . .

… We think that, in substance, the effect of the second proviso to subparagraph (C) is to allow recognitional or organizational picketing to continue if it meets two important restrictions: (1) it must be addressed to the public and be truthful and (2) it must not induce other unions to stop deliveries or services. The picketing here met those criteria….

[**The court affirmed the Board's dismissal of the complaint.**]

Case Questions

1. Why was the union picketing the cafeteria? How long had it been picketing?
2. What kind of picketing is allowed under the proviso to Section 8(b)(7)(C)? What two conditions must be met for picketing to fall under the proviso's protection?
3. Does the picketing in this case fall under the proviso?

was held to violate Section 8(b)(7)(C) because the NRLB will not accept petitions for certification of one-person units, so the union could not file a petition for an election within a reasonable period of time.

As Smitley emphasizes, not all recognitional picketing violates Section 8(b)(7). The proviso in Section 8(b)(7)(C) allows recognitional picketing directed at the public to inform them that the picketed employer does not have a contract with the union. Such picketing for publicity may continue beyond 30 days, unless it causes other employees to refuse to work. Picketing to protest substandard wages paid by an employer, as long as the union does not have a recognitional object, is not subject to Section 8(b)(7). Such picketing may continue indefinitely and is not unlawful, even if it has the effect of disrupting deliveries to the employer, according to *Houston Building & Construction Trades Council.*[16] Similarly, picketing to protest unfair practices by the employer, when there is no recognitional objective, is not prohibited, according to *UAW Local 259.*[17]

---

[16] 136 NLRB 321 (1962).

[17] 133 NLRB 1468 (1961).

Concept *Summary* 16.2

RECOGNITIONAL PICKETING

Section 8(b)(7)—Recognitional Picketing

- Picketing to force an employer to recognize a union as representative of its employees when:
  - another union has been legally recognized;
  - a representation election has been held within the last 12 months; or
  - the union pickets for a reasonable period of time without filing a petition for an election.
- Exceptions: publicity or picketing to advise the public that an employer does not have a contract with a labor organization

Section 8(b)(4): Secondary Boycotts

Section 8(b)(4), which deals with secondary boycotts, is one of the most complex provisions of the NLRA. Section 8(b)(4) contains the following provisions:

[It is an unfair practice for a labor organization] (4) (i) to engage in, or to induce or encourage any individual employed by any person engaged in commerce or in an industry affecting commerce to engage in, a strike or refusal in the course of his employment to use, manufacture, process, transport, or otherwise handle or work on any goods, articles, materials, or commodities or to perform any services; or (ii) to threaten, coerce, or restrain any person engaged in commerce or in an industry affecting commerce, where in either case an object thereof is:

(A) forcing or requiring any employer or self-employed person to join any labor or employer organization or to enter into any agreement which is prohibited by Section 8(e);

(B) forcing or requiring any person to cease using, selling, handling, transporting, or otherwise dealing in the products of any other producer, processor, or manufacturer, or to cease doing business with any other person, or forcing or requiring any other employer to recognize or bargain with a labor organization as the representative of his employees unless such labor organization has been certified as the representative of such employees under the provisions of Section 9: Provided, That nothing contained in this clause (B) shall be construed to make unlawful, where not otherwise unlawful, any primary strike or primary picketing;

(C) forcing or requiring any employer to recognize or bargain with a particular labor organization as the representative of his employees if another labor organization has been certified as the representative of such employees under the provisions of Section 9;

(D) forcing or requiring any employer to assign particular work to employees in a particular labor organization or in a particular trade, craft, or class rather than to employees in another labor organization or in another trade, craft, or class, unless such employer is failing to conform to an order or certification of the Board determining the bargaining representative for employees performing such work:

Provided, That nothing contained in this Subsection (b) shall be construed to make unlawful a refusal by any person to enter upon the premises of any employer (other than his own employer), if the employees of such employer are engaged in a strike ratified or approved by a representative of such employees whom such employer is required under this Act: Provided further, That for the purposes of this paragraph (4) only, nothing contained in such paragraph shall be construed to prohibit publicity, other than picketing, for the purpose of truthfully advising the public, including consumers and members of a labor organization, that a product or products are produced by an employer with whom the labor organization has a primary dispute and are distributed by another employer, as long as such publicity does not have an effect of inducing any individual employed by any person other than the primary employer in the course of his employment to refuse to pick up, deliver, or transport any goods, or not to perform any services, at the establishment of the employer engaged in such distributions. . . .

When considering Section 8(b)(4), the courts and the Board generally consider the intention behind the provisions rather than its literal wording. The intention is to protect employers who are not involved in a dispute with a union from being pressured by that union. For example, if the union representing the workers of a toy manufacturing company goes on strike, it is free to picket the manufacturer (the primary employer). But if the union pickets the premises of a wholesaler who distributes the toys of the primary employer, such picketing may be secondary and prohibited by Section 8(b)(4)(B). Whether the picketing is prohibited depends on whether the union's picketing has the objective of trying to force the wholesaler to cease doing business with the manufacturer.

Most secondary picketing situations, however, are more complicated than this simple example. For instance, if the primary employer's location of business is mobile, such as a cement-mix delivery truck, is the union allowed to picket a construction site where the cement truck is making a delivery? What if the union has a dispute with a subcontractor on a construction site? Can it picket the entire construction site?

Primary picketing by a union is against an employer with which it has a dispute. Section 8(b)(4) does not prohibit such picketing, even though it is intended to persuade customers to cease doing business with the primary employer. It is important, therefore, to identify which employer is the primary employer—the employer with whom the union has the dispute. It is helpful to consider three questions when confronting a potential secondary picketing situation.

- With whom does the union have the dispute? This question identifies the primary employer.
- Is the union picketing at the primary employer's premises or at the site of a neutral employer?
- What is the object of the union's picketing? If the union is picketing at a secondary employer to force that employer to cease doing business with the primary employer, then it is illegal. But if the picketing is intended only to inform the public that the secondary employer handles the primary product, it is legal.

The objective of the picketing is the key to its legality: Does the picketing have an objective prohibited by Section 8(b)(4)?

Ambulatory Situs Picketing

ambulatory *situs* picketing
union picketing that follows the primary employer's mobile business

When the primary employer's business location is mobile, picketing by a union following that mobile location is called **ambulatory *situs* picketing**. The following NLRB decision sets out the conditions under which the union may engage in ambulatory *situs* picketing.

» CASE 16.4

SAILORS' UNION OF THE PACIFIC AND MOORE DRY DOCK CO.
92 NLRB 547 (NLRB, 1950)

Facts: Samsoc, a shipping company, contracted with Kaiser Gypsum to ship gypsum from Mexico in the ship *Phopho*. Samsoc replaced the *Phopho* crew with a foreign crew. The union demanded bargaining rights for the ship, but Samsoc refused. The union therefore requested permission from Moore to post pickets alongside the ship at the dry dock, but Moore refused. The union then posted pickets at the entrances to the dry dock. The signs carried by the picketers clearly indicated that the union's dispute was with the ship and not with the dry-dock company. When the pickets were posted, the dry-dock workers refused to work on the ship but did perform other work. The dry-dock company filed an unfair practice charge with the NLRB, alleging that the union's picketing at the dry dock violated Section 8(b)(4)(B).

Issue: Does picketing directed against the primary employer, but taking place at a secondary location, violate Section 8(b)(4)(B)?

Decision: Picketing at the premises of the primary employer is traditionally recognized as primary action, even though it is intended to induce and encourage third persons to cease doing business with the picketed employer. The *Phopho* was the place of employment of the seamen, and it was the *situs* of the dispute between Samsoc and the union over working conditions aboard the vessel. If Samsoc, the ship's owner, had its own dock at which the *Phopho* had been docked while undergoing conversion by Moore Dry Dock employees, it is clear that picketing by the union at the dock site would be primary picketing, even though the union might have expected that the picketing would be more effective in persuading Moore employees not to work on the ship. In the case here, however, the *Phopho* was not tied up at its own dock, but at Moore's dock, and the union picketing was going on in front of the gates at Moore's premises. The location of the primary employer is not limited to a fixed location—here it is ambulatory. Thus, the *situs* may come to rest temporarily at the premises of another employer. How can the union

picket to follow the *situs* while it is stationed at the premises of a secondary employer, if the only way to picket is in front of the secondary employer's premises? The situation requires balancing the right of a union to picket at the site of its dispute against the right of a secondary employer to be free from picketing in a controversy in which it is not directly involved.

The NLRB rules for ensuring that the picketing at the secondary location is legally permitted primary picketing are as follows:

- the union's picketing at the secondary location is limited to the times when the *situs* of the labor dispute is located at the secondary employer's premises;
- at the time of the picketing, the primary employer is engaged in its normal business at the *situs*;
- the picketing is limited to places reasonably close to the location of the *situs*; and
- the picketing clearly discloses that the union's dispute is with the primary employer and not the secondary employer.

All these conditions were met in the present case:

- during the entire period of the union's picketing at Moore's shipyard, the *Phopho* was tied up at a dock there;
- while the ship was at the dry dock, its crew was engaged in getting the ship ready for sea, which is part of the normal business of a ship, so the *Phopho* was engaged in its normal business;
- when Moore refused to allow the union to place pickets alongside the ship, the union posted its pickets at the shipyard entrance which was as close to the *Phopho* as they could get under the circumstances; and
- the union's picketing and other conduct clearly indicated that its dispute was solely with the primary employer, the owners of the *Phopho*.

The NLRB therefore dismissed the unfair labor practice complaint because it held that the union's picketing at Moore's premises was primary in nature, and did not violate Section 8(b)(4)(B).

Reserved Gate Picketing: Secondary Employees at the Primary Site

The *Moore Dry Dock* case deals with the legality of picketing at a secondary, or neutral, location. What about the legality of picketing that affects secondary employees at a primary site? The following case, also called the *General Electric* case, deals with that situation.

≫ CASE 16.5

LOCAL 761, INTERNATIONAL UNION OF ELECTRICAL RADIO & MACHINEWORKERS [GENERAL ELECTRIC] v. NLRB
366 U.S. 667 (1961)

Facts: General Electric Corporation operates a huge plant known as Appliance Park near Louisville, Kentucky, where it manufactures household appliances. The lot on which the plant is located is surrounded by a large drainage culvert, and access to the lot is limited to five roadways, known as gates, that cross the culvert. At any given time, there are employees of various contractors present at the GE plant. Those employees perform a variety of tasks:

- some do construction work on new buildings;
- some install and repair ventilating and heating equipment;
- some engage in retooling and rearranging operations necessary to the manufacture of new models; and
- others do general maintenance work.

In order to isolate the GE employees from the effects of any labor disputes involving the contractors, GE requires that the employees of the contractors use Gate 3-A; Gate 3-A is limited to use only by the contractors and GE employees are not permitted to use it. A large sign has been posted at the gate which states: "*Gate 3-A for Employees of Contractors Only—G.E. Employees Use Other Gates*," and guards at the gate enforce the ban on GE employees using the gate.

The union representing the GE employees went on strike against GE, and initially placed pickets at all gates, including Gate 3-A. The signs carried by the pickets at all gates read: "Local 761 on Strike G.E. Unfair." Because of the picketing at Gate 3-A, almost all of the employees of independent contractors refused to enter the company premises. GE filed a complaint with the NLRB, alleging that union's picketing at Gate 3-A, used exclusively by the employees of the contractors, violated Section 8(b)(4)(ii)(B). The ALJ hearing the complaint recommended that the

complaint be dismissed because the picketing at Gate 3-A was primary in nature.

The NLRB reversed the ALJ's decision and held that, because only the employees of the independent contractors used Gate 3-A, the union's object in picketing there was encourage those employees to engage in a concerted refusal to work "with an object of forcing the independent contractors to cease doing business with the Company," in violation of Section 8(b)(4)(ii)(B). On review, the Court of Appeals for the District of Columbia granted enforcement of the Board's order. The union then appealed to the U.S. Supreme Court.

Issue: Does the union picketing at the gate used only by the employees of the contractors violate Section 8(b)(4)(ii)(B)?

Decision: Section 8(b)(4)(B) of the National Labor Relations Act provided that it shall be an unfair labor practice for a labor organization:

> to engage in, or to induce or encourage the employees of any employer to engage in, a strike or a concerted refusal in the course of their employment to use, manufacture, process, transport, or otherwise handle or work on any goods, articles, materials, or commodities or to perform any services, where an object thereof is: [(B)] forcing or requiring ... any employer or other person ... to cease doing business with any other person....

The Supreme Court noted that Section 8(b)(4)(B) could not be literally construed because to do so would ban most primary strikes. Congress included a proviso in Section 8(b)(4)(B) that states "*Provided*, That nothing in this clause (B) shall be construed to make unlawful, where not otherwise unlawful, any primary strike or picketing." The prohibition in Section 8(b)(4)(B) is directed toward secondary boycotts, which involve union pressure or sanctions directed not at the primary employer, who is a party to the dispute, but at some third party who has no involvement in the dispute. A union involved in a strike with the primary employer is free to use persuasion, including picketing, not only on the primary employer and his employees, but also on secondary employers who were customers or suppliers of the primary employer, and persons dealing with them, and even employees of secondary employers, as long as the union does not "induce or encourage the employees of any [other] employer to engage in a strike or a concerted refusal in the course of their employment." Section 8(b)(4)(B) does not speak generally of secondary boycotts, but rather condemns specific union conduct directed to specific objectives: inducing employees to engage in a strike or concerted refusal, of which an object must be to force or require their employer or another person to cease doing business with a third person.

While the distinction between legitimate "primary activity" and prohibited "secondary activity," is critical, it is not always a "bright line." The objectives of any picketing include a desire to influence others from withholding from the employer their services or trade; but primary picketing which induces secondary employees to respect a primary picket line is not the equivalent of picketing that has an object of inducing those employees to engage in concerted conduct against their employer in order to force him to refuse to deal with the struck employer. Under the *Moore Dry Dock* analysis, whether picketing at a gate used exclusively by employees of independent contractors who work at the primary employer's premises depends upon the type of work that is being performed by those employees who use the separate gate. The NLRB has only applied the separate gate analysis to situations where the independent workers were performing tasks unconnected to the normal operations of the struck employer, usually construction work on the buildings of the primary employer. The Court of Appeals of the Second Circuit upheld the NLRB application of Section 8(b)(4)(B) to a separate-gate situation. The court there held that

> there must be a separate gate marked and set apart from other gates; and the work done by the employees who use the separate gate must be unrelated to the normal operations of the primary employer, and the work must be of a kind that would not, if done when the plant were engaged in its regular operations, necessitate curtailing those operations.

The Supreme Court adopted the analysis of the Second Circuit, but in this case, neither the NLRB nor the court of appeals considered whether the employees who used Gate 3-A performed work necessary to the normal operations of General Electric. If that is so, then the gate would not be considered a separate gate, and the mixed use of the gate would allow the striking union to picket that gate as part of its actions directed against the primary employer. The Supreme Court therefore remanded the case to the NLRB to consider whether the work performed by the employees using Gate 3-A was related to the normal operations of GE, the primary employer.

Common Situs Picketing

common *situs* picketing
union picketing of an entire construction site

The *General Electric* case made the nature of the work performed by the secondary employees at the primary site the key to whether the union may target secondary employees with picketing. In the construction industry, subcontractors and the general contractor are all working on the same project: erecting a building. Does this mean a union that has a dispute with the general contractor may picket the entire construction site (such picketing is known as **common *situs* picketing**)? Should the NLRB apply the *General Electric* separate gate approach to picketing at construction sites, or does the legality of common *situs* picketing require a different approach? In *Building and Construction Trades Council of New Orleans, AFL-CIO and Markwell and Hartz, Inc.,*[18] the NLRB held that the *Moore Dry Dock* approach applied to common *situs* picketing. The following case illustrates the application of the *Moore Dry Dock* doctrine to a case of common *situs* picketing.

---

[18] 155 NLRB 319 (1965).

CASE 16.6

INTERNATIONAL UNION OF OPERATING ENGINEERS, LOCAL 150, AFL-CIO v. NLRB

47 F.3d 218 (7th Cir. 1995)

Coffin, Circuit Judge

Local 150 of the International Union of Operating Engineers, AFL-CIO, seeks review of a decision by the National Labor Relations Board (Board) that the Union violated the secondary boycott provisions of the National Labor Relations Act (NLRA), Section 8(b)(4)(i), (ii)(B). The Board, which cross-petitions for enforcement of its order, found that the Union . . . picketed neutral gates at a multi-employer workplace in an effort to force the uninvolved employers to pressure the struck employer into settling the dispute more quickly. . . .

LTV Steel operates a large steel making plant in East Chicago, Indiana. Located on the grounds of the 1,150-acre facility are two companies that serve as subcontractors to LTV for the processing and disposal of slag, a by-product of the steelmaking process. The strike at issue in this case was aimed at one of those companies, Edward C. Levy Co. (Levy), whose collective bargaining agreement with Local 150 expired at the end of September 1991. Employees of the other slag processing firm, the Heckett Division of Harsco Corp. (Heckett), also are represented by Local 150. . . .

The LTV plant has three entrances, designated as the East Bridge gate, the West Bridge gate, and the Burma Road gate. The East and West Bridge gates are the entrances normally used for access to the facility by employees and vendors. The ALJ found that the Burma Road entrance is used only in strike situations, as part of a so-called "reserved gate" system. Such a system is common where employers share a site but only one is experiencing labor strife. One entrance is "reserved" for the exclusive use of traffic related to the struck firm, and all picketing must be directed there. This system is designed to keep neutral parties out of the dispute, and avoids the need for them to cross picket lines.

The strike against Levy began on October 12, 1991, and ended on October 18. On the first day of the strike, LTV posted signs at each of the three gates. All of them identified the East and West Bridge gates as "neutral" gates reserved for the use of LTV Steel and all persons having business with the company, except for anyone connected with Levy. The signs directed Levy's traffic to the Burma Road gate, "which has been reserved solely and exclusively

for Levy's employees, their suppliers, their delivery men, their subcontractors and all others having business with Levy." LTV expected the Union to picket only at this gate.

It is undisputed that no one from LTV gave written notice, or any other formal notification, of the gate arrangement to the Union, which established picket lines on public property near each of the three gates. The signs posted by LTV at the East and West Bridge gates could be seen by the picketers, but the words probably were not visible. Two company officials testified, however, that they told picketers at both the East and West Bridge locations on October 12 that a Levy gate had been set up at the Burma Road entrance and that the picketing should be confined to that location. An LTV security officer also testified that he informed four picketers near the East Bridge gate entrance that they would have to picket at Burma Road. . . .

Burma Road . . . is a distinctly non-road-like path that lies between the Amoco Oil gate and the EJ & E property. A large pole placed there by Amoco usually blocks the entrance to Burma Road from Front Street, but this was removed at LTVs request during the strike. The truck traffic generated by Levy made the location of the road "obvious" as the strike progressed.

Burma Road is central to this case because the Board maintains that, once the Levy reserved gate was established, the Union was legally permitted to picket only at that location. The Union claims that it . . . received no notice of the reserved gate system. . . .

Also of significance is the role of Heckett's employees during the strike. Heckett and Levy are direct competitors and, consequently, there apparently was some concern on the part of the Union about whether LTV would look to Heckett for help during a strike by Levy. Heckett's employees, meanwhile, were concerned about what the Union expected of them if a strike were called against Levy; their contract had a no-strike provision and they feared losing their jobs if they did not report to work.... Several Heckett employees testified that they were told either before the strike, or at its outset, that a neutral gate would be set up. On two occasions, however, Union officials at least implicitly urged members to respect picket signs established at their worksite, thereby disdaining the reserved gate system. . . .

About 53 of the 69 Union members employed by Heckett worked during the strike. On October 14, during the strike, the Union filed internal charges against them for "refus[ing] to honor the picket line," in violation of the Union's by-laws.

. . . the Board found that various of the Union's actions constituted unfair labor practices under the NLRA: (1) picketing at neutral gates; (2) distributing pamphlets encouraging employees of neutral employers to stay out of work; (3) bringing internal charges against members employed by a neutral employer; and (4) applying to employees of a neutral employer the Union bylaw barring members from working on a job where a strike has been called.

The Union challenges only the finding that it violated the NLRA by picketing at the East and West Bridge gates. . . .

The question before us, therefore, is whether substantial evidence in the record supports the Board's finding that the Union's picketing ran afoul of the NLRA's secondary boycott provisions. Union conduct violates section 8(b)(4) of the NLRA "if any object of that activity is to exert improper influence on secondary or neutral parties...." Whether the Union was motivated by a secondary objective is a question of fact, and is to be determined through examination of "the totality of [the] union's conduct in [the] given situation."

. . . Because not all union conduct that interferes with uninvolved employers is banned, the distinction between permissible "primary" activity and unlawful "secondary" activity "is often more nice than obvious." This is particularly true where the primary and secondary employers occupy a common work site. As an evidentiary tool for determining the dispositive point—the union's intent—the NLRB has adopted the so-called *Moore Dry Dock* standards. Under these standards, a union's picketing is presumed to be lawful primary activity if (1) it is "strictly limited to times when the situs of the dispute is located on the secondary employer's premises"; (2) "the primary employer is engaged in its normal business at the situs"; (3) it is "limited to places reasonably close to the location of the situs"; and (4) it "discloses clearly that the dispute is with the primary employer."

The third [*Moore Dry Dock*] standard is the one of significance in this case. When an employer implements a valid reserved gate system, and a union continues to picket a gate designated exclusively for neutrals, a violation of the third Dry Dock criterion is established because the picketing is not limited to the "location" of the dispute as permissibly confined. This gives rise to a presumption of illegitimate,

secondary intent. The question remains, however, "a factual inquiry into the union's actual state of mind under the totality of the circumstances."

. . . Under these standards, we have little difficulty affirming the Board's determination that the Union violated section 8(b)(4) by intentionally enmeshing neutrals in its dispute with Levy. The ALJ's most crucial finding, that the Union knew about the reserved gate system, yet "consciously chose" to ignore it, is amply supported by the record. The evidence recounted by the ALJ showed that Union officials anticipated the establishment of a reserved gate system and had indicated to some Heckett employees that the Union itself was working toward setting up a safe gate. In addition, Union officials knew that Levy was using the Burma Road entrance, and it is undisputed that [the Burma Road] gate was used only during strikes as part of a reserved gate system. Thus, the fact that the Union sent pickets to Burma Road by itself reflects knowledge that a reserved gate system was in place. Moreover, while the wording on the signs posted at the East and West Bridge gates may not have been visible to picketers and supervising Union officials, they certainly could see that signs had been posted and so must have realized that the anticipated reserved gates had been designated. Indeed, LTV officials testified that they told Union members at both the East and West Bridge gates to move to the Levy gate at Burma Road. . . .

The Union contends that, in the absence of formal notice of a reserved gate system, it may not be penalized for failing to confine its picketing to the Burma Road location. We acknowledge that it would be better if employers gave written or other formal notice of such a system, even when it appears that the Union must have gained actual knowledge through an informal method. In these circumstances, however, we cannot say that the ALJ improperly imposed responsibility on the Union based, among other factors, on its having received sufficient notice of the system. . . . Moreover, misuse of the reserved gate system was not the only evidence of the Union's intent to engage in secondary activity. As the Board found, the Union unlawfully distributed pamphlets to Heckett employees advising them that they had the right not to work "no matter how many gates the employer sets up." In addition, on the first day of the strike, a picketer who identified himself as picket captain, told LTV's labor relations manager that a Union official had directed that all three gates be picketed and that the Union's "intent was to impact not only Levy employees but Heckett employees, iron workers and other employees." This intent also was reflected in statements made by Union official Cisco at a November meeting, in which he suggested that the strike would have been shorter if the Heckett employees had not crossed the picket line. Finally, the fact that the Union brought charges against those employees for crossing the line lends further support to the finding of a secondary objective.

. . . In sum, we believe the ALJ permissibly found that the Union received adequate notice of a validly established reserved gate system, and "chose to ignore it." This conclusion, particularly when taken together with the Union's distribution of leaflets encouraging Heckett employees to honor the picket line, the disciplinary action against the 53 employees who did work, and the statements made by Union representatives, provides more than substantial evidence to support the Board's determination that Local 150's picketing activity was intended to implicate secondary parties and thus was unlawful under section 8(b)(4).

The Union's petition for review is therefore denied, and the Board's cross-application for enforcement of its order is granted.

Case Questions

1.   Was the union ever formally notified by LTV about the reserved gate arrangement set up in response to the strike against Levy? Did the court determine that the union was aware of the reserved gate arrangement? Why?

2.   What is the relevance of the third *Moore Dry Dock* standard—the requirement that the union picketing be limited to places reasonably close to the *situs* of the dispute (the operations of the struck employer, Levy)? Where was the *situs* of Levy's operations in this case?

3.   What is the significance of the union's efforts to get Heckett employees to honor the picket line against Levy? What is the significance of the union's efforts to discipline the Heckett employees who crossed the picket line?

The NLRB had adopted a requirement that a union notifying an employer of its intention to engage in common *situs* picketing must affirmatively declare its intention to conform with the requirements of *Moore Dry Dock*, but that requirement was rejected by the U.S. Court of Appeals for the Ninth Circuit in *United Ass'n of Journeymen, Local 32 v. NLRB*,[19] and by the U.S. Court of Appeals for the D.C. Circuit in *Sheet Metal Workers' Int. Ass'n, Local 15 v. NLRB*.[20]

Ally Doctrine

Not all union picketing directed against employers other than the primary employer is prohibited. The secondary boycott prohibitions were intended to protect neutral employers from union pressure. If any employer is not neutral—because it is performing the work normally done by the workers of the primary employer, who are now on strike—may the union picket that other employer? That is the issue addressed in the following case on page 531.

Publicity: "Consumer" Picketing

The second proviso to Section 8(b)(4) allows the union to use "… publicity, other than picketing, for the purpose of truthfully advising the public" that the secondary employer is handling the product of the primary employer. Such publicity is legal unless it has the effect of inducing other employees to refuse to perform their services at the secondary employer's location. This proviso allows the union to distribute handbills addressed to the public, asking for the public to support the union in its strike by refusing to buy the primary product or by refraining from shopping at the secondary employer.

---

[19] 912 F.2d 1108, 1110 (9th Cir.1990).

[20] 491 F.3d 429 (D.C. Cir. 2007).

CASE 16.7

NLRB v. Business Machine & Office Appliance Mechanics Conference Board, IUE, Local 459 [Royal Typewriter Co.]

228 F.2d 553 (2d Cir. 1955), *cert. denied*, 351 U.S. 962 (1956)

Lumbard, J.

This case arose out of a labor dispute between the Royal Typewriter Company and the Business Machine and Office Appliance Mechanics Conference Board, Local 459, IUE-CIO, the certified bargaining agent of Royal's typewriter mechanics and other service personnel. The National Labor Relations Board now seeks enforcement of an order directing the Union to cease and desist from certain picketing and to post appropriate notices. . . .

On about March 23, 1954, the Union, being unable to reach agreement with Royal on the terms of a contract, called the Royal service personnel out on strike. The service employees customarily repair typewriters either at Royal's branch offices or at its customers' premises. Royal has several arrangements under which it is obligated to render service to its customers. First, Royal's warranty on each new machine obligates it to provide free inspection and repair for one year. Second, for a fixed periodic fee Royal contracts to service machines not under warranty. Finally, Royal is committed to repairing typewriters rented from it or loaned by it to replace machines undergoing repair. Of course, in addition Royal provides repair service on call by non-contract users.

During the strike Royal differentiated between calls from customers to whom it owed a repair obligation and others. Royal's office personnel were instructed to tell the latter to call some independent repair company listed in the telephone directory. Contract customers, however, were advised to select such an independent from the directory to have the repair made, and to send a receipted invoice to Royal for reimbursement for reasonable repairs within their agreement with Royal. Consequently many of Royal's contract customers had repair services performed by various independent repair companies. In most instances the customer sent Royal the unpaid repair bill and Royal paid the independent company directly. Among the independent companies paid directly by Royal for repairs made for such customers were Typewriter Maintenance and Sales Company and Tytell Typewriter Company. . . .

During May, 1954, the Union picketed four independent typewriter repair companies who had been doing work covered by Royal's contracts pursuant to the arrangement

described above. The Board found this picketing unlawful with respect to Typewriter Maintenance and Tytell. Typewriter Maintenance was picketed for about three days and Tytell for several hours on one day. In each instance the picketing, which was peaceful and orderly, took place before entrances used in common by employees, deliverymen and the general public. The signs read substantially as follows (with the appropriate repair company name inserted):

> NOTICE TO THE PUBLIC ONLY EMPLOYEES OF ROYAL TYPEWRITER COMPANY ON STRIKE TYTELL TYPEWRITER COMPANY EMPLOYEES ARE BEING USED AS STRIKEBREAKERS BUSINESS MACHINE & OFFICE APPLIANCE MECHANICS UNION, LOCAL 459, IUE-CIO

Both before and after this picketing, which took place in mid-May, Tytell and Typewriter Maintenance did work on Royal accounts and received payment directly from Royal. Royal's records show that Typewriter Maintenance's first voucher was passed for payment by Royal on April 20, 1954, and Tytell's first voucher was passed for payment on May 3, 1954. After these dates each independent serviced various of Royal's customers on numerous occasions and received payment directly from Royal. . . .

On the above facts the Trial Examiner and the Board found that ... the repair company picketing violated Section 8(b)(4) of the National Labor Relations Act.... We are of the opinion that the Board's finding with respect to the repair company picketing cannot be sustained. The independent repair companies were so allied with Royal that the Union's picketing of their premises was not prohibited by Section 8(b)(4).

We approve the "ally" doctrine which had its origin in a well reasoned opinion by Judge Rifkind in the *Ebasco case, Douds v. Architects, Engineers, Chemists & Technicians, Local 231*. Ebasco, a corporation engaged in the business of providing engineering services, had a close business relationship with Project, a firm providing similar services. Ebasco subcontracted some of its work to Project and when it did so Ebasco supervised the work of Project's employees and paid Project for the time spent by Project's employees on

Ebasco's work plus a factor for overhead and profit. When Ebasco's employees went on strike, Ebasco transferred a greater percentage of its work to Project, including some jobs that had already been started by Ebasco's employees. When Project refused to heed the Union's requests to stop doing Ebasco's work, the Union picketed Project and induced some of Project's employees to cease work. On these facts Judge Rifkind found that Project was not "doing business" with Ebasco within the meaning of Section 8(b)(4) and that the Union had therefore not committed an unfair labor practice under that Section. He reached this result by looking to the legislative history of the Taft-Hartley Act and to the history of the secondary boycotts which it sought to outlaw. He determined that Project was not a person "wholly unconcerned in the disagreement between an employer and his employees" such as Section 8(b)(4) was designed to protect. . . .

Here there was evidence of only one instance where Royal contacted an independent (Manhattan Typewriter Service, not named in the complaint) to see whether it could handle some of Royal's calls. Apart from that incident there is no evidence that Royal made any arrangement with an independent directly. It is obvious, however, that what the independents did would inevitably tend to break the strike. As Judge Rifkind pointed out in the *Ebasco* case: "The economic effect on Ebasco's employees was precisely that which would flow from Ebasco's hiring strikebreakers to work on its own premises. . . .

Moreover, there is evidence that the secondary strikes and boycotts sought to be outlawed by Section 8(b)(4) were only those which had been unlawful at common law. And although secondary boycotts were generally unlawful, it has been held that the common law does not proscribe union activity designed to prevent employers from doing the farmed-out work of a struck employer. Thus the picketing of the independent typewriter companies was not the kind of a secondary activity which Section 8(b)(4) of the Taft-Hartley Act was designed to outlaw. Where an employer is attempting to avoid the economic impact of a strike by securing the services of others to do his work, the striking union obviously has a great interest, and we think a proper interest in preventing those services from being rendered. This interest is more fundamental than the interest in

bringing pressure on customers of the primary employer. Nor are those who render such services completely uninvolved in the primary strike. By doing the work of the primary employer they secure benefits themselves at the same time that they aid the primary employer. The ally employer may easily extricate himself from the dispute and insulate himself from picketing by refusing to do that work. A case may arise where the ally employer is unable to determine that the work he is doing is "farmed-out." We need not decide whether the picketing of such an employer would be lawful, for that is not the situation here. The existence of the strike, the receipt of checks from Royal, and the picketing itself certainly put the independents on notice that some of the work they were doing might be work farmed-out by Royal. Wherever they worked on new Royal machines they were probably aware that such machines were covered by a Royal warranty. But in any event, before working on a Royal machine they could have inquired of the customer whether it was covered by a Royal contract and refused to work on it if it was. There is no indication that they made any effort to avoid doing Royal's work. The Union was justified in picketing them in order to induce them to make such an effort. We therefore hold that an employer is not within the protection of Section 8(b)(4) when he knowingly does work which would otherwise be done by the striking employees of the primary employer and where this work is paid for by the primary employer pursuant to an arrangement devised and originated by him to enable him to meet his contractual obligations.

Enforcement denied.

Case Questions

1. Against whom was the union on strike? Why did the union picket the independent typewriter repair shops?

2. Was the union's picketing at the independent repair shops primary or secondary? Explain your answer.

3. What is the rationale for the "ally" exception to the secondary picketing prohibitions of Section 8(b)(4)? How does that rationale apply to the facts in this case? Explain.

In the case of *NLRB v. Fruit and Vegetable Packers, Local 760 (Tree Fruits)*,[21] the Supreme Court held that the publicity proviso did not, by negative implication,

---

[21] 377 U.S. 58 (1964).

prohibit peaceful picketing by a union at a supermarket that sold apples packed by the employer against whom the union was on strike. The union's picketing was directed at consumers and asked only that they refuse to buy the apples; it did not ask them to refrain from shopping at the market. The Supreme Court found that such picketing was not prohibited because it was directed at the primary product rather than the neutral supermarket.

In *Tree Fruits*, the primary product, the apples, was only one of many products sold by the supermarket. May the union engage in consumer picketing when the secondary employer sells only one product—the primary product? In *NLRB v. Retail Store Employees Union, Local 1001, Retail Clerks Int. Association (Safeco)*,[22] the union striking against Safeco Title Insurance Co. conducted consumer picketing of local title companies, asking consumers to cancel their Safeco policies. The local title companies sold title insurance, performed escrow services, and conducted title searches; over 90 percent of their gross income was derived from the sale of Safeco title insurance. The Supreme Court held that the consumer picketing was in violation of Section 8(b)(4) because, unlike that in *Tree Fruits*, it was "reasonably calculated to induce customers not to patronize the neutral parties at all.... Product picketing that reasonably can be expected to threaten neutral parties with ruin or substantial loss simply does not square with the language or the purpose of Section 8(b)(4)(ii)(B)." The Court also stated that if "secondary picketing were directed against a product representing a major portion of a neutral's business, but significantly less than that represented by a single dominant product.... The critical question would be whether, by encouraging customers to reject the struck product, the secondary appeal is reasonably likely to threaten the neutral party with ruin or substantial loss."

The effect of the *Safeco* decision is to restrict *consumer picketing* (also known as *product picketing*) to situations in which the primary product accounts for less than a substantial portion of the business of the neutral party at whose premises the picketing takes place. Other problems under consumer picketing have involved cases in which the primary product has become mixed with the product of the neutral or secondary employer. In such merged product cases, the public is unable to separate the primary product from the secondary product; hence, a call to the public to avoid the primary product becomes, in effect, a call to avoid the secondary employer's product altogether. For example, if a union representing striking bakery workers pickets a fast-food restaurant, urging customers not to eat the sandwich buns supplied by the struck bakery, the effect of the union's consumer picketing may be to urge consumers to boycott the restaurant totally, according to *Teamsters Local 327*.[23] In *Kroger Co. v. NLRB*,[24] the union representing striking paper workers picketed grocery stores, asking consumers to refrain from using paper bags to pack their groceries. The picketing was held to violate Section 8(b)(4) because the bags had lost their separate identity and had become "merged" with the products (groceries) of the neutral grocery stores.

---

[22] 447 U.S. 607 (1980).

[23] 170 NLRB 91 (1968), *enforced* 411 F.2d 147 (6th Cir. 1969).

[24] 647 F.2d 634 (6th Cir. 1980).

CONSUMER AND PUBLICITY PICKETING

You are the human resources manager for FoodMart, a regional grocery retailer. The FoodMart employees are members of the Retail Clerks Union, and FoodMart and the union are engaged in negotiations to renew their collective agreement. The retail grocery business is extremely competitive, and a number of low-cost, low-overhead chains compete directly with FoodMart. The employees of the low-cost grocery chains are not unionized, and their wages are barely above the minimum wage. FoodMart employees' wages average around $9.25 per hour, and FoodMart also offers generous benefit packages, including medical insurance and pensions. As a result, FoodMart's labor costs are much higher than the low-cost chains, and FoodMart has seen its profit margins decline. FoodMart had considered proposing wage and benefit reductions to the union; the union had publicly vowed not to agree to any wage concessions.

To avoid a strike, the CEO suggests that you offer the union a guarantee not to reduce wages and benefits if the union agrees to begin a campaign of consumer and publicity picketing and hand-billing in front of the low-cost grocery stores—to inform the public how the low-cost chains treat their employees. What arguments can you make in favor of such a proposal? What arguments can you make against it? Should you make such an offer to the union? Prepare a memo to the CEO outlining the positive and negative aspects of the proposal, and recommending a course of action, with appropriate supporting reasons.

The Publicity Proviso

The publicity proviso of Section 8(b)(4) purports to allow publicity, other than picketing, for the purposes of truthfully advising the public that the products of the employer against whom the union is striking are being distributed by another employer. How far does that proviso go in allowing consumer appeals by a union? This question is addressed by the following Supreme Court decision.

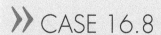

CASE 16.8

EDWARD J. DEBARTOLO CORP. v. FLORIDA GULF COAST BUILDING TRADES COUNCIL
485 U.S. 568 (1988)

Facts: The Florida Gulf Coast Building Trades Council, a group of construction unions, engaged in hand billing at the entrances to a shopping mall in Tampa, Florida, to protest the presence of High Construction Co., a nonunion contractor constructing a department store in the mall. The hand-billing was peaceful. The union's handbills asked mall customers not to shop at any of the stores in the mall "until the Mall's owner publicly promises that all construction at the Mall will be done using contractors who pay their employees fair wages and fringe benefits." The handbills made clear that the union was seeking only a consumer boycott against the other mall tenants, not a secondary strike by the employees of the mall tenants.

DeBartolo, the mall owner, tried to get the union to change the language of the handbills to state that the union's dispute did not involve DeBartolo or the mall lessees other than Wilson, and to get the union to limit its distribution to the immediate vicinity of construction site. DeBartolo then filed a complaint with the NLRB, charging the union with engaging in unfair labor practices under Section 8(b)(4) of the NLRA.

The NLRB's General Counsel issued a complaint—which the NLRB eventually dismissed—concluding that the hand-billing was protected by the publicity proviso of Section 8(b)(4). The Court of Appeals for the Fourth Circuit affirmed the Board, but the Supreme Court reversed, holding that the hand-billing did not fall within the proviso's limited scope of exempting "publicity intended to inform the public that the primary employer's product is 'distributed by' the secondary employer" because DeBartolo and the other tenants, as opposed to Wilson, did not distribute products of High. The Court remanded the case to the NLRB for a determination whether the hand-billing was in violation of Section 8(b)(4), and, if so, whether it was protected by the First Amendment.

On remand, the NLRB held that the union's hand-billing was in violation of Section 8(b)(4)(ii)(B), reasoning that "hand-billing and other activity urging a consumer boycott constituted coercion." Because it held that the hand-billing was prohibited by Section 8(b)(4), the NLRB also held that it was not necessary to consider whether the hand-billing was protected by the First Amendment. On review, the court of appeals held that the hand-billing was protected by the First Amendment, and refused to enforce the NLRB order. DeBartolo again appealed to the U.S. Supreme Court.

Issue: Is peaceful hand-billing a violation of Section 8(b)(4), or is the hand-billing protected by the First Amendment?

Decision: The Supreme Court noted that the handbills here truthfully revealed the existence of a labor dispute and urged potential customers of the mall not to patronize the retailers doing business in the mall. The hand-billing was peaceful, and no picketing or patrolling was involved; it was expressive activity arguing that substandard wages should be opposed by abstaining from shopping in a mall where such wages were paid. The court of appeals was correct that the NLRB's interpretation of Section 8(b)(4)(ii) raises concerns under the First Amendment.

The Court noted that the main issue here was whether the hand-billing must be held to "threaten, coerce, or restrain any person" to cease doing business with another, within the meaning of Section 8(b)(4)(ii)(B). The Court stated that more than mere persuasion is necessary to prove a violation of 8(b)(4)(ii), which requires a showing of threats, coercion, or restraints. The Court held that the handbills involved in this case did not constitute "threats, coercion or restraints." There was no suggestion that the handbills had any coercive effect on customers of the mall. There was no violence, picketing, or patrolling and only an attempt to persuade customers not to shop in the mall. The NLRB here found that the hand-billing "coerced" mall tenants, explaining that "[a]ppealing to the public not to patronize secondary employers is an attempt to inflict economic harm on the secondary employers by causing them to lose business … such appeals constitute 'economic retaliation' and are therefore a form of coercion." The Court noted, however, that its decision in *Tree Fruits* held that any kind of hand-billing, picketing, or other appeals to a secondary employer to cease doing business with the employer involved in the labor dispute was not "coercion" within the meaning of Section 8(b)(4)(ii)(B) just because it has some economic impact on the neutral. *Tree Fruits* involved a union picketing a retailer, asking the public not to buy a product produced by the primary employer and sold by the retailer. The impact of this picketing was not coercion within the meaning of Section 8(b)(4) even though, if the appeal succeeded, the retailer would lose revenue. *Tree Fruits* held that Congress did not intend to prohibit all peaceful consumer picketing at secondary sites.

It is also clear that the language of Section 8(b)(4)(ii), standing alone, does not give any indication that hand-billing, without picketing, "coerces" secondary employers. The loss of customers because they read a handbill urging them not to patronize a business, and not because they are intimidated by a line of picketers, is the result of mere persuasion, and the neutral who reacts is doing no more than what its customers honestly want it to do.

Section 8(b)(4) should not be read as prohibiting publicity that does not involve picketing, and that includes making appeals to customers of a retailer as they approach the store, to urge a complete boycott of the retailer because he handles products produced by nonunion shops. Interpreting Section 8(b)(4) as not reaching the hand-billing involved in this case is necessary to avoid raising the question of the constitutionality of a prohibition on otherwise peaceful publicity. The Supreme Court affirmed the decision of the court of appeals.

Sheet Metal Workers Int. Assoc., Local 15 v. NLRB[25] held that union conduct including leafleting, staging a mock funeral procession, and displaying a huge inflatable rat to protest the use of nonunion labor at a construction site was protected by the First Amendment, as with the *DeBartolo* decision. A union distributing handbills and displaying a huge banner reading "labor dispute" on public property outside firms that were employing nonunion contractors was not picketing and did not violate Section 8(b)(4)(ii)(B), according to *Overstreet v. United Brotherhood of Carpenters and Joiners of America, Local Union No. 1506.*[26] The case of *Int. Longshoremen's Association v. NLRB*[27] involved requests by U.S. union officials to Japanese unions asking for support in a dispute with nonunion shipping firms. The Japanese unions responded by stating that they would refuse to unload any cargo that had been loaded by nonunion workers. The U.S. Court of Appeals for the D.C. Circuit held that the Japanese unions were not acting as agents of the U.S. unions, and the U.S. unions' requests for support did not violate Section 8(b)(4). But not all union hand-billing or publicity activity is protected. In *Warshawsky & Co. v. NLRB,*[28] union hand-billing directed at employees of neutral subcontractors and intended to induce them to walk off the job was held to be an effort to induce a secondary boycott in violation of Section 8(b)(4). A union protesting the use of nonunion carpenters at a residential complex by using a sound system to broadcast a protest message at excessive volume levels was held to violate Section 8(b)(4)(ii)(B) because it caused, or threatened to cause, disruption to a secondary employer's operation in *Metropolitan Regional Council of Philadelphia (Society Hill Towers).*[29]

Section 8(b)(4)(D): Jurisdictional Disputes

Section 8(b)(4)(D) prohibits a union from picketing an employer in order to force that employer to assign work to that union. If the picketing union is not entitled to that work by reason of a certification or NLRB order, such picketing violates Section 8(b)(4)(D). For example, the union representing plasterers and the union representing stonemasons on the construction site of an apartment complex both might demand the right to lay the ceramic tiles in hallways and bathrooms. If either union picketed to force such assignment of the work, it would be a violation of Section 8(b)(4)(D).

When a Section 8(b)(4)(D) complaint is filed with the Board, Section 10(k) requires that the Board give the parties involved 10 days to settle the dispute. If the parties are unable to settle the jurisdictional dispute in 10 days, the Board must then make an assignment of the work in dispute. Once the Board awards the work, the successful union may picket to force the employer to live up to the Board order. Section 10(l) requires that the Board seek an injunction against the picketing when a complaint alleging a violation of Section 8(b)(4)(D) is filed.

---

[25] *Sheet Metal Workers Int. Assoc., Local 15*, 356 NLRB No. 162 (2011), on remand from 491 F.3d 429 (D.C. Cir. 2007).

[26] 409 F.3d 1199 (9th Cir. 2005).

[27] 56 F.3d 205 (D.C. Cir. 1995).

[28] 182 F.3d 948 (D.C. Cir. 1999).

[29] 335 NLRB 814 (2001), enforced by 50 Fed. Appx. 88 (3d Cir. 2002).

Concept *Summary* 16.3

SECONDARY PICKETING

Section 8(b)(4)—Secondary Picketing

- Picketing to pressure a neutral party—one with whom the union does not have a dispute—with the object to:
  - Force an employer to join a labor organization
  - Force any person to cease doing business with another person
  - Force an employer to recognize a union when another union has been certified as bargaining representative
  - Force an employer to assign work to employees of one union rather than another
- Exceptions:
  - Individuals are allowed to refuse to cross a picket line
  - Publicity, other than picketing, to advise the public the products of the primary employer are being distributed by another employer

Section 8(e): Hot Cargo Clauses

hot cargo clause
provision in collective bargaining agreements that purports to permit employees to refuse to handle the product of any employer involved in a labor dispute

Hot cargo clauses are provisions in collective bargaining agreements purporting to permit employees to refuse to handle the product of any employer involved in a labor dispute. Section 8(e), inserted into the NLRA as one of the 1959 Landrum-Griffin amendments, prohibits the negotiation and enforcement of such clauses:

> (e) It shall be an unfair labor practice for any labor organization and any employer to enter into any contract or agreement, express or implied, whereby such employer ceases or refrains or agrees to cease or refrain from handling, using, selling, transporting or otherwise dealing in any of the products of any other employer, or to cease doing business with any other person, and any contract or agreement entered into heretofore or hereafter containing such an agreement shall be to such extent enforceable and void: *Provided*, That nothing in this subsection (e) shall apply to an agreement between a labor organization and an employer in the construction industry relating to the contracting or subcontracting of work to be done at the site of the construction, alteration, painting, or repair of a building, structure, or other work: *Provided further*, That for the purposes of this subsection (e) and section 8(b)(4)(B) the terms "any employer," "any person engaged in commerce or an industry affecting commerce," "any person" when used in relation to the terms "any other producer, processor, or manufacturer," "any employer," or "any other person" shall not include persons in the relation of a jobber, manufacturer, contractor, or subcontractor working on the goods or premises of the jobber or manufacturer or performing parts of an integrated process of production in the apparel and clothing industry: *Provided further*, That nothing in this Act shall prohibit the enforcement of any agreement which is within the foregoing exception.

It can be seen that the provisos to Section 8(e) exempt the garment industry and the construction industry from its provisions. The garment industry is completely exempted; the construction industry is exempted to the extent of allowing unions to negotiate hot cargo clauses that relate to work normally done at the work site.

The objective of Section 8(e) is to prohibit language in a collective agreement that purports to authorize conduct that is prohibited by Section 8(b)(4), such as refusing to handle goods produced by a nonunion employer or by an employer who is being struck by a different union. The courts have allowed contract language that authorizes conduct that is primary, such as refusing to cross a primary picket line and refusing to perform the work normally done by the employees of an employer who is the target of a primary strike. One issue that has been problematic under Section 8(e) is whether work preservation clauses outside the construction industry are prohibited by Section 8(e). The courts have consistently held that when unions seek to retain the right to perform work that they have traditionally done or to acquire work that is similar to work they have traditionally done, and such activity to enforce the clauses is directed against the employer with the right of control over the working conditions at issue, such activity is primary. In *NLRB v. International Longshoremen's Association*,[30] the Supreme Court considered a union rule penalizing shippers who used prepacked containers to ship cargo that had traditionally been loaded and unloaded by union members at the docks. The Court held that, even though the use of containers had eliminated most of the traditional loading work done by longshoremen, the language that sought to preserve such "unnecessary" work was a legitimate work preservation clause under Sections 8(e) and 8(b)(4). The union's objective through the language was the preservation of work similar in nature to that traditionally performed by the longshoremen, and the employers had the power to control the assignment of such work. A neutrality agreement, by which an employer agrees that all business entities it controls will allow unions access for organizing and to recognize the union if a majority of employees sign authorization cards, was not in violation of Section 8(e) because it did not require the employer to cease doing business with any company refusing to accept the neutrality agreement, according to *Heartland Ind. Partners LLC*.[31] A collective agreement provision that required the employer to recognize the union upon a showing of majority support and to apply the terms of the collective-bargaining agreement within its operations performing bargaining unit work to the extent that the employer controlled the operation was held to have the primary objective of preserving unit work was not a violation Section 8(e).[32]

16-2d Remedies for Secondary Activity

As mentioned, the NLRB is required to seek an immediate injunction against the picketing when a complaint alleging a violation of Section 8(b)(4), Section 8(b)(7), or Section 8(e) is filed. The injunction is intended to prevent the activity in question until its legality can be determined. If the Board holds the conduct illegal, it will issue a cease-and-desist order against it.

Section 303 of the NLRA also provides that any person suffering harm to business or property by reason of activity that violates Section 8(b)(4) may sue in federal court to recover damages for the injuries sustained and legal fees. Either the primary or secondary employer may sue under Section 303, and they may file a suit regardless of whether an unfair labor practice charge has been filed with the NLRB.

---

[30] 473 U.S. 61 (1985).

[31] 348 NLRB 1081 (2006).

[32] *Road Sprinkler Fitters*, 357 NLRB No. 176 (2011).

16-3   National Emergencies

Sections 206 to 210 of the NLRA, which were added by the Taft-Hartley Act of 1947, provide for injunctions forestalling strikes when they threaten the national health or safety. When a strike or threatened strike poses such a threat, the president is authorized to appoint a board of inquiry to report on the issues involved in the dispute. The U.S. attorney general can secure an injunction to forestall the strike for up to eighty days, while the Federal Mediation and Conciliation Service (FMCS) attempts to resolve the dispute. The parties are not bound by the FMCS recommendations, and if no agreement is reached, the NLRB is required to poll the employees to determine if they will accept the employer's last offer. If the last offer is rejected, the injunction is dissolved, and the president may refer the issue to Congress for "appropriate action."

The emergency provisions of the Taft-Hartley Act have been invoked only rarely in recent years. President George W. Bush's action to stop a lockout of longshoremen in West Coast ports in October 2002 was the first use of the Taft-Hartley emergency provisions since 1978. The emergency provisions allow the president to delay a strike but do not address the causes of the strike. As a result, the dispute remains despite the invocation of the emergency provisions, and the strike or lockout may resume after the delay period under the injunction expires.

THE **WORKING** LAW

FMCS Statement on Tentative West Coast Ports Agreement Between the ILWU and the PMA

WASHINGTON, D.C.—Federal Mediation and Conciliation Service Acting Director Allison Beck today issued the following statement on a tentative agreement reached between representatives of the International Longshore and Warehouse Union (ILWU) and the Pacific Maritime Association covering operations at 29 U.S. ports on the Pacific coast:

"I am extremely pleased to announce today that after extensive negotiations and mediation provided by the FMCS and with the support and assistance of Secretary of Labor Tom Perez, Secretary of Commerce Penny Pritzker, and Los Angeles Mayor Eric Garcetti, representatives of the ILWU and PMA have tentatively agreed to a new contract, resolving all outstanding issues that divided them and that have affected operations at U.S. west coast ports. Due to the complexity of the issues the parties had to address, these have been lengthy and at times difficult negotiations. The parties persevered over a long and challenging process and were ultimately successful in averting any further situations that could have been disruptive to shipping operations and to the nation's economy."

"As a result of their efforts, shippers can expect that normal operations will be restored as soon as possible at our nation's west coast ports. At the FMCS, we are proud and honored that we were able to assist the parties and contribute to this successful negotiation."

"I want especially to acknowledge the extraordinary contributions of FMCS Deputy Director Scot Beckenbaugh, who led our Agency's efforts in assisting the ILWU and PMA in their negotiation, and I especially want to thank Secretary Perez and Secretary Pritzker for their leadership these past few days. We are grateful for their efforts and for their commitment to bringing this significant negotiation to a positive resolution."

Source: Federal Mediation & Conciliation Service, February, 20, 2015, available at http://www.fmcs .gov/internet/itemDetail.asp?categoryID=39&itemID=24920.

CHAPTER REVIEW

» Key Terms

» Summary

- When collective bargaining fails to produce an agreement in a labor dispute, either party may resort to pressure tactics to try to force the other side to settle the dispute. Union pressure involves strikes and calls for a boycott, while employers may resort to lockouts. The right to strike is not constitutionally guaranteed, but a strike is protected activity under the NLRA. Picketing, which usually accompanies a strike, is subject to several controls under the NLRA and related legislation.

- The Norris-La Guardia Act restricts the ability of the federal courts to issue injunctions against union conduct in a labor dispute; the term *labor dispute* is defined broadly in the Norris-La Guardia Act and includes strikes that are politically motivated. State courts can regulate violent picketing or picketing in violation of state laws, but when an unfair labor practice complaint has been filed concerning the legality of union picketing on private property, the *Babcock & Wilcox* approach should be used to decide the issue.

- The NLRA prohibits recognitional picketing, but publicity picketing directed to inform the public of a labor dispute is protected. Similarly, secondary picketing—union picketing directed at neutral employers who are not involved in the labor dispute—is an unfair labor practice. Exceptions to the prohibition on secondary picketing include consumer picketing and other publicity activities, such as hand-billing; employers who are allies of the struck employer may also be picketed by the union involved in the labor dispute.

- Hot cargo clauses—contract language that would allow unions to engage in secondary activity—are illegal under Section 8(e) of the NLRA; exceptions to Section 8(e) allow work preservation clauses and exclude the garment industry from the prohibitions of both Section 8(e) and Section 8(b)(4).

- Remedies for illegal secondary activity include injunctions under Section 10(l) and civil suits for damages under Section 303 of the NLRA.

» Problems

» Questions

1. In what situations can the states regulate picketing? Explain your answer.

2. What is recognitional or organization picketing? Under what circumstances is it prohibited by the NLRA?

3. What is primary picketing? What is secondary picketing? What factors determine the legality of picketing against neutral employers?

4. What is the ally doctrine? How does it affect the legality of picketing under Section 8(b)(4)?

5. What is a hot cargo clause? Why are hot cargo clauses prohibited by the NLRA?

» Case Problems

6. Alpha Theta of Alpha Delta Pi Building Association (Alpha Theta) is a nonprofit corporation that owns a sorority house near the University of Washington campus. In August 2009, Alpha Theta hired Marquise Construction to work on the basement of the sorority house. About three weeks after Marquise began its work, approximately 30 individuals from the local Carpenters' Union Regional Council (union) began marching and picketing up and down the street in front of the property, protesting Marquise's use of nonunion workers. The picketers also whistled and chanted as they marched. Alpha Theta claimed that defendant's agents have verbally harassed other contractors and employees of plaintiff, temporarily blocked the sidewalk in front of the property, and endangered the safety of Alpha Theta's president by distributing approximately 1,000 fliers with her name and personal mobile telephone number. Alpha Theta filed suit in state court for an injunction to stop the union's actions, claiming that it would disrupt the pledging season by discouraging prospective members from visiting the sorority house.

Should the state court issue an injunction against the union's actions? Is the union conduct protected under the NLRA? Explain your answer. [See *Alpha Theta of Alpha Delta Pi Bldg. Ass'n v. Pacific Northwest Regional Council of Carpenters*, 187 L.R.R.M. (BNA) 2211, 158 Lab.Cas. P 10,092 (W.D. Wash. 2009).]

7. Theater Techniques, Inc. (TTI) was a supplier of theatrical props and scenery for Broadway shows. TTI had a subcontract with Nolan Studios to paint scenery and props provided by TTI. Nolan Studios' employees were represented by Local 829, United Scenic Artists, whose collective agreement gave the union jurisdiction over the sculpting and painting of props. When some props from TTI arrived at Nolan already fabricated, the union employees refused to paint them unless Nolan paid a premium rate for the work. Nolan did not inform the union that TTI had contractual control over the disputed work, but Nolan did file a complaint with the NLRB, charging the union with violating Section 8(b)(4)(B) by refusing to handle the props from TTI to force Nolan to stop doing business with TTI.

How should the Board decide the unfair labor practice complaint filed by Nolan? Explain your answer. [See *United Scenic Artists, Local 829 v. NLRB*, 762 F.2d 1027 (D.C. Cir. 1985).]

8. Service Employees International Union, Local 6 [the Union] sought to organize BAGS, Inc. a company that performs baggage handling services as a subcontractor to Alaska Airlines, Inc. at the Seattle–Tacoma Airport. The Union staged protest actions with an object of forcing Alaska to cease doing business with a contractor, BAGS, Inc. ("BAGS") and/or forcing BAGS to recognize and bargain with the Union. On April 18, 2013, the Union made an unannounced visit to the Alaska ticket counter to present Alaska with customer comment forms filled out by its supporters earlier in another area of the Airport. Alaska's ground operations manager came to the ticketing area to meet the group of approximately 40 people after being

alerted to their presence while attending a manager's meeting that morning. He observed a news television camera recording the group. The majority of the group assembled in front of two unmanned check-in kiosks. A smaller number of people stood in front of the oversized baggage drop, which was in use at the time. It does not appear that any customers were delayed in checking into their flights or attempted to use or avoided using the oversized baggage drop during the Union's visit. The Union's point person introduced himself to the manager and stated that a number of people were going to read something to him. The ground operations manager responded "ok, that's fine," and then about 20 people came up one at a time to read their customer comment forms, which contained complaints about BAGS and other airport contractors. The group met with the operations manager for about 30 minutes, and the manager thanked them for their time and stated that he would make sure the comment forms got into the right hands. After someone thanked the manager for his time, the group walked to a common corridor in the departure level, chanted for an unspecified amount of time, and then disbanded. At no time did the Union attempt to speak with any customers or engage in any overtly disruptive conduct, and only one Alaska employee was spoken to briefly prior to management's arrival. Alaska Airlines and BAGS, Inc. then filed an unfair practice complaint with the regional NLRB office, alleging that the Union demonstration had violated Section 8(b)(4)(ii)(B).

How should the NLRB rule on the complaint? What factors will the NLRB consider in deciding this complaint? [See SEIU Local 6 (Bags, Inc.), 2013 WL 6385018 (N.L.R.B.G.C., Nov. 19, 2013).]

9. Delta Air Lines subcontracted the janitorial work of its offices at the Los Angeles International Airport to the National Cleaning Company. National entered into a collective bargaining agreement with the Hospital and Service Employees Union, Local 399. Delta later lawfully terminated its contract with National and made a new contract with Statewide Maintenance Company, a nonunion employer. Consequently, National fired five of the six janitors who had cleaned Delta's offices.

In furtherance of its recognitional dispute with Statewide Maintenance, the union began distributing handbills at Delta's Los Angeles airport facilities in front of the downtown Los Angeles office. One or two persons usually distributed the flyers at each facility. The hand-billing caused no interruptions in deliveries or refusals by Delta's employees to do their work.

There were four handbills altogether. The first stated, "Please do not fly Delta Airlines. Delta Airlines unfair. Does not provide AFL-CIO conditions of employment. (signed by union)." The other side said, "It takes more than money to fly Delta. It takes nerve. Let's look at the accident record." There followed a list of 55 accidents involving Delta over the years, along with the total number of deaths and injuries.

The second handbill, distributed a week later, contained all the information on side two of the first handbill but not the information from side one. The third handbill, another week later, again consisted of two sides. Side one said:

> Please Do Not Fly Delta Airlines. This airline has caused members of Service Employees Union, Local 399, AFL-CIO, at Los Angeles International Airport, to become unemployed. In their place they have contracted with a maintenance company which does not provide Local 399 wages, benefits and standards. We urge all union members to protest Delta's action to the Delta office in your region. If you are concerned about the plight of fellow union members … Please Do Not Fly Delta Airlines.

Side two contained the same accident information as the previous two broadsides.

Handbill four contained the same accident information as the prior three, with the following prefatory statement:

> As members of the public and in order to protect the wages and conditions of Local 399 members and to publicize our primary dispute with the Statewide Building Maintenance Company, we wish to call to the attention of the consuming public certain information about Delta Airlines from the official records of the Civil Aeronautics Board of the United States Government.

Simultaneous with the hand-billing activities, the union published copies of flyers one and three in two union newspapers, along with an advertisement stating simply, "Do Not Fly Delta."

Analyze each of the four handbills. What, if anything, in each constituted an illegal secondary boycott? What, if anything, was protected by the NLRA's publicity proviso? Is the same true with respect to the newspaper ads? [See *Service Employees Local 399 v. NLRB*, 117 L.R.R.M. 2717, 743 F.2d 1417 (9th Cir. 1984).]

10. Shortly after the Soviet invasion of Afghanistan in 1979, the United States imposed an embargo on exports to the Soviet Union. However, some grain shipments were exempted from the embargo. Nevertheless, the International Longshoremen's Association (ILA), apparently disagreeing with the exemptions, adopted a resolution that its longshoremen would not handle any goods exported to or arriving from the Soviet Union.

Sovfracht Chartering Corporation, a Soviet government maritime agency, chartered a Belgian ship (*The Belgium*) to transport exempt and duly licensed grain from Houston to Russia. The Houston stevedore companies had to hire all longshoremen from ILA hiring halls. When TTT Stevedores, an employer party to an ILA collective bargaining agreement, sought to load the Soviet-bound grain on board *The Belgium*, it was informed that the ILA local would not provide any of its members to do the work. When informed of this decision, Sovfracht canceled *The Belgium's* stop in Houston.

Was the ILA guilty of a secondary boycott? If so, against whom? What arguments can be made that this action was not illegal activity under the NLRA? [See *ILA v. NLRB*, 723 F.2d 963, 115 L.R.R.M. 2093 (D.C. Cir. 1983).]

11. The Iron Workers Union had been engaged in organizing the employees of Stokrr's Multi-Ton Corporation. When Stokrr's refused to recognize the union, the union called a strike of the company's employees. Perkins Trucking Company handled and transported Stokrr's products. Three days into the strike, pickets gathered around a Perkins truck as it attempted to make a pickup at the Stokrr's facility. One of the union pickets jumped on the running board of the Perkins truck and yelled at the driver, "We're going to rape your wife…. I'm going to break your legs." The picket then pointed at the driver's face and stated, "Just remember what I look like, because I know who you are. I'm going to get you…. [W]e're going to get all your trucks, you run a lot of them." At that point, the police assisted the Perkins truck through the picket line to the loading dock.

Sometime later, 8 to 12 strikers arrived at the Perkins terminal at 7 a.m. carrying placards. But they engaged in no picketing of the terminal facility; they stood around, 5 to 10 feet from the terminal gate. They told the assistant shop steward of the union at Perkins that they were "individuals" trying to gain information for their "personal use" and that they wanted to know if Perkins was handling any of Stokrr's freight. They were told that Perkins had not handled any Stokrr's freight for "the last couple of weeks." At about 8 a.m., the strikers departed.

Based on these facts, could it be said that Perkins was an ally of Stokrr's? What provisions of the NLRA, if any, did the union violate? [See *Iron Workers, Local 455*, 243 NLRB 340, 102 L.R.R.M. 1109 (1979).]

12. Point Ruston, LLC ("Point Ruston"), is a general construction contractor and property developer formed to provide management, development, and oversight services for the Point Ruston project., a master-planned, mixed-use development constructed on a site along the shore of the Puget Sound, near Tacoma, Washington. From 1890 to 1986, the site contained a lead and copper smelter. The EPA officially designated the land as a superfund site on the National Priorities List, because the site contained certain levels of arsenic and lead. In 2006, Point Ruston purchased the property during a bankruptcy proceeding, and assumed environmental remediation liabilities for the property and other adjacent sites. In the spring of 2008, Point Ruston entered into an agreement with Rain City Contractors, Inc. ("Rain City") to provide construction of concrete foundations and other concrete structures. While all other contractors retained by

Point Ruston in 2008 were union contractors, Rain City was not a unionized employer. After Point Ruston contracted with Rain City, the Carpenters Regional Council, a labor organization, informed Point Ruston that it had a labor dispute with Rain City, "and that if Point Ruston continued to use Rain City on the project then the Regional Council would have a dispute with Point Ruston as well." In February and March of 2009, the Carpenters began demonstrating by placement of large banners and leafleting to hotels owned by Silver Cloud, in Seattle, Washington. Silver Cloud owns hotels and has an option to build a hotel on the Point Ruston property at some point in the future. Silver Cloud does not have any relationship with Rain City, and Silver Cloud had not exercised its option to build a hotel at the Point Ruston site.

On February 4, 2009, the Carpenters sent Jim Korbein, CEO of Silver Cloud, a notice regarding its labor dispute with Rain City. This letter informed Korbein that, if Silver Cloud used Rain City to perform work on the hotel for which it had an option to build at the Point Ruston site, it too would have a labor dispute with the Carpenters. The letter stated that the Carpenters wanted Korbein "to use [its] managerial discretion to not allow Rain City ... to perform any work on any of your projects unless and until they generally meet area labor standards...." The letter further informed Korbein that the Carpenters would be engaged in "lawful demonstrations, including jobsite picketing and highly visible lawful banner displays, including distribution of handbills at the jobsite and premises of property owners, developers, general contractors, leasing/sales offices, tenants, clients and other firms involved with any project where sub-area standards contractors are employed." The letter cautioned that the Carpenters did "not want Silver Cloud ... to become embroiled in our labor dispute. That is why as a courtesy we are providing you with this notice." The letter concluded by stating that Silver Cloud could avoid "becoming publicly involved in this dispute" by agreeing to "comply with the requests" made in the letter: "Doing so will provide the greatest protection against Silver Cloud...."

Between February 11, 2009, and March 23, 2009, the Carpenters set up a large banner at the Silver Cloud stadium hotel in Seattle, located adjacent to the Mariners' and Seahawks' sports stadiums. This hotel location is over 30 miles from the Point Ruston site. The Carpenters used three people to hold the banner up and on occasion lashed the sign to the light poles. The banner contained three large block print statements, each one on top of the other: "POINT RUSTON, SILVER CLOUD HOTEL, GOT ARSENIC?" At each end of the banner, in smaller print, was the statement "Labor Dispute." The Banner did not include Rain City's name. On February 11, 2009, and continuing through March 23, 2009, the Carpenters passed out handbills to passers-by of the Silver Cloud hotels. The handbill stated, in extra-large print, "SHAME ON Silver Cloud Inns & Hotels For Desecration of the American Way of Life." In smaller font size, the relevant portion of the handbill's body reads as follows:

> Shame on SILVER CLOUD INN for contributing to the erosion of area standards for area carpenter craft workers. While SILVER CLOUD INN may not be the entity that chose the "Rat" [Rain City], they are certainly choosing to benefit from the "Rat's" practices. [Carpenters] has a labor dispute with RAIN CITY ... which is a subcontractor for POINT RUSTON .... RAIN CITY .... Please call JIM KORBEIN, CEO with SILVER CLOUD ... and tell him that you want him to do all he can to change this situation and see that Area Standards are met on all his construction projects.

Silver Cloud files suit against the Carpenters Regional Council under Section 303 of the NLRA, seeking damages for harm to its business caused by the Carpenters Council activities directed against it. Does Silver Cloud have to file an unfair labor practice charge alleging a violation of Section 8(b)(4)(ii)(B) before filing suit in federal court under Section 303? Did the conduct of the Carpenters Regional Council violate Section 8(b)(4)(ii)(B)? What defenses can the Carpenters Regional Council raise? How should the court rule on the suit? [See *Point Ruston, LLC v. Pacific Northwest Regional Council of the United Brotherhood of Carpenters and*

Joiners of America, 2010 WL 3522124 (W.D. Wash. Sept. 8, 2010).]

13. Zellers worked as an elevator installer; he was a member of Local 123 of the Elevator Constructors. Zellers was employed by Eggers Construction Co. and was working at a neutral construction site. The elevator construction crew was directed to use a separate, neutral gate at the work site because another union had set up a picket line at a different gate at the work site. When he saw the other picket line, Zellers refused to enter the work site, even though there was no picket line at the gate he was required to use. Because of his refusal to enter the gate, Zellers was suspended by Eggers. The Elevator Constructors Union filed a grievance protesting the suspension of Zellers. Eggers then filed an unfair labor practice complaint with the NLRB, alleging that the union filing the grievance was in violation of Section 8(b)(4) because it sought to authorize Zellers' refusal to work in order to force the general contractor to get rid of the employer subject to the strike by the other union.

How should the board rule on Eggers's unfair labor practice complaint? Explain your answer. [See *NLRB v. Elevator Constructors*, 134 L.R.R.M. 2137 (8th Cir. 1990).]

14. The Truck Drivers' Union was engaged in a primary labor dispute with Piggyback Services, Inc., a nonunion employer. The dispute began when the Santa Fe Railroad awarded Piggyback a subcontract to ramp and deramp intermodal freight (freight carried inside trailers and containers on railroad flat-cars) at Santa Fe's Richmond, California, rail terminal. That work had been performed by union members for a wholly owned subsidiary of Santa Fe. Piggyback had initially agreed to hire the former union workers, but later reneged on that promise, and the union began picketing and distributing handbills at Santa Fe's Richmond rail terminal.

In an effort to insulate itself from the union's labor dispute with Piggyback, Santa Fe designated a gate, Gate 1, as the sole entrance to the Richmond facility for employees, customers, visitors, and suppliers of Piggyback. Santa Fe also posted signs at four other entrances to the Richmond facility,

designated as Gate 2, Gate 3, Gate 4, and Gate 5, stating that these "neutral" gates were reserved for the exclusive use of Santa Fe's employees, customers, visitors, and suppliers, and that Gate 1 was available only for Piggyback's employees, customers, visitors, and suppliers.

Although Piggyback employees entered only through Gate 1, and the union fully acknowledged that it had no labor dispute with Santa Fe, the union began picketing at the four neutral gates. Handbills distributed by the union at neutral locations urged neutral employees and customers entering the Santa Fe railway yard to either honor the picket line or, alternatively, to cease all work related to Piggyback's day-to-day operations. The union sent letters to the presidents of the seven unions that represented Santa Fe employees. The letters requested that union members employed by Santa Fe not perform work directly related to Piggyback's operations at the Richmond terminal. A similar letter was sent by the union to United Parcel Services (UPS), Santa Fe's primary unionized intermodal trucking customer.

The UPS drivers and other Santa Fe customers honored the picket line by refusing to deliver intermodal freight to the Richmond terminal. In response, Santa Fe established a drop-off site about a mile-and-a-half from Gate 3 for use by UPS and other Santa Fe customers. Although no Piggyback employees were stationed at the UPS drop-off site, the union expanded its activity to that location. The union also picketed at the two railroad spur lines where intermodal freight cars entered the railway yard.

Santa Fe filed an unfair labor practice complaint with the NLRB, alleging that the union picketing violated Section 8(b)(4). How should the NLRB rule on the complaint? Why? Explain your answer. [See *NLRB v. General Truck Drivers, Warehousemen, Helpers and Automotive Employees of Contra Costa County, Local No. 315*, 20 F.3d 1017 (9th Cir. 1994).]

15. Aircraft Service International, Inc. [ASI] provides aircraft refueling and maintenance services at the Seattle–Tacoma International Airport. On September 14, 2012, ASI indefinitely suspended

Popescu, who worked as a fueler. Popescu and the other fuelers claimed that he was suspended because of his outspoken actions to promote workplace safety, including testifying at a public hearing held by the Seattle Port Commission, which operates the airport. ASI claimed that he was suspended pending an investigation into reports that he engaged in inappropriate conduct in the workplace. After the suspension, Popescu and the other fuelers decided to organize a "group response" and got together with a local labor coalition to press for his reinstatement. After two weeks of unsuccessful efforts to secure Popescu's reinstatement, the fuelers began distributing strike ballots on September 28. The fuelers voted overwhelmingly to go on strike to get Popescu rehired and to protest "retaliation and intimidation by ASIG." The fuelers and the labor coalition held a press conference soon after to publicize the fuelers' vote to go on strike. Two days after the press conference, ASI filed suit in federal district court seeking to enjoin any anticipated strike. The district court granted an injunction against the proposed strike, concluding that the Railway Labor Act [which governs railroads and airline companies] overrode the Norris-La Guardia Act. The fuelers and the labor coalition then appealed to the U.S. Court of Appeals for the 9th Circuit, seeking to have the injunction overturned on the grounds that ASI had not complied with the requirements of Section 8 of the Norris-La Guardia Act that the employer seeking an injunction must "make every reasonable effort to settle such dispute either by negotiation or with the aid of any available governmental machinery of mediation or voluntary arbitration."

Has ASI made any reasonable efforts to avoid the labor dispute here? Should the Court of Appeals affirm or reverse the trial court's grant of an injunction? Explain. [See *Aircraft Services Int. v. Working Washington*, 739 F.3d 1069 (9th Cir. 2015).]

» Hypothetical Scenarios

16. The United Brotherhood of Carpenters has a dispute with Brady Contracting over Brady's use of nonunion employees on construction jobs. The union claims that Brady's wages and benefits are below the area standards paid by unionized contractors. Brady is currently constructing several retail stores in the Phoenix area. The union sent letters to the various retail store owners, urging them not to work with Brady until Brady agreed to pay area standard wages and benefits. The union also informed the retailers that the union would begin an "aggressive public information campaign" against Brady, including displaying banners at the retail stores. The union then set up protests at several retail stores—it displayed large banners reading "Shame on [the name of the retailer]" and "Labor Dispute." The banners were displayed on public property about 20 feet from the retail store. Union members also distributed handbills that explained that the union's dispute was with Brady and not the retailer. Brady and two retailers filed unfair labor practice charges with the NLRB. Does the union conduct here violate Section 8(b)(4)? Explain your answer.

17. Midwest Moving Co. is a nonunion commercial moving and storage business. The International Brotherhood of Teamsters, Local 55, has been trying, without any success, to organize Midwest's employees. Midwest signed a contract to relocate Morgan Stanley's local office to an office building in downtown Chicago. The union learns of the upcoming job and notifies the building owner that it intends to picket at the building when Midwest employees are present there. The building owner informed the union that Midwest would be required to use the loading dock at the rear of the building, and would only have access to the loading dock after 6:00 p.m. and before 8:00 a.m. the next day. Shortly before 6:00 p.m., several union members began distributing handbills on the sidewalk in front of the building, and as the Midwest trucks approached, several other union members carrying picket signs began to walk back and forth in the alley near the loading dock at the rear of the building. The picketing was peaceful, but Midwest complained that the picketing made it difficult for the Midwest trucks to approach the loading

dock. The building owner and Midwest both filed complaints about the picketing with the NLRB. Is the union picketing here primary or secondary? Why? Is the picketing in violation of Section 8(b)(4)? Explain.

18. Local 15 of the United Food and Commercial Workers Union went on strike against Gold Medal Bakery when negotiations for a new contract reached an impasse. The bakery's cookies are sold at FoodCo grocery stores in the Syracuse area. The union posts members holding signs saying "Don't Buy Gold Medal Cookies" and "Don't Eat Scab Cookies" in front of the local FoodCo stores. As a result of the union actions, sales of Gold Medal Cookies fall sharply. FoodCo files an unfair labor practice charge against the union with the NLRB. Is the union's conduct legal under the NLRA? Explain.

19. State Electric, a nonunion contractor, is doing the electrical work at the construction site of a church. The employees of a number of other contractors are also working at the construction site. The Electricians' Union begins picketing the construction site, but pickets at all gates into the site even though State Electric employees are restricted to Gate 1. When the union begins picketing, the employees of the other contractors at the site refuse to work. Has the union violated Section 8(b)(4)? Explain. What, if any, actions should the union take to make sure the picketing is legal? Why?

20. Speedy Delivery, Inc. is a local parcel delivery service. Its drivers are represented by Local 33 of the Service Employees International Union. The Teamsters Union, Local 747, approaches the manager of Speedy Delivery and demands that the company recognize it as the bargaining representative for its employees. When the manager refuses, the Teamsters begin picketing around Speedy Delivery's warehouse and garage. The picketing causes several UPS and FedEx truck drivers to refuse to make deliveries to Speedy Delivery. Does the Teamster's picketing violate the NLRA? If so, which section? Why?

CHAPTER 17

The Enforcement and Administration of the Collective Agreement

The signing of a collective agreement by a union and an employer may mark the end of the bargaining process; it is also the beginning of a continuing relationship between them. The agreement creates rights for and imposes obligations on both parties. The parties are bound to uphold the terms of the contract for its duration. How can union and management ensure that the "other side" will honor the contract? What means are available to enforce the contract in the event of a breach by either side? How can disputes over the interpretation of the agreement be resolved? This chapter discusses the means available for the enforcement and administration of the collective agreement.

Section 301 of the National Labor Relations Act (NLRA) provides that suits for violations of contracts between an employer and a labor union may be brought in federal and state courts. Therefore, either the union or employer could bring a lawsuit over the other side's failure to live up to the contract. However, lawsuits are a cumbersome means of resolving most contract disputes; they are also expensive and time consuming. For these reasons, lawsuits are impractical for resolving disputes over how collective agreements should be interpreted or applied.

Either party to the agreement could resort to pressure tactics to try to resolve a contract dispute. The union could go on strike, or the employer could lock out the employees to force the other side to live up to the contract. The employer generally is not willing to lock out employees and cease production over minor matters. Nor are union members likely to strike, lose wages, and risk being replaced over insignificant issues.

17-1 Arbitration

arbitration
the settlement of disputes by a neutral adjudicator chosen by the parties

Because of the shortcomings of both lawsuits and pressure tactics as a way to resolve contract disputes, the parties usually agree, as a part of their collective agreement, to establish their own process for resolving disputes peacefully. The peaceful settlement process usually involves **arbitration**. Arbitration is the settlement of disputes by a neutral adjudicator chosen by the parties to the dispute. It provides a means to resolve contractual disputes relatively inexpensively and expeditiously. Arbitration also provides flexibility because the parties are free to tailor the arbitration process to suit their particular situation. The parties generally incorporate arbitration as the final step of the grievance procedure. In return for

549

the agreement by each party to arbitrate their dispute, they give up their right to strike or lock out over such issues.

17-1a   Interest Arbitration Versus Rights Arbitration

interest arbitration
arbitration that is used to create a new collective agreement or to renew an existing agreement

In a labor relations setting, arbitration may be used either to settle a dispute over the creation of a new collective agreement or over the interpretation and administration of an existing agreement. When arbitration is used to create a new agreement (or renew an existing one), it is known as **interest arbitration**—the parties seek to protect their economic interests through favorable contract terms. Interest arbitration is common in the public sector, where employees are generally prohibited from striking. Interest arbitration replaces pressure tactics as a means to resolve the negotiating impasse in the public sector. It is much less common in the private sector.

rights arbitration
arbitration to resolve a dispute involving the interpretation or application of an existing collective agreement; arbitration that defines the rights and obligations of each party under the agreement

If the dispute involves interpreting an existing agreement rather than creating a new one, the arbitration to resolve it is known as **rights arbitration**. Rights arbitration is the means to define the rights and obligations of each party under the agreement. It is very common in both the public and private sectors. Even though rights arbitration is not required by the NLRA, more than 90 percent of all collective agreements provide for rights arbitration as the means to resolve disputes over the interpretation and/or application of the collective agreement. This chapter is concerned with rights arbitration, and unless otherwise specified, the term *arbitration* refers to rights arbitration.

17-1b   Rights Arbitration and the Grievance Process

grievance process
the process set up by a collective agreement to deal with complaints that arise under the collective agreement

Rights arbitration is generally used as the final step in the **grievance process**—a process set up to deal with complaints under the collective agreement. Like rights arbitration, the grievance process is created by the parties to the agreement. It is not required by statute. Because it is voluntarily created by the parties under the collective agreement, the grievance process can be tailored to fit their particular situation or desires.

grievance
a complaint that one party to a collective agreement is not living up to the obligations of the agreement

A **grievance** is simply a complaint that either party to the agreement is not living up to the obligations of the agreement. Most grievances are filed by employees complaining about the actions of the employer (or its agents), but management may also file grievances under the agreement.

Grievance procedures vary widely; the parties to an agreement can devise whatever procedure is best suited to their purposes. The following is an example of a four-step grievance procedure, with arbitration as the final step.

ARTICLE XIII: GRIEVANCE PROCEDURE

SECTION 1. Any grievance or dispute between the Company and the Union involving the interpretation or application of any terms of this Agreement shall be adjusted according to the following procedure:

Step One: The employee who believes he has suffered a grievance or been unjustly treated may raise the alleged grievance with his Foreman or Assistant Foreman in an attempt to settle the same. The said employee may be accompanied or represented if he so desires by the Steward. The Foreman shall have two (2) working days to settle the grievance.

Step Two: If the matter is not satisfactorily settled in Step One, it may be taken to the Second Step by the Union's reducing it to writing, on a mutually agreed upon form provided by the Company. Any grievance taken to the Second Step must be signed by a Steward, a Chief Steward, or a Local Union Committee member. Two (2) copies will be delivered to the Supervisor, who will sign and date the grievance upon receipt of it. A meeting will be arranged within four (4) working days following receipt of the form, between the Supervisor, Plant Superintendent, Grievant, Steward, or in his absence, Chief Steward. A written answer shall be given within four (4) working days from the date of the meeting even though an oral decision is given at the meeting. If the answer is not received during the time period, the grievance shall be deemed settled in favor of the grievant or Union.

Step Three: The Steward, or Chief Steward in his absence, may appeal the Second Step decision by completing the "Appeal to Third Step" portion of the grievance form and by delivering the same to the Industrial Relations Department within five (5) working days (excluding Saturday and Sunday) after the decision in the Second Step. The Industrial Relations Department shall arrange a meeting within five (5) working days (excluding Saturday and Sunday) following receipt of the appeal, between the representative designated by the Company, the Shop Grievance Committee, and the International Representative. A written answer shall be given within five (5) working days (excluding Saturday and Sunday) from the date of the meeting even though an oral decision is given at the meeting. Any failure by either party to meet the time limits required shall deem the grievance settled in favor of the other party.

Step Four: Any grievance or dispute involving the interpretation or application of this Agreement, which has not been satisfactorily settled in the foregoing steps, may, at the request of either party, be submitted to an arbitrator or arbitration board selected as hereinafter provided, by written notice delivered to the other party within four (4) calendar weeks subsequent to the decision in Step Three. Any failure, by either party, to meet such time limits shall be deemed a waiver of the grievance. Unless the parties mutually agree upon arbitration by the State Board of Mediation and Arbitration, the matter shall be referred to the American Arbitration Association for arbitration under its rules. The fees and expenses of the arbitrator thus selected shall be divided equally between the parties.

SECTION 2. The arbitration board or the arbitrator is not authorized to add to, modify, or take away from the express terms of this Agreement and shall be limited to the interpretation or application of the provisions of the Agreement of the determination as to whether there is a violation of it. Any decision of the arbitration board or the arbitrator within the scope of the above authority shall be final and binding on both parties.

SECTION 3. Time limits above set forth must be complied with strictly.

SECTION 4. The Company or the Union may institute a grievance at Step Three on any matter concerning general application, and process it through Step Four.

It can be seen that the actual grievance procedure is a series of meetings between union and management representatives. As the grievance remains unresolved and moves through the various steps of the procedure, the rank of the representatives involved increases. Either party may request that a grievance unresolved at Step Three be submitted to arbitration.

Concept *Summary* 17.1

RIGHTS ARBITRATION VERSUS INTEREST ARBITRATION

Rights Arbitration	Interest Arbitration
Used to resolve disputes over the enforcement of a collective agreement—to determine the rights and obligations of the parties under the collective agreement	Used to create or renew the terms of a collective agreement
Arbitration clause is quid pro quo for a union agreeing not to strike during the term of the agreement	Used in the public sector to resolve contract disputes involving employees who are prohibited from striking

17-2   The Courts and Arbitration

As noted, arbitration as a means to resolve grievances is a voluntary mechanism; the parties to the contract have agreed to use it. But what happens if either party refuses to submit a dispute to arbitration? What remedies are available to the party seeking arbitration? The following *Lincoln Mills* case deals with an attempt to use Section 301 of the NLRA to force management to arbitrate a union grievance.

As *Lincoln Mills* indicates, if the parties have agreed to arbitration as a means of resolving disputes, the courts will require them to use it. What is voluntary about arbitration, then, is its existence—whether the agreement provides for arbitration. Once the parties have agreed to use arbitration, the courts will enforce that agreement.

What should the role of the court be when it is asked to order that a dispute be arbitrated or when it is asked to enforce an arbitration award? Those issues were addressed by the Supreme Court in three cases that came to be known as the *Steelworkers Trilogy*. In *United Steelworkers of America v. Warrior & Gulf Navigation Co.*,[1] the Supreme Court held that when a court is asked to order arbitration under Section 301, an order to arbitrate the grievance should not be denied "unless it may be said with positive assurance that the arbitration clause is not susceptible of an interpretation that covers the asserted dispute. Doubts should be resolved in favor of coverage." In a more recent decision, the Supreme Court again affirmed the holding of *Warrior & Gulf Navigation*. In *AT&T Technologies v. Communications Workers of America*,[2] the Court held that it is the role of the courts, not of the arbitrators, to resolve questions of whether a grievance is subject to arbitration. A dispute

---

[1] 363 U.S. 574 (1960).

[2] 475 U.S. 643 (1986).

between an employer and a union over the date upon which a collective agreement was ratified was to be decided by a court and not by arbitration.[3]

The collective agreement's arbitration clause may also affect the right of individual employees to bring employment discrimination suits. (See the discussion on this topic in Chapter 8.) In *Alexander v. Gardner Denver Co.*,[4] the Supreme Court held that an employee who had lost in arbitration under the collective agreement was still able to bring a Title VII suit in court. The Court held that the arbitration dealt with the employee's rights under the collective agreement, which were distinct from the employee's statutory rights under Title VII. In *Wright v. Universal Marine Supply*,[5] the Supreme Court held that the arbitration clause of a collective agreement must contain a "clear and unmistakable waiver" of the individual employee's rights to sue in order to waive the individual employee's right to sue over employment discrimination claims. More recently, the Supreme Court decided the case of *14 Penn Plaza v. Pyett*[6] involving age discrimination claims filed by employees covered by a collective agreement that included an arbitration clause specifically covering any claims under Title VII, the Age Discrimination in Employment Act, and other EEO legislation. The Court held that the employees were required to arbitrate their age discrimination claims. The Court noted that *Alexander* did not apply where the collective bargaining agreement's arbitration provision expressly included statutory claims as well as contractual claims arising under the terms of the collective agreement. The effect of the decision in *14 Penn Plaza v. Pyett* may be limited, however, because the Court specifically refrained from holding that employees must arbitrate their statutory EEO claims when the union controls access to arbitration and could prevent the employees from pursuing their EEO claims through arbitration.

≫ CASE 17.1

TEXTILE WORKERS UNION OF AMERICA V. LINCOLN MILLS OF ALABAMA
353 U.S. 448 (1957)

Facts: The Textile Workers Union entered into a collective bargaining agreement with the employer, Lincoln Mills. The agreement provided that there would be no strikes or work stoppages, and contained a grievance procedure. The last step in the grievance procedure was arbitration, which could be invoked by either party. The union processed several grievances concerning work loads and work assignments through the various steps in the grievance procedure, but the employer denied them.

The union then requested arbitration, and the employer refused. The union then filed suit under Section 301 of the NLRA to compel the employer to arbitrate the grievances. The trial court ordered the employer to arbitrate the grievances under the arbitration provisions of the collective bargaining agreement. The employer appealed, and the court of appeals reversed the trial court decision. The union then appealed to the U.S. Supreme Court.

---

[3] *Granite Rock Co. v. Int. Brotherhood of Teamsters*, 130 S.Ct. 2847 (2010).

[4] 415 U.S. 147 (1974).

[5] 525 U.S. 70 (1998). Applying the holding in *Wright*, the U.S. Court of Appeals for the Sixth Circuit held that an employee who had arbitrated a claim of employment discrimination was not prevented from bringing a court suit over the same discrimination claim because the collective agreement's general nondiscrimination clause was not a "clear and unmistakable waiver," in *Kennedy v. Superior Printing Co.*, 215 F.3d 650 (6th Cir. 2000).

[6] 129 S.Ct. 1456 (2009).

Issue: Does Section 301 authorize a court to order the parties to a collective agreement to arbitrate a grievance?

Decision: The Court looked to the wording of Section 301, which provides:

(a) Suits for violation of contracts between an employer and a labor organization representing employees in an industry affecting commerce as defined in this chapter, or between any such labor organizations, may be brought in any district court of the United States having jurisdiction of the parties, without respect to the amount in controversy or without regard to the citizenship of the parties.

Previous decisions involving Section 301 hold that Section 301(a) authorizes federal courts to fashion a body of federal law for the enforcement of collective bargaining

agreements, including enforcing of promises to arbitrate grievances under collective bargaining agreements. The agreement to arbitrate grievance disputes, contained in this collective bargaining agreement, should be enforced. The agreement to arbitrate grievances is the quid pro quo for an agreement not to strike. Section 301 expresses a federal policy that federal courts should enforce these agreements to arbitrate in order to ensure that industrial peace can be promoted. In enforcing agreements to arbitrate under Section 301, the courts should to apply substantive federal law, fashioned from the policy of the national labor laws. The Court also noted that the Norris–La Guardia Act, which restricts federal courts issuing injunctions in labor disputes, does not apply to suits seeking to order arbitration under Section 301. The Supreme Court reversed the decision of the court of appeals and remanded the case.

The limited role of the court ordering arbitration was emphasized in *United Steelworkers v. American Mfg Co.*,[7] the second case in the trilogy. In that case, the Supreme Court held that

[t]he function of the court ... is confined to ascertaining whether the party seeking arbitration is making a claim which on its face is governed by the contract. Whether the moving party is right or wrong is a question of contract interpretation for the arbitrator.... *The courts, therefore, have no business weighing the merits of the grievance.* [emphasis added]

The duty to arbitrate arises from the collective agreement between the parties, but does the duty to arbitrate continue to exist after the expiration of the collective agreement? In *Litton Financial Printing Div., Litton Business Systems v. NLRB*,[8] the Supreme Court held that the duty to arbitrate continues after the expiration of the agreement if the grievance arises "under the agreement." In other words:

• it involves facts and occurrences that arose prior to expiration;

• it concerns post-expiration action that infringes a right accrued or vested under the agreement; or

• it involves disputed contract rights that survive the expiration of the collective agreement.

When one of the parties refuses to comply with the arbitrator's award or decision after the grievance has been arbitrated, the other party may seek to have the award judicially enforced. What is the role of the court that is asked to enforce the arbitration decision? This was the subject of the final case in the trilogy, *United Steelworkers v. Enterprise Wheel & Car Co.*[9] In that case, the Supreme Court held that the court is required to enforce the

---

[7] 363 U.S. 564 (1960).

[8] 501 U.S. 190 (1991).

[9] 363 U.S. 593 (1960).

arbitrator's decision unless it is clear to the court that the arbitrator has exceeded the authority given to him or her by the collective agreement. The Court stated that "the question of interpretation of the collective agreement is a question for the arbitrator. It is the arbitrator's construction which was bargained for; and so far as the arbitrator's decision concerns the construction of the contract, the courts have no business overruling him because their interpretation of the contract is different from his." In *Major League Baseball Players Association v. Garvey*,[10] the Supreme Court emphasized that even when the court vacates an arbitration award, the court must remand the issue back to arbitration for resolution rather than settling the merits of the dispute according to the court's own judgment.

Under the *Enterprise Wheel & Car* decision, the court should refuse to enforce an arbitration decision that violates the law. How should the court react when an employer claims that an arbitration decision conflicts with the "policy" behind the law?

CASE 17.2

EASTERN ASSOCIATED COAL CORPORATION V. UNITED MINE WORKERS OF AMERICA, DISTRICT 17

531 U.S. 57 (2000)

Justice Breyer Delivered the Opinion of the Court

... Eastern Associated Coal Corp., and respondent, United Mine Workers of America, are parties to a collective-bargaining agreement with arbitration provisions. The agreement specifies that, in arbitration, in order to discharge an employee, Eastern must prove it has "just cause." Otherwise the arbitrator will order the employee reinstated. The arbitrator's decision is final.

James Smith worked for Eastern as a member of a road crew, a job that required him to drive heavy truck-like vehicles on public highways. As a truck driver, Smith was subject to Department of Transportation (DOT) regulations requiring random drug testing of workers engaged in "safety-sensitive" tasks.

In March 1996, Smith tested positive for marijuana. Eastern sought to discharge Smith. The union went to arbitration, and the arbitrator concluded that Smith's positive drug test did not amount to "just cause" for discharge. Instead the arbitrator ordered Smith's reinstatement, provided that Smith (1) accept a suspension of 30 days without pay, (2) participate in a substance-abuse program, and (3) undergo drug tests at the discretion of Eastern (or an approved substance-abuse professional) for the next five years.

Between April 1996 and January 1997, Smith passed four random drug tests. But in July 1997 he again tested positive for marijuana. Eastern again sought to discharge Smith. The union again went to arbitration, and the arbitrator again concluded that Smith's use of marijuana did not amount to "just cause" for discharge, in light of two mitigating circumstances. First, Smith had been a good employee for 17 years. And, second, Smith had made a credible and "very personal appeal under oath... concerning a personal/family problem which caused this one time lapse in drug usage."

The arbitrator ordered Smith's reinstatement provided that Smith (1) accept a new suspension without pay, this time for slightly more than three months; (2) reimburse Eastern and the union for the costs of both arbitration proceedings; (3) continue to participate in a substance-abuse program; (4) continue to undergo random drug testing; and (5) provide Eastern with a signed, undated letter of resignation, to take effect if Smith again tested positive within the next five years.

Eastern brought suit in federal court seeking to have the arbitrator's award vacated, arguing that the award contravened a public policy against the operation of dangerous machinery by workers who test positive for drugs. The

---

[10] 532 U.S. 504 (2001).

District Court, while recognizing a strong regulation-based public policy against drug use by workers who perform safety-sensitive functions, held that Smith's conditional reinstatement did not violate that policy. And it ordered the award's enforcement.

The Court of Appeals for the Fourth Circuit affirmed on the reasoning of the District Court. [Eastern appealed to the U.S. Supreme Court.] …

Eastern claims that considerations of public policy make the arbitration award unenforceable…. Eastern does not claim here that the arbitrator acted outside the scope of his contractually delegated authority. Hence we must treat the arbitrator's award as if it represented an agreement between Eastern and the union as to the proper meaning of the contract's words "just cause." … We must then decide whether a contractual reinstatement requirement would fall within the legal exception that makes unenforceable "a collective bargaining agreement that is contrary to public policy." The Court has made clear that any such public policy must be "explicit," "well defined," and "dominant." It must be "ascertained 'by reference to the laws and legal precedents and not from general considerations of supposed public interests.'" And, of course, the question to be answered is not whether Smith's drug use itself violates public policy, but whether the agreement to reinstate him does so. To put the question more specifically, does a contractual agreement to reinstate Smith with specified conditions run contrary to an explicit, well-defined, and dominant public policy, as ascertained by reference to positive law and not from general considerations of supposed public interests?…

We agree, in principle, that courts' authority to invoke the public policy exception is not limited solely to instances where the arbitration award itself violates positive law. Nevertheless, the public policy exception is narrow and must satisfy the principles set forth in … *Misco*. Moreover, in a case like the one before us, where two political branches have created a detailed regulatory regime in a specific field, courts should approach with particular caution pleas to divine further public policy in that area.

Eastern asserts that a public policy against reinstatement of workers who use drugs can be discerned from an examination of that regulatory regime, which consists of the Omnibus Transportation Employee Testing Act of 1991 and DOT's implementing regulations. The Testing Act … requires the Secretary of Transportation to promulgate regulations requiring "testing of operators of commercial motor vehicles for the use of a controlled substance." It mandates suspension of those operators who have driven a commercial motor vehicle while under the influence of drugs. And DOT's implementing regulations set forth sanctions applicable to those who test positive for illegal drugs.

In Eastern's view, these provisions embody a strong public policy against drug use by transportation workers in safety-sensitive positions and in favor of random drug testing in order to detect that use. Eastern argues that reinstatement of a driver who has twice failed random drug tests would undermine that policy—to the point where a judge must set aside an employer–union agreement requiring reinstatement.

Eastern's argument, however, loses much of its force when one considers further provisions of the Act that make clear that the Act's remedial aims are complex. The Act says that "rehabilitation is a critical component of any testing program"…. Neither the Act nor the regulations forbid an employer to reinstate in a safety-sensitive position an employee who fails a random drug test once or twice. The congressional and regulatory directives require only that the above-stated prerequisites to reinstatement be met.

Moreover, when promulgating these regulations, DOT decided not to require employers either to provide rehabilitation or to "hold a job open for a driver" who has tested positive, on the basis that such decisions "should be left to management/driver negotiation." That determination reflects basic background labor law principles, which caution against interference with labor-management agreements about appropriate employee discipline….

We believe that these expressions of positive law embody several relevant policies. As Eastern points out, these policies include Testing Act policies against drug use by employees in safety-sensitive transportation positions and in favor of drug testing. They also include a Testing Act policy favoring rehabilitation of employees who use drugs. And the relevant statutory and regulatory provisions must be read in light of background labor law policy that favors determination of disciplinary questions through arbitration when chosen as a result of labor-management negotiation.

The award before us is not contrary to these several policies, taken together. The award does not condone Smith's conduct or ignore the risk to public safety that drug use by truck drivers may pose. Rather, the award punishes Smith by suspending him for three months, thereby depriving him of nearly $9,000 in lost wages; it requires him to pay the arbitration costs of both sides; it insists upon further substance-abuse treatment and testing; and it makes clear (by requiring Smith to provide a signed letter of resignation) that one more failed test means discharge.

The award violates no specific provision of any law or regulation. It is consistent with DOT rules requiring completion of substance-abuse treatment before returning to work, for it does not preclude Eastern from assigning Smith to a non-safety-sensitive position until Smith completes the prescribed treatment program. It is consistent with the Testing Act's … driving license suspension requirements, for those requirements apply only to drivers who, unlike Smith, actually operated vehicles under the influence of drugs. The award is also consistent with the Act's rehabilitative concerns, for it requires substance-abuse treatment and testing before Smith can return to work.…

Regarding drug use by persons in safety-sensitive positions, then, Congress has enacted a detailed statute. And Congress has delegated to the Secretary of Transportation authority to issue further detailed regulations on that subject. Upon careful consideration, including public notice and comment, the Secretary has done so. Neither Congress nor the Secretary has seen fit to mandate the discharge of a worker who twice tests positive for drugs. We hesitate to infer a public policy in this area that goes beyond the careful and detailed scheme Congress and the Secretary have created.

We recognize that reasonable people can differ as to whether reinstatement or discharge is the more appropriate remedy here. But both employer and union have agreed to entrust this remedial decision to an arbitrator. We cannot find in the Act, the regulations, or any other law or legal precedent an "explicit," "well defined," "dominant" public policy to which the arbitrator's decision "runs contrary." We conclude that the lower courts correctly rejected Eastern's public policy claim.

The judgment of the Court of Appeals is affirmed.

Case Questions

1. Why did the arbitrator order the reinstatement of Smith? What penalties did Smith suffer as a result of testing positive for drug use?

2. What does the employer use to define the public policy it claims requires that Smith be discharged? Does the Court read those materials as defining the same public policy as claimed by the employer?

3. Does the Court enforce the arbitrator's award here? Why?

In *Paperworkers v. Misco, Inc.*,[11] the Supreme Court held that a court may refuse to enforce an arbitration award only if the award violates "explicit" public policy as defined by reference to legislation and court decisions rather than "general considerations of supposed public interests."

17-2a Judicial Enforcement of No-Strike Clauses

The decisions in the *Steelworkers Trilogy* emphasized that arbitration was a substitute for industrial strife. The *Lincoln Mills* decision stated that the employer's agreement to arbitrate disputes is the quid pro quo for the union's agreement not to strike over arbitrable disputes.

no-strike clause
a provision in a collective agreement by which the union agrees not to strike over disputes of interpretation of the agreement during the term of the agreement

Many agreements contain **no-strike clauses** by which the union agrees not to strike over disputes of interpretation of the agreement during the term of the agreement. In *Teamsters Local 174 v. Lucas Flour*,[12] the Supreme Court held that a no-strike clause will be implied by the court, even when the agreement itself is silent on the matter, if the agreement contains an arbitration provision. The implied no-strike clause covers any dispute that is subject to arbitration under the agreement.

If the collective agreement contains an express no-strike clause, or even an implied one under *Lucas Flour*, can a federal court enforce that clause by enjoining a strike in violation of the no-strike clause? What about the anti-injunction provisions of the

11 484 U.S. 29 (1987).
12 369 U.S. 95 (1962).

Norris–La Guardia Act? This issue was presented to the Supreme Court in *Boys Markets, Inc. v. Retail Clerks Union, Local 770.*[13] The Court in *Boys Markets* held that the Norris–La Guardia Act did not prevent a federal court from issuing an injunction to stop a strike over an issue that was subject to the arbitration clause of a collective agreement.

Injunctions under the doctrine of *Boys Markets* may also be issued against employers for breaches of the collective agreement that threaten the arbitration process. In *Oil, Chemical and Atomic Workers International Union, Local 2–286 v. Amoco Oil Co.,*[14] the court affirmed an injunction preventing an employer's unilateral implementation of a drug testing program, pending the outcome of arbitration to determine the employer's right to institute such a program under the collective bargaining agreement.

The decision in *Boys Markets* allowing federal courts to enjoin strikes in violation of no-strike clauses does not mean that a union may never go on strike during the term of a collective agreement. The *Boys Markets* holding is limited to strikes over issues subject to arbitration under the agreement. In *Jacksonville Bulk Terminals, Inc. v. Int. Longshoremen's Assn.,*[15] the Supreme Court refused to enjoin a refusal by longshoremen to handle cargo destined for the Soviet Union in protest over the Soviet invasion of Afghanistan. The Court held that the strike was over a political dispute that was not arbitrable under the collective agreement. The policy behind that decision was first set out in the Supreme Court decision of *Buffalo Forge Co. v. United Steelworkers of America,*[16] which held that the use of an injunction to stop a strike, as in *Boys Markets*, is appropriate only when the cause of the strike is a dispute that is subject to arbitration under the collective agreement.

Concept *Summary* 17.2

COURTS AND ARBITRATION

- The courts will enforce a no-strike clause where the dispute is subject to the arbitration clause
- The courts will enforce an agreement to arbitrate unless the grievance is clearly not within the scope of the arbitration agreement
- When ordering arbitration, the court is not to rule on the merits of the grievance
- The courts are required to enforce an arbitration award unless the arbitrator has exceeded her or his authority under the collective agreement or violates explicit public policy

Remedies for Breach of No-Strike Clauses

As the preceding cases demonstrate, an employer may enjoin strikes that violate a no-strike clause when the strike is over an arbitrable issue. But even when an injunction will not be issued, an employer may still recover damages for breach of the no-strike clause through a suit under Section 301. In the *Lucas Flour* case, the Supreme Court upheld a damage award for a strike in violation of the implied no-strike clause.

---

[13] 398 U.S. 235 (1970).
[14] 885 F.2d 697 (10th Cir. 1989).
[15] 457 U.S. 702 (1982).
[16] 428 U.S. 397 (1975).

Section 301 Suits The Supreme Court had held that suits under Section 301 are governed by the appropriate state statutes of limitations, according to *UAW v. Hoosier Cardinal Corp.*[17] More recently, in *DelCostello v. Teamsters*,[18] the Court held that suits under Section 301 by an individual employee against the employer for breach of the collective agreement and against the union for breach of the duty of fair representation were subject to the six-month limitation period under Section 10(b) of the NLRA.

Section 301, while allowing damage suits for breach of no-strike clauses, places some limitations upon such suits. Section 301(b) specifies that "any money judgment against a labor organization in a district court of the United States shall be enforceable only against the organization as an entity and its assets, and shall not be enforceable against any individual member or his assets." In *Atkinson v. Sinclair Refining Co.*,[19] the Supreme Court held that Section 301 does not authorize damage suits against individual union officials when their union is liable for violating a no-strike clause. In *Complete Auto Transit, Inc. v. Reis*,[20] the Court held that individual employees are not liable for damages from a wildcat strike not authorized by their union in breach of the collective agreement. If the employer cannot recover damages from the individuals responsible for such a strike, what other steps can the employer take against those individuals?

In *Carbon Fuel Co. v. United Mine Workers*,[21] the Supreme Court held that an international union was not liable for damages resulting from a strike by one of its local unions when the international had neither instigated, authorized, supported, nor encouraged the strike. Why would the employer seek damages from the international when the local had gone on strike?

The result of the *Complete Auto Transit and Carbon Fuel* cases is to deprive the employer of the right to recover damages from either the union or the individual union members when a strike by the individual union members is not authorized by the union. The remedy of damages is available to the employer only when the union has called or authorized the strike in breach of the collective agreement.

When the employer can pursue arbitration over the union violation of the agreement, the court will stay a suit for damages pending arbitration according to the Supreme Court decision in *Drake Bakeries Inc. v. Bakery Workers Local 50*.[22] The employer's obligation to arbitrate such disputes continues despite the union's breach of its contractual obligations, according to *Packinghouse Workers Local 721 v. Needham Packing Co.*[23]

Section 301 and Other Remedies Can a court hear a suit alleging a breach of contract under Section 301 even though the contract is silent about judicial remedies? In *Groves v. Ring Screw Works*,[24] the collective agreement provided for arbitration in discharge cases only upon agreement of both parties. It also provided that if a grievance was not resolved through the grievance procedure, the union could go on strike over the issue. Two employees who were discharged by the employer filed suit for wrongful discharge in state court; their union joined

---

[17] 383 U.S. 696 (1966).

[18] 462 U.S. 151 (1983).

[19] 370 U.S. 238 (1962).

[20] 451 U.S. 401 (1981).

[21] 444 U.S. 212 (1979).

[22] 370 U.S. 254 (1962).

[23] 376 U.S. 247 (1964).

[24] 498 U.S. 168 (1990).

the suits as a plaintiff. The employer argued that the union could not file suit because the contract did not require arbitration. The Supreme Court reversed the court of appeals. The Court unanimously held that a contract giving the union the right to strike or the employer the right to lock out does not automatically strip federal courts of the authority to resolve contractual disputes. The union was not precluded from filing suit against the employer to enforce the contract, even though the contract was silent about judicial remedies.

Section 301 Preemption of Other Remedies In *Allis-Chalmers Corp. v. Leuck*,[25] the Supreme Court held that if the resolution of a state law claim depends on the interpretation of a collective agreement, the application of the state law is preempted by federal law. A suit under state law alleging bad-faith handling of a disability benefits claim was preempted by Section 301 because the collective agreement set out provisions for handling disability claims. In *I.B.E.W. v. Hechler*,[26] the Supreme Court held that an employee's tort suit against the union for failure to provide a safe place to work was precluded by Section 301 because her claim was "nothing more than a breach of the union's federal duty of fair representation." However, where state law remedies exist independently of any collective agreement and do not require interpretation of the agreement, the state law remedy is not preempted. In *Lingle v. Norge Division of Magic Chef, Inc.*,[27] the Supreme Court held that an employee who was discharged for filing a workers' compensation claim could file suit under state law for compensation and punitive damages. Her suit was not preempted by Section 301.

California law requires that employers pay discharged employees all wages owed to them immediately at the time of the discharge. The California State commissioner of labor interpreted that law as not applying to employees covered by a collective agreement containing an arbitration clause. In *Livadas v. Bradshaw*,[28] the U.S. Supreme Court held that the commissioner's interpretation was preempted by Section 301 because it denied employees benefits for engaging in activity—pursuing arbitration and other remedies under the collective agreement—protected under federal labor law.

17-2b　The NLRB and Arbitration

As the preceding cases have demonstrated, the courts favor the policy of voluntary resolution of disputes between labor and management. The courts will therefore refrain from deciding issues that are subject to arbitration, instead deferring to the arbitrator's resolution of such issues. If a grievance under an agreement involves conduct that may also be an unfair labor practice under the NLRA, what is the role of the National Labor Relations Board (NLRB)? Should the Board, like the courts, defer to arbitration? Or should the Board decide the issue to ensure that the parties' statutory rights are protected?

The NLRB had previously taken the position that it would defer to arbitration on unfair labor practice complaints, even if they involved claims of violations of Sections 8(a)(1) and 8(a)(3). Over the years, several courts of appeals have criticized the NLRB's broad deferral policy.

---

[25] 471 U.S. 202 (1985).

[26] 481 U.S. 851 (1987).

[27] 486 U.S. 399 (1988).

[28] 512 U.S. 107 (1994).

In its decision in *Babcock & Wilcox Construction Co.*,[29] the NLRB adopted a new approach to determining whether the NLRB should defer resolution of an unfair practice complaint to an arbitrator's decision under the relevant collective bargaining approach. The approach is intended to enable the NLRB to determine whether the arbitrator has actually resolved the unfair labor practice issue in a manner consistent with the act, without placing an undue burden on unions, employers, arbitrators, or the arbitration system itself. The approach also is used to determine whether the NLRB should defer to the settlement of a grievance by the union and the employer.

The NLRB will defer a meritorious unfair labor practice charge to the arbitration process where the following conditions are met:

1. The arbitrator must be explicitly authorized to decide the statutory issue.

2. The arbitrator must have been presented with and considered the statutory issue, or have been prevented from doing so by the party opposing deferral.

3. NLRB law must reasonably permit the award.

4. The proponent of deferral has the burden to show that the standards for deferral have been met.

The Board will consider an arbitration procedure to be unworkable if an employer, through prohibited means, precludes employee access to it. For instance, the Board has held that where an employer discharges employees or threatens reprisals against employees who attempt to file grievances, the grievance-resolution procedure is not actually open for use by disputants.[30] Deferral is not appropriate for an alleged unfair labor practice violation that "strikes at the foundation of the grievance and arbitration mechanism upon which we have relied in the formulation of the [deferral] doctrine." In *Community Convalescent Hospital*,[31] the Board subsequently revoked its deferral where additional delay and the employer's imposition of preconditions were evidence of bad faith and an unwillingness to arbitrate the dispute.

17-3   Changes in the Status of Employers

17-3a   Successor Employers

When a new employer takes over a unionized firm, what is the obligation of the successor employer to recognize the union, to adhere to the collective agreement, and to arbitrate grievances that arose under the collective agreement?

---

[29] 361 NLRB No. 132 (Dec. 15, 2014). The new approach is explained more fully in the Office of the General Counsel's Memorandum GC 15-02, issued February 10, 2015. The memo is available at http://www.nlrb.gov/reports-guidance/general-counsel-memos.

[30] *Jos. T. Ryerson & Sons, Inc.,* 199 NLRB 461 (1972); and *U.S. Postal Service*, 228 NLRB 1235 (1977).

[31] 206 NLRB 962 (1973).

In *John Wiley & Sons, Inc. v. Livingston*,[32] the Supreme Court held that the successor employer must arbitrate a grievance arising under the collective agreement where there was a "substantial continuity of identity in the business enterprise" and the employer retained a majority of the employees from the former unionized work force. The union in Wiley sought only to force the new employer to arbitrate; it did not seek to force the employer to bargain with it. In *NLRB v. Burns International Security Services, Inc.*,[33] the Supreme Court dealt with a case where the union sought to force the new employer to recognize the union and to abide by the collective agreement. The Supreme Court held that the successor employer was not bound by the prior collective agreement but was required to recognize and bargain with the union because it had retained enough employees from the prior, unionized work force to constitute a majority of the new employer's work force.

What factors should be considered when determining whether a "substantial continuity of identity" of the operation exists, and at what point in the hiring process does the presence of a union's supporters constituting a majority of the work force trigger the duty to bargain with the union? The Supreme Court addressed these issues in the *Fall River Dyeing* case.

Following *Fall River Dyeing*, a court held that an employer who assumed operation of a steel mill that had been closed for two years and that had drastically reduced the number of employees and restructured job classifications was not a successor employer because of the lack of a substantial continuity of operation with the former employer, according to *CitiSteel USA v. NLRB*.[34] However, a two-year hiatus in operations did not preclude the NLRB from holding that the new employer was a successor in *Pennsylvania Transformer Technology, Inc. v. NLRB*.[35]

CASE 17.3

FALL RIVER DYEING & FINISHING CORP. V. NLRB
482 U.S. 27 (1987)

Blackmun, J.

... For over 30 years before 1982, Sterlingwale operated a textile dyeing and finishing plant in Fall River, Massachusetts. Its business consisted basically of two types of dyeing, called, respectively, "converting" and "commission." Under the converting process, which in 1981 accounted for 60 to 70 percent of its business, Sterlingwale bought unfinished fabrics for its own account, dyed and finished them, and then sold them to apparel manufacturers. In commission dyeing, which accounted for the remainder of its business, Sterlingwale dyed and finished fabrics owned by customers according to their specifications. The financing and marketing aspects of

converting and commission dyeing are different. Converting requires capital to purchase fabrics and a sales force to promote the finished products. The production process, however, is the same for both converting and commission dyeing.

In the late 1970s the textile-dyeing business, including Sterlingwale's, began to suffer from adverse economic conditions and foreign competition. After 1979, business at Sterlingwale took a serious turn for the worse because of the loss of its export market, and the company reduced the number of its employees. Finally, in February 1982, Sterlingwale laid off all its production employees, primarily because it no longer had the capital to continue

---

[32] 376 U.S. 543 (1964).

[33] 406 U.S. 272 (1972).

[34] 53 F.3d 350 (D.C. Cir. 1995).

[35] 254 F.3d 217 (2001).

the converting business. It retained a skeleton crew of workers and supervisors to ship out the goods remaining on order and to maintain the corporation's building and machinery. In the months following the layoff, Leonard Ansin, Sterlingwale's president, liquidated the inventory of the corporation and, at the same time, looked for a business partner with whom he could "resurrect the business."...

For almost as long as Sterlingwale had been in existence, its production and maintenance employees had been represented by the United Textile Workers of America, AFL-CIO, Local 292 (Union).

In late summer 1982, however, Sterlingwale finally went out of business. It made an assignment for the benefit of its creditors [who held] ... a first mortgage on most of Sterlingwale's real property and ... a security interest on Sterlingwale's machinery and equipment....

During this same period, a former Sterlingwale employee and officer, Herbert Chace, and Arthur Friedman, president of one of Sterlingwale's major customers ... formed petitioner Fall River Dyeing & Finishing Corp. Chace, who had resigned from Sterlingwale in February 1982, had worked there for 27 years, had been vice-president in charge of sales at the time of his departure, and had participated in collective bargaining with the Union during his tenure at Sterlingwale. Chace and Friedman formed petitioner with the intention of engaging strictly in the commission-dyeing business and of taking advantage of the availability of Sterlingwale's assets and workforce. Accordingly, Friedman [acquired] ... Sterlingwale's plant, real property, and equipment, and [sold] them to petitioner. Petitioner also obtained some of Sterlingwale's remaining inventory at the liquidator's auction. Chace became petitioner's vice-president in charge of operations and Friedman became its president. In September 1982, petitioner began operating out of Sterlingwale's former facilities and began hiring employees.... Petitioner's initial hiring goal was to attain one full shift of workers, which meant from 55 to 60 employees. Petitioner planned to "see how business would be" after this initial goal had been met and, if business permitted, to expand to two shifts. The employees who were hired first spent approximately four to six weeks in start-up operations and an additional month in experimental production.

By letter dated October 19, 1982, the Union requested petitioner to recognize it as the bargaining agent for petitioner's employees and to begin collective bargaining. Petitioner refused the request, stating that, in its view, the request had "no legal basis." At that time, 18 of petitioner's 21 employees were former employees of Sterlingwale.

By November of that year, petitioner had employees in a complete range of jobs, had its production process in operation, and was handling customer orders; by mid-January 1983, it had attained its initial goal of one shift of workers. Of the 55 workers in this initial shift, a number that represented over half the workers petitioner would eventually hire, 36 were former Sterlingwale employees. Petitioner continued to expand its workforce, and by mid-April 1983 it had reached two full shifts. For the first time, ex-Sterlingwale employees were in the minority but just barely so (52 or 53 out of 107 employees).

Although petitioner engaged exclusively in commission dyeing, the employees experienced the same conditions they had when they were working for Sterlingwale. The production process was unchanged and the employees worked on the same machines, in the same building, with the same job classifications, under virtually the same supervisors. Over half the volume of petitioner's business came from former Sterlingwale customers,...

On November 1, 1982, the Union filed an unfair labor practice charge with the Board, alleging that in its refusal to bargain petitioner had violated Section 8(a)(1) and (5) of the National Labor Relations Act. After a hearing, the Administrative Law Judge (ALJ) decided that, on the facts of the case, petitioner was a successor to Sterlingwale.... Thus, in the view of the ALJ, petitioner's duty to bargain rose in mid-January because former Sterlingwale employees then were in the majority and because the Union's October demand was still in effect. Petitioner thus committed an unfair labor practice in refusing to bargain. In a brief decision and order, the Board, with one member dissenting, affirmed this decision. The Court of Appeals for the First Circuit, also by a divided vote, enforced the order....

... [I]n *NLRB v. Burns International Security Services, Inc.*, this Court first dealt with the issue of a successor employer's obligation to bargain with a union that had represented the employees of its predecessor.... These presumptions [of majority support developed in Burns are based not so much on an absolute certainty that the union's majority status will not erode following certification, as on a particular policy decision. The overriding policy of the NLRA is "industrial peace." The presumptions of majority support further this policy by "promot[ing] stability in collective-bargaining relationships, without impairing the free choice of employees." In essence, they enable a union to concentrate on obtaining and fairly administering a collective-bargaining agreement without worrying that, unless it produces immediate results, it will lose majority support and will be decertified.... The presumptions also remove any temptation on the part of the employer to avoid good-faith bargaining in the hope that, by delaying, it will undermine the union's support among the employees....

The rationale behind the presumptions is particularly pertinent in the successorship situation and so it is understandable that the Court in Burns referred to them. During a transition between employers, a union is in a peculiarly vulnerable position. It has no formal and established bargaining relationship with the new employer, is uncertain about the new employer's plans, and cannot be sure if or when the new employer must bargain with it. While being concerned with the future of its members with the new employer, the union also must protect whatever rights still exist for its members under the collective bargaining agreement with the predecessor employer. Accordingly, during this unsettling transition period, the union needs the presumptions of majority status to which it is entitled to safeguard its members' rights and to develop a relationship with the successor.

The position of the employees also supports the application of the presumptions in the successorship situation. If the employees find themselves in a new enterprise that substantially resembles the old, but without their chosen bargaining representative, they may well feel that their choice of a union is subject to the vagaries of an enterprise's transformation.... Without the presumptions of majority support and with the wide variety of corporate transformations possible, an employer could use a successor enterprise as a way of getting rid of a labor contract and of exploiting the employees' hesitant attitude towards the union to eliminate its continuing presence.

In addition to recognizing the traditional presumptions of union majority status, however, the Court in Burns was careful to safeguard "the rightful prerogative of owners independently to rearrange their businesses." If the new employer makes a conscious decision to maintain generally the same business and to hire a majority of its employees from the predecessor, then the bargaining obligation of Section 8(a)(5) is activated. This makes sense when one considers that the employer intends to take advantage of the trained workforce of its predecessor....

We now hold that a successor's obligation to bargain is not limited to a situation where the union in question has been recently certified. Where, as here, the union has a rebuttable presumption of majority status, this status continues despite the change in employers. And the new employer has an obligation to bargain with that union so long as the new employer is in fact a successor of the old employer and the majority of its employees were employed by its predecessor.

We turn now to the three rules, as well as to their application to the facts of this case, that the Board has adopted for the successorship situation.

In Burns we approved the approach taken by the Board and accepted by courts with respect to determining whether a new company was indeed the successor to the old. This approach, which is primarily factual in nature and is based upon the totality of the circumstances of a given situation, requires that the Board focus on whether the new company has "acquired substantial assets of its predecessor and continued, without interruption or substantial change the predecessor's business operations." Hence, the focus is on whether there is "substantial continuity" between the enterprises. Under this approach, the Board examines a number of factors: whether the business of both employers is essentially the same; whether the employees of the new company are doing the same jobs in the same working conditions under the same supervisors; and whether the new entity has the same production process, produces the same products, and basically has the same body of customers.... In conducting the analysis, the Board keeps in mind the question whether "those employees who have been retained will understandably view their job situations as essentially unaltered."...

[W]e find that the Board's determination that there was "substantial continuity" between Sterlingwale and petitioner and that petitioner was Sterlingwale's successor is supported by substantial evidence in the record. Petitioner acquired most of Sterlingwale's real property, its machinery and equipment, and much of its inventory and materials. It introduced no new product line. Of particular significance is the fact that, from the perspective of the employees, their jobs did not change. Although petitioner abandoned converting dyeing in exclusive favor of commission dyeing, this change did not alter the essential nature of the employees' jobs because both types of dyeing involved the same production process. The job classifications of petitioner were the same as those of Sterlingwale; petitioner's employees worked on the same machines under the direction of supervisors most of whom were former supervisors of Sterlingwale. The record, in fact, is clear that petitioner acquired Sterlingwale's assets with the express purpose of taking advantage of its predecessor's workforce....

For the reasons given above, this is a case where the other factors suggest "substantial continuity" between the companies despite the 7-month hiatus. Here, moreover, the extent of the hiatus between the demise of Sterlingwale and the start-up of petitioner is somewhat less than certain. After the February layoff, Sterlingwale retained a skeleton crew of supervisors and employees that continued to ship goods to customers and to maintain the plant. In addition, until the assignment for the benefit of the creditors late in the summer, Ansin was seeking to resurrect the business or to find a buyer for Sterlingwale. The Union was aware of these efforts. Viewed from the employees' perspective, therefore, the hiatus may have been much less than seven months. Although petitioner hired the employees through advertisements, it often relied on recommendations from supervisors, themselves formerly employed by Sterlingwale, and intended the advertisements to reach the former Sterlingwale workforce. Accordingly, we hold that, under settled law, petitioner was a successor to Sterlingwale. We thus must consider if and when petitioner's duty to bargain arose.

In *Burns*, the Court determined that the successor had an obligation to bargain with the union because a majority of its employees had been employed by Wackenhut. The "triggering" fact for the bargaining obligation was this composition of the successor's workforce. The Court, however, did not have to consider the question when the successor's obligation to bargain arose: Wackenhut's contract expired on June 30 and Burns began its services with a majority of former Wackenhut guards on July 1. In other situations, as in the present case, there is a start-up period by the new employer while it gradually builds its operations and hires employees. In these situations, the Board, with the approval of the Courts of Appeals, has adopted the "substantial and representative complement" rule for fixing the moment when the determination as to the composition of the successor's workforce is to be made. If, at this particular moment, a majority of the successor's employees had been employed by its predecessor, then the successor has an obligation to bargain with the union that represented these employees. In deciding when a "substantial and representative complement" exists in a particular employer transition, the Board examines a number of factors. It studies "whether the job classifications designated for the operation were filled or substantially filled and whether the operation was in normal or substantially normal production." In addition, it takes into consideration "the size of the complement on that date and the time expected to elapse before a substantially larger complement would be at work ... as well as the relative certainty of the employer's expected expansion."...

We conclude ... that in this situation the successor is in the best position to follow a rule the criteria of which are straightforward. The employer generally will know with tolerable certainty when all its job classifications have been filled or substantially filled, when it has hired a majority of the employees it intends to hire, and when it has begun normal production. Moreover, the "full complement" standard advocated by petitioner is not necessarily easier for a successor to apply than is the "substantial and representative complement." In fact, given the expansionist dreams of many new entrepreneurs, it might well be more difficult for a successor to identify the moment when the "full complement" has been attained, which is when the business will reach the limits of the new employer's initial hopes, than it would be for this same employer to acknowledge the time when its business has begun normal production—the moment identified by the "substantial and representative complement" rule. We therefore hold that the Board's "substantial and representative complement" rule is reasonable in the successorship context. Moreover, its application to the facts of this case is supported by substantial record evidence. The Court of Appeals observed that by mid-January petitioner "had hired employees in virtually all job classifications, had hired at least fifty percent of those it would ultimately employ in the majority of those classifications, and it employed a majority of the employees it would eventually employ when it reached full complement." At that time petitioner had begun normal production. Although petitioner intended to expand to two shifts, and, in fact, reached this goal by mid-April, that expansion was contingent expressly upon the growth of the business. Accordingly, as found by the Board and approved by the Court of Appeals, mid-January was the period when petitioner reached its "substantial and representative complement." Because at that time the majority of petitioner's employees were former Sterlingwale employees, petitioner had an obligation to bargain with the Union then.

We also hold that the Board's "continuing demand" rule is reasonable in the successorship situation. The successor's duty to bargain at the "substantial and representative complement" date is triggered only when the union has made a bargaining demand. Under the "continuing demand" rule, when a union has made a premature demand that has been rejected by the employer, this demand remains in force until the moment when the employer attains the "substantial and representative complement."

Such a rule, particularly when considered along with the "substantial and representative complement" rule, places a minimal burden on the successor and makes sense in light of the union's position. Once the employer has concluded that it has reached the appropriate complement, then, in order to determine whether its duty to bargain will be triggered, it has only to see whether the union already has made a demand for bargaining. Because the union has no established relationship with the successor and because it is unaware of the successor's plans for its operations and hiring, it is likely that, in many cases, a union's bargaining demand will be premature. It makes no sense to require the union repeatedly to renew its bargaining demand in the hope of having it correspond with the "substantial and representative complement" date, when, with little trouble, the employer can regard a previous demand as a continuing one.

The reasonableness of the "continuing demand" rule is demonstrated by the facts of this case. Although the Union had asked Ansin to inform it about his plans for Sterlingwale so that it could become involved in the employer transition, the Union learned about this transition only after it had become a *fait accompli*. Without having any established relationship with petitioner, it therefore is not surprising that the Union's October bargaining demand was premature. The Union, however, made clear after this demand that, in its view, petitioner had a bargaining obligation: the Union filed an unfair labor practice in November. Petitioner responded by denying that it had any duty to bargain. Rather than being a successor confused about when a bargaining obligation might arise, petitioner took an initial position—and stuck with it—that it never would have any bargaining obligation with the Union.

The judgment of the Court of Appeals is affirmed.

It is so ordered.

Case Questions

1. What is the NLRB's substantial and representative complement rule? How does it apply to the facts in this case? Explain.

2. What factors does the NLRB consider when determining if there is a substantial continuity of operation between the former employer and a successor employer? How do those factors apply to the facts here?

3. What is the NLRB's continuing demand rule? How does it apply to the facts in this case? Explain.

An employer that intends to rehire most of the employees from the predecessor firm may lawfully recognize the union that represented the previous firm's workers, and negotiate with the union over the terms upon which it will hire those workers, according to *Road & Rail Services., Inc.*[36] Where a successor employer has rehired most of the employees from the previous employer, it is a violation of Section 8(a)(5) for the successor employer to unilaterally change the terms of employment for the individuals it hires from the previous employer, as held by *Rosedev Hospitality, Secaucus LP.*[37] A successor employer who discriminatorily refuses to rehire the unionized employees from the prior firm violates Section 8(a)(3), according to *Planned Bldg. Servs. Inc.*[38]

In *Trafford Dist. Center v. NLRB*,[39] where a company formed after a bankrupt employer surrendered its assets was determined by the NLRB to be an "alter ego" of the original employer, the successor firm was held to violate Sections 8(a)(1) and 8(a)(5) when it refused to honor the terms of the union's collective agreement with the predecessor employer.

A successor employer can be held liable for the remedy of an unfair labor practice committed by the old employer. In *NLRB v. Winco Petroleum*,[40] a successor was held subject to a bargaining order remedy even though the successor itself was not guilty of a refusal to bargain.

---

[36] 348 NLRB No. 77 (2006).

[37] 349 NLRB 202 (2007).

[38] 347 NLRB 670 (2006).

[39] 478 F.4d 172 (4d Cir. 2007).

[40] 668 F.2d 974 (8th Cir. 1982).

ethical	DILEMMA

TO RETAIN OR NOT TO RETAIN?

Immense Multinational Business (IMB) is planning to purchase the entire plant, assets, and operation of CastCo, a small manufacturing company. The employees at CastCo are represented by the International Molders Union, but IMB's employees are not unionized. IMB plans to maintain most of the operations at CastCo and is considering whether to retain the former CastCo employees as well. What are the benefits of retaining the former CastCo production workers? Are there any arguments against retaining the CastCo workers? Are there any legal restrictions on the decision whether to retain the CastCo workers? How should IMB proceed here?

You, the recently promoted director of human resources for IMB's manufacturing operations, are asked by the CEO to prepare a memo discussing these issues and recommending a course of action. Be sure to support your recommendation.

The incumbent union in a successorship situation is entitled to a rebuttable presumption of continuing majority status, the new employer has a legally enforceable duty to recognize and bargain with a union that represented its predecessor's employees, and the Board will bar any challenge to the union's representative status for a similar reasonable period of time.[41]

17-4   Bankruptcy and the Collective Agreement

The prior cases dealt with the obligations of successor employers. When an employer experiencing financial difficulties seeks protection from creditors under the bankruptcy laws, can the employer also reject the collective agreement?

When a corporation files a petition for the protection of the bankruptcy laws, the financial obligations of the corporation are suspended pending the resolution of the issue by the bankruptcy courts. What happens when a unionized employer files a petition for bankruptcy? Is the employer required to adhere to the terms and conditions of the collective agreement? In the case of *NLRB v. Bildisco & Bildisco*[42] the Supreme Court held that an employer who files for reorganization under Chapter 11 of the Bankruptcy Act does not violate Section 8(a)5 by unilaterally changing the terms of the collective agreement after filing the bankruptcy petition. The Court also held that the bankruptcy court may allow the employer to reject the collective agreement if the court finds that the agreement "burdens the estate" of the employer and if "the equities balance in favor of rejecting the labor contract."

Following the Supreme Court's *Bildisco* decision, Congress amended the Bankruptcy Code to deal with the rejection of a collective agreement. The changes, enacted in

---

[41] *Lamons Gasket Co.*, 457 NLRB No. 72 (2011).

[42] 465 U.S. 514 (1984).

Public Law 98-353 (1984), 11 U.S.C. Section 1113, allow the employer petitioning for bankruptcy protection to reject the collective agreement only when the following conditions are met:

1. The employer has made a proposal for contractual modifications, necessary to permit reorganization and treating all interested parties equitably, to the union.

2. The employer must provide the union with such relevant information as is necessary to evaluate the proposal.

3. The employer must offer to "confer in good faith in attempting to reach mutually satisfactory modifications."

4. The bankruptcy court finds that the union has rejected the employer's proposal "without good cause."

5. The court concludes that "the balance of equities clearly favors rejection" of the agreement.

The bankruptcy court is required to hold a hearing on the employer's petition within fourteen days and to issue its determination on the rejection issue within thirty days after the hearing.

THE **WORKING** LAW

Reorganizations of GM and Chrysler Gave UAW a Unique Role as Union and Investor

General Motors (GM) and Chrysler both emerged from bankruptcy in the summer of 2009. GM and Chrysler had struggled for years in the face of declining sales, increased foreign competition, and soaring retiree health care and benefit costs. In 2007, GM agreed with the United Auto Workers (UAW) to transfer the company's health care liabilities to a union-run trust (a Voluntary Employee Beneficiary Association, or VEBA) and to reduce wages and benefits for new employees. But the general economic crisis of 2008 and 2009 caused a drastic fall in auto sales and dried up credit for would-be customers. GM lost $80 billion from 2005 to 2009. In May 2009, the UAW agreed to accept wage and benefit concessions and to eliminate restrictive work rules as part of the reorganization of the company, and also agreed to take GM stock in lieu of half of the $20.4 billion that GM owed to the VEBA. The union also agreed to similar concessions at Chrysler and agreed not to go on strike against GM or Chrysler until 2015.

As a result of the reorganization in bankruptcy, a new corporation, the Vehicle Acquisitions Holding LLC, was created to assume most of the assets of the former company. This "new General Motors" is owned by the U.S. and Canadian governments and the UAW. The liabilities of the "old General Motors" were retained by GM, which will eventually be liquidated under the bankruptcy courts. In return for bailouts from the U.S. Treasury of about $50 billion, the U.S. government received a 60.8 percent ownership stake in new General Motors, and the Canadian government received 11.7 percent in return for providing $9.5

billion. The UAW-operated VEBA received 17.5 percent, with warrants to purchase an additional 2.5 percent, $6.5 billion worth of preferred stock, and a note for $6.5 billion. The unsecured bondholders received a 10 percent stake in return for having lent the company $27 billion. Challenges to GM by some bondholders to the bankruptcy reorganization were rejected by the Bankruptcy Court of the Southern District of New York in *In re General Motors Corp.*

GM offered its workers a buyout and early retirement program in an effort to reduce its workforce. Workers who agreed to retire were given cash payments of between $20,000 and $115,000, with the largest payouts going to workers with at least 20 years of service who agreed to give up retirement benefits other than pensions. The retiring workers also received a voucher worth $25,000 toward the purchase of a new vehicle. In the case of Chrysler, the shares were divided as follows:

- The VEBA received 55 percent
- The U.S. government received 10 percent in return for providing a bailout of $25.5 billion
- The Italian automaker Fiat, in return for agreeing to operate the reorganized Chrysler, initially received 20 percent of the shares.

Fiat took full ownership of Chrysler in 2014 by purchasing the remaining shares owned by the UAW for $4.35 billion.

The reorganization agreements of Chrysler and GM placed the UAW in an unusual position—acting as a union representing the firms' employees but also serving as a major investor in the firms. The alternative to the union's acceptance of the reorganization plans would most likely have been liquidation of the firms, which would mean huge job losses.

Some analysts predict that the UAW's new role would make the union more willing to work with management to increase profitability—a higher stock price would provide the VEBA with billions more to cover retiree health care costs in the years ahead. But other industry experts feel it will be difficult for the union to give up its traditional focus on preserving jobs for its members rather than increasing profits and share price. The financial future of the union and its members will depend upon the stock performance of Chrysler and General Motors. It remains to be seen whether the UAW would be willing to go on strike against either of the companies, if the strike could affect the price of the shares of stock held by the VEBA to cover the health care costs of retirees.

Sources: "The bankruptcy of General Motors: A giant falls," *The Economist*, June 4, 2009; "GM nears bankruptcy: Chapter 11 beckons," *The Economist*, May 21, 2009; "Chrysler and General Motors: End game," *The Economist*, April 30, 2009; David Kiley, "A mucky road for the UAW," *Business Week*, May 11, 2009; "Rescue plan would give U.S. most of GM's stock," *The Washington Post*, May 27, 2009; Nick Bunkley, "Union workers at G.M. ratify concessions," *The New York Times*, May 30, 2009; Steven Greenhouse, "G.M.'s new owners, labor and government, adjust to roles," *The New York Times*, June 2, 2009; Michael J. de la Merced, "Court ruling clears path for new G.M.," *The New York Times*, July 6, 2009; Nick Bunkley, "After 6,000 take buyouts, G.M. to lay off thousands," *The New York Times*, August 4, 2009; "Business this week," *The Economist*, March 3, 2012; "Business this week," *The Economist*, April 7, 2012; "Fiat, trust differ over Chrysler stock value," *Automotive News*, October 8, 2012; Jaclyn Trop, "Fiat, in deal with union, will buy rest of Chrysler," *The New York Times*, January 2, 2014; and "Fiat–Chrysler merger complete," *The Buffalo News*, January 3, 2014.

The provisions of Section 1113 apply to an employer's attempt to reject a collective bargaining agreement that has expired, but the provisions of the agreement still remain in effect.[43] Section 1113 also applies to employers under the NLRA and also to employers under the Railway Labor Act, such as railroads and airlines. In addition to the bankruptcy filings of Chrysler and General Motors, fluctuating oil prices and the economic crisis have caused numerous airlines to go through Chapter 11 bankruptcy proceedings, including:

- Aloha Airlines
- ATA Airlines
- Comair
- Delta Air Lines
- Frontier Airlines
- Era Aviation
- Hawaiian Airlines
- Independence Air
- Mesaba Airlines
- Northwest Airlines
- United Airlines
- U.S. Airways
- American Airlines

The results have been significant wage and benefit reductions for the labor unions involved. The Northwest pilots agreed to a pay cut of 24 percent over a five-and-a-half-year contract. A bankruptcy court approved the imposition of a proposal lowering the Northwest flight attendants' take-home pay by up to 40 percent. The Delta pilots agreed to a new contract with a 14 percent pay cut, in addition to concessions in a 2004 agreement in which Delta's pilots had agreed to a 33 percent wage cut. The following case involves American Airlines' request to reject its collective agreement with the union representing its pilots; the case focuses on whether American Airlines negotiated in good faith and whether the union rejected the proposals "without good cause" as required under Section 1113.

›› CASE 17.4

IN RE AMR CORPORATION
477 B.R. 384, aff'd. by 523 B.R. 415 (S.D.N.Y. 2014)

Facts: American Airlines, Inc. [American] filed under Section 1113 of the Bankruptcy Code for bankruptcy court permission to reject the collective bargaining agreements between American and its pilots, flight attendants and some of its transit workers. These employees are represented by three unions: (1) the Association of Professional Flight Attendants [APFA]; (2) the Allied Pilots Association [APA]; and (3) the Transit Workers Union of America [TWU].

---

[43] *In re Trump Entertainment Resorts*, 519 B.R. 76 (Bankr. D. Del. 2014).

American has approximately 65,000 active employees, 70% of whom are represented by one of three labor unions under nine separate collective bargaining agreements. American has suffered losses of approximately $6.6 billion since 2003 and cumulative losses of more than $10 billion since 2001. American has maintained negative net margins since 2003, averaging –4.6% over the period of 2003–2011. American has a much higher percentage of secured debt than do the other network carriers, and has run out of unencumbered assets to pledge as collateral for additional financing. American's poor financial performance over the last few years stands in sharp contrast not only to that of the lower cost carriers [LCCs] but also to other large network carriers. American lost $1.06 billion in 2011, the only network carrier that failed to earn a profit last year. While other airlines maintained positive net margins in 2011, American had net margins of –4.4%. While American ranked first in the world in terms of overall capacity in 2000, it now ranks fourth in the world and third in the United States, behind Delta and United. Because American's smaller route network relative to United/Continental and Delta, American is at a greater competitive disadvantage in attracting passengers, particularly time-sensitive, high-yield business travelers who value larger networks that offer more non-stop flight options and more convenient connecting options with less travel time. American's financial weakness has hurt its ability to invest in products and services that may have enabled it to counter further erosion of its revenue.

The decline in American's financial performance results from many factors, including but not limited to: (1) increased price and service competition from the LCC's, other large network carriers and foreign fare carriers; (2) high labor costs and low productivity; and (3) mergers and restructurings of other carriers. American's overall costs per available seat mile [CASM, a common industry metric] significantly exceed those for most of its competitors. A significant reason for this difference is labor costs, American's largest controllable cost. American's labor CASM is approximately 24% higher than the average of the other network carriers and 79% higher than the average of the LCCs with which American competes. Several factors contribute to American's high unit labor cost, including relatively high wage scales for employees, pilots and flight attendants; generous benefits; and a more senior workforce. American has maintained the highest pension accounting costs per ASM and that American's labor CASM is 21% higher than the average of other large network carriers and 70% higher than the LCC average. In the last decade, the airline industry also has been reshaped by mergers and bankruptcy restructurings, all of which have made it more difficult for American to compete. All of American's major network competitors have already filed for bankruptcy, some more than once.

On November 29, 2011, American filed for bankruptcy, together with its parent AMR Corporation, and other affiliates. In their bankruptcy filings, the American explained that they have been unable to match its competitors' abilities to adequately deal with the variables associated with the airline industry because the "airline industry is labor intensive" and because of their higher labor-related costs.

On February 1, 2012, American began the process leading up to its Section 1113 application. It unveiled its new business plan, labeled the "Plan for Success," for the six year period from 2012 through 2017 [Business Plan]. The Business Plan contains a detailed business model, a network plan and a fleet plan, including details about the markets in which American plans to operate and the equipment it intends to use to serve those markets. The fundamental principles behind the Business Plan include:

- Concentration on the five key hub markets for American: Dallas-Fort Worth, Miami, Chicago, Los Angles, and New York;
- Expanding American international presence, particularly through the use of joint business agreements and codesharing;
- Increasing passenger feed to American's hub and across its network through codesharing with domestic air carriers and increased use of regional jets;
- Implementing a long-term fleet plan sufficient for both replacement and growth;
- Creating a capital structure that allows American to grow and compete, attract capital at favorable rates and withstand external shock to the business; and
- Setting up a sustainable cost structure.

The Business Plan is designed to enable American to better compete for its share of "high value" customers and restore its unit revenue to levels consistent with those of other network carriers.

At the same time as it unveiled its Business Plan, American also provided term sheets for the Business Plan, including the projections for the six year period. In discussing these term sheets with the Unions, American explained that it was seeking a 20% reduction in costs from each labor group, or $1.25 billion in average annual costs over a six year period from all labor groups. Of this number, American sought $370 million from the pilots,

$230 million from the flight attendants, and $390 million from its transit workers. At this time, American proposed to terminate its pension plan for all employees and institute uniform plans for active employee medical, future retiree medical, and pensions. During and after the February 1st meeting with American, the Unions requested information regarding the Business Plan and the term sheets. On March 21, 2012, American delivered a new term sheet to the pilots. The overall requested amount of average labor concessions of $1.25 billion sought from all Unions did not change, but the new term sheet included two substantial changes from the Company's initial term sheet: American's decision to freeze its defined pension plans rather than terminate them and to lower the monthly cost share of American's medical plan for active employees from 23% to 21%.

On March 27, 2012, American filed its Motion seeking authority to reject some nine collective bargaining agreements with the three Unions pursuant to Section 1113 of the Bankruptcy Code. After the filing of the Motion, American continued to negotiate with the TWU and, to a lesser extent, the APA and the APFA.

Section 1113(b) requires that a debtor take a number of procedural steps prior to the rejection of a collective bargaining agreement. The debtor must provide the union with its proposed modifications to a collective bargaining agreement prior to filing an application with a court to reject the union's agreement. The proposed modifications must be (1) "based on the most complete and reliable information available at the time of the proposal;" (2) "necessary to permit the reorganization of the debtor;" and (3) "assure that all creditors, the debtor and all of the affected parties are treated fairly and equitably." The debtor must also provide the union with the relevant information necessary for the union to evaluate the proposal. Section 1113(b)(2) requires that, between the time that the debtor's 1113 proposal and the hearing date on any 1113 application, the debtor must bargain in good faith with the union in an attempt to reach an agreement. Section 1113(c) sets forth additional substantive requirements for rejection of a collective bargaining agreement. First, the debtor must establish that it made a proposal that fulfills the requirements of subsection (b)(1). Second, the debtor must show that the union refused to accept the proposal without good cause. Third, the debtor must prove that the balance of the equities favors rejection of the agreement. The Debtor bears the burden of proof to show that it complied with on the elements of Section 1113.

Issue: Has American met the requirements under Section 1113 to reject its collective agreements?

Decision: Section 1113(b)(2) requires that after a proposal is made, but before a hearing on rejection, the debtor meet with the union at reasonable times to negotiate in good faith. Section 1113(c)(2) also requires that a collective bargaining agreement can only be rejected if the union has refused to accept the proposal without good cause.

American did make some changes to its initial proposal to the APA; those changes demonstrate good faith bargaining. One of these changes was particularly significant: American decided to freeze its pensions rather than terminate them. The Unions had objected to the termination of the pension plan, and the freezing of the pension plan is a significant improvement over termination. American did not seek to offset the added costs from the pension freeze through additional labor cost reductions. That change presents a significant additional hurdle to American's re-emergence from bankruptcy, because American will be required to make significant cash contributions that had not originally been factored into the initial Business Plan. Freezing the pension plans would result in significant pension underfunding liability upon emergence from bankruptcy. American must compete against LCCs that do not carry the same pension obligations. Retaining the pension liabilities and the related ongoing cash payments affects American's credit profile. American's unwillingness to move on the other savings requested in its initial proposal was not necessarily a failure to confer in good faith. Parts of a debtor's Section 1113 proposal may be non-negotiable if they are essential to its reorganization. Thus, it is not bad faith to adhere to a necessary cost-saving target. American made clear to the unions that it is open to ways to achieve its labor ask that are different from those it proposed provided that the same overall monetary reduction is achieved.

American concedes that its current proposal goes further than the pre-petition concessions it sought from the unions. Those pre-petition negotiations were an attempt to balance the twin goals of lowering American's costs and enhancing productivity while at the same time trying to reach a consensual deal with the unions that could avert a Chapter 11 filing. Those proposals were designed to be acceptable to the unions, as opposed to fully addressing American's financial issues. In contrast, the Section 1113 proposals were designed as part of a comprehensive Business Plan for a reorganized entity that will be profitable going forward. American noted that, in hindsight, the pre-petition proposals would have been inadequate, as they were based on assumptions that have not yet come to pass: improvement in the economy, stabilization of fuel prices, and convergence with other airline costs.

The APA claimed that American refused to negotiate over certain terms of its proposal, such as the scope clause and sick leave. The APA specifically argues that American has not shown that these particular terms are essential to its reorganization and that the APA's counterproposals would enable American to achieve the revenue enhancements contemplated in the Business Plan. But the court held that the APA objection was not based on American's refusal to negotiate, but rather American's refusal to adopt the APA's counterproposals. The APA the objection conflates the requirement to negotiate in good faith with the requirement of necessity. The APA admits that reasonable people can disagree on the issues between itself and the American, but there is no evidence on the record that American has taken these positions in bad faith or to stalemate negotiations. American has shown flexibility in the allocation of concessions; it was willing to consider any reasonable alternative suggestions the union might have to the American's cost reduction proposals so long as the total cost reduction total was met. The failure to come to an agreement shows that both sides have become entrenched, and under the circumstances, the court did not find that American's failure to adopt the proposals of the APA constituted a failure to negotiate in good faith.

Under Section 1113(c)(2) a collective bargaining agreement can only be rejected if the union has refused to accept the proposal without good cause. The union must come forward with evidence of its reasons for declining to accept the debtor's proposal in whole or in part. If a union insists on economically unworkable terms without offering a compromise that will provide the debtor with necessary savings, the court will find that the union has not acted with good cause. The APA argued that it put forth two alternatives that would permit the American to reorganize. First, it states that it negotiated a contingent labor agreement with U.S. Airways that would generate $240 million in annual savings. But the merger transaction with U.S. Airways had been discussed and the court rejected the argument that an agreement on labor costs between the unions and U.S. Airways constituted a viable alternative that would permit American to reorganize. The APA also contended that it put forward a package that would allow American, as a stand-alone company, to generate between $260 and $270 million in annual savings. In *Maxwell Newspapers, Inc.* [981

F.2d 85 (2d Cir. 1992)], the court held that "a union will not have good cause to reject an employer's proposal that contains only those modifications essential for the debtor's reorganization, that is, the union's refusal to accept it will be held to be without good cause. On the other hand … where the union makes compromise proposals during the negotiating process that meet its needs while preserving the debtor's savings, its rejection of the debtor's proposal would be with good cause." The court here held that the APA's reliance on its counterproposal was not a good cause basis for the APA to reject American's proposals. American has stated that it needs at least $370 million in cuts to successfully reorganize, excluding changes to the scope clauses. The APA admits that its counterproposal will generate only between $260 and $270 million in annual savings. Because the APA failed to provide cuts in that amount, its rejection of American's proposals lacked good cause.

The APA's counterproposal for sick leave was also problematic. While the APA would consent to a medical verification program, it would not require verification until a pilot has been out for 30 days of uninterrupted sick leave, at which time the employer would have to make a demand for substantiation. If the pilot then returned to work, no substantiation would be required, but the pilot could again call in sick the next day and restart the 30 day period. The APA proposal would also establish a sell-back program for unused pilot sick leave. Rather than saving money, this proposed program could cost American additional money because pilots could sell either 30 or 60 hours of sick for pay depending on whether the pilot had accrued more than 1,000 hours of sick time.

The U.S. Court of Appeals for the Second Circuit has set forth a non-exclusive list of factors to consider when determining whether the equities clearly favor rejection of a collective bargaining agreement:

(1) the likelihood and consequences of liquidation if rejection is not permitted;

(2) the likely reduction in the value of creditors' claims if the bargaining agreement remains in force;

(3) the likelihood and consequences of a strike if the bargaining agreement is voided;

(4) the possibility and likely effect of any employee claims for breach of contract if rejection is approved;

(5) the cost-spreading abilities of the various parties, taking into account the number of employees covered by the bargaining agreement and how various employees' wages and benefits compare to those of others in the industry; and

(6)   the good or bad faith of the parties in dealing with the debtor's financial dilemma.

When balancing these factors, a court must examine them in relation to the debtor's attempts to reorganize. The first two factors favor rejection of the collective bargaining agreement. It is clear that rejection of the agreement is necessary for American to successfully reorganize. The court noted that the existing APA agreement is a burden that American is unable to maintain on an ongoing basis and the APA itself has recognized that continuation of the status quo is not a viable option. American suffered losses of approximately $6.6 billion since 2003 and cumulative losses of more than $10 billion since 2001. American lost $1.06 billion in 2011, the only network carrier that failed to earn a profit last year. Leaving the agreement intact would severely impact the return that creditors would receive on their claims. The diminished likelihood of a strike also weighs in favor of approving rejection of the agreement. Following the rejection of a collective bargaining agreement, it would be unlawful for a union to strike until the bargaining process set forth in the Railway Labor Act had been exhausted. After rejection of the agreement, both management and a union under the Railway Labor Act would be required to continue negotiating in good faith. A strike is an inherent risk in every § 1113 motion, and in the end, it makes little difference if the debtors are forced out of business because of a union strike or because of the continuing obligation to pay union benefits to avoid one. The unions may have the legal right to strike, but that does not mean that they must exercise that right.

The Court must also consider the possibility and likely effect of any employee claim for breach of contract in the event of rejection. It is unlikely that the unions would have rejection claims for breach of contract here, because, as the Second Circuit observed [in *Northwest Airlines Corp.*, 483 F.4d 160 (2007)] "a debtor who rejects a contract pursuant to [Section 1113] abrogates rather than breaches the [collective bargaining agreement] at issue." Even if that were not the case, rejection would relegate employee damage claims "to the status of unsecured debt.... Absent rejection, and assuming they have the money, the Debtors [would] have to pay these claims, as they accrue, on an administrative basis. From the viewpoint of the other creditors, rejection is preferable."

The court also considered the cost-spreading abilities of the various parties, taking into account the number of employees covered by the agreement and how various employees' wages and benefits compare to those of others in the industry. It is undoubted that the sacrifices the union employees are being asked to make will affect them deeply. However, American's Section 1113 proposal to each union requested the same sacrifice, together with non-union employees, of 20% across the board. This request for across the board reduction must be viewed in light of the fact that the wages and benefits of APA are above industry standard, a point conceded by the APA.

Finally, the court examined the good or bad faith of the parties in dealing with American's financial dilemma. American has asserted that the APA has shown bad faith by abandoning negotiations with American while pursuing an agreement with U.S. Airways. Given that negotiations subsequently resumed and continued even after the close of the trial, however, the court did not find bad faith on the side of either party and this factor is in equipoise. For all these reasons, the court concluded that the balance of the equities clearly favored the rejection of the APA agreement.

However, the court concluded that American's proposed changes to furlough and codesharing have not been justified by either reference to the Business Plan or the practices of American's competitors. Given the significance of these two provisions collectively to American's proposal, the court found that American has not shown that the proposal is necessary as required by Section 1113. Because of this the court initially denied American's motion to reject the collective bargaining agreements of the APA. The court did allow American the option to remedy those two factors and submit new application under Section 1113.

Note: American did submit a new application addressing the factors identified by the court, and pursuant to that application, the court did authorize American to reject the collective bargaining agreement with the APA, effective as of September 5, 2012 [*In re AMR Corp.*, 2012 WL 3834798 (Bkrtcy. S.D.N.Y., Sept. 5, 2012)].

In *Wheeling Pittsburgh Steel Corp. v. United Steelworkers*,[44] the Third Circuit Court of Appeals held that it was an error to allow the employer to void the collective agreement

---

[44] 791 F.2d 1074 (1986).

where the employer did not give any persuasive rationale for asking the unionized employees to take disproportionate cuts for a five-year period without any provision for improvement if the employer's position improved. In *Teamsters Local 807 v. Carey Trans.*,[45] the Second Circuit Court of Appeals upheld rejection of the agreement where unionized employees were expected to take cuts greater than those for non-union employees because the union wages were 60 percent higher than industry average, whereas the other employees' compensation was barely competitive.

The NLRB has made it clear that filing a petition for bankruptcy protection does not affect the employer's obligation to recognize and bargain with the union, according to *Airport Bus Service*.[46] In *Willis Elec.*,[47] the NLRB held that an employer unilaterally abrogating an agreement without obtaining bankruptcy court relief is guilty of violating Section 8(a)(5); economic necessity is not a defense for such conduct. In *NLRB v. Superior Forwarding, Inc.*,[48] the court of appeals held that a bankruptcy court may enjoin the NLRB from proceeding with hearings on unfair labor practice charges that arise from an employer's unilateral modification of a collective agreement, when the unfair labor practice proceedings would threaten the assets of the employer.

17-4a   Bankruptcy and Retiree Benefits

From the 1950s through the 1970s, employers were willing to negotiate with unions for generous health care benefit provisions for retired employees; this was particularly true in the automobile and steel industries. But from the 1980s on, the costs of such retiree benefits, known as "legacy costs," became a significant financial burden on the employers. The steel and automobile industries began to face strong competition from foreign firms, the costs of medical care increased substantially, and the number of retirees grew. It was estimated that the costs of retiree health care benefits added $1,400 to the cost of each car produced by General Motors,[49] while the European and Japanese automakers were not saddled with such legacy costs. The huge retiree medical costs added to the other financial problems that forced General Motors and Chrysler into bankruptcy.[50] In many cases, firms facing bankruptcy unilaterally stopped paying the retiree benefits. In response to such actions, Congress amended the Bankruptcy Code to include Section 1114, which creates a procedure for modification or rejection of retiree benefit obligations similar to that under Section 1113 for the rejection of collective agreements. Section 1114[51] requires that the bankrupt employer make a proposal for modification to the representative of the retirees (either a labor union or a committee appointed by the trustee in bankruptcy). The employer must also provide the retirees' representative with the information upon which the proposal

---

[45] 816 F.2d 82 (1987).

[46] 274 NLRB 561 (1984).

[47] 269 NLRB 1145 (1984).

[48] 762 F.2d 695 (8th Cir. 1985).

[49] "The Bankruptcy of General Motors: A Giant Falls," *The Economist*, June 4, 2009.

[50] As noted in the "Working Law" feature in this chapter, the companies eventually agreed with the United Auto Workers Union to have a union-operated trust, known as a Voluntary Employee Beneficiary Association, or VEBA, assume the responsibility of paying future retiree medical benefits in return for a huge cash payment from the firms.

[51] 11 U.S.C. § 1114.

is based and demonstrate the necessity of the modification for the reorganization of the employer. The employer must negotiate in good faith with the representative over the proposed modification. If the representative does not agree to the modification, the employer can ask the bankruptcy court to order the modification. Before the court can order the modification, the employer must convince the court that the modification is necessary to permit the reorganization of the employer, that the proposed modification treats all affected parties fairly and equitably, and that the retirees' representative refused to accept the proposal without good cause.

In the case of General Motors, the company and the United Auto Workers Union agreed to have the retiree benefits assumed by a VEBA. However, some of the retirees of some subsidiaries of the "old General Motors" were represented by other unions (non-UAW unions) and were not included in the agreement setting up the VEBA. As part of its emergence from bankruptcy, the productive assets of the former General Motors Corporation were purchased by a newly created firm ("new General Motors"), while the liabilities, including those for retiree benefits, remained with the old General Motors. The non-UAW unions objected to the proposal for the new General Motors to emerge from bankruptcy, because the new General Motors would only agree to pay reduced benefits to their retirees. The bankruptcy court, in *In re General Motors Corp.*,[52] held that the obligation to comply with the requirements of Section 1114 applied only to the bankrupt employer (old General Motors in this case) and not the corporation purchasing the productive assets of the firm (new General Motors). The court stated that old General Motors had complied with the requirements of Section 1114. If, in the future, old General Motors fails to comply with its obligations under the modification, the unions could ask the court to take appropriate action. The court noted:

> The Court fully realizes that UAW retirees will get a better result, after all is said and done, than . . . [non-UAW] Retirees will, but that is not by reason of any violation of the Code or applicable case law. It is because as a matter of reality, the Purchaser ["new GM"] needs a properly motivated workforce to enable New GM to succeed, requiring it to enter into satisfactory agreements with the UAW—which includes arrangements satisfactory to the UAW for UAW retirees. And the Purchaser is not similarly motivated, in triaging its expenditures, to assume obligations for retirees of unions whose members, with little in the way of exception, no longer work for GM.
>
>   The Court has also considered . . . that in pre-bankruptcy planning, GM and the U.S. Treasury focused on the duties to . . . [non-UAW] Retirees, and made a conscious decision that . . . [non-UAW] retirees would not be offered as good a deal as others. . . . The U.S. Treasury, in making hard decisions about where to spend its money and make New GM as viable as possible, made business decisions that it was entitled to make, and the fact that there were so few . . . [non-UAW] employees still working for GM was an understandable factor in that decision. The Court's responsibility is not to make fairness judgments as to those decisions, but merely to gauge those decisions under applicable law.[53]

---

[52] 407 B.R. 463 (Bkrtcy. S.D.N.Y. 2009).

[53] 407 B.R. 463 at 512.

CHAPTER REVIEW

» Key Terms

arbitration	549	**rights arbitration**	550	**grievance**	550
interest arbitration	550	**grievance process**	550	**no-strike clause**	557

» Summary

- Arbitration is the usual method by which the parties to a collective agreement enforce that agreement. The existence of an arbitration clause is voluntary; the NLRA does not require that the parties include an arbitration clause in the agreement. But if the parties do agree to an arbitration clause, it becomes legally enforceable through Section 301 of the NLRA, and arbitration becomes the preferred means of interpreting and enforcing the agreement. When asked to order arbitration, a court should not consider the merits of the grievance but rather only whether the grievance is within the scope of the arbitration clause. When asked to enforce an arbitration award under Section 301, the court should not substitute its judgment for that of the arbitrator but rather only consider whether the arbitrator acted within the scope of his or her authority under the agreement. Courts should refuse to enforce an arbitration award only when the arbitrator exceeded the authority granted under the agreement or when the arbitration award violates "clear and explicit public policy."

- Section 301 also allows a court to enforce a no-strike clause in a collective agreement; despite the Norris–La Guardia Act, a court may grant an injunction to stop a strike that is over an issue subject to arbitration under a collective agreement.

Suits under Section 301 may be used to seek damages for violations of the agreement, including the no-strike clause. Remedies under Section 301 may preempt any state law remedies or actions that involve the interpretation or application of the collective agreement.

- The NLRB may defer unfair labor practice complaints to arbitration under certain circumstances, as outlined by the General Counsel, and will recognize arbitration decisions as resolving unfair labor practice charges when the contract has the statutory right incorporated in it or the parties present the statutory issue to the arbitrator, and the arbitrator correctly enunciates the applicable statutory principles and applies them in deciding the issue. Successor employers may be required to recognize and bargain with the union that had represented the employees of the former employer when there is a substantial continuity of operation and the employees from the former unionized employer make up a majority of the successor's employees. Section 1113 of the Bankruptcy Code sets out the procedure to be followed by an employer seeking to reject a collective agreement after having filed a petition for bankruptcy protection with the bankruptcy court.

» Problems

» Questions

1. What is rights arbitration? What is interest arbitration? Why is arbitration used to resolve contract disputes between unions and employers?

2. When will a court enforce a contractual promise to arbitrate disputes over the interpretation and application of a collective agreement? When should a court refuse to enforce an arbitrator's decision?

3. What remedies are available to an employer against workers striking in violation of a no-strike clause? Against a union striking in violation of a no-strike clause?

4. When will the NLRB defer consideration of an unfair labor practice complaint to arbitration?

5. When is a successor employer obligated to recognize and bargain with the union representing the employees of the former employer?

» Case Problems

6. Union member Bobby Reeves was employed as a driver by Allied, a commercial and residential solid waste disposal company, since 2004. This employment was governed by a collective bargaining agreement ("CBA") between the union and Allied. Under the CBA, Allied retained "the right to suspend, discipline, or discharge for just cause ...; [and] to make and enforce reasonable rules and regulations ... except as expressly abridged by the specific provisions of this Agreement." The CBA also contained a grievance procedure that culminated in final binding arbitration.

Reeves had been a safe driver for Allied since he began working there in 2004 until he had a bad run of accidents in the fall of 2011. On October 25, 2011, he knocked over a telephone box with the Allied truck he was driving. The following day, he was issued a written disciplinary report for this incident, which Allied viewed as preventable. On November 5, 2011, he hit a wooden enclosure with a dumpster he was hoisting with the Allied truck he was driving and caused minor damage. Although Reeves reported the incident immediately, no disciplinary report was issued for this incident at the time. On November 7, 2011, the Allied truck he was driving was damaged while he was driving it through a wheel-washing facility. The arm of the truck was down when it should have been up and was bent as Reeves drove through the washer. The next day, he was issued another written disciplinary report for the wheel-washing accident, which Allied also viewed as preventable. Reeves was suspended for three days pending an investigation and then on November 14, 2011, was terminated. The Union grieved his termination and pursued the issue to arbitration. After holding a hearing, the arbitrator decided in the Union's favor, approved the three-day suspension, and ordered Allied to reimburse Reeves the pay and benefits he suffered because of his termination.

Allied filed a lawsuit seeking to vacate the arbitrator's decision, and the Union answered and filed a counterclaim to confirm the arbitrator's award. What arguments can Allied make to support its claim that the arbitration award should be vacated? What arguments can the union make to support its claim that the award should be enforced? On what grounds can a court refuse to enforce an arbitration award? How should the court rule here? Explain. [See *Allied Waste Transportation, Inc. d/b/a Allied Waste Services of Edwardsville v. Teamsters Local Union No. 50*, 2013 WL 5587401 (S.D. Ill. Oct. 10. 2013).]

7. An employee of the Du Pont Company's plant in East Chicago attacked his supervisor and another employee and destroyed some company equipment, all for no apparent reason. He was discharged by the company. He was subsequently arrested, and he spent 30 days under observation in a hospital psychiatric ward. Two psychiatrists subsequently testified in court that the employee was temporarily insane at the time of the incident, and therefore he was acquitted of the criminal charges. They also testified that the worker had recovered and was not likely to suffer another mental breakdown.

Following his acquittal, the worker's discharge was challenged by the union on the ground that the employee was not responsible for the assaults due to temporary mental incapacity. Therefore, argued the union, he was not dismissed for "just cause" as called for under the "security of employment" clause in the collective bargaining agreement.

The company refused to reinstate the employee, and the union moved the grievance to arbitration. The arbitrator ruled in the union's favor and ordered the grievant reinstated to his job. Du Pont filed suit in a federal court in Indiana to overturn the arbitrator's ruling.

If you represented the company in front of the federal judge, what arguments would you make for overturning the arbitrator's award? If you represented the union, what counterarguments would you make in response? How should the judge have ruled? [See *E. I. Du Pont De Nemours & Co. v. Grasselli Employees Independent Ass'n. of E. Chicago*, 790 F.2d 611 (7th Cir. 1986).]

8. In the mid-1980s, Eastern Airlines experienced severe financial difficulties. After intense negotiations, Eastern and its pilots' union, ALPA, ratified a collective bargaining agreement. On February 24, 1986, the parent corporation of Continental Airlines, acquired Eastern. The ALPA believed that the acquisition constituted a "merger" within the meaning of certain "labor protective provisions" (LPPs) contained in the collective bargaining agreement. The LPPs in the collective bargaining agreement protected the pilots' seniority rights in the event of a merger between Eastern and another airline carrier by requiring the integration of Eastern's seniority lists with the merging carrier's list. The ALPA requested a meeting with Eastern and Continental to discuss the integration of the seniority lists of Eastern's and Continental's pilots. Despite ALPA's requests, both Eastern and Continental refused to bargain with ALPA about the integration of the seniority lists. Consequently, ALPA requested that Eastern submit the dispute to arbitration to determine whether an alleged merger occurred between Eastern and Continental that triggered the LPP seniority integration provision. Eastern, however, filed for bankruptcy in March,

1989, but did not seek to reject the collective bargaining agreement under Section 1113 of the Bankruptcy Code. Eastern refused to submit to arbitration, claiming that it was not required to do so under the bankruptcy laws. The ALPA filed suit in bankruptcy court to compel Eastern to arbitrate the dispute.

Should Eastern be required to arbitrate the dispute under the collective agreement, or does the bankruptcy filing end any obligation to arbitrate based on the collective agreement? Explain your answer. [See *In re Ionosphere Clubs, Inc.*, 922 F.2d 984 (2d Cir. 1990); and *In re Continental Airlines*, 125 F.3d 120 (3d Cir. 1997), *cert. denied*, 522 U.S. 1114 (Feb 23, 1998).]

9. Safeway Stores, Inc., discharged a journeyman meat cutter for disobeying an order and threatening a supervisor with physical harm. United Food and Commercial Workers Local 400 filed a grievance on behalf of the employee, and a few days later, representatives of the company and the union met to discuss the grievance. Unable to reach an informal resolution, the union submitted the grievance to arbitration.

The arbitrator found that the grievant was guilty of disobeying a direct order and that he had compounded his offense by threatening his supervisor with bodily harm. However, the arbitrator refused to sustain the discharge because he also found that the company had not fully disclosed to the union or the grievant all the reasons for the discharge. At the grievance meeting, the company had stated that the reason for the discharge was the incident of insubordination. But during the arbitration hearing, the personnel director testified that his decision to discharge the grievant was based not only on his acts of insubordination but also on his past disciplinary record and a newspaper clipping he had seen concerning the grievant's conviction for assault and battery of his former girlfriend.

The company refused to abide by the arbitrator's decision and sought to have it overturned in the U.S. District Court for the District of Columbia. If you had been the federal judge sitting in this case, would you have affirmed or overturned the arbitrator's award? Explain. [See *Safeway Stores*,

Inc. v. United Food and Commercial Workers Local 400, 621 F. Supp. 1233 (D.D.C. 1985).]

10. *The Cleveland Press* and *The Plain Dealer*, the two daily newspapers in Cleveland, Ohio, were part of a multiemployer bargaining group that had signed a collective bargaining agreement with the Cleveland Typographical Union, Local 53. The contract stated that each covered employee was entitled to "a regular full-time job … for the remainder of his working life."

When the Cleveland Press went out of business, 89 former press employees sued the parent company, E. W. Scripps Company, and The Plain Dealer to enforce the lifetime employment guarantee in their collective bargaining agreement. In addition to their Section 301 action, the plaintiffs also charged that the two defendants had conspired to create a daily newspaper monopoly in the city of Cleveland. The defendants replied, among other defenses, that the plaintiffs had no standing to sue on this second basis.

Should the federal judge enforce the contract guarantee of lifetime jobs? If you say yes, what kind of a remedy should the judge fashion? What evidence do you see to support the plaintiffs' antitrust allegation? If defendants violated the Sherman Act, what impact should this have on their case? [See *Province v. Cleveland Press Publishing Co.*, 787 F.2d 1047 (6th Cir. 1986).]

11. Nolde Bros. Bakery's collective bargaining agreement with the Bakery & Confectionery Workers Union, Local 358, provided that any grievance between the parties was subject to binding arbitration. During negotiations over the renewal of the agreement, the union gave notice of its intention to cancel the existing agreement. Negotiations continued for several days past the termination date, and the union threatened to strike. The employer informed the union that it was permanently closing its plant. The employer paid the employees their accrued wages and vacation pay but refused to pay severance pay as called for in the collective agreement. The employer argued that its duty to pay severance pay and its duty to arbitrate the claim for severance pay expired with the collective agreement. The union sued under Section 301 to force the employer to arbitrate the question of whether the employer was required to pay severance pay.

How should the court decide the union's suit? Is the employer required to arbitrate the matter? Explain your answer. [See *Nolde Bros. v. Bakery & Confectionery Workers Local 358*, 430 U.S. 243 (1977).]

12. The Grissom family owned and operated a motor lodge and restaurant franchised by the Howard Johnson Co.; they employed 53 employees, who were represented by the Hotel & Restaurant Employees Union. The Grissoms sold their business to the Howard Johnson Co. Howard Johnson hired 49 employees, nine of whom were former employees of the Grissoms. The union requested that Howard Johnson recognize it and meet the obligations of the prior collective agreement, but Howard Johnson refused. The union then sought arbitration of the question of the successor's obligations under the agreement; it filed a suit under Section 301 to compel Howard Johnson to arbitrate.

Is Howard Johnson required to recognize and bargain with the union? Is Howard Johnson required to arbitrate the question of the successor's obligation? Explain your answer. [See *Howard Johnson Co. v. Hotel & Restaurant Employees Detroit Local Joint Board*, 417 U.S. 249 (1974).]

13. The underlying dispute in this case arose when Waller Brothers, which operates a stone quarry engaged in removing and processing stone and packing the stone in boxes for shipment, purchased an Instapak machine, which sprays protective padding around the stone being packed for shipment. Before the purchase of the Instapak, the stone was packed with strips of synthetic material as padding. Employees called "craters" pack the stone for shipment.

The union claims that it was entitled to negotiate a new wage rate for an Instapak machine operator, whereas the company maintains that the operation of the machine is only a function of the crater job classification, which is subject to a previously negotiated wage rate. The company takes the position that both the no-strike clause and the provision for mandatory grievance arbitration contained in the collective bargaining agreement apply to this dispute. The union for its part relies on the portion of the contract that provides that wage rates are not subject to arbitration and that the union expressly reserves the right to strike in the event of a disagreement on wages.

If the union calls a strike and the company goes into court seeking a *Boys Markets* injunction, should the court grant or deny it? [See *Waller Bros. Stone Co. v. District 23*, 620 F.2d 132 (6th Cir. 1980).]

14. HMC Management Corp., an apartment rental and management company, discharged two of its employees for substandard work performance. The employees, represented by the Carpenters Union, filed grievances. The employer subsequently decided to rehire one of the employees but not the other one. When the grievance filed by the employee who was not rehired was arbitrated, the arbitrator acknowledged that the employer had sufficient reason to discharge the two employees but held that the employer had acted improperly when it rehired one employee but not the other. The arbitrator ordered that the employer reinstate the other employee. The employer filed suit in federal court to have the arbitration award vacated.

    Should the court enforce or vacate the arbitrator's decision? Explain your answer. [See *HMC Mgt. Corp. v. Carpenters District Council*, 750 F.2d 1302 (5th Cir. 1985).]

15. The appellate court judge who wrote the decision of the three-judge panel in this case began his opinion as follows:

    Coffin, Chief Judge—This tempest has been brewed in a very small teapot. The dispute which precipitated the filing in this court of more than 80 pages of briefs and an extensive appendix began on July 30, 1974, when appellee Anheuser-Busch posted a notice prohibiting employees at its Merrimack, New Hampshire, brewery from wearing tank-top shirts on the job. Tank-tops are sleeveless shirts which leave exposed the shoulders, arms and underarms of the wearer. Beginning on July 31, when three employees were sent home after refusing to doff their tank-tops for other shirts, the emotional temperature rose, with over a dozen more employees, including shop stewards, being sent home a few days later. The issue peaked by August 14, when thirteen of the eighteen employees in the Brewery Department wore tank-tops, refused to put on other shirts, and went home. Approximately thirty employees in the Maintenance Department wore tank-tops on August 15. On August 16 no maintenance employees reported for work and production at the brewery was halted.

    The brewery filed a lawsuit in federal district court seeking injunctive relief and damages against the employees' union on the grounds that the collective bargaining agreement contained a no-strike clause and an arbitration clause.

    The union responded that (1) the employees' actions were individual, not concerted, activity; (2) the employees were entitled to wear the tank-tops pending arbitration of the controversy; and (3) the employer should not be permitted to hide behind a *Boys Markets* injunction after management's overreaction had itself precipitated the crisis.

    How do you think the court ruled in this dispute? [See *Anheuser-Busch v. Teamsters Local 633*, 511 F.2d 1097 (1st Cir.), *cert. denied*, 423 U.S. 875 (1975).]

16. Stikes, an employee of Chevron Corp., was discharged for refusing to allow the employer to search her car under a company antidrug policy, adopted in 1984, that required workers to submit to random searches of person and property. Stikes was a member of the bargaining unit represented by the Oil, Chemical and Atomic Workers Union; the collective agreement covering the bargaining unit provided for arbitration of discharge cases. Rather than submit a grievance over her discharge, Stikes filed a suit against Chevron in the state court. The suit charged Chevron with wrongful discharge, intentional infliction of emotional distress, unfair business practice, and violation of rights to privacy under the state constitution. Chevron argued that the suit was preempted by Section 301 because it was a suit to enforce the collective agreement.

    Does Stikes have a right to sue under state law over her discharge, or is her suit preempted by Section 301? Explain your answer. [See *Stikes v. Chevron USA Inc.*, 914 F.2d 1265 (9th Cir. 1990).]

» Hypothetical Scenarios

17. The employees of Robinson Ford Sales, a local auto dealer, are represented by Local 303 of the United

Automobile Workers Union. Because of slumping sales, the dealership announces that it must change the medical insurance provided to the employees under the collective agreement by doubling the copays and deductibles that the employees are required to pay. The union objects that the change violates the collective agreement, and demands that the dealership submit the dispute to arbitration under the collective agreement arbitrations procedures. The dealership refuses to do so, and the union files suit under Section 301 of the NLRA to force the employer to submit the dispute to arbitration. The trial court refuses to order Robinson to arbitrate the dispute, holding that Robinson's reduced business was a legitimate reason for making the changes. The union then appeals to the federal court of appeals. Should the court of appeals order the employer to arbitrate the dispute? What factors should the court consider when deciding whether to order arbitration?

18. West World Holding, Inc. owned an office building in Boise. The maintenance and cleaning employees for the building were represented by Service Employees International Union, Local 32, and the union and employer had a collective agreement governing the terms and conditions of employment for those employees. West World sold the building to Maiden LLC, a Denver-based real estate company, on August 27, 2007. Maiden announced that it would retain all maintenance and cleaning employees who had worked for West World. Local 32 then requested that Maiden bargain with the union over whether to continue to adhere to the terms of collective agreement with West World. Maiden refused to recognize the union and made unilateral changes to the terms and conditions of employment for the workers. The union filed an unfair labor practice charge against Maiden over its refusal to recognize the union. How should the NLRB rule—is Maiden required to recognize and bargain with the union? Is Maiden bound by the previous collective agreement? Explain your answer.

19. Crucible Metals Foundry makes structural steel for the construction industry but has been losing orders because new construction has been affected by the lack of availability credit funding. Crucible is forced to file for reorganization under Chapter 11 of the Bankruptcy Code. Crucible submits a proposal to the union representing its production workers that would eliminate the pension and medical insurance benefits that the employees and retirees presently enjoy under the current collective agreement. Crucible argues that the costs of those programs are prohibitively expensive and the firm can no longer afford them. The union is reluctant to agree to the proposal. What steps must Crucible pursue to reject the requirements of the collective agreement?

20. Sievers, a union steward at Spina Manufacturing Co., was fired when he filed a grievance over the employer's change to its overtime pay policies. Sievers argued that the action was in violation of the collective agreement and also violated the federal Fair Labor Standards Act. The union filed unfair labor practice charges with the NLRB, claiming that the discharge was a violation of Sections 8(a)(1) and 8(a)(3) of the NLRA. The employer argued that dispute over the discharge should be arbitrated under the collective agreement's arbitration provisions, and that the NLRB should defer the dispute to arbitration. Should the NLRB refer the dispute to arbitration? What factors will the NLRB consider in making it decision?

21. Michaels, a police officer with the Shelbyville Police Department, was dismissed for violating the city's sexual harassment policy. Michaels and the union representing the police officers filed a grievance over the discharge and ultimately submitted the grievance to arbitration under the collective agreement covering police officers. The arbitrator held that Michaels had violated the sexual harassment policy, but because of Michaels' previously unblemished record, reduced the discharge to a suspension without pay for three months. The city objects to the arbitration award and brings an action in the federal district court to have the arbitrator's decision vacated. What factors should the court consider in deciding this case? How should the court decide? Why?

CHAPTER 18

The Rights of Union Members

Unions, as bargaining agents representing bargaining units of employees, have significant power and control over individual employees. Those employees are precluded from dealing with the employer on matters of wages and working conditions; the employees must go through the union in dealing with the employer. Because employees are dependent on the union, they must be protected from the arbitrary or unreasonable exercise of union power. This chapter explores the legal controls of unions to protect the rights of union members.

18-1 Protection of the Rights of Union Members

duty of fair representation
legal duty on the part of the union to represent fairly all members of the bargaining unit

The legal controls on unions are the result of actions by the courts, the National Labor Relations Board (NLRB), and Congress. The courts and the NLRB have imposed a **duty of fair representation** on the part of the union—an obligation to represent fairly all members of the bargaining unit. Congress has legislated a *union members' "bill of rights"* to guarantee that union internal procedures are fair and has prohibited certain practices by unions that interfere with employees' rights under the National Labor Relations Act (NLRA).

In 1947, the Taft-Hartley Act added a list of union unfair labor practices to the NLRA, which included the following:

- Section 7 was amended to give employees the right to refrain from engaging in concerted activity, as well as the right to engage in such activity.

- Section 8(b)(1)(A) prohibits union activity that interferes with, restrains, or coerces employees in the exercise of their Section 7 rights.

- Section 8(b)(2) prohibits unions from causing an employer to discriminate against employees in terms and conditions of employment because they are not union members.

- Section 8(b)(5) protects employees from unreasonable union dues and initiation fees.

- The Landrum-Griffin Act of 1959 added the union member's bill of rights to the NLRA.

Those provisions will be discussed in detail later in this chapter.

18-1a The Union's Duty of Fair Representation

The duty of fair representation is a judicially created obligation on the part of the union to represent fairly all employees in the bargaining unit. The duty was developed by the courts because of the union's role as exclusive bargaining agent for the bargaining unit. The initial cases dealing with the duty of fair representation arose under the Railway Labor Act; subsequent cases applied the duty to unions under the NLRA as well. In the following case, the Supreme Court developed the concept of the duty of fair representation.

CASE 18.1

STEELE V. LOUISVILLE & NASHVILLE R.R.

323 U.S. 192 (1944)

Stone, C. J.

The question is whether the Railway Labor Act ... imposes on a labor organization, acting by authority of the statute as the exclusive bargaining representative of a craft or class of railway employees, the duty to represent all the employees in the craft without discrimination because of their race, and, if so, whether the courts have jurisdiction to protect the minority of the craft or class from the violation of such obligation.

... Petitioner, a Negro, is a locomotive fireman in the employ of respondent railroad, suing on his own behalf and that of his fellow employees who, like petitioner, are Negro firemen employed by the Railroad. Respondent Brotherhood, a labor organization, is as provided under Section 2, Fourth of the Railway Labor Act, the exclusive bargaining representative of the craft of firemen employed by the Railroad and is recognized as such by it and the members of the craft. The majority of the firemen employed by the Railroad are white and are members of the Brotherhood, but a substantial minority are Negroes who, by the constitution and ritual of the Brotherhood, are excluded from its membership. As the membership of the Brotherhood constitutes a majority of all firemen employed on respondent Railroad and as under Section 2, Fourth, the members, because they are the majority, have chosen the Brotherhood to represent the craft, petitioner and other Negro firemen on the road have been required to accept the Brotherhood as their representative for the purposes of the Act.

On March 28, 1940, the Brotherhood, purporting to act as representative of the entire craft of firemen, without informing the Negro firemen or giving them opportunity to be heard, served a notice on respondent Railroad and on twenty other railroads operating principally in the southeastern part of the United States. The notice announced the Brotherhood's desire to amend the existing collective bargaining agreement in such a manner as ultimately to exclude all Negro firemen from the service. By established practice on the several railroads so notified only white

firemen can be promoted to serve as engineers, and the notice proposed that only "promotable," i.e., white, men should be employed as firemen or assigned to new runs or jobs or permanent vacancies in established runs or jobs.

On February 18, 1941, the railroads and the Brotherhood, as representative of the craft, entered into a new agreement which provided that not more than 50 percent of the firemen in each class of service in each seniority district of a carrier should be Negroes; that until such percentage should be reached all new runs and all vacancies should be filled by white men; and that the agreement did not sanction the employment of Negroes in any seniority district in which they were not working....

... [W]e think that Congress, in enacting the Railway Labor Act and authorizing a labor union, chosen by a majority of a craft, to represent the craft, did not intend to confer plenary power upon the union to sacrifice, for the benefit of its members, rights of the minority of the craft, without imposing on it any duty to protect the minority. Since petitioner and the other Negro members of the craft are not members of the Brotherhood or eligible for membership, the authority to act for them is derived not from their action or consent but wholly from the command of the Act....

Section 2, Second, requiring carriers to bargain with the representative so chosen, operates to exclude any other from representing a craft. The minority members of a craft are thus deprived by the statute of the right, which they would otherwise possess, to choose a representative of their own, and its members cannot bargain individually on behalf of themselves as to matters which are properly the subject of collective bargaining....

The fair interpretation of the statutory language is that the organization chosen to represent a craft is to represent all its members, the majority as well as the minority, and it is to act for and not against those whom it represents. It is a principle of general application that the exercise of a granted power to act in behalf of others involves the assumption toward them of a duty to exercise the power in their interest and behalf, and that such a grant of power will not be deemed to dispense with all duty toward those for whom it is exercised unless so expressed.

We think that the Railway Labor Act imposes upon the statutory representative of a craft at least as exacting a duty to protect equally the interests of the members of the craft as the Constitution imposes upon a legislature to give equal protection to the interests of those for whom it legislates. Congress has seen fit to clothe the bargaining representative with powers comparable to those possessed by a legislative body both to create and restrict the rights of those whom it represents, but it also imposed on the representative a corresponding duty. We hold that the language of the Act to which we have referred, read in the light of the purposes of the Act, expresses the aim of Congress to impose on the bargaining representative of a craft or class of employees the duty to exercise fairly the power conferred upon it in behalf of all those for whom it acts, without hostile discrimination against them.

This does not mean that the statutory representative of a craft is barred from making contracts which may have unfavorable effects on some of the members of the craft represented. Variations in terms of the contract based on differences relevant to the authorized purposes of the contract in conditions to which they are to be applied, such as differences in seniority, the type of work performed, the competence and skill with which it is performed, are within the scope of the bargaining representation of a craft, all of whose members are not identical in their interest or merit. Without attempting to mark the allowable limits of differences in the terms of contracts based on differences of conditions to which they apply, it is enough for present purposes to say that the statutory power to represent a craft and to make contracts as to wages, hours and working conditions does not include the authority to make among members of the craft discriminations not based on such relevant differences. Here the discriminations based on race alone are obviously irrelevant and invidious. Congress plainly did not undertake to authorize the bargaining representative to make such discriminations. . . .

The representative which thus discriminates may be enjoined from so doing, and its members may be enjoined from taking the benefit of such discriminatory action. No more is the Railroad bound by or entitled to take the benefit of a contract which the bargaining representative is prohibited by the statute from making. In both cases the right asserted, which is derived from the duty imposed by the statute on the bargaining representative, is a federal right implied from the statute and the policy which it has adopted. . . .

So long as a labor union assumes to act as the statutory representative of a craft, it cannot rightly refuse to perform the duty, which is inseparable from the power of representation conferred upon it, to represent the entire membership of the craft. While the statute does not deny to such a bargaining labor organization the right to determine eligibility to its membership, it does require the union, in collective bargaining and in making contracts with the carrier, to represent non-union or minority union members of the craft without hostile discrimination, fairly, impartially, and in good faith. Wherever necessary to that end, the union is required to consider requests of non-union members of the craft and expressions of their views with respect to collective bargaining with the employer and to give to them notice of and opportunity for hearing upon its proposed action. . . .

We conclude that the duty which the statute imposes on a union representative of a craft to represent the interests of all its members stands on no different footing and that the statute contemplates resort to the usual judicial remedies of injunction and award of damages when appropriate for breach of that duty.

The judgment is accordingly reversed and remanded. . . .
So ordered.

Case Questions

1. Is Steele a member of the union? Why?
2. To what conduct by the union and the railroad did Steele object?
3. To which employees does the union owe a duty of fair representation? What is the source of the union's duty of fair representation?.

The *Steele* case held that the duty of fair representation arose out of the union's exclusive bargaining agent status under Section 2, Ninth, of the Railway Labor Act. In *Syres v. Oil Workers Local 23*,[1] the Supreme Court held that the duty of fair representation also extended to unions granted bargaining agent status under Section 9(a) of the NLRA.

---

[1] 350 U.S. 892 (1955).

Unions, in representing employees, must make decisions that affect different employees in different ways. For example, in negotiating a contract, the union must decide whether to seek increased wages or improved benefits—trade-offs must be made in fashioning contract proposals. Older employees may be more concerned with pensions, whereas younger employees may be more concerned with increased wages. Should the courts monitor the union's negotiation proposals to ensure that all workers are fairly represented? In *Ford Motor Co. v. Huffman*,[2] the Supreme Court held that unions should be given broad discretion by the courts in negotiation practices; the courts should ensure only that the union operates "in good faith and honesty of purpose in the exercise of its discretion."

---

ethical DILEMMA

UNION MEMBERSHIP BENEFITS AND COSTS

You are the human resource manager of the Springfield plant of Immense Multinational Business; the plant production employees are represented by a union, and the collective agreement has a union shop clause requiring employees in the bargaining unit to join the union and to maintain their membership in good standing.

You have just hired a new production employee, Waylon Smithers, who asks you if he is required to join the union. He also asks you what benefits he may receive by becoming a union member and what the negative aspects of union membership are. How should you respond to him? Prepare a short memo outlining your response to his questions, supporting your comments with appropriate references.

The courts also give unions some leeway in exercising their contractual duties. In *Steelworkers v. Rawson*,[3] the Supreme Court held that the allegations that the union had been negligent in its duty under the collective agreement to conduct safety inspections did not amount to a breach of the duty of fair representation because mere negligence, even in the performance of a contractual duty, does not amount to a breach of the duty of fair representation. Where a union's work assignments were not irrational, the union did not breach duty of fair representation even though the work assignments had the effect of favoring skilled workers over unskilled workers.[4] However, a union's negligent failure to follow hiring hall rules may be a breach of the duty of fair representation, according to *Jacoby v. NLRB*.[5]

Although the courts allow unions broad latitude in negotiations, they may be more concerned with union decisions involving individual employee grievances. In *Vaca v. Sipes*,[6] the Supreme Court held that an individual does not have an absolute right to have a grievance taken to arbitration, but the union must make decisions about the merits of a grievance in good faith and in a nonarbitrary manner.

---

[2] 345 U.S. 330 (1953).

[3] 495 U.S. 362 (1990).

[4] *Bowerman v. Int, Union, U.A.W., Local 12*, 646 F.3d 360 (6th Cir. 2011).

[5] 233 F.3d 611 (D.C. Cir. 2000).

[6] 386 U.S. 171 (1967).

In *Vaca*, the union refused to arbitrate the employee's grievance. If the union decides to arbitrate the grievance but mishandles the employee's claim, does it violate the duty of fair representation? What if the union gives the grievance only perfunctory handling? The following case addresses these questions.

» CASE 18.2

HINES v. ANCHOR MOTOR FREIGHT, INC.
424 U.S. 554 (1976)

Facts: Two truck drivers employed by Anchor Motor Freight, Inc., were discharged for allegedly submitting expense claims in excess of the actual costs of their motel rooms. The relevant collective agreement provided that discharge required just cause. At a grievance meeting between the union and the employer, the employer presented the following:

- the motel receipts submitted by the employees that showed charges in excess of the rates shown on the motel's registration cards;
- a notarized statement of the motel clerk asserting the accuracy of the registration cards; and
- an affidavit of the motel owner affirming that the registration cards were accurate and that inflated receipts had been supplied to the employees.

The union claimed petitioners were innocent and opposed the discharges. The grievance over the discharge was then submitted to arbitration under the collective agreement. The two employees suggested that the union investigate the motel, but the union responded that "there was nothing to worry about" and that they need not hire their own attorney.

At the arbitration hearing, Anchor presented its case. Then both the union and employees were afforded an opportunity to present their case. The employees denied the claim of dishonesty, but neither they nor the union presented any other evidence contradicting the documents presented by the company. The arbitration panel upheld the discharges.

The employees then retained an attorney and sought rehearing based on a statement by the motel owner that the discrepancy between the receipts and the registration cards could have been attributable to the motel clerk's recording on the cards less than what was actually paid and pocketing the difference between the amount receipted and the amount recorded. The arbitration panel unanimously denied rehearing "because there was no new evidence presented which would justify reopening this case." It was later discovered that the motel clerk was in fact the culprit.

The discharged employees filed suit against both the union and the employer. They alleged that because their discharge was not for good cause, the employer was in violation of the collective agreement. They also alleged that the union violated its duty of fair representation by arbitrarily failing to make an effort to investigate the employer's charges of dishonesty. The union relied upon the decision of the arbitration panel, and the employer claimed that the employees had been properly discharged for just cause. The employer also claimed that the employees, diligently and in good faith represented by the union, had unsuccessfully resorted to the grievance and arbitration machinery provided by the contract, and that the adverse decision of the arbitration panel was binding upon the union and employees under the collective agreement.

During pretrial discovery proceedings, the motel clerk revealed that he had falsified the records and had pocketed the difference between the sums shown on the receipts and the registration cards. The trial court granted summary judgment for the employer and the union on the ground that the decision of the arbitration panel was final and binding on the employees and that they had failed to show that the union had acted arbitrarily or in bad faith. The court stated that the union's conduct of the investigation and arbitration may have demonstrated bad judgment on the part of the union, but it was insufficient to prove a breach of the duty of fair representation.

The employees then appealed to the U.S. Court of Appeals, which reversed the decision of the trial court and held that the employees had presented sufficient evidence to support a finding of bad faith or arbitrary conduct on the part of the union. An appeal was taken to the U.S. Supreme Court.

Issue: Can the union be sued for breach of the duty of fair representation when the employer's discharge of the employees was held by the arbitration panel not to be in violation of the collective agreement?

Decision: The Supreme Court noted that, in order to prevail against either the employer or the union, the employees must show not only that their discharge was in violation of the collective agreement requirement of just cause but must also carry the burden of demonstrating a breach of the duty of fair representation by the union. Such a showing requires more than just demonstrating mere errors in judgment. The employees are not entitled to relitigate their discharge merely because they offer newly discovered evidence that the charges against them were false and that in fact they were fired without cause. The grievance processes cannot be expected to be error-free. The finality provision of the collective agreement regarding arbitration has sufficient force to surmount occasional instances of mistake.

However, an arbitration decision may be reopened where the employees' representation by the union has been dishonest, in bad faith, or discriminatory. Here, in order to prevail, the employees must show that the arbitration decision was in error because it was undermined by the union's breach of the duty of fair representation. If they can make such a showing, then they are entitled to remedies against both the employer for violating the collective agreement and the union for breach of the duty of fair representation. The employer is not immunized from liability for discharge without just cause by reason of the union's breach of the duty of fair representation.

The Supreme Court reversed the court of appeals' decision affirming the dismissal of the suit against the employer.

Union Dues and the Duty of Fair Representation

A union owes a duty of fair representation to all employees in the bargaining unit it represents, whether or not the employees are members of the union. As you recall from Chapter 14, Section 8(a)(3) allows the employer and union to agree on a union security clause (unless there is a state right-to-work law that prohibits mandatory union membership or union dues). Union security clauses generally involve either a **union shop** clause, which requires employees to become union members within thirty days of their employment, or an **agency shop** clause, which requires employees to pay union dues and fees.

Negotiating a union security clause that incorporates the language of Section 8(a)(3) of the NLRA is not a violation of the union's duty of fair representation, as held in *Marquez v. Screen Actors Guild.*[7] An employer who unilaterally ceases to deduct union dues from employees under a union security clause violates Sections 8(a)(1) and 8(a)(5), according to *NLRB v. Oklahoma Fixture Co.*[8] Where the collective agreement contains a union shop agreement, a proviso to Section 8(a)(3) states that an employer may not discharge an employee for failing to join the union if union membership is denied for a reason other than failure to pay union dues or fees. In *NLRB v. General Motors Corp.,*[9] the Supreme Court held that the effect of that proviso is to reduce an employee's obligation under a union shop clause to "a financial core"—that is, simply to pay union dues and fees. According to the Supreme Court's decision in *Communications Workers of America v. Beck,*[10] unions may not use the dues or fees of employees who are not union members to pay for union activities not related to collective bargaining. Such employees are entitled to a reduction in dues and fees by the percentage of union expenditures that go for non–collective bargaining expenses. Employees who are not union members may not be charged for the portion of union dues spent on organizing activities outside the appropriate bargaining unit, according to *United Food and Commercial Workers Union, Local*

union shop
a union security provision in a collective agreement that requires employees to become union members within thirty days of their employment

agency shop
a union security provision in a collective agreement that requires employees to pay union dues and fees, but does not require that they become union members

---

[7] 525 U.S. 33 (1998).

[8] 332 F.3d 1284 (10th Cir. 2003).

[9] 373 U.S. 734 (1963).

[10] 487 U.S. 735 (1988).

1036 v. NLRB.[11] However, in *Lehnert v. Ferris Faculty Ass'n,*[12] the Supreme Court held that employees who are not union members but are subject to an agency fee provision under a collective agreement can be charged a pro rata share of the costs of union activities related to bargaining, litigation, preparation for a strike, and other union activities that may not directly benefit members of bargaining unit; they are not required to pay the costs of lobbying activity by the union. In *Chicago Teachers Union, Local No. 1 v. Hudson,*[13] the Supreme Court held that the union is required to provide objecting members with information relating to the union expenditures on collective bargaining and political activities and must include an adequate explanation of the basis of dues and fees. The objecting members must also be provided with a reasonable opportunity to challenge, before an impartial decision maker, the amount of the dues or fees; the union must hold in escrow the disputed amounts pending the resolution of the challenges. Unions may require that disputes over the amount of agency fees charged to nonmembers be arbitrated. However, the objecting nonmembers, unless they have specifically agreed to arbitrate their dispute, are not required to exhaust the arbitration process before filing suit in federal court, as held in *Air Line Pilots Association v. Miller.*[14] A state law that requires public sector unions to get affirmative authorization of the use of agency shop fees for political purposes does not violate the unions' First Amendment rights, according to the Supreme Court decision in *Davenport v. Washington Education Association.*[15] Where a union increases the fee, or imposes a new fee for the union's political activities, it must inform nonmembers in the bargaining unit of the increase or new fee, and allow the nonmembers to choose whether to pay it.[16] In *Ysursa v. Pocatello Education Ass'n,*[17] the Supreme Court upheld the constitutionality of an Idaho state law that prohibited public sector employees from authorizing voluntary payroll deductions for union political activities.

Shortly after taking office in 2001, President George W. Bush signed Executive Order 13201,[18] which applied to all firms doing business with the federal government. The order required those firms to post notices in the workplace informing employees subject to a union security agreement that they have the right to refuse to pay the portion of their union dues that is expended for activities unrelated to collective bargaining, contract administration, or grievance adjustment. However, on January 30, 2009, President Barack Obama issued Executive Order 13496,[19] which revoked Executive Order 13201. The new executive order requires employers to post a notice, the content of which will be established by the Secretary of Labor, informing employees of their rights under the National Labor Relations Act.[20]

---

[11] 249 F.3d 1115 (2001).

[12] 500 U.S. 507 (1991). *Abood v. Detroit Bd. of Ed.*, 431 U.S. 209 (1977) held that a public sector union may not require nonmembers to fund its political and ideological activities.

[13] 475 U.S. 292 (1986).

[14] 523 U.S. 866 (1998).

[15] 551 U.S. 177 (2007).

[16] *Knox v. Service Employees Int. Union, Local 1000*, 132 S. Ct. 2277 (2012).

[17] 555 U.S. 353 (2009).

[18] 66 FR 11221, 2001 WL 169257 (Feb. 17, 2001).

[19] 74 FR 6107, 2009 WL 248091 (Jan. 30, 2009).

[20] Note that the imposition of a separate but similar posting requirement issued by the NLRB was invalidated by *National Ass'n of Mfrs. v. NLRB*, 717 F.3d 947 (D.C. Cir. 2013).

CASE 18.3

INTERNATIONAL BROTHERHOOD OF TEAMSTERS, LOCAL 776, AFL-CIO (CAROLINA FREIGHT CARRIERS CORPORATION)

324 NLRB 1154 (NLRB 1997)

Michael O. Miller, ALJ

... Since before 1994, the Employer had recognized Respondent [union] (and the Teamsters National Freight Industry Negotiating Committee) as the exclusive collective-bargaining representative of its employees in a unit appropriate for collective-bargaining purposes. The collective-bargaining agreement includes a "Union Shop" clause which."... [a]ll present employees who are not members of the Local union and all employees who are hired hereafter [to] become and remain members in good standing of the Local Union as a condition of employment on and after the thirty-first (31st) day following the beginning of their employment...."

It further provides that an employee "who has failed to acquire, or thereafter maintain, membership in the Union ... shall be terminated seventy-two (72) hours after his Employer has received written notice from ... the Local Union."

... Carolina hired Timothy Blosser on May 2, 1994, as a casual dock laborer. As a casual, he had no set or guaranteed hours; his schedule was determined each week....

The following case illustrates how the NLRB applies the Beck decision.

On May 27, the Union sent Blosser a registered letter outlining what it asserted were his union membership and financial obligations. That letter stated:

Our Constitution states that after thirty (30) calendar days, you are required to join the Local Union.... Your initiation fee is $200.00 plus the first month's dues which is two times your hourly rate, plus one dollar ($1.00) assessment for the death benefit....

According to our records, your first day of employment at Carolina Freight was May 2, 1994. Therefore, per the terms of our agreement with Carolina Freight and as outlined above, you are hereby notified that you must come into the Local Union office and join and/or become a member in good standing in the Local Union on, but not before June 2, 1994.

Upon failure to comply on this date, we shall contact your employer to inform him that you are not eligible to work. If you have any questions regarding Teamsters Local Union No. 776 or are no longer employed by the above-mentioned company, please feel free to call.

The letter omitted any reference to employee rights to opt out of full membership or pay less than the full amount of dues.

On June 1, Blosser responded to the Union's demand ... he described, as a violation of the duty of fair representation, a union's maintenance and application of a union-security clause requiring membership in good standing without advising the unit employees that their obligation was limited to the payment of uniform initiation fees and dues.

... Blosser asserted that nonmembers "do not have to pay a fee equal to union dues," that they "can only be required to pay a fee that equals their share of what the union can prove is its costs of collective bargaining, contract administration, and grievance adjustment with their employer."

... The Union replied on June 3, notifying Blosser that "the fees established by our auditor is [sic] 87% of the two times the hourly rate, and $1.00 for the death benefit, plus the $200.00 initiation fee." Accordingly, the dues, he was told, would be $26.10 per month. He had, he was told, seven days to comply before the employer would be informed not to assign him work.

The correspondence continued. Blosser replied, insisting that, "before the union demands fees, an independent accountant's verification of the union's cost of collective bargaining, NOT the union's interpretation" must be provided. Because no such verification had been provided, Blosser asserted that no payment could be demanded and that he would await receipt of that verification. He also asserted that the initiation fee should similarly be reduced by the appropriate percentage, 87 percent according to the Union's calculation. Finally, he requested a copy of the collective bargaining agreement.

On June 20, the Union sent Blosser the "latest auditor's verification of the core fees," those for 1993, noting that the computations of the core fees using the 1994 financial information was [sic] in process. The computation showed the Union's expenses and the portion of those expenses, if any, which were chargeable under Beck. It concluded that the expenses chargeable to protesting members amounted to 86.7 percent of the total expenses.

Blosser was also told that copies of the National Master Freight Agreement and the supplement applicable to Carolina are "given to all members when they become members of the Union." A hope was expressed that his dues and initiation fee would be received within 72 hours.

On June 24, the Union sent Blosser a computer-generated letter reiterating his obligation to pay the initiation fee and dues. The sums demanded were the full dues and initiation fee; there was no reference to any adjustments.... It also reiterated his obligation to "become a member in good standing" with no reference to his right to choose financial core membership and it threatened to notify his employer that he was ineligible to work if he did not comply within 72 hours.

Blosser wrote back on June 27, asserting that he was entitled to the independent auditor's complete audit or his complete review, as well as his opinion letter, for the Local's expenses as well as those of the Union's District and National levels, where some of the dues money goes. He also threatened to file an additional unfair labor practice charge if he did not get a copy of the collective-bargaining agreement, to which he claimed entitlement as a member of the unit.

On June 29, the Union gave him a copy of the contract. The other information he sought, the Union stated, was "being investigated as to the legality;" he was promised a subsequent response. Blosser never became a member of the [union]; neither did he pay it any fees or dues. He voluntarily left Carolina's employ on June 29.

... The union-security clause in Respondent's collective-bargaining agreement requires all employees "to become and remain members in good standing." On May 27, and on June 24, the Union demanded that Blosser "join and/or become a member in good standing in the Local Union." At no time was he told that he had a right to be and remain a nonmember. By failing to so inform him, Respondent breached the duty of fair representation owed to him as a member of the bargaining unit and thereby violated Section 8(b)(1)(A)....

As set forth [by the NLRB] in *California Saw & Knife Works* (1995), a union, when it seeks to enforce a union-security clause, is required to inform the employees [who choose not to join the union] of their rights under Beck. Thus, they must tell the employees that they are not required to pay the full dues and fees, give those employees information upon which to intelligently decide whether to object, and apprise them of the union's internal procedures for filing objections. Respondent did none of those when it made repeated demands upon Blosser that he join the Union and pay dues. It thus failed in its duty of fair representation, in violation of Section 8 (b)(1)(A).

In its various demands that he pay the dues and the initiation fee and join the Union, Respondent gave Blosser only three to seven days in which to decide and act, on pain of the loss of his job if he failed to comply. At the times it did so, Respondent had not yet provided him with the Beck notifications to which he was entitled. General Counsel argues that by failing to give Blosser a reasonable time within which to satisfy his dues obligation, Respondent further breached its duty of fair representation.

... the complaint further alleges this conduct more generally as unlawful restraint and coercion. I agree. By threatening to cause his termination if he did not join the Union in an unreasonably short time and without the information necessary for him to reasonably decide whether to assume objector status, Respondent has restrained and coerced him in violation of Section 8(b)(1)(A).

Respondent's repeated demands upon Blosser continued to seek payment of the full $200 initiation fee, even after it acknowledged that some portion of the dues were [sic] not chargeable to objectors as representational expenses.... The complaint expressly raised the issue of the Union's attempt to collect the full initiation fee from Blosser. Respondent offered no evidence that funds derived from initiation fees were expended differently than those derived from periodic dues and presented no argument on brief that initiation fees should be exempt from the Beck apportionment. Accordingly, I find that by seeking to require Blosser, a nonmember objector, to pay the full initiation fee, Respondent breached its duty of fair representation and thereby violated Section 8(b)(1)(A).

In its computation of "core fees," the Union included, as chargeable to objecting employees, its organizing expenses. The complaint alleges that by the inclusion of such expenses the Union has breached its duty of fair representation.... It is axiomatic that the organizing of other bargaining units, at least within the same industry and/or geographical area, strengthens a union's hand in bargaining with the employer of objecting employees. Successful organization of the employees of an employer's competitors precludes that employer from arguing, at the bargaining table, that the lesser wages and benefits paid by his union-free competition prevents him from granting wage and benefit increases sought by the union which represents his employees. It also tends to increase the support which his employees will receive should they find it necessary to engage in economic action, such as a strike. Organizing of other employees thus inures "to the benefit of the members of the local union by virtue of their membership in the parent organization."

Moreover, in order to avoid the "free rider" problem . . . it is essential that a union be permitted to charge objecting nonmembers for its expenses in organizing other units. The bargaining unit in which the objector finds him or herself has already been organized. The expense of that organizational effort was borne by the union (and its members in previously organized units) sometime in the past; it can no longer be charged to current employees. Only by permitting a union to pass along the cost of its current organizing efforts to the members of its already organized units can it equitably recoup those expenses.

It may be that some organizing expenses are too remote, in terms of industry or geography, to pose more than a theoretical benefit to the objector's bargaining unit. However ... I find that organizing expenses are not "necessarily nonchargeable ... as a matter of law" and recommend dismissal of this allegation.

... Having found that the Respondent has engaged in certain unfair labor practices, I find that it must be ordered to cease and desist and to take certain affirmative action designed to effectuate the policies of the Act....

[On review by the NLRB, the Board affirmed the judge's rulings, findings, and conclusions and adopted the recommended order.]

Case Questions

1. What information does the NLRB require a union to provide to employees who choose not to become members? What information did the union provide to Blosser?

2. Why is the union allowed to include organizing expenses in the expenses chargeable to nonmembers? What is the free rider problem?

3. How was the union's conduct coercive? What unfair labor practices did the union commit? Explain.

Liability for Breach of the Duty of Fair Representation

Most cases involving the duty of fair representation arise from action by the employer; after the employee has been disciplined or discharged, the union's alleged breach of the duty compounds the problem.

How should the damages awarded in such a case be divided between the employer and the union? Which party should bear primary liability? In *Vaca v. Sipes*,[21] the Supreme Court held that an employer cannot escape liability for breach of the collective agreement just because the union has breached its duty of fair representation.

Where the employee has established a breach of the collective agreement by the employer and a breach of the duty of fair representation by the union, the employer and the union must share liability. In *Bowen v. U.S. Postal Service*,[22] the Supreme Court held that the employer is liable for back pay for the discharge of an employee in breach of the collective agreement, whereas the union breaching the duty of fair representation by refusing to grieve the discharge is responsible for any increase in damages suffered by the employee as a result of the breach of the duty of fair representation. In *Chauffeurs, Teamsters and Helpers, Local No. 391 v. Terry*,[23] the Supreme Court held that to recover damages against both the employer and the union, the employee must prove both that the employer's actions violated the collective agreement and that the union's handling of the grievance breached the duty of fair representation.

The NLRB has held that when an employee has established that the union improperly refused to process a grievance or handled it in a perfunctory manner, the Board is prepared to resolve doubts about the merits of the grievance in favor of the employee, according to *Rubber Workers Local 250 (Mack-Wayne Enclosures)*.[24]

---

[21] 386 U.S. 171 (1967).

[22] 459 U.S. 212 (1983).

[23] 494 U.S. 558 (1990).

[24] 279 NLRB 1074 (1986).

THE **WORKING** LAW

Notice of Employee Rights under Federal Labor Laws Required by Executive Order 13496

EMPLOYEE RIGHTS

UNDER THE NATIONAL LABOR RELATIONS ACT

The NLRA guarantees the right of employees to organize and bargain collectively with their employers, and to engage in other protected concerted activity. Employees covered by the NLRA* are protected from certain types of employer and union misconduct. This Notice gives you general information about your rights, and about the obligations of employers and unions under the NLRA. Contact the National Labor Relations Board, the Federal agency that investigates and resolves complaints under the NLRA, using the contact information supplied below, if you have any questions about specific rights that may apply in your particular workplace.

Under the NLRA, you have the right to:

- Organize a union to negotiate with your employer concerning your wages, hours, and other terms and conditions of employment.
- Form, join or assist a union.
- Bargain collectively through representatives of employees' own choosing for a contract with your employer setting your wages, benefits, hours, and other working conditions.
- Discuss your terms and conditions of employment or union organizing with your co-workers or a union.
- Take action with one or more co-workers to improve your working conditions by, among other means, raising work-related complaints directly with your employer or with a government agency, and seeking help from a union.
- Strike and picket, depending on the purpose or means of the strike or the picketing.
- Choose not to do any of these activities, including joining or remaining a member of a union.

Under the NLRA, it is illegal for your employer to:

- Prohibit you from soliciting for a union during non-work time, such as before or after work or during break times; or from distributing union literature during non-work time, in non-work areas, such as parking lots or break rooms.
- Question you about your union support or activities in a manner that discourages you from engaging in that activity.
- Fire, demote, or transfer you, or reduce your hours or change your shift, or otherwise take adverse action against you, or threaten to take any of these actions, because you join or support a union, or because you engage in concerted activity for mutual aid and protection, or because you choose not to engage in any such activity.
- Threaten to close your workplace if workers choose a union to represent them.
- Promise or grant promotions, pay raises, or other benefits to discourage or encourage union support.
- Prohibit you from wearing union hats, buttons, t-shirts, and pins in the workplace except under special circumstances.
- Spy on or videotape peaceful union activities and gatherings or pretend to do so.

Under the NLRA, it is illegal for a union or for the union that represents you in bargaining with your employer to:

- Threaten you that you will lose your job unless you support the union.
- Refuse to process a grievance because you have criticized union officials or because you are not a member of the union.
- Use or maintain discriminatory standards or procedures in making job referrals from a hiring hall.
- Cause or attempt to cause an employer to discriminate against you because of your union-related activity.
- Take other adverse action against you based on whether you have joined or support the union.

If you and your coworkers select a union to act as your collective bargaining representative, your employer and the union are required to bargain in good faith in a genuine effort to reach a written, binding agreement setting your terms and conditions of employment. The union is required to fairly represent you in bargaining and enforcing the agreement.

Illegal conduct will not be permitted. If you believe your rights or the rights of others have been violated, you should contact the NLRB promptly to protect your rights, generally within six months of the unlawful activity. You may inquire about possible violations without your employer or anyone else being informed of the inquiry. Charges may be filed by any person and need not be filed by the employee directly affected by the violation. The NLRB may order an employer to rehire a worker fired in violation of the law and to pay lost wages and benefits, and may order an employer or union to cease violating the law. Employees should seek assistance from the nearest regional NLRB office, which can be found on the Agency's website: **www.nlrb.gov**.

Click on the NLRB's page titled "About Us," which contains a link, "Locating Our Offices." You can also contact the NLRB by calling toll-free: **1-866-667-NLRB (6572)** or (TTY) **1-866-315-NLRB (6572)** for hearing impaired.

*The National Labor Relations Act covers most private-sector employers. Excluded from coverage under the NLRA are public-sector employees, agricultural and domestic workers, independent contractors, workers employed by a parent or spouse, employees of air and rail carriers covered by the Railway Labor Act, and supervisors (although supervisors that have been discriminated against for refusing to violate the NLRA may be covered).

This is an official Government Notice and must not be defaced by anyone.

U.S. Department of Labor

Source: U.S. Department of Labor, available at http://www.dol.gov/olms/regs /compliance/EmployeeRightsPoster11x17_Final.pdf.

Enforcing the Duty of Fair Representation

In *Miranda Fuel Co.*,[25] the NLRB held that a breach of the duty of fair representation by a union was a violation of Section 8(b)(1)(A) of the NLRA. The Board reasoned that "Section 7 … gives employees the right to be free from unfair or irrelevant or invidious treatment by their exclusive bargaining agent in matters affecting their employment." Although the Court of Appeals for the Second Circuit refused to enforce the Board's order in *Miranda*,[26] other courts of appeals have affirmed NLRB findings of Section 8(b)(1)(A) violations in subsequent duty of fair representation cases. The NLRB continues to hold that breach of the duty of fair representation by a union is an unfair labor practice.

The NLRB does not have exclusive jurisdiction over claims of the breach of the duty of fair representation; federal courts also may exercise jurisdiction over such claims according to the Supreme Court in *Breininger v. Sheet Metal Workers Local 6*.[27] The cases developing the duty of fair representation that we have seen so far have involved lawsuits filed against both the union and the employer. Such suits are filed under Section 301 of the NLRA, may be filed either in state or federal courts, and are subject to federal labor law, not state contract law. In *Steelworkers v. Rawson*,[28] the Supreme Court held that a wrongful death suit brought under state law against a union by the heirs of miners killed in an underground fire was preempted by Section 301. According to the Supreme Court in *Chauffeurs, Teamsters and Helpers, Local No. 391 v. Terry*, an employee who seeks back pay as a remedy for a union's violation of the duty of fair representation is entitled to a jury trial.

In *DelCostello v. Teamsters*,[29] the Supreme Court held that the time limit for bringing a suit under Section 301 alleging a breach of the duty of fair representation is six months. In cases where the employee is required to exhaust internal procedures, the six-month time limit does not begin to run until those procedures have been exhausted, according to *Frandsen v. BRAC*.[30] A suit against a union for failing to enforce an arbitration award is an action for breach of the duty of fair representation and is subject to the six-month limitations period, as held by *Carrion v. Enterprise Association, Metal Trades Branch Local Union 638*.[31]

Exhausting Internal Remedies

We have seen that the duty of fair representation may be enforced by either a Section 301 suit or a Section 8(b)(1)(A) unfair labor practice proceeding. Before either action can be initiated, however, the employee alleging breach of the duty of fair representation must attempt to exhaust internal remedies that may be available.

Because most complaints of breaches of the duty of fair representation result from employer actions, such as discharge or discipline, which are then compounded by the union's breach of its duty, the affected employee may have the right to file a grievance under the collective bargaining agreement to challenge the employer's actions. When contractual remedies—the grievance procedure and arbitration—are available to the employee, he or she must first attempt to use those procedures. This means that the employee must file a

---

[25] 140 NLRB 181 (1962).

[26] 326 F.2d 172 (1963).

[27] 493 U.S. 67 (1989).

[28] 495 U.S. 362 (1990).

[29] 462 U.S. 151 (1983).

[30] 782 F.2d 674 (7th Cir. 1986).

[31] 227 F.3d 22 (2d Cir. 2000).

grievance and attempt to have it processed through to arbitration before filing a Section 301 suit or a Section 8(b)(1)(A) complaint. The requirement of exhausting contractual remedies flows from the policy of fostering voluntary settlement of disputes. This policy is behind the court's deferral to arbitration (recall the *Steelworkers Trilogy* from Chapter 17) and the NLRB deferral to arbitration (recall the discussion of that policy in Chapter 17).

The requirement of exhausting contractual remedies is not absolute. In *Glover v. St. Louis–San Francisco Railway*,[32] the Supreme Court held that employees need not exhaust contract remedies when the union and employer are cooperating in the violation of employee rights. In such cases, attempts to get the union to file a grievance or to process it through to arbitration would be an exercise in futility.

Aside from contractual remedies, an employee may have available internal union procedures to deal with complaints against the union. Some union constitutions provide for review of complaints of alleged mistreatment of union members by union leaders. For example, if local union officials refuse to submit the employee's grievance to arbitration, the employee may appeal that decision to the membership of the local. An appeal to the international union leadership may also be available. Should an employee be required to exhaust such internal union remedies before filing a suit or unfair practice complaint alleging breach of the duty of fair representation?

In *Clayton v. United Auto Workers*,[33] the Supreme Court held that an employee is not required to exhaust internal union remedies when the internal union appeals procedure cannot result in reactivation of the employee's grievance or award the complete relief sought by the employee. In such cases, the employee may file a Section 301 suit or a Section 8(b)(1)(A) complaint without exhausting the internal union remedies. If such remedies could provide the relief sought by the employee, they must be pursued before filing under Section 301 or Section 8(b)(1)(A).

If the alleged breach of the duty of fair representation involves claims of discrimination based on race, sex, religion, or national origin, the affected employees may also have legal remedies under Title VII of the Civil Rights Act of 1964. Just as in *Alexander v. Gardner-Denver* (see Chapter 8), the remedies under Title VII are separate from any remedies under Section 301 or Section 8(b)(1)(A). The affected employees may then file a complaint with the Equal Employment Opportunity Commission under Title VII as well as filing under Section 301 and/or Section 8(b)(1)(A).

Remedies available under an action for breach of the duty of fair representation depend on whether the employee pursues the claim under Section 301 or Section 8(b)(1)(A). Under Section 301, an action against both the employer and the union can be brought. An employee may recover monetary damages (but not punitive damages) and legal fees and may get an injunction (such as ordering the union to arbitrate the grievance or ordering the employer to reinstate the employee). Under Section 8(b)(1)(A), the NLRB can order the union to

- pay compensation for lost wages, benefits, and legal fees;
- arbitrate the grievance; and
- "cease and desist" from further violations.

If the employee's complaint involves action by both the employer and the union, Section 301 would be preferable; if only the union is involved, either Section 301 or Section 8(b)(1)(A) is appropriate.

---

[32] 393 U.S. 324 (1969).
[33] 451 U.S. 679 (1981).

Concept *Summary* 18.1

THE DUTY OF FAIR REPRESENTATION

- Unions must not act arbitrarily, discriminatorily, or in bad faith when representing members of the bargaining unit
- Enforced through Section 8(b)(1)(A) or Section 301
  - Section 8(b)(1)(A)—NLRB unfair labor practice action against the union
  - Section 301—suits in court against union and/or employer
  - Must first exhaust internal remedial procedures unless they do not provide the remedies sought

18-2   Rights of Union Members

In addition to being protected by the duty of fair representation, union members have certain rights against the union guaranteed by statute. The union members' bill of rights under the Labor Management Reporting and Disclosure Act and Section 8(b)(1) establishes those rights.

18-2a   Union Discipline of Members

Section 8(b)(1)(A) prohibits union actions that restrain, coerce, or interfere with employee rights under Section 7. Section 8(b)(1)(A), however, does provide that "This paragraph shall not impair the right of a labor organization to prescribe its own rules with respect to the acquisition or retention of membership therein."

In *NLRB v. Allis-Chalmers Mfg. Co.*,[34] the Supreme Court held that a union could impose fines against members who crossed a picket line and worked during an authorized strike. In *NLRB v. Boeing Co.*,[35] the Supreme Court held that a union may file suit in a state court to enforce fines imposed against members. However, if union members legally resign from the union before crossing the picket line and return to work during a strike, the union cannot impose fines against them, as held by the Supreme Court in *NLRB v. Textile Workers Granite State Joint Board*.[36] Where the process used by a union to determine the amount of fines levied against members does not allow the fines to be apportioned between the members' conduct before and after they resigned from the union, the NLRB will rescind the entire amount of the fines, according to *Sheet Metal Workers Ass'n*.[37]

In response to the *Textile Workers Granite State Joint Board* decision, a number of unions adopted rules that limited the right of members to resign from the union during a strike. Such rules violate Section 8(b)(1)(A) according to the Supreme Court decision in *Pattern Makers' League of North America v. NLRB*.[38] Where workers in a right-to-work state resign from the union but continue to work in the bargaining unit, and later decide to rejoin the union, a union rule requiring them to pay a "reinitiation" fee equal to the amount of union dues that they would have paid had they remained in the union did not violate Section 8(b)(1)(A), as held in *Lee v. NLRB*.[39]

---

[34] 388 U.S. 175 (1967).

[35] 412 U.S. 67 (1973).

[36] 409 U.S. 213 (1972).

[37] 338 NLRB 116 (2002).

[38] 473 U.S. 95 (1985).

[39] 325 F.3d 749 (6th Cir. 2003).

18-2b Union Members' Bill of Rights

The Labor Management Reporting and Disclosure Act (LMRDA) seeks to ensure that union members are guaranteed certain rights when subjected to internal union proceedings. Section 101 of the LMRDA is commonly called the union members' bill of rights.

Union Disciplinary Procedures

Procedural safeguards against improper disciplinary action are provided by Section 101(a)(5), which states:

> No member of any labor organization may be fined, suspended, expelled, or otherwise disciplined except for nonpayment of dues by such organization or by any officer thereof unless such member has been (A) served with written specific charges; (B) given a reasonable time to prepare his defense; (C) afforded a full and fair hearing.

Section 102 of the LMRDA allows any person whose rights under the act have been violated to bring a civil suit in the federal courts for such relief as may be appropriate. In *Wooddell v. International Brotherhood of Electrical Workers, Local 71*,[40] the Supreme Court held that a union member suing under the LMRDA, alleging discrimination against him by the union in job referrals through the union hiring hall, was entitled to a jury trial.

When a union member alleges that his or her rights have been violated by union disciplinary action, what standards should the court apply to determine if the union procedure was reasonable? This question was addressed by the following *Boilermakers v. Hardeman* case.

To have a valid claim under Section 101(a)(5) and Section 102, the union member must been subjected to discipline by the union. In *Breininger v. Sheet Metal Workers Local 6*,[41] the Supreme Court held that Breininger's suit over the union's failure to refer him under a hiring hall agreement because he supported a political rival of the union business manager did not state a claim under the LMRDA. The Court held that the failure to refer him was not "discipline" within the meaning of the act. Where a union pursuing disciplinary action against a member did not allow the member to record the disciplinary hearing and allowed a biased decision maker to sit as a member of the hearing board, the union was held to have violated the LMRDA due process requirements, according to *Knight v. Longshoremen, ILA*.[42]

» CASE 18.4

BOILERMAKERS V. HARDEMAN
401 U.S. 233 (1971)

Facts: George Hardeman was a boilermaker and a member of Local Lodge 112 of the International Brotherhood of Boilermakers. He went to the union hiring hall to see Herman Wise, business manager of the local, who was the official responsible for referring workers for jobs. An employer who was a friend of Hardeman had promised to ask for him by name for a job. He sought an assurance from Wise that he would be referred for the job, but Wise refused to make a definite commitment. Hardeman threatened violence if no work was forthcoming in the next few days. Hardeman returned to the hiring hall the next day and waited for a referral, but there was none. He returned to

---

[40] 502 U.S. 93 (1991).

[41] 493 U.S. 67 (1989).

[42] 457 F.3d 331 (3d Cir. 2006).

the hiring hall the next day, and when Wise came out of his office, Hardeman handed him a copy of a telegram asking for Hardeman by name. As Wise was reading the telegram, Hardeman began punching him in the face.

The union brought disciplinary charges against Hardeman. He was tried on charges of creating dissension and working against the interest and harmony of the local, and of threatening and using force to restrain an officer of the lodge from properly discharging the duties of his office. The trial committee found him guilty of the charges, and the local sustained the finding and voted his expulsion for an indefinite period. Hardeman then sought an internal union appeal of this action, but the verdict and the penalty were upheld. Five years later, Hardeman filed suit against the union, alleging that it violated Section 101(a)(5) by denying him a full and fair hearing in the union disciplinary proceedings. After a jury trial, Hardeman was awarded damages of $152,150. On appeal, the U.S. Court of Appeals for the Fifth Circuit affirmed the trial decision. The union then appealed to the U.S. Supreme Court.

Issue: What standards should the courts use to review whether union disciplinary procedures are reasonable under Section 101(a)?

Decision: The union claimed that the NLRB had exclusive jurisdiction over the subject matter of this lawsuit because it involves an allegation of discrimination against Hardeman in job referrals, which is arguably an unfair labor practice under Sections 8(b)(1)(A) and 8(b)(2) of the NLRA and that the federal courts must defer to the exclusive competence of the NLRB. The Court rejected that claim, holding that Hardeman's suit alleged that his expulsion was unlawful under Section 101(a)(5), and he sought compensation for the consequences of the claimed wrongful expulsion. The issue presented by Hardeman's suit was whether the union disciplinary proceedings had denied him a full and fair hearing within the meaning of Section 101(a)(5)(c). Congress explicitly referred claims under Section 101(a)(5) not to the NLRB, but to the federal district courts, as stated in Section 102. The internal union procedures resulted in Hardeman being convicted on both charges, and he was expelled from the union.

When the trial court was considering Hardeman's suit against the union, the trial judge held that whether Hardeman was rightfully or wrongfully expelled was a question of law for the judge to determine. The judge assumed that the transcript of the union disciplinary hearing contained evidence adequate to support conviction of using threats or force against an officer of the union, but held that there was no evidence in the transcript to support the charge of creating dissension and working against the interest and harmony of the local.

Because the union tribunal had returned only a general verdict, and since one of the charges was thought to be supported by no evidence whatsoever, the trial judge held that Hardeman had been deprived of the full and fair hearing guaranteed by Section 101(a)(5), and the court of appeals affirmed. The Supreme Court disagreed, holding that neither the language nor the legislative history of Section 101(a)(5) could justify the substitution of judicial authority for the union's authority to interpret its regulations when determining whether the scope of offenses warrant discipline of union members. The Court stated that Section 101(a)(5) was not intended to authorize courts to determine the scope of offenses for which a union may discipline its members, and it is not appropriate for a court to construe the union's written disciplinary rules in order to determine whether particular conduct may be punished at all. Here, Hardeman was given a detailed statement of the facts relating to the fight which formed the basis for the disciplinary action against him, which complied with the notice requirement of Section 101(a)(5). Section 101(a)(5)(c) guarantees union members a "full and fair" disciplinary hearing, and the parties and the lower federal courts are in full agreement that this guarantee requires the charging party to provide some evidence at the disciplinary hearing to support the charges made. The courts have repeatedly held that conviction on charges unsupported by any evidence is a denial of due process, and Section 101(a)(5)(c) imports a similar requirement into union disciplinary proceedings. In this case, there is no question that the charges were adequately supported by "some evidence."

The Supreme Court reversed the court of appeals' decision affirming the trial court verdict.

Free Speech and Association

Whereas Section 101(a)(5) guarantees union members' procedural rights in union disciplinary proceedings, the other provisions of Section 101(a) provide for other basic rights in participating in union activities. These rights take precedence over any provisions of union constitutions or bylaws that are inconsistent with Section 101 rights. Section 101(b) states that any such inconsistent provisions shall have no effect.

Section 101(a)(2) provides for the rights of freedom of speech and assembly for union members. Every union member has the right to meet and assemble with other members and to express any views or opinions, subject to the union's reasonable rules for the conduct of meetings. As long as any item of business is properly before a union meeting, a union member may express his or her views on that item of business. The latitude given to union members to express their opinions at union meetings is very broad. Any restrictions on such expression must be reasonable and required for the orderly conducting of union meetings. Violations of these rights give rise to civil liability. In *Hall v. Cole*,[43] a union member was expelled from the union after introducing a series of resolutions alleging undemocratic actions and questionable policies by union officials. The union claimed such resolutions violated a rule against "deliberate and malicious vilification with regard to the execution or duties of any office." The member filed suit under Section 102, alleging violations of his rights guaranteed by Section 101(a)(2). The Supreme Court upheld the trial decision ordering that the member be reinstated in the union and awarding him $5,500 in legal fees.

In *Sheet Metal Workers International Association v. Lynn*,[44] an elected business agent of the union filed suit under Section 102 over his removal from office because of statements he made at a union meeting opposing a dues increase sought by the union trustee. The Supreme Court held that his removal from office constituted a violation of the free speech provisions of Section 101(a)(2).

In *United Steelworkers of America v. Sadlowski*,[45] the Supreme Court held that a union rule prohibiting contributions from nonmembers in campaigns for union offices did not violate a union member's right of free speech and assembly under Section 101(a)(2), even though it had the effect of making a challenge to incumbent union officers much more difficult.

The courts have recognized some other limits on union members' rights of free speech and assembly. A union member cannot preach "dual unionism"—that is, advocate membership in another union during his union's meeting. Furthermore, the remarks of a union member are subject to libel and slander laws. The right of free assembly does not protect a group of members who engage in a wildcat strike that violates the union's no-strike agreement with the employer.

Right to Participate in Union Affairs

The right of union members to participate in all membership business, such as meetings, discussions, referendums, and elections, is guaranteed by Section 101(a)(1) of the LMRDA. This right to participate is subject to the reasonable rules and regulations of the union's constitution and bylaws. Any provisions that are inconsistent with these rights are of no effect by reason of Section 101(b).

The provisions of the LMRDA allow a union to require that members exhaust internal union remedies before pursuing external action for violation of the rights granted by the LMRDA. Section 101(a)(4) does provide, however, that the internal union proceedings cannot last longer than four months. If the proceedings take longer than four months, the member is not required to pursue them before instituting external proceedings.

---

[43] 412 U.S. 1 (1973).

[44] 488 U.S. 347 (1989).

[45] 457 U.S. 102 (1982).

Election Procedures

Title IV of the LMRDA requires that union elections be conducted according to certain democratic procedures. Section 401 sets the following requirements:

- National and international labor organizations must elect their officers at least every five years

- Every local union must hold elections at least every three years

- Elections shall be by secret ballot or at a convention of delegates chosen by secret ballot

- There must be advance notice of the election, freedom of choice among candidates, and publication and one year's preservation of the election results

- Dues and assessments cannot be used to support anyone's candidacy

- Every candidate has the right to inspect lists of members' names and addresses

- Each candidate has the right to have observers at polling places and at the counting of the ballots

In the case of *International Organization for Masters, Mates & Pilots v. Brown*,[46] the Supreme Court held that labor unions must cooperate with all reasonable requests from candidates for union office to distribute campaign literature despite union rules restricting such requests. In that case, the Court decided that a union refusal to provide a membership list to a candidate because of a union rule prohibiting preconvention mailings was in violation of the LMRDA.

The election provisions of the LMRDA also prohibit unduly restrictive eligibility requirements that enable incumbents to become entrenched in office. Such eligibility requirements are the subject of the following case.

CASE 18.5

HERMAN V. LOCAL 1011, UNITED STEELWORKERS OF AMERICA

207 F.3d 924 (7th Cir. 2000), *cert. denied*, 531 U.S. 1010 (2000)

Posner, Chief Judge

Section 401(e) of the Labor–Management Reporting and Disclosure Act [LMRDA] makes all union members in good standing eligible to run for office in the union's elections subject to "reasonable qualifications uniformly imposed." The constitution of the steel-workers international union conditions eligibility for local office on the member's having attended at least eight of the local's monthly meetings (or been excused from attendance at them, in which event he must have attended one-third of the meetings from which he was not excused) within the two years preceding the election. Noting that the rule disqualifies 92 percent of the almost 3,000 members of Local 1011 of the steelworkers union, the district judge,

at the behest of the Secretary of Labor ... declared the rule void.

The Act's aim was to make the governance of labor unions democratic. The democratic presumption is that any adult member of the polity, which in this case is a union local, is eligible to run for office....

As an original matter we would think it, not absurd, but still highly questionable, to impose a meeting-attendance requirement on aspirants for union office, at least in the absence of any information, which has not been vouchsafed us, regarding the character of these meetings. All we know is that they are monthly and that the union's constitution requires that all expenditure and other decisions of the union's hierarchy be approved at these meetings; yet despite

---

[46] 498 U.S. 466 (1991).

the formal power that the attendants exercise, only a tiny percentage of the union's membership bothers to attend—on average no more than 3 percent (fewer than 90 persons). We are not told whether an agenda or any other material is distributed to the membership in advance of the meeting to enable members to decide whether to attend and to enable them to participate intelligently if they do attend. We do not know how long the meetings last or what information is disseminated at them orally or in writing to enable the attenders to cast meaningful, informed votes. For all we know the only attenders are a tiny coterie of insiders not eager to share their knowledge with the rest of the union's members....

All we know for sure about this case, so far as bears on the reasonableness of the meeting-attendance requirement, is that the requirement disqualifies the vast majority of the union's members, that it requires members who have not been attending meetings in the past to decide at least eight months before an election that they may want to run for union office (for remember that the meetings are monthly and that a candidate must have attended at least eight within the past two years unless he falls within one of the excuse categories), and that the union itself does not take the requirement very seriously, for it allows members who have attended no meetings to run for office, provided that they fall into one of the excuse categories. The categories are reasonable in themselves—service with the armed forces, illness, being at work during the scheduled time of the meeting, and so forth—and they expand the pool of eligibles from 95 union members to 242, of whom 53 attended not a single meeting. But if the meeting-attendance requirement were regarded as a vital condition of effective officership, equivalent in importance to the LMRDA's requirement that the candidate be a union member in good standing, the fact that a member was without fault in failing to satisfy it would not excuse the failure.... So many of the union's members are excused from the meeting-attendance requirement that there could be an election for officers of Local 1011 at which none of the candidates satisfied the requirement.

The requirement is paternalistic. Union members should be capable of deciding for themselves whether a candidate for union office who had not attended eight, or five, or for that matter any meetings within the past two years should by virtue of his poor attendance forfeit the electorate's consideration. The union's rule is antidemocratic in deeming the electors incompetent to decide an issue that is in no wise technical or esoteric—what weight to give to a candidate's failure to have attended a given number of union meetings in the recent past. . . . And

since most union members interested in seeking an office in the union are likely to attend meetings just to become known ... the rule is superfluous.

... Under conditions of pervasive apathy, a requirement of attending even a single meeting might disqualify the vast bulk of the membership. That is true here. Only 14 percent of the members attended even one meeting within the last two years. Yet the Department of Labor does not argue that therefore even a one-meeting requirement would be unreasonable.

... We think the proper approach, and one that is consistent with the case law ... is to deem a condition of eligibility that disqualifies the vast bulk of the union's membership from standing for union office presumptively unreasonable. The union must then present convincing reasons, not merely conjectures, why the condition is either not burdensome or though burdensome is supported by compelling need. This approach distinguishes ... between impact and burden. A requirement that to be eligible to be a candidate a member of the union have attended one meeting of the union in his lifetime would not be burdensome even though it might disqualify a large fraction of the union membership simply because very few members took any interest in the governance of the union. That defense is unavailable here, however. Requiring attendance at eight meetings in two years imposes a burden because it compels the prospective candidate not only to sacrifice what may be scarce free time to sit through eight meetings, but also, if he is disinclined to attend meetings for any reason other than to be able to run for union office, to make up his mind whether to run many months before the election.

The burden is great enough in this case to place the onus of justification on the union. The only justification offered is that the requirement of attending eight meetings in two years encourages union members who might want to run for office, perhaps especially opponents of the incumbents, to attend union meetings (since otherwise they may not be eligible to run), thus bolstering attendance at the meetings and fostering participatory democracy. The slight turnout at the meetings suggests that this goal, though worthy, cannot be achieved by the means adopted; the means are not adapted to the end, suggesting that the real end may be different. So far as appears, the union has given no consideration to alternative inducements to attend meetings that would not involve disqualifying from office more than nine-tenths of its members.... Under the rule challenged in this case, a union member who wanted to be sure of qualifying for eligibility to run for office might have to start attending meetings as much as a year in advance of the election, because he might miss one or more meetings for reasons that the union does not recognize as excusing (such as vacation or family leave) and because the union might cancel one or more meetings. And yet a year before the election an issue that might move a union member to incur the time and expense of running for office might not even be on the horizon....

The district court was right to invalidate the meeting-attendance requirement as unreasonable, and the judgment is therefore.

AFFIRMED.

Case Questions

1. What does the election rule require of members who want to run for union office? Why would the union impose such a requirement?

2. Why has the Secretary of Labor (Herman) challenged the election-eligibility rule?

3. What does the court mean by distinguishing "between impact and burden" of the challenged rule? How does the court's approach apply to the rule at issue in this case?

Concept *Summary* 18.2

THE UNION MEMBERS' BILL OF RIGHTS

- Rules regarding acquisition and retention of membership must be reasonable
- Union internal disciplinary procedure requirements
  - Must provide specific written charges
  - Must allow a reasonable time to prepare defense
  - Must provide for a full and fair hearing
- Union members are accorded freedom of speech and association
- Union members have the right to participate in union meetings, discussions, referenda, and elections
- Requirements for union election procedures
  - National unions must hold elections for officers at least every five years
  - Local unions must hold elections at least every three years
  - Elections must be by secret ballot or at a convention of delegates chosen by secret ballot
  - Advance notice of elections, a choice of candidates, and preservation of election results for at least one year
  - Union dues or assessments cannot be used to support any candidacy
  - Candidates have the right to a list of members' names and addresses, and to have observers present at polling places and the counting of the ballots

18-2c Other Restrictions on Unions

Duties of Union Officers

The provisions of the LMRDA and the Taft-Hartley amendments to the NLRA imposed a number of duties on union officers to eliminate financial corruption and racketeering and to safeguard union funds. All officials handling union money must be bonded, and persons convicted of certain criminal offenses are barred from holding union office for five years.

Unions are also subjected to annual reporting requirements by the LMRDA. The union reports, filed with the Secretary of Labor, must contain the following information:

- the name and the title of each officer;
- the fees and dues required of members;

- provisions for membership qualification and issuing work permits;
- the process for electing and removing officers;
- disciplinary standards for members;
- details of any union benefit plans; and
- authorization rules for bargaining demands, strikes, and contract ratification.

Any changes in the union constitution, bylaws, or rules must be reported. In addition, detailed financial information must be reported annually; these financial reports must contain information on the following:

- assets and liabilities at the beginning and end of the fiscal year;
- union receipts and their sources;
- salaries paid by the union in excess of $10,000 total;
- any loans by the union in excess of $250; and
- any other union disbursements.

All reports and information filed with the Secretary of Labor must also be made available to union members.

Union officials must report any security or financial interest in, or any benefit received from, any employer whose employees are represented by the union and anything of value received from any business dealing connected with the union. The LMRDA imposes on union officers a duty to refrain from dealing with the union as an adverse party in any manner connected with their duties and to refrain from holding or acquiring any personal or pecuniary interest that conflicts with the interests of the union, according to *Chathas v. Local 134 I.B.E.W.*[47] Employers are required to make annual reports of any expenditures or transactions with union representatives and payments to employees or consultants for the purpose of influencing organizational or bargaining activities.

Welfare and Pension Plans

Section 302 of the Taft-Hartley Act, along with the Employee Retirement Income Security Act (ERISA), controls the operation and administration of employee welfare and pension plans. Persons administering such funds must handle them to protect the interests of all employees. Union officials serving as trustees or administrators of such funds may receive only one full-time salary. They must also be careful to keep their roles as trustee and union official separated.

Section 304 of the Taft-Hartley Act, along with the federal election laws, control union political contributions and expenditures. Union dues or assessments may not be used to fund political expenditures. However, the union may establish a separate political fund if it is financed by voluntary contributions from union members. Members must be kept informed of the use of such funds and must not be subject to any reprisals in connection with the collection of contributions. State laws may affect public sector unions; a law requiring public sector unions to get affirmative authorization of the use of agency shop fees for political purposes was valid and did not violate the unions' First Amendment rights, as held by *Davenport v. Washington Education Association.*[48]

---

[47] 233 F.3d 508 (7th Cir. 2000), *cert. denied*, 533 U.S. 949 (2001).

[48] 551 U.S. 177 (2007).

CHAPTER REVIEW

» Key Terms

duty of fair representation   583   **union shop**   5 8 8   **agency shop**   5 8 8

» Summary

- The duty of fair representation was developed by the Supreme Court to ensure that unions protected the rights of the employees they represent. The NLRB has determined that a breach of the duty of fair representation is an unfair labor practice in violation of Section 8(b)(1)(A) of the NLRA. Section 301 may also be used to bring a suit for breach of duty of fair representation in the courts. Although unions have some leeway to exercise judgment as to how to represent their members, actions that are discriminatory, arbitrary, or in bad faith are violations of the duty of fair representation.

- Unions owe the duty of fair representation to all employees in the bargaining unit, not just to union members. Employees subject to a union security clause may not be terminated for failing to join the union, as long as membership is denied to them for reasons other than failure to pay union dues or fees. Nonmembers who pay union dues and fees are entitled to a reduction in those dues and fees reflecting union expenditures on matters not related to collective bargaining. Failure to inform such employees of their rights, or to allow them the reductions, is a violation of the duty of fair representation.

- Unions are entitled to make and enforce reasonable rules for internal discipline and maintenance of membership; however, unions cannot enforce such rules against employees who resign from the union. Rules that restrict the right of employees to resign from the union may violate Section 8(b)(1)(A).

- The Labor Management Reporting and Disclosure Act (LMRDA) sets out a bill of rights for union members, guaranteeing them certain procedural rights for internal union proceedings. Union officials must comply with the financial and reporting requirements of the LMRDA, and elections for union officers are subject to the requirements of Section 401 of the LMRDA.

» Problems

» Questions

1. What is meant by the duty of fair representation? What standard of conduct by a union is required by the duty of fair representation? Who is protected by the duty of fair representation? What remedies are available for a breach of the duty of fair representation?

2. What is the union member's bill of rights?

3. Can bargaining unit employees who are not union members be required to pay union dues and fees? What information must the union provide to such employees?

4. When can a union enforce its disciplinary rules against employees who resign from the union? When can a union restrict the right of members to resign? Explain your answers.

5. What restrictions are placed on union officers by the Taft-Hartley Act and the Labor Management Reporting and Disclosure Act amendments to the NLRA?

» Case Problems

6. Before she was terminated for two alleged incidents of profanity, Cheryl Beck was employed as a scanning coordinator by Fry's Food Stores. Her employment was governed by the collective bargaining agreement between Local 99, United Food and Commercial Workers Union, and Fry's. The collective bargaining agreement prohibited the use of "profane, abusive or threatening language toward fellow employees." The collective bargaining agreement also provided that an employee could not be disciplined without "just cause." On April 13, 2001, Beck had a conversation with Bob Evans in the parking lot of Fry's Prescott store before reporting to work. Evans, an employee with whom Beck previously had a romantic relationship, had recently been promoted. The conversation became heated when Beck implied that Evans's recent promotion was due to favoritism, not merit. Evans subsequently submitted a statement to Fry's management accusing Beck of using profanity in the course of this conversation. No one else witnessed the incident.

Acting upon Evans's statement, Fry's suspended Beck. Beck reported this suspension to Barbara Cleckner, Local 99's field representative. A meeting was scheduled on April 20, 2001, among Beck, Cleckner, and Fry's, for the administration of any discipline. Prior to the meeting, Fry's management informed Cleckner that it intended to terminate Beck on the ground that

Beck had a "history of a foul mouth." In eight and a half years of working for Fry's and its predecessor Smith's, Beck had not previously been disciplined for using profanity. In her meeting with Cleckner prior to the scheduled meeting with Fry's management, Beck maintained that any statements made in the course of her conversation with Evans were not actionable because the conversation occurred while Beck was off duty. At the April 20, 2001 meeting, Fry's issued Beck a "Final Written Warning," which provided, in relevant part, that "any further conduct [involving] the use of profanity, inappropriate comments or malicious gossip will result in termination." Beck asked Cleckner to file a grievance contesting the warning. Cleckner promised to file Beck's requested grievance, but she never did so.

On July 5, 2001, Beck had an argument with Cecil Carr, the store secretary, over a pay error. Carr asserted that Beck used profanity in the course of the argument, an accusation Beck denied. Fry's credited Carr's version of the incident and terminated Beck on July 9, 2001. At Beck's request, Local 99 filed a grievance contesting Beck's termination. Beck provided Local 99 with a six-page statement setting forth the basis for her grievance. A representative from Fry's Human Resources Department conducted an investigation of the events leading up to Beck's termination and provided Local 99 with copies of relevant notes, records, and employee statements gathered in the course of that investigation. In September, Local 99 contacted its attorney to determine whether it was legally required to demand arbitration of Beck's grievance. The attorney provided an opinion letter stating that, in his view, a single incident of alleged profanity would not constitute just cause for discharge. However, the attorney opined that an arbitrator would "almost certainly" conclude that termination for a second incident of profanity constituted just cause when the first incident resulted in an unchallenged written warning less than three months earlier. Local 99 subsequently informed Beck that it would not arbitrate her grievance. Beck then filed suit against Local 99, alleging that the union had breached its duty of fair representation to her.

How should the court rule on her suit? Why? [See *Beck v. United Food and Commercial Workers Union, Local 99*, 506 F.3d 874 (9th Cir. 2007).]

7. After being on sick leave for half a year because of high blood pressure, Owens attempted to return to work. Owens's family physician had approved his return to work, but Owens's employer's company physician felt that Owens's blood pressure was too high to return, and the employer discharged him. Owens filed a grievance over his discharge, which the union processed through the grievance procedure in the collective agreement. In preparation for taking Owens's grievance to arbitration, the union had Owens examined by another physician. That doctor also believed that Owens should not return to work. In light of its doctor's opinion, the union decided not to take Owens's grievance to arbitration. Owens demanded that his grievance be arbitrated, but the union refused. Owens then sued the union and the employer in state court, alleging breach of the collective agreement and of the duty of fair representation.

   How should the court decide Owens's claims against the union? Against the employer? Explain your answers. [See *Vaca v. Sipes*, 368 U.S. 171 (1967).]

8. Darryl White, worked for Detroit Edison as a pipefitter at the River Rouge power plant; he was a member of the utility workers' union. Under the collective agreement governing the workers at the power plant, employees are probationary for the first year of employment, but after completing one year, employees can only be discharged for just cause. While still a probationary employee, White was disciplined for being away from his work area without permission on two occasions. White did not file a grievance in response to the discipline. After he completed his probationary period, White left work early without permission on June 1 and June 7. After inquiring into those early absences, Detroit Edison placed White on "decision-making" leave, which is paid leave where an employee is provided the opportunity to consider the future status of his or her employment with Detroit Edison. Decision-making leave is considered serious discipline, and

it puts an employee on notice that any subsequent inappropriate behavior may result in more severe discipline, including discharge. White filed a grievance over his being placed on leave. After a hearing on White's grievance, at which he was represented by the union, the hearing panel upheld the discipline of placing him on leave.

Between September and the next April, White had some difficulty with his supervisors. Two fact-finding hearings were conducted on separate incidents: in one case, a refusal by White to do work because of safety concerns; in another case, an accusation that White engaged in disruptive behavior during a briefing. Neither hearing resulted in White receiving any additional discipline. Also during this time, White was subjected to two counseling sessions for arguing with a supervisor and for failing to tell his supervisors where he could be reached. The counseling sessions were not considered discipline, nor did they result in any discipline.

On July 23, White finished an assignment at approximately 5:00 p.m. and waited for another assignment until 7:00 or 7:30 p.m., and then went on his double-shift lunch break. After his lunch, White continued to relax in the break room, waiting for another assignment. White waited until 11:30 p.m. without working or receiving another assignment; he then punched out of work and went home. The following day, July 24, White began working on an assignment in the morning. Before White was done with his first job, his supervisor, Wallace Cash, assigned White to another job. White said that he could not get to the second job immediately because he was not finished with the first job. White testified that after lunch, at around 12:15 or 12:30 p.m., he went to check the status of his second job, and found that he could not begin because insulation was still being removed at the job site. White left the job site, and a coworker subsequently began the job without White. White eventually did return to the job site and began work on this second job at around 2:00 p.m.

On July 29, 2003, the employer held a fact-finding hearing to consider the events of July 23 and 24, 2003. White was present at the hearing and was represented by Local 223. The hearing panel concluded that White was absent from his work location without permission for approximately three and a half hours on July 23 and approximately two and a half hours on July 24. Because this misconduct occurred while White was still on decision-making leave probation, Detroit Edison terminated White's employment. He received an official letter dated August 22, 2003, informing him that he was discharged. White filed a grievance over his discharge, but after a hearing on the grievance, the discharge was upheld. White then asked the union to take his case to arbitration; the union reviewed White's request and decided against taking White's case to arbitration, notifying White of its decision on March 10, 2004. White then appealed the local union's decision ruling to the National Union.

On July 28, 2004, after providing both the local union and White an opportunity to submit additional information, the national union decided to uphold the local union's refusal to take White's case to arbitration. White then filed suit in federal court against Detroit Edison, the local union, and the national union. He alleged (1) that Detroit Edison breached the collective bargaining agreement by terminating his employment without just cause, and (2) that the local union and the national union breached their duties of fair representation by not submitting White's grievance to arbitration.

How should the court rule on his suit against the unions and the employer? Explain. [See *White v. Detroit Edison*, 472 F.2d 420 (6th Cir. 2006).]

9. The plaintiff, Joan Taschner, worked for Thrift-Rack, Inc., in its warehouse for nine years, from 1973 until September 1982. Teamsters Local Union 384 was at all times relevant to this action the exclusive bargaining representative for the employees of Thrift-Rack.

In September 1982, the plaintiff successfully cross-bid for an outside job of driver-salesperson. While working outside as a driver, she developed a severe neurodermatitis condition and allergic reaction requiring a doctor's supervision and medication. As a result, she was unable to perform her outside job as a driver.

The plaintiff twice requested Thrift-Rack to transfer her to her prior warehouse position, which was still open, or to any other warehouse position. The company, however, rejected her requests on grounds that the plaintiff's claims were not provided for in the collective agreement and were in violation of past practice.

In response to the company's refusal to transfer her, the plaintiff filed a grievance with Local 384. That grievance was denied by the union agent, James Hill, on grounds that no cross-bidding was allowed, that there were two separate seniority lists for union members who were employed by the company, and that an employee must be working in a unit to be allowed to bid for a job in that unit. Plaintiff requested to take her grievance to arbitration, but that request was denied by Hill. Subsequently, the warehouse position was awarded to another employee with less seniority, no experience, and lower qualifications than the plaintiff possessed.

On November 2, 1982, Thrift-Rack again refused the plaintiff's request to transfer to any warehouse position, although there were still warehouse jobs open, some of which may not have been bid upon by warehouse workers. The company refused to give her any work, informing her that there was no work available for her and telling her to go home. Thereafter, the plaintiff called Thrift-Rack every day for about one week. She reported that she was still on medication and could not drive, but that she was available for any other work. She specifically requested transfer to any position in the warehouse. Thrift-Rack continued to refuse to transfer her to any position in the warehouse.

What recourse did the plaintiff have against her union? [See *Taschner v. Hill*, 589 F. Supp. 127, 118 L.R.R.M. 2044 (E.D. Pa. 1984).]

10. Plaintiff Feist received a Coast Guard license as a third assistant engineer in 1974 and was accepted into the applicant program of the Merchant Engineers' Beneficial Association (MEBA) in 1975. From 1975 on, he served aboard vessels as a licensed third engineer, completed additional schooling, and worked the required number of days to achieve what is known as Group I status. The plaintiff paid all MEBA dues and had satisfied the requirement of a $2,500 initiation fee for membership. The

plaintiff claims that in May 1979 he was informed that the District Investigating Committee had voted to deny him membership in the MEBA. Plaintiff's application was denied a second time on September 7, 1979, and again on February 13, 1981. Plaintiff filed suit against the MEBA, alleging that he had satisfied the requirements of membership in the MEBA and had been wrongfully denied membership status and the right to a full hearing, all in violation of the LMRDA.

Acceptance into membership of the MEBA is governed by Article 3 of the National Constitution, Articles 3 and 4 of the District Constitution, and Rules and Regulations No. 3, promulgated by the National Executive Committee. Rules and Regulations No. 3 states, in pertinent part, "The MEBA reserves the absolute right in its own discretion, for any reason whatsoever (a) at any time prior to acceptance into membership to terminate any applicant's status as such, or (b) to reject the application for membership." The plaintiff sued the union, demanding that he be admitted to membership.

How should the federal court have ruled on the plaintiff's demand? [See *Feist v. Engineers' Beneficial Ass'n.*, 118 L.R.R.M. 2419 (E.D. La. 1983).]

11. Tyrone White was a member of the Multnomah County Oregon, Employees Union, Local 88 of the American Federation of State, County and Municipal Employees, AFL-CIO ("Union"). In 2004, he was appointed by Marla Rosenberg, the Union president at that time, to serve as shop steward for the Department of School and Community Partnerships ("DSCP"), a work group represented by the Union. In January 2005, Rebecca Steward replaced Ms. Rosenberg as Union president. In September 2005, several Union members who were African Americans complained to White, as shop steward, about an article in the July 15, 2005, Union newsletter. The article, entitled "Tarred and feathered: No labor in labor–management," criticized labor–management cooperation in DSCP. White, who is also an African American, met with Val Andreas, the author of the article, and told her that he and others within his department were offended by the article. He asked her to retract the characterization and to apologize

to his department. Ms. Andreas responded that "Tar and feather" originated in Europe and was not offensive. A few months later, Mr. White met with Ms. Andreas and Union Executive Board member Jackie Tate and urged them to apologize to his department for being racially insensitive and to retract the article.

In late 2005, Ms. Tate requested that Ms. Steward remove Mr. White as shop steward for several reasons, including failure to attend shop steward meetings. In January 2006, Ms. Steward removed Mr. White as an appointed shop steward under Article VIII, § III of the Union's constitution, which provides that a shop steward who misses four meetings in one year may be replaced at the discretion of the president. White does not dispute that he missed more than four shop steward meetings in each of the past couple of years, but he claims that Ms. Steward removed him from his appointed position as shop steward without procedural safeguards and in retaliation for his vocal opposition to the "Tarred and feathered" article. Mr. White continues to be a member of the Union and retains all rights of union membership, including the right to attend general membership meetings and to express his opinions in those meetings, the right to run for elected office, the right to vote for elected officers, and the right to vote to ratify collective bargaining agreements. He filed suit against the Union, alleging that his removal as shop steward was in violation of Section 101(a)(5) of the LMRDA.

How should the court rule on his suit? Explain. [See *White v. Multnomah County Oregon*, 2007 WL 1575234 (D. Ore. May 29, 2007).]

12. Russell Blunden was a candidate for the office of president of Local 951 of the United Food and Commercial Workers Int. Union. Election. Blunden ran against the incumbent president, Robert Potter. The election was conducted by mail ballots which were sent out to approximately 33,000 union members on August 16, 2004. After the ballots were sent out, the Potter slate used a telephone service to make approximately 27,000 campaign calls. The local union did not inform Blunden of the availability of union membership records or lists of the members' telephone numbers. The ballots were

tallied on September 7, 2004. Robert Potter won the election. Blunden challenged the election results by letter to the union's general election chairman and the international union. After the union denied his challenge, he filed his complaint with the Secretary of Labor. The Secretary of Labor filed suit against Local 951, seeking a judgment declaring that the 2004 election was void and directing the union to conduct a new election.

Should the court set aside the election results? Explain. [See *Chao v. Local 951, United Food and Commercial Worker Int. Union*, 2007 WL 208537 (W.D. Mich.), 181 L.R.R.M. (BNA) 2420.]

13. Suit was filed as a class action by 10 employees of the Kroger Company. These employees claimed that Teamsters International and Teamsters Local 327, which represented their bargaining unit, breached the union's duty to represent all members of the collective bargaining unit fairly. The employees also charged that Kroger conspired with the union to "reduce" the conditions and benefits of their employment. More specifically, the plaintiffs claimed that Local 327 failed to represent the members of the union fairly in negotiating a collective bargaining agreement with Kroger, with the result that the union "bargained away substantial benefits relating primarily to seniority." The complaint charged the International Union with failing to furnish a skilled negotiator to aid in the negotiations when requested to do so by the negotiating committee.

The complaint also alleged that the business agent and president of Local 327 conspired with Kroger in formulating an agreement that contained terms and conditions that were contrary to union policies and that diminished the rights of the plaintiffs and the class they sought to represent (all the unit members in two Kroger warehouses in the Nashville, Tennessee, area). The complaint further alleged that Local 327 and its business agent and president fraudulently changed the results of a membership vote on the proposed collective bargaining agreement to reflect ratification when in fact the proposed agreement had been rejected. Finally, the complaint asserted that the agreement negotiated by Local 327 and Kroger contained a provision that

discriminated against female members of the unit by prescribing a lower wage scale for the unit employees in one of the warehouses than for the employees in the other. Virtually all employees in the warehouse with the lower wage rate were women.

Did the union breach its duty of fair representation? [See *Storey v. Teamsters Local 327*, 759 F.2d. 517, 118 L.R.R.M. 3273 (6th Cir. 1985).]

14. In 1983, General Motors Corporation signed a collective bargaining agreement with the International Brotherhood of Electrical Workers, under the wage provisions of which new employees joining the bargaining unit were to be paid at a different (lower) hourly rate than current members. A so-called two-tier wage scale resulted from the arbitration of a postal service dispute that same year. Since then, a number of other unions have accepted two-tier systems as concessions in their collective bargaining agreements. Labor negotiators commonly refer to such two-tier wage concessions as "selling the unborn."

Can you articulate an argument on behalf of these "unborn" (new employees) that two-tier labor contracts violate the union's duty of fair representation? Do you see an equal employment opportunity implication to such an agreement? [See "IRRA panelists address two-tier implications for fair representation and equal opportunity," No. 1 DLRA–5 (1985).]

15. Fontana, the president of the National Association of Letter Carriers, Branch 1100, attended a union seminar in Las Vegas, Nevada. Another union officer in attendance reported back to other branch officers that Fontana had failed to attend classes at the seminar and had charged personal expenses on his union credit cards. The branch officers subsequently accused Fontana of misappropriating union funds. Political tensions grew, and Fontana filed numerous charges against other officers for insubordination and violations of the branch's by-laws. Those other branch officers brought charges against Fontana, and the branch membership found Fontana guilty and removed him as branch president. Fontana retained his membership in the branch.

Several months later, three branch members filed additional charges against Fontana, charging him with "misconduct based on his disrupting the Branch by repeatedly filing frivolous charges against other members" and "misuse of his position of influence." The written charges did not cite any specific incidents or actions, but rather made only general allegations. Committees were appointed to investigate these charges and present reports of their findings to the branch membership. One month later, the branch membership found Fontana guilty of the additional charges and suspended his membership. Fontana appealed the decision to the national union, and the national union's Committee on Appeals reversed Fontana's suspension with respect to the charges but continued the suspension, however, because he had failed to pay union dues while the appeal was pending. On May 10, 1994, Fontana brought suit in federal court against the branch, individual members of the branch, and the national union under the LMRDA.

Did the union's disciplinary procedures here satisfy the requirements under Section 101(a)(5) of the LMRDA? Explain your answer. [See *Johnson v. National Ass'n of Letter Carriers Branch 1100*, 182 F.3d 1071 (Cal. 1999).]

» Hypothetical Scenarios

16. Local 1357 of the International Brotherhood of Electrical Workers (IBEW) found Kellerman, the business manager and financial secretary of the local, guilty of spending $80,499.92 without proper documentation and authorization, in violation of the IBEW constitution and the local's by-laws, rules, and policies. Kellerman was barred from holding office for five years and ordered to make restitution of $80,499.92 to the local or face expulsion from the union. Three years later, Kellerman announced his intention to seek election as business manager of the local. The local election committee ruled that he was not eligible for election because the five-year restriction on his holding office had not expired. Kellerman sued the local union, alleging that the restriction on his eligibility to run for office violated the LMRDA. How should the court rule on Kellerman's suit? Why?

17. Darryl Green worked as a utility worker for National Edison and was a member of Local 222 of the Utility Workers of America Union. The collective agreement between National Edison and the union provided that employees who have been employed for one year or longer can only be discharged for just cause, but employees with less than one year's service are probationary workers and can be discharged at will. On March 12, 2007, while still a probationary employee, Green was disciplined for being away from his work area without permission on two occasions. As penalty for those violations, consistent with the collective agreement, the employer extended Green's probationary period. Several months later, on two consecutive days, Green left work early without permission. The employer terminated Green because he was still a probationary employee and had violated the employer's work rules.

Green filed a grievance challenging his discharge, and the local union pursued the grievance through the preliminary stages of the grievance procedure under the collective agreement. The employer denied the grievance and refused to reinstate Green. Green then asked the local union to take his grievance to arbitration, the final step of the grievance procedure. At a meeting of the local, Green presented his request for arbitration, but the membership of the local voted not to take his grievance to arbitration. Green appealed that decision to the national union, which upheld the local decision not to arbitrate his grievance. Green then filed suit against both the employer and the local and national unions. He alleged that the employer violated the collective bargaining agreement by terminating his employment without just cause, and that the local and national unions had breached their duties of fair representation by not submitting his grievance to arbitration. How should the court rule on his suit against the employer and the unions? Explain your answer.

18. Martin and Harris are employed by Stith Mfg. Co. but are not members of the union that represents the Stith production workers. However, they are required to pay an agency fee to the union under

the collective agreement between the union and the employer. A portion of the agency fees they pay go into a "strike pay" fund that is used to support workers who go on strike. When negotiations to renew the expiring collective agreement break down, the union votes to go on strike. Harris and Martin oppose the strike and continue working during the strike. They also refuse to pay the portion of the agency fee that goes to the strike pay fund. Can the union require that they pay the portion of the agency fee that is paid into the strike pay fund? Explain your answer.

19. Under a labor agreement governing construction work at job sites in California, Steamfitters Local Union No. 342 had the exclusive right to dispatch workers to contractor Contra Costa Electric. Shears, a member of the union for 27 years, was registered for employment through the union's hiring hall. Because of his skills and experience, his name was placed on the highest priority "A" list, meaning that he would be among the first employees dispatched for any job. Due to an innocent computer filing error, the union mistakenly dispatched several lower-priority individuals ahead of Shears. When it discovered the error, the union immediately dispatched Shears to the job site. Shears filed an unfair labor practice charge with the NLRB, claiming that the union breached its duty of fair representation to him by failing to dispatch him to the job site earlier. How should the NLRB rule on his complaint? Why? Explain your answer.

20. McKelvie was hired as a production worker by Onondaga Pottery Works. The employer has a collective agreement with the Ceramic Workers Union that contains a union shop provision. McKelvie is glad to have a job after being unemployed for several months, but she strongly objects to joining the union and paying union dues. She asks you for advice—can she be forced to join the union? Can she be forced to pay union dues? Explain your answers.

CHAPTER 19

Public Sector Labor Relations

The rights of public sector employees to organize and bargain collectively are relatively recent legal developments. The National Labor Relations Act (NLRA) excludes employees of the federal, state, and local governments from its coverage. Only in the last several decades have Congress, the executive branch, and the states adopted legal provisions allowing public employees some rights to organize and bargain collectively. Furthermore, during the first dozen years of the 21st century, public employee unions have come under attack in several states. In these states, Republican governors and GOP-dominated legislatures have sought to withdraw collective bargaining rights and to rescind benefits from their unionized employees. They have sometimes succeeded in doing so. This chapter examines the legal provisions that enable public employees to engage in labor relations activities and the recent trend toward repealing and amending many of those laws. Labor relations legislation affecting the federal sector is examined in some detail, and the recent developments in state legislation are also surveyed.

19-1 Government as Employer

Although many labor relations issues in the public sector are similar to those in the private sector, there are also significant differences. Actions taken by government employers with regard to their employees may raise issues regarding the constitutional rights of those employees. Both the U.S. Constitution and the various state constitutions regulate and limit government action affecting citizens. Because public sector workers are simultaneously both citizens and employees, employers must respect their constitutional rights. The public sector employer may therefore be limited in its attempts to discipline or regulate its employees by constitutional requirements, such as "due process of law." The private sector employer faces no similar constitutional problems.

Another area in which public sector labor relations differ from the private sector involves the idea of sovereignty. The government, as government, is sovereign; it cannot vacate or delegate its sovereignty. The government may be obligated by law to perform certain functions and provide certain services, and government officials are given authority to take such actions and make such decisions as are necessary to perform those functions. Collective bargaining involves sharing decision-making power between the employer and the union; the employer and the union jointly determine working conditions, rates of pay, benefits, and so on. For the public sector employer, collective bargaining may involve delegating to the union the authority relating to the employer's statutory obligations. Bargaining may also affect the financial condition of the employer, requiring tax increases or cutbacks in the level of public services provided by the government employer. Because of this concern over sharing or delegating government sovereignty with the union, public sector labor relations statutes may narrowly define terms and conditions of employment and limit the matters that are subject to collective bargaining to avoid the government employer abdicating its legal authority. In the federal government, for example, most employees have their wages set by statute. Collective bargaining in the federal service is precluded from dealing with any matter that is "provided for by Federal statute." Some state public sector labor relations statutes do not provide for collective bargaining at all but rather for consultation or "meeting and conferring" on working conditions.

A third area in which public sector employment differs from the private sector is the right to strike. The right to strike is protected by Section 7 of the NLRA for private sector workers. Public sector workers, in general, do not have the right to strike. The activities of the government employer are usually vital to the public interest. Disruptions of these activities because of labor disputes could imperil the welfare of the public. For that reason, the right to strike by public sector workers may be prohibited (as in the federal government and most states) or be limited to certain employees whose refusal to work would not endanger the public safety or welfare (as in several states).

The following case involves a challenge to the prohibitions of strikes by federal employees. The union representing postal clerks argues that such a prohibition violates their members' constitutional rights to strike.

CASE 19.1

POSTAL CLERKS V. BLOUNT

325 F. Supp. 879 (U.S.D.C., D.C. 1971), aff'd, 404 U.S. 802 (1971)

Per Curiam

This action was brought by the United Federation of Postal Clerks (hereafter sometimes referred to as "Clerks"), an unincorporated public employee labor organization which consists primarily of employees of the Post Office Department, and which is the exclusive bargaining representative of approximately 305,000 members of the clerk craft employed by defendant. Defendant Blount is the Postmaster General of the United States. The Clerks seek declaratory and injunctive relief invalidating portions of 5 U.S.C. Section 7311, 18 U.S.C. Section 1918, an affidavit required by 5 U.S.C. Section 3333 to implement the above statutes, and Executive Order 11491. The Government, in response, filed a motion to dismiss or in the alternative for summary judgment, and plaintiff filed its opposition thereto and cross motion for summary judgment....

5 U.S.C. Section 7311(3) prohibits an individual from accepting or holding a position in the federal government or in the District of Columbia if he

(3) participates in a strike ... against the Government of the United States or the government of the District of Columbia....

Paragraph C of the appointment affidavit required by 5 U.S.C. Section 3333, which all federal employees are required to execute under oath, states:

I am not participating in any strike against the Government of the United States or any agency thereof, and I will not so participate while an employee of the Government of the United States or any agency thereof.

18 U.S.C. Section 1918, in making a violation of 5 U.S.C. Section 7311 a crime, provides:

Whoever violates the provision of Section 7311 of Title 5 that an individual may not accept or hold a position in the Government of the United States or the government of the District of Columbia if he ...

(3) participates in a strike, or asserts the right to strike, against the Government of the United States or the District of Columbia … shall be fined not more than $1,000 or imprisoned not more than one year and a day, or both.

Section 2(e)(2) of Executive Order 11491 exempts from the definition of a labor organization any group which:

asserts the right to strike against the Government of the United States or any agency thereof, or to assist or participate in such strike, or imposes a duty or obligation to conduct, assist or participate in such a strike.

Section 19(b)(4) of the same Executive Order makes it an unfair labor practice for a labor organization to:

call or engage in a strike, work stoppage, or slowdown; picket any agency in a labor–management dispute; or condone any such activity by failing to take affirmative action to prevent or stop it; …

Plaintiff contends that the right to strike is a fundamental right protected by the Constitution, and that the absolute prohibition of such activity by 5 U.S.C. Section 7311(3), and the other provisions set out above thus constitutes an infringement of the employees' First Amendment rights of association and free speech and operates to deny them equal protection of the law. Plaintiff also argues that the language to "strike" and "participate in a strike" is vague and overbroad and therefore violative of both the First Amendment and the Due Process Clause of the Fifth Amendment. For the purposes of this opinion, we will direct our attention to the attack on the constitutionality of 5 U.S.C. Section 7311(3), the key provision being challenged….

At common law no employee, whether public or private, had a constitutional right to strike in concert with his fellow workers. Indeed, such collective action on the part of employees was often held to be a conspiracy. When the right of private employees to strike finally received full protection, it was by statute, Section 7 of the National Labor Relations Act, which "took this conspiracy weapon away from the employer in employment relations which affect interstate commerce" and guaranteed to employees in the private sector the right to engage in concerted activities for the purpose of collective bargaining. It seems clear that public employees stand on no stronger footing in this regard than private employees and that in the absence of a statute, they too do not possess the right to strike. The Supreme Court has spoken approvingly of such a restriction, and at

least one federal district court has invoked the provisions of a predecessor statute, 5 U.S.C. Section 118p-r, to enjoin a strike by government employees. Likewise, scores of state cases have held that state employees do not have a right to engage in concerted work stoppages in the absence of legislative authorization. It is fair to conclude that, irrespective of the reasons given, there is unanimity of opinion on the part of courts and legislatures that government employees do not have the right to strike. Congress has consistently treated public employees as being in a different category than private employees. The National Labor Relations Act and the Labor-Management Relations Act of 1947 (Taft-Hartley) both defined "employer" as not including any governmental or political subdivisions, and thereby indirectly withheld the protections of Section 7 from governmental employees. Congress originally enacted the no-strike provision separately from other restrictions on employee activity by attaching riders to appropriations bills, which prohibited strikes by government employees….

Given the fact that there is no constitutional right to strike, it is not irrational or arbitrary for the Government to condition employment on a promise not to withhold labor collectively, and to prohibit strikes by those in public employment, whether because of the prerogatives of the sovereign, some sense of higher obligation associated with public service, to assure the continuing functioning of the Government without interruption, to protect public health and safety, or for other reasons. Although plaintiff argues that the provisions in question are unconstitutionally broad in covering all Government employees regardless of the type or importance of the work they do, we hold that it makes no difference whether the jobs performed by certain public employees are regarded as "essential" or "nonessential," or whether similar jobs are performed by workers in private industry who do have the right to strike protected by statute. Nor is it relevant that some positions in private industry are arguably more affected with a public interest than are some positions in the Government service….

Furthermore, it should be pointed out that the fact that public employees may not strike does not interfere with their rights, which are fundamental and constitutionally protected. The right to organize collectively and to select representatives for the purposes of engaging in collective bargaining is such a fundamental right. But, as the Supreme Court noted in *Local 232 v. Wisconsin Employment Relations Board*, "The right to strike, because of its more serious impact upon the public interest, is more vulnerable to regulation than the right to organize and select representatives for lawful purposes of collective bargaining which this Court has characterized as a 'fundamental right' and which, as the Court has pointed out, was recognized as such in its decisions long before it was given protection by the National Labor Relations Act."

Executive Order 11491 recognizes the right of federal employees to join labor organizations for the purpose of dealing with grievances, but that Order clearly and expressly defines strikes, work stoppages and slowdowns as unfair labor practices. As discussed above, that Order is the culmination of a longstanding policy. There certainly is no compelling reason to imply the existence of the right to strike from the right to associate and bargain collectively. In the private sphere, the strike is used to equalize bargaining power, but this has universally been held not to be appropriate when its object and purpose can only be to influence the essentially political decisions of Government in the allocation of its resources. Congress has an obligation to ensure that the machinery of the Federal Government continues to function at all times without interference. Prohibition of strikes by its employees is a reasonable implementation of that obligation.

Accordingly, we hold that the provisions of the statute, the appointment affidavit and the Executive Order, as construed above, do not violate any constitutional rights of those employees who are members of plaintiff's union. The Government's motion to dismiss the complaint is granted.

Order to be presented.

Case Questions

1. Do public sector employees have a constitutional right to strike? Is the right to strike protected at common law?

2. Does the right of employees to organize and join unions for purposes of collective bargaining include the right to strike?

3. Are the legislative prohibitions against strikes by federal employees constitutional? What is the rationale behind such prohibitions?

Concept *Summary* 19.1

CHARACTERISTICS OF PUBLIC SECTOR LABOR RELATIONS

- Public employers must respect their employees' constitutional rights
- Public employers have sovereignty as government entities
  - May restrict the scope of collective bargaining that affects their statutory obligations
- Dispute resolution involves mediation and interest arbitration
  - Most public employees do not have the right to strike

19-2   Federal Government Labor Relations

19-2a   Historical Background

It is not clear exactly when federal employees began negotiating over the terms of their employment, but informal bargaining began as long ago as 1883. In that year, the Pendleton Act, known as the Civil Service Act, was passed. It granted Congress the sole authority to set wages, hours, and other terms and conditions of federal employment. This act led to informal bargaining and congressional lobbying by federal employees seeking higher wages and better working conditions.

In 1906, President Theodore Roosevelt halted the informal bargaining by issuing an executive order forbidding federal employees or their associations from soliciting increases in pay, either before Congress and its committees or before the heads of the executive agencies. Employees violating the order faced dismissal.

In the years following the executive order, Congress passed several laws that gave limited organization rights to some federal workers. The Lloyd–La Follette Act of 1912 gave postal workers the right to join unions. In 1920, the federal government negotiated the terms of a contract with the union representing construction workers building the government-sponsored Alaskan Railroad.

It was not until 1962, however, with the issuing of Executive Order 10988 by President Kennedy, that large numbers of federal employees were given the right to organize. The executive order recognized the right of federal workers to unionize and to present their views on terms and conditions of employment to the agencies for which they worked.

Executive Order 10988 was supplemented by Executive Order 11491, which was issued in 1969 by President Nixon. That order placed the entire program of employee–management relations under the supervision and control of the Federal Labor Relations Council.

The Federal Service Labor–Management Relations Act of 1978 (FSLMRA), which was enacted as part of the Civil Service Reform Act of 1978, was the first comprehensive enactment covering labor relations in the federal government. The FSLMRA took effect in January 1979.

19-2b The Federal Service Labor–Management Relations Act

Federal Labor Relations Authority (FLRA)
the federal agency created under the Federal Service Labor–Management Relations Act to administer federal employee labor relations

The FSLMRA, which was modeled after the NLRA, established a permanent structure for labor relations in the federal public sector. It created the **Federal Labor Relations Authority (FLRA)** to administer the act, and it granted federal employees the right to organize and bargain collectively. It also prohibited strikes and other defined unfair practices.

Coverage

The FSLMRA covers federal employees who are either employed by a federal agency or who have ceased to work for the agency because of an unfair labor practice. Most federal agencies are covered, but some are specifically exempted. The following agencies are excluded from FSLMRA coverage:

- the FBI
- the CIA
- the National Security Agency
- the General Accounting Office
- the Tennessee Valley Authority
- the FLRA itself, and
- the Federal Service Impasses Panel

Furthermore, any agency that the president determines is investigative in nature or has a primary function of intelligence and would thus not be amenable to FSLMRA coverage because of national security may be excluded. The FSLMRA also excludes certain employees from coverage, including:

- noncitizens working outside the United States for federal agencies;
- supervisory and managerial employees;

- certain foreign service officers; and
- any federal employee participating in an illegal strike.

The Thurmond Act of 1969 prohibits military personnel from belonging to a union. That act makes it a felony for enlisted personnel to join a union and for military officers or their representatives to recognize or bargain with a union. The Thurmond Act does not apply to civilian employees of the military.

Employees covered by the FSLMRA are granted the right to form, join, or assist any labor organization or to refrain from such activity freely and without reprisal. Employees may act as representatives of a labor organization and present the views of the organization to the heads of agencies, the executive branch, and Congress.

Postal Service Employees

The employees of the U.S. Postal Service are not subject to the FSLMRA. The Postal Service Reorganization Act, which created the U.S. Postal Service as an independent agency, provides that postal service employees are subject to the NLRA, with some limitations. The National Labor Relations Board (NLRB) is authorized to determine appropriate bargaining units, hold representation elections, and enforce the unfair labor practice provisions of the NLRA for postal service employees. The postal service unions bargain with the U.S. Postal Service over wages, hours, and conditions of employment, but postal service workers are not permitted to strike. Instead, the Postal Service Reorganization Act provides for fact-finding and binding arbitration if an impasse exists after 180 days from the start of bargaining. Supervisory and managerial employees of the Postal Service are not covered by the NLRA provisions.

Administration

The FSLMRA created the FLRA, which assumed the duties of its predecessor, the Federal Labor Relations Council created by Nixon's Executive Order 11491. The FLRA, therefore, is the central authority responsible for the administration of the FSLMRA.

The FLRA is composed of three members who are nominated by the president and confirmed by the Senate. The members serve five-year terms. The FLRA is empowered to do the following:

- Determine the appropriateness of units for representation
- Supervise or conduct elections to determine if a labor organization has been selected as the exclusive representative by majority of the employees in the appropriate unit
- Resolve issues relating to the duty to bargain in good faith
- Resolve complaints of unfair labor practices

The FLRA has the authority to hold hearings and issue subpoenas. It may order any agency or union to cease and desist from violating the provisions of the FSLMRA, and it can enlist the federal courts in proceedings against unions that strike illegally. The FLRA may take any remedial actions it deems appropriate in carrying out the policies of the act.

Representation Issues

Under the FSLMRA, a union becomes the exclusive representative of an appropriate unit of employees when it has been selected by a majority of votes cast in a representation election. When selected, the union becomes the sole representative of the employees in the unit and is authorized to negotiate the terms and conditions of employment of the employees in the unit. The union must fairly represent all employees in the unit without discrimination or regard to union membership. The FLRA is authorized to settle questions relating to issues of representation, such as the determination of the appropriate unit and the holding of representation elections.

Appropriate Representation Units The FLRA is empowered to determine the appropriateness of a representation unit of federal employees. The FLRA ensures the employees the fullest possible freedom in exercising their rights under the FSLMRA in determining the unit, and it ensures a clear and identifiable community of interest among the employees in the unit to promote effective dealing with the agency involved. The FLRA may determine the appropriateness of a unit on an agency, plant, installation, functional, or other basis.

Units may not include:

- Any management or supervisory employees
- Confidential employees
- Employees engaged in personnel work except those in a purely clerical capacity
- Employees doing investigative work that directly affects national security
- Employees administering the FSLMRA
- Employees primarily engaged in investigation or audit functions relating to the work of individuals whose duties affect the internal security of an agency

Any employees engaged in administering any provision of law relating to labor–management relations may not be represented by a labor organization that is affiliated with an organization representing other individuals under the act. An appropriate unit may include professional and nonprofessional employees only if the professional employees, by majority vote, approve their inclusion.

Representation Elections The procedures for representation elections under the FSLMRA closely resemble those for elections under the NLRA. The act allows for the holding of consent elections to determine the exclusive representative of a bargaining unit. It also provides that the FLRA may investigate the question of representation, including holding an election, if a petition is filed by any person alleging that 30 percent of the employees in a unit wish to be represented by a union for the purpose of collective bargaining. In addition, when a petition alleging that 30 percent of the members of a bargaining unit no longer wish to be represented by their exclusive representative union, the FLRA will investigate the representation question.

If the FLRA finds reasonable cause to believe that a representation question exists, it will provide, upon reasonable notice, an opportunity for a hearing. If, on the basis of the hearing, the FLRA finds that a question of representation does exist, it will conduct a representation election by secret ballot. An election will not be held if the unit has held a valid election within the preceding 12 months.

When an election is scheduled, a union may intervene and be placed on the ballot if it can show that it is already the unit's exclusive representative or that it has the support of at least 10 percent of the employees in the unit. The election is by secret ballot, with the employees choosing between the union(s) and no representation. If no choice receives a majority of votes cast, a runoff election is held between the two choices receiving the highest number of votes. The results of the election are certified; if a union receives a majority of votes cast, it becomes the exclusive representative of the employees in the unit.

A union that has obtained exclusive representation status is entitled to be present at any formal discussions between the agency and unit employees concerning grievances, personnel policies and practices, or other conditions of employment. The exclusive representative must also be given the opportunity to be present at any examination of an employee in the unit in connection with an agency investigation that the employee reasonably believes may result in disciplinary action, provided that he or she has requested such representation. (This right is the equivalent of the *Weingarten* rights established by the NLRB for organized employees in the private sector. See Chapter 14.)

Consultation Rights If the employees of an agency have not designated any union as their exclusive representative on an agency-wide basis, a union that represents a substantial number of agency employees may be granted consultation rights. Consultation rights entitle the union to be informed of any substantive change in employment conditions proposed by the agency. The union is to be permitted reasonable time to present its views and recommendations regarding the proposed changes. The agency must consider the union recommendations before taking final action, and it must provide the union with written reasons for taking the final action.

Collective Bargaining

The FSLMRA requires that agencies and exclusive representatives of agency employees meet and negotiate in good faith. Good faith is defined as approaching the negotiations with a sincere resolve to reach a collective bargaining agreement, meeting at reasonable times and convenient places as frequently as may be necessary, and being represented at negotiations by duly authorized representatives prepared to discuss and negotiate on any condition of employment.

In *National Federation of Federal Employees, Local 1309 v. Dept. of the Interior,*[1] the Supreme Court held that the FLRA had the power to determine whether federal employers were required to engage in "midterm" bargaining—bargaining during the term of a collective agreement over subjects that were not included in the agreement. The FLRA, on remand from the Supreme Court, decided that the FSLMRA required employers to engage in midterm bargaining and the refusal to do so was an unfair labor practice under the FSLMRA.[2]

Conditions of Employment The act defines "conditions of employment" as including personnel policies, practices, and matters—whether established by rule, regulation, or otherwise—that affect working conditions. However, the act excludes the following from being defined as conditions of employment:

* Policies relating to prohibited political activity
* Matters relating to the classification of any position
* Policies or matters that are provided for by federal statute

---

[1] 526 U.S. 86 (1999).

[2] *U.S. Dept. of the Interior v. National Federation of Federal Employees, Local 1309,* 56 FLRA 45, *reconsideration denied,* 56 FLRA 279 (2000).

Wages Wages for most federal employees are not subject to collective bargaining because they are determined by statute. Federal blue-collar employees are paid under the coordinated Federal Wage System, which provides for pay comparable to pay for similar jobs in the private sector. Federal white-collar employees are paid under the General Schedule (GS), and increases and changes in GS pay scales are made by presidential order. However, in *Fort Stewart Schools v. Federal Labor Relations Authority,*[3] the Supreme Court considered the question of whether schools owned and operated by the U.S. Army were required to negotiate with the union representing school employees over mileage reimbursement, paid leave, and a salary increase. The school declined to negotiate, claiming that the proposals were not subject to bargaining under the FSLMRA. The school claimed that "conditions of employment" under the FSLMRA included any matter insisted upon as a prerequisite to accepting employment but did not include wages. The Supreme Court upheld an order of the FLRA that the school was required to bargain over wages and fringe benefits. Whereas the wages of most federal employees are set by law under the GS of the Civil Service Act, the school employees' wages are exempted from the GS. Wages for the school employees, therefore, were within the conditions of employment over which the school was required to bargain. Section 7106 of the FSLMRA, which provides that "nothing in this chapter shall affect the authority of any management official of any agency to determine the … budget … of the agency…." did not exempt wages and fringe benefits from the duty to bargain. Agency management seeking to avail themselves of that provision to avoid bargaining over a proposal must demonstrate that the proposal would result in significant and unavoidable increases in costs.

Management Rights The FSLMRA contains a very strong management-rights clause, which also restricts the scope of collective bargaining. According to that clause, collective bargaining is not to affect the authority of any management official or any agency to determine the mission, budget, organization, number of employees, or internal security practices of the agency. In addition, management's right to hire, assign, direct, lay off, retain or suspend, reduce in grade or pay, or take disciplinary action against any employee is not subject to negotiation. Decisions to assign work, contract out work, or select candidates to fill positions are not subject to negotiation. The act also precludes bargaining over any actions necessary to carry out the mission of the agency during emergencies.

The duty to bargain extends to matters that are the subject of any rule or regulation as long as the particular rule or regulation is not government-wide. However, if the agency determines there is a compelling need for such a regulation, it can refuse to bargain over that regulation. The exclusive representative must be given an opportunity to show that no compelling need exists for the regulation. Disputes over the existence of a compelling need are to be resolved by the FLRA.

CASE 19.2

U.S. DEPARTMENT OF THE NAVY V. FEDERAL LABOR RELATIONS AUTHORITY
665 F.3d 1339 (D.C. Cir. 2012)

Facts: In the mid-1990s, the Naval Undersea Warfare Center Division in Newport, Rhode Island, began providing employees with bottled water. It did so after an EPA report indicated that water fountains in some Navy

---

[3] 495 U.S. 641 (1990).

buildings in Newport contained components manufactured with lead. Beginning in 2005, however, the Navy replaced the problematic water fountains, tested the tap water, and determined it safe to drink. The Navy then stopped providing bottled water; it did not negotiate with employee unions before removing the bottled water. The Navy reasoned that an agency has no duty or authority to bargain over or grant benefits that are prohibited by federal appropriations law. And the Navy concluded that providing bottled water when safe and drinkable tap water was available would violate the legal prohibition against use of appropriated funds for employees' personal expenses.

The unions representing civilian employees at the Newport facilities objected to the removal of the bottled water and filed grievances with the Navy. When negotiations did not yield a compromise, the unions sought binding arbitration. An arbitrator sided with the unions and ordered the Navy to continue providing bottled water on the ground that bottled water had become a condition of employment. The Federal Labor Relations Authority affirmed the arbitrator's decision, holding that the Navy had a duty to bargain with the unions before removing the bottled water.

Issue: Did the Navy have an obligation to bargain with the unions about the elimination of bottled water, and if not, should the arbitrator's award be vacated?

Decision: The Circuit Court of Appeals for the District of Columbia held that federal appropriations law barred the Navy from providing bottled water to its civilian employees when perfectly safe tap water was available. The appellate panel explained that the Appropriations Clause of the U.S. Constitution is "a bulwark" of the separation of powers, because in its absence the executive branch would have unbounded power to spend the taxpayers' dollars. The Clause forbids the federal bureaucracy from spending public funds even accidentally, where statutory authority is lacking.

Federal collective bargaining rights do not trump this hard-and-fast-rule. A federal agency cannot bargain and contract with a labor union to spend money where Congress hasn't given its approval. The FLRA is entitled to a high level of deference when it interprets the FSLMRA. But the FLRA gets no deference when it ventures to interpret other federal laws.

The "necessary expense doctrine" comes into play when it's unclear whether a specific expenditure is legally authorized or not. In this case, continued providing by the Navy of the bottled water clearly was no longer a necessary expense. The Navy, therefore, would have violated the law had it continued to provide the bottled water or if it had negotiated with the unions to that result. Consequently, it had no such duty to bargain before it changed this condition of employment, and the FLRA was out of bounds when it sought to enforce the arbitrator's award to the contrary.

The agency's duty to bargain includes the obligation to furnish, upon request by the exclusive representative, data and information normally maintained by the agency. Such data must be reasonably available and necessary for full and proper discussion of subjects within the scope of bargaining. Data related to the guidance, training, advice, or counsel of management or supervisors relating to collective bargaining are excluded from the obligation to provide information. The duty to bargain in good faith also includes the duty to execute a written document embodying the terms of agreement, if either party so requests.

Impasse Settlement

Federal Service Impasse Panel
federal body created under the Federal Service Labor–Management Relations Act to resolve impasses in collective bargaining in the federal service

The FSLMRA created the **Federal Service Impasse Panel**, which is authorized to take any actions necessary to resolve an impasse in negotiations. The Federal Mediation and Conciliation Service, created by the Taft–Hartley Act, also assists in the resolution of impasses by providing mediation services for the parties. If the mediation efforts fail to lead to an agreement, either party may request that the Federal Service Impasse Panel consider the dispute. The panel may either recommend procedures for resolving the impasse or assist the parties in any other way it deems appropriate. The formal impasse resolution procedures may include hearings, fact-finding, recommendations for settlement, or directed settlement. The parties may also seek binding arbitration of the impasse with the approval of the panel.

Grievance Arbitration The FSLMRA provides that all collective agreements under it must contain a grievance procedure. The grievance procedure must provide for binding arbitration as the final step in resolving grievances. If arbitration is invoked, either party may appeal the arbitrator's decision to the FLRA for review within 30 days of the granting of the award. Upon review, the FLRA may overturn the arbitrator's award only if it is contrary to a law, rule, or regulation or is inconsistent with the standards for review of private sector awards by the federal courts (see Chapter 17). If no appeal is taken from the arbitrator's award within 30 days of the award, the arbitrator's award is final and binding.

When a grievance involves matters that are subject to a statutory review procedure, the employee may choose to pursue the complaint through the statutory procedure or through the negotiated grievance procedure. Examples would be grievances alleging discrimination in violation of Title VII of the Civil Rights Act of 1964, where the griever can elect to pursue the complaint through the grievance process or through the procedure under Title VII. Performance ratings, demotions, and suspensions or removals that are subject to civil service review procedures may be pursued either through the civil service procedures or the grievance procedure.

Unfair Labor Practices
The FSLMRA prohibits unfair labor practices by agencies and unions. The unfair labor practices defined in the act are similar to those defined by Sections 8(a) and 8(b) of the NLRA.

Agency Unfair Practices
Unfair labor practices by agencies under the FSLMRA include:

*   Interfering with or restraining the exercise of employees' rights under the act
*   Encouraging or discouraging union membership by discrimination in conditions of employment
*   Sponsoring or controlling a union
*   Disciplining or discriminating against an employee for filing a complaint under the act
*   Refusing to negotiate in good faith
*   Refusing to cooperate in impasse procedures

It is also an unfair labor practice for an agency to enforce any rule or regulation that conflicts with a preexisting collective bargaining agreement.

Union Unfair Labor Practices
Union unfair labor practices under the FSLMRA include:

*   Interfering with or restraining the exercise of employees' rights under the act
*   Coercing or fining a member for the purpose of impeding job performance
*   Discriminating against an employee on the basis of race, color, creed, national origin, gender, age, civil service status, political affiliation, marital status, or disability
*   Refusing to negotiate in good faith
*   Refusing to cooperate in impasse procedures

It is also an unfair labor practice for a union to call or condone a strike, work slow-down, or stoppage or to picket the agency if the picketing interferes with the agency's operations. Informational picketing that does not interfere with agency operations is allowed.

Unfair Labor Practice Procedures

When a complaint alleging unfair labor practices is filed with the FLRA, the General Counsel's Office of the FLRA investigates the complaint and attempts to reach a voluntary settlement. If no settlement is reached and the investigation uncovers evidence that the act has been violated, a complaint is issued. The complaint contains a notice of the charge and sets a date for a hearing before the FLRA. The party against whom the complaint is filed has the opportunity to file an answer to the complaint and to appear at the hearing to contest the charges.

If the FLRA finds, by a preponderance of evidence, that a violation has occurred, it will issue written findings and an appropriate remedial order. FLRA decisions are subject to judicial review by the federal courts of appeals.

Unfair Labor Practice Remedies

The FLRA has broad authority for fashioning remedial orders for unfair labor practices. Remedial orders may include cease-and-desist orders, reinstatement with back pay, renegotiation of the agreement between the parties with retroactive effect, or any other actions deemed necessary to carry out the purposes of the act.

When a union has been found by the FLRA to have intentionally engaged in a strike or work stoppage in violation of the act, the FLRA may revoke the exclusive representation status of the union or take any other disciplinary action deemed appropriate. Employees engaging in illegal strikes are subject to dismissal. The FLRA may also seek injunctions, restraining orders, or contempt citations in the federal courts against striking unions.

The following case involves the review of an FLRA order revoking the exclusive representation status of the air traffic controllers' union because of its involvement in an illegal strike.

 CASE 19.3

PROFESSIONAL AIR TRAFFIC CONTROLLERS ORG. v. FLRA
685 F.2d 547 (D.C. Cir. 1982)

Facts: The Professional Air Traffic Controllers Organization (PATCO) was the exclusive bargaining representative for air traffic controllers employed by the Federal Aviation Administration (FAA) since the early 1970s. PATCO and the FAA began negotiations for a new contract in early 1981, and a tentative agreement was reached in June. That proposed agreement was overwhelmingly rejected in a vote by the PATCO membership. Following the rejection, the parties resumed negotiations in late July, and PATCO announced a strike deadline of August 3, 1981. When the negotiations failed to reach an agreement, PATCO went on strike against the FAA on August 3, 1981. Of the 9,304 air traffic controllers scheduled to work on August 3, only 2,308 reported for work, resulting in a significantly reduction in the number of private and commercial flights in the U.S. President Reagan warned the strikers that if they did not return to work by August 5, they would be terminated. Approximately 11,000 air traffic controllers were fired.

In addition, the FAA filed an unfair labor practice charge against PATCO with the Federal Labor Relations Authority (FLRA). An FLRA regional director issued a complaint on the unfair labor practice charge, alleging that the strike was prohibited by federal law and seeking revocation of PATCO's certification under the Civil Service Reform Act. The FLRA held that PATCO had called or participated in an illegal strike, and revoked PATCO's certification as exclusive bargaining representative of the air traffic controllers. PATCO then sought judicial review of the FLRA decision before the U.S. Court of Appeals for the D.C. Circuit.

Issue: Did PATCO engage in an illegal strike, and should PATCO's certification have been revoked?

Decision: Federal employees have long been forbidden from striking against their employer, the federal government. Section 7311(2) of Title 5 of the U.S. Code prohibits a person who "participates in a strike ... against the Government of the United States" from accepting or holding a position in the federal government. Violating that prohibition is a criminal offense. Newly hired federal employees are required to execute an affidavit attesting that they have not struck and will not strike against the government.

In addition, since the beginning of formal collective bargaining between federal employee unions and the federal government, unions have been required under Executive Order No. 10988 to disavow using the strike as an economic weapon. Since 1969, striking has been expressly designated a union unfair labor practice.[4] The Civil Service Reform Act, passed in 1978, added a new provision that authorized the FLRA to "revoke the exclusive recognition status" of a recognized union or "take any other appropriate disciplinary action" against any labor organization when that union has called, participated in, or condoned a strike, work stoppage, or slowdown against a federal agency in a labor–management dispute.

Here, the FLRA held that PATCO had called or participated in a strike in violation of federal law, and revoked PATCO's status as exclusive bargaining representative for the air traffic controllers. The court of appeals held that the FLRA was fully justified in taking official notice of proceedings in the District Court for the District of Columbia that found PATCO and its president, Robert Poli, in contempt of court for violating the restraining order against the strike. Before the FLRA, PATCO offered no evidence to indicate that it even attempted to end the strike. The court of appeals therefore affirmed the FLRA finding that the strike was an unfair labor practice.

The court then considered whether the FLRA properly exercised its discretion under the act to revoke the exclusive recognition status of PATCO. The FLRA has substantial discretion under Section 7120(f) to decide whether or not to revoke the certification of a union found guilty by the FLRA of striking or condoning a strike against the government. On judicial review of the FLRA's exercise of its remedial discretion, the court has a limited role. The court will uphold the remedial orders of the FLRA "unless it can be shown that the order is a patent attempt to achieve ends other than those which can fairly be said to effectuate the policies of the Act." Here, the court of appeals had little trouble deciding that the FLRA did not abuse its discretion. The FLRA could take official notice that PATCO has repeatedly violated legal prohibitions against striking and other job actions in the past. PATCO openly defied the restraining orders and injunctions directed at the strike of August 3, 1981. PATCO made no attempt to end the strike. Even after the striking controllers had been terminated and the FLRA had ordered revocation of its exclusive recognition status, PATCO failed to satisfy the FLRA request that it end the strike and promise to abide by the no-strike provisions of the Civil Service Reform Act. PATCO was a repeat offender that has willfully ignored statutory proscriptions and judicial injunctions. The court affirmed the FLRA order finding PATCO had violated the legal prohibitions against strikes by federal employees, and revoking PATCO's certification as exclusive bargaining representative of the federal air traffic controllers.

19-2c   Judicial Review of FLRA Decisions

As the *U.S. Navy* and *PATCO* cases illustrate, final orders, other than bargaining unit determinations (as well as most, but not all, arbitration awards), are subject to review in the federal courts of appeals. The party seeking review has 10 days from the issuance of the FLRA decision to file a petition for review with the court of appeals for the appropriate circuit. Unless specifically authorized by the appeals court, the filing of a petition for review does not operate to stay the FLRA order.

---

[4] 5 U.S.C § 7120(f).

Upon review, the court may affirm, enforce, modify, or set aside the FLRA order. Findings of fact by the FLRA are deemed conclusive if they are supported by substantial evidence. The order of the court of appeals is subject to discretionary review by the Supreme Court.

Concept *Summary* 19.2

THE FEDERAL SERVICE LABOR MANAGEMENT RELATIONS ACT

- Covers employees of most federal agencies, but some agencies are exempted
- Administered by the Federal Labor Relations Authority (FLRA)
- Duty to bargain in good faith—but statutory management rights clause restricts scope of bargaining
- Impasses in negotiations resolved through mediation, the Federal Service Impasse Panel, or arbitration
- Imposes mandatory grievance arbitration
- Defines unfair labor practices by agencies and unions
- Prohibits strikes, work stoppages, or work slowdowns by employees and unions

19-2d The Hatch Act

The Hatch Act[5] was enacted in 1939. Its long title is "An Act to Prevent Pernicious Political Activities." As that mouthful suggests, it prohibits certain political activity by federal employees. Federal employees are prevented from taking an active part in the management of political campaigns and from running for office in a partisan political campaign. The act also restricts federal employees from engaging in political activity while on the job. The purposes of the restrictions on the political activities of federal employees are to:

- avoid the appearance of political bias in government actions;
- prevent the coercion of federal employees to engage in political action or to support political positions; and
- avoid politicizing the federal civil service.

In 1940 the act's reach was extended to include employees of state and local governments, whose positions are funded primarily by federal appropriations. In 1947 and again in 1974 the act survived challenges, based upon First Amendment free-speech arguments, in the U.S. Supreme Court. More recently, the act's restrictions on political activity by federal employees were held to be constitutional in *Burrus v. Vegliante*.[6] That case also held that the American Postal Workers Union's use of bulletin boards in nonpublic areas of post offices to display political materials violated the Hatch Act prohibitions against political activities on the job. Most states have legislation similar to the Hatch Act to restrict political activities by state government employees.

---

[5] 5 U.S.C. § 7321 *et seq.*

[6] 336 F.2d 82 (2d Cir. 2003).

19-2e Union Security Provisions

A union that is granted exclusive representation rights under the FSLMRA must accept as a member any unit employee who seeks membership. A union may not require union membership as a condition of employment. This means that the collective agreement may not contain a closed shop or union shop provision. For the government employer to require that employees join a union in order to retain their jobs would violate the employees' constitutional rights of association protected by the First Amendment (or Fourteenth Amendment if the employer is a state or local government agency).

Agency shop provisions, which require that an employee pay union dues or fees but do not require union membership, do not raise the same constitutional problems. However, if the employee's dues money is spent by the union on matters other than those relating to collective bargaining or representation issues, the employee is, in effect, forced to contribute to causes and for purposes that he or she may oppose. Does this "forced contribution" violate the employee's constitutional rights?

In *Abood v. Detroit Board of Education*,[7] the Supreme Court held that union expenditures for expression of political views, in support of political candidates, or for advancement of ideological causes not related to its duties as bargaining agent can be financed only from dues or assessments paid by employees who do not object to advancing such ideas and who are not coerced into doing so. To do otherwise violates the First Amendment rights of the employees who object to such expenditures. The Court held that employees who object to political expenditures by the union are entitled to a refund of that portion of their dues payments that represents the proportion that union political expenditures bear to the total union expenditures. A state law requiring public sector unions to get affirmative authorization of the use of agency shop fees for political purposes was valid and did not violate the unions' First Amendment rights, according to *Davenport v. Washington Education Association*.[8] In *Ysursa v. Pocatello Education Association*,[9] the Supreme Court held that a state law prohibiting the use of payroll deductions of public employees for political purposes was not in violation of the First Amendment.

In *Chicago Teachers Union, Local No. 1 v. Hudson*,[10] the Supreme Court addressed the procedures that the union must make available for employees who object to union expenditures of their dues or fees. The Court held that the union is required to provide objecting members with information relating to the union expenditures on collective bargaining and political activities and must include an adequate explanation of the basis of dues and fees. The members must also be provided a reasonably prompt opportunity to challenge—before an impartial decision maker—the amount of the dues or fees, and the union must hold in escrow the amounts in dispute pending the resolution of the challenges by the members.

The *Abood* and *Chicago Teachers Union* cases hold that individuals who object to a union's political activities are not required to pay that portion of union dues and fees that fund such nonbargaining activities. What standards should a court use to determine which union expenditures are related to its collective bargaining activities? The Supreme Court

---

[7] 431 U.S. 209 (1977).

[8] 551 U.S. 177 (2007).

[9] 555 U.S. 353 (2009).

[10] 475 U.S. 292 (1986).

considered this question in the case of *Lehnert v. Ferris Faculty Association.*[11] The Court set out three criteria for determining which activities can be funded by dues and fees of objecting individuals:

- The activity must be germane to collective bargaining
- It must be justified by the government's interest in promoting labor peace and avoiding "free riders" who benefit from union activities without paying for union services
- It must not significantly add to the burdening of free speech inherent in allowing a union shop or agency shop provision

Using these criteria, the *Lehnert* Court held that the teachers' union could not charge objecting individuals for lobbying, electoral activities, or political activities beyond the limited context of contract implementation or negotiation. In addition, the union could not charge for expenses incurred in conducting an illegal work stoppage or for litigation expenses unless the litigation concerned the individual's own bargaining unit. The union could charge objecting individuals for:

- national union programs and publications designed to disseminate information germane to collective bargaining;
- information services concerning professional development, job opportunities, and miscellaneous matters that benefited all teachers, even though they may not directly concern members of the individual's bargaining unit;
- participation by local delegates at state or national union meetings at which representation policies and bargaining strategies are developed; and
- expenses related to preparation for a strike.

The Court also held that the union could not charge the objecting individuals for public relations efforts designed to enhance the reputation of the teaching profession generally because such efforts were not directly connected to the union's collective bargaining function.

It should be noted that private sector employees have the same right to object to political expenditures by their unions; in *Communications Workers of America v. Beck*[12] (see Chapter 18), the Supreme Court stated that

> We conclude that Section 8(a)(3) … authorizes the exaction [from nonmembers or objecting employees] of only those fees and dues necessary to "performing the duties of an exclusive representative of the employees in dealing with the employer on labor–management issues."

The FSLMRA provides that union dues may be deducted from an employee's pay only if authorized by the employee. The employer may not charge a service fee for deductions to either the employee or the union. Employee authorizations for dues deduction may not be revoked for a period of one year from their making.

It is worth noting that in a still more recent decision, the Supreme Court held that political action committees (PACs) have a constitutional right to spend as much money as they wish to promote political candidates of their choosing. In light of the restrictions

[11] 500 U.S. 507 (1991).
[12] 487 U.S. 735 (1988).

placed upon public-employee unions in the preceding decisions, this latter case has been sharply criticized by organized labor and the political left as unfairly tilting the political playing field in favor of wealthy individuals and corporations.[13]

19-2f Federal Labor Relations and National Security

The terrorist attacks of September 11, 2001, brought about a profound government emphasis on protecting national security. President George W. Bush, responding to pressure from Congress, created the Department of Homeland Security (DHS) and gave it responsibility for a broad range of agencies and functions within the federal government, including Customs and Border Protection, Citizen and Immigration Services, the U.S. Coast Guard, and the Transportation Security Administration. As part of the administrative reorganization involved with the creation of DHS, the Bush administration sought to increase management flexibility and control over employees and working conditions. The Homeland Security Act of 2002 authorized the Secretary of Homeland Security and the director of the Office of Personnel Management to adopt regulations to create a human resource management system. The act also stated that any regulations adopted had to "ensure that employees may organize, bargain collectively and participate through labor organizations of their choosing in decisions which affect them...." Pursuant to the authority granted under the Homeland Security Act, DHS adopted the Department of Homeland Security Human Resources Management System, a human resource management system that restricted bargaining over personnel actions and limited the role of the FLRA in handling labor relations matters. The unions representing the affected DHS employees challenged the human resource management system as violating the legislative requirement to protect collective bargaining rights and illegally restricting the statutory authority of the FLRA and the Merit System Protection Board (MSPB), which administers the federal civil service system and regulations. The U.S. Court of Appeals for the District of Columbia agreed.[14]

The Department of Defense (DoD) also sought more flexibility and control in its human resource management system for its civilian employees. The National Defense Authorization Act for fiscal year 2004 authorized the DoD to establish a National Security Personnel System (NSPS) to restructure labor relations between management and employees. The act also provided that the NSPS would supersede all collective bargaining agreements for the bargaining units in the DoD until 2009. Several unions representing the DoD civilian employees challenged the resulting NSPS as going beyond the legislative authority granted to DoD.

In early 2010, the NSPS announced that the DoD was on track to transition the majority of its 220,000 civilian employees out of the NSPS by September 2010, more than a year ahead of the deadline. The 2010 National Defense Authorization Act called for the termination of NSPS by January 2012, bringing an end to a controversial personnel system that has been operational for less than four years. In the spring of 2010, the majority of employees began to transition back to the decades-old General Schedule system but with an assurance in regard to pay. The law required the DoD to take all actions necessary for

---

[13] *Citizens United v. Federal Election Commission*, 558 U.S. 310 (2010).

[14] *National Treasury Employees Union v. Chertoff*, 452 F.3d 839 (D.C. Cir. 2006).

the orderly termination of NSPS and the transition of all employees and positions from NSPS to legacy personnel systems or, if applicable, to the personnel systems that would have applied if NSPS had never been established. The law mandated that no employee would suffer loss in pay during the transition process, which was completed by January 1, 2012. The law also required DoD to establish a new performance management system and consider development of additional staffing flexibilities and a workforce incentive fund.

THE **WORKING** LAW

Airport Screeners Seek Bargaining Rights

The legislation that established the Transportation Security Administration (TSA), the federal agency in the Department of Homeland Security that employs some 45,000 officers who work as airport screeners, states that the Administrator of the TSA has the authority to decide whether or not to allow its employees to engage in collective bargaining. The Bush administration took the position that collective bargaining rights for TSA employees would weaken travel security protection by adding an additional layer of procedures to TSA operations and would limit the agency's ability to respond quickly in emergencies because it would be required to negotiate changes in security procedures with unions representing its employees. Proponents for collective bargaining rights argue that collective bargaining can ensure that the agency is run more effectively and that current TSA employees complain of hostile work environments, favoritism, and fear of retaliation by managers for reports of violations of regulations. They also point out that staffing levels at some airports are very low, so that employees are required to work through break times, work extra shifts, and work on scheduled days off. A survey of the "Best Places to Work" in the federal government for 2009 ranked the TSA near the bottom of federal agencies, although the ratings for employee job satisfaction for the TSA had increased by nearly 23 percent.

In February 2011 TSA administrator John S. Pitole issued a "Determination" in which he stated, "The failed Christmas Day terrorist attack just over a year ago and the recent air cargo plot reminded us all of the challenges we face in protecting our nation against a creative and determined enemy. The Transportation Security Administration's mission to protect transportation security systems is critical to our national interests. While we continue to step up to the challenges of this mission, I am engaged in a full examination of how we can continue to evolve towards an agile, high performance organization that is better able to protect the traveling public from constantly changing threats."

He added, "As part of my top-to-bottom review of TSA, and in line with a commitment I made during the Senate confirmation process, I have conducted a full assessment of the impact union representation and collective bargaining might have on TSA's counter-terrorism mission. I have also considered the recent decision under the Federal Service Labor–Management Relations Statute (5 U.S.C. Chapter 71) issued by the Federal Labor Relations Authority (FLRA or Authority)—an independent government agency that oversees federal labor relations—directing an election about exclusive representation for purposes other than collective bargaining (65 FLRA No. 53 (2010))."

He then outlined a framework for labor relation within his agency. This framework is unique to TSA in that it allows for bargaining at the national level only. It prohibits local-level bargaining at individual airports—except on the nonsecurity employment issues identified in the Determination, such as shift bids, transfers, and awards. Administrator Pistole's Determination prohibits bargaining on any topics that might affect security, such as:

- Security policies, procedures, or the deployment of security personnel or equipment
- Pay, pensions, and any form of compensation
- Proficiency testing
- Job qualifications
- Discipline standards

The following two decisions of the U.S. Court of Appeals for the District of Columbia involve the legal challenges to the DHS and the Department of Defense human resources management systems by the unions representing their employees.

CASE 19.4

NATIONAL TREASURY EMPLOYEES UNION V. MICHAEL CHERTOFF, SECRETARY, UNITED STATES DEPARTMENT OF HOMELAND SECURITY
452 F.3d 839 (D.C. Cir. 2006)

Edwards, Senior Circuit Judge

When Congress enacted the Homeland Security Act of 2002 ("HSA" or the "Act") and established the Department of Homeland Security ("DHS" or the "Department"), it provided that "the Secretary of Homeland Security may, in regulations prescribed jointly with the Director of the Office of Personnel Management, establish, and from time to time adjust, a human resources management system." [5 U.S.C. § 9701 (Supp. II 2002)] Congress made it clear, however, that any such system "shall—(1) be flexible; (2) be contemporary; (3) not waive, modify, or otherwise affect [certain existing statutory provisions relating to ... merit hiring, equal pay, whistle blowing, and prohibited personnel practices], [and] (4) ensure that employees may organize, bargain collectively, and participate through labor organizations of their own choosing in decisions which affect them, subject to any exclusion from coverage or limitation on negotiability established by law." The Act also mandated that DHS employees receive "fair treatment in any appeals that they bring in decisions relating to their employment." Section 9701 does not mention "Chapter 71," which codifies the Federal Services Labor–Management Statute and delineates the framework for collective bargaining for most federal sector employees.

In February 2005, the Department and Office of Personnel Management ("OPM") issued regulations establishing a human resources management system ... [the] Department of Homeland Security Human Resources Management System ("Final Rule" or "HR system"). The Final Rule ... defines the scope and process of collective bargaining for affected DHS employees, channels certain disputes through the Federal Labor Relations Authority ("FLRA" or the "Authority"), creates an in-house Homeland Security Labor Relations Board ("HSLRB"), and assigns an appellate role to the Merit Systems Protection Board ("MSPB") in cases involving penalties imposed on DHS employees.

Unions representing many DHS employees filed a complaint in [District of Columbia] District Court ... challeng[ing] aspects of the Final Rule. ... the District Court found that the regulations would not ensure collective bargaining, would fundamentally and impermissibly alter FLRA jurisdiction, and would create an appeal process at MSPB that is not fair. Based on these rulings, the District Court enjoined DHS from implementing [certain sections] ... of the regulations. However, the District Court rejected the Unions' claims that the regulations impermissibly restricted the scope of bargaining and that DHS lacked authority to give MSPB an intermediate appellate function in cases involving mandatory removal offenses. ... The case is now before this court on appeal by the Government and cross-appeal by the Unions. We affirm in part and reverse in part.

We hold that the regulations fail in two important respects to "ensure that employees may ... bargain collectively," as the HSA requires. First, we agree with the District Court that the Department's attempt to reserve to itself the right to unilaterally abrogate lawfully negotiated and executed agreements is plainly unlawful. If the Department could unilaterally abrogate lawful contracts, this would nullify the Act's specific guarantee of collective bargaining rights, because the agency cannot "ensure" collective bargaining without affording employees the right to negotiate binding agreements.

Second, we hold that the Final Rule violates the Act insofar as it limits the scope of bargaining to employee-specific personnel matters. The regulations effectively eliminate all meaningful bargaining over fundamental working conditions (including even negotiations over procedural protections), thereby committing the bulk of decisions concerning conditions of employment to the Department's exclusive discretion. In no sense can such a limited scope of bargaining be viewed as consistent with the Act's mandate that DHS "ensure" collective-bargaining rights for its employees. The Government argues that the HSA does not require the Department to adhere to the terms of Chapter 71 and points out that the Act states that the HR system must be "flexible," and from this concludes that a drastically limited scope of bargaining is fully justified. This contention is specious. Although the HSA does not compel the Government to adopt the terms of Chapter 71 as such, Congress did not say that Chapter 71 is irrelevant to an understanding of how DHS is to comply with its obligations and Chapter 71 gives guidance to its meaning. It is also noteworthy that the HSA requires that the HR system

be "contemporary" as well as flexible. We know of no contemporary system of *collective bargaining* that limits the scope of bargaining to employee-specific personnel matters, as does the HR system, and the Government cites to none. We therefore reverse the District Court on this point.

We affirm the District Court's judgment that the Department exceeded its authority in attempting to conscript FLRA into the HR system. The Authority is an independent administrative agency, operating pursuant to its own organic statute and long-established procedures. Although the Department was free to avoid FLRA altogether, it chose instead to impose upon the Authority a completely novel appellate function, defining FLRA's jurisdiction and dictating standards of review to be applied by the Authority. In essence, the Final Rule attempts to co-opt FLRA's administrative machinery, prescribing new practices in an exercise of putative authority that only Congress possesses. Nothing in the HSA allows DHS to disturb the operations of FLRA....

The allowance of unilateral contract abrogation and the limited scope of bargaining under DHS's Final Rule plainly violate the statutory command in the HSA that the Department "ensure" collective bargaining for its employees. We therefore vacate any provisions of the Final Rule that betray this command. DHS's attempt to co-opt FLRA's administrative machinery constitutes an exercise of power far outside the Department's statutory authority. We therefore affirm the District Court's decision to vacate the provisions of the Final Rule that encroach on the Authority.

The judgments of the District Court are affirmed in part and reversed in part, and the case is hereby remanded for further proceedings consistent with this opinion.

So ordered.

CASE 19.5

AMERICAN FEDERATION OF GOVERNMENT EMPLOYEES, AFL-CIO v. ROBERT M. GATES, SECRETARY OF DEFENSE

486 F.3d 1316 (D.C. Cir. 2007)

Kavanaugh, Circuit Judge

This case arises out of a contentious dispute over the collective-bargaining rights of hundreds of thousands of civilian employees of the Department of Defense. Our limited judicial task is to determine whether the Department of Defense has acted consistently with its statutory authority in promulgating certain regulations. The primary legal question we must decide is whether the National Defense Authorization Act for Fiscal Year 2004 authorizes DoD to curtail collective-bargaining rights that DoD's civilian employees otherwise possess under the Civil Service Reform Act of 1978. We hold that the National Defense Authorization Act grants DoD *temporary* authority to curtail collective bargaining for DoD's civilian employees. By its terms, the Act authorizes DoD to curtail collective bargaining through November 2009. But after November 2009, with certain specified exceptions, DoD again must ensure collective bargaining consistent with the Civil Service Reform Act of 1978. We reverse the District Court's judgment, and we uphold the DoD regulations at issue in this appeal....

To put together the pieces of the statutory puzzle in this case, one must first appreciate the difference between Chapter 71 and Chapter 99 of Title 5 of the U.S. Code. Chapter 71 of Title 5 codifies the Civil Service Reform Act of 1978 and establishes the right of federal civilian employees, including civilian employees at the Department of Defense, "to engage in collective-bargaining with respect to conditions of employment through representatives chosen by employees." The Act generally requires agency management to "meet and negotiate" in good faith with recognized unions over conditions of employment "for the purposes of arriving at a collective-bargaining agreement." The Act exempts various matters from collective bargaining, such as hiring, firing, suspending, paying, and reducing the pay of employees. Therefore, the Civil Service Reform Act ensures collective bargaining for federal employees, albeit more limited than the collective bargaining rights for private employees.

Chapter 99 of Title 5 codifies a section of the National Defense Authorization Act for Fiscal Year 2004 and sets out a new labor relations framework for Department of Defense employees. Chapter 99 differs from the Chapter 71 model in several respects. In particular, Section 9902(a) of Chapter 99 establishes procedures for DoD, in coordination with the Office of Personnel Management, to "establish, and from time to time adjust, a human resources management system for some or all of the organizational or functional units of the Department of Defense." The "human resources management system" is called the "National Security Personnel System." Within the National Security Personnel System, the Act authorizes DoD to establish a "labor relations system" to structure bargaining between management and employees....

After Congress enacted the National Defense Authorization Act in November 2003, DoD began developing the National Security Personnel System. On February 14, 2005, DoD published a proposed system in the Federal Register. After various DoD employee representatives submitted comments, DoD held several meetings with employee representatives in the spring of 2005. On November 1, 2005, DoD promulgated final regulations setting up the National Security Personnel System....

The regulations curtail the scope of Chapter 71 collective bargaining in several ways relevant to this appeal:

- The regulations permit certain DoD officials to issue "implementing issuances" to abrogate any provision of an existing collective bargaining agreement or effectively take any topic off the table for future bargaining purposes. DoD may also promulgate "issuances" that take topics off the table. (Issuances and implementing issuances are documents issued to carry out DoD policies; implementing issuances relate to the National Security Personnel System, while issuances relate to any DoD policy.) Under the regulations, both issuances and implementing issuances can have prospective effect, but only implementing issuances can abrogate existing collective bargaining agreements.
- The regulations broaden the scope of "management rights"—that is, actions that management can take without collective bargaining—beyond the management rights already provided in Chapter 71. In particular, the regulations permit DoD "to take whatever other actions may be necessary to carry out the Department's mission."
- The regulations curtail bargaining over (i) the procedures DoD must follow when exercising management rights and (ii) the "appropriate arrangements" that DoD must make for employees affected by exercises of management rights.
- The regulations limit collective-bargaining rights over pay and benefits for employees of certain DoD units known as "non-appropriated fund instrumentalities." These employees' compensation is not set by statute and is therefore traditionally subject to collective bargaining....

[S]ubsection (m) of Section 9902 grants DoD expansive authority to curtail collective bargaining through November 2009.... After November 2009, however, the authority in subsection (m) runs out, and collective bargaining under Chapter 71 again will structure the Department's labor relations ... In effect, therefore, the Act sets up a temporary, experimental period through November 2009 during which DoD has broad leeway to restructure its labor relations system. But after November 2009, assuming that Congress has not amended the statute in the meantime, the Chapter 71 collective-bargaining requirements ... again will apply and govern labor relations for DoD's civilian workers (subject to targeted exceptions).

... In sum, we hold that the plain language of the National Defense Authorization Act authorizes DoD to curtail collective bargaining for DoD's civilian employees through November 2009. For purposes of our analysis, we find the relevant statutory terms plain.... Because we conclude that the National Defense Authorization Act authorizes DoD to curtail collective bargaining, we reverse the contrary judgment of the District Court....

We reverse the judgment of the District Court and uphold the DoD regulations at issue in this appeal.

So ordered.

Case Questions

1.   As noted, the court of appeals held that the DHS regulations were invalid but upheld the Department

of Defense regulations. Because the intent and the effects of the regulations in both cases were similar, how can you explain the different results in the two decisions?

2.   In the *DHS* decision, what reasons did the court give for holding that the regulations failed to ensure the rights of the employees to bargain collectively?

3.   In the *Department of Defense* case, how did the NSPS limit the scope of collective bargaining for the civilian employees? Were the restrictions on collective bargaining legal? Explain.

Note that the National Defense Authorization Act for Fiscal Year 2008[15] amended Section 9902 to eliminate subsection (m) and to require that the DoD bargain collectively within the National Security Personnel System (NSPS). The amended legislation also ensures that no collective bargaining agreement is superseded under the NSPS.

19-3   State Public Sector Labor Relations Legislation

In 1954, Wisconsin adopted a public employee labor relations law covering state, county, and municipal employees. Since that first legal provision for state public sector labor relations, approximately 40 states have adopted provisions relating to public sector labor relations. The various state laws differ widely in their treatment of issues such as employee coverage, impasse resolution procedures, and restrictions on the scope of bargaining. Because of the diversity of statutes, it is not possible to discuss them in detail; thus, the remaining portion of this chapter discusses certain general features of state public sector labor relations statutes. In recent years, as a response to the negative economic impact the recession has had on state finances, state legislatures and governors have made public sector unions the target of legislation restricting collective bargaining rights and automatic payroll deduction of union dues. In Wisconsin the governor and legislature essentially repealed its pioneering laws. This chapter outlines the current movement to reverse the trend started by Wisconsin some six decades ago.

19-3a   Coverage of State Laws

As noted, approximately 40 states have provisions for some labor relations activity by state or local employees. Most of these states have adopted statutes that provide for organizing rights and for collective bargaining by public employees. Some states that have no statutes dealing with public sector labor relations allow voluntary collective bargaining by public employees based on court decisions. Other states, while not restricting the rights of public

---

[15] Pub.L. No. 110-181, § 1106 (2008).

employees to join unions, prohibit collective bargaining by public employees based on statutory prohibitions or court decisions.

In states that have public sector labor relations statutes, the pattern of coverage of those statutes varies. Some statutes cover all state and local employees. Others may cover only local or only state employees. Some states have several statutes, with separate laws covering teachers, police, and firefighters. Some states also allow for the enactment of municipal labor relations legislation. New York City, for example, has established an Office of Collective Bargaining by passage of a city ordinance.

The courts have generally held that there is no constitutionally protected right to bargain collectively. For that reason, the courts have upheld restrictions or prohibitions on the right to bargain. The right to join unions or to organize, however, has been held to be protected by the constitutional freedom of association under the First and Fourteenth Amendments. Because the right to organize is constitutionally protected, restrictions on that right of public employees have consistently been struck down by the courts.

But while public employees in general may have the right to organize, many states exclude supervisors and managerial or confidential employees from unionizing. Other states may allow those employees to organize but provide for bargaining units separate from other employees. The courts have generally upheld exclusions of managerial, supervisory, and confidential employees from organizing and bargaining.

19-3b Representation Issues

Most of the state statutes authorizing public sector labor relations provide for exclusive bargaining representatives of the employees. The statutes generally create a Public Employee Relations Board (PERB) to administer the act and to determine representation issues and unfair labor practice complaints.

Bargaining Units

Determining appropriate bargaining units is generally the function of the PERB agency created by the particular statute. Some statutes provide for bargaining by all categories of public employees, whereas other statutes may specifically define appropriate units, such as teachers within a particular school district. When the PERB is entrusted with determining the appropriate unit, it generally considers community interest factors such as the nature of work, similarity of working conditions, efficiency of administration, and the desires of the employees. Some statutes require determination based on efficiency of administration. Police and law enforcement officers and firefighters are generally in separate district-wide units (or statewide units for state law enforcement officers). Faculty at public universities may be organized in statewide units or may bargain on an institution unit basis. In general, PERB agencies seek to avoid a proliferation of small units.

Representation Elections

The procedures for holding representation elections for units of public employees generally resemble those under the FSLMRA and the NLRA. The union seeking representation rights petitions the PERB requesting an election. The union must demonstrate some minimum level of employee support within the unit. If the parties fail to reach agreement on the bargaining unit definition, the eligibility of employees to vote, and the date and other details of the election, the PERB settles such issues after holding hearings on them.

The elections are by secret ballot, and the results are certified by the PERB. Either party may file objections to the election with the PERB; the PERB then reviews the challenges and possibly orders a new election when the challenges are upheld.

Bargaining

As noted, a majority of states have provisions requiring, or at least permitting, some form of collective bargaining. Some statutes may use the term "meet and confer" rather than collective bargaining, but in actual operation, the process is not substantially different from collective bargaining.

The scope of bargaining subjects may be restricted to protect the statutory authority of, or to ensure the provision of essential functions by, the public employer. The public employer may also be legally prohibited from agreeing with the union on particular subjects. For example, state law may require a minimum number of evaluations of employees annually, and the employer may not agree to fewer evaluations.

Public sector labor relations statutes generally have broad management-rights clauses. As a result, the subjects of "wages, hours and other terms and conditions" of employment may be defined more narrowly than is the case in the private sector under the NLRA.

The state PERBs generally classify subjects for bargaining as mandatory, permissive, and illegal subjects. Mandatory topics involve the narrowly defined matters relating to wages, hours, and other terms and conditions of employment. Permissive subjects generally are those related to government policy, the employer's function, or matters of management rights. Illegal subjects may include matters to which the employer is precluded by law from agreeing. Some states may prohibit bargaining over certain items that may be classified as permissive in other states.

In *Central State University v. A.A.U.P., Central State Chapter*,[16] the U.S. Supreme Court upheld the constitutionality of an Ohio law that required state public universities to set instructional workloads for professors and exempted those workloads from collective bargaining. In 2011 the newly elected Republican governor of Wisconsin proposed the so-called Budget Repair Law, and the state legislature enacted it. This law sharply curtailed public employees' collective bargaining rights, while increasing their individual contributions into their healthcare and pension plans. Upon the signing of the bill by Governor Scott Walker on March 10, 2011, a county district attorney mounted a legal challenge, which wound up before the state's Supreme Court.

CASE 19.6

MADISON TEACHERS, INC. V. WALKER
358 Wis.2d 1 (Wisconsin Sup. Ct. 2014)

Facts: In March 2011, the Wisconsin Legislature passed Act 10, a budget repair bill proposed by Governor Scott Walker. The Act significantly altered Wisconsin's public employee labor laws; it prohibits general employees from collectively bargaining on issues other than base wages, prohibits municipal employers from deducting labor organization dues from paychecks of general employees, imposes annual recertification requirements, and prohibits fair share agreements requiring non-represented general employees to make contributions to labor organizations. In August 2011,

[16] 526 U.S. 124 (1999).

Madison Teachers, Inc. and Public Employees Local 61 sued Governor Walker, challenging several provisions of Act 10. The plaintiffs alleged that four aspects of Act 10—the collective bargaining limitations, the prohibition on payroll deductions of labor organization dues, the prohibition of fair share agreements, and the annual recertification requirements—violate the constitutional associational and equal protection rights of the employees they represent. The Dane County Circuit Court invalidated several provisions of Act 10, including the provisions relating to collective bargaining limitations, union recertifications, and the prohibitions on fair share agreements and payroll deductions of labor organization dues. The court of appeals certified the case to the Supreme Court of Wisconsin.

Issue: On appeal, the unions raised the following issues: (1) whether Act 10 impermissibly infringes on the associational rights of general employees; (2) whether Act 10 impermissibly infringes on the equal protection rights of represented general employees when compared to non-represented general employees. The unions' central argument is that the following provisions of Act 10 violate the associational rights of general employees and their certified representatives that are guaranteed under Article I, Sections 3 and 4 of the Wisconsin Constitution:

1. The provision prohibiting collective bargaining between municipal employers and the certified representatives for municipal general employee bargaining units on all subjects except base wages.
2. The provisions limiting negotiated base wage increases to the increase in the Consumer Price Index, unless a higher increase is approved by a municipal voter referendum.
3. The provisions prohibiting fair share agreements that previously required all represented general employees to pay a proportionate share of the costs of collective bargaining and contract administration.
4. The provision prohibiting municipal employers from deducting labor organization dues from the paychecks of general employees.
5. The provision requiring annual recertification elections of the representatives of all bargaining units, requiring 51% of the votes of the bargaining unit members (regardless of the number of members who vote), and requiring the commission to assess costs of such elections.

Decision: Before the enactment of Act 10, general employees were permitted under MERA to collectively bargain over a broad array of subjects, including wages, working conditions, work hours, and grievance procedures. Act 10 limits collective bargaining between municipal employers and the certified representatives of general employees to the single topic of "total base wages and excludes any other compensation...." Moreover, Act 10 prohibits collective bargaining for base wage increases that exceed an increase in the Consumer Price Index unless approved in a municipal voter referendum. The plaintiffs argue this limitation penalizes general employees who choose to be represented by a certified representative because Act 10 imposes no limitations whatsoever on the terms that non-represented general employees may negotiate with their municipal employers. Consequently, the plaintiffs contend, Act 10 unconstitutionally burdens the associational rights of general employees because they must surrender their association with a certified representative in order to negotiate anything beyond base wages.

General employees have no constitutional right to negotiate with their municipal employer on the lone issue of base wages, let alone on any other subject. As the United States Supreme Court made clear:

> [While t]he public employee surely can associate and speak freely and petition openly, and he is protected by the First Amendment from retaliation for doing so.... [,] the First Amendment does not impose any affirmative obligation on the government to listen, to respond or, in this context, to recognize the association and bargain with it. *Smith v. Ark. State Highway Emps., Local 1315*, 441 U.S. 463, 465, 99 S.Ct. 1826, 60 L.Ed.2d 360 (1979) (citations omitted).

The plaintiffs have insisted at every stage of litigation in this case that they are not arguing a constitutional right exists to collectively bargain. It is evident, however, that they really are, for without such a constitutional right, their challenge fails.

Put differently, general employees are not being forced under Act 10 to choose between a tangible benefit and their constitutional right to associate. Instead, Act 10 provides a benefit to represented general employees by granting a statutory right to force their employer to negotiate over base wages, while non-represented general employees, who decline to collectively bargain, have no constitutional or statutory right whatsoever to force their employer to collectively bargain on any subject. For this reason, the plaintiffs' argument must be rejected. The plaintiffs' associational rights are in no way implicated by Act 10's modifications to Wisconsin's collective bargaining framework. At issue in this case is the State's implementation of an exclusive representation system for permitting public employers and public employees to negotiate certain employment terms in good faith. It is a prerogative of a state to establish workplace policy in a non-public process in consultation with only select groups—here, an organization selected by the affected workforce itself—and not others.

Not at issue in this case is the plaintiffs' constitutional right to associate to engage in protected First Amendment activities. The plaintiffs remain free to advance any position, on any topic, either individually or in concert, through any channels that are open to the public. Represented municipal employees, non-represented municipal employees, and certified representatives lose no right or ability to associate to engage in constitutionally protected speech because their ability to do so outside the framework of statutory collective bargaining is not impaired. Act 10 merely provides general employees with a statutory mechanism to force their employer to collectively bargain; outside of this narrow context, to which the plaintiffs freely concede public employees have no constitutional right, every avenue for petitioning the government remains available.

General employees may feel inclined to collectively bargain under Act 10 in order to compel their employer to negotiate on the issue of base wages, but this creates no unconstitutional inhibition on associational freedom. The defendants are not barring the plaintiffs from joining any advocacy groups, limiting their ability to do so, or otherwise curtailing their ability to join other "like-minded individuals to associate for the purpose of expressing commonly held views...." The limitations on permissible collective bargaining subjects imposed by Act 10 do not force general employees to choose between their constitutional right to associate and the benefit of collective bargaining. Therefore, the court held that Wis. Stat. §§ 111.70(4)(mb), 66.0506, and 118.245 do not violate Plaintiffs' right to freedom of association.

Fair share agreements are negotiated arrangements between municipal employers and certified representatives that require all general employees, including non-represented general employees, to pay the proportional share of the cost of collective bargaining and contract administration. Act 10 prohibits these agreements. See Wis. Stat. § 111.70(1)(f), (2). The plaintiffs argue this creates a financial burden on certified representatives and represented general employees to bear the full cost of collective bargaining for the benefit of the entire bargaining unit, while allowing non-represented general employees in the bargaining unit to enjoy the benefits of representation as

"free riders." For the certified representative and its members to choose the statutory "privilege" of collective bargaining, the plaintiffs argue they must accept the financial penalty as a condition of their associational choices to serve as the certified representative and be represented general employees. The plaintiffs contend these burdens will dissuade labor organizations from becoming certified representatives and general employees from becoming represented general employees, and are therefore unconstitutional.

The court rejected the unions' argument. First, labor organizations "have no constitutional entitlement to the fees of nonmember-employees." *Davenport v. Wash. Educ. Ass'n*, 551 U.S. 177, 127 S.Ct. 2372 (2007). Further, as the United States Supreme Court recently reaffirmed in *Harris v. Quinn*, fair share agreements "unquestionably impose a heavy burden on the First Amendment interests" of municipal employees who do not wish to participate in the collective bargaining process. *Harris v. Quinn*, 573 U.S. ——, 134 S.Ct. 2618 (2014).

Even setting aside the question of whether fair share agreements are constitutionally permissible, it is evident that the prohibition of fair share agreements does not infringe on the associational rights of general employees or certified representatives in any respect. The First Amendment does not compel the government to subsidize speech. By logical extension, the First Amendment does not compel the government to compel its employees to subsidize speech. The court concluded that Wis. Stat. § 111.70(1)(f) and the third sentence of § 111.70(2), examined in isolation, do not violate the plaintiffs' right to freedom of association.

Prior to Act 10, general employees could petition WERC to hold an election to designate a labor organization as the general employees' certified representative. The voting requirement for certification was a simple majority of employees in the collective bargaining unit. Once a labor organization was certified, it would remain the general employees' certified representative until thirty percent of the employees requested a decertification election. Act 10, however, requires the certified representative of a collective bargaining unit to undergo an annual certification election in which the representative must obtain the vote of an absolute majority of the general employees in the bargaining unit to retain status as the employees' certified representative. Wis. Stat. § 111.70(4)(d)3.b. Further, Act 10 requires that the certified representative pay the cost of administering the related certification elections. Certification requirements for certified representatives have existed in Wisconsin's labor laws since 1959. The certification requirements imposed by Act 10 are certainly more stringent than under the prior laws, but it is impossible for these increased "organizational penalties" to violate the plaintiffs' associational rights, when there are no associational rights at stake. The certification requirements apply solely to collective bargaining, which is wholly distinct from an individual's constitutional right to associate. Therefore, the court held that Wis. Stat. § 111.70(4)(d)3.b., examined in isolation, does not infringe on the plaintiffs' constitutional right to associate.

Prior to Act 10, municipal employers could deduct labor organization dues from the paychecks of general employees at the employee's request. Act 10 prohibits this practice. Wis. Stat. § 111.70(3g). The plaintiffs argue this prohibition hampers certified representatives and general employees both organizationally and financially, creating an unconstitutional burden on their associational rights. The prohibition on an employer's authorization to deduct labor organization dues from the paychecks of general employees does not infringe on an employee's constitutional right to associate. Further, this prohibition does not penalize employees because no constitutional right exists for the deduction of dues from a paycheck to support membership in a voluntary organization. Accordingly, Wis. Stat. § 111.70(3g), examined in isolation, does not infringe on the plaintiffs' constitutional right to associate.

Even when viewed together, the contested provisions of Act 10 are not unconstitutional. Each provision of Act 10 that the plaintiffs contend infringes upon the associational rights of certified representatives and general employees does not, in fact, do so, because in each instance, there is no constitutional associational right implicated. Viewing the provisions as a whole does not change our analysis. Each of the plaintiffs' arguments fails for largely the same reason:

collective bargaining requires the municipal employer and the certified representative to meet and confer in good faith. Wis. Stat. § 111.70(1)(a). The Wisconsin Constitution does not. Indeed, it is uncontested that it would be constitutional for the State of Wisconsin to eliminate collective bargaining entirely. Thus, the plaintiffs' contention that several provisions of Act 10, which delineate the rights, obligations, and procedures of collective bargaining, infringe upon general employees' constitutional right to freedom of association is unfounded. No matter the limitations or "burdens" a legislative enactment places on the collective bargaining process, collective bargaining remains a creation of legislative grace and not constitutional obligation. The restrictions attached to the statutory scheme of collective bargaining are irrelevant in regards to freedom of association because no condition is being placed on the decision to participate. If a general employee participates in collective bargaining under Act 10's statutory framework, that general employee has not relinquished a constitutional right. They have only acquired a benefit to which they were never constitutionally entitled. The First Amendment cannot be used as a vehicle to expand the parameters of a benefit that it does not itself protect.

The court held that the plaintiffs' associational rights argument was without merit, and rejected the plaintiffs' argument that several provisions of Act 10, which delineate the rights, obligations, and procedures of collective bargaining, somehow infringe upon general employees' constitutional right to freedom of association. The court concluded that Wis. Stat. §§ 111.70(4)(mb), 66.0506, 118.245, 111.70(1)(f), 111.70(3g), 111.70(4)(d) 3 and the third sentence of § 111.70(2) do not violate the plaintiffs' associational rights, and upheld the validity of Act 10 in its entirety. The decision and order of the circuit court was reversed.

19-3c   Bargaining and Open-Meeting Laws

open-meeting ("sunshine") laws
laws that require that meetings of public bodies be open to the public

Some states have adopted **open-meeting, or "sunshine," laws** that require meetings of public bodies be open to the public. Such laws could present a problem for collective bargaining by public employers because they may allow members of the general public to take part in the bargaining process. In some states, such as Ohio, collective bargaining is exempted from the open-meeting law. In other states, however, the right of the public to participate in the bargaining is legally protected.

Impasse Resolution Procedure

Because most state laws restrict or prohibit strikes by public employees, they must provide some alternative means for resolving bargaining impasses. Most statutes provide for a process that includes fact-finding, mediation, and ultimately, interest arbitration.

Mediation is generally the first step in the impasse resolution process. The mediator may be appointed by the PERB at the request of either party. The mediator attempts to offer suggestions and to reduce the number of issues in dispute.

If the mediation is unsuccessful, fact-finding is the second step. Each party presents its case to the fact-finder, who will issue a report defining the issues in dispute and establishing the reasonableness of each side's position. The fact-finder's report may be released to the public in an attempt to bring the pressure of public opinion upon the parties to force a settlement.

If no resolution is reached after mediation and fact-finding, the statutes generally provide for interest arbitration (see Chapter 18). The arbitration may be either voluntary or compulsory, and it may be binding or nonbinding. Compulsory, binding arbitration is generally found in statutes dealing with employees who provide essential services, such as firefighters and police. Nonbinding arbitration awards may be disregarded by the public employer if it so chooses. Binding arbitration awards bind both parties to the arbitrator's settlement of the dispute.

In several states, the arbitration of bargaining disputes has been challenged as being an illegal delegation of the public employer's legal authority to the arbitrator. Most state courts have upheld the legality of arbitration; examples are Maine, Michigan, Minnesota, New York, Oklahoma, Pennsylvania, and Washington. In some states, however, courts have held compulsory arbitration to be illegal. Such was the case in Colorado, South Dakota, Texas, and Utah.

Some statutes allow for judicial review of arbitration awards, generally on grounds of whether the award is unreasonable, arbitrary, or capricious.

Strikes by State Workers

Most state public sector labor relations statutes prohibit strikes by public employees. Statutes in other states, such as Hawaii, Michigan, Pennsylvania, and Vermont, allow strikes by employees whose jobs do not immediately affect the public health, safety, and welfare. Still other states' statutes allow for strikes in situations in which the public employer refuses to negotiate or to abide by an arbitration award.

Penalties for illegal strikes vary from state to state. New York's Taylor Law, which prohibits all strikes by public employees, provides for fines and the loss of dues check-off provisions for unions involved in illegal strikes. Employees who participate in illegal strikes in New York may face probation, loss of job, and loss of pay. The court may issue injunctions or restraining orders against illegal strikes.

Disciplining public sector employees, even those who have taken part in illegal strikes, may pose constitutional problems for the public sector employer. The employer must ensure that any disciplinary procedure ensures the employees "due process," including adequate notice of and an opportunity to participate in a hearing on the proposed penalty.

State and municipal employees in the following states are accorded a limited right to strike:

- Alaska
- Hawaii

- Idaho
- Illinois
- Minnesota
- Montana
- Oregon
- Pennsylvania
- Vermont

ethical DILEMMA

PROPERTY TAXES VERSUS PUBLIC-EMPLOYEE BENEFITS

In 2011, New Jersey residents stagger under the highest property taxes in the nation. Meanwhile, teachers and other public employees regularly retire at 80 percent of their most recent base salaries, plus full medical benefits. The U.S. debt clock shows state revenue at less than $80 billion, while it estimates spending at $108 billion. Debt, it claims, equals nearly $94 billion, or about 18.5 percent of state GDP. New Jersey Governor Chris Christie released his 2012 budget in February 2011. A press release from the governor's press secretary stated:

> Advancing his vision for a New Normal in state budgeting, Governor Chris Christie … presented a $29.4 billion budget for Fiscal Year 2012 that cuts real spending for a second consecutive year. The Governor's Budget proposal includes $200 million in focused tax cuts, provides additional property tax relief, increases school aid and funds a reformed state pension system, while preserving or increasing funding to protect our state's most vulnerable citizens. The Fiscal Year 2012 Budget marks a departure from the Trenton tradition of budgeting to meet deficit projections that embrace wish-list spending by legislators and assume continuous funding increases that irresponsibly ignore actual revenue sources and the fiscal health of the state.

Specifically with respect to public employees, the release stated:

> Governor Christie will continue to insist that the shared sacrifice be spread among state employees as well, including in payment of a fair share of medical costs. By increasing co-payments and premiums to levels still below what federal employees pay, the state will save $323 million that will be used to pay for other critically important programs—and prevent increases in some of the highest sales, income and property taxes in the nation.

What do you think is the appropriate balance between homeowners' and business property taxes and the pension and health care benefits given by the Garden State to its public employees, such as police, firefighters and teachers? What are the possible repercussions, if any, of reducing these benefits going forward? (Might the very property owners who seek tax relief, suffer indirectly?) Are there other ways in which Governor Christie and the state legislature might afford property owners some tax relief, while not shifting the burden onto the backs of public employees?

19-4   Public Employees and First Amendment Free Speech Rights

The employment practices of public employers may also be matters of public concern—citizens and taxpayers may want to express their views on matters such as benefits for domestic partners, family leave, pension benefits, and even workforces. Public employees have a dual role—they are employees who are affected by such practices or policies, and they are also citizens (and taxpayers). Do the public employees, as citizens, have the right to speak out on matters relating to their employer's practices? Can a public employer prohibit its employees from speaking out on such issues? Does the First Amendment freedom of speech protect those employees from disciplinary action by the employer? The following two cases involve the question of whether or not a school board can allow a teacher to comment at a public meeting on matters currently being negotiated with the teachers' union, and whether an employee of a district attorney who reports concerns about improper actions by other employees to his supervisor is protected by the First Amendment.

CASE 19.7

CITY OF MADISON JOINT SCHOOL DISTRICT NO. 8 V. WISCONSIN EMPLOYMENT RELATIONS COMMISSION
429 U.S. 167 (1976)

Burger, C. J.

The question presented on this appeal from the Supreme Court of Wisconsin is whether a State may constitutionally require that an elected board of education prohibit teachers, other than union representatives, to speak at open meetings at which public participation is permitted, if such speech is addressed to the subject of pending collective-bargaining negotiations.

The Madison Board of Education and Madison Teachers, Inc. (MTI), a labor union, were parties to a collective-bargaining agreement during the calendar year of 1971. In January 1971 negotiations commenced for renewal of the agreement and MTI submitted a number of proposals. One among them called for the inclusion of a so-called "fair share" clause, which would require all teachers, whether members of MTI or not, to pay union dues to defray the costs of collective bargaining. Wisconsin law expressly permits inclusion of "fair share" provisions in municipal employee collective-bargaining agreements. Another proposal presented by the union was a provision for binding arbitration of teacher dismissals. Both of these provisions were resisted by the school board. The negotiations deadlocked in November 1971 with a number of issues still unresolved, among them "fair share" and arbitration.

During the same month, two teachers, Holmquist and Reed, who were members of the bargaining unit, but not members of the union, mailed a letter to all teachers in the district expressing opposition to the "fair share" proposal. Two hundred teachers replied, most commenting favorably on Holmquist and Reed's position. Thereupon a petition was drafted calling for a one-year delay in the implementation of "fair share" while the proposal was more closely analyzed by an impartial committee. The petition was circulated to teachers in the district on December 6, 1971. Holmquist and Reed intended to present the results of their petition effort to the school board and the MTI at the school board's public meeting that same evening.

Because of the stalemate in the negotiations, MTI arranged to have pickets present at the school board meeting. In addition, 300 to 400 teachers attended in support of the union's position. During a portion of the meeting devoted to expression of opinion by the public, the president of MTI took the floor and spoke on the subject of the ongoing negotiations. He concluded his remarks by presenting to the board a petition signed by 1,300–1,400 teachers calling for the expeditious resolution of the negotiations. Holmquist was next given the floor, after John Matthews, the business representative of MTI, unsuccessfully attempted to dissuade him from speaking. Matthews had also spoken to a member of the school board before the meeting and requested that the board refuse to permit Holmquist to speak. Holmquist stated that he represented "an informal committee of 72 teachers in 49 schools" and that he desired to inform the board of education, as he had already informed the union, of the results of an informational survey concerning the "fair share" clause. He then read the petition that had been circulated to the teachers in the district that morning and stated that in the 31 schools from which reports had been received, 53 percent of the teachers had already signed the petition.

Holmquist stated that neither side had adequately addressed the issue of "fair share" and that teachers were confused about the meaning of the proposal. He concluded by saying: "Due to this confusion, we wish to take no stand on the proposal itself, but ask only that all alternatives be presented clearly to all teachers and more importantly to the general public to whom we are all responsible. We ask simply for communication, not confrontation." The sole response from the school board was a question by the president inquiring whether Holmquist intended to present the board with the petition. Holmquist answered that he would. Holmquist's presentation had lasted approximately 2½ minutes.

Later that evening, the board met in executive session and voted a proposal acceding to all of the union's demands with the exception of "fair share." During a negotiating session the following morning, MTI accepted the proposal and a contract was signed on December 14, 1971.

In January 1972, MTI filed a complaint with the Wisconsin Employment Relations Commission (WERC) claiming that the board had committed a prohibited labor practice by permitting Holmquist to speak at the December 6 meeting. MTI claimed that in so doing the board had engaged in negotiations with a member of the bargaining unit other than the exclusive collective-bargaining representative, in violation of Wis. Stat. Sections 111.70(3)(a)(1), (4) (1973). Following a hearing the Commission concluded that the board was guilty of the prohibited labor practice and ordered that it "immediately cease and desist from permitting employees, other than representatives of Madison Teachers Inc., to appear and speak at meetings of the Board of Education, on matters subject to collective bargaining between it and Madison Teachers, Inc." The Commission's action was affirmed by the Circuit Court of Dane County.

The Supreme Court of Wisconsin affirmed. The court recognized that both the Federal and State Constitutions protect freedom of speech and the right to petition the

government, but noted that these rights may be abridged in the face of "a clear and present danger that [the speech] will bring about the substantive evils that [the legislature] has a right to prevent." The court held that abridgment of the speech in this case was justified in order "to avoid the dangers attendant upon relative chaos in labor management relations."

The Wisconsin court perceived "clear and present danger" based upon its conclusion that Holmquist's speech before the school board constituted "negotiation" with the board. Permitting such "negotiation," the court reasoned, would undermine the bargaining exclusivity guaranteed the majority union under Wis. Stat. Section 111.70(3)(a)(4) (1973). From that premise it concluded that teachers' First Amendment rights could be limited. *Assuming, arguendo,* that such a "danger" might in some circumstances justify some limitation of First Amendment rights, we are unable to read this record as presenting such danger as would justify curtailing speech.

The Wisconsin Supreme Court's conclusion that Holmquist's terse statement during the public meeting constituted negotiation with the board was based upon its adoption of the lower court's determination that, "[e]ven though Holmquist's statement superficially appears to be merely a 'position statement,' the court deems from the total circumstances that it constituted 'negotiating.'" This cryptic conclusion seems to ignore the ancient wisdom that calling a thing by a name does not make it so. Holmquist did not seek to bargain or offer to enter into any bargain with the board, nor does it appear that he was authorized by any other teachers to enter into any agreement on their behalf. Although his views were not consistent with those of MTI, communicating such views to the employer could not change the fact that MTI alone was authorized to negotiate and to enter into a contract with the board.

Moreover the school board meeting at which Holmquist was permitted to speak was open to the public. He addressed the school board not merely as one of its employees but also as a concerned citizen, seeking to express his views on an important decision of his government. We have held that teachers may not be "compelled to relinquish the First Amendment rights they would otherwise enjoy as citizens to comment on matters of public interest in connection with the operation of the public schools in which they work." ... Where the State has opened a forum for direct citizen involvement, it is difficult to find justification for excluding teachers who make up the overwhelming proportion of school employees and who are most vitally concerned with the proceedings. It is conceded that any citizen could have presented precisely the same points and provided the board with the same information as did Holmquist.

Regardless of the extent to which true contract negotiations between a public body and its employees may be regulated—an issue we need not consider at this time—the participation in public discussion of public business cannot be confined to one category of interested individuals. To permit one side of a debatable public question to have a monopoly in expressing its views to the government is the antithesis of constitutional guarantees. Whatever its duties as an employer, when the board sits in public meetings to conduct public business and hear the views of citizens, it may not be required to discriminate between speakers on the basis of their employment, or the content of their speech....

The WERC's order is not limited to a determination that a prohibited labor practice had taken place in the past; it also restrains future conduct. By prohibiting the school board from "permitting employees ... to appear and speak at meetings of the Board of Education" the order constitutes an indirect, but effective, prohibition on persons such as Holmquist from communicating with their government. The order would have a substantial impact upon virtually all communication between teachers and the school board. The order prohibits speech by teachers "on matters subject to collective bargaining." As the dissenting opinion below noted, however, there is virtually no subject concerning

the operation of the school system that could not also be characterized as a potential subject of collective bargaining. Teachers not only constitute the overwhelming bulk of employees of the school system, but they are the very core of that system; restraining teachers' expressions to the board on matters involving the operation of the schools would seriously impair the board's ability to govern the district....

The judgment of the Wisconsin Supreme Court is reversed, and the case is remanded to that court for further proceedings not inconsistent with this opinion.

Reversed and remanded.

Case Questions

1. Why did the Wisconsin Supreme Court characterize Holmquist's statement as constituting negotiation? Did the U.S. Supreme Court agree with that characterization? Why?

2. Was Holmquist addressing the school board in his capacity as an employee, as a concerned citizen, or as both? Why is it relevant here? Explain your answer.

3. When can the First Amendment rights of the freedom of speech and the right to petition the government be limited? Were those circumstances applicable to the facts in this case? Explain.

The *City of Madison* decision recognized that public employees are also citizens who enjoy First Amendment protection of freedom of speech—they may not be prohibited from speaking out in a public forum on matters of public interest, even if those matters relate to labor relations policies affecting those employees. But how far does the First Amendment protection extend? Does it cover all work-related speech of public employees? That is the question addressed by the Supreme Court in the following case.

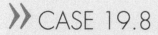

›› CASE 19.8

GARCETTI V. CEBALLOS
547 U.S. 410 (2006)

Facts: Richard Ceballos was a deputy district attorney for the Los Angeles County District Attorney's Office. In February 2000, a defense attorney contacted Ceballos

about a pending criminal case and told him that there were inaccuracies in an affidavit used to obtain a critical search warrant. The attorney informed Ceballos that he had filed a motion to challenge the warrant, and asked Ceballos to review the case. Ceballos determined the affidavit contained serious misrepresentations. He informed his supervisors and prepared a memo explaining his concerns and recommending dismissal of the case. A meeting was held to discuss Ceballos' concerns about the affidavit. The meeting allegedly became heated, and Ceballos was criticized for his handling of the case. The supervisor decided to proceed with the prosecution, and at a hearing on the motion to challenge the warrant, Ceballos was called by the defense and testified about his observations about the affidavit. The trial court rejected the challenge to the warrant.

Ceballos claimed that in the aftermath of these events he was subjected to a series of retaliatory employment actions, including reassignment to a trial deputy position, transfer to another courthouse, and denial of a promotion. Ceballos initiated an employment grievance, but the grievance was denied. Ceballos then filed suit, claiming that his employer had violated the First and Fourteenth Amendments by retaliating against him based on his memo. The trial court granted the employer's motion for summary judgment, but on appeal, the U.S. Court of Appeals for the Ninth Circuit reversed the trial court, holding that Ceballos allegations of wrongdoing in his memorandum constituted protected speech under the First Amendment. The employer appealed to the U.S. Supreme Court.

Issue: Does the First Amendment protect a government employee from discipline based on speech made pursuant to the employee's official duties?

Decision: The court of appeals held that Ceballos' memo was "inherently a matter of public concern" but did not consider whether the speech was made in Ceballos's capacity as a citizen or as part of his professional duties. The Supreme Court, however, stated that there were two questions to ask to determine whether constitutional protection is accorded to speech by a public employee.

The first question is whether the employee spoke as a citizen on a matter of public concern. If the employee is not speaking as a citizen but rather in the course of official duties, the employee's speech is not protected by the First Amendment. If the employee is speaking as a citizen, then the possibility of a First Amendment claim arises. In that case, the court considers the second question, whether the government employer had an adequate justification for treating the employee differently from any other member of the general public. Government has broader discretion to restrict speech when it is acting in its role as employer, but any restrictions it can impose must be directed at speech that has some potential to affect the employer's operations. When public employees speak out, they may express views that contravene governmental policies or impair the proper performance of governmental functions.

At the same time, the First Amendment limits the ability of a public employer to impose restrictions on employees in their capacities as private citizens. So long as employees are speaking as citizens about matters of public concern, the employer can only impose speech restrictions that are necessary for their employers to operate efficiently and effectively. However, when public employees make statements pursuant to their official duties, the employees are not speaking as citizens for First Amendment purposes, and the Constitution does not protect their communications from employer discipline.

In this case, Ceballos believed the affidavit used to obtain a search warrant contained serious misrepresentations, and he conveyed his opinion and recommendation in a memo to his supervisor. His expressions were made pursuant to his duties as a calendar deputy, not as a citizen, and his conduct was not protected by the First Amendment. The Supreme Court reversed the decision of the court of appeals.

CHAPTER REVIEW

» Key Terms

Federal Labor Relations Authority (FLRA)   6 1 7

Federal Service Impasse Panel   6 2 2

open-meeting ("sunshine") laws   6 3 9

» Summary

- Labor relations in the public sector differ from those in the private sector in several ways: (1) government employees are also citizens who have certain rights under the federal and appropriate state constitutions, which may limit disciplinary procedures by government employers; (2) government sovereignty requires that the scope of collective bargaining be restricted; and (3) the right of public employees to strike may be limited or completely prohibited. While legislation in some states permits certain public employees to strike, federal government employees are prohibited from striking. A union that authorizes or conducts a strike against the federal government may have its status as exclusive bargaining representative revoked, and federal employees who go on strike are subject to discharge.

- The Federal Service Labor–Management Relations Act (FSLMRA) regulates federal labor relations; it grants federal employees the right to join or assist unions. Certain federal employees, including members of the armed forces and those involved in intelligence work

or national security matters, are excluded from coverage of the FSLMRA. The FSLMRA requires employers and unions to negotiate in good faith, but the act also contains a broad management-rights clause and restricts the scope of collective bargaining subjects. The Federal Labor Relations Authority (FLRA) administers the FSLMRA; the FLRA determines appropriate representation units, conducts representation elections, and hears complaints of unfair labor practices under the FSLMRA.

- State public sector labor relations legislation varies widely; some states grant certain public employees the right to strike, and most states require that employers negotiate, or "meet and confer," with the unions representing public employees. The scope of collective bargaining under state public sector legislation is generally restricted by broad management-rights clauses. State public sector labor relations laws are generally administered by a state Public Employee Relations Board (PERB), which conducts representation elections and decides unfair labor practice complaints.

» Problems

» Questions

1. In what ways does the role of government as employer raise constitutional issues not found in the private sector?

2. Which federal employees are covered by the FSLMRA? Which federal agencies are excluded from the act's coverage?

3. What restrictions are placed on the scope of collective bargaining under the FSLMRA? What procedures are available for impasse settlement under the FSLMRA?

4. What legal issues are raised by union security clauses in the public sector? Explain why these issues arise.

5. To what extent may states restrict the right of state public employees to join unions? To what extent may the right of state public sector employees to bargain collectively be restricted?

» Case Problems

6. In April 1978, public employee Dorothea Yoggerst heard an unconfirmed report that her boss, the director of the Illinois Governor's Office of Management and Human Development, had been discharged. While still at work, she asked a coworker, "Did you hear the good news?"

   Yoggerst was orally reprimanded by her supervisor. Subsequently, a written memorandum of the reprimand was placed in her personnel file. Two months later, she resigned her job, citing this alleged infringement of her First Amendment right of free speech as her reason for leaving. Yoggerst sued four defendants, including the supervisor who reprimanded her and the personnel director.

   An earlier case heard by the Supreme Court, *Connick v. Myers*, involved the firing of a public employee for distributing to her coworkers a questionnaire that challenged the trustworthiness of her superiors. In that case, the high court enunciated a two-prong test: (1) Did the speech in question address a matter of public concern? (2) How

did the employee's right to speak her mind compare to the government's interest in efficient operations? The U.S. Court of Appeals applied this same test in the *Yoggerst* case.

   How do you think the courts ruled in these two cases? [See *Yoggerst v. Hedges and McDonough*, 739 F.2d 293 (7th Cir. 1984); *Connick v. Myers*, 461 U.S. 138 (1983); and *Garcetti v. Ceballos*, 547 U.S. 410 (2006).]

7. On March 3, 2011, the Ohio Legislature passed a massive revision of the state's public sector collective bargaining act. The chief changes are described as follows:

   • S.B. 5 places significant restrictions on the subjects that can be brought to the bargaining table for public employees. Specifically, bargaining will not be permitted about health insurance benefits, employer assistance toward the employee share of pension contributions, privatization of public services, staffing levels, and certain other management rights.

   • S.B. 5 prohibits strikes by all public employees. Previously, Ohio collective bargaining law prohibited strikes only by police officers, firefighters, and other specified employees whose jobs have a direct impact on public safety. S.B. 5 makes it illegal for all public employees to strike and imposes extraordinary penalties if public employees do strike. Striking employees can be terminated and can be subjected to substantial financial penalties.

   • S.B. 5 establishes a new procedure for dispute resolution in bargaining. Under existing law, if contract negotiations reach a stalemate, the parties typically first have a hearing before a neutral fact-finder. The fact-finder issues recommendations for resolving the dispute, but either the union or the employer can reject those recommendations. In the case of police, firefighters, and other specified safety employees who are prohibited from striking, the dispute then goes to a hearing before another neutral person whose decision is binding. The theory is that since those employees do not have the leverage of the threat of a strike, there has to be a neutral person to break the deadlock in the bargaining. S.B. 5 eliminates the binding arbitration step and prohibits all employees from striking. In cases where bargaining reaches a stalemate, the fact-finding proceeding will be followed first. If either party rejects the fact-finder's report, the employer's last best offer and the union's last best offer will be presented to the legislative body (i.e., City Council in the case of a municipality) which will conduct a public hearing and then vote to accept either the last best offer of the union or the last best offer of the employer. [Mike Underwood, "Ohio Senate Passes Massive Reform to Public Sector Collective Bargaining Law," *Employer Law Report* (Mar. 3, 2011).]

In a November 8, 2011 election, Ohio voters had the opportunity to decide whether or not to repeal this legislation. How do you think the majority voted? Why?

8. In 2003, New York amended its Clean Indoor Air Act to prohibit indoor smoking in all "places of employment," including workplaces of "the legislative, executive and judicial branches of state government and any political subdivision of the state." *N.Y. Pub. Health Law § 1399-* o(1), -n(2). Accordingly, the New York Division of Military and Naval Affairs (DMNA) issued a new smoking policy that prohibited all smoking in National Guard facilities in New York.

The Association of Civilian Technicians, New York State Council, which represents the civil technicians working at the Guard facilities, filed a grievance charging that the DMNA had violated their collective bargaining agreement by failing to negotiate the terms of the new smoking policy. When the grievance was not resolved, the union invoked its right to binding arbitration and added an allegation that DMNA's unilateral implementation of the policy constituted an unfair labor practice because it was taken in clear and patent breach of the collective bargaining agreement's negotiation provisions.

The parties were unable to stipulate to the issues before the arbitrator. She reviewed their proposed issues and found that, "[a]t the heart of this case is a dispute over the interpretation and application of the language of the Parties' Collective Bargaining Agreement." She then framed the issues as, "Did the Agency violate the Collective Bargaining Agreement when it issued a new smoking policy letter on 23 July 2003?" and "If so, what should the remedy be?" She concluded that the DMNA had not violated the collective bargaining agreement because the smoking ban was a statutory requirement and therefore did not fall within the agreement's requirement that rules "within the purview" of the DMNA be negotiated.

The union challenged this award in court. How do you think the court ruled on the challenge? [See *Association of Civilian Technicians, N.Y. State Council v. Federal Labor Relations Authority*, 507 F.3d 697 (2d Cir. 2007).]

9. In February 2010, the Central Falls, Rhode Island, school board decided to fire all its teachers at the end of that academic year. According to the *Providence Journal*, "Just an hour after the rally, the Central Falls school Board of Trustees, in a brief but intense meeting, voted 5–2 to fire every teacher at the school. In all, ninety-three names were read aloud in the high school auditorium—seventy-four classroom teachers, plus reading specialists, guidance counselors, physical education teachers, the school psychologist, the principal and three assistant principals." [Jennifer D. Jordan, "Every Central Falls teacher fired, labor outrage," *Providence Journal*, February 24, 2010.]

What arguments might the teachers and their union raise in order to prevent this proposed action? How do you think these arguments would fare in court?

10. Marjorie Rowland began working at Stebbins High School in Yellow Springs, Ohio, in August 1974. The school principal subsequently asked her to resign when it was learned that she had stated she was bisexual. When she refused, the school suspended her but was forced to rehire her by a preliminary injunction issued by a federal district

judge. The administration assigned her to a job with no student contact and, when her contract expired, refused to renew it. Rowland sued.

How do you think the court ruled on Rowland's suit? Why? [See *Rowland v. Mad River Local School District*, 730 F.2d 444 (6th Cir. 1984).] Do you believe that the outcome might be different if the case arose today? [See *Commission on Human Rights & Opportunities v. City of Hartford*, 2010 WL 4612700 (Conn. Super. 2010).]

11. On June 28, 2011, the New Jersey Pension and Health Care Benefits Act (Chapter 78) was enacted into law, *L.* 2011, *c.* 78—a law that applies to all public employees, including Supreme Court justices and Superior Court judges then in service. Article VI, Section 6, Paragraph 6 of the New Jersey Constitution provides that justices and judges "shall receive for their services such salaries as may be provided by law, which shall not be diminished during the term of their appointment" (the No–Diminution Clause). Under Chapter 78, over a course of seven years, sitting justices and judges will be subject to a more than 400 percent increase in their pension contributions and a more than 100 percent increase in their health care contributions. Because the increased individual contributions are imposed without any corresponding salary increase, the take-home salaries of justices and judges will decrease in the range of $17,000 or more, representing a more than 10 percent decline in their disposable income.

Do the proposed increases in judges' pension and health care contributions constitute a violation of the New Jersey constitution? [See *Depascale v. State of New Jersey*, 47 A.3d 690 (N.J. Supreme 2012).]

12. The Denver firefighters are city employees, subject to the supervision and control of the city manager, who is appointed by the mayor. In 1971, Denver voters passed an amendment to the City Charter, granting Denver firefighters the right to collectively bargain with the city over certain working conditions.

The plaintiff in this case was the firefighters' exclusive bargaining agent, and the parties have had a collective bargaining agreement every year since the amendment. The parties' relevant collective bargaining agreement had been in effect since January 1, 2010, and expired on December 31, 2012.

The dispute underlying this appeal arose from defendants' proposed unilateral creation and implementation of a discipline matrix for the Fire Department. As described by the parties, a discipline matrix is a system that lists prohibited conduct and the corresponding disciplinary sanctions to be imposed through a progressive system based on the severity and frequency of an employee's misconduct.

The Fire Department previously did not have a discipline matrix, but it did have a code of conduct and a system for imposing discipline, which had been in place for decades. Under the old disciplinary system, when a firefighter violated the code of conduct, the fire chief issued a written report containing the charges, the evidence of and reasons for the charges, and the specific disciplinary action ordered. The city manager then reviewed the report and could approve, modify, or disapprove the recommended disciplinary action.

Defendants' proposed creation and implementation of a discipline matrix unilaterally changed the current discipline system.

Should the city government be allowed to unilaterally change the disciplinary system as a management right and/or act of sovereign immunity? Or should this be declared, as a matter of first impression for the court, a mandatory subject for collective bargaining? What are some of the policy considerations that might drive the court's decision? [See *Denver Firefighters Local No. 858 v. City and County of Denver*, 292 P.3d 1101 (Colo. App. 2012).]

13. The Combined Federal Campaign (CFC) is an annual charitable fund-raising drive conducted in the federal workplace during working hours largely through the voluntary efforts of federal employees. Participating organizations confine their fund-raising activities to a 30-word statement submitted by them for inclusion in the campaign literature.

Volunteer federal employees distribute to their coworkers literature describing the campaign and the participants, along with pledge cards. Designated funds are paid directly to the specified recipient.

The CFC is a relatively recent idea. Prior to 1957, charitable solicitation in the federal workplace occurred on an ad hoc basis. Federal managers received requests from dozens of organizations seeking endorsements and the right to solicit contributions from federal employees at their work sites. In facilities where solicitation was permitted, weekly campaigns were commonplace.

In 1957, President Eisenhower established the forerunner of the CFC to bring order to the solicitation process and to ensure truly voluntary giving by federal employees. The order established an advisory committee and set forth general procedures and standards for a uniform fund-raising program. It permitted no more than three charitable solicitations annually and established a system requiring prior approval by a committee on fund raising for participation by "voluntary health and welfare" agencies.

A number of organizations joined in challenging these criteria, including the NAACP Legal Defense and Educational Fund, Inc., the Sierra Club Legal Defense Fund, the Puerto Rican Legal Defense and Education Fund, the Federally Employed Women Legal Defense and Education Fund, the Indian Law Resource Center, the Lawyers Committee for Civil Rights under Law, and the Natural Resources Defense Council. Each of the groups attempts to influence public policy through one or more of the following means: political activity, advocacy, lobbying, and litigation on behalf of others.

On what grounds did these organizations challenge the regulations? How do you think the Supreme Court ruled? [See *Cornelius v. NAACP Legal Defense and Educational Fund*, 473 U.S. 788 (1985).]

14. Defendants, the County of Wayne and the Wayne County Chief Executive Officer (CEO), appealed the trial court's orders granting partial summary disposition in favor of the plaintiff, Michigan AFSCME Council 25, on its claim that the defendants unlawfully imposed a wage reduction for county employees and denied the

defendants' motion for reconsideration regarding the applicability of governmental immunity.

The plaintiff and defendants were participants in a collective bargaining agreement (CBA). After the CBA expired, the parties unsuccessfully engaged in negotiations to reach a successor agreement. On October 21, 2010, the plaintiff filed this action, alleging that the defendants were in violation of the Wayne County Charter and had engaged in improper collective bargaining practices. In a December 1, 2010, letter to the plaintiff, Mark Dukes, director of Wayne County's Labor Relations Division, declared that negotiations had reached an impasse and indicated that the county would be implementing the terms of its "last best offer" (LBO), which required union employees to accept a 20 percent wage decrease and other concessions. The LBO was issued through the Labor Relations Division, under the authority of the CEO, and was not submitted to or approved by the Wayne County Commission. The county filed a counterclaim for a declaratory judgment and injunctive relief. Council 25 alleged that the CEO violated Wayne County ordinances by issuing the wage decrease without Commission approval.

In light of all you've learned in this chapter about the dual capacity of state and local governments, as both sovereign entities and employers, how should the appellate court rule? [See *AFSCME Local 25 v. County of Wayne*, 824 N.W.2d 271 (Mich. App. 2012).]

15. The American Federation of State, County and Municipal Employees, District Council 33, Local 934 ("appellant"), and appellee, the Philadelphia Housing Authority ("PHA"), are parties to a collective bargaining agreement (CBA) governing the wages, hours, and working conditions of PHA's employees. The CBA includes a provision that an employee can be terminated only for just cause. Thomas Mitchell, a warehouseman employed by PHA, was accused of sexually harassing a coworker, Stephanie Broadnax, and was fired following an internal PHA investigation. Thereafter, the appellant filed a grievance on Mitchell's behalf. When the grievance procedures of the CBA were exhausted

without a resolution satisfactory to appellant and Mitchell, the appellant filed a demand for arbitration. Arbitration hearings were conducted on August 27, 2003, and February 17, 2004. The issue before the arbitrator was "whether [PHA] had just cause to terminate [Mitchell's] employment, and, if not, what would be the appropriate remedy." The arbitrator made extensive factual findings.

The arbitrator concluded that Mitchell was not credible, and that Broadnax's testimony regarding Mitchell's inappropriate conduct was credible. The arbitrator specifically found that Mitchell had been adequately informed about PHA's prohibition against sexual harassment, and that his behavior toward Broadnax was "lewd, lascivious and extraordinarily perverse." Although he found that Mitchell's misconduct was "unacceptable," the arbitrator also found that after the "verbal warning" given to Mitchell by his superior, Mitchell engaged in no further inappropriate sexual harassment of Broadnax. The arbitrator then concluded that PHA did not have just cause to terminate Mitchell's employment. PHA was directed to reinstate Mitchell and make him whole.

PHA filed a petition to vacate the arbitrator's award, which the trial court denied. On PHA's further appeal, the Commonwealth Court reversed, holding that PHA's legal obligation to protect its employees constituted a "core function" of the agency that PHA could not bargain away and, therefore, the arbitrator's award requiring Mitchell's reinstatement was not rationally derived from the CBA and could not be enforced.

How should the Pennsylvania Supreme rule on this case? As with Case Problem 14, this case presents the difficult issue of balancing a governmental entity's dual capacity, inherent in its role as a public employer. In this case, the court is also confronted with a public policy against illegal conduct, embodied in both federal and state statutes, as well as in an ordinance of the City of Philadelphia. Does this fact sway your opinion one way or the other, and should it also sway the state's highest court? [See *Philadelphia Housing Authority v. AFSCME*, 52 A.3d 1117 (Pa. Supreme 2012).]

» Hypothetical Scenarios

16. The school teachers and teachers' aides in the Syracuse City School District, in Syracuse, New York, are represented by the Syracuse United Teachers, a union affiliated with the New York State United Teachers. The teachers' union and the Syracuse School District have not had a contract for three years, and negotiations have been at an impasse. The School District has proposed eliminating 75 teacher positions and 200 teachers' aide positions because of declining tax revenues. The teachers' union calls for a one-day strike on the first day of the school year to protest the proposed job cuts. What legal remedies, if any, can the Syracuse School District pursue against the teachers and against the teachers' union? Explain. Would your answers be different if the public school district were located in Vermont rather than in New York? Why?

17. Houseman and Harmon have a contract with the Kentucky State Police to train forensic lab specialists. The state police received a large federal grant as part of the economic stimulus package and decided to use the grant to train more forensic lab specialists for the police crime lab. Rather than solicit bids from companies interested in conducting the training, the state police awarded a no-bid contract to National Forensic Science Center, a Florida company. Houseman and Harmon wrote a letter to the director of the police crime lab criticizing the no-bid contract as overpriced and a waste of taxpayers' money. They also sent a copy of the letter to the local newspaper, which did a story on the no-bid contract. The director of the crime lab then suspended Houseman and Harmon. They claimed that their suspension was in retaliation for their letter about the no-bid contract and was in violation of their First Amendment rights. Was it? Explain.

18. The nonprofessional employees at the federal Government Services Administration Center are represented by the National Federation of Federal Employees Union, Local 144. The depot had provided child-care services for both military and civilian

employees through an on-site day-care center. The staff members at the day-care center were members of Local 144, and many other union members sent their children to the day-care center. In April 2009, the depot's director of personnel sent a letter to all employees informing them that the day-care center would be closed in three months. The union then notified the director that it was requesting negotiations over the decision to close the day-care center. The director responded that the decision was not subject to bargaining under the Federal Service Labor–Management Relations Act. The union then filed an unfair labor practice complaint with the FLRA. Was the refusal to bargain over the closure of the day-care center a violation of the FSLMRA? Explain.

19. The staff auditors and clerks at the Federal Internal Revenue Service Processing Center in Andover, Massachusetts, are represented by the National Treasury Employees Union. During the months of February, March, and April, the employees are required to work 12-hour shifts to process the huge volume of income tax returns. In January 2009, the director of the processing center notifies the employees that as of February 15, they will be required to work double shifts. The union officials plan a "sick-out" to protest—the workers will take turns calling in sick and refuse to work at least one day a week. Does the union's action violate federal law? What, if any, actions can be taken against the union? What, if any, actions can be taken against the employees? Explain.

20. During contract negotiations, the faculty union representing the professors at Springfield State University, a public university located in Springfield, Ohio, presented the school administration with a demand that the teaching load for faculty be limited to no more than three courses per semester. The college administration refused to bargain over the proposal because it involves a matter of inherent management rights. Must the university administration bargain over teaching loads for faculty? Explain your answer.

PART 4

EMPLOYMENT LAW ISSUES

CHAPTER 20

Occupational Safety and Health

Observing that increased responsibilities and anemic staffing have hampered Uncle Sam's ability to protect workers, President Barack Obama pledged in the first months of his presidency to step up federal enforcement of workplace safety. Obama's first budget, released in late February 2009, and passed in substantial part in early April 2009, increased funding to the Occupational Safety and Health Administration (OSHA).

"For the past eight years, the department's labor law enforcement agencies have struggled with growing workloads and shrinking staff," the 134-page budget proposal said. 'The president's budget seeks to reverse this trend, restoring the department's ability to meet its responsibilities to working Americans under the more than 180 worker protection laws it enforces."

The funding increase was aimed at enabling OSHA to "vigorously enforce workplace safety laws and whistleblower protections, and ensure the safety and health of American workers," according to the White House document. (The extra money also was intended to beef up enforcement of wage and hour regulations and to enforce equal opportunity aspects of federal contracting.)

On October 20, 2011, then Secretary of Labor Hilda L. Solis issued the following statement:

"We are encouraged by the reported decline in incidence rates for workplace injuries and illnesses, which is reflective of the joint effort of government, business, unions and other organizations. Nevertheless, 3.1 million injuries and illnesses in the workplace is too high. Serious injuries and illnesses can knock a working family out of the middle class. Workers should not have to sacrifice their health and safety to earn a paycheck.

"We remain concerned that more workers are injured in the health care and social assistance industry sector than in any other, including construction and manufacturing, and this group of workers had one of the highest rates of injuries and illness at 5.2 cases for every 100 workers. The Department of Labor's Occupational Safety and Health Administration will continue to work with employers, workers and unions in this industry to reduce these risks.

"Illness and injury rates for public sector workers also continue to be alarmingly high at 5.7 cases for every 100 workers, which is more than 60 percent higher than the private sector rate. We must continue to work with state and local governments to ensure the safety of our public employees.

"A report like this also highlights the importance of accurate record keeping. Employers must know what injuries and illnesses are occurring in their workplaces in order to identify and correct systemic issues that put their workers at risk. We are concerned with poor record-keeping practices and programs that discourage workers from reporting injuries and illnesses. That's why OSHA is working hard to ensure the completeness and accuracy of these data, which are compiled by the nation's employers.

"As our economy continues to rebound and grow, we must ensure that safety and health are a part of that growth. Let's all remember that no job is a good job unless it is also a safe job."[1]

Twenty-four states have accepted Congress's invitation to enact their own workplace safety programs, leaving it to the federal agency to try to oversee safety in the remaining 26, plus the American territories—notably Puerto Rico, the Virgin Islands, and Guam. Federal funding assistance for the state-run OSHA programs dramatically trails inflation, rising only about 1 percent in the aggregate since 2001.

THE **WORKING** LAW

Occupational Safety and Health Administration (OSHA) Enforcement

The Occupational Safety and Health Administration's (OSHA) mission is to promote and to assure workplace safety and health, and to reduce workplace fatalities, injuries and illnesses. With over four decades of working to ensure safe and healthy workplaces, OSHA has continually served a vital role in assuring safe and healthful working conditions for men and women. Since the passage of the OSH Act of 1970, workplace deaths have fallen nearly 65 percent and occupational injury and illness rates have dropped 67 percent. OSHA continues to respond to new challenges from emerging industries, new technologies, and an ever-changing workforce by utilizing strategic mechanisms such as Site Specific Targeting (SST), National Emphasis Programs (NEPs), the Severe Violator Enforcement Program, and Corporate Settlement Agreements.

OSHA Inspection Activity

In FY 2013 OSHA conducted 39,228 total inspections. This number includes 185 significant and egregious (instance-by-instance) enforcement actions. In addition, OSHA conducted 22,170 programmed inspections. These inspections indicate that OSHA devoted more resources to proactively target the industries and employers that experienced the greatest number of workplace injuries and illnesses. OSHA also conducted 17,058 unprogrammed inspections, including employee complaints, injuries/fatalities, and referrals. Fatality inspections decreased by 8.2 percent in FY 2013.

---

[1] "Statement from Secretary of Labor Hilda L. Solis on reported decline in workplace injuries and illnesses," OSHA News Release 11-1547-NAT, October 20, 2011, available at https//www.osha.gov/pls/oshaweb/owadisp .show_document?p_table=NEWS_RELEASES&p_id=20883.

OSHA Inspection Statistics	FY 2009	FY 2010	FY 2011	FY 2012	FY 2013
Total Inspections	39,004	40,993	40,614	40,961	39,228
Total Programmed Inspections	24,323	24,773	23,329	23,078	22,170
Total Unprogrammed Inspections	14,681	16,220	17,285	17,883	17,058
Fatality Investigations	836	830	851	900	826
Complaints	6,661	8,027	8,765	9,573	9,505
Referrals	4,375	4,634	4,776	4,864	4,024
Other Unprogrammed Insps*	2,809	2,729	2,893	2,546	2,703

* Other Unprogrammed Inspections include: Fatality/Catastrophe, Monitoring, Follow-Up, Unprogrammed Related, and Unprogrammed Other Inspections.

Note: FY 2011 includes OSHA Information System (OIS) data and OSHA's Integrated Management Information System (IMIS) data, which is of limited comparability to previous years that only include IMIS data.

OSHA Violation Statistics	FY 2009	FY 2010	FY 2011	FY 2012	FY 2013
Total Violations	87,663	96,742	85,514	78,723	78,196
Total Serious Violations	67,668	74,885	62,115	57,112	58,316
Total Willful Violations	401	1,519*	594	423	319
Total Repeat Violations	2,762	2,758	3,229	3,034	3,139
Total Other-than-Serious	16,615	17,244	19,306	18,054	16,290

* It should be noted that the significant increase in willful violations in FY 2010 is due to a number of significant enforcement actions in the refinery industry, including an action against British Petroleum North America, which has been subsequently settled.

Referrals or Significant Aid to Prosecutors Addressing OSHA-Related Matters

	2010	2011	2012	2013
Criminal Referrals	14	10	13	3

OSHA continues to make referrals or provide significant aid to prosecutors addressing OSHA-related matters. These actions include referrals under Title 29 of the United States Code, Section 666(e), for employee deaths caused by willful conduct violating an OSHA standard, obstruction of justice, aiding state and local investigations, and prosecutions on safety and health related matters. Fraud related matters, such as training card fraud, are also included. A criminal referral is made by the DOL Office of the Solicitor to the Department of Justice.

Source: "Occupational Safety and Health Administration (OSHA) enforcement," United States Department of Labor, available at https://www.osha.gov/dep/2013_enforcement_summary.html.

20-1   Policy and Processes of the Occupational Safety and Health Act

The Occupational Safety and Health Act (OSH Act) was enacted by Congress in 1970. The statute has two broad goals:

- To ensure safe and healthful working conditions for working men and women

- To provide a framework for research, education, training, and information in the field of occupational safety and health

The act requires employers to furnish their employees a workplace that is free from recognized hazards that cause, or are likely to cause, serious injury or death. A recognized hazard is one that is known to be hazardous, taking into account the standard of knowledge of the industry.

The act also requires that employers meet the various health and safety standards set under the act and keep records of injuries, deaths, accidents, illnesses, and particular hazards.

The Occupational Safety and Health Act applies to all employees who work for an employer that is engaged in a business affecting interstate commerce. This broad coverage reaches almost all employers and employees in the United States and its territories, with some exceptions. The act does not apply to the federal and state governments in their capacity as employers, nor does it apply to domestic servants or self-employed persons.

The act contains no specific industry-wide exemptions. However, if other federal agencies exercise statutory authority to prescribe or enforce standards or regulations affecting occupational safety or health, the Occupational Safety and Health Act does not apply. For this exemption to operate, it must be shown that the working conditions of the affected employees are covered by another federal statute that has the protection of employees as one of its purposes. The other agency must also have exercised its jurisdiction to make regulations or standards applying to specific working conditions that would otherwise be covered by the act. An example of such a situation involves the workers on offshore oil platforms. Their working conditions were governed by health and safety regulations enacted and enforced by both the U.S. Coast Guard and the U.S. Geological Survey. In *Marshall v. Nichols*,[2] the court held that the Occupational Safety and Health Administration was precluded from exerting its jurisdiction over offshore oil platforms because of the coverage by the Coast Guard and the Geological Survey.

20-1a   Administration and Enforcement

The Occupational Safety and Health Act created three federal agencies for administration and enforcement. The Occupational Safety and Health Administration (OSHA) is the primary agency created for enforcement of the act. An independent agency within the Department of Labor, it has the authority to:

- promulgate standards;

- conduct inspections of workplaces;

- issue citations for violations; and

- recommend penalties.

---

[2] 486 F. Supp. 615 (E.D. Texas 1980).

OSHA acts on behalf of the Secretary of Labor.

The National Institute of Occupational Safety and Health (NIOSH) is an agency created to conduct research and promote the application of the research results to ensure that no worker will suffer diminished health, reduced functional capacity, or decreased life expectancy as a result of his or her work experience.

The Occupational Safety and Health Review Commission (OSHRC) is a quasi-judicial agency created to adjudicate contested enforcement actions of OSHA. Whereas OSHA may issue citations and recommend penalties for violations of the act, only OSHRC can actually assess and enforce the penalties. The decisions of OSHRC can be appealed to the U.S. courts of appeals. OSHRC has three members appointed by the president for overlapping six-year terms and a number of administrative law judges who have career tenure.

Standards, Feasibility, and Variances

To reach the goal of providing hazard-free workplaces for all employees, the act provides for the setting of standards regulating the health and safety of working conditions. The Secretary of Labor is granted authority under the act to promulgate occupational safety and health standards through OSHA. The act provides for the issuance of three kinds of standards: interim standards, permanent standards, and emergency standards.

- *Interim standards* are those that the Secretary of Labor had power to issue for the first two years following the effective date of the act. These standards were generally modeled on various preexisting industry consensus standards. The Secretary, in adopting previously accepted national consensus standards, was not required to hold public hearings or any other formal proceedings.

- *Permanent standards* are both newly created standards and revised interim standards. These standards are developed by OSHA and NIOSH and are frequently based on suggestions made by interested parties, such as employers, employees, states and other political subdivisions, and labor unions. The Secretary of Labor is also empowered to appoint an advisory committee to assist in the promulgation of permanent standards. This committee has 90 days from its date of appointment, unless a longer or shorter period is prescribed by the Secretary, to make its recommendations regarding a proposed rule.

After OSHA has developed a proposed rule that promulgates, modifies, or revokes an occupational safety or health standard, the Secretary must publish a notice in the *Federal Register*. Included in this notice must be a statement of the reasons for adopting a new standard, changing an existing standard, or revoking a prior standard. Interested parties are then allowed 30 days after publication to submit written data, objections, or comments relating to the proposed standards. If the interested party files written objections and requests a public hearing concerning these objections, the Secretary must publish a notice in the *Federal Register* specifying the time and place of the hearing and the standard to which the objection has been filed.

Within 60 days after the expiration of the period for comment or after the completion of any hearing, the Secretary must issue a rule promulgating, modifying, or revoking the standard or make a determination that the rule should not be issued. If adopted, the rule must state its effective date. This date must ensure a sufficient period for affected employers and employees to be informed of the existence of the standard and of its terms.

• The Secretary of Labor may, under special circumstances, avoid the procedures just described by issuing temporary *emergency standards.* These standards are issued when the Secretary believes that employees are exposed to grave dangers from substances or agents determined to be toxic or physically harmful. Actual injury does not have to occur before a temporary emergency standard can be promulgated, although there must be a genuinely serious emergency.

Emergency standards take effect immediately upon publication in the *Federal Register.* After publication, the Secretary must then follow the procedure for formally adopting a permanent standard to make the emergency standard into a permanent standard. That new permanent standard must be issued within six months after its publication as an emergency standard.

Appeals of Standards   After a standard has been promulgated by the Secretary, any person adversely affected by it can file a challenge to the validity of the standard. Such challenges must be filed with the appropriate federal court of appeals before the 60th day after the issuance of the standard.

Upon reviewing the standard, the court of appeals will uphold the standard if it is supported by substantial evidence. The Secretary must demonstrate that the standard was in response to a significant risk of material health impairment.

Feasibility   The act grants the Secretary authority to issue standards dealing with toxic materials or harmful physical agents. A standard must be one that most adequately ensures, to the extent feasible and on the basis of the best available evidence, that no employee will suffer material impairment of health or functional capacity, even if the employee has regular exposure to the hazard. The feasibility of a standard must be examined from two perspectives: technological feasibility and economic feasibility. Further, OSHA can force an industry to develop and diffuse new technology to satisfy precise permissible exposure limits to toxic materials or harmful physical agents that have never before been attained, if OSHA can present substantial evidence showing that companies acting vigorously and in good faith can develop the technology. The standard also must satisfy the requirement of economic feasibility.

Burden of Proof   The Secretary must carry the burden of proving both technological and economic feasibility when promulgating and enforcing standards governing toxic materials and harmful physical agents. However, the Secretary does not have to establish that the cost of a standard bears a reasonable relationship to its benefits, as established in the case of *American Textile Mfr.'s Inst. v. Donovan.*[3]

In general, the Secretary bears the burden of proving by "substantial evidence on the record considered as a whole" that the cited employer violated the act. The prima facie case which the Secretary must prove to make an OSHA citation "stick" is well illustrated in the following case.

---

[3] 452 U.S. 490 (1981).

CASE 20.1

CHAO V. GUNITE CORP.

442 Fed.3d 550 (7th Cir. 2006)

After issuing a number of citations against Gunite Corporation for violations of occupational safety and health regulations, the Secretary of Labor failed to convince the Occupational Safety and Health Review Commission to uphold four of the charges. The Secretary has petitioned this court to reverse the Commission's decision. We conclude that the Secretary is correct: the Commission's decision is not supported by substantial evidence in the record and therefore the case must be remanded to the agency with instructions to affirm the citations.

I

Gunite's foundry in Rockford makes brakes and wheels for heavy trucks. Its process involves melting scrap iron and then pouring the molten iron into molds created from a mixture of sand, clay, and water. The molds then pass along a series of interconnecting conveyor belts that transport and cool the iron pieces. As they move along the conveyer belts, the castings are shaken from the molds; in the process, dust containing respirable silica becomes airborne. The amount of this dust is enormous; the process uses some 400 tons of sand per hour. Breathing silica is dangerous for the foundry's workers, as it can lead to silicosis, a deadly disease that primarily affects the lungs. The Occupational Safety and Health Administration (OSHA) has accordingly set ceilings called permissible exposure limits, or PELs, on the amount of silica that may be present in the air.

Gunite's foundry was built in the first half of the twentieth century. From the start, it has been plagued with the problem of controlling the amount of silica dust escaping into the air. In 1977 and again in 1981, OSHA cited Gunite for violations of the silica PEL. That problem has intensified since the installation of the conveyer belt system in 1989. The plant manager described the initial installation of the conveyor belts as "a disaster." In order to control the airborne dust, the plant first tried spraying water to keep the dust down. When that failed to make a difference, Gunite installed covers over the conveyer belts. They too were ineffective, even though they were still being used several years later when OSHA entered the picture. In 1990, one of Gunite's insurers reported that employee exposure to silica exceeded a different measure, the "threshold limit value" set by the American Conference of Governmental Industrial Hygienists. Two upgrades later, Gunite still had

too much silica in the air. Another insurer measured the air four times between June 1996 and March 1998 and found that foundry employees—including those at the positions listed in the citations at issue before us—were being exposed to levels of respirable silica in excess of OSHA's PEL. That insurer, Kemper-NATLSCO, recommended in 1996 that Gunite require its employees to wear individual respirators until the company could implement feasible engineering and administrative controls to limit employee exposure. Gunite seems to have ignored that recommendation; two reports from Kemper-NATLSCO in 1997 indicated that employees still were not being required to wear the individual respiratory protection. In 1996 and 1997, Gunite recorded three cases of silicosis in its OSHA logs. Gunite itself describes its efforts to deal with excess silica from 1991 through 1998 as involving four major engineering projects that together were intended to bring the foundry into compliance with the silica PEL and other federal regulations. The last of these, installation of new covers and a ventilation system over the conveyor belts, was planned and being implemented in 1998 during the OSHA inspection, though it did not become fully functional until March 1999.

Since 1971, OSHA regulations have required facilities with excess respirable silica to use engineering or administrative controls "whenever feasible" to attain compliance with the PEL. Only when feasible engineering or administrative controls are insufficient to bring silica levels below the PEL may a company turn to individualized protective equipment to supplement those controls. This "hierarchy of controls" privileges engineering and administrative controls because they "make respiratory protection automatic, while respirators are dependent on use and constant attention and are subject to human error."

The OSHA inspection leading to the citations involved in the Secretary's petition took place between May and October of 1998. During the inspection, OSHA representatives took samples that showed that workers in four positions at the foundry were exposed to about 1.6 times the PEL for respirable silica in an eight-hour shift. OSHA assigned three members of its Health Response Team (HRT) to Gunite's case and asked them to evaluate Gunite's administrative and engineering controls. The HRT came up with a list of proposed administrative and engineering controls that it concluded would alleviate the airborne silica problem. The team based its recommendations for engineering controls "on general principles of ventilation and industrial hygiene which have been shown to be effective in reducing contaminant levels in a variety of industries." One control measure highlighted in the report was the use of "clean air islands," which are devices that blow clean air at the at-risk employees; the fresh air creates a bubble around each employee that does not contain dangerous levels of silica. Other measures on the list included installing physical barriers to block the areas where the most dust was kicked up into the air and improving housekeeping and maintenance. Finally, the report mentioned the new system of covers for the conveyor belts that Gunite was in the process of implementing during the OSHA inspection, although it opined that the new system would solve the problem for only three of the four employee positions that were overexposed to silica.

Based on its investigation of the foundry, the Secretary issued three citations containing various items, each alleging violations of federal regulations. Among those were six items based on the sampling results and the HRT's report alleging that Gunite had committed serious and willful violations of 29 C.F.R. § 1910.1000(c) (the air contaminant regulation) by exposing employees to respirable silica in amounts in excess of OSHA's PEL and of 29 C.F.R. § 1910.1000(e) by failing to implement feasible engineering or administrative controls. Another item alleged a violation of 29 C.F.R. § 1910.134(e)(4) (1997) by failing to inspect to ensure proper respirator use. The Secretary also alleged a willful violation of 29 C.F.R. § 1910.95(g)(6) for failure to obtain annual audiograms. Of these charges, only four are at issue in this petition: items 8a and 8b of citation 1, which charge serious violations of § 1910.1000(c) and(e) for overexposing three "mold station" workers (a metal pourer, coreset/blowoff operator, and mold line technician) to respirable silica and for failing to determine and implement feasible administrative or engineering controls to achieve compliance with the PEL; and items 3a and 3b of citation 2, which charged willful violations of the same standards for overexposing a sprue pulloff operator, who works at a different location in the factory closer to the finishing process.

Gunite appealed the citations, contending before the administrative law judge (ALJ) that it should not be liable because it was already implementing a new system designed to alleviate the respirable silica problem and because of the availability of individual respirators, which it contended both alleviated overexposures and qualified as an administrative control. In the pre-hearing documents made part of the record by the ALJ, the Secretary designated two members of the HRT team—industrial hygienist Keith Motley and mechanical engineer Lee Hathon—as experts. They were expected to testify about their qualifications, their observations of Gunite's foundry, and "administrative and engineering controls to reduce respirable silica" for the locations identified as having overexposures, as well as the contents of the HRT report. Motley's expertise included 12 years of experience as part of the HRT responsible for addressing respirable hazards, while Hathon had served 10 years on the HRT and had participated in investigations "at several foundries and other industries where airborne silica is a hazard." Gunite objected to both Motley's and Hathon's testimony about actual silica levels as "not probative of exposures of the cited employees to the cited levels of respirable silica dust." Nevertheless, Gunite did "not deny that [Motley's and Hathon's] opinions are probative relative to the question of engineering controls for some of the cited work areas," although the company reserved the right to disagree substantively with their opinions "in some respects." At the hearing, the parties stipulated to the admission of the HRT report and agreed that the Secretary would not call the HRT members for direct examination, leaving their testimony in the form of the report itself and other pre-hearing filings made part of the administrative record. The Secretary, however, planned to and did present them for cross-examination.

Both Motley and Hathon were cross-examined about their qualifications, about their preparation of the HRT report, and about the recommended engineering controls. Motley testified about his tour of the plant, during which he was able to observe first hand the problem areas and ventilation systems. When he asked to see the plans for the new ventilation system, he was shown the actual parts that Gunite was putting in place. Motley also described the team's particular recommended solutions to the airborne silica problem, including a way generally to filter the plant's air before recirculating it. He explained how clean air islands work and how they might alleviate the problems. Hathon's testimony was similar. After answering questions about his own training and credentials, Hathon testified that he had previously examined at least seven foundries similar to Gunite's in terms of size, age of the building, and products produced; that he had toured the areas of Gunite's foundry with overexposures; and that the HRT report was designed specifically to address the problems of the Gunite foundry.

Another witness, Julia Evans, an OSHA compliance officer, testified that an administrative control such as employee rotation likely would have eliminated the overexposure. Evans also testified that Gunite's planned improvements likely would solve the silica problem at three of the four employee stations.

Finally, Gunite's own witness, Leroy Cator, the 50-year veteran employee in charge of the abatement process, testified that "[c]lean air islands are probably effective and I don't question that." However, he also said that they are difficult to implement because of temperature control issues, and that they had not been recommended by the outside engineers working with Gunite. Instead, those engineers recommended systemic approaches that would improve the air for many employees rather than individualized approaches. He admitted, however, that clean air technology was used elsewhere in the foundry, near the pouring line.

The ALJ affirmed the four citations (as well as the others not at issue here), finding that "except for clean air islands, Gunite has not challenged [the HRT's] recommendations." The ALJ also found that Gunite's future plans to solve the problem did not relieve the company of liability. Likewise, the use of respirators did not alleviate Gunite's obligation to implement systemic administrative or engineering controls that would make individual respirators unnecessary.

Gunite appealed the ALJ's determination to the Commission, which by a divided vote affirmed some of the citations, but vacated the four now before us. The majority found that the Secretary had failed to prove that the proposed engineering and administrative controls would produce a "significant reduction" in respirable silica:

The Secretary's case for establishing technological feasibility rests primarily on OSHA's HRT report and supporting testimony by compliance officer Evans and HRT members Lee Hathon and Keith Motley. Neither compliance officer Evans nor the HRT members were qualified as experts. The HRT report identified deficiencies in Gunite's controls and recommended additional controls, including general ventilation to reduce plantwide levels of air contaminant and specific controls to address areas where sampling results showed employee exposure in excess of the PEL....

We conclude that the evidence of record as a whole is insufficient to prove that the controls suggested by the Secretary would produce a significant reduction in airborne respirable silica in the foundry. Because neither compliance officer Evans nor any of the HRT members were presented by the Secretary as expert witnesses, the record lacks sufficient evidence to establish that the proposed controls were technologically feasible. Moreover, the testimony failed to quantify the expected or anticipated amount of silica dust reduction. At most, the HRT report provided a list of control technologies for Gunite to experiment with in the hope that some of them or some combination of them would reduce employee

exposure to some undefined levels. The Commission then found that because the Secretary had failed to show a technologically feasible engineering control, the use of respirators by employees was sufficient. (Somewhat inexplicably, the Commission found that the evidence of the respirator use on the day the air was tested was sufficient to vacate those items, even though elsewhere it affirmed a separate item by finding that "Gunite's lax enforcement of respirator use in the foundry constituted willfulness.")

The dissenting commissioner found that the HRT report was "comprehensive" and that it recommended a number of feasible administrative and engineering controls. She also concluded that the witnesses' credentials made their testimony "sufficiently reliable" and that Gunite had failed to challenge the witnesses' expertise. Furthermore, she wrote, "[T]he fact that the Secretary did not present the HRT members as experts does not diminish the probative value of their testimony.... To the extent that the majority would find dispositive the lack of 'expert' testimony from the Secretary in order to meet her burden, and since this issue has not been previously briefed, I would remand."

II

This court has jurisdiction under 29 U.S.C. § 660(b) to review on the Secretary's petition "any final order" of the Commission. The Commission's "function is to act as a neutral arbiter." Where the Commission reverses an ALJ, it is the Commission's order alone that is reviewed. In reviewing the Commission's conclusions in enforcement actions, we follow the dictates of the Administrative Procedure Act, 5 U.S.C. § 701 *et seq.*, and review interpretations of law with deference to determine only whether they are "arbitrary or capricious" or contrary to law. Where, however, a dispute exists between the Secretary and the Commission about an interpretation of OSHA or regulations adopted under its umbrella, the Secretary's interpretation is entitled to deference if it "sensibly conforms to the wording and purpose" of the relevant provisions. In reviewing the facts, we uphold the Commission if its findings are "supported by substantial evidence on the record considered as a whole." Our deference to the Commission includes deference to its credibility determinations, except in extraordinary circumstances.

The Secretary bears the burden of proof in demonstrating the feasibility of administrative and engineering controls "when the compliance remedy is based upon a very general statutory or regulatory command that does not describe for the employer any specific methods for compliance." As the Commission itself has noted, however, "[t]he test of whether administrative and/or engineering controls are technologically feasible is whether the controls are 'achievable' and capable of producing a significant reduction in exposure to air contaminants." Although a significant reduction is required, it is not necessary to show that the control would achieve full compliance. "The Secretary need not propose or prove the feasibility of a detailed abatement program. [She] need only show that some controls are feasible in an employer's plant." There is no magic percentage of reduction that is required; all that is required is that the administrative or engineering control be systemic—so that, unlike with respirators, an individual employee's mistake cannot eviscerate her protection—and that it produce a significant reduction in silica.

In this case, the Commission found that the Secretary failed to carry her burden on feasibility, but it is hard to discern why it came to this conclusion. On one reading of the opinion, it seems that the Commission might be saying that the Secretary failed either to present any evidence of feasibility or that she failed to present necessary expert evidence of feasibility, and thus failed to meet her burden of proof. This, at least, is the way one might understand the portions of the Commission's opinion stating that "neither compliance officer Evans nor any of the HRT members were presented by the Secretary as expert witnesses...." and "the Secretary offered no expert testimony in attempting to meet her burden of proof." In the alternative, the opinion might be interpreted as finding that the Secretary's witnesses lacked expertise, as where the Commission writes that "[n]either compliance officer Evans nor the HRT members were qualified as experts." Or the Commission might have been faulting the Secretary for failing to jump through some procedural hoops in presenting her evidence or designating her experts.

Our problem with the Commission's opinion is twofold. First, it did not adequately explain why it concluded that the Secretary failed to satisfy her burden. It is neither proper nor feasible for us to fill in the blanks with our own guesses. Second, even if we somehow succeeded in constructing a rationale for the Commission's result, we conclude that its factual conclusions are contrary to the "substantial evidence on the record considered as a whole." Finally, nothing in the record hints at any purely procedural failing in the Secretary's handling of the case. The Commission generally follows the Federal Rules of Civil Procedure, 29 C.F.R. § 2200.2(b), but it does so in a manner designed to "secure an expeditious, just and inexpensive determination of every case." It is the role of the ALJ, among other things, to "[r]ule upon offers of proof and receive relevant evidence" and "introduce into the record documentary or other evidence"; the judge may also ask the parties to state their positions on issues. Witnesses generally

must testify under oath or affirmation and must be subject to cross-examination, 29 C.F.R. § 2200.69, and the Federal Rules of Evidence govern the proceedings. Gunite has not pointed to any particular problem under those rules, and so we conclude that the Commission could not have rejected the ALJ's opinion on this ground.

The other three possibilities all, in one way or the other, attack the sufficiency of the evidence the Secretary presented to support the citations. In applying the substantial evidence rule, our point of reference is the Commission's opinion. As we have said before, "[w]e cannot uphold a decision by an administrative agency … if … the reasons given by the trier of fact do not build an accurate and logical bridge between the evidence and the result."

If we interpret the Commission's decision as holding that the Secretary utterly failed to present any evidence of feasibility that could satisfy her burden of proof, we can easily reject that conclusion as contrary to the record as a whole. This would be obvious if the Secretary had presented Hathon and Motley as witnesses on direct, but the method of proceeding to which all parties agreed does not change the result. The parties stipulated that the HRT report would be admitted into evidence, and it was. Then, as agreed, the Secretary presented both Motley and Hathon for cross-examination. Their testimony on cross covered much of the same material that a direct examination normally would have covered; their credentials, their inspection of the foundry, and the basis for their report and conclusions. Furthermore, the ALJ specifically made part of the record the pre-trial pleadings, which also covered much of the same ground. Even the Commission acknowledged that "Gunite challenged only the feasibility of clean air islands" and not the many other recommended controls, which included basic housekeeping, employee hygiene, and employee rotation. Indeed, the parties agreed that the already planned—but not implemented—improvements would significantly decrease the silica exposure for the molding line employees. In the absence of any rebuttal or specific evidence about nonfeasibility from Gunite, the Secretary's evidence is more than sufficient to carry her burden. In administrative litigation as elsewhere, if both sides agree on a matter, such as the fact that the planned changes would significantly decrease the level of silica in the foundry's atmosphere, there is no requirement that evidence be introduced to support that fact or conclusion. A contrary rule would bog down the administrative process with unnecessary evidence on uncontested facts. The feasibility inquiry is governed by "realism and common sense." While the Commission majority tried to distinguish *Sherwin-Williams* and

Castle & Cooke Foods by suggesting that expert testimony may be unnecessary only where the feasibility challenged is economic (as it was in those cases) rather than technological (as in Gunite's case), we see no principled distinction between the two issues. "Realism and common sense" are equally applicable in both realms.

If we think instead that the Commission took the position that Hathon and Motley were not experts, lacked expertise, or were somehow not properly designated as experts, that interpretation likewise collapses in the face of the record. We have said that a court excluding expert testimony must "articulate with reasonable specificity the reasons why it believes the testimony is insufficiently reliable to qualify for admission," because otherwise the lack of such explication makes it difficult (or impossible) for us meaningfully to review the court's decision. Here, the Commission's opinion suggests less an evaluation of the witnesses' testimony and more "an utter disregard for uncontroverted sworn testimony" and other evidence presented by the Secretary. Especially in administrative adjudication, there is no magical set of procedures for designating someone as an expert witness. As we observed in *United States v. Williams*, 81 F.3d 1434, 1442 (7th Cir. 1996), the "difference between an expert witness and an ordinary witness is that the former is allowed to offer an opinion, while the latter is confined to testifying from personal knowledge." The test is whether the witness has "specialized knowledge that the lay person cannot be expected to possess" and reasonably applies that knowledge to the relevant facts. In this case, both the Secretary and Gunite recognized Hathon's and Motley's expertise, as Gunite admitted that their testimony would be probative on the issue of feasible engineering controls.

Gunite's argument on appeal is primarily limited to a reminder that the court should defer to the Commission's decision when that decision is supported by substantial evidence, but its brief is remarkably short on specific evidence that might have supported this particular ruling. If the Commission had made a reasoned decision supported by substantial evidence in the record, we would defer to that decision, even if we ourselves might have preferred another outcome. Such deference extends to credibility determinations about witnesses, including expert witnesses. Nonetheless, deference has its limits. In order for us to uphold an administrative commission's decision, there must be "an accurate and logical bridge between the evidence and the result." That same bridge is necessary between the evidence in the record and the credibility determination about expert testimony. The Commission's opinion in this case does not meet those standards. No matter how we look at it, the opinion is not supported by substantial evidence.

***

For these reasons, we REVERSE the Commission's decision and REMAND the case with instructions to affirm the four contested citations.

Case Questions

1. Why should the Secretary of Labor bear the burden of proof in demonstrating the feasibility of administrative and engineering controls? Wouldn't a safer workplace result from holding employers strictly liable for conditions that do not comply with OSHA regulations?

2. Why do you think the Commission found that the Secretary failed to carry her burden of proof on the feasibility of administrative and engineering controls? Do you agree with their findings?

3. Should courts second guess OSHA's experts when it comes to determining whether unsafe conditions exist in a workplace? Or in determining the appropriate burden of proof to place on the Secretary of Labor, should judges defer to the agency's judgment in these matters? Why did the court not accord the Commission such deference in this decision?

Variances If an employer, or a class of employers, believes that the OSHA standard is inappropriate to its particular situation, an exemption, or variance, may be sought. This variance may be temporary or permanent.

- A *temporary variance* may be granted when the employer is unable to comply with a standard by its effective date because of the unavailability of professional or technological personnel or of materials or equipment necessary to come into compliance with the standard. The employer must show that all possible actions have been taken to protect employees and that all actions necessary for compliance are being undertaken. A temporary variance can be granted only after the affected employees have been given notice of the request and an opportunity for a hearing. Temporary variances can be granted for a one-year period and may then be renewed for two six-month periods.

- *Permanent variances* are granted when the employer establishes by a preponderance of the evidence that its particular procedures provide as safe and healthful a workplace as the OSHA standard would provide. The affected employees must be informed of the request for the permanent variance and may request a hearing. If the variance is granted, either the employees or OSHA may petition to modify or revoke the variance.

The Secretary of Labor also has authority to issue experimental variances involving new or improved techniques to safeguard worker safety or health.

Concept *Summary* 20.1

OSHA's ORGANIZATIONAL STRUCTURE AND STANDARDS

- Administration and enforcement:
  - ◦ Occupational Health and Safety Administration: Enforcement
  - ◦ National Institute of Occupational Safety and Health: Research
  - ◦ Occupational Safety and Health Review Commission: Adjudication
- Standards of enforcement:
  - ◦ Standards: Interim, permanent, emergency
  - ◦ Standards may be challenged in federal court
  - ◦ The Secretary of Labor has the burden of proving a standard's feasibility
  - ◦ Variances may be allowed to employers under appropriate circumstances

20-1b Employee Rights

In addition to being granted the right to a workplace free from recognized hazards, employees under the Occupational Safety and Health Act are protected from retaliation or discrimination by their employer because they have exercised any rights granted by the act. Section 11(c)(1) of the act provides that:

> No person shall discharge or in any manner discriminate against any employee because such employee has filed any complaint or instituted or caused to be instituted any proceeding under or related to this Act or has testified or is about to testify in any such proceeding or because of the exercise by such employee on behalf of himself or others of any right afforded by this Act.

In March 2015, the U.S. Department of Labor issued a Final Rule allowing employees to submit oral complaints of retaliation, in addition to the existing ability to submit written complaints. Employees who believe that they have been subject to retaliation for exercising their rights under OSHA must file a written or oral complaint with OSHA within 180 days of learning of the alleged retaliation. Upon receiving the complaint, OSHA begins an investigation into it; the employee making the complaint must make a *prima facie* showing that: (1) the employee had engaged in an activity protected under OSHA; (2) the employer knew or suspected that the employee had engaged in protected activity; (3) the employee suffered an adverse employment action; and (4) the circumstances of the adverse employment action were sufficient to raise the inference that the protected activity was a contributing factor in the adverse action.[4] If the employee makes such a showing, the employer then has the burden to demonstrate, by clear and convincing evidence, that is would have taken the same adverse action in the absence of the employee's protected activity. OSHA is required to issue written findings as to whether there is reasonable cause to believe that the employer has retaliated against the employee within 60 days of the filing of the complaint. If OSHA finds reasonable cause, it must issue a preliminary order that includes all relief necessary to make the employee whole, including reinstatement. A preliminary order requiring reinstatement is effective immediately, and the reinstatement stands during the administrative appeals process. Once a preliminary order is issued, the parties to the complaint have 30 days to request a hearing before an administrative law judge (ALJ). Once the ALJ has issued a decision, the parties have 14 days to file objections with the Administrative Review Board (ARB), which then has 30 days to decide whether to grant a review. If the ARB grants a review, its decision becomes the final order, and the parties then have 60 days to seek judicial review of that order in a U.S. Court of Appeals. If no final decision has been issued after 180 days from the date the complaint was filed with OSHA, the employee may then file suit in the appropriate federal district court.

In addition to protecting employees against retaliation, OSHA also gives employees the right to refuse to work in the face of a dangerous condition. Pursuant to Section 11(c)(1), the Secretary of Labor has adopted a regulation that protects employees from discrimination because they refuse to work in the face of a dangerous condition. The right to refuse can be exercised when employees are exposed to a dangerous condition posing the risk of serious injury or death and when there is insufficient time, due to the nature of the hazard, to resort to the regular statutory procedures for enforcement. When possible, the employees should attempt to have the employer correct the hazardous condition before exercising their right to refuse. The dangerous condition triggering the employees' refusal must be of such a nature that a reasonable person, under the circumstances facing the employees, would conclude that there is a real danger of death or serious injury. As the following case illustrates, a worker who refuses to perform her duties does so at her own risk, and the refusal to work may or may not be found reasonable by the courts.

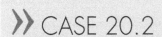

≫ CASE 20.2

HERBERT V. ALTIMETER, INC.
230 Or. App. 715, 218 P.3d 542 (2009)

Facts: The defendant is a trucking company based in Eugene. The defendant hired the plaintiff as a long-haul truck driver in January 2006. Truck drivers are required to undergo a medical history examination and a physical examination to receive Department of Transportation certification. The plaintiff was certified as physically fit to

---

[4] 29 C.F.R. § 1980.104(e)(2).

drive commercial vehicles at the time that she was hired by defendant. The defendant assigned her to truck number 4003.

In the first week of operating her assigned truck, the plaintiff reported to Tony Note, one of defendant's vice-presidents, that there was a noticeable smell of exhaust and oil in the cab. A number of repairs followed within the next few weeks: a flex-pipe and band clamps were replaced; a "blow by tube" was replaced (by the plaintiff herself) to address the oil smell in the cab; two head gaskets were replaced because the gaskets were leaking either internally or externally; another new flex-pipe was installed to address an exhaust leak; and an air hose and a turbo clamp were replaced to address exhaust and oil leaks. Approximately two months later, on April 13, another oil leak was recorded on the truck's maintenance log.

On April 19, the plaintiff was on the road waiting to make a delivery in Arizona the next morning. The plaintiff had been idling her truck's engine all day in order to run the air conditioner due to the extremely hot weather. She testified that the smell of exhaust in the truck was overwhelming and seemed to be causing her dog to be very lethargic. She was concerned about her health, so, in the evening, she turned off the truck to stop the exhaust smell from coming into the cab. Later, when she tried to restart the motor (in order to cool off), the starter locked up, and it was necessary for service to be called in to restart it. The service provider told the plaintiff that the starter was beginning to fail and that it probably was not a good idea to turn off the engine. The plaintiff called Tony to inform him of the problem. He advised her not to turn the motor off and to make her delivery the following morning.

The following morning, the plaintiff made her Arizona delivery and picked up a new load for delivery in Nevada. Once there, as directed, she went to a truck service center to have the starter checked. While waiting at the service center, the plaintiff again kept the engine running, both to keep the cab cool and because she was worried that they might not get to it and was concerned about "whether the starter would start or not." Earlier that day, the plaintiff had called Mike Note, the vice-president of operations, and reported that she was not feeling well—that she was nauseated, light-headed, and fatigued. When she learned from the truck service center that it would not be possible to have the truck serviced until after midnight, the plaintiff called Tony and told him that she was not feeling well and did not feel that she could stay up all night waiting. Tony agreed that she could turn the engine off for the night and sleep.

The next morning the truck started and the plaintiff delivered her load in Nevada. She spoke with Mike that morning and told him that she still was not feeling well. She testified that she felt very ill that day and that she was "gravely concerned" about her health because she was not feeling well, her dog was very lethargic, and she had been breathing the exhaust in the truck for "almost a week straight" at that point.

On April 22, the plaintiff returned to Eugene. She reported the exhaust leak to Tony and turned in a repair request. Tony sent the truck to the repair shop. Although the repair personnel found no indication of problems with the starter or exhaust, Tony advised them to replace the starter and the exhaust band clamps.

On the same day, on her doctor's advice, the plaintiff had a blood test for carbon monoxide exposure. On April 24, the plaintiff's doctor gave her a copy of the test result, which revealed a 9.6 percent level of carboxyhemoglobin. He also gave her a note indicating that her level of carboxyhemoglobin was "consistent with excess exhaust fume exposure = markedly elevated!" Because 48 hours had passed since the blood draw, and the plaintiff had not been back in her truck, her doctor ordered a second blood test for comparison.

After seeing her doctor, the plaintiff took the result of the first test and the doctor's note to Mike and told him that she was concerned about her exposure to carbon monoxide. Mike told her that she might be able to drive truck number 4010, assigned to Tony, to complete a delivery to Portland. He also told her that, if she liked that truck, he would not object if she wanted to keep it. Later that day, Tony called the plaintiff and asked her what was going on. According to the plaintiff, she had a "similar conversation" with Tony to the one that she had with Mike. In that conversation, Tony told her that "there had to be some other health issues going on" and that she was a safety risk and should not be driving. He then suspended the plaintiff.

Also on April 24—after the exhaust band clamps on the plaintiff's truck had been replaced—Tony arranged to have the carbon monoxide levels in the cab tested by a Eugene-area diesel mechanic, using a gas monitor borrowed from the Springfield Fire Department. The truck was driven for approximately 20 minutes, and the gas monitor continuously showed no carbon monoxide in the cab of the truck. The mechanic also did not smell any exhaust in the cab.

On April 25, the plaintiff's doctor received the result of the second blood test, which revealed a 7.6 percent level of carboxyhemoglobin in the plaintiff's blood. The plaintiff's doctor considered that to be a significant change and concluded that it was attributable to the fact that she had not been exposed to exhaust in her truck for two days. He wrote her a second note:

"Due to exposure to engine fumes to excess in current truck[,] this patient needs to be in another rig. She has side effects including nausea, burning eyes and throat, weakness, muscle tingling etc."

On April 26, the plaintiff brought the second note to a meeting with Tony. Tony was upset with the plaintiff and told her that he had spent thousands of dollars on her truck, that her truck could not possibly be having exhaust problems, and that she must have some other health issues. The plaintiff asked Tony, "What's the bottom line here? Are you letting me go?" He said, "Yes." The plaintiff asked if there was another truck she could drive, to which he responded, "No." The plaintiff took out the doctor's second note and asked Tony if he wanted to read it, to which he also responded, "No." Tony told the plaintiff that she "shouldn't be driving a truck anymore" and that she was "a risk." Tony also told the plaintiff that a test had been performed and had revealed no carbon monoxide in the truck and that her truck's diesel engine did not emit carbon monoxide. At the end of their conversation, the plaintiff cleared out her truck and turned in her keys.

The plaintiff initiated a complaint with the Bureau of Labor and Industries (BOLI), and defendant filed a response. The plaintiff later dismissed the BOLI complaint and then initiated this civil action. In her complaint, the plaintiff alleged in four counts that her termination constituted an unlawful employment practice. Each count advanced a different legal theory of discrimination: retaliation for complaining about unsafe working conditions (OSHA retaliation); retaliation for invoking the workers' compensation system; retaliation for requesting a reasonable accommodation under the disability discrimination statutes; and perceived disability discrimination.

At trial, the plaintiff testified to the events described above and reported that her symptoms had dissipated a few days after she stopped driving truck number 4003. She also testified that, although she is a heavy smoker, she had never experienced similar symptoms associated with smoking.

The plaintiff offered expert testimony from a diesel mechanic. He testified that exhaust leaks around the flex-pipe and band clamps are very common in the trucking industry, that exhaust leaks can be very hard to find and

remedy, and that such leaks can create a risk of carbon monoxide poisoning. He further testified that a review of truck 4003's maintenance log showed that an exhaust problem was reported before the plaintiff began working for defendant; specifically, that the truck had a "big exhaust leak" in October 2005. In November 2005, a flex-pipe and the head gaskets were replaced. The witness also stated that carbon monoxide is emitted by diesel engines as a result of incomplete combustion. He noted a report of white smoke associated with truck 4003 in May 2005, which, he testified, could be caused by incomplete combustion.

The plaintiff called Tony as a witness. He testified that he was aware that a safety regulation required that he take a truck offline and repair it if it leaked carbon monoxide into the cab. He acknowledged that the plaintiff filled out a maintenance request for an exhaust leak before she was terminated. He stated that he felt that the plaintiff could not safely drive any truck until the cause of her symptoms was determined, treated, and alleviated. He confirmed that the truck had had an exhaust leak in 2005, before the plaintiff's employment began. He testified that the plaintiff's employment "concluded" when they reached an "impasse over whether or not she would be allowed to drive another truck versus checking out the cause of her symptoms and treatment for them." He further testified that he did not follow the plaintiff's doctor's advice because the plaintiff's truck did not emit carbon monoxide and, therefore, the truck could not have been the source of the plaintiff's health problems. He acknowledged that he could have requested an independent fitness-for-duty exam for the plaintiff but did not do so.

The plaintiff also offered at trial defendant's response to her BOLI complaint. Written by Tony, it stated that, among other reasons, the plaintiff's "employment was terminated as a result of [h]er insistence that the employer assign her to another truck and complete disregard for all the reasons why this was neither necessary nor possible."

At the close of the plaintiff's case-in-chief, defendant moved for a directed verdict on all four counts in the complaint. The trial court, without elaboration, granted the motion and dismissed the complaint.

Issue: Was the plaintiff's termination a retaliatory discharge?

Decision: The court picked through the plaintiff's arguments, beginning with her count concerning OSHA retaliation. ORS 654.062(5) provides that it is an unlawful employment practice to retaliate against an employee who has opposed any practice forbidden by the Oregon Safe Employment Act or makes a complaint related to that act.

The plaintiff argued that she presented sufficient evidence that she was terminated because she complained to her employer about an exhaust leak and carbon monoxide poisoning. Specifically, she argued that the evidence showed that, shortly before she was terminated, she complained about an exhaust leak, reported her symptoms, and provided the test results and her doctor's notes, all of which indicated carbon monoxide poisoning.

The defendant responded that the plaintiff failed to introduce any evidence showing that the defendant terminated her *because* she made the safety complaint. The defendant cited the evidence that, after the plaintiff reported a possible exhaust leak, the defendant inspected the truck, sent it to a repair shop for further inspection and repairs, and had it tested for carbon monoxide emissions, implying that the defendant was responsive to the plaintiff's complaint and thus would not have terminated her in retaliation for it. The defendant contended further that, during the

plaintiff's conversations with Tony on April 24 and 26, in which the plaintiff was suspended and then terminated, her complaints about the exhaust leak were never mentioned.

Although the evidence on which the defendant relied supported an inference that a jury would be entitled to draw, it is not the only reasonable inference to which the record gives rise. The plaintiff introduced evidence that she was terminated within a few days of reporting what she believed to be an unsafe working condition that was affecting her health. She also offered evidence that the defendant was unhappy with the plaintiff because her repair requests were costing the defendant thousands of dollars. Together, those facts were considered by the court to constitute circumstantial evidence that the defendant had an impermissible retaliatory motive in terminating the plaintiff's employment. A jury could reasonably have found that the plaintiff's decision to report an unsafe work environment was a substantial factor in her termination. Thus, concluded the court, the trial court erred in granting the defendant's motion for a directed verdict on the count concerning OSHA retaliation.

Even where the employee has a legitimate reason for refusing the work order, the remedy for illegal discipline may be delayed so long that it is mooted for all practical purposes. Some union critics have criticized the lengthy procedures involved in resolving a complaint under Section 11(c), and suggest that if more than one employee was involved in the safety-related activity, they may get the matter resolved sooner by contacting the National Labor Relations Board.

The United States is not the only nation that attempts to afford workers this right of refusal. Other industrialized nations may have better approaches to the problem. In Canada, occupational safety and health is a matter of provincial rather than federal law; the Province of Ontario, for example, has adopted a fairly detailed approach, which is embodied in the following employer's policy.

CARLTON UNIVERSITY'S POLICY

Work Refusal Procedures

The Occupational Health and Safety Act of Ontario provides employees the right to refuse work for safety reasons. These procedures follow the requirements of the Act.

Right to Refuse Work

Under the Occupational Health and Safety Act, a worker may refuse to work or do particular work if he/she has reason to believe that,

Any equipment, machine, device or thing he/she is to use or operate is likely to endanger himself/herself or another worker.

The physical condition of the workplace in which he/she works or is to work is likely to endanger himself/herself.

Any equipment, machine, device or thing he/she is to operate or the physical condition of the workplace in which he/she works is in contravention of the Act and such contravention is likely to endanger himself/herself or another worker.

Procedures for Work Refusal

First Stage Refusal

(a) Upon refusing to do unsafe work, the worker must immediately report the circumstances of the refusal to the supervisor. The supervisor should contact the Department of University Safety.

(b) The supervisor must immediately investigate the report in the presence of the worker and a worker representative from the [Joint Occupational Health and Safety Committee]. The worker representative must be made available and must attend the investigation without delay; time spent by this representative is deemed to be work time, for which the person shall be paid at his/her regular or premium rate, as may be proper. If these workers are not available, a worker selected because of his/her knowledge, experience and training should be called.

The worker representatives from the Joint Occupational Health and Safety Committee to be contacted for a work refusal are the certified members:

Colleen Neely, CUASA 520-2600 ext. 8198

Troy Giles, Physical Plant 520-2600 ext. 3668

(c) Until the investigation is completed, the worker must remain in a safe place near the work station.

(d) During the investigation, supervisors must record as many details as possible regarding the refusal, using the attached Employer's Report.

(e) The Ministry of Labour is only called if the refusal progresses to the second stage.

Second Stage Refusal

(a) If the worker is dissatisfied with the results of the investigation and has reasonable grounds to believe that the circumstances are still such that the work is dangerous, then he/she may continue to refuse to work.

(b) Upon the continuance of the worker's refusal to work, the supervisor should notify the Department of University Safety, who will immediately notify a Ministry of Labour Officer. Until the ministry is notified, the work cannot be reassigned to another worker and the worker must remain near the work station.

(c) The Ministry of Labour Officer will investigate the work refusal in the presence of the employer, the worker and the worker's representative.

(d) Pending the investigation and decision of the officer,

(i) The worker must continue to remain at a safe place near the work station during his/her normal working hours unless the supervisor assigns the worker reasonable alternative work during those hours, or, if such an assignment is not practicable, the supervisor may give the worker other directions (which may include being sent home).

(ii) No other worker shall be assigned to the work that is being investigated unless that worker has been advised of the other worker's refusal and reasons for it, in the presence of the worker representative, and has signed a statement of being advised of the refusal.

(e) Supervisors must take great care that they do not intentionally penalize any worker for exercising, or seeking to exercise their rights under the Act.

(f) After the investigation, the officer will decide whether the machine, device, thing or workplace is likely to endanger the worker or another person. This decision will be given in writing, as soon as practical, to the employer, the worker and the worker's representative.

(g) If the inspector does not consider the refusal to be based on reasonable grounds, the worker is expected to return to work. If, however, the worker maintains that he/she has reasonable grounds for refusing such work, the inspector cannot order a return to work. If, however, no reasonable grounds exist for such further refusal, the worker may be subject to disciplinary action by the employer.

Employer Reprisals Prohibited

If a worker has acted in compliance with the Act, its regulations or an order made under them, the employer (or any person acting on its behalf) may not, because the worker so acted,

(a) Dismiss or threaten to dismiss the worker;

(b) Discipline or threaten to discipline the worker;

(c) Impose any penalty on the worker;

(d) Intimidate or coerce a worker.

If a worker complains that the employer (or a person acting on its behalf) has improperly taken any of these actions, he/she may file a grievance.

Work refusals can be avoided with a workplace commitment to health and safety, advising workers of hazards, providing safety training, and keeping the lines of communication open to encourage an atmosphere where workers feel free to raise health and safety concerns at any time, knowing management will treat them seriously.

Supervisor Notification to Human Resources and University Safety

Before imposing discipline or sending workers home during or after a work refusal, supervisors must consult with the Director of Human Resources and the Director of University Safety.

Canada's procedures are more complex and detailed than those under the U.S. Occupational Safety and Health Act, raising the question as to which approach accords employees greater protection.

Concept *Summary* 20.2

REFUSAL TO WORK

- Employee may refuse to obey a work order, if the order poses a reasonable threat to the employee's health and safety
- Right to refuse is not uniquely American; other nations also recognize this right, for instance, Canada
- Retaliation for reasonable refusal is prohibited
- Terminated employee may challenge discharge in federal agencies and courts

20-1c Inspections, Investigations, and Record Keeping

OSHA's occupational safety and health standards are enforced through physical inspections of workplaces. Practical realities in enforcing the act have forced OSHA to prioritize the inspection process. Thus, inspections are targeted in the following order:

- first to the investigation of complaints of imminent danger,
- then to investigation of fatal and catastrophic accidents,
- then to investigation of complaints filed by employees alleging hazardous working conditions,
- then to investigation of high-hazard industries, and finally
- random general investigations.

Reporting and Record-Keeping Requirements

OSHA relies on several sources of information to determine when and where inspections will occur. First, employers with eight or more employees are required under the act to keep records of and to make periodic reports to OSHA on occupational injuries and illnesses. As of January 1, 2015, employers must notify OSHA within 24 hours of an employee suffering a serious injury that involves an amputation, the loss of an eye, or any incident resulting in at least one employee being admitted to a hospital for in-patient care. Employers must report any employee fatality within eight hours. States that operate their own state OSHA programs are required to adopt the new reporting requirements by January 1, 2016. Occupational injuries must be recorded if they involve or result in:

- death;
- loss of consciousness;
- medical treatment other than minor first aid;
- one or more lost workdays;
- the restriction of work or motion; or
- transfer to another job.

Second, the employer is required to maintain accurate records of employee exposures to potentially toxic materials or harmful physical agents required to be monitored under the act. Third, any employee or representative of an employee who believes that a violation of a safety or health standard exists that threatens physical harm, or believes that an imminent danger exists, may request an inspection.

Inspections

The compliance officer conducting the inspection may enter without delay and at reasonable times any factory, business establishment, construction site, or workplace covered by the act. This inspection may include all pertinent conditions, structures, machines, apparatus, devices, equipment, and materials on the inspection site. The office is also given authority to question privately any employer, owner, operator, agent, or employee.

The act allows the employer and a representative authorized by the employees to accompany the inspector during the physical inspection of the work site.

In *Marshall v. Barlow's Inc.*,[5] the Supreme Court held that an employer subject to an OSHA inspection may insist upon a search warrant. As a result of *Marshall v. Barlow's*, the compliance officer now must request permission to enter the workplace or other area that is to be the subject of the search. If the employer refuses entry or forbids the continuation of an inspection, the compliance officer must terminate the inspection or confine it to those areas where no objection has been raised. Following such a refusal, an ex parte application for an inspection warrant can be obtained from either a U.S. district judge or a U.S. magistrate.

ethical DILEMMA

WHEN THE OSHA INSPECTION FINDS THAT THE ENDANGERED WORKERS ARE ILLEGALLY IN THE U.S.

A story appeared in the national newspaper *USA TODAY* on June 7, 2006, regarding the vital, but illegal, immigrant workers who labored on post–Hurricane Katrina reconstruction in New Orleans. A study conducted by professors at Tulane University and the University of California at Berkeley found that the workers were distinctly vulnerable to exploitation due to their illegal status.

Despite the fact that under federal labor law illegal workers are to be afforded the same protections as their legal counterparts, these illegal workers often worked in unsafe conditions without the benefit of safety gear and typically earned much less—$6.50 less on average—than documented workers performing the same duties. Immigrant workers can, however, sue their employers regardless of their legal status.

- Do you agree that illegal immigrant workers should receive the same protections under the federal Occupational Safety and Health Act as American workers and legal immigrants?
- If OSHA inspects a site for safety violations and the inspector suspects that illegal workers are employed at the site, should she or he be required to report this suspicion to the U.S. Immigration and Customs Enforcement (ICE) agency?
- What if the OSHA inspection was prompted by a call or complaint from one of the illegal workers? Does this change your answer?

---

[5] 436 U.S. 307 (1973).

Sometimes the legitimacy of the inspection becomes entwined with the even knottier question of jurisdiction. In the following case, the question of jurisdiction is raised in relation to OSHA regulations on vertical tandem lifts. The National Maritime Safety Association makes the argument that OSHA's authority is limited to requiring, not prohibiting, workplace practices, and furthermore that the Occupational Safety and Health Act made an unconstitutional delegation of power to OSHA.

CASE 20.3

NATIONAL MARITIME SAFETY ASS'N V. OCCUPATIONAL SAFETY & HEALTH...
649 F.3d 743 C.A.D.C. (2011), *cert. denied*, 132 S.Ct. 1960 (April 16, 2012)

On December 10, 2008, the Occupational Safety and Health Administration (OSHA), an agency of the United States Department of Labor, published a final rule regulating vertical tandem lifts (VTLs). The National Maritime Safety Association (NMSA), a trade association representing marine terminal operators, petitions for review of the VTL Standard and argues, among other claims, that OSHA's authority is limited to requiring, not prohibiting, workplace practices; and if the Standard is otherwise valid, the Occupational Safety and Health Act (OSH Act or Act) has made an unconstitutional delegation of legislative power to OSHA.

I.
On September 16, 2003, OSHA issued a notice of proposed rulemaking announcing its intention to regulate VTLs. The proposed rule would have permitted VTLs of two containers with a total weight (including cargo) of 20 tons. It would have prohibited platform containers with upright end frames from being lifted in a VTL unit but would have allowed empty platform containers with the end frames folded down to be lifted as a VTL unit. It would have also imposed a wind speed restriction on VTL operations and would have required the employer to examine the interbox connectors before each use.

After receiving comments and holding public hearings, OSHA published the final VTL Standard in 2008. Like the proposed rule, the Standard permits only two-container VTL lifts. Unlike the proposed rule, however, the Standard permits VTLs of empty containers only so that a two-container VTL can have a mass *at most* of approximately 9200 kg or 9.2 metric tons. Further departing from the proposed rule, the final Standard categorically bans VTLs of platform containers. The Standard additionally requires "that interbox connectors and containers, including, in particular, their corner castings [connection points], ... be inspected immediately before being used in a VTL" despite OSHA's

acknowledgment that this requirement "may make ship-to-shore VTLs impractical." Finally, the Standard imposes a "safe work zone" requirement, which requires the employer to "establish a safe work zone within which employees may not be present when vertically connected containers are in motion.... sufficient to protect employees in the event that a container drops or overturns." As discussed more fully below, OSHA also determined that "unregulated VTL operations" pose a "significant risk" to worker safety.

NMSA petitioned for review of the Standard on February 6, 2009.

***

C. "Safe Work Zone" Requirement
The "safe work zone" requirement directs the employer to "establish a safe work zone within which employees may not be present when vertically connected containers are in motion." The safe work zone must be "sufficient to protect employees in the event that a container drops." If an employer establishes a safe work zone as the Standard requires, the NMSA asserts, employees will not face any danger and the Standard's other requirements are therefore not "reasonably necessary or appropriate" to protect worker safety. According to the NMSA, OSHA has a duty to explain why it did not simply "adopt the 'safe work zone' requirement without some or all of the other requirements in the VTL Standard." The NMSA further argues that, because employees are not at risk when an employer complies with the safe work zone requirement, OSHA lacks jurisdiction to impose additional requirements because no risk to employees remains. The NMSA is mistaken. While the safe work zone requirement adequately protects employees located on the ground, it does not necessarily protect the crane operator who moves the containers. If a container were to separate during a VTL, the separation could jar the crane and injure the operator. The safe work

zone requirement, therefore, does not make the VTL Standard's other requirements unnecessary or inappropriate and we believe OSHA has supported the requirement with substantial evidence.

D. OSHA's Authority to Prohibit Workplace Practices

The NMSA takes issue with OSHA's statement in the VTL Standard that it "*permits* VTLs of no more than two empty containers." OSHA, according to the NMSA, lacks statutory authority to permit or ban workplace practices, arguing that OSHA can regulate only *how* workplace practices are performed, not *what* workplace practices are performed. OSHA's unquestioned authority to ensure safe workplace practices, however, includes the authority to prohibit unsafe practices. OSHA might be stymied in its responsibility to require certain practices if it could not also prohibit noncompliant practices.

E. Non-Delegation Challenge

The United States Constitution vests "[a]ll legislative Powers herein granted … in a Congress of the United States." The Constitution "permits no delegation of those powers, and so … when Congress confers decisionmaking authority upon agencies *Congress* must lay down by legislative act an intelligible principle to which the person or body authorized to act is directed to conform." In *Benzene*, the Supreme Court interpreted the OSH Act to require OSHA, before issuing a standard under the Act, to "determine that [the standard] is reasonably necessary and appropriate to remedy a significant risk of material health impairment." The limiting construction was necessary because a plurality of the Court believed that without the construction "the statute would make such a sweeping delegation of legislative power that it might be unconstitutional." That the Court did not invalidate the Act manifests that the Court believes the Act, as interpreted in *Benzene*, contains an intelligible principle for promulgating health standards. But here the NMSA challenges, as an unconstitutional delegation of legislative power, the Act's grant of authority to issue safety standards.

The delegation of power to OSHA under the OSH Act to set health or safety standards that are "reasonably necessary or appropriate to provide safe or healthful employment and places of employment," is no broader than other delegations that direct agencies to act in the "public interest," e.g., *Nat'l Broad. Co. v. United States*, 319 U.S. 190, 215–16, 63 S.Ct. 997, 87 L.Ed. 1344 (1943) (internal quotation marks omitted), or in a way that is "fair and equitable," *Yakus v. United States*, 321 U.S. 414, 420–23, 64 S.Ct. 660, 88 L.Ed. 834 (1944), or in a manner "requisite to protect the public health," *Whitman*, 531 U.S. at 472–76, 121 S.Ct. 903 (internal quotation marks omitted), or when "necessary to avoid an imminent hazard to the public safety," *Touby v. United States*, 500 U.S. 160, 163, 165, 111 S.Ct. 1752, 114 L.Ed.2d 219 (1991) (internal quotation marks omitted). See also *Am. Power & Light Co. v. SEC*, 329 U.S. 90, 104, 67 S.Ct. 133, 91 L.Ed. 103 (1946) (authorizing SEC to reorganize corporate structures to ensure they are not "unduly or unnecessarily complicate[d]" and do not "unfairly or inequitably distribute voting power among security holders" (internal quotation marks omitted)); *Michigan Gambling Opposition v. Kempthorne*, 525 F.3d 23, 30–31 (D.C. Cir. 2008) (authorization to obtain land "for Indians" contains intelligible principle), *cert. denied*, 555 U.S. 1137, 129 S.Ct. 1002, 173 L.Ed.2d 293 (2009). See generally *Whitman*, 531 U.S. at 472–76, 121 S.Ct. 903." In light of these precedents, one cannot plausibly argue that [29 U.S.C. §652(8)'s "reasonably necessary or appropriate to provide safe or healthful employment and places of employment"] standard is not an intelligible principle." *Touby*, 500 U.S. at 165, 111 S.Ct. 1752. Accordingly, we reject the NMSA's non-delegation challenge.

III.

For the foregoing reasons, we deny the NMSA's petition for review in large part, finding that Congress presented intelligible principle to warrant delegation of power to OSHA.

Case Questions

1. Why is the NMSA incorrect in its claim that OSHA does not have the power to prohibit workplace practices? Do you agree with the court's reasoning?

2. The NMSA argued that because employees are not at risk when an employer complies with the safe work zone requirement, OSHA lacks jurisdiction to impose additional requirements because no risk to employees remains. Why is this line of reasoning incorrect?

3. The court found that Congress presented intelligible principals to warrant the delegation of power to OSHA. Do you agree? Why? Why not?

Concept *Summary* 20.3

INSPECTIONS AND RECORD KEEPING

- OSHA annually inspects thousands of workplaces
- Employers must report any workplace fatalities to OSHA within eight hours, and report incidents resulting in serious injury within 24 hours
- Employers must maintain records of work-related injuries for OSHA inspection
- If an employer refuses entry, the OSHA inspector must get a search warrant from a federal judge
- Illegal immigrants are entitled to the same health and safety protections as American workers
- An ethical dilemma may exist when an OSHA inspector, in the workplace to ensure workers' health and safety, discovers that some workers are illegal aliens

20-2   Citations, Penalties, Abatement, and Appeal

de minimis violation
a technical violation, but so insignificant as to require no fine or remediation

When an inspection leads to the discovery of a violation of a standard under the act, the employer is issued either a written citation describing the particular nature of the violation or a notice of de minimis violations. A **de minimis violation** is one that has no direct or immediate relationship to the health or safety of the workers or the workplace affected, and no citations or proposed penalties are issued.

If a citation is issued, the employer must be notified by certified mail within a reasonable time, but in no event longer than six months after the identification of the violation, of any proposed penalty to be assessed. The employer then has 15 working days within which to notify OSHA that it intends to contest the citation or the proposed penalty. If the employer does not contest, the citation becomes final and is not subject to appeal or review.

The citation must set a reasonable time for the abatement of the violation, usually not to exceed 30 days. The employer is required to post the citation, or a copy, prominently at or near each place the violation occurred. The employees or representatives of the employees may file a notice challenging the period of time set in the citation for the abatement.

If the employer challenges the citation, the penalty assessed, or the period for abatement, a hearing is held before an administrative law judge, who makes findings of fact and conclusions of law that affirm, modify, or vacate the citation. This order becomes final 30 days after it is filed with OSHA unless, within that time, a member of OSHRC exercises the statutory right to direct review by the full commission. Any party to the proceeding may file a petition requesting this discretionary review. A final order of the commission may be appealed to the appropriate U.S. court of appeals.

The penalty and citation may be separately challenged by the employer. However, if only the penalty is contested, the violation is not subject to review.

When the citation and proposed penalty are contested, the employer has an absolute defense to the citation if it can prove that compliance to the standard is impossible.

A showing that the standards are merely impractical or difficult to meet will not excuse performance.

In the event the violation is not corrected within the allowed time, the employer is notified by certified mail of the failure to abate and of the proposed penalty. This notice and proposed penalty are final unless, here again, the employer files a notice of contest within 15 working days. If the order is not contested, it is deemed a final order and is not subject to judicial review.

If the employer has made a good-faith effort to comply with the abatement requirements of the initial citation but the abatement has not occurred because of factors beyond the reasonable control of the employer, a petition for modification of abatement can be filed. If OSHA or an employee objects to the requested extension or modification, a hearing is held before OSHRC.

If the employer files a petition for modification, the petition must state in detail the steps taken by the employer to abate the hazard; the additional time necessary to abate; the reasons additional time is necessary, including unavailability of technical or professional personnel or equipment; and interim steps being taken to protect employees.

If the employer fails to correct a cited violation after it has become final, a fine may be imposed of not more than $1,000 per day. If the violation is found to be willful or a repeat violation, or it results in the death of an employee, OSHA can impose fines of up to $70,000. In the past, OSHA had a practice of imposing a large fine and then allowing the offender to negotiate a reduction in the fine. In 1990, Congress amended the act to prohibit OSHA from reducing a fine for a willful violation below $7,000. The act also provides for criminal penalties of up to six months imprisonment, with the maximum increased to 12 months for a repeat violation.

In his proposed budget for fiscal year 2016, President Obama asked Congress to increase the civil penalties for violations of the Occupational Safety and Health Act, noting that the civil penalties had been increased only once since the law was passed in 1970. The budget proposal also requested that Congress apply the Federal Civil Penalties Inflation Act to the OSHA civil penalties, which would adjust those penalties to keep pace with inflation.

Concept *Summary* 20.4

CITATIONS, PENALTIES, ABATEMENT, AND APPEAL

- A citation is an OHSA charge that an employer has committed a serious or a de minimis violation of the Occupational Safety and Health Act
- A citation, like a traffic ticket, will include a penalty, usually a fine that varies in amount with the seriousness of the violation
- The citation also will require the employer to abate, that is, eliminate the hazard within a specified time frame
- The employer may appeal the citation, if it disagrees with OSHA

20-2a   Workplace Violence

Workplace violence has emerged as an important safety concern in the 21st century. Its most extreme form—homicide—is the second leading cause of fatal occupational injury in the United States. Every year, almost 1,000 workers are murdered and about 1.5 million are assaulted in their places of employment. Concern about workplace violence has intensified exponentially in the wake of the terrorist attacks and anthrax events of autumn 2001. Businesses based primarily in office buildings, which once thought themselves above and beyond the workplace safety concerns of heavy industry and hermetically sealed from the violent intrusions endemic to convenience food stores and other retail establishments, now find themselves in need of policies and procedures to deal with all manner of threats from inside and outside their organizations. Most large businesses have felt compelled to go so far as to develop evacuation plans in anticipation of the day when it is their high-rise office building or corporate office park that is the target of a terrorist attack or a biological or chemical incursion.

Workplace violence can be classified as follows:

- Violence by emotionally enraged persons
- Violence by an angry spouse or relative of an employee
- Random acts of violence
- Violence against law enforcement or security
- Terrorism and hate crimes

Persons who commit workplace violence often share one or more of the following characteristics:

- A history of violence
- Psychosis
- Romantic obsession
- Chemical dependence
- Depression
- Paranoia or pathological blaming
- Impaired neurological functioning
- Elevated frustration with the work environment
- Interest in or obsession with weapons
- Personality disorder

Other documented indicators of a potential for workplace violence are the following:

- Alcohol abuse
- Drug abuse
- Impaired judgment
- Emotional difficulties
- Financial problems
- Legal problems

- Strained family relations
- Occupational failure
- Threats
- Absenteeism
- Deterioration of personal appearance, attitude, and behavior
- Deterioration of interpersonal relations
- Inefficiency

Documenting Behavior

Incidents of workplace violence or possible violent behavior should be documented as follows:

- Record incidents promptly.
- Indicate date, time, and location.
- Detail the behavior.
- List all persons and work products involved.
- Identify the performance standards and disciplinary rules violated.
- Record the consequences of the action.
- Record management's response.
- Record the employee's reaction to management's response.

A Supervisor's Response

Supervisors should respond as follows to indicators of potential workplace violence:

- Don't try to diagnose the behavior personally.
- Don't discuss drinking unless it occurs on the job.
- Don't moralize.
- Don't be misled by sympathy-evoking tactics.
- Don't cover up for a friend.
- Don't put the individual into an isolated work area.
- Don't ignore the problem or the signs of trouble.
- Do remember that chemical dependence is progressive and likely will only get worse over time.
- Do bring to the attention of suspected employees the company's employee assistance program.
- Do make it clear that your organization is concerned with job performance and that, if performance does not improve, the job is in jeopardy.
- Do explain that the employee must make the personal decision to seek help.
- Do emphasize that the employee assistance program is confidential.

Prevention

The following should be done to prevent workplace violence:

- Develop a written policy.

- Form a crisis management team.

- Develop policies on counseling, suspension, and termination.

- Immediately investigate all incidents, such as threats.

- Contact specialists for assistance.

- Be flexible: Revise plans, policies, and procedures as information develops.

Evacuation Plans

In the words of labor lawyer Louis Lessig of the New Jersey law firm Brown & Connery, "Employers of all sizes are now drafting and revising emergency evacuation procedures. But, in order to adequately prepare, it is necessary to know in advance which employees, if any, will need assistance."[6] In line with Lessig's observation, the EEOC recently released guidelines concerning the creation of emergency plans that comply with the Americans with Disabilities Act. The guide lists three ways in which employers can obtain the information Lessig says they need:

- The employer can ask about a new hire's needs in this regard after making an offer of employment and prior to the commencement of work.

- The employer is allowed to send out periodic surveys to all employees to ascertain such special needs; however, self-identification must be strictly voluntary and be used only in conjunction with construction of the emergency plan.

- The employer may ask all employees with declared disabilities if they will require such special assistance in the event of an evacuation of the work site.

Also worth noting is the ADA provision that while, in general, medical information must be maintained in confidentiality, relevant information can be provided by the employer to:

- Health care workers

- Emergency coordinators

- Floor captains

- A colleague designated to provide the special assistance required

Packages and Mail

In light of incidents involving the mailing of parcels or letters containing dangerous or hazardous substances, employers and employees should be alert to such dangers. The OSHA has issued the following guidelines.

---

[6] See Lessig blog, http://www.lessig.org/blog.

GENERAL MAIL HANDLING	THINGS THAT SHOULD TRIGGER SUSPICION
• Be observant for suspicious envelopes and packages • Open all mail with a letter opener or by the method least likely to disturb the contents • Do not blow into envelopes • Do not shake or pour out the contents • Keep hands away from nose and mouth • Wash hands after handling the mail	• Discoloration, crystallization, strange odor, or oil stains • Powder or residue • Protruding wires or aluminum foil • Excessive tape or string • Unusual size or unusual weight for its size • Lopsided or oddly shaped envelope • Postmark that does not match return address • Restrictive endorsement such as Personal or Confidential

In the wake of the many workplace-violence incidents of the past two decades, many employers have adopted "zero-tolerance policies" when it comes to worker violence or threats of violence. Other employers, perhaps subscribing to the old adage that "every dog is entitled to one bite," will give an employee who exhibits violent or threatening behavior but does no immediate harm a second chance before terminating him. Regardless of the policy or approach, the employer faces a dilemma, because the terminated employee may be expected to challenge his firing, pointing when possible to an alleged discriminatory motive on the part of his supervisor or the company's HR office, as exemplified by the following case.

CASE 20.4

TOMICK V. UNITED PARCEL SERVICE, INC.

511 F. Supp. 2d 235 (D. Conn. 2007)

This action arises from the events leading to Tomick's termination by UPS after nearly twenty years of employment. Counts one and two allege common law claims of negligent infliction of emotional distress and intentional infliction of emotional distress, respectively. Counts three and seven allege violations of Connecticut General Statutes §§ 31-51x and 46a-60(a)(1), respectively.

The complaint alleges that in 1984 UPS hired Tomick as a driver. In January 2003, Tomick injured his back and was unable to work while recuperating from that injury. Although he was diagnosed with fifteen percent permanent partial disability, his doctor released him to return to work. UPS agreed, as part of a "reasonable accommodation," to supply Tomick with a driver's helper upon his return.

On December 2, 2004, which was presumably Tomick's first day back at work, he expected a driver's helper, but UPS did not provide one. Nevertheless, he commenced his delivery route. He began feeling "intolerable" back pain, at which point he called his wife. Thereafter he called UPS to report that he was unable to complete his delivery route. He said that he needed to see his physician, and that he was going to drive the UPS truck, which was presumably stocked with the undelivered customer packages, to his home. Tomick alleges that UPS later called his home and left a message for Tomick to return the truck that afternoon. Tomick did so, and a confrontation ensued.

Tomick asked his supervisors why he was not given a driver's helper. Trudelle accused him of acting "irrationally." Trudelle then suggested Tomick was under the influence of drugs and alcohol and insisted that Tomick be driven immediately to a drug testing clinic and that he submit to a substance abuse test. Tomick refused to do so, and countered that he needed to see his physician immediately. He attempted to leave, but Trudelle and fellow supervisor Ray Congdon prevented him from getting into his vehicle. Tomick accused Trudelle of verbally abusing his wife and threatened him.

Trudelle accused Tomick of workplace violence and threatened to terminate Tomick if Tomick did not submit to an immediate fitness-for-duty observation, including a controlled substance test, at UPS' testing facility. Tomick agreed on the condition that the test be performed at his hospital where he could simultaneously receive treatment from his physician for his back pain. Trudelle rejected this condition and terminated Tomick. Congdon interceded and everyone agreed that the evaluation could be performed at Tomick's hospital. The two men traveled together to the hospital.

During the fitness-for-duty observation, the physician characterized Tomick as a "pleasant man, cooperative, and alert." The doctor concluded that a physical drug test was unnecessary and declared Tomick fit for work. The doctor did, however, prescribe pain medication.

The next day, Tomick returned to work, whereupon he was called into a meeting with Trudelle, fellow supervisor Victor Birch and union steward John Fitzgerald to discuss the events. Trudelle asked Tomick to submit to a controlled substance test. Tomick agreed. The supervisors then left the room, returned several minutes later, and fired Tomick for engaging in workplace violence the previous day. Tomick filed this action.

Discussion. In deciding a motion to dismiss, the allegations of the complaint are accepted as true and are construed in a light most favorable to the plaintiff. A "complaint should not be dismissed for failure to state a claim unless it appears beyond doubt that the plaintiff can prove no set of facts in support of his claim which would entitle him to relief." "The issue is not whether a plaintiff will ultimately prevail but whether the claimant is entitled to offer evidence to support the claims. Indeed it may appear on the face of the pleadings that a recovery is very remote and unlikely but that is not the test."

***

IV. Perceived Disability under Connecticut General Statutes § 46a-60(a)(1)

UPS asserts that Connecticut law does not recognize a claim for "perceived disability" under Connecticut General Statutes § 46a-60(a)(1). In support, they rely on *Beason v. United Techs. Corp.*, 337 F.3d 271, 279 (2d Cir. 2003), wherein the court unambiguously concluded "that no cause of action for perceived disability discrimination presently exists under Connecticut law." Tomick contends that the Connecticut Supreme Court implicitly recognized this cause of action in *Ann Howard's Apricots Rest. v. Comm'n on Human Rights & Opportunities*, 237 Conn. 209, 676 A.2d 844 (1996).

In *Ann Howard's Apricots Rest.*, the "principal issue on appeal is whether the trial court properly determined that a hearing officer for the commission on human rights and opportunities had abused her discretion in failing to strike the direct testimony of a defendant who died before he could be fully cross-examined." The court did not decide whether there is a cause of action in Connecticut of perceived disability discrimination. The court, did, however, discuss the hearing officer's findings, which may have included a finding of perceived disability.

The language on which Tomick relies is dicta. The Connecticut Supreme Court has not expanded the legislatively created rights codified in General Statutes § 46a-60 (a)(1), notwithstanding its recognition, stated in the form of dicta, of the limits of the law. Moreover, the Connecticut General Assembly has not chosen to expand those rights that act although its limitation has been pointed out by the Supreme Court. Accordingly, count seven is dismissed.

IT IS SO ORDERED.

Case Questions

1. Why did Tomick's employment discrimination claim fail?

2. Do you think Tomick might have prevailed if Connecticut law recognized his claim?

3. Do you think the employer acted fairly in terminating Tomick's employment?

Concept *Summary* 20.5

WORKPLACE VIOLENCE

- Incidents of workplace violence have become increasingly common in the United States
- In the 21st century, employers must adopt policies and procedures aimed at protecting employees from violence
- Employees themselves must be aware of and trained in practices and procedures to detect and respond to threats
- The employer's dilemma is that in protecting employees from potentially violent coworkers, they run the risk of discrimination-based suits from terminated employees, who deny they posed a threat

CHAPTER REVIEW

» Key Term

de minimis violation   677

» Summary

- The Occupational Safety and Health Act was enacted by Congress in response to the large number of workplace deaths, diseases, and injuries occurring in the United States every year. Scholars and critics disagree about how effective the OSH Act has been in reducing or preventing such occurrences.

- The OSH Act empowers the Occupational Safety and Health Administration to promulgate rules and set standards for workplace safety. These rules are subject to challenge in our federal courts.

- The Occupational Safety and Health Administration is also empowered to enforce the law and the regulations by means of workplace inspections and citations. Its agents are not required to meet the same strict search warrant requirements imposed upon police officers by the 4th Amendment to the U.S. Constitution. Furthermore, while OSHA's jurisdiction can sometimes become entangled with that of other agencies, such as the Environmental Protection Agency and the U.S. Coast Guard, recent case law suggests that in this post-9/11 world of heightened health and safety concerns, the U.S. Supreme Court is prepared to allow OSHA a substantial amount of leverage in conducting inspections and enforcing the OSH Act and its implementing regulations.

- Not only is OSHA's jurisdiction over workplace safety not exclusive, but in some major areas—workplace smoking being a very significant one—private litigation has played a significant role in securing employee rights and recompensing employee injuries.

- In addition to employee-to-employee violence and third-party threats, such as terrorism, the risk posed by flu pandemics and other health hazards

involved in conducting global business are all too real. An employee returning from a trip abroad or a customer coming from overseas can infect a firm's entire work force, quite literally putting the organization out of business. No company can afford to be blasé about such possibilities today. Both OSHA and the CDC are acutely concerned with anticipating and, if necessary, meeting such challenges. Another emerging area of OSHA concern is workplace violence, a complicated issue that implicates multiple government agencies, professions, and causes. Here, too, the September 11, 2001, terrorist attacks and the anthrax crisis that followed have led many corporations to develop policies and procedures for dealing with a wide range of health and safety threats that might come from within as well as from outside their workplaces, including in the case of many larger corporations and organizations, detailed work site evacuation plans.

» Problems

» Questions

1. What agencies were created by the Occupational Safety and Health Act, and what are the roles of those agencies?

2. Describe the procedures used to create permanent standards under OSHA.

3. Can employees exercise the right to refuse to work under OSHA without fear of reprisal? If so, give an example.

4. What is the purpose of workplace inspections under OSHA? What is the effect of the *Barlow's* case on that purpose?

5. Is OSHA's authority limited to mandating workplace practices? Can OSHA prohibit workplace practices as well? If so, explain why.

6. What procedures must be followed in issuing a citation under OSHA? What penalties may be imposed for violations of OSHA?

» Case Problems

7. An employee filed a complaint with the Occupational Safety and Health Administration, accusing her employer—a printing plant—of assorted safety violations. A few days after filing the complaint, she held a lunchtime meeting with her coworkers in an effort to get them to protest their work conditions. Later that same afternoon, she was called to her supervisor's office, where she was fired.

   The Department of Labor brought this action, claiming that the employee's termination was retaliatory. The company contended that during the meeting with her supervisor, the employee became loud, abusive, and even threatened him.

   If the threatening and abusive language can be proven, should this constitute an independent reason for the discharge, such that the DOL's claim of retaliatory firing should be defeated? Does the lunchtime meeting with her coworkers implicate any other federal labor statute in your consideration of this case? Does this consideration change the outcome? [See *Herman v. Crescent Publishing Group, Inc.*, 2000 WL 1371311 (S.D.N.Y.).]

8. The U.S. Department of Labor's Wage and Hour Division audited an employer and determined that the company had committed violations of the minimum wage and overtime provisions of the federal Fair Labor Standards Act (see Chapter 22). The company wished to appeal this determination.

   The firm's human resources director called the main number of the Department of Labor's offices in the corporation's home city. She was put through to an official in the OSHA office in the local federal building. This OSHA official, responding to the human resources director's inquiry, advised her that she need not count weekends and holidays when calculating the deadline date for filing her company's appeal. It turned out that this information was incorrect, and as a result, the appeal was dismissed by the Wage and Hour Division's appellate office as untimely.

   Should a court order the Department of Labor to honor the appeal, since one of its agencies gave the human resources manager the incorrect information upon which her company relied to its detriment? What are the policy considerations' pro and con regarding such a ruling? Is there a constitutional issue involved in this case? [See *Atlantic Adjustment Co. v. U.S. Dept. of Labor*, 90 F. Supp. 2d 627 (E.D. Pa. 2000).]

9. Following an explosion and fire at an employer's petrochemical facility, OSHA investigators interviewed numerous employees of the company. While OSHA's investigation was still pending, the company sent the agency a Freedom of Information Act (FOIA) request, asking for transcriptions of all witness statements taken by the investigators. When OSHA declined to provide these statements, the company sued, seeking a writ of mandamus that would require the agency to comply with the FOIA request.

   What policy considerations favor requiring OSHA to provide the company with copies of these statements? What policy considerations are against requiring disclosure? Do these policy considerations change in any way as the underlying case progresses from the investigative to later stages in OSHA's procedures? Are there constitutional considerations involved? [See *Cooper Cameron Corp. v. U.S. Dept. of Labor*, 118 F. Supp. 2d 757 (S.D. Texas 2000); see also *Freedom of Information Act*, 5 U.S.C. 552 (West 2000).]

10. Because the availability of new plots was becoming very limited, a cemetery company in a major metropolitan area began selling single plots wherein a husband and wife ultimately would be interred one on top of the other. When the first spouse died, a grave was excavated to a depth sufficient to leave room for the future interment of the surviving spouse. To "square off" the corners of the grave, a member of the cemetery's grounds crew would enter the newly dug grave with a spade or trowel to perform the task.

   One of the groundskeepers filed a complaint with OSHA claiming that it was unsafe to work in the graves without shoring. An inspector from OSHA decided that the double graves were deep enough to require proper shoring before a grave-digger enters them to square them off. The cemetery's general manager replied that no other cemetery's procedure included shoring and that if required to do so, his company would become uncompetitive.

   What recourse does the general manager have? (This case problem is drawn from the experience of one of the authors in legal practice.)

11. Employees of the state's Department of Environmental Management (DEM) complained to the state's attorney general that their agency was not properly implementing the requirements of the federal Solid Waste Disposal Act. DEM fired them after it learned of their complaint.

   The Solid Waste Disposal Act contains a whistleblower protection clause. See 42 U.S.C. 6971 (West 2000). The employees sued in federal court to collect damages from the state under this provision. The state moved to dismiss the action on the basis of its sovereign immunity.

What is sovereign immunity, and when do you think a state should be able to rely upon this legal principle to avoid liability? Should the fact that this case creates a potential clash between state and federal government influence the court's decision on whether or not to dismiss the action? [See *Rhode Island v. United States*, 16 BNA IER Cases 1258 (D.R.I. 2000).]

12. Sami Al-Arian was a tenured professor of computer engineering at the University of South Florida. Early in 2002, the university terminated his employment, citing his public statements, reported by the media and broadcast on TV, in support of Islamic *jihad*. The university claimed in terminating Al-Arian that he posed a threat to the safety of other university employees.

    Do you think the university was justified in firing the Palestinian professor? What arguments could you make in favor of his reinstatement if you were his attorney? Did OSHA have any jurisdiction in this case? Would OSHA have had grounds to issue a citation for a safety violation if the university had failed to fire the professor and his presence on campus had in fact resulted in a violent third-party action that killed or injured university employees? [See *U.S. v. Al-Arian*, 308 F. Supp. 2d 1322 (M.D. Fla. 2004).]

13. About one year later, Al-Arian was charged by federal law enforcement officials with raising money to support a terrorist organization, Palestinian Islamic Jihad, allegedly responsible for more than 100 murders in Israel and the Israeli-occupied territories.

    Does this indictment strengthen the university's case for firing Al-Arian? Is your answer the same whether or not the university knew of these indictable activities prior to the indictment? [See *West's Termination of Employment Bulletin*, May 2003, at 11.]

14. We have seen in this chapter that OSHA shares responsibility for workplace health and safety with a variety of other federal agencies (such as the U.S. Coast Guard), as well as state and local governmental bodies and even private rights of action (as in the secondhand smoke cases). In this case,

the Teamsters Union was endeavoring to unionize the Overnite Transportation Company's Bedford, Illinois, facility. In furtherance of those organizing efforts, Teamster-paid pickets appeared at the work site armed with ax handles disguised as picket signs. In the ensuing confrontation, some of the company's employees, mainly security guards, were injured.

    Which governmental body should have jurisdiction over this case: OSHA, the National Labor Relations Board, the U.S. District Court, or an appropriate state court? [See *Overnite Transportation Co. v. International Brotherhood of Teamsters, Chauffeurs, Warehousemen and Helpers of America*, 773 N.E.2d 26 (Ill. App. 2002).]

15. Plaintiff drove a bus for defendant Diversified Paratransit, Inc., which was in the business of transporting developmentally disabled adults and children from their homes and care providers to various day-care centers and schools. One such adult client harassed the plaintiff regularly, including exposing himself to her and ultimately grabbing her and trying to kiss her. Her complaints to her employer were largely ignored. Following the incident involving physical contact, she quit her job.

    Does the plaintiff have the right to file an OSHA complaint in this case? Does she have a private right of action to sue her employer? If so, what is her legal theory? Does the lawsuit have any OSHA preemption problems? [See *Salazar v. Diversified Paratransit, Inc.*, 126 Cal. Rptr. 2d 475 (Cal. App. 2002).]

16. The plaintiff in this case was employed by United Engineers and Constructors at its chemical weapons incinerator on the Johnston Atoll in the South Pacific. Due to the types of weapons handled at the facility, the court observed, "the working conditions ... are probably as dangerous as any undertaken in the world." Plaintiff had previously been employed at the Pine Bluff Arsenal in Arkansas, where he had made more than 1,000 "toxic entries"—that is, entries into a contaminated area of a plant, requiring protective clothing and other precautions. Upon his arrival at the atoll, he concluded that the company's managers and his coworkers failed to appreciate the risks they

were running. In particular, he concluded that the basic training and the safety equipment were both inadequate. Consequently, he began complaining. His complaints were vindicated by the subsequent issuance of two "serious" citations by OSHA following the agency's inspection of the facility in reaction to plaintiff's complaints. The citations related to unapproved respirators and the standby team's use of improper equipment. (A "serious" violation means that the hazard poses a "substantial probability of death or serious physical harm.")

Disputes between plaintiff and his superiors continued. The situation came to a climax when plaintiff refused to work in a toxic area because the company had failed to provide him with a new set of corrective lenses for his face mask. Plaintiff was discharged for insubordination. He again filed an OSH Act complaint, and the agency's regional investigator made an initial finding that the complaint had merit. However, after several local attempts to amicably resolve the dispute, the case was forwarded to the OSHA regional solicitor in San Francisco with a recommendation that the case be adjudicated. However, the regional solicitor decided to dismiss the case due to a possible jurisdictional dispute with the U.S. Army, which conducted its own inspection and investigation but failed to act. Instead, the army turned the file over to the Department of Labor, where OSHA gave the case one final review but still refused to take adjudicative action.

Based on these facts, what are the policy considerations in favor and against allowing the plaintiff to pursue a lawsuit against OSHA, seeking a writ of mandamus from a federal judge, and requiring OSHA to adjudicate plaintiff's retaliation claim against the employer? [See *Wood v. Department of Labor*, 275 F.3d 107 (D.C. Cir. 2001).]

» Hypothetical Scenarios

17. The Hot Zone Thermometer Company manufactured outdoor thermometers in a small factory in the Bronx. The company employed illegal aliens of various backgrounds to do the assembly work. This work, among other things, involved injecting liquid mercury into the glass tubes, sealing the tubes, and affixing them to the wooden frames of the 12-inch devices. Inevitably, workers came into contact with the mercury. The owners of the company knew how dangerous mercury is but declined to provide protective equipment, such as rubber gloves and masks, or even to warn the workers. On a tip, OSHA and ICE raided the factory. ICE arrested the illegal workers. OSHA cited the company for serious violations. The story was front-page news in the tabloid *New York Post*. The New York district attorney has decided it would really help her reelection campaign if she prosecuted the owners of Hot Zone under the city's criminal code.

Do you think that the district attorney should be allowed to prosecute the owners criminally, or should health and safety enforcement such as this be limited to the citations and fines permitted under the Occupational Safety and Health Act? If you believe that criminal prosecutions should be permitted under some circumstances, where would you draw that line?

18. Columbia Iron & Steel, Inc., operates a foundry where pipes and other plumbing fixtures are cast. Much of the raw material used in the manufacturing process comes from scrap metal of all kinds, including galvanized pipe containing zinc. While overexposure to zinc fumes can result in the so-called "zinc shakes," this is a temporary condition. When a worker appears in the plant's clinic with zinc shakes, the doctor typically prescribes a week of sick leave, after which the employee is cleared to return to work. However, women workers are a different story. While not absolutely proven, it is widely accepted in the medical profession that exposure to zinc in the early stages of pregnancy can result in spontaneous abortion or severe birth defects. Consequently, the company has a rule against women of childbearing age working in the "hot end" of the foundry, where exposure to zinc fumes is likely to occur. However, hot-end work pays much better than quality assurance and packing work at the cold end of the plant. A number of young women working in the foundry contend that it should be left up to them whether or

not to risk exposure to zinc by working in the hot end of the plant, if they are otherwise qualified to do the work.

What is your view of their position? If OSHA has regulations that apply to iron foundries, and if those regulations do not address the potential risk that concerns the company, how does this affect your answer? If the women are willing to waive any rights they may have against the company in the event that their reproductive systems are harmed in the hot end, what are the public policy considerations, pro and con, permitting such a waiver?

19. Geraldine Jones is a clerk in the Sack-of-Suds convenience store. She works on the night shift alone. OSHA has issued recommendations for prevention of workplace violence, many of which relate directly to Jones's situation. However, the OSHA publication specifically states,

> These recommendations are not a new standard or regulation and do not create any new OSHA duties. Under the Occupational Safety and Health Act of 1970 (the OSH Act, or the Act), the extent of an employer's obligation to address workplace violence is governed by the General Duty Clause. The fact that a measure is recommended in this document but not adopted by an employer is not evidence of a violation of the General Duty Clause. The recommendations provide information about possible workplace violence prevention strategies. They describe a variety of tools that may be useful to employers designing a violence prevention program.

The Sack-of-Suds owners decline to provide any training or protection for employees such as Jones. The company's iron-clad rule for clerks is that no more than $50 is to be kept in the register at any one time. All other cash is to be stuffed through the slot in a floor safe, which Jones is unable to open. One night an armed robber entered her store and demanded the money. When Jones could only produce a little less than $50 from her cash drawer, the thief became infuriated, beating Jones severely. If Jones complains to OSHA, will the agency be able to make a citation and fine stick against the company on these facts?

20. The High-Flier Aircraft Company manufactures small aircraft in a plant which features a 50-foot-high, arched roof; this accommodates an overhead crane to move the aircraft fuselages from one end of the assembly line to the other. During the recent economic downturn, orders for executive jets for corporate CEOs have been way down. Grateful for an order for a top-of-the-line plane from a *Fortune* 500 company, High-Flier's employees are determined to produce a top-flight aircraft within the short timeline provided in the sales contract. Consequently, when the crane breaks down and the line is forced to stop, Fred Smith, the plant's head maintenance mechanic, is determined to repair the crane without wasting the time involved in following the normal maintenance procedure, which requires lowering the boom to floor level. Instead, Fred climbs to the top of the crane. Finding no convenient place to fix a safety line, he goes to work "without a net," so to speak. He slips and falls to his death. When OSHA proposes to cite the company for Fred's death and impose a significant fine, the company appeals on the ground that Fred failed to follow plant procedure but instead took it upon himself to risk his life at the top of the crane. What should the federal court rule in this case?

21. Responding to a call alleging safety violations from a janitorial employee at the Toddler Togs garment factory, an OSHA inspector drives up to the back of the factory. A group of workers on break is sitting around on the loading dock, smoking and eating snacks. The inspector introduces himself. One of the employees identifies herself as the caller. She invites him to come into the shipping area, where he sees several violations, which he subsequently cites. The plant manager first learns of the inspection when he receives the citations via certified mail. Is the inspection legal? If the plant manager learns the identity of the janitor involved, are there legal grounds for disciplining her?

CHAPTER 21

The Employee's Safety Nets: Unemployment and Workers' Compensation, Social Security, and Retirement Plans

Not until the 1900s, and for a substantial number of Americans not even until the 1930s, did the government assist workers affected by unemployment, on-the-job injury, work-related disability, or old age. Until that time, Americans (like workers around the world then and millions even today) relied on their families, ethnic communities, churches, and social clubs for aid when their incomes were temporarily or permanently disrupted. For instance, Irish coal miners in Pennsylvania in the 1870s might have belonged to the Ancient Order of Hibernians, a benevolent society with a fund dedicated to assisting the widows and orphans of miners killed in the "pits." Increasingly, too, workers organized and looked to their unions for help in times of trouble. But before Congress passed the National Labor Relations Act (NLRA) in 1935, most unions were mere shadows of what they would later become.

Congress did occasionally become involved in the welfare of employees in private industry, even before the groundbreaking legislation of the 1930s. The Railway Labor Act (governing labor relations), which was passed in 1926, and the **Federal Employment Liability Act (FELA)**, which was passed in 1908, predate the NLRA and workers' compensation laws, respectively. The FELA was enacted in recognition of the incredible number of casualties in the railroad industry (about 25,000 deaths annually around the turn of the last century) and of the virtual hopelessness of injured workers trying to sue their employers in those days.

Suppose a railroad worker in 1900 was hit by a railcar that rolled in deadly silence down the track because of a faultily set brake. The injured, perhaps permanently disabled, worker might hold the railroad responsible and seek to sue it for monetary damages. To do so, he would first have to find a lawyer willing to take the case. Having little or no savings, he might find it difficult to obtain an attorney prepared to take on one of the great financial juggernauts of the era. If he did, he faced a daunting set of defenses that the railroad company could raise. The railroad's lawyers most likely would first argue that the hapless employee, by taking the job, had assumed the risk of injury. They would then seek to establish that he somehow had been contributorily negligent, such as by not being alert while in the rail yard. Finally, they would invoke the fellow-servant doctrine; that is, they would say

Federal Employment Liability Act (FELA) a federal law designed to protect and compensate railroad workers injured on the job

that he was not injured by their client, "the railroad," but by a coworker who had negligently failed to set the brake properly.

As you can see, any worker who recovered what his injuries deserved from the railroad had to have been both very persistent and very lucky. For most workers, or their widows and orphans, the alternative was one of the forms of charity previously mentioned, perhaps in combination with some modest form of public dole. But being employed in the key industry of industrialized America, railroad workers were the first who were able to exert unified pressure to better their circumstances. Theirs was the first major industry to be organized by several railway brotherhoods, such as the Brotherhood of Railway Clerks. Once organized, they successfully lobbied for passage of the FELA.

Although the FELA still requires an injured railroad worker to file suit in a federal or state court, it substantially reduces the burden of proof placed upon the employee/plaintiff, while depriving the railroad/defendant of some of its most potent defenses. Thus, injured employees generally win their cases under the FELA, which is still in force today.

Not until the New Deal era of the 1930s did such legislation become widespread in the United States. The Pennsylvania Superior Court summarized the development of such U.S. laws in a 1946 unemployment compensation decision, *Bliley Electric Company v. Unemployment Compensation Board of Review*:[1]

> The statute, almost ten years old, introduced into our law a new concept of social obligation, extended the police power of the State into a virgin field, and created a body of rights and duties unknown to the common law. England was the first common law country to operate a similar system, and its experience began as an experiment in 1911. Its law, revised as trial exposed error, became the basis for the American unemployment compensation system, although in detail there are vast variances between the American and British systems. Wisconsin passed an act in 1932, but it required the enactment of the Social Security Act by Congress on August 14, 1935 to induce other states to adopt the system. All of the states have enacted conforming legislation, and their statutes include the basic requirements laid down by the Act of Congress, but they differ widely and sharply in respect to the details, which Congress left open to state legislation.

The model for the genesis of unemployment benefits identified by the Pennsylvania Superior Court also matches the historical pattern for social security and workers' compensation. Although the roots of these laws can be traced to the second decade of the 20th century (just a bit behind England and Germany), the widespread availability of these important benefits is indebted to President Franklin Roosevelt's New Deal.

All three social welfare programs—social security pensions, workers' compensation, and unemployment compensation—descend from a common history and came into being about the same time. A major distinction between unemployment and workers' compensation versus social security is that the states have primary responsibility for the first two (with some notable exceptions), whereas social security is a federally supervised program applied uniformly across the country. But despite this difference, plus many distinctions between the various states' systems of unemployment or workers' compensation, the common threads, like the common ancestry, make it possible to discuss each of these forms of worker welfare in general terms. Wherever you wind up working in the United States, you will find that state's systems readily recognizable.

---

[1] 45 A.2d 898, 901 (1946).

Last but not least in this chapter is the Employee Retirement Income Security Act (ERISA), a latecomer to the "security net" outlined in the preceding paragraphs. In 1974, the act was passed by Congress in response to numerous instances of pension fund mismanagement and abuse. Retired employees had their pension benefits reduced or terminated because their pension plan had been inadequately funded or depleted through mismanagement. In other instances, employees retiring after as many as 20 years or more of service with an employer were ineligible for pensions because of complex and strict eligibility requirements. ERISA is intended to prevent such abuses and to protect the interests of employees and their beneficiaries in employee benefit plans.

21-1   Unemployment Compensation

The economic crisis of late 2008, extending into 2012, starkly underlined the significance of unemployment compensation. The national unemployment rate approached 10 percent in the depths of the severe recession, a level unseen since the "stagflation" days of the 1970s, and only dipped below 8 percent again in September 2012. Most of the job casualties of this downturn were able to collect weekly unemployment compensation checks for anywhere from 26 to 52 weeks, depending upon the individual states' laws, financial circumstances, and the availability of federal bailout supplements to state funds.

However, not every out-of-work employee was entitled to this benefit. Eligibility for **unemployment compensation** requires that the "idleness" occur in a specific set of circumstances: The employee must be out of work through no fault of his or her own and be available for suitable work if and when it becomes available.

The concept of fault is an attenuated one; that is, only a high level of fault, termed **willful misconduct**, will serve to disqualify the out-of-work worker from these benefits. Incompetence is considered to be an unfortunate condition, not a basis for affixing guilt, under this branch of employment law. So although an at-will employee, or even one protected by a "good cause" provision in a labor contract, may properly be dismissed for poor performance, that alone will not disqualify him or her from receiving unemployment benefits.

"Willful misconduct" is an issue of constant debate and redefinition in the unemployment compensation systems of our 50 states. For example, is absenteeism "misconduct"? If it is, when is it "willful"? The employee who is "excessively" (itself a tough term to define) absent or tardy may be lazy, or he or she may have children to get to day care or a bus to catch that is unreliable. In the latter instance, the employee can probably still be discharged but most likely will not be denied benefits until she or he can find another job.

Even if the conduct is clearly willful and wrong, it still may not be enough to disqualify the applicant for unemployment benefits. If, for instance, the misconduct is not readily discernible to the average worker and the employer failed to promulgate a rule or give a warning for prior infractions, an unemployment referee may be reluctant to deny benefits. The following case deals with whether an employer's drug testing policy must specifically state that refusal to submit to a drug test is grounds for discharge.

unemployment compensation
benefits paid to employees out of work through no fault of their own and who are available for suitable work if and when it becomes available

willful misconduct
the high level of fault that disqualifies an out-of-work worker from unemployment benefits

» CASE 21.1

ARCHITECTURAL TESTING, INC. V. UNEMPLOYMENT COMPENSATION BOARD OF REVIEW
940 A.2d 1277 (Pa. Commonwealth Ct. 2008.)

Facts: George W. Yohe worked for Architectural Testing, Inc. [employer] since November 2001. His position involved construction-type work on mechanical lifts at up to 60 feet in height, and in close proximity to other workers. The employer had an established substance abuse policy which stated in pertinent part:

> The use, possession, or distribution of alcohol or illegal drugs or the illegal distribution of legal drugs is not tolerated on company property, in company vehicles, or at any job site. Any employee aware of or suspicious of abuse to [*sic*] this policy is obligated to report the issue to management immediately.
>
> A drug & alcohol screening is performed for all newly hired employees and all employees involved in an accident in which property damage, personal injury, or the potential for personal injury has occurred. Additionally, a drug & alcohol screening may be requested from any employee that demonstrates cause for concern regarding use of drugs or alcohol.
>
> Any employee whose screening detects use of an illegal drug may be immediately terminated. ...

On May 30, 2006, the employer discharged Yohe for failing to submit to a drug test. He then applied for unemployment compensation benefits, but his claim was denied based on Section 402(e)(1) of the Unemployment Compensation Law (UCL), which relates to a claimant's ineligibility for benefits "due to failure to submit and/or pass a drug test conducted pursuant to an employer's established substance abuse policy." Yohe appealed the denial, and after a hearing, the Unemployment Compensation Referee affirmed the denial of benefits. Yohe then appealed to the Unemployment Compensation Board of Review [Board], which reversed the Referee and granted benefits to Yohe. The Board held that because the employer's substance abuse policy did not provide for disciplinary action for an employee who refused to submit a drug test, Section 402(e)(1) did not render Yohe ineligible for benefits. The Board also found that employer's concerns, which led

to the drug test, "were based on speculation and hearsay reports." The employer then appealed to the Commonwealth Court.

Issue: Must an employee's refusal to take a drug test be in violation of a written drug testing policy that specifically states that an employee can be discharged for refusing to take a drug test in order for the employee to be disqualified from receiving unemployment benefits?

Decision: Before the court, the employer argued that Yohe's refusal to submit to a drug test, despite an established policy allowing the employer to request a drug test upon reasonable grounds for suspicion, constituted willful misconduct under Section 402(e)(1) of the law. Section 402(e)(1) states that a claimant will not be eligible for unemployment compensation benefits if he is unemployed "due to failure to submit and/or pass a drug test conducted pursuant to an employer's established substance abuse policy. ..." The case here turns on the phrase "conducted pursuant to an employer's established substance abuse policy." The Board appeared to interpret this phrase to mean that in order to terminate an employee for refusing a drug test, the employer must have an established policy which explicitly sets out the consequences for refusal of a drug test. However, the court held that such an interpretation goes against the plain meaning of the law. Under the plain meaning of Section 402(e)(1), an employer's established substance abuse policy only needs to set forth when an employee may be required to submit to a drug test. Section 402(e)(1), by its language, does not require the policy to set forth the consequences for refusal of a drug test.

The Board's reading of the statute added an extra requirement that does not appear in the text itself. Had the legislature wished to require that employers' substance abuse policies set forth the consequences for failure to submit or pass drug tests, it could have done so. Instead, it only required that the drug test be conducted pursuant to an established policy. To accept the Board's rule that in order to discharge an employee for refusal to submit to a drug test, the employer must have a substance abuse policy which explicitly provides for such discharge would render 402(e)(1) redundant given that such a situation would already satisfy the requirements to show willful misconduct.

The Board's reading of the statute also leads to an absurd, unreasonable result. Here the employer has an established substance abuse policy providing for employee drug testing and for discharge of an employee for failure to pass a drug test. The Board's reading of Section 402(e) (1), would produce the absurd result where, in such a situation, an employee who knows he cannot pass a drug test may avoid discharge by simply refusing to take a drug test that the employer is attempting to conduct pursuant to its

established substance abuse policy. Therefore, the court held that in order for a claimant to be rendered ineligible for benefits under Section 402(e)(1) of the law, the employer need only have an established substance abuse policy which permits it to conduct drug tests; the employer's policy need not explicitly state that an employee may be discharged for refusal to submit to such a test, even though well-drafted policies will do so. The employer believed it had cause for concern regarding Yohe's use of drugs and alcohol, and therefore, pursuant to its established substance abuse policy, requested him to submit to a drug test. He refused, and is therefore ineligible for benefits under Section 402(e)(1). The Commonwealth Court reversed the order of the Board granting unemployment benefits to Yohe.

Besides being guilty of willful misconduct, a claimant may be denied benefits if he or she voluntarily quit the job. Under normal conditions, an employee cannot quit his job and then apply for unemployment benefits. In other words, when a worker is discontented, he or she is expected to stick with his or her current job until he or she finds another—not quit and collect benefits pending reemployment.

However, in some compelling circumstances, the law will allow an employee to leave the employment. In these cases, quitting is considered involuntary because it amounts to a constructive discharge from the job. Some such cases have involved extreme instances of sexual or racial harassment by the employee's immediate supervisor to the extent that the boards and courts held that no worker should be required to submit to such abuse or risk denial of unemployment compensation. Others have concerned an employee's extreme allergic reaction to substances in the workplace. In all such cases, the employee must remain available for alternative jobs that the state employment agency might direct him or her to apply for. (In some instances, such as when an allergy is so severe and general that the employee cannot work at all, workers' compensation might be the more appropriate remedy.)

21-1a Litigating Unemployment Claims

Unemployment compensation litigation usually starts with a terminated worker's application for benefits. The unemployment claim is usually evaluated in the first instance by an unemployment office or agency in the area where the worker resides. Regardless of whether the decision is favorable or unfavorable, an appeal is possible. The worker's motive for appealing an unfavorable decision is obvious. But why would an employer challenge the grant of benefits to someone it had let go? The answer is that unemployment benefits are paid for by a tax on the wages of the workers and an equal levy on the employer's total payroll. In most jurisdictions, this tax is variable, rising and falling with the particular company's experience in drawing upon the state fund. Consequently, if undeserving dischargees are permitted to receive benefits, the employer will experience a gradual increase in these payroll taxes.

Challenged decisions go to a referee and from there can usually be appealed into the state court system. A case can potentially go all the way to a state's supreme court, which typically reviews a few selected cases of special significance each year.

Some organizations and their human resources operations consider eligibility for unemployment compensation to be a ministerial matter to be administered by a low- or mid-level staffer on a case-by-case basis. Other, more sophisticated employers recognize that unemployment compensation claims must be considered within the context of the company's total human resource strategy. These executives understand that unemployment compensation claims can:

- impact the organization's bottom line (as when substantial turnover accompanied by increased claims substantially enlarges the company's payroll taxes);

- create a record which is helpful to the claimant when later pursuing a discrimination or other type of wrongful discharge claim against the corporation; and

- be included in a severance/release agreement between the company and an employee departing under less than amicable circumstances.

However, using the terminated employee's potential eligibility for unemployment benefits, and the company's ability to oppose the former employee's claim, presents some danger to the employer who abuses this leverage. The following case, *Label Systems Corp. v. Aghamohammadi*, illustrates this risk.

CASE 21.2

LABEL SYSTEMS CORP. V. AGHAMOHAMMADI

70 Conn. 291, 852 A.2d 703 (Connecticut Supreme Court, 2004)

This appeal arose out of a dispute between two former employees, the defendants, Samad Aghamohammadi and Pamela Markham, and their former employer, the plaintiff, Label Systems Corporation (Label Systems), as well as its president, Kenneth P. Felis. Label Systems commenced this action against the defendants, who counterclaimed against Label Systems and filed a third-party complaint against Felis. A jury found the defendants liable for conversion (theft), and awarded Label Systems compensatory and punitive damages. In addition, the jury found Label Systems and Felis liable for vexatious litigation in relation to a prior action, and awarded the defendants compensatory damages. The trial court rendered judgment in accordance with the jury's verdict. The plaintiffs appealed, and the defendants cross-appealed to the Appellate Court. The state supreme court took jurisdiction under a special jurisdictional statute.

The jury had rendered its verdict on the following facts in evidence: Label Systems, a corporation located in Bridgeport, was in the business of manufacturing and producing,

among other things, labels, stickers and holograms. The defendants were a married couple, both of whom were employed by Label Systems. Aghamohammadi, an immigrant from Iran, began his employment with Label Systems in 1985, and advanced to the position of head of the finishing department. In that capacity, Aghamohammadi was responsible for the examination and inspection of finished products for defects, packaging finished products for shipment and shipping products to customers. Markham began her employment at Label Systems in 1982, and served as the office manager and bookkeeper, where she was primarily responsible for paying Label Systems' bills, managing its finances, and overseeing its medical plan. Both defendants were regarded as valuable and trusted employees by Felis. During their employment, the defendants were provided with a company car, which they used for their commute from Waterbury to Bridgeport. In November, 1992, while driving the company car, their sole means of transportation, the defendants were rear-ended by another car. Subsequently, the defendants received a check in the amount of $1095.01 from the other driver's insurance company. Because Markham was nearing the end of a difficult pregnancy, her first, the defendants did not want to be without the car, and they chose to delay having it repaired until after her delivery. Accordingly, the defendants cashed the insurance check and deposited the proceeds into their personal checking account. In early 1993, Felis equipped the defendants' house with computer equipment so that Markham could work from home after the baby was born, and he built and furnished a nursery in the office for Markham to use after she returned to work.

On February 15, 1993, upon their arrival at work, the defendants were met outside by Felis and other members of his staff. Felis gave the defendants letters of termination that accused them of willful and felonious misconduct in the course of their employment, terminated their employment, and refused to allow them to enter the facility to collect their personal belongings.

The defendants surrendered the company car to Felis, and departed in an awaiting limousine, which had been arranged by Felis. Later that evening, Aghamohammadi was arrested based upon Felis' claim that Aghamohammadi had threatened him when receiving his letter of termination. Label Systems immediately stopped paying a salary to both defendants, and terminated their health insurance.

On February 23, 1993, Markham gave birth to the defendants' first child. On March 10, 1993, Label Systems filed a three-count complaint against the defendants, alleging conversion, breach of duties of loyalty, and appropriation of trade secrets. The defendants had requested unemployment benefits immediately following their termination, and on April 7, 1993, over the objection of Label Systems, separate awards of unemployment benefits were made to both defendants. The defendants were unable to extend their health insurance at their own expense, however, because of the alleged willful and felonious misconduct underlying the termination of their employment. On April 22, 1993, Felis, on behalf of Label Systems, appealed from the decisions awarding unemployment benefits to the defendants, claiming that the defendants were terminated for willful and felonious misconduct, and, therefore, that they were precluded from receiving such benefits. Over the course of the next four months, three separate hearings were held in which the plaintiffs offered testimony and evidence in support of their claim of willful and felonious misconduct by the defendants. On August 18, 1993, after the third hearing, both appeals were unilaterally withdrawn by the plaintiffs.

In April, 1994, in response to the withdrawal of the appeals, the defendants counterclaimed against Label Systems, and filed a third-party complaint against Felis, both of which alleged vexatious litigation, abuse of process, intentional infliction of emotional distress, negligent infliction of emotional distress, slander per se, slander, interference with contractual relations, wrongful discharge and intentional interference with prospective contractual relations. In July, 2001, the actions proceeded to trial, where the jury found the defendants liable for conversion, rejected all of Label Systems' remaining claims, and awarded Label Systems $50 in compensatory damages. In addition, the jury found that the defendants had converted Label Systems' property under circumstances warranting punitive damages, in an amount to be set by the trial court according to the prior agreement of the parties. In regard to the counterclaims and third-party complaint, the jury found the plaintiffs liable for vexatious litigation, rejected all of the remaining claims, and awarded Markham $160,000 and Aghamohammadi $60,000 in compensatory damages. These awards were doubled automatically pursuant to General Statutes § 52-568 (1), which provides for the doubling of damages for groundless or vexatious actions. The trial court denied several post-trial motions filed by both parties, awarded Label Systems $19,460.17 in punitive damages, and rendered judgment in accordance with the jury's verdict. This appeal followed....

In regard to the appeal from Markham's award, the plaintiffs advanced two reasons supporting their belief, prior to the time of termination, that Markham had engaged in willful and felonious misconduct. First was Felis' belief that Markham had met with Henry J. Behre, Jr., a former employee of Label Systems, and provided him with confidential company information to assist him with his arbitration action then pending against Label Systems for back wages. As the trial court properly noted, however, the jury reasonably could have credited Markham's testimony that she had never disclosed any confidential information to Behre, as well as Behre's testimony that Felis had disclosed the information to Behre in earlier conversations. In addition, it was well within the province of the jury not to credit the testimony of Felis. Second was Felis' belief that Markham had leaked information to Behre concerning a financial investment made in Label Systems by RPM, Inc. (RPM). The jury reasonably could have declined to credit this testimony, and instead credit the testimony of Behre that Felis not only told him of RPM's investment in Label Systems, but that the letter that had terminated his employment relationship with Label Systems had the logo of both companies at the top of the page, thereby making the relationship between the companies obvious. This letter was admitted into evidence, and the jury was able to examine it firsthand. Indeed, Felis testified that in 1992, RPM had circulated a memo to all of its operating companies, including Label Systems, that highlighted RPM's concern with having its logo directly next to each individual operating company's logo on items such as stationery and invoices.

In regard to the appeal from Aghamohammadi's award, Felis testified that, at the time of Aghamohammadi's termination, Felis believed that Aghamohammadi was responsible for an alleged shortage of materials at Label Systems, and that Aghamohammadi was a partner with Behre in an undisclosed business venture, Mecca Trading and Shipping (Mecca). With respect to Mecca, Aghamohammadi testified that he had disclosed Mecca to Felis previously, had offered to make Felis a partner in the business, and that Felis allowed him to make limited use of Label Systems equipment and facilities in his spare time for activities relating to Mecca. To the contrary, Felis testified that Aghamohammadi never disclosed Mecca's existence to him, and that he discovered Mecca's existence just prior to terminating the defendants. It was entirely reasonable, therefore, for the jury to credit Aghamohammadi's testimony over Felis' testimony. With respect to the alleged shortage of materials, Aghamohammadi testified that he was not responsible for any alleged shortage, and that he never stole or misappropriated any material from Label Systems. Indeed, Felis testified that he could not identify whether the alleged shortages occurred with raw product, partially finished product or finished product.

In sum, our review of the record reveals that there was sufficient evidence from which the jury could "reasonably and legally have reached their conclusion." Accordingly, we conclude that the trial court did not abuse its discretion in denying the plaintiffs' motion for a directed verdict on the vexatious litigation claim....

In regard to Aghamohammadi, the jury reasonably could have credited his testimony that the initiation of the appeal, the accusation of willful and felonious misconduct, and the concomitant threatened loss of benefits, collectively caused him such emotional harm as to give up all hope of being successful in the United States, and to plead with his wife to move back to his native country of Iran. Thus, we agree with the trial court that Aghamohammadi's feelings, "as he expressed and visibly displayed them to the jury," reasonably supported the jury's award of $60,000 and that the jury's award "reflects a thoughtful exercise of judgment and discretion."

The award of $120,000 to Markham, while certainly more substantial than the award to Aghamohammadi, also is reasonably supported by the evidence presented at trial. Specifically, viewed in the light most favorable to Markham, the jury reasonably could have found that she had endured mental and emotional suffering due to the vexatious appeal of the unemployment awards for the same reasons as we discussed with regard to Aghamohammadi. In addition, the jury could have found that the emotional damage to Markham was exacerbated, in comparison to Aghamohammadi, by virtue of the fact that she recently had given birth and had a prior history of depression. Indeed, Markham's testimony provided reasonable support for the jury's conclusion that the appeal deeply distressed her, both while the appeal was pending and for a long period after it was withdrawn summarily. If the jury thought Markham was embellishing her testimony, or exaggerating the impact the appeal had on her well-being, it could have rejected her claim or awarded her a smaller amount in damages. In its memorandum of decision, however, the trial court noted that when "the court saw her give that testimony, it knew at once that the jury would be moved by it." Accordingly, while we agree that the damages awarded to Markham were "ample," we nevertheless are unable to conclude that the trial court abused its discretion by denying the plaintiffs' motion for remittitur [reduction].

Case Questions

1. Were the defendants, husband and wife, guilty of any wrongdoing?

2. If so, why were they awarded unemployment compensation in the first place?

3. Do you agree that the plaintiffs were guilty of "vexatious litigation" when they opposed the defendants' unemployment compensation claim?

4. Why did the plaintiffs oppose the defendants' unemployment compensation? Was their motive purely personal animosity or were they pursuing a broader corporate strategy with regard to the defendants or in terms of overall company human resources policy?

5. In retrospect, given the length and outcome of the litigation, what advice would you have given the company?

Concept *Summary* 21.1

UNEMPLOYMENT COMPENSATION

- Typically administered by the states, not the federal government
- Intended to assist employees out of work through no fault of their own
- Disqualifications for an out-of-work employee include:
  - Willful misconduct
  - Voluntary quitting
- Litigating unmeritorious claims:
  - Keeps payroll taxes down
  - May prevent subsequent wrongful discharge claims

21-2 Workers' Compensation

workers' compensation
benefits awarded to an employee when injuries are work related

Workers' compensation, as it has been instituted in virtually every state, is a statutory trade-off. As noted earlier in the case of the injured railway worker, the employer loses several highly successful defenses to the injured employee's claim: assumption of risk, contributory negligence, and the fellow-servant doctrine. In return, employers get immunity from suits by injured employees, with some limited exceptions. Typically, the exceptions are failure to carry the requisite compensation insurance; intentional, as opposed to accidental, injuries to employees; and those rare circumstances in which the employer—a hospital, for example—deals with, and harms, the employee in its capacity as a third-party provider of a service and not as employer.

For the worker, typical compensation schemes permit easy access to benefits, relatively simple adjudication of disputed claims, plus the possibility of an additional, perhaps more substantial, recovery in a related third-party tort action against, say, the manufacturer of the machine that caused the work-related injury. Employers and insurance carriers often complain about fraudulent claims, usually involving hard-to-disprove back injuries. Perhaps the only possible response to claims of fraud is that any system conceived and run by human beings will be subject to some abuses. The concept of workers' compensation is eminently fair, and in practice, it has spared millions of injured workers and their families untold hardship.

To be eligible for workers' compensation, an employee's injury must be work related. Sometimes factual circumstances make it difficult to determine whether the worker's injury or illness is really work related and therefore covered by workers' compensation or falls outside the exclusive jurisdiction of the act. Some examples include:

- Injuries intentionally inflicted upon one employee by another
- Injuries occurring when the employee is "on the road," especially if the trip began from the employee's home
- Chronic illnesses such as lung disease, especially if contributing factors include workplace hazards (e.g., dust) in combination with personal behavior (e.g., smoking)

One of the most difficult issues for the courts in recent years has been in utero injury to a fetus as the result of the mother's on-the-job accident. Should workers' compensation be the child's exclusive remedy, just as it is the mother's, or should the parents be able to sue for larger damages on the child's behalf?

Some state legislatures and courts have answered this question in the affirmative, as shown in the Ethical Dilemma. This dilemma arises from a long tradition in Anglo-Saxon law that generally denies legal standing to fetuses as full-fledged human beings. But what to do, then, if the fetus is injured "on the job" but survives to become a full-fledged "person" in the eyes of the law?

ethical DILEMMA

IN UTERO WORKPLACE INJURIES

In *Meyer v. Burger King Corporation*,[2] Sonrise Management, Inc. (Sonrise) was the management company for a Burger King Corporation restaurant located in Lacey, Washington. Verona Meyer (Verona) was employed by Sonrise at this Burger King. On April 26, 1995, Verona was working her shift at the restaurant. She was approximately 35 weeks pregnant at the time. While in the course and scope of her employment on that day, she lost her footing and struck her lower abdomen on the corner of a table known as the "Whopper board." Later that evening, Verona went to the hospital and delivered her baby, Patricia. Verona and Gary Meyer, her husband, claimed that blunt trauma to Verona's abdomen from the Whopper board had caused an abruption of the placenta, in which the placenta partially detached from Verona's uterine wall. The Meyers further claimed that, because of the placental abruption, there was a loss of oxygen to Patricia while she was *in utero*, and this loss of oxygen in turn resulted in Patricia being born several hours later with severe injuries.

In April 1998, the Meyers, on behalf of themselves and their daughter, Patricia, filed suit against Sonrise for negligence. The complaint alleged that both Verona and Patricia were injured in the course of Verona's employment because of unsafe working conditions. The Meyers claimed damages for Patricia's injuries, which allegedly included permanent mental and physical disabilities, and for their own subsequent losses due to destruction of the parent/child relationship.

The Washington State Supreme Court wrote, "We must determine whether the exclusionary provision of the [Workers' Compensation] Act bars Patricia's claims and those of her parents. This is a question of law which we review *de novo*."

The court then reviewed how numerous "sister" courts around the nation have dealt with this difficult issue:

- "The most analogous representative case is *Cushing ex rel. Brewer v. Time Saver Stores, Inc.*,[3] where the Louisiana Court of Appeals held the exclusivity provision of Louisiana's workers' compensation statute did not bar a child's claim for damages

---

[2] 144 Wash.2d 160, 26 P.3d 925 (2001).

[3] 552 So.2d 730 (La. Ct. App. 1989).

for prenatal injuries suffered as a result of the mother's fall at work. In that case, the mother was performing recordkeeping duties in the store's back room. The room was without furniture, so the woman was compelled to sit on boxes and use crates and plywood as a surface for an adding machine. The boxes shifted, the mother fell, and the adding machine fell on her abdomen, causing an abruption of the placenta. Her baby was born prematurely 12 days later with severe birth defects, including permanent brain damage. The Louisiana court reasoned the exclusivity provision of the statute barred actions that depend on the injuries of the employee, such as loss of support or loss of consortium (i.e., because the mother/father or husband/wife suffered an injury, the family suffered a loss based upon that injury). The *Cushing* court found the child's injuries in no way derived from the mother's injuries because '[w]hether mom is there to continue bringing home a pay check or to participate in the child's life has no relevance to this child's alleged brain damage. The court held the workers' compensation statute was not intended to nor does it purport to affect the rights of an employee's child who is injured on the employer's job site."

- "The Colorado Supreme Court reached the same conclusion in *Pizza Hut of Am., Inc. v. Keefe*.[4] In that case, the court reasoned the fact the mother and child were injured in the same event does not render the damage to the child derivative of the mother's injury because the child's right of action arises out of the child's own personal injuries and not merely the personal injuries suffered by the mother. When the employee's child is *born*, it stands in the same position as any other nonemployee member of the public. Workers' compensation laws would not bar a claim by a child who was injured while visiting his or her parent in the workplace. Therefore, the exclusivity provisions of workers' compensation statutes do not bar claims by a nonemployee child who sustains prenatal injuries in the workplace, as it does not bar claims asserted by third party victims. A nonemployee's injury is neither collateral nor derivative of an employee's injury merely because both resulted from the same negligent conduct by the employer. Thus, a child still in the womb can sustain independent injuries arising from the same event allegedly caused by the negligence of the employer."

- "Most recently, the Hawaii Supreme Court reached a similar conclusion. In *Omori v. Jowa Hawai'i Co.*,[5] a pregnant employee who worked at a convenience store had her water break prematurely. Her doctor ordered her to stop working. However, the convenience store manager refused to allow her time off. Her job included lifting boxes, stacking shelves, and various cleaning duties. Allegedly, as a consequence of being forced to continue working, the mother suffered a premature rupture of the membrane and the child was born prematurely with severe physical injuries. The mother brought suit on behalf of the child for his injuries and also for loss of consortium with the child. The court found the child's injuries were independent of any injury to the worker and held Hawaii's workers' compensation statute *did not bar* a child from bringing an action against the mother's employer for prenatal injuries, *nor* a claim by the parents for loss of consortium."

---

[4] 900 P.2d 97 (Colo. 1995).

[5] 91 Hawai'i 146 981 P.2d 703 (1999).

The Washington Supreme Court, following the lead of these other courts, declined to limit the child's remedy to the provisions of the Workers' Compensation Act. In a concurring opinion, one justice attempted to square the decision with the U.S. Supreme Court's 1974 [*Roe v. Wade*[6]] precedent, which ruled that an unborn fetus lacks legal rights. "The common thread throughout all these cases is a limited recognition of a *person's* retroactive right to recover for prenatal injuries. The United States Supreme Court has likewise upheld recovery for prenatal injuries for children later born alive, while clarifying that 'the unborn have never been recognized in the law as persons in the whole sense.' While upholding Patricia's right to a remedy because she is a person exercising her retroactive right to recover for prenatal injuries, we do not recognize a fetus as a 'person[ ] in the whole sense' and thus do not affect the jurisprudence established under *Roe*." The justices, besides reconciling *Roe*, expressly rejected the employer's arguments that:

- the fetus's injury occurred simultaneously with the mother's;
- the company could not bar pregnant employees from the workplace without committing illegal discrimination; and
- it could not take steps to protect the unborn child in the way that it could guard against injury to its customers' children.

21-2a   Federal Preemption of Workers' Compensation Claims

Although workers' compensation has been left primarily to the states to administer, the system does brush up against various federal acts for compensating workers for whom Congress now deems, or at some time in the past considered, deserving of special protection. Railroad workers have long had recourse to the FELA; sailors come under the Jones Act[7]; and many other maritime workers are covered by the Longshoremen's and Harbor Workers' Compensation Act.[8] U.S. government workers have their own Federal Employees Compensation Act.[9] In all cases, these acts supersede state workers' compensation laws.

The FELA has given rise to some difficult litigation. Suppose a railroad subsidiary is a trucking company that picks up and delivers goods to the railroad's freight yard, where the subsidiary's drivers are supervised by the railroad yardmaster. Does this make the railroad a joint employer of the driver? If so, can a driver injured at the yard claim workers' compensation benefits against the trucking subsidiary and then turn around and sue the railroad for even more money, such as for pain and suffering, under the FELA? The answer to this question typically turns on the railroad's right to control the driver's activities, as well as the legal relationship between the two companies.

A similar problem can arise when a worker contends that although the employer's liability under state law is limited to paying workers' compensation, separate employer liability exists under a preemptive federal law. In the 1990 case of *Adams Fruit Co., Inc. v. Barrett*,[10]

---

[6] 410 U.S. 113 (1973).

[7] 46 U.S.C. Section 688.

[8] 33 U.S.C. Section 901 *et seq.*

[9] 5 U.S.C. Section 1801.

[10] 494 U.S. 638 (1990).

the Supreme Court held that workers could bring suit for violations of specific federal legislation despite the fact that they had received benefits under the state workers' compensation law. The Court held that the specific federal legislation superseded the exclusivity provisions of the state workers' compensation law.

On the other hand, although ERISA (discussed in detail later in this chapter) has sweeping preemptive impact on most state laws, it specifically exempts state workers' compensation laws from its preemptive powers.

Concept *Summary* 21.2

WORKERS' COMPENSATION

- The fifty states administer workers' compensation laws
- Employers give up common law defenses
- Employees give up right to sue for tort damages
- Applicability is limited to job-related injuries
  - ○ Sometimes it is difficult to determine whether an injury is actually job related
- Some federal laws preempt workers' compensation laws
  - ○ ERISA is not one of them

21-3 Social Security

Nearly one in every seven Americans receives social security benefits. The Social Security system was originally entitled "old age and survivor's insurance" (OASI), and the notion that it really was insurance was a significant component of Franklin Roosevelt's success in selling the program to Congress and the country. During the decades that followed, the Social Security system rode out recurrent crises, as the baby boomers born after World War II retired in ever larger numbers and the deficit-ridden federal government borrowed from the Social Security fund. Today, at least for the foreseeable future, Social Security remains relatively sound, even in the face of the record deficits being run by Uncle Sam in an effort to reverse the financial meltdown that began in late 2008 to early 2009. The system's benefits fall into three major categories—retirement insurance benefits, Medicare, and disability.

21-3a Retirement Insurance Benefits

The original and still the main purpose of Social Security is to provide partial replacement of earnings when a worker decides it is time to retire. Although benefits have increased substantially in the last two decades, both in relative and absolute terms, this retirement benefit was never intended to totally replace what that worker was earning prior to retirement. And yet, for many Americans over 65, Social Security is the main, or even the only, source of income. This is true in part because the other major piece of federal legislation dealing with pensions, ERISA, goes a long way toward protecting an employee's accrued pension benefits. But, as you will learn, ERISA does not require an employer to establish a pension plan for its employees in the first place. And many workers still do not have significant pension plans where they work. Social Security is often the only safety net when it is no longer possible to continue working.

Monthly benefits are payable to a retired insured worker from age 62 onward. Under some circumstances, a spouse or children may also be eligible. For a person to be "fully insured" by Social Security, he or she must accrue a minimum of 40 quarters (that is, 10 years) of contributions. These contributions are shared by the employer and the employee, who has no choice but to have the tax taken directly out of each paycheck, until a maximum amount of taxable income (for social security purposes only) has been earned in a calendar year.

21-3b Medicare, Medicaid, and the Affordable Care Act

In addition to basic benefits, retired Americans receive a form of health insurance under the Social Security system. Medicare benefits cover a portion of the costs of hospitalization and the medical expenses of insured workers and their spouses aged 65 and older, as well as younger disabled workers in some circumstances. This insurance is divided into two parts, designated by the federal bureaucracy as A and B.

Part A is hospital insurance for inpatient hospital care, inpatient skilled nursing care, and hospice care. Part B is supplementary medical insurance, which helps defray the costs of doctors' services and other medical expenses not covered by part A.

A worker who applies for social security benefits and is receiving them at age 65 is automatically covered under part A. The same is true for someone who has been receiving social security disability benefits (discussed briefly in section Disability) for at least 24 months. Part B is not entirely free. One-fourth of the premium is paid by the beneficiary, whereas the other three-fourths are covered by the federal government's general revenues.

On March 23, 2010, President Barack Obama signed into law a 1,000-page statute, which marked the culmination of efforts by the Democratic Party to overhaul the U.S. health care system. These efforts began with an abortive effort by President Clinton and his wife Hilary in 1993. The Patient Protection and Affordable Health Care Act touched upon almost every aspect of health care and health insurance in America. The most controversial of its myriad provisions was the so called "mandate," requiring all Americans by 2014 to either have health insurance or pay a penalty to the IRS. Also deemed highly objectionable by many states was an expansion of Medicaid, which they felt was being forced upon them, whether they wanted it or not.

During the ensuing two years, more than half of the 50 states, as well as numerous private parties, mounted legal challenges to all or key parts of what was soon rechristened "Obamacare." Federal district and appellate courts divided sharply over the constitutionality of Obamacare. In 2012, the consolidated cases reached the nation's highest judicial forum. The U.S. Supreme Court held an unprecedented three days of hearings in the spring of that year.

Then, on June 28, 2012, by a vote of 5–4, the Court upheld the Affordable Care Act (Obamacare) mandate,[11] thus blessing the massive statute in almost all its essentials. While a majority of the justices ruled the ACA failed to pass muster under the Constitution's Commerce Clause, Obamacare was rescued by Chief Justice Roberts's decision to join the

---

[11] *National Federation of Independent Businesses v. Sebelius*, 132 S.Ct. 2566 (2012).

four liberal justices in finding that the mandate met the requirements of a constitutionally enacted tax. As a result:

- Individuals will have to (1) be covered by a group health insurance plan; (2) buy health insurance on their own, e.g., via State Exchange; or (3) pay a penalty along with their annual federal income tax to the U.S. Treasury, starting in 2014.

- Unmarried children will be able to continue coverage under their parents' group health insurance plans to age 26, if they lack group health insurance of their own.

- States will have to establish Health Insurance Exchanges by 2014.

But what does the decision mean for employers? The Philadelphia-headquartered law firm of Morgan Lewis offered the following guidance to its clients in the wake of the landmark decision:

- For purposes of 2012 and 2013 compliance, employers should determine if they are appropriately aggregating monthly group health plan valuation data in order to support 2012 Form W-2 reporting requirements.

- Companies also should get ready to receive and distribute or apply any medical loss ratio rebates associated with their 2011 insured health coverages.

- Employer group health plans should finalize their "Summary of Benefits and Coverage" materials to be included in their 2013 open-enrollment packages.

- Such plans also should complete updates of their SPDs and plan documents to describe 2011 and 2012 ACA changes they have made in their plan designs.

- Open-enrollment materials, payroll systems, and admin systems should reflect the 2013 plan–year cap of $2,500 on salary-deferral contributions into health care spending accounts.

- The creators of such plans need to understand and determine the patient-centered-outcomes trust fund fees that will be due in 2013.

- They should also take steps to identify whether or not they are both affordable and available to full-time employees, so that they can avoid the 2014 shared-responsibility penalties that can result if employees are driven to buying alternative insurance via state exchanges.

- Creators of plans should review potential design changes to retiree drug programs, reflective of the change in Medicare D subsidy tax rules.

- And, finally, they should consider design changes to blunt the impact of the Cadillac-Plan Tax that hits in 2018.

From the New York–headquartered firm of Proskauer Rose the following additional advice was forthcoming, as executives and human resources professionals scratched their heads:

- Employers should brace for expansion of FICA liability by 3.8 percent on the compensation of high-income individuals in 2013.

- They should also brace for the 9 percent Medicare payroll tax increase.

- And they should be ready to provide employees with a notice of availability of state exchanges starting in March of 2014.

Presenters in a Proskauer-sponsored June 29, 2012, webinar on Obamacare also cautioned about the potential for a variety of new lawsuits under the various provisions of the ACA. These included:

- *Workforce Realignment.* Many employers currently classify employees who work fewer than 40 hours per week as part-time. Part-time under the ACA is fewer than 30 hours. Some employers may decide to restructure jobs so that employees fall below the ACA threshold for purposes of health care coverage and shared-responsibility penalties. According to Proskauer, such realignment could stimulate a suit under 29 USC 1140, the section of ERISA, which prohibits improper interference with benefits. Such a suit would be ripe for class-action status.

- *Retiree-Only Plans.* Since the ACA allows for lesser benefits for retirees than active employees, employers may be tempted to sever retirees from "mixed" plans. Retirees typically are well-organized classes of claimants, who have demonstrated the willingness and ability to obtain counsel and pursue their former employers in court when their benefits have been diminished. Those who retired under the umbrellas of collective bargaining agreements have proven themselves to be particularly litigious.

- *Independent Review Organizations.* Such bodies function to determine claims of employees of affiliated employers. Lawsuits are most likely to arise where an IRO has incorrect plan information for a particular employer in its database, thus for example, paying a claim where the employer's plan does not in fact provide coverage. Whether or not an IRO is a fiduciary under the ACA is an open issue at the moment.

- *Grandfathered Plans.* If a plan is grandfathered, it will be able to avoid providing certain ACA-mandated benefits. But if the plan loses grandfather status, perhaps for a technical error, this may be yet another opportunity for aggrieved employees to launch a class action.

- *Whistleblowing.* The ACA beefs up ERISA's whistleblower protections by allowing special damages for the first time.

- *Religious Employers.* The application of the ACA's mandatory benefits in the area of women's preventive services including birth control and abortion coverage to religious institutions, religiously affiliated corporations, and some closely held for-profit corporations would substantially burden their exercise of religious freedom, according to the Supreme Court's decision in *Burwell v. Hobby Lobby Stores, Inc.*[12]

State Medicaid Expansion

The Supreme Court's decision in *National Federation of Independent Businesses v. Sebelius* also held that the ACA's Hobbs's Choice—expand their Medicaid or face stiff federal penalties—could not stand. Thus, each state must decide whether to opt in or out of Obamacare's Medicaid expansion provisions. In the wake of this aspect of the massive court opinion, the states have been weighing their options.

---

[12] 134 S.Ct. 2751 (2014).

Urban Institute and Kaiser Family Foundation   Opting out of the PPACA's Medicaid expansion appears to be more a function of political philosophy than fiscal responsibility. Despite the fact that many southern states run by conservative governors have pledged to opt out of the expansion, a recent study by the Kaiser Family Foundation shows that those are the states that would benefit most dramatically in terms of reducing their uninsured population.[13] "Overall, the Medicaid expansion is expected to result in a decrease in the number of uninsured of 11.2 million people, of 45 percent of the uninsured adults below 133 percent of poverty. States with low coverage levels and higher uninsured rates will see larger reductions (Alabama 53.2 percent and Texas 49.4)."[14]

The Urban Institute more recently concluded that the number of states which would realize savings by opting into Medicaid expansion could range anywhere from 21 to 45. However, the organization clearly agrees with Kaiser that those southern states, where Republican governors are uniting against involvement, would benefit the most.[15]

21-3c Disability

Under the social security system, a worker is considered disabled when a severe physical or mental impairment prevents that person from working for a year or more or is expected to result in the victim's death. The disability does not have to be work related (as is the case for workers' compensation disability), but it must be total. In other words, if the injured or ailing worker can do some sort of work, though not necessarily the same work as before the disability, then this program probably will not apply. Under some circumstances, a disabled worker's spouse, children, or surviving family members are also eligible for benefits.

Just as older workers must accrue 40 quarters of credit to be fully insured, so too, younger people must earn some social security credits to qualify for disability benefits. For instance, before reaching age 24, a member of the work force would need six credits (six quarters of work subject to social security tax) during the preceding three years. A worker who becomes disabled between ages 31 and 42 must be credited with 20 quarters on his or her account.

After 24 months of disability, Medicare is made available, just as in the case of retired Americans. Additionally, the Social Security system provides services intended to get disabled people back into the work force and off the benefit rolls. Usually, vocational rehabilitation services are provided by state rehabilitation agencies in cooperation with the federal Social Security Administration. The law provides that disability benefits can continue during a nine-month return-to-work trial period. Generally, if the trial is successful, benefits will be continued during a three-month "adjustment period" and then stopped.

---

[13] "STUDY: Uninsured in Republican-controlled southern states would benefit most from medicaid expansion," ThinkProgress.org, July 6, 2012, available at http://thinkprogress.org/health/2012/07/06/511727 /southern-states-uninsured-medicaid-benefit.

[14] Holahan and Headen, "Medicaid coverage and spending in health reform," Kaiser Family Foundation (Kaiser Commission), May 2010, available at http://www.scribd.com/doc/99236333/Medicaid-Coverage-and-Spending-in-Health-Reform-National-and-State-by-State-Results-for-Adults-at-or-Below-133-FPL.

[15] Buettgens, Dorn, and Carroll, "Consider savings as well as costs," Urban Institute, July 2011, available at http://www.urban.org/UploadedPDF/412361-consider-savings.pdf.

Related to this aspect of the Social Security system is supplemental security income, a program financed by general funds from the U.S. Treasury (not Social Security taxes) and aimed at aiding legally blind, elderly, or partially disabled workers.

Such benefits are difficult to obtain, as exemplified by the following *Baker v. Commissioner of Social Sec.* case, in which the Court of Appeals affirms the administrative law judge (ALJ)'s denial of benefits. As a general rule, benefits will be denied if the claimant is found capable of doing almost any job that is available in the U.S. economy, whether or not the job relates to his or her prior career. Furthermore, the courts are inclined to accord great deference to the expertise of ALJs, who deal with these claims day in and day out.

>> CASE 21.3

BAKER V. COMMISSIONER OF SOCIAL SEC.
384 Fed. Appx. 893 (11th Cir. 2010).

Facts: John L. Baker appeals the magistrate judge's order affirming the Administrative Law Judge's ("ALJ") denial of disability insurance and supplemental social security income benefits on behalf of the Commissioner of Social Security. On appeal, Baker argues that his use of a cane renders him unable to perform the full range of work at the "sedentary" exertional level. He also argues that the ALJ inappropriately relied on the Medical Vocational Guidelines at 20 C.F.R. pt. 404, subpt. P, app. 2 ("Grids"), rather than a vocational expert's testimony, to determine whether he was disabled.

Issue: Did the ALJ commit a reversible error in deciding that Baker could perform the full range of work at the "sedentary" exertional level?

Decision: When an ALJ denies benefits and the Appeals Council "denies review, we review the ALJ's decision as the Commissioner's final decision." We review the ALJ's decision "to determine whether it is supported by substantial evidence." We do not reweigh the evidence, decide the facts anew, or make credibility determinations. We review *de novo* the legal principles on which the ALJ's decision is based.

An individual claiming disability benefits carries the burden of demonstrating that he is disabled. The social security regulations outline a five-step, sequential evaluation process to determine whether a claimant is disabled. It is undisputed that Baker meets steps one through three.

At step four, the ALJ must evaluate the claimant's residual functional capacity ("RFC") and the claimant's ability to return to his past relevant work. RFC is that which an individual is still able to do despite the limitations caused by his impairments. There are 3 types of limitations: (1) exertional limitations affect an individual's ability to meet the seven strength demands of the job; (2) non-exertional limitations affect an individual's ability to meet the non-strength demands of the job; and (3) limitations that are both exertional and non-exertional. The ALJ must use "all the relevant medical and other evidence" to determine if the claimant can return to his past relevant work.

If the ALJ assesses the claimant's RFC and determines that the claimant cannot return to his past relevant work, then the ALJ moves on to step five. At step five, the ALJ must determine if there are other jobs in the national economy to which a claimant could adjust, considering the claimant's RFC, age, education, and work experience. The ALJ considers the physical requirements of a job, as divided into five exertional levels: sedentary, light, medium, heavy, and very heavy. "[I]n order for an individual to do a full range of work at a given exertional level, such as sedentary, the individual must be able to perform substantially all of the exertional and nonexertional functions required to work at that level." According to the regulations:

Sedentary work involves lifting no more than 10 pounds at a time and occasionally lifting or carrying articles like docket files, ledgers, and small tools. Although a sedentary job is defined as one which involves sitting, a certain amount of walking and standing is often necessary in carrying out job duties. Jobs are sedentary if walking and standing are required occasionally and other sedentary criteria are met.

The ALJ may approach step five in one of two ways. First, an ALJ may apply the Grids, which provide adjudicators with a guideline for jobs available in the national economy for someone of the claimant's characteristics. Second, the ALJ may consult a vocational expert. A vocational expert is an expert on the kinds of jobs an individual can perform based on his capacity and impairments.

Generally, after determining the claimant's RFC and ability to return to past relevant work, the ALJ can use the Grids to determine if other jobs exist in the national economy that a claimant is able to perform and, consequently, whether the claimant is disabled. However, an ALJ must consult a vocational expert upon finding either (1) that the claimant is not able to perform a full range of work at a given residual functional level or (2) that the "claimant has nonexertional impairments that significantly limit basic work skills." If the ALJ concludes that the claimant can perform a full range of work at a given level, and also that the claimant has no non-exertional limitations that significantly limit basic work skills, the ALJ may rely exclusively on the Grids to determine if the claimant is disabled.

Baker argues that the ALJ erred in finding that he had the RFC to perform the full range of sedentary work. The parties dispute whether the ALJ determined if Baker's cane was "medically necessary," but this issue is not dispositive. Even an individual using a medically required hand-held assistive device can perform sedentary work, depending on the facts and circumstances of the case. The ALJ determined that Baker "requires a cane for ambulation but is able to walk effectively with it." However, Baker argues, the ALJ did not perform a function-by-function analysis of the effects of Baker's cane on specific basic sedentary work skills. Baker argues that the ALJ made no finding about the effects of Baker's cane on balancing, prolonged versus brief ambulation, standing, lifting and carrying with one hand, balancing on level terrain, and stooping.

The ALJ found that Baker's cane was needed for ambulation, but that Baker was able to walk effectively with its assistance. Although some of the reporting physicians noted that Baker requires a cane to walk, no physician of record rendered an opinion that suggests that the cane limits his ability to comply with the exertional requirements of sedentary work. Rather, the ALJ found that there was no loss of motion or deformity of major joints, that Baker only had "mild" lumbar paravertebral muscle spasms, and had no sensory or reflex deficits. The only restrictions placed on Baker by his physician were no repetitive motions and no heavy lifting. Further, the ALJ discredited Baker's testimony concerning the limits on his physical capacity. Substantial evidence supports the ALJ's determination that Baker has the RFC to perform the full range of sedentary work.

Baker also argues that the ALJ erred by relying solely on Grids and by failing to consult a vocational expert regarding whether Baker's cane use erodes the sedentary occupational base. He argues that because the ALJ determined that Baker's cane is "medically required," he was obligated to determine whether use of a cane constitutes a non-exertional impairment that significantly limits Baker's ability to perform all the basic exertional and non-exertional sedentary tasks.

The ALJ permissibly relied on the Grids to determine that Baker is not disabled. The ALJ discounted Baker's testimony concerning the incapacitating effects of his impairment. Ultimately, the ALJ considered the medical and other evidence of record and concluded that Baker "has the residual functional capacity to perform the full range of sedentary work." Baker required the cane for walking-an exertional function and one of the "strength requirements" of a job. Other than his own discredited testimony, the record contains no evidence to suggest that Baker's use of a cane is a non-exertional limitation that significantly impaired the basic work skills required to perform at a sedentary level. Because the ALJ concluded that Baker had the RFC to perform the full range of sedentary work that was unimpaired by his use of a cane, the ALJ did not err by relying on the Grids to determine that Baker was not disabled.

Accordingly, we affirm the magistrate judge's order upholding the Commissioner's denial of benefits.

AFFIRMED.

Concept *Summary* 21.3

SOCIAL SECURITY

- A federally funded and administered program initiated during the New Deal
- Consists of three parts:
  - Pensions
  - Medical benefits
  - Long-term disability insurance

21-4 Employee Retirement Income Security Act (ERISA)

Employee Retirement Income Security Act (ERISA)
an act that sets standards for pension plans including fiduciary conduct, information disclosure, plan taxation, and remedies for employees

The **Employee Retirement Income Security Act**, known as **ERISA**, imposes standards of conduct and responsibility upon pension fund fiduciaries (persons having authority or control over the management of pension fund assets). The act also requires that pension plan administrators disclose relevant financial information to employees and the government. The act sets certain minimum standards that pension plans must meet to qualify for preferential tax treatment, and it provides legal remedies to employees and their beneficiaries in the event of violations.

The provisions of ERISA apply to employee benefit plans established by employers. The act recognizes two types of benefit plans: welfare plans and pension plans. Welfare plans usually provide participating employees and their beneficiaries with medical coverage, disability benefits, death benefits, vacation pay, and/or unemployment benefits. Welfare plans may also include apprenticeship programs, prepaid legal services, day care centers, and scholarship funds. Pension plans are defined as including any plan intended to provide retirement income to employees and resulting in deferral of income for such employees.

ERISA's main focus is on pension plans. It seeks to ensure that all employees covered by pension plans receive the benefits due them under the plans. ERISA does not require an employer to provide a pension plan for its employees. However, if a pension plan is offered, ERISA sets the minimum standards and requirements that the pension plan must meet.

The provisions of ERISA do not apply to employee benefit plans that are established by federal, state, or local government employers. Nor does the act apply to plans covering employees of tax-exempt churches or to plans maintained solely for the purpose of complying with state workers' compensation, unemployment compensation, or disability insurance laws. Neither does ERISA apply to plans maintained outside the United States primarily for the benefit of nonresident aliens. But these exemptions are relatively narrow; ERISA's reach is very broad.

The two main features of ERISA—the imposition of standards for fiduciary conduct and responsibility and the setting of minimum standards for pension plan requirements—have different bases for their coverage. The fiduciary duties and conduct standards apply to any employee benefit plan established or maintained by an employer engaged in interstate commerce or in an industry or activity affecting interstate commerce. They also apply to plans established and maintained by unions representing employees engaged in an industry or activity affecting interstate commerce.

The minimum standards for pension plans must be met for the employee pension plans to qualify for preferential tax treatment. Because such tax treatment enables an employer to deduct contributions to qualified benefit plans immediately but does not consider the payments as income to participating employees until they receive the payments after retirement, most employers seek to "qualify" their plans by complying with ERISA's minimum standards. Such compliance, however, is not required. Some employers who view the ERISA requirements as too stringent have chosen not to qualify their pension and other benefit plans for preferential tax treatment. Those employers are still subject to the fiduciary duties of ERISA if they are engaged in, or affect, interstate commerce (which today includes the vast majority of enterprises).

21-4a   Preemption

Despite the broad preemptive power that the federal courts have given to ERISA, as originally recognized and explained by the U.S. Supreme Court in *Shaw v. Delta Airlines, Inc.*,[16] several courts have allowed plaintiffs raising claims of discrimination in employee benefit plans to pursue them under state antidiscrimination laws. The following *Ruby v. Sandia Corp.* case stands as a recent example of such an exception from ERISA's broad reach.

CASE 21.4

RUBY V. SANDIA CORP.

699 F. Supp. 2d 1247 D.N.M. (2010)

Factual Background

For purposes of resolving a motion to dismiss under rule 12(b)(6) of the Federal Rules of Civil Procedure, the Court must accept all well-pled facts as true. Accordingly, the Court has relied on Ruby's Complaint in outlining the facts pertinent to this motion. Sandia Corporation operates the Sandia National Laboratories, a federally owned research facility in Bernalillo County, New Mexico. Ruby, a physicist, accepted employment with Sandia Labs in November 1985. In 1989, Ruby was promoted to Senior Member of the Technical Staff ("SMTS"), and in 1999, he was promoted to Principal Member of the Technical Staff ("PMTS"). In early 2004, Sandia Labs brought in a new manager, Dr. Jeffrey Nelson, who was assigned as Ruby's supervisor.

At the time Nelson was hired, Ruby's retirement benefits were close to vesting. May 16, 2007, Nelson informed Ruby that he could accept placement on a Performance Improvement Plan ("PIP") or be terminated from his employment. Ruby accepted the PIP, and was given tasks such as

developing a comprehensive research program for accelerated aging of Thin-Film materials, devices, and systems and developing a concentrating photovoltaic systems research program within sixty days. Ruby did not meet the tasks and was demoted to SMTS in September 2007. Ruby was placed on another PIP as a SMTS. Ruby set goals and work assignments for himself, which were Nelson approved, and submitted a twenty-page report to Sandia Labs management documenting his accomplishments and describing how he satisfied the goals set pursuant to the second PIP. Ruby subsequently received a letter stating that he had not satisfied the goals under the second PIP. Sandia Labs terminated Ruby's employment on January 28, 2008, citing the failure to meet the second PIP as the grounds for termination. As a result of his termination, Ruby filed a complaint with the New Mexico Human Rights Commission ("NMHRC") pursuant to the NMHRA. The NMHRC, in its finding of probable cause, determined that Ruby attempted to meet his PIP requirements, that evidence showed that a younger

---

[16] 463 U.S. 85 (1983).

female employee who was having employment issues was allowed to transfer to another department and Ruby was not offered the same option, and that there was sufficient evidence to believe discrimination occurred.

Procedural Background

On July 2, 2009, after the NMHRC found sufficient evidence to believe that discrimination had occurred, Ruby filed a Complaint against Sandia Labs in the Second Judicial District Court of Bernalillo County, New Mexico, alleging that Sandia Labs wrongfully discriminated against him based on his age, in contravention of the NMHRA, and engaged in conduct that constituted the common-law torts of wrongful termination and prima-facie tort. In his Complaint, Ruby raised these causes of actions predicated on the averments that Sandia Labs treated him differently than younger employees to save money and that, but for his age, Sandia Labs would not have treated him unfairly. Ruby alleges that he "was treated less favorably by Sandia management than other younger employees with respect to employment decisions because of his age."

On August 8, 2009, Sandia Labs filed a Notice of Removal. Sandia Labs also filed its motion to dismiss contemporaneously with its Notice of Removal. Both Sandia Labs' Notice of Removal and its motion to dismiss are predicated solely on the argument that ERISA preempts Ruby's state-law claims. In its motion to dismiss, Sandia Labs argues that the Court should grant its motion because all of Ruby's claims relate to an employee-benefit plan which ERISA governs, seek benefits which that plan provides, and are, therefore, completely preempted by § 502 of ERISA. Specifically, Sandia Labs argues that Ruby's Complaint does not allege any other motive for Sandia Labs' alleged wrongful termination of his employment other than preventing Ruby from receiving a full retirement service pension. Sandia Labs relies on: (i) the provision in ERISA which states that ERISA "shall supersede any and all State laws insofar as they may now or hereafter relate to any employee benefit plan described in section 1003(a) of this title and not exempt under *1255 section 1003(b) of this title," in which the Supreme Court held that ERISA preempted the state claims of an employee who had lost his job and sued in state court under various tort and contract theories based on the allegation that the principal reason for his termination was that his pension benefits vested in another four months, were preempted by ERISA. Sandia Labs argues that, because ERISA preempts all four of Ruby's claims, the

Court should dismiss them with leave to amend the state claims into an ERISA claim.

On August 31, 2009, Ruby filed his response to Sandia Labs' motion to dismiss. In his response, Ruby argues that ERISA does not preempt his state-law claims. Ruby relies on the provision in ERISA which states that nothing in ERISA is to be construed so as to "alter, amend, modify, invalidate, impair, or supersede any law of the United States ... or any rule or regulation issued under any such law." Ruby contends that the Supreme Court's holding in *Shaw v. Delta Air Lines, Inc.* makes clear that state human rights laws are preempted with respect to ERISA benefit plans only insofar as they prohibit practices that are lawful under federal law. Ruby argues that, because the NMHRA's age discrimination provisions are co-extensive with the Age Discrimination in Employment Act, a finding of ERISA preemption as to Ruby's claims for age discrimination would both "modify" and "impair" the enforcement of rights under the ADEA, and because Ruby seeks to vindicate rights that the ADEA promotes, even though he brought his claims through state-law causes of action, ERISA does not preempt his claims. Ruby also contends that his claims do not relate to any employee-benefit plan the ERISA preemption provision contemplates. Ruby argues that *Ingersoll-Rand Co. v. McClendon* does not apply, because he has asserted claims predicated on laws prohibiting age discrimination, which he contends are laws of general applicability and not dependant on an ERISA plan. Ruby contends that his claims have only an incidental impact on any ERISA plan and that such a tenuous connection is insufficient grounds to support a claim of preemption.

In its reply to Ruby's response to the motion to dismiss, Sandia Labs makes a distinction between express preemption and complete preemption. Sandia Labs argues that the "courts have recognized two types of preemption under ERISA: (1) express preemption under § 1144(a), which occurs when a law 'relates to' an employee benefit plan governed by ERISA; and (2) complete preemption, which occurs when the allegations in the complaint give rise to an ERISA cause of action." Sandia Labs argues that complete preemption applies to Ruby's four state-law claims. Sandia Labs also argues that Ruby's reliance on *Shaw v. Delta Air Lines, Inc.* is misplaced, because it addressed express preemption, not complete preemption, and because the plaintiff in *Shaw v. Delta Air Lines, Inc.* was not asserting a claim based upon alleged conduct that ERISA expressly prohibits, as Sandia Labs contends is the case in the matter before the Court.

Ruby has also filed a motion to remand, requesting that the Court enter an order remanding the case to state court. In the motion to remand, Ruby argued that, because Sandia Labs' notice of removal is predicated solely on ERISA preemption, and because Ruby contends that ERISA does not preempt his claims, that the Court does not have jurisdiction. In Sandia Labs' response, it argues that removal was not only proper, but essential, because ERISA completely preempts Ruby's claims, and because Congress vests exclusive jurisdiction over ERISA violations in federal court.

In his reply to the motion to remand, Ruby addressed the arguments that Sandia Labs raised in its reply to the motion to dismiss. Ruby argued that his state-law age-discrimination claims do not fall within the ambit of § 502's civil-enforcement provision. Ruby also argues that, even if his claims are viable under § 502, complete preemption does not apply because his claims arise from an independent legal duty. Ruby argues that his claims stem solely from the NMHRA, which prohibits an employer from discharging an employee based on his age, unlike § 510 of ERISA, which makes it "unlawful … to discharge … a participant or beneficiary … for the purpose of interfering with the attainment of any right to which such participant may become entitled under the plan."

At the hearing, Matthew L. Garcia, Ruby's counsel, conceded that Ruby has alleged that part of the reason Sandia Labs terminated Ruby was in an effort to save money, "including denying Dr. Ruby retirement benefits." He argued, however, that Sandia Labs also had discriminatory motives on the basis of age and retaliatory motives. Mr. Garcia contended that Ruby's claims do not meet both prongs of the test for § 502's complete preemption. He argued that Sandia Labs' actions implicated an independent legal duty, and therefore complete preemption is not applicable. Garcia conceded that, if ERISA preempts any of Ruby's claims, § 502 most likely preempts the claims for wrongful termination and prima-facie tort. He asserted that, if the Court finds that ERISA preempts some claims, the Court should still permit Ruby to keep his state NMHRA claims, and that Ruby would like the Court to exercise supplemental jurisdiction over all of the claims, rather than send some claims to state court while retaining the claims that the Court finds ERISA preempts.

Luis G. Stelzner, Sandia Labs' counsel, stated at the hearing that Sandia Labs cannot assert jurisdiction under § 514 express preemption in this case. Mr. Stelzner explained, however, that Ruby's claims fall within the scope of § 514 because he is a participant in Sandia Labs' benefits plan and the Complaint alleges that Sandia Labs interfered with the attainment of his benefits. He also argues that Ruby's claims fall within the scope of § 502's civil-enforcement provision.

Mr. Stelzner conceded that, if Ruby's Complaint had not mentioned his retirement benefits, his claims would not have triggered ERISA preemption. He argued, however, that the sole motive alleged in Ruby's Complaint is Sandia Labs' desire to save money by denying Ruby retirement benefits and that, although Mr. Garcia argued that Ruby was terminated because of discriminatory motives on the basis of age, such a motive was not pled in the Complaint. He also argued that, as pled, Ruby's claims cannot be brought based on an independent legal duty, because he only pled a benefits-defeating motive, which ERISA exclusively covers. Like Mr. Garcia, Mr. Stelzner also expressed a strong preference that, if the Court finds that ERISA preempts only some claims, the Court should exercise supplemental jurisdiction over all of the claims.

Analysis

Sandia Labs moves the Court to dismiss Ruby's four state-law claims because ERISA completely preempts them. Ruby moves the Court to remand his case to state court because, he argues, ERISA does not completely preempt his claims. Complete preemption is an exception to the well-pleaded complaint rule that permits removal of a complaint alleging state-law claims if "federal preemption makes the state law claim necessarily federal in character.…" Thus, even if a complaint alleges state-law claims, a state-law claim may be converted into an ERISA claim for purposes of removal and the well-pleaded complaint rule if ERISA completely preempts the claim. Because the Court finds that Ruby's NMHRA claims for age discrimination and retaliation arise from independent legal duties separate from those ERISA creates, the Court finds that ERISA does not completely preempt those claims. Because the Court finds that ERISA completely preempts Ruby's claims for wrongful termination and prima-facie tort, the Court will convert those claims into a federal claim under ERISA's civil-enforcement provisions. Because complete preemption by ERISA converts the state-law claims into a federal claim upon which relief can be granted, the Court denies Sandia Labs' motion to dismiss and will grant Ruby leave to amend his Complaint to properly plead his preempted state claims under ERISA and to add additional state and/or federal claims. Further, because both parties have requested the Court to maintain supplemental jurisdiction if the Court finds complete preemption for some of the claims, the Court will deny the

Plaintiff's motion to remand and will maintain jurisdiction over all Ruby's claims.

Conclusion

IT IS ORDERED that the Defendant's Motion to Dismiss Pursuant to Fed.R.Civ.P. 12(b)(6) is denied. Claim III and Claim IV of the Plaintiff's Complaint for Damages Arising Under the New Mexico Human Rights Act and New Mexico Common Law are converted into a federal ERISA claim, and the Court treats Claims III and IV as an ERISA claim pursuant to the civil enforcement provision, 29 U.S.C. § 1132. The Plaintiff shall have ten days from the filing of this Order to amend his state-law claims for wrongful termination and prima-facie tort to properly frame his causes of action to comply with ERISA's civil-enforcement provision. The Plaintiff's Motion to remand is denied. The Court also grants the Plaintiff leave to amend his complaint to add additional state and/or federal claims.

Case Questions

1. What triggered the ERISA preemption? Why did Sandia Labs reason that this preemption should apply to all of Ruby's claims?

2. Why did the court find that ERISA does not completely preempt Ruby's claims for age discrimination and retaliation?

3. What was the court's reasoning in deciding to maintain jurisdiction over all of Ruby's claims? Does this benefit Ruby's case?

21-4b Fiduciary Responsibility

ERISA imposes standards of conduct and responsibility on fiduciaries of benefit plans established or maintained by employers and unions engaged in or affecting interstate commerce. The act requires that all such plans must be in writing and must designate at least one named fiduciary who has the authority to manage and control the plan's operation and management. The plan must also provide a written procedure for establishing and carrying out a funding policy that is consistent with the plan's objectives and with ERISA's requirements. The written provisions must also specify the basis on which contributions to the fund and payments from the fund will be made. Finally, the written plan must describe the procedure for allocation of responsibility for administering and operating the benefit plan.

ERISA requires that all assets of the benefit plan must be held in trust for the benefit of participating employees and their beneficiaries. The plan must establish a procedure for handling claims on the fund by participants and their beneficiaries. Any individual with a claim against the fund must exhaust these internal procedures before seeking legal remedies from the courts.

Fiduciary

fiduciary
any person exercising discretionary authority over benefit plan administration, management, or disposition of plan assets; or who renders investment advice regarding the plan

ERISA defines a **fiduciary** as including any person exercising discretionary authority or control respecting the management of the benefit plan, or disposition of plan assets; or who renders, or has authority or responsibility to render, investment advice (for which he or she is compensated) with respect to any money or property of the plan; or who has any discretionary authority or responsibility in the administration of the plan. Persons not normally considered fiduciaries, such as consultants or advisers, *may* be found to be fiduciaries when their expertise is used in a managerial, administrative, or advisory capacity by the plan.

THE **WORKING** LAW

US Labor Department Seeks Public Comment on Proposal to Protect Consumers from Conflicts of Interest in Retirement Advice

WASHINGTON—The U.S. Department of Labor has released a proposed rule that will protect 401(k) and IRA investors by mitigating the effect of conflicts of interest in the retirement investment marketplace. A White House Council of Economic Advisers analysis found that these conflicts of interest result in annual losses of about 1 percentage point for affected investors—or about $17 billion per year in total.

Under the proposals, retirement advisers will be required to put their clients' best interests before their own profits. Those who wish to receive payments from companies selling products they recommend and forms of compensation that create conflicts of interest will need to rely on one of several proposed prohibited transaction exemptions.

"This boils down to a very simple concept: if someone is paid to give you retirement investment advice, that person should be working in your best interest," said Secretary of Labor Thomas E. Perez. "As commonsense as this may be, laws to protect consumers and ensure that financial advisers are giving the best advice in a complex market have not kept pace. Our proposed rule would change that. Under the proposed rule, retirement advisers can be paid in various ways, as long as they are willing to put their customers' best interest first."

Today's announcement includes a proposed rule that would update and close loopholes in a nearly 40-year-old regulation. The proposal would expand the number of persons who are subject to fiduciary best interest standards when they provide retirement investment advice. It also includes a package of proposed exemptions allowing advisers to continue to receive payments that could create conflicts of interest if the conditions of the exemption are met. In addition, the announcement includes a comprehensive economic analysis of the proposals' expected gains to investors and costs.

The proposed "best interest contract exemption" represents a new approach to exemptions that is broad, flexible, principles-based and can adapt to evolving business practices. It would be available to advisers who make investment recommendations to individual plan participants, IRA investors and small plans. It would require retirement investment advisers and their firms to formally acknowledge fiduciary status and enter into a contract with their customers in which they commit to fundamental standards of impartial conduct. These include giving advice that is in the customer's best interest and making truthful statements about investments and their compensation.

If fiduciary advisers and their firms enter into and comply with such a contract, clearly explain investment fees and costs, have appropriate policies and procedures to mitigate the harmful effects of conflicts of interest, and retain certain data on their performance, they can receive common types of fees that fiduciary advisers could otherwise not receive under the law. These include commissions, revenue sharing, and 12b-1 fees. If they do not, they generally must refrain from recommending investments for which they receive conflicted compensation, unless the payments fall under the scope of another exemption.

In addition to the new best interest contract exemption, the proposal also includes other new exemptions and updates some exemptions previously available for investment advice to plan sponsors and participants. For example, the proposal includes a new exemption for principal transactions. In addition, the proposal asks for comment on a new "low-fee exemption" that would allow firms to accept conflicted payments when recommending the lowest-fee products in a given product class, with even fewer requirements than the best interest contract exemption.

Finally, the proposal carves out general investment education from fiduciary status. Sales pitches to large plan fiduciaries who are financial experts, and appraisals or valuations of the stock held by employee-stock ownership plans, are also carved out.

Source: News Release 15-0655-NAT, "US Labor Department seeks public comment on proposal to protect consumers from conflicts of interest in retirement advice," Department of Labor, April 14, 2015, available at http://www.dol.gov/opa/media/press/ebsa/EBSA20150655.htm.

Concept *Summary* 21.4

ERISA

- ERISA
  - ○ Regulates employee benefits, especially pensions
  - ○ Does not require an employer to provide any employee benefits, not even pensions
  - ○ Has wide preemptive power but does not preempt all state laws
- State banking, insurance, and workers' compensation laws are generally not preempted
  - ○ Imposes strict fiduciary duties on employers and plan administrators
- 2008 amendments to ERISA seek primarily to provide relief to retirees who must draw upon their diminished pension funds

CHAPTER REVIEW

» Key Terms

» Summary

- The American worker's safety net consists primarily of unemployment compensation, workers' compensation, Social Security, and retirement plans.

- Employees who lose their jobs through no willful fault of their own are entitled to unemployment compensation benefits while they look for alternative employment. Unemployment compensation is administered at the state level and is funded by payroll taxes imposed on employers and employees alike.

• Workers' compensation benefits are mandated by state law and provide medical insurance and income supplements for employees who are injured on the job. Workers injured while commuting to and from work are not covered. The advantage to the employer is that covered employees cannot sue their employers for negligence, but rather must be content with the benefits prescribed by the state system.

• Social Security is a federal program that provides minimum pension benefits for retirees, as well as benefits for permanently disabled workers. The program, dating from the New Deal of the 1930s, is funded by taxes on employers and employees. Participation is mandatory.

• In sharp contrast to unemployment, workers' compensation, and Social Security, neither the federal nor the state governments require private employers to provide pensions. However, if an employer does provide a pension plan, it is regulated by ERISA. Additionally, this sweeping federal law also regulated many other employee benefit plans.

» Problems

» Questions

1. In his opinion on the Affordable Care Act, Chief Justice Roberts made it clear that he was only ruling on the constitutionality of the act and nothing more. Do you think that the Affordable Care Act is a wise and effective law that should be retained? Or should it be repealed, in whole or in part?

2. Part-time employees under the Affordable Care Act are those who work fewer than 30 hours. How does this classification open employers up to potential lawsuits?

3. In what way does the Affordable Care Act affect ERISA?

4. Most state workers' compensation laws do not apply to injuries sustained when employees are commuting to and from work. What are the pros and cons of this rule?

5. Are there any arguments to be made for eliminating the rule that employees who are guilty of willful misconduct are ineligible for unemployment compensation benefits? New Jersey law only applies this ineligibility to the first six weeks of unemployment. What do you think of this rule?

6. Do you think that the Social Security system is economically sustainable in the 21st century?

» Case Problems

7. Plaintiff was fired by his employer, along with a coworker, as a result of a fistfight that the two of them conducted on the company's premises. The plaintiff subsequently sued the employer for wrongful discharge, claiming that he was only defending himself and that the state's public policy favoring victim compensation in cases of violent crime created a cause of action. The state also has a well-established common-law rule favoring at-will employment.

   What are the arguments for and against a wrongful discharge cause of action in this case? (Review Chapter 2, if necessary, in answering this question.)

   Is the plaintiff entitled to receive unemployment compensation benefits under this set of facts? How does your answer to this question affect your answer to the preceding question, if at all?

   Are the plaintiff's injuries arguably compensable under the state's workers' compensation act? How should the workers' compensation act be factored into the court's consideration of the plaintiff's public policy wrongful discharge claim? [See *Quebedeaux v. Dow Chemical Company*, 820 So.2d 542 (La. Supreme 2002).]

8. Plaintiff/employee suffered mental and emotional trauma but no physical injuries as the result of an armed robbery that occurred in the store while the plaintiff was on the job. Her posttraumatic stress disorder was manifest by nausea, cramps, confusion, and the side effects of her prescribed medication. She sued her employer for negligence in failing to maintain appropriate security measures in the store.

   What are the arguments for and against an employer defense of workers' compensation exclusivity with regard to plaintiff's injuries? How should the court rule? [See *Rivers v. Grimsley Oil Company, Inc.*, 842 So.2d 975 (Fla. App. 2003).]

9. Plaintiff was injured on the job when she was attacked by a coworker. She sued the employer on the basis of negligent hiring and negligent supervision. The employer sought dismissal of the lawsuit on the ground that the attack was a work-related accident that is covered by the exclusivity provisions of workers' compensation and that workers' compensation benefits should be the plaintiff's sole remedy in this case.

   What are the arguments for and against the employer's defense? How should the court rule? [See *Caple v. Bullard Restaurants, Inc.*, 152 N.C. App. 421, 567 S.E.2d 828 (2002).]

10. Plaintiff/truck driver was fired after he tested positive for use of marijuana on the job. Under applicable federal interstate trucking regulations, the driver had the right to a second test at the employer's expense within 72 hours of the positive result. The employer failed to advise the employee of this right. However, the employee paid for his own test, which came up negative. The employer then refused to consider the results of that second test and let the discharge stand.

    When the plaintiff applies for unemployment compensation, if the referee considers only the employer's evidence of a positive drug test, should the plaintiff be found guilty of willful misconduct and denied benefits? Should the referee allow the plaintiff/employee to submit evidence of his personally purchased drug test? How much weight should the referee give this test? [See *Southwood Door*

Company v. Burton, 847 So.2d 833 (Miss. Supreme 2003).]

11. A terminated sales representative claimed he was fired because he was HIV positive. The company contended that he was let go due to intentional disrespect for his supervisors and contravention of company rules. On appeal of the unemployment referee's decision, the state superior court ruled that plaintiff's supervisor knew nothing of his health condition. This ruling became a final judgment on the unemployment compensation claim, which therefore was denied due to plaintiff's willful misconduct.

    Should this judgment collaterally stop the plaintiff from relitigating his disability discrimination claim against the former employer under the state's antidiscrimination statute? [See *Shields v. Bellsouth Advertising and Publishing Co.*, 273 Ga. 774, 545 S.E.2d 898 (Ga. Supreme 2001).]

12. Plaintiff suffered a heart attack. He applied for Social Security disability insurance (SSDI). His claim was initially rejected, but he appealed and was successful on appeal. The social security administrative law judge found that plaintiff was unable to perform the work he had done in the past. During the pendency of this social security claim, plaintiff was also a part of an unfair labor practice complaint against his employer. The National Labor Relations Board administrative law judge found that plaintiff and his coworkers had been the victims of their employer's unfair labor practices and therefore would ordinarily be entitled to back-pay awards for any periods of unemployment related to the unfair labor practices. However, the employer contended that plaintiff should not be eligible for any back pay under the National Labor Relations Act because he had a total-disability claim concurrently pending with the Social Security Administration and would not have reported for work during the pendency of that claim anyway.

    What do you think? [See *Performance Friction Corporation*, 335 NLRB No. 86, 2001 WL 1126575 (NLRB).]

13. A medical center sued a major insurance company in state court, contending that the insurance carrier

had breached its contract with the center's hospital by failing to reimburse it for the full contractual amounts when the hospital rendered services to the carrier's insured patients. The insurance company removed the case to federal district court, claiming that the controversy was essentially federal in nature, involving a welfare benefit plan regulated by ERISA. The medical center moved to have the case remanded to state court, pointing out that ERISA exempts from its coverage, among other things, insurance contracts.

Who is right? [See *Lake-view Medical Center v. Aetna Health Management, Inc.*, 2000 WL 1727553 (E.D. La.).]

14. The administrator of a major corporation's employee benefit plans filed suit, seeking to preempt claims by obtaining a declaratory judgment that certain sales personnel were not actually employees and therefore were not entitled to benefits under the plans. The personnel in question performed sales services for the marketing subsidiary of the parent corporation. The evidence showed that these personnel were paid neither wages nor salaries but instead earned fees by selling magazine subscriptions. These salespeople claimed they were subject to substantial supervision such as:

- review of sales presentations;
- review of correspondence;
- occasional accompaniment by managers to meetings with clients; and
- management direction on the handling of clients.

They were required to file periodic reports but were not required to work any particular hours or any particular number of hours in a week. Nor did they have to obtain advance approval to take a vacation. The company claims they are independent contractors and therefore not entitled to employee benefits.

What do you say? [See *Administrative Committee of Time Warner, Inc. v. Biscardi*, 2000 WL 1721168 (S.D.N.Y.).]

15. Cypress Mountain Coals Corporation entered into a collective bargaining agreement with the United Mine Workers of America under which the company agreed, among other things, to add disability pensions to its existing obligations under the union's multiemployer pension plan. The plan documents were silent as to whether or not an injured employee could qualify if his disability was not exclusively caused by a mining accident. A year after the collective agreement was consummated, Cypress employee Donald Miller was injured in a mine accident. But when he applied for a disability pension, the company denied his application, contending that his disability was partly caused by preexisting conditions. The union sued Cypress for breach of the collective agreement and the pension plan.

Which law should the court apply in determining this controversy, the NLRA or ERISA, or both? Is state workers' compensation law implicated here in any way? And what about the collective bargaining agreement's grievance/arbitration clause? (In considering this last question, review Chapter 1, if necessary.) [See *United Mine Workers of America v. Cypress Mountain Coals Corp.*, 171 BNA L.R.R.M. 2512 (6th Cir. 2002).]

16. Petitioner Metropolitan Life Insurance Company (MetLife) is an administrator and the insurer of Sears, Roebuck & Company's long-term disability insurance plan, which is governed by the Employee Retirement Income Security Act of 1974 (ERISA). The plan gives MetLife (as administrator) discretionary authority to determine the validity of an employee's benefits claim and provides that MetLife (as insurer) will pay the claims. Respondent Wanda Glenn, a Sears employee, was granted an initial 24 months of benefits under the plan following a diagnosis of a heart disorder. MetLife encouraged her to apply for, and she began receiving, Social Security disability benefits based on an agency determination that she could do no work. But when MetLife itself had to determine whether she could work, in order to establish eligibility for extended plan benefits, it found her capable of doing sedentary work and denied her the benefits.

In challenging MetLife's decision, Glenn contends that the court should consider MetLife's conflict of interest as both the administrator and the payor under the plan. Do you agree? If so, how much weight should the judge give this factor in assigning burdens of proof? [See *Metropolitan Life Insurance Company v. Glenn*, 128 S.Ct. 2343 (2008).]

» Hypothetical Situations

17. A ski instructor and member of the ski patrol in the Oregon Cascades resort region was married to a woman who was HIV positive. When she developed full-fledged AIDS, she applied for and was awarded Social Security disability benefits. After the instructor's employer learned of his wife's total-disability status under the Social Security program and the cause of her disability, it demanded that the plaintiff submit to a blood test to ascertain whether he was HIV positive. When he refused, he was fired. What rights do you think the plaintiff has under federal employment laws based on these facts?

18. A discharged U.S. Navy officer filed claims for back pay and reinstatement, claiming that he was wrongfully discharged after he refused, on religious grounds, to sign reenlistment papers that required him to use his Social Security number as his personal military identification number. He argued that the Navy erroneously listed his discharge as "voluntary" and that in fact he was constructively discharged. Should the officer be reinstated with back pay?

19. Plaintiff was employed in one of the defendant's stores. She suffered a back injury and made a workers' compensation claim. When she was partially recovered, she returned to the store on a light-duty assignment that allowed her to work four hours per day. Upon her return, coworkers made fun of her injury and mocked her limitations, sometimes implying by their barbs that the injury was faked. The plaintiff sued for disability discrimination under the state's antidiscrimination statute, retaliation under the state's workers' compensation act, and intentional infliction of emotional distress.

    How should a court rule on each of these claims as against plaintiff's employer? Does it make a difference whether the store manager was aware of her coworkers' behavior? Whether she complained to higher company officials about it? Whether the manager took part in the behavior?

    If a court finds retaliation for pursuing a workers' compensation claim, should this finding insulate the employer from liability under the state's antidiscrimination statute? Under state tort law?

20. In March 2009, the entire United States was in a furor over the fact that the beleaguered insurance giant AIG, which had just received hundreds of millions of dollars in bailout money from the U.S. government, had paid out $165 million in performance and retention bonuses to key executives. If you were attorney general of the United States, how would you have advised President Obama with regard to recovering these funds? Are the employee benefits covered by ERISA? Did the CEO of AIG have a fiduciary duty with regard to these funds under ERISA to the employees who claimed they were entitled to the bonuses? Did the CEO have a fiduciary duty to the United States, which owned 79 percent of AIG at that time?

21. Suppose that a unionized employee is fired on the grounds that her disability is work related and therefore, even with reasonable accommodations, she cannot perform the fundamental duties of her position. The terminated employee subsequently files for and receives disability benefits under the Social Security Act. She also files a grievance through her union under the grievance/arbitration provision of the collective bargaining agreement, and she files a disability discrimination claim in state court. You are the human resources director of the company. Advise the CEO on how to respond to these actions. Consider and deal with the following issues:

    • Does the former employee's successful receipt of Social Security disability benefits preclude her claim of having a non-job-related disability?

    • Is this claim essentially a workers' compensation matter, subject to the exclusive remedies of the state workers' compensation act?

    • Does it matter whether or not she received unemployment compensation benefits when she was first fired?

    • Can the employer require her to submit her claim to arbitration, as her exclusive remedy?

    • Does ERISA figure into this case in any way?

CHAPTER 22

The Fair Labor Standards Act

Although the Fair Labor Standards Act (FLSA) was first enacted in 1938, the issue of the minimum wage remains the subject of a current public and political campaign regarding the plight of low-paid workers. President Obama has called for the minimum wage to be raised to $10.10 per hour from the current figure of $7.25. Across the country, public demonstrations aimed primarily at fast-food employers seek to raise the prevailing wage to a "liveable wage" of $15 per hour. In response to such public pressure, McDonald's Corp. announced on April 1, 2015, that it would raise the pay of the employees at company-owned restaurants to at least $1.00 more per hour than the local minimum wage where company-owned restaurants are located, starting on July 1, 2015. It should be noted that the pay raise announced by McDonald's does not apply to privately owned franchises, which account for about 90 percent of the company's more than 14,300 locations. The McDonald's announcement came after Walmart, Target, and TJ Maxx had pledged to increase the wages of their lowest-paid employees. A number of states and some municipalities have also raised their minimum wages above the federal minimum wage.

In addition to concerns about the minimum wage, there are other issues of FLSA enforcement. The U.S. Department of Labor estimates that at least 70 percent of employers are not in compliance with the FLSA. Wage and hour cases have surpassed EEO cases as the most common workplace-law class actions filed in federal courts (accounting for 6,081 suits in 2010 alone, an 18 percent increase from 2009). Wage class actions now outnumber discrimination class actions as well. Thus, the DOL has increased its number of investigators, is seeking increased funding, and now regularly pursues company-wide compliance rather than site-specific relief.

Faced with such facts and figures, Americans can no longer take for granted the sanctity of the minimum wage, their entitlement to premium pay or compensatory time off for hours worked in excess of 40 per week, or that child and/or "sweated" labor is a historical artifact to be experienced only in the display cases of the Smithsonian Institution's Museum of American History. To the contrary, a thorough understanding and appreciation of the FLSA have assumed new urgency in the new millennium.

22-1 Background of the FLSA

In 1931, Congress passed the Davis-Bacon Act, which provides that contractors working on government construction projects must pay the prevailing wage rates in the geographic area, as determined by the secretary of labor. The Davis-Bacon Act is still in force.

The federal government attempted the general regulation of wages and hours through the National Industrial Recovery Act (NIRA). NIRA, passed in 1933, was an attempt to improve general conditions during the Great Depression. NIRA provided for the development of "codes of fair competition" for various industries. The codes, to be developed by trade associations within each industry, would specify the minimum wages to be paid, the maximum hours to be worked, and limitations on child labor. When approved by the president, the codes would have the force of law. The Supreme Court held that the NIRA was an unconstitutional delegation of congressional power in the 1935 case of *Schecter Poultry Corp. v. U.S.*[1]

In 1936, the Walsh-Healy Act was passed. Like the Davis-Bacon Act, it regulates working conditions for government contractors. The Walsh-Healy Act sets minimum standards for wages for contractors providing at least $10,000 worth of goods to the federal government. It also requires that hours worked in excess of 40 per week be paid at time-and-a half the regular rate of pay. The Walsh-Healy Act, like Davis-Bacon, is also still in force.

In 1937, the Supreme Court was presented with a case that challenged the legality of a Washington state law that set a minimum wage for women. In several prior cases, the Court had held minimum wage laws to be unconstitutional, as it had done with the NIRA. Though the *West Coast Hotel* case is now 78 years old, the principles it enunciates are as pertinent to the body of employment law as they ever were.

>> CASE 22.1

WEST COAST HOTEL CO. v. PARRISH
300 U.S. 379 (1937)

Facts: This case questioned of the constitutionality of a minimum wage law of the State of Washington. The act, entitled "Minimum Wages for Women," authorized the fixing of minimum wages for women and minors. It provided:

> SECTION 1. The welfare of the State of Washington demands that women and minors be protected from conditions of labor which have a pernicious effect on their health and morals. The State of Washington, therefore, exercising herein its police and sovereign power declares that inadequate wages and unsanitary conditions of labor exert such pernicious effect.
>
> SEC. 2. It shall be unlawful to employ women or minors in any industry or occupation within the State of Washington under conditions of labor detrimental to their health or morals; and it shall

be unlawful to employ women workers in any industry within the State of Washington at wages which are not adequate for their maintenance.

> SEC. 3. There is hereby created a commission to be known as the "Industrial Welfare Commission" for the State of Washington, to establish such standards of wages and conditions of labor for women and minors employed within the State of Washington, as shall be held hereunder to be reasonable and not detrimental to health and morals, and which shall be sufficient for the decent maintenance of women.

The appellant was in the hotel business. The appellee Elsie Parrish was employed as a chambermaid and (with her husband) brought this suit to recover the difference between the wages paid her and the minimum wage fixed pursuant

---

[1] 295 U.S. 495 (1935).

to the due process clause of the Fourteenth Amendment of the Constitution of the United States. The Supreme Court of the State, reversing the trial court, sustained the statute and directed judgment for the plaintiffs. West Coast Hotel appealed to the U.S. Supreme Court.

Issue: In reviewing the case, the Court was required to revisit one of its long-standing precedents, *Adkins v. Children's Hospital*,[2] in which New York's minimum wage for women had been struck down, and ask whether this case was wrongly decided and therefore ought to be overruled.

Decision: The Court explained that the principle which must control its decision was the due process clause of the Fourteenth Amendment, which in effect applies the analogous due process clause of the Fifth Amendment (which limits the federal government) to the states. The due process violation alleged by those attacking minimum wage regulations for women was deprivation of freedom of contract. "What is this freedom?" the Court inquired. The Constitution does not speak of freedom of contract. It speaks of liberty and prohibits the deprivation of liberty without due process of law. In prohibiting that deprivation, the Constitution does not recognize an absolute and uncontrollable liberty. Liberty under the Constitution is subject to the restraints of due process, just as the states themselves are subject to the due process limitation on its legislation. State regulation of private enterprise, if it is reasonable in relation to its subject matter, and is adopted in the interests of the community, meets the due process standard.

The Court then went on to ask, rhetorically, "What can be closer to the public interest than the health of women and their protection from unscrupulous and overreaching employers?" The answer was that the protection of women

is a legitimate goal of the exercise of state power. The legislature of the state was clearly entitled to consider the situation of women in employment, the fact that they are in the class receiving the least pay, that their bargaining power is relatively weak, and that they are the ready victims of those who would take advantage of their necessitous circumstances. The legislature then was entitled to adopt measures to reduce the evils of the "sweating system," the exploiting of workers at wages so low as to be insufficient to meet the bare cost of living, thus making their very helplessness the occasion of a most injurious competition. The legislature had the right to consider that its minimum wage requirements would be an important aid in carrying out its policy of protection.

Perhaps feeling that such a "radical" (in the eyes of conservatives) decision required a "belt and suspenders," the majority added an additional "compelling consideration," which they said recent economic experience (i.e., the Great Depression) had brought into a strong light. The exploitation of a class of workers who are in an unequal position with respect to bargaining power and are thus relatively defenseless against the denial of a living wage is not only detrimental to their health and well-being but casts a direct burden for their support upon the community. What these workers lose in wages the taxpayers were called upon to pay through public assistance (at that time called "the dole").

The majority opinion ended by overruling an earlier case that had held that minimum wage laws violated the due process clauses and therefore were unconstitutional. "Our conclusion is that the case of *Adkins v. Children's Hospital*, should be, and it is, overruled. The judgment of the Supreme Court of the State of Washington is Affirmed."

22-2   Origin and Purpose of the Fair Labor Standards Act

The *Schecter Poultry* decision and the *West Coast Hotel* case were the main factors behind the FLSA. The *Schecter* case, which struck down the National Industrial Recovery Act, forced the federal government to attempt direct regulation of hours and wages in general. The *West Coast Hotel* case demonstrated that some regulation of working conditions was viewed by the Supreme Court as a valid exercise of government power.

After the *West Coast Hotel* decision, President Roosevelt told Congress, "All but the hopelessly reactionary will agree that to conserve our primary resources of manpower,

[2] 261 U.S. 525 (1923).

Government must have some control over maximum hours, minimum wages, the evil of child labor, and the exploitation of unorganized labor."

The FLSA was passed by Congress and signed into law on June 25, 1938. The Supreme Court held the FLSA to be constitutional in the 1941 case of *U.S. v. Darby Lumber Co.*[3] The FLSA, as amended over the years, continues in force today. It is the essential, although unglamorous, foundation for more recent federal regulation of working conditions through OSHA, ERISA, and even ADEA. The FLSA deals with four areas: minimum wages, overtime pay provisions, child labor, and equal pay for equal work. (The Equal Pay Act is an amendment to the FLSA. See Chapter 7 for a discussion of the provisions of the Equal Pay Act.)

22-2a Coverage

The FLSA, as amended, provides for three bases of coverage. Employees who are engaged in interstate commerce, including both import and export, are covered. In addition, employees who are engaged in the production of goods for interstate commerce are subject to the FLSA. The "production" of goods includes "any closely related process or occupation directly essential" to the production of goods for interstate commerce. Finally, all employees employed in an "enterprise engaged in" interstate commerce are subject to the FLSA, regardless of the relationship of their duties to commerce or the production of goods for commerce. This basis, the "enterprise" test, is subject to minimum dollar-volume limits for certain types of businesses. Employees of small employers would have to qualify for FLSA coverage under one of the other two bases of coverage. Employers and employees not covered by FLSA are generally subject to state laws, similar to the FLSA, which regulate minimum wages and maximum hours of work.

In 1966, the FLSA was extended to cover some federal employees and to include state and local hospitals and educational institutions. In 1974, FLSA coverage was extended to most federal employees, to state and local government employees, and to private household domestic workers.

The Congressional Accountability Act of 1995[4] extended the coverage of Fair Labor Standards Act to the employees of the House of Representatives, the Senate, the Capitol Guide Service, the Capitol Police, the Congressional Budget Office, the Office of the Architect of the Capitol, the Office of the Attending Physician, and the Office of Technology Assessment.

The extension of FLSA coverage to state and local government employees spawned a controversy under provisions of the U.S. Constitution. In the 1976 decision of *National League of Cities v. Usery*,[5] the Supreme Court held that federal regulation of the working conditions of state and local government employees infringed upon state sovereignty. The question was addressed again, in 1985, by the Supreme Court in *Garcia v. San Antonio Metropolitan Transit Authority*,[6] which overruled *National League of Cities*, stating, "We perceive nothing in the overtime and minimum-wage requirements of the FLSA ... that

---

[3] 312 U.S. 100.

[4] Pub. L. 104-1, 109 Stat. 3 (January 23, 1995).

[5] 426 U.S. 833.

[6] 469 U.S. 528.

is destructive of state sovereignty or violative of any constitutional provision." One event that helped persuade the Court to overrule *National League of Cities* a mere nine years after it was decided was an intervening congressional amendment of the FLSA permitting states and municipalities to provide their nonexempt employees with compensatory time off in lieu of overtime pay.

This FLSA amendment generated even more litigation. The Supreme Court felt compelled to speak yet again on this contentious problem of federal regulation of public employers' wage and hour obligations. This time, the justices were asked to determine whether a public employer, faced with a potential obligation to pay off accrued compensatory time in cash, could force its employees to take time off.

CASE 22.2

CHRISTENSEN v. HARRIS COUNTY
529 U.S. 576 (2000)

Thomas, J.

Under the Fair Labor Standards Act of 1938 (FLSA), States and their political subdivisions may compensate their employees for overtime by granting them compensatory time or "comp time," which entitles them to take time off work with full pay. If the employees do not use their accumulated compensatory time, the employer is obligated to pay cash compensation under certain circumstances. Fearing the fiscal consequences of having to pay for accrued compensatory time, Harris County adopted a policy requiring its employees to schedule time off in order to reduce the amount of accrued compensatory time. Employees of the Harris County Sheriff's Department sued, claiming that the FLSA prohibits such a policy. The Court of Appeals rejected their claim. Finding that nothing in the FLSA or its implementing regulations prohibits an employer from compelling the use of compensatory time, we affirm.

I.

A

The FLSA generally provides that hourly employees who work in excess of 40 hours per week must be compensated for the excess hours at a rate not less than 1½ times their regular hourly wage. Although this requirement did not initially apply to public-sector employers, Congress amended the FLSA to subject States and their political subdivisions to its constraints, at first on a limited basis, and then more broadly. States and their political subdivisions, however, did not feel the full force of this latter extension

until our decision in *Garcia v. San Antonio Metropolitan Transit Authority*, 469 U.S. 528, which overruled our holding in *National League of Cities v. Usery*, 426 U.S. 833, that the FLSA could not constitutionally restrain traditional governmental functions.

In the months following *Garcia*, Congress acted to mitigate the effects of applying the FLSA to States and their political subdivisions, passing the Fair Labor Standards Amendments of 1985. Those amendments permit States and their political subdivisions to compensate employees for overtime by granting them compensatory time at a rate of 1½ hours for every hour worked. To provide this form of compensation, the employer must arrive at an agreement or understanding with employees that compensatory time will be granted instead of cash compensation.

The FLSA expressly regulates some aspects of accrual and preservation of compensatory time. For example, the FLSA provides that an employer must honor an employee's request to use compensatory time within a "reasonable period" of time following the request, so long as the use of the compensatory time would not "unduly disrupt" the employer's operations. The FLSA also caps the number of compensatory time hours that an employee may accrue. After an employee reaches that maximum, the employer must pay cash compensation for additional overtime hours worked. In addition, the FLSA permits the employer at any time to cancel or "cash out" accrued compensatory time hours by paying the employee cash compensation for unused compensatory time. And the FLSA entitles the employee to cash payment for any accrued compensatory time remaining upon the termination of employment.

B

Petitioners are 127 deputy sheriffs employed by respondents Harris County, Texas, and its sheriff, Tommy B. Thomas (collectively, Harris County). It is undisputed that each of the petitioners individually agreed to accept compensatory time, in lieu of cash, as compensation for overtime.

As petitioners accumulated compensatory time, Harris County became concerned that it lacked the resources to pay monetary compensation to employees who worked overtime after reaching the statutory cap on compensatory time accrual and to employees who left their jobs with sizable reserves of accrued time. As a result, the county began looking for a way to reduce accumulated compensatory time. It wrote to the United States Department of Labor's Wage and Hour Division, asking "whether the Sheriff may schedule non-exempt employees to use or take compensatory time." The Acting Administrator of the Division replied:

> "[I]t is our position that a public employer may schedule its nonexempt employees to use their accrued FLSA compensatory time as directed if the prior agreement specifically provides such a provision....
>
> "Absent such an agreement, it is our position that neither the statute nor the regulations permit an employer to require an employee to use accrued compensatory time." Opinion Letter from Dept. of Labor, Wage and Hour Div. (Sept. 14, 1992), 1992 WL 845100 (Opinion Letter).

After receiving the letter, Harris County implemented a policy under which the employees' supervisor sets a maximum number of compensatory hours that may be accumulated. When an employee's stock of hours approaches that maximum, the employee is advised of the maximum and is asked to take steps to reduce accumulated compensatory time. If the employee does not do so voluntarily, a supervisor may order the employee to use his compensatory time at specified times.

Petitioners sued, claiming that the county's policy violates the FLSA because § 207(o)(5)—which requires that an employer reasonably accommodate employee requests to use compensatory time—provides the exclusive means of utilizing accrued time in the absence of an agreement or understanding permitting some other method. The District Court agreed, granting summary judgment for petitioners and entering a declaratory judgment that the county's policy violated the FLSA. The Court of Appeals for the Fifth Circuit reversed, holding that the FLSA did not speak to the issue and thus did not prohibit the county from implementing its compensatory time policy.

II.

Both parties, and the United States as *amicus curiae*, concede that nothing in the FLSA expressly prohibits a State or subdivision thereof from compelling employees to utilize accrued compensatory time. Petitioners and the United States, however, contend that the FLSA implicitly prohibits such a practice in the absence of an agreement or understanding authorizing compelled use. Title 29 U.S.C. § 207(o)(5) provides:

> An employee ...
>
> (A) who has accrued compensatory time off ..., and
>
> (B) who has requested the use of such compensatory time, shall be permitted by the employee's employer to use such time within a reasonable period after making the request if the use of the compensatory time does not unduly disrupt the operations of the public agency.

Petitioners and the United States rely upon the canon *expressio unius est exclusio alterius*, contending that the express grant of control to employees to use compensatory time, subject to the limitation regarding undue disruptions of workplace operations, implies that all other methods of spending compensatory time are precluded.

We find this reading unpersuasive. We accept the proposition that "[w]hen a statute limits a thing to be done in a particular mode, it includes a negative of any other mode." But that canon does not resolve this case in petitioners' favor. The "thing to be done" as defined by § 207(o)(5) is not the expenditure of compensatory time, as petitioners would have it. Instead, § 207(o)(5) is more properly read as a minimal guarantee that an employee will be able to make some use of compensatory time when he requests to use it. As such, the proper *expressio unius* inference is that an employer may not, at least in the absence of an agreement, deny an employee's request to use compensatory time for a reason other than that provided in § 207(o)(5). The canon's application simply does not prohibit an employer from telling an employee to take the benefits of compensatory time by scheduling time off work with full pay.

In other words, viewed in the context of the overall statutory scheme, § 207(o)(5) is better read not as setting forth the exclusive method by which compensatory time can be used, but as setting up a safeguard to ensure that an employee will receive timely compensation for working overtime. Section 207(o)(5) guarantees that, at the very minimum, an employee will get to use his compensatory time (i.e., take time off work with full pay) unless doing so would disrupt the employer's operations. And it is precisely this concern over ensuring that employees can timely "liquidate" compensatory time that the Secretary of Labor identified in her own regulations governing § 207(o)(5):

> "Compensatory time cannot be used as a means to avoid statutory overtime compensation. An employee has the right to use compensatory time earned and must not be coerced to accept more compensatory time than an employer can realistically and in good faith expect to be able to grant within a reasonable period of his or her making a request for use of such time."

At bottom, we think the better reading of § 207(o)(5) is that it imposes a restriction upon an employer's efforts to prohibit the use of compensatory time when employees request to do so; that provision says nothing about restricting an employer's efforts to require employees to use compensatory time. Because the statute is silent on this issue and because Harris County's policy is entirely compatible with § 207(o)(5), petitioners cannot prove that Harris County has violated § 207.

Our interpretation of § 207(o)(5)—one that does not prohibit employers from forcing employees to use compensatory time—finds support in two other features of the FLSA. First, employers remain free under the FLSA to decrease the number of hours that employees work. An employer may tell the employee to take off an afternoon, a day, or even an entire week. Thus, under the FLSA an employer is free to require an employee to take time off work, and an employer is also free to use the money it would have paid in wages to cash out accrued compensatory time. The compelled use of compensatory time challenged in this case merely involves doing both of these steps at once. It would make little sense to interpret § 207(o)(5) to make the combination of the two steps unlawful when each independently is lawful.

III.

In an attempt to avoid the conclusion that the FLSA does not prohibit compelled use of compensatory time, petitioners and the United States contend that we should defer to the Department of Labor's opinion letter, which takes the position that an employer may compel the use of compensatory time only if the employee has agreed in advance to such a practice. [A] court must give effect to an agency's regulation containing a reasonable interpretation of an ambiguous statute.

Here, however, we confront an interpretation contained in an opinion letter, not one arrived at after, for example, a formal adjudication or notice-and-comment rulemaking. Interpretations such as those in opinion letters—like interpretations contained in policy statements, agency manuals, and enforcement guidelines, all of which lack the force of law—do not warrant … deference. Instead, interpretations contained in formats such as opinion letters are "entitled to respect" … but only to the extent that those interpretations have the "power to persuade." As explained above, we find unpersuasive the agency's interpretation of the statute at issue in this case.

Of course, the framework of deference … does apply to an agency interpretation contained in a regulation. But in this case the Department of Labor's regulation does not address the issue of compelled compensatory time. The regulation provides only that "[t]he agreement or understanding [between the employer and employee] may include other provisions governing the preservation, use, or cashing out of compensatory time so long as these provisions are consistent with [§ 207 (o)]." Nothing in the regulation even arguably requires that an employer's compelled use policy must be included in an agreement. The text of the regulation itself indicates that its command is permissive, not mandatory.

As we have noted, no relevant statutory provision expressly or implicitly prohibits Harris County from pursuing its policy of forcing employees to utilize their compensatory time. In its opinion letter siding with the petitioners, the Department of Labor opined that "it is our position that neither the statute nor the regulations permit an employer to require an employee to use accrued compensatory time." Opinion Letter. But this view is exactly backwards. Unless the FLSA prohibits respondents from adopting its policy, petitioners cannot show that Harris County has violated the FLSA. And the FLSA contains no such prohibition. The judgment of the Court of Appeals is affirmed.

It is so ordered.

Case Questions

1. Why do you suppose the FLSA amendment, permitting states and municipalities to give their employees compensatory time off in lieu of paying overtime pay, helped persuade the Supreme Court that the FLSA unconstitutionally infringed upon state sovereignty? How does this amendment relate to the age-old constitutional principle that "the power to tax is the power to destroy"?

2. Explain the reasoning as to why the FLSA does not forbid public employers from forcing their employees to take compensatory time off, even when those employees would prefer not to do so.

3. Why should a public employee mind being ordered to take some time off?

4. Suppose that Harris County had lost this case. Could the county, in order to prevent its employees from accumulating more compensatory time, lay them off? If so, would this in effect force such employees to fall back on their accumulated comp time anyway?

5. If such employees were represented by a labor union, what should the union's position appropriately be with respect to this controversy? In light of the court's ruling, what provisions might that union try to negotiate into the relevant collective bargaining agreement to provide its members with as much discretion in their use of comp time as legally possible?

Concept *Summary* 22.1

BACKGROUND AND JURISDICTION OF THE FLSA

- New Deal legislation, enacted after Supreme Court reversed its position on the constitutionality of minimum wage laws
- Remains a vital part of U.S. employment and labor law system in light of human trafficking and sweat-shop persistence in 21st century
- Regulates:
  - Minimum wages
  - Overtime pay
  - Child labor
  - Equal pay for equal work
- Applies to public as well as private sector workers
  - But public employers may provide compensatory time in lieu of overtime pay

22-2b Minimum Wages

minimum wage
the wage limit, set by the government, under which an employer is not allowed to pay an employee

The government regulation of the **minimum wage** is an attempt to reduce poverty and bring the earnings of workers closer to the cost of living. The setting of the minimum wage was also an attempt to maintain the purchasing power of the public to lift the country out of the economic depths of the Great Depression.

The concept of a minimum wage may seem simple: The employer may not pay employees less than the minimum wage per hour. In 1938, the minimum wage was set at $0.25 per hour, and it was raised to $0.40 per hour through the next seven years. The federal minimum wage for covered nonexempt employees is currently $7.25 per hour; it was last raised on July 24, 2009.

Although the concept of the minimum wage seems simple, administering it may present some problems because of the wide variation in methods of compensating employees. For example, many employees are paid on an hourly basis, whereas others receive a weekly or monthly salary. Waiters and waitresses often rely on tips from customers for a large percentage of their earnings. Machinists and sewing machine operators are usually paid on a "piece-rate" basis; that is, they earn a certain amount of money for each piece completed. Salespeople usually earn a commission, which may or may not be supplemented by a base salary. Musicians may be paid a flat rate per engagement, and umpires or referees may be paid by the game.

Such atypical compensation methods are subject to regulations developed by the administrator of the Wage and Hour Division of the Department of Labor (DOL). The regulations are designed to ensure that all workers receive at least the minimum wage. If a worker is a "tipped worker"—that is, one who receives tips from customers—the employer is allowed to reduce the minimum wage paid to that worker by up to 40 percent, with the difference to be made up by tips received. The earnings of workers who are paid on a piece-rate basis must average out to at least the minimum wage; the time period over which the earnings are averaged cannot be longer than a single workweek. This means that the earnings of such an employee may be less than the minimum wage for any single hour, as long as the total earnings for the week average out to the minimum wage. Some persons being paid for the work may not even be viewed as employees at all for purposes of Fair Labor Standards Act coverage.

Employers may have an incentive to characterize some workers as independent contractors rather than employees. If a worker is an independent contractor, they are not covered by the minimum wage and overtime provisions of the FLSA, and the employer may not be required to make income tax deductions, Social Security, and workers' compensations contributions on behalf of those workers. The U.S. Department of Labor has recently made the misclassification of workers one of its top enforcement priorities, and the Internal Revenue Service and U.S. Government Accountability Office estimated that employee misclassification will cost the federal government over $7 billion in payroll taxes lost over the 10 years. A number of states have entered into memoranda of understanding to implement and improve detection and enforcement of employee misclassification. The following case addresses the issue of whether exotic dancers are employees or independent contractors.

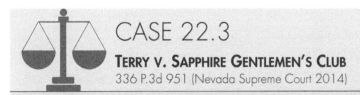

CASE 22.3

TERRY V. SAPPHIRE GENTLEMEN'S CLUB

336 P.3d 951 (Nevada Supreme Court 2014)

Facts: Sapphire Gentlemen's Club [Sapphire] contracts for semi-nude entertainment with approximately 6,600 performers. Under those contracts, the performers may determine their own schedules, subject to a minimum shift length of six hours any day they decide to work; set prices for their private performances (provided that they comply with the club's established minimum charge); control the "artistic aspects" of their performances (though the club DJ chooses the music they dance to, and they must obey club rules as to body positioning and physical contact with customers); and perform at other venues should they wish to. The performers also agree to abide by certain "house rules," including a minimum standard of coverage by their costumes and a minimum heel height; payment of a "house fee," which ranges in amount, any night they work; and performing two dances per shift on the club stage unless they pay an "off-stage" fee. Sapphire does not pay wages to the performers, whose income is entirely dependent upon tips and dancing fees paid by Sapphire patrons. The performers filed suit against the Sapphire challenging their work arrangements, claiming that they were "employees" within the meaning of state minimum wage laws and were thus guaranteed a minimum wage. The district court found that the performers were not "employees" within the meaning of the state legislation and granted summary judgment for Sapphire. The performers appealed to the Nevada Supreme Court.

Issue: Are the performers at Sapphire Gentlemen's Club employees within the meaning of the state minimum wage laws and thus entitled to the minimum wages guaranteed by state and federal law?

Decision: The state legislature has long used federal minimum wage laws as a platform for the state's minimum wage scheme, and for practical reasons the two schemes should be harmonious in terms of which workers are entitled to protection. The court here therefore adopted the Fair Labor Standards Act's "economic realities" test for employment in the minimum wage context. Sapphire argued that the performers had no "contract of hire" and alternatively that the performers were not "in the service of" Sapphire. The court rejected those arguments. First, the signed entertainment agreement, which describes in detail the terms under which Sapphire permits the performers to dance at its facility, is an express contract of hire, despite that therein the parties state that they "intend that the relationship created will be only that of Sapphire and Entertainer and not any other legal relationship." Given the purpose of remedial legislation such as minimum wage laws, a putative employer's self-interested disclaimers of any intent to hire cannot control the realities of an employment relationship. Thus, Sapphire's protestations that the performers "never intended to

be employees" and agreed to be independent contractors are beside the point.

The court noted that the state legislature has long relied on the federal minimum wage law to lay a foundation of worker protections that Nevada could build upon. The parallels between the state and federal laws are part of a larger national pattern of laws that have emerged to deal with common problems in the minimum wage context, and many other states have adopted the economic realities test to determine whether an employment relationship exists under their respective state minimum wage laws. The economic realities test fashioned by the federal courts examines the totality of the circumstances and determines whether, as a matter of economic reality, workers depend upon the business to which they render service for the opportunity to work. The state legislature has not clearly signaled its intent that Nevada's minimum wage scheme should deviate from the federally set course, the state and federal minimum wage laws should be harmonious in terms of which workers qualify as employees under them. The Nevada Supreme Court therefore adopted the FLSA's economic realities test for employment in the context of Nevada's minimum wage laws.

In applying the economic realities test, there are some factors which courts nearly universally consider:

1. the degree of the alleged employer's right to control the manner in which the work is to be performed;

2. the alleged employee's opportunity for profit or loss depending upon his managerial skill;

3. the alleged employee's investment in equipment or materials required for his task, or his employment of helpers;

4. whether the service rendered requires a special skill;

5. the degree of permanence of the working relationship; and

6. whether the service rendered is an integral part of the alleged employer's business.

The court then examined the district court's summary judgment regarding the performers' relationship with Sapphire. As to the "control" factor considered under the totality of the circumstances, at first look, the facts may appear mixed. Sapphire did not produce a set schedule for performers, theoretically allowing them to work any day they wished for as long as they wished, provided that they met a six-hour shift minimum or received permission to depart early. Additionally, though the club set a two stage-dance minimum for performers not paying the off-stage fee, and discouraged performers from refusing to give a lap dance if a customer requested one, the decision of whether or not to stage dance ultimately lay in the discretion of the performers, as did their acceptance or rejection of a patron's invitation for a private dance. While Sapphire required performers to accept "dance dollars"—from which the club took a cut—whether or not they preferred to, performers were also permitted to accept cash, to which the club laid no claim. But Sapphire's supposed lack of control may actually reflect "a framework of false autonomy" that gives performers "a coercive 'choice' between accruing debt to the club or redrawing personal boundaries of consent and bodily integrity." Put differently, Sapphire emphasizes that performers may choose not to dance on stage at Sapphire so long as they also "choose to pay an optional 'off-stage fee,'" and similarly that a performer may "choose not to dance for a patron she knows will pay with dance dollars, she may make that choice," though the performer may not ask that patron to pay in cash, and in making either choice the performers also risk taking a net loss for her shift. But by forcing them to make such choices, Sapphire is actually able to heavily monitor the performers, including dictating their appearance, interactions with customers, work schedules, and minute-to-minute movements when working, while ostensibly ceding control to them. This reality undermines Sapphire's characterization of the choices it offers performers and the freedom it suggests that these choices allow them; the performers are, for all practical purposes, "not on a pedestal, but in a cage."

The weight of other economic realities factors add to this characterization. First, given that the performers risked little more than their daily house fees, personal grooming expenditures, costume costs, and time, and that the one who "takes the risks ... reaps the returns," their opportunity for profit was limited accordingly. That a performer might increase her profits through "hustling," that is using her interpersonal skills to solicit larger tips, is not dispositive— "[a]s is the case with the zealous waiter at a fancy, four star restaurant, a dancer's stake, her take and the control she exercises over each of these are limited by the bounds of good service...." [citations omitted].

With regard to the relative investment of the parties, Sapphire provides all the risk capital, funds advertising, and covers facility expenses. The performers' financial contributions are limited to those noted above—their costume and appearance-related expenses and house fees. Thus, the performers are "far more closely akin to wage earners toiling for a living, than to independent entrepreneurs seeking a return on their risky capital investments," and this factor also weighs in the performers' favor.

All work requires some skill, so in the economic realities context, courts look specifically for workers' "special" skills; namely, whether their work requires the initiative demonstrated by one in business for himself or herself. Sapphire suggests that the performers' ability to "hustle" clients is one such skill. But Sapphire does not interview the performers for any indication of their hustling prowess; it is not apparent that their work actually requires such initiative. In any case, though it may well be that a good "hustle" is a considerable boon in the field, "the ability to develop and maintain rapport with customers is not the type of 'initiative' contemplated by this factor." Sapphire argued that the dancers are itinerant because they have the freedom to ply their dancing trade at a multitude of gentlemen's clubs, and so the factor looking to the permanency of the relationship should weigh in its favor. Sapphire did allow the performers to work at other venues, and different performers testified that they continued schooling or other employment during their tenure at Sapphire. But that the performers "were free to work at other clubs or in other lines of work does not distinguish them from countless workers in other areas of endeavor who are undeniably employees, such as waiters, ushers, and bartenders. The ultimate inquiry is the nature of the performers' dependence on the club, and '[e]ven if the freedom to work for multiple employers may provide something of a safety net, unless a worker possesses specialized and widely-demanded skills, that freedom is hardly the same as true economic independence.' Thus, though the temporary nature of the relationship at issue weighs against it being that of employer/employee, this factor carries little persuasive value in the context of dancers and the clubs at which they perform, and cannot alone tilt the scales in Sapphire's favor.

Sapphire argued that exotic dancing is customarily performed by independent contractors, and therefore, is "not an integral part of Sapphire's business." Even assuming it is true that "exotic dancing" is typically performed by independent contractors, the court noted that was a tenuous proposition given that most other precedents demonstrate that it is performed by employees. Sapphire was not able to cite any authority supporting the application of the "normal work" test to this factor in the economic realities context. The court held that to do so simply made no sense; if we are examining whether work is "integral" to an employer's business, the test must be whether it is "useful, necessary, or even absolutely indispensable" to the business. Given that Sapphire billed itself as the "World's Largest Strip Club," and not as a sports bar or night club, the court held that the women strip-dancing there were useful and indeed necessary to its operation.

The court then held that, based on the review of the totality of the circumstances of the working relationship's economic reality, Sapphire qualified as an employer under the state legislation, and the performers therefore qualified as employees under the law. In so holding, the court noted that its decision was in accord with the great weight of authority, which has almost "without exception ... found an employment relationship and required ... nightclub[s] to pay [their] dancers a minimum wage."

The court therefore reversed the district court's grant of summary judgment in favor of Sapphire and remanded the case for further proceedings consistent with this opinion.

Case Questions

1.   How would the performers' status as independent contractors affect Sapphire's obligations toward them? Why would Sapphire have an economic incentive to classify them as independent contractors and not employees?

2.   Why does the court hold that the individual "entertainment agreements" between the individual performers and Sapphire are not definitive in determining the relationship between the performers and the club?

3.   Why does the court look to federal courts' use of the "economic realities" test to determine whether the performers were employees for the purposes of state minimum wage law?

Another FLSA issue with which the DOL and courts have wrestled is whether employees are to be paid for the time required for an employee to prepare to perform the job and the time required to end the day's performance. This issue has arisen, for instance, in the following situations:

•   Where the shifts of incoming and outgoing retail clerks must effectuate a transfer of the store's cash register between their shifts;

•   Where miners and factory workers must don uniforms or equipment in a locker room at the start of their shifts and perhaps shower and change at the end of their workdays.

The FLSA did not initially define "work" or "workweek"; in some early FLSA decisions, the Supreme Court interpreted those terms broadly. The Court found that the time spent traveling between mine portals and underground work areas, and the time spent walking from time clocks to work benches, were compensable under the FLSA. Congress responded by passing the Portal-to-Portal Act. The Portal-to-Portal Act exempted employers from liability for future claims based on two categories of work-related activities as follows:

(a)   Except as provided in subsection (b) [which covers work compensable by contract or custom], no employer shall be subject to any liability or punishment under the Fair Labor Standards Act of 1938, as amended, ... on account of the failure of such employer ... to pay an employee overtime compensation, for or on account of any of the following activities of such employee engaged in on or after the date of the enactment of this Act—

(1)   walking, riding, or traveling to and from the actual place of performance of the principal activity or activities which such employee is employed to perform, and

(2)   activities which are preliminary to or postliminary to said principal activity or activities,

which occur either prior to the time on any particular workday at which such employee commences, or subsequent to the time on any particular workday at which he ceases, such principal activity or activities.[7]

The following case involves the application of the Portal-to-Portal Act to determine whether certain activities are compensable under the FLSA.

CASE 22.4

SALAZAR v. BUTTERBALL, LLC
644 F.3d 1130 (10th Cir. 2011)

Facts: Butterball's Longmont plant produces turkey products, including cooked ready-to-eat (RTE) turkey products. Butterball acquired the plant from ConAgra Foods in 2006. Butterball retained the same workforce, management, and pay practices that were in place during ConAgra's ownership.

The plaintiffs worked at various times in the plant's deboning, evisceration, packaging, and quality assurance departments. They were required to don various items of apparel and equipment prior to their shifts and to doff such items after their shifts. Generally, production employees wore frocks, aprons, plastic sleeves, gloves, cotton glove liners, boots or overshoes, hard hats, earplugs, and safety glasses. When working in the deboning and evisceration areas, plaintiffs also wore mesh gloves, knife holders, and arm guards. As the parties have done, we refer to these items collectively as personal protective equipment, or PPE.

Butterball, continuing ConAgra's practice, has never paid most production employees for donning and doffing time. The plaintiffs are aware that they have never been paid for donning and doffing time.

Production employees at the plant are represented by United Food and Commercial Workers Local 7 (UFCW 7 or the Union). ConAgra and UFCW 7 entered into

a collective bargaining agreement (CBA) for the period of February 6, 2005 through February 2, 2008. Butterball and UFCW 7 entered into a new CBA for the period of February 3, 2008 through February 2, 2009. As of April 1, 2009, the Union was working without a contract, and the current status of negotiations is not evident from the record presented. Neither CBA discusses donning and doffing pay or how hours worked are to be calculated.

On December 16, 2005, the Union filed a grievance claiming that employees should be paid for donning and doffing time. ConAgra denied the grievance and the Union demanded arbitration on November 13, 2006. However, arbitration did not occur. Butterball presented evidence that the grievance had been resolved by April 2008. On the other hand, the plaintiffs presented evidence that the Union considered the grievance to be pending, at least as of June 1, 2007. It is undisputed that the issue of donning and doffing pay was not discussed during negotiations of either CBA.

The FLSA, Portal-to-Portal Act, and 29 U.S.C. § 203(o)
Congress enacted the FLSA in 1938 "to establish nationwide minimum wage and maximum hours standards." *Moreau v. Klevenhagen*, 508 U.S. 22, 25, 113 S.Ct. 1905, 123 L.Ed.2d

---

[7] § 4, 61 Stat. 86–87 (codified at 29 U.S.C. § 254(a)).

584 (1993). Generally, the FLSA mandates that employees be paid a minimum wage and paid at an overtime rate for hours worked in excess of forty in a workweek. The statute does not define "work" or "workweek," and the Supreme Court's early FLSA decisions interpreted those terms broadly. *IBP, Inc. v. Alvarez*, 546 U.S. 21, 25, 126 S.Ct. 514, 163 L.Ed.2d 288 (2005). In *Anderson v. Mt. Clemens Pottery Co.*, 328 U.S. 680, 690–91, 66 S.Ct. 1187, 90 L.Ed. 1515 (1946), the Supreme Court held that the "workweek" included "all time during which an employee is necessarily required to be on the employer's premises, on duty or at a prescribed workplace...." Congress enacted the Portal-to-Portal Act, 29 U.S.C. §§ 251–62, in response to *Mt. Clemens* and other judicial decisions that, in Congress's view, interpreted the FLSA "in disregard of long-established customs, practices, and contracts between employers and employees, thereby creating wholly unexpected liabilities." 29 U.S.C. § 251(a).

Among other things, the Portal-to-Portal Act provided that employers could not be liable under the FLSA for failure to compensate time an employee spent performing activities that were preliminary or postliminary to "the principal activity or activities which such employee is required to perform." The Supreme Court interpreted this provision to mean that activities performed prior or subsequent to a regular work shift are compensable if they are "an integral and indispensable part of the principal activities for which covered workmen are employed...." *Steiner v. Mitchell*, 350 U.S. 247, 256, 76 S.Ct. 330, 100 L.Ed. 267 (1956). In 2005, the Supreme Court held that, assuming donning and doffing was an integral and indispensable activity, any post-donning and pre-doffing walking time (i.e., between locker rooms and production areas) would be compensable under the Portal-to-Portal Act.

Congress amended the FLSA again in 1949 enacting, among other provisions, what is now 29 U.S.C. § 203(*o*). Section 203(*o*) defines hours worked:

> Hours worked.—In determining for the purposes of sections 206 and 207 of this title [minimum wage and maximum hours] the hours for which an employee is employed, there shall be excluded any time spent in changing clothes or washing at the beginning or end of each workday which was excluded from measured working time during the week involved by the express terms of or by custom or practice under a bona fide collective-bargaining agreement applicable to the particular employee.

Colorado Wage Order 27

The Colorado Minimum Wage Act, Colo.Rev.Stat. §§ 8-6-101-8-6-119, prohibits employment of workers "for wages which are inadequate to supply the necessary cost of living and to maintain the health of workers so employed" or "under conditions of labor detrimental to [workers'] health or morals." Colo.Rev.Stat. § 8-6-104. The Act also delegates to the Colorado Department of Labor the authority to set minimum wage and maximum hour standards. Colo.Rev.Stat. § 8-6-106. Pursuant to this authority, the Colorado Department of Labor issued Wage Order 27, which prescribes minimum wage and overtime requirements *1136 for employees in the retail and service, food and beverage, commercial support service, and health and medical industries. 7 Colo.Code Regs. § 1103-1:1.

Procedural History

Plaintiffs filed a complaint in the United States District Court for the District of Colorado, seeking to bring a collective action under the FLSA and a class action under Colorado law for compensation for time spent "donning, doffing, and sanitizing gear and equipment, and walking to and from the production floor." Aplt. App., Vol. I at 12–13. Butterball moved for summary judgment on both claims. A magistrate judge issued a Report and Recommendation determining that plaintiffs' PPE was clothes under 29 U.S.C. § 203(*o*) and there was a custom or practice of nonpayment, and that Butterball was not subject to Wage Order 27. The district court adopted the Report and Recommendation and entered summary judgment in Butterball's favor. Plaintiffs appeal....

III.

Plaintiffs contend that Butterball violated the FLSA by failing to compensate them for donning and doffing time. Butterball argues that it is not required to compensate donning and doffing time for the following reasons: it is not work under the FLSA; it is excluded from FLSA "hours worked" by 29 U.S.C. § 203(*o*); it is not compensable pursuant to the Portal-to-Portal Act, specifically 29 U.S.C. § 254(a); and it is de minimis.

The district court based its FLSA ruling on § 203(*o*), and we do the same. Section 203(*o*) excludes "any time spent changing clothes or washing" from "the hours for which an employee is employed" if such time "was excluded from measured working time during the week involved by the express terms of or by custom or practice under a bona fide collective-bargaining agreement applicable to the particular employee." 29 U.S.C. § 203*(o)*. We hold that donning and doffing the PPE at issue in this case is changing clothes and that there is a custom or practice of excluding donning and doffing time from measured working time under the collective bargaining arrangement between the Union and Butterball. We, therefore, affirm the district court's ruling that Butterball did not violate the FLSA by failing to pay plaintiffs for donning and doffing time.

The Supreme Court addressed a similar issue in *Integrity Staffing Solutions, Inc. v. Busk*.[8] That case involved hourly warehouse workers who retrieved products from warehouse shelves and packaged them for delivery to Amazon.com customers, and who were required to undergo a security screening before leaving the warehouse each day; the employees often spent up to 25 minutes waiting to be screened. The Supreme Court held that time spent by employees waiting for and undergoing security screenings before leaving workplace was not compensable under FLSA.

Concept *Summary* 22.2

MINIMUM WAGE

- The minimum wage is the lowest amount that an employer may pay per hour to employees who are paid by the hour
- This minimum has risen steadily since the FLSA was first enacted and reached $7.25 per hour on July 24, 2009
- Issues regarding eligibility for minimum wages include:
  - Whether the workers actually are "employees" under the FLSA (as with incarcerated prisoners)
  - Whether waiting and down time are compensable hours of work

overtime pay
employees covered by the FLSA are entitled to overtime pay, at one-and-a-half times their regular pay rate, for hours worked in excess of 40 hours per workweek

workweek
a term the FLSA uses to signify seven consecutive days; the law does not require that the workweek start or end on any particular day of the calendar week

22-2c   Overtime Pay

In addition to being entitled to earn the minimum wage, employees covered by the FLSA are entitled to **overtime pay** at one-and-a-half times their regular pay rate for hours worked in excess of 40 hours per **workweek**.

The term *workweek* has special significance under the FLSA. It is a "term of art" with a fairly precise meaning. A workweek consists of seven consecutive days, but the law does not require that the workweek start or end on any particular day of the calendar week. For instance, a workweek may run from Tuesday to Monday or from Friday to Thursday. The starting day of the workweek may be changed from time to time, provided that the purpose of the change is not to avoid the requirements of the law (such as avoiding the payment of overtime to a group of workers).

---

[8] 135 S.Ct. 513 (2014).

As with the minimum wage, regulations have been developed to compute the hourly wages of workers paid by commission, piece-rate, and so forth for the purpose of calculating overtime pay. A more difficult question is deciding whether certain hours, not strictly part of working hours, should be included in working time for the calculation of wages and overtime. The Portal to Portal Act of 1947, which amended the FLSA, provides that preliminary or postwork activities are to be included in compensable time only if they are called for under contract or industry custom or practice.

22-2d Exemptions from Overtime and Minimum Wage Provisions

exempt employee
employee whose hours of work and compensation are not stipulated by the FLSA

Not all employees under the FLSA are entitled to overtime pay or subject to the minimum wage. The FLSA sets out four general categories of employees who are exempt from the minimum wage and overtime requirements of the statute. Such **exempt employees** include executives, administrators, professionals, and outside salespeople.

ethical DILEMMA

CONVENIENCE STORE CLERK'S CONUNDRUM

College sophomore Suzy Smart works part-time in the Handi Mart convenience store near campus. The manager at Handi Mart requires that each clerk arrive 15 minutes prior to the start of the shift so that the clerk going off duty can review the sales figures and cash status with the replacement before leaving. The clerk going off duty punches her timecard after this review, but the oncoming clerk is not allowed to clock in until the review is completed and she has agreed that the sales and cash figures are accurate. Sometimes this exercise takes more than 15 minutes; no matter how long it takes, the clerk coming on duty may not punch her timecard and start earning wages until the process is completed.

This semester, Suzy is taking a course on labor and employment law. After reading the text chapter concerning minimum wage and overtime rules under the FLSA, she realizes that the store manager is violating the law by not allowing the oncoming clerk to punch the time clock as soon as she arrives. She brings this up with the store manager.

The store manager tells Suzy that he is not allowed by the parent corporation of Handi Mart to compensate two clerks for the same period of time, no matter how brief, because this is classified by the corporation as a "single coverage" store. Furthermore, he adds ominously, if Suzy complains to the Wage and Hour Division of the U.S. DOL, he probably will be forced by the company to lay off Suzy and the other part-timers and cover the evening shifts himself. "You may get everyone a few dollars in back pay," he adds, "but you'll also cost everybody their jobs. Remember, some of your coworkers are single parents who need this extra income to make ends meet." Should Suzy file a minimum wage complaint with the U.S. DOL?

Executive Employees

The regulations under the FLSA provide the following test:

(1) Employee is compensated on a salary basis at a rate of not less than $455 per week (or $380 per week, if employed in American Samoa by an employer other than the Federal Government), exclusive of board, lodging, or other facilities;

(2) Her or his primary duty is management of the enterprise in which the employee is employed or of a customarily recognized department or subdivision thereof;

(3) She or he customarily and regularly directs the work of two or more other employees; and

(4) She or he has the authority to hire or fire other employees or to make suggestions and recommendations as to the hiring, firing, advancement, promotion or any other change of status of other employees are given particular weight.[9]

Administrative Employees

The regulations under the FLSA set out the following test:

(1) Employee is compensated on a salary or fee basis at a rate of not less than $455 per week (or $380 per week, if employed in American Samoa by an employer other than the Federal Government), exclusive of board, lodging, or other facilities;

(2) Her/his primary duty is the performance of office or non-manual work directly related to the management or general business operations of the employer or the employer's customers; and

(3) Her/his primary duty includes the exercise of discretion and independent judgment with respect to matters of significance.[10]

Professional Employees

Employees in bona fide professional positions are exempted from the FLSA's overtime and minimum wage provisions if they meet the following test:

(1) Employee is compensated on a salary or fee basis at a rate of not less than $455 per week (or $380 per week, if employed in American Samoa by an employer other than the Federal Government), exclusive of board, lodging, or other facilities; and

(2) Her/his primary duty is the performance of work:
   (a) Requiring knowledge of an advanced type in a field of science or learning customarily acquired by a prolonged course of specialized intellectual instruction; or
   (b) Requiring invention, imagination, originality, or talent in a recognized field of artistic or creative endeavor.[11]

---

[9] Title 29, Subpart B, 541.100, Electronic Code of Federal Regulations, available at http://www.ecfr.gov/cgi-bin/text-idx?c=ecfr&sid=48d6ee3b99d3b3a97b1bf189e1757786&rgn=div5&view=text&node=29:3.1.1.1.23&idno=29.

[10] Title 29, Subpart C, 541.200, Electronic Code of Federal Regulations, available at http://www.ecfr.gov/cgi-bin/text-idx?c=ecfr&sid=48d6ee3b99d3b3a97b1bf189e1757786&rgn=div5&view=text&node=29:3.1.1.1.23&idno=29.

[11] Title 29, Subpart D, 541.300, Electronic Code of Federal Regulations, available at http://www.ecfr.gov/cgi-bin/text-idx?c=ecfr&sid=48d6ee3b99d3b3a97b1bf189e1757786&rgn=div5&view=text&node=29:3.1.1.1.23&idno=29.

Outside Salespeople

The regulations under the FLSA exempt outside salespeople from both the overtime and minimum wage provisions. To be exempt, the following requirements must be met:

(1) Employee's primary duty is:

   (a) making sales within the meaning of section 3(k) of the Act, or

   (b) obtaining orders or contracts for services or for the use of facilities for which a consideration will be paid by the client or customer; and

(2) S/he is customarily and regularly engaged away from the employer's place or places of business in performing such primary duty.

   (a) The term "primary duty" is defined at Section 541.700. In determining the primary duty of an outside sales employee, work performed incidental to and in conjunction with the employee's own outside sales or solicitations, including incidental deliveries and collections, shall be regarded as exempt outside sales work. Other work that furthers the employee's sales efforts also shall be regarded as exempt work including, for example, writing sales reports, updating or revising the employee's sales or display catalogue, planning itineraries and attending sales conferences.

   (b) The requirements of subpart G (salary requirements) of this part do not apply to the outside sales employees described in this section.[12]

An employer that wants to pay a category of employees a salary and treat them as falling outside the minimum wage and overtime rules cannot end its inquiry with the FLSA, however. When Congress determines that the federal government should regulate some aspect of our lives, it also decides whether the new federal statute will preempt the field or whether (alternatively) the 50 states may continue to play a role. In such enterprises as TV and radio broadcasting and airline travel, Uncle Sam has taken over regulating almost all activities. In others, such as ERISA (see Chapter 21), Congress has claimed the largest part of pension and benefits regulation, leaving only insurance and banking to state laws. But in some important areas of employment law, such as job discrimination (see Chapters 6–10), Congress actually has encouraged the states to supplement federal efforts with their own laws. The same is true for the FLSA. The states may supplement the federal wage and hours laws and regulations, provided state law expands the rights accorded to workers by the federal scheme.

Sometimes state involvement in wage and hour issues can make the law quite confusing. For instance, what if workers from New Mexico and Arizona are sent to do a job in California? Which law should apply, if the federal law and the laws of the several states provide differing rights with respect to overtime pay? This issue troubled the U.S. Court of Appeals for the Ninth Circuit in 2008 and 2009. In 2008, the court awarded overtime pay to such out-of-state workers.[13] Then on February 17, 2009, the court thought better of its decision, withdrew it, and certified the case to the California Supreme Court for its opinion.[14] The California Supreme Court responded as follows:

   (1) The California Labor Code overtime compensation statutes apply by their terms to work performed in California by nonresidents; (2) under conflict-of-laws principles,

---

[12] Title 29, Subpart F, 541.500, Electronic Code of Federal Regulations, available at http://www.ecfr.gov/cgi-bin/text-idx?c=ecfr&sid=48d6ee3b99d3b3a97b1bf189e1757786&rgn=div5&view=text&node=29:3.1.1.1.23&idno=29.

[13] *Sullivan v. Oracle Corporation*, 547 F.3d 1177 (9th Cir. 2008).

[14] 557 F.3d 979 (9th Cir. 2009).

Labor Code overtime compensation provisions applied to full days and weeks of work performed in California by nonresidents; (3) The California Unfair Competition Law [UCL] applies to a failure to pay overtime for work performed in California by nonresidents; but (4) UCL did not apply to employer's alleged failure to pay Fair Labor Standards Act (FLSA) overtime for work performed outside California.[15]

After the California Supreme Court answered those questions, the Ninth Circuit then held that application of California Labor Code provision requiring California-based employer to pay overtime to out-of-state employees did not violate due process or dormant commerce clause of the U.S. Constitution.[16]

THE **WORKING** LAW

Presidential Memorandum—Updating and Modernizing Overtime Regulations

MEMORANDUM FOR THE SECRETARY OF LABOR

SUBJECT: Updating and Modernizing Overtime Regulations

The Fair Labor Standards Act (the "Act"), 29 U.S.C. 201 et seq., provides basic rights and wage protections for American workers, including Federal minimum wage and overtime requirements. Most workers covered under the Act must receive overtime pay of at least 1.5 times their regular pay rate for hours worked in excess of 40 hours per week.

However, regulations regarding exemptions from the Act's overtime requirement, particularly for executive, administrative, and professional employees (often referred to as "white collar" exemptions) have not kept up with our modern economy. Because these regulations are outdated, millions of Americans lack the protections of overtime and even the right to the minimum wage.

Therefore, I hereby direct you to propose revisions to modernize and streamline the existing overtime regulations. In doing so, you shall consider how the regulations could be revised to update existing protections consistent with the intent of the Act; address the changing nature of the workplace; and simplify the regulations to make them easier for both workers and businesses to understand and apply.

This memorandum is not intended to, and does not, create any right or benefit, substantive or procedural, enforceable at law or in equity by any party against the United States, its departments, agencies, or entities, its officers, employees, or agents, or any other person.

Nothing in this memorandum shall be construed to impair or otherwise affect the authority granted by law to a department or agency, or the head thereof.

You are hereby authorized and directed to publish this memorandum in the Federal Register.

BARACK OBAMA

Source: "Presidential memorandum—updating and modernizing overtime regulations," The White House, March 13, 2014, available at https://www.whitehouse.gov/the-press-office/2014/03/13/presidential-memorandum-updating-and-modernizing-overtime-regulations.

---

[15] 51 Cal.4th 1191, 254 P.3d 237 (Cal. 2011).

[16] 662 F.3d 1265 (9th Cir. 2011).

On July 6, 2015, the U.S. Department of Labor published the Notice of Proposed Rulemaking about the proposed changes to the eligibility rules for overtime under the Fair Labor Standards Act.[17] The main focus of the proposed changes is to increase the salary-level threshold for the "white-collar" exemptions for executive, administrative, professional, outside sales or computer employees from $455 per week (or $23,660 per year) to $970 (or ($50,440 per year) in 2016. Employees who satisfy certain job duty tests related to their classification as executive, administrative, professional, outside sales, or computer employees and whose weekly pay is above $970 will be exempt from the FLSA requirement to pay overtime for hours of work exceeding 40 hours per workweek. The salary-level threshold has not been updated for ten years, and the proposed $970 weekly figure would represent the 40th percentile of weekly earnings for full-time salaried workers. The Department of Labor estimates the proposed rule change would mean that 4.6 million workers currently classified as exempt from overtime would become eligible for overtime pay. The proposed rule changes would also increase the salary-level threshold for the exemption for highly compensated employees from the present figure of $100,000 annual compensation to the figure of $122,148 annual compensation.

Concept *Summary* 22.3

OVERTIME PAY

- Employees who are paid by the hour generally are entitled to one-and-a-half times their hourly rates for work in excess of 40 hours in a single workweek
- Exemptions from the minimum wage and overtime roles:
  - Salaried employees who earn at least the minimum weekly salary specified by the U.S. Department of Labor and who are bona fide executives, administrators, or professionals
  - Outside sales people, who are paid mainly by commissions
- The FLSA allows the states to regulate wages and hours, including overtime provisions, provided the state rules are more generous to employees than the federal law
- The blend of federal and state jurisdiction over wage and hour matters, such as overtime entitlements, can create confusing legal issues

22-2e Limitations on Child Labor

The problems of child labor are graphically demonstrated by photographs from the late 19th and early 20th centuries showing children who had spent their youth toiling in coal mines or factories. The children, often immigrants, were subjected to the same hazardous

---

[17] The notice, some 295 pages in all, appears at 80 FR 38516 (July 6, 2015).

conditions and occupational diseases as were their parents. They received little or no formal education. Their wages were usually meager and, as a result, drove down the wages of adult workers who held the same, or similar, jobs.

The social and economic problems of child labor were recognized by government; many states passed legislation attempting to limit child labor. Those early laws were restricted in their effectiveness, though, and the number of children employed continued to rise until about 1910. Congress made several attempts to enact federal limitations on child labor. In 1916, a law prohibiting the shipment in interstate commerce of goods produced by factories or mines employing child labor was passed. The Supreme Court, however, in the 1918 case of *Hammer v. Dagenhart*,[18] held that the law was unconstitutional because it exceeded the limited power granted to the federal government under the commerce clause of the Constitution.

National Industrial Recovery Act (NIRA)
an act primarily designed to regulate and revitalize industry; promoted fair trade practices

The **National Industrial Recovery Act (NIRA)** provided that the codes of fair competition for each industry could limit child labor, but in 1935, the NIRA was held unconstitutional by the Supreme Court in *Schecter Poultry v. U.S.* In 1936, the Walsh-Healy Act prohibited contractors under government contracts from using child labor to produce, manufacture, or furnish materials for the contract. The Fair Labor Standards Act of 1938 at last provided for general federal regulation of child labor.

The FLSA and Child Labor

The FLSA does not prohibit all child labor; rather, it proscribes only "oppressive" child labor. The act prohibits the interstate shipment of goods from establishments employing oppressive child labor. It also prohibits oppressive child labor in any enterprise with two or more employees engaged in the production of goods for interstate commerce. The definition of "oppressive child labor" is crucial to the administration of the act. The act defines oppressive child labor by using age restrictions and identifying hazardous occupations.

Employing minors under age 18 in any occupation identified as hazardous by the secretary of labor is prohibited. At present, a number of occupations have been identified as hazardous by the secretary of labor, including the following:

- coal mining or mining other than coal;
- occupations in or about plants manufacturing explosives or articles containing explosive components;
- occupations involving operation of motor-driven hoisting apparatus;
- logging or saw milling occupations;
- occupations involving exposure to radioactive substances;
- occupations of motor-vehicle operator or helper;
- occupations involving operation of power-driven woodworking machines;
- occupations involving operation of power-driven metalworking, forming, punching, or shearing machines;

---

[18] 247 U.S. 251.

- occupations in or about slaughtering or meatpacking plants or rendering plants;

- occupations involving the manufacture of brick, tile, or related products;

- occupations involving the operation of circular saws, handsaws, and guillotine shears;

- occupations involving wrecking, demolition, and ship-breaking.

Minors aged 16 to 18 may work in certain nonhazardous occupations, and minors aged 14 to 16 may be employed in non-manufacturing or non-mining occupations for limited hours outside school hours. Minors under age 14 can be employed only in agriculture under specific limitations and with parental consent.

The regulations limiting work by minors aged 14 to 16 further specify that the minors' hours between 7 a.m. and 7 p.m. may not exceed 18 hours per week when school is in session or 40 hours per week when school is not in session; nor may they exceed three hours per day when school is in session or eight hours per day when school is not in session.

Specific exemptions from the category of oppressive child labor include the employment of:

- newspaper carriers who are engaged in delivering papers to consumers;

- minors who are hired as actors or performers in movies, radio, television, or theatrical productions; and

- minors who are employed by their parents, or persons standing in the place of parents, in occupations other than manufacturing, mining, or others identified as hazardous by the secretary of labor.

Although child labor cases have become relatively rare in recent years, the DOL strictly enforces the FLSA provision. In the following case, the secretary of labor argues about the line between "student" and "employee" at a boarding school.

≫ CASE 22.5

SOLIS v. LAURELBROOK SANITARIUM AND SCHOOL, INC.
642 F.3d 518 (6th Cir. 2011)

Facts: Founded in 1950 by a group of Seventh-Day Adventists, Laurelbrook is a nonprofit corporation located in Dayton, Tennessee. Laurelbrook follows the philosophy and teachings of the Seventh-Day Adventist Church and its founder, Ellen G. White, which include the view that children are to receive an education with a practical training component.

In conformity with its beliefs, Laurelbrook operates a boarding school for students in grades nine through twelve, an elementary school for children of staff members, and a 50-bed intermediate-care nursing home that assists in the students' practical training (the Sanitarium). The school has been approved and accredited by the Tennessee Department of Education since the 1970s. The State of Tennessee accredits certain private schools through independent authorized accrediting agencies. The E.A. Sutherland Education Association (EASEA) is one such agency, whose purpose is to consider and adjudicate requests for accreditation from self-supporting (as opposed to denominational) schools, like Laurelbrook, which are operated by members of the Seventh-Day Adventist Church. Laurelbrook is currently accredited through EASEA.

Students in Laurelbrook's boarding school learn in both academic and practical settings, spending four hours of each school day in the classroom and four hours learning practical skills. The two aspects of the education are integrated, and all teachers instruct in both settings. Laurelbrook's stated mission is the "education of young people, providing a balanced program of spiritual, academic and vocational training to high school students (grades nine through twelve) with a goal of reproducing the character of God and preparing for His service." Students learn practical skills, in part, so they can later serve as missionaries in foreign lands. Boarding students keep busy with "wholesome activities" that teach them practical skills about "work, responsibility, [and] the dignity of manual labor," and that contribute to maintaining Laurelbrook's operations.

Laurelbrook offers the following vocational courses: Agriculture, Building Arts, Grounds Management, Mechanical Arts, Office Procedures, Plant Services, Water Services, Certified Nursing Assistant ("CNA"), Child Development, Environmental Services, and Food Service. The Sanitarium is an integral part of Laurelbrook's vocational training program. As part of their training, students are assigned to the Sanitarium's kitchen and housekeeping departments. Students sixteen and older may participate in the CNA program, which is approved by the State of Tennessee licensing authority. Students who receive their CNA certification may then be assigned to the Sanitarium to provide medical assistance to patients. Students assist patients in relation to the students' training and in line with Laurelbrook's guiding philosophy of education. Laurelbrook receives Medicaid funding for the care it provides at the Sanitarium.

The Sanitarium is staffed such that if the students were not training there, staff members could continue to provide the same patient services. But since the Sanitarium is integral to the education the school provides, Laurelbrook would not operate the Sanitarium if the school did not exist. In other words, the Sanitarium's sole purpose is to serve as a training vehicle for students. Therefore, the district court reasoned, students do not displace adult workers or other employees who might be willing to work at the Sanitarium.

Many of Laurelbrook's practical training courses (16 of 25) are approved by the Tennessee Department of Education for transfer credit. Several others are approved as "special courses," meaning a transferee school can accept the courses at its discretion. Students learn to use tools associated with specific trades, and the learning experience is similar to that received in vocational training courses at public schools. Adult staff members adequately supervise students and provide reasonable safeguards to protect them from hazardous activities. Laurelbrook has performed reasonably well in ensuring student safety.

Students do not receive wages for duties they perform. They are not entitled to a job with Laurelbrook upon graduation, and are expected to move on after graduation.

Laurelbrook provides "important tangible benefits and intangible training" and its students "reap great benefits" from the training and education provided. Any benefits Laurelbrook derives from its students are "secondary to its religious mission" of providing academic and practical training. Therefore, the district court reasoned, any such benefits are "much less" than those received by the students.

Laurelbrook does not compete for labor. Its vocational program compares favorably with programs operated by public high schools in the area. But because Laurelbrook operates a boarding school, it cannot compare perfectly with a public school where students are only in school for part of the day. Laurelbrook is responsible for its boarding students at all times, and its efforts to keep the students gainfully occupied are in keeping with its religious mission to teach students moral character.

In February 2007, the Secretary brought this action to enjoin future violations of 29 U.S.C. §§ 212(a), 212(c), and 215(a)(4), as well as Child Labor Regulation 3, 29 C.F.R. §§ 570.31–.37. The district court conducted a seven-day bench trial between August 19, 2008 and April 6, 2009, and subsequently denied the Secretary's request for a permanent injunction in a written order. The basis for the decision was that Laurelbrook students were not "employees" under the FLSA, thus rendering the Act inapplicable to Laurelbrook's entire operation. To reach this result, the district court considered the benefits each party received from the work performed, and concluded that the primary benefit of the work students performed at Laurelbrook ran to themselves, not Laurelbrook.

The Secretary appealed.

Issue: Does the student vocational training practiced at Laurelbrook violate the child labor provision of the FLSA?

Decision: Students received primary benefit of work they performed in boarding school's practical training courses, during which students worked in school run nursing home, including in nursing home's kitchens or as part of nursing home's certified nursing assistant (CNA) program, and therefore, were not employees under the Fair Labor Standards Act (FLSA), as would violate the child labor provisions; students did not displace compensated workers, instructors had to spend extra time supervising students at the expense of performing productive work, nursing home was sufficiently staffed such that it could run even if students did not perform work, students were provided hands-on training comparable to that of a public school vocational course, students learned to operate tools normally used in the trades they were learning, courses had been considered and approved by a state accrediting agency, and students received intangible benefits, including value of hard work and respect for the elderly and infirm. Fair Labor Standards Act of 1938, § 1 et seq., 29 U.S.C.A. § 201 et seq.

The district court applied the proper test when it asked which party to the relationship received the primary benefit of the students' activities. We find the district court's findings of fact amply supported by the evidence adduced at trial, and agree with its application of the primary benefit test to conclude that the students at Laurelbrook are not employees for purposes of the FLSA. Accordingly, the judgment of the district court is affirmed.

Concept *Summary* 22.4

CHILD LABOR

- The FLSA does not forbid all child labor
- Rather, the FLSA regulates when and how children may be employed
- The FLSA and its regulations pay particular attention to child labor in dangerous industries and involving dangerous equipment
- Sweatshops, including those that use child labor, persist in the United States and abroad, posing a continuing challenge to U.S. law enforcement officials and wage and hour regulators

22-2f Enforcement and Remedies Under the FLSA

The FLSA is enforced by the Department of Labor (DOL). The Wage and Hour Division of the DOL performs inspections and investigations and issues rules and regulations. The secretary of labor is authorized to file suit on behalf of employees seeking to collect wages and overtime and may also recover liquidated damages in an amount equal to the amount of wages owed. The secretary may also seek injunctions against violations of the act. Criminal proceedings for willful violations may be instituted by the Department of Justice.

Employees may file suit to recover back wages and overtime plus liquidated damages in an equal amount. They may also seek reinstatement and may recover legal fees. The statute of limitations for violations is two years; for willful violations it is extended to three years. The Supreme Court discussed the definition of "willful" in *McLaughlin v. Richland Shoe Co.*[19] The Court defined "willful" as "that the employer either knew or showed reckless

---

[19] 486 U.S. 128 (1988).

disregard as to whether its conduct was prohibited by the FLSA." Employees generally may not release employers for less than the full amount owing, nor may employees waive their rights to compensation under the act.

The child labor prohibitions are enforced by the prohibition of interstate shipment of goods produced by child labor and by fines. Fines may also be levied against employers who keep inadequate wage and hour records.

The following case involves a discussion of the standard used by the court in determining whether to award liquidated damages.

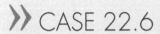

» CASE 22.6

MUMBY v. PURE ENERGY SERVICES
636 F.3d 1266 (10th Cir. 2011)

Facts: Pure Energy, a subsidiary of a Canadian oilfield services company, has provided services to U.S. gas and oil wells since 2004. Its field employees, which include Plaintiffs, work twelve-hour shifts, seven days per week, with one week off for every three weeks worked. Thus, employees work approximately eighty-four hours per workweek.

During the events leading to this litigation, Pure Energy paid its field employees under a "day rate" compensation plan, whereby employees received a single daily payment regardless of the number of hours actually worked. Pure Energy defined its "day rate" not by the relevant regulation, 29 C.F.R § 778.112, but rather as a daily rate consisting of a defined regular rate for the first eight hours and an overtime rate for the remaining four hours of the day. For those employees paid in this fashion, Pure Energy did not keep track of either daily or weekly hours worked.

Pure Energy's pay scheme, however, violated the FLSA, which requires employers to compensate their employees "for a workweek longer than forty hours … at a rate not less than one and one-half times the regular rate at which [the employee] is employed." For an employee to be correctly paid under a day rate, a weekly "regular rate" is first calculated "by totaling all the sums received at such day rates … and dividing by the total hours actually worked." The employee "is then entitled to extra half-time pay at this [regular] rate for all hours worked in excess of 40 in the workweek."

Since its field employees' work schedules exceeded forty hours per week, Pure Energy should have paid overtime for all hours worked over forty. Instead, Pure Energy paid

only what it believed was a day rate which included, by its calculations, four hours of overtime per day. This formula did not comply with 29 C.F.R. § 778.112. Even by its own erroneous calculation, four hours of overtime per day falls well short of the FLSA-mandated overtime owed for all hours over forty where the employee works eighty-four hours each week.

In 2005, after one year of U.S. operations, Pure Energy began transferring *1269 management of its U.S. operations from Canada to the United States. When it transferred payroll functions to its new domestic management team, it hired a new manager, Cindy Rucker, to run payroll operations in compliance with U.S. labor standards. At the time of her hiring, Ms. Rucker was aware of the FLSA, but she was unfamiliar with day rates. When she expressed concerns about the company's compensation policy, Pure Energy's management referred Ms. Rucker to a Colorado attorney, Paul Hurcomb.

In January 2006, after speaking with Ms. Rucker and reviewing some of Pure Energy's employment offer letters, Mr. Hurcomb advised Ms. Rucker that Pure Energy's day rate policy complied with the FLSA so long as the company itemized regular and overtime rates and did not have its field employees work more than twelve hours per day. Mr. Hurcomb also discussed with Ms. Rucker that any weekly hours over forty had to be paid as overtime, regardless of the day rate. Mr. Hurcomb did not perform any legal research regarding day rates or the FLSA. Although he essentially stated the forty-hour overtime requirement correctly, his other advice was incorrect.

After receiving Mr. Hurcomb's advice, Ms. Rucker confirmed with management that Pure Energy was paying its employees correctly so long as it broke down the day rate into regular and overtime hourly rates and did not exceed twelve-hour shifts. However, until it changed its compensation policies in late 2007 to finally comply with the FLSA, Pure Energy continued to underpay its field employees for overtime. Field employees also continued to occasionally work more than twelve hours per day without additional compensation, in violation of Mr. Hurcomb's advice.

In 2007, a group of field employees sued Pure Energy for its violation of the FLSA, based on, inter alia, its failure to pay sufficient overtime. See *Condos v. Pure Energy Servs. (USA), Inc.*, 07–CV–00127–ABJ (D. Wyo. filed June 12, 2007). The district court granted the *Condos* plaintiffs partial summary judgment, finding that Pure Energy had failed to pay the overtime required by the FLSA. Shortly thereafter, Pure Energy and the *Condos* plaintiffs settled.

Plaintiffs in this case are similarly situated to the plaintiffs in *Condos*, and as such, Pure Energy has already admitted it owes Plaintiffs back pay for missed overtime. There were only two issues at summary judgment: first, whether Plaintiffs may be awarded compensatory damages under the extended three-year statute of limitations for Pure Energy's "willful" violation of the

FLSA; and second, whether Pure Energy should be required to pay liquidated damages. The district court denied Pure Energy's motion and granted Plaintiffs' motion in part, reserving judgment on the liquidated damages issue until after trial. The parties agreed to have the court rule on liquidated damages based on their existing briefs, and the district court then found Pure Energy liable for the full amount of liquidated damages. An appeal followed.

Issue: Was the court within its discretion in awarding the plaintiffs liquidated damages?

Decision: The court found that Pure Energy failed to compensate Plaintiffs for weekly overtime despite being put on notice. It applied its compensation policy in reckless disregard of FLSA requirements, and is therefore subject to the three-year statute of limitations for damages. The same facts that support the district court's conclusion that Pure Energy's failure to fully compensate Plaintiffs' weekly overtime was willful also support the district court's conclusion that Pure Energy's belief that it was complying with the FLSA was unreasonable. Moreover, even if the district court had found Pure Energy acted reasonably, it retained discretion to award liquidated damages.

The FLSA also prohibits retaliation against employees who invoke the statute's protections. Section 215(a)(3) makes it illegal for an employer "to discharge or in any other manner discriminate against any employee because such employee has filed any complaint or instituted or caused to be instituted any proceeding under or related to this chapter, or has testified or is about to testify in any such proceeding, or has served or is about to serve on an industry committee...."[20] The Supreme Court held in *Kasten v. Saint-Gobain Performance Plastics Corp.*[21] that an oral complaint by an employee was covered by the "filed any complaint" language of the FLSA anti-retaliation provisions. Following *Kasten*, the U.S. Court of Appeals for the Second Circuit held that an oral complaint triggered the FLSA protections against retaliation.[22]

---

[20] 29 U.S.C. § 215(a)(3).

[21] 563 U.S. 1 (2011).

[22] *Greathouse v. JHS Security Inc.*, 784 F.3d 105 (2nd Cir. 2015).

Concept *Summary* 22.5

FLSA ENFORCEMENT

- The U.S. Department of Labor is charged with enforcing the FLSA
- The DOL's Wage and Hour Division is the component of the cabinet-level department which specifically creates and enforces the regulations that operationalize the FLSA's broad principles
- The Wage and Hour Division can investigate violations and sue on behalf of employees
- A private right of action is available for aggrieved workers
  - Remedies include liquidated damages and attorney fees

CHAPTER REVIEW

» Key Terms

minimum wage	728	workweek	735	National Industrial Recovery Act (NIRA)	741
overtime pay	735	exempt employee	736		

» Summary

- The Fair Labor Standards Act (FLSA) is the primary federal law governing minimum wages, overtime compensation, and child labor in the United States. It does not preempt similar state laws that provide employees with greater protections in these key categories. The FLSA has been declared by the Supreme Court not to be an unconstitutional taking of employers' property or an unconstitutional interference with the right to make contracts.

- Minimum hourly wages need not be paid to bona fide executives, administrators, professionals, and outside salespeople, who typically receive salaries and commissions. Hourly workers, who are entitled to at least the federal minimum wage, cannot be

penalized by deductions for tools, uniforms, or cash register losses.

- Executives, administrators, professionals, and outside salespeople also are not entitled to overtime pay. Hourly employees are entitled to at least one-and-a-half times their regular hourly pay rates for all hours over 40 in any workweek.

- FLSA child labor provisions limit the use of children and teens in dangerous workplaces. Since the law does not extend to American corporations' activities outside the United States and its territories, critics of corporate practices in third-world countries recently have accused a number of major corporations of exploiting child labor, as well as workers generally, in offshore operations.

» Problems

» Questions

1. How has the DOL changed its approach to pursuing compliance with the FLSA from a company? How does this new approach affect employers?

2. Do the DOL and/or the federal courts have jurisdiction to award liquidated damages? In what circumstances?

3. What are the major exceptions from the overtime and minimum wage requirements of the FLSA? What are the tests used to determine whether an employee falls under one of those exemptions?

4. What is meant by "oppressive child labor"? What is the significance of oppressive child labor under the FLSA?

5. How does the DOL decide under the FLSA whether or not a child's labor makes the child an employee?

6. What remedies are available for violations of the minimum wage and overtime provisions of the FLSA? What penalties may be imposed for violations of the child labor prohibitions?

» Case Problems

7. The employer is a not-for-profit corporation that provides services to mentally retarded and developmentally disabled individuals. It operates residential group homes for its clientele. Each such geographically separate house is under the sole charge of a house manager. The house manager's job includes (1) managing the house's budget, (2) hiring and managing other employees at the house, and (3) maintaining employment records. However, these house managers also perform nonmanagerial tasks such as transporting clients, assisting them with bathing and dressing, and numerous other chores normally performed by their subordinates.

    Should these house managers be classified as exempt executive employees for purposes of minimum wage and overtime pay under the FLSA?

[See *Department of Labor, Wage and Hour Division, Opinion Letter of July 14, 2000*, 2000 WL 1537209.]

8. Company A sells airtime and infomercials on television. It employs telephone callers at $9 per hour. Company B, which is owned by the same parent company, does telephone collection calling of its clients' debtors, paying the same hourly rate of $9.

    Employee C works 40 hours per week for Company A. He also is employed evenings for a total of 10 hours per week for Company B.

    Should Company B be required to pay Employee C time-and-one-half for overtime compensation? [See *Department of Labor, Wage and Hour Division, Opinion Letter of July 14, 2000, Attachment 1*, 2000 WL 1537209.]

9. A volunteer ambulance company contracts with a for-profit corporation to provide drivers and emergency medical technicians (EMTs). The for-profit company then bills the volunteer ambulance company for the services of these employees. Sometimes, however, these very same drivers and EMTs provide their services to the volunteer ambulance company as volunteers in their off-duty hours.

    Should the volunteer ambulance company be required to pay these drivers and EMTs either minimum wages and/or overtime compensation for their "volunteer" hours? [See *Department of Labor, Wage and Hour Division, Opinion Letter of May 22, 2000*, 2000 WL 1537253.]

10. The employer established a performance-based bonus plan under which workers who were not exempt from the minimum wage and overtime provisions of the FLSA were evaluated on various productivity criteria. At year's end, some of the company's top performers were given lump-sum, one-time bonuses. Who received the bonuses and the amounts of the bonuses were determinations made by the CEO at her sole discretion. The company was under no advance contractual obligation to give any bonuses or to give any particular employees a bonus.

Should the employer be permitted to exclude these lump-sum bonuses when calculating a recipient's hourly rate of pay for purposes of determining whether she or he has been receiving the proper amount when entitled to overtime compensation? [See *Department of Labor, Wage and Hour Division, Opinion Letter of May 19, 2000*, 2000 WL 1537273.]

11. A company allowed its employees to take a half-hour lunch break. However, the break was uncompensated, and the employees were not permitted to leave the employer's premises during the break. Nevertheless, these employees did leave their positions on the production line and eat in an employee lunchroom. They also went outdoors at their discretion.

    Should the employer be required under the FLSA to compensate these hourly production workers for their 30-minute lunch breaks? What about maintenance workers who might be recalled early from their lunch breaks if an equipment breakdown required it? [See *Brown v. Howard Industries, Inc.*, 116 F. Supp. 2d PN764 (S.D. Miss. 2000).]

12. Pursuant to the FLSA exception, which allows public employers to give their hourly workers compensatory time in lieu of overtime pay, a town provided its police officers with compensatory time credits in place of overtime premiums. However, when police officers tried to "cash in" their compensatory entitlements, the chief of police—following the instructions of the town council—approved such requests only when a police officer's absence on "comp time" did not require the town to pay a replacement officer overtime/comp time.

    Should the town be permitted to restrict the police officers' enjoyment of their comp time entitlements in this fashion? [See *Canney v. Town of Brookline*, 2000 WL 1612703 (D. Mass.).]

13. The employee, an immigrant, filed a claim with state's labor commission, claiming unpaid overtime entitlements. The employer then reported her immigration status to the Immigration and Naturalization Service (now the Bureau of Citizenship and Immigration Services in the Department of Homeland Security), which upon

investigation found that the employee in fact was in violation of INS regulations.

    Should the employee be permitted to pursue a lawsuit against the employer, alleging retaliation in violation of Section 215(a)(3) of the FLSA, which makes it illegal to punish an employee for exercising her rights under the FLSA? Does your answer change if the Immigration Control and Enforcement (ICE) agency fails to find that the employee is working in violation of ICE regulations? What if the reporting employer honestly believed in good faith that the violation existed?

    What are the competing public policy considerations for and against permitting such a lawsuit under these two different sets of facts? [See *Contreras v. Corinthian Vigor Insurance Brokerage, Inc.*, 2000 WL 1521369 (N.D. Cal.).]

14. The employee was employed as a "floating" pharmacist by a small chain of drug stores. As the floater, he was shifted from store to store to fill in for ill and vacationing regular pharmacists. He was paid an hourly wage of $27 but no overtime, even though he sometimes worked more than 40 hours in a single week. When he sued for his unpaid overtime compensation, the company contended that he is a professional employee and therefore not entitled to overtime compensation under the FLSA.

    Is the company correct? What different or additional facts, if any, might cause you to change your answer? [See *Iheanacho v. Safeway, Inc.*, 2000 WL 1364239 (D. Oregon).]

15. A university provided free housing for its male security guards but not for its female guards. The university claimed that its purpose was to ensure round-the-clock availability of public safety officers on the campus in case of emergencies, and therefore the housing was for its benefit and convenience and not an added form of compensation to the male officers. University officials also claimed that it would be unduly expensive to try to make the facilities coed to accommodate the female guards. The female guards brought suit under the Equal Pay Act provisions of the FLSA (see Chapter 4).

    Who should win? [See *Stewart v. S.U.N.Y. Maritime College*, 2000 WL 1218379 (S.D.N.Y.).]

16. A local bus company makes its money by transporting passengers to and from the local train station and to bus depots, where they catch interstate buses. The company runs no buses outside state lines but is strictly local. Nevertheless, the company is regulated by the U.S. Department of Transportation. The FLSA exempts interstate transportation activities.

    The local bus company admits it never pays its drivers overtime compensation when they exceed 40 hours of work in a week. But it argues that it is exempt because it is engaged in interstate transportation.

    Do you agree? [See *United Transportation Local Union 759 v. Orange Newark Elizabeth Bus, Inc.*, 111 F. Supp. 2d 514 (D.N.J. 2000).]

» Hypothetical Scenarios

17. Clara is the supervisor in charge of a fast-food restaurant. She has six cooks, dishwashers, and waitresses under her supervision. However, she herself often has to cook at the grill, load and run the dishwasher, and even occasionally wait on tables during particularly busy times or when workers call in sick. She is paid a weekly salary of $500. Do you think she should be exempt from the FLSA's minimum wage and overtime provisions?

18. Jerry is a security officer. He is paid by the hour to help protect celebrities. A typical evening shift involves riding in the limousine with a famous performer, accompanying her into the arena where she is performing, then sitting around backstage, while the show is proceeding. While the performer is on stage, Jerry and his fellow guards have no particular duties to perform. They usually play cards or watch the concert. However, they are not allowed to leave the performance venue. They continue to wear their Bluetooth head sets and must respond immediately if called upon to do so.

Should they continue to receive their hourly wages for the time they are just sitting around backstage?

19. Cindy is a saleswoman. Four days a week she is "in the field," making sales calls. A typical work day, Monday through Thursday, begins with her reviewing her schedule at her kitchen table over her morning coffee. She then spends the rest of her days making her calls, returning home in the late afternoon, where she does about an hour's worth of paperwork, submitting orders electronically to the home office. On Fridays, however, she is required to report to the home office, where she attends a mandatory sales meeting and works at her desk the remainder of the day. Is Cindy an outside salesperson who is exempt from the minimum wage and overtime provisions of the FLSA? Does your answer apply to Fridays, too?

20. Henry is an avid adherent of a religious cult, which requires members to turn over all their property to the church elders. He lives in a communal setting owned and maintained by the church, which provides his food and clothing. He is required to work a 10-hour day in one of several church-affiliated enterprises. He is paid nothing for this work. Is the church violating the FLSA where Henry is concerned? Does the fact that he does the work not only voluntarily but gladly affect your answer?

21. Maggie is 10 years old. Her parents are legal migrant farm workers. While her parents are picking fruit in the fields, the agribusiness which employs them provides day care for children such as Maggie. However, Maggie and the other children are often required to work in the farm kitchens, preparing meals, including operating such electrical equipment such as meat slicers, as they help prepare the meals that are then delivered to the workers in the fields. Is Maggie's work subject to the FLSA's child labor provisions? How about the FLSA's minimum wage requirements?

GLOSSARY

A

academic freedom   The college professors' right to take unpopular positions in the classroom and in scholarly work without fear of reprisals by the university.

administrative law judges (ALJs)   Formerly called trial examiners, these judges are independent of both the Board and the general counsel.

affirmative action plan   Program which involves giving preference in hiring or promotion to qualified female or minority employees.

after-acquired evidence   Evidence, discovered after an employer has taken an adverse employment action, that the employer uses to justify the action taken.

agency shop   A union security provision in a collective agreement that requires employees to pay union dues and fees, but does not require that they become union members.

agency shop agreement   Agreement requiring employees to pay union dues, but not requiring them to join the union.

Alien Tort Claims Act   Federal statute that provides a cause of action for aggrieved aliens in U.S. courts.

ambulatory *situs* picketing   Union picketing that follows the primary employer's mobile business.

arbitration   The settlement of disputes by a neutral adjudicator chosen by the parties.

authorization cards   Cards signed by employees indicating that they authorize the union to act as the employees' bargaining agent and to seek an election on behalf of the employees.

B

bargaining unit   Group of employees being represented by a union.

Bennett Amendment   The provision of Section 703(h) that allows pay differentials between employees of different sexes when the pay differential is due to seniority, merit pay, productivity-based pay, or a factor other than sex.

bona fide occupational qualification (BFOQ)   An exception to the civil rights law that allows an employer to hire employees of a specific gender, religion, or national origin when business necessity—the safe and efficient performance of the particular job—requires it.

business necessity   The safe and efficient performance of the business or performance of a particular job requires that employees be of a particular sex, religion, or national origin.

C

captive-audience speech   Meeting or speech held by the employer during working hours, which employees are required to attend.

closed shop   An employer who agrees to hire only those employees who are already union members.

collective bargaining   Process by which a union and employer meet and confer with respect to wages, hours, and other terms and conditions of employment.

common law   Judge-made law as opposed to statutes and ordinances enacted by legislative bodies.

common *situs* picketing   Union picketing of an entire construction site.

comparable worth   A standard of equal pay for jobs of equal value; not the same as equal pay for equal work.

confidential employee   Person whose job involves access to confidential labor relations information.

consent election   Election conducted by the regional office giving the regional director final authority over any disputes.

construct validity   A method of demonstrating that an employment selection device selects employees based on the traits and characteristics that are required for the job in question.

contract bar rule   A written labor contract bars an election during the life of the bargaining agreement, subject to the "openseason" exception.

contract compliance program   Regulations which provide that all firms having federal government contracts or subcontracts exceeding $10,000 must include a no-discrimination clause in the contract.

convention International law, usually sponsored by the United Nations or other multinational organizations, to which a number of nations agree to adhere.

criminal conspiracy A crime that may be committed when two or more persons agree to do something unlawful.

criterion-related validity A method of demonstrating that an employment selection device correlates with the skills and knowledge required for successful job performance.

D

de minimis violation A technical violation, but so insignificant as to require no fine or remediation.

decertification petition Petition stating that a current bargaining representative no longer has the support of a majority of the employees in the bargaining unit.

defamation An intentional, false, and harmful communication.

disparate impact The discriminatory effect of apparently neutral employment criteria.

disparate treatment When an employee is treated differently from others due to race, color, religion, gender, or national origin.

drug testing Testing of human blood and/or urine for the presence of controlled or illegal substances.

duty of fair representation Legal duty on the part of the union to represent fairly all members of the bargaining unit.

E

eavesdropping Surreptitiously listening to others' conversations.

economic strike A strike over economic issues such as a new contract or a grievance.

election of remedies The requirement to choose one out of two or more means afforded under the law for the redress of an injury to the exclusion of the other(s).

Employee Assistance Program (EAP) Includes a range of psychological, health, fitness and legal services aimed at helping employees solve problems that interfere with job performance.

Employee Retirement Income Security Act (ERISA) An act that sets standards for pension plans including fiduciary conduct, information disclosure, plan taxation, and remedies for employees.

employment-at-will Both the employee and the employer are free to unilaterally terminate the relationship at any time and for any legally permissible reason, or for no reason at all.

English-only rules Employer work rules requiring that employees speak English in the workplace during working hours.

Equal Pay Act of 1963 Federal legislation that requires that men and women performing substantially equal work be paid equally.

ex parte proceedings Court hearing in which one party, usually the defendant, is not present and is not able to take part.

Excelsior list A list of the names and addresses of the employees eligible to vote in a representation election.

exempt employee Employee whose hours of work and compensation are not stipulated by the FLSA.

express contract A contract in which the terms are explicitly stated, usually in writing but perhaps only verbally, and often in great detail. In interpreting such a contract, the judge and/ or the jury is asked only to determine what the explicit terms are and to interpret them according to their plain meaning.

F

failing firm exception An exception to the WARN notice requirement for layoffs that occurs when the employer can demonstrate that giving the required notice would prevent the firm from obtaining capital or business necessary to maintain the operation of the firm.

featherbedding The practice of getting paid for services not performed or not to be performed.

Federal Employment Liability Act (FELA) A federal law designed to protect and compensate railroad workers injured on the job.

Federal Labor Relations Authority (FLRA) The federal agency created under the Federal Service Labor–Management Relations Act to administer federal employee labor relations.

Federal Service Impasse Panel Federal body created under the Federal Service Labor– Management Relations Act to resolve impasses in collective bargaining in the federal service.

fiduciary Any person exercising discretionary authority over benefit plan administration, management, or disposition of plan assets; or who renders investment advice regarding the plan.

forty-eight-hour rule NLRB requirement that a party filing a petition for a representation election must provide evidence to support the petition within 48 hours of the filing.

Four-Fifths Rule A mathematical formula developed by the EEOC to demonstrate disparate impact of a facially neutral employment practice on selection criteria.

front pay Monetary damages awarded to a plaintiff instead of reinstatement or hiring.

G

genetic testing Examination of chromosomes, genes, and proteins in human cells in a search for defects.

global corporate responsibility   Philosophy which says that corporations should behave as good global citizens.

global unions   International labor organizations, which typically attempt to organize employees of globalized industries.

globalization   The integration of national economies into a worldwide economy, due to trade, investment, migration, and information technology.

grievance   A complaint that one party to a collective agreement is not living up to the obligations of the agreement.

grievance process   The process set up by a collective agreement to deal with complaints that arise under the collective agreement.

H

hiring hall   A job-referral mechanism operated by unions whereby unions refer members to prospective employers.

honesty test   Employment test used by employers as a screening device to evaluate employees or applicants on various workplace behaviors such as truthfulness, perceptions about employee theft, admissions of theft, and drug use.

hostile environment harassment   Harassment which may not result in economic detriment to the victim, but which subjects the victim to unwelcome conduct or comments and may interfere with the employee's work performance.

hot cargo clause   Provision in collective bargaining agreements that purports to permit employees to refuse to handle the product of any employer involved in a labor dispute.

I

Immigration Reform and Control Act (IRCA) of 1986   The most recent major overhaul of U.S. immigration law.

impasse   A deadlock in negotiations.

implied contract   A contractual relationship, the terms and conditions of which must be inferred from the contracting parties' behavior toward one another.

independent contractor   A person working as a separate business entity.

individual employee rights   Rights enjoyed by workers as individuals, as against collective rights secured by unionization; sources are statutes and court decisions.

information technology   The study, design, development, implementation, support, or management of computer-based information systems.

in-house union   Union created and controlled by the employer.

injunction   A court order to provide remedies prohibiting some action or commanding the righting of some wrongdoing.

intentional infliction of emotional distress   Purposely outrageous conduct causing emotional harm.

interest arbitration   Arbitration that is used to create a new collective agreement or to renew an existing agreement.

International Labor Organization (ILO)   A United Nations subsidiary agency dealing with international labor standards, workers' rights, and global employment issues.

L

laboratory conditions   The conditions under which a representative election is held; the NLRB tries to ensure that neither the employer nor the union unduly affects the employees' free choice.

libel   A written falsehood.

Lilly Ledbetter Fair Pay Act   Statute that extends time in which an employee may file suit under several federal employment statutes.

lockout   An employer's temporary withdrawal of employment to pressure employees to agree to the employer's bargaining proposals.

M

malice   Knowledge or reckless disregard of the falsity of a communication.

managerial employee   Person involved in the formulation or effectuation of management policies.

mandatory bargaining subjects   Those matters that vitally affect the terms and conditions of employment of the employees in the bargaining unit; the parties must bargain in good faith over such subjects.

mass layoffs   Layoffs creating an employment loss during any 30-day period for 500 or more employees or for 50 or more employees who constitute at least one-third of the full-time labor force at a unit of the facility.

minimum wage   The wage limit, set by the government, under which an employer is not allowed to pay an employee.

N

National Industrial Recovery Act (NIRA)   An act primarily designed to regulate and revitalize industry; promoted fair trade practices.

negligent hiring   When an employer hires an employee that the employer knows (or should have known through reasonable checks) could cause injury to others.

negligent infliction of emotional distress   Carelessly outrageous conduct causing emotional harm.

network   Group of computers, all interconnected to one another.

non-suspect class   A basis of discrimination, classification, or differential by government action which is neutral with regard to race, color, gender, religion, or national origin, and which is related to legitimate government interests; examples of non-suspect classes are age, veteran status, or personal achievement.

no-strike clause   A provision in a collective agreement by which the union agrees not to strike over disputes of interpretation of the agreement during the term of the agreement.

O

open-meeting ("sunshine") laws   Laws that require that meetings of public bodies be open to the public.

overtime pay   Employees covered by the FLSA are entitled to overtime pay, at one-and-a-half times their regular pay rate, for hours worked in excess of 40 hours per workweek.

P

patrolling   The movement of persons back and forth around an employer's premises.

permissive bargaining subjects   Those matters that are neither mandatory nor illegal; the parties may, but are not required to, bargain over such subjects.

picketing   Placing persons outside an employer's premises to convey information to the public via words, signs, or distributing literature.

Pregnancy Discrimination Act of 1978   An act that amended Title VII to include pregnancy discrimination in the definition of sex discrimination.

pressure tactics   Union pressure tactics involve strikes and calls for boycotts, while employers may resort to lockouts.

prima facie case   A case "on the face of it" or "at first sight"; often used to establish that if a certain set of facts is proven, then it is apparent that another fact is established.

protected health information (PHI)   Information specifically identified by federal law as subject to privacy protection.

public policy exception   Although the employee is employed at-will, termination is illegal if a clear and significant mandate of law (statutory or common) is damaged if the firing is permitted to stand unchallenged.

Q

qualified individual with a disability   An individual with a disability who is able to perform, with reasonable accommodation, the requirements of the job in question, despite the disability.

qualified privilege   Immunity from a suit in the absence of malice.

quid pro quo harassment   Harassment where the employee's response to the harassment is considered in granting employment benefits.

R

Racketeer Influenced and Corrupt Organizations Act (RICO) A federal law designed to criminally penalize those that engage in illegal activities as part of an ongoing criminal organization (e.g., the Mafia).

reasonable suspicion   Justifiably suspecting a person, based on facts or circumstances, of inappropriate or criminal activities.

retaliatory demotion   Reduction in rank, salary, or job title as a punishment.

rights arbitration   Arbitration to resolve a dispute involving the interpretation or application of an existing collective agreement; arbitration that defines the rights and obligations of each party under the agreement.

right-to-work laws   Laws which prohibit union security agreements.

runaway shop   Situation in which an employer closes in one location and opens in another to avoid unionization.

S

Seniority   The length of service on the job.

sexual harassment   Unwelcome sexual advances, requests for sexual favors, or other verbal or physical conduct of a sexual nature that the employee is required to accept as a condition of employment, the employee's response to such conduct is used as a basis for employment decisions, or such conduct creates a hostile working environment.

slander   A spoken falsehood.

strict liability   Plaintiff prevails without proving negligence.

strict scrutiny test   A constitutional analysis used by courts hearing equal protection claims involving governmental discrimination based on a "suspect class." This test requires the government to demonstrate that the discriminatory treatment was necessary to achieve a compelling government purpose and that the governmental action was "narrowly tailored" to achieve the compelling purpose.

strike   The organized withholding of labor by workers—the traditional weapon by which workers attempt to pressure employers.

substance abuse   Long-term use or dependence on alcohol or drugs.

supervisor   Person with authority to direct, hire, fire, or discipline employees in the interests of the employer.

surveillance Monitoring of behavior.

suspect class A basis of discrimination, classification, or differential treatment—such as race, color, gender, religion, or national origin—by government action for which there is little legitimate justification for treating persons because of such characteristics.

system administrator Person employed by an organization's IT department to manage and oversee a network of computers.

T

Title VII of the Civil Rights Act of 1964 Legislation that outlawed discrimination in terms and conditions of employment based on race, color, sex, religion, or national origin.

tort A private or civil wrong or injury, caused by one party to another, either intentionally or negligently.

tortious interference with contract Unprivileged intrusion into a contractual relationship.

trade secret Proprietary information protected by common law or state statute.

twenty-four-hour silent period The twenty-four-hour period prior to the representation election, during which the parties must refrain from formal campaign meetings.

U

undue hardship An accommodation that requires significant difficulty or expense for the employer.

unemployment compensation Benefits paid to employees out of work through no fault of their own and who are available for suitable work if and when it becomes available.

unfair labor practice strike A strike to protest employer unfair practices.

unfair labor practices (ULPs) Actions by employers or unions that interfere with the rights of employees under the National Labor Relations Act.

Uniform Guidelines on Employee Selection Procedures Regulations adopted by the EEOC and other federal agencies that provide for methods of demonstrating a disparate impact and for validating employee selection criteria.

union security agreement Contract provisions requiring employees to join the union or pay union dues.

union shop A union security provision in a collective agreement that requires employees to become union members within thirty days of their employment.

union shop agreement Agreement requiring employees to join the union after a certain period of time.

union shop clause Clause in an agreement requiring all present and future members of a bargaining unit to be union members.

V

voluntary **recognition** An employer agreeing to recognize a union with majority support as the exclusive bargaining agent for the workers in the bargaining unit, without holding a certification election.

W

weingarten **rights** The right of employees to have a representative of their choice present at meetings that may result in disciplinary action against the employees.

whipsaw strike Strike by a union selectively pitting one firm in an industry against the other firms.

whistleblower An employee who reports or attempts to report employer wrongdoing or actions threatening public health or safety to government authorities.

willful misconduct The high level of fault that disqualifies an out-of-work worker from unemployment benefits.

workers' compensation Benefits awarded to an employee when injuries are work related.

workweek A term the FLSA uses to signify seven consecutive days; the law does not require that the workweek start or end on any particular day of the calendar week.

Y

yellow-dog contract An employment contract requiring employees to agree not to join a union.

CASE INDEX

SUBJECT INDEX